COLLECTIVE BARGAINING
AND
LABOR ARBITRATION

Materials on Collective Bargaining, Labor Arbitration
and Discrimination in Employment

SECOND EDITION

CONTEMPORARY LEGAL EDUCATION SERIES

Collective Bargaining
and
Labor Arbitration

MATERIALS ON COLLECTIVE BARGAINING,
LABOR ARBITRATION AND
DISCRIMINATION IN EMPLOYMENT

SECOND EDITION

DONALD P. ROTHSCHILD
Professor of Law
George Washington University

LEROY S. MERRIFIELD
Lobingier Professor of Jurisprudence and Comparative Law
George Washington University

HARRY T. EDWARDS
Professor of Law
University of Michigan

THE BOBBS-MERRILL COMPANY, INC.
PUBLISHERS
INDIANAPOLIS • NEW YORK • CHARLOTTESVILLE, VIRGINIA

Dedication

The authors wish to dedicate this book to Professor Emeritus Russell A. Smith whose materials started this course and casebook. Each of us is personally grateful for Russ' guidance in this field, and most particularly for his friendship. Without his leadership and generosity these materials would not have been developed.

Donald P. Rothschild
Leroy S. Merrifield
Harry T. Edwards

Preface to Second Edition

We have sought in this volume to provide teaching materials for use primarily in law schools, but also in schools of business administration, departments of economics and other college and university departments where there is advanced curricular attention to labor and industrial relations. The typical basic course in "Labor Law" or "Labor and Industrial Relations" cannot, without undue dilution, deal adequately with the problems associated with the negotiation and enforcement of the collective bargaining agreement, as well as the current "external" law affecting collective bargaining. We think this subject is worthy of independent examination by law students and others who contemplate careers in labor relations law or practice, and even by students who are preparing for some other vocation in view of the increasing importance, in today's pluralistic society, of the process of informal dispute settlement.

The subtitle of this volume indicates that our materials deal with "collective bargaining, labor arbitration and discrimination in employment." Actually, because of the usual constraints inherent in the preparation of course materials, and having in mind certain primary objectives, we have found it necessary or desirable to give relatively greater emphasis to certain aspects of the broad subject range of the subtitle than to others. With respect to negotiation, we concentrate on the "how to" aspects of the process, because of the prolix materials dealing with the conceptual basis of bargaining. With respect to the administration of collective bargaining agreements, we emphasize the arbitration process because of its general acceptance and the stature accorded to it by the developing federal labor law. Our treatment of the Agreement itself has been substantially reduced from the first edition, because of the inherent complexity of the subject matter, such as seniority, and the many forms of compensation (*e.g.*, incentives, fringes, pensions, etc.). Since the last ten years have brought considerable attention to the critical areas of discrimination in employment, we have added a new dimension to our materials covering its impact on collective bargaining. We feel that the challenge of the next decade to the process will come from its capacity to resolve the issues raised in this section.

Since our first edition, we have been able to experiment with the pedagogical problems inherent in using these materials for an elective course. Our usage, along with the constructive criticism that we have received from some of our users, has convinced us of the importance of the subject matter in the materials, if not on the form of its presentation. Our goal in this edition is to provide materials that will assist the student in understanding the process of negotiation, and the drafting and administration of collective bargaining agreements. Secondly, we feel that it is of utmost importance in such a course to present the current challenges to the system posed by the significant issues in laws which are "external" to the process itself. We hope that those using this second edition will be aware of what Professor Russell A. Smith, to whom this book is dedicated, calls the "agenda items" in collective bargaining, as well as to the pressure in our society impacting on the process. Frankly, we feel that this awareness is more significant than the pedigogical impediments which naturally flow from such an ambitious exposition.

The authors are grateful to Linda Edith Rosenzweig, Esq., for her research and editing, and particularly for her work on Chapter 2. We also appreciate the research assistance of Lynne Darcy, student at the University of Michigan Law School; Howard A. Lowdon, student at the National Law Center, George Washington University; and Eliza Patterson, Esq. Our thanks go to Robert Folks and Debra Braun for the careful preparation of the manuscript. We are indebted to The Bureau of National Affairs, Inc., Washington, D.C., for their generous permission to reprint materials. We have cited arbitration cases from their publication, Labor Arbitration Reports, as — L.A. — (arbitrator, date).

Donald P. Rothschild
Leroy S. Merrifield
Harry T. Edwards

Preface to First Edition

We have sought in this volume to provide teaching materials for use primarily in law schools, but also in schools of business administration, departments of economics and other college and university departments where there is curricular attention to labor and industrial relations. The typical basic course in "Labor Law" or "Labor and Industrial Relations" cannot, without undue dilution, deal adequately with the problems associated with the negotiation and enforcement of the collective bargaining agreement. We think this subject is worthy of independent examination by law students and others who contemplate careers in labor relations law or practice and even by students who are preparing for some other vocation in view of the obvious importance, in today's pluralistic society, of the institution of collective bargaining.

The subtitle of the volume indidates that our materials deal with "the negotiation, enforcement and content of the labor agreement." Actually, because of the usual constraints inherent in the preparation of course materials, and having in mind certain primary objectives, we have found it necessary or desirable to give relatively greater emphasis to certain aspects of the broad subject range of the subtitle than to others. Thus, with respect to collective bargaining our principal concerns are the relevant legal framework and the substantive content of negotiations rather than the techniques of bargaining. With respect to the administration and enforcement of the labor agreement, we concentrate on the arbitration process rather than on the intra-plant uses of the grievance procedure. Even so we have had to be selective, as for example, in our summary treatment of the subjects of health and welfare plans, pension programs, and supplemental unemployment benefit provisions.

We have in mind that teaching methods will vary in the use of these materials as, indeed, they have even among ourselves in using them in their previous mimeographed form. The three major subdivisions of the volume differ measurably in the kinds of materials presented, and this in itself will probably tend to induce pedagogical variances in their use. Throughout the volume, but especially in Part Three, are interspersed illustrative "problems" with the thought that they could be a focus of class discussion of the subjects to which they relate. One of us has used this "problem solving" technique to cover the materials, and found it to be an effective teaching method. Some teachers may be inclined to use some parts of the materials, especially those in Parts Two and Three, primarily or in part as resource aids to the student in connection with assigned special projects. These could include the negotiating or drafting of certain parts of the labor agreement in the context of a basic hypothetical set of facts prepared by the instructor, the preparation or decision of selected actual or hypothetical grievance arbitration cases, reporting on important current collective bargaining developments, and reporting on subject areas of bargaining not fully treated in the volume (e.g., "automation," impacts of Title VII of the Civil Rights Act of 1964, or collective bargaining in the public sector). Another of us has used this technique and has found it both interesting to students as a different kind of learning process, and productive. We have in mind, in this connection, the preparation of a set of problem materials in multilithed form, which can be made available to teachers who may want to consider this approach.

It may well be (and we express the hope) that this volume will be of interest to the lawyer or other labor relations practitioner who is embarking on his career. A major objective, especially in the preparation of Part Three, has been to achieve in the user of the volume some degree of awareness of what we call the "agenda" items which parties should consider and, if deemed important, place on the "table," in negotiating contract provisions relating to identified subject areas.

It is obvious that these objectives are extremely ambitious. To the extent that we have succeeded, we are indebted to the following people and institutions. We appreciate the assistance of our colleagues Professor Jerome Barron, Dean Robert Kramer, at the National Law Center, George Washington University, for their counsel and assistance. Our thanks to the following students who served as research assistants during the preparation of this volume: Mr. Craig Dunbar, Mrs. Arlene Mendelson, Miss Alexis Panagokos, and also to Anna Chambliss, and Paula Young who helped in the preparation of the manuscript. We are indebted to The Bureau of National Affairs, Inc., Washington, D. C., particularly Mr. Donald F. Farwell, for their generous permission to reprint materials. We have cited arbitration cases from their publication, Labor Arbitration Reports, as — L.A. — (arbitrator, date).

Professor Smith wishes to thank his wife Berta and family, Professor Merrifield wishes to thank his wife Marian and children, Louis, Eric, Randall and Karen; and Professor Rothschild wishes to thank his wife Ruth and children, Nancy, Judy and Jimmy—their patience, sacrifice and cooperation have made possible the contribution of each of us.

Russell A. Smith
Leroy S. Merrifield
Donald P. Rothschild

Summary Table of Contents

Table of Contents

PART ONE. COLLECTIVE BARGAINING

PART THREE. THE SUBJECT MATTER OF COLLECTIVE BARGAINING AGREEMENTS

PART FOUR. DISCRIMINATION IN EMPLOYMENT

Table of Cases

Principal cases are those in italics.

A

C

I

L

M

O

V

W

PART ONE
COLLECTIVE BARGAINING

Chapter 1

CHARACTERISTICS AND THOUGHTS ON COLLECTIVE BARGAINING

A. WHAT IS IT?

It is easy to understand A. H. Raskin's cynical observation "I am a great believer in collective bargaining; the only trouble is that after thirty years of watching it at close range in dozens of industries, large and small, I am not sure I know what it is." [1] The difficulty in defining the term arises from the eclectic uses of the phrase. It is used to define the relationship of a management organization to the representative of a group of its employees. This relationship implies a joint decision-making process of the terms and conditions of employment. Collective bargaining also can be analyzed in terms of the power relationship which exists between management and the union or unions with which it deals under a contractual arrangement or legal duty. Obviously the use of collective power to determine the rights, duties and obligations of management and its employees can lead to conflict resolution, as in the case of strikes and lockouts. However, bargaining can continue throughout the use of a threatened strike or lockout, and even beyond where there is not a total breakdown of the relationship. Collective bargaining is also defined as a continuous process through which management and unions negotiate, interpret and enforce an agreement concerning wages, hours or other terms and conditions of employment. In this latter sense it is a process of communication, agreement and cooperation under what has been analogized to a treaty between the parties governing the rules of the workplace. [2] This treaty-making and treaty-enforcing system of industrial jurisprudence [3] is distinguishable from a conflict-oriented process.

The fact is that the term "collective bargaining" includes all of these relationships, and more, which operate within the complex

---

[1] A. H. Raskin & J. T. Dunlop, "Two Views of Collective Bargaining," in Challenges to Collective Bargaining 155 (Am. Assembly 1967) [hereinafter cited as Challenges to Collective Bargaining].

[2] Cox, "The Legal Nature of Collective Bargaining Agreements," 57 Mich. L. Rev. 1 (1958), p. 30.

[3] N. Chamberlain & J. Kuhn, Collective Bargaining 121-22 (2d ed. 1965) [hereinafter cited as Collective Bargaining], citing Professor Sumner Slichter of Harvard University.

pattern of industrialization that exists in the country.[4] In a seminar conducted by the Graduate School of Business of the University of Chicago,[5] it was suggested that in examining the complex field of labor-management relations, the emphasis be placed on the structure of the bargaining relationship.

Many of the forces playing on contemporary systems of collective bargaining, it is suggested here, can be analyzed and understood in terms of bargaining "structure." The notion of "structure," however, is inherently vague and needs some definition in its own right. The concept of collective bargaining structure encompasses the following elements:

1. The *size of the bargaining unit* with respect to the number of employees and establishments directly involved in a given collective bargaining relationship.

2. The *scope of the bargaining unit* with respect to the various occupational groups, plants, firms, and industries involved in a given collective bargaining relationship. In many instances the scope of the bargaining unit is coextensive with particular labor and product markets and thus has an implicit geographical dimension. Clearly the size and scope of the bargaining unit will tend to be closely related.

3. The *distribution of decision-making power* within the bargaining agencies — both union and management — as they deal with each other across the bargaining table. In some situations the analysis of decision-making power must be expanded to include government, which may exercise its influence over the parties through formal or informal means.

4. The *relationships between bargaining units* and the mechanisms by which substantive determinations in one unit are transmitted to other units.

. . .

Despite the term's initial ambiguity, all the papers submitted for the seminar approached the problems of bargaining structure from one or more of the aspects listed above; but the greatest emphasis was placed on the scope of the bargaining unit and the distribution of decision-making power within the bargaining agencies.

The current interest in bargaining structure, as it has been defined here, reflects certain broad assessments of post-World War II trends in collective bargaining. First, it has been asserted

---

[4] J. T. Dunlop, Industrial Relations Systems 7-18 (1958) [hereinafter cited as Industrial Relations Systems].

[5] Univ. of Chi. Grad. School of Business, the Structure of Collective Bargaining xv-xvii (Weber ed., 3d series, 1961). Reprinted with permission of the publisher. © 1961 by the Free Press of Glencoe, Inc.

that the size and scope of the de facto bargaining unit have become so great that effective collective bargaining, including the right of the union to strike and the right of management to resist vigorously the union's demands, may be precluded by the serious economic and social consequences of such actions. This observation gives rise to fears of increased governmental intervention in collective bargaining to reduce the undesirable social consequences of private actions. The more extreme analyses foresee compulsory arbitration being substituted for voluntary collective bargaining.

Second, it has been argued that in some cases the scope of the bargaining unit encompasses so many divergent interests that the bargaining agents cannot accurately and sensitively represent the specific needs and interests of their constituents. Instead, management and the union may seek a consensus so broad that they neglect or ignore problems of great importance to particular management and worker groups. On the other hand the expanded scope of the bargaining unit may necessitate intensive "internal bargaining" within unions and managements, thereby increasing rigidities in the bargaining process.

Third, it has been stated that the centralization of decision-making in many unions and companies has resulted in efforts to resolve at the firm or industry level those issues that can best be treated at the plant or local level. This "displacement" of bargaining issues to higher levels of decision-making may in turn enlarge the scope of possible conflict arising from disputes relating to such issues.

Fourth, developments in bargaining structure along the lines just indicated have elicited renewed interest in the venerable "labor monopoly" issue. It has been alleged that the emergence of expanded bargaining units, centralized decision-making within these units, and an interlocking system of "pattern" agreements have all had an increasingly deleterious effect on the allocation of resources and the efficient operation of the economy. Behind this assertion lies the additional fear of the establishment of a syndicalistic type of collusion between organized labor and management, at the expense of the public.[5]

Fifth, it has been frequently pointed out that we are in a period of extensive technological advance, which has given rise to significant changes in the occupational composition of the labor force and in the organization of product markets. Hence it is important to preserve the adaptability of bargaining structures,

---

[5] The classic statement of this argument is found in Henry C. Simons, "Some Reflections on Syndicalism," *Journal of Political Economy,* Vol. LII (March, 1944).

as unions and management strive to adjust their approaches to collective bargaining under these new economic and technological conditions.

Underlying all these issues is what might be called, for want of a better term, a concern for the preservation of democratic values in industrial society by maintaining a diffusion of power within and between the major competing economic groups. As stated by the participants in the seminar, this essentially means preserving the individual's opportunity to dissent within the institutional framework of modern industrial relations.

Finally, the phrase collective bargaining should be described in terms of the participants in the process.

J. T. DUNLOP, INDUSTRIAL RELATIONS SYSTEMS 7-18 (H. Holt & Co. 1958) [6]

The Actors in a System

The actors are: (1) a hierarchy of managers and their representatives in supervision, (2) a hierarchy of workers (nonmanagerial) and any spokesmen, and (3) specialized governmental agencies (and specialized private agencies created by the first two actors) concerned with workers, enterprises, and their relationships. These first two hierarchies are directly related to each other in that the managers have responsibilities at varying levels to issue instructions (manage), and the workers at each corresponding level have the duty to follow such instructions (work).

The hierarchy of workers does not necessarily imply formal organizations; they may be said to be "unorganized" in popular usage, but the fact is, that wherever they work together for any considerable period, at least an informal organization comes to be formulated among the workers with norms of conduct and attitudes toward the hierarchy of managers. In this sense workers in a continuing enterprise are never unorganized. The formal hierarchy of workers may be organized into several competing or complementary organizations, such as works councils, unions, and parties.

The hierarchy of managers need have no relationship to the ownership of the captial assets of the work place; the managers may be public or private or a mixture in varying proportions. In the United States, for instance, consider the diverse character of management organizations in the executive departments of the federal government, local fire departments, the navy yards, the Tennessee Valley Authority, municipal transit operations and local

---

[6] Industrial Relations Systems reprinted with permission of publisher. © 1958 by Holt, Rinehart and Winston, Inc.

utilities, government-owned and privately operated atomic-energy plants, railroads and public utilities, and other private enterprises. The range of combinations is greater where governments own varying amounts of shares of an enterprise and where special developmental programs have been adopted. The management hierarchy in some cases may be contained within an extended or a narrow family, and its activities largely explained in terms of the family system of the society.

The specialized government agencies as actors may have functions in some industrial-relations systems so broad and decisive as to override the hierarchies of managers and workers on almost all matters. In other industrial-relations systems the role of the specialized governmental agencies, at least for many purposes, may be so minor or constricted as to permit consideration of the direct relationships between the two hierarchies without reference to governmental agencies, while in still other systems the worker hierarchy or even the managerial hierarchy may be assigned a relatively narrow role. But in every industrial-relations system these are the three actors.

NOTE:

(1) *Selected Bibliography:*

    American Assembly, Challenges to Collective Bargaining (1967)

    BNA, Collective Bargaining Today (1971)

    N. Chamberlain & J. Kuhn, Collective Bargaining (2d ed. 1965)

    U. Chi. Grad. School of Business, Collective Bargaining (Weber ed., 3d series 1961)

    H. Davey, Contemporary Collective Bargaining (2d ed. 1959)

(2) *Problems:*

(a) Which characteristics would you look at in a specific collective bargaining relationship in order to prepare for bargaining?

(b) What factors outside the employer-union relationship impact on the collective bargaining process?

(c) How would you expect these characteristics and outside factors to affect any agreement arising out of such a bargaining relationship?

B. INCIDENCE AND SCOPE OF BARGAINING

As indicated in the prior section, the term "collective bargaining" includes the negotiation, drafting, administration and interpretation of written agreements between employers and unions, or associations representing their employees, which set forth their joint understanding as to wages, hours and other terms and conditions of employment. The incidence of this process in our country establishes its significance. In 1976, some 175,000 labor agreements fixed wages, hours, job rights and other working conditions for approximately 24 million workers.[7] Although these workers represent slightly less than one-fourth of the total labor force and about 28 percent of all employees in non-agricultural establishments,[8] the impact of the agreements they work under extends beyond the workers covered. The extent of this influence can be seen by examining the pattern of union organization. Union membership totals are not necessarily identical with collective bargaining coverage, because not all workers in plants covered by contracts belong to a union and not all union members are governed by contract. However, the figures are close.[9] Despite the fact that only a minority of workers are union members, the impact of organization is significant because it is a substantial and powerful minority. In industry, for example, "trade unions are dominant in nearly all of the large plants and enterprises of the country — those where technology is most advanced, where capital is used most abundantly, where the productivity of labor is highest, and where technological progress is most rapid." [10] In addition, membership in the public sector continues to grow both proportionally and absolutely within the work force.[11] As the total of federal, state, and local government union and association membership grows, its effect on all of us who depend upon government services is apparent.[12]

1. Incidence

BUREAU OF LABOR STATISTICS NEWS RELEASE (LABOR DAY WEEKEND ED. 1978) [13]

Union and Association Membership

U. S. membership in labor organizations (excluding Canada) declined from 22.8 million in 1974 to 22.5 million in 1976 (table 2). As a proportion of the total labor force, membership declined by more than 1 percentage point between 1974 and 1976 continuing the long term decline that had been briefly reversed in 1974.

[7] U.S. Bureau of Labor Statistics, Dep't of Labor [hereinafter cited as B.L.S.] News Release #77-771 (Labor Day Weekend Ed. 1978).

[8] *Id.*

[9] B.L.S. Bull. No. 1596, Directory of National and International Labor Unions in the United States 69 (1968). *See also* B.L.S. Bull. No. 1596 (1975).

[10] S. Slichter, J. Healy & E. Livernash, The Impact of Collective Bargaining on Management 2 (1960) [hereinafter cited as Impact of Collective Bargaining].

[11] B.L.S. News Release #77-771, *supra* note 7.

[12] R. Smith, H. Edwards, & R. T. Clark, Jr., Labor Relations Law in the Public Sector 5-9 (1974).

[13] B.L.S. News Release #77-771, *supra* note 7.

Membership in the U.S. represented 23.2 percent of the labor force in 1976 and 28.3 percent of employment in nonagricultural establishments.

Table 2. U. S. union and association membership, 1970-76[1]

Year	Total membership (thousands)[1]	Total labor force		Employees in nonagricultural establishments	
		Number (thousands)	Percent union members	Number (thousands)	Percent union members
1970	21,248	85,903	24.7	70,920 [2]	30.0 [2]
1971	21,327	86,929	24.5	71,222 [2]	29.9
1972	21,657	88,991	24.3	73,714 [2]	29.4
1973	22,239	91,040	24.4	76,896 [2]	28.9
1974	22,809	93,240	24.5	78,413 [2]	29.1
1975	22,298	94,793	23.5	77,051	28.9
1976	22,463	96,917	23.2	79,443	28.3

[1] Membership includes total reported membership excluding Canada. Also included are members of directly affiliated local unions. Members of single-firm unions are excluded.
[2] Revised.

Membership in the public sector continued to increase with a 600,000 gain in State and local government, offsetting a 100,000 reduction in the number of Federal employees who belonged to labor organizations. As was true in earlier years, employee association members outnumbered union members at the State and local level.

Table 3. Union and association membership by employment sector, 1968-76[1]
(In thousands)

Year	Total	Private sector			Government	
		Manu-facturing	Nonmanu-facturing	Total	Federal [2]	State and local
Unions and Associations						
1968	22,015	9,218	8,940	3,857	1,391	2,466
1970	22,558	9,173	9,305	4,080	1,412	2,668
1972	23,059	8,920	9,619	4,520	1,383	3,137
1974	24,194	9,144	9,705	5,345	1,433	3,911
1976	24,036	8,463	9,721	5,853	1,332	4,521
Associations						
1968	1,805	0	103	1,702	–	1,702
1970	1,869	0	107	1,762	–	1,762
1972	2,221	0	161	2,060	–	2,060
1974	2,610	0	185	2,425	–	2,425
1976	3,031	0	188	2,843	–	2,843

[1] Includes membership outside the United States, except members of locals directly affiliated with the AFL-CIO.
[2] Fewer than 50,000 were in the Federal government.

Some 6.5 million union and association members were employed in white-collar occupations in 1976, a 579,000 member increase or about 10 percent. With the decrease in total membership of labor organizations, the proportion represented by white-collar members rose by 2.6 percentage points, to 26.9 percent. About three-fifths of all organized white-collar workers are members of unions.

The increasing number of women in labor organizations peaked in 1974 at slightly over 6 million or 25 percent of total membership. In 1976, women members of labor organizations declined by about 50,000 or 0.1 percent. This decline resulted from a 400,000 reduction in union rolls and a 350,000 gain in the number of new women members recruited by associations. Both constituted a significant proportion of the overall membership change in the two types of organizations: over two-thirds of the union loss and over four-fifths of the association increase.

. . .

Union Membership Developments

For the first time since the 1960-62 period, the U.S. membership of unions declined, by 767,000 or about 4 percent from 1974 to 1976. Much of this decline is a reflection of the state of the economy, particularly in manufacturing and construction in 1975 and 1976 where average production work employment declined by approximately 1.4 million workers. However, the labor force and overall nonagricultural employment continued to grow. Thus, the union penetration rate declined from 21.7 percent of the labor force in 1974 to 20.1 percent in 1976. The nonagricultural union penetration rate fell from 25.8 percent to 24.5 percent over the same period.

. . .

After an increase of more than 200,000 members in the U.S. and Canadian manufacturing industries between 1972 and 1974, total membership in the sector declined by 681,000 in 1976. This substantial decrease was somewhat offset by a small gain in nonmanufacturing industries and an 89,000 membership increment in government (table 6). Successful organizing drives at the State and local government levels increased membership by 181,000. Well over 100,000 of this gain was accounted for by American Federation of State, County, and Municipal Employees whose 1976 membership reached three-quarters of a million. Federal union membership declined by somewhat under 100,000.

Table 6. Union membership by employment sector, 1968-1976[1]

(in thousands)

| Year | Total | Private sector | | Government | | |
		Manu-facturing	Nonmanu-facturing	Total	Federal	State and local
1968	20,210	9,218	8,837	2,155	1,351	804
1970	20,689	9,173	9,198	2,318	1,370	947
1972	20,838	8,920	9,458	2,460	1,355	1,105
1974	21,585	9,144	9,520	2,920	1,391	1,529
1976	21,006	8,463	9,533	3,009	1,300	1,710

[1] Includes membership outside the United States, except members of locals directly affiliated with the AFL-CIO.

NOTE: Because of rounding, sums of individual items may not equal totals.

Between 1974 and 1976, union white-collar membership continued its long-term upward trend, increasing by 95,000 to almost 3.9 million or 18.4 percent of all members in 1976. In 1974, white-collar members constituted 17.4 percent of all members; in 1972, 16.5 percent.

After many years of growth, women union membership declined by 400,000 over the 2-year period. Women constituted 20.0 percent of all members in 1976, down from 21.3 percent in 1974 and 21.7 percent in 1972.

AFL-CIO affiliates reported 16.6 million members in 1976, compared with 16.9 million in 1974. The Federation represented 78 percent of all union members in 1976 and 1974, and 79 percent in 1972.

Unions with Largest Gains in Members over Decade

Eight national and international unions increased their membership by 100,000 or more in the past decade, in contrast to 14 organizations that achieved that increase between 1964-74 and 13 between 1962-72. The Teamsters union, which reported the largest increase in the 1964-74 decade, was replaced as the most successful recruiter of new members by the State, County, and Municipal Employees (469,000) and the Teachers (321,000) unions. Three other unions reported 200,000 or more new members: Teamsters, Steelworkers, and Service Employees. A 257 percent increase in the Teachers' rolls was considerably higher than the percent increase recorded by any other union, as was the case in the previous 10 years (table 7). Two unions, down from three between 1964-74, more than doubled their membership over the decade — State, County and Municipal Employees, and Teachers.

Twelve large unions, those with 100,000 members or more, reported membership losses over the decade.

Table 7. Unions that gained 100,000 members or more, 1966-76

Union	Membership (in thousands)			Increase 1966-76 [1]	
	1966	1974	1976	Number (in thousands)	Percent
State, County Employees	281	648	750	469	166.9
Teachers	125	444	446	321	256.8
Teamsters (Ind.)	1,651	1,973	1,889	238	14.4
Steelworkers	1,068	1,300	1,300	232	21.7
Service Employees	349	500	575	226	64.8
Retail Clerks	500	651	699	199	39.8
Communications Workers	321	499	483	162	50.0
Laborers	475	650	627	152	32.0

[1] Includes several unions where a portion of the membership gain was due to a merger with one or more other unions. Excludes merged unions where the membership of the smaller organization represented a significant proportion of the total and the combined membership did not increase 100,000.

NOTE:

Problems: The BLS statistics indicate that despite an increase in the total labor force (and overall nonagricultural employment), membership in unions declined about 4 percent from 1974 to 1976. BLS attributes "most of this decline . . . [to] the state of the economy, particularly in manufacturing and construction of 1975 and 1976, where average production work employment declined approximately 1.4 million workers." How did the state of the economy affect the collective bargaining process in these industries? What other factors contributed to the decline in these industries? Does this relate to the current political activities of the unions operating in these industries?

2. Scope of Collective Bargaining Agreements

In 1964, BLS began a comprehensive study of subject areas covered in collective bargaining agreements, and has published a number of pamphlets, known as the "Bulletin 1425 Series," indicating their findings.[14]

A tentative list of the subjects in the new series follows. The listing does not indicate an order or priority or the subjects to be studied as a group.

ESTABLISHMENT AND ADMINISTRATION OF THE AGREEMENT

* Arbitration and mediation (Bulletin #1425-6)
  Bargaining unit and plant supplements

---

[14] The Bulletin 1425 series on major collective bargaining agreements is available from the Superintendent of Documents, U.S. Government Printing Office, Washington, D.C. 20402.

* Pamphlets already published under Bulletin number.

Contract duration and reopening and renegotiation provisions
Contract enforcement
* Grievance procedures (Bulletin #1425-1)
Special bargaining committees
Strikes and lockouts
Union security and the checkoff

FUNCTIONS, RIGHTS, AND RESPONSIBILITIES

* Administration of seniority (Bulletin #1425-14)
Advance notice and consultation
* Management rights and union-management cooperation (Bulletin #1425-5)
* Plant movement, transfer and relocation allowances (Bulletin #1425-10)
Regulation of technological change
* Subcontracting (Bulletin #1425-8)
Union activities on company time and premises

WAGE DETERMINATION AND ADMINISTRATION

Allowances
* Deferred wage increases and escalation clauses (Bulletin #1425-4)
General provisions
* Hours, overtime and weekend work (Bulletin #1425-15)
Incentive systems and production bonus plans
Individual wage adjustments
Job classification and job evaluation
* Paid vacation and holiday provisions (Bulletin #1425-9)
Production standards and time studies
Rate structure and wage differentials

JOB OR INCOME SECURITY

* Administration of negotiated pensions, health and insurance plans (Bulletin #1425-12)
Attrition arrangements
Employment and income guarantees
Hiring and transfer arrangements
* Layoff, recall and worksharing procedures (Bulletin #1425-13)
Promotion practices
Regulation of overtime, shift work, etc.
Relocation allowances
Reporting and call-in pay
* Seniority in promotion and transfer provisions (Bulletin #1425-11)

---

* Pamphlets already published under Bulletin number.

* Severance pay and layoff benefit plans (Bulletin #1425-2)
Special funds and study committees
* Supplemental unemployment benefit plans (Bulletin #1425-3)
* Training and retraining provisions (Bulletin #1425-7)

The Bureau of National Affairs, Inc. (BNA) maintains a file of over 5,000 labor agreements from which they select a sample of 400 to utilize in their Collective Bargaining Negotiations and Contracts reporting service.[15] This looseleaf service provides sample contract provisions under the following major headings: [16]

Amendment and Duration
Discharge, Discipline, and Resignation
Insurance
Pensions
Grievances and Arbitration
Income Maintenance
Hiring — New Employees
Hours and Overtime
Holidays
Layoff, Rehiring, and Worksharing
Leave of Absence
Management and Union Rights
Promotion, Demotion, and Transfers
Recognition — Parties to Contract
Seniority
Strikes and Lockouts
Training and Apprenticeship
Union Security
Vacations
Wages, Working Conditions and Safety

Its sample indicates that as of 1973, 70 percent of all contracts have three-year terms, while one-year contracts represent only 5 percent (most of which are found in non-manufacturing industries), and two-year agreements account for 21 percent.[17] Three-year contracts predominate in all industries except petroleum, leather and utilities.[18] Reopening of collective bargaining agreements prior to their scheduled expiration date is allowed in 17 percent of the sample (as of 1973) to renegotiate wages, fringes, occurrences beyond the

---

* Pamphlets already published under Bulletin number.
[15] Two Vols., Collective Bargaining Negotiations and Contracts (BNA) [hereinafter cited as (vol.) C.B.N.C. (sec.) (date)].
[16] 2 C.B.N.C. § 32:i (5/22/75); for full index, see 2 C.B.N.C. § 32:11 (2/14/74).
[17] 2 C.B.N.C. § 36:1 (12/19/74).
[18] 2 C.B.N.C. § 36:2 (12/19/74).

control of the parties, and other subjects by mutual consent (in declining frequency by the order listed).[19]

Eighty-two percent of the contracts provide for extension past their expiration date unless action is taken to amend or terminate the agreements.[20] However, less than one-quarter of the sample provide for the exact status of a collective bargaining agreement when renewal negotiations extend beyond the expiration date.[21] The National Labor Relations Act (NLRA), as amended, requires parties to collective bargaining agreements to give 60 days notice of any intention to amend or terminate the agreement,[22] and failure to give such notice automatically renews most contracts under contract renewal provisions.

Joint study committees to facilitate contract renegotiations are found in only three percent of the sample of all collective bargaining agreements, but this is an increasing trend.[23] Furthermore, the Taft Hartley Amendment to the NLRA requires that the Federal Mediation and Conciliation Service (FMCS) and any state or territorial mediation services be informed of the existence of a dispute within 30 days after notice of renegotiation is served on either party if no agreement has been reached.[24] Such notice gives

---

[19] 2 C.B.N.C. § 36:3 (12/14/74).

[20] 2 C.B.N.C. § 36:4 (12/19/74).

[21] 2 C.B.N.C. § 36:5 (12/19/74).

[22] 29 U.S.C. 158, § 8:

 (d) For the purposes of this section, to bargain collectively is the performance of the mutual obligation of the employer and the representative of the employees to meet at reasonable times and confer in good faith with respect to wages, hours, and other terms and conditions of employment, or the negotiation of an agreement, or any question arising thereunder, and the execution of a written contract incorporating any agreement reached if requested by either party, but such obligation does not compel either party to agree to a proposal or require the making of a concession: Provided, That where there is in effect a collective-bargaining contract covering employees in an industry affecting commerce, the duty to bargain collectively shall also mean that no party to such contract shall terminate or modify such contract, unless the party desiring such termination or modification—
  (1) serves a written notice upon the other party to the contract of the proposed termination or modification sixty days prior to the expiration date thereof, or in the event such contract contains no expiration date, sixty days prior to the time it is proposed to make such termination or modification; . . . .

[23] 2 C.B.N.C. § 36:6 (12/19/74).

[24] 29 U.S.C. 158(d):

 (3) notifies the Federal Mediation and Conciliation Service within thirty days after such notice of the existence of a dispute, and simultaneously therewith notifies any State or Territorial agency established to mediate and conciliate disputes within the State or Territory where the dispute occurred, provided no agreement has been reached by that time; and . . . .

the government agency an opportunity (within 60 days after notice or expiration of the contract whichever occurs later) to mediate and conciliate the dispute before the parties can resort to strike or lockout.[25]

Almost one-quarter of BNA's sample agreements contain successorship provisions, which are clauses that provide that a change in management does not invalidate the contract and that the new management must assume the contractual obligations of its predecessor.[26]

NOTE:

Problem: The following clause was entered into in order to give an employer the most favorable terms given by the union to any employer:

> In the event the Union enters into any agreement with another employer or employers containing more favorable terms and/or conditions (including wage rates) than those contained herein, the Union agrees that such more favorable terms and conditions shall automatically be extended to employers covered by this agreement.

(a) Would you expect to find such a clause in a manufacturing or non-manufacturing industry? Why?

(b) What does the answer to the last question indicate about the use of sample contract provisions in different industrial contexts?

(c) Is there a practical reason to attempt to analyze a collective bargaining relationship for the purpose of proposing specific provisions in a collective bargaining contract?

C. ACHIEVEMENTS AND SHORTCOMINGS

It is difficult to disagree with Professor (and former U.S. Secretary of Labor) John Dunlop's conclusion that,

> In our industrial relations system, collective bargaining purports to accomplish three major functions: (a) it is a system to establish, revise and administer many of the rules of the work place; (b) it is a procedure to determine the compensation of employees and to influence the distribution of the economic pie;

---

[25] 29 U.S.C. 158(d):

> (4) continues in full force and effect, without resorting to strike or lockout, all the terms and conditions of the existing contract for a period of sixty days after such notice is given or until the expiration date of such contract, whichever occurs later: . . . .

[26] 2 C.B.N.C. § 36:6 (12/19/74).

(c) it is a method for dispute settlement during the life of agreements and on their expiration or reopening, before or after, resort to the strike or lockout. These are basic purposes which every industrial society and economy must somehow perform.[27]

However, this expectation seems to increase the ongoing argument of the achievements and shortcomings of the process in our industrial setting. Professor Dunlop analyzes the debate in the following manner:

The popular debate about collective bargaining has been conducted with reference to five main issues, or five groups of charges and defenses:

1. Strife vs. Peace — The charge is made that collective bargaining exhausts the parties and the community in strife and conflict. Unions are depicted as the most powerful organizations in the community in that they, and they alone, can deprive the community of essential goods and services.

The defense is made that the extent of strife in collective bargaining is declining, and there is even talk of the withering away of the strike. The average level of strike activity in the six years 1960-65, as a percentage of working time, was one-half the level of the preceding decade. The extent of violence in labor disputes has been very materially reduced over the past generation. The occasional withdrawal of services or a lockout is said to be inherent in the free market, a refusal to buy or sell. In fact, the community has never been seriously hurt by a work stoppage. The alternatives to collective bargaining are likely to prove of greater mischief to the community.

2. Economic Distortion vs. Standardized Competition — The detractors of collective bargaining contend that it leads to labor and management combining against the public interest. Producers combine to push up wages and prices against the interests of the consumer. Moreover, the allocation of resources in the economy is distorted so that there are too few workers at too high wages in organized sectors and too many workers at too low wages in sectors without collective bargaining. The national product for everyone is lower as a result.

The defenders argue that collective bargaining "takes wages out of competition" and compels employers to compete among each other on the basis of managerial efficiency rather than on their capacity to depress wage rates. It places competing employers on an equal basis and assures that competitors are confronted with the same price for labor services.

---

[27] Challenges to Collective Bargaining 169, *supra* note 1.

3. Disruptive Inflation vs. Plea of Not Guilty — Charles E. Lindblom wrote that "Unionism is not disruptive simply because it causes inflation and unemployment, for these are problems in a non-union economy as well. Rather it is disruptive because it will cause an amount of lasting unemployment or a degree of continuing inflation which will become so serious that the competitive price system will be abandoned in the search for remedies." The experience with incomes policies in Western countries suggests that free collective bargaining, full employment and a reasonable degree of price stability are incompatible.

The proponents of collective bargaining plead not guilty to the charge of constituting a significant independent influence creating inflation. The finger should be pointed rather to monetary or fiscal policy of governments or to high profits which may appropriately stimulate larger wage demands. The relative stability of labor costs in manufacturing over the past five or six years is cited to support this defense.

4. Stifle vs. Stimulate Management — The indictment is made that collective bargaining constricts management with a variety of artificial rules leading to excessive manning, inefficient operations and loss of prerogatives essential for an enterprise to grow and adapt in a dynamic economy. In the absence of collective bargaining management would be more efficient and productivity would grow faster. On the other hand, according to the late Sumner Slichter,

> Unions have greatly improved the management of American enterprises by accelerating the shift from personal management to management based upon policies and rules, and they have given the workers in industries the equivalent of civil rights. The strong upward pressure of unions on wages has been an important influence stimulating technological change and raising real wages — though other influences have been even more important.

Collective bargaining procedures facilitate orderly introduction of change.

5. Union Dictatorship vs. Industrial Democracy — The advent of the union at the work place is seen by its critics as installing an abritrary union boss over the members to replace the management boss over the employees. The union officer is depicted as having vast powers over the member in disposing of grievances and setting wages and other conditions of work.

Collective bargaining is described, in contrast, as the introduction of industrial democracy at the work place. Through elected representatives, the individual worker participates in the determination of wages and working conditions. Our labor organizations are among the most democratic of institutions in the society; indeed, they may be much too responsive to the immediate wishes of the rank and file on wage and technological displacement issues. The Landrum-Griffin law has accentuated these problems by making union officers even less willing to take unpopular positions with the rank and file.

. . .

These conflicting views on collective bargaining are not readily reconciled. There are no doubt individual collective bargaining relationships which can be found to fit each of the above conflicting categories. In a large country with more than 150,000 agreements diversity should not be surprising. Some of these pro's and con's arise from inherent conflicting tendencies within collective bargaining. Some tension and inner conflict is normal to institutions as well as to personalities. Some of these opposing appraisals involve appeals to contending social and economic values — price stability, economic growth, full employment, industrial peace, union democracy, distributional equity and freedom from government regulation. These goals are scarcely entirely compatible, and a degree of one can be achieved only at the price of giving up a degree of another. Finally, some of the popular views sketched in apposition are simply in error or are gross oversimplifications.

It is perhaps foolhardy for anyone to state an over-all appraisal in capsule form. Professor Slichter once put it this way:

> Our system . . . gives the American worker better protection of his day-to-day interests than is received by workers anywhere else; it puts American employers under greater pressure than the employers of any other country to raise productivity; and, though it gives unions a wonderful opportunity to whipsaw employers, it gives employers a freedom to bargain which they like and for which they seem willing to pay a big price. Hence, we seem justified in being grateful that we have been favored by fortune and perhaps also in taking modest pride that we have pursued opportunist policies with considerable flexibility and good sense.

My own summary appraisal would state that our collective bargaining system must be classified as one of the more successful distinctive American institutions along with the family farm, our higher educational system and constitutional government of checks and balances. The industrial working class has been assimilated into the mainstream of the community, and has altered to a degree the values and direction of the community, without disruptive conflict or alienation and with a stimulus to economic efficiency. This is no mean achievement in an industrial society. The institution faces, however, new challenges in the generation ahead; discussion considers these questions in a final section.[28]

. . .

R. Heath Larry, President of the National Association of Manufacturers (formerly top executive with United States Steel Corporation), characterizes these challenges from management's standpoint as follows:

... [I]n terms of the basic competitive struggle between employers and unions over "how much," and the establishment of a balance of power consistent with the nation's need to alleviate a growing inflationary bias in our economy, the law relating to these central aspects of the bargaining process is both ambivalent and contradictory.

These characterizations are evidenced in several ways. In the first place, at the very time that the public and the Congress first became concerned about the abuses of labor power, and were translating that concern into the provisions of the Taft-Hartley Act, Congress had just taken action which was destined to add immeasurably to the power of unions in their pursuit of higher wages. Just months before it acted on the Taft-Hartley Act, Congress adopted the Employment Act of 1946.[38] This Act committed the government to the pursuit of full employment without a corollary commitment to currency and price stability. The increasing practice of the Keynesian concepts of looser fiscal and monetary policies to support high demand [39] began to erode the earlier potential for periodically rising unemployment which acted as an economic brake upon employees' aspirations and union power. One cannot philosophically be against full employment. But, so long as this Act continues to reflect the economic and social policy of the United States, the economic scenario which was the justification for the Wagner Act's change in the power balance will never again return.[40]

---

[28] *Id.* at pp. 170-72.

[38] 15 U.S.C. §§ 1021-25 (1970).

[39] While John Maynard Keynes was primarily an economic theoretician rather than an economic advocate, his writings have often been cited as the rationale for using fiscal and monetary policies to achieve a continued high level of employment. He outlined his theories in a book entitled, The General Theory of Employment, Interest and Money, published in 1936. Keynes' theories are often contrasted with those of earlier laissez-faire or classical economists such as Adam Smith and David Ricardo.

[40] So long as the government is committed to maintaining full employment, the vast unemployment, with the corresponding decrease in the price that labor can

Secondly, the public seems to support the continued existence of a number of conditions which virtually equate the right to strike with the right to win the strike. These conditions accord strikers such a degree of economic amnesty from the consequences of their strike so as to virtually insure an uneven contest.[41] Inevitably these conditions support an inflationary bias. Yet the public occasionally becomes so concerned with the impact of bargaining upon employment costs and prices that our lawmakers claim to find broad support for price and wage controls [42] despite the fact that such controls are invariably pronounced disastrous in terms of the distortions which they impose upon the economy.

Thirdly, when some of our lawmakers are not busy thinking about impaling the competitive market system upon a reconstituted fence of wage and price controls, they speculate about the potential for lower prices through increased market competition, something they apparently believe can come about by breaking up "large" corporations.[43] Yet, they address little attention to the other side of the equation where the principal cost pressures arise. "Big" unions, permitted by law to span entire industries, whose avowed purpose is to keep the wages and working conditions of employees out of competition, and whose power enables them to ratchet nominal wages even higher, regardless of competition and regardless of what happens to productivity trends, are rarely considered for such drastic action.

The need to resolve this ambivalence is becoming critical. The nation can no longer continue to absorb the impact of major settlements which embody a significant inflationary bias. Nor can

---

demand for its services, that occurred during the depression will probably never be approached again.

[41] Under the National Labor Relations Act, 29 U.S.C. §§ 158(a)(1), (a)(3) (1970), an employer is prohibited from discharging an employee who engages in a strike. In NLRB v. Mackay Radio & Tel. Co., 304 U.S. 333 (1938), the Supreme Court ruled that an employer may "replace" a striker with another employee and refuse to discharge the replacement at the end of the strike to make room for the striker. The employer's replacement right has been increasingly restricted. E.g., NLRB v. Fleetwood Trailer Co., 389 U.S. 375 (1967); NLRB v. Erie Resistor Corp., 373 U.S. 221 (1963); Mastro Plastics Corp. v. NLRB, 350 U.S. 270 (1956). In addition to the legal protection referred to above, the striking employee may be eligible for economic assistance at the public expense in the form of welfare benefits, food stamps, and unemployment compensation. E.g., Carney, The Forgotten Man on the Welfare Roll: A Study of Public Subsidies for Strikers, 1973 WASH. U.L.Q. 469.

[42] See, e.g., Economic Stabilization Act of 1970, 12 U.S.C. § 1904 note (1970) (now expl. d).

[43] See, e.g., The Industrial Reorganization Act, S. 1167, 93d Cong., 1st Sess. (1973).

it continue to absorb the impact of strikes which enforce inflationary demands and which interrupt the operations of a major segment of our interrelated economy for any period of time, thereby limiting the supply of goods while attempting to increase the supply of consumer money chasing these goods.

. . .

There can be no question that during our current surge of inflation we have suffered from many other pressures which have simultaneously flooded us — the delayed impact of having failed to tax during the Vietnam period as if we were really at war; the delayed impact of the years during which our exchange rates vis-à-vis Europe and Japan were misaligned; the delayed impact of too many years in which emphasis had been placed upon consumer incomes and spending at the expense of savings and capital expansion; the impact of the decisions of some less-developed countries to change the relative values between their energy and other raw materials and our finished goods; the impact of certain misconceived grain transactions upon the whole gambit of food prices, and so on. Nevertheless, it must be recognized that as the shock waves of these rising prices become integrated into the permanent cost structure of our economy through their reflection in wage costs, those wage costs cannot escape accepting a certain portion of the responsibility for even today's multifaceted inflation.

Cost-of-living clauses applicable to employees' wages and benefits may be politically understandable but they are economically insidious. Unless they are applied to virtually all other income accounts, including rents, interests, dividends, etc., the capital foundation of the economy can become seriously weakened. Shortages will emerge, and prices will be further driven up by demand exceeding supply.[50] The point is this: whenever hourly employment costs rise faster than output per man-hour, no matter what the reason, they add to unit labor costs and hence to rising pressures on prices. They have done so in all but two of the last twenty-two years, with an inescapable inflationary impact.[51] We must not forget that employment

---

[50] The practice of inserting cost-of-living clauses into a collective bargaining agreement is generally referred to as "indexing," and denotes a type of inflation accounting by which the "real" value of all types of income is readjusted and realigned in relation to some specific index, such as the cost-of-living, wholesale price or some other index chosen by the government.

[51] U.S. Bureau of Labor Statistics, Dep't of Labor, as published in Council of Economic Advisors, Economic Report of the President Transmitted to the Congress February, 1974, at 287.

costs constitute seventy-five to eighty percent of *all* costs for finished goods and services in our economy.[52]

. . .

This emphasis upon the impact of labor is never very popular politically, and this is a political world. There is, therefore, a natural tendency to reach for remedies which do not confront labor's impact head on. Yet, given the multiple contributing causes and deep roots of today's inflation, treating it mainly by use of the traditional monetary and fiscal tools will simply hasten a recession or depression of sufficient magnitude to risk a complete political and social upheaval. Certain other institutions, including particularly collective bargaining, simply must produce less in the way of upward cost pressures than they have in the past. The motivation to find answers may lie in the fact that our failure to deal with inflation will produce the same risk of political and social upheaval, but for different reasons.[60] We are, therefore, driven to ask whether a sufficient showing of responsibility can reasonably be expected of the parties under the law as it now exists; and, if not, what changes in the law could be effective in dealing with either the problem of strikes, or inflation.

. . .

Thirty years ago, Philip Murray, the astute and powerful first president of the United Steel Workers, acknowledged that the use of raw power of unions in pursuit of the chase was really futile, because the setting of wages was really an economic function; *i.e.,* that the value of wages would be inseparable from the country's rate of productivity growth.[71] Somehow over the years we have lost the message. Yet the data accumulated over the decades since he wrote have continued to bear him out. Whether wages in nominal dollars have increased much or little, the line tracing output per man-hour has almost exactly

---

[52] National Income and Product Tables appearing in U.S. Dep't of Commerce, Survey of Current Business, September, 1974, at 89.

[60] Many influential persons from South America, including Pedro Beltrans, former editor of La Prensa, pled with the United States to realize, before it is too late, the insidious problems which go with a long-continued inflation. We have, of course, seen government after government fall, throughout South America, because of the problem.

[71] Over two decades ago, Philip Murray participated in the writing of a book in which the following enlightened statements appear:

The employees and their union representatives must realize that the determination of wages and conditions of work is an economic function and not an arbitrary process dependent upon the exercise of sheer power.

M. Cooke & P. Murray, Organized Labor & Procedure 188 (1940).

paralleled the line tracing real compensation per man-hour in the total private economy.[72]

The lesson is simple, yet hard to learn. We can only pay ourselves what we produce. An effort to do more turns out in the long run to be illusory and inflationary. And worse, when the productivity curve falls flat, as it has recently, while the number of people keeps growing, there is no way we can avoid a relative decline in living standards. Likewise, when the scarcity of goods drives prices up, there is no way by which adding to consumer incomes (wages) can maintain purchasing power or help to bring forth more goods at lower prices.[29]

NOTE:

Problem: What new collective bargaining systems have you read, or heard about which attempt to minimize disruption, economic distortion and/or the deprivation of individual rights? What do these attempts indicate about the flexibility of the process?

---

[72]   OUTPUT PER MAN-HOUR AND REAL COMPENSATION
          PER MAN HOUR, TOTAL PRIVATE ECONOMY, 1950-70
INDEX 1950 = 100
RATIO SCALE

[29] Larry, "Inflation, Labor and Law," 13 Duquesne L. Rev. 203, 211-13, 217-18, 223-24, (1974). Reprinted with permission of publisher; © 1974.

Chapter 2

THE LEGAL FRAMEWORK OF COLLECTIVE BARGAINING *

The statutory basis of the mutual obligation to bargain in good faith arises out of the National Labor Relations Act.[1] Section 8(a)(5) makes it an unfair labor practice for an employer to refuse to bargain collectively with the representative(s) of its employees; Section 8(b)(3) makes a union guilty of an unfair labor practice for refusing to bargain collectively with an employer whose employees it represents. Read together, Sections 8(a)(5), 8(b)(3) and 8(d) of the Act as amended provide the basis from which the legal framework of collective bargaining is established through the administrative law process of the National Labor Relations Board (NLRB).[2]

The Wagner Act of 1935 created the NLRB, the five-member adjudicatory body that enforces the law. Since an unjustified refusal to bargain is an alleged violation under Section 8 of the Act, the Board adjudicates such charges in unfair labor proceedings. These

---

* Ms. Linda E. Rosenzweig, who received both her J.D. and LL.M. degrees from the National Law Center of the George Washington University and who is currently at the National Labor Relations Board, Washington, D.C., prepared the initial draft of Chapter 2, at the request of the authors.

[1] 49 Stat. 435 (1935), as amended by 61 Stat. 141 (1947), 29 U.S.C. § 152 *et seq.* (1970). Many states have enacted labor relations statutes which govern the employer-union-employee relationship. In this casebook, however, examination of the legal framework will be focused on federal law. More specifically, the discussion will deal with the law that has evolved under the National Labor Relations Act as amended. The regulation of employment relations in the railroad and interstate air carrier industries are covered by the Railway Labor Act, 45 U.S.C. § 151 *et seq.* (1970), which is beyond the scope of these materials.

[2] Section 8(d), 29 U.S.C. § 158(d), provides that "[f]or the purposes of this section to bargain collectively is the performance of the mutual obligation of the employer and the representative of the employees to meet at reasonable times and confer in good faith with respect to wages, hours, and other terms and conditions of employment, or the negotiation of an agreement, or any question arising thereunder, and the execution of a written contract incorporating any agreement reached if requested by either party, but such obligation does not compel either party to agree to a proposal or require the making of a concession; . . . ."

Section 8(a)(5), 29 U.S.C. § 158(a)(5) provides: It shall be an unfair labor practice for an employer to refuse to bargain collectively with the representatives of his employees. . . .

Section 8(b)(3), 29 U.S.C. § 158(b)(3) provides: It shall be an unfair labor practice for a labor organization or its agents to refuse to bargain collectively with an employer. . . .

For a thorough study of the legislative development of the duty to bargain, *see* Smith, The Evolution of the "Duty to Bargain" Concept in American Law, 39 Mich. L. Rev. 1065, 1107-08 (1941).

arise when a charge is filed against an employer or union alleging a violation of this duty, and an investigation of the charge results in the issuance of a complaint by the Board's Regional Director. A hearing is thereafter held before an Administrative Law Judge who prepares a decision, which includes findings of fact, conclusions of law and a recommended order. If no exceptions are filed, the Board adopts the Administrative Law Judge's decision. If exceptions are filed, the Board will consider the case on the record. If the Board finds by a "preponderance of the testimony" that an unfair labor practice has been committed, it issues a cease-and-desist order, accompanied by other appropriate action. Since the Board's order is not self-enforcing, the Board can seek an enforcement order from a United States court of appeals if the party against whom the order is issued does not comply. The aggrieved party can also ask for judicial review. A final possibility exists for review by the United States Supreme Court upon petition for writ of certiorari.

The rules and decisions arising from this administrative process fill in the interstices of the statute, and together constitute the legal framework. Obviously, Congress recognized the need for flexibility in a constantly changing arena of labor-management relations, since it provided the parties with only a sketchy guideline for the duty it imposed. In *Pine Industrial Relations Comm., Inc.,*[3] the Board acknowledged that its role is not to establish ideal bargaining conditions, but rather, to determine whether parties are meeting their obligation to bargain in good faith. And, indeed Congress made clear in Section 8(d) that the Board's authority would not extend to forcing the parties either to agree to proposals or to make concessions. The purpose of this Chapter is to present the issues that arise from the obvious tension created by the tenuous but significant distinction between the duty to meet at reasonable times and confer in good faith, and the absence of legal compulsion to agree or concede to anything.

The minimum requirements as well as the boundaries of the parties' duty to bargain — how the duty to bargain arises ("majority rule"), how the parties must approach the bargaining table ("in good faith"), when they are obligated to negotiate ("at reasonable times"), over what matters the parties are required to ("mandatory"), permitted to ("permissive"), or proscribed from ("illegal") bargaining, and what specific conduct is regarded as unlawful — creates the need to strike a delicate balance in order to satisfy the Act.

---

[3] 118 NLRB 1055, 1061 (1957).

A. HOW THE DUTY ARISES

The concept of exclusive representation is fundamental to the legal framework of collective bargaining.[4] The employer's obligation to bargain does not mature until a labor organization makes a clear request for negotiations and a majority of the employees in an "appropriate bargaining unit"[5] demonstrates their desire to be represented by that organization for purposes of collective bargaining. Section 9(c) of the Act authorizes the NLRB to conduct secret-ballot elections for workers who seek certification of a union. The Act, however, does not require a union to utilize a particular procedure to establish its majority support, and proof of majority status may be established by: stipulation between the parties, cross-check on union membership cards, membership lists, or polling workers. An employer may voluntarily recognize and bargain with a union if, independent of a Board-conducted election, it has knowledge of the union's majority status.

The appropriateness of an employer's acceptance or rejection of a union's claim that it has attained majority status may be tested in an unfair labor practice proceeding before the NLRB. An employer may lawfully insist that a union establish its majority status in an NLRB election and certification if the employer has good faith doubt of the union's claim of majority support. If an employer is found to have erred in its decision regarding recognition, a remedial order requiring the employer to conduct itself properly will issue; but if it has acted in good faith,[6] no other penalty will be assessed.

---

[4] Section 9(a), 29 U.S.C. § 159(a) (1970) provides:

Representatives designated or selected for the purposes of collective bargaining by the majority of the employees in a unit appropriate for such purposes, shall be the exclusive representatives of all the employees in such unit for the purposes of collective bargaining in respect to rates of pay, wages, hours of employment, or other conditions of employment: *Provided,* That any individual employee or a group of employees shall have the right at any time to present grievances to their employer and to have such grievances adjusted, without the intervention of the bargaining representative, as long as the adjustment is not inconsistent with the terms of a collective-bargaining contract or agreement then in effect: *Provided* further, That the bargaining representative has been given opportunity to be present at such adjustment.

[5] In representation cases presented to the NLRB, the Board must determine: (1) what is an appropriate unit of employees for bargaining purposes; and (2) whether the majority of the unit employees desire to be represented by a labor organization, and if so, which organization. Numerous factors are considered in determining the appropriate bargaining unit, which is a subject area beyond the scope of these materials. *See* Smith, Merrifield and St. Antoine, *Labor Relations Law* 227-46 (5th ed. 1974).

[6] However, whether an employer's refusal to bargain was in good faith comes into question only if the bargaining representative occupied majority status when it sought the employer's recognition. NLRB v. Heck's, Inc., 386 F.2d 317 (4th Cir. 1967).

A union may establish an employer's obligation to bargain with it by yet another means — the unfair labor practice proceeding — and be certified. While authorization cards have not been consistently viewed with approval as a reliable basis for the issuance of bargaining orders,[7] the Supreme Court in *NLRB v. Gissel Packing Co.*[8] approved the use of the cards where the employer has committed an unfair labor practice.

NOTES:

(1) The *Gissel* doctrine was further refined by the Board in *Steel-Fab, Inc.*, 212 NLRB 363 (1974) and *Trading Post, Inc.*, 219 NLRB No. 76 (1975). In *Steel-Fab* the NLRB held that a *Gissel* bargaining order may issue even absent a finding of a section 8(a)(5) duty to bargain violation, where an employer's acts, violative of section 8(a)(3), is so serious that a fair election seems unlikely. In *Trading Post*, the Board held that it had the authority to issue retroactive bargaining orders which relate back to the date of which the union presented authorization cards and demanded recognition.

In *Pinter Bros.*, 227 NLRB 921 (1977), a decision applying the *Gissel* doctrine, the Board approved of the combination of election ballots and of authorization cards from employees who either didn't vote or whose ballot had been challenged.

(2) Should the NLRB certify as the exclusive bargaining agent a union which had engaged in past discriminatory practices on the basis of race or sex? *See Handy Andy, Inc.*, 228 NLRB 447 (1977), and *Bell & Howell*, 213 NLRB 407 (1974), *infra*, Chapter 18 at —.

(3) In *Linden Lumber Div. v. NLRB*, 419 U.S. 301 (1974), the Supreme Court held that, unless an employer has committed an unfair labor practice that impairs the electoral process, it cannot be required to bargain without an election. The Court further held that the burden is on the union to go forward and invoke the Board's election procedure. However, a bargaining order will issue, absent an election, where an employer obtains independent knowledge of the union's majority status or agrees to an alternative means of ascertaining employees' support of the union.

(4) *Problems:* (a) Does an employer have a duty to bargain with a duly certified bargaining agent if, shortly after the election which resulted in certification, the Union loses a majority of employees from its membership? *See e.g., Brooks v. NLRB,* 348 U.S. 96 (1954).

(b) What quantum of proof must be presented by an employer to

---

[7] *See* NLRB v. Joy Silk Mills, Inc., 185 F.2d 732 (D.C. Ct. App. 1950), *cert. denied,* 341 U.S. 914 (1951). *But see* Aiello Dairy Farms Co., 110 NLRB 1365 (1954), reversing Bernel Foam Products Inc., 146 NLRB 1277 (1964).

[8] 395 U.S. 575 (1969).

demonstrate a union's loss of support? May subjective evidence be relied on to bolster objective facts tending to show lack of majority support? *Retired Persons Pharmacy v. NLRB,* 519 F.2d 486 (2d Cir. 1975); *Hirsh v. Pick-Mt. Laurel Corp.,* 436 F. Supp. 1342 (D.N.J. 1977).

B. HOW IT IS CARRIED OUT

1. Elements of Good Faith

Section 8(d) of the NLRA requires both the employer and the exclusive bargaining agent of its employees to meet and bargain over "wages, hours and other terms and conditions of employment" — those matters which vitally affect the working conditions of employees. Although Section 8(d) further provides that the bargaining obligation imposed by the Act does not require the parties to agree to any proposal or to make a concession, it does obligate the parties to bargain in "good faith." As Professor Cox so aptly notes, the obligation to bargain collectively would be meaningless absent the qualifying term "good faith."

COX, "THE DUTY TO BARGAIN IN GOOD FAITH," 71 Harv. L. Rev. 1401, 1412-15 (1958)

It was not enough for the law to compel the parties to meet and treat without passing judgment upon the quality of the negotiations. The bargaining status of a union can be destroyed by going through the motions of negotiating almost as easily as by bluntly withholding recognition. The NLRB reports are filled with cases in which a union won an election but lacked the economic power to use the strike as a weapon for compelling the employer to grant it real participation in industrial government. As long as there are unions weak enough to be talked to death, there will be employers who are tempted to engage in the forms of collective bargaining without the substance.

The concept of "good faith" was brought into the law of collective bargaining as a solution to this problem. One who merely went through the outward motions knowing that they were a sham could be said to lack good faith and held to violate section 8(5) despite the formal appearances. . . . [T]he duty to bargain in good faith is an "obligation . . . to participate actively in the deliberations so as to indicate a present intention to find a basis for agreement . . . ." Not only must the employer have "an open mind and a sincere desire to reach an agreement" but "a sincere effort must be made to reach a common ground." [49]

---

[49] *Id.* at 686, quoting in part from NLRB v. Reed & Prince Mfg. Co., 118 F.2d 874, 885 (1st Cir.), *cert. denied,* 313 U.S. 595 (1941).

The books abound with similar statements.[50] In making them both the NLRB and the courts were seeking primarily to advance the policies of protecting unions and compelling recognition. In order to distinguish the real from the sham they established a subjective test making the employer's state of mind the decisive factor. So much is clear. The difficult problem is to identify the state of mind precisely. Such phrases as "present intention to find a basis for agreement" and "sincere effort ... to reach common ground" suggest that willingness to compromise is an essential ingredient of good faith. The inference becomes even stronger when the phrases are read against the background of the old National Labor Relations Board opinions which assert the duty "to match their proposals, if unacceptable, with counter-proposals; and to make every reasonable effort to reach an agreement." [51] A man may wish to negotiate an agreement provided that his terms are met but be quite unwilling to compromise; or he may be so anxious to reach an agreement that he is willing to accept whatever terms he can get. Which state of mind — which of all the intermediate states of mind — is necessary to bargain "in good faith" ?

Congress, in creating the duty to bargain in good faith, failed to clearly define the term "good faith." As a minimum, it would seem that the Act proscribes a superficial pretense at negotiating — often called "sham" or "surface" bargaining — which, when engaged in by an employer, essentially denies recognition to a union. Manifestations of such activity may be subtle and hard to detect. Further, a more difficult problem is presented by the fact that a finding that a party lacked good faith may necessitate the delving into the mind of the negotiating party.

Absent a statutory definition of "good faith" it is necessary to look to the National Labor Relations Board and the courts for guidance. Over the years they have attempted to provide insight as to what Congress intended in requiring the parties to bargain in "good faith," while at the same time eschewing anything more than minimal governmental intrusion into the negotiation process.

What is good faith bargaining? The Board has described the test as "dependent in part upon how a reasonable man might be expected to react to the bargaining attitude displayed by those across the

---

[50] See, *e.g.*, NLRB v. Boss Mfg. Co., 118 F.2d 187, 189 (7th Cir. 1941) ("Collective bargaining requires that the parties involved deal with each other with an open and fair mind and sincerely endeavor to overcome obstacles or difficulties existing between the employer and the employees . . . ."); Globe Cotton Mills v. NLRB, 103 F.2d 91, 94 (5th Cir. 1939) ("[T]here is a duty on both sides, though difficult of legal enforcement, to enter into discussion with an open and fair mind, and a sincere purpose to find a basis of agreement . . . .").

[51] Houde Engineering Corp., 1 N.L.R.B. (old) 35 (1934).

table." [9] To fulfill the statutory duty, a party must demonstrate more than a "willingness to enter upon a sterile discussion of union-management differences." [10] Rather, it requires an attitude of "sincerity, candor, and [a] willingness to negotiate toward the possibility of effecting compromises and does not connote stubbornness." [11] Thus, when an employer approaches the bargaining table with a mind "hermetically sealed" [12] against the thought of reaching an agreement, it fails to satisfy its duty under the Act.

2. Indicia of Bad Faith

a. Hard Bargaining

Is it easier and more objective for the Board to determine whether a party has bargained in bad faith? Is this approach to the regulation of good faith bargaining appropriate under the Act? *See e.g., NLRB v. Pacific Grinding Wheel Co.,* 98 LRRM 2246 (9th Cir. 1978).

The legislative history behind the Wagner Act indicates major Congressional concern over the NLRB's involvement in the substantive matters of bargaining. Nonetheless, the "good faith" concept often leads the Board to an examination not only of the mechanics of bargaining, but of the substance of the discussion between the parties. It has been held that under certain circumstances the content of the various proposals and counterproposals of the negotiating parties may be relevant as evidence of lack of good faith.[13] For example, where either party makes patently unreasonable demands which do not have the slightest chance of acceptance and look like fictitious bargaining, this may provide a foundation for the Board finding that party guilty of bad faith.[14] However, it is a mistake to assume that the Board or the courts will find an unfair labor practice solely from an examination of the substantive proposals. The Board negated such a possibility in the *Dierks Forests* case by holding:

> Admittedly, the Respondent here engaged in a course of "hard bargaining" and, as noted by the Trial Examiner, the Union was

---

[9] Times Publishing Co., 72 NLRB 676, 682-83 (1947).
[10] NLRB v. American National Ins. Co., 343 U.S. 395, 402 (1952).
[11] NLRB v. General Corp., 354 F.2d 625, 628 (7th Cir. 1965).
[12] NLRB v. Boss Mfg. Co., 118 F.2d 187, 189 (7th Cir. 1941).
[13] *See, e.g.,* Majure v. NLRB, 198 F.2d 735 (5th Cir. 1952) (employer refused to consider specific requests for increased compensation); NLRB v. Century Cement Mfg. Co., 208 F.2d (2d Cir. 1953) (refusal to consider seniority promotions); White v. NLRB, 255 F.2d 564 (5th Cir. 1958) (absence of concessions must be accompanied by other acts).
[14] *See, e.g.,* Vanderbilt Products Inc. v. NLRB, 297 F.2d 833 (2d Cir. 1961).

disappointed when it made concessions but failed to receive a *quid pro quo* from Respondents. But the Board has been admonished by the Supreme Court that it may not "either directly or indirectly compel concessions or otherwise sit in judgment upon the terms of collective bargaining agreements." [15]

Moreover, the Board has acknowledged that "there comes a point in any negotiations where the positions of the parties are set and beyond which they will not go." [16] This affirms the right to make a final offer at a subsequent stage of negotiations even though the company engages in "non-coercive and factual communications" to the employees.

During negotiations in 1960 with the International Union of Electrical, Radio and Machine Workers, AFL-CIO (IUE), the General Electric Company employed a bargaining technique commonly known as "Boulwareism," after Lemuel R. Boulware, a former GE vice-president who first developed it. After a contract was signed by both parties, IUE filed unfair labor practice charges with the NLRB. In *General Electric Co.,*[17] the Board agreed with the Administrative Law Judge's findings that GE had not bargained in good faith thereby violating Sections 8(a)(1) and 8(a)(5), as evidenced by (1) its failure to furnish certain information requested by the union during contract negotiations; (2) its attempts at solicitation of locals to deal separately with the company and refrain from supporting the strike; (3) its presentation of the insurance proposal on a "take-it-or-leave-it" basis; and (4) *its overall approach to and conduct of bargaining.*

At the outset the company presented the union with a "fair, firm offer," with the understanding that nothing was being withheld for later trading. G.E. represented that its offer would be modified only if new facts were disclosed. The proposal was subsequently "marketed" to G.E.'s employees and the general public, emphasizing the company's policy of firmness.

The U.S. Court of Appeals in *NLRB v. General Electric Co.*[18] found that by employing this combination of bargaining strategy and communications, G.E. "in effect painted itself into a corner of

---

[15] Dierks Forests, Inc., 148 N.L.R.B. 923 (1964); *see also* H.K. Porter Co. v. NLRB.

[16] Philip Carey Mfg. Co., Miami Cabinet Div. v. NLRB, 331 F.2d 720 (6th Cir. 1964). *See also* American Aggregate Co., 125 N.L.R.B. 96 (1959), *enforced,* 285 F.2d 529 (5th Cir. 1960), *contempt proceedings dismissed,* 335 F.2d 253 (5th Cir. 1964).

[17] 150 NLRB 192 (1964).

[18] 418 F.2d 736 (2d Cir. 1969), *cert. denied,* 397 U.S. 985 (1970), *rehearing denied,* 397 U.S. 1059 (1970).

unbending firmness on all bargaining matters." [19] The majority concluded that the company's overall approach to negotiations violated its duty to bargain in good faith.

Although the distinction between the "frozen position" theory predicated in the *General Electric* case and "hard bargaining" seems conceptually sound, its use is deceptive. If this means that either party is proscribed from taking a "frozen position" prior to the commencement of serious negotiations but may do so during negotiations, it is subject to the challenge of "game playing." If, however, the policy behind this distinction is to move the parties one step further toward reasoned negotiation without controlling the substance of their proposals, unless patently unreasonable, it may be justified. Under the latter approach, the Board's rule of good faith bargaining in the *General Electric* case may be viewed as proscribing techniques that are inherently destructive of meaningful interchange. However, the lines drawn are difficult to apply.

b. The "Totality of Conduct"

Scrutiny of the "totality of conduct" engaged in by a party is the well-ensconced standard utilized to determine the quality of the party's negotiations. Although specific conduct may not by itself violate sections 8(a)(5) or 8(b)(3), an evaluation of the entire course of bargaining conduct may support an inference of bad faith.[20] Consider the following case. It is an example of a thorough examination of an employer's total course of bargaining in the context of an unfair labor practice proceeding. Distill a "totality of conduct" test from the case.

NLRB v. TOMCO COMMUNICATIONS, INC.

United States Court of Appeals Ninth Circuit
567 F.2d 871 (1978)

Burns, District Judge.
In this application for enforcement, the National Labor Relations Board (the Board) represents the charging party, the United Electrical, Radio, and Machine Workers of America, Local 1412 (the Union), against Tomco Communications, Inc. (the Company).

---

[19] The Court stated, however, that:
    We do not today hold an employer may not communicate with his employees during negotiations. Nor are we deciding that the "best offer first" bargaining technique is forbidden. Moreover, we do not require an employer to engage in "auction bargaining," or, as the dissent seems to suggest, compel him to make concessions, "minor" or otherwise. . . . 418 F.2d at 762.
[20] *See* Continental Insurance Co. v. NLRB, 495 F.2d 44 (2d Cir. 1974), *enforcing* 204 NLRB 1013 (1973).

The Board found that the Company had violated § 8(a)(5) and (1) of the National Labor Relations Act (the Act), 29 U.S.C. § 158(a)(5) and (1), by failing to bargain in good faith; and § 8(a)(3) and (1) of the Act, 29 U.S.C. § 158(a)(3) and (1), by locking out Union members to enhance its unlawful bargaining position and to discourage their support of the Union.

Pursuant to these findings, the Board ordered the Company to cease and desist from discouraging membership in the Union by locking out employees in support of an unlawful bargaining position, to bargain collectively, to offer reinstatement and reimbursement for consequential loss of wages suffered by the locked out employees, and to post notices and preserve evidence of compliance. The Board's decision is reported at 220 N.L.R.B. 636, 90 L.R.R.M. 1321 (1975).

. . .

FACTS

The Company is a manufacturer of electronic components in Mountain View, California. On November 2, 1973, following a Board-conducted election, the Union was certified as the collective bargaining representative of the Company's nine production and maintenance employees.

Beginning on November 9, 1973, the Company and the Union met in negotiations for a collective bargaining agreement. The Company was represented principally by Charles Goldstein, an attorney in a law firm it had retained, the Union by Paul Chown, an international representative of the Union. It was agreed that the negotiators would indicate any accords reached by initialling the appropriate draft provision, but that the entire contract would not become effective until . atified by the Union's membership and Company directors.

The Union submitted a proposed contract for discussion. No agreement was reached on any of its 25 articles. However, Goldstein did set forth the Company's responsive position on each proposal. He also recommended that bargaining on economic issues generally be deferred until the next meeting, when he promised to return with a management counter-proposal. This Company draft became the basis of negotiations at all subsequent meetings.

Chown and Goldstein met again on December 5 and 6. On the first day they discussed the Company's proposed draft and reached tentative agreement on six items — discharges (in which the Company gave up incorporation of a list of specific acts to be deemed just cause); bulletin boards (in which the Union agreed to a requirement that Union notices be approved by management); seniority; recognition; non-discrimination; and military leave. Further discussions, but no further agreements, took place on December 6.

By the end of this second session, the parties had sufficiently disclosed their positions to reveal the major issues on which they never agreed. Goldstein indicated that the Union was "shooting very high" in its demand for wage increases of between 85 cents and $1.05 an hour, and doubted the Company's willingness to continue with 12 days of annual sick leave when it believed the current allowance was being abused. He opposed the Union's demand for security in the form of a union shop. He opposed inclusion of a clause continuing past practices, suggesting that each "practice" be dealt with individually instead and that the Union furnish a list of the existing benefits it had in mind. He indicated that a requested dues check-off might be acceptable, provided the Company were indemnified for erroneous deductions (a concept that Chown said was "new" to him). Finally, he objected to the Union's proposed grievance procedure, involving shop stewards who would have unlimited freedom to investigate and process grievances. The Union, for its part, had resisted a no-strike clause which Goldstein demanded in return for a management consent to submit disputes to arbitration.

The next meeting took place on December 14. Chown submitted a revised proposal on four subjects — seniority, grievance processing, representation, and management rights. Goldstein offered to accept the Union's grievance procedure if the Union would accept the Company's management rights and no-strike clauses. This offer was rejected. Wages and Union Security were again discussed, but the parties did not succeed in narrowing their differences.

Negotiations resumed on January 7 and 8, 1974, now in the presence of a state conciliator. The parties agreed to an additional fourteen provisions, including those governing hours of work and overtime (a matter in which both sides made concessions); safety and health; performance of work by supervisors; benefit plans; a luncheon period; and the contract preamble (in which the Union dropped its insistence that the agreement bind successors and assigns). On the still unresolved issue of economic benefits, the Company proposed a wage increase of 10 cents an hour for 7 of the 9 bargaining unit employees and a wage review for the remaining two employees. The Union turned down this proposal in favor of its original demand, which was likewise rejected. Later, the Union repeated the position that it would accept nothing short of a union shop.

At this point, members of the bargaining unit apparently became concerned about the prospect of an agreement. Several witnesses testified to talk among the employees of a slowdown or of not reporting to work. Simultaneously, the amount of sick leave claimed in January rose 1100% from the level of previous months. Employees and their spouses also began to contact the president of the

Company, Thomas Olson, to get him to change the bargaining position taken by his negotiator, Goldstein. On January 15 Goldstein wrote to Chown complaining of the above-mentioned activity.

On January 28, again in the presence of the state conciliator, the parties met for what proved to be their final bargaining session. Chown denied any knowledge of a "sick-out" and stated that he was in no position to know about such employee behavior. The two sides reviewed their positions, then conferred separately with the conciliator. The Company emerged from the conference with a modified wage proposal that would have given an hourly increase of 10 cents to all bargaining unit employees. Neither side, however, would agree to the other's wage demands. Thereupon, the Company announced that the typewritten contract brought to the January 7-8 session, as modified by handwritten emendations made in those meetings, and as orally modified at the January 28 meeting by its revised wage proposal, constituted its "last, best, and final" offer. Goldstein gave the Union until 5:00 P.M. on the following day to accept the proposal. Failing that, he warned, the Company would take economic action. No arrangements were made for further negotiations, and in the next twenty-four hours no further communications passed between Chown and Goldstein.

On January 29 the Company distributed notices to the bargaining unit employees. These told of its final offer and stated that employees would not be permitted to work until the offer was accepted. The Company maintained a lockout thenceforth, despite offers by the Union to return to work and to negotiate further (but not, to accept the Company's final proposals) at various intervals in the next six months.

On this record, the administrative law judge ruled that the Company committed a last-minute violation of the Act. He found that the Company had bargained in good faith in all negotiations until January 28; however, by its declaration of final terms on that day, it retracted the December 14 offer to trade away its grievance procedure — *i. e.,* it insisted on its own grievance procedure — and this insistence violated § 8(a)(5).

The Board drew the same legal conclusion from altogether different facts. It ruled that the Company had been guilty of *general* bad faith, or "surface bargaining," and pitched its decision on the combined effect of the Company's (1) *non*-grievance proposals (its wage-benefit offerings and management rights clause in particular) and (2) bargaining tactics.

Both the administrative law judge and the Board held that the Company's lockout was illegal because it was in support of an unlawful bargaining position. The Board ruled, in addition, that the lockout was illegal because it was designed to penalize the employees for their unionization and collective bargaining.

DISCUSSION

I. *Bargaining Faith*

Section 8(a)(5) of the Act makes it an unfair labor practice for an employer "to refuse to bargain collectively with the representatives of his employees." "To bargain collectively," § 8(d) explains, is to observe

> the mutual obligation . . . to meet at reasonable times and confer in good faith with respect to wages, hours, and other terms and conditions of employment, or the negotiation of an agreement . . . .

The critical issue in this case is whether the Company did confer in good faith as described in § 8(d) so as to meet the requirements of § 8(a)(5). Once that determination is made, the legality or illegality of the supporting lockout under § 8(a)(3) follows swiftly.

The Board found against the Company on the issue of bargaining faith. By settled law, we must affirm that decision to the extent it rests on findings of fact for which there is "substantial" evidence on the record as a whole. 29 U.S.C. § 160(e); *Universal Camera Corp. v. NLRB,* 340 U.S. 474, 488, 71 S.Ct. 456, 95 L.Ed. 456 (1951); *Queen Mary Restaurants Corp. v. NLRB,* 560 F.2d 403, 407 (9th Cir. 1977).[2]

Substantiality of evidence, however, must take into account whatever in the record fairly detracts from its weight. *Universal Camera, supra,* 340 U.S. at 488, 71 S.Ct. 456. In reaching our decision, we have borne in mind the finding of the administrative law judge that the Company negotiated in good faith during all but the last day of the bargaining period. This finding is in direct conflict with the critical portion of the Board's determination. It is to be considered along with the probability of testimony itself, for, as the Supreme Court has stated,

> [e]vidence supporting a conclusion may be less substantial when an impartial, experienced examiner who has observed the witnesses and lived with the case has drawn conclusions different from the Board's than when he has reached the same conclusion.

Id. at 496, 71 S.Ct. at 469. This is especially true where the issue,

---

[2] Actually, "good faith" is described as a question of mixed law and fact. *NLRB v. Holmes Tuttle Broadway Ford, Inc.,* 465 F.2d 717, 719 (9th Cir. 1972). Where the issues are not purely factual, the Act does not explicitly direct the courts to exercise a particular measure of review. Manifestly, however, the measure of our oversight increases as the Board's determination approaches the purely legal. *NLRB v. Marcus Trucking Co.,* 286 F.2d 583, 591-92 (2d Cir. 1961). As our opinion makes clear, however, even a "substantial evidence" review does not change the result in this case.

like good faith, calls for an assessment of the credibility of witnesses. *Id.*

Our examination of the basis for the Board's ruling leads us to conclude that neither the proposals nor the tactics of the Company, nor the sum of its conduct, amounts to substantial evidence of bad faith.

A. Inferences from Bargaining Proposals

Economic Items

"Particularly in the benefit or 'economic' areas," the Board found, the proposals of the Company showed "an intention . . . to penalize the employees for having engaged in protected concerted activity." 220 N.L.R.B. at 636. We disagree. There is uncontroverted testimony that at the time of negotiations the wages of bargaining unit employees were comparable to those of other employees in the area engaged in similar work. Once negotiations began, wages and benefits in the form of cash or a cash equivalent were mandatory subjects of bargaining. *NLRB v. Wooster Div. of Borg-Warner Corp.,* 356 U.S. 342, 348-49, 78 S.Ct. 718, 2 L.Ed.2d 823 (1958); *NLRB v. Katz,* 369 U.S. 736, 744, 745-46, 82 S.Ct. 1107, 8 L.Ed.2d 230 (1962) (sick leave, incentive pay); *Singer Mfg. Co. v. NLRB,* 119 F.2d 131, 136 (7th Cir.), *cert. denied,* 313 U.S. 595, 61 S.Ct. 1119, 85 L.Ed. 1549 (1941) (paid holidays, vacation). Under § 8(d) the Company was to bargain on these matters in good faith but it was not required to agree to the Union's proposals or to make concessions. The record shows that the Company did discuss its economic package seriously at every meeting after November 9, and, as a result of bargaining, changed its position on vacation leave and wages. Its final offer called for a wage increase of 10 cents an hour, one additional paid holiday, and a bonus of 10 hours' pay for every 90-day period of perfect attendance and punctuality. Despite a reduction in paid sick leave from 12 to 6 days, the Board's own calculations show that these terms would have represented some improvement in economic benefits.[3]

In the Board's opinion, nevertheless, it is a mark against the Company that "it was offering no major improvements in wages and working conditions." Brief of Petitioner at 27. As we discuss at greater length below, that reasoning betrays inappropriately partisan

---

[3] The Board assumed a work year of 2080 hours and wages of $5.00 an hour. 220 N.L.R.B. at 637 n. 6. Using these figures, the wage and holiday proposals would have represented definite increases of $208.00 and $40.00 in annual benefits respectively; the bonus proposal a possible increase of $200.00; and the sick leave proposal a possible decrease of $240.00. Each employee thus stood to gain between $8.00 (assuming he was sick in each quarter and for 12 or more days of the year) and $448.00 (assuming no absences and complete punctuality).

expectations. The right to union representation under the Act does not imply the right to a better deal. The proper role of the Board is to watch over the process, not guarantee the results, of collective bargaining. *H. K. Porter v. NLRB,* 397 U.S. 99, 109, 90 S.Ct. 821, 25 L.Ed.2d 146 (1970).

Non-Economic Items

The Board's finding of bad faith also rests on several of the non-benefit items that appeared in the Company's final offer — the terms that outlined the scope of the management prerogative (management rights, integration, and waiver-of-past-practices clauses), and those that defined the means of registering protest and dissent (no-strike and grievance-and-arbitration clauses). We consider these in order.

1. An employer may insist on a management rights clause to impasse without violating the Act. *NLRB v. American Nat'l Ins. Co.,* 343 U.S. 395, 409, 72 S.Ct. 824, 96 L.Ed. 1027 (1952). The Board cites *American National Insurance,* but in the next breath accuses the Company of making "proposals clearly designed to force the Union into abandoning its *statutory rights and duties.*" 220 N.L.R.B. at 636 (emphasis added). We are not sure what force the accusation has, that the Supreme Court has not already answered. If the point is merely that

> absent contractual waiver, the Union has a right to a meaningful opportunity to bargain over any change the Company might wish to make in the employees' wages, hours, or other conditions of employment during the term of the contract,

Brief of Petitioner at 24, we agree, and simply point out the Board's own reference to the possibility of "contractual waiver." If the point is that the Union has a *duty* of representation to its members, which forbids it to concede ·certain prerogatives to management, and correspondingly forbids management to insist upon these prerogatives, we find the doctrine novel. The Board cites no statutory or case law in its support.

Apparently, even the Board would not complain if there were "significant economic benefits to compensate for the loss [of representation rights during the contract term]." *Id.* at 20-21. But if the only question is whether a waiver price is right, then the Board is again insinuating its judgment on the terms of an agreement that the parties themselves must reach.

2. An integration, or "zipper," clause seeks to close out bargaining during the contract term and to make the written contract the exclusive statement of the parties' rights and obligations. It is nothing but a diluted form of waiver, and so is governed by the same

principles that apply to a management functions clause. The existence and utility of an integration clause have been recognized by the Supreme Court. *See NLRB v. C & C Plywood Corp., supra* n. 4, 385 U.S. at 423, 87 S.Ct. 559. The Company could rightly insist on its inclusion in the contract.

3. The original proposal of the Union contained a continuation-of-past-practices clause. The Company felt that its operations in the past had been quite loosely handled, and that it would be difficult to know what past practices the Union might rely on in the future. It therefore rejected the Union proposal and insisted on a clause waiving all past practices as a basis for the agreement. The Company did offer to consider specific practices if the Union would submit a list of what it had in mind. The Union failed to do this. We agree with the administrative law judge that the Company's action was reasonable under the circumstances.

4. A no-strike clause is a common feature of collective bargaining agreements. Frequently, indeed, it is *quid pro quo* for a binding arbitration clause and therefore a fundamental element of the federal policy favoring arbitration of labor disputes. *See Gateway Coal Co. v. United Mine Workers of America,* 414 U.S. 368, 377, 94 S.Ct. 629, 38 L.Ed.2d 583 (1974); *Boys Markets, Inc. v. Retail Clerks Local 770,* 398 U.S. 235, 247-48, 90 S.Ct. 1583, 26 L.Ed.2d 199 (1970). The Board reasons backward from the association of these terms, to argue that a no-strike clause is evidence of bad faith when, and to the extent that, the range of subjects on which employees may not strike is broader than that for which arbitration of grievances is available. We cannot agree that a no-strike clause has only derivative value. An agreement to arbitrate may be sufficient, but it is not necessary, consideration for an agreement not to strike. *See Drake Bakeries v. Bakery Workers,* 370 U.S. 254, 261 and n. 7, 82 S.Ct. 1346, 1351, 8 L.Ed.2d 474 (1962) (rejecting the "flat and general rule that these two clauses are properly to be regarded as exact counterweights"). Moreover, the policy favoring arbitration is only an aspect of the broader federal policy favoring the substitution of collective bargaining for industrial strife. No-strike clauses are a mandatory subject of collective bargaining, *Borg-Warner, supra,* 356 U.S. at 350, 78 S.Ct. 718; *American National Insurance, supra,* 343 U.S. at 408 n. 22, 72 S.Ct. 824; *NLRB v. Bricklayers & Masons Internat'l U., Local No. 3,* 405 F.2d 469, 470 n. 1 (9th Cir. 1968), and the Company was entitled to insist upon its term.

5. The Company's grievance-and-arbitration clause is the source of more confusion than any other term. It was the sole basis on which the administrative law judge found that the Company violated the Act. One cannot tell from the law judge's decision, however, whether he found that the Company (a) insisted on its proposal in good faith, unaware that aspects of the grievance procedure were permissive

subjects of bargaining; or (b) hardened its bargaining position, in bad faith, on an otherwise mandatory subject. More confusing still, the Board chose to affirm the law judge's findings and conclusions "only to the extent consistent [with its opinion]" — which omitted any mention whatsoever of the grievance proposal. Under these conditions, we examine the matter afresh.

We find that we do not need to decide whether the proposed grievance procedure was in all respects a mandatory subject (and therefore bargainable to impasse), for the article was not a cause of impasse in this case, and under the circumstances the Company was under no obligation to bargain until it became so.

Unlike the other terms discussed, Article XVIII ("Grievance and Arbitration") was the subject of a bargaining offer and negotiable until the end of the meeting on January 28. We therefore view it in a very different light. The record shows that by the time it lost its negotiability, the parties had reached an irremediable impasse on other issues. The Company and the Union met on seven occasions over a period of two months. They discussed all proposals and explained all positions. On January 7, they felt it appropriate to enlist the services of a state labor conciliator. Transcript of Hearing (Tr.) at 87-91. As the meeting that day closed, a union negotiator was heard to remark, "It looks like a strike," or words to that effect. *Id.* at 279. The conciliator also commented that "the Union wants a shop steward system, but the real main point is money." *Id.* at 328. From then on the employees engaged in a partial sick-out. The crucial meeting on January 28 was arranged through the efforts of the conciliator, who opened by saying that the situation appeared to be at an impasse. *Id.* at 348. Later, after conferring with each side separately, he expressed the equivalent opinion that the minimum expectations of the employees were a great deal higher than the employer's proposals. *Id.* at 356. At this point the Company was offering wage increases of 10 cents an hour, while the Union was demanding increases of between 85 cents and $1.05 an hour. The Company altered its wage proposal to include increases for all employees. The rejection of this new offer, viewed against the background of preceding events, gave the Company ample ground to believe that further bargaining would be fruitless. Goldstein then announced that the proposals on the table constituted the Company's "best, last, and final offer." This stroke, which made the grievance article non-negotiable, came at a time when it was no longer important.

Those who bargain collectively are normally under an obligation to continue negotiating to impasse on all mandatory issues. *Chambers Mfg. Co.,* 124 N.L.R.B. 721 (1959), *enf'd,* 278 F.2d 715 (5th Cir. 1960). The law relieves them of that duty, however, when a single issue looms so large that a stalemate as to it may fairly be said to cripple the prospects of any agreement. *Cheney California Lumber Co. v. NLRB, supra* n. 10, at 380; *NLRB v. Wire Products Manufacturing Corp.*, 484 F.2d 760, 766 (7th Cir. 1973); *Taft Broadcasting Co.*, 163 N.L.R.B. 475, 478 (1967), *enf'd sub nom. AFTRA v. NLRB*, 129 U.S.App.D.C. 399, 395 F.2d 622 (1968). The record leaves no doubt that wages and related benefits were a central and irreconcilable issue in this case. A further discussion of grievance procedures would have served no useful purpose, and therefore was not called for.

A proposal, not the cause of impasse, may nevertheless contain terms so hostile to the role of the other side's bargaining representative that it constitutes evidence of bad faith. This is not the case here. An employer may reasonably believe that labor disputes will be more easily settled at the first stage by direct contact between the aggrieved employee and his foreman than by the intervention of a union to represent the worker; that a shop steward committee of six is a cumbersome vehicle to represent a labor force of nine; and that the international representative of the union would be more skilled and professional in handling grievances than a member of the local union. Whether the employer is entitled to insist on his beliefs is, as we have said, a question reserved. But the beliefs themselves, as embodied in the Company's grievance and arbitration proposals, do not support a charge of bad faith in negotiations. The Company's previous willingness to accept the shop steward system in exchange for its management rights and no-strike clauses, and its willingness to have an employee act as agent of the international union representative when the latter was unavailable, put to rest any remaining doubts of its good faith on this subject.

B. Inferences from Bargaining Tactics

1. The Board finds evidence of bad faith in the interrelationship of terms in the Company's final offer. It notes that (1) under the Company's salary proposal, the wages of all employees would rise by 10 cents the first years, but there would be no further guarantee of wage improvement as the Company had discretion to reclassify employees within their wage range; (2) under the attendance and punctuality bonus, excused absences such as the first day of sickness would not count as days worked; and (3) under the management rights clause, the Company had the exclusive and unreviewable right to discharge employees, although the article on discipline provided that discharges should be for just cause. On the basis of these offsetting provisions the Board accuses the Company of conducting a "shell game."

If, in fact, the contradictions were intentional, and if they were enforceable in the Company's favor, they amount in our judgment to evidence of sharp draftsmanship at most. The terms of the contract were there for the Union to read. It was not compelled to accept them. That no agreement was ever reached on wages, or an attendance bonus, or management rights, is some indication that these terms were not inherently deceptive. There is no evidence that the Company ever falsely described its written proposals. There is no evidence that it ever subsequently altered non-initialled terms to nullify concessions made elsewhere in the contract. While we would accept that some of the terms are harsh — in particular the manner in which sickness served to disqualify an employee from bonus eligibility — that does not give the Board or the courts the power to strike them.

2. Finally, the Board finds evidence of bad faith in the relationship between the Company's final offer and its earlier proposals. It notes that the "last, best, and final" offer omitted (1) a dues check-off provision, which on November 9 the Company had said it would consider if the Union would accept a corollary hold-harmless clause; (2) a ten-day statute of limitations for the filing of grievances, which on December 5 the Company had noted in writing as a possible revision of the three-day period proposed; and (3) the Union's grievance procedure involving shop stewards, which on December 14 the Company had offered to trade for Union acceptance of the Company's management rights and no-strike provisions. In the Board's opinion these omissions represent a "retrenchment on previous concessions." Brief of Petitioner at 33.

We question how many of these "offers" were really "firm." According to Chown, the Company took the position that if it *were* to agree to a dues check-off clause, then the clause would have to contain an indemnification proviso. Tr. at 19. By Goldstein's account, his notation on a second issue was that the statute of limitations *might* be ten days. Tr. at 327. These witnesses portray a carefully guarded management position, in all respects consistent with the beatitude that, in bargaining, it is more blessed to receive than to give unconditional offers. We are inclined to believe that the Company's offers were less firm than the Board assumes.

In addition, we question the Board's unreflective treatment of "offers" as if they were "concessions." The negotiators agreed to indicate any and all accords by their initials. All initialled clauses were included in the Company's last offer. Absent abuse not present here, it is perfectly legitimate for a party to retract a proposal before the other side has accepted it. It may do so because the offer was germane only to the context in which it was made, or because it feels a different offer is more likely to be accepted, or because it has further determined the relative bargaining strengths of the opposed sides. The law does not require that each offer and indication of possible acceptance be included in the final contract before a legal impasse is reached. To do so would hamper the ability of parties to explore their respective positions early in their negotiations. "To bargain collectively" does not impose an inexorable ratchet, whereby a party is bound by all it has ever said.

C. The Board's Analysis

The Board would have us look at the sum of the evidence, not merely pieces, to decide whether the Company was bargaining in good faith. Clearly, it would be disingenuous to decline.

> A state of mind such as good faith is not determined by a consideration of events viewed separately. The picture is created by a consideration of all the facts viewed as an integrated whole.

NLRB v. Stanislaus Imp. & H. Co., 226 F.2d 377, 381 (9th Cir. 1955). Equally clearly, our judic...l review of the Board's decision is most problematic at the stage of holistic analysis. Nevertheless, we do not find the requisite substantial evidence of bad faith in the record as a whole.

The cases of surface bargaining on which the Board relies are factually distinguishable, . . . all involve much more aggravated behavior on the part of management than is present here.

Our divergence from the Board is most apparent in the evaluation of bargaining proposals. As Petitioner argues,

> the Board 'must take some cognizance of the reasonableness of the position taken by an employer in the course of bargaining negotiations' if it is not to be 'blinded by empty talk and by the mere surface motions of collective bargaining . . .' [Authorities omitted.]

Holmes Tuttle Broadway Ford, supra, 465 F.2d at 719. The issue is how proposals most appropriately should be evaluated, to determine "reasonableness."

The Board's approach is best illustrated when it condemns the Company's final offer as "terms which no self-respecting union could be expected to accept." 220 N.L.R.B. at 637. The quotation is from *Reed and Prince, supra,* 205 F.2d at 139, a case with whose result we have no quarrel, but which contains language we have questioned once before. *See NLRB v. MacMillan Ring-Free Oil Co.,* 394 F.2d 26, 29 (9th Cir. 1968). The utility and appropriateness of a "self-respecting union" standard are still doubtful. As an analytic tool, the phrase seems rather better suited to conclude inquiry than to advance it. As a test of good faith under the National Labor Relations Act, it directs first attention to the bargaining position of the party whose interests are opposed to the employer. Thus, it comes perilously close to determining what the employer should give by looking at what the employees want. More relevant in judging of good faith and reasonableness, it seems to us, are other factors such as the employer's economic position and the past level of employee benefits. By those standards, as we have indicated, the Company's proposals cannot be characterized as surface bargaining.

A finding of bad faith would require the Company to yield despite the Union's inability to enforce its will through the classic economic weapons of labor relations. But the obligation to bargain collectively "does not compel either party to agree to a proposal or require the making of a concession." 29 U.S.C. § 158(d); *American National Insurance, supra,* 343 U.S. at 404, 72 S.Ct. 824; *Queen Mary Restaurants, supra,* 560 F.2d at 411. Nor may the Board, "directly or indirectly, compel concessions or otherwise sit in judgment upon the substantive terms of collective bargaining agreements." *American National Insurance, supra,* 343 U.S. at 404, 72 S.Ct. at 829, *cited in H. K. Porter, supra,* 397 U.S. at 106, 90 S.Ct. 821; *NLRB v. Insurance Agents' Union,* 361 U.S. 477, 487, 80 S.Ct. 419, 4 L.Ed.2d 454 (1960). While the parties' freedom of contract is not absolute under the Act,

> allowing the Board to compel agreement when the parties themselves are unable to agree would violate the fundamental premise on which the Act is based — private bargaining under governmental supervision of the procedure alone, without any official compulsion over the actual terms of the contract.

H. K. Porter, supra, 397 U.S. at 108, 90 S.Ct. at 826.

On the central issue of bargaining intent, the events in question resolve into a case of hard bargaining between two parties who were possessed of disparate economic power: a relatively weak Union and a relatively strong Company. The Company naturally wished to use its advantage to retain as many rights as possible. That desire is not inconsistent with its statutory duty to bargain in good faith. *Chevron Oil Co. v. NLRB,* 442 F.2d 1067, 1073 (5th Cir. 1971).

II. *Lockout*

Our ruling on the lockout is controlled by the decision of the Supreme Court in *American Ship Building v. NLRB,* 380 U.S. 300, 85 S.Ct. 955, 13 L.Ed.2d 855 (1965). *American Ship Building* held that a lockout after impasse, when used as a means of bringing pressure in support of an employer's lawful bargaining position, does not violate § 8(a)(3) or (1). *Id.* at 318, 85 S.Ct. 955. As the Company's bargaining position was lawful, so was the lockout in support of its position.

. . .

III. *Conclusion*

We find that there is not substantial evidence on the record as a whole to support the Board's ruling (1) that the Company went through the motions of bargaining as a pretense to avoid reaching agreement, or (2) that it locked out its employees to discourage union support. Accordingly, we deny the petition for enforcement.

NOTES:

(1) As the *Tomco* court states, the use of economic weapons, like a lockout or strike, to exert pressure during negotiations is not, in and of itself, inconsistent with the obligation to bargain in good faith. In *NLRB v. Insurance Agents' International Union, AFL-CIO,* 361 U.S. 477 (1960), the Supreme Court, pointing out that Congress did not intend the Board to regulate the substantive terms of the labor agreement, held that the role of the NLRB is not to sit in judgment upon every economic weapon wielded by the parties in the course of bargaining. *See also* Senator Walsh's testimony prior to the passage of the NLRA, 79 Cong. Rec. 7660 (1934).

(2) *Problem:* Is a lockout inherently destructive of employees rights? May an employer lockout its workers before an impasse in negotiations is reached? In answering this question, is it material whether the employer had a legitimate and substantial reason for the lockout? *See Lane v. NLRB,* 418 F.2d 1208 (D.C. Cir. 1969); *American Ship Bldg. v. NLRB,* 280 U.S. 300 (1965) (lockout is lawful even though employer's sole motivating reason was to weaken the union's position).

(3) How does the *G.E.* approach to "firm, final offer" tactics differ from the employer's announcement in *Tomco, supra,* that its wage increase proposal was its "last, best, and final" order? Is it that hard bargaining becomes unlawful where a company's take-it-or-leave-it approach is combined with a well-publicized policy of inflexibility?

c. Unilateral Action

While contract negotiations are being conducted, an employer may not unilaterally implement any changes that affect matters within the ambit of "mandatory" subjects of collective bargaining, without first consulting the union. In *NLRB v. Katz,*[21] the Supreme Court found a *per se* violation of the duty to bargain where an employer unilaterally granted merit increases and changed its policy concerning sick leave and wage increase during contract negotiation with the union over these matters. The court held that this action

---

[21] 369 U.S. 736 (1962).

was a "circumvention of the duty to negotiate which frustrates the objectives of Section 8(a)(5) much as does a flat refusal." [22]

NOTE:

Problem: Does a union violate its duty to bargain in good faith under Section 8(b)(3) by establishing during the term of an agreement a union rule that unilaterally imposes a low production ceiling? *N.Y. District Council No. 9, International Brotherhood of Painters v. NLRB,* 453 F.2d 783 (2d Cir. 1971), *cert. denied,* 408 U.S. 930 (1972).

d. Refusal to Reduce an Agreement to Writing

The courts have long held that a refusal to sign a written agreement, once an agreement has been reached, is evidence that a party is merely going through the motions of bargaining. In *H.J. Heinz Co. v. NLRB,* 311 U.S. 514 (1941), the Supreme Court, describing a signed agreement as the "final step in the bargaining process," upheld the Board's finding that an employer who refused to sign a written embodiment of the negotiated agreement was guilty of a *per se* violation of the duty to bargain. Such conduct demonstrates a refusal to recognize the union as a legitimate representative of the employees and "tends to frustrate the aim . . . of industrial peace through collective bargaining." *Id.* at 523. Section 8(d) of the Act, which codified this doctrine,[23] specifically states that the parties to contract negotiations must execute a written agreement if either side so requests. However, a party may lawfully refuse to sign any agreement reached at the bargaining table if both sides clearly understand that the approval of another party first must be secured.[24]

In situations where the NLRB has found an employer's unlawful refusal to sign a contract, it has granted a union one of the following remedies: (1) execution of a contract based on the agreed upon terms, or (2) new negotiations conducted with the understanding that any agreement reached will be incorporated in a signed contract.[25] Further, the Board has ordered an employer to reimburse

---

[22] *Id.* at 743.

[23] "[I]t carries the law beyond the requirement of formal negotiation and beyond a subjective test designed to protect the union against being talked to death into an effort to realize at least in part the third purpose of the Wagner Act — a partnership of management and labor in governing the terms and conditions of employment." Cox, The Duty of Bargain in Good Faith, 71 Harv. L. Rev. 1401, 1423 (1958).

[24] Painters Local 850 *and* Morganstern Glass & Mirror Co., 177 NLRB 155 (1969).

[25] NLRB v. Warrensburg Board & Paper Corp., 340 F.2d 920 (2d Cir. 1965).

employees, with interest, for benefits they would have received *but for* the employer's failure to sign the contract.[26]

C. WHAT THE PARTIES BARGAIN ABOUT

1. Subject Matter at the Bargaining Table

Section 8(d) of the National Labor Relations Act, when read with Sections 8(a) (5) and 8(b) (3), imposes on employers and unions the mutual obligation to bargain collectively "with respect to wages, hours, and other terms and conditions of employment." In *NLRB v. Borg-Warner Corp.,*[27] the Supreme Court characterized the substantive issues that arise in the course of bargaining as: (1) mandatory, (2) permissive, and (3) illegal.

A matter falling within the scope of Section 8(d) is a mandatory subject for bargaining, and must be bargained about before any unilateral action is taken with respect to such a matter. Further, a party may insist to the point of impasse, upon the inclusion of a mandatory subject in a collective bargaining agreement, since Section 8(d) does not compel either party to make concession. A "non-mandatory" or "permissible" topic is one that may be bargained about and included in a collective agreement if the parties wish, but may not be pressed to the point of impasse or made a necessary condition of reaching an agreement. In *Borg-Warner,* the company was found to have committed an unfair labor practice by refusing to enter into an agreement unless the union agreed to two proposals involving non-mandatory subjects.[28] Of course, neither party may insist upon a clause which would be unlawful under the Act, such as a provision for a closed shop.

The NLRB and the courts have construed very broadly the statutory language in Section 8(d), and the tendency has been for the scope of subject matters that are recognized as "mandatory" bargaining topics to grow and expand. For instance, the statutory term "wages" has been held to include all emoluments of value, such as merit increases, pensions, stock purchase plans, Christmas bonuses, and employee discounts. Also, the statutory language "terms and conditions of employment" has been construed to cover contract provisions directly affecting the employment relationship, such as seniority, discipline, no-strike provisions, nondiscriminatory exclusive hiring hall arrangements, and the contracting-out of work

---

[26] NLRB v. Beverage-Air Co., 402 F.2d 411 (4th Cir. 1968).

[27] 356 U.S. 342 (1958).

[28] The company insisted that the agreement include two provisions: (1) that all of its employees, before striking, vote on the company's final offers in future contract negotiations; and (2) that the local union, rather than the certified international, was to be a party to the contract.

presently being performed by the employees. On the other hand, matters considered too remote from the employment relationship, or regarded as a prerogative of employers or unions have been held to be "non-mandatory" or "permissible," such as performance bonds, contributions to an industry promotion fund, change of a party's negotiator and rehiring of replaced economic strikers.

ALLIED CHEMICAL & ALKALI WORKERS LOCAL 1 v. PITTSBURGH PLATE GLASS CO.

United States Supreme Court
404 U.S. 157, 92 S. Ct. 383, 30 L. Ed. 2d 341 (1971)

Mr. Justice Brennan delivered the opinion of the Court.

Under the National Labor Relations Act as amended, mandatory subjects of collective bargaining include bargaining to include provisions for pension and insurance benefits for active employees, and an employer's mid-term unilateral modification of such benefits constitutes an unfair labor practice. This case presents the question whether a mid-term unilateral modification that concerns, not the benefits of active employees, but the benefits of already retired employees also constitutes an unfair labor practice. The National Labor Relations Board, one member dissenting, held that changes in retired employees' retirement benefits are embraced by the bargaining obligation and that an employer's unilateral modification of them constitutes an unfair labor practice in violation of §§ 8(a)(5) and (1) of the Act. 71 L.R.R.M. 1433 (1969). The Court of Appeals for the Sixth Circuit disagreed and refused to enforce the Board's cease-and-desist order, 427 F.2d 936 (1970). We granted certiorari, 401 U.S. 907 (1971). We affirm the order of the Court of Appeals.

. . . .

The Board found that bargaining over pensioners' rights has become an established industrial practice. But industrial practice cannot alter the conclusions that retirees are neither "employees" nor bargaining unit members. The parties dispute whether a practice of bargaining over pensioners' benefits exists and, if so, whether it reflects the views of labor and management that the subject is not merely a convenient but a mandatory topic of negotiations. But even if industry commonly regards retirees' benefits as a statutory subject of bargaining, that would at most, as we suggested in Fibreboard Corp. v. Labor Board, 379 U.S. 203, 211 (1964), reflect the interests of employers and employees in the subject matter as well as its amenability to the collective-bargaining process; it would not be determinative. Common practice cannot change the law and make into bargaining unit "employees" those who are not.

Even if pensioners are not bargaining unit "employees," are their benefits, nonetheless, a mandatory subject of collective bargaining as "terms and conditions of employment" of the active employees who remain in the unit? The Board held, alternatively, that they are, on the ground that they "vitally" affect the "terms and conditions of employment" of active employees principally by influencing the value of both their current and future benefits. 71 L.R.R.M. at 1438. The Board explained: "It is not uncommon to group active and retired employees under a single health insurance contract with the result that . . . it is the size and experience of the entire group which may determine insurance rates." *Ibid.* Consequently, active employees may "benefit from the membership of retired employees in the group whose participation enlarges its size and might thereby lower costs per participant." *Ibid.* Furthermore, the actual value of future benefits depends upon contingencies, such as inflation and changes in public law, which the parties cannot adequately anticipate and over which they have little or no control. By establishing a practice of representing retired employees in resolving those contingencies as they arise, active workers can insure that their own retirement benefits will survive the passage of time. This, in turn, the Board contends, facilitates the peaceful settlement of disputes over active employees' pension plans. The Board's arguments are not insubstantial, but they do not withstand careful scrutiny.

Section 8(d) of the Act, of course, does not immutably fix a list of subjects for mandatory bargaining. See, *e.g., Fibreboard Corp. v. Labor Board, supra,* at 220-221 (Stewart, J., concurring); Richfield Oil Corp. v. Labor Board, 231 F.2d 717, 723-724 (CADC 1956). But it does establish a limitation against which proposed topics must be measured. In general terms, the limitation includes only issues which settle an aspect of the relationship between the employer and employees. See, *e.g., Labor Board v. Borg-Warner Corp.,* 356 U.S. 342 (1958). Although normally matters involving individuals outside the employment relationship do not fall within that category, they are not wholly excluded. In Teamsters Union v. Oliver, 358 U.S. 283 (1959), for example, an agreement had been negotiated in the trucking industry, establishing a minimum rental which carriers would pay to truck owners who drove their own vehicles in the carriers' service in place of the latter's employees. Without determining whether the owner-drivers were themselves "employees," we held that the minimum rental was a mandatory subject of bargaining, and hence immune from state antitrust laws, because the term "was integral to the establishment of a stable wage structure for clearly covered employee-drivers." United States v. Drum, 368 U.S. 370, 382 n. 26 (1962). Similarly, in *Fibreboard Corp. v. Labor Board, supra,* at 215, we held that "the type of 'contracting out' involved in this case — the replacement of employees in the existing bargaining unit with those of an independent contractor to do the same work under similar conditions of employment — is a statutory subject of collective bargaining. . . ." As we said there, *id.,* at 213, "the work of the employees in the bargaining unit was let out piecemeal in *Oliver,* whereas here the work of the entire unit has been contracted out."

The Board urges that *Oliver* and *Fibreboard* provide the principle governing this case. The Company, on the other hand, would distinguish those decisions on the ground that the unions there sought to protect employees from outside threats, not to represent the interests of third parties. We agree with the Board that the principle of *Oliver* and *Fibreboard* is relevant here; in each case the question is not whether the third-party concern is antagonistic to or compatible with the interests of bargaining unit employees, but whether it vitally affects the "terms and conditions" of their employment. But we disagree with the Board's assessment of the significance of a change in retirees' benefits to the "terms and conditions of employment" of active employees.

The benefits which active workers may reap by including retired employees under the same health insurance contract are speculative and insubstantial at best. As the Board itself acknowledges in its brief, the relationship between the inclusion of retirees and the overall insurance rate is uncertain. Adding individuals increases the group experience and thereby generally tends to lower the rate, but including pensioners, who are likely to have higher medical expenses, may more than offset that effect. In any event, the impact one way or the other on the "terms and conditions of employment" of active employees is hardly comparable to the loss of jobs threatened in *Oliver* and *Fibreboard.* In *Fibreboard,* after holding that "the replacement of employees in the existing bargaining unit with those of an independent contractor to do the same work under similar conditions of employment" is a mandatory subject of bargaining, we noted that our decision did "not encompass other forms of 'contracting out' or 'subcontracting' which arise daily in our complex economy." 379·U.S. at 215. The inclusion of retirees in the same insurance contract surely has even less an impact on the "terms and conditions of employment" of active employees than some of the contracting activities which we excepted from our holding in *Fibreboard.*

The mitigation of future uncertainty and the facilitation of agreement on active employees' retirement plans which the Board said would follow from the union's representation of pensioners are equally problematical. To be sure, the future retirement benefits of active workers are part and parcel of their overall compensation and hence a well-established statutory subject of bargaining. Moreover, provisions of those plans to guard against future contingencies are equally subsumed under the collective bargaining obligation. Under the Board's theory, active employees undertake to represent pensioners in order to protect their own retirement benefits, just as if they were bargaining for, say, a cost-of-living escalation clause. But there is a crucial difference. Having once found it advantageous to bargain for improvements to pensioners' benefits, active workers are not forever thereafter bound to that view or obliged to negotiate in behalf of retirees again. To the contrary, they are free to decide, for example, that current income is preferable to greater certainty in their own retirement benefits or, indeed, to their retirement benefits altogether. By advancing pensioners' interests now, active employees, therefore, have no assurance that they will be the beneficiaries of similar representation when they retire. The insurance against future contingencies which they may buy in negotiating benefits for retirees is thus a hazardous and, therefore, improbable investment, far different from a cost-of-living escalation clause that they could contractually enforce in court. . . . We find, accordingly, that the effect which the Board asserts bargaining in behalf of pensioners would have on the negotiation of active employees' retirement plans is too speculative a foundation on which to base an obligation to bargain.

Nor does the Board's citation of industrial practice provide any ground for concluding otherwise. The Board states in its brief that "[n]either the bargaining representative nor the active employees . . . can help but recognize that the active employees of today are the retirees of tomorrow — indeed, such a realization undoubtedly underlies the widespread industrial practice of bargaining about benefits of those who have already retired . . . and explains the vigorous interest which the Union has taken in this case." But accepting the Board's finding that the industrial practice exists, we find nowhere a particle of evidence cited showing that the explanation for this lies in the concern of active workers for their own future retirement benefits.

We recognize that "classification of bargaining subjects as 'terms [and] conditions of employment' is a matter concerning which the Board has special expertise." Meat Cutters v. Jewel Tea, 381 U.S. 676, 685-686 (1965). The Board's holding in this case, however, depends on the application of law to facts, and the legal standard to be applied is ultimately for the courts to decide and enforce. We think that in holding the "terms and conditions of employment" of active employees to be *vitally* affected by pensioners' benefits, the Board here simply neglected to give the adverb its ordinary meaning. Cf. Labor Board v. Brown, 380 U.S. 278, 292 (1965).

The question remains whether the Company committed an unfair labor practice by offering retirees an exchange for their withdrawal from the already negotiated health insurance plan. After defining "to bargain collectively" as meeting and conferring "with respect to wages, hours, and other terms and conditions of employment,"

§ 8(d) of the Act goes on to provide in relevant part that "where there is in effect a collective-bargaining contract covering employees in an industry affecting commerce, the duty to bargain collectively shall also mean that no party to such contract shall terminate or modify such contract" except upon (1) timely notice to the other party, (2) an offer to meet and confer "for the purpose of negotiating a new contract or a contract containing the proposed modifications," (3) timely notice to the Federal Mediation and Conciliation Service and comparable state or territorial agencies of the existence of a "dispute," and (4) continuation "in full force and effect [of] . . . all the terms and conditions of the existing contract . . . until [its] expiration date. . . ." The Board's trial examiner ruled that the Company's action in offering retirees a change in their health plan did not amount to a "modification" of the collective-bargaining agreement in violation of § 8(d), since the pensioners had merely been given an additional option which they were free to accept or decline as they saw fit. The Board rejected that conclusion on the ground that there were several possible ways of adjusting the negotiated plan to the Medicare provisions and the Company "modified" the contract by unilaterally choosing one of them. The Company now urges, in effect, that we adopt the views of the trial examiner. We need not resolve, however, whether there was a "modification" within the meaning of § 8(d), because we hold that even if there was, a "modification" is a prohibited unfair labor practice only when it changes a term that is a mandatory rather than a permissive subject of bargaining.

Paragraph (4) of § 8(d), of course, requires that a party proposing a modification continue "in full force and effect . . . all the terms and conditions of the existing contract" until its expiration. Viewed in isolation from the rest of the provision, that language would preclude any distinction between contract obligations that are "terms and conditions of employment" and those that are not. But in construing § 8(d), " 'we must not be guided by a single sentence or member of a sentence, but look to the provisions of the whole law, and to its object and policy.' " Mastro Plastics Corp. v. Labor Board, 350 U.S. 270, 285 (1956). . . . Seen in the light, § 8(d) embraces only mandatory topics of bargaining. The provision begins by defining "to bargain collectively" as meeting and conferring "with respect to wages, hours, and other terms and conditions of employment." It then goes on to state that "the duty to bargain collectively shall also mean" that mid-term unilateral modifications and terminations are prohibited. Although this part of the section is introduced by a "proviso" clause, see n. 21, *supra,* it quite plainly is to be construed *in pari materia* with the preceding definition. Accordingly, just as § 8(d) defines the obligation to bargain to be with respect to mandatory terms alone, so it prescribes the duty to maintain only mandatory terms without unilateral modification for the duration of the collective-bargaining agreement.

The relevant purpose of § 8(d) which emerges from the legislative history of the Act together with the text of the provision confirms this understanding. The section stems from the 1947 revision of the Act, an important theme of which was to stabilize collective-bargaining agreements. The Senate bill, in particular, contained provisions in §§ 8(d) and 301(a) to prohibit unilateral mid-term modifications and terminations and to confer federal jurisdiction over suits for contract violations. See S. 1126, 80th Cong., 1st Sess., §§ 8(d), 301(a), in 1 LMRA 114-116, 151. The bill also included provisions to make it an unfair labor practice for an employer or labor organization "to violate the terms of a collective-bargaining agreement." *Id.,* §§ 8(a)(6), 8(b)(5), in 1 LMRA 111-112, 114. In conference the Senate's proposed §§ 8(d) and 301(a) were adopted with relatively few changes. See H. R. Conf. Rep. No. 510, *supra,* at 34-35, 65-66, in 1 LMRA 538-539, 569-570. The provisions to make contract violations an unfair labor practice, on the other hand, were rejected with the explanation that "[o]nce parties have made a collective bargaining contract the enforcement of that contract should be left to the usual processes of the law and not to the National Labor Relations Board." *Id.* at 42, in 1 LMRA 546. The purpose of the proscription of unilateral mid-term modifications and terminations in § 8(d) cannot be, therefore, simply to assure adherence to contract terms. As far as unfair-labor-practice remedies are concerned, that goal was to be achieved through other unfair-labor-practice provisions which were rejected in favor of customary judicial procedures. See Dowd Box Co. v. Courtney, 368 U.S. 502, 510-513 (1962).

The structure and language of § 8(d) point to a more specialized purpose than merely promoting general contract compliance. The conditions for a modification or termination set out in paragraphs (1) through (4) plainly are designed to regulate modifications and terminations so as to facilitate agreement in place of economic warfare. Thus, the party desiring to make a modification or termination is required to serve a written notice on the other party, offer to meet and confer, notify mediation and conciliation agencies if necessary, and meanwhile maintain contract relations. Accordingly, we think we accurately described the relevant aim of § 8(d) when we said in *Mastro Plastics Corp. v. Labor Board, supra,* at 284, that the provision "seeks to bring about the termination and modification of collective-bargaining agreements without interrupting the flow of commerce or the production of goods. . . ."

If that is correct, the distinction that we draw between mandatory and permissive terms of bargaining fits the statutory purpose. By once bargaining and agreeing on a permissive subject, the parties, naturally, do not make the subject a mandatory topic of future bargaining. When a proposed modification is to a permissive term, therefore, the purpose of facilitating accord on the proposal is not at all in point, since the parties are not required under the statute to bargain with respect to it. The irrelevance of the purpose is demonstrated by the irrelevance of the procedures themselves of § 8(d). Paragraph (2), for example, requires an offer "to meet and confer with the other party for the purpose of negotiating a new contract or a contract containing the proposed modifications." But such an offer is meaningless if a party is statutorily free to refuse to negotiate on the proposed change to the permissive term. The notification to mediation and conciliation services referred to in paragraph (3) would be equally meaningless, if required at all. We think it would be no less beside the point to read paragraph (4) of § 8(d) as requiring continued adherence to permissive as well as mandatory terms. The remedy for a unilateral mid-term modification to a permissive term lies in an action for breach of contract, see n. 20, *supra,* not in an unfair-labor-practice proceeding.

As a unilateral mid-term modification of a permissive term such as retirees' benefits does not, therefore, violate § 8(d), the judgment of the Court of Appeals is

Affirmed.

Mr. Justice Douglas dissents.

NOTES:

(1) What is the significance of the dichotomy between mandatory and permissive subjects of bargaining? Is this distinction consistent with Congressional intent that the Board not intrude into the regulation of the substance of collective bargaining? Does this characterization lead to a freezing of those topics on which the parties have to bargain and a blocking of the natural evolution of collective bargaining subjects in response to the changing needs and conditions of the parties?

(2) In *United Mine Workers* (Lone Star Steel Co.), 231 NLRB No. 88 (1977), the Board found that the Union's insistence to the point of impasse upon the inclusion of a successorship clause did not violate Section 8(b)(3) of the Act. Relying on the previous case, *Pittsburgh Plate Glass,* the Board attempted to clarify the distinction between subjects of bargaining as follows:

The touchstone in such cases is "not whether the third-party concern is antagonistic to or compatible with the interests of bargaining-unit employees, but whether it *vitally* affects the 'terms and conditions' of their employment [emphasis supplied]." The Court has found in certain instances that third-party concern did vitally affect the terms and conditions of employment of bargaining unit employees, whereas in Pittsburgh Plate Glass, supra, it did not. The instant case is distinguishable from the foregoing in that the successorship clause does not purport to deal with *individuals* outside the employment relationship, but rather with successor employers, who are likewise outside that relationship. Notwithstanding this distinction, we are persuaded that a successor's assumption of any collective-bargaining agreement negotiated between the Union and Lone Star would be vital to the protection of Starlight employees' previously negotiated wages and working conditions, as it is clear that the general rules governing successorship guarantee neither employees' wages nor their jobs.

Does the Act permit the Board to ignore this distinction?

(3) May an employer insist to the point of impasse upon a management rights clause which gives it final control over certain subject matters ordinarily determined by collective agreements and by impartial arbitration? Is such a withdrawal of items from the bargaining table consistent with the obligation to bargain in good faith over the range of subjects specified by the Act? *See NLRB v. American National Insurance Co.,* 343 U.S. 395 (1952).

2. Duty to Furnish Information

Integral to the duty to bargain is the requirement that an employer furnish relevant information in its possession to the union. The purpose of this requirement is to enable the union to bargain intelligently, to understand and discuss issues raised by the employer's opposition to union's demands, and to administer a contract. The collective bargaining process is frustrated when an employer states that it cannot afford to pay higher wages but refuses to substantiate its claims with relevant financial records.[29] Accordingly, the Board fashioned the rule that an employer's refusal to provide such data to a union is a *per se* violation of Section 8(a)(5) of the Act. In *NLRB v. Truitt Mfg. Co.,*[30] the Supreme Court, although equivocating on the Board's *per se* approach, held that the employer's refusal to substantiate its claim of inability to pay increased wages may support a finding of failure to bargain in good faith.

If an employer does not claim inability to pay, can a union make the employer's profit position relevant anyway? Is a union entitled to place in issue, and hence require data concerning, other possible grounds for urging wage increases, such as employee productivity? The Board has found information concerning job classifications,

---

[29] *See, e.g.,* Pine Industrial Comm. Inc., 118 NLRB 1055 (1957).
[30] 351 U.S. 149 (1956).

seniority, insurance and welfare plans, time studies, employment method, production and operating statistics, productivity and other profit-sharing information relevant.

a. Inability to Pay.

WESTERN MASS. ELECTRIC CO. v. NLRB

United States Court of Appeals, First Circuit
570 F.2d 1340 (1978)

Campbell, Circuit Judge: — These cross-petitions for review and enforcement of two orders of the National Labor Relations Board present the same legal issue in different factual contexts: whether an employer is guilty of an unfair labor practice when in the course of negotiating a new collective bargaining agreement it refuses to divulge to the union its prior costs in subcontracting out work that members of the bargaining unit are capable of performing.

. . .

Facts — the Complaint Against WMECO

This dispute arose during negotiations between Local 455 and WMECO concerning a collective bargaining agreement to take the place of the one expiring on July 1, 1975. WMECO traditionally had subcontracted out some work that is regular employees can and on occasion do perform, such as overhead line work, underground excavation and line installation, and tree trimming. The collective bargaining agreement then in effect required WMECO to use its own employees when performing certain underground cable work in the Berkshire area (the "Berkshire restriction"), but otherwise allowed the company free rein with regard to subcontracting. During the fall of 1974 WMECO had, at the unions' request, launched an experiment of using regular employees to perform certain tree trimming work that ordinarily would have been contracted out. The company ended the experiment after a few months, informing the union both that the regular employees were not cheaper than the subcontractors, and that it did not intend to compete with its subcontractors.

At the first negotiating session over the new collective bargaining agreement on May 20, 1975, the company proposed to eliminate the Berkshire restriction. According to testimony of the union's bargaining agent, the company stated that the restriction was inefficient and uneconomical. At the next session on June 2, the union submitted its own proposal with regard to subcontracting. The union wanted to forbid subcontracting whenever regular employees were laid off or not fully utilized. Some layoffs had occurred before bargaining began, and the company warned the union that more might be expected. At the meeting where it presented its proposal, the union requested information as to total hours worked by subcontractors during the existing agreement and the amounts paid to these workers. A union spokesman explained to company negotiators that the union believed regular employees could do the work more cheaply than the subcontractors. According to the spokesman, one of the company negotiators asked if the union's proposal would apply even to short term subcontracting and, when informed that it did, declared that such a restriction would be inefficient and uneconomical.

At a negotiating session on June 24, the company orally informed the union of the hours worked by subcontractors, but refused to provide the cost information on the ground that it was not relevant. On June 26 the union renewed its request for the cost data in writing. On June 30 both parties withdrew their respective proposals as to subcontracting, but the union did not waive its claim to the information. The parties reached a new agreement on July 3, and during that day the company provided the union with a letter in response to the request for cost information. It stated:

> The company feels that the cost of such outside contracting is not material to negotiations and, consequently, that we do not have to supply it.
> Our refusal is not based on economic reasons, but on the fact that such information is not relevant to negotiations.

These proceedings followed.

Facts — The Complaint Against CL&P

Beginning in the spring of 1976, CL&P and Locals 420 and 457 entered into negotiations over a collective bargaining agreement to replace the one expiring on June 1. The existing agreement contained the following clause:

Article XVI
Work regularly performed by employees covered by this Agreement will not be contracted out if it would result in loss of continuity of employment or opportunities for permanent promotions to job classifications covered by this Agreement.

At least since 1972 the locals had requested information from the company respecting subcontracting, and the company consistently had refused to disclose cost data on the ground that such information was not relevant to bargaining. Before negotiations on the 1976 contract began, the locals sent a letter to the company requesting the following information:

> 1. The name of each and every contractor & or subcontractor who performed work during the year 1975.

2. The type of work performed.

3. The number of people employed by the contractors on such work.

4. Total manhours worked by contractors [sic] employees.

5. A list of equipment used to perform the work.

6. The total cost of each job contracted out and a breakdown of the costs to the Company to complete the work.

The letter indicated the union's intention "to propose to the Company areas where our members can perform work now being performed by contractors more economically . . . ." The company agreed to provide most of the information, but refused to comply with the last two requests. With regard to the demand for cost information, the company replied, "There are many reasons why contractors are used on various projects. Therefore, the Company does not consider the cost data relevant for bargaining on this matter." The locals renewed their request for this information, and the company held to its earlier position.

The parties exchanged initial proposals for a new collective bargaining agreement on April 26, and among those forwarded by the union was a change in the existing subcontracting restriction. Although most of the promised information was provided to the locals in the course of negotiations in May, the company remained adamant in refusing to pass on subcontracting cost data. A new collective bargaining agreement was executed July 15, in which the previous subcontracting limitation clause was carried over without change. By that time the locals had already begun to seek relief from the Labor Board.

Principles Applicable to Both Cases

The sole issue in each of these appeals is whether in the circumstances of each case the company violated its duty to bargain in good faith by refusing to disclose subcontracting cost information. This court recently addressed the principles applicable to the compulsory exchange of financial information between union and employer during bargaining in *Teleprompter Corp. v. NLRB,* 570 F.2d 4 (1st Cir. 1977). In our discussion of "the general obligation of an employer to provide information that is needed by the bargaining representative for the proper performance of its duties," *NLRB v. Acme Industrial,* 385 U.S. 432, 435-36, 87 S.Ct. 565, 568, 17 L.Ed.2d 495, 64 LRRM 2069 (1967), we observed:

"The 'general obligation' described in Acme extends in varying degrees of intensity throughout the many aspects of management-union relations, with accommodation being made between the union's urgent need for some types of information, such as wage data, and the employer's greater relative interest in preserving the confidentiality of other information, such as profitability data."

Teleprompter Corp., supra, 570 F.2d at 8. Information pertaining immediately to the mandatory subjects of bargaining — wages, hours, and other terms and conditions of employment, *see* 29 U.S.C. § 158(d) — is presumptively relevant and must be disclosed unless it "plainly appears irrelevant." *NLRB v. Yawman and Erbe Mfg. Co.,* 187 F.2d 947, 949 (2d Cir. 1951). Other kinds of information which a union believes might be useful in bargaining "need not be disclosed in the course of contract negotiations unless the bargaining representative first makes a showing that it is specially relevant to the bargaining taking place." *Teleprompter Corp., supra,* 570 F.2d at 9 (citing *International Woodworkers v. NLRB,* 105 U.S.App.D.C. 37, 263 F.2d 483 (1959)). In such cases, a union must do more than merely claim that the data would be helpful in performing its tasks. *Id.* But if an employer itself puts the information in contention — as by asserting an economic inability to pay an increase in wages where a union seeks profitability data — then the employer must divulge the information. *Id.* at 9 (citing *NLRB v. Truitt Mfg. Co.,* 351 U.S. 149, 152-53, 76 S.Ct. 753, 100 L.Ed. 1027 (1955)).

Neither of the Labor Board decisions at issue here treated the cost data sought by the unions as directly related to a mandatory subject of bargaining and therefore presumptively relevant. For example, the ALJ wrote in the CL&P case: "I agree with the [employer's] contention that not all information is presumptively relevant to the bargaining process, and that in areas such as contracting and subcontracting an employer is not obligated to furnish information unless such precise relevance has been established." The ALJ in the WMECO decision applied a similar analysis.[4] Rulings of the Board and case law support this conclusion. Following the decision of the Supreme Court in *Fibreboard Paper Products Corp. v. NLRB,* 379 U.S. 203, 85 S.Ct. 398, 13 L.Ed.2d 233 (1965), that con- tracting out of unit work that results in the extinction of the bar- gaining unit is a mandatory subject of bargaining, the Labor Board quickly sought to cut off precipitous extension of that ruling to other forms of subcontracting.[5] In *Westinghouse Electric Corp.,* 150 NLRB 1574

---

[4] He wrote:

"Though a union need not make a special showing of relevancy and necessity to obtain information about employment of employees within the bargaining unit, where the request for information concerns matters outside the bargaining unit, as in the case at bar, the Union must ordinarily demonstrate more precisely the relevancy of the data requested."

[5] The court in Fibreboard made clear its holding was limited to the facts of the case:

"We are thus not expanding the scope of mandatory bargaining to hold, as

(1965), the Board held that an employer was per- mitted unilaterally to implement contracting out of work capable of being performed by unit employees when the subcontract- ing was part of the employer's usual method of conducting its operations and did not have a significant impact on unit em- ployees' job interests. *Id.* at 1576. Subsequent judicial decisions have made clear the importance of impact on the bargaining unit as a factor in determining whether particular subcontracting consti- tutes an issue over which bargaining is compulsory. Where an em- ployer decision to contract out work takes away jobs previously performed by members of the bargaining unit, the employer must bargain over the decision. *UAAAIW v. NLRB,* 127 U.S.App.D.C. 97, 381 F.2d 265 *cert. denied,* 389 U.S. 857, 88 S.Ct. 82, 19 L.Ed.2d 122 (1967). Where subcontracting does not divert from the bargaining unit jobs performed by unit employees, however, an employer need not bargain with the union over the decision. .

[Citation omitted.]

It is not enough that the unit employees may be concerned about lost work; if diminution in available work cannot be attributed to the subcontracting, it cannot be made an issue over which bargaining is compulsory.

Although the parties are thus agreed that the employers here were not guilty of an unfair labor practice unless the unions have shown that the information requested was precisely relevant to the bargaining that took place, they vigorously dispute whether that showing was made out in either case. Because the facts of the two cases differ, separate analysis is necessary.

Analysis and Conclusions as to WMECO

As noted above, at various times both before and during its bargaining with the union, WMECO indicated that restrictions on its power to subcontract were uneconomical. It cited economics as a reason (although not the only one) for discontinuing its experiment of using unit employees for tree trimming, and criticized the union's proposal to limit subcontracting as uneconomical. Once having made such assertions, the duty to bargain in good faith required WMECO to provide, upon demand, such information as was reasonably

---

we do now, that the type of 'contracting out' involved in this case — the replacement of employees in the existing bargaining unit with those of an independent contractor to do the same work under similar conditions of employment — is a statutory subject of collective bargaining under § 8(d). Our decision need not and does not encompass other forms of 'contracting out' or 'subcontracting' which arise daily in our complex economy."

379 U.S. at 215, 85 S.Ct. at 405.

necessary to substantiate them. *Teleprompter Corp., supra,* 570 F.2d at 11.

WMECO protests on this appeal that the union never made clear the reasons why it wanted the cost information, thereby preventing WMECO from evaluating the propriety of the request in light of the obligations imposed by law. The Labor Board found, however, that the circumstances of the negotiations with the union gave WMECO adequate notice that the requested information was related to various assertions by WMECO that restrictions on subcontracting were uneconomical. There was sufficient evidence to support a finding that WMECO had tied subcontracting to economics at the first bargaining session in 1975, and that at the very next session, the union both responded to the company's proposal and requested the cost information. Again at that second session the company made clear its belief that cost and subcontracting issues were bound together. In light of these findings, the company appears to have had a sufficient basis for understanding the purpose of the union's request.

There is, it is true, some force to WMECO's further argument that the rationale expressed by the Labor Board in its decision was broader than that sanctioned by case law. The Board appears, at times, to have proceeded on the broader and, we believe, improper theory that subcontracting costs are always relevant in a collective bargaining context, once a union has made clear its intent to capture work previously contracted out. *See infra.* It did not seek to rely on *Truitt Mfg. Co., supra,* or other cases dealing with the relevance of information needed to substantiate an employer's assertions in the course of bargaining. But, although the Board may have applied a different rationale, ample basis exists in this record for a finding that the union needed subcontracting cost information to verify statements made by WMECO as to the economic necessity of removing restrictions on subcontracting. The evidence is clear that WMECO put costs in contention, and "the exact formulation used by the Employer in conveying this message is immaterial." *New York Printing Pressmen v. NLRB,* 538 F.2d 496, 500, 92 LRRM 3207 (2d Cir. 1976). The special relevance of the information thus being established, it is unnecessary to determine whether other rationales would be available to support the Labor Board's result. In these circumstances, nothing would be gained by remanding to the Labor Board for reevaluation. *Compare Associated Grocers of New England, Inc. v. NLRB,* 562 F.2d 1333, 1337, 96 LRRM 2630 (1st Cir. 1977). There is ample record support for the Board's order that WMECO disclose the subcontracting cost data which the union requested for bargaining purposes.

WMECO also attacks the portion of the Board's order that requires disclosure of subcontracting cost information for contract administration purposes. The ALJ did not address the union's claim that it needed the data to police WMECO's compliance with the contract, and on the basis of the record before him we are unable to see how the information would be relevant to this purpose. The Labor Board nevertheless found, in summary fashion, that the information was necessary for contract administration and modified the cease and desist order accordingly.

This action remains entirely unexplained, and indeed seems inexplicable in light of the Board's previous holding directly to the contrary in *Southwestern Bell Telephone Co.,* 173 NLRB 172 (1968). There the Board held that subcontracting cost information was irrelevant to the union's contract administration needs. It noted then, as is true in this case, that finding out whether the employer violated a contract restriction on subcontracting requires knowledge only of the extent and nature of that activity, not of the employer's purposes or motivations. In sum, there is absolutely no support in the record or findings of the Board for this portion of the order, and it therefore must be modified to delete all references to contract administration. As modified, the order will be enforced.

Analysis and Conclusions as to CL&P

The record is quite different with regard to CL&P. Unlike WMECO, officials of CL&P never made any statements indicating that existing or proposed restrictions on subcontracting were uneconomical. There is no assertion that the information was necessary for substantiation purposes. Instead, the Labor Board advances a far broader theory. It argues that at least where job security is a genuine concern of the union, all information about an employer's subcontracting practices are relevant whether or not the subcontracting is responsible for work lost to the unit. According to the ALJ, in conclusions adopted by the Board,

"The [employer] further argues that the record evidence supports its contention that the Unions were not concerned in reality with protecting the work of the bargaining unit, but were really intent on capturing additional work. The [employer's] argument in this respect is bottomed on the phraseology of the Union's proposed amendment to Article XVI; and supposed admissions of the Union's [sic] agents in their testimony. It can be readily conceded that the Unions' proposed amendment would have further restricted the [employer's] authority to contract out work, but I find no persuasive evidence to support the contention that the Unions' agents admitted that the capture of additional work was their real objective. Even if established, however, I fail to perceive that such evidence would have any material bearing on the issue of relevancy. I know of no authority, and the [employer] has cited none, to substantiate the proposition that information is relevant only where the bargaining agent intends to use it solely for the purpose of maintaining the *status quo,* or that information is not relevant where the union intends to use it to expand the work potential of the bargaining unit employees."

Because unit employees were capable of doing the work currently contracted out, the Board argues cost information about the work must be disclosed.

Whether or not the locals' agents admitted their purpose was to capture additional work, the record is clear that CL&P's existing subcontracting practices did not divert any unit work, and that the aforementioned Article XVI protected the employees from such encroachment. The conclusion is inescapable that the work which was the object of the locals' interest was non-unit work that the locals sought to capture, possibly to mitigate the effects of work reduction attributable to entirely independent causes. It is in light of this fact that the locals' demand for cost information must be evaluated.

The Labor Board seeks to support its analysis of the relevance of this information by relying on two distinct lines of authority. It attempts to compare this case to other situations where information about employees outside the bargaining unit has been held relevant to the concerns of representatives of those within the unit. *See NLRB v. Rockwell-Standard Corp.,* 410 F.2d 953 (6th Cir. 1969); *NLRB v. Goodyear Aerospace Corp.,* 388 F.2d 673 (6th Cir. 1968); *International Telephone and Telegraph Corp.* v. NLRB, 382 F.2d 366 (3d Cir. 1967), *cert. denied,* 389 U.S. 1039, 88 S.Ct. 777, 19 L.Ed.2d 829 (1968); *Curtiss-Wright Corp. v. NLRB,* 347 F.2d 61 (3d Cir. 1965); *Ohio Power Co.,* 216 NLRB 987 (1975), *enforced,* 531 F.2d 1381 (6th Cir. 1976) (mem.); *Hollywood Brands, Inc.,* 142 NLRB 304, *enforced,* 324 F.2d 956 (5th Cir. 1963) (mem.), *cert. denied,* 377 U.S. 923, 84 S.Ct. 1221, 12 L.Ed.2d 215 (1964). The Board also cites to cases where employers have been forced to divulge cost data relating to employee benefits. *NLRB v. General Electric Co.,* 418 F.2d 736 (2d Cir. 1969), *cert. denied,* 397 U.S. 965, 90 S.Ct. 995, 25 L.Ed.2d 257 (1970); *Sylvania Electric Products, Inc. v. NLRB,* 358 F.2d 591 (1st Cir.), *cert. denied,* 385 U.S. 852, 87 S.Ct. 87, 17 L.Ed.2d 80 (1966). None of the cases cited, however, apply to the problem presented here.

Rockwell-Standard, Goodyear, and *Curtiss-Wright* involved union investigations into the suspected diversion of bargaining unit work to employees who were outside the unit. The unions needed wage, job description, and related data for the outside employees to determine whether they were doing work properly performed by unit employees. *See also Acme Industrial, supra.* Here, by contrast, diversion of unit work is not a concern. In *International Telephone and Telegraph Corp., supra,* the unit sought seniority data about an entire class of non-unit employees who were potentially eligible to be transferred into the bargaining unit, thereby altering the seniority structure of the unit. Disclosure was ordered only as to those employees who were about to be transferred. *See also NLRB v. Western Electric, Inc.,* 559 F.2d 1131 (8th Cir. 1977). The union in *Ohio Power Co., supra,* expressly disclaimed any interest in cost information. In *Hollywood Brands, Inc., supra,* the Board ordered disclosure of the wages paid employees in factories outside the unit. This information was made relevant by statements of the employer expressing its intention to standardize wages throughout its factories. None of these situations exist here.

The other line of cases cited by the Labor Board also involved circumstances different from the case at bar. In both *General Electric* and *Sylvania* the union demanded to know the cost to the employer of particular benefit packages proposed as substitutes for wage increases in the course of collective bargaining. Both courts held that this data would significantly aid the bargaining process by enabling the unions to evaluate the desirability of an increase in benefits as against an equivalent wage increase. But the information demanded related to benefits to be received by the employees. Although the cost of the benefits was not itself a mandatory subject of bargaining, *see Sylvania Electric Products, Inc. v. NLRB,* 291 F.2d 128 (1st Cir.), *cert. denied,* 368 U.S. 926, 82 S.Ct. 360, 7 L.Ed.2d 190 (1961), the benefits themselves were and the cost information was shown to be closely related to them. Here, by contrast, the cost information relates to a subject which all agree is not a mandatory subject of bargaining, namely subcontracting that does not itself reduce the work traditionally performed by bargaining unit employees.

Although the ALJ professed to know of no authority supporting a distinction between restrictions on subcontracting that are necessary to preserve the status quo, and restrictions motivated only by a desire to capture additional work for the unit, just such a distinction appears to have been drawn to determine when particular forms of subcontracting do and do not constitute mandatory subjects of bargaining. The line of cases beginning with Fibreboard, and including the Board's own Westinghouse Electric decision, indicate that whether or not a union seeks only to preserve the status quo is a critical difference with respect to the duty to bargain. It should follow that this distinction is highly relevant, if not dispositive, in information demand cases as well. Just as a union cannot compel an employer to bargain over subjects that fall outside the ambit of "wages, hours, and other terms and conditions of employment," it cannot bootstrap a demand for information relating to these non-mandatory matters by its unilateral assertion of interest. Some action of the employer is necessary to make this kind of information relevant to bargaining.

On the facts of this case, we can find no action of CL&P to justify disclosure of the information requested. Although CL&P voluntarily provided the locals with some information about its subcontracting practices, throughout the negotiations it consistently reserved its rights as to the cost information. CL&P did not hamstring the locals by insisting on bargaining over subcontracting while withholding pertinent information. In short, the Board does not and, the record indicates, cannot point to any statement, compromise or suggestion attributable to CL&P that raised costs as an issue. Instead CL&P has been confronted with a unilateral attempt by the locals to put subcontracting costs into contention. Under the principles expressed above, CL&P was under no obligation to respond, and its refusal to provide the information cannot be held an unfair labor practice. The order of the Board against CL&P will not be enforced.

NOTE:

1. The Court in *Western Mass. Electric Co., supra,* found a distinction drawn between restrictions on subcontracting that seek to preserve the status quo and those motivated by a desire to capture additional work for the unit. Is the Court actually distinguishing between "mandatory" and "non-mandatory" subjects of bargaining in granting a union's demand for information?

b. Administration of the Collective Bargaining Agreement

The duty to supply information applies not only at the active negotiations stage, but also to the administration of collective bargaining agreements already in force. In *NLRB v. Acme Industrial,*[31] the Supreme Court held that where a company's relocation of major machinery could affect employee rights under the contract, a union's request for the facts behind the move was granted. ("There can be no question of the general obligation of an employer to provide information that is needed for the proper performance of its duties.") In *Erbe Mfg. Co.,* the Second Circuit fashioned a discovery-type rule declaring "information must be disclosed unless it plainly appears irrelevant."[32] Furthermore, the existence of a grievance procedure will not preclude a union from seeking relevant information in a Board proceeding.[33]

---

[31] 385 U.S. 432 (1967).
[32] 187 F.2d 947, 949 (2d Cir. 1951).
[33] *See, e.g.,* NLRB v. Detroit Edison Co., 560 F.2d 722 (6th Cir. 1977).

NOTES:

(1) In *NLRB v. Detroit Edison Co.*, 560 F.2d 722 (6th Cir. 1977), the Court of Appeals for the Sixth Circuit enforced a Board's order directing the employer to furnish the union with the psychological aptitude test used in determining eligibility for promotion together with the scores of employees who took the test. In so holding, the Court stated:

> It is the duty of an employer generally to provide to the authorized representative of its employees information which the representative needs to perform its duties. *N.L.R.B. v. Acme Industrial Company*, 385 U.S. 432, 435-36, 87 S. Ct. 565, 17 L. Ed. 2d 495 (1967); *N.L.R.B. v. Truitt Manufacturing Company*, 351 U.S. 149, 76 S. Ct. 753, 100 L. Ed. 1027 (1956); *Kayser-Roth Hosiery Co., Inc. v. N.L.R.B.*, 447 F.2d 396 (6th Cir. 1971); *N.L.R.B. v. Rockwell-Standard Corp.*, 410 F.2d 953 (6th Cir. 1969). Referring to permissible Board action directing an employer to deliver such requested information to a union, the Court in *Acme Industrial Company*, 385 U.S. *supra*, at 437, 87 S. Ct. at 568, said: "It was only acting upon the probability that the desired information was relevant, and that it would be of use to union in carrying out its statutory duties and responsibilities." Matters related to seniority and eligibility for promotion under a collective bargaining agreement satisfy the test of probability of relevance to the duties and responsibilities of the union representing employees under that agreement. Since Detroit Edison unilaterally selected the standardized tests to be included in the examination for Instrument Man B and unilaterally determined the cutoff point below which no applicant would be considered eligible for promotion to that classification, the union was entitled to information about the tests.

A union's right to information in the possession of the employer is not unlimited. An employer would undoubtedly resist furnishing information valuable to competitors or revealing its potential to resist a strike. Both the NLRB and the courts have distinguished an employer's refusal to furnish financial data showing profitability from an employer's refusal to supply information relating to wages. *See Teleprompter Corp. v. NLRB*, 470 F.2d 4 (1st Cir. 1977) ("financial data need not be disclosed in contract negotiations unless the bargaining representative *first* makes a showing that it is specially relevant to the bargaining taking place").

(2) Can a union waive its right to relevant information by agreement? The Board has answered this question affirmatively, but will insist upon the showing of a clear, express waiver, which will not be easily inferred.

(3) To what extent must one party provide affirmative assistance to the other in preparing for negotiations? In *NLRB v. Milgo Industrial, Inc.,* 567 F.2d 450 (2d Cir. 1977), the Court refused to enforce part of a NLRB order to furnish information where the employer failed to supply the union with a copy of the company's health plan. It found that the Union was not denied access to the document where:

> Milgo informed the Union of the title of its Blue Cross-Blue Shield plan, which was in common use; if the Union did not have a copy in its files, a telephone call to Blue Cross-Blue Shield would have obtained one.

3. The Impact of External Law

During the past decade, Congress enacted several laws which attempt to fill a vacuum left by the collective bargaining process. The Occupational Safety and Health Act of 1970 (OSHA),[34] the Employee Retirement Income Security Act of 1974 (ERISA)[35] and the 1978 amendments to the Age Discrimination in Employment Act (ADEA)[36] are examples of such federal legislation regulating employees' benefits and working conditions.

There has been a great deal of debate, but little agreement, regarding the impact of external law on collective bargaining.[37] None of these laws require the inclusion of substantive provisions in a collective bargaining agreement. These laws, however, may provide an impetus to unions to negotiate for comprehensive safety clauses, and better pension and retirement programs. These laws should strengthen a union's position that it has a substantial interest in the negotiation of such provisions.

D. WHEN THE PARTIES MUST BARGAIN

1. Meeting at Reasonable Times

Section 8(d) of the Act requires the parties to meet "at reasonable times" for the purpose of collective bargaining. This requirement has been interpreted to include the obligation to meet at reasonable intervals and for reasonable periods of time.[38] A finding that a party has failed to comply with this procedural obligation may be

---

[34] 29 U.S.C. §§ 651-678 (1970).

[35] 29 U.S.C. § 1001 *et seq.* (Supp. V, 1975).

[36] 29 U.S.C. §§ 621-634 (1970), as amended.

[37] *See* Part Two, *infra,* pp. 437-494.

[38] Tennessee Chair Co., 126 NLRB 1357 (1960); B.F. Diamond Constr. Co., 163 NLRB 161 (1967), *enforced,* 410 F.2d 462 (5th Cir. 1969), *cert. denied,* 396 U.S. 835 (1969) (one month intervals between bargaining sessions unreasonable).

considered a *per se* refusal to bargain, without regard to the good or bad faith of the party.

Dilatory tactics — that is, delay in scheduling meetings,[39] in supplying requested information,[40] or in the execution of an agreement[41] — may be deemed violative of a party's duty to bargain. Similarly condemned is the failure to invest a negotiator with sufficient authority to engage in bargaining with the intent to reach an agreement.[42] However, the duty to prevent unreasonable delay is bilateral, and a refusal to bargain will not be found where both parties were equally dilatory.[43]

2. Duration of the Bargaining Obligation

Once a bargaining obligation has been rightfully established, a reasonable period in which it can have a fair chance to succeed must be afforded.[44] To promote stable labor relations, the NLRB does not permit a certified union's majority status to be questioned for one year following its certification.[45] When an employer voluntarily recognizes a union as the majority's representative, there is an irrebuttable presumption of the union's continuing majority status for a reasonable time.[46]

NOTES:

(1) Is there a duty to bargain during the life of a contract? In an early case, *Jacobs Mfg. Co.,* 94 NLRB 1214 (1951), *affirmed, NLRB v. Jacobs Mfg. Co.,* 196 F.2d 680 (2d Cir. 1952), the Board ordered the company to discuss union pension plan proposals which were neither incorporated into the collective bargaining agreement nor discussed during negotiations. However, a different result may obtain where the subject was discussed in negotiations.

Although in the *Jacobs* case, the agreement included a provision for the reopening of the contract, subsequent decisions have required mid-term bargaining even in the absence of such provisions. *See Elizabethtown Water Co.,* 234 NLRB No. 68 (1978). For an

---

[39] Solo Cup Co., 142 NLRB 1290 (1963), *enforced,* 332 F.2d 447 (4th Cir. 1964).
[40] Rhodes-Holland Chevrolet Co., 146 NLRB 1304 (1964).
[41] Local 717, Ice Cream Drivers (Ice Cream Council, Inc.), 145 NLRB 865 (1964).
[42] National Amusements, Inc., 155 NLRB 1485 (1965).
[43] Dunn Packing Co., 143 NLRB 1149 (1963).
[44] Franks Bros. v. NLRB, 321 U.S. 702 (1944).
[45] Section 9(c)(3) of the Act, 29 U.S.C. § 159(c)(3) prohibits the Board from conducting more than one representation election for a bargaining unit in a year. After a year has passed since certification, clear evidence must be presented to prove the union's loss in majority status.
[46] Brennan's Cadillac, 321 NLRB No. 34 (1977), relying on the principles established in Keller Plastics, 157 NLRB 583 (1966).

interesting discussion on the effect of recent federal legislation on the duty to bargain over welfare and retirement plans during the term of a contract, *see* Smith, Impact of 1978 ADEA Amendments on Collective Bargaining, 98 LRR 146 (1978). *See also* Anderson, The Duty to Bargain During Term of Contract, 1967 Lab. Rel. Yearbk. 242 (BNA).

3. Defense to the Bargaining Obligation — Waiver

A party may be found to have waived its right to bargain over particular subject matter if certain requirements are met. The "waiver" defense is often raised in an NLRB unfair labor practice proceeding by a party charged with the unlawful refusal to bargain for implementing unilateral changes that affect matters over which the party was under an obligation to negotiate.

A party may be deemed to have waived its rights as a result of the totality of its past practices, a single act or even its failure to act. However, the Board will not easily infer a party's relinquishment of its bargaining rights. Where a contractual waiver is alleged, the Board will require the language to indicate a "clear and unmistakable" waiver.[47] The language must be specific; a generally worded clause will not be considered a waiver of a party's rights to bargaining over a subject. However, in a 1974 decision, the NLRB departed from past holdings in rejecting a strict application of the "clear and unequivocal" waiver rule. In the *Radioear Corp.* case,[48] the Board found a conscious waiver of a union's right to bargain over certain bonuses where the contract included a clause providing that the document embodied the complete agreement of the parties (called a "zipper" clause). The Board majority stated that in determining the continuing bargaining obligation of the parties, a variety of factors should be considered, including: (1) the bargaining history of the parties; (2) the precise wording and completeness of the clause; and (3) the proposals rejected or accepted during the course of the bargaining. If, however, the Board finds that the waiver clause was exacted as the price of the contract or agreement to negotiate, such a clause will not be enforced.[49]

E. THE EXTENT OF GOVERNMENT INTERVENTION

As stated in the introduction to this chapter, in administering the Act, the Board must be mindful of the two, sometimes conflicting,

---

[47] Timken Roller Bearing Co. v. NLRB, 325 F.2d 746 (6th Cir. 1963, *cert. denied*, 376 U.S. 971 (1964).

[48] Radioear Corp., 214 NLRB 362 (1974). *See also* NLRB v. Auto Crane Co., 536 F.2d 310 (10th Cir. 1976) (unilateral implementation of wage increase and employee thrift plan by employer was permissible in light of broad zipper clause).

[49] Shell Oil Co., 93 NLRB 161 (1951).

philosophies underlying the legal framework. On one hand, Congress sought to encourage collective bargaining between labor and management as the means of establishing mutually satisfactory working conditions; on the other hand, it did not intend the Board to intervene in the collective bargaining process and assist a party in an "economically disadvantageous position." [50]

To carry out its Congressional mandate, the Board at times must exercise restraint in its regulation of the parties' conduct. Has the NLRB crossed the threshold into the conference room and now looks over the negotiator's shoulder? Was Professor Cox correct when he questioned whether the NLRB's "next step [is] to take a seat at the bargaining table?" [51] Can the Board avoid "intervention"?

The following opinion was written by a former member of the Board.

WALTHER, THE BOARD'S PLACE AT THE BARGAINING TABLE, 28 Labor Law Journal 131-33 (1977)

The declared purpose of the National Labor Relations Act is to promote and protect the "friendly adjustment of industrial disputes" through the practice of collective bargaining.

A cursory glance at the Act thus shows that it is concerned to a great extent with maneuvering the parties to the bargaining table. The Board under the Act, is constituted as the midwife of the bargaining relationship. It oversees the birth of that bargaining relationship and attempts to prevent any miscarriages. But once the parties have passed the threshold into the bargaining arena, the Board has accomplished much of what it can do. After that threshold is passed, the Board's further involvement with the collective bargaining process is limited to defining the subjects about which the parties must bargain and to seeing that the bargaining is not simply a charade. Although these are not negligible tasks, they do not compare in importance to the Board's task of getting the parties safely to the table for meaningful bargaining.

No matter what happens at or on the way to the bargaining table, the Board cannot go so far as to compel the making of a concession or the agreement to any proposal.[1] Even where, as sometimes happens, the employer engages in patently illegal activity which undermines the union's support and destroys its bargaining strength, the Board must limit itself (perhaps through imposition of a bargaining order) to bringing the parties to the bargaining table; anything beyond this is not permitted.

---

[50] NLRB v. Wooster Division of Borg-Warner Corp., 356 U.S. 342, 348 (1958).
[51] Cox, The Duty to Bargain in Good Faith, 71 Harv. L. Rev. 1401, 1403 (1959).
[1] H.K. Porter Co., Inc. v. NLRB, 397 U.S. 99 (1970).

To those who argue that this is lamentable or unfair, it is sufficient to observe that collective bargaining, as envisioned by the Act, is at heart a consensual process. There are good reasons, practical and otherwise, why this should be so. The collective bargaining agreement is an excellent vehicle for the adjustment of disputes (and correlatively for promoting employees' welfare) primarily because it is a privately negotiated, consensual document. Its strengths lie in the fact that it is self-enforcing and flexible — strengths which themselves derive from the fact that the agreement is the product of the parties' consent.

Only an agreement consented to by both parties and negotiated without undue interference from an outside agency will be truly self-enforcing. Similarly, only an agreement negotiated in the absence of substantive restraints will be sufficiently flexible to effectively meet the difficult unforeseen problems that can and will arise in the collective bargaining relationship. The parties alone know what they want. Absence of control by the Board is thus warranted if the agreement is to best balance each party's expectations.

Additionally, only by making collective bargaining a free and cooperative action of the parties can the Act achieve what the Act intends the collective bargaining relationship to achieve. It is paradoxically the Act's insistence upon consent in collective bargaining that has made the Act such an effective regulatory device. Like every piece of comprehensive social legislation, the National Labor Relations Act has both a regulative and an educative function — two functions which, because they work in tandem, are inseparable. Each function complements and is dependent upon the other.

Unless the public had become, through time, educated in and acquiescent to the goals of the Act, the Board, as the agency empowered to enforce the Act, would have found itself mired in a hopeless regulative task. That this has not happened is a tribute to the Act's educative successes. The fact that the Act stops short of compelling consent to the terms of collective bargaining agreements has, I feel, been chiefly responsible for these educative successes and has brought about the widespread acceptance of unionization and collective bargaining that is vital to the realization of the Act's objectives.

Where, therefore, an employer — through the employment of illegal tactics — effectively undermines the union's bargaining power before being shepherded to the bargaining table, the Board can perhaps attempt to mitigate the effect of this unlawful conduct by devising a remedy which restores to the union some of its bargaining power.[2] But forcing either party to make bargaining concessions and making the Board the final arbiter of what goes into a collective bargaining agreement would irreparably damage the collective bargaining process and would in the long run do more harm than good.

It follows from the above that, just as the Board cannot compel the making of a concession, so the Board should be very reluctant to disturb the terms of the collective bargaining agreement once negotiated. A collective bargaining agreement is a fragile latticework of trade-offs and compromise, which often represents the results of months of negotiation. If the Board voids a provision of the agreement, it upsets the delicate balance arranged by the parties and in the process makes it probable that one of the parties will be disproportionately prejudiced by the Board's action. Obviously, such a result should be avoided if possible.

This is not to say that the Board should stand idly by if a negotiated agreement clearly sacrifices employee rights or is written in blatant disregard for the provisions of the Act. However, where the parties' agreement represents a reasonable accommodation between competing employer and union interests and does not trample on the employees' rights guaranteed by the Act, the Board should not intrude.

NOTES:

(1) For early discussions of government regulation of the subject matter of collective bargaining, *see* Cox and Dunlop, Regulation of Collective Bargaining by the National Labor Relations Board, 63 Harv. L. Rev. 389 (1950); Findling & Colby, Regulation of Collective Bargaining by the National Labor Relations Board — Another View, 51 Colum. L. Rev. 170 (1951).

(2) At times the Board is confronted with a case where it must strike a delicate balance between a party's freedom to contract and the furtherance of the policies underlying the labor laws' duty to bargain in good faith. In *H.K. Porter Co. v. NLRB,* 397 U.S. 99 (1970), the employer refused to bargain about a contract clause providing for the check-off of union dues. The Board held that the employer had not acted in good faith, finding that the refusal was motivated by the desire to frustrate agreement. The Board, in a supplemental order affirmed by the Court of Appeals, ordered the company to agree to the union check-off provision it previously refused to bargain about. The Supreme Court, while stating that the

---

[2] See my dissent in *Atlas Tack Corporation,* 226 NLRB No. 38 (1976), 1976-77 CCH NLRB ¶ 17,442.

NLRB has the power to require the parties to negotiate, held that the Board cannot compel them to agree to any substantive contractual provision of a collective bargaining agreement. Justice Black, speaking for the Court majority said:

> "The object of this Act was not to allow governmental regulation of the terms and conditions of employment, but rather to ensure that employers and their employees could work together to establish mutually satisfactory conditions. The basic theme of the Act was that through collective bargaining the passions, arguments, and struggles of prior years would be channeled into constructive, open discussions leading, hopefully, to mutual agreement. But it was recognized from the beginning that agreement might in some cases be impossible, and it was never intended that the Government would in such cases step in, become a party to the negotiations and impose its own views of a desirable settlement. . . . While the parties' freedom of contract is not absolute under the Act, allowing the Board to compel agreement when the parties themselves are unable to agree would violate the fundamental premise on which the Act is based — private bargaining under governmental supervision of the procedure alone, without any official compulsion over the actual terms of the contract. *H.K. Porter v. NLRB*, 397 U.S. at 108.

(3) However, in some circumstances, the usual cease-and-desist order issued by the NLRB may be inadequate to remedy an employer's "clear and flagrant" violation of its bargaining duty. In *IUE v. NLRB* [Tiidee Products, Inc.], 426 F.2d 1243 (D.C. Cir. 1970), *cert. denied*, 400 U.S. 950 (1970), the Court of Appeals for the District of Columbia remanded the case to the Board for further consideration of an appropriate remedy, which might include back pay to compensate the employees for the benefits denied them by the employer's refusal to bargain. In reaching this result, the majority stressed that remand was limited to consideration of past damages, and not to compulsion of a future contract term, thus distinguishing the case from the Supreme Court's decision in *H.K. Porter*. The same court held that the Board had not abused its discretion in refusing to grant make-whole relief, however, where employers declined to bargain in good faith efforts to challenge a union's certification or other representational determinations. *IBEW v. NLRB* (Presto Mfg. Co.), 417 F.2d 1144 (D.C. Cir. 1969), *cert. denied*, 396 U.S. 1004 (1970); *United Steelworkers v. NLRB* (Quality Rubber Mfg. Co.), 430 F.2d 519 (D.C. Cir. 1970).

In *Ex-Cell-O Corp.*, 185 NLRB 107 (1970), *aff'd, Ex-Cell-O Corp. v. NLRB*, 449 F.2d 1058 (D.C. Cir. 1971), the Board held that it did not have the authority to make employees whole for the loss of wages and fringe benefits that they might have received absent a refusal to bargain. The Board found such a remedy too speculative to formulate. Further, it stated that the fashioning of more adequate, compensatory remedies in these cases is a matter for Congress, and not the Board. *Compare Phelps Dodge Corp. v. NLRB*, 313 U.S. 177 (1941).

The "make whole" remedy was interred, at least for the foreseeable future, in *Tiidee Products, Inc.*, 194 N.L.R.B. No. 198, 79 L.R.R.M. 1175 (1972). On remand, a unanimous Board rejected a reimbursement order, even where the employer's refusal to bargain was a "clear and flagrant" violation of law. Nonetheless, the Board thought such a violation did merit a remedy going beyond the customary cease and desist order. It therefore required the employer to reimburse both the NLRB and the union for their litigation expenses, to mail copies of the NLRB's notice to each employee's home, to keep the union supplied with an employee name-and-address list for one year, and to give the union reasonable access to company bulletin boards. In this and subsequent decisions the Board has distinguished between situations where the company's defense in such NLRB proceedings fell in the "frivolous" or "bad faith" category, *e.g., Tiidee Products, supra,* rather than the "debatable" category. *Heck's Inc.*, 215 NLRB 765 (1974).

(4) In *Textile Workers Union v. Darlington Mfg. Co.*, 380 U.S. 263 (1965), the Supreme Court refused to hold that the employer violated the NLRA by shutting down its business completely. In so doing, the Court declared:

> We are not presented here with the case of a "runaway shop," whereby Darlington would transfer its work to another plant or open a new plant in another locality to replace its closed plant. Nor are we concerned with a shutdown where the employees, by renouncing the union, could cause the plant to reopen. Such cases would involve discriminatory employer action for the purpose of obtaining some benefit from the employees in the future. We hold here only that when an employer closes his entire business, even if the liquidation is motivated by vindictiveness toward the union, such action is not an unfair labor practice. 380 U.S. at 272 (footnotes omitted).

(5) *Problem:* After ten months of fruitless negotiations with a union over a new contract, may a company unilaterally decide to discontinue the operation of one of its plants without violating Section 8(a)(5)? What if the employer stipulates that this decision was motivated solely by "economic considerations"? Although this type of decision necessarily involves employment security, does requiring an employer to bargain about this kind of decision encroach upon its managerial prerogatives? Did Congress intend such

"interference" with business decisions? For an analysis of some of the considerations involved, *see* Rabin, Fibreboard and the Termination of Bargaining Union Work; The Search for Standards in Defining the Scope of the Duty to Bargain, 71 Colum. L. Rev. 803 (1971); and Schwarz, Plant Relocation or Partial Terminations — A Choice Between Bargaining Equality and Economic Efficiency, 14 U.C.L.A. L. Rev. 1089 (1967).

Chapter 3

THE NEGOTIATION PROCESS

A. SKILL DEVELOPMENT

Over twenty years ago Professor Archibald Cox asked the incisive question, "Can the NLRB effectively regulate the actual conduct of collective negotiations"?[1] His answer is still instructive today. He explained then that:

> The decisions imposing an obligation to bargain in good faith have often been criticized on the ground that since it is futile to legislate a state of mind, the duty is easily evaded. There are undoubtedly labor-relations advisers who have made good the promise to talk a union to death without either signing a contract or involving the employer in unfair-labor-practice proceedings; but section 8(a)(5) seems on the whole to have been remarkably effective. The law can influence men's attitudes, up to a point, by declaring a higher standard of conduct than the legal machinery can enforce. A good many companies would have done no more if listening politely had satisfied their legal obligations. Many empty discussions were gradually and unconsciously transformed into a bona fide exchange of ideas leading to mutual persuasion. . . .[2]

As he indicated, the legal framework can serve as a basis upon which negotiations can proceed, but it does not follow that the law can be used to explain the negotiation process. Nor is it true that there is a single or preferred way of learning about it — other than the "catch 22" method, "experience"!

The famous 1965 Brookings Institute study by Professors Slichter, Healy and Livernash indicate the principal impediment to learning the skill of negotiation.

> The representation of employees and management in collective bargaining takes an almost indefinite variety of forms. The simplest case of employee representation is that of local union dealing with an employer. Even this is handled in various ways. Representation is usually by a business agent or a bargaining committee. Business agents who are in a strong position locally may handle the negotiations themselves and may not submit the result to ratification by the rank and file — indeed,

---

[1] Cox, The Duty to Bargain in Good Faith, 71 Harv. L. Rev. 1401, 1439 (1958).
[2] *Id.* at 1438-39.

some business agents would refuse to negotiate without the authority to make a binding settlement. Other business agents negotiate subject to the approval of the rank and file, which is expected as a matter of course. Some local unions negotiate through specially-elected bargaining committees that report to the membership. The men on the bargaining committee are likely to be the active leaders in the union.[3]

Management is also represented in a seemingly endless variety of configurations. As we indicated in Chapter 1, the patterns of industrialization in this country are so diverse that almost each one creates a management-employee relationship that is unique unto itself. The natural consequences of this diversity is that the negotiation process used by these parties is also not uniform. This fact however does not invalidate the study of the process, because, as one of the authors stated in his casebook, *The Lawyer as Negotiator,*[4]

> Despite our considerable investment in the teaching of the art of negotiation and notwithstanding our sometimes passionate commitment to that cause, we too harbor doubts about exactly what we teach to whom. We suspect that different students learn quite different things in a course dealing with the art of negotiation. We suggest only that these doubts are no greater than those which should afflict the teachers of more traditional law school courses about what they teach to whom. Ultimately we reject the proposition that negotiation is unteachable, and we also reject the proposition that it is a skills course that has no place in academe. Without conceding that understanding of the art of negotiation lacks intellectual vigor, we maintain that it is the obligation of law schools not only to impart substantive knowledge and intellectual skills to their students but also to do what they can to impart less intellectual, if more basic, skills.[5]

Nor should the multiplicity of expertise and skills which are actually used in negotiation impede development of courses training for the process. Whether the skill used in the negotiation process is acquired through formal education, such as business, economics, law or social science, or whether it is based on experience in industry or a union, it is still a basic skill used in the process.[6] Furthermore, economists,[7]

---

[3] S. Slichter, S. Healy, & E. Livernash, The Impact of Collective Bargaining on Management 919 (1960) [hereinafter cited as Impact of Collective Bargaining].

[4] H. Edwards & J. White, The Lawyer as Negotiator (1977) [hereinafter cited as Lawyer as Negotiator].

[5] *Id.* at 1.

[6] *See generally* Lawyer as Negotiator, *supra* note 4.

[7] *See e.g.,* Schelling, The Strategy of Conflict: Prospectus, 2 Journ. Conflict Resolution 206 (Sept. 1958); C. Stevens, Strategy and Collective Bargaining (1963)

psychologists,[8] sociologists,[9] and many other social scientists, as well as lawyers,[10] have contributed much to developing an ana- lytical framework of labor negotiations. Any attempt to dissect the scholarship according to speciality, or to search for primacy in the field is fruitless. This does not indicate that our book pretends to be a comprehensive multidisciplinary approach. There are many educational disadvantages in attempting to put together such materials, not the least of which is the necessity of cutting others' work to such an extent that the result becomes a survey of the prolix scholarship in the field, which is difficult to use as a tool in developing either intellectual or more basic skills.

The intendment of this chapter is basically to provide techniques that will improve a person's skills for the preparation, negotiation and drafting of a collective bargaining agreement. We will indicate some of the tools that can be of assistance in the practice of negotiation. Nonetheless, we are compelled to admit that this is only one of many valid approaches to skill development in the negotiation process. If pressed to indicate why we selected this one over the others, we would probably have to rely on the outlandish answer — "experience"!

B. THE PROCESS OF NEGOTIATION

1. In General

Negotiation of a collective bargaining agreement is at the heart of collective bargaining. Most negotiations are concerned with revising existing agreements where permitted as a modification during their term or at expiration. The negotiation of a new agreement is much less frequent and presents different strategic and substantive problems to all parties. However, in either case "... the procedures employed by unions and management have their necessary influence on the decisions which the parties reach." [11] In most cases these

---

[hereinafter cited as Strategy and Collective Bargaining]; and J. Stahl, Bargaining Theory (1972).

[8] See e.g., O. Bantos, Process and Outcome of Negotiations (1974); Compare Holzman, Theories of Choice and Conflict in Psychology and Economics, 2 Journ. Conflict Resolution 310 (Dec. 1958).

[9] See e.g., O. Bantos, Process and Outcome of Negotiations (1974); R. Walton & R. McKersie, A Behavioral Theory of Labor Negotiations (1965) [hereinafter cited as Behavioral Theory].

[10] See e.g., Smith, Evolution of the Duty to Bargain Concept in American Law, 39 Mich. L. Rev. 1065 (1941); Compare Cox, The Duty to Bargain in Good Faith, 71 Harv. L. Rev. 1401 (1958); and see generally Feller, A General Theory of the Collective Bargaining Agreement, 6 Cal. L. Rev. 663 (1973).

[11] N. Chamberlain & J. Kuhn, Collective Bargaining 51 (2d ed. 1965) [hereinafter cited as Collective Bargaining].

procedures are dictated in part by the bargaining structure of the parties.

2. Representation in Negotiations

Where the bargaining unit is single employer/single plant, the organization for negotiations is a simple matter.[12] The person who represents the company in negotiations may be a line executive who uses as advisors, production personnel, a public relations expert and a company lawyer. Where multiplant or multiemployer, bargaining is called for by union organizations,[13] the configuration on the employer side is more complex. Although many employers will rely on respected senior member firm executives in addition to staff assistance, others will use an executive secretary of a trade association to represent management.[14] On the union side, the negotiating committee,

> . . . may be a standing committee, such as the union's executive board, or, at the other extreme, a committee elected specially, almost always includes, in any case, certain ex officio members such as the president, one or more vice presidents, the secretary, the chief steward. If the local has a business agent, he (or she) will certainly accompany the negotiators.

> Also accompanying the negotiators in most cases will be someone who is not a member of the local union: the international representative.[15]

In 1966 the International Union of Electrical Workers formed a coalition with seven other members of the AFL-CIO Industrial Union Department, with the avowed purpose of evolving national goals and of adopting a "coordinated approach" to negotiations with the General Electric Corporation.[16] Since this configuration of union representatives in negotiation has been sustained by the courts, it must also be included as a current bargaining structure for unions.

---

[12] E. Beal, E. Wickersham & P. Kinast, The Practice of Collective Bargaining (4th ed. 1972) [hereinafter cited as Practice of Collective Bargaining].

[13] See R. Smith, L. Merrifield & T. St. Antoine, Labor Relations Law 241-43 (5th ed. 1974).

[14] Practice of Collective Bargaining 214-17 supra note 12.

[15] Id. at 214.

[16] See Northrup, Boulwarism vs. Coalitionism in the 1966 GE Negotiations, 5 Mgt. Pers. Q. 2 (1966); and Cooper, Boulwarism and the Duty to Bargain in Good Faith, 20 Rutgers L. Rev. 653 (1966); Compare Cohen, Coordinated Bargaining and Structures of Collective Bargaining, 26 Lab. L.J. 375 (1974); and Kuhn, A New View of Boulwarism: The Significance of the GE Strike, 21 Lab. L.J. 582 (1970).

S.H. SLICHTER, J.J. HEALY AND E.R. LIVERNASH, THE IMPACT OF COLLECTIVE BARGAINING ON MANAGEMENT 919-25 (Brookings Institution, 1960) [17]

a. Union Representation in Negotiations

. . . .

Many unions use lawyers in several ways in their negotiations. Sometimes they are used as advisors to the regular union negotiators; sometimes the lawyers assume the principal burden of negotiating. Two genreal types of lawyers represent unions. One tries to dominate the local union and to make it dependent on him, frequently by persuading the union to take extreme positions so that it is in constant trouble with the employer. A second type of lawyer may be described as the constructive type. He is a true expert in industrial relations and interested in negotiating the kind of labor-management contract that will benefit both the union and the employer. There is an increasing number of this latter type who are devoted to the trade union movement and are of great assistance to many local unions that for one reason or another receive little guidance from their national unions.

Most national unions, especially the older ones, exercise some control over the freedom of local unions to involve themselves in the hazards and costs of strikes. In its milder form this control involves refusal of the national to support strikes financially unless its prior approval has been obtained. The stricter degree of control requires the national approval for a strike. Before a national either agrees to share in the cost of the strike or to permit the local to conduct a strike, the national is likely to try to settle the dispute through the intervention of a national vice-president or international representative. Although national intervention sometimes undermines real bargaining by the local union representatives, more often than not the international representative provides constructive leadership and guidance that may be lacking or limited in perspective at the local level.

When a union negotiates a master contract covering several plants of a multiplant company, the union is usually represented by a negotiating committee of representatives from each plant, though actual negotiations may be conducted by a small part of the committee or by several subcommittees. Negotiations covering 15 or 20 plants usually mean a very large negotiating group. If the union committee has representatives from each plant, management is likely to want to have representatives from each plant.

---

[17] Impact of Collective Bargaining, *supra* note 3. Reprinted with permission of the Publisher. © 1960 by the Brookings Institute.

If negotiations are to be conducted reasonably, there must be unified leadership among the negotiators who speak for the union and accept or reject company propositions. In an important negotiation in 1955 there was divided leadership in the union committee. The members of the committee could not agree to accept anything the company offered, and a strike resulted. Only with great difficulty and with the help of an outside conciliator was agreement finally reached.

Large committees have both advantages and disadvantages. The advantages involve the educational and democratic value of keeping reasonably large numbers of representatives closely informed on the content of negotiation and of securing some degree of participation by them. The major disadvantage is the difficulty of conducting negotiations with large groups. In many situations negotiations begin with large committees on each side, but bargaining teams are reduced after an initial exploration of issues. If teams are not reduced, settlement is likely to take place in informal meetings of key individuals outside of the formal meetings. In some cases small committees conduct the negotiations in the presence of larger groups in a sort of fish-bowl atmosphere. Also negotiations may take place in small committees that continuously report to larger groups. Unions with strong democratic traditions have difficulties in devising representative mechanisms that are not a stumbling block in achieving settlements. Some managements welcome large committees on the ground that representation from every plant gives the company a better chance to spread information about the company and about the management's viewpoint. If the union has a large committee, some managements want a large committee also. Managements say that they want someone present from each plant who has first-hand information of any local conditions that the union negotiators may bring up. . . .

b. Management Representation in Negotiations

Management may be represented in negotiations by operating officers, employers' associations, lawyers or industrial relations consultants, industrial relations staffs, or combinations thereof.

Representation by Operating Officers

This was the original method of representation, and it is still, frequently used, especially in companies too small to have industrial relations departments. Negotiations by operating officers help keep the terms of labor-management agreements properly related to operating conditions and problems. This method has the great disadvantage that operating men can ill afford to take time from their jobs to engage in bargaining, and they are not necessarily capable bargainers. Nothing is more likely to produce bad bargains for employers than impatience on the part of management representatives to get back to their regular jobs. A labor relations staff is selected partly to obtain individuals skilled in the art of negotiation.

Representation Through Associations of Employers

The association may be quite informal, consisting of little more than a bargaining committee (as when contractors in small communities negotiate with unions), or it may be a formal organization with dues and a professional staff. There are two general types of association — specialized organizations confined to employers in a given industry, such as the associations in the construction industry, the printing trades, the tool and die industry, the coal industry, and general associations covering plants in various industries throughout a city or area. Especially in industries where there are numbers of small competing employers, the competitive equality made possible by bargains between associations of employers and unions is important alike to the employers and their employees. . . .

Representation Through Lawyers and Industrial Relations Consultants

Some companies, finding themselves suddenly organized and without an industrial relations staff (or a staff experienced in labor law), turn to lawyers for representation. Some of the lawyers are tough and sharp, but they are employed to fight the union, not to develop good relations with it. As management and unions learn how to get along together, the demand for representation through anti-union lawyers seems to be diminishing. But many employers who are too small to have their own industrial relations departments and who do not have the services of an employers' association use labor consultant services or attorneys who do not specialize in fighting unions. There are today a considerable number of law firms and labor consultants well qualified either to advise employers during negotiations or to take on the responsibility of negotiating for them.

Representation Through Industrial Relations Staffs

In the largest companies there is a strong tendency for the responsibility for conducting negotiations to be assigned to the director of industrial relations and his staff. In large companies it is recognized that handling industrial relations is sufficiently important to call for a man of stature who is well qualified to negotiate for the company. The practice of handling negotiations through the industrial relations staff is steadily spreading to companies of medium size. In a large company the negotiating team is likely to include such members of the industrial relations staff as are needed, plus some one from finance and the legal department, and some representation from operations. The addition of a representative from the legal department is important because with the growth of arbitration, management (as well as the union) wants to be sure that the language finally adopted means precisely what it is intended to mean.

Representation Through Plant Managers and the Industrial Relations Staff

Some companies follow the policy of building up the importance of the plant managers by giving them the responsibility of conducting negotiations with unions. The managers are assisted by the industrial relations staff. The practice of concentrating responsibility for negotiations in plant managers is usually found in multiplant companies where the plants are numerous and small and where separate local agreements are made for each plant. In one large company with many small plants a representative from the national industrial relations staff of the company regularly sits with the manager during negotiations.

There is reason to believe that the efforts of some multiplant companies to transfer negotiations to plant managers are not entirely successful. Some managers enjoy negotiating, but many do not, and even those that like to negotiate find themselves handicapped by the fact that the union committee has far more time for negotiating than the manager can take from running the plant. Hence, if the plant is large enough to have an industrial relations department, this department is likely sooner or later to take over negotiations. Of course, most important is not who represents the company, but whether a wise position is taken by the company representatives with respect to the several interests of the firm.

3. The Role of the Lawyer

There has been some skepticism about the use of lawyers in collective bargaining. Willard Wirtz stated in 1948:

> There is some feeling that lawyers have developed such a deep affection for the status quo, for the certainty of precedent, and for the formalism of the courtroom, that they have become by nature disqualified for participation in this new type of industrial government.[18]

This feeling still persists to some extent, but the fact is that lawyers are increasingly used either as advisors or as direct participants in

---

[18] Wirtz, Collective Bargaining: The Lawyer's Role in Negotiation and Arbitration, 34 A.B.A. J. 547, 548 (1948).

handling labor relations problems of all kinds including the negotiation and administration of labor agreements.

This is a development primarily of the last decade or two. Previously, the lawyer's role was predominately, that of an advisor or an advocate in purely legal matters, such as litigation relating to strikes, picketing, and boycotts or before administrative tribunals, such as the National Labor Relations Board. It was in this latter context, that Wirtz made his observations in 1948.

Even today, the role of the lawyer in labor relations matters necessarily depends to a substantial degree on the attitude of his/her clients concerning what his/her role should be, and this may well depend on the client's own labor relations posture and attitude. If an employer is in the pre-organizational phase of union-management relations, and is hostile to unionization and determined to invoke all the legal rights and related techniques available to fend off unionization, the lawyer obviously is in a different position than in the case of an employer involved in a day-to-day good faith relationship ensuing upon a completion of the organizational phase.

The lawyer's role in the pre-organizational phase is typically the traditional one of legal advice and representation in adversary proceedings. His/her role in the post-organizational phase in relation to collective bargaining and contract administration is quite different. Whether she/he can operate effectively, or more effectively than others, depends on his/her ability to develop the additional skills and knowledge which are required of the labor relations expert. An increasing number of lawyers have met this challenge and have become very effective negotiators and labor relations advisors. If a lawyer approaches a collective bargaining relationship with the kind of adversarial posture which she/he brings to "one-shot" courtroom litigation, she/he is not likely to be an effective or constructive representative of his/her client.

This is not to suggest that a representative in collective bargaining for either side should not be aggressive. His/her job is to achieve the best bargain she/he can for his/her client. Nor is it to suggest that collective bargaining negotiations are always or even typically conducted in an atmosphere of calm rationality. Sometimes they are heated and the participants are intemperate. But a lawyer-representative of a party, like any other member of a negotiating team, has to learn to be a good and vigorous representative while inflicting the minimum amount of psychological damage and, if at all possible, help develop or sustain a good relationship with the other party. Lawyers presumably are possessed of special analytical skills, in addition to knowledge of relevant law, and of the ability to absorb and marshal facts and articulate ideas persuasively and clearly both orally and in writing. If, in addition, the lawyer acquires a knowledge of labor relations problems either through experience or special study, and has the personality and attitude which will permit him/her to establish the respect of the other party in collective bargaining, she/he should be a useful member or even leader of the negotiating team of his/her client.

Moreover, it should be recognized that the collective bargaining process actually involves two sets of negotiations in addition to those conducted across the bargaining table. On each side there will frequently, probably typically, be differences of opinion among those responsible for developing the party's bargaining positions on a wide variety of issues. These differences must be reconciled and a consolidated, consistent set of proposals prepared for presentation to the other side. A lawyer having the insight gained from the perspective of extensive experience, and some of the talents of the mediator, can be very useful in helping to resolve these internal conflicts and develop bargaining positions. Almost inevitably this will be an important part of the lawyer's role if she/he is to be involved at all in the area of collective bargaining. The same is true with respect to questions arising during the term of a labor agreement concerning its interpretation and application.

In this latter area it is important to take note of the fact that the vast majority of collective bargaining agreements provide for arbitration of issues of contract interpretation or application ("grievances") as the terminal point of the contract grievance procedure. An arbitration proceeding is a quasi-judicial proceeding where adversarial skills obviously are needed if a party is to be effectively represented. This is a phase of labor relations activity in which a party would naturally think of using a lawyer, and many lawyers do represent their clients in arbitration proceedings, although more so on the management than on the union side.

C. ORGANIZING FOR NEGOTIATION

Selection of the Team

Although various members of the bargaining team may be selected for their specific expertise, the chief spokesperson of the bargaining team should possess a wide range of abilities. In his *Employer's Guide to Successful Labor Relations*,[19] N. A. Levin advises that,

> A word should be said here to allay a fear which sometimes besets management. Facing a serious contest with a union, a company picks the best man it can to be its advocate. It is often a shock to management when their labor relations counsel meets with the union organizer for what they expect to be a

---

[19] N. A. Levin, Successful Labor Relations 276 (1967). Reprinted with permission of Publisher. © 1967, Fairchild Publications, Inc.

confrontation as dramatic as a TV gunfight, only to see the two men exchange pleasantries and discuss mutual friends. This is no indication of divided loyalty on the part of management's negotiator. Such a person deals with union representatives constantly and therefore knows many of them. To effectively do his job he must have their respect. In return, he will respect those who are honest and capable. Abuse or rudeness to a union organizer is pointless, and the management counsel who treats his adversaries with dignity will in turn be afforded the respect and credibility that can aid in attaining a fair settlement.

In general the same qualities required of a labor relations counselor in representation proceedings and collective bargaining sessions are appropriate for the advisor in arbitration or grievance-settlement situations. In arbitrations, particularly, management should be represented by a man who is well versed in presenting a case and in cross-examination. The representative in an arbitration must be an advocate, not a judge. An arbitration is a proceeding between adversaries. Management's spokesman must concern himself with putting forth his viewpoint and in such capacity he should stand vigorously on his client's side. Final judgment is reserved for the arbitrator. For this reason management should select a representative trained in the techniques of litigation since arbitration is a trial of issues.

For negotiation, election campaigns grievance processing and arbitration, research is necessary. The information which the company's experts must have falls into two categories — economic and technical. Effective employer representation is predicated on collecting and marshalling economic and statistical facts about an industry, area or company. This includes research into comparative wage rates, the ratio of labor costs to over-all expenses and volume, a background knowledge of the nature and number of firms in the industry and an awareness of their rate of growth, of decline, figures pertaining to membership in the union, and many other matters. Technical know-how requires an understanding of the company's operations and the working of the plant or store. The negotiators must know how many men are needed on a job, how the operation is best performed, how machinery functions, what customer's requirements are, what prevailing work hours and performance standards exist, and so on.

Aid and advice on negotiations, representation matters and contract administration are rendered either by an attorney or by a non-lawyer labor relations counselor.

CHAMBERLAIN AND KUHN, COLLECTIVE BARGAINING 70-73 (2d ed. 1965) [20]

Conference Organization

Collective negotiations, particularly in smaller companies, are sometimes conducted without formal organization. Other bargaining sessions have been organized more systematically. The chief purpose of this more formal constitution is to provide a moderator who, even though he is a member of one of the partisan groups, is given the task of bringing some procedural order into negotiations, which otherwise may easily break down into a series of undirected and sometimes impertinent arguments. Where the number of representatives is large, a chairman may be necessary, if only to preserve order by recognizing speakers. A perceptive negotiator and labor student mentioned recently that he has noted a subtle change in the organization of bargaining conferences:

> Up until the last decade bargaining sessions were widely regarded as the province of the union and the union spokesman tended to be the dominant figure in the sessions. Now, with the unions' very strong interest in protecting the status quo, I observe more of a tendency for the session to be regarded as a joint affair, but with the management spokesman tending to act as chairman, to the extent that function is performed at all.

Because a moderator chosen from among the bargainers does not have to be neutral, occasional use has been made of an impartial chairman. This practice is more common abroad than in the United States. It occurs in this country most frequently when a conciliator is brought into the picture and acts as a chairman, though not formally selected to fill that role. Officials of the Federal Mediation and Conciliation Service or of state mediatory agencies are called upon to help, particularly in negotiations between managers of smaller companies and local unions. Unfortunately the conciliator is usually introduced only after an impasse has been reached, and he is thus placed at a decided disadvantage. Not only must he perform the customary chairmanship tasks of preserving order and encouraging agreement through procedural devices, but he must as well attempt to provide a solution to end the deadlock. Conciliators are in almost unanimous agreement that the earlier they participate in negotiations, the more likely they are to succeed in helping the parties reach agreement. They become more familiar with the issues and thus are better prepared to suggest compromise solutions; also, a neutral party capable of exercising to the greatest advantage the functions of conference chairman may steer the conference to

---

[20] Reprinted with permission of Publisher. © 1965 McGraw-Hill.

agreement — avoiding deadlock altogether — by suggesting and enforcing procedural devices which avert argument. These devices may include appointing a subcommittee to investigate a particular question and report back to the full conference, supplying the conferees with information they may not have at hand, or calling in outside expert opinion to settle factual disputes.

In addition to the chairman, a conference secretary is sometimes appointed, though less frequently. Generally, each party will name one of its own members to take notes, although sometimes no record of any sort will be made. At the other extreme, court recorders are sometimes hired to make a verbatim transcript of proceedings. Although once favored and used in a fair number of negotiations, verbatim transcripts are much less popular today. A complete record was usually made so that future arbitrators could refer to it for an interpretation of what the conferees really meant when they finally agreed upon some clause, just as federal courts turn to the *Congressional Record* to interpret the intent behind legislation. A conference record was to help establish beyond dispute just what agreements or commitments the parties might have made that were not reflected in any written contract. The keeping of verbatim records has drawbacks, however. The insistence by only one of the parties upon such a record often has been considered by the other to be suggestive of distrust, arousing a feeling of antagonism. Other objections have been based on the belief that frankness is inhibited when every remark goes into the record and on the discovery that the verbatim account is not always useful in interpreting the meaning of contract provisions but all too often requires a "secondary interpretation" itself.

The use of joint conference subcommittees for a variety of purposes is one organizational device which has proved particularly helpful. The spokesman for a large manufacturer explained the role of subcommittees in negotiations in this way:

> The role of the subcommittee varies substantially, based on the bargaining situation. But in any major situation today [1962] where there are complex employee benefit plans involved, it would seem almost imperative to arrange for subcommittees in order to make meaningful progress. Aside from the formal subcommittees of the main national negotiating team which were established on highly technical issues such as pensions, insurance and supplemental unemployment benefits, there were times when it was advisable to establish committees to discuss issues affecting a group of company locations or a group of company employees. For example, certain company and union personnel joined together to discuss and attempt to resolve an issue of the assignment of certain type of work in parts depots. The issue was

not common to all company employees but was more or less common at all parts depots. Certain issues involving skilled maintenance and construction employees throughout the company were discussed in subcommittee meetings. While the meetings of these subcommittees did not necessarily lead to agreement on these issues, reports were issued to the main table ultimately leading to resolution of the issues.

The manager of labor relations in another large firm pointed out the benefits of subcommittees but also indicated a trouble point:

> They are particularly helpful in solving knotty or highly technical problems of the agreement. We may agree on the pattern in our top-level negotiations without fixing the details. The major task of the technical subcommittees, then, is to apply the principles we had negotiated to the particular context. This has led to some disagreements, primarily as a result of the efforts of union technicians to apply "frosting to the cake," in the words of the union president.

Subcommittees have also been fruitfully used when issues prove to be too comprehensive or complex to allow of settlement during the conference itself but can be deferred to postconference deliberation. In this latter use, the subcommittee's agreement sometimes requires the ratification of the original conference or a succeeding conference before being submitted to the union membership or before becoming effective.

Conference Procedure

In the actual negotiations between the bargaining parties, there may be no ordered procedure or only a very informal procedure. This is particularly true of local negotiations. Describing his own experience, one union representative remarked: "There is no order at a conference. If the boss wants to go fishing, the union goes fishing with him. If he wants to talk about baseball, you talk about baseball. If the union is strong, the reverse may be true." This lack of procedural plan is in part due to a belief by some that any semblance of parliamentary order makes the conference stilted, puts every man on his guard, and renders agreement more difficult. Nevertheless, most bargainers have developed certain broad patterns of negotiating to which they adhere.

Preliminary informal meetings of the bargaining parties have occasionally been held to establish the order and scope of bargaining conferences. More informally, there is sometimes only an agreement between the parties on the order in which issues shall be discussed.

Especially in large-scale negotiations, the conference may begin with an opening statement by leaders on both sides, perhaps with a general discussion by other participants. This opening session sometimes offers the only real opportunity for including all conferees in the negotiations, if their number is large, the actual bargaining then being delegated to a subcommittee. Such preliminary discussion is usually followed by a presentation of specific proposals, most often by the union, since it is usually the union which is pressing for changes. This presentation consists of a reading of the desired terms followed by a brief justification. If the other party has not yet had an opportunity to consider the demands or prepare a counterproposal, there follows an adjournment to allow for this. Upon resumption and a reading of the counterproposal, bargaining will begin in earnest.

When the chairman of each committee knows within what limits it may make concessions, this bargaining may take place across the table in open meeting. The more common procedure, however, is for the side receiving a proposition to caucus following conference discussion, in order to prepare its response. These caucuses may consume a large part of the conference time. A national official of one union has added that frequently there is more wrangling in the committee caucus than there is in actual negotiations between the two parties.

An issue which cannot be settled after an initial discussion is generally tabled for the time being. In the course of agreement on other matters, some settlement of the tabled proposition may become apparent, or, in the light of other concessions, the party which had proposed it may withdraw or compromise it. In reaching a conference agreement, unit voting is almost invariably employed; that is to say, each party votes as a group. In reaching agreement within the group, sometimes a unanimous vote of all committeemen is required, while in other cases a simple majority is sufficient.

As agreement is reached clause by clause, some negotiators begin the construction of the new contract, so that the progress of the conference is clearly indicated. Until the conclusion of the entire contract and its approval in its entirety by both parties, however, any agreement upon particular issues is recognized as only tentative, for the clauses of a contract may be interrelated. The settlement of one may affect the determination of another, and a concession on one clause won early in the conference may be traded for a concession on another, more important issue sometime later.

NOTES:

(a) One of an employer's primary assets in the legal process is delay. As Chapter 2 reveals, the whole concept of "good faith bargaining" leaves open large questions of definitions and of proof. May a lawyer assist his/her client in "going through the motions" of bargaining in such a way that she/he will escape an unfair practice charge, but will also avoid concluding an agreement with the other side?

(b) The ABA Code of Professional Responsibility provides that "a lawyer shall not . . . assert a position . . . or take other action on behalf of his client when he knows or when it is obvious that such action would serve merely to harass or maliciously injure another." More specifically, she/he is forbidden to "counsel or assist his client in conduct that [he] knows to be illegal or fraudulent." Does this prohibition cover delays in bargaining? Does it cover recommending a "frozen position"? What should the lawyer's reaction be if the client asks him/her to actually assist in some way in a proposed illegal tactic? And should the lawyer's response differ if she/he is convinced that the client is responding to (1) illegal pressure from the union, or (2) a serious financial crisis in which additional labor costs may drive him/her out of business?

(c) In general, to what extent may a lawyer properly assist his/her client in either escaping the duty to bargain altogether, or exercising that duty in such a way as to win maximum tactical advantage?

D. PREPARING FOR NEGOTIATIONS

1. Assembling Information

As the 1965 Brookings Institute study suggested, "[t]he success of the parties in reaching agreement depends mainly on an understanding of each other and each others problems, but negotiations that are well planned and well conducted help bring about a meeting of minds." [21] Bruce Morse in advising management *How to Negotiate the Labor Agreement* observes that "many strikes have occurred because management did not take the time and energy or did not exercise the skill necessary to do the right kind of preparatory and selling job." [22] The preparation necessary for organizing, preparing and conducting negotiations for either party, regardless of tactical considerations, should include (a) assembling information; (b) drawing up demands; and (c) solidifying positions within the team, within the company or union, and within the community in which the company operates.

In assembling information there are at least three types of data that are extremely useful in preparing for negotiations: (a) bargaining history between the parties; (b) relevant economic data (both external and internal to the company); and (c) financial data and other "intelligence."

---

[21] Impact of Collective Bargaining, *supra* note 3 at 918.

[22] B. Morse, How to Negotiate the Labor Agreement vii (rev. ed. 1971) [hereinafter cited as How to Negotiate].

a. Bargaining History

Whether the process of negotiation is viewed as a strategy or game [23] or as a union or business management technique,[24] the collective bargaining agreement which results from the process is an ongoing document. Many of its provisions are the result of "demands" made over a period of several past contract negotiations. Accordingly, a "negotiation log" should be separately kept by union and management. All proposals brought up during each negotiation should be classified by: (1) date; (2) specific proposal; (3) to whom made; (4) the stated reason for proposal; (5) whether the proposal was agreed to, resolved by compromise, or dropped; and (6) a brief summary of the ensuing discussion. The format of the negotiation log, whether a looseleaf workbook [25] or a formal bargaining book,[26] is of no consequence, but it should contain information about the past bargaining history in summary form.

Furthermore, the collective bargaining agreement negotiated is analogous to a treaty in that it establishes the: "(1) rules governing compensation in all its forms; (2) the duties and performance expected from workers including rules of discipline and failure to achieve these standards and (3) rules defining the rights and duties of workers, including new or laid-off workers, to particular positions or jobs." [27] A separate section of the bargaining history log should be kept by supervisors from management staff — personnel specialists, foremen, managers, etc., for use by the management team; and also by representatives from the union — stewards, local business agents or elected officers, for use by the union team. This section should contain a looseleaf copy of the last prior agreement with written suggestions as to where, how and why it should be revised by words, sentences, and/or clauses. It is important that those planning for negotiation have a written record of the "line administration" of the contract. Although informed on-line personnel may be selected for the negotiating team and may thus be able to convey their personal knowledge during negotiations, the advantages of having this information in writing over the term of the contract are many. Priorities should be established well in advance of negotiations, because agenda items may be varied by the procedures used in negotiations, and important items may be

---

[23] *See generally* Strategy and Collective Bargaining, *supra* note 7.

[24] *See generally* Nat'l Industrial Conference Be. Inc., Preparing for Collective Bargaining, Studies in Personnel Policy No. 172 (1959) [hereinafter cited as Preparing for Collective Bargaining].

[25] How to Negotiate, *supra* note 22 at 2.

[26] Preparing for Collective Bargaining, *supra* note 24 at 35-39 (Examples A-G).

[27] J. T. Dunlop, Industrial Relations Systems 15 (1958) [hereinafter cited as Industrial Relations Systems].

obscured by this process. Intra-team priority squabbles during negotiations may cause trade-offs of important problem areas. Inter-team pressures may also cause memories to fade. Thus, a section kept by those who administer the agreement should be a part of the bargaining history of the contract.

As a part of the ongoing administration of the contract, grievance records should also be kept as a record of the bargaining history. Even though a thorough analysis of serious problems raised by grievances is important information to have for negotiations, this topic will be covered in this chapter in the next section involving drawing-up demands.

b. Use of Economic Data in Negotiations

Economic information is a significant force in collective bargaining. Major employers and unions bargaining on behalf of large numbers of workers have entered a sophisticated era of bargaining backed by economists or other specialized experts who handle data peculiar to their industry.

This section attempts to provide an overview of the types of economic information that labor and management might use in negotiations. Effective use of economic data requires a great deal of care and sophistication.[28] It is important that negotiators be able to evaluate and utilize their own and their opponents data. This skill requires that they understand how the data was derived so as to be able to adjust for any resulting biases. A proper use of the data also requires a knowledge of exactly what the figures are a measurement of, and of what they are not. Selection and interpretation are equally important. As the AFL-CIO's Research Department admonishes: "It is not enough merely to put some facts on the table; the most appropriate ones must be chosen and they must be put in perspective." [29]

The importance of various types of economic data will vary widely by negotiation, by union and by industry. In most cases, however, its presentation will include national economic data indicative of the overall economic context in which collective bargaining occurs as well as data pertaining to the economic condition of the specific industry, locality and company. Such data will include wages and wage supplements at every level.

---

[28] The sophisticated economic analysis necessary for the thorough preparation which is generally considered the key to a successful outcome of collective bargaining is beyond the scope of this book. The interested reader may find such an analysis in M. Friedman, The Use of Economic Date in Collective Bargaining (1976) [hereinafter cited as Friedman] a copy of which may be obtained from the International Association of Fire Fighters (IAFF), 1750 New York Avenue, N.W., Washington, D.C. 20006.

[29] 1 C.B.N.C. § 14:31, No. 700.

(1) National Economic Data

At the broadest level, economic information is used by management and labor to assess the economic environment in which they operate, and to indicate a general range for a reasonable settlement. Economic policy statements by federal, state, and local governments often provide the most explicit information concerning the state of the economy. Perhaps more useful to negotiators are data on employment and unemployment, the cost of living, family-budget requirements for a reasonable standard of living, and productivity levels. In addition to this "general" use of national economic data, federal, state and local governments often find it appropriate to suggest that collective bargaining address certain of the major social and economic problems in our society. Such suggestions have been made in recent years with respect to such matters as inflation, affirmative action, employment opportunities for youth, veterans and the handicapped. When a union and a company seek to negotiate contractual arrangements which deal with public policies, information about the nature and magnitude of the problem being addressed is critical. And, in attempting to respond constructively to such requests, private business and labor must consider the macro-economic impact of their negotiated agreements.

(a) Employment Statistics

Employment and unemployment statistics are utilized by both parties in assessing the economic environment in which they operate. The number, employment status, educational and skill level of certain groups, as well as other demographic characteristics, are important factual matters which affect the approach business and labor take to certain contract issues.

The U.S. Department of Labor's Bureau of Labor Statistics (BLS) publishes employment and unemployment statistical data from three sources: [30] (1) the Current Population Survey (CPS) frequently referred to as the Household Survey; (2) the Survey of Establishments; and (3) Unemployment Insurance data.[31]

---

[30] BLS Periodicals and reference handbooks may be ordered from the U.S. Government Printing Office (G.P.O.), Washington, D.C. 20402. News releases and reports can be purchased from the Superintendent of Documents, G.P.O., *supra.* It is also possible to be placed on the Bureau's mailing list for press releases and announcements issued by the Washington Office by checking the appropriate box on a form supplied on request, and returning it to the U.S. Department of Labor, Bureau of Labor Statistics, Washington, D.C. 20212.

[31] For information on the concepts, methodology and scope of Household Data, Establishment Data, and State and Area Unemployment Data, *see* Explanatory Notes, U.S. Bureau of Labor Statistics, U.S. Department of Labor, catalogue No.

The *Current Population Survey* includes personal interviews of about 56,000 persons conducted each month by the Bureau of Census for BLS. It provides monthly employment and unemployment totals for the entire country and yearly totals for the fifty states and the District of Columbia cross-classified by a variety of demographics such as sex, race, marital status, primary occupation and primary industry of employment. This "Household Survey" presents primarily an overview of the employment situation in the economy as a whole. It does not permit a careful measurement of the employment situation in particular industries, and/or areas, and therefore provides little direct guidance in specific negotiations.

2. Employment status by sex, age, and race, seasonally adjusted[32]

[Numbers in thousands]

Employment status	Annual average		1978		
	1976	1977	Jan.	Feb.	Mar.
TOTAL					
Total noninstitutional population[1] ..	156,048	158,559	159,937	160,128	160,313
Total labor force	96,917	99,534	101,228	101,217	101,536
Civilian noninstitutional population[1]	153,904	156,426	157,816	158,004	158,190
Civilian labor force	94,773	97,401	99,107	99,093	99,414
Employed	87,485	90,546	92,881	93,003	93,266
Agriculture	3,297	3,244	3,354	3,242	3,310
Nonagricultural industries . .	84,188	87,302	89,527	89,761	89,956
Unemployed	7,288	6,855	6,226	6,090	6,148
Unemployment rate	7.7	7.0	6.3	6.1	6.2
Not in labor force	59,130	59,025	58,709	58,911	58,776
Men, 20 years and over					
Civilian noninstitutional population[1]	64,561	65,796	66,467	66,556	66,645
Civilian labor force	51,527	52,464	53,153	53,142	53,242
Employed	48,486	49,737	50,673	50,759	50,833
Agriculture	2,359	2,308	2,394	2,283	2,289
Nonagricultural industries . .	46,128	47,429	48,279	48,476	48,544
Unemployed	3,041	2,727	2,480	2,383	2,409
Unemployment rate	5.9	5.2	4.7	4.5	4.5
Not in labor force	13,034	13,332	13,314	13,414	13,403

70-11379, Employment and Earnings, June 1978; and BLS free pamphlet, How the Government Measures Unemployment. For a comprehensive discussion of the differences between household and establishment survey employment data, *see* Gloria P. Green, Comparing Employment Estimates from Household and Payroll Surveys, U.S. Bureau of Labor Statistics, U.S. Department of Labor, catalog No. 15-26485, Monthly Labor Review, (Dec. 1969). Reprints of this article are available upon request from the BLS.

[32] Source: U.S. Bureau of Labor Statistics, U.S. Dep't of Labor, catalog No. 15-26485, Monthly Labor Review, May 1978.

Employment status	Annual average		1978		
	1976	1977	Jan.	Feb.	Mar.
Women, 20 years and over					
Civilian noninstitutional population[1]	72,917	74,160	74,892	74,996	75,093
Civilian labor force	34,276	35,685	36,595	36,654	36,849
Employed	31,730	33,199	34,348	34,569	34,722
Agriculture	511	537	517	604	628
Nonagricultural industries	31,218	32,662	33,831	33,965	34,094
Unemployed	2,546	2,486	2,247	2,085	2,127
Unemployment rate	7.4	7.0	6.1	5.7	5.8
Not in labor force	38,641	38,474	38,297	38,342	38,244
Both sexes, 16-19 years					
Civilian noninstitutional population[1]	16,426	16,470	16,457	16,453	16,452
Civilian labor force	8,970	9,359	9,252	9,297	9,323
Employed	7,269	7,610	7,860	7,675	7,711
Agriculture	427	399	443	355	393
Nonagricultural industries	6,842	7,211	7,417	7,320	7,318
Unemployed	1,701	1,642	1,499	1,622	1,612
Unemployment rate	19.0	17.7	16.0	17.4	17.3
Not in labor force	7,455	7,218	7,098	7,156	7,129
WHITE					
Civilian noninstitutional population[1]	135,569	137,595	138,687	138,834	138,997
Civilian labor force	83,876	86,107	87,425	87,360	87,532
Employed	78,021	80,734	82,650	82,697	82,880
Unemployed	5,855	5,373	4,775	4,663	4,652
Unemployment rate	7.0	6.2	5.5	5.3	5.3
Not in labor force	51,692	51,488	51,262	51,474	51,465
BLACK AND OTHER					
Civilian noninstitutional population[1]	18,335	18,831	19,129	19,170	19,194
Civilian labor force	10,897	11,294	11,725	11,785	11,871
Employed	9,464	9,812	10,238	10,391	10,402
Unemployed	1,433	1,482	1,487	1,394	1,469
Unemployment rate	13.1	13.1	12.7	11.8	12.4
Not in labor force	7,438	7,535	7,404	7,385	7,323

The *Survey of Establishments* is conducted by BLS in cooperation with state employment security agencies of approximately 160,000 businesses. It is compiled from payroll records reported on a voluntary basis. Results compiled for the country, each state, and 226 metropolitan areas are a primary source of employment data on an industry and area basis.

B-2. Employees on nonagricultural payrolls, by industry[33]
[in thousands]

SIC Code	Industry	All employees					Production workers[1]				
		Apr. 1977	May 1977	Mar. 1978	Apr.ᴾ 1978	Mayᴾ 1978	Apr. 1977	May 1977	Mar. 1978	Apr.ᴾ 1978	Mayᴾ 1978
—	TOTAL	81,332	82,029	83,734	84,867	85,552	—	—	—	—	—
—	PRIVATE SECTOR	66,042	66,684	67,894	69,001	69,682	54,222	54,787	55,492	56,491	57,097
—	MINING	838	844	716	887	901	632	636	521	671	682
10	METAL MINING	96.9	97.2	95.5	95.2	—	74.8	75.0	73.9	73.8	—
101	Iron ores	25.5	26.1	24.7	25.0	—	20.5	21.0	19.7	20.0	—
102	Copper ores	36.5	36.7	36.0	35.3	—	28.1	28.2	27.9	27.5	—

[33] Source: U.S. Bureau of Labor Statistics, Dep't of Labor, catalog No. 70-11379, Employment and Earnings, June 1978.

Unemployment Insurance Data are compiled monthly by the Employment and Training Administration of the U.S. Department of Labor from records of state and federal unemployment insurance claims filed and benefits paid. Since this survey covers only the two-thirds of the labor force, covered by unemployment insurance, the data can only be used to estimate state and area unemployment rates.

21. Unemployment insurance and employment service operations[34]
[All items except average benefits amounts are in thousands]

Item	1977											1978	
	Feb.	Mar.	Apr.	May	June	July	Aug.	Sept.	Oct.	Nov.	Dec.	Jan.	Feb.
All programs:													
Insured unemployment	4,448	3,972	3,506	3,105	2,939	3,065	2,751	2,643	2,649	2,853	3,226	3,780	3,637
State unemployment insurance program:[1]													
Initial claims[2]	1,995	1,483	1,357	1,325	1,429	1,688	1,467	1,255	1,350	1,582	2,010	2,272	
Insured unemployment (average weekly volume)	3,647	3,173	2,752	2,414	2,291	2,465	2,322	2,089	2,071	2,274	2,644	3,191	3,272
Rate of insured unemployment	5.5	4.8	4.1	3.6	3.4	3.6	3.4	3.1	3.0	3.3	3.9	4.6	4.7
Weeks of unemployment compensated	12,423	13,328	9,923	8,793	8,761	7,988	8,891	7,617	6,776	7,571	8,846	11,085	....
Average weekly benefit amount for total unemployment	$80.48	$79.59	$78.63	$77.08	$77.00	$75.89	$77.17	$77.52	$79.60	$79.80	$81.54	$85.52	....
Total benefits paid	$975,618	$1,038,503	$763,713	$666,014	$660,812	$593,583	$671,337	$577,165	$525,773	$599,474	$703,041	$909,859	....

[34] Source: U.S. Bureau of Labor Statistics, Dep't of Labor, catalog No. 15-26485, Monthly Labor Review, May 1978.

Employment and unemployment data from these three surveys are published after the data are compiled along with other relevant information about employment in a number of BLS publications. For example:

Labor Force Development [35] is a quarterly press release which analyzes overall trends in the nation's labor force. Since it is based on data from the *Household Survey,* it includes information about disadvantaged persons — discouraged workers, Vietnam veterans, Latinos and poverty area residents;

Monthly Labor Review [36] includes analytical articles, reports and statistical analysis based on BLS employment statistics;

Employment and Earnings [37] contains detailed household data on the labor force, including insured and uninsured employment statistics nationally and by state or area;

Employment and Earnings, States and Areas, 1939-1975 [38] is a series of detailed reports providing historical data by industry on employment for each state and the District of Columbia; and,

Employment and Wages, [39] a quarterly report, presents tabular summaries of employment data for workers covered by State unemployment insurance laws.

The paradox in some of the uses to which management and unions put these unemployment and employment statistics is illustrative of the limitations of their value in negotiations. For example, in wage negotiations it is not uncommon for management to use a basic "supply and demand argument" to defend small compensation increases, citing high official unemployment rates as evidence of the excess supply of labor. In this context, unions will minimize unemployment statistics. On the other hand, when matters of public policy, especially unemployment relief, are under discussion the parties may switch sides with unions exaggerating unemployment rates and management insisting that the true rate is much lower than the statistics indicate.

---

[35] U.S. Bureau of Labor Statistics, Dep't of Labor, List No. 365, Labor Force Developments.

[36] U.S. Bureau of Labor Statistics, Dep't of Labor, catalog No. 15-26485, Monthly Labor Review [hereinafter cited as Monthly Labor Review].

[37] U.S. Bureau of Labor Statistics, Dep't of Labor, catalog No. 70-11379, Employment and Earnings [hereinafter cited as Employment and Earnings].

[38] U.S. Bureau of Labor Statistics, Dep't of Labor, Bull. No. 1370-12, Employment and Earnings, States and Areas, 1939-75.

[39] U.S. Bureau of Labor Statistics, Dep't of Labor, List No. 301, Employment and Wages.

(b) Compensation

There is no area of collective bargaining in which the parties devote as much attention to economic data as in "compensation." Economic data on the cost of living, family-budget requirements for a reasonable standard of living and productivity provide a general background guide to negotiators as to the adequacy, reasonableness, and true value of compensation adjustments. These data break down into two major categories — "external" and "internal." External data are those figures which arise outside of the relationship of the parties negotiating a collective bargaining agreement. The data pertaining to the negotiating company will inevitably be compared by the negotiators to current compensation levels in the industry, area, or both, at the time of the negotiations; or compared to compensation trends over a specified period of time. These levels and trends will usually be discussed by negotiators on the basis of economic data derived from the following sources:

The Cost Of Living — In negotiating economic demands the union's goal is to achieve a better standard of living for their members. The standard of living that one is able to maintain is determined not by the actual number of dollars received, but, rather by what those dollars will buy. And, as everyone is aware today, rising prices erode workers' purchasing power potential. Only if wages increase more than prices will workers' standard of living improve. Therefore, the compensation data relevant to negotiators is "real wages," actual money wages deflated by an index of the price level.[40] The *Consumer Price Index (CPI)* compiled monthly by the Bureau of Labor Statistics [41] is the most widely utilized index and is available monthly in four publications: *BLS News; Monthly Labor Review; Employment Earnings;* and *CPI Detailed Report.*[42] The *Handbook of Labor Statistics* is an annual volume produced by the BLS which also contains current and historical price data. The Consumer Price Index is a monthly statistical measure of the average change in prices in a fixed market basket of goods and services. Effective with the January 1978 index, the Bureau of Labor Statistics began publishing the index for two groups of the population. One index, a new CPI for all urban consumers, covers eighty percent of the total noninstitutional population; and the other index, a revised CPI for urban wage earners and clerical workers, covers about half the new index population. The *All Urban Consumers Index* includes, in addition to wage earners and clerical workers, professional, managerial, and technical workers, the self-employed, short-term workers, the unemployed, retirees, and others not in the labor force.

---

[40] P.A. Samuelson, Economics 573 (10th ed. 1976).

[41] U.S. Bureau of Labor Statistics, Dep't of Labor, List No. 302, Consumer Price Index.

[42] For information on how to obtain, *see* note 31 *supra.*

23. Consumer Price Index for All Urban Consumers and revised CPI for Urban Wage Earners and Clerical Workers, U.S. city average—general summary and groups, subgroups, and selected items[43]
[1967 = 100 unless otherwise specified]

General summary	All Urban Consumers							Urban Wage Earners and Clerical Workers (revised)						
	1977					1978		1977					1978	
	Feb.	Sept.	Oct.	Nov.	Dec.	Jan.	Feb.	Feb.	Sept.	Oct.	Nov.	Dec.	Jan.	Feb.
All items	177.1	184.0	184.5	185.4	186.1	187.2	188.4	177.1	184.0	184.5	185.4	186.1	187.1	188.4
Food and beverages	183.8	190.2	190.1	191.2	191.9	194.6	197.3	183.8	190.2	190.1	191.2	191.9	194.5	197.1
Housing	181.4	189.5	190.4	191.4	192.4	193.8	195.0	181.4	189.5	190.4	191.4	192.4	193.8	195.0
Apparel and upkeep	150.8	156.2	157.2	158.5	158.2	155.7	154.5	150.8	156.2	157.2	158.5	158.2	155.4	154.5
Transportation	173.2	178.4	178.6	178.7	178.8	179.0	179.4	173.2	178.4	178.6	178.7	178.8	179.1	179.5
Medical care	195.8	206.3	207.2	208.1	209.3	211.2	213.3	195.8	206.3	207.2	208.1	209.3	211.2	213.2
Entertainment	164.8	169.7	170.3	170.4	171.0	171.9	172.9	164.8	169.7	170.3	170.4	171.0	171.7	173.7
Other goods and services	168.8	174.4	176.0	177.2	177.8	178.5	179.0	168.8	174.4	176.0	177.2	177.8	178.4	179.1
Commodities	170.9	176.6	177.0	177.9	178.3	179.2	180.2	170.9	176.6	177.0	177.9	178.3	179.1	180.1
Commodities less food and beverages	162.5	167.7	168.4	169.1	169.5	169.6	169.8	162.5	167.7	168.4	169.1	169.5	169.5	169.8
Nondurables less food and beverages	164.8	170.4	171.3	172.2	172.5	171.7	171.5	164.8	170.4	171.3	172.2	172.5	171.6	171.6
Durables	159.7	164.5	165.0	165.5	165.9	166.6	167.2	159.7	164.5	165.0	165.6	165.9	166.7	167.1
Services	188.7	197.7	198.5	199.5	200.5	202.0	203.5	188.7	197.7	198.5	199.5	200.5	202.0	203.6
Rent, residential	150.2	155.3	156.1	157.0	157.9	158.8	159.7	150.2	155.3	156.1	157.0	157.9	158.8	159.7
Household services less rent	205.5	216.7	217.8	219.0	220.0	221.8	223.7	205.5	216.7	217.8	219.0	220.0	221.7	223.8
Transportation services	183.3	191.0	191.3	192.0	192.9	193.7	194.7	183.3	191.0	191.3	192.0	192.9	194.0	195.1
Medical care services	209.4	221.1	222.0	223.0	224.2	226.5	228.7	209.4	221.1	222.0	223.0	224.2	226.5	228.6
Other services	168.8	175.0	175.8	176.8	177.5	178.8	179.9	168.8	175.0	175.8	176.8	177.5	178.6	180.3

[43] Source: U.S. Bureau of Labor Statistics, Dep't of Labor, catalog No. 15-25485, Monthly Labor Review, May 1978.

The CPI is based on prices of food, clothing, shelter, fuel, drugs, transportation fares, doctor's fees, and other goods and services that people buy for day-to-day living. The quantity and quality of these items is kept essentially unchanged between major revisions so that only price changes will be measured. Prices are collected from over 18,000 tenants, 24,000 retail establishments, and 18,000 housing units for property taxes in 85 urban areas across the country. All taxes directly associated with the purchase and use of items are included in the index. Because CPIs are based on the expenditures of two population groups in 1972-73, they may not accurately reflect the experience of individual families and single persons with different buying habits.

22. Consumer Price Index for Urban Wage Earners and Clerical Workers, annual averages and changes, 1967-77[44]

[1967 = 100]

Year	All items		Food and beverages		Housing		Apparel and upkeep		Transportation		Medical care		Entertainment		Other goods and services	
	Index	Percent change	Index	Percent change	Index	Percent change	Index	Percent change	Index	Percent change	Index	Percent change	Index	Percent change	Index	Percent change
1967	100.0	....	100.0	....	100.0	....	100.0	....	100.0	....	100.0	....	100.0	....	100.0	....
1968	104.2	4.2	103.6	3.6	104.0	4.0	105.4	5.4	103.2	3.2	106.1	6.1	105.7	5.7	105.2	5.2
1969	109.8	5.4	108.8	5.0	110.4	6.2	111.5	5.8	107.2	3.9	113.4	6.9	111.0	5.0	110.4	4.9
1970	116.3	5.9	114.7	5.4	118.2	7.1	116.1	4.1	112.7	5.1	120.6	6.3	116.7	5.1	116.8	5.8
1971	121.3	4.3	118.3	3.1	123.4	4.4	119.8	3.2	118.6	5.2	128.4	6.5	122.9	5.3	122.4	4.8
1972	125.3	3.3	123.2	4.1	128.1	3.8	122.3	2.1	119.9	1.1	132.5	3.2	126.5	2.9	127.5	4.2
1973	133.1	6.2	139.5	13.2	133.7	4.4	126.8	3.7	123.8	3.3	137.7	3.9	130.0	2.8	132.5	3.9
1974	147.7	11.0	158.7	13.8	148.8	11.3	136.2	7.4	137.7	11.2	150.5	9.3	139.8	7.5	142.0	7.2
1975	161.2	9.1	172.1	8.4	164.5	10.6	142.3	4.5	150.6	9.4	168.6	12.0	152.2	8.9	153.9	8.4
1976	170.5	5.8	177.4	3.1	174.6	6.1	147.6	3.7	165.5	9.9	184.7	9.5	159.8	5.0	162.7	5.7
1977	181.5	6.5	188.0	6.0	186.5	6.8	154.2	4.5	117.2	7.1	202.4	9.6	167.7	4.9	172.2	5.8

[44] *Id.*

The major use of the CPI collective bargaining is that it provides a gauge of the impact of rising prices on the purchasing power of workers' incomes.

Table 4. Composition of change in real earnings (production or nonsupervisory workers on private nonfarm payrolls)[45]

Month	(1) Average hourly earnings	(2) Average weekly hours	(3) Average weekly earnings	(4) Consumer price index[1]	(5) Real average weekly earnings	(6) Average tax effect[2]	(7) Real spendable earnings[3]
	Percent change from preceding month, seasonally adjusted						
1978							
Jan.	1.3	−1.7	−0.4	0.8	−1.2	1.8	−2.9
Feb.	0.5	0.6	1.1	0.6	0.5	0.2	0.3
March[P]	0.7	0.8	1.6	0.8	0.8	0.2	0.5
April[P]	1.1	0.3	1.4	0.8	0.5	0.2	0.3

Note: The following relationships hold approximately:
    column (1) + column (2) = column (3)
    column (3) − column (4) = column (5)
    column (5) − column (6) = column (7)

p = preliminary
[1] Beginning with the January 1978 data, earnings in current dollars are adjusted by the revised Consumer Price Index for Urban Wage Earners and Clerical Workers to derive real earnings. See "Changes in the Spendable Earnings and Real Earnings Series for 1978" in the March 1978 issue of Employment and Earnings.

The CPI shows *changes* in prices, in terms of index points, for the geographic area to which the index applies. In using CPI to calculate the real income of the workers, the negotiators will relate it to changes in total wages, take-home pay, and to wage increases already given. The union will use this to indicate that the rise in the cost of living has wiped out an important segment of wage increases or has actually resulted in the loss of real income. Management will use the data to prove that the company's wage rates have increased more than the cost of living.[46] Negotiators generally use CPI in terms of the composite index of all items with reference to the area reported nearest to the locale to which the bargaining relates. Regional CPIs cross-classified by population size were introduced with the May 1978 issue of the *Monthly Labor Review*.[47]

---

[45] Table 4 illustrates the BLS calculation of real earnings. Source: BLS News, USDL-78-502.
[46] *Id.*
[47] Source: U.S. Bureau of Labor Statistics, Dep't of Labor, catalog No. 15-26485, Monthly Labor Review, May 1978.

24. Consumer Price Index for All Urban Consumers: Cross-classification of region and population size class by expenditure category and commodity and service group
[December 1977 = 100]

Category and group	Size class A (1.25 million or more)			Size class B (385,000 – 1.250 million)			Size class C (75,000 – 385,00)			Size class D (75,000 or less)		
	1977		1978	1977		1978	1977		1978	1977		1978
	Oct.	Dec.	Feb.	Oct.	Dec.	Feb.	Oct.	Dec.	Feb.	Oct.	Dec.	Feb.
Northeast												
Expenditure category												
All items	....	100.0	101.0	....	100.0	100.9	....	100.0	101.2	....	100.0	101.0
Food and beverages	....	100.0	102.8	....	100.0	102.5	....	100.0	102.4	....	100.0	102.5
Housing	....	100.0	100.8	....	100.0	101.1	....	100.0	101.7	....	100.0	101.3
Apparel and upkeep	....	100.0	97.3	....	100.0	94.2	....	100.0	96.7	....	100.0	95.7
Transportation	....	100.0	100.2	....	100.0	100.7	....	100.0	100.5	....	100.0	100.3
Medical care	....	100.0	101.9	....	100.0	101.6	....	100.0	102.5	....	100.0	101.8
Entertainment	....	100.0	101.9	....	100.0	101.2	....	100.0	100.7	....	100.0	101.3
Other goods and services	....	100.0	100.5	....	100.0	100.7	....	100.0	100.5	....	100.0	100.3
Commodity and service group												
Commodities	....	100.0	100.8	....	100.0	100.7	....	100.0	100.8	....	100.0	100.6
Commodities less food and beverages	....	100.0	99.6	....	100.0	99.8	....	100.0	100.1	....	100.0	99.8
Services	....	100.0	101.2	....	100.0	101.3	....	100.0	101.9	....	100.0	101.5

These indexes will enable users in local areas for which an index is not published to get a better approximation of the CPI for their area by using the appropriate population size class measure for their region. The cross-classified indexes are published bimonthly. The time span over which the change in the cost of living is measured is critical. In an effort to justify large pay increases, for example, unions will choose a period of rapid price increases. Management, on the other hand, will choose a time span in which the union pay increases were particularly high. In response the union will argue that the pay increases during that period were peculiarly high because of attempts to close a gap, to "catch-up," but that when measured from an earlier base year, the union's gains fall short of what they should have been. Misconceptions surrounding the CPI often lead to erroneous inter-area comparisons. Local area CPIs can be used to determine whether prices in one area are rising faster or slower than in other areas or in the nation as a whole. But, since the index shows only price changes, not price levels, it is impossible to tell from the separate indexes whether prices are higher in one area than another.[48]

The cost of living may actually be referred to in the contract. This may take either of two forms. The cost of living may be stipulated as a reason for reopening the contract for renegotiation of wages; or a methodology for automatic wage revision based upon changes in the cost of living. This latter type of wage revision is normally termed an "escalator" or "COLA" provision. Ideally, the escalator clause seeks to maintain, throughout the term of the agreement, the full buying power of the wage or salary that is established at the outset of the agreement. That is, the clause is written so that, as the price level (the CPI) changes, the wage or salary will change proportionally. Some escalators are designed to protect the wage or salary of each individual employee. They usually provide that, at each adjustment (usually every three months), each employee's wage or salary shall be increased by the same percentage the CPI has increased. The more common escalator clauses are designed to protect the average straight-time rate of the bargaining unit. When the cost-of-living adjustments are made, every member of the unit receives the same amount, rather than percentage increase.[49]

------

[48] *See* Friedman *supra* note 28.

[49]

(a) *Sample Escalator Clause — Straight Percentage*

"*Section 1* — In addition to the basic salary scales specified in this Agreement, all employees covered by this Agreement shall be paid a cost-of-living allowance, to be determined on the basis of changes in the Consumer Price Index — All Items, for the United States (1967 = 100), published by the Bureau of Labor Statistics of the U.S. Department of Labor.

Family Budgets — The Urban Family Budgets, which are also known as the "City Worker's Family Budgets," represent another

---

"*Section 2* — The cost-of-living allowance shall be based on changes in the Consumer Price Index between May 1974 and each of the following months:

1974:	August
	November
1975:	February
	May
	August
	November
1976:	February
	May

"*Section 3* — The percentage change, if any, between the Consumer Price Index for May 1974 and for each of the months listed above shall be applied to the basic salary for each classification, computed to the nearest dollar, in order to determine the cost-of-living allowance that shall be paid to each employee during each subsequent quarterly (three month) period.

"*Section 4* — The cost-of-living allowance shall be paid beginning with the start of the first pay period that commences following publication of the Consumer Price Index for each of the months listed above.

"*Section 5* — The cost-of-living allowances shall be used in the computation of straight-time, overtime, and all other allowances and benefits.

"*Section 6* — This cost-of-living provision shall be applied to increase or reduce pay, but in no event shall it operate to reduce the salaries below the basic salary scales specified in this Agreement.

"*Section 7* — No adjustments, retroactive or otherwise, shall be made due to any revision which may later be made in the published figures for the Consumer Price Index."

(b) *Sample Escalator Clause — Dollars-for-Points*

"*Section 1* — In addition to the basic salary scales specified in this Agreement, all employees covered by this Agreement shall be paid a cost-of-living allowance, to be determined on the basis of changes in the Consumer Price Index — All Items, for the United States (1967 = 100), published by the Bureau of Labor Statistics of the U.S. Department of Labor.

"*Section 2* — The cost-of-living allowance shall be based on changes in the Consumer Price Index between May 1974 and each of the following months:

1974:	August
	November
1975:	February
	May
	August
	November
1976:	February
	May

"*Section 3* — The cost-of-living allowance for each employee covered by the Agreement shall be one dollar per week for each 0.62 points change in the Consumer Price Index between May 1974 and each of the months listed above.

"*Section 4* — The cost-of-living allowance shall be paid beginning with the start of the first pay period that commences following publication of the Consumer Price Index for each of the months listed above.

type of benchmark employed in negotiating economic demands. These family budgets are compiled by the BLS and are designed to show how much it costs a family to live at three different standards: (1) a lower budget level, (2) an intermediate budget level, and (3) a higher budget level.[50] BLS compiles the data for "urban" United States as a whole (broken into metropolitan and non-metropolitan areas) and for forty individual large metropolitan areas. In addition, family budget data are compiled regionally (Northeast, Northcentral, South and West) for non-metropolitan areas with populations ranging from 25,000 to 50,000. This data is published monthly in *BLS News* and in the *Handbook of Labor Statistics*.[51]

"*Section 5* — The cost-of-living allowance shall be used in the computation of straight-time, overtime, and all other allowances and benefits.

"*Section 6* — This cost-of-living provision shall be applied to increase or reduce pay, but in no event shall it operate to reduce the salaries below the basic salary scales specified in this Agreement.

"*Section 7* — No adjustment, retroactive or otherwise, shall be made due to any revision which may later be made in the published figures for the Consumer Price Index."

[50] The sources of data, methods of calculation and quantities of goods and services for each budget level are described in detail in "Three Standards of Living for an Urban Family of Four Persons" (Spring 1967), U.S. Bureau of Labor Statistics, Dep't of Labor, Bull. No. 1570-5. Copies may be obtained under accession number PB 227542/LK at a cost of $4.75 from the National Technical Information Service, U.S. Department of Commerce, Springfield, Virginia 22151.

[51] Table 2 is a copy of the family budget which appeared in U.S. Bureau of Labor Statistics, U.S. Dep't of Labor, USDL-78-393 BLS News (April 28, 1978).

Table 2. Annual costs of an intermediate budget for a 4-person family,[1] autumn 1977

Area	Total Budget[2]	Family Consumption								
		Total Consumption	Food			Total	Housing[3]			
			Total	Food at Home	Food Away from Home		Total[4]	Shelter		House-Furnishings & Operations
								Renter[5]	Homeowner[6]	
Urban United States	$17106	$13099	$4098	$3427	$671	$4016	$3127	$2023	$3495	$889
Metropolitan areas[11]	17498	13299	4160	3454	706	4130	3254	2103	3638	875
Nonmetropolitan areas[12]	15353	11880	3823	3304	519	3510	2560	1669	2856	950
Northeast:										
Boston, Mass.	20609	15302	4426	3733	693	5585	4700	2361	5479	885
Buffalo, N.Y.	18298	13683	4229	3524	705	4239	3324	2163	3711	915
Hartford, Conn.	17796	14041	4413	3659	754	4438	3568	2234	4012	870
Lancaster, Pa.	16322	12473	4222	3560	662	3655	2824	2027	3089	831
New York-Northeastern, N.J.	19972	14702	4653	3830	823	5071	4184	2353	4794	887
Philadelphia, Pa.-N.J.	17792	13268	4572	3790	782	3914	3066	1837	3476	848
Pittsburgh, Pa.	16516	12553	4266	3532	734	3563	2703	1729	3028	860
Portland, Maine	17578	13648	4448	3816	632	4155	3238	2190	3587	917
Nonmetropolitan areas[12]	17052	12974	4147	3599	548	4168	3320	1824	3819	848

[1]The family consists of an employed husband, age 38, a wife not employed outside the home, an 8-year-old girl, and a 13-year-old boy.

[2] Total budget costs include personal income taxes, social security, other items and total consumption.

[3]Housing includes shelter, housefurnishings and household operations. the higher budget also includes an allowance for lodging away from home city.

[4]The average costs of shelter were weighted by the following proportions: **Lower budget,** 100 percent for families living in rented dwellings; intermediate budget, 25 percent for renters, 75 percent for homeowners; higher budget, 15 percent for renters, 85 percent for homeowners.

[5]Renter costs include average contract rent plus the costs of required amounts of heating fuel, gas, electricity, water, specified equipment, and insurance on household contents.

[6]Homeowner costs include interest and principal payments plus taxes; insurance on house and contents; water, refuse disposal, heating fuel, gas, electricity, and specified equipment; and home repair and maintenance costs.

[11]As defined in 1960-61. For a detailed description of these and previous geographical boundaries, see the 1967 edition of *Standard Metropolitan Statistical Areas,* prepared by the Office of Management and Budget.

[12] Places with population of 2,500 to 50,000.

There are several ways in which to utilize the figures representing family budgets. The most obvious involves the direct comparison between salary and the current budget requirements. Because the budgets are designed to show how much it costs to live at the prescribed standards, such comparisons give added credibility to union demands concerning the workers' income needs.

Typically, unions use the intermediate budget to demonstrate a lag in their pay scales, arguing that members should be able to live at least at the level represented by this budget, especially since it is a very modest standard. If the union salary exceeds the cost of the intermediate budget, the comparison will be keyed to the higher budget which, the union will claim, also represents only a modest living standard, and that the company should maintain the highest of these "modest" figures.

To demonstrate the impact of rising prices on workers' standard of living, the union will compare the increase in the cost of the budget over a selected period of time and the increase in the workers' salary during the same period. The union will argue that the increase in salary should exceed the budget-cost increase, because workers are entitled to an improvement in their standard of living that matches the trend of national economic advancement and/or the productivity increases in their particular industry.

Local unions in metropolitan areas other than the forty covered areas must rely on the national estimates or, if there are credible reasons for doing so, on the estimates for one of the forty areas. Local unions in nonmetropolitan areas must rely on the regional estimate for their region or on the national estimate for nonmetropolitan areas. In the forty metropolitan areas for which separate budgets are published, inter-city comparisons can be used to establish comparative salary values. Unions use such comparisons when they want to eliminate salary differences between areas with similar budgetary requirements.[52]

Productivity Figures — Productivity, the amount produced per hour of work, is also a basic and important consideration in bargaining. This is so because of the logical linkage between increases in productivity and increases in pay. For example, if output per work-hour is increasing at a rate of three percent per year, then each hour is likewise worth an additional three percent per year to match the increase in productivity.

Productivity data are compiled by the Bureau of Labor Statistics from data compiled from the Establishment Survey and from

---

[52] For interarea comparisons of living costs at three hypothetical standards of living, *see* the family budget data published in the Handbook of Labor Statistics, 1977, U.S. Bureau of Labor Statistics, Dep't of Labor, Bull. No. 1966 tables 122-133.

estimates of compensation and output supplied by the U.S. Department of Commerce and the Federal Reserve Board. This data is published by the BLS in the *Monthly Labor Review* and in *Employment and Earnings.*[53]

---

[53] BLS also publishes a chartbook, U.S. Bureau of Labor Statistics, Dep't of Labor, Bull. No. 1926, Productivity and the Economy, which shows what productivity is and how it interacts with other aspects of the economy. Table 31 is a copy of the productivity data published in the Monthly Labor Review, May 1978.

31. Indexes of productivity and related data, selected years, 1950-77
[1967 = 100]

Item	1950	1955	1960	1965	1969	1970	1971	1972	1973	1974	1975	1976	1977
Private business sector:													
Output per hour of all persons	59.7	69.2	78.1	94.7	103.7	104.5	107.8	111.0	113.1	109.9	111.8	116.5	119.4
Compensation per hour	41.6	54.9	71.4	88.4	115.1	123.3	131.5	138.9	150.3	164.3	180.2	196.5	213.9
Real compensation per hour	57.7	68.5	80.5	93.6	104.8	106.0	108.4	110.9	112.9	111.2	111.8	115.3	117.9
Unit labor cost	69.6	79.3	91.4	93.4	111.0	118.1	121.9	125.2	132.9	149.5	161.1	168.7	179.1
Unit nonlabor payments	73.2	80.6	85.4	95.8	104.6	105.9	113.2	119.4	125.4	130.9	152.1	159.9	164.7
Implicit price deflator	70.8	79.8	89.3	94.2	108.8	113.9	118.9	123.2	130.3	143.1	158.0	165.6	174.2
Nonfarm business sector:													
Output per hour of all persons	65.5	73.2	80.3	95.7	103.1	103.3	106.3	109.5	111.4	108.1	109.9	114.3	116.8
Compensation per hour	44.5	57.8	73.7	89.1	114.3	121.9	129.9	137.4	148.1	162.0	176.6	193.1	210.0
Real compensation per hour	61.7	72.1	83.1	94.3	104.1	104.8	107.1	109.7	111.3	109.7	110.2	113.3	115.7
Unit labor cost	67.9	79.0	91.7	93.2	110.9	118.1	122.2	125.5	133.0	149.8	161.7	168.9	179.8
Unit nonlabor payments	71.5	80.2	84.5	95.8	104.5	106.2	113.4	117.9	118.3	125.3	147.7	157.4	162.7
Implicit price deflator ..	69.1	79.4	89.2	94.1	108.7	114.0	119.2	122.9	128.0	141.5	156.9	165.0	174.0

BLS productivity data substantiates the view that the rise in the nation's productivity since World War II has been at an annual rate of about three percent. Because of this growth, the nation's total output of goods and services (The Gross National Product (GNP)) has been able to rise at a faster pace than the nation's population. This means there are more goods and services per person. The influence of national productivity figures on collective bargaining received a tremendous impetus from the General Motors agreements in 1948. In that settlement, the United Automobile Workers and GM agreed that workers should share in the nation's increased productivity. It was agreed that hourly wages would automatically be raised by three cents — the equivalent of 2% — each year. This was known as the "annual improvement factor." This was raised to 2.5% in 1950, and 3% in 1955.

Productivity changes within individual industries or companies, although less important than nation-wide productivity, also play a prominent role in shaping wage settlements. For some industries data are compiled by the BLS and are published in the *Monthly Labor Review*.[54] U.S. Bureau of Labor Statistics, Department of Labor, Bull. No. 1938, *Productivity Indexes for Selected Industries* (1976 edition) provides a compilation of productivity indexes for sixty-one industries for 1939, 1947-1975. These measures show changes from year to year in amount of labor time required to produce a unit of output.[55]

---

[54] The April, 1977 issue of the Monthly Labor Review for example contained data on "Productivity in Grain Mill Products and in Sawmills"; and the February 1977 issue contained a "Report on Productivity Gains in Selected Industries."

[55] 1 C.B.N.C. § 10:231 (6/29/78).

INDEXES OF OUTPUT PER EMPLOYEE-HOUR IN SELECTED INDUSTRIES, 1971-77, AND PERCENT CHANGES, 1976-77

(1967 = 100)

Industry	1971	1972	1973	1974	1975	1976	1977[1]	Percent Change 1976-77
Mining[2]								
Iron mining, crude ore	117.1	124.4	126.7	118.1	117.0	119.3	112.8	−5.5
Iron mining, usable ore	112.4	118.8	119.9	108.7	107.0	106.7	99.9	−6.4
Copper Mining, crude ore	121.2	118.1	117.2	117.6	128.9	143.2	136.3	−4.8
Copper mining, recoverable metal	104.9	102.5	97.0	89.0	96.4	112.8	111.1	−1.5
Coal mining	91.0	84.2	83.9	82.6	74.9	73.4	72.5	−1.2
Bituminous coal and lignite mining	91.3	83.9	83.4	82.1	74.7	72.9	72.5	−0.5
Nonmetallic minerals	117.2	121.7	127.5	124.8	122.5	125.3	123.4	−1.5
Crushed and broken stone	121.9	128.2	139.5	136.9	137.6	133.6	128.3	−4.0
Manufacturing								
Canning and preserving	112.6	114.8	126.6	122.6	124.8	132.4	(3)	(3)
Grain mill products	114.1	116.9	115.8	123.9	124.9	131.7	(3)	(3)
Flour and other grain mill products	110.0	114.3	111.9	116.2	116.8	119.6	111.1	−7.1
Cereal breakfast foods	106.7	112.8	111.9	105.3	107.7	112.8	(3)	(3)
Rice milling	102.8	115.3	100.3	115.2	111.7	109.7	(3)	(3)
Blended and prepared flour	112.1	103.6	103.5	116.4	104.7	108.2	(3)	(3)
Wet corn milling	106.9	138.9	123.3	150.6	152.7	168.7	(3)	(3)
Prepared feeds for animals and fowls	119.9	115.9	118.5	127.1	129.5	138.3	(3)	(3)
Bakery products	108.1	113.7	113.1	112.9	112.7	112.8	115.9	2.7

Frequently, however, this data is calculated roughly by the negotiators themselves by comparing changes in employment and changes in output, usually production or sales, to show the increase in output per employee or per manhour.

The debate as to whether or to what extent increased productivity should be translated into increased compensation revolves around two issues: what causes increased productivity, and who should receive its benefits? It is difficult to quantify the respective contributions of labor, capital and management; and existing economic data is of little use in settling the normative issue of who should receive the benefits of increased productivity. Unions argue that in order for workers to obtain a "fair and equitable" share of the benefits of the nation's or the industry's productivity gains, wages should be adjusted by an amount that reflects not only advancements in the cost of living and family-budget requirements, but also the rate of productivity improvement. Management's position is that labor is not the only factor contributing to increased productivity, and increases that result from economics of scale, management efficiency or new technology should not be the basis for increasing employee compensation.

Wage-Price Guidelines — President Carter asked unions to hold their annual wage and fringe benefit increases in the private sector to 7 percent or less and companies to hold price increases to .5 percentage points less than their average adjustments in 1976 and 1977 in order to contain inflation in 1979. As BNA reported in 99 LRR 169-170 (10-30-78):

> About 25 to 30 percent of the nation's 94.9 million workers will be exempt from the wage guidepost, the Administration source said. Low-wage workers earning less than $4 an hour, as well as workers covered by existing wage contracts, will not be expected to comply with the 7 percent cap. All other worker groups, however, will be held to the new standard.
>
> In the case of a new collective bargaining contract, wage and fringe increases must average no more than 7 percent annually over term to comply with the standard. "Mild front-loading" will be allowed, however, with first-year increases up to 8 percent deemed acceptable.
>
> Increases under cost-of-living provisions will be considered in determining compliance. Evaluation of c-o-l clauses will be made on the assumption of a 6 percent rate of price inflation over the life of the contract. Thus, a c-o-l provision granting wage adjustments equal to 50 percent of increases in the Consumer Price Index would be treated as a wage boost of 3 percent — allowing an additional guaranteed increase of 4 percent.

Increases above the 7 percent standard will be allowed "to the extent they they reflect changes in work rules and practices that. show demonstrable productivity growth," according to a White House white paper. Violation of the standard is also justified in order to "maintain a close historical tandem relationship to another employee whose wage adjustment occurred prior to announcement of the program," the white paper also says.

Officials explicitly noted that the wage standard applies to average pay increases for groups of workers, rather than individual workers. Companies will be expected to divide their work forces into groups of management employees, workers covered by collective bargaining agreements, and all other employees, with wage adjustments for each group expected to satisfy the 7 percent standard. The division is necessary, the White House explained, "to take account of the differing institutional arrangements for setting wage rates and in order to prevent an equitable distribution of the wage moderation."

Administration planners determined that a single standard for price increases would be impractical because rates of price increases vary markedly from industry to industry. As an alternative, they settled on a single standard for a rate of deceleration. The 1976-77 period was chosen as the base for the price guidepost "as being representative of basic underlying cost and productivity trends." A senior Administration source noted that the inflation rate in those years was about 1.5 point below the 1978 rate.

Firms that cannot meet the 0.5 point deceleration standard because of "unavoidable" cost increases must demonstrate that their before-tax profit margins are no higher than in the best two of the last three years, the Administration source said. In no event will average price boosts of more than 9.5 percent be deemed acceptable by the Administration. In addition, if wage increases in a given firm decline by more than 0.5 point, a commensurate deceleration in price increases is expected to reflect a full passthrough of the moderation.

Although the standards are not mandatory in the sense that there are no legal penalties for violation, the Administration is planning to use "a panoply of tools" to secure compliance. A company or union in violation of the standards "will feel the pressure the public can exert, through new competition to drive prices down, or removal of government protections and privileges which they now enjoy," the President promised in his address.

Violation of the standards will be interpreted as "an indication of inflationary conditions in the market concerned" and will result in actions including lifting of import restrictions, a request to regulatory agencies to review rate levels, possible reinterpretation of Davis-Bacon and Service Contract Act wage standards, and the focusing of public attention on violators of the wage-price standards.

(2) "External" Financial Data

Useful external wage data usually fall into the broad categories of the results of recent bargaining settlements across the nation, in the industry, trade or area, or current levels of wage rates for similar work nationally, in the same industry or trade, or in the area.[56] Information on the position taken by competitors is best secured directly from interviews with other companies. It is therefore not uncommon for companies, especially where there is a trade association, to exchange the "internal" data which they have prepared for their own negotiations. When this information has been gathered for representative firms in the industry, area, or both, it is possible to determine the prevailing practice for each item.

Information on recent major settlements is provided regularly by the labor press and to some extent by the daily press. A national union's newspaper, its bulletins on bargaining and other material usually provide reports on that union's own settlements.[57] The Industrial Union Department of the AFL-CIO annually publishes a comparative survey of major collective bargaining activities. A general picture of wages and wage supplements bargained across the country in the previous year appears in the March issue of the AFL-CIO monthly magazine, *The American Federationist.* The research departments of the AFL and the CIO can also provide information on current happenings, trends, issues and actions in the field of labor.[58]

Similar information can be obtained from a number of private and industrial research and informational institutions and associations which conduct forums, make surveys and publish authoritative articles and books. Among the industrial organizations are the National Association of Manufacturers, the U.S. Chamber of Commerce, the local Associated Industry groups, the American Management Association and the International Personnel Management Association. Among the private institutions are the American Arbitration Association, the Brookings Institute, the

---

[56] 1 C.B.N.C. § 14:31-32 (No. 700).

[57] The AFL-CIO News, an official weekly paper is a useful source of information. It can be purchased from the Pamphlet Division, AFL-CIO Department of Publications, 815 16th St., N.W., Washington, D.C. 20006 for $2.00 a year.

[58] AFL-CIO, Dep't of Research, 815 16th Street, N.W., Washington, D.C. 20006.

National Bureau of Economic Research, and the various labor relations centers of the colleges and universities.[59]

(3) "Internal" Financial Data

Economic conditions in the negotiating industry or company are especially relevant in defining the economic setting in which collective bargaining occurs. This includes not only profit and wage developments, but also sales, production and new order trends, investment plans, new products and methods, price increases of the company's and its competitor's products, and ever more frequently, foreign trade developments. Trade journals, industry association reports, and publications by such industrial organizations as the National Association of Manufacturers, the U.S. Chamber of Commerce,[60] the Society for the Advancement of Management and the American Management Association are plentiful sources for such information. Financial information about many companies can also be obtained commercially in many forms from Standard and Poors, 345 Hudson Street, New York, N.Y. 10016, and Dun & Bradstreet, Inc., P.O. Box 803, Church Street Section, New York, N.Y. 10008. Periodic reports on many industries from the U.S. Department of

---

[59] *Contact, e.g.,*

National Association of Manufacturers
1776 F Street, N.W.
Washington, D.C.

U.S. Chamber of Commerce
1615 H Street, N.W.
Washington, D.C.

American Management Associations
1800 K Street, N.W.
Washington, D.C.

International Personnel Management Association
1776 Mass. Ave., N.W.
Washington, D.C.

American Arbitration Association
1730 Rhode Island Ave., N.W.
Washington, D.C.

Brookings Institution
1775 Mass. Ave., N.W.
Washington, D.C.

National Bureau of Economic Research
1750 N.Y. Ave., N.W.
Washington, D.C.

[60] The Chamber of Commerce of the United States publishes a Monthly magazine, Nation's Business, which forecasts, analyzes and interprets trends and developments in business and in the government. It may be purchased from the Chamber of Commerce of the United States, 1615 H Street, N.W., Washington, D.C. 20062.

Commerce also are useful source materials as are the articles and statistics which regularly appear in the BLS monthly periodicals.

Having already prepared data on the national economic condition of the industry and nation as a whole, the negotiator is equipped with a general background guide with which to evaluate the adequacy and reasonableness of compensation adjustments. Nevertheless, effective negotiation requires a good deal more preparation.

Compensation

Information on compensation is perhaps the most important material in preparing for negotiations. "Compensation," although often used interchangeably with "wages" or "salaries," is normally, considered to include the cost to the employer of both wages (or salaries) and wage supplements (fringe benefits). Data on compensation levels and trends in the industry and area are frequently used as a scale against which negotiators compare compensation data pertaining to the negotiating company. Crucial to adequate preparation therefore is the accumulation of data, from within the company. The following material is reasonably representative of the information negotiators should obtain and evaluate.[61]

Wage Data — A list of all employees, or classifications of employees, including hiring dates and rates of pay, should be compiled. To avoid confusion and facilitate comparisons, wage rates should be related to job descriptions rather than title. Average hourly, straight-time hourly, weekly and straight-time weekly earnings should be calculated. Where there is an incentive plan, job evaluation plan, plans for employee upgrading or plans for employee progression within a wage rate range, a description of the plan is useful.

Hours Data — The number of hours in a normal and an average workday and workweek should be known. This data is needed to convert earning figures, which are usually known in terms of hourly and weekly rates, into take-home pay so that they are meaningful in terms of the standard of living which they allow the workers to maintain. This data is also useful in determining job comparability.

Employee Data — The number of employees, subdivided into male and female by shift, should be known. This data is useful in determining the comparability of jobs as well as in discussions of public policy regarding employment opportunities for women. Information on the age distribution of employees is useful particularly when negotiating pension and health care plans. A list

---

[61] Friedman *supra* note 28 at 7; W. Randle, Collective Bargaining Principles and Practices 166-68, 179-81 (1951).

of available employee services such as credit unions, recreational facilities, magazines, etc., is helpful in discussions of job comparability. Where many services are available, the employer may use this information to justify wages lower than the prevailing practice.[62]

The turnover rate of employees for the past several years should be obtained and reviewed. From the union's point of view, the higher the employee turnover rate, the more credible is their claim that the company's wages are not sufficient to keep the workers with the company. Conversely, the lower the turnover rate, the more reasonable is the company's claim that its wages are adequate.

Wage Supplement (Fringes) Data — There is a growing emphasis upon wage supplements in collective bargaining. To the extent that the union has chosen to take its compensation in the form of wage supplements, salary figures underestimate the true standard of living of the workers. Meaningful negotiations require therefore that the negotiators compile a list of existing wage supplements along with the current company practice for the respective fringes. A typical list might include the following:

---

[62] Mills & Medoff, Data Needs in Collective Bargaining 19, 20 (1978).

Employee Benefits as Per Cent of Payroll, by Type of Benefit and Industry Groups, 1975[63]

Type of benefit	TOTAL, ALL INDUSTRIES	Manufacturing industries														
		Total, all manufacturing	Food, beverages & tobacco	Textile products & apparel	Pulp, paper, lumber & furniture	Printing & publishing	Chemicals & allied products	Petroleum industry	Rubber, leather & plastic products	Stone, clay & glass products	Primary metal industries	Fabricated metal products (excl. mach. & trans. equipment)	Machinery (excluding electrical)	Electrical machinery, equipment & supplies	Transportation equipment	Instruments & miscellaneous manufacturing industries
Total employee benefits as per cent of payroll	35.4	36.1	36.2	27.8	32.7	32.2	42.2	39.2	40.4	35.1	40.6	35.1	36.1	35.0	39.9	34.8
1. Legally required payments (employer's share only)	8.0	8.8	9.0	8.8	8.4	7.4	7.9	6.4	9.3	9.4	9.5	9.3	8.3	8.1	10.3	8.1
a. Old-Age, Survivors, Disability and Health Insurance	5.7	5.8	5.8	5.8	5.8	5.5	5.8	5.2	5.8	5.8	5.8	5.8	5.8	5.6	5.8	5.8
b. Unemployment Compensation	1.0	1.2	1.2	1.5	1.1	1.2	0.8	0.6	1.2	1.4	1.0	1.2	1.1	1.5	1.3	1.3
c. Workmen's compensation (including estimated cost of self-insured)	1.2	1.7	1.9	1.1	1.5	0.6	1.2	0.5	2.2	2.1	2.7	2.2	1.4	0.9	3.2	1.0
d. Railroad Retirement Tax, Railroad Unemployment and Cash Sickness Insurance, state sickness benefits insurance, etc.**	0.1	0.1	0.1	0.4	•••	0.1	0.1	0.1	0.1	0.1	•••	0.1	•••	0.1	•••	•••
2. Pension and other agree-upon payments (employer's share only)	11.6	11.6	11.7	7.3	9.7	9.4	13.3	13.5	15.6	11.4	15.8	11.1	12.2	9.9	14.1	10.3
a. Pension plan premiums and pension payments not covered by insurance type plan (net)	5.5	4.9	5.7	2.9	3.5	4.1	6.5	9.3	6.7	4.7	7.2	4.4	4.7	3.8	5.3	4.4
b. Life insurance premiums, death benefits, accident and medical insurance premiums, hospitalization insurance, etc. (net)	5.2	6.1	5.1	4.1	5.6	4.9	5.8	3.7	8.0	6.3	8.1	6.2	6.9	5.5	7.8	5.4
c. Salary continuation or long term disability	0.2	0.2	0.2	0.1	0.2	0.1	0.2	0.1	0.4	0.1	•••	0.2	0.3	0.3	0.3	0.2

---

[63] 1 C.B.N.C. § 10:404 (11/4/76). It may also include:

1. Description of shift differentials.

Perhaps the most important preparatory work in this area is the cost calculation. Calculation of the present cost of existing wage supplements and the projected cost of these plus the additional fringes demanded by the union is crucial to successful negotiations.

There are basically four types of data used by negotiators to demonstrate these costs: (1) annual cost of all employees, (2) cost per employee per year, (3) cost as a percent of payroll, (4) cents-per-hour cost per employee. In present bargaining it is considered a virtual necessity to determine past, present and future wage supplement costs expressed in cents-per-hour to facilitate comparisons with direct wages.

Other Financial Data — As indicated in Chapter 2, it is the established position of the National Labor Relations Board (NLRB) that if during negotiations an employer pleads an inability to pay the increased wages demanded by the union, she/he must back up his/her pleas, upon demand by the union, with sufficient information and explanation to enable the union to understand and evaluate the employer's position. The U.S. Supreme Court has similarly held that a refusal to attempt to substantiate a claim of inability to pay increased wages may support a finding of a failure to bargain in good faith.[64] Although ultimately the reason for the employer's inability to pay does not matter, the union's position is weaker to the extent it can be shown that the inability results from higher labor costs rather than other factors such as material and/or selling costs, inefficient manufacturing facilities, price controls, or a disadvantageous supply and demand situation. On the other hand, where the company's financial difficulties are due to non-wage matters, the union is less likely to go along with sub-standard wages. And, where wages are a relatively small part of total costs, the company, although doing poorly, may still be able to pay reasonable wage increases without materially affecting its financial position. One of the most frequently employed types of financial data therefore

----

1. Description of shift differentials.
2. Description of overtime payment plan.
3. Description of pension plan.
4. Description of group insurance plan.
5. Description of employee compensation plan if separate.
6. Description of safety program.
7. Policy on vacations.
8. Policy on call-in and/or call-back pay.
9. Policy on sick leave.
10. Policy on termination pay.
11. Policy on holiday pay.
12. Policy on rest periods.
13. Policy on wash-up or clean-up time.
14. Policy on use of bulletin board.
15. Policy on pay for grievance and negotiating work.

[64] NLRB v. Truitt Mfg. Co., 351 U.S. 149 (1956).

shows the distribution of the sales dollar into compensation, raw material, overhead, etc. In addition to information supplied by the employer, the union may find the financial statement of the company in financial reporting services such as Dun & Bradstreet, Moody's and Standard and Poor's.[65]

Accounting data, which is not audited, although cited in connection with arguments concerning how much a company can afford to pay, is known to be subject to such easy manipulation that it is not given much weight by the union. Earnings reports are regarded with particular skepticism. They do not necessarily tell what a company can afford to pay. For example, a company can be near bankruptcy for lack of adequate cash flow and still show substantial earnings.

The most relevant data to be used in wage comparisons in collective bargaining are actual pay scales. Average earnings statistics measure something other than basic job rates and their use, although frequent, can be misleading unless their limitations are kept in mind.

Average earnings statistics are affected by the distribution of workers. An industry with a relatively high percentage of high-wage workers will have higher than average earnings even though its wage rates paid for the same job may be identical to those of another industry. Similarly, when an industry increases the proportion of workers in its lowest-paid jobs, as is generally the case in times of rising employment, average earnings will decrease even though there is no decrease in wage rates.

Financial Data and Other "Intelligence"

Although a great deal of information about the company or companies and the union or unions is readily available, each side is at a bargaining disadvantage unless they have on hand at the negotiation information which the "other side" has at their disposal and upon which they may rely. The last section is devoted to the use of economic data, but internal financial data as well as other background information can be very relevant to the posture taken by the other party/ies during negotiations. For example, the company's position on wages may be affected by profits and sales, orders and prospects as well as a macro view of the economy as it pertains to the industry. These factors may affect the company's willingness to make concessions as well as withstand a strike just as well as its ability to pay. Although the background of the company's negotiators is probably far less important to the nature of negotiations, this too can be a factor in understanding at least some of the tactics involved in bargaining. Informal financial data is

---

[65] *See* text page 120 *supra.*

available from the company, for example, in shareholders' reports, at consumer affairs offices, and public relations offices, etc. Unions have a tendency to look with a jaundiced eye at this type of information when furnished by the company. Financial information about many companies can also be obtained commercially in many forms from Standard and Poors, 345 Hudson Street, New York, N.Y. 10016 and Dun & Bradstreet, Inc., P.O. Box 803, Church Street Section, New York, New York 10008.

On the other side, company negotiators may want copies of the international union's contribution, by-laws, administrative policies, and financial reports which are available from the specific union, Library of Public Disclosure Office (Reference Pension Reports) and the U.S. Department of Labor, 200 Constitution Ave., N.W., Washington, D.C. 20210. Information about the local union's background, number of employees claimed, amount of dues and initiation fees, general position and attitude, as well as the demands it is making on a national and regional basis, is also useful.

2. Drawing Up Demands

a. Proposals and Counterproposals

Proposals and counterproposals can arise in a variety of contexts. In most cases they arise from a preexisting collective bargaining relationship, under an existing contract — a renewal negotiation. In such cases the desire for new provisions can arise from a mid-contractual request or at the end of a term. They can be motivated by new desires, problem areas or changing patterns within the industry. Or, as previously indicated, a newly certified or recognized union may request bargaining for a collective bargaining agreement through its first negotiation with the company. In each circumstance the nature of the demands and responses will vary. Furthermore the bargaining may arise under a crises or non-crises environment. As Chamberlain and Kuhn indicate,

> In most negotiations continuous exploration of issues does not take place except through the grievance procedures. The parties meet more or less formally, laying on the bargaining table proposals and counterproposals. Since the union usually initiates the bargaining negotiations, it generally has to prepare a set of "demands" for submission to the company. Where a bargaining relationship is already well established, the demands or proposals may simply be suggested modifications of isolated clauses in the existing collective agreement. In other instances, a completely new contract will be presented, ready for signature, though not all paragraphs will have undergone change. This

latter practice involves, of course, an examination of the entire document by the other party to ascertain what it is that has been changed, and why.

In a conference between representatives of a local union and a plant management, the process of drafting the union's proposal is not a particularly complicated one. Possible changes are generally discussed at stewards' and union meetings, with shop officers and members having an opportunity to make suggestions from the floor. Other unions sometimes post suggestion boxes into which members drop comments. In a few cases, members may be invited to submit their ideas by mail. The material received by any of these methods is considered by a committee, usually specially chosen for the purpose. It generally includes the elected officers and often contains representatives of each of the major departments or occupations represented in the membership. The proposal finally drawn up by this committee is sometimes submitted to the union membership for ratification before presentation to the employer.

In community, regional, or national negotiations, the business of drafting the proposal becomes more complex. In the first, the local unions involved often submit suggestions by their memberships to the district council or joint board or to the officials representing the union in negotiations, who exercise their own judgement in determining what should be included in, and what excluded from, the union's demands. Sometimes in order to satisfy the desires of all constituents, no demands are excluded except those actually conflicting with others, although the committee will decide which will be pressed in conference and which will be conveniently forgotten.

In national or industry-wide negotiations, the union's proposal is generally drawn up at a regular convention or in a special conference convened solely for that purpose. The local unions' wishes are made known through formal resolutions addressed to the conference or convention, and committees or subcommittees are appointed to consider all resolutions bearing on a particular phase of the collective agreement, such as wages, hours, seniority, and so on. Approval by the full conference, committee, or convention of the final draft is required.

The impression should not be given, however, that the union members usually take an active part in determining the demands to be pressed upon an employer.

Democratic participation in making up union proposals can lead to serious difficulties. The experience of the Communications Workers of America is illustrative. Prior to 1957 the union's collective bargaining program was discussed and decided by the annual convention on the convention floor. According to an officer of the union:

Frequently, well intentioned but emotional speeches made at a union convention resulted in CWA's making demands in subsequent bargaining completely out of keeping with the then current economic facts of life. In addition, there was a tendency to be constantly changing national bargaining items which did not afford the opportunity of continued pressure year after year, in order to achieve worthwhile objectives which were not obtainable in a single year's bargaining. The inherent weakness of this method of determining national bargaining policy was compounded by the fact that CWA conventions are public forums and detailed public records are kept. It cannot be otherwise in a democratic organization. However, as a result, our most intimate and strategic union discussions and decisions were available and were used by managements throughout the communications industry. Union negotiators came to the bargaining table completely in the dark with respect to what management had in mind.

To overcome the handicap of too much democracy in the formulation of its proposals, the CWA placed responsibility for working out its bargaining policy with a committee of sixty members elected by delegates to the national convention in special geographic and national bargaining unit caucuses.

In most other unions, too, experience has demonstrated the wisdom of giving the responsibility for bargaining proposals to the union officers, who may work with rank-and-file committees. They are responsible, that is, for the articulation of those demands which strike some balance between what they believe their members are most desirous of obtaining and what can actually be obtained. Other considerations may enter as well, but if it is a democratic union the officers must necessarily be guided either by what they infer to be the wishes of their constituents or by what they believe will be acceptable to them.

As control of union affairs has become centralized in the hands of the national office, the degree of discretion which local unions and even joint boards and district councils may exercise in drafting some bargaining proposals has become limited. This result has come about in a number of ways. The national union may prepare a standard contract, which becomes the basis for all local negotiations; it may adopt minimum standards in certain particulars; or it may require that certain standard clauses be inserted in all contracts negotiated by affiliated locals. In some instances, the national union must approve a local proposal before it can be presented to the employer. The curtailment of local discretion in major wage decisions is simply another manifestation of the union drive, formally noted by the Webbs about sixty years ago, to standardize the conditions of employment of all workers who are potential competitors for the job.[1]

We have been speaking here of the union's initial proposal. What of the employer who may wish to make "demands" upon the union or who is faced with the drafting of a counterproposal? Individual companies commonly leave this task to a specially selected bargaining committee, including at least one of the major operating officials. A company's position is generally outlined in discussions between top company officials or in executive committees; less frequently, nonoperating members of the board of directors may be involved. Where a company operates more than one plant, usually representatives from all plants will be heard before a company position is adopted. In some companies where an effective communications system is at work, representatives of particular departments will be given their say before the company commits itself by making an offer to the union. In a few large enterprises formal meetings of plant and departmental representatives will approach the size of, and perform the same purposes as, a union conference at which proposals are formulated.

In some bargaining conferences a trade association may represent a group of employers. In these cases a specially elected committee or the standing board of governors will usually formulate the association's position. There are, however, a few examples of employers' associations which hold conventions to draft proposals for industry-wide negotiations in a manner closely resembling that of unions.[66]

Professor Getman classifies the intial union demands under: [67]

1. *Institutional Proposals* — Union security clause, dues checkoff, and superseniority for union officials.

2. *Non-Pecuniary Proposals* — Seniority, grievance machinery, work protection and work scheduling.

---

[1] Sidney Webb and Beatrice Webb, *Industrial Democracy*, rev. ed., London: Longmans, Green & Co., Ltd., 1920, pp. 715-739. The object of such standardization is, of course, to prevent the exploitation of the weakest members of the group, which might serve to drag down the wages and conditions of their fellow workers. A more recent and limited study of the effects of centralization on collective bargaining is Robert R. France, *Union Decisions in Collective Bargaining*. Princeton University, Princeton, N.J., 1955.

[66] Collective Bargaining, *supra* note 11 at 52. Reprinted with permission of Publisher. © 1965 McGraw-Hill.

[67] J. Getman, Labor Relations 180-186 (1978).

3. *Wage Related Proposals* — Wages and other benefits ("fringes").[68]

Management demands, since they are most often "responsive" to union demands, will vary considerably. Certainly, management rights or prerogatives are of critical importance. In fact, one can accurately view the entire collective bargaining process as an attempt to achieve a balance between union security and management rights. Certainly, management is acutely interested in maintaining flexibility in its operation. Thus, as more "competitive" advantages are based on seniority, management flexibility tends to lessen.

Employers often desire changes to "write out" ambiguities in the agreement, and to resolve problems arising through grievances. However, their attitude toward binding arbitration is not uniform, and depends on the stability of the bargaining relationship.[69] The mere presence of binding arbitration provisions in the vast majority of collective bargaining agreements does not necessarily parallel management attitudes, but is a function of external law on the collective bargaining process, as explained in Part Two of this book.

Insofar as management responses to a union's wage related proposals are concerned, they can probably be categorized as traditionally motivated — management desires wages that are sufficiently high to maintain and attract new workers, and sufficiently low to enable the employer to utilize its capital resources in a competitive manner.

Finally, both parties may, depending on the tactics used, make demands for tradeability purposes or engage in "take-it-or-leave-it" bargaining as permitted by law.[70]

b. Specific Use of Information

Basically broad demands will originate from the bargaining history (for example, the log book, including the negotiation history, and staff suggestions), and the economic data. Specific demands may arise from grievance records and what is sometimes called a "clause book." [71] The latter material is simply one method of utilizing existing contract clauses to improve existing contract language by making it more understandable and less ambiguous. Accordingly, we will cover this method in our section on drafting.

c. Grievance Records

As stated earlier, grievance records are part of the information

---

[68] *Id.* at 180-184.

[69] Rothschild, "Arbitration and the National Labor Relations Board: An Examination of Preferences and Prejudices and Their Relevance," 28 Ohio St. L.J. 195 (1967).

[70] *See* Chapter 2 *supra* at 32.

[71] B. Morse, How to Negotiate the Labor Agreement 2-5 (Rev. ed. 1971).

both parties want to assemble. These records should be analyzed by: (1) department; (2) date; (3) who filed them; (4) subject; (5) contract clause reference; (6) disposition; and (7) grievance step. Grievances should not be viewed from a perspective of "won" or "lost," but rather as problems arising from poor or ambiguous clauses, and corrective demands made to obviate the problem.

Another aspect of problems arising in grievances (including arbitration) is the difficulty arising from an arbitrator's decision which may be contrary to the desire of either party and which may have to be negotiated "out" of the bargaining history of the contract. In such cases, either party may demand that the contract be changed to eliminate the result ordered by the arbitrator. Such a demand could also arise on the basis of the grievance records.

3. Communications

Although in mature bargaining relationships when the parties enter into "serious" negotiations, privacy is a desideratum in order to maintain flexibility, communication is generally an important element of negotiations. Other than direct communication between the parties, each may want to appeal to the public. Both will want to communicate with the employees. And, both may want to "signal" each other in an indirect fashion.

Initially, each side may utilize the media to appeal to the public for understanding and support. This forum also presents an opportunity for each side to signal the other as to their overall expectations from bargaining.

During bargaining, the union may directly circularize its members, or on occasion hold bargaining meetings. Union stewards who are elected officials also maintain constant communication with their constituents. Employers, on the other hand, are more likely to communicate with employees through "leaks" since unions may fiercely resent company communications.

In what may be classified as an atypical approach, Lemuel Boulware in 1946 developed a strategy or "marketing" technique that became General Electric's collective bargaining approach to its employees. This approach requires opening up the lines of communication with the employees in order to be able to put on the table a "full and fair" offer. The Boulware concept of "truthful collective bargaining-making" a final offer based on thorough research subject to rebuttal by the union, ran afoul of the Board's good faith bargaining requirements, because it tended to undermine the union's role in bargaining.[72] However, the notion about keeping the other side fully informed about plans, programs and proposals is utilized by many parties in collective bargaining.

---

[72] *See* Chapter 2, p. 32 *supra.*

If negotiations break down, each party may resort to public opinion to try to arouse public support in order to create disfavor which the other will be unwilling to incur. Public support may also lead to government intervention in the impasse.

If a final contract is agreed to, communication is limited until final ratification occurs and then each side will go public with the results of the agreement in order to state its "victories" together with the potential costs of achieving them!

E. NEGOTIATIONS

1. Bargaining Environment

As indicated in the last section, preparation and organization are critical to the success of negotiations. However, in actual negotiations other factors will affect the atmosphere and environment under which the bargaining takes place, such as the history of prior relations between the parties. This history will undoubtedly be the result of the company's attitude toward unionization, and, conversely, the compulsion that may be operating on union leadership.[73] The economic circumstances at the time of negotiations, under which both parties are operating, are usually significant factors. The attitudes, skills and experience of the negotiators are also variables that affect the negotiations procedures. In sum, there is a bargaining environment which has independent significance in negotiations.

In their work on *A Behavioral Theory of Labor Negotiations*,[74] Walton and McKersie identify four distinct bargaining processes which occur during negotiations. "Distributive bargaining" is directed towards maximizing fixed *benefits for one side,* and is based primarily on economic theory. The leverage for such bargaining derives from a risk-benefit analysis of deadline bargaining (strike threat). "Interpretive bargaining" is a problem solving process for the purpose of increasing *mutual benefits.* "Attitudinal structuring" has the goal of obtaining and maintaining a *desired working relationship* with the other side, and is based on psychological theories. "Intra-organizational bargaining" attempts to achieve successful negotiations through *compromise* on the basis of the appropriate role models. Richard Peterson and Lane Tracy correctly point out that this is not a unified model of all aspects of labor negotiations, but instead ". . . four separate bargaining models, each drawing on a different theoretical base and involving a different set of variables." [75] They illustrate their contention of the variable aspect

---

[73] H. Davey, Contemporary Collective Bargaining 108 (2d ed. 1959) [hereinafter cited as Contemporary Collective Bargaining].

[74] Behavioral Theory, *supra* note 9.

[75] Peterson & Tracy, "Testing a Behavioral Theory Model of Labor Negotiations," 16 Industrial Relations 35, 37 (1977).

of negotiations by accepting Walton and McKersie's thesis of four goals of bargaining under different conditions, behaviors, and moderators, as illustrated by the following chart.

Model of Conditions and Behaviors Related to Walton and McKersie's Four Goals of Bargaining

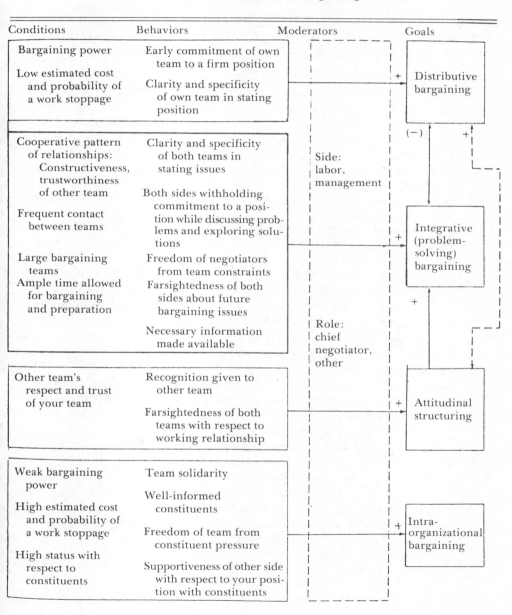

They conclude that the behavioral theory is valid and helps explain the dynamics of collective bargaining.[76] Their point that "collective bargaining is an interpersonal, attitudinal process as well as an economic one and that there are several distinct goals for the process" is well taken.

2. The Agenda

As could be expected from the variable nature of negotiations, there is no agreement as to how the agenda for negotiations should be established. Harold Davey believes in a pre-planned agenda. His recommendations for bargaining are as follows:

1. Both the union and management negotiating committees should be kept reasonably small. If the union or company committee is too large and everyone insists on participating, much time will be consumed, tempers will become frayed, and much irrelevant material may be introduced.

2. One person should be in charge of conducting the negotiations for each side. Division of authority in negotiation is fatal to orderly procedure and usually impedes the agreement-making process.

3. The parties should agree in advance on the time of day and desired length for bargaining sessions. Each side can then make its plans accordingly.

4. Careful advance preparation for negotiations should be made. If possible, the parties should exchange demands or proposals for study before the actual bargaining sessions begin. A frequent source of trouble is the springing of a complicated new proposal during negotiations.

5. Advance agreement should be secured on the procedures to be followed in bargaining sessions. This eliminates many unnecessary arguments over correct procedure, such as whether subject X is "in order at this time." Advance agreement on procedures provides a healthy common basis for accord on substantive issues at the bargaining table.

6. Company and union negotiators should have authority to make decisive commitments in the course of negotiations. Company negotiators should have the power to bind their principals. In most unions the negotiated terms are subject to ratification or rejection by the membership. In the vast majority of cases, however, the rank and file do not exercise their veto power. Realistically, therefore, it is possible for union negotiators to make binding commitments. Company negotiators must have similar power.

---

[76] *Id.* at 50.

7. Negotiations should begin with a well-planned agenda that includes a complete statement of all disputed issues together with a listing of proposals and counterproposals on the disputed points.

8. There should be, if possible, an agreed statement as to relevant factual information. Agreement on such a statement will be easier if the parties have already made effective use of the prenegotiation conference.

9. The negotiators should first eliminate the least controversial issues and reduce agreement on these to writing before proceeding to negotiation of the tougher issues.

10. The difficult issues may be divided into those that involve money outlays and those that are noneconomic demands.

11. Noneconomic issues may be taken up individually and decided in each case on their intrinsic merits, instead of allowing the cruder measure of the economic strength of the principals to determine whether a particular demand will be accepted or rejected.

12. Use of the basket approach on economic issues is recommended. If the prenegotiation conference has produced agreement on relevant factual information as to the economic state of the industry and the financial condition of the plant, it may be possible to reach agreement on a lump sum available for disposition of income demands (wage increase, paid holidays not worked, call-in pay). The negotiations can then proceed on the basis of allocation of this over-all total in terms of the relative urgency of the competing demands for economic benefits.[77]

Carl Stevens, in *Strategy and Collective Bargaining Negotiations,* indicates the general rule in establishing the agenda is otherwise.[78]

THE AGENDA RULE — AGENDA SET BY INITIAL DEMAND AND COUNTERPROPOSAL

Characteristically in collective bargaining the initial demand and counterproposal set the agenda for each periodic agreement conference. That is, there is no systematic negotiation of the agenda prior to the beginning of substantive contract negotiations.

As with other rules for play of the negotiation game, there are possible alternatives to the agenda rule. In some international negotiations, for example, it is customary to decide upon the agenda itself by negotiation before the beginning of substantive negotiation. In some collective bargaining relationships there are preagreement

---

[77] Contemporary Collective Bargaining, *supra* note 73 at 111-12.
[78] C. Stevens, Strategy and Collective Bargaining Negotiation 38-45 (1963). Reprinted with permission of Publisher. ©1963 McGraw-Hill.

conference procedures which tend in the direction of agenda negotiation.

The problem of the tactical significance of agenda composition is related to the institution of the "large demand" since the agenda is brought into being by the bargaining demand and counterproposal. Nevertheless, these phenomena ought to be distinguished. Suppose that "n" items are to be negotiated by the parties in one or more plays — that is, in one or more separate forums. The tactics of agenda design are concerned with the distribution of these n items among the one or more plays. The large demand institution is more concerned with the number n itself. The above supposed demand would have been larger, for example, if we had supposed that n + 1 items were to be negotiated by the parties in one or more plays (but this need not affect the composition of the agenda pertaining to other than one play). Since the agenda for each play is brought into being by demand and counterdemand, a decision to increase the magnitude of a demand will alter the compensation of the agenda pertaining to that play. However, in this case the alteration of the composition of the agenda is essentially a by-product of the initial bargaining demand decision, the latter made on grounds not peculiarly concerned with the tactics of agenda composition.

Interest in the agenda rule for collective bargaining negotiation inheres in the possibility that agenda composition has tactical significance. There is no *prima facie* case that agenda composition has significant tactical implications in collective bargaining negotiation. Nevertheless, this possibility should be explored. Schelling has expressed the opinion that whether two or more items are negotiated simultaneously or in separate forums may affect the outcome. For example, negotiating items simultaneously may facilitate the use of threat, by bringing to bear on one proposition the threat of adverse action on others. Also, multi-item negotiations may play a generally enabling role in cases where the principal means of compensation available to the parties is concession on some other item. In such a case, if two simultaneous negotiations can be brought into a contingent relationship, a means of compensation may be made available, where otherwise none might exist. These suggestions are aspects of the proposition frequently encountered in the literature on collective bargaining that items may be included in bargaining demands because of their trading value.

It is sometimes suggested that in a bilateral-conflict relationship such as collective bargaining there may be a tactical advantage attached to "first move," especially if this can be seized by commitment. However, the above considerations suggest that there may be an offsetting asymmetry of tactical advantage stemming from agenda composition inherent in any procedure in which the demand and counterproposal are not presented simultaneously. For example, in a nonsimultaneous procedure, the party with "first move" may "waste" a potentially useful threat by attempting to exploit it in circumstances which turn out to be inappropriate in the light of the counterproposition. Suppose that a union, aiming for a substantial wage increase, thinks that the company will offer little or nothing. The union might include a union security demand in the agenda for this forum, hoping to trade it for a tolerable wage increase. If, however, the company's "real" position on the wage increase is much more generous than the union had expected (a fact which might have been inferred had the company made the initial proposal), the union security demand "turns out to have been" used in a context in which its trading value significance was not tactically required. The party with "second move" may be able to avoid such waste. Moreover, the party with "second move" (the counterproposer) can judiciously avail himself of means to compensation and, thus perhaps induce agreements which would not otherwise be possible. A company, wishing to eliminate an objectionable clause from the collective agreement, might attach this demand to an agenda which contained union demands on which it is willing to make a concession. Thus, the company, in making its demand, does so in a context known to contain at least potential means of compensation. Where the demand and counterproposal procedure is simultaneous, the company might attach its demand to an agenda which contained no other union propositions it was willing to concede and which therefore contained no means (agreeable to the company) for compensating the union for accepting its own demand.

Why do the parties to collective bargaining negotiation not engage in prenegotiation agenda negotiation rather than simply accept whatever agenda eventuates from the initial demand and counterproposal? One answer to this lies in the nature of the political relationship between the negotiators and their constituents, especially on the union side, a matter to be discussed subsequently. Another answer probably lies in the nature of those sanctions available to the parties which underlie their bargaining relationship; namely, the strike or lockout. Just as A's refusal to accept a given B demand may be backed if necessary by the strike, so A's refusal to admit a given B item to the agenda may be backed by the strike or lockout if this be necessary. What is to be gained by striking an opponent during prenegotiation if he may be struck as well during the course of substantive negotiations?

Another answer is that the continuing nature of the collective bargaining relationship may greatly attenuate the tactical implications of agenda composition. In a continuing relationship such as collective bargaining it may not be possible to achieve *de facto* isolation of the agenda for one play from the (anticipated) agendas for subsequent plays. Indeed, and this is another explanation of large initial bargaining proposals, some demands may be included in this year's agenda largely for "educational" purposes: that is, included not so much with the intention of obtaining them this year as with the intention of familiarizing the bargaining opponent with demands to be pursued in earnest at a future date. A recent case in point has been the guaranteed annual wage (GAW) demand. For many years before the UAW finally negotiated a GAW plan with the automobile industry in 1955, many major CIO unions made demands for the GAW, only to drop these in favor of other benefits more directly felt by their members. Hence, in the years just prior to 1955, a question existed as to the "seriousness" of the GAW demand.

More generally, many demands and counterdemands tend to be in the air before they make a formal appearance at the bargaining table. The mere exclusion of a pension demand, for example, from this year's agenda may not keep the expectation of such a demand on next year's agenda from having a strong influence upon this year's negotiation. Even if the agenda pertaining to any one play of the collective bargaining game is not neutral with respect to the outcome of that play, it would not be of great significance in collective bargaining if the agendas pertaining to a succession of plays were collectively neutral with respect to the grand total outcome. However, since some significance attaches to the order in which items are negotiated, nonneutrality of the agenda *vis-à-vis* the whole series of plays seems probable.

. . .

ADDITIONS TO INITIAL DEMANDS

Another aspect of agenda composition is the proscription that, generally speaking, a party to collective bargaining negotiation does not during the course of negotiation make demands in excess of those contained in his initial proposal. This proscription applies both to increasing the magnitude of a given item and to adding additional items to those contained in the initial proposal.

Since negotiation sessions are frequent and the initial bargaining demands can be "large" in any event, there is no general necessity to provide for subsequent increases in demands. Moreover, the practice of adding to demands during the course of negotiation is not compatible with the negotiation process. How can a party really begin to negotiate until he knows what his opponent's maximum asking price will be? Certainly the basic bargaining processes of changing position, rewarding by concession, threatening by adherence, and so on, could scarcely begin until the total demands to be served during a given play of the negotiation game were on the table.

The above considerations do not rule out the possibility that certain special functions might be served by such subsequent changes in position. One such function, for example, would be the exploitation of information about one's opponent gained during the course of negotiations. The fact that negotiation sessions are frequent greatly reduces the importance of serving this function *vis-à-vis* any particular contract negotiations; that is, it can be served during the next contract negotiations. One legitimate aspect of this function *vis-à-vis* a particular set of negotiations is the case in which the initial demander gets new ideas from the counterproposal — ideas which suggest that some redesign of the initial demand would facilitate agreement.

Much more dubious is the practice whereby a party attempts during the final stages of negotiation to exploit the fact of near agreement by tacking a last-minute demand, as a sort of "rider," onto a virtually wrapped-up package. Such an attempt, even if successful, would surely degenerate the atmosphere prevailing during subsequent negotiations sessions. However, Peters, discussing "bad faith" on the part of negotiators, cites the case of a union negotiator who habitually uses this tactic. Peters classifies this tactic as, while not perhaps properly considered bad faith, a borderline case — certainly to be regarded as bad practice.

"PACKAGE" SETTLEMENTS (TENTATIVE PROPOSALS) RULE

The outcome of collective bargaining negotiation is by agreement. Characteristically, such agreement must be upon all the items comprising the agenda. Agreement upon all items is defined as mutual assent to a disposition for each of the agenda items. This may involve overt agreement in the sense of settling upon a wage rate somewhere between the initial demands of the parties. But it may also involve other kinds of disposition such as covert agreement in the sense of the parties' refraining from further mention of an agenda item. Or it may be agreement by the parties to submit a disputed item to arbitration. Such a provision for package settlements is fairly straightforward. The items comprising a package are to a considerable extent commensurable in terms of cost, and, to a considerable extent, it is the total cost of the package that matters. In consequence, agreement on all the items is what matters.

Discussion of the package settlement provision, relating as it does to termination of negotiations, should perhaps have been delayed till the end of this chapter (where we will deal more generally with the rule for termination). Nevertheless, an aspect of the package settlement relating to tentative proposals during the course of negotiation is involved with the matter of agenda composition, and, in consequence, it facilitates matters to bring it into the discussion at this juncture.

The agenda-related point of interest is that even though a number of items are on the "same" agenda, they may in a sense be accorded separate "forums." In some collective bargaining negotiation, a division is made between "cost" and "noncost" items, and an effort is made to get the latter out of the way first. The union in particular is apt to favor seriatim treatment in an effort to wrap up fringe items before attention is given subjects of major importance. According to Peters, the motivation for this is the union's knowledge that the employer is aware that a strike is unlikely over subordinate differences. However, so long as the major issues have not been settled, the union exerts strike pressure in the negotiations.

The significance of the attempt to distribute items on the "same" agenda among separate forums by pressing for seriatim treatment is conditioned by a provision strongly implied by the package settlement rule: Any agreements or proposals relating to individual items made during the course of negotiations are understood to be provisional and may be withdrawn (without prejudice) if final agreement upon all items in dispute is not reached prior to a strike or lockout. This tentative-proposals provision is not quite a necessary consequence of package settlements. Even with package settlements, it could be understood that all interim agreements and concessions were binding in the sense that they would comprise part of the final agreement if and when such was achieved.

Perhaps the most interesting aspect of the tentative-proposals provision is its ambiguous status as a "rule." Dunlop and Healy have observed that withdrawal of an offer is more a matter of ritual than of fact in the sense that, barring serious defeat of one side or the other in a strike or lockout, offers already made are seldom effectively withdrawn. The ambiguous status of this "rule" would seem to reflect a basic institutional ambiguity in the negotiation situation. On the one hand, such a rule is very understandable. Agreements and concessions during the course of negotiations are expected to induce mutual agreement. These are made as "promises" against a *quid pro quo* — namely, concessions and agreement by the opposite number. If agreement is not reached prior to strike or lockout, earlier concessions have not served their function. They become essentially gratuitous. In such circumstances, it seems reasonable that they be withdrawn.

On the other hand, free withdrawal without prejudice of prior agreements and proposals in the event of strike or lockout would seem to decrease the efficiency of the negotiation process. If the parties characteristically returned to their initial positions in the event of a strike or lockout, whatever function the prestrike negotiations had served in bringing the "real" positions of the parties closer would be nullified; that is, the efficiency of the negotiation process as a whole will be enhanced if strike negotiations are concerned with settling a residual difference between the parties inherited from the prestrike negotiations, rather than with settling the entire initial difference between the parties.

The negotiator needs to balance two considerations. On the one hand he needs to wait until he has enough information about the intentions of his opponent — until he can decide whether his opponent will take the first step in narrowing the range. On the other hand, by seizing the initiative and taking a committed position, he increases the probability that his opponent will move first.

Communicating Flexibility versus Actual Concession. Here we assume that Party does not intend to communicate extreme firmness in his present position. His choice now centers on whether to merely communicate some degree of flexibility or to actually make a concession. What factors does Party consider in deciding this question at any particular time? This is the question of pacing the convergence process and controlling its final point of intersection.

Peters emphasizes the importance of sophisticated treatment of this tactical decision area:

> In skillful hands the bargaining position performs a double function. It conceals, and it reveals. The bargaining position is used to indicate — to unfold gradually, step by step — the maximum expectation of the negotiator, while at the same time concealing, for as long as necessary, his minimum expectation.

NOTES:

(a) *Compare* Gallo and McClintock, "Cooperative and Competitive Behavior in Mixed-Motive Games," 9 J. Conflict Resolution 68 (1965); Howard, "Theory of Meta-Games," 11 Gen'l Systems 167 (1966); and McClintock, Gallo and Harrison, "Some Effects of Variations in Other Strategy in Game Behavior," L.J. Abnormal Soc. Psych. 305 (1965).

(b) *Problems:* (1) Which of Walton and McKersie's four bargaining goals is Stevens referring to in his "agenda rule"? Is his "game theory" compatible with their theory of attitudinal structuring and intra-organizational bargaining goals?

(2) Can the Davey and Stevens views be rationalized on the basis of Walton and McKersie's differing bargaining structures? What is the underlying premise of Stevens' agenda rule insofar as offer and acceptance in negotiation is concerned?

3. Strategy

Just as with procedures, there is no established rule for the strategy and tactics used in negotiations. It is probably true that the strategy selected will be a function of the bargaining environment, the structure of the bargaining teams, the behavior of the parties, and the goals desired.

Walton and McKersie summarize tactics within their "analytical framework" in terms of resistance points.[79]

> A brief review of some propositions implicit in the model of distributive bargaining will suggest the various ways by which the negotiator can influence the outcome by directly influencing the other's perceptions of utilities (including values associated with the issue and strike action). We view these from the point of view of one negotiator, Party, whose general tactical assignment can be thought of as inducing Opponent to adopt a relatively lower (less ambitious) resistance point and to take explicit bargaining positions throughout negotiations consistent with the lower resistance point.
>
> First, *Opponent's resistance point varies directly with the utilities he attaches to possible outcomes.* Thus, Opponent's resistance point will be lower if he places a lower value on the conceivable outcomes, that is, if the whole or a major portion of his utility function is shifted appropriately. Party can manipulate Opponent's view of Opponent's utility function so that Opponent does not see as much advantage in maintaining his position. Opponent must be convinced that a proposal of his own is of less value to him than he originally thought or that a demand of Party is less unpleasant to him than he first thought.
>
> According to our analysis of subjectively expected utilities (to which the resistance-point decision rule was coordinated), the resistance point also varies directly with subjective probabilities. Since the later value varies inversely with one's own strike costs, directly with the other's strike costs, and inversely with the other's utilities for the outcomes, we have the following additional derived propositions:
>
> Second, *Opponent's resistance point varies inversely with his subjective strike costs.* Thus, Opponent's resistance point will be lower if he places a higher estimate on his own strike costs. Party can manipulate Opponent's view of his strike costs so that Opponent is somehow convinced that a strike would provoke a

---

[79] R. Walton & R. McKersie, A Behavorial Theory of Labor Negotiation 58 (1965). Selected portions from Chapter III reprinted with permission of Publisher. Copyright © 1965 by McGraw-Hill.

higher cost than he had originally assumed (either because of increased rate or increased duration).

Third, *Opponent's resistance point varies directly with Party's subjective costs of a strike.* Thus, Opponent's resistance point will be lower if he places a lower estimate on Party's strike costs. Party can convince Opponent that the former will experience a low rate of costs and perhaps that Party would derive some positive by-products from the strike which would tend to offset these costs.

Fourth, *Opponent's resistance point varies inversely with Party's utilities of possible outcomes.* Thus, Opponent's resistance point will be lower if he places a higher estimate on how much Party values the conceivable outcomes. Party can convince Opponent that Party attaches greater importance to issues than Opponent had earlier realized.

The explicit positions that Opponent takes at any time during negotiations, as well as his resistance point, are assumed to be subject to the influence of these basic parameters. Therefore, Party can influence the process and the outcome of bargaining by manipulating Opponent's subjective assessment of any or all of the four utility parameters. . . .

The authors detail the tactical assignments implied in these propositions.

Assessing Opponent's Utilities for Outcomes and Strike Costs

Party's first tactical assignment is to assess Opponent's utilities and strike costs and if possible ascertain his resistance point. Party may know that the parties hold differing objectives regarding the resolution of an agenda item; that is, he knows that he is dealing with a distributive issue. But what is not so obvious to Party is just how important the objective is to Opponent, particularly in terms of how much gain (loss) on the issue would be minimally acceptable to him. Moreover, while a negotiator usually knows whether a strike would be costly to the other party, he does not know *how* costly!

Knowledge about the relevant parameters is critical in deciding whether to maintain or abandon a position. Such knowledge enables Party to make in turn intelligent probability assessments. These assessments tell him how far he has to go in further manipulating the parameters in order to bring about movement on Opponent's part. They also tell him whether he had better consider altering his own position.

Tactics to Elicit Clues. When we turn to the problem of obtaining more direct clues about Opponent's resistance point, we must consider the ongoing negotiation process. Sometimes the efforts flow along ethically questionable channels and involve cloak-and-dagger operations, e.g., utilizing an informant from Opponent's headquarters or bugging Opponent's caucus room. . . .

Informal conferences with negotiators of the other party are sometimes employed in order to sound them out regarding reactions to various types of proposals. Typically, however, reliance is placed on bargaining-table tactics. Some of these tactics are intended to elicit reactions that become data in estimating the resistance point. The most obvious way is to ask questions designed to clarify both the meaning of the proposal and its underlying rationale. Sometimes Party will direct such questions to some of the "less-coached" members of Opponent's team.

. . . .

By probing Opponent's team members regarding a specific proposal, Party can determine how well prepared they are, using this information as one basis for inferring how seriously they are advancing their proposal.

Tactics involving personal abuse may be introduced to induce or provoke Opponent into revealing more than he wishes. . . .

Tactics of exaggerated impatience which make it appear as if the negotiations were rushing headlong into their final stages may force the inexperienced negotiator into prematurely revealing the bargaining room he has allowed himself. . . .

The tactics discussed above — personal abuse and exaggerated impatience — are not without their risks. In his excitement the other negotiator may take a stronger position than he had originally planned and then become obliged to maintain that position.

Testing techniques are particularly useful for assessing Opponent's resistance point late in negotiations. Sometimes in order to test Opponent's position, Party will suggest calling in a mediator. If Opponent accepts the suggestion, this is taken as an indication that he sees the problem as one of exploring a way by which the positions of the parties can be brought together; he would presumably have some "give" left himself. If he rejects the bid, this may indicate that he has no room to move unless he had reason to believe that Opponent is just looking for an excuse to move all the way himself. Another tactic is for a union to bring the parties up to a strike deadline, arrange a last-minute postponement, and then bargain up to the new deadline in order to test and retest the company's limits.

Tactics to Record and Analyze Reactions. Even in the absence of "baiting" tactics, the verbal and nonverbal behaviors of members of Opponent's negotiating team are often rich with clues about the degree of interest they have in the items being discussed or passed over and about their expectations regarding these issues. . . .

In a continuous relationship the negotiators learn in various subtle ways how to assess the position and intentions of the other person. . . .

Several tactics are used to take full advantage of this source of data regarding Opponent's resistance point.

First, Party may have a man-to-man policy in composing his own negotiating team. Many managements find it useful to have one management committeeman for each union committeeman, so that the latter can be under constant observation during negotiation proceedings. . . .

Second, Party may be even more sophisticated in this practice by making a continually revised assessment about the influence of each member of Opponent's negotiating team. Since negotiations are not an isolated event but occur as part of a continuing labor-management relationship, most members of the negotiating committee are known to the opposite group. Respective individuals work together during contract administration, on problems and grievance handling. This type of familiarity enables each side to better assess the intentions of the other side. . . .

Modifying Opponent's Perceptions of Party's Utilities

This tactical assignment is to conceal or misrepresent the utilities for Party inherent in the agenda items. In a sense, this becomes the countermeasure to the first tactical assignment. If we assume that all of the verbal and nonverbal behaviors of Party are being scanned by Opponent for clues about Party's utilities, then Party has two responses. He can be inscrutable, that is, behave in a minimal or irrelevant way, or he can disguise his utilities by deliberately misrepresenting them. Of course, sometimes the best Party can hope to do is to accurately represent the importance of some particular demand, if, for example, Opponent is very likely to underestimate it.

Minimizing Clues. The earlier discussion of assessing Opponent's resistance point suggests certain tactical countermeasures which Party can take to minimize the number of revealing clues he admits. It is especially important for Party to minimize clues early in negotiations rather than fashion misleading ones, to the extent that he has not already developed clear notions about what his ultimate resistance point is in these negotiations. The point is that the negotiation process itself is a mechanism whereby Party gathers much of the information he needs to test the appropriateness of his own resistance point.

Perhaps a basic step in this direction is for Party to maintain a low rate of activity and interaction. He makes a deliberate effort to remain quiet, letting members from Opponent's committee do most of the talking. Another way in which Party sometimes ensures that minimum clues, or rather appropriate clues, will be produced is by using a single spokesman or a chairman who controls the participation of other members of his committee. . . .

Conveying Deliberate Impressions. Party will attempt to communicate those facts which create the most advantageous impressions of his inherent demands and threats. When it is advantageous, he will provide Opponent with information which gives the latter a better appreciation of the basic importance of an issue. Party advances cogent reasoning and engages in emotional behavior in order to underscore the importance of a particular issue to him. For example, Party can convey the appropriate impression by informing Opponent of the costs that he faces. Several tactics have this as their purpose.

One tactic adopted by management with more frequency in recent years is to take the initiative by introducing positive demands of its own, and the function of these demands is to focus attention on difficulties encountered under the *status quo.* It allows management to focus attention on areas in which they can demonstrate basic costs or difficulties — areas which the union might not anticipate or fully consider. Even though these demands will relate to only a portion of the bargaining agenda, the tactic tends to create the appropriate overall impression.

Another tactic for Party is to ensure himself that he has informed Opponent of all Party's costs associated with a given demand. . . .

The tactical use of economic cost information can get rather involved and contains liabilities. All the observer can be certain about is that *prior* to the signing of the settlement, the company is trying to convince the union that a given set of demands will cost too much, while the union is seeking to convince the company that the costs will not be as great. . . .

When the importance of a demand is not merely underscored or slightly overstated but rather is grossly exaggerated, this tactic contains important risks. . . .

Clearly there are other risks in communicating misinformation. The point may come in distributive bargaining when Party would like to talk about his true feelings and his true perceptions as a way of closing a negative settlement gap. But it is very difficult to be oblique in one negotiation and accepted as a faithful reporter in the next negotiation. Moreover, unless one is consistent in the types of arguments he advances, his positions lose credibility. In certain situations one can influence perceptions by communicating cost information. Such information may give Opponent a better appreciation of the inherent importance of an issue. But if the use of cost information is turned on and off, then when it is not advanced, Opponent will assume that Party's position is weak and his arguments are designed to mislead.

Many other difficulties emerge from the tactical use of information. Opponent will be able to counter with tactics of his own. What then results is a buildup of misinformation on top of misinformation. Instead of negotiations progressing to more common perceptions, they may lead in the opposite direction. Such a spiraling of misinformation can lead to greater uncertainty and miscalculation.

Aside from the question of how communicating misinformation affects the distributive bargaining process, certain value judgments are involved. There is a fine line between misrepresentations which are viewed as "natural" and those which are viewed as "lies" and consequently provoke hostility. Since collective bargaining is a continuing relationship, abuses along these lines will eventually receive their due.

Modifying Opponent's Perceptions of His Own Utilities

The objective of this tactical assignment is to alter Opponent's subjective utility function either by changing his view of the value of his own demands to himself or by changing his view of the unpleasantness of Party's proposals. We see these efforts to revise Opponent's utilities as primarily consisting of bringing to bear the right information and arguments at the right point within Opponent's organization. We shall first discuss the substantive aspect of these tactics, i.e., the types of information and arguments employed, and then turn to the procedural aspects of these tactics, i.e., the problem of introducing these arguments into Opponent's decision-making apparatus.

Tactical Arguments. In the preceding tactical assignment Party attempted to selectively report the consequences of a certain demand for him. In the present tactical assignment Party is enlightening Opponent about the consequences Opponent will face if the latter should succeed in maintaining his position on a certain issue. The distinction can be characterized as follows: In the first instance Party was communicating, "Here is why I definitely·can't concede this item to you in a settlement." In the second instance, the one we are concerned with here, Party is saying, "Even though I'm not saying whether you could have it or not, here is why for your own good you should not insist upon this item."

Generally, this maneuver takes the form of a union trying to convince the company that the union's demands are costless and the company trying to convince the union that the union's demands are valueless to the union. Stated in terms of a general example, the union would say something like this to the company, "Your proposal to cut crew size will not save you money; morale will suffer and overall output will drop significantly." Similarly, the company says something like this, "Your proposal for a change in the seniority system is really not going to be that valuable to you because of the repercussions that will take place in your own organization."

Negotiators use colloquial and colorful language in their effort to force the other person to reassess the cost and value of different issues. Such phrases as the following are frequently encountered: "it could backfire"; "it might come back to haunt you"; "you can't have your cake and eat it too"; "the cost of this proposal will eventually be shifted to you"; "increases in cost will hurt our ability to compete, meaning fewer jobs and less security for you"; and "don't kill the goose that lays the golden egg." But whatever the language, the intent is the same, namely, to force the other person to reappraise the utility of a given issue.

The disadvantages to Opponent of his position may be more or less immediate and may be more or less certain in their effect. Some undesirable consequences possibly not considered by Opponent may be shown to be "part and parcel" of his demand. . . .

Procedural Tactics. The foregoing material dealt with the content of the arguments. How does Party introduce these arguments most effectively into Opponent's organization? There are several possibilities. First, Party may invite a higher official from Opponent's organization to participate in negotiations. Such officials may have wider experience in the industry, may better understand Party's language, may be better aware of the bigger picture; hence, if Party's logics are good, they may have more impact on the higher official. It is in this vein that the union often asks to speak to the company president or to a higher authority than that represented in the company's bargaining team. Management may seek to involve a representative of the international union for the same reason.

Second, Party may communicate directly with Opponent's principals. Employees, for instance, may be less familiar with the issues and hence more easily convinced by illogical but persuasive arguments, or the principals may be assumed to have some doubt about their bargaining agent or the importance of the union's bargaining positions and hence can be reached by arguments that are couched in terms of what is in the workers' best interest. Letters sent to employees' homes telling them about the "generous company offer" represent this kind of procedural approach.

Third, in situations which have features opposite to those above, it is sometimes tactical for management to try to deal strictly with local union officials. This is used when many of the union's demands are believed to have originated at higher levels of the organization and may contain mixed blessings for the local unit of the organization. . . .

Manipulating Strike Costs of Party and Opponent

In this section we consider two remaining tactical assignments which operate on strike costs: increasing Opponent's potential strike costs and minimizing Party's. They are considered together for reasons of convenience inasmuch as single tactics chosen by negotiators often operate simultaneously on both sides of the power equation. In the discussion of the distributive model we indicated that we would be limiting our treatment of the costs of disagreeing to that of strike costs. However, it should be understood that pressure can be inflicted in ways other than precipitating a strike. . . .

A frequently used device is to physically exhaust Opponent to the point at which his fatigue overwhelms his desire to attain his objective. This is often characteristic of the closing phases of negotiations. . . .

In deciding how to place an opponent at a strike disadvantage, many structural and strategic questions are involved. In the short run it is difficult for a negotiator to manipulate the rate of cost that his opponent will experience should open conflict develop. However, in the long run many possibilities are available. Some of these are suggested by the factors outlined in the model chapter. For example, changes can be made in the structure of collective bargaining. Each side can attempt to alter the structure in a favorable direction. Companies may move toward industry-wide bargaining or move to strengthen one another's position through the development of mutual-aid arrangements. On the union side action may be taken toward the development of cooperating councils. . . .

Over the long run either party can maneuver the expiration date in its favor. However, it may be necessary to forego certain short-run gains in order to achieve a more favorable expiration. Obviously Party's objective is to have the contract expire when costs of conflict are greatest for Opponent and least for himself.

Beyond manipulating the structural factors, many other steps can be taken by each side to gain the favorable side of the power equation. These tactics work on both the rate of strike cost and the amount of total resources available for withstanding a strike. A few of these tactics can be quickly summarized for the union and the company.

Union Tactics. First, the union can attempt to increase membership solidarity. The union can strive to bring all the employees within the bargaining unit, to quell factionalism, and to take other steps designed to create solid support for a strike.

Second, the union can increase the availability of other activities and benefits. Prior to the strike the union can survey the availability of alternate employment and make arrangements for various kinds of supplementary benefits. Over the long run the union can push for legislation that would provide state unemployment compensation to striking workers.

Third, the union can build strike funds and enter into mutual assistance pacts. Funds are usually collected and paid out by national headquarters. . . .

Fourth, the union can encourage employees to increase their personal savings and place an upper limit on their fixed weekly financial commitments, such as regular payments for durable goods purchased on time. Both efforts limit the employees' dependence on continuous income. . . .

Company Tactics. First, the company may take steps to keep the plant open. It may go so far as to hire strikebreakers and proceed to replace the work force. Short of this the company can attempt to operate the plant with supervisors and regular employees who have been encouraged to return to work.

Second, the company can build inventories. The objective is to continue shipments during the course of the strike. Whether this can be done depends on the location of the firm's warehouses and the general questions of how easy and inexpensive it is to store materials. It also involves the question of who normally stores the inventories — customers or suppliers?

Third, the company can transfer production to alternate plants not represented by the union. If a plant is only one of several company plants which have similar production facilities, the company can reduce the cost of a strike by transferring production to other plants. The net cost of supplying customers from alternate production facilities will depend upon added transportation costs, amount of excess capacity available, how much adaptation of other production facilities is required, etc. Still an additional production capability may be achieved by subcontracting operations to another firm or otherwise arranging for them to supply customers.

Fourth, the company can secure financial resources in order to withstand a long strike. Many things can be done to avoid capitulation because of the lack of financial resources. Extra cash can be acquired. Resources from other parts of the company can be shifted into the plant.

Commitment Tactics

The strategies of commitment are based on a simple proposition well expressed by Schelling [20] along these lines: *If Party can make an irrevocable commitment to a position near Opponent's resistance point* [21] *in a way that is unambiguously visible to Opponent, Party can squeeze the range of indeterminateness down to the point most favorable to himself. . . .*

The practical idea of a commitment strategy is for Party to develop his position in such a way that Opponent believes Party is firmly committed to an outcome most favorable to himself but at the same time leave himself an avenue of retreat known only to himself which will permit him to demonstrate that he never was in fact committed to this preferred outcome, should it develop that this becomes untenable.

Determining Appropriate Degree of Commitment

A central issue in distributive bargaining strategy is the question of how rapidly in the sequence of bargaining moves does one approach a particular point which he will pose as his final position. The execution of one's commitment strategy is comprised of the tactical decisions which the negotiator must make about when to actually make a concession, when to indicate flexibility, and when to hold firm. These tactical decisions have several aspects, since at any given point in the bargaining sequence he will indicate his current position, the degree of resoluteness he attaches to that position, and the course of action he intends to follow should his position not be acceded to.

Communicating Firmness versus Flexibility. Here we assume that Party does not intend to make a concession at this precise moment but considers that he must communicate something about his current position. The need to communicate may grow

[20] T. C. Schelling, "An Essay on Bargaining," American Economic Review, Vol. 46 (June, 1956), p. 283.

[21] The assumption is that there is a positive initial settlement range. If there is a negative gap capable of being closed, the propitious commitment for Party would be one near his own current resistance point. For purposes of simpler exposition in discussing commitment tactics, we shall make the constant assumption that there is a positive gap between the resistance points of the two parties.

out of a preference to take the initiative, or it may be necessary to respond to an initiative by Opponent. What factors does Party consider in deciding how much firmness should be communicated at any particular point in time?

Limits to firmness. Certain considerations limit how early in the bargaining sequence one can make an irrevocably firm commitment. Stated more generally, these considerations influence how much firmness one dare communicate at any point in time. To the extent that Party is uncertain about Opponent's perceptions of utilities and strike costs, maximal commitments by Party run the risk of violating Opponent's resistance point. By taking a maximally committed position, a negotiator makes it more difficult for himself to abandon an untenable position — he can do so only by risking internal dissension within his own organization and embarrassment at the main bargaining table. By its very nature firm commitment requires that the initiating party go through with the consequences.

Therefore commitment does more than indicate the utility of an outcome — it also shapes and increases utility associated with that outcome. The negotiator who becomes identified with a particular position has gone on record with respect to the importance that he gives to his position. As a result the act of taking a committed position arbitrarily changes his utilities. This explains why negotiators often hold to positions which incur the costs of protracted strike action. The costs of the strike action are less than the cost of "losing face." What started out as an inconsequential issue to both sides takes on increased importance.

Reasons for flexibility. The point of the discussion above is that firmness contains risks. However, Party's reasons for wishing to convey flexibility rather than firmness in his current position may be of a more positive nature. Party may desire to communicate the possibility that he will reduce his demands or concede something to Opponent's demands. Party may, for example, wish to make this change contingent upon some concession by Opponent, or Party may have other reasons for wishing to suggest that he has the latitude to accommodate Opponent's position without actually making that a binding promise.

Party may desire flexibility in his present position for another reason — in order to increase his demands later should that become feasible or necessary. Some of the factors which might contribute to this are as follows: First, there is the possibility that a strike might ensue, in which case it might be better to increase one's demands. If a strike is going to occur, it is desirable to possess as much trading room as possible. It may also be necessary to win more benefits to justify the strike to the membership. For these reasons the union negotiator will often remain vague about his position in the event that he needs to take a higher position than he initially envisioned. This is facilitated by the ground rule often adopted specifying that "nothing is final until everything is wrapped up." Second, Party may wish to add a new demand or otherwise increase his position during negotiations as a credibility tactic. We shall see in the next section that one sometimes convinces the other that he is serious by this technique — "You will see what will happen if you persist in your position! " Third, the possibility exists that a pattern that would justify higher demands may develop during negotiations. Fourth, Party might concede more in one area than is presently contemplated, making it necessary to tighten up on a position in a related area.

Remaining flexible and not taking a committed position has the advantage of allowing the negotiator to continue to test the feasibility of various positions. Flexibility enables the negotiator to increase his aspiration as well as to reduce his aspiration in the light of the unfolding negotiations. In effect, a flexible position minimizes the risk of a strike.

The negotiator needs to balance two considerations. On the one hand he needs to wait until he has enough information about the intentions of his opponent — until he can decide whether his opponent will take the first step in narrowing the range. On the other hand, by seizing the initiative and taking a committed position, he increases the probability that his opponent will move first.

NOTE:

Problems: (a) Since the tactics Walton and McKersie refer to as distributive bargaining involve dividing up the "economic pie", is there an assumption about the use of, or knowledge about economic data in the existence of resistance points? How valid is this assumption in light of our discussion of the use of economic data in bargaining?

(b) Since the leverage for the resistance point is the likelihood and cost of a strike, can the strike deadline effectively be removed from collective bargaining in the private sector? What could take its place?

(c) Do "bid and auction" tactics preclude Boulware's notion of "honest collective bargaining"? Should collective bargaining for wages, hours, and terms and conditions be a "game" of strategy? Does such a process adequately protect the "public interest"?

4. Costing Contract Proposals *

The need of both labor and management to determine, with considerable accuracy, the financial consequences of labor contract proposals is of critical importance to the success of the collective bargaining process. Knowing the financial impact of each contract proposal is essential to negotiators to enable them to judge the value of each item, and to intelligently trade one item for another.

The common practice in labor negotiations is to evaluate contract proposals in terms of the following four expressions of cost: [80]

1. *Total Annual Cost:* This is the total sum expended by the company over a year for a given item.

2. *Annual Cost per Employee:* This is determined by dividing the total annual cost by the number of employees covered by the particular program.

3. *Percent of Payroll:* This is the total annual cost of proposal divided by the total annual payroll.

4. *Cents per Hour:* This is derived by dividing the total annual cost by the total productive hours worked by all employees covered by the program during the year. This is perhaps the most frequently used of the four expressions of cost.

Although used in collective bargaining, these four expressions of cost have little relevance for corporate decision-making. The data are deficient in that they emphasize the direct cost of the contract changes instead of their effect on profit. While the primary goal of negotiators may be to minimize the cents-per-hour cost of a contract, the primary goal of a firm is to maximize profits. Because labor costs are among the largest incurred by most corporations, their impact on profits is significant. But, it is important to remember that it is this impact, rather than costs as traditionally expressed, which is relevant for corporate decision-making.

Traditional cost calculations fail to measure the impact of the contract proposals on profits because they use data based on the previous year's operations rather than on projections of the level and nature of operations during the period covered by the new contract. Such calculations fail to take into account the ability of a firm to minimize the adverse financial impact of a change in labor costs by

---

* This section was written by Ms. Eliza Patterson, B.A. University of Michigan; J.D. Harvard Law School. The material was taken largely from three sources; Division of Research, Planning and Development, Office of Technical Services, Federal Mediation and Conciliation Service, Elementary Steps in Costing a Contract (1975) [hereinafter cited as Costing a Contract]; M. Granof, *How to Cost Your Labor Contract* (1973); M. Friedman, *The Use of Economic Data in Collective Bargaining* (1976).

[80] National Industrial Conference Board, Studies in Personnel Policy No. 128, Computing the Cost of Fringe Benefits, 7 (1952).

adjusting price, volume of production, product mix, capital-labor mix and work and production scheduling. However, whether negotiators will rely on rough estimates of the cost of proposals or will utilize the most accurate calculations possible is largely a function of scale. Large firms with actuarial resources are more equipped to project figures than to rely on an "historical estimate." The decision of how detailed costing should be also turns on the cost effectiveness of such projections. The purpose of this section is to alert negotiators to potential error rather than attempt to advise the parties of "better" costing practice.

a. Economic Variables in New Proposals

Negotiators must consider that the level of such economic variables as price, volume, product mix and capital-labor mix at which profits will be maximized will vary with changes in labor costs. The impact of a new labor contract on profits will stem, therefore, not only from the negotiated contract revisions but also from accompanying adjustments in these economic variables to their new profit-maximizing levels.

(1) Price and Production Volume

As labor costs rise, firms and industries with little or no competition, management may, in order to maintain profits, attempt to pass on part of the increase to customers in the form of higher prices. The severity of consumer reaction will depend on what is known as the "elasticity of demand." [81] The greater the elasticity, the more pronounced the response to a price increase will be in terms of a decline in demand for the firm's products. Hence, a firm may be required to reduce production volume below previously planned levels, thereby also reducing the amount of labor employed.[82] In such cases, the result of a new contract may be a rise in per unit labor costs and price, but a decline in total labor costs and total revenue. As long as labor costs decline more than revenue, profits will increase. The optimum price and volume levels will be those at which revenue exceeds costs by the greatest amount.

(2) Product Mix

A firm which produces more than one product may be able to minimize the adverse effect on profits of a contract change by

---

[81] For a complete definition of the concept of elasticity of demand, *see* P. Samuelson, Economics 382 (10th ed. 1976).

[82] How a particular firm's labor requirements respond to changes in production volume depends to a large degree upon a firm's production process. The greater the number of workers assigned to perform a function generally categorized as "overhead" the less labor requirements will vary.

changing its product mix. It is unlikely that a contract settlement will cause the labor costs of each product to increase by equal proportions relative to other costs. A contract change increasing labor costs might therefore make some products comparatively less profitable. To maximize profits the firm will probably increase production of the relatively more profitable products and decrease production of the relatively less profitable products. As a result, management may have to change the size, structure and composition of its labor force.

(3) Capital-Labor Mix

In order to determine the ultimate influence of a contract settlement on profits, negotiators should be aware of opportunities to reduce the burden of higher labor costs by substituting capital for labor. If a firm has been operating under its old contract with the optimum proportion of labor to the capital,[83] an increase in labor costs relative to capital costs would induce management to increase its use of capital relative to labor.

b. Costing Wage Rates and Compensation for Nonworking Time

Negotiators should be aware of the consequences of evaluating contract revisions from an historical, rather than a future perspective. Furthermore, the indirect implication of any modification should be included in the analyses negotiators accord provisions pertaining to wage rates (including cost-of-living adjustments and premium pay), as well as to compensation for nonproductive time such as vacations, holidays and relief time. The following material is illustrative.

(1) Wage Rates

(a) Direct Wages

As FMCS explains: [84]

Wage rates and wage increases vary greatly by industry, occupation and union status. Wage rates and wage rate changes are published monthly by the Bureau of Labor Statistics.[1] Shown below are a few simple methods for calculating wage increases.

There are at least two basic methods by which to calculate the direct cents per hour cost of a wage increase.

Method 1. If a wage increase of $.45 per hour is granted, the cost

---

[83] To maximize profits a firm will employ each of its resources up to the point at which the marginal physical product of a dollar's worth of every resource yields the same amount of output.

[84] Costing a Contract, *supra* note * on p. 154 at pp. 3-6. Reprinted with permission of the Federal Mediation and Conciliation Service.

[1] Two Bureau of Labor Statistics publications which contain such information are *Monthly Labor Review* and *Employment and Earnings*.

is then $.45. If the increase is not a flat across the board increase, but rather an average increase of $.45, then the increases are weighted.

> 100 workers with increases of $.40
> 80 workers with increases of $.45
> 50 workers with increases of $.50

$$100 \times \$.40 = \$\ 40$$

$$
\begin{array}{ll}
80 \times\ .45 = & 36 \\
50 \times\ .50 = & 25
\end{array}
\qquad \frac{101}{230} = \$.44
$$

$$
\begin{array}{cc}
\overline{230} & \overline{\$101}
\end{array}
$$

1. Hourly cost per employee = $.44
2. Total annual cost = $210,496
   Average hourly increase × number of hours paid × number of employees − .44 × 2080 × 230 = $210,496
3. Annual cost per employee = $915.20

$$\frac{\text{Annual Total Cost}}{\text{No. of Employees}} \qquad \frac{\$210,496}{230} = \$915.20$$

Method 2. This method takes into account hours paid for but not worked. The total increase in wages is divided by either the total projected or total estimated number of productive hours to be worked. Assume a standard number of paid hours, 2080, for the workers in this above example:

$$
\begin{array}{rl}
100 \times 2080 \times \$.40 = & \$\ 83,200 \\
80 \times 2080 \times\ .45 = & 74,880 \\
50 \times 2080 \times\ .50 = & 52,000 \\
\hline
\text{Total Increase in Wages} - & \$210,080
\end{array}
$$

This is then divided by the total number of projected productive hours. (Assume each employee works 2000 hours per year.)

> Total number of productive hours = number of employees x number of productive hours for each worker.

$$230 \times 2000 = 460,000$$

$$\frac{\text{Average cost}}{\text{Productive hours}} \qquad \frac{\$210,080}{460,000} = \$.46 \text{ per hour}$$

(Note: If productive hours had been determined to be 1,900, the increase would have been $.48. Generally, the previous year's average number of productive hours per employee is used.)

Method 3. In order to determine the average hourly cost of a wage increase of a multi-year contract, calculate the increase by the number of years or months each increase will be in effect and divide by the total number of years or months of the contract.

A three-year contract provides for the following increases. (This calculation utilizes 2080 hours per year as does Method 1 above.)

$$December\ 1,\ 1975 = \$\ .50\ per\ hour$$
$$December\ 1,\ 1976 =\quad .45\ per\ hour$$
$$December\ 1,\ 1977 =\quad \underline{.40}\ per\ hour$$
$$\$1.35$$

	In Years			In Months	
$ per hr.	yrs. in effect		$ per hr.	mos. in effect	
.50	×	3 = $1.50	.50	×	36 = $18.00
.45	×	2 = .90	.45	×	24 = 10.80
.40	×	1 = .40	.40	×	12 = 4.90
		$2.80			$33.60

$\dfrac{\$2.80}{3}$ years = $.93 per hour $\dfrac{\$33.60}{36}$ months = $.93 per hour

Method 4. An alternative method for calculating the average hourly cost of the wage increase over the life of the contract is to sum the total wage increase over the period in which it is in effect and then divide this sum by the total time period of the contract.

For example:

	$ per hour		mos. in effect
First 12 months	$ .50	×	12 = $ 6.00
Second 12 months $.50 + $.45	.95	×	12 = 11.40
Third 12 months $.50 + $.45 + $.40	1.35	×	12 = 26.20
			$33.60

$\dfrac{\$33.60}{36\ \ months}$ = $.93 per hour

(Note: This method assumes 2080 hours per year as does Method 1 above.)

The technique of computing increases by the number of months for which an increase is to remain in effect is particularly useful when the company is attempting to stay within certain cost limitations and the union is influenced by the total package increase as opposed to the actual money in hand. For example, a $1.50 total wage increase over three years of $.25 at six-month intervals may be more acceptable than one which is front loaded but does not yield as high a wage increase over the same period than a $.50 — $.50 — $.20 package. In fact, the first package may even become an acceptable compromise if the company is willing to increase the wage rate over the period by the $1.50 amount but is unable or unwilling to front load the package in, say, a $.50 — $.50 — $.50 fashion.

This approach has often been used in instances where the parties desire to create or expand a differential between different bargaining units. The parties can stay within the same average cost for all bargaining units, and end up with varying wage rates. By applying this method in certain situations, such as delaying a second or third year increase for a month or two, it is often possible to persuade the parties to apply the savings to a fringe demand costing one or two cents per hour.

Method 5. This method determines the average yearly wage increase over the term of the contract and is frequently used by the parties to describe a wage settlement. The same three-year contract and increases given in Method 3 applies to this example.

In Years			In Months		
$ per hr.		yrs. in effect	$ per hr.		yrs. in effect
.50	×	3 = $1.50	.50	×	36 = $18.00
.45	×	2 = .90	.45	×	24 = 10.80
.40	×	1 = .40	.40	×	12 = 4.80
		$2.80			$33.60

$\dfrac{\$2.80}{6 \text{ years}} = \$.47 \text{ per hour}$ $\dfrac{\$33.60}{72 \text{ months}} = \$.47 \text{ per hour}$

Appendix 1 gives the cost of 1½¢ to 50¢ hourly increases over periods ranging from one day to three years, and is particularly useful in demonstrating to the parties long-term costs of hourly increases.

The cents-per-hour figure arrived at by these traditional methods is only an estimate for corporate decisionmaking because it is based exclusively on historical information. The most accurate calculation for determining the effect of a proposed cents-per-hour wage increase requires that the anticipated productive hours be derived, not from previous years records, but rather from forecasts of labor productivity and of future production volume estimated in corporate profit plans. The number of productive hours required to produce this projected amount of output is calculated by dividing the projected volume by the forecasted productivity of labor for the estimated period.

(b) The Effect of an Increase in Direct Wages on Fringe Benefit Costs

It is generally recognized that an increase in direct wages will result in an increase in the cost of those fringe benefits, the costs of which are a function of the direct wage rate. Examples of some of these benefits are: [85]

1. *Social Security and Unemployment Insurance Contributions.* The employer's contribution is computed as a percentage of each employee's wage up to a fixed amount annually. To the extent that the annual earnings of some employees are less than the fixed amounts, an increase in wages will require an increase in Social Security and unemployment insurance contributions.

2. *Life Insurance.* Often the amount of insurance coverage for which the employer pays is based on the annual earnings of the employee. As the earnings of the employee increase, so too will the amount and cost of the coverage.

3. *Overtime Premium and Shift Premium.* Overtime premium is almost always, and shift premium is sometimes, computed as a percentage of base wages. As the base wage rate goes up, so also will required overtime and shift premiums.

4. *Pension Benefits.* Pension benefits are often computed as a percentage of employee's average annual earnings over a number of years. An increase in wages will increase the cost of providing pension benefits.

The effect of the wage increase on these fringe benefits is known by several terms: "roll-up," "creep" or "add-on." Those benefits which are stated in fixed dollar amounts are not subject to any "roll-up." For example, cost-of-living clauses are frequently stated in flat cents-per-hour amounts, and thereby do not vary with fluctuations in wages and are not subject to roll-up.

In evaluating the financial impact of roll-up most companies base the roll-up percentage on historical payroll data. For example, assume a firm currently pays its employees at the rate of $4.00 per hour and that the current cost of those fringe benefits, which are a function of the $4.00 wage rate, is $1.00 per hour. The company is considering a direct wage rate increase of $0.80 per hour, as well as increases of $0.40 per hour in fringe benefits. Assume also that the company employs 500 workers each of whom works 2,000 hours per year; the company uses 1,000,000 hours of labor per year. The

---

[85] M. Granof, How to Cost Your Labor Contract 35 (1973).

annual cost of the increase in the base-wage rate would be computed as follows:

(1) Using historical payroll data the firm determines the cost of direct wages and those fringe benefits which are a function of the direct wage rate:
Cost of direct wages:

$4.00 x 1,000,000 work hours = $4,000,000.
Cost of fringe benefits:

$1.00 x 1,000,000 work hours = $1,000,000.

(2) The firm then computes the roll-up percentage by dividing the total cost of the fringes which are a function of the direct rate by the cost of direct wages:

$1,000,000/$4,000,000 = 25%.

(3) The direct cost of the proposed increase in the base-wage rate is calculated by multiplying the proposed direct hourly wage increase by the previous years work hours data:

$0.80 x 1,000,000 work hours = $800,000.

(4) The increase in the cost of fringes attributable to the increase in the direct wage rate is computed by multiplying the direct cost of the proposed increase in the base-wage rate by the roll-up percentage:

$800,000 x 25% = $200,000.

(5) Finally the direct cost of the increase in the base-wage rate is added to the cost of automatic increases in fringe benefits:

$800,000 + $200,000 = $1,000,000.

The roll-up percentage based on historical payroll data as calculated above fails to take into account increases in fringe benefits being negotiated concurrently with increases in direct wages. To do so it is necessary to add to the cost of the direct wage increase not only an amount representing an increase in the cost of current fringe benefits resulting from the increase in the base-wage rate, but also an amount representing the increases in newly negotiated fringe benefits attributable to the change in the base-wage rate. The ratio of the cost of proposed fringes to the cost of direct wages is called the "package roll-up" percentage. Accordingly, a more accurate analysis is achieved therefore by adding the following calculations to those outlined above:

(6) Management should compute the cost of proposed

increases in the fringes themselves which are currently being negotiated:

$$\$0.40 \times 1,000,000 \text{ work hours} = \$400,000.$$

(7) The package roll-up percentage is determined by dividing the cost of changes in benefits calculated in step 6 by the cost of direct wages:

$$\$400,000/\$4,000,000 = 10\%$$

(8) The increase in costs of the new fringes which result from the increase in the base-wage rate is computed by multiplying the package roll-up percentage by the increased cost of the direct wages:

$$\$800,000 \times 10\% = \$80,000.$$

(9) Therefore, the financial impact of a proposed increase in the base-wage rate is computed by adding the direct cost of the increase in the base-wage rate (per step 3), $800,000; the increase in costs of both existing fringes, $200,000; and new fringes attributable to the increase in the base-wage rate, $80,000 (per steps 4 and 8):

$$\$800,000 + \$200,000 + \$80,000 = \$1,080,000.$$

(c) Cost-of-Living Adjustments

Cost-of-living adjustments (COLA) are increases or decreases in wages based upon movement of a price index, usually the Consumer Price Index (CPI), compiled by the U.S. Department of Labor's Bureau of Labor Statistics.[86] These adjustments are designed to protect the "real" wages of employees from the effects of inflation. A typical cost-of-living provision, for example, might require a one-cent-per-hour increase for each 0.3 point quarterly increase in the CPI. Determining the financial impact of cost-of-living adjustments presents special analytical problems. The amount of the increase to be granted over the life of the contract is not only variable, but it is a variable beyond the control of management.

Typically companies assume for purposes of calculations that they will be required to grant the maximum increase in rates possible under the contract. For example, assume an agreement lasting 15 months and covering 200 employees with a COLA provision requiring a $0.01 hourly wage increase for each 0.3 point quarterly rise in the CPI. Assume that the CPI increased 1.2 points in each

---

[86] See 1 C.B.N.C. § 10:101 et seq. (12/19/74); BLS, CPI for 1978, id. at § 10:153 (6/15/78).

quarter. Assume further that the first quarterly adjustment will take place 3 months after the effective contract date and will be in effect for 12 months. The second increase would then begin 6 months after the start of the contract and would be in effect for 9 months or ¾ of a year. The third increase would then be in effect for 6 months (½ year), and the fourth would be in effect for 3 months (¼ year). The estimated cost of each of the four quarterly increases would be calculated as follows:

	Hourly Increase		Number of Hours Paid		Number of Employees	
First quarterly adjustment:	$0.03	×	2080*	×	200	= $12,480
Second quarterly adjustment:	$0.03	×	¾(2080)	×	200	= $ 9,360
Third quarterly adjustment:	$0.03	×	½(2080)	×	200	= $ 6,240
Fourth quarterly adjustment:	$0.03	×	¼(2080)	×	200	= $ 3,120
Estimated Total Cost of the COLA						$31,200

Relying on the assumption that the maximum increase will be granted enables the firm to avoid the task of projecting the trend of consumer prices. It may, however, lead the firm to make artificial bargaining decisions. By overstating the cost of the COLA, a company may forego accepting smaller increases in the base-wage rate or in fringe benefits.

A more accurate calculation of the financial impact of COLA provisions is obtained by multiplying an estimate of the cents-per-hour rates which will have to be paid in each quarter, derived from explicit forecasts of the behavior of the appropriate price index, times the anticipated number of productive hours for which it will be in effect, derived from estimates of projected production volume and labor productivity. The total cost of the COLA would be the sum of the quarterly adjustments figured in this manner.

(d) Overtime Premiums and Shift Differentials

It is a widely accepted practice in the United States to pay workers both a premium for "overtime," hours in addition to the normal number of hours per day or week, and a "shift differential," usually stated in cents-per-hour, for working either an evening or a night shift. The cost of a change in contract provisions relating to overtime

---

* This figure is obtained as follows: 40 hrs/week x 52 weeks/year = 2080.

premiums and shift differential is calculated by multiplying the increase in rates times the number of labor hours which would be affected by such change.

Most firms assume that the number of overtime or non-day-shift labor hours will be the same during each year of the new contract as it was during the preceding year of the old contract. Whether a firm can properly assume that its mix of labor hours compensated for at straight-time and premium rates (the labor-rate mix) will remain constant is a function of the stability of demand for its products, the extent to which increases in production volume require increases in labor, and the ability to the firm to increase labor in ways other than overtime. Where the labor-rate mix does not remain stable, the financial impact of changes in premium pay provisions is dependent on determinations of the optimum levels of employment. Such determinations involve decisions as to whether to hire additional workers or to request that current employees work overtime, and whether to add additional shifts or extend existing shifts. A firm should therefore take into account its anticipated production volume and its plans for fulfilling that volume in projecting labor-rate mix.

A more accurate procedure for costing overtime premiums and shift differential provisions is to multiply the negotiated increases in overtime premiums and shift differentials by the anticipated number of hours to be compensated at premium rates. This hours data can be derived from the firm's employment policies, production schedules, and anticipated production volume.

(2) Compensation for Time-Off

Firms normally pay wages for a certain amount of time during which employees do not work. It is common, for example, to grant paid vacations and holidays and to provide a certain amount of relief time each day.

In general, the cost of granting additional time-off with pay is calculated by multiplying the base-wage rate times the additional hours demanded. This implicitly assumes that the additional time-off will cause a decline in production and that such decline will be offset by additional work hours of labor compensated at straight-time rates. This assumption is often incorrect. In some cases production will not decline at all and the cost of additional time-off will be zero. When production is lost, it may be made up by temporary employees or current employees working overtime at rates other than straight-time rates. If the firm is already operating at capacity, it may not be possible to recover the lost production, in which case the cost is the lost profit.

The overall impact of increased compensation by reason of modifications in time-off provisions is more accurately calculated by multiplying the number of hours required to recover lost production by the rate at which they will be compensated. In addition, where an expanded physical plant is required to maintain production volume, the cost of such expansion and the cost of hiring and training any new employees required should be added.

The number of units of production lost can be derived from monthly production forecasts and statistics of labor productivity. Estimates of the number of new employees, the number of hours, and the rates of pay required to recover lost production can be made by reviewing employment policies followed in the past.

(a) Vacations

The contract changes in vacation provisions most frequently proposed by unions involve increases in the number of days of vacation. Normally, the first step in evaluating changes in vacation policy is to determine the number of employees in each category by years of service,[87] the number of additional days to which they will be entitled, and the rates at which they will be paid. Thereafter most firms simply multiply the number of additional vacation hours by the appropriate wage rate. For example, take the case of a firm with the following vacation eligibility and rates of pay:

No. of Workers	Base Wage Rate	Years of Service
50	$4.00 per hour	1
100	$4.50 per hour	2
65	$5.00 per hour	3

The additional cost for this firm of providing an additional week of vacation for each year of service would be calculated as follows:

No. of Employees		No. of Additional Vacation Hours		Base Wage Rate	
50	×	40	×	$4.00 =	$ 8,000
100	×	80	×	$4.50 =	36,000
65	×	120	×	$5.00 =	39,000
				Total Additional Cost =	$83,000

This costing technique fails to consider the effect on profits of the services lost and is therefore only a rough estimate for corporate decision makers. The relevant financial impact of additional vacation time is more accurately determined by paying attention, not to the amount of vacation pay that employees will draw, but rather to the cost of maintaining production at planned volumes in spite of the additional vacation days. This impact is determined by the following procedures:

---

[87] The amount of vacation to which an employee is entitled is usually determined according to a sliding scale of years of service with the company (by seniority).

(1) Determine the number of employees whose absence would be unlikely to decrease production and who will therefore not be replaced. The cost of granting these workers additional vacation time will be near zero.

(2) Determine the number of hours employees will be required to work overtime. The cost to the company will be the number of overtime hours times the overtime wage rate.

(3) Determine the number of additional employees who will have to be hired and the number of hours they will be required to work. The cost to the firm is the number of hours paid to the new employees times the wage rate they receive plus such hiring cost as advertising, employment agency fees, application blanks, interviews, indoctrination and training, and break-in time.[88] When permanent rather than temporary employees are hired the cost of the fringe benefits they will receive should also be added.

(4) Determine the number of employees who are irreplaceable. The cost of an increase in the number of vacation days for these employees will be the profit lost because of lost production and resulting lost sales.

(5) The cost of maintaining planned production volume in spite of additional vacation days is the sum of the four costs calculated above.

(b) Holidays

The problems involved in evaluating the financial impact of an additional holiday are similar to those of evaluating the impact of an extra day of vacation. The probable effects on production and the adjustments made as a result are, however, likely to be different.

Most firms determine the cost of an additional holiday by simply multiplying the number of additional holiday hours by the appropriate base-wage rate. For example, if the firm has 10 workers earning $4.50 an hour and 15 workers earning $4.00 per hour, the cost of granting 2 additional paid holidays (16 hours) would be $8,400, calculated as follows:

$$10 \times \$4.50 \times 16 = \$ \ 720$$
$$15 \times \$4.00 \times 16 = \$ \ \underline{960}$$

Total Annual Cost $\underline{\$1,680}$

This calculation is also just a rough estimate of the overall financial impact of an additional holiday. It fails to recognize the ways in which lost production will be recouped. Holidays, unlike vacations, provide time-off to all employees simultaneously. It is more likely in the case

---

[88] F. Gaudet, Labor Turnover: Calculation and Cost 39 (1960).

of holidays that granting additional days may require a firm to shut-down completely or operate at a fraction of capacity thereby causing a loss of production, sales and profits. Because it is seldom feasible to hire temporary employees for only a few days, especially holidays, it is likely that the lost production will be made up by increasing production on some other day, by requiring existing employees to work overtime, or by hiring more permanent employees. If a firm is operating at capacity, however, it can only make up lost production by expanding its plant and hiring additional workers. In such cases, to compute the financial impact of granting additional holidays, anticipated interest charges on the capital required to finance construction of the additional plant facilities necessary to maintain production at planned levels must be added to anticipated payroll costs.

Firms in industries with continuous operations have less flexibility. Since they are unable to discontinue operations they will require many of their employees to work on holidays and will be required to pay them at premium rates.[89]

(c) Relief Time

The cost of granting additional relief time is generally calculated in the same manner used to cost other provisions involving pay for time not worked, *i.e.*, by multiplying the total number of additional hours of relief time by the appropriate base-wage rate. The implicit assumption that additional relief time will cause a decline in production which will be offset by additional person hours of labor compensated at straight-time rates may be particularly inappropriate when costing relief-time provisions. The productivity of many employees is not a direct function of the time on the job. Employees have considerable leeway in adjusting their required output to the time available. Therefore, it is unlikely that additional amounts of relief time will affect production volume. Additional rest time may actually increase efficiency and production. To the extent production is lost it is also unlikely that it will be recouped by replacing the exact number of additional hours lost paid at straight-time rates.

If operations on an entire production line cease during the relief period then lost time can be made up by placing in service additional equipment and hiring new employees, or by requiring current employees to work additional hours at overtime rates. The firm may, rather than shut down an assembly line, replace the workers with special relief employees. The hours for which these workers must be

---

[89] Computation of the financial impact of hiring new permanent employees and of requiring more labor hours at premium rate has been discussed above.

employed and paid rarely equals the exact number of hours of relief time granted.

The more accurate costing procedure requires that a detailed analysis be made of the amount of production likely to be lost and how the firm intends to recoup, giving consideration to the possibilities discussed above. The cost is then calculated by multiplying the number of hours that will be required to recover lost production times the rate at which it will be compensated, plus, where appropriate the cost of placing additional equipment in service and of hiring new employees.

c. Costing Indirect Benefits

Complete analysis of proposals requires that negotiators examine not only the provisions dealing with compensation and compensated time-off, but also those pertaining to indirect benefits such as pensions, accident and sickness insurance and supplementary unemployment benefits (SUB).

(1) Pensions

The problem with determining the financial impact of pension plans is that the total amount to be paid to each employee cannot be accurately determined until the employee qualifies for benefits, *e.g.,* she/he retires. The computations are based on estimates of such variables as employee longevity, employee turnover, future interest earnings on investments in the pension fund, and mortality rates for workers and their beneficiaries. Variation will also be provided by the distinction between definite payment and variable annuity plans.

Most companies merely collect the necessary demographic data and then delegate the costing task to outside actuaries. In compiling the data most firms make the assumption that the historical patterns of employee turnover and retirement will continue. The validity of this assumption is questionable. The proportions of workers who will take advantage of liberalized early retirement provisions, for example, will be affected by such variables as the availability of other work, trends in consumer prices and the prosperity of the industry. In fact, modifications in pension plans may themselves affect employees' decisions whether and when to terminate their employment with the firm. Legal changes in mandatory retirement also affect assumptions.[90]

(2) Insurance

The problem of costing insurance plans is that the eventual cost

---

[90] *See* Age Discrimination in Employment Act Amendments of 1978, Public Law 95-256; R. MacDonald, Mandatory Retirement and the Law (AEI 1978).

is a function of many hard-to-predict variables. As with pension plans, most firms merely compile the demographic data and delegate the task of costing to outside actuaries.

The commonly made assumption that historical patterns of employee behavior will continue may result in inaccurate cost calculations. For example, modifications in medical insurance coverage have themselves frequently influenced employee decisions as to whether and when to seek medical care.

(3) Supplementary Unemployment Benefits (SUB)

SUB plans are designed to provide workers with financial protection against layoffs. The plans generally follow a basic pattern. The firm makes a cents-per-hour contribution to a special fund until the fund reaches an agreed-upon level expressed in terms of dollars per employee covered. The right of each employee to draw upon the fund depends on his/her length of service. The amount the employee receives is expressed as a percent of current pay and depends on the level of the fund.

The common practice is to determine the cost of SUB plans by multiplying the maximum possible cents-per-hour contribution to the fund times the number of workers employed in the previous year. In most cases the contributions which will be required are not obvious from the contract provision or level of the fund at the time of the negotiations. It is possible that the fund will reach and remain above the maximum level with no additional funding for at least part of the contract period. In such a case the total cost during the period after which the maximum is reached is likely to be zero.

A more accurate costing procedure is to multiply the anticipated number of hours on which contributions will be paid times the appropriate anticipated cents-per-hour contribution. This data may be derived from projections of future levels of employment, the number and eligibility status of workers who will be laid off, and the average length of their layoff.

d. Spillover

If management accepts a proposal for bargaining unit employees, it will probably be necessary to grant to non-bargaining unit employees ("exempt employees") certain of the increases in wages and benefits it has negotiated for the bargaining unit. For example, if a firm grants additional holidays and intends to close its plant on these days, exempt employees will also have to be given the day off. If all employees are covered by the same pension and/or insurance plans, exempt as well as covered employees will be affected by modifications in the plans. If historical wage differentials exist between bargaining unit and exempt employees, a negotiated wage increase may affect the exempt employees' rates.

Many firms do not bother to quantify the cost of probable wage and salary increases to exempt employees. Of those that do, most determine the percentage by which the total compensation of covered employees will increase under the new contract and apply that percentage to the current annual compensation of exempt employees.

The assumption that exempt employees will be given the same percentage increases and similar improvements in benefits as bargaining unit employees may not be correct. It is possible, especially when historical wage differentials do not exist, that exempt employees will receive a smaller percentage wage increase than that negotiated with the bargaining unit employees. And, the policy regarding benefits for exempt employees may be different than that for bargaining unit employees.

It is advisable therefore to obtain projections of which specific wage or benefit increases are likely to be granted to exempt employees. A reasonably accurate determination of the financial impact attributed to spillover can then be calculated by costing these provisions for the appropriate number of exempt employees according to the same procedures, including the calculation of roll-up and package roll-up where applicable, as for covered employees.

F. IMPASSE RESOLUTION

1. Strikes and Lockouts

Just as there is a cost in agreement, there is a cost in disagreement. In fact, a widely recognized tactic in negotiation is for one party to make the cost of disagreement high to the other party.[91] Although the actual calling of a strike is a union responsibility, the decision to strike is a function of the negotiations. A strike can arise from the danger of being called on a bluff just as it can arise from a total impasse. In many instances union members will strengthen the hand of the negotiators by taking a strike vote, which does not necessarily mean that there will be a strike but does create a real strike threat. Furthermore, a strike vote is an actual indication that the membership is willing to support a strike, if one is actually called. The threat of a strike creates a "strike deadline" in negotiations when management is put to the election of "fishing or cutting bait" insofar as reaching agreement is concerned. Although there are some important legal differences between a strike and a lockout,[92] the

---

[91] Collective Bargaining, *supra* note 11 at 173-82.
[92] *See* R. Gorman, Labor Law: Basic Text 355 (1976).

lockout as it is presently practiced constitutes another way of responding to a deadline. In the case of a lockout, an employer will withhold employment until resolution of the impasse. The cost to a company of ignoring a deadline and taking a strike or engaging in a lockout depends on a variety of factors:

(a) What are the legal effects of a strike — is it an "unfair labor practice" strike (all strikers have reinstatement privileges)? Is it an economic strike (strikers have a limited right to reinstatement)? Is it an unprotected strike (no right to reinstatement)?

(b) Does the union have a significant strike fund to pay employees who are out of work? Are outside funds — for example, state funds — available?

(c) What effect will a strike have on an employer's costs? Profit? Will the union be able to effectively halt the employer's business?

(d) What will a strike do to an employer's customers? Will picketing affect the employer's operation? Are customers likely to switch business to competitors?

(e) Will the public support a strike? Is the government likely to intervene?

The union is going to be faced with a similar analysis of the cost-effectiveness of a strike. For example, the union will have to evaluate how the loss of employee wages will affect membership support for a strike. The union will also consider:

(a) The legal protection afforded a striking union, or conversely, an employer's right to enjoin a strike. Recently the trend has been to enforce no-strike/no-lockout provisions that are found in a majority of collective bargaining agreements.[93]

(b) The total cost of a strike. Like everything else, these costs have increased dramatically. One author estimates the income loss from strikes to have increased from $293 million in 1961 to over one billion in 1971. At the same time he estimated the loss of tax revenues from strikes to have increased from $47 million to $210 million[94] during the same period.

(c) The public unwillingness to support a strike. Whatever the actual increased costs of a strike, it is true that public support of strikes, in general, has decreased over the past decade.[95]

---

[93] *See* Boys Markets, Inc. v. Retail Clerks Local 770, 398 U.S. 235 (1970) (purpose of arbitration is to provide settlement mechanism without resort to strikes or lockouts). *Cf.* Buffalo Forge Co. v. United Steelworkers of America, AFL-CIO, 96 S. Ct. 3141 (1976) (if sympathy strike were found by arbitrator to violate no-strike clause).

[94] W. Baer, Strikes 7 (1975).

[95] BNA, Collective Bargaining Today 23 (1971); Henderson, Creative Collective

Accordingly, both companies and unions are going to look carefully at the ramifications of engaging in a strike or lockout.

In 1974, the American Society for Personnel Administration prepared the following Strike Preparation Manual for companies: [96]

A. Preparation for a possible strike prior to commencing negotiations

1. Initial questions which must be answered by the company about the company:

a) How do your wages, benefits and working conditions compare with others in your area and industry?

b) Is your company in a position to take a strike?

c) If necessary, will it take a strike?

d) What advantages exist if a strike does occur? (Do you have excess inventory; is sales volume and forecast low, etc.?)

e) Assuming all production is shut down or substantially reduced, how long can you stand a strike?

f) Determine what anticipated union demands the company can accept or reject.

g) When will you indicate to the union that you are prepared to take a strike and over what issues?

h) Can you continue to obtain supplies, keep up production, develop sales and continue to do business during a strike?

i) What instructions will you give to supervisors?

j) When should you initially alert customers, stockpile products or transfer inventories?

2. Initial questions which the company must answer about the union:

a) What is your labor relations history? Has the attitude of employees become hostile; if so, why?

b) Do the union negotiators/representatives control the membership or does the membership control the negotiators?

c) Can you anticipate the severity of the union's demands?

d) What percentage of your employees might "go out?"

e) Does the union pay strike benefits? If so, how much and when do payments begin?

f) Are strikers eligible for state unemployment compensation, food stamps, welfare?

g) If applicable would other unions respect your union's picket line?

Bargaining 30-32 (Healy ed. 1965) [Creative Collective Bargaining]; Straus, Alternatives to the Strike, in 25th Ann. Proc. Conf. on Labor (1973) [hereinafter cited as Alternatives to the Strike].

[96] 1 C.B.N.C. § 14:511 (10/24/74). Reprinted with permission of publisher. © Bureau of National Affairs, Inc.

B. Second stage strike preparations during final weeks of bargaining

1. Urgent questions which must be answered by the company about the company:

  a) Does the negotiations committee have true authority?

  b) Does your management honestly believe its position is morally right?

  c) When is it the right time to communicate your position to all employees?

  d) Is the company really prepared to hold out when it begins to hurt?

  e) Will you continue to operate during a strike and with what personnel?

  f) What is the priority sequence for scheduling production during a strike situation?

  g) What are the company's chances of winning?

2. Urgent questions which the company must answer about the union:

  a) What do you think the union is really after?

  b) What promises has the union made to rank and file?

  c) Do union negotiators/representatives control the membership or does the membership control the negotiators?

  d) What is the strength of the union to take a strike and for how long a period?

  e) How big is the union's "war chest"?

  f) How long can employees be expected to hold out in spite of installment payments, rent, living expenses, etc.?

  g) Many labor leaders concede that sometimes a strike is a much needed catharsis. A strike is sometimes call for purposes other than the reason announced relative to a particular issue. Therefore, it is well to realize that a strike may be the result of unrest within the labor organization; a proving ground for union leadership; a sharing of hardship which may help weld the union organization; a high-level confrontation precipitated by inadequate means of problem resolution at lesser levels of the organizations. Are these, or similar causes, possible factors of consideration for your "probable strike?"

C. Preparation For A Probable Strike: Preparatory departmental assignment and responsibilities

1. Industrial relations activities:

  a) Coordinate with *all* departments and appropriate company officials to insure their awareness of the contract expiration date, general status of current negotiations and pre-strike assignments and responsibilities.

  b) Again review stability and strike history of union.

c) Develop confidential master schedule for layoff of non-striking personnel where no production work is available.

d) Prepare a final plan for the approval of top management on the feasibility of, and plans for, operating the plant during a strike.

e) Coordinate appropriate arrangements for the transfer of work to other plants or divisions when required.

f) Coordinate initial plans for an orderly shut-down of operations and plant supporting facilities. This plan will be utilized subsequent to or coincidental with a strike, and subsequent to the time it may be determined that the plant will not be producing.

g) Consider establishing in-plant printing and mailing services and be sure they are adequately supplied. Insure that a primary or alternate printing and mailing service is available outside the plant.

h) Maintain an up-to-date list of all employees by name and address, categorized as follows: all hourly-rated employees, all non-exempt employees, all exempt employees.

i) Update list of all officers, stewards and members of the local union organization. This list should include addresses, telephone numbers and pictures, if possible.

j) Maintain a list of appropriate union officials, business agents, regional directors, etc., together with their addresses and telephone numbers.

k) Prepare two sets of mailing envelopes pre-addressed to all employees and separated as in (h) above.

l) Maintain a list of the officials in the community and county, particularly the Chief of Police, Sheriff's Office, City Attorney, etc. In the event of a strike, these individuals must be contacted and made aware of the situation and, when appropriate, the company's position.

m) Establish and maintain appropriate contact with governmental agencies — Federal Mediation and Conciliation Service and State Mediation Service.

n) Provide instruction to foremen and related supervisory personnel in regard to their responsibilities and conduct during the strike.

o) Prepare to contact State Unemployment Benefits Agency to prevent payment of benefit claims by strikers, if state law bars benefits to strikers.

p) Establish a management team of observers to man each entrance to the plant where picket lines may be established. Observers should be instructed to record all incidents, listing date, time, names, etc. Provide tape recorders.

q) Arrange for and have available the services of management personnel to act as photographers, preferably individuals who have had experience in strike situations. However, photographers acting for the company must be instructed not to take pictures of peaceful picketing or other peaceful activities. To do so may constitute an unfair labor practice charge and convert the strike to an unfair labor practice strike. Thus, picture-taking must be confined to the pictorial recording of incidents of mass picketing, violence or other unlawful acts.

r) Have available a sketch of the facility, indicating all entrances and exits, fence lines, window locations and building locations with dimensions drawn to scale.

s) Insure that management has selected one company representative to handle communications and act as sole spokesman with the media and inquiring public, and be sure that your communication releases do not exaggerate the facts.

2. Legal department consultation:

Consultation with a labor lawyer is most important and future success or failure relative to certain incidents may be dependent upon their interpretation from a labor law viewpoint. The counsel, either in-house or outside legal counsel, should make all necessary pre-strike plans for possible legal action which may result from a strike situation. This is critical with regard to possible injunctions to prevent violence, limiting the number of pickets, plus insuring free entrance to, and exit from the facility.

3. Manufacturing responsibilities:

a) Plan for operating the plant with non-strikers, salaried employees, replacement employees or a combination thereof.

b) Plan for an orderly shut-down of the facility should the decision be made not to operate during a strike.

c) Plan for plant maintenance during a strike.

d) Consider requirements for property protection, heating, fire protection, etc., during a strike.

e) Be prepared to inform vendors and customers regarding shipment or nonshipment of supplies and finished goods.

f) Make necessary arrangements with railroads, steamship companies and over-the-road trucking companies for the shipping and receiving of goods or products.

g) Attempt to arrange for independent operators to handle truck shipments.

h) Prepare to remove all key items from the plant including the property of customers.

i) Be prepared to locate some company vehicles in a secure location distant from the plant. Should a strike occur, they can then be used without being driven through the picket line.

4. Marketing — sales department assignments:

a) Plan for alternate warehouse facilities remote from

company premises. If possible, arrangements should be made with customers to advance-ship products previously sold.

b) Letters or telegrams should be drafted which would adequately explain the situation to customers should a strike occur.

c) Review all customer contracts for penalty provisions which may be applicable to a labor dispute and advise appropriate managers accordingly.

d) Be prepared to contact governmental and commercial customers to notify them of a strike and make any arrangements which may be dictated by an existing contract.

5. Purchasing department:

a) Be prepared to notify all vendors and sub-contractors of the circumstances.

b) In conjunction with manufacturing department, arrange for cancellation, delivery or re-scheduling of unneeded vendor or sub-contractor shipments.

c) In conjunction with manufacturing, arrange for common carriers to handle special shipments.

d) Review Interstate Commerce Commission regulations regarding the duty of truckers licensed by the I.C.C. to pick up and deliver goods at the premises. Be prepared to remind trucking officials of their responsibilities.

e) Plan to expedite vendor or sub-contractor shipments of materials required for strike priority projects.

f) Arrange for a location distant from the facility for storage transfer of key items.

g) Have all telephone work or modifications completed prior to strike.

h) Plan for "in-facility" feeding and living requirements.

i) Provide for rubbish pickup.

j) Provide camera equipment and tape recorders as required by the Industrial Relations department.

6. Plant engineering/maintenance department assignments:

a) Plan to organize required crews to provide necessary plant services on an emergency basis (boilers, lighting, maintenance, etc.)

b) Develop sources to obtain replacement or temporary replacement personnel.

c) Plan to maintain night lighting and perimeter fencing.

d) Plan to establish and maintain any required eating or sleeping facilities.

e) Provide protection shields for all outside electrical transformers. (Transformers are most secure when located at ground level or below the surface.)

f) Perform all annual facility maintenance and safety checks.

Be particularly sure to arrange for immediate checks which involve the services of local utility companies.

7. Accounting/controllers department assignments:

a) Arrange to pay all wages due striking personnel *except vacation allowances* immediately after strike occurs.

b) Provide necessary petty cash and dispensing systems to handle immediate needs.

c) Set up appropriate accounting procedure to record all losses to the company as a result of the strike for use in possible future legal action.

d) Take necessary steps to pay overtime to employees who may continue working during a strike. Bear in mind exempt or non-exempt status of work and appropriate overtime pay provisions.

e) In absence of office manager or equivalent official, be responsible for incoming visitors and customers, and arrange for the possible necessity that they be escorted in and out of the facility.

f) Estimate the cost of a strike in per-day terms and be prepared to accurately compute the actual daily cost, should the anticipated strike occur.

8. Plant protection and security responsibilities:

a) Plan to provide adequate protection for property, facilities, equipment, vendors, company shipments and all non-striking personnel.

b) Be prepared to notify local law enforcement agencies to obtain coverage and maintain contacts during the strike.

c) Develop strike surveillance activities and locations for placement of photographers for best surveillance coverage to document all "incidents".

d) Obtain telephone message equipment to record pertinent strike information.

e) Update list of "authorized" personnel in the event of strike.

f) Update gate procedures and consider installing gate and fence telephones where needed.

g) Prepare parking arrangements inside fenced areas.

h) Review and/or provide for medical and first aid facilities.

i) Review entrances and exits to plant facilities.

j) Review night lighting, possible effects of glass or window breakage and location of fire fighting equipment.

k) Arrange for supplemental guard service.

l) Prepare for providing 24 hour guard/security service of the plant and grounds.

D. "Must do" items to be considered by company negotiators

a) Negotiations with the union for a settlement should continue on a good faith basis after a strike becomes apparent.

The company must determine if it places its best offer on the table when the strike appears evident or does it save something in anticipation of the strike settlement?

b) Do you stand on one final offer?

c) Consider sweetening your offer/position just before the deadline to gain additional voting support for the package.

d) Consider the value of an extended contract.

e) Request the assistance of a mediator.

f) Check to see if proper notice was given to state and federal mediation services.

g) Determine if the company is willing to present its position to the press.

h) Inquire about the use of mail ballots or on-premises voting.

E. Steps to take: Strike

Contract negotiations have failed from the standpoint that the parties have not been able to reach a timely and mutually acceptable settlement of the issues — economic, non-economic or a combination of both. The union is leaving (or has left) the plant and is in the process of doing what it has to do — establish picket lines, answer questions and coordinate efforts of the rank and file, display strength and solidarity, etc.

I. THE PLANT MANAGER MUST:

a) Put into effect the measures appropriate for your *individual* strike situation as anticipated on the basis previously formulated for a "probable" strike.

b) Formalize a Strike Committee comprised of the department heads to whom specific responsibilities were assigned during the "probable" strike period.

c) Discuss with all department heads the why of the strike and review their assigned roles and responsibilities.

d) Establish a Strike Log and formalize a Strike Operations Center. Designate who will be the "keeper" of the log and who is to be the operations center spokesman for the company.

e) The following items must be again considered, decided, reviewed, and appropriately generated into action: Do we continue operating? Yes or no right now? Yes or no a week or 10 days from now? If you decide to try to continue operating the plant: Will you encourage employees to cross the picket line? Will you attempt to hire *replacement* or interim production employees? Will you use salaried and/or sales employees to operate the plant?

II. Pay and benefits

a) Immediately arrange to pay strikers any *wages* which they are due.

b) Discontinue the payment of fringe benefits, specifically insurance and pension premiums, providing the previous contract does not prohibit same and it is done on a non-discriminatory basis.

c) Do not pay vacation pay.

d) Notify the local employment service office in writing that a strike has occurred and indicate the name and address of each striking employee.

e) Review the files of employees currently drawing accident and sickness benefits, paying particular attention to the "expected" date of return to work for each employee so involved. Payments should cease on the "expected" date unless additional medical statements verify a continuing disability.

III. Communications

a) Advise all appropriate agencies and offices of the strike.

b) Advise all employees via a husband-wife home-addressed letter as to the company's position during negotiations, industry competitive position, cost of the union's demands, factual outline of the company's final position and the cost of its final offer.

c) Encourage the employees to return to work.

d) Inform all employees of their rights during a strike.

e) Review and approve for release by your designated "media man" all public and employee communications.

IV. The law

a) Know how to correctly replace or terminate strikers under state and federal law.

b) Know what the reinstatement rights and requirements are of replaced strikers.

c) Over-extend yourself to insure all individuals receive fair and equal treatment.

d) Be alert for and knowledgeable of actions by strikers which may constitute unprotected union activities.

e) Be keenly aware of conditions or actions by the company which could lead to unfair labor practice charges against the company and possibly convert the strike from an economic strike to an unfair labor practice strike.

f) Know the "rights" of strikers.

V. Verification

Maintain your Strike Log as accurately as possible (by day, by hour) and in a confidential manner for possible future legal actions. Pictures taken or recordings made of unprotected activities or incidents are to be referenced to the log.

VI. Conduct

Communicate, observe, and enforce (by law agencies if necessary) the following:

a) People working in or having any business with the company have a right to pass freely in and out of the plant.

b) Pickets must not block a door, passageway, driveway, crosswalk or other entrance or exit to a struck plant.

c) Profanity on streets and sidewalks is a violation of the law.

d) Company officials, with the assistance of local law enforcement agents, should make every effort to permit individuals and vehicles to move in and out of the plant in a normal manner.

e) Union officials or pickets have a right to talk to people going in or out of a struck plant. Intimidation, threats and coercion are not permitted, either by verbal remarks or physical action.

f) Sound trucks should not be permitted to be unduly noisy — it should have a permit and must be kept moving.

g) If acts of violence or trespassing occur on company premises, plant officials should file complaints or seek injunctions. In cases of violence on one's person, the aggrieved person should sign a warrant for the arrest of the person or persons causing such violence.

h) Fighting, assault, battery, violence, threats, or intimidation are not permissible under the law, nor is the carrying of knives, firearms, clubs or other dangerous weapons.

VII. DO NOT:

a) Offer extra rewards to non-strikers and make statements that returning strikers will not have the same reward, or attempt to withhold the "extras" from strikers once the strike has ended and some or all strikers are reinstated.

b) Threaten employees or strikers.

c) Promise benefits to individual or groups of strikers in an attempt to end the strike or undermine the union.

d) Threaten employees with discharge for taking part in a lawful strike.

e) Discharge non-strikers who refuse to take over a striker's job.

VIII. Continuing negotiations

a) Indicate a continuing cooperative attitude with and toward the mediator. (If the services of a state or federal mediator were not used during pre-strike negotiations, seriously consider making contact and express your willingness to resume bargaining when the union indicates a possibly significant revision of its demands.)

b) Advise the bargaining committee that the company will be willing to resume negotiations at any time, but that there is little sense in meeting without purpose. Therefore, the union should understand that the company is firm on its final position but that any consideration by the union of a change in its demands will certainly be cause for a prompt resumption of negotiations.

IX. Plant operations

a) Supervisory employees should assist wherever possible and do whatever is necessary, should the plant be shut down.

b) When the plant continues to operate, supervisory employees should render all assistance possible — from advice and encouragement to manual, physical labor.

c) Continue to employ non-striking employees in productive capacities. Consider lay-off of non-strikers subsequent to the time when all productive operations cease.

d) Insure that all non-striking employees are kept busy to avoid idleness and reduce verbal speculation and rumor.

e) Stress safety. If a plant operates during a strike it necessarily means that some, if not many or all, employees on the job are unfamiliar with both equipment and surroundings. Should the decision be made that the plant will not operate, many employees will still be confronted with new responsibilities and strange situations. Thus, in either case, safety must be discussed, practiced and impressed upon all personnel.

F. Strike Settlement

Terms and agreements:

Strike settlement agreements must be written, preferably in Memorandum of Understanding form, to cover all aspects of the terms of settlement. Part or all of the points addressed in the Memorandum will later be incorporated into the contract. Therefore, in addition to the terms of settlement relative to bargainable economic or non-economic issues, any agreements concerning the following points must be specified:

1. Terms of reinstatement for striking employees.

2. Seniority and status of employees who did not strike.

3. Status of replacement employees hired during the strike.

4. Status of striking employees who may have been disciplined or discharged during the strike.

5. Intended disposition of court suits filed during the strike.

6. Language to preclude the initiation of grievances arising from strike actions or activities.

7. Effective date that insurance coverages will resume, and on what basis.

8. Retroactivity — Specify any and all items or issues for which retroactivity is granted.

The following outline on planning and conducting strikes was prepared by the Office and Professional Employees International Union and distributed to the union's staff representatives and business agents at an April 1976 meeting.[97]

[97] 1 C.B.N.C. § 14:541 (11/18/76). Reprinted with permission of publisher. ©
Bureau of National Affairs, Inc.

A. PLANNING FOR STRIKE POSSIBILITY

1. Exhaust all attempts for settlement
2. Investigate all national and local laws affecting strikes
3. Confer with other affected Unions and Central Labor Council
4. Make sure required 60-day notice to employer (90 days to Health Care Institutions), 30-60 day notices to Federal Mediation and Conciliation Service, and to State Mediation Services, where appropriate, have been complied with
5. Obtain strike authorization. Submit form, "Application for Strike Sanction from International President."
6. Form committees to handle administrative functions
   a. Publicity Committee — News releases, public statements
   b. Clerical Committee — Typists, handbills, telephones
   c. Fund Raising Committee
7. Soften Financial Hardship
   a. Determine methods for raising strike funds
   b. Survey temporary and part-time employment opportunities
   c. Arrange loan extensions
   d. Publicize credit union loan possibilities
   e. Contact community agencies able to assist

B. PRE-STRIKE PROCEDURES

1. Determine property limits of employer
   a. Where needed, establish strike shelter in vicinity
2. Select Picket Captains
3. Draw up picketing schedule
4. Promulgate picket line rules of conduct
   a. No alcoholic drinking
   b. Prohibit boisterous activity
   c. Picket line conduct toward individuals crossing line
   d. Conduct toward news media agents
5. Provide for physical needs of pickets
   a. Brief pickets on clothing requirements
   b. Furnish coffee, water, sandwiches, when necessary
   c. Arrange for sanitary facilities
6. Establish lines of communication from strike leaders to members
   a. Schedule picket line visitations by Union officals
   b. Keep pickets informed

C. STRIKE PUBLICITY

1. Purpose
   a. Explain Union's position to members
   b. Present Union's case to public

2. Principal Media
   a. Local newspapers, press releases
   b. Radio stations — taped interviews discussing strike issues
   c. Television stations — News bulletins more likely broadcast if press can thereby be "scooped."
3. Means of disseminating news
   a. Press releases. Utilize "who, what, where, when, how" approach. Be direct, factual, no editorializing
   b. Press conference — refreshments, when appropriate
   c. Handbills to public — limit to one page
   d. Handbills to strikers — report latest developments
   e. Paid advertisements — be brief, simple, to the point
   f. Imaginative picket line activities — costumes, children, displays, etc.

D. NIGHT PRECEDING STRIKE

1. Call mass meeting of all employees
   a. Present status of negotiations and outstanding issues
   b. Set forth duties and responsibilities
   c. Obtain pledges of support and unity
2. Final pre-strike meeting of strike officials
   a. Tactical review of assignments with Union officers, picket captains, committee members

E. STANDARD STRIKE PROCEDURE

1. Assemble at pre-determined area
2. Approach employer site and assume picket positions
3. Reduce number of pickets where possible while maintaining effectiveness
4. Promote sympathetic public relations with news media and community
5. Persuade scabs, unions, companies to honor picket line
6. Make application for Strike Benefit Funds
7. Properly administer Benefits in accordance with Fund's "Rules and Regulations."

F. MAINTAIN SETTLEMENT EFFORTS

1. Use facilities of Federal Mediation and Conciliation Service
2. Seek assistance of community leaders, officials of O.P.E.I.U. and other labor organizations

G. THE STRIKE SETTLEMENT

1. Reduce to writing resolution of all strike issue and any pending law suits or N.L.R.B. charges
2. Any settlement conditioned on reinstatement of all strikers or satisfactory agreement to arbitrate reinstatement

H. AFTER STRIKE SETTLEMENT

1. Acknowledge with gratitude all strike donations and support of other Unions
2. Resolve to support other striking Unions
3. Notify the International Union of the settlement
4. Notify all news media of details of the settlement

2. Mediation

The most obvious strike-avoidance program is mediation — techniques for maintaining communication between the parties in order to resolve problems. Use of mediation can be for the purpose of preventing impasses through joint labor management committees, consultation, continuing liaison, or training and assistance. Or, it can arise from a mediator's intervention in contract negotiation disputes. Preventative techniques will be covered in the next section as alternatives to strike deadline bargaining. For the purposes of outline only, this section will address the role of a mediator in crisis bargaining.

The third-party intervention sequence ranges from conciliation (bringing the two parties together to discuss this dispute), to mediation (direct third-party intervention by a go-between to resolve disputes), to fact finding (with or without recommendations), to arbitration (voluntary or binding). William Simkin, former director of FMCS describes this range of activity as follows:

> Conciliation is conceived of as a mild form of intervention limited primarily to scheduling conferences, trying to keep the disputants talking, facilitating other procedural niceties, carrying messages back and forth between the parties, and generally being a "good fellow" who tries to keep things calm and forward-looking in a tense situation.
>
> Mediation is frequently thought of as a slightly more affirmative function. The mediator may make suggestions. He may even make procedural or, on rare occasions, substantive recommendations. But since he has no power and authority, these somewhat more aggressive tactics are considered to be without significant potency.
>
> Fact-finding without recommendations is sometimes depicted as a masterful analysis of statistics, arguments, and contentions — so skillfully presented in written form that all sensible disputants should readily see the way to a mutually agreeable solution.
>
> Fact-finding with recommendations is thought to embody all the preceding virtues normally associated with facts plus a very specific recipe for settlement that the parties should adopt and

around which public sentiment will rally if the disputing parties should be so presumptuous as to raise questions.

Voluntary arbitration goes one more step toward potency. It is fact-finding plus. Since the arbitrator will be impressively wise after his fact-finding, the parties will agree in advance to accept his decision. This is a right and proper thing to do. The judgment will certainly resolve the issues in a satisfactory way, and all doubts about continuation of the dispute will be removed by the commitment to accept the decision.

Compulsory arbitration, by individual arbitrators or by a court, is admittedly a last resort and a somewhat repugnant device. It is imposed on a union and a company, usually by government decree, when one or both of the parties are very stubborn. They will not yield either to the logic of facts or to the public interest and agree to arbitrate voluntarily. The public need being paramount, it must prevail in the face of the irrational behavior exhibited by the disputants.[98]

However, as Mr. Simkin pointed out, other than the distinction between mediation and arbitration [99] the rest of the techniques are used interchangeably depending on the circumstances of the impasse.

Typically, a mediator is a representative of the government, state or federal, although occasionally parties will engage a private mediator. At the federal level mediation in interstate railway and airline disputes is a function of the National Mediation Board pursuant to provisions of the Railway Labor Act.[100] For other branches of industry affecting interstate commerce the basic mediation function is vested in the Federal Mediation and Conciliation Service, an independent agency established in 1947 by the Taft-Hartley Act.[101] Mediation is also provided for by some forty-five states and by Puerto Rico, as well as by some municipalities.[102] The mediation functions as thus provided are on occasion supplemented in critical situations by the intervention of higher level government officials.[103]

Ordinarily strictly local disputes (*i.e.,* those not involving an employer engaged in interstate commerce) are left to state and local mediation, at least where available. But where interstate commerce

---

[98] W. Simkin, Mediation and the Dynamics of Collective Bargaining 25-26 (1971) [hereinafter cited as Mediation]. Reprinted with permission of publisher. © Bureau of National Affairs, Inc.

[99] *Id.* at 27.

[100] The Railway Labor Act, 45 U.S.C. § 152(3), (4); F.C.A. 45 § 152(3), (4).

[101] 61 Stat. 136, 29 U.S.C. § 158(d), Section 8(d).

[102] U.S. Dep't of Labor, Growth of Labor Law in the United States 232-33 (1962).

[103] Mediation, *supra* note 98 at ch. X.

is involved and the Federal Mediation and Conciliation Service has statutory mediatory jurisdiction, and if a state has a mediation service, the mediation function is frequently performed by a "team" consisting of one or more federal and state mediators.[104]

Since mediation is an art form rather than a scientific skill, it is much easier to define a mediator's role in terms of what she/he should not do. As Mr. Simkin explains,

> Inclusion of a mediator among the participants at a bargaining table does not alter the fundamental fact that it continues to be essentially a two-party process. The intervention adds a new element. That is unavoidable. But the new element is a person whose function is to assist, not supplant, the parties and the process. . . . It is imperative that the mediator understand his function. If he does not demonstrate that he understands it, a great disservice can be done. The mediator who attempts to create the impression that he is the most important person at the bargaining table is of no help to anybody.[105]

A mediator is a consultant who has specialized skills in conflict situations which are utilized through a variety of techniques. The late Willoughby Abner, former mediator and arbitrator, described a mediator's options,

> The degree of his involvement and the options he elects to pursue depend on the developing circumstances of each case. His role at one stage may be essentially passive — doing little more than chairing the meeting, keeping the negotiations rolling and controlling tempers. He may simply pass along proposals and counter proposals. The mediator may decide to separate the parties for a variety of reasons. It is in the separate caucuses that the most meaningful progress and groundwork for progress is usually made. It is where confidential and privileged information may be communicated to the mediator, ideas explored without commitment, previous positions re-examined without embarrassment. It provides an opportunity to both "sell" and "unsell" as well as to get each party to adopt a solution as its own. At any point during this process, the mediator may drop an idea, suggest a procedure, make a substantive suggestion, informally or formally, and at the outer range of his options, make an informal or even formal recommendation to the parties, orally or in writing. Formal recommendations are infrequently made and only when the mediator believes that such recommendations will close the remaining gap and be accepted by both parties. The right of a mediator to refuse to make recommendations is as critical as his right to make them. The choice must be that of the

---

[104] *See* Note, Code of Conduct for Labor Mediators, 57 LRRM 104, 105.
[105] Mediation, *supra* note 98 at 30-31.

mediator alone. Diminishing his choice by either requiring recommendations or precluding them would adversely affect the mediation process as well as the bargaining process. For example, if the parties knew in advance the mediator had to make recommendations if agreement otherwise could not be reached, positions would likely be less flexible and genuine bargaining more difficult. On the other hand, precluding the right of the mediator to make recommendations would deprive him of a potential device (expertly though sparingly employed) which could spur genuine bargaining in certain cases and help breach the final gap to settlement in others.[106]

The function of the mediator is to assist the parties to effectuate bargaining without reaching an impasse, and to facilitate social change by peaceful methods. There is a growing feeling that this function can be better accomplished through non-crises intervention, and FMCS mediators are now devoting increased attention to "preventive mediation."

3. Other Techniques for Minimizing Crises in Collective Bargaining

Although there are continuous recommendations and experimentations on techniques to improve collective bargaining by minimizing crises,[107] current theories and practices can be categorized according to (a) pre-crises bargaining; (b) continuous bargaining; and (c) third-party impasse resolution activities. The premise underlying these techniques is that strikes and lockouts have become too expensive for the parties and too costly to the public to depend upon the "strike threat" as leverage in deadline bargaining.[108]

a. Pre-Crises Bargaining

Some unions and managements have found it helpful to minimize crises by utilizing preventative mediation. As previously indicated these programs can include (1) joint labor management committees; (2) consultation; (3) continuing liaison; and (4) training or assistance. For example, Wayne Horvitz, Director of FMCS helped establish the Joint Labor Management Committee (JLMC) of the Retail Food Industry. It lists as its objectives:

A primary objective of the committee is to achieve fair and equitable noninflationary contract settlements. To facilitate this

---

[106] Willoughby Abner, Dispute Mediation in the Federal Government, Address delivered 1968 Biennial Convention of the National Federation of Federal Employees, St. Louis, Mo., Sept. 11, 1968.

[107] *See, e.g.,* Ann. N.Y.U. Proc. Conf. on Labor (Matthew Bender); Ann. Inst. Southwest. Leg. Found. Labor Law Develop. (Matthew Bender) for yearly coverage.

[108] Alternatives to the Strike *supra* note 95 at 37.

objective, the Steering Committee has unanimously approved (1) Collective Bargaining Procedures for the Retail Food Industry, (2) Data Collection and Analysis, (3) Targeted and Monitored Negotiations, (4) Prenegotiation Conferences, (5) Criteria for Collective Bargaining Settlements in the Retail Food Industry, and (6) A Policy Declaration on Noninflationary Settlements. Fair and equitable noninflationary settlements can be achieved by proper usage of the foregoing, fully recognizing that the factors employed may vary in individual situations. We have a mutual interest in demonstrating to the public that labor and management in the retail food industry are engaging in responsible collective bargaining.[109]

In order to achieve these objectives, JLMC established prenegotiation conferences, monitored ongoing negotiations, and established subcommittees for research and training purposes.

Professor Matthew Kelly indicates that early settlement (prior to the old contract termination date) which then becomes effective on ratification is another variation of pre-crises bargaining, without the use of third-party intervention. The potential cost of early adoption of new terms is deemed to be outweighed by the advantage of avoiding the strike threat.

b. Continuous Bargaining

There are a number of variations to ongoing bargaining as distinguished from deadline bargaining. However, continuous bargaining is not new. Since collective bargaining is a continuous process, the notion is that negotiations should take place on a systematic, ongoing basis throughout the term of a contract. This concept also has been widely adopted where particular subject matter is so complex (pensions, automation, etc.) that it does not lend itself to deadline bargaining. The Armour Automation Committee, established in the early 1960's, is an early use of the formal ad hoc study of bargaining issues.[110] The Human Relations Committee in basic steel and the Glass Container Manufacturers Institute are two other early examples of continuous study and negotiation of critical problems in bargaining.[111]

"Coordinated bargaining," discussed earlier in Chapter 3 is highly controversial.[112] However, it has been used "... as a joint undertaking of some labor and management to lessen tension and

---

[109] Statement of Concepts, Joint Labor Management Committee (Letter dated 8/24/77).

[110] Creative Collective Bargaining *supra* note 95 ch. 6, p. 135.

[111] *Id.,* ch. 7, p. 192.

[112] *See* Chapter 3, *supra* p. 80.

minimize potential for crises." [113] The technique used is for industry and union representatives to negotiate about common economic and industry-related items as a "package," and then negotiate all other issues separately. Thus, it too has been used to remove issues from deadline bargaining that are better solved in a non-crisis atmosphere.

c. Third-Party Impasse Resolution

Like many other techniques for minimizing crises in collective bargaining, the use of arbitration ("interest arbitration") is not new but it has never had wide acceptance.[114] However, it was accepted in the 1974 Experimental Negotiating Agreement (ENA) between the Steelworkers and the major steel companies, as Elliot Bredhoff, Special Counsel to the United Steelworkers explains:

The essential feature of the Experimental Negotiating Agreement is that there would not be a nationwide strike or lockout if the parties failed to agree on the terms of new collective bargaining contracts. Instead, nationwide disputes would be submitted to an Impartial Arbitration Panel for solution. However, there would be a right to strike at the plant level in support of local collective bargaining issues. Because customers knew that there could not be a nationwide steel strike, an absence of stockpiling in 1973 and 1974 was anticipated.

In consideration for this understanding, the companies agreed to important benefits for their employees. The minimum guarantees included in the ENA were:

(1) *Bonus.* Each member having employee status as of August 1, 1974, would receive a $150 bonus, "in consideration of the contribution made by employees to stability of steel operations. . ."

The companies agree to this bonus in recognition of the production savings anticipated from the avoidance of stockpiling. Customers, knowing that no nation-wide steel strike can occur and, therefore, that no stockpiling need be undertaken, do not feel compelled to purchase as much foreign steel as before. As a result, American steel companies retain a larger share of the market. Additionally, because customers may purchase steel as needed, rather than accelerating their orders, the steel companies can schedule production on a normal basis. Thus, the companies are spared the expensive start-up costs of marginal facilities, the attendant overtime costs and, following

---

[113] M. Kelly, Techniques for Minimizing Crisis, cited in J. Getman, Labor Relations 234 (1978).

[114] *E.g.,* The New York hotel industry has used such a model since the 1930's, Creative Collective Bargaining, *supra* note 95 at 78.

a strike-free settlement, SUB costs which result from crisis buying.

The union understandably felt that the employees, whose surrender of their ultimate economic weapon was the direct cause of this financial benefit to the companies, should share in that financial benefit, and the bonus reflects that sharing. Reluctance of the companies to commit themselves to such a sharing in 1967 was a significant reason for the union's decision to reject the arbitration approach at that time.

(2) *The "guaranteed" wage increase.* There was *no* limit to the amount of wage increase, or any other benefit, which the Union could seek in negotiations. The agreement *did,* however, provide a guaranteed "floor," which employees were assured of receiving regardless of what developed in negotiations. The guaranteed minimum consisted of increases of 3% in the wage scales, including incentive rate scales at the beginning of each of the three contract years, starting August 1, 1974.

(3) *Cost of living adjustment.* The Agreement provided that the cost of living adjustment would continue throughout the three-year agreement. There will be no "floor" or "ceiling" on cost of living adjustments which can become payable during the 1974 agreement.

(4) *Protection of certain important contractual provisions.* There are certain fundamental safeguards in the collective bargaining agreements which each side wanted to insulate and preserve. Accordingly, the ENA listed a series of issues which could not be submitted to the Impartial Arbitration Panel. These provisions, in addition to the wage, bonus and cost of living provisions described above, included: (a) the local working conditions provisions; (b) the union shop and checkoff provisions; (c) the no strike and no lockout provisions; and (d) the management rights provisions.[115]

The 1974 and 1977 negotiations in the basic steel industry seems to justify Steelworkers President Abel's exuberant prediction that,

> The ENA, which was the result of a determination by both sides to find a better way to negotiate, may well prove to be the most valuable new tool devised for resolving labor-management problems related to the collective bargaining process. It can add a fresh dimension to industries that are afflicted with "boom-bust" problems associated with normal negotiations.[116]

---

[115] Bredhoff, New Methods of Bargaining and Dispute Settlement, 27th Ann. Proc. N.Y.U. Conf. on Lab. 1, 8-9 (Riff ed. 1975). Reprinted with permission of Publisher. Copyright © 1975 Matthew Bender.

[116] *Id.* at 16.

It may be that the Steelworkers' prior experiences with third-party impasse resolutions [117] together with current industry problems create a unique disposition to this technique. Certainly the Kaiser Plan's Long Range Committee's commitment to finding alternatives to strike deadline bargaining would seem to support the steel industry's and Steelworkers' experimentations in creative collective bargaining techniques.[118]

Nonetheless, each of those attempts to minimize crises in collective bargaining has the objective of reaching agreement with a minimum of disruption to the parties and the public.

---

[117] Creative Collective Bargaining, *supra* note 95 at 194.
[118] *Id.* at 244.

Chapter 4
THE COLLECTIVE BARGAINING AGREEMENT

A. THE WRITTEN AGREEMENT

1. Drafting

Once the parties have agreed to the terms of a new agreement, either through their own negotiations or the intervention of a third party, their last negotiation task is to finalize the written agreement. As a matter of practice, many persons actually negotiate the final terms of the clauses as they go along so that at the point of agreement, the contract is finalized for all intents and purposes. Others negotiate on the basis of a rough draft which includes all terms but not in final form. This leaves finalization as the last aspect of negotiations. In either event, the actual contract language should be finalized during negotiations.

2. Use of Checklists

As previously indicated, the preparation for negotiation is of critical importance, and today the parties spend a considerable amount of time and money in marshalling factual information prior to the beginning of negotiations. Naturally, the parties will use the information all during the negotiations and in drafting the specific language of the agreement. For example, the bargaining history, economic data and financial data will be used to formulate proposed language or changes in existing language. The greivance records, together with staff recommendations, also will be used to write out previous problems that have existed with written agreements. In point of fact, the use of this information has to a large extent replaced the "free-wheeling and dealing" impression of collective bargaining, if indeed it ever existed.

However, the method by which information is put to use varies in every negotiation. Some negotiators prepare checklists of issues to be discussed by topic. In Part Three of this book, we will use checklists to demonstrate the issues involved in the subject matter of the agreement. This checklist approach utilizes the information gathered prior to negotiation in order to raise viable issues during the process of negotiating or renegotiating collective bargaining agreements. Other negotiators use bargaining books which contain the present clauses, the change desired and reason for the proposed change. The National Industrial Conference Board recommended this usage in their interesting pamphlet, *Preparing for Collective Bargaining* (Studies in Personnel, Policy Number 172 published in

1959) at page 35. Whatever method selected, the purpose is to create a more orderly bargaining process based on factual information in order to create a more positive environment in which to draft a better agreement.

When the parties achieve agreement based upon a discussion of the agenda items contained in a checklist or "bargaining book," there still is no uniform way to actually draft the contract. Some negotiators use secretaries or typists on the spot to assist in drafting the agreement. Others use tape recorders. Still others use the old contract, if one exists, as a scratch sheet for the new terms. In our experience, a "clause book" which contains clauses from the present agreement, from the past agreement, and from other agreements in the same or similar industry is of great value in drafting a good written agreement.

B. THE CLAUSE BOOK

The clause book technique serves several constructive purposes. It identifies historical changes in specific clauses of the contract. This graphically demonstrates the progression in the contractual agreement between the parties. It also prevents time-consuming discussions of when changes were made in specific clauses, including additions, deletions and modifications.

Further, the clause book provides the specific language used in prior contracts compared with language used that negotiators prefer. The following clauses taken from the contract between Retail Store Employees Union, Local No. 876, Retail Clerks Int'l Ass'n (AFL-CIO) and United Super Market Association (Detroit, Michigan) illustrates how a clause book might be assembled.

RETAIL STORE EMPLOYEES UNION, LOCAL NO. 876, RETAIL CLERKS INT'L ASS'N
(AFL-CIO, WITH UNITED SUPER MARKET ASSOCIATION (DETROIT, MICHIGAN)

TOPIC	1974-1977	1977-1980	COMPARATIVE CLAUSE RETAIL STORE EMPLOYEES UNION LOCAL 400 WITH SAFEWAY STORES (WASH., D.C.)
Article 5 *Dispute Procedure* Subsect. D.	D. Grievances must be taken up promptly and no grievance shall be considered or discussed which is presented later than thirty (30) calendar days after such has happened, with the exception of wage claims.	D. Grievances must be taken up promptly and no grievance shall be considered or discussed which is presented later than thirty (30) calendar days after such has happened, with the exception of wage claims. Wage claims shall be defined as, and limited to, the following: a. Overdue progression step increases b. Incorrect wage rates c. Computer error d. Errors in the mathematical calculation of wages or wage rates or failure to pay for holidays, sick pay, vacations, etc. e. Improper recall of laid-off employees. In the case of a grievance contesting a discharge, the time limit shall be fourteen (14) days.	18.6 All complaints must be filed, in writing, within thirty (30) days after occurrence of the matter in dispute or disagreement, provided that any complaints in reference to dismissal must be filed, in writing, to the Employer within ten (10) days from the date of dismissal. Complaints not filed within the limits herein specified shall have no right of appeal by any party involved.

Contracts and contract clauses are available from unions, companies, BNA's, and the Bureau of Labor Statistics Bulletin Series 1425 (by subject matter). Accordingly, parties negotiating a new contract can also utilize the "clause book" concept to write a new agreement. The use of this technique not only facilitates the drafting of a *specific* contract, but comports with the *ongoing* nature of the agreement and insures the best drafting information available to the parties.

NOTE:

Problem: Use the provisions under the current contract in the sample clause book, and assume that the collective bargaining agreement provides *inter alia,* that:

> Either party to this Agreement shall have the right to refer to an impartial arbitrator any grievance which has not been satisfactorily settled in the foregoing steps. . . .

Assume further that a dispute arose over the discharge of an employee for falsification of records, and the Union filed a grievance. Prior to reaching the terminal step of arbitration, the employee was reinstated when it was admitted by the Union and the employee that his discharge was for "cause." The Union agreed that "settlement shall constitute a final notice to the grievant that any future violation of Company rules is cause for immediate discharge," and that "in such event the Union and grievant waive all rights to submit the grievance to arbitration proceedings."

One year later, the employee was involved in a fight with the Company's foreman during working hours, and the Company discharged the employee. The Union filed a grievance against the foreman which went to the final step of arbitration, at which point the Company claims that the Union waived its right to arbitrate the particular dispute.

Does the prior settlement and/or waiver make the issue not arbitrable? *Compare National Cash Register Co.,* 47 L.A. 248 (M. Nichols, 1966) *with Speer Carbon Co.,* 41 L.A. 1232 (J. Waldron, 1963). Should provision be made regarding "settlement," "waiver" and "relitigation"? Draft such provisions. Are they likely to be included in a collective bargaining agreement? Why?

C. THE COLLECTIVE BARGAINING AGREEMENT

Collective bargaining agreements are enforceable at law in this country, as the following section of the Taft-Hartley Act indicates:

SUITS BY AND AGAINST LABOR ORGANIZATIONS

Section 301. (a) Suits for violation of contracts between an employer and a labor organization representing employees in an industry affecting commerce as defined in this Act, or between any such labor organizations, may be brought in any district court of the United States having jurisdiction of the parties, without respect to the amount in controversy or without regard to the citizenship of the parties.

(b) Any labor organization which represents employees in an industry affecting commerce as defined in this Act and any employer whose activities affect commerce as defined in this Act shall be bound by the acts of its agents. Any such labor organization may sue or be sued as an entity and in behalf of the employees whom it represents in the courts of the United States. Any money judgment against a labor organization in a district court of the United States shall be enforceable only against the organization as an entity and against its assets, and shall not be enforceable against any individual member or his assets.[1]

However, as Part Two of these materials illustrates, enforcement is not free from difficulty. Prior to consideration of these problems, it is desirable to investigate the nature of collective bargaining agreements, and some of the technical problems that confront the courts in classifying them within our legal framework in this country.

PROFESSOR ARCHIBALD COX, THE LEGAL NATURE OF COLLECTIVE BARGAINING AGREEMENTS [2] **(Address at Eleventh Annual Summer Institute of the University of Michigan Law School, Summer 1959)**

. . . .

There are rules applicable to "common" or "commercial" contracts which can be helpful in resolving cases arising under collective bargaining agreements because they furnish the conceptual tools of analysis even though the ultimate answer turns less on the concepts than on evaluation of functional aspects of the agreement. This point is illustrated by the question whether the

---

[1] 61 Stat. 136, Sec. 301(a)-(c). *See* Textile Workers Union v. Lincoln Mills, 353 U.S. 448 (1957) for judicial construction of this section.

[2] 57 Mich. L. Rev. 1 (1958). Reprinted by permission of the publisher. Copyright © by the Michigan Law Review, University of Michigan.

union or the individual employee is the proper party to sue to enforce or to settle a claim under a collective bargaining agreement.

One early conceptual view was that although a collective bargaining agreement gave no rights to individual workers whenever a man went to work his individual contract incorporated the union agreement as a local custom or usage so that every failure to pay wages in accordance with the collective agreement was a breach of the individual contract of employment. Of course the parties to an ordinary commercial contract may stipulate that their agreement does not include local usages but this difficulty was surmounted by saying that under the Railway Labor and National Labor Relations Acts the collective agreement is included in each individual's contract of employment by force of law somewhat as a carrier's tariff or the statutory provisions of an insurance policy. Under this view, which was adopted by the Court of Appeals for the Third Circuit and followed by Justice Reed in the *Westinghouse* case [3] the legal relation between the employer, the union and the employees is conceived as two bilateral contracts. One contract — between the employer and the union — is made up partly of promises running to the benefit of the union as an organization, like the check-off or closed shop clauses which the union alone can enforce, and partly of provisions relating to wages, hours and job security which the employer promises to incorporate in a second bilateral contract — the contract of hire between the employer and the individual employees. Under this theory the union may sue for breach of the first contract but since it is not a party to the second contract, only the individual may sue for the breach of promises running to his benefit. And since the claim for compensation is the individual's it must follow that the union has no power to make a binding settlement.

A second theory holds that a collective bargaining agreement is a third-party contract with the employer as promisor, the union as promisee, and the employees as third-party beneficiaries. In the *Westinghouse* case Circuit Judge Staley argued that this description does not fit the facts because such promises as the union shop and check-off do not benefit individual workers but surely some of the promises in an instrument may run to the benefit of third parties while others benefit the promisee alone. The other objection to the third-party beneficiary theory — that the individual's labor is the sole consideration for the obligation to pay wages — is hardly an accurate description of the facts. In negotiating a collective agreement the employer promises a given wage scale as part of a package deal in return for various undertakings by the union including the promise

---

[3] [Association of Westinghouse Salaried Employees v. Westinghouse Elec. Corp., 210 F.2d 623 (3d Cir. 1954), *aff'd,* 348 U.S. 437 (1955), *rehearing denied,* 349 U.S. 925 (1956), *rev'd,* Smith v. Evening News Ass'n, 371 U.S. 195, 199 (1962). *Eds.*]

not to strike and it is rather likely that he would have agreed to the same wage scale without the union's promises. The individual's furnishing labor is consideration, but not the only consideration for the employer's promise to pay. Under this theory either the union or the employee may sue for breach of the promises inuring to the benefit of individual workers. When the individual sues, judgment may be entered for the amount due him. When the union sues, the decree may be for specific performance or the company can be required to pay the money into the registry of court for distribution to individual workers in supplementary proceedings. In a suit by either an individual or the union alone, the judgment would not bind the absent party but the employer could protect himself against a second suit by impleading the absent party.

Third, the legal situation under a collective bargaining agreement may be somewhat loosely compared to a trust with a chose in action as the *res*. In this view the bargaining representative, which is subject to fiduciary obligations, holds the employer's promises in trust for the benefit of the individuals. The trust is a common legal device for handling situations in which a single obligee is empowered to play a continuing role in the administration of contracts intended for the benefit of a large and ever changing group of beneficiaries who may have divergent interests. Massachusetts business trusts and mortgage indentures furnish familiar illustrations. According to this analogy the union would ordinarily be the only proper party to bring an action for breach of the collective agreement and the judgment would bind the individuals. The union can enter into binding settlements with the employer. The individual's remedy is to show that the union's handling of the claim did not meet its fiduciary obligations. In the latter case the individual could sue the union to compel it to perform its duties or he could join the union and the company as co-defendants and seek a judgment for the money alleged to be due him.

Such theories are highly useful in determining rights and remedies under collective bargaining agreements. They furnish tools of analysis. They help us to perceive the implications of particular issues — to see the relation between problems — so that we may achieve consistency and integrity instead of an illogical mass of *ad hoc* decisions. They remind us of the flexibility and adaptability of the common law. They become dangerous only when artificially selected concepts are allowed to dictate the decision. Any of the three theories is a sound abstraction. In the final analysis one must deal with the underlying questions of policy which make one theory more appropriate than another. Logic cannot replace wisdom.

Thus we are led back to consideration of the functional nature of a collective bargaining agreement. What are its purposes? What does it do? What legal conclusions about the right to enforce and settle claims against the employer result in better performance of the functions of the agreement?

In the community of the shop the collective bargaining agreement serves a function fairly comparable to the role of the Federal Trade Commission Act or National Labor Relations Act in the whole community. It is an instrument of government as well as an instrument of exchange. The point is highly important both in evolving substantive law and, as I shall seek to show later, in matters of interpretation.

The governmental nature of a collective bargaining agreement results partly from the number of people affected and the diversity of their interests. Harry Shulman aptly suggested other determining conditions:

> [The collective bargaining agreement] is not the typical offer and acceptance which normally is the basis for classroom or text discussions of contract law. It is not an undertaking to produce a specific result; indeed, it rarely speaks of the ultimate product. It is not made by parties who seek each other out to make a bargain from scratch and then go his own way. The parties to a collective agreement . . . meet in their contract negotiations to fix the terms and conditions of the collaboration for the future.[4]

Perhaps "collaboration" is too optimistic a word. Perhaps there is a "typical" contract only in the sense that economists have a model. The point which Shulman caught and I am seeking to emphasize is that the collective agreement governs complex many-sided relations between large numbers of people in a going concern for very substantial periods of time. "The trade agreement thus becomes, as it were, the industrial constitution of the enterprise setting forth the broad general principles upon which the relationship of employer and employee is to be conducted."[5]

. . . .

The governmental nature of a collective bargaining agreement should have the predominant influence in its interpretation. The generalities, the deliberate ambiguities, the gaps, the unforeseen contingencies, the need for a rule although the agreement is silent — all require a creativeness quite unlike the attitude of one construing a deed or a promissory note or a three-hundred page corporate trust indenture. Perhaps the requisite attitude can be

---

[4] The quotation is from a mimeographed address entitled, The Role of Arbitration in the Collective Bargaining Process which is used in courses in the Harvard Trade Union Program. I believe that it must have been delivered at a meeting of the National Academy of Arbitrators, but apparently it has not been published.

[5] NLRB v. Highland Park Mfg. Co., 110 F.2d 632, 638 (4th Cir. 1940).

suggested by likening the interpretation of a collective agreement to the construction of a basic statute creating an administrative agency, although the analogy may assume too readily that the "look-in-dictionary" school of statutory interpretation has given way to willingness to read basic statutes "not as theorems of Euclid but with some imagination of the purposes which lie behind them." [6]

The interpretation of a statute is the proliferation of a purpose. In a sense it is misleading to speak of the legislative intent. No one supposes that the tens of senators and hundreds of representatives who vote for a bill have one common state of mind. I trust also that arbitrators who speak of "the intent of the parties" do not mean to imply that they are concerned with the secret unexpressed intent of either party. Those who listen seriously to the testimony of negotiators concerning what they understood or supposed or intended run the risk of imposing upon one side the unilateral suppositions of the other. The true standard of interpretation must be objective. To speak of intent as if the congressmen or negotiators had reached a conclusion upon the specific issue is also misleading. The troublesome issues during the administration of a statute or contract are usually those which the authors either refused to face or failed to anticipate. Yet to speak of intent, when the word is properly understood, serves two useful functions. It reminds the interpreter that the statute or contract is a purposive instrument. The metaphor also cautions the interpreter that it is his duty to effectuate the will of the Congress — or of the parties to the contract — even though he himself might reach an infinitely wiser decision. What the interpreter must strive to do, therefore, is to give the instrument the application which the author would have provided if he had consciously determined the issue.

In the case of a statute the best guide to this meaning is its policy or purpose. Behind the words there usually lies a general aim, an objective, which embodies specific meanings, half-understood, half-unarticulated; and by these one may judge specific cases.

Life overflows its molds and the will outstrips its own universals. Men cannot know their own meaning till the variety of its manifestations is disclosed in its final impacts and the full content of no design is grasped till it has got beyond its general formulation and become differentiated in its last incidence. It should be, and it may be, the function of the profession to manifest such purposes in their completeness if it can achieve the genuine loyalty which comes not from obedience, but from the

---

[6] Lehigh Valley Coal Co. v. Yensavage, 218 F. 547, 553 (2d Cir. 1914), *cert. denied*, 235 U.S. 705 (1915).

according will, for interpretation is a mode of the will and understanding is a choice.[7]

Many questions of interpretation can be handled in this fashion under collective bargaining agreements. The most ambiguous phrase may be directed to a practical problem, and it is an obvious mistake to read the words without attention to the problem. Because the problems are usually unfamiliar and are often subtle, counsel may find it hard to persuade the judge to read the provisions of a labor contract "not as theorems of Euclid, but with some imagination of the purposes which lie behind them." It may sometimes be extraordinarily difficult to convey a sense of purpose through testimony, briefs and oral argument; but these are all familiar tasks of advocacy which hardly affect the nature of the issues.

Unfortunately, many of the most important questions of interpretation are not solvable by reference to the fundamental purposes of the collective agreement — at least not in the sense in which that term is usually understood. The difficulty arises from the fact that management and labor often have conflicting aims and objectives, and the interpretation put upon the contract may depend upon which objective is chosen as the major premise. The point is illustrated by a dispute which I heard as arbitrator some years ago over the meaning of a clause in the grievance procedure. The clause stipulated that a grievance which could not be settled with the foreman should be taken up in a second step — "Between the Shop Committee (including the steward in the department where the grievance originated) and the Division Superintendent."

The contract was executed after a long strike which almost wiped out the local union. The International took the president of the local out of the plant in an effort to rebuild and put her on a full-time salary with the sole task of serving the employees in the mill in question. As an employee she had been on the shop committee. TWUA wished her to continue to be present at the second step of the grievance procedure. The company objected on the ground that one who was not an employee could not be a member of the "shop committee." There is some force to the verbal argument but it can be countered with the contention that the clause should not be taken as an exclusive list of the persons who might participate because this interpretation would exclude everyone on the company's side except the division superintendent. Verbally the case was a stand-off. The president of the local union had some familiarity with the ways of collective bargaining; she was self-possessed, quick and articulate. The employees on the shop committee were unusually inexperienced and inarticulate. If one started from the premise that the grievance

---

[7] Hand, The Speech of Justice, 29 Harv. L. Rev. 617, 620 (1916).

procedure was intended to be a forum in which both sides of a question should be presented effectively in the hope of reaching a reasoned decision, the local president should be allowed to attend with, or as a member of, the shop committee. The third and fourth steps would be handled by officials of the International Union. I assume that this was roughly the purpose which the union attributed to the grievance procedure. The employer's reputation was strongly anti-union. At this particular mill, one of its few unionized plants, the union had almost disintegrated because of the strike. It seems realistic to suppose that the company hoped that the union's administration of the contract would be so inefficient and inept that the employees would lose interest. From this premise one would logically come to the view that Step 2 should be narrowly interpreted in order to keep the union ineffective. Thus the issue really turned upon whether one took the union's purpose or the company's purpose as the guiding premise. I ruled for the union and would do so again, but candor compels me to recognize that the conception of the collective bargain as an instrument intended to operate effectively was imposed upon the parties from outside in defiance of the employer's intent, which must have been known to the union, because the arbitrator chose to be guided by the national labor policy or perhaps by a personal predilection for effective union participation.

Although the preceding illustration may seem unimportant, the type of conflict which it illustrates lies at the bottom of many of the toughest problems of interpretation. Let me use two common examples, one involving discharge and the other subcontracting, in order to bring out the difficulty.

Suppose that an employee is discharged for what the union thinks is insufficient cause during the term of a collective bargaining agreement which contains most of the customary provisions, including recognition, seniority, grievance, and arbitration clauses but which imposes no express limitation upon the management's power to discharge. Of course the exact words of the contract make a difference but one reading the opinions gets the feeling that it is not the language which leads courts to deny relief while arbitrators examine the merits of the discharge. In *Coca-Cola Bottling Co. of Boston* Saul Wallen reasoned that ". . . the meaning of the contract, when viewed as a whole, is that a limitation on the employer's right to discharge was created with the birth of the instrument. Both the necessity for maintaining the integrity of the contract's component parts and the very nature of collective bargaining agreements are the basis for this conclusion." [8]

---

[8] Coca-Cola Bottling Co., *reprinted in* A. Cox & D. Bok, Cases and Materials on Labor Law (6th ed. 1965).

There is little force to the argument that the implication of a clause limiting discharges to cases of just cause is necessary to preserve the integrity of a seniority clause or grievance procedure. The integrity of the seniority and grievance clauses would not be affected by the arbitrary and capricious discharge of a junior employee who had no grievance.

Mr. Wallen's reliance upon "the very nature of collective bargaining agreements" cuts much deeper. He thereby asserts that a company which signs a collective bargaining agreement automatically assumes some obligations and submits certain management actions to the jurisdiction of the arbitrator even though the agreement says nothing about them. The dissenting member of the arbitration board spoke the truth when he protested that the majority "have taken a contract which contained no language which could possibly be construed as a limitation on the Company's right of discharge and have implied a very stringent limitation on that right," [9] but this assertion did not meet the basic contention that employees had rights cognizable by the arbitrator in addition to those which the contract expressly gave them.

Some of the subcontracting cases which have been so much debated in recent years raise the same kind of issues although others may turn upon narrower reasoning. Suppose that a manufacturer of heavy steam valves is a party to a contract which makes no mention of subcontracting but contains, in addition to the arbitration clause, such customary provisions as a recognition clause, a seniority clause, a discharge clause and a schedule of wage rates. The manufacturer sublets the machining of certain parts to an independent concern instead of following his previously unbroken practice of doing all his own production. There are layoffs and a reduction of overtime. The union protests that the contract has been violated and takes the case to arbitration. There is precedent for the view that subcontracting is a reserved right of management. There are also decisions upholding the union's contention on grounds reminiscent of Mr. Wallen's reasoning in the *Coca-Cola* case:

> ... the Recognition clause, where considered together with the Wage clause, the Seniority clauses, and other clauses establishing standards for covered jobs and employees limits the Company's right to subcontract during the term of the Contract. ... To allow the Company, ... to lay off the employees and transfer the work to employees not covered by the agreed standards would subvert the contract and destroy the meaning of the collective bargaining relation.

I suggested earlier that the collective bargaining agreement, unlike

---

[9] A. Cox, Cases on Labor Law 590 (4th ed. 1958).

most other contracts, is an instrument of government because it regulates diverse affairs of many people with conflicting interests over a substantial period of time. One can phrase the basic problem of interpretation in the discharge and subcontracting cases by saying that the parties differ with respect to the kind of government which they propose to establish. Is it a monarchy except insofar as the employer has assumed the obligations explicitly stated or fairly implied from the contract? Or has the whole realm of matters of mutual concern to employer and employees been brought within the joint authority of the company and union under a regime in which the legislative process is performed in annual contract negotiations and the executive and judicial process is carried out under a grievance procedure ending in arbitration? Usually the realm of matters of mutual concern is divided, part to be regulated by the employer and part to be governed by joint authority under the regime established by the contract. The issue then becomes, which matters are regulated by one form of government and which by the other. Did the Coca-Cola contract move discharges into the area of collective bargaining, i.e., of joint responsibility, or were they left to the sole responsibility of management? What about subcontracting? It is to the basic conflict over the size of the area subject to joint responsibility that I refer when I speak of the lack of a common purpose on the part of both management and labor to which questions of interpretation can be referred. Going a step further, I suggest that this is the very essence of large parts of a collective bargaining agreement — it has the nature of an armed truce in a continuing struggle, yet the armistice line has not been put on a map.

. . . .

Every collective bargaining agreement is by its very nature the product of conflicting desires concerning the sphere of joint government established by the collective agreement. Sometimes the sphere is expressly delineated with all the rest reserved as management prerogatives but as often as not the impossibility of making an explicit compromise, coupled with the impossibility of not reaching an agreement, results in a more or less ambiguous silence. The task of finding where the boundaries would have been drawn if the parties who signed the contract had drawn them explicitly is then a problem of interpretation within the jurisdiction of the arbitrator who is given power to decide questions concerning the interpretation and application of the agreement. For it is the agreement that draws the boundary line even though it does not draw it expressly. The interpreter must remember that the contract goes a distance but also that it stops, because it is a product of competing wills and its policy inheres as much in its limitations as in its affirmations. Nor is the interpreter left wholly without guidance.

Even a vague management-functions clause suggests that the boundaries may be narrower than under a contract without it. An integrated writing clause bespeaks narrow interpretation. Surely an open-ended arbitration clause indicates a wider area of joint sovereignty than a clause limiting the arbitrator in the interpretation and application of the contract. In the discharge case it would not be implausible to conclude, if the words of the contract are otherwise blind, that review of discharges to determine whether there is just cause is more consistent with a contract granting other forms of job security and industrial justice than is the reservation of untrammelled power to discharge for any reason which the employer deems sufficient. The plausibility is less, if indeed there is any, in the case of subcontracting or shift schedules.

These last suggestions are the common stuff of arbitration decisions, but there is need for a coherent rationalization if this conception of the arbitrator's task is to find its way into the law of collective bargaining agreements. The suggestions made here are hardly a beginning. A single word may be added in conclusion. In the final analysis the arbitrator or the judge must make a choice. He may be an activist and impose his view upon the agreement when its words leave scope, bringing doubtful territory into the joint realm because he thinks that he knows that this is fair and good industrial relations. A wise and respected man may do much good through this conception of the arbitrator's function. It may also be right to follow the quieter role which Learned Hand assigns a judge in interpreting a statute the reach of which was sharply disputed.

> . . . But the judge must always remember that he should go no further than the government would have gone, had it been faced with the case before him. If he is in doubt, he must stop, for he cannot tell that the conflicting interests in the society for which he speaks would have come to a just result, even though he is sure that he knows what the just result should be. He is not to substitute even his juster will for theirs; otherwise it would not be the common-will which prevails, and to that extent the people would not govern.[10]

The parties can make the choice when they select their arbitrator.

NOTES:

(1) Much has been written on the legal nature of the collective agreement, with most commentators noting its unique characteristics and the difficulties and dangers of adopting traditional doctrines

---

[10] Hand, How Far Is a Judge Free in Rendering a Decision?, in Law Series 1, Lecture 14, at 5 (National Advisory Council on Radio in Education, 1933).

developed in other fields of contract law. *See* Chamberlain, Collective Bargaining and the Concept of Contract, 48 Colum. L. Rev. 829 (1948); Cox, Rights Under a Labor Agreement, 69 Harv. L. Rev. 601 (1956); Feller, A General Theory of the Collective Bargaining Agreement, 61 Calif. L. Rev. 663 (1973); Gregory, The Law of the Collective Agreement, 57 Mich. L. Rev. 635 (1959); Gregory, The Collective Bargaining Agreement: Its Nature and Scope, 1949 Wash. U.L.Q. 3; Rice, Collective Labor Agreements in American Law, 44 Harv. L. Rev. 572 (1931); Shulman, Reason, Contract, and Law in Labor Relations, 68 Harv. L. Rev. 999 (1955).

(2) The Supreme Court has been eclectic in its approach to common-law doctrines; it refuses to confine itself to any single theory, but draws upon whatever elements may be helpful in a variety of theories. For example, consider the following well-known comments by Mr. Justice Jackson in *J.I. Case Co. v. NLRB,* 321 U.S. 332, 334-35 (1944):

> Contract in labor law is a term the implications of which must be determined from the connection in which it appears. Collective bargaining between employer and the representatives of a unit, usually a union, results in an accord as to terms which will govern hiring and work and pay in that unit. The result is not, however, a contract of employment except in rare cases; no one has a job by reason of it and no obligation to any individual ordinarily comes into existence from it alone. The negotiations between union and management result in what often has been called a trade agreement, rather than in a contract of employment. Without pushing the analogy too far, the agreement may be likened to the tariffs established by a carrier, to standard provisions prescribed by supervising authorities for insurance policies, or to utility schedules of rates and rules for service, which do not of themselves establish any relationships but which do govern the terms of the shipper or insurer or customer relationship whenever and with whomever it may be established. Indeed, in some European countries, contrary to American practice, the terms of a collectively negotiated trade agreement are submitted to a government department and, if approved, become a governmental regulation ruling employment in the unit.
>
> After the collective trade agreement is made, the individuals who shall benefit by it are identified by individual hirings. The employer, except as restricted by the collective agreement itself and except that he must engage in no unfair labor practice or discrimination, is free to select those he will employ or discharge. But the terms of the employment already have been traded out. There is little left to individual agreement except the act of hiring. This hiring may be by writing or by word of mouth or may

be implied from conduct. In the sense of contracts of hiring, individual contracts between the employer and employee are not forbidden, but indeed are necessitated by the collective bargaining procedure.

But, however engaged, an employee becomes entitled by virtue of the Labor Relations Act somewhat as a third party beneficiary to all benefits of the collective trade agreement, even if on his own he would yield to less favorable terms. The individual hiring contract is subsidiary to the terms of the trade agreement and may not waive any of its benefits, any more than a shipper can contract away the benefit of filed tariffs, the insurer the benefit of standard provisions, or the utility customer the benefit of legally established rates.

(3) In England, the traditional view has been that a collective bargaining agreement is not a legally enforceable contract but only a "gentlemen's agreement," the terms of which become embodied in an individual worker's contract of employment. In 1968, the Royal Commission on Trade Unions and Employers' Associations, headed by Lord Donovan, concurred with this traditional view that collective agreements are not contracts, for the reason that the parties usually do not intend to make a legally binding contract. In 1969, the question had, for the first time, to be faced explicitly by a court. In *Ford Motor Co. v. Amalgamated Union of Engineering and Foundry Workers,* [1969] 2 Q.B. 303, where the employer was seeking an injunction against a number of striking unions, the court relied heavily upon the Donovan Commission report in holding that a collective agreement is not a legally binding contract because such was not the intention of the parties.

The Conservative Government's Industrial Relations Act of 1971 provided in Section 34(1) that a written collective agreement is conclusively presumed to be a legally enforceable contract, unless the parties have inserted an express term that the agreement is not intended to be legally enforceable. However, when the Labor Government came into power, the Industrial Relations Act of 1971 was repealed, and Section 18 of the Trade Union and Labor Relations Act of 1974 reversed the presumption, so that collective agreements are not legally enforceable unless the parties expressly provide to the contrary.

(4) The Supreme Court has increasingly emphasized what may be described as the "constitutional" or "governmental" quality of the labor agreement, as discussed in Professor Cox's article above. Thus, the collective agreement has been described as "not an ordinary contract" but rather a "generalized code" for "a system of industrial self-government." In analogizing the plant or industrial community to a political society, it might be said that the collective agreement

serves as a sort of basic legislation or constitution, and the grievance and arbitration procedure for the resolution of day-to-day disputes arising under the agreement constitutes a sort of judicial system.

Before going in detail into the developing federal law of labor arbitration, it is desirable to examine some background material on the different kinds of labor arbitration systems and their legal status at common law and modern statutes.

(5) *Problem:* Does the analogy between a collective bargaining agreement and a statute pertain to the records that negotiators keep regarding prior contract clauses? How? Extend the analogy to the use of such information in a subsequent breach of contract suit.

PART TWO
LABOR DISPUTE ARBITRATION

Chapter 5

ARBITRATION PROCEDURES, TECHNIQUES, AND ETHICAL CONSIDERATIONS

A. SCOPE

The intention of this Chapter is to provide a basic understanding of the practices, techniques, and ethical considerations in grievance arbitration [1] for the purpose of providing students with a knowledge of how arbitration procedures work. It is not intended to serve as a treatise on the procedural and substantive aspects of this process. For an in-depth study of arbitration procedures and techniques, you should refer to O. Fairweather, *Practice & Procedure in Labor Arbitration* (BNA 1973); and F. Elkouri & E. Elkouri, *How Arbitration Works* (3d ed. 1973). This Chapter should be used simply as a detailed outline of the process. We believe our coverage is important because arbitration is an informal procedure with great flexibility and variation, and a basic notion of the process is important. It is well established that unless required by the contract, strict observance of legal rules of evidence is not necessary.[2] Accordingly, the actual practice used in arbitration requires exposition based on experience. The American Arbitration Association (AAA) has "Voluntary Labor Arbitration Rules" (referred to by AAA number in this Chapter) which are useful in demonstrating their recommended procedures which cover approximately 20% of labor arbitrations.[3]

> **Rule 1. Agreement of Parties** — The parties shall be deemed to have made these Rules a part of their arbitration agreement whenever, in a collective bargaining agreement or submission, they have provided for arbitration by the American Arbitration Association (hereinafter AAA) or under its Rules. These Rules shall apply in the form obtaining at the time the arbitration is initiated.

---

[1] As stated in the last Chapter grievance or "rights" arbitration should be distinguished from "interests" arbitration which concerns the substantive rights to be included in the contract, *see generally* Proc. of 26th Ann. Meet. Nat'l Acad. Arb. (Dennis & Somers ed. 1973).

[2] F. Elkouri & E. Elkouri, How Arbitration Works 254 (3d ed. 1973) [hereinafter cited as How Arbitration Works]

[3] Proc. of 29th Ann. Meet. Nat'l Acad. Arb., 379 (App. F.) (Dennis & Somers ed. 1976).

B. THE ARBITRATOR'S JURISDICTION

Labor arbitration is a voluntary process established by contract.[4] Both the scope of the arbitration and the arbitrator's jurisdiction is established by agreement. When a dispute, claim or grievance arises out of or relates to the interpretation or application of a collective bargaining agreement and is taken to arbitration by a "joint submission," [5] there is no problem of jurisdiction since by submitting the dispute to arbitration the parties have identified the dispute and agreed to its arbitration. When one party invokes the arbitration clause in the grievance procedures by a "demand" for arbitration [6] the other may assert lack of jurisdiction — for example, the dispute is not covered (or is even expressly excluded) by the arbitration clause in the contract.

The threshold issue in arbitration, therefore, is whether the arbitrator has jurisdiction over the dispute. Substantive jurisdiction will be covered in Chapter 7 under the emerging federal law of collective bargaining. Procedural jurisdiction is usually a question of contract, but state arbitration statutes and the U.S. Arbitration Act should also be consulted to determine whether any additional statutory prerequisites exist and if so, whether they have been satisfied.[7]

C. INITIATING AN ARBITRATION PROCEEDING

A grievance arbitration proceeding is the last step in grievance administration — it takes place after the parties have exhausted every step in the grievance procedure provided in the collective bargaining agreement to no avail. Then as a last resort, they call upon an

---

[4] 29 U.S.C. 203 (d) Final adjustment by a method agreed upon by the parties is hereby declared to be the desirable method for settlement of grievance disputes arising over the application or interpretation of an existing collective bargaining agreement. The Service is directed to make its conciliation and mediation services available in the settlement of such grievance disputes only as a last resort and in exceptional cases.

[5] AAA, Labor Arbitration: Procedures & Techniques, Glossary of Terms (29-10M-9/69) [hereinafter cited as Procedures & Techniques] defines a Submission Agreement. A submission agreement is a jointly signed document stating the nature of the dispute and affirming the parties' intention to arbitrate and to abide by the award.

[6] Demand for Arbitration. A demand for arbitration is a formal request made by one party to the other for arbitration of a particular dispute under the arbitration clause of a contract. *Id.*

[7] *See* U.S. Arbitration Act, Title 9, U.S. Code §§ 1-14, first enacted February 12, 1925 (43 Stat. 883), codified July 30, 1947 (61 Stat. 669), and amended September 3, 1954 (68 Stat. 1233). Chapter 2 added July 31, 1970 (84 Stat. 692); Matto, The Applicability of State Arbitration Statutes to Proceedings Subject to LMRA Section 301, 27 Ohio St. L.J. 692 (1966).

arbitrator to render a judicial type decision after a hearing about the dispute which they agree to abide by in advance.

As previously indicated, labor-management disputes are brought to arbitration in one of two ways, either by a submission agreement which describes an existing controversy which both parties want settled by an impartial person, or by a demand for arbitration filed by either party to a contract, provided that contract has an arbitration clause.

As the AAA points out,

> The advantage of a future dispute arbitration clause is that it leaves nothing to chance. When a controversy arises, the parties may be in no mood to agree and it is sometimes difficult to get *both* parties to submit to the procedures of arbitration. But when they are subject to a clause, arbitration may be initiated without delay by either party.

> The agreement to arbitrate, if it does not refer to established rules and procedures, may not by itself answer all questions. Among the problems that remain are:

> How shall arbitrators be appointed?

> When and where shall hearings take place? And who will make these decisions if the parties cannot agree?

> Shall the arbitration board consist of one or of three neutral arbitrators?

> If a tripartite board is preferred (see Glossary of Terms), what shall the remedy be if the two party-appointed arbitrators cannot agree upon an impartial member of the board?

> Who may represent the parties? Shall witnesses be sworn?

> How shall requests for adjournments be handled? May briefs be filed?

> How are hearings closed and under what conditions may they be reopened?

> When will the award be rendered? To whom delivered?

> How much should the arbitrator be paid? [8]

Since well over 90% of all collective bargaining agreements contain arbitration clauses, the vast majority of arbitrations are requested by one party — usually the union, who initiates the procedures.

AAA rules provide:

7. Initiation Under an Arbitration Clause in a Collective Bargaining Agreement — Arbitration under an arbitration clause in a collective bargaining agreement under these Rules may be initiated by either party in the following manner:

---

[8] Procedures & Techniques, *supra* note 5 at 5-6.

(a) By giving written notice to the other party of intention to arbitrate (Demand), which notice shall contain a statement setting forth the nature of the dispute and the remedy sought, and

(b) By filing at any Regional Office of the AAA three copies of said notice, together with a copy of the collective bargaining agreement, or such parts thereof as relate to the dispute, including the arbitration provisions. After the Arbitrator is appointed, no new or different claim may be submitted to him except with the consent of the Arbitrator and all other parties.

8. Answer — The party upon whom the demand for arbitration is made may file an answering statement with the AAA within seven days after notice from the AAA, in which event he shall simultaneously send a copy of his answer to the other party. If no answer is filed within the stated time, it will be assumed that the claim is denied. Failure to file an answer shall not operate to delay the arbitration.

9. Initiation under a Submission — Parties to any collective bargaining agreement may initiate an arbitration under these Rules by filing at any Regional Office of the AAA two copies of a written agreement to arbitrate under these Rules (Submission), signed by the parties and setting forth the nature of the dispute and the remedy sought.

A "demand for arbitration" should include a brief statement of the issue to be arbitrated and the relief sought, and it should be signed by the complaining party. It should indicate the grievance provision under which arbitration is sought, and quote the specific language of the arbitration clause. Since jurisdiction is a threshold issue, care should be taken to avoid issues that have not gone through the appropriate grievance steps. A statement of the issues and of the relief sought in the demand for arbitration is usually the same one set forth in the written statement of grievance, on the basis of which the grievance machinery was invoked initially under the contract.

D. SELECTION OF AN ARBITRATOR

To many parties the current successful acceptance of grievance arbitration in collective bargaining agreements is due in large part to the right given to both parties to jointly select their arbitrators.[9] A common method of selecting an arbitrator is to make an "ad hoc" appointment for each case (or a small number of cases). In 1972

---

[9] Rothschild, Arbitration and the National Labor Relations Board: An Examination of Preferences and Prejudices and Their Relevance, 28 Ohio St. L.J. 195 (1967).

approximately 75% of appointments were made in this manner.[10] Of these ad hoc appointments, about 55% came from an appointing agency (FMCS, AAA); 43% directly from the parties, and the balance from other sources.[11] A smaller but increasing percentage of agreements provide for a "permanent arbitrator" or a "permanent panel" of arbitrators. In 1972 about 25% of all cases involved permanently appointed arbitrators.[12] A permanent arbitrator usually serves for the term of the contract. Still other parties use state agencies or select their arbitrator from the public, as the occasion arises, by mutual agreement.

The AAA charges each party $50.00 for administering an arbitration, while the arbitrators on its roster pay $100.00 dues per year. FMCS arbitrators are made available without charge either to the parties or the arbitrators.

AAA rules for selection provide that:

12. Appointment from Panel — If the parties have not appointed an Arbitrator and have not provided any other method of appointment, the Arbitrator shall be appointed in the following manner: Immediately after the filing of the Demand or Submission, the AAA shall submit simultaneously to each party an identical list of names of persons chosen from the Labor Panel. Each party shall have seven days from the mailing date in which to cross off any names to which he objects, number the remaining names indicating the order of his preference, and return the list to the AAA. If a party does not return the list within the time specified, all persons named therein shall be deemed acceptable. From among the persons who have been approved on both lists, and in accordance with the designated order of mutual preference, the AAA shall invite the acceptance of an Arbitrator to serve. If the parties fail to agree upon any of the persons named or if those named decline or are unable to act, or if for any other reason the appointment cannot be made from the submitted lists, the Administrator shall have power to make the appointment from other members of the Panel without the submission of any additional lists.

13. Direct Appointment by Parties — If the agreement of the parties names as Arbitrator or specifies a method of appointing an Arbitrator, that designation or method shall be followed. The notice of appointment, with the name and address of such Arbitrator, shall be filed with the AAA by the appointing party.

---

[10] O. Fairweather, Practice and Procedure in Labor Arbitration 66-67 (1973) [hereinafter cited as Practice & Procedure].

[11] Proc. of 26th Ann. Meet. Nat'l Acad. Arb., 297 (App. F) (Dennis & Somers ed. 1973).

[12] *Id.*

If the agreement specifies a period of time within which an Arbitrator shall be appointed, and any party fails to make such appointment within that period, the AAA may make the appointment.

If no period of time is specified in the agreement, the AAA shall notify the parties to make the appointment and if within seven days thereafter such Arbitrator has not been so appointed, the AAA shall make the appointment.

. . . .

15. Number of Arbitrators — If the arbitration agreement does not specify the number of Arbitrators, the dispute shall be heard and determined by one Arbitrator, unless the parties otherwise agree.[13]

16. Notice to Arbitrator of His Appointment — Notice of the appointment of the neutral Arbitrator shall be mailed to the Arbitrator by the AAA and the signed acceptance of the Arbitrator shall be filed with the AAA prior to the opening of the first hearing.

18. Vacancies — If any Arbitrator should resign, die, withdraw, refuse or be unable or disqualified to perform the duties of his office, the AAA shall, on proof satisfactory to it, declare the office vacant. Vacancies shall be filled in the same manner as that governing the making of the original appointment, and the matter shall be reheard by the new Arbitrator.

FMCS practices are very similar to those cited above. Other procedures vary somewhat, but all of these processes have led to the selection of a fairly small, select group of arbitrators who because of their being in great demand are forced to "slow up" the process in scheduling hearings. A 1974 survey indicates that the average age of arbitrators is 58.4 years (over 82% are 50 years old or older); and that the overwhelming number of arbitrators hold at least a bachelors degree (over 50% hold masters or other graduate degrees).[14] This has led to various attempts to increase the pool of qualified arbitrators,[15] and develop expedited procedures,[16] about which

---

[13] Otherwise the parties might select a Tripartite Board — A board consisting of a representative of each party and an impartial arbitrator. *See* How Arbitration Works 81-87, *supra* note 2.

[14] Proc. of 29th Meet. Nat'l Acad. Arb., pp. 377-78 (App. F) (Dennis & Somers ed. 1976).

[15] McDermott, "Evaluation of Programs Seeking to Develop Arbitrator Acceptability," *in* Proc. of 27th Ann. Meet. Nat'l Acad. Arb., 329 (Dennis & Somers ed. 1974).

[16] See Hoellering, Expedited Grievance Arbitration: The First Steps, *in* Proc. of 27th Ann. Meet. Ind. Rel. Res. Ass'n 324 (Mad. Wisc. Assoc. 1975).

more will be said later. The National Academy of Arbitrators is a nonprofit and honorary association of arbitrators established in 1947 to foster high standards of conduct and competence through educational proceedings, annual meetings, and an annual publication.[17] It has devoted substantial efforts to raising standards and increasing the pool of qualified arbitrators.[18]

Although arbitrators come from a wide variety of backgrounds — in addition to professional arbitrators, professors, lawyers, judges, public office holders, ministers, economists, etc., those who are consistently selected have a substantial expertise in labor-management dispute settlements.

Agency Requirements

Both the AAA and the FMCS have fairly stringent requirements for admission to their panels. Indeed, in April 1976 the FMCS revised its standards of eligibility of arbitrators for admission to and retention on its roster. The revised standards require conformance to the Code of Professional Responsibility, and state: "All applicants and arbitrators . . . must be able to demonstrate acceptable ability in analysis, recommendations, and decision writing," to conduct a fair and impartial due-process hearing in an orderly manner, and to "be physically and mentally equipped to withstand the tensions of an adversary proceeding, and be able to speak and write in a clear and concise manner. Applicants also should be able to demonstrate experience, competence, and acceptability in a decision-making role in the solution of labor relations disputes."

Actual arbitration experience is preferred, with frequency, complexity, and variety of issues taken into account. Those who do not possess these qualifications may substitute other relevant experience and/or participation in acceptable orientation and training programs for arbitrators, examples of which are spelled out. Party advocates or representatives generally are not eligible. There also is a requirement that arbitrators "keep current with developments that are relevant to arbitration practice." The FMCS intends to certify for two years applicants who meet these qualifications. Those currently on the roster will be certified for three years "following an evaluation of their continuing compliance with the standards." The Service plans periodic review thereafter.[19] Arbitrators are chosen for their ability, impartiality and integrity.

---

[17] How Arbitration Works *supra* note 2 at 24.

[18] *Supra* note 13.

[19] Coulson, Certification and Training of Labor Arbitrators: Should Arbitrators Be Certified?, *in* Proc. of 30th Ann. Meet. Nat'l Acad. Arb., 173, 211-12 (Dennis & Somers ed. 1977).

First, they are screened by the agencies based on stated requirements. Then the parties select them on the basis of information obtained through contact with others whom they know have used a specific arbitrator, or they can use a variety of written information to find out about specific arbitrators. BNA prepares a "Directory of Arbitrators," and Prentice Hall publishes "Who's Who in Arbitration." FMCS provides biographical data on those arbitrators whose names are supplied to the parties for selection. And, both BNA and CCH publish awards by arbitrators with a finder's index.[20]

An arbitrator's duty to disclose and ethical obligations will be covered in Chapter 7. But, it is important to note as part of a consideration of the importance of the selection process that the connection between contract disputes and current laws that impact on the collective bargaining process (covered in Chapter 7 and Part Four of this book) is increasing pressures for the selection of qualified arbitrators. Conversely, the impact of external laws on the arbitration process is increasing pressures on the arbitrators selected to expand their decision making process!

E. THE HEARING

1. Costs

The preparation and presentation of the case is within the control of each party, and the expenses involved in this stage are borne by each party. They include the time and expenses of participants, and the investigation of facts. If lawyers are involved, their fees (unless a full-time employee of either party) are going to raise the cost of arbitration substantially. A stenographic report of the testimony at a hearing is controversial because it is also costly. Most arbitrators take their own notes. When requested, the transcript of the hearing is paid for by the party or parties ordering it.

The arbitrator's bill is shared by the parties, and usually ranges from $175 up per day. The following AAA form indicates the usual costs involved in an:

---

[20] BNA, Labor Arbitration Reports [hereinafter cited as L.A.]; CCH Labor Arbitration Awards [hereinafter cited as L.A.A.].

ARBITRATOR'S COMPENSATION

Number of hearing days ____ @ $ _____ $ _____
Study and preparation days __ @ $ _____ $ _____
Other (specify) _____ @ $ _____ $ _____

FEE TOTAL $ _____

To be filled out by the Arbitrator

ARBITRATOR'S EXPENSES

Transportation $ _____
Hotel $ _____
Meals $ _____
Other (specify) $ _____ $ _____

TOTAL $ _____

Payable by Employer $ _____
Payable by Union $ _____
Date _____ Arbitrator's Signature _____

In 1963 it was estimated that the costs of just the arbitrator's fees, the lawyer's fee and the court reporter were $640 to the union and $1,025 to the company (the difference attributed to lawyers' costs).[21] Today this figure has undoubtedly doubled.[22] In addition, as previously indicated, AAA charges an administration fee to each party, and the costs of a neutral room, if one is used, must also be added to the expenses of a hearing. Furthermore, if the arbitrator's award involves back pay or other costs, this will have to be added to the cost of an arbitration.

The AAA rule is as follows:

44. Expenses — The expenses of witnesses for either side shall be paid by the party producing such witnesses.

Expenses of the arbitration, other than the cost of the stenographic record, including required traveling and other expenses of the Arbitrator and of AAA representatives, and the expenses of any witnesses or the cost of any proofs produced at the direct request of the Arbitrator, shall be borne equally by the parties unless they agree otherwise, or unless the Arbitrator in his award assesses such expenses or any part thereof against any specified party or parties.

2. Checklist of Procedures

One author uses the following checklist for conduct of the hearing.

---

[21] R.W. Fleming, The Labor Arbitration Process 50 (1965).
[22] Estimate based on Consumer Price Index 1. C.B.N.C. § 10:126 (4/20/78) [Eds.].

CHECKLIST FOR HEARING

(1) Introduction
(2) Swearing-in ceremonies
(3) Parties' preferences:
    (a) Will there be a transcript?
    (b) Will witnesses be sworn?
    (c) Will witnesses be sequestered?
    (d) Is there a presentation of joint documentary exhibits?
    (e) Are there stipulations?
(4) Opening statement by initiating party
(5) Opening statement by other side
(6) Presentation of case-in-chief (initiating party) — evidence, witnesses, and arguments
                -Cross-
(7) Presentation of case-in-chief (defending party)
                -Cross-
(8) Summation by initiating party
(9) Summation by defending party
(10) Close of hearing
    (a) Will parties present post-hearing briefs?
    (b) Announce time of decision

The AAA uses the following form for keeping a record of the hearing:

3. Record of the Hearing

American Arbitration Association

VOLUNTARY LABOR ARBITRATION TRIBUNAL

In the Matter of the Arbitration between

CASE NUMBER:

RECORD OF HEARING

Hearing held at _____ Date_____Hearing No._____
        Name(s) of Arbitrator(s) _____

Oath Administered   ☐   Waived   ☐

Case Initiated by Demand   ☐   Submission ☐

APPEARANCES

_____   _____

(Union)   (Attorney or Representative)

_____   _____

(Company)   (Attorney or Representative)

STENOGRPHIC RECORD ordered by   Union ☐   Company ☐

Name of Stenographer_____Date promised_____

Estimated cost_____

NAMES OF WITNESSES (check, if sworn)		ADDRESS	CALLED BY
_____	☐	_____	_____
_____	☐	_____	_____
_____	☐	_____	_____
_____	☐	_____	_____
_____	☐	_____	_____
_____	☐	_____	_____
_____	☐	_____	_____

EXHIBITS

Brief Description	No.	Submitted by	Return to

REMARKS

_____
_____
_____
_____
_____
_____
_____
_____
_____
_____

                            A.M.   A.M.

Hearing commenced at_____P.M.   Concluded at_____P.M.

                                             A.M.

Hearing No. _____ set for _____ at _____P.M.

Briefs to be filed by Union ☐   (date)_____
            by Company ☐   (date)_____
Reply Briefs,   by Union ☐   (date)_____
            by Company ☐   (date)_____

                                           A.M.

Hearing declared closed by the Arbitrator(s) on _____ at _____ P.M.
Number of copies of Award desired by: Union_____Company_____
Award Due Date _____ 19_____
          Signature_____

4. Conduct of Hearing

There are certain preliminary matters which the arbitrator may have to deal with prior to the hearing. The following AAA rules are illustrative:

19. Time and Place of Hearing — The Arbitrator shall fix the time and place for each hearing. At least five days prior thereto the AAA shall mail notice of the time and place of hearing to each party, unless the parties otherwise agree.

20. Representation by Counsel — Any party may be represented at the hearing by counsel or by other authorized representative.

. . . .

23. Adjournments — The Arbitrator for good cause shown may adjourn the hearing upon the request of a party or upon his own initiative, and shall adjourn when all the parties agree thereto.

24. Oaths — Before proceeding with the first hearing, each Arbitrator may take an Oath of Office, and if required by law, shall do so. The Arbitrator may, in his discretion, require witnesses to testify under oath administered by any duly qualified person, and if required by law or requested by either party, shall do so.

. . . .

34. Waiver of Oral Hearing — The parties may provide, by written agreement, for the waiver of oral hearings. If the parties are unable to agree as to the procedure, the AAA shall specify a fair and equitable procedure.

35. Extensions of Time — The parties may modify any period of time by mutual agreement. The AAA for good cause may extend any period of time established by these Rules, except the time for making the award. The AAA shall notify the parties of any such extension of time and its reason therefor.

As the arbitrator's checklist indicates, there are also hearing procedures that the arbitrator must decide upon. The first procedural question that normally presents itself is which party should present its case first.

26. Order of Proceedings — A hearing shall be opened by the filing of the oath of the Arbitrator, where required, and by the recording of the place, time and date of hearing, the presence of the Arbitrator and parties, and counsel if any, and the receipt by the Arbitrator of the Demand and Answer, if any, or the Submission.

Exhibits, when offered by either party, may be received in evidence by the Arbitrator. The names and addresses of all witnesses and exhibits in order received shall be made a part of the record.

The Arbitrator may, in his discretion, vary the normal procedure under which the initiating party first presents his claim, but in any case shall afford full and equal opportunity to all parties for presentation of relevant proofs.

However, even though a grievant is comparable to a plaintiff in a law suit,[23] she/he does not uniformly present his/her case first. For example, it is common practice to have the company present its case first in a discharge case. The reason has to do with the responsibility usually placed upon the company to prove that the discharge of the grievant was for "just cause" to the satisfaction of the arbitrators — the company must sustain its burden of proof.[24]

Another preliminary issue may arise when a witness fails to show up, and the arbitrator must determine whether to hold an ex parte proceeding. The AAA rules provide that:

> **27. Arbitration in the Absence of a Party** — Unless the law provides to the contrary, the arbitration may proceed in the absence of any party, who, after due notice, fails to be present or fails to obtain an adjournment. An award shall not be made solely on the default of a party. The Arbitrator shall require the other party to submit such evidence as he may require for the making of an award.

However, arbitrators are extremely reluctant to hold such a hearing.[25] An analogous and more common issue concerns the receipt of evidence by affidavit. The AAA's rule states:

> **29. Evidence by Affidavit and Filing of Documents** — The Arbitrator may receive and consider the evidence of witnesses by affidavit, but shall give it only such weight as he deems proper after consideration of any objections made to its admission.
>
> All documents not filed with the Arbitrator at the hearing but which are arranged at the hearing or subsequently by agreement of the parties to be submitted, shall be filed with the AAA for transmission to the Arbitrator. All parties shall be afforded opportunity to examine such documents.

Once again, although the rule is permissive, it should be considered by the arbitrator on a case-by-case basis, since it raises issues of hearsay.

5. Receipt of Evidence

Since arbitration is an informal proceeding conducted by an expert in labor-management disputes chosen to make a relatively narrow decision based on contract, the technical rules of evidence are not often applied. In fact, the AAA rules expressly state:

> **28. Evidence** — The parties may offer such evidence as they

---

[23] B. Siegel, Proving Your Arbitration Case 10 (1977) [hereinafter cited as Proving Your Case].

[24] *Id.* at 11. *See* Practice & Procedure p. 192 *et seq. supra* note 10.

[25] Practice & Procedure, *supra* note 10 at 145.

desire and shall produce such additional evidence as the Arbitrator may deem necessary to an understanding and determination of the dispute. When the Arbitrator is authorized by law to subpoena witnesses and documents, he may do so upon his own initiative or upon the request of any party. The Arbitrator shall be the judge of the relevancy and materiality of the evidence offered and conformity to legal rules of evidence shall not be necessary. All evidence shall be taken in the presence of all of the Arbitrators and all of the parties except where any of the parties is absent in default or has waived his right to be present.

However, a major reason for the rules of evidence is to insure that relevant proof is admitted. Therefore, in the case of testimony most arbitrators require first-hand knowledge — that based upon personal observation.

Similarly, although it is commonplace for arbitrators to accept hearsay testimony into evidence — testimony about a statement made out of court by someone other than the witness, presented for the purpose of demonstrating the truth of matters contained in the out-of-court statement, most arbitrators guardedly admit such evidence. They usually reserve the right to decide on its reliability in light of the surrounding circumstances under which it was made and offered; and the weight, if any, which should be accorded to the hearsay evidence. Opinion testimony is also permitted under the same guarded reservation as hearsay evidence. Although there is substantial controversy about the extent to which an arbitrator should inject himself/herself into a hearing by asking questions, it is common practice where the purpose is to clarify the nature of the evidence being presented.

Inspections are permitted under the AAA rules.

30. Inspection — Whenever the Arbitrator deems it necessary, he may make an inspection in connection with the subject matter of the dispute after written notice to the parties who may, if they so desire, be present at such inspection.

In sum, an arbitrator will sift through the evidence presented at a hearing to determine its weight and relevancy after all of the case is in. It is therefore important for the parties to effectively present their case of the hearing.

F. HOW TO PRESENT A CASE IN ARBITRATION

1. *The Opening Statement.* The opening statement should be prepared with utmost care, because it lays the groundwork for the testimony of witnesses and helps the arbitrator understand the relevance of oral and written evidence. The statement, although

brief, should clearly identify the issues, indicate what is to be proved, and specify the relief sought.

The question of the appropriate remedy, if the arbitrator should find that a violation of the agreement did in fact take place, deserves careful attention at the outset. A request for relief should be specific. This does not necessarily mean that if back pay is demanded, for instance, it is essential for the complaining party to have computed an exact dollar-and-cents amount. But it *does* mean that the arbitrator's authority to grant appropriate relief under the contract should not be in doubt.

Because of the importance of the opening statement, some parties prefer to present it to the arbitrator in writing, with a copy given to the other side. They believe that it may be advantageous to make the initial statement a matter of permanent record. It is recommended, however, that the opening statement be made orally even when it is prepared in written form, for an oral presentation adds emphasis and gives persuasive force to one's position.

While opening statements are being made, parties are frequently able to stipulate facts about the contract and the circumstances which gave rise to the grievance. Giving the arbitrator all the uncontested facts early in the hearing saves time throughout, thereby reducing costs.

2. *Presenting Documents.* Documentary evidence is often an essential part of a labor arbitration case. Most important is the collective bargaining agreement itself, or the sections that have some bearing on the grievance. Documentary evidence may also include such material as records of settled grievances, jointly signed memoranda of understanding, correspondence, official minutes of contract negotiation meetings, personnel records, medical reports and wage data. Every piece of documentary evidence should be properly identified, with its authenticity established. This material should be physically presented to the arbitrator (with a copy made available to the other side), but an oral explanation of the significance of each document should not be omitted. In many instances, key words, phrases and sections of written documents may be underlined or otherwise marked to focus the arbitrator's attention on the essential features of the case. Properly presented, documentary evidence can be most persuasive; it merits more than casual handling.

3. *Examining Witnesses.* Each party should depend on the *direct examination* of his own witnesses for presentation of facts. After a witness is identified and qualified as an authority on the facts to which he will testify, he should be permitted to tell his story largely without interruption. Although leading questions may be permitted in arbitration, testimony is more effective when the witness relates facts in his own language and from his own knowledge. This does not mean, however, that questions from counsel may not be useful in

emphasizing points already made or in returning a witness to the main line of his testimony.

4. *Cross-Examining Witnesses.* Every witness is subject to cross-examination. Among the purposes of such cross-examination are: disclosure of facts the witnesses may not have related in direct testimony; correction of misstatements; placing of facts in their true perspective; reconciling apparent contradictions; and attacking the reliability and credibility of witnesses. In planning cross-examination, the objective to be achieved should be kept in mind. Each witness may therefore be approached in a different manner, and there may be occasions when cross-examination will be waived.[26]

5. *Maintaining the Right Tone.* The atmosphere of the hearing often reflects the relationship between the parties. While the chief purpose of the arbitration hearing is the determination of the particular grievance, a collateral purpose of improving that relationship may also be achieved by skillful and friendly conduct of the parties. Thus, a better general understanding between the parties may be a by-product of the arbitration. To this end, the parties should enter the hearing room with the intention of conducting themselves in an objective and dignified manner. The arbitration hearing should be informal enough for effective communication, but without loss of that basic sense of order that is essential in every forum of adjudication.

The hearing is no place for emotional outbursts, long speeches with only vague relevancy to the issue, for bitter, caustic remarks, or personal invective. Apart from their long-run adverse effect on the basic relationship between the parties, such immoderate tactics are unlikely to impress or persuade an arbitrator. Similarly, over-technical and over-legalistic approaches are not helpful.

A party has every right to object to evidence he considers irrelevant, as the arbitrator should not be burdened with a mass of material that has little or no bearing on the issue. But objections made merely for the sale of objecting often have an adverse effect, and they may give the arbitrator the impression that one simply fears to have the other side heard.

6. *The Summary.* Before the arbitrator closes the hearing, he will give both sides equal time for a closing statement. This is the occasion to summarize the factual situation and emphasize again the issue and the decision the arbitrator is asked to make.

As arbitration is a somewhat informal proceeding, arguments may be permitted to some extent during all phases of the hearing. There may be times, however, when the arbitrator will require parties to

---

[26] Many arbitrators also permit redirect and recross examination, Proving Your Case 40, *supra* note 23.

concentrate on presenting evidence and put off all arguments until the summary. In either event, all arguments should be stated fully.

Finally, as this will be the last chance to convince the arbitrator, the summary is the time to refute all arguments of the other side.[27]

G. THE AWARD

Much has been written about the arbitrator's award. We also will have more to say about this aspect of arbitration in Chapter 7 under the subjects of judicial and Board review; Part Three, when we discuss substantive arbitration awards; and Part Four concerning the impact of discrimination in employment contracts. In addition to these important aspects of the impact of an arbitrator's award under federal common, and statutory law, it is important to note that as a matter of industrial practice an arbitrator's award should: be timely, within the scope provided for by the arbitration clause; dispose of all claims submitted finally and conclusively; and be based upon the collective bargaining agreement.

AAA rules provide:

31. Closing of Hearings — The Arbitrator shall inquire of all parties whether they have any further proofs to offer or witnesses to be heard. Upon receiving negative replies, the Arbitrator shall declare the hearings closed and a minute thereof shall be recorded. If briefs or other documents are to be filed, the hearings shall be declared closed as of the final date set by the Arbitrator for filing with the AAA. The time limit within which the Arbitrator is required to make his award shall commence to run, in the absence of other agreement by the parties, upon the closing of the hearings.

32. Reopening of Hearings — The hearings may be reopened by the Arbitrator on his own motion, or on the motion of either party, for good cause shown, at any time before the award is made, but if the reopening of the hearing would prevent the making of the award within the specific time agreed upon by the parties in the contract out of which the controversy has arisen, the matter may not be reopened, unless both parties agree upon the extension of such time limit. When no specific date is fixed in the contract, the Arbitrator may reopen the hearings, and the Arbitrator shall have 30 days from the closing of the reopened hearings within which to make an award.

. . . .

37. Time of Award — The award shall be rendered promptly by the Arbitrator and, unless otherwise agreed by the parties, or

---

[27] Procedures & Techniques, *supra* note 5 at 17-19.

specified by the law, not later than thirty days from the date of closing the hearings, or if oral hearings have been waived, then from the date of transmitting the final statements and proofs to the Arbitrator.

38. Form of Award — The award shall be in writing and shall be signed either by the neutral Arbitrator or by a concurring majority if there be more than one Arbitrator. The parties shall advise the AAA whenever they do not require the Arbitrator to accompany the award with an opinion.

39. Award Upon Settlement — If the parties settle their dispute during the course of the arbitration, the Arbitrator, upon their request, may set forth the terms of the agreed settlement in an award.

40. Delivery of Award to Parties — Parties shall accept as legal delivery of the award the placing of the award or a true copy thereof in the mail by the AAA, addressed to such party at his last known address or to his attorney, or personal service of the award, or the filing of the award in any manner which may be prescribed by law.

Under federal common law either party is entitled to request clarification or modification of an award, for example, where it is incomplete.[28] Despite a long held doctrine ("functus officio") that once an award is rendered the power of an arbitrator ends, the ruling case law now holds otherwise, and there is a trend to clarify awards where needed.[29]

H. EXPEDITED ARBITRATION

As Robert Coulson, President of the American Arbitration Association explains:

> Recently there has been increasing concern over rising costs and delays in grievance arbitration. The Labor-Management Committee of the American Arbitration Association recommended the establishment of an expedited procedure, under which cases could be scheduled promptly and an award rendered within five days of the hearing. Simplified procedures would also reduce the cost.
>
> In return for giving up their right to some of the procedural advantages of traditional labor arbitration, the parties could get a quick decision, at a reduced cost.

---

[28] Enterprise Wheel & Car Corp. v. United Steelworkers, 296 F.2d 327, 331-32 (4th Cir. 1959), *affirmed in part,* United Steelworkers v. Enterprise Wheel & Car Corp., 363 U.S. 593, 597-98 (1960).

[29] Practice & Procedure, *supra* note 10 at 551.

These Expedited Rules [AAA] provide such a procedure for use in appropriate cases.[30]

1. Agreement of Parties — These Rules shall apply whenever the parties have agreed to arbitrate under them, in the form obtaining at the time the arbitration is initiated.

2. Appointment of Neutral Arbitrator — The AAA shall appoint a single neutral Arbitrator from its Panel of Labor Arbitrators, who shall hear and determine the case promptly.

3. Initiation of Expedited Arbitration Proceeding — Cases may be initiated by joint submission in writing, or in accordance with a collective bargaining agreement.

4. Qualifications of Neutral Arbitrator — No person shall serve as a neutral Arbitrator in any arbitration in which that person has any financial or personal interest in the result of the arbitration. Prior to accepting an appointment, the prospective Arbitrator shall disclose any circumstances likely to prevent a prompt hearing or to create a presumption of bias. Upon receipt of such information, the AAA shall immediately replace that Arbitrator or communicate the information to the parties.

5. Vacancy — The AAA is authorized to substitute another Arbitrator if a vacancy occurs or if an appointed Arbitrator is unable to serve promptly.

6. Time and Place of Hearing — The AAA shall fix a mutually convenient time and place of the hearing, notice of which must be given at least 24 hours in advance. Such notice may be given orally.

7. Representation by Counsel — Any party may be represented at the hearing by counsel or other representative.

8. Attendance at Hearings — Persons having a direct interest in the arbitration are entitled to attend hearings. The Arbitrator may require the retirement of any witness during the testimony of other witnesses. The Arbitrator shall determine whether any other person may attend the hearing.

9. Adjournments — Hearings shall be adjourned by the Arbitrator only for good cause, and an appropriate fee will be charged by the AAA against the party causing the adjournment.

10. Oaths — Before proceeding with the first hearing, the Arbitrator shall take an oath of office. The Arbitrator may require witnesses to testify under oath.

---

[30] R. Coulson, Labor Arbitration: What You Need to Know 105 (1973).

11. No Stenographic Record — There shall be no stenographic record of the proceedings.

12. Proceedings — The hearing shall be conducted by the Arbitrator in whatever manner will most expeditiously permit full presentation of the evidence and the arguments of the parties. The Arbitrator shall make an appropriate minute of the proceedings. Normally, the hearing shall be completed within one day. In unusual circumstances and for good cause shown, the Arbitrator may schedule an additional hearing, within five days.

13. Arbitration in the Absence of a Party — The arbitration may proceed in the absence of any party who, after due notice, fails to be present. An award shall not be made solely on the default of a party. The Arbitrator shall require the attending party to submit supporting evidence.

14. Evidence — The Arbitrator shall be the sole judge of the relevancy and materiality of the evidence offered.

15. Evidence by Affidavit and Filing of Documents — The Arbitrator may receive and consider evidence in the form of an affidavit, but shall give appropriate weight to any objections made. All documents to be considered by the Arbitrator shall be filed at the hearing. There shall be no post hearing briefs.

16. Close of Hearings — The Arbitrator shall ask whether parties have any further proofs to offer or witnesses to be heard. Upon receiving negative replies, the Arbitrator shall declare and note the hearing closed.

17. Waiver of Rules — Any party who proceeds with the arbitration after knowledge that any provision or requirement of these Rules has not been complied with and who fails to state his objections thereto in writing shall be deemed to have waived his right to object.

18. Serving of Notices — Any papers or process necessary or proper for the initiation or continuation of an arbitration under these Rules and for any court action in connection therewith or for the entry of judgment on an Award made thereunder, may be served upon such party (a) by mail addressed to such party or its attorney at its last known address, or (b) by personal service, or (c) as otherwise provided in these Rules.

19. Time of Award — The award shall be rendered promptly by the Arbitrator and, unless otherwise agreed by the parties, not later than five business days from the date of the closing of the hearing.

20. Form of Award — The Award shall be in writing and shall be signed by the Arbitrator. If the Arbitrator determines that an opinion is necessary, it shall be in summary form.

21. Delivery of Award to Parties — Parties shall accept as legal delivery of the award the placing of the award or a true copy thereof in the mail by the AAA, addressed to such party at its last known address or to its attorney, or personal service of the award, or the filing of the award in any manner which may be prescribed by law.

22. Expenses — The expenses of witnesses for either side shall be paid by the party producing such witnesses..

23. Interpretation and Application of Rules — The Arbitrator shall interpret and apply these Rules insofar as they relate to his powers and duties. All other Rules shall be interpreted and applied by the AAA, as Administrator.

The AAA has made special arrangements to reduce the cost of arbitration under these rules. Details are available at the AAA regional office administering the case.[31]

NOTE:

For discussions of some problems of procedure in arbitration, see Fleming, Problems of Procedural Regularity in Labor Arbitration, 1961 Wash. U.L.Q. 221; R. W. Fleming, The Labor Arbitration Process ch. 6 (University of Illinois Press, 1965); Smith & Jones, Management and Labor Appraisals and Criticism of the Arbitration Process: A Report with Comments, 62 Mich. L. Rev. 1115 (1964); Straus, Labor Arbitration and Its Critics, 20 Arb. J. 197 (1965); Problems of Proof in Arbitration, Proc. of 19th Ann. Meet. Nat'l Acad. Arb. (Jones ed. 1967).

1. Some Problems of Proof and Procedure

a. *Applicability of Legal Rules of Evidence in General*

Arbitrators exercise a great deal of discretion in determining what shall be received in evidence, especially if the method of conducting the hearing is not prescribed by the parties or by statute. Generally speaking, they do not apply (at least fully) the strict rules of evidence used by the courts and by some administrative tribunals, although practice varies depending on the attitude of the arbitrator and that of the parties. A common response by the arbitrator to an objection to the receipt of evidence on grounds which might successfully be

---

[31] *Id.* For copies write 140 West 51st St., New York, N.Y. 10020.

urged in a court is to "receive it for what it is worth." This has occasioned a considerable amount of criticism, but the other, and perhaps predominant view, as expressed by the late Harry Shulman, is that "the more serious danger is not that the arbitrator will hear too much irrelevancy, but rather that he will not hear enough of the relevant." Shulman, Reason, Contract, and Law in Labor Relations, 68 Harv. L. Rev. 999, 1017 (1955).

For a summary of criticisms see Smith & Jones, Management and Labor Appraisals and Criticisms of the Arbitration Process: A Report with Comments, 62 Mich. L. Rev. 1115, 1127-30 (1964). *See generally, Practice & Procedure* 209-11; *How Arbitration Works* 252; R. W. Fleming, *The Labor Arbitration Process* 165 (1965); *Problems of Proof in Arbitration, Proceedings of the Nineteenth Annual Meeting of the National Academy of Arbitrators* at 86 et seq. (D. Jones ed. 1966) (an interesting and valuable series of reports by tripartite regional committees which had been commissioned by the Academy to consider "problems of proof"); and Jones, Evidentiary Concepts in Labor Arbitration: Some Modern Variations on Ancient Legal Themes, 13 U.C.L.A. L. Rev. 1241 (1966).

William E. Simkin expressed some very interesting views on the subject of evidence in arbitration: ". . . I think there are a lot of things that a typical lawyer has to unlearn before he becomes an arbitrator. I would like to outline two or three of those things: In the first place, I don't think he has much use for his training as to rules of evidence. We don't have any rules of evidence in arbitration, by and large, and I think it is a good thing. One of the fundamental purposes of an arbitration hearing is to let people get things off their chest, regardless of the decision. The arbitration proceedings is the opportunity for a third party, an outside party, to come in and act as a sort of father confessor to the parties, to let them get rid of their troubles, get them out in the open, and have a feeling of someone hearing their troubles. Because I believe so strongly that that is one of the fundamental purposes of arbitration, I don't think you ought to use any rules of evidence. You have to make up your own mind as to what is pertinent or not in the case. Lots of times I have let people talk for five minutes, when I knew all the time that they were talking — it had absolutely nothing to do with the case — just completely foreign to it. But there was a fellow testifying, either as a worker or a company representative, who had something that was important for him to get rid of. It was a good time for him to get rid of it. . . ." [Conference on Training of Law Students in Labor Relations, Vol. III, Transcript of Proceedings at 636, 637 (1948)].

b. Admissibility and Significance of Employee's Past Record

There are some evidentiary and procedural problems which, although in some instances not peculiar to the arbitration process, have been more troublesome than questions concerning the applicability of the legal rules of evidence. Included in this category are the admissibility and significance, in a discharge or discipline case, of the aggrieved employee's past record in the plant; or his record subsequent to the disciplinary action but prior to the arbitration hearing.

In *Harshaw Chemical Co.,* 32 L.A. 23 (1958), an employee was discharged for insubordination and use of profane language against a supervisor. In the arbitration proceeding, the employer sought to justify the discharge by evidence of the past misconduct of the dischargee. The union objected to the admissibility of the employee's past work record on the ground that the Employer was bound by the language of the termination notice which stated the cause of the discharge. In overruling the union's objection, Arbitrator Louis S. Belkin declared:

> The question of the use of the employee's past work record by the company in making its determination to discharge him is one which has several ramifications. In the opinion of the undersigned it would be inconceivable that the company do anything else. We have here a matter of equity and fairness. In order to be fair and equitable the totality of an employee's record, good or bad, must be weighed. This would certainly be applicable where the record is good. It must also apply where the opposite is true. It must also apply insofar as an arbitrator is concerned.
>
> I could not decide this matter if I had no knowledge of an employee's work performance and work record. This is a matter of discharge or reinstatement and thus transcends the realm of the ordinary grievance. I shall hold therefore that despite the wording of the notice the company may show evidence of the employee's record.
>
> This does not mean nor is it intended to mean that the union is barred from asserting its claim that the notice shows that the company's use of the employee's work record is an afterthought. The union may offer proof, if it can, that when the employee was discharged the foreman did not know of his past record and thus only the immediate incident was in his mind. It may offer proof, if it can, that this is the first time an employee's record of absenteeism or tardiness was used in a discharge for insubordination.
>
> These, however, are matters of evidence going to motivations. They are matters of proof and issues for argument. They do not

and cannot obviate the requirement and necessity for viewing the whole record of performance.

It is generally accepted that evidence of the grievant's past record is admissible in order to determine the propriety of the penalty imposed. *Lone Star Cement Corp.,* 39 L.A. 652 (1962) (Oppenheim, arbitrator); *American Forest Products Corp.,* 44 L.A. 20 (1965) (Lucas, arbitrator); *Foremost Dairies, Inc.,* 44 L.A. 148 (1965) (Tatum, arbitrator); *Robertshaw-Fulton Controls Co.,* 36 L.A. 4 (1961) (Hilpert, arbitrator). However, with respect to the use of past record to establish the guilt or innocence of the grievant or the likelihood of the commission of the alleged misconduct, arbitrators are in disagreement. *E.g.,* for decisions admitting past record see *Lake Shore Tire & Rubber Co.,* 3 L.A. 455 (1946) (Gorder, Chairman, Board of Arbitrators); *Mueller Brass Co.,* 3 L.A. 285 (1946) (Wolf, arbitrator); *National Malleable & Steel Casting Co.,* 12 L.A. 262 (1949) (Pedrick, arbitrator). For opposite rulings see *Bird & Son, Inc.,* 30 L.A. 948 (1958) (Sembower, arbitrator); *Capital Airlines, Inc.,* 27 L.A. 358 (1956) (Guthrie, referee); *Chicago Newspaper Publishers Ass'n,* 38 L.A. 491 (1962) (Sembower, arbitrator). For discussions *see generally* R. W. Fleming, *The Labor Arbitration Process* 166-70 (1965); *Practice & Procedure* 233-236; *How Arbitration Works* 119 (3d ed. 1973).

For arbitral rulings on the admissibility and significance of grievant's record after the disciplinary action but prior to the arbitration hearing *see Westinghouse Electric Corp.,* 26 L.A. 836 (1956) (Simkin, arbitrator); *Southern Bell Telephone & Telegraph Co.,* 25 L.A. 270 (1955) (McCoy, arbitrator); *Robertshaw-Fulton Controls Co.,* 36 L.A. 4 (1961) (Hilpert, arbitrator).

c. Calling a Witness Associated with the Other Side

Another interesting problem is created by the right or propriety, in a discipline or discharge case (or any other type of case, for that matter) of "calling" as a witness some person associated "with the other side" (*e.g.,* the employer calling a bargaining unit employee, or the union calling a supervisory employee). If this is done, the question arises whether the person thus called becomes an "adversary" witness who may, in effect, be subjected to what amounts to cross-examination by the party calling the witness.

For interesting comments of some arbitrators regarding this problem and what they did about it see footnotes 16-18 in Wirtz, Due Process of Arbitration, in The Arbitrator and the Parties, Proceedings of the Eleventh Annual Meeting of the National Academy of Arbitrators 1, 18-19 (BNA 1958). In Douglas Aircraft Co., 28 L.A. 198 (1957), the Company moved to have the grievant excluded from the arbitration hearing on the ground that it is poor industrial relations practice to allow the grievant to hear adverse testimony by fellow unit employees and his supervisor. The arbitrator, E. Jones, denied the motion, ruling that the grievant had a legal right to be present in the hearing. In so ruling, the arbitrator discounted the Company's claim that the fellow employees might otherwise refrain from telling the whole truth.

d. The Right to Information

The right of a party to have access to documentary information in the possession of the other party (*e.g.*, in a discipline or discharge case, the internal records of the employer pertaining to the case, or in any type of case the transcript or other record of interviews conducted by the other party with witnesses to the event giving rise to the grievance) has created a number of difficult issues.

For discussions of this problem see generally R. W. Fleming, The Arbitration Process 170-75 (1965); Jones, Accretion of Federal Power in Labor Arbitration — The Example of Arbitral Discovery, 116 U. Pa. L. Rev. 830 (1968); Jones, Blind Man's Bluff and the Now-Problems of Apocrypha, Inc. and Local 711 — Discovery Procedures in Collective Bargaining Disputes, 116 U. Pa. L. Rev. 571 (1968). In *Chesapeake & Potomac Telephone Co. of W. Va.,* 21 L.A. 367 (1954), an employee was discharged for chronic alcoholism that allegedly rendered him unfit for the job. The union protested the discharge as without just cause. In the arbitration proceeding, the union, after its prior request had been rejected by the employer, filed a motion for discovery and inspection of the grievant's employment and medical records. The union argued that the records were relevant and necessary to the presentation of its case while the employer contended that it had no obligation to furnish any record to the union. After ruling that the Board of Arbitration had authority to compel the employer to produce records and documents in its possession, Harry J. Dworkin (Chairman) observed:

> Apart from specific rules, it is a salutary principle of arbitration procedure that both parties to the dispute be accorded a full and complete hearing and an opportunity to present such evidence, documentary or otherwise, as is germane to the issues, without regard to whether one or another party has possession or custody of such evidence. The object and purpose of arbitration is to arrive at a fair and just decision, and to this end parties should be assisted in obtaining competent and material evidence where such production may reasonably be had. The laudatory aim and purpose of arbitration would be defeated and impaired were a party to be denied his just rights solely because the other party to the dispute refused to disclose material evidence which

it had under its control. Fortunately, in the great majority of arbitration disputes, the parties are usually willing to provide any data or evidence requested by either the arbitrator or a party. . . .

. . . .

Although the arbitration board is of the opinion that the Union's request in the instant case should be granted, it should extend only to such documents and writings which appear to be relevant and pertinent to the issues presented for ultimate determination. The exercise of the arbitrator's authority should be reasonable, and a party is entitled to be protected against "fishing expeditions" and the examination of files and records which may not be considered as being pertinent. In the exercise of this authority, the arbitrator should be guided by the principle of "sound discretion."

Accordingly, the request for the disclosure of the employment application is denied, as is the request for the reports of the supervisors on the ground that such records would not be of any probative value, and would involve the disclosure of confidential reports, including personal opinions. These records at most would disclose the mental process of the supervisors and would be of no factual value.

The requests for the work records, absence records, and medical records are of a documentary character which would be directly related to the issues in dispute, and therefore as to this request, the Motion for Discovery is granted.

For other illustrative cases see *American Telephone & Telegraph Co.,* 6 L.A. 31 (1947); I. *Hirst Enterprises, Inc.,* 24 L.A. 44 (1954); *Clay City Paper Co.,* 20 L.A. 538 (1952).

e. The Right to Confront Witnesses

Another issue which arises in arbitration is the right of a party to be confronted at the hearing with the direct testimony (in lieu of "hearsay") of a person whose complaint has resulted in some protested employer action. For example, in a disciplinary action resulting from a complaint made by a female customer of the employer against the aggrieved employee concerning the alleged misconduct of the employee on the customer's premises or disciplinary action resulting from reports made to the employer by unidentified "spotters" as in public conveyances operated by the employee or in retail stores where employee-clerks are observed, does the aggrieved employee have the right to confront the customer or the "spotter"?

See generally *Practice & Procedure* 159-163; F. Elkouri & E. Elkouri, *How Arbitration Works* 269-272; R. W. Fleming, *The Labor Arbitration Process* 175-81 (1965); Wirtz, Due Process of

Arbitration, in The Arbitrator and the Parties, Proceedings of the Eleventh Annual Meeting of the National Academy of Arbitrators 1, 16-18 (BNA 1958). Arbitrators seem to distinguish cases involving disciplinary action arising from a complaint by an employee whose identity the employer is unwilling to divulge and those involving disciplinary action as a result of a report of an unidentified professional "spotter" or investigator. Arbitrators generally require the appearance of the complaining employee witness. *E.g.,Murray Corp. of America,* 8 L.A. 713 (1947) (Wolf, arbitrator); *Bower Roller Bearing Co.,* 22 L.A. 320 (1954) (Bowles, arbitrator); *Lockheed Aircraft Corp.,* 13 L.A. 433 (1949) (Aaron, arbitrator); *Hooker Chemical Corp.,* 36 L.A. 857 (1961) (Kates, arbitrator). But reports by "spotters" or investigators have been admitted into evidence. The justification for this was explained by G. H. Hildebrand, Chairman, Board of Arbitration, in the case of *Los Angeles Transit Lines,* 25 L.A. 740 (1955), as follows:

(1) These reports are a record of specific acts and events. Obviously they are relevant to the issue being tried. (2) The superintendent of detectives, Forkner, was a qualified witness. He testified extensively regarding the selection and training of the operatives, the nature of their work and assignments, and the instructions that control the preparation of their reports. (3) The reports were made in the regular course of business, at or near the time of the act and event. The basic assignment of the operatives is to ride company vehicles as trained observers and to report on adherence to or infractions of company rules. A regular reporting form is used and the purpose and procedure governing each report is uniform, though the factual content may vary and though it may emerge either from a casual spotcheck or a more intensive special assignment. . . . (4) The information was obtained by trained observers, who are taught to be accurate and objective. In selecting them, the company tries to obtain persons capable of these qualities and who do not know any company employees. The operatives are not supposed to have personal contacts with the employees, and are shielded from such contacts by various safeguards. No reason was submitted to show that they had incentive to falsify the facts. The reports they rendered are succinct, specific and dispassionate; and they are uniform as to quality. They were prepared within twenty-four hours after the acts were observed. They were not prepared after the charge of NAP had been made and the issue joined.

On these criteria, the spotters' reports comply with the requirements of the business records statute and could be admitted in a court proceeding. However, we have here a collective bargaining relationship and not a non-recurring adversary proceeding in a court of law. Arbitration is an extension of the bargaining relationship. While an arbitration proceeding has adversary elements, the existence and continuance of the bargaining relationship must be kept in mind. Both parties must be fully satisfied that a fair decision has been reached, since their relationship will continue in the future. The rules of evidence and the determination of facts are admittedly more informal in an arbitration than in a court of law. Accordingly, the union has properly urged that for an issue as severe as discharge, the standards of proof must be even more exacting than in a court proceeding. This contention goes not against hearsay evidence as such, as the union thinks, but to the tests of admissibility of such evidence.

Beyond the specific requirements of the business records statute, two tests are decisive in an arbitration proceeding. (1) It must be shown that the reports were prepared before the decision to discharge had been taken and the issue joined between the parties. This condition was satisfied here. (2) There must be no tangible basis for believing that the company is biased against the employee and has set out to get him. In this case no serious charge of this sort has been made and no factual evidence submitted even to raise the question. Thus the spotters' reports pass these additional tests, which are decisive. But precisely because they are decisive, the ruling in favor of their admissibility should not be taken to mean that all spotters' reports, of this company or of any other transit company, are automatically admissible.

The company has also argued for the admissibility and weight of these reports on a plea of necessity — that the spotter system and disciplinary action based on spotters' reports are essential to the control of its employees. It is true that there are no practical alternative means by which supervision can exert its responsibilities in this industry. It is also obvious that control is essential, for the safety of the public, as well as protection of the property and efficiency of the company. However, the necessity for the system would not justify its sloppy or unfair use in disciplinary procedure.

The company also pleads from necessity to justify its failure to present seven of its operatives at the hearing and the restricted conditions under which X128 appeared, holding that if they were to be seen and identified their confidential status would be ended and the effectiveness of the system destroyed. As a practical matter for this industry, this claim has substantial merit, though the risk might have been reduced if the method by which X128 was produced had been applied to the others. However, the main issue is admissibility of hearsay, not the appearance of the operatives. Nor can I agree that the decision of Arbitrator Benjamin Aaron in *Lockheed Corp.,* 13 L.A. 433, is applicable here — that a discharged employee accused of bookmaking was entitled to a confrontation and cross-examination of his accusers. In that case the charge involved a criminal offense and was made by fellow employees whose names were kept secret by the company. The charge was general and not supported by a valid offer of proof, although the company was willing to allow the arbitrator to interview the informants privately, which he refused to do. Here we do not have a criminal charge, expressed in vague and general language and with no factual evidence made known to the opposing party; nor does the charge derive from anonymous fellow employees with possible grudges to bear as unsuccessful bettors.

Accord, Shenango Valley Transportation Co., 23 L.A. 362 (1954) (Brecht, Chairman, Bd. of Arbitration).

f. The Privilege Against Self-Incrimination and Improper Search and Seizure

There is also a question of whether the rules applicable in criminal proceedings are applicable in arbitration proceedings. For example, is the "privilege" against self-incrimination — may the disciplined employee, called as a witness, properly refuse to answer the question whether he did or did not commit the act charged against him — applicable? Does an employee have a privilege against improper search and seizure — as of an employee's locker to ascertain whether he has stolen Company property?

(1) Arbitrators have ruled that the privilege against self-incrimination has no place in grievance arbitrations. Wirtz, Due Process of Arbitration, in The Arbitrator and the Parties, Proceedings of the Eleventh Annual Meeting of the National Academy of Arbitrators 1, 19-20 (BNA 1958). The reason is the tendency of arbitrators to differentiate due process in a criminal proceeding from due process in an arbitration hearing. As arbitrator, James Hill, explained in Wirtz, Due Process of Arbitration, *supra,* "the typical disciplinary case is a matter not to be viewed primarily as a question of penalty for misconduct, but as a problem of whether or not, all things considered, the individual has proved an unsatisfactory employee." For illustrative cases expressing related views *see Simoniz Co.,* 44 L.A. 658 (1964) (McGury, arbitrator); *Lockheed Aircraft Corp.,* 27 L.A. 709 (1956) (Maggs, arbitrator); *Southern Bell & Telegraph Co.,* 25 L.A. 270 (1955) (McCoy, arbitrator). For discussions of this problem see generally F. Elkouri & E. Elkouri, How Arbitration Works 182-83 (rev. ed. 1960); R. W. Fleming, The Labor Arbitration Process 181-86 (1965); Jones,

Evidentiary Concept in Labor Arbitration: Some Modern Variations on Ancient Legal Themes, 13 U.C.L.A. L. Rev. 1241, 1286-90 (1966).

(2) For a discussion of the problems related to the admissibility of evidence procured by means of an allegedly illegal search and seizure see R. W. Fleming, The Labor Arbitration Process 186-90 (1965). *See also* the various Area Reports, in Problems of Proof in Arbitration, Proceedings of the Nineteenth Annual Meeting of the National Academy of Arbitrators 86-339 (BNA 1967).

g. An Employee's Right of Privacy

Should some kinds of evidence be excluded because they constitute improper invasions of the employee's asserted "right of privacy"? For example, should evidence of alleged employee misconduct derived from electronic devices such as closed circuit television or wiretaps or hidden tape records or microphones or evidence obtained through the use of lie detectors be excluded?

See generally R. W. Fleming, *The Labor Arbitration Process* 190-97 (1965). For a penetrating article on the use of lie detector tests and its admissibility in arbitration proceedings see Burkey, Lie Detectors in Labor Relations, 19 Arb. J. 193 (1964). In *Needham Packing Co.,* 44 L.A. 1057, 1080, 1095 (1965), the Board of Arbitration (Davey, Chairman), held inadmissible the recordings of telephone conversations between a Company counsel and a union officer to prove the existence of a controverted agreement on the ground that the conversations were recorded without the knowledge and consent of the union officer. The recordings were rejected in spite of the claim that they were the best evidence of the contents of the conversations.

Arbitrators are generally in agreement that the results of lie detector tests are incompetent evidence and therefore inadmissible to prove the guilt or innocence of the grievant. *E.g., Spiegel, Inc.,* 44 L.A. 405 (1965) (Sembower, arbitrator); *Saveway Inwood Service,* 44 L.A. 709 (1965) (Kornblum, arbitrator); *American Maize Products Co.,* 45 L.A. 1155 (1965) (Epstein, arbitrator). *But see Westinghouse Electric Co.,* 43 L.A. 450 (1964) (Singletary, arbitrator) (result of polygraph test admitted as corroborative evidence). In rejecting lie detector evidence, arbitrators often cite the courts' refusal to admit it on the ground that it is both unreliable and inaccurate. For grounds contributing to the lack of reliability and accuracy of lie detector tests *see* Burkey, Lie Detectors in Labor Relations, *supra* at 205. In *Warwick Electronics, Inc.,* 45 L.A. 95 (1966), the issue presented was whether an employer could properly discipline an employee for refusal to take a polygraph test. Without ruling on the admissibility of the result of such a test, the arbitrator, C. R. Daugherty, held that under the bargaining agreement, the union promised "to cooperate fully" with the employer in the investigation of theft of company's property and in so promising waived the employee's right to refuse to submit to the test. The arbitrator sustained the employer's action.

2. A Problem

On September 1, 1969, four men were working on the fifth floor of the plant including grievant who had sixteen years seniority. At 10 p.m. an explosive device was thrown into an area where two of the four men were sitting, and *A* was seriously injured. Although both men saw the device fall, they could not see the grievant nor a fourth man working on the same floor. The Company, after interviewing the four men, as well as the seven other men working in the building, could not ascertain who was responsible. All eleven employees were then asked, and agreed, to submit to a polygraph test. The Union, which does not approve of the tests as a matter of policy, admits that each man was advised at the laboratory of his right to refuse to submit, but alleges that refusal to submit would be admissible and damaging evidence. The opinion of the Director of the Polygraph Laboratory was that the "polygraph charts indicate conclusively that the grievant caused the explosion." Accordingly, the Company discharged the grievant under Art. VIII, Sec. 1 of the collective bargaining agreement which provides,

> "The management of the work and direction of the working forces including the right to hire, promote, transfer, suspend, or discharge for proper cause, are vested exclusively in the Company, and the Union agrees not to attempt to abridge these rights."

Company Position: The Company argues that: (1) The polygraph test indicates conclusively that the grievant was responsible for the explosion, because grievant was the only one of the eleven employees stated to be responsible for the explosion; (2) There were only four employees on the fifth floor where the explosion occurred, and all but grievant were within 15 feet of each other in the area where the device actually landed; (3) After the explosion, all employees on the fifth floor ran to the place where the explosion occurred except the grievant; (4) The talk among the employees in the department was that grievant caused the explosion; (5) Grievant admitted that he heard nothing despite the fact that the explosion was loud enough to affect *A*'s hearing; and (6) Grievant refused to testify at the arbitration hearing.

Union Position: The Union challenges the evidence adduced, namely (1) There is no evidence as to which direction the explosion came from; (2) No witness saw the explosive device thrown; (3) Grievant was out of sight of the desk area where the explosion occurred and was performing his normal job; (4) Other people, unseen and unknown, had access to the area of the explosion from the roof, the area between the ceiling and the roof, and several doors; (5) The Company relies primarily on the result of the polygraph test which the Union claims is inadmissible because grievant was coerced into taking the test which is an invasion of privacy, and because due to unreliable results it should be inadmissible in court or arbitration proceedings; and (6) The Company has not submitted any corroborative evidence proving the guilt or complicity of grievant in the explosion incident.

Should the arbitrator sustain the discharge? Is refusal to take a polygraph or the results if taken admissible evidence? Evaluate the evidence in light of Gorske's concepts of burden and quantum of proof in disciplinary cases. *Compare American Maize-Products Co.,* 45 L.A. 1155 (A. Epstein, 1965) *and Publishers' Ass'n of New York City,* 43 L.A. 400 (J. Altieri, 1964) *with Westinghouse Electric Corp.,* 43 L.A. 450 (A. Singletary, 1964). For an excellent analysis of the use of lie detector results in arbitration proceedings *see* Arbitrator John F. Sembower's decision in *Spiegel, Inc.,* 44 L.A. 405 (1965); Practice & Procedure 261-264.

I. THE CODE OF PROFESSIONAL RESPONSIBILITY FOR ARBITRATORS OF LABOR-MANAGEMENT DISPUTES

1. Background

Since 1951 arbitrators have operated under a Code of Ethics adopted by the National Academy of Arbitrators, the American Arbitration and the Federal Mediation and Conciliation Service.[32] However, much has changed about labor arbitration since 1951. Widespread adoption of the process by parties to collective bargaining agreements with the imprimatur of the federal courts has created what Professor David Feller calls the "Golden Age of Arbitration." [33] In 1974, when the same three organizations adopted a revision of the 1951 Code — "The Code of Professional Responsibility for Arbitrators of Labor-Management Disputes," more than five times more persons were holding themselves out as qualified to serve as arbitrators than in 1951.[34] One result of increased labor arbitration has been a heavy demand for specific arbitrators which has led to what Professor Harold Davey refers to

---

[32] Elson, Ethical Responsibilities of the Arbitrator, in Proc. of 24th Ann. Meet. Nat'l Acad. Arb., 194 (Dennis & Somers ed. 1971) [hereinafter cited as Ethical Responsibilities].

[33] Feller, The Coming End of Arbitration's Golden Age, in Proc. of 29th Ann. Meet. Nat'l Acad. Arb. (Dennis & Somers ed. 1976).

[34] Miller, Presidential Reflections, in Proc. of 28th Ann. Meet. Nat'l Acad. Arb. 1, 5 (Dennis & Somers ed. 1975).

as the "sins of arbitrators." [35] More recently, Mr. Justice Douglas' adulation has given way to charges of serious misconduct, rigged awards, agreed cases, excessive fees and other procedural irregularities.[36] These charges have probably received more attention than their occurrence warrants, because of the scrutiny given all professionals since the scandals of Watergate.

Nor has interest in ethical concerns been confined to "outsiders." In pressing for a new code, academy members stressed the importance of ethics in the procession. Alex Elsen in making his case for the Code of Professional Responsibility cited an earlier speech:

> "It consists of a membership composed solely of those who are willing and anxious to follow an enlightened consensus on what activities and acts are permissible, demanded, or precluded to the practitioner — basically without fear of organized sanction against the individual. . . . The concern of the classic professions is to see that established emphases upon function, service, and codes of behavior are not chiseled away — our concern is to see that more and more emphasis is put upon performance of function, that more and more we build, through our individual behavior as arbitrators, those codes of right and wrong which keep our efforts focused on performance of function." [37]

Herbert Sherman's articles on an "Arbitrator's Duty to Disclose" are another example of ongoing study of ethical obligations.[38]

The significance of these concerns in contemporary labor arbitration cannot be overemphasized. The arbitration process has grown not only in reputation and size, but in complexity as well. The current impact of external law on the arbitration process and upon the professional responsibility of arbitrators has dramatic significance for at least the next decade of arbitration.[39] The student of this process is well advised to pay considerable attention to the ramifications of the Code of Professional Responsibility.

---

[35] Davey, Situation Ethics and The Arbitrator's Role, in Proc. of 26th Ann. Meet. Nat'l Acad. Arb., 162, 169-70 (Dennis & Somers ed. 1973).

[36] Ethical Responsibilities, *supra* note 32 at 196. *See also* P. Hays, Labor Arbitration: Dissenting View (1966).

[37] Ethical Responsibilities, *supra* note 32 at 196 quoting William Louks Speech at the 13th Annual Meeting of the Academy.

[38] Sherman, The Arbitrator's Duty of Disclosure — A Sequel, in Proc. of 24th Ann. Meet. Nat'l Acad. Arb., 203 (Dennis & Somers ed. 1971); Sherman, The Arbitrator's Duty of Disclosure, 31 U. Pitt. L. Rev. 377 (1970).

[39] Edwards, Labor Arbitration at the Crossroads: The Common Law of the Shop v. External Law, 1977 Arb. J. 65 (1977).

2. The Code

Preamble

Background

Voluntary arbitration rests upon the mutual desire to management and labor in each collective bargaining relationship to develop procedures for dispute settlement which meet their own particular needs and obligations. No two voluntary systems, therefore, are likely to be identical in practice. Words used to describe arbitrators (Arbitrator, Umpire, Impartial Chairman, Chairman of Arbitration Board, etc.) may suggest typical approaches but actual differences within any general type of arrangement may be as great as distinctions often made among the several types.

Some arbitration and related procedures, however, are not the product of voluntary agreement. These procedures, primarily but not exclusively applicable in the public sector, sometime utilize other third party titles (Fact Finder, Impasse Panel, Board of Inquiry, etc.). These procedures range all the way from arbitration prescribed by statute to arrangement substantially indistinguishable from voluntary procedures.

The standards of professional responsibility set forth in this Code are designed to guide the impartial third party serving in these diverse labor-management relationships.

Scope of Code

This Code is a privately developed set of standards of professional behavior. It applies to voluntary arbitration of labor-management grievance disputes and of disputes concerning new or revised contract terms. Both "ad hoc" and "permanent" varieties of voluntary arbitration, private and public sector, are included. To the extent relevant in any specific case, it also applies to advisory arbitration, impasse resolution panels, arbitration prescribed by statutes, fact-finding, and other special procedures.

The word "arbitrator," as used hereinafter in the Code, is intended to apply to any impartial person, irrespective of specific title, who serves in a labor-management dispute procedure in which there is conferred authority to decide issues or to make formal recommendations.

The Code is not designed to apply to mediation or conciliation, as distinguished from arbitration, nor to other procedures in which the third party is not authorized in advance to make decisions or recommendations. It does not apply to partisan representatives on tripartite boards. It does not apply to commercial arbitration or to other uses of arbitration outside the labor-management dispute area.

Format of Code

Bold Face type, sometimes including explanatory material, is used to set forth general principles. *Italics* are used for amplification of general principles. Ordinary type is used primarily for illustrative or explanatory comment.

Application of Code

Faithful adherence by an arbitrator to this Code is basic to professional responsibility.

The National Academy of Arbitrators will expect its members to be governed in their professional conduct by this Code and stands ready, through its Committee on Ethics and Grievances, to advise its members as to the Code's interpretation. The American Arbitration Association and the Federal Mediation and Conciliation Service will apply the Code to the arbitrators on their rosters in cases handled under their respective appointment or referral procedures. Other arbitrators and administrative agencies may, of course, voluntarily adopt the Code and be governed by it.

In interpreting the Code and applying it to charges of professional misconduct, under existing or revised procedures of the National Academy of Arbitrators and of the administrative agencies, it should be recognized that while some of its standards express ethical principles basic to the arbitration profession, others rest less on ethics than on considerations of good practice. Experience has shown the difficulty of drawing rigid lines of distinction between ethics and good practice and this Code does not attempt to do so. Rather, it leaves the gravity of alleged misconduct and the extent to which ethical standards have been violated to be assessed in the light of the facts and circumstances of each particular case.

1

Arbitrator's Qualifications
and Responsibilities
to the Profession

A. General Qualifications

1. Essential personal qualifications of an arbitrator include honesty, integrity, impartiality and general competence in labor relations matters.

An arbitrator must demonstrate ability to exercise these personal qualities faithfully and with good judgment, both in procedural matters and in substantive decisions.

a. Selection by mutual agreement of the parties or direct designation by an administrative agency are the effective methods of appraisal of this combination of an individual's potential and performance, rather than the fact of placement on a roster of an administrative agency or membership in a professional association of arbitrators.

2. An arbitrator must be as ready to rule for one party as for the other on each issue, either in a single case or in a group of cases. Compromise by an arbitrator for the sake of attempting to achieve personal acceptability is unprofessional.

B. Qualifications for Special Cases

1. An arbitrator must decline appointment, withdraw, or request technical assistance when he or she decides that a case is beyond his or her competence.

a. An arbitrator may be qualified generally but not for specialized assignments. Some types of incentive, work standard, job evaluation, welfare program, pension, or insurance cases may require specialized knowledge, experience or competence. Arbitration of contract terms also may require distinctive background and experience.

b. Effective appraisal by an administrative agency or by an arbitrator of the need for special qualifications requires that both parties make known the special nature of the case prior to appointment of the arbitrator.

C. Responsibilities to the Profession

1. An arbitrator must uphold the dignity and integrity of the office and endeavor to provide effective service to the parties.

a. To this end, an arbitrator should keep current with principles, practices and developments that are relevant to his or her own field of arbitration practice.

2. An experienced arbitrator should cooperate in the training of new arbitrators.

3. An arbitrator must not advertise or solicit arbitration assignments.

a. It is a matter of personal preference whether an arbitrator includes "Labor Arbitrator" or similar notation on letterheads, cards, or announcements. *It is inappropriate, however, to include memberships or offices held in professional societies or listings on rosters of administrative agencies.*

b. *Information provided for published biographical sketches, as well as that supplied to administrative agencies, must be accurate.* Such information may include membership in professional organizations (including reference to significant offices held), and listings on rosters of administrative agencies.

2

Responsibilities to
the Parties

A. Recognition of Diversity in Arbitration Arrangements

1. An arbitrator should conscientiously endeavor to understand and observe, to the extent consistent with professional responsibility, the significant principles governing each arbitration system in which he or she serves.

a. Recognition of special features of a particular arbitration arrangement can be essential with respect to procedural matters and may influence other aspects of the arbitration process.

2. Such understanding does not relieve an arbitrator from a corollary responsibility to seek to discern and refuse to lend approval or consent to any collusive attempt by the parties to use arbitration for an improper purpose.

B. Required Disclosures

1. Before accepting an appointment, an arbitrator must disclose directly or through the administrative agency involved, any current or past managerial, representational, or consulative relationship with any company or union involved in a proceeding in which he or she is being considered for appointment or has been tentatively designated to serve. Disclosure must also be made of any pertinent pecuniary interest.

a. The duty to disclose includes membership on a Board of Directors, full-time or part-time service as a representative or advocate, consultation work for a fee, current stock or bond ownership (other than mutual fund shares or appropriate trust arrangements) or any other pertinent form of managerial, financial or immediate family interest in the company or union involved.

2. When an arbitrator is serving concurrently as an advocate for or representative of other companies or unions in labor relations matters, or has done so in recent years, he or she must disclose such activities before accepting appointment as an arbitrator.

An arbitrator must disclose such activities to an administrative agency if he or she is on that agency's active roster or seeks

placement on a roster. Such disclosure then satisfies this requirement for cases handled under that agency's referral.

a. It is not necessary to disclose names of clients or other specific details. It is necessary to indicate the general nature of the labor relations advocacy or representational work involved, whether for companies or unions or both, and a reasonable approximation of the extent of such activity.

b. *An arbitrator on a administrative agency's roster has a continuing obligation to notify the agency of any significant changes pertinent to this requirement.*

c. When an administrative agency is not involved, an arbitrator must make such disclosure directly unless he or she is certain that both parties to the case are fully aware of such activities.

3. An arbitrator must not permit personal relationships to affect decision-making.

Prior to acceptance of an appointment, an arbitrator must disclose to the parties or to the administrative agency involved any close personal relationship or other circumstance, in addition to those specifically mentioned earlier in this section, which might reasonably raise a question as to the arbitrator's impartiality.

a. Arbitrators establish personal relationships with many company and union representatives, with fellow arbitrators, and with fellow members of various professional associations. There should be no attempt to be secretive about such friendships or acquaintances but disclosure is not necessary unless some feature of a particular relationship might reasonably appear to impair impartiality.

4. If the circumstances requiring disclosure are not known to the arbitrator prior to acceptance of appointment, disclosure must be made when such circumstances become known to the arbitrator.

5. The burden of disclosure rests on the arbitrator. After appropriate disclosure, the arbitrator may serve if both parties so desire. If the arbitrator believes or perceives that there is a clear conflict of interest, he or she should withdraw, irrespective of the expressed desires of the parties.

C. Privacy of Arbitration

1. All significant aspects of an arbitration proceeding must be treated by the arbitrator as confidential unless this requirement is waived by both parties or disclosure is required or permitted by law.

a. Attendance at hearings by persons not representing the parties or invited by either or both of them should be permitted only when the parties agree or when an applicable law requires or permits. Occasionally, special circumstances may require that an arbitrator rule on such matters as attendance and degree of participation of counsel selected by a grievant.

b. *Discussion of a case at any time by an arbitrator with persons not involved directly should be limited to situations where advance approval or consent of both parties is obtained or where the identity of the parties and details of the case are sufficiently obscured to eliminate any realistic probability of identification.*

A commonly recognized exception is discussion of a problem in a case with a fellow arbitrator. *Any such discussion does not relieve the arbitrator who is acting in the case from sole responsibility for the decision and the discussion must be considered as confidential.*

Discussion of aspects of a case in a classroom without prior specific approval of the parties is not a violation provided the arbitrator is satisfied that there is no breach of essential confidentiality.

c. *It is a violation of professional responsibility for an arbitrator to make public an award without the consent of the parties.*

An arbitrator may request but not press the parties for consent to publish an opinion. Such a request should normally not be made until after the award has been issued to the parties.

d. It is not improper for an arbitrator to donate arbitration files to a library of a college, university or similar institution without prior consent of all the parties involved. When the circumstances permit, there should be deleted from such donations any cases concerning which one or both of the parties have expressed a desire for privacy. As an additional safeguard, an arbitrator may also decide to withhold recent cases or indicate to the donee a time interval before such cases can be made generally available.

e. *Applicable laws, regulations, or practices of the parties may permit or even require exceptions to the above noted principles of privacy.*

D. Personal Relationships with the Parties

1. An arbitrator must make every reasonable effort to conform to arrangements required by an administrative agency or mutually desired by the parties regarding communications and personal relationships with the parties.

> a. *Only an "arm's-length" relationship may be acceptable to the parties in some arbitration arrangements or may be required by the rules of an administrative agency. The arbitrator should then have no contact of consequence with representatives of either party while handling a case without the other party's presence or consent.*
>
> b. *In other situations, both parties may want communications and personal relationships to be less formal. It is then appropriate for the arbitrator to respond accordingly.*

E. Jurisdiction

1. An arbitrator must observe faithfully both the limitations and inclusions of the jurisdiction conferred by an agreement or other submission under which he or she serves.

2. A direct settlement by the parties of some or all issues in a case, at any stage of the proceedings, must be accepted by the arbitrator as relieving him or her of further jurisdiction over such issues.

F. Mediation by an Arbitrator

1. When the parties wish at the outset to give an arbitrator authority both to mediate and to decide or submit recommendations regarding residual issues, if any, they should so advise the arbitrator prior to appointment. If the appointment is accepted, the arbitrator must perform a mediation role consistent with the circumstances of the case.

> a. Direct appointments, also, may require a dual role as mediator and arbitrator of residual issues. This is most likely to occur in some public sector cases.

2. When a request to mediate is first made after appointment, the arbitrator may either accept or decline a mediation role.

> a. *Once arbitration has been invoked, either party normally has a right to insist that the process be continued to decision.*
>
> b. *If one party requests that the arbitrator mediate and the other party objects, the arbitrator should decline the request.*
>
> c. *An arbitrator is not precluded from making a suggestion that he or she mediate. To avoid the possibility of improper*

pressure, the arbitrator should not so suggest unless it can be discerned that both parties are likely to be receptive. In any event, the arbitrator's suggestion should not be pursued unless both parties readily agree.

G. Reliance by an Arbitrator on Other Arbitration Awards or on Independent Research

1. An arbitrator must assume full personal responsibility for the decision in each case decided.

a. *The extent, if any, to which an arbitrator properly may rely on precedent, on guidance of other awards, or on independent research is dependent primarily on the policies of the parties on these matters, as expressed in the contract, or other agreement, or at the hearing.*

b. When the mutual desires of the parties are not known or when the parties express differing opinions or policies, the arbitrator may exercise discretion as to these matters, consistent with acceptance of full personal responsibility for the award.

H. Use of Assistants

1. An arbitrator must not delegate any decision-making function to another person without consent of the parties.

a. *Without prior consent of the parties, an arbitrator may use the services of an assistant for research, clerical duties, or preliminary drafting under the direction of the arbitrator, which does not involve the delegation of any decision-making function.*

b. *If an arbitrator is unable, because of time limitations or other reasons, to handle all decision-making aspects of a case, it is not a violation of professional responsibility to suggest to the parties an allocation of responsibility between the arbitrator and an assistant or associate. The arbitrator must not exert pressure on the parties to accept such a suggestion.*

I. Consent Awards

1. Prior to issuance of an award, the parties may jointly request the arbitrator to include in the award certain agreements between them, concerning some or all of the issues. If the arbitrator believes that a suggested award is proper, fair, sound, and lawful, it is consistent with professional responsibility to adopt it.

a. *Before complying with such a request, an arbitrator must be certain that he or she understands the suggested settlement adequately in order to be able to appraise its terms. If it appears that pertinent facts or circumstances may not have been disclosed, the arbitrator should take the initiative to assure that all significant aspects of the case are fully understood. To this end, the arbitrator may request additional specific information and may question witnesses at a hearing.*

J. Avoidance of Delay

1. It is a basic professional responsibility of an arbitrator to plan his or her work schedule so that present and future commitments will be fulfilled in a timely manner.

a. When planning is upset for reasons beyond the control of the arbitrator, he or she, nevertheless, should exert every reasonable effort to fulfill all commitments. If this is not possible, prompt notice at the arbitrator's initiative should be given to all parties affected. Such notices should include reasonably accurate estimates of any additional time required. To the extent possible, priority should be given to cases in process so that other parties may make alternative arbitration arrangements.

2. An arbitrator must cooperate with the parties and with any administrative agency involved in avoiding delays.

a. An arbitrator on the active roster of an administrative agency must take the initiative in advising the agency of any scheduling difficulties that he or she can foresee.

b. Requests for services, whether received directly or through an administrative agency, should be declined if the arbitrator is unable to schedule a hearing as soon as the parties wish. If the parties, nevertheless, jointly desire to obtain the services of the arbitrator and the arbitrator agrees, arrangements should be made by agreement that the arbitrator confidently expects to fulfill.

c. An arbitrator may properly seek to persuade the parties to alter or eliminate arbitration procedures or tactics that cause unnecessary delay.

3. Once the case record has been closed, an arbitrator must adhere to the time limits for an award, as stipulated in the labor agreement or as provided by regulation of an administrative agency or as otherwise agreed.

a. If an appropriate award cannot be rendered within the required time, it is incumbent on the arbitrator to seek an extension of time from the parties.

b. If the parties have agreed upon abnormally short time limits for an award after a case is closed, the arbitrator should be so advised by the parties or by the administrative agency involved, prior to acceptance of appointment.

K. Fees and Expenses

1. An arbitrator occupies a position of trust in respect to the parties and the administrative agencies. In charging for services and expenses, the arbitrator must be governed by the same high standards of honor and integrity that apply to all other phases of his or her work.

An arbitrator must endeavor to keep total charges for services and expenses reasonable and consistent with the nature of the case or cases decided.

Prior to appointment, the parties should be aware of or be able readily to determine all significant aspects of an arbitrator's bases for charges for fees and expenses.

a. *Services Not Primarily Chargeable on a Per Diem Basis*

By agreement with the parties, the financial aspects of many "permanent" arbitration assignments, of some interest disputes, and of some "ad hoc" grievance assignments do not include a per diem fee for services as a primary part of the total understanding. *In such situations, the arbitrator must adhere faithfully to all agreed-upon arrangements governing fees and expenses.*

b. *Per Diem Basis for Charges for Services*

(1) *When an arbitrator's charges for services are determined primarily by a stipulated per diem fee, the arbitrator should establish in advance his or her bases for application of such per diem fee and for determination of reimbursable expenses.*

Practices established by an arbitrator should include the basis for charges, if any, for:

(a) hearing time, including the application of the stipulated basic per diem hearing fee to hearing days of varying lengths;

(b) study time;

(c) necessary travel time when not included in charges for hearing time;

(d) postponement or cancellation of hearings by the parties and the circumstances in which such charges will normally be assessed or waived;

(e) office overhead expenses (secretarial, telephone, postage, etc.);

(f) the work of paid assistants or associates.

(2) *Each arbitrator should be guided by the following general principles:*

(a) *Per diem charges for a hearing should not be in excess of actual time spent or allocated for the hearing.*

(b) *Per diem charges for study time should not be in excess of actual time spent.*

(c) *Any fixed ratio of study days to hearing days, not agreed to specifically by the parties, is inconsistent with the per diem method of charges for services.*

(d) *Charges for expenses must not be in excess of actual expenses normally reimbursable and incurred in connection with the case or cases involved.*

(e) *When time or expense are involved for two or more sets of parties on the same day or trip, such time or expense charges should be appropriately prorated.*

(f) *An arbitrator may stipulate in advance a minimum charge for a hearing without violation of (a) or (e) above.*

(3) *An arbitrator on the active roster of an administrative agency must file with the agency his or her individual bases for determination of fees and expenses if the agency so requires. Thereafter, it is the responsibility of each such arbitrator to advise the agency promptly of any change in any basis for charges.*

Such filing may be in the form of answers to a questionnaire devised by an agency or by any other method adopted by or approved by an agency.

Having supplied an administrative agency with the information noted above, an arbitrator's professional responsibility of disclosure under this Code with respect to fees and expenses has been satisfied for cases referred by that agency.

(4) *If an administrative agency promulgates specific standards with respect to any of these matters which are in addition to or more restrictive than an individual arbitrator's standards, an arbitrator on its active roster must observe the agency standards for cases handled under the auspices of that agency, or decline to serve.*

(5) *When an arbitrator is contacted directly by the parties for a case or cases, the arbitrator has a professional responsibility to respond to questions by submitting his or her bases for charges for fees and expenses.*

(6) *When it is known to the arbitrator that one or both of the parties cannot afford normal charges, it is consistent with professional responsibility to charge lesser amounts to both parties or to one of the parties if the other party is made aware of the difference and agrees.*

(7) *If an arbitrator concludes that the total of charges derived from his or her normal basis of calculation is not compatible with the case decided, it is consistent with professional responsibility to charge lesser amounts to both parties.*

2. An arbitrator must maintain adequate records to support charges for services and expenses and must make an accounting to the parties or to an involved administrative agency on request.

3

Responsibilities to
Administrative Agencies

A. General Responsibilities

1. An arbitrator must be candid, accurate, and fully responsive to an administrative agency concerning his or her qualifications, availability, and all other pertinent matters.

2. An arbitrator must observe policies and rules of an administrative agency in cases referred by that agency.

3. An arbitrator must not seek to influence an administrative agency by any improper means, including gifts or other inducements to agency personnel.

   a. It is not improper for a person seeking placement on a roster to request references from individuals having knowledge of the applicant's experience and qualifications.

   b. Arbitrators should recognize that the primary responsibility of an administrative agency is to serve the parties.

4

Prehearing Conduct

1. All prehearing matters must be handled in a manner that fosters complete impartiality by the arbitrator.

   a. The primary purpose of prehearing discussions involving the arbitrator is to obtain agreement on procedural matters so that the hearing can proceed without unnecessary obstacles. If differences of opinion should arise during such discussions and, particularly, if such differences appear to impinge on substantive matters, the circumstances will suggest whether the matter can be resolved informally or may require a prehearing conference or, more rarely, a formal preliminary hearing. When an administrative agency handles some or all aspects of the arrangements prior to a hearing, the arbitrator will become involved only if differences of some substance arise.

   b. *Copies of any prehearing correspondence between the arbitrator and either party must be made available to both parties.*

5

Hearing Conduct

A. General Principles

1. An arbitrator must provide a fair and adequate hearing which assures that both parties have sufficient opportunity to present their respective evidence and argument.

a. *Within the limits of this responsibility, an arbitrator should conform to the various types of hearing procedures desired by the parties.*

b. An arbitrator may: encourage stipulations of fact; restate the substance of issues or arguments to promote or verify understanding; question the parties' representatives or witnesses, when necessary or advisable, to obtain additional pertinent information; and request that the parties submit additional evidence, either at the hearing or by subsequent filing.

c. *An arbitrator should not intrude into a party's presentation so as to prevent that party from putting forward its case fairly and adequately.*

B. Transcripts or Recordings

1. Mutual agreement of the parties as to use or non-use of a transcript must be respected by the arbitrator.

a. *A transcript is the official record of a hearing only when both parties agree to a transcript or an applicable law or regulation so provides.*

b. An arbitrator may seek to persuade the parties to avoid use of a transcript, or to use a transcript if the nature of the case appears to require one. *However, if an arbitrator intends to make his or her appointment to a case contingent on mutual agreement to a transcript, that requirement must be made known to both parties prior to appointment.*

c. If the parties do not agree to a transcript, an arbitrator may permit one party to take a transcript at its own cost. The arbitrator may also make appropriate arrangements under which the *other* party may have access to a copy, if a copy is provided to the arbitrator.

d. Without prior approval, an arbitrator may seek to use his or her own tape recorder to supplement note taking. The arbitrator should not insist on such a tape recording if either or both parties object.

C. Ex Parte Hearings

1. In determining whether to conduct an ex parte hearing, an arbitrator must consider relevant legal, contractual, and other pertinent circumstances.

2. An arbitrator must be certain, before proceeding ex parte, that the party refusing or failing to attend the hearing has been given adequate notice of the time, place, and purposes of the hearing.

D. Plant Visits

1. An arbitrator should comply with a request of any party that he or she visit a work area pertinent to the dispute prior to, during, or after a hearing. An arbitrator may also initiate such a request.

a. *Procedures for such visits should be agreed to by the parties in consultation with the arbitrator.*

E. Bench Decisions or Expedited Awards

1. When an arbitrator understands, prior to acceptance of appointment, that a bench decision is expected at the conclusion of the hearing, the arbitrator must comply with the understanding unless both parties agree otherwise.

a. *If notice of the parties' desire for a bench decision is not given prior to the arbitrator's acceptance of the case, issuance of such a bench decision is discretionary.*

b. *When only one party makes the request and the other objects, the arbitrator should not render a bench decision except under most unusual circumstances.*

2. When an arbitrator understands, prior to acceptance of appointment, that a concise written award is expected within a stated time period after the hearing, the arbitrator must comply with the understanding unless both parties agree otherwise.

6

Post Hearing Conduct

A. Post Hearing Briefs and Submissions

1. An arbitrator must comply with mutual agreements in respect to the filing or nonfiling of post hearing briefs or submissions.

a. An arbitrator, in his or her discretion, may either suggest the filing of post hearing briefs or other submissions or suggest that none be filed.

b. When the parties disagree as to the need for briefs, an arbitrator may permit filing but may determine a reasonable time limitation.

2. An arbitrator must not consider a post hearing brief or submission that has not been provided to the other party.

B. Disclosure of Terms of Award

1. An arbitrator must not disclose a prospective award to either party prior to its simultaneous issuance to both parties or explore possible alternative awards unilaterally with one party, unless both parties so agree.

a. Partisan members or tripartite boards may know prospective terms of an award in advance of its issuance. Similar situations may exist in other less formal arrangements mutually agreed to by the parties. In any such situation, the arbitrator should determine and observe the mutually desired degree of confidentiality.

C. Awards and Opinions

1. The award should be definite, certain, and as concise as possible.

a. When an opinion is required, factors to be considered by an arbitrator include: desirability of brevity, consistent with the nature of the case and any expressed desires of the parties; need to use a style and form that is understandable to responsible representatives of the parties, to the grievant and supervisors, and to others in the collective bargaining relationship; necessity of meeting the significant issues; forthrightness to an extent not harmful to the relationship of the parties; and avoidance of gratuitous advice or discourse not essential to disposition of the issues.

D. Clarification or Interpretation of Awards

1. No clarification or interpretation of an award is permissible without the consent of both parties.
2. Under agreements which permit or require clarification or interpretation of an award, an arbitrator must afford both parties an opportunity to be heard.

E. Enforcement of Award

1. The arbitrator's responsibility does not extend to the enforcement of an award.

2. In view of the professional and confidential nature of the arbitration relationship, an arbitrator should not voluntarily participate in legal enforcement proceedings.

3. A Problem

HOLODNAK v. AVCO CORP.

381 F. Supp. 191 (D. Conn. 1974, *modified,* 514 F.2d 285
(2d Cir.), *cert. denied,* 423 U.S. 892 (1975).

Lumbard, Circuit Judge:

Michael Holodnak brings this action against Avco-Lycoming Division of Avco Corporation and Local 1010 of the United Auto Worker of America, challenging his dismissal on May 28, 1969, for publishing an article critical of company and union practices. He claims $79,569.88 in damages with interest and counsel fees of $50,000.

In his first cause of action, Holodnak argues that the award of arbitrator Burton Turkus, upholding his discharge, should be vacated under § 10 of the Federal Arbitration Act, 9 U.S.C. § 10, because of the "evident partiality" of the arbitrator and because the arbitrator exceeded his power, principally by making an award in disregard of Holodnak's First Amendment rights.[1] In his second cause of action, Holodnak maintains that his discharge violated his contractual rights under the collective bargaining agreement, and he should therefore be reinstated and fully compensated for losses suffered, pursuant to § 301 of the Labor Management Relations Act (LMRA), 29 U.S.C. § 185. In his final cause of action, Holodnak asserts that Local 1010 breached its duty of fair representation, thereby entitling him to reinstatement and monetary damages, also under § 301 of the LMRA.[2]

---

[1] Holodnak also argues that the arbitrator exceeded his powers since the maximum allowable penalty for violation of the plant conduct rule which the plaintiff was accused of violating is a written warning. The plaintiff is mistaken in this as the plant conduct rules specifically provide for discharge. See p. 194 *infra.*

[2] Courts of appeals, however, have made it clear that a suit against a union for breach of the duty of fair representation is not an action under § 301; rather, it is a breach of a duty implied from the grant to the union of exclusive power to represent employees of the collective bargaining unit in § 9(a) of the National Labor Relations Act, 29 U.S.C. § 159(a). Jurisdiction is under 28 U.S.C. § 1337. See Retana v. Apartment, Motel, Hotel, & Elevator Operators, Local 14, 453 F.2d 1018, 1021-1022 (9th Cir. 1972); De Arroyo v. Sindicato de Trabajadores Packinghouse, 425 F.2d 281, 283 n. 1 (1st Cir.), *cert. denied,* 400 U.S. 877, 91 S.Ct. 117, 27 L.Ed.2d 114 (1970).

Holodnak's allegations were substantially denied by both defendants, who also raised three special defenses: that the plaintiff had failed to state a claim upon which relief could be granted; that the suit was barred by the statute of limitations; and, that, under the contract between Avco and Local 1010, the arbitrator's conclusion that there was "just cause" for Holodnak's discharge was final and binding.

On July 17, 1970, Judge Zampano denied motions by the defendants Avco and Local 1010 to dismiss. After discovery and a pre-trial conference, cross motions for summary judgment by the plaintiff and the defendant Avco were heard by Magistrate Latimer who recommended denial, which was so ordered by Judge Zampano. A two-day trial without a jury then commenced before this court on April 29, 1974.

I.

On May 28, 1969, at approximately 9:30 a. m., Holodnak received a written notice that he was to report to Avco's labor relations office for a "disciplinary hearing." At 10 a. m., accompanied by his shop steward, Frank Guida, and committeeman Joe Mezick, Holodnak entered the labor relations office, where several management officials were present. William Ashlaw, a company representative showed Holodnak a copy of an article written by the plaintiff and published in the AIM Newsletter of May 15, 1969. The article is reproduced as an appendix to this opinion. The newsletter, a biweekly, was published in New Haven by the American Independent Movement, whose activities included running a candidate for Congress. The AIM Newsletter's circulation was approximately 750. There was no evidence concerning how many, if any, of Avco's employees received this publication.

Ashlaw informed Holodnak that this article violated plant conduct rule 19 which provided:

> The below listed rules constitute prohibited conduct. Offenses under these rules may be cause for suspension or discharge.
>
> . . .
>
> 19. Making false, vicious or malicious statements concerning any employee or which affect the employee's relationship to his job, his supervisors, or the Company's products, property, reputation, or good will in the community.[4]

Ashlaw read several paragraphs from the article aloud. The article, which was two printed pages, generally criticized both Avco and

---

[4] The plant conduct rules were incorporated by reference into the collective bargaining agreement, which allowed Avco to promulgate rules of conduct. Article XVI, § 4.

Union officials. Holodnak wrote that the "current course of moderation, charted by the Shop Committee, is alienating and frustrating the membership to no end." He accused the company, "like all large corporations," of engaging in "union busting tactics, which run the gamut from sweet talk, giving special privileges to company oriented candidates, . . . to making it miserable for and sometimes firing the really dedicated unionists, and last but not least, buying off whatever other effective opposition may be left with a foremanship." Turning then to the tactics which the workers might employ, the plaintiff noted that it is "probably true that wildcat strikes are not the answer, but wildcats wouldn't even be tempting if we had a good solid union that knows where it's at and that does not, through the grievance procedure, compromise away our rights. Yet it is comforting to have wildcats in our arsenal of weapons, just in case."

The process for resolving grievances came under particular attack. Holodnak wrote that "the company gets away with its devious and unfair labor practices because the company is above the law, (even the more naive realize this) and the biased judges and arbitrators, for all practical purposes, belong to the company. The most recent example was the firing of the twenty-two so-called 'hard core of miscreants.' From his Heavenly perch the 'impartial' Arbitrator, backing up the company, pronounced his God-like opinion upon us poor sinful mortals while praising the pure-as-the-snow 'patient company' to the high heavens."

Holodnak concluded by emphasizing "that nothing has ever been accomplished by so-called 'reasonable people' . . . The labor movement itself would have never been born if the workers had been 'reasonable.' "

Ashlaw asked Holodnak whether he subscribed to the views expressed in the article and Holodnak said he did. Ashlaw then questioned a company security officer about the American Independent Movement and asked whether it was on the Attorney General's subversive list. The security officer answered that it was not. At the end of the meeting, despite a request by committeeman Joe Mezick to have a lesser charge carrying a reduced penalty brought against Holodnak, Ashlaw asked for Holodnak's badge and informed him that he was discharged. Holodnak had worked at the Avco plant for nine years, first as a tool-and-die maker and then as a small-parts inspector.

Following his discharge, the plaintiff contacted George Johnson, an attorney for AIM. It was agreed that Holodnak should permit the union to pursue the normal three-stage grievance procedure and then, if necessary, resort to arbitration. The grievance procedure proved unsuccessful and an arbitration hearing at the union's request was scheduled. Prior to this hearing, Holodnak asked that Edward

Burstein, the attorney for Local 1010, represent him. Although union members were usually represented by a committeeman at arbitration proceedings, the union attorney did so from time to time. On July 8, 1969, Johnson, the AIM attorney who was advising Holodnak, spoke with Burstein on the phone and offered his assistance. Burstein expressed his pleasure at Johnson's offer, but never communicated with him again.

On July 17, 1969, the arbitration was held before arbitrator Burton Turkus at the Howard Johnson Motor Inn in West Haven, Connecticut. Here Burstein met the plaintiff for the first time. In the course of their ten or fifteen minute meeting, Burstein read the controversial article for the first time.

When the arbitration began, Burstein asked to be informed which rule Holodnak had been accused of violating.[5] After being informed, Burstein indicated Holodnak's right of free speech was at stake. But later when the arbitrator asked whether Holodnak would be attacking Plant Conduct Rule 19 on First Amendment grounds, Burstein agreed that rule 19 was a "fair and reasonable rule, regulation, policy requirement" and that the rule did not infringe on "the exercise of free speech." [6]

As the arbitration proceeded, the company representative, along with Arbitrator Turkus, inquired into the plaintiff's political and social views as well as his personal background. He was asked about the books he read, the candidates he supported for political office, and his views on "corporatism." Most striking was the extent to which the arbitrator participated in this irrelevant and, at times, offensive questioning. Thus, at one point he asked Holodnak

---

[5] At the arbitration, plaintiff indicated that he was satisfied to have Edward Burstein representing him and that he had discussed his grievance with Burstein. At trial, Holodnak indicated that he did not realize at the time the degree to which Burstein inadequately represented him. There is no reason to consider his comments at the arbitration in any way binding.

[6] Both the Company and the union claim that Burstein's statements are inadmissible because of Conn.Gen.Stat. § 52-172, which allows the declarations of a deceased to be admitted in actions by or against the estate of the deceased. Since Burstein has since died and his estate is not a party to this action, it is claimed that his statements are not admissible in any other proceeding. Section 52-172, however, was intended to do away with the rule that a party was disqualified to testify in an action against the deceased's estate. See generally, C. McCormick, Evidence § 65 (2d ed. 1972). This section, recommended by the ABA in 1938 as a model, *id.* at 144 n. 32, certainly was not intended to bar testimony where there had been no bar previously. Antedomenico v. Antedomenico, 142 Conn. 558, 115 A.2d 659 (1955), and Mooney v. Mooney, 80 Conn. 446, 68 A. 985 (1908), cited by the union, merely stand for the proposition that § 52-172 does not allow the admission of otherwise inadmissible hearsay. Here there is no reason not to consider Burstein's comments as recorded at the arbitration proceeding and his brief on Holodnak's behalf.

In any event, this court is not necessarily bound by Connecticut rules of evidence. See Fed.R.Civ.P. 43(a).

whether he had travelled to Cuba in 1960 and had written articles based on his experiences and his views of the "Castro system." He questioned Holodnak repeatedly about his motives for writing the article which had led to his discharge.

Emphasis throughout the proceeding seemed to be on instructing Holodnak on the mistake of his ways. At one point the arbitrator told him, referring to Holodnak's comments suggesting that the union was not doing all that it might, "[N]ow you know differently, don't you." At another point, the arbitrator instructed him:

> "Well, don't you know, as a fact, when you wrote the article, that you have here a very militant and zealous union that seeks the protection of the rights of its membership and seeks to endorse (sic) all Company obligations under the contract. Didn't you know that when you wrote the article?"

Throughout this line of questioning the union attorney made no objection. Indeed, the record of the arbitration reveals only the most half-hearted efforts on his part to object to the irrelevant and improper statements made by the arbitrator and the counsel for Avco.

Testimony at the trial revealed that Holodnak's article was less vituperative and critical of company and union practices than numerous other articles and leaflets, many of which had been distributed at the plant by the union. These leaflets included the descriptions of company officials as "the Mickey Mouse managers of Stratford's Disneyland" with "a superb talent for being both inconsistent and incompetent." The supervision at the plant is described in one circular as "the political cesspool of mahogany row" that "has no regard for human dignity." General foremen are depicted as "brainless" and the grievance proceedings as a "weekly farce." Two union officials who testified at trial, Frank Guida and Joe Mezick, made clear that Holodnak's article was not nearly as harsh in its criticisms as much of the material circulated among workers at the plant.

After the conclusion of the arbitration hearing, the parties submitted post-arbitration briefs. The brief submitted by attorney Burstein on behalf of Holodnak was harsh in its characterization of Holodnak. Holodnak was described as "politically conscious to an inordinate degree." It stated that: "It is said, 'A little knowledge is a dangerous thing', and so it is with Michael Holodnak — that which he knows is but a scintilla of what he doesn't know!" Then Burstein repudiated much of Holodnak's testimony at the arbitration: "Testimony throughout is replete with examples of this man's superficial knowledge, which because it was gleaned informally, is oftimes wrong and even childlike in its naivete." Burstein "respectfully submitted that grievant really knew not what he was doing . . . and that the arbitrator should consider this in making his decision as to whether the termination was proper and just." Burstein then argued only briefly that there was no evidence that Holodnak's comments had been false, vicious, or malicious and that the company had waived any right to discharge an employee for violation of rule 19.

Pursuant to Article V, § 1.a. of the collective bargaining agreement then in force, which gave Avco the right to discharge for "just cause," arbitrator Turkus, on December 18, 1969, rendered a one-sentence award which stated that the proof "establishes the just cause for the discharge . . . with conclusive finality." Article IV, § 1.b. of the collective bargaining agreement further provided that the "decision of the *Arbitrator* shall be final and binding."

At the time of the plaintiff's discharge, the Avco plant in Stratford was owned by the government, as was virtually all the machinery and the land upon which it was located. Military personnel were present at all times to guarantee quality control of the plant's output. Eighty percent of the production of the plant was in the form of military hardware: nose cones for missiles, helicopter engines, and constant speed drives for fighter planes. The plant in Stratford as well as one in South Carolina is part of the Avco-Lycoming Division of the Avco Corporation, a widely diversified comglomerate.

[The Court found that the plaintiff's action to vacate the arbitrator's award was not time barred.]

. . .

III.

The next question is whether the arbitrator's award, "final and binding" under the collective bargaining agreement, may be vacated by this court.[7]

In his first cause of action, Holodnak seeks to vacate the arbitrator's award pursuant to 9 U.S.C. § 10. One of the grounds urged for setting aside the award is the arbitrator's "evident partiality." It is settled that upon judicial review of an arbitrator's award, "the court's function in . . . vacating an arbitration award is severely limited," *Amicizia Societa Navegazione v. Chilean Nitrate & Iodine Sales Corp.,* 274 F.2d 805, 808 (2d Cir.), *cert. denied,* 363 U.S. 843, 80 S.Ct. 1612, 4 L.Ed.2d 1727 (1960), and is confined to determining

---

[7] Both the plaintiff and the defendants assume that the provisions of the Federal Arbitration Act are applicable to this labor arbitration. While there has been considerable debate on whether the Act applies to labor arbitration, the Second Circuit is of the view that it does. *See* Bell Aerospace Co. v. Local 516, UAW, 500 F.2d 921 (2d Cir. 1974); International Assn. of Machinists v. General Electric Co., 406 F.2d 1046, 1049-1050 (2d Cir. 1969).

whether one of the grounds for vacation specified in 9 U.S.C. § 10 is available, *Office of Supply, Republic of Korea v. New York Navigation Co.,* 469 F.2d 377 (2d Cir. 1972). One such ground is the arbitrator's partiality.

"[W]hen a claim of partiality is made, the court is under an obligation to scan the record to see if it demonstrates 'evident partiality' on the part of the arbitrators." *Saxis Steamship Co. v. Multifacs International Traders, Inc.,* 375 F.2d 577, 582 (2d Cir. 1967); *Ballantine Books, Inc. v. Capital Distributing Co.,* 302 F.2d 17 (2d Cir. 1962). The transcript of the arbitration here discloses substantial evidence of partiality on the part of the arbitrator, if not open hostility toward the plaintiff. Throughout the proceeding, the arbitrator permitted inquiries to be made into the books Holodnak read, his political views, and his personal background. The arbitrator himself participated in questioning the plaintiff about a trip to Cuba in 1960 and his views on Castroism. Repeatedly, he showed an undue concern for the plaintiff's motives in writing the article published in the AIM Newsletter and what Holodnak was trying to "signal" to his readers. Indeed, at times the arbitrator openly badgered the plaintiff, as when he persistently questioned Holodnak about his statement that "reasonableness" on the part of workers in pressing their demands might not be the best way to achieve their goals. This line of questioning culminated with an exchange:

> (Arbitrator): Well, it was the general tenor and purport of the article to indicate that the Union officials of this Union were supine and were not doing the job that they were supposed to do. Isn't that the whole purpose of your article?
> (Holodnak): Well, at that time I thought that was true, that they weren't quite doing the job.
> (Arbitrator): But now you know differently, don't you?

Later the arbitrator took issue with Holodnak's view that the union should be more agressive in handling grievances:

> (Arbitrator): Well, don't you know, as a fact, when you wrote this article, that you have here a very militant and zealous union that seeks the protection of rights of its membership and seeks to endorse (sic) all Company obligations under the contract? Didn't you know that when you wrote the article?
> (Holodnak): Well, I didn't say that they didn't enforce it. I'm pointing out the shortcoming here. I know there are some good things they do, a lot of good things.
> (Arbitrator): Well, certainly when you wrote this article, you knew that there was no shortcoming, that this was not a supine Union that sat by and allowed the Company to do whatever it wanted; you knew that when you wrote it."

The arbitrator seemed compelled to convince Holodnak that he was wrong in criticizing the grievance system to which the arbitrator himself had been appointed as the permanent umpire.

The clear bias revealed by the arbitrator's comments throughout the arbitration proceeding requires that the award be vacated. 9 U.S.C. § 10.

IV.

Because the plaintiff seeks not only vacation of the arbitrator's award, but also reinstatement and damages, his claims under § 301 of the LMRA, 29 U.S.C. § 185, must be considered. Section 301 provides for private suits for violation of collective bargaining agreements. The right to bring suit is not restricted to the representative union, but may be exercised by an employee in his own behalf. *Smith v. Evening News Association,* 371 U.S. 195, 200-201, 83 S.Ct. 267, 9 L.Ed.2d 246 (1962). Here there is no problem of a failure to exhaust grievance and arbitration procedures, since Holodnak has pursued fully the recourse provided in the collective bargaining agreement. Such procedures having been exhausted, the plaintiff may properly seek relief for breach of contract under the collective bargaining agreement pursuant to § 301 of the LMRA. *See Republic Steel Corp. v. Maddox,* 379 U.S. 650, 85 S.Ct. 614, 13 L.Ed.2d 580 (1965).

Ordinarily, an employee may not challenge in the courts the decision of an arbitrator where based on an interpretation of the collective bargaining agreement following a fair hearing of his grievance. *United Steel-Workers of America v. Enterprise Wheel & Car Corp.,* 363 U.S. 593, 598-599, 80 S.Ct. 1358, 4 L.Ed.2d 1424 (1960). However, where the union has failed to provide him with fair representation in the course of the grievance or arbitration process, the arbitrator's award is not binding on the employee and he may maintain an action under § 301 of the LMRA against the employer and the union. *Vaca v. Sipes,* 386 U.S. 171, 184-186, 87 S.Ct. 903, 17 L.Ed.2d 842 (1967). The reason is that the employee's grievance can hardly have been given due consideration by the arbitrator when it was not fairly presented by his representative union. *Id.* at 185, 87 S.Ct. 903.[8] Here there can be little question that Holodnak was not

[8] In Margetta v. Pam Pam Corp., 354 F. Supp. 158 (N.D.Cal. 1973), the district court held that the reasoning of Vaca v. Sipes, *supra,* did not apply to cases in which the grievant had actually exhausted all the remedies provided by the collective bargaining agreement and then claimed that he had been unfairly represented. The court rejects this view. The clear import of *Vaca* is that the grievant must be afforded meaningful representation and denial of such representation requires that the grievant be permitted an opportunity to bring his own action in the district court. *See* Griffin v. UAW, 469 F.2d 181 (4th Cir. 1972); Andrus v. Convoy Co., 480 F.2d 604, 606 (9th Cir.), *cert. denied,* 414 U.S. 989, 94 S.Ct. 286, 38 L.Ed.2d 228 (1973); Harris v. Chemical Leaman Tank Lines, Inc., 437 F.2d 167, 171 (5th Cir. 1971).

fairly represented at the arbitration by his union's attorney, Edward Burstein.

In *Vaca v. Sipes,* Mr. Justice White said, "A breach of the statutory duty of fair representation occurs only when a union's conduct toward a member of the collective bargaining unit is arbitrary, discriminatory, or in bad faith." 386 U.S. at 190, 87 S.Ct. at 916. It is clear that the union's representation of Holodnak constitutes a breach of the duty of fair representation. The harsh and unfair description of Holodnak contained in Burstein's brief is at best a misguided attempt to plead for mercy from the arbitrator, *cf. Bazarte v. United Transportation Union,* 429 F.2d 868 (3d Cir. 1970), and is at worst an indication of the union's bad faith. This need not be decided since the union breached its duty of fair representation because of the perfunctory manner in which the union handled the arbitration. See *Vaca, supra,* 386 U.S. at 191, 87 S.Ct. 903.

Although the Second Circuit has not yet passed upon the point, see, *e.g., Pyzynski v. New York Cent. R. R.,* 421 F.2d 854 (2d Cir. 1970), other courts of appeals have held that arbitrary conduct in handling a meritorious grievance in a perfunctory manner is a breach of the duty of fair representation.[9] *See Griffin v. UAW, supra,* 469 F.2d at 182-183; *Retana v. Elevator Operators, supra,* 453 F.2d at 1024 n. 10; *De Arroyo v. Sindicato de Trabajadores Packinghouse, supra,* 425 F.2d at 283-284. *See generally* Clark, *supra* note 9. There is little doubt that Burstein represented Holodnak in a perfunctory manner. Although he recognized that important free speech rights were involved, he conceded, probably because of inadequate preparation, that rule 19, which is certainly vague and easily susceptible to an overbroad interpretation, was reasonable. Although the collective bargaining agreement did give the company the right to promulgate rules of conduct, Burstein should have argued that the parties to the agreement did not intend to allow

---

[9] The description of the duty of fair representation contained in Amalgamated Association of Street Employees v. Lockridge, 403 U.S. 274, 301, 91 S.Ct. 1909, 29 L.Ed.2d 473 (1971), which emphasized bad faith, does not change this conclusion. That case was concerned with pre-emption of a claim by the National Labor Relations Board and gave no indication that it intended to change the duty of fair representation as stated in *Vaca.* See Clark, The Duty of Fair Representation: A Theoretical Structure, 51 Texas L.Rev. 1119, 1126 (1973).

NLRB pre-emption of Holodnak's claims is no problem here. While the company's dismissal of him is arguably an unfair labor practice, see NLRB v. Nu-Car Carriers, Inc., 189 F.2d 756, 760 (2d Cir. 1951), *cert. denied,* 342 U.S. 919, 72 S.Ct. 367, 96 L.Ed. 687 (1952), Holodnak may nonetheless sue under § 301, see Smith v. Evening News Assn., *supra.* Likewise, while the union's breach of its duty of fair representation may be an unfair labor practice, see NLRB v. Miranda Fuel Co., 326 F.2d 172 (2d Cir. 1963), Holodnak may still sue the union in district court for the breach. See Vaca v. Sipes, *supra.*

dismissal for conduct such as Holodnak's.[10] Burstein should have emphasized the important free speech considerations and demanded that rule 19 be strictly construed so that it was at least limited to situations in which the false, vicious or malicious statements concerned any *particular* employee or situations in which the statements were *proved* to have affected the employee's relationship to his job or the company's reputation in the community. Finally, Burstein made no effort to distinguish what might be considered to be factual statements in Holodnak's article from statements of opinion and rhetorical hyperbole. Indicative of this passive approach by Burstein is the minimal effort on his part to object when the arbitration proceeding became an inquisition into Holodnak's beliefs.

The union was not faced with the task of balancing the interests of one set of employees it represents with another. Holodnak's right was the right of all its members to express their views on labor-management relations. Under these circumstances, the court must hold that the union's representation of Holodnak was sadly lacking and was arbitrary.

V.

Even though the union failed in its duty to provide fair representation, the question remains whether Holodnak has a meritorious claim under § 301 of the LMRA.

The crux of Holodnak's § 301 claim is that his discharge by Avco was in breach of Article V, Section 1 of the Collective Bargaining Agreement of April 16, 1967, between the company and the union, which provided that "The Company shall have the right to discharge or discipline employees for just cause." Holodnak maintains that his discharge was not for "just cause" since it was due to his exercising of his First Amendment rights by authorship of the article published in the AIM Newsletter.

In determining whether Holodnak was fired without "just cause" this court must take due account of Holodnak's First Amendment rights. *See Shelley v. Kraemer,* 334 U.S. 1, 68 S.Ct. 836, 92 L.Ed. 1161 (1948). There is no doubt that Holodnak was discharged because of what he wrote in the article. If Holodnak's dismissal

---

[10] It is now clear that a union cannot bargain away its members' rights under § 7 of the National Labor Relations Act, 29 U.S.C. § 157, to distribute pro- or anti-union literature in the plant so long as production or discipline is not disturbed. NLRB v. Magnavox Co., 415 U.S. 322, 94 S.Ct. 1099, 39 L.Ed.2d 358 (1974). If Holodnak's conduct was protected by § 7, *see* note 9 *supra,* then presumably the union here could not validly agree to any infringement of his rights. This, of course, would be a matter for determination, in the first instance, by the NLRB.

infringed his First Amendment rights, the court must hold his discharge was without "just cause" and Avco breached the collective bargaining agreement.

The First Amendment is a protection against governmental infringement of speech. There is no First Amendment protection, however, from infringement by a private employer. *NLRB v. Edward G. Budd Mfg. Co.,* 169 F.2d 571, 577 (6th Cir. 1948), *cert. denied,* 335 U.S. 908, 69 S.Ct. 411, 93 L.Ed. 441 (1949); *cf. Buckley v. American Fed. of Television & Radio Artists,* 496 F.2d 305 (2d Cir. 1974).

The parties here have disputed whether the links between Avco and the federal government are so substantial as to provide the requisite degree of governmental action to enable Holodnak to challenge his discharge on First Amendment grounds. The evidence adduced at trial reveals that Avco is a major defense contractor. Beverly Warren, Avco vice president and chief operating officer at the Stratford plant, testified that approximately 80% of the work done at the plant at the time of the plaintiff's discharge was defense-related and primarily directed toward producing aircraft engines, missile nose cones, and constant speed drives for the military. Nearly all the land, buildings, machinery, and equipment at the Stratford plant were owned by the government. The Department of Defense maintained a large task force at the plant to oversee operations, assure contract compliance and guarantee quality control.

The question of how much government involvement constitutes "state action" does not lend itself to a simple answer. Rather, as the Supreme Court emphasized in *Burton v. Wilmington Parking Authority,* 365 U.S. 715, 81 S.Ct. 856, 6 L.Ed.2d 45 (1961), the task is one of "sifting facts and weighing circumstances," *id.* at 722, 81 S.Ct. 856, a procedure, which as Judge Friendly has recently noted, "has survived much better than attempts at more definitive formulations." *Wahba v. New York University,* 492 F.2d 96, 101-102 (2d Cir. 1974).

In the *Burton* case, a restaurant located in an automobile parking building had refused to serve a customer because of his race. The building in which the restaurant was located was owned by the State of Delaware with the restaurant as a lessee. Reversing the Supreme Court of Delaware and holding that there was "state action," the Supreme Court emphasized that the land and building were publicly owned, the cost of land acquisitions, construction, and maintenance had been defrayed by public funds, and the restaurant was an "indispensable part of the State's plan to operate its project as a self-sustaining unit," 365 U.S. at 723-724, 81 S.Ct. at 861. Many of these same factors are present here. Not only were the land, buildings, and equipment all owned by the government, but the production at the plant was almost entirely for the military.

Wahba v. New York University, supra, on which *Avco* relies is clearly distinguishable on its facts. As the court of appeals stressed, "decisions dealing with one form of state involvement and a particular provision of the Bill of Rights [are not] at all determinative in passing upon claims concerning different forms of government involvement and other constitutional guarantees." 492 F.2d at 100.

Here we are concerned with substantial governmental involvement at Avco's Stratford plant. The fact that Avco-Lycoming Division also operated a second plant in South Carolina engaged in other production and is part of a far-flung conglomerate does not alter the conclusion that there is governmental action. The right here involves the basic right of freedom of speech and press and the firing of Holodnak for expressing his views is "offensive." *See Wahba, supra,* 492 F.2d at 102. For present purposes, the court concludes that there was sufficient governmental action for the First Amendment to apply.

In light of this governmental presence, the plaintiff's discharge for writing an article must be analyzed to determine if First Amendment rights have been infringed. The First Amendment does not guarantee an absolute right of free speech. Concerning discharges of public employees, the Supreme Court has held that the interest of the employee in free speech must be balanced against the employer's interest in job efficiency. *Pickering v. Board of Education,* 391 U.S. 563, 568, 88 S.Ct. 1731, 20 L.Ed.2d 811 (1968). *See also Linn v. Plant Guards, Local 114,* 383 U.S. 53, 86 S.Ct. 657, 15 L.Ed.2d 582 (1963).

[The Court then held *Arnett v. Kennedy,* 416 U.S. 134 (1974) and *Birdwell v. Hazelwood School District,* 352 F. Supp. 613 (E.D. Mo. 1972) inapposite.]

. . .

Since the cases cited by defendants are not in point, the court must balance the competing interests as suggested in *Pickering.* Read fairly, Holodnak's article is an analysis of why unions lose their militancy. It is largely composed of Holodnak's opinions concerning labor-management relations at Avco and as such is a matter of employee interest clearly protected. [11] Furthermore, many of the statements in the article that could be read as statements of facts are more reasonably read as rhetorical hyperbole, and as such are constitutionally protected. *Greenbelt Cooperative Publishing Assn. v. Bresler,* 398 U.S. 6, 11-14, 90 S.Ct. 1537, 26 L.Ed.2d 6 (1970); *cf. Watts v. United States,* 394 U.S. 705, 89 S.Ct. 1399, 22 L.Ed.2d 664 (1969). Finally, as noted above, none of the statements

---

[11] "Under the First Amendment there is no such thing as a false idea. However pernicious an opinion may seem, we depend for its correction not on the conscience of judges and juries but on the competition of other ideas." Gertz v. Robert Welch, Inc., 418 U.S. 323, 94 S.Ct. 2997, 3007, 41 L.Ed.2d 789 (1974).

concerned any particular person. Thus it must be concluded that Holodnak's article was constitutionally protected regardless of the truth or falsity of the few statements of facts in it. See generally *Gertz v. Robert Welch, Inc., supra; New York Times Co. v. Sullivan, supra.*

Against Holodnak's interest in having his say, Avco's interest in maintaining efficiency in production is insufficient. As noted above, vituperative articles such as Holodnak's were quite common at Avco and evidently they have not interfered with production. Avco strongly argues that Holodnak's article favored wildcat strikes, which were a problem at Stratford. But the article in fact questions the effectiveness of such strikes and does not advocate them. While Holodnak's belief, expressed at the arbitration hearing, that workers had a constitutional right to engage in a wildcat strike was mistaken, *see Boys Markets, Inc. v. Retail Clerks, Local 770,* 398 U.S. 235, 90 S.Ct. 1583, 26 L.Ed.2d 199 (1970), his article falls far short of being "incitement to imminent lawless action." *Brandenburg v. Ohio,* 395 U.S. 444, 449, 89 S.Ct. 1827, 23 L.Ed.2d 430 (1969).

The balance, therefore, clearly tips in favor of Holodnak's right to free speech. It is noteworthy that even in private enterprise where the guarantees of the First Amendment do not apply, federal statutes have given employees the right to speak their minds on labor relations. Section 7 of the National Labor Relations Act, 29 U.S.C. § 157, gives employees the "right to self-organization, to form, join, or assist labor organizations, to bargain collectively through representatives of their own choosing, and to engage in other concerted activities for the purpose of collective bargaining or other mutual aid or protection. . . ." Interference with these rights by an employer is an unfair labor practice. 29 U.S.C. § 158(a)(1). Only recently in *NLRB v. Magnavox Co., supra,* 415 U.S. 322, 94 S.Ct. 1099, 39 L.Ed.2d 358, the Supreme Court upheld a finding of an unfair labor practice where a company rule forbade the distribution of pro- and anti-union literature within the plant, even though the collective bargaining agreement authorized the rule. *See also Republic Aviation Corp. v. NLRB,* 324 U.S. 793, 65 S.Ct. 982, 89 L.Ed. 1372 (1945). Of course, the question of whether Holodnak's discharge is an unfair labor practice is not for a district court to decide. *See* notes 9 & 10, *supra.* But *Magnavox* by analogy supports the conclusion that the First Amendment can allow no greater restrictions by a public employer on the right of employees to write articles which are circulated outside the plant and which in no way interfere with production.

Moreover, Congress has shown its interest in ensuring the right of employees to speak out on matters of union representation in § 101(a)(2) of the Labor-Management Reporting and Disclosure Act, 29 U.S.C. § 411(a)(2), which provides: "Every member of any labor organization shall have the right to meet and assemble freely with other members; and to express any views, arguments or opinions . . . ."

While this statute is principally concerned with preserving the right of the worker to speak out on union matters without being punished by the union, it clearly evidences a concern by Congress that the worker should be free to speak his mind on the important question of the quality of representation he is receiving. This is precisely what Holodnak sought to do. *Cf. Cole v. Hall,* 462 F.2d 777 (2d Cir. 1972), aff'd, 412 U.S. 1, 93 S.Ct. 1943, 36 L.Ed.2d 782 (1973).

In light of the foregoing, the court must conclude that Avco's dismissal of Holodnak infringed on his First Amendment rights and that Holodnak was not discharged for "just cause" as required by Article V, § 1.a. of the collective bargaining agreement.[12]

In conclusion, we would do well to remember what the Supreme Court said 34 years ago in *Thornhill v. Alabama,* 310 U.S. 88, 103, 60 S.Ct. 736, 744, 84 L.Ed. 1093 (1940): "Free discussion concerning the conditions in industry and the causes of labor disputes appears to us indispensable to the effective and intelligent use of the processes of popular government to shape the destiny of modern industrial society."

VI.

Attached to plaintiff's post-trial memorandum is a revised financial loss statement. In addition to seeking reinstatement, plaintiff claims $49,569.88 in back wages. The plaintiff also seeks $30,000 in

---

[12] This resolution makes unnecessary the determination of other issues presented here. Although Holodnak did not state as one of his claims the denial of his constitutional rights, this theme ran throughout the trial and the post-trial briefs. Reliance on the First Amendment rather than LMRA § 301 and 9 U.S.C. § 10 as a basis for his claims would presumably require resolution of the issue of whether the rationale of Bivens v. Six Unknown Named Agents, 403 U.S. 388, 91 S.Ct. 1999, 29 L.Ed.2d 619 (1971), which allowed damage actions to remedy violations of the Fourth Amendment, extends to actions charging violations of the First Amendment. See Wahba v. New York University, *supra,* 492 F.2d at 103-104. The court expresses no views on this question, as well as the question of whether an action under the First Amendment can be used to bypass the tight restrictions on judicial review of a labor arbitrator's award. See generally Alexander v. Gardner-Denver Co., 415 U.S. 36, 94 S.Ct. 1011, 59 L.Ed.2d 147 (1974).

It is also unnecessary to consider other possible grounds for vacating the arbitration award and granting Holodnak relief. One of these would be to hold that since the arbitrator is an instrument of national labor policy, he is not a mere "private" person, but rather one acting on behalf of the government who must take into account First Amendment rights. *Cf.* Buckley v. AFTRA, *supra,* 496 F.2d at 309-310. Closely related to this is the argument that the labor laws express a public policy encouraging free association and communication among employees and that courts are free to review and vacate an arbitration award which conflicts with that policy. *Cf.* Local 453, Electrical Workers v. Otis Elevator Co., 314 F.2d 25 (2d Cir.), *cert. denied,* 373 U.S. 949, 83 S.Ct. 1680, 10 L.Ed.2d 705 (1963).

punitive damages for wilful discharge. Finally, $50,000 in attorney fees are requested.

Holodnak is entitled to $9,113.24 in back pay. At trial, he was unable to offer any evidence that he had sought equivalent employment during the last four years. He frankly conceded that he had not looked for employment, although he was a skilled laborer, and had relied to some extent on a disability pension. Only during the first year after being discharged did he make any effort to obtain other employment. Holodnak was under a duty to mitigate damages. *Schneider v. Electric Auto-Lite Co.,* 456 F.2d 366, 373 (6th Cir. 1972); *De Arroyo v. Sindicato de Trabajadores Packinghouse, supra,* 425 F.2d at 292; *cf. N. L. R. B. v. Mastro Plastics Corp.,* 354 F.2d 170, 178 (2d Cir. 1965), *cert. denied,* 384 U.S. 972, 86 S.Ct. 1862, 16 L.Ed.2d 682 (1966). Accordingly, damages for back pay are awarded only to the extent of $9,113.24. This figure is comprised of $7,012.40 for normal hours worked and $2,101.84 for overtime from May 29, 1969 to April 14, 1970, as a small-parts inspector *A.* The union was on strike for the remainder of the year following discharge. Interest is awarded on this amount at a rate of 6% from the date of judgment. No pre-judgment interest is awarded. *Lodge 743 v. United Aircraft Corp.,* 336 F.Supp. 811, 815 (D.Conn. 1971).

As to the apportionment of damages between Avco and Local 1010, Vaca v. Sipes, *supra,* makes clear that damages should be apportioned according to fault. "[D]amages attributable solely to the employer's breach of contract should not be charged to the union." 386 U.S. at 197, 87 S.Ct. at 920. *See also De Arroyo v. Sindicato de Trabajadores Packinghouse, supra; Richardson v. Communications Workers,* 443 F.2d 974 (8th Cir. 1971). Since essentially all the loss suffered here was due to Avco's improper discharge of the plaintiff, it must be held liable for plaintiff's back pay and interest thereon.

Holodnak also seeks $30,000 in punitive damages. Whether such damages are recoverable under LMRA § 301 is still an open question. A closely divided Third Circuit has held that punitive damages are not available under § 301 and the Ninth Circuit apparently agrees. *Local 127, Shoe Workers v. Brooks Shoe Manufacturing Co.,* 298 F.2d 277 (3d Cir. 1962) (en banc); *Williams v. Pacific Maritime Assn.,* 421 F.2d 1287 (9th Cir. 1970). Two district courts, however, have said that punitive damages may be available under § 301. *Zamora v. Massey-Ferguson, Inc.,* 336 F.Supp. 588 (S.D.Iowa 1972); *Patrick v. I.D. Packing Co.,* 308 F.Supp. 821 (S.D.Iowa 1969); *Sidney Wanzer & Sons, Inc. v. Milk Drivers, Local 753,* 249 F.Supp. 664 (N.D.Ill.1966). In the context of other statutory provisions, the Supreme Court has held that the NLRB does not have the power to impose punitive damages, *Republic Steel Corp. v. NLRB,* 311 U.S. 7, 61 S.Ct. 77, 85 L.Ed. 6 (1940), and that punitive damages are not available under LMRA § 303(b), 29 U.S.C.

§ 187(b), which allows a person injured by unlawful secondary boycotts to recover the "damages by him sustained and the costs of the suit." *Local 20, Teamsters v. Morton,* 377 U.S. 252, 84 S.Ct. 1253, 12 L.Ed.2d 280 (1964).

The determination of whether punitive damages are available is, of course, a question of federal law. *Textile Workers v. Lincoln Mills,* 353 U.S. 448, 77 S.Ct. 912, 1 L.Ed.2d 972 (1957). The language of § 301, which only gives the district courts jurisdiction over suits for violation of collective bargaining agreements, does not provide the answer. Two justifications have been given for allowing punitive damages. One is that such damages may be awarded in special instances to further the policy of federal labor laws when other remedies may be lacking. *Sidney Wanzer & Sons, supra,* 249 F. Supp. at 668-671. The other is that while punitive damages are not normally available in contract actions, they are when an independent right apart from plaintiff's contractual rights has been infringed. *Local 127, Shoe Workers v. Brooks Shoe, supra,* 298 F.2d at 282-283 (Staley, J., dissenting on this point).

The justification given in *Wanzer* is doubtful given the sweeping rejection of a deterrence as a rationale for penalties in *Republic Steel Corp. v. NLRB, supra,* 311 U.S. at 12, 61 S.Ct. 77, even though *Wanzer* attempted to distinguish that case. This matter need not be decided here since there is no evidence that punitive damages are necessary to deter future violations by Avco.

The rationale of the *Brooks Shoe* dissent is more in point and is more persuasive. Generally in contract cases punitive damages are available when the defendant's actions might also be tortious. See 5 A. Corbin, Contracts § 1077 (1964). There is no reason to believe that the district courts cannot apply general contract principles in § 301 actions where such principles are consistent with federal labor law policies. *See Textile Workers v. Lincoln Mills, supra,* 353 U.S. at 457, 77 S.Ct. 912. Unlike the NLRB, with which the Supreme Court was concerned in *Republic Steel,* the federal courts are not administrative agencies with limited expertise but are forums that often balance a wide range of concerns in rendering decisions.

Here Avco acted in a manner that interfered with Holodnak's rights under the First Amendment and the federal labor laws. As noted above, no substantial explanation for the discharge can be given. Avco's actions must be either viewed as an irrational reaction to the article or as a calculated attempt to remove an employee who was considered to be a trouble maker. In either event, such wilful behavior, contrary as it is to the policies of the Constitution and federal law, cannot be tolerated. Punitive damages are damages available in civil rights actions for gross disregard of rights. See, *e.g., Lee v. Southern Home Sites Corp.,* 429 F.2d 290, 294 (5th Cir. 1970); *Chubbs v. City of New York,* 324 F.Supp. 1183, 1191

(E.D.N.Y.1971); *Stamps v. Detroit Edison Corp.,* 365 F.Supp. 87, 119, 124 (E.D.Mich.1973). Since Avco has acted wilfully in a manner that violated Holodnak's constitutional and statutory rights, the court holds that punitive damages are available and that the award to Holodnak of $10,000 in such damages from Avco is appropriate.

Plaintiff also seeks reinstatement at his former job at Avco. While reinstatement is a proper remedy in some circumstances, *see De Arroyo v. Sindicato de Trabajadores Packinghouse, supra,* 425 F.2d at 292, the court does not feel that this remedy is appropriate here. Holodnak's failure to seek work for several years casts doubt upon his contention that he is willing in good faith to return to work. Moreover, Holodnak's physical condition, observed at trial, makes it doubtful that he is physically capable of returning to doing the work he had been doing. In short, in the absence of any showing that Holodnak is now capable of doing the work he had been doing, in light of his failure to attempt to secure employment, there is no basis for ordering his reinstatement.

As for plaintiff's request for counsel fees, this is generally a matter reserved to the discretion of the court. *De Arroyo v. Sindicato de Trabajadores Packinghouse, supra,* 425 F.2d at 292-293 (1st Cir. 1970); *Local 4076, United Steelworkers of America, AFL-CIO,* 338 F.Supp. 1154 (W.D.Pa.1972). The court has power to award counsel fees despite the absence of express statutory authorization. *Cf. Cole v. Hall, supra.* As in *Cole,* which was a suit brought under the Labor-Management Reporting and Disclosure Act, the rights vindicated here as a result of Holodnak's action will be of great benefit to all employees at the Avco plant. Benefits such as those achieved here "would be lost in most instances without the discretionary authority in courts to grant counsel fees," since individual employees generally lack the resources to take on the company or the union, 462 F.2d at 780. The alleged wrong inflicted on the employee, the loss of employment in violation of contractual rights; the anticipated recovery, perhaps too insubstantial to sustain competent counsel's best efforts, and the ultimate purpose of making the employee whole, all suggest that the employee should retain his lost earnings for himself. *Vaca v. Sipes,* 386 U.S. at 210, 87 S.Ct. 903 (Mr. Justice Black dissenting); *De Arroyo v. Sindicato de Trabajadores Packinghouse, supra.*

While violation of Holodnak's rights was caused primarily by Avco's actions, it cannot be said that the union's breach of its duty of fair representation did not contribute to Holodnak's need for counsel to assert his rights. On all the circumstances of the case, a fair apportionment of the liability for counsel fees and expenses is that Avco pay two-thirds and the union one-third.

The amount of counsel fees which should be awarded is a matter which the court is unable at present to determine. Counsel for plaintiff is directed to offer detailed proof of the extent of time devoted in preparation and trial of this case and the expenses incurred by all attorneys for whose services compensation is sought, within fifteen days of the filing of this opinion. Avco and the union may file objections thereto ten days after receipt of a copy thereof.

Accordingly, it is ordered that Avco compensate the plaintiff $9,113.24 in back pay plus $10,000 in punitive damages with interest at 6% from the date of judgment. Additionally, Avco and the union are to pay the plaintiff's attorney fees in an amount to be determined.

. . .

NOTE:

(1) The U.S. Court of Appeals for the Second Circuit reversed the award of punitive damages, but affirmed the District Court in all other respects, 514 F.2d 825 (2d Cir. 1975).

(2) "Study Time," a quarterly newsletter of AAA stated in its January 1976 case for "the other side" as taken from Avco's brief —

Burton Turkus was not a party to the litigation and has made no public pronouncements about it. But from the company's appeal brief, we glean the following:

1. During the arbitration hearing, Holodnak admitted he was advocating wildcat strikes, and admitted also that he knew that course of action was expressly contrary to the union contract and an arbitrator's cease-and-desist order.

2. The union's decision to press the grievance to arbitration was unanimous. Holodnak admitted during the court trial that he thought, during the arbitration hearing, that he was being properly represented. Only later, when it was suggested to him that a First Amendment issue might be involved, did he come to think that his representation might not have been adequate.

3. Holodnak at first claimed his disciplinary record with Avco was clean, but under cross-examination admitted that he had been disciplined on a number of occasions for violation of company rules.

4. Judge Lumbard had found Holodnak's representation inadequate in that the union's attorney had met him only a few minutes before the start of the hearing. Actually, the union's attorney scheduled to represent Holodnak had died before the hearing, making it necessary to designate someone else. The new attorney was, in fact, thoroughly briefed on the Holodnak case, having spent time with UAW staff members for days prior to the hearing.

5. No one raised any Fifth Amendment issues at the arbitration hearing, all the participants apparently relying on previous case

law which held that there could be government involvement only in establishments open to the public. It was assumed, in accordance with legal and arbitration precedents, that Constitutional issues concern what the government may or may not do to suppress speech, not what a private employer may do. Following citation and discussion of four leading cases, Avco's brief states: "The First Amendment is *not applicable* to proscribe private interference with speech in any form, whether picketing, handbilling, or otherwise, *unless* the private entity displays, among other things, a functional equivalency to a government facility open generally to access by the public. . . . To suggest that Avco's military contracts alone constitute a significant governmental presence is to say that any private corporation which sells a substantial portion of its output at a single plant to the government is a party coming within the ambit of the First Amendment. The standard . . . would bring under the umbrella of the 'governmental action' the majority of major manufacturing corporations in the United States."

6. Judge Lumbard found heavy involvement of the government in Avco because of the amount of Defense Department contracts. Actually, 85 percent of the business of the plant where Holodnak worked was non-government connected.

7. A few lines taken from the transcript seem to show Arbitrator Turkus questioning Holodnak vigorously, in a manner intended to extract admission that his accusations against the company and the union were unfounded, and that Holodnak's political views were objectionable. But when the same exchange of questions and answers is read in the context of surrounding material, it appears that the arbitrator was trying to get the grievant to express his views in a manner that could justify mitigation of the penalty. Moreover, the arbitrator specifically excluded from consideration Holodnak's radical views. "Well, he has a perfect right to feel antagonistic toward the capitalistic system if that's his belief. What I am concerned with is whether or not he violated Article 19." — from the transcript of the arbitration hearing. The arbitrator's reference apparently was to *Rule* 19, quoted above.

8. A reading of the entire transcript of the arbitration hearing and the trial reveals that: Holodnak was aware of the wildcat strike situation and of two cease-and-desist orders by arbitrators; he admitted he had no information at the time he wrote the article of union-busting activities by the employer; he was unable to give any instances of Avco buying off unionists with the offer of foremanships, as alleged; he could not cite any example of arbitral bias; he would not have written the article had he known at the time what they knew by the time the hearing took place;

and he agreed that the hearing was fair and that he was fairly represented.

9. Judge Lumbard found it evidence of bad representation that Holodnak's attorney concentrated on winning conversion of the discharge to a suspension, rather than achieving full vindication. He would have had the union argue that, as First Amendment rights were involved, it did not matter whether Holodnak had made false and malicious statements in violation of a company rule. On balance, however, taking into account the fact that no one had thought that First Amendment rights were relevant to what a private employer does under the circumstances of this case, it was not unreasonable for the attorney with a "losing" case to try to salvage something for the grievant. "He failed," Avco's brief stated, "but so far as we know failure by counsel in an endeavor properly undertaken does not warrant the harsh treatment accorded him by the lower court."

The Moral: Let's Not Rush to Judgment

The nine paragraphs above were, as indicated, taken from Avco's brief. It is possible for others to read the transcripts or interview persons involved in that interesting case and reach conclusions different from those offered. And it might be that if the arbitrator were not constrained by the doctrine of *functus officio,* he too would have a version to relate that might affect one's judgment as to whether the *Holodnak* case was one of bad arbitration, or a bad decision by a judge. At any rate, we hope that writers and researchers will study the facts and law independently, and not accept uncritically what has already been written.

(3) *Problems:* (a) Do you agree with the court's decision in light of the Code of Professional Responsibility? Be specific. What is the legal basis for the court's finding of partiality? Does this comport with the Code's description of an arbitrator's control of a hearing?

(b) What are the implications of the court's decision for those persons representing grievants in arbitration procedures? Is there a duty to adequately, as distinguised from "fairly," represent grievants?

(c) Is the court's application of constitutional law (rather than contract law) to the facts of this case under the doctrine of "state action" an indication of the potential of judicial review through laws external to the contract? What are the implications to the arbitration process from the application of external law? Do these implications relate to *Avco's* argument that the court's decision would reach almost all major U.S. corporations?

Chapter 6

THE FEDERAL LAW OF ARBITRATION [1]

A. NATURE AND KINDS OF LABOR DISPUTE ARBITRATION

The arbitration process is a method by which the parties to a dispute settle it through adjudication outside the normal judicial system.[2] In some countries it is established by statute, and is a part of the judicial system, although functioning with specialized jurisdiction.[3] In other countries it is the product of voluntary agreement by the parties to submit their dispute to a privately selected third party, or parties, for determination.[4]

Labor dispute arbitration falls into two quite distinct categories.[5] One, referred to by legalists as "rights" arbitration, but more

---

[1] This book is a companion volume in the Contemporary Legal Education Series to Smith, Merrifield, and St. Antoine, Cases and Materials on Labor Relations Law. While that book is designed primarily for the basic course in labor law, it includes substantial coverage of the enforcement of the collective agreement through arbitration, particularly for schools that do not have a second course in labor law on collective bargaining and labor arbitration. Of course, the law of labor arbitration is an even larger component of this book. There is thus an overlap in coverage, and some of the materials herein are drawn from the labor relations law book. A school which has both a basic course in labor law and a course in collective bargaining and labor arbitration can make the allocation which suits its particular situation.

[2] *See also* F. Elkouri & E. Elkouri, How Arbitration Works 2 (3d ed. 1973) [hereinafter cited as How Arbitration Works]; C. Updegraff, Arbitration and Labor Relations (3d ed. 1970) [hereinafter cited as Arbitration]; 6 C.J.S. Arbitration & Awards 1, at 152 (1937). For a court definition of voluntary arbitration *see* Gates v. Arizona Brewing Co., 54 Ariz. 266, 269, 95 P.2d 49 (1939).

[3] *See, e.g.,* Denmark: W. Galenson, The Danish System of Labor Relations 209-32 (1952); Norway: W. Galenson, Labor in Norway 237-52 (1949); Sweden: T.L. Johnston, Collective Bargaining in Sweden 138-54 (1962). *See also* Canada: A.W.R. Carrothers, Labour Arbitration in Canada 12-36 (1961) (where provincial law may require the parties to include in their collective bargaining agreement arbitration of "grievance" disputes); H.D. Woods, Shadows over Arbitration, in Proceedings of the 30th Annual Meeting of the National Academy of Arbitrators 1-14 (1977).

[4] *See, e.g.,* Great Britain: O. Kahn-Freund, Legal Framework, in The System of Industrial Relations in Great Britain 87-101 (A. Flanders & H.A. Clegg, eds., 1954). See also the prevailing law in Canada where "interests" disputes may only be arbitrated by voluntary agreement of the parties. Carrothers, *supra* note 2, at 13.

[5] How Arbitration Works 47-67; Arbitration 294-95. *See also* Fleming, Reflections on the Nature of Labor Arbitration, 61 Mich. L. Rev. 1245, 1249 (1963), where he classified the various classes of arbitration cases as (1) contract interpretation cases; (2) "legislation" cases; (3) "policy" cases; and (4) "interest" cases. For examples of each class *see* pp. 1249-55. In Britain, no distinction is made between "rights" disputes and "interests" disputes in practice; each dispute is simply treated as a problem to be solved. *See* B. Aaron in Forward to K.W. Wedderburn and P.L. Davies, Employment Grievances and Disputes Procedures in Britain vii (1969).

colloquially as "grievance" arbitration, involves, typically, a dispute arising during the term of a collective bargaining agreement and concerning a problem with respect to its interpretation or application. The second, sometimes termed "interest" arbitration, involves unresolved issues concerning the substantive terms to be included in a collective bargaining agreement.

In the United States grievance arbitration, except in the case of industries subject to the Railway Labor Act, is voluntary, in the sense that the parties determine by agreement, usually as a part of the contract grievance procedure, to submit unresolved disputes in this category to arbitration. It is also non-statutory, subject to the qualification that there are numerous state statutes which relate to the arbitration process and to the further qualification that the process has become subject to regulation, as a matter of federal substantive law, by virtue of the Supreme Court's interpretations of Section 301 of the Taft-Hartley Act of 1947.[6] In contrast with some foreign countries, contract term ("interest") arbitration is not compelled by law in the United States except for a few state statutes which prescribe arbitration as the method for resolving collective bargaining impasses in the case of certain industries, principally public utilities, and in some areas of public employee unionism.

The use of the arbitration process as a means for reducing industrial strife has, in this country, been largely restricted to the area of disputes arising during the term of collective bargaining agreements (i.e., to "grievances"). In this category, however, there is wide acceptance of the use of arbitration. Of 1,717 major collective bargaining agreements analyzed, about 94% provided for the arbitration of grievances.[7] Hence, the fact is that thousands of disputes are settled in voluntary arbitration proceedings without resort to strike action or other economic pressure, or to litigation. In contrast, however, there is relatively little use of arbitration to resolve contract term ("interest") disputes. Less than 2% of the 1,717 major agreements contained any provision for the resolution of disputes concerning the terms of the next agreement between the parties by this method.[8] And there is relatively little resort to "ad hoc" use of arbitration as a means of resolving collective bargaining impasses. There has, however, been some use of this process, and it may be that its use will increase in the future, partially in response to increasing discontent, both by the parties and by the public, with strikes.

---

[6] Textile Workers Union v. Lincoln Mills, 353 U.S. 448 (1957).

[7] U.S. Bureau of Labor Statistics, Dep't of Labor, Bull. No. 1425-26, Major Collective Bargaining Agreements: Arbitration Procedure 5 (1966).

[8] Id. at 95. But see, R.W. Fleming, Interest Arbitration Revisited, in Proceedings of the 26th Annual Meeting of the National Academy of Arbitrators (1974).

The advantages of arbitration over the alternatives (litigation, strike action or yielding to the position of the charged party) as a means of resolving grievances are fairly obvious, at least in theory. As compared with litigation,[9] arbitration is said to involve substantial savings in time and expense and the opportunity to make use of the "expertise" of adjudicators who are experienced in labor relations matters. Moreover, the process, being voluntary, can be shaped by the parties to suit their particular needs and desires. As compared with the resolution of disputes through strike action, the advantages of arbitration are clear enough. A solution to the controversy is obtained without the costs, direct and indirect, of economic strife. Despite the generally wide-spread acceptance of these evaluations, there are some who are skeptics or at least critics.[10] One of our tasks will be to indicate, and provide an opportunity to appraise, these differing views.

A threshold question, which should occur to the student at this point, is what accounts for the sharp difference in general attitude in this country toward grievance as contrasted with contract term arbitration.[11] It is perhaps readily apparent why unions would prefer arbitration to litigation, generally speaking, as a means of ultimate enforcement of the collective bargaining agreement. But why are they willing to sacrifice the right to strike in the one area but not the other? And why do managements, in general, share with unions an adverse reaction to the use of arbitration to settle contract term disputes?

A common explanation is that there is less "risk" in submitting grievances to arbitration than in submitting contract terms to arbitration. The function of the arbitrator in a grievance case is thought to be quasi-judicial and confined within the framework of what the parties have already negotiated into the collective bargaining agreement. Hence there are standards to guide him. On the other hand, it is thought that in the arbitration of "interest"

---

[9] One significant deficiency of litigation as a solution to industrial disputes was described by Professor Harry Shulman in this way: "[L]itigation results in a victory, perhaps, results in a decision in any event, which disposes of the particular controversy, but which does not affirmatively act to advance the parties' cooperative effort, which does not affirmatively act to affect their attitudes in their relations with one another. Arbitration can be made to do that." Conference on Training of Law Students in Labor Relations, Vol. III, Transcript of Proceedings 709 (1947). For a concise analysis of the differences between labor arbitration and the court system as adjudicatory processes *see* Fleming, Reflections on the Nature of Labor Arbitration, 61 Mich. L. Rev. 1245, 1258-71 (1963).

[10] *E.g.,* P. Hays, Labor Arbitration: A Dissenting View 112-13 (1966).

[11] In 1964, ninety-eight arbitrators rendered decisions in 3980 cases, of which 3747 were grievance and 183 were contract cases. *See* Survey of Arbitration in 1964 in Proceedings of the 18th Annual Meeting of the National Academy of Arbitrators 243 (BNA 1965).

disputes there is a lack of meaningful standards for arbitral determination, and hence a fear of giving carte blanche to a third party who has no continuing responsibilities with respect to the operation of the enterprise or the interests of the employees.[12] There is also the thought that better labor-management relations will result from a negotiated agreement, however difficult the negotiations may be, than from a settlement imposed by a third party.

These views are not universally held throughout the world. In Great Britain, for example, the arbitration of new contract terms is considerably more common than the arbitration of grievances, and the British apparently feel that outsiders are better equipped to deal with basic wage and hour issues of broad applicability than with individual grievances occurring in a particular local setting.[13] Doubtless the general attitudes now prevailing in the United States will remain substantially as they are for the foreseeable future, but they should nevertheless be critically appraised. Is there empirical evidence in support of the view that in "interest" arbitration there is a lack of meaningful standards to guide the arbitrator? [14] Is there evidence that labor relations are better following negotiated settlements than following settlements imposed by arbitration? Is there any indication on the basis of accumulated experience that contract term arbitration involves any substantial risk of results differing measureably from what could have been expected to result from negotiations?

B. LABOR ARBITRATION SYSTEMS

1. Arbitration Under the Railway Labor Act

The Railway Labor Act creates special machinery to deal with various kinds of labor disputes, including disputes concerning the

---

[12] Davey, Hazards in Labor Arbitration, 1 Ind. & Lab. Rel. Rev. 386, 396 (1948). In Twin City Rapid Transit Co., 7 Lab. Arb. Rep. 848 (1947), Arbitrator Whitley P. McCoy described the task of the arbitrator in an arbitration of "interest" disputes as follows: "Arbitration of contract terms differs radically from arbitration of grievances. The latter calls for a judicial determination of existing contract rights; the former calls for a determination, upon considerations of policy, fairness, and expediency, of what the contract rights ought to be. In submitting this case to arbitration, the parties have merely extended their negotiations — they have left it to this board to determine what they should, by negotiation, have agreed upon. We take it that the fundamental inquiry, as to each issue, is: What should the parties themselves, as reasonable men, have voluntarily agreed to?"

[13] I. Sharp, Industrial Conciliation and Arbitration in Great Britain 444 (1950); Gratch, Grievance Settlement Machinery in England, 12 Lab. L.J. 861, 863 (1961); R.W. Rideout, Principles of Labour Law 46-54 (2d ed. 1976).

[14] The Elkouris believe that there are sufficient standards that can be used in the arbitration of "interests" disputes. For an examination of these standards see F. Elkouri & E. Elkouri, How Arbitration Works 745-796 (3d ed. 1973).

interpretation or application of collective bargaining agreements (more frequently called "working rules") in the interstate railroad and airline industries. The National Mediation Board functions as a mediating agency in handling "interest" disputes, and the statute creates, for the railroad industry, a "National Railroad Adjustment Board" (and, alternatively permits the establishment of ad hoc adjustment boards) with jurisdiction over contract grievances. Provision is likewise made for the creation of special adjustment boards in the airline industry with similar jurisdiction. In addition, the Act imposes upon the Mediation Board the duty to urge parties involved in "interest" disputes to agree voluntarily to submit unresolved issues to arbitration. If any such agreement is entered into, the arbitration procedures are those specified in the Act.

Adjudication of grievance disputes by an adjustment board under the Act is voluntary in the sense that appeal is apparently optional. But if either party does refer the case, the Board's jurisdiction attaches and it is directed to dispose of the matter. Upon failure of the carrier to abide by an award an appeal may be made to the appropriate federal district court where the award will be enforced or set aside. In a district court the findings and order of the adjustment board are "conclusive on the parties," except for failure to comply with legal requirements or for fraud or corruption in the procedure.

The National Railroad Adjustment Board is divided into four jurisdictional divisions. The members are appointed one-half by the carriers and one-half by the appropriate unions, and are compensated by the parties whom they represent. Because of the even division of members, deadlocks are common. In any such case, the division may select a "referee" (*i.e.,* a neutral third party to serve as chairman) but if it fails to do so, the Mediation Board designates the referee. This entire system is unique in American industry, and, on the whole, the railroad phase of it functions in a world of its own with little reference to it in other arbitration contexts and with its own accumulated body of decisional "precedent." [15]

---

[15] For articles and other materials on the resolution of disputes under the Railway Labor Act see Kaufman, The Railroad Labor Dispute: A Marathon of Maneuver and Improvisation, 18 Ind. & Lab. Rel. Rev. 196 (1965); Kroner, Minor Disputes Under the Railway Labor Act: A Critical Appraisal, 37 N.Y.U.L. Rev. 41 (1962); Larson, Collective Bargaining Under the Railway Labor Act, in Southwestern Legal Foundation, Labor Law Developments, Proceedings of the Eleventh Annual Institute on Labor Law 179 (1965); Mangum, Grievance Procedures for Railroad Operating Employees, 15 Ind. & Lab. Rel. Rev. 474 (1962); C. Rehmus, The Railway Labor Act at Fifty (1976).

2. Private Arbitration

SIMKIN & KENNEDY, ARBITRATION OF GRIEVANCES, DIVISION OF LABOR STANDARDS, U. S. DEPARTMENT OF LABOR, Bulletin 82 (1946) [16]

Types of Grievance Arbitration Systems

Several types of machinery or procedure for impartial settlement of grievances are in common use. Differences can usually be traced to the length of time the system has been in effect, to differing collective bargaining practices, to size of the company or industry, and to problems inherent in the technology of the industry. Some apparent differences are matters of language rather than basic differences in procedure or function.

Arbitrator's Tenure

The first major distinction between types of grievance arbitration systems relates to the tenure of the third party.

a. *Temporary Arbitrator.* — Throughout this pamphlet the term *temporary* is used to designate a third party who is selected for a single case or for a specific group of cases after it has become clear that the grievance or grievances in question must be submitted to arbitration. The arbitrator is selected with a specific case or group of cases in mind, and there is no commitment whatever to use that same person again. Third parties selected in this manner are sometimes called *ad hoc* arbitrators. The majority of labor agreements providing for arbitration specify this type.

b. *Permanent Arbitrator.* — The term *permanent* arbitrator is used in connection with a third party who is selected for a longer period of time. The word *permanent* is in italics since it is obviously a relative term. A *permanent* arbitrator is seldom selected for a term longer than the duration of the contract, although he may be reselected for succeeding contracts. Sometimes he is selected for a term shorter than the life of the contract, such as a 6-month term. . . .

Terms Used to Describe Third Parties

a. *Impartial Chairman.* — In some industries, such as men's and women's clothing and hosiery, which have a long history of impartial settlement of grievances, the third party who is engaged to make the decisions at the final step of the grievance procedure is called an impartial chairman. Technically, the individual who carries this title in these industries is not a chairman of any official body or organization, and he makes his decisions as an individual. But the

---

[16] Prepared by William E. Simkin and Van Dusen Kennedy, both experienced labor arbitrators. Simkin was named Director of the Federal Mediation and Conciliation Service in 1961.

title does describe his function, which is to preside over the collective bargaining agreement and its observance by both parties. This function frequently includes informal mediation.

An impartial chairman is named for the life of an agreement or for a specified period of time and therefore is a *permanent* arbitrator. Almost invariably he is selected by mutual agreement.

Other employers and unions which have adopted impartial settlement procedures more recently also use the title "impartial chairman" to designate the third party in the process. There has been some tendency, however, to make him an impartial chairman of a tripartite arbitration board or adjustment board. See below.

b. *Tripartite Board.* — An arbitration board, adjustment board, or appeals board is made up of at least one named representative of each party to the contract and a third member called the impartial chairman or chairman. On such boards, the question at issue is discussed by all members of the board after the hearing. If the board does not reach a unanimous decision, either the union or management representative usually will concur with the chairman to give a majority decision. In a few instances a majority decision may be required, but most contracts providing for tripartite boards give the chairman the right and obligation to make a final decision, regardless of whether or not it is concurred in by other members of the board. . . .

c. *Umpire.* — Some employers and unions have chosen to call the impartial third party in their agreements an umpire instead of an impartial chairman. This is true in certain automobile, rubber, and shipbuilding companies. Almost invariably the umpire sits alone. Usually he is retained for the life of the agreement or for a specific period of time, although there are many instances where he is selected only for a specific case or group of cases. Therefore, the term *umpire* is in common use with both *permanent* and *temporary* systems. . . .

d. *Arbitrator.* — The more general term *arbitrator* is typically used in connection with a third party selected only for one case or for a group of cases and therefore is almost synonymous with the *temporary* arbitrator referred to heretofore. However, there are instances where a *permanent* third party is referred to in the contract as arbitrator rather than impartial chairman or umpire. . . .

Temporary arbitrators are also used frequently in cases where there is no contract provision for arbitration but where a conciliator secures agreement to arbitrate a specific grievance.

Analysis of Systems Used

Every person experienced in arbitration, from the point of view of union labor, employer, or arbitrator, undoubtedly has some preference for one or another system. Each has its proper place.

Before setting up an arbitration system, however, it may be helpful to weigh in advance some of the advantages and disadvantages of each. Here is a summary based on the authors' experience.

Single Permanent Arbitrator (Impartial Chairman or Umpire)

This type of arbitrator is selected for a specific period of time.

Advantages: a. The arbitrator gradually becomes familiar with, and eventually expert in, the contract clauses, wage payment plans, industrial techniques, and processes of the industry.

b. Decisions will be consistent one with another. Because of this, precedents will be established, the parties will know what to expect from the arbitrator, and similar cases in the future will be resolved by agreement at an early stage of the grievance procedure. It is pointless to "whip a dead horse" by pushing a second time the same type of grievance which has been lost once.

c. No time is lost in choosing an arbitrator after the initial selection. Less time is usually consumed in making arrangements for hearings. The grievance procedure is shortened to the advantage of both parties, particularly in discharge or seniority cases where an employee's job status is in doubt and back pay may be involved.

d. The *permanent* arbitrator becomes acquainted with the personalities of both sides of the table.

e. As a result of (a) and (b) above, time required for the presentation of evidence at hearings is shortened substantially. The parties do not have to educate the arbitrator each time, and there is less tendency for one or both parties to stray from the subject at hand or belabor a point. To illustrate, one of the writers of this pamphlet averages approximately eight grievance cases per day of hearings where he is the *permanent* umpire or impartial chairman, in contrast to an average of approximately two cases per day when he is retained on a temporary basis and is not familiar with the parties or the industry.

f. The *permanent* arbitrator requires less time for investigation and preparation of opinions due to familiarity with the industry and with the parties.

g. The *permanent* arbitrator seldom requires a verbatim transcript.

h. As a result of (e), (f), and (g) above, the direct cost of each arbitration (fees and expenses of the arbitrator and expense of a transcript, if taken), and the indirect costs (time spent by the representatives of the parties and the union or company cost for time of witnesses, etc.), are substantially less than for a series of temporary arbitrators.

i. There is less tendency for either party to throw in a few admittedly weak cases with the thought that a green arbitrator will split the difference and by this means give favorable decisions on the more important cases, or even give favorable decisions on some of the weak cases.

j. The arbitrator must live with the parties and with his own decisions. He cannot blithely toss off a decision, knowing that he may never see the parties again. A really bad decision may come back to haunt him. If any emphasis on responsibility is needed, tenure provides it.

k. When a *permanent* arbitrator can secure the full confidence of both parties, they may sometimes request him to step out of his semi-judicial role and assist them in the mediation of potential disputes.

Disadvantages: a. Because of tenure, it becomes more important to select an individual in whom both parties will have confidence. The parties may become saddled with a "lemon" with no convenient way of removing him.

b. While total arbitration costs should be less, when a *permanent* impartial chairman or umpire is selected, the parties usually obligate themselves to at least a minimum predetermined cost for his services.

c. There is a danger that the ready availability of a *permanent* arbitrator may result in failure to exhaust all possibilities of settlement at earlier stages of the grievance procedure.

d. The fact that the parties usually must pay a *permanent* arbitrator a minimum fee may tempt them not to exhaust all other means of settlement but instead to make the arbitrator earn his money by deciding at least a few cases.

e. It is sometimes difficult to find any one individual who is experienced in all types of potential grievances. For example, one individual may be particularly qualified to handle seniority cases but may be inexperienced in incentive pay cases.

Permanent Tripartite Board

Most of the pros and cons of a *permanent* umpire or impartial chairman apply with equal force to an arbitration board, adjustment board, or appeals board whose impartial chairman is retained for a specified period of time. In addition there are the following advantages and disadvantages.

Advantages: a. The tripartite board gives the parties a better opportunity to keep the third member fully informed of their real positions (sometimes a modification of their official positions), and to be in on the actual making of the decision. Representatives of the parties can also give valuable assistance on technical phases of the case and special industry practices.

b. Unanimous decisions and even majority decisions of a tripartite board have more weight than a decision of the third party alone. At least one party is then semi-officially committed to support each decision, even if it is a modification of that party's original position.

Disadvantages: a. The cost is inevitably greater. The parties must pay their own representatives, and in addition more time is usually spent in hearings and deliberations.

b. It is sometimes a disadvantage that the third member either is required by the agreement or feels it is advisable to secure a majority vote. Conceivably, he may be forced to compromise his own best judgment in a case in order to secure that vote.

Temporary Arbitrator or Umpire

Some of the advantages and disadvantages of this type of arbitration are obvious from the preceding discussion. Here are some additional considerations:

Advantages: a. The system permits easy change of the third party if the arbitrator proves to be incompetent.

b. It facilitates selection of an arbitrator especially qualified for the grievance dispute in question. For example, the parties can judge the experience and qualifications of prospective arbitrators in handling disputes over incentive pay.

c. It is well adapted to situations where arbitration is an entirely new idea to both parties and they wish to experiment, or where experience has shown that practically all disputes can be resolved by the parties.

d. A *temporary* system does not eliminate the possibility of continuous re-selection of the same individual thus securing many of the benefits of a *permanent* system without some of its liabilities.

Disadvantages: a. The time and effort required to select an arbitrator for each case or group of cases delays conclusion of the grievance or grievances, sometimes to the detriment of plant morale.

b. Frequently, out of desperation, a person is selected who has little or no experience or real qualification for the case. Such a selection may be made because he is the only person available who has not issued a decision somewhere, sometime, which the union or the company does not like. Good arbitrators are few and far between who have not incurred somebody's wrath at some time in their career or who have not issued decisions elsewhere on similar issues which may influence one party to "blackball" them for a specific case in spite of excellent qualifications in every other respect.

c. When *temporary* arbitrators are used, there is little precedent established. Either party may want to take a chance on the same type of case again.

d. There is no necessary consistency in the decisions. If a contract interpretation has any precedent value, it persists only until the next time it is tested before a different arbitrator. Resultant conflicting decisions from two or more arbitrators may create more disputes than have been resolved.

e. There is a tendency for the party losing the majority of cases before a *temporary* arbitrator to seek a change of luck and to insist on a different arbitrator for the next case, regardless of the fairness of the decisions.

f. Each new arbitrator must be educated in local conditions, requiring much hearing time and time for investigation and writing decisions, thus adding to the cost.

g. There is some tendency for temporary arbitrators to be unduly legalistic in their approach. . . .

NOTES:

(1) In an address before the Second Annual Meeting of the National Academy of Arbitrators in January, 1949, Dr. George W. Taylor said: "The arbitrator who serves for the term of an agreement is apt to be consistent and he should have a broader understanding of the problems to be solved. In addition, the parties will usually give facts to the permanent arbitrator rather than the arguments ordinarily supplied to the *ad hoc* man. And there should be no 'short sale' of the greater chance for developing an agreed-upon or acquiesced-in settlement when the same arbitrator serves throughout the term of an agreement. . . ." [Effectuating the Labor Contract Through Arbitration (1949)]. The National Academy of Arbitrators is a professional association of labor dispute arbitrators. The Academy was founded in 1947, and has held annual meetings, the *Proceedings* of which contain much valuable material concerning the labor dispute arbitration process.

(2) Apart from private arrangements made by the parties directly with arbitrators, two important sources of *ad hoc* arbitrators are the American Arbitration Association and the Federal Mediation and Conciliation Service. Both maintain panels or lists of persons who are known to be available for and qualified and experienced in arbitration. The parties select their own arbitrators from lists supplied upon request by the AAA or the FMCS. In a survey of arbitration in 1964 by the National Academy of Arbitrators, it was found that among the sources of *ad hoc* arbitrators, selection by the parties led with 42.5%, the FMCS was second with 24.9% and the AAA was third with 19.2%. The remainder was distributed among the other sources of *ad hoc* arbitrators, like, for instance, state agencies. *See* Survey of Arbitration in 1964, Proceedings of the Eighteenth Annual Meeting of the National Academy of Arbitrators 243, 245, 251-52 (BNA 1965). For comparative data see Survey of Arbitration in 1962, Proceedings of the Seventeenth Annual Meeting of the National Academy of Arbitrators 292, 296, 314 (BNA 1964). *See also* R. Fleming, The Labor Arbitration Process 27 (1965).

(3) For the detail as to selection procedures see F. Elkouri & E. Elkouri, How Arbitration Works 87-90 (3d ed. 1973); MacDonald,

The Selection and Tenure of Arbitrators in Labor Disputes, N.Y.U. First Annual Conference on Labor 145, 162-76 (1948). *See also* Jones & Smith, Management and Labor Appraisals and Criticisms of the Arbitration Process: A Report with Comments, 62 Mich. L. Rev. 1115, 1132-40 (1964). The appointing agencies have been criticized for their methods of listing and designating available arbitrators. The following types of complaints are most frequent: (1) The agencies are not sufficiently selective in placing individuals on their rosters of available arbitrators; (2) the names of the same arbitrators appear too frequently on the lists or "panels" sent to the parties; (3) insufficient information is supplied to the parties about the people included on the panels; and (4) the agencies at times improperly include the name of an "objectionable" arbitrator upon a panel list. *See* Jones & Smith, *supra* at 1132-33.

In order to develop (and increase the supply of) competent, acceptable and experienced arbitrators, the two major appointing agencies, with the active support and assistance of the National Academy of Arbitrators, have undertaken a unique program of training new arbitrators. For comments and evaluation of this program see Jones & Smith, *supra* at 1136-37; Straus, Report to the Annual Meeting of the American Arbitration Association, 20 Arb. J. 1, 3 (1965); Straus, Labor Arbitration and Its Critics, 20 Arb. J. 197, 209 (1965). For statistical data and analysis of this training program see Survey of Arbitration in 1962, Proceedings of the Seventeenth Annual Meeting of the National Academy of Arbitrators 292, 294, 309-10 (BNA 1964).

(4) There is a marked and steady increase in the FMCS arbitration caseload every year. In 1966, the Service reported receipt of 5,654 requests for panels; 13,005 in 1972; and 23,474 in 1977. (See the Annual Reports of the Federal Mediation and Conciliation Service.)

(5) The National Academy of Arbitrators has encouraged the publication of studies of a number of permanent arbitration systems. *See* The John Deere-UAW Permanent Arbitration System, in Critical Issues in Labor Arbitration (BNA 1957); Wolff, Crane and Cole, The Chrysler-UAW Umpire System, in The Arbitrators and the Parties (BNA 1958) (which is followed by comparative comments by the (then) Umpires at General Motors and Ford, Nathan P. Feinsinger and Harry H. Platt). *See also* Kennedy, Effective Labor Arbitration (1948), discussing the system in the full-fashioned hosiery industry; and Arbitration of Labor-Management Grievances (U.S. Dep't of Labor, Bull. 1159, 1954), discussing the Bethlehem Steel system.

(6) There are three methods of compensating arbitrators: Per diem basis; retainer basis; or flat rate basis. For a discussion of these types of compensation see MacDonald, The Selection and Tenure of Arbitrators in Labor Disputes, N.Y.U. First Annual Conference on Labor 145, 152-56 (1948). For interesting statistics on arbitrators'

fees see Fleming, The Labor Arbitration Process: 1943-1963, Proceedings of the Seventeenth Annual Meeting of the National Academy of Arbitrators 33, 42-46 (BNA 1964); R. W. Fleming, The Labor Arbitration Process 36-40 (1965); and Survey of Arbitration in 1962, Proceedings of the Seventeenth Annual Meeting of the National Academy of Arbitrators 292, 315 (BNA 1964).

(7) The last two decades have produced a torrent of writing on labor arbitration. Works emphasizing the legal problems of arbitration, including its relationship to the courts, will be cited in the sections to follow. At this point attention will be paid to books and articles concentrating on the practice and procedure of arbitration. A useful periodical is the American Arbitration Association's Arbitration Journal. Texts of selected arbitration awards are published in BNA's Labor Arbitration Reports, CCH's Labor Arbitration Awards, and Prentice-Hall's Labor Arbitration Service, looseleaf services with bound cumulations. In addition to the contrasting appraisals by Judge Paul Hays in Labor Arbitration: A Dissenting View (1966) and R. W. Fleming in The Labor Arbitration Process (1965), general studies of arbitration include F. Elkouri & E. Elkouri, How Arbitration Works (3d ed. 1973); M. Stone, Labor-Management Contracts at Work (1961); M. Stone, Managerial Freedom and Job Security (1964); C. Updegraff, Arbitration and Labor Relations (3d ed. 1970); M. Trotta, Arbitration of Labor-Management Disputes (1974); R. Coulson, Labor Arbitration — What You Need to Know (2d ed. 1978); N. Levin, Arbitrating Labor Cases (1973).

Some of the many articles of general interest are: Aaron, Some Procedural Problems in Arbitration, 10 Vand. L. Rev. 649, 733 (1957); American Arbitration Association, Procedural and Substantive Aspects of Labor-Management Arbitration, 12 Arb. J. (n.s.) 67 (1957); Bailer, Lurie & O'Connell, Arbitration Procedure and Practice, in N.Y.U. Fifteenth Annual Conference on Labor 331, 341, 349 (1962) (three separate papers); Davey, The Arbitrator Views the Agreement, 12 Lab. L. J. 1161 (1961); Fleming, Reflections on the Nature of Labor Arbitration, 61 Mich. L. Rev. 1245 (1963); Fuller, Collective Bargaining and the Arbitrator, 1963 Wis. L. Rev. 1; Jones, Evidentiary Concept in Labor Arbitration: Some Modern Variations on Ancient Legal Themes, 13 U.C.L.A. L. Rev. 1241 (1966); Jones & Smith, Management and Labor Appraisals and Criticisms of the Arbitration Process: A Report with Comments, 62 Mich. L. Rev. 1115 (1964); McCoy, Some Pitfalls in Arbitration, 11 Lab. L.J. 23 (1960); Seward, Arbitration and the Functions of Management, 16 Ind. & Lab. Rel. Rev. 235 (1963).

C. THE LEGAL STATUS OF ARBITRATION

1. At Common Law

In many states voluntary arbitration may be conducted under either statutory or common law rules.[17] Most arbitrations are in fact conducted outside of or at least without reference to the statute, if any, and the legal status of the proceeding may then rest upon common law principles. Many state arbitration statutes are very general in nature and it is necessary to fill in details by resort to the common law. The basic principles of common law arbitration have been summarized by the United States Department of Labor as follows:

> Common law arbitration rests upon the voluntary agreement of the parties to submit their dispute to an outsider. The submission agreement may be oral and may be revoked at any time before the rendering of the award. The tribunal, permanent or temporary, may be composed of any number of arbitrators. They must be free from bias and interest in the subject matter, and may not be related by affinity or consanguinity to either party. The Arbitrators need not be sworn. Only existing disputes may be submitted to them. The parties must be given notice of hearings and are entitled to be present when all the evidence is received. The arbitrators have no power to subpoena witnesses or records and need not conform to legal rules of hearing procedure other than to give the parties an opportunity to present all competent evidence. All arbitrators must attend the hearings, consider the evidence jointly and arrive at an award by a unanimous vote. The award may be oral, but if written, all the arbitrators must sign it. It must dispose of every substantial issue submitted to arbitration. An award may be set aside only for fraud, misconduct, gross mistake, or substantial breach of a common law rule. The only method of enforcing the common law award is to file suit upon it and the judgment thus obtained may be enforced as any other judgment.[18]

The common law rule that an agreement to arbitrate future disputes will not be enforced by the courts and is revocable at will

---

[17] *See* Jones, Judicial Review of Arbitral Awards — Common Law Confusion and Statutory Clarification, 31 S. Cal. L. Rev. 1 (1957). *See also* F. Elkouri & E. Elkouri, How Arbitration Works 35-41 (3d ed. 1973); C. Updegraff & W. McCoy, Arbitration of Labor Disputes 19-21 (2d ed. 1961). Although it is usually held that the statute supplements and does not abrogate the common law, at least one state, Washington, has declared that its statute completely supersedes the common law rules. Puget Sound Bridge & Dredging Co. v. Lake Washington Shipyards, 1 Wash. 2d 401, 96 P.2d 257 (1939).

[18] D. Ziskind, Labor Arbitration Under State Statutes 3 (U.S. Dep't of Labor 1943).

by either party is still accepted in many states.[19] The rule of non-enforceability applies only to an executory agreement to arbitrate.[20] The National War Labor Board (of World War II) consistently rejected the common law view that arbitration is to be regarded with hostility because it is an attempt to supplant the courts. Instead, the Board accepted the view that agreements for arbitration of future disputes are favored and that aid should be given to their enforcement.[21]

2. State Arbitration Statutes

Many states have statutes which are or may be applicable to labor dispute arbitration. New York is such a state, because its Civil Practice Act makes it possible to obtain a court order directing the arbitration of an unresolved dispute.[22] In general there are three types: (1) General statutes, used principally in commercial disputes, but often applicable, with some limitations, to labor disputes; (2) statutes designed specifically for labor disputes, and prescribing arbitration procedures, containing detailed provisions for judicial review and providing for enforcement of awards; (3) statutes which merely "promote" arbitration by directing state officials to

---

[19] Gregory and Orlikoff, The Enforcement of Labor Arbitration Agreements, 17 U. Chi. L. Rev. 233 (1950); and Comment, Arbitration of Labor Contract Interpretation Disputes, 43 Ill. L. Rev. 678 (1948). *But see* United Ass'n of Journeymen & Apprentices of Plumbing and Pipefitting Industry, Local 525 v. Stine, 76 Nev. 189, 351 P.2d 965 (1960) (agreement to arbitrate future dispute enforced despite the common law).

[20] Red Cross Line v. Atlantic Fruit Co., 264 U.S. 109 (1924). The nonenforceability rule has sometimes been applied with apparent displeasure. In Gatliff Coal Co. v. Cox, 142 F.2d 876 (6th Cir. 1944), the law of Kentucky, that an agreement between parties to arbitrate all of the disputes thereafter to arise under their collective bargaining agreement, is invalid and unenforceable, was applied but the court said (at 881):

"It may be that the courts in refusing to specifically enforce arbitration agreements because against public policy, have placed too great faith in the law alone and that no unrighteous purpose would be served by upholding such contracts because their enforcement would often determine disputes and controversies, thus avoiding the formalities, the delay and expense and the vexation of ordinary litigation. An agreement that all differences arising under a contract shall be submitted to arbitration relates to the law of remedies and the law that governs remedies is the law of the forum. Such a contract, whatever form it may assume, affects in its operation the remedy alone.... The rule prevails in Kentucky that parties may not, by contract, deprive themselves of the right to resort to courts for the settlement of their controversies. It is our duty to expound, not to make the law of the state."

[21] *See* Freidin & Ulman, Arbitration and the National War Labor Board, 58 Harv. L. Rev. 309, 315 (1945).

[22] Article 84, § 1448 (now § 7501), Civil Practice Act, as amended in 1940 and as further amended in 1963. *See also* Association of Master Painters v. Brotherhood of Painters, 64 N.Y.S.2d 405 (Sup. Ct. 1946).

encourage its use.[23] Some of these statutes are applicable only to controversies which might be the subject of a legal action, thereby removing from their coverage "interest" arbitration.[24]

In 1955 the Conference of Commissioners on Uniform State Laws promulgated a Uniform Arbitration Act, applicable to labor disputes as well as commercial disputes. By 1977, twenty states had adopted the Act but several excepted collective bargaining agreements from the coverage of the Act.[25]

One of the problems with respect to grievance arbitration, whether conducted under common law principles or in the light of an applicable state statute, has been the extent to which a court should be authorized either to intercept the arbitration process, or to review an award, on the basis of alleged lack of arbitral jurisdiction or authority with respect to the subject matter of the dispute. As will be noted, this has given rise to a considerable amount of litigation and to extensive discussion. Obviously, to the extent that judicial review is available and utilized, one of the asserted virtues of the arbitration process is lost.

There is a substantial question with respect to the extent of the continuing relevance of state common law and statutory provisions relating to the arbitration process in view of the development of federal substantive law under Section 301 of the Taft-Hartley Act. State law may, however, retain some significance as to procedural matters, at least, and as a possible guide in the ultimate shaping of the federal law.[26]

It may be that ultimately it will be considered desirable to enact a federal statute regulating the labor dispute arbitration process. Since 1947 there has been on the federal statute books an enactment entitled, "United States Arbitration Act," [27] which makes "valid, irrevocable, and enforceable" agreements to arbitrate disputes concerning any maritime transaction and disputes arising out of a "transaction involving commerce." The statute contains procedural and other provisions similar to those contained in many of the state statutes. However, Section 1 of the Act provides that "nothing herein contained shall apply to contracts of employment of seamen, railroad employees, or any other class of workers engaged in foreign or

---

[23] D. Ziskind, Labor Arbitration Under State Statutes 2, 3 (U.S. Dep't of Labor 1943).

[24] Balk, The Enforcement of Agreements to Arbitrate Labor Disputes, 3 N.Y.U. Intra. L. Rev. 1, 3 (1947).

[25] Uniform Laws Ann. 1 (Supp. 1977).

[26] Smith & Clark, Reappraisal of the Role of the States in Shaping Labor Relations Law, 1965 Wis. L. Rev. 411, 456. *See also* Comment, The Applicability of State Arbitration Statutes to Proceedings Subject to LMRA Section 301, 27 Ohio St. L.J. 692 (1966).

[27] 9 U.S.C. §§ 1-14; F.C.A. 9 §§ 1-14.

interstate commerce." The federal courts have been in disagreement concerning the applicability of this statute to arbitration provisions contained in collective bargaining agreement.[28] The issue has not been resolved by the Supreme Court except by negative implication in the *Lincoln Mills* case, *infra*.[29]

The National Academy of Arbitrators in 1960 proposed the enactment of a "United States Labor Arbitration Act," [30] which in many respects differed both from the Uniform Arbitration Act and the United States Arbitration Act. Some of the problems which led to the Academy's promulgation have since been dissipated, at least measurably, by later decisions of the Supreme Court delineating the role of the court vis-a-vis that of the arbitrator. But problems of substance and procedure are by no means fully resolved nor are they likely to be for some time. It may yet be considered desirable to enact a federal statute dealing specifically with the labor dispute arbitration process as generally practiced.

D. THE IMPACT OF SECTION 301 OF THE LABOR-MANAGEMENT RELATIONS ACT (Taft-Hartley Act)

TEXTILE WORKERS UNION v. LINCOLN MILLS

United States Supreme Court
353 U.S. 448, 77 S. Ct. 912, 1 L. Ed. 2d 972 (1957)

Mr. Justice Douglas delivered the opinion of the Court.

Petitioner-union entered into a collective bargaining agreement in 1953 with respondent-employer, the agreement to run one year and from year to year thereafter, unless terminated on specified notices. The agreement provided that there would be no strikes or work stoppages and that grievances would be handled pursuant to a specified procedure. The last step in the grievance procedure — a step that could be taken by either party — was arbitration.

---

[28] UE, Local 205 v. General Elec. Co., 233 F.2d 85 (1st Cir. 1956), *aff'd on other grounds,* 353 U.S. 547 (1957); UE, Local 475 v. Signal-Stat Corp., 235 F.2d 298 (2d Cir. 1956), *cert. denied,* 354 U.S. 911 (1957). *Contra,* Street, Elec. Ry. & Motor Coach Employees, Div. 1210 v. Pennsylvania Greyhound Lines, 192 F.2d 310 (3d Cir. 1951). *See* Burstein, The United States Arbitration Act — A Reevaluation, 3 Vill. L. Rev. 125 (1958).

[29] Despite the Supreme Court's tacit rejection of the United States Arbitration Act as the basis of federal court jurisdiction over labor arbitration contracts, it possibly may be looked to for guidance in developing federal law on arbitral practice and arbitral awards.

[30] For the text and explanatory notes of the proposed United States Labor Arbitration Act see Proceedings of the Thirteenth Annual Meeting of The National Academy of Arbitrators 159 (BNA 1960).

This controversy involves several grievances that concern work loads and work assignments. The grievances were processed through the various steps in the grievance procedure and were finally denied by the employer. The union requested arbitration, and the employer refused. Thereupon the union brought this suit in the District Court to compel arbitration.

The District Court concluded that it had jurisdiction and ordered the employer to comply with the grievance arbitration provisions of the collective bargaining agreement. The Court of Appeals reversed by a divided vote. 230 F.2d 81....

The starting point of our inquiry is § 301 of the Labor Management Relations Act of 1947....

There has been considerable litigation involving § 301 and courts have construed it differently. There is one view that § 301(a) merely gives federal district courts jurisdiction in controversies that involve labor organizations in industries affecting commerce, without regard to diversity of citizenship or the amount in controversy. Under that view § 301(a) would not be the source of substantive law; it would neither supply federal law to resolve these controversies nor turn the federal judges to state law for answers to the questions. Other courts — the overwhelming number of them — hold that § 301(a) is more than jurisdictional — that it authorizes federal courts to fashion a body of federal law for the enforcement of these collective bargaining agreements and includes within that federal law specific performance of promises to arbitrate grievances under collective bargaining agreements. Perhaps the leading decision representing that point of view is the one rendered by Judge Wyzanski in *Textile Workers Union v. American Thread Co.,* 113 F. Supp. 137 (1953). That is our construction of § 301(a), which means that the agreement to arbitrate grievance disputes, contained in this collective bargaining agreement, should be specifically enforced.

From the face of the Act it is apparent that § 301(a) and § 301(b) supplement one another. Section 301(b) makes it possible for a labor organization, representing employees in an industry affecting commerce, to sue and be sued as an entity in the federal courts. Section 301(b) in other words provides the procedural remedy lacking at common law. Section 301(a) certainly does something more than that. Plainly, it supplies the basis upon which the federal district courts may take jurisdiction and apply the procedural rule of § 301(b). The question is whether § 301(a) is more than jurisdictional.

The legislative history of § 301 is somewhat cloudy and confusing. But there are a few shafts of light that illuminate our problem.

The bills, as they passed the House and the Senate, contained provisions which would have made the failure to abide by an agreement to arbitrate an unfair labor practice. S. Rep. No. 105, 80th

Cong., 1st Sess., pp. 20-21, 23; H.R. Rep. No. 245, 80th Cong., 1st Sess., p. 21. This feature of the law was dropped in Conference. As the Conference Report stated, "Once parties have made a collective bargaining contract, the enforcement of that contract should be left to the usual processes of the law and not to the National Labor Relations Board." H.R. Conf. Rep. No. 510, 80th Cong., 1st Sess., p. 42.

Both the Senate and the House took pains to provide for "the usual processes of the law" by provisions which were the substantial equivalent of § 301(a) in its present form. Both the Senate Report and the House Report indicate a primary concern that unions as well as employees should be bound to collective bargaining contracts. But there was also a broader concern — a concern with a procedure for making such agreements enforceable in the courts by either party. At one point the Senate Report, *supra* at 15, states, "We feel that the aggrieved party should also have a right of action in the Federal courts. Such a policy is completely in accord with the purpose of the Wagner Act which the Supreme Court declared was 'to compel employers to bargain collectively with their employees to the end that an employment contract, binding on both parties, should be made. . . .' "

Congress was also interested in promoting collective bargaining that ended with agreements not to strike. The Senate Report, *supra* at 16 states:

"If unions can break agreements with relative impunity, then such agreements do not tend to stabilize industrial relations. The execution of an agreement does not by itself promote industrial peace. The chief advantage which an employer can reasonably expect from a collective labor agreement is assurance of uninterrupted operation during the term of the agreement. Without some effective method of assuring freedom from economic warfare for the term of the agreement, there is little reason why an employer would desire to sign such a contract.

"Consequently, to encourage the making of agreements and to promote industrial peace through faithful performance by the parties, collective agreements affecting interstate commerce should be enforceable in the Federal courts. Our amendment would provide for suits by unions as legal entities and against unions as legal entities in the Federal courts in disputes affecting commerce."

Thus collective bargaining contracts were made "equally binding and enforceable on both parties." Id. at 15. As stated in the House Report, *supra* at 6, the new provision "makes labor organizations equally responsible with employers for contract violations and provides for suit by either against the other in the United States district courts." To repeat, the Senate Report, *supra* at 17, summed up the philosophy of § 301 as follows: "Statutory recognition of the collective agreement as a valid, binding, and enforceable contract is a logical and necessary step. It will promote a higher degree of responsibility upon the parties to such agreements, and will thereby promote industrial peace."

Plainly the agreement to arbitrate grievance disputes is the *quid pro quo* for an agreement not to strike. Viewed in this light, the legislation does more than confer jurisdiction in the federal courts over labor organizations. It expresses a federal policy that federal courts should enforce these agreements on behalf of or against labor organizations and that industrial peace can be best obtained only in that way.

To be sure there is a great medley of ideas reflected in the hearings, reports, and debates on this Act. Yet, to repeat, the entire tenor of the history indicates that the agreement to arbitrate grievance disputes was considered as *quid pro quo* of a no strike agreement. And when in the House the debate narrowed to the question whether § 301 was more than jurisdictional, it became abundantly clear that the purpose of the section was to provide the necessary legal remedies. Section 302 of the House bill, the substantial equivalent of the present § 301, was being described by Mr. Hartley, the sponsor of the bill in the House:

"Mr. Barden. Mr. Chairman, I take this time for the purpose of asking the Chairman a question, and in asking the question I want it understood that it is intended to make a part of the record that may hereafter be referred to as history of the legislation.

"It is my understanding that Section 302, the section dealing with equal responsibility under collective bargaining contracts in strike actions and proceedings in district courts contemplates not only the ordinary lawsuits for damages but also such other remedial proceedings, both legal and equitable, as might be appropriate in the circumstances; in other words, proceedings could, for example, be brought by the employers, the labor organizations, or interested individual employees under the Declaratory Judgments Act in order to secure declarations from the Court of legal rights under the contract.

"Mr. Hartley. The interpretation the gentleman has just given of that section is absolutely correct." 93 Cong. Rec. 3656-3657.

It seems, therefore, clear to us that Congress adopted a policy which placed sanctions behind agreements to arbitrate grievance disputes [42] by implication rejecting the common-law rule discussed

---

[42] Association of Westinghouse Salaried Employees v. Westinghouse Corp., 348 U.S. 437 (1955), is quite a different case. There the union sued to recover unpaid wages on behalf of some 4,000 employees. The basic question concerned the standing of the union to sue and recover on those individual employment contracts. The question here concerns the right of the union to enforce the agreement to arbitrate which it has made with the employer.

in *Red Cross Line v. Atlantic Fruit Co.,* 264 U.S. 109 (1924), against enforcement of executory agreements to arbitrate. We would undercut the Act and defeat its policy if we read § 301 narrowly as only conferring jurisdiction over labor organizations.

The question then is, what is the substantive law to be applied in suits under § 301(a)? We conclude that the substantive law to apply in suits under § 301(a) is federal law which the courts must fashion from the policy of our national labor laws. See Mendelsohn, Enforceability of Arbitration Agreements Under Taft-Hartley Section 301, 66 Yale L.J. 167. The Labor Management Relations Act expressly furnishes some substantive law. It points out what the parties may or may not do in certain situations. Other problems will lie in the penumbra of express statutory mandates. Some will lack express statutory sanction but will be solved by looking at the policy of the legislation and fashioning a remedy that will effectuate that policy. The range of judicial inventiveness will be determined by the nature of the problem. See *Board of Commissioners v. United States,* 308 U.S. 343, 351 (1939). Federal interpretation of the federal law will govern, not state law. *Cf. Jerome v. United States,* 318 U.S. 101, 104 (1943). But state law, if compatible with the purpose of § 301, may be resorted to in order to find the rule that will best effectuate the federal policy. *See Board of Commissioners v. United States, supra,* at 351-352. Any state law applied, however, will be absorbed as federal law and will not be an independent source of private rights.

It is not uncommon for federal courts to fashion federal law where federal rights are concerned. *See Clearfield Trust Co. v. United States,* 318 U.S. 363, 366-367 (1943); *National Metropolitan Bank v. United States,* 323 U.S. 454 (1945). Congress has indicated by § 301(a) the purpose to follow that course here. There is no constitutional difficulty. Article III, § 2 extends the judicial power to cases "arising under . . . the Laws of the Untied States. . . ." The power of Congress to regulate these labor-management controversies under the Commerce Clause is plain. *Houston Texas R. Co. v. United States,* 234 U.S. 342 (1914); *NLRB v. Jones & Laughlin Corp.,* 301 U.S. 1 (1936). A case or controversy arising under § 301(a) is, therefore, one within the purview of judicial power as defined in Article III.

The question remains whether jurisdiction to compel arbitration of grievance disputes is withdrawn by the Norris-La Guardia Act, 47 Stat. 70, 29 U.S.C. § 101. Section 7 of that Act prescribes stiff procedural requirements for issuing an injunction in a labor dispute. The kinds of acts which had given rise to abuse of the power to enjoin are listed in § 4. The failure to arbitrate was not a part and parcel of the abuses against which the Act was aimed. Section 8 of the Norris-La Guardia Act does, indeed, indicate a congressional policy toward settlement of labor disputes by arbitration, for it denies injunctive relief to any person who has failed to make "every reasonable effort" to settle the dispute by negotiation, mediation, or "voluntary arbitration." Though a literal reading might bring the dispute within the terms of the Act (*see* Cox, Grievance Arbitration in the Federal Courts, 67 Harv. L. Rev. 591, 602-604), we see no justification in policy for restricting § 301(a) to damage suits, leaving specific performance of a contract to arbitrate grievance disputes to the inapposite procedural requirements of that Act. Moreover, we held in *Virginian R. Co. v. System Federation,* 300 U.S. 515 (1937), and in *Graham v. Brotherhood of Firemen,* 338 U.S. 232, 237 (1949), that the Norris-La Guardia Act does not deprive Federal courts of jurisdiction to compel compliance with the mandates of the Railway Labor Act, 45 U.S.C. § 151. The mandates there involved concerned racial discrimination. Yet those decisions were not based on any peculiarities of the Railway Labor Act. We followed the same course in *Syres v. Oil Workers,* 350 U.S. 892 (1955), which was governed by the National Labor Relations Act, 29 U.S.C. § 151. There an injunction was sought against racial discrimination in application of a collective bargaining agreement; and we allowed the injunction to issue. The congressional policy in favor of the enforcement of agreements to arbitrate grievance disputes being clear, there is no reason to submit them to the requirements of § 7 of the Norris-La Guardia Act. . . .

The judgment of the Court of Appeals is reversed and the cause is remanded to that court for proceedings in conformity with this opinion.

Reversed.

Mr. Justice Black took no part in the consideration or decision of this case.

Mr. Justice Burton, whom Mr. Justice Harlan joins, concurring in the result.

This suit was brought in a United States District Court under § 301 of the Labor Management Relations Act of 1947, 61 Stat. 156, 29 U.S.C. § 185, seeking specific enforcement of the arbitration provisions of a collective-bargaining contract. The District Court had jurisdiction over the action since it involved an obligation running to a union — a union controversy — and not uniquely personal rights of employees sought to be enforced by a union. *Cf. Association of Westinghouse Salaried Employees v. Westinghouse Elec. Corp.,* 348 U.S. 437 (1955). Having jurisdiction over the suit, the court was not powerless to fashion an appropriate federal remedy. The power to decree specific performance of a collectively bargained agreement to arbitrate finds its source in § 301 itself, and in a Federal District Court's inherent equitable powers, nurtured by a congressional policy to encourage and enforce labor arbitration in industries affecting commerce.

I do not subscribe to the conclusion of the Court that the substantive law to be applied in a suit under § 301 is federal law. At the same time, I agree with Judge Magruder in *International Brotherhood v. W. L. Mead, Inc.,* 230 F.2d 576 (1st Cir. 1956), that some federal rights may necessarily be involved in a § 301 case, and hence that the constitutionality of § 301 can be upheld as a congressional grant to Federal District Courts of what has been called "protective jurisdiction."

[Mr. Justice Frankfurter dissented in a rather unusual 86-page opinion, including the entire relevant legislative history of § 301 of the Taft-Hartley Act and its predecessor bill, the Case bill, in order to prove the point which he had made in *Westinghouse* — that § 301 did not create substantive rights but was only procedural.]

NOTES:

(1) In *Association of Westinghouse Salaried Employees v. Westinghouse Elec. Corp.,* 348 U.S. 437 (1955), the Supreme Court avoided the constitutional question reached and decided in *Lincoln Mills* by holding that § 301 was not intended to authorize a union to sue on behalf of employees for accrued wage claims, which were described as "uniquely personal rights." Five years after *Lincoln Mills,* in *Smith v. Evening News Ass'n,* 371 U.S. 195, 199 (1962), the Court declared that *Westinghouse* was "no longer authoritative as a precedent." The lower federal courts have accordingly allowed unions to maintain actions to enforce the rights of employees in a distribution of the assets of a negotiated pension fund, *UAW v. Textron, Inc.,* 312 F.2d 688 (6th Cir. 1963), and to secure for employees wages due under a cost-of-living adjustment clause in a labor contract, *Retail Clerks, Local 1222 v. Alfred Lewis, Inc.,* 327 F.2d 442 (9th Cir. 1964). *See UAW v. Hoosier Cardinal Corp.,* 383 U.S. 696, 699-700 (1966). In *Hoosier Cardinal* the Supreme Court also held that § 301 suits are governed by state statutes of limitations.

(2) The Supreme Court has held that Section 301 did not divest the state courts of jurisdiction over suits to enforce the collective agreement. State and federal courts have concurrent jurisdiction to handle such suits. *Dowd Box Co. v. Courtney,* 368 U.S. 502 (1962). But a state court, exercising jurisdiction over cases within the purview of Section 301, must apply principles of federal substantive law rather than state law. *Teamsters Local 174 v. Lucas Flour Co.,* 369 U.S. 95 (1962). The Court said: "The dimensions of § 301 require the conclusion that substantive principles of federal labor law must be paramount in the area covered by the statute.

Comprehensiveness is inherent in the process by which the law is to be formulated under the mandate of *Lincoln Mills,* requiring issues raised in suits of a kind covered by § 301 to be decided according to the precepts of federal labor policy. The Supreme Court itself formulated an important precept of federal collective agreement law in the *Lucas Flour* case: that where the agreement provides for mandatory arbitration of an issue, the union has a duty not to strike over that issue. This duty applies even in the absence of an express no-strike clause. The agreement to arbitrate implies the obligation not to strike over an arbitrable issue arising during the term of the contract. In the *Lucas Flour* case, the union had struck over a concededly arbitrable issue (whether an employee had been discharged for good cause); the Supreme Court affirmed the state court's award of damages to the employer, but not on the theory which had been used by the state court.

(3) The weight of authority is that an action for a declaratory judgment can be brought under § 301; *e.g., Jersey Central Power & Light Co. v. Electrical Workers,* 508 F.2d 687 (3d Cir. 1975), *vacated on other grounds,* 96 S. Ct. 2196 (1976); *Black-Clawson Co., Inc. v. Machinists Lodge 355,* 313 F.2d (2d Cir. 1962); *Radio Corp. v. Association of Professional Engineering Personnel,* 291 F.2d 105 (3d Cir. 1961), *cert. denied,* 368 U.S. 898 (1961).

(4) *Interest arbitration* — Is an agreement to arbitrate the terms of a new contract enforceable under § 301? A pre-*Lincoln Mills* case held that § 301 would not support a suit to enforce such an agreement; the statute was not thought to encompass such "quasi-legislative" arbitration. *Boston Printing Pressmen's Union v. Potter Press,* 141 F. Supp. 553 (D. Mass. 1956), *aff'd,* 241 F.2d 787 (1st Cir. 1957), *cert. denied,* 355 U.S. 817 (1957). Since that decision, however, several courts have indicated that an interest arbitration provision is enforceable under § 301. *Builders Ass'n of Kansas City v. Kansas City Laborers,* 336 F.2d 867 (8th Cir. 1964), *cert. denied,* 377 U.S. 917 (1964); *A. Seltzer & Co. v. Livingston,* 253 F. Supp. 509 (S.D.N.Y. 1966), *aff'd,* 361 F.2d 218 (2d Cir. 1966); *Winston-Salem Printing Pressman v. Piedmont Publishing Co.,* 393 F.2d 221 (4th Cir. 1968); *Chattanooga Mailers v. Chattanooga News-Free Press,* 524 F.2d 1305 (6th Cir. 1975). Of what relevance to this issue are cases holding that an interest arbitration clause is not a mandatory subject of bargaining and hence that a party may not insist on such a clause to the point of impasse without committing an unfair labor practice? *NLRB v. Columbia Printing Pressmen,* 524 F.2d 1161 (5th Cir. 1976); *NLRB v. Greensboro Printing Pressmen,* 549 F.2d 308 (4th Cir. 1977); *NLRB v. Massachusetts Nurses Ass'n,* 557 F.2d 894 (1st Cir. 1977).

E. ARBITRABILITY (ENFORCEMENT OF THE AGREEMENT TO ARBITRATE)

UNITED STEELWORKERS v. AMERICAN MANUFACTURING CO.

United States Supreme Court
363 U.S. 564, 80 S. Ct. 1343, 4 L. Ed. 2d 1403 (1960)

Mr. Justice Douglas delivered the opinion of the Court.

This suit was brought by petitioner union in the District Court to compel arbitration of a "grievance" that petitioner, acting for one Sparks, a union member, had filed with the respondent, Sparks' employer. The employer defended on the ground (1) that Sparks is estopped from making his claim because he had a few days previously settled a workmen's compensation claim against the company on the basis that he was permanently partially disabled, (2) that Sparks is not physically able to do the work, and (3) that this type of dispute is not arbitrable under the collective bargaining agreement in question.

The agreement provided that during its term there would be "no strike," unless the employer refused to abide by a decision of the arbitrator. The agreement sets out a detailed grievance procedure with a provision for arbitration (regarded as the standard form) of all disputes between the parties "as to the meaning, interpretation and application of the provisions of this agreement." [1]

The agreement reserves to the management power to suspend or discharge any employee "for cause." [2] It also contains a provision that the employer will employ and promote employees on the

---

[1] The relevant arbitration provisions read as follows:

"Any disputes, misunderstandings, differences or grievances arising between the parties as to the meaning, interpretation and application of the provisions of this agreement, which are not adjusted as herein provided, may be submitted to the Board of Arbitration for decision . . .

"The arbitrator may interpret this agreement and apply it to the particular case under consideration but shall, however, have no authority to add to, subtract from, or modify the terms of the agreement. Disputes relating to discharges or such matters as might involve a loss of pay for employees may carry an award of back pay in whole or in part as may be determined by the Board of Arbitration.

"The decision of the Board of Arbitration shall be final and conclusively binding upon both parties, and the parties agree to observe and abide by same."

[2] "The Management of the works, the direction of the working force, plant layout and routine of work, including the right to hire, suspend, transfer, discharge or otherwise discipline any employee for cause, such cause being: infraction of company rules, inefficiency, insubordination, contagious disease harmful to others, and any other ground or reason that would tend to reduce or impair the efficiency of plant operation; and to lay off employees because of lack of work, is reserved to the Company, provided it does not conflict with this agreement. . . ."

principle of seniority "where ability and efficiency are equal." [3] Sparks left his work due to an injury and while off work brought an action for compensation benefits. The case was settled, Sparks' physician expressing the opinion that the injury had made him 25% "permanently partially disabled." That was on September 9. Two weeks later the union filed a grievance which charged that Sparks was entitled to return to his job by virtue of the seniority provision of the collective bargaining agreement. Respondent refused to arbitrate and this action was brought. The District Court held that Sparks, having accepted the settlement on the basis of permanent partial disability, was estopped to claim any seniority or employment rights and granted the motion for summary judgment. The Court of Appeals affirmed, 264 F.2d 624, for different reasons. After reviewing the evidence it held that the grievance is "a frivolous, patently baseless one, not subject to arbitration under the collective bargaining agreement." Id. at 628. . . .

Section 203(d) of the Labor Management Relations Act, 1947, 61 Stat. 154, 29 U.S.C. § 173(d) states, "Final adjustment by a method agreed upon by the parties is hereby declared to be the desirable method for settlement of grievance disputes arising over the application or interpretation of an existing collective-bargaining agreement. . . ." That policy can be effectuated only if the means chosen by the parties for settlement of their differences under a collective bargaining agreement is given full play.

A state decision that held to the contrary announced a principle that could only have a crippling effect on grievance arbitration. The case was *International Ass'n of Machinists v. Cutler-Hammer, Inc.,* 271 App. Div. 917, 67 N.Y.S.2d 317, aff'd 297 N.Y. 519, 74 N.E.2d 464. It held that "If the meaning of the provision of the contract sought to be arbitrated is beyond dispute, there cannot be anything to arbitrate and the contract cannot be said to provide for arbitration." 271 App. Div. at 918, 67 N.Y.S.2d at 318. The lower courts in the instant case had a like preoccupation with ordinary contract law. The collective agreement requires arbitration of claims that courts might be unwilling to entertain. In the context of the plant or industry the grievance may assume proportions of which judges are ignorant. Yet, the agreement is to submit all grievances to arbitration, not merely those that a court may deem to be meritorious. There is no exception in the "no strike" clause and none therefore should be read into the grievance clause, since one is the

---

[3] This provision provides in relevant part:

"The Company and the Union fully recognize the principle of seniority as a factor in the selection of employees for promotion, transfer, lay-off, reemployment, and filling of vacancies, where ability and efficiency are equal. It is the policy of the Company to promote employees on that basis."

quid pro quo for the other. The question is not whether in the mind of the court there is equity in the claim. Arbitration is a stabilizing influence only as it serves as a vehicle for handling any and all disputes that arise under the agreement.

The collective agreement calls for the submission of grievances in the categories which it describes, irrespective of whether a court may deem them to be meritorious. In our role of developing a meaningful body of law to govern the interpretation and enforcement of collective bargaining agreements we think special heed should be given to the context in which collective bargaining agreements are negotiated and the purpose which they are intended to serve. *See Lewis v. Benedict Coal Corp.,* 361 U.S. 459, 468. The function of the court is very limited when the parties have agreed to submit all questions of contract interpretation to the arbitrator. It is confined to ascertaining whether the party seeking arbitration is making a claim which on its face is governed by the contract. Whether the moving party is right or wrong is a question of contract interpretation for the arbitrator. In these circumstances the moving party should not be deprived of the arbitrator's judgment, when it was his judgment and all that it connotes that was bargained for.

The courts, therefore, have no business weighing the merits of the grievance, considering whether there is equity in a particular claim, or determining whether there is particular language in the written instrument which will support the claim. The agreement is to submit all grievances to arbitration, not merely those which the court will deem meritorious. The processing of even frivolous claims may have therapeutic values of which those who are not a part of the plant environment may be quite unaware.

The union claimed in this case that the company had violated a specific provision of the contract. The company took the position that it had not violated that clause. There was, therefore, a dispute between the parties as to "the meaning, interpretation and application" of the collective bargaining agreement. Arbitration should have been ordered. When the judiciary undertakes to determine the merits of a grievance under the guise of interpreting the grievance procedure of collective bargaining agreements, it usurps a function which under that regime is entrusted to the arbitration tribunal.

Reversed.

[Mr. Justice Brennan, Mr. Justice Harland, and Mr. Justice Frankfurter concurred in an opinion which appears with *United Steelworkers v. Warrior & Gulf Nav. Co., infra.*]

Mr. Justice Whittaker, believing that the District Court lacked jurisdiction to determine the merits of the claim which the parties had validly agreed to submit to the exclusive jurisdiction of a Board of Arbitrators (*Textile Workers v. Lincoln Mills,* 353 U.S. 448), concurs in the result of this opinion.

Mr. Justice Black took no part in the consideration or decision of this case.

UNITED STEELWORKERS v. WARRIOR & GULF NAVIGATION CO.

United States Supreme Court
363 U.S. 574, 80 S. Ct. 1347, 4 L. Ed. 2d 1409 (1960)

Mr. Justice Douglas delivered the opinion of the Court.

Respondent transports steel and steel products by barge and maintains a terminal at Chickasaw, Alabama, where it performs maintenance and repair work on its barges. The employees at that terminal constitute a bargaining unit covered by a collective bargaining agreement negotiated by petitioner union. Respondent between 1956 and 1958 laid off some employees, reducing the bargaining unit from 42 to 23 men. This reduction was due in part to respondent contracting maintenance work, previously done by its employees, to other companies. The latter used respondent's supervisors to lay out the work and hired some of the laid-off employees of respondent (at reduced wages). Some were in fact assigned to work on respondent's barges. A number of employees signed a grievance which petitioner presented to respondent, the grievance reading:

"We are hereby protesting the Company's actions, of arbitrarily and unreasonably contracting out work to other concerns, that could and previously has been performed by Company employees.

"This practice becomes unreasonable, unjust and discriminatory in lieu [*sic*] of the fact that at present there are a number of employees that have been laid off for about 1 and ½ years or more for allegedly lack of work.

"Confronted with these facts we charge that the Company is in violation of the contract by inducing a partial lockout, of a number of the employees who would otherwise be working were it not for this unfair practice."

The collective agreement had both a "no strike" and a "no lockout" provision. It also had a grievance procedure which provided in relevant part as follows:

"Issues which conflict with any Federal statute in its application as established by Court procedure or matters which are strictly a function of management shall not be subject to arbitration under this section.

"Should differences arise between the Company and the Union or its members employed by the Company as to the meaning and application of the provisions of this Agreement, or should any local trouble of any kind arise, there shall be no suspension of work on account of such differences but an earnest effort shall be made to settle such differences immediately in the following manner:

"A. For Maintenance Employees:

"First, between the aggrieved employees, and the Foreman involved;

"Second, between a member or members of the Grievance Committee designated by the Union, and the Foreman and Master Mechanic.

. . . .

"Fifth, if agreement has not been reached the matter shall be referred to an impartial umpire for decision. The parties shall meet to decide on an umpire acceptable to both. If no agreement on selection of an umpire is reached, the parties shall jointly petition the United States Conciliation Service for suggestion of a list of umpires from which selection will be made. The decision of the umpire shall be final."

Settlement of this grievance was not had and respondent refused arbitration. This suit was then commenced by the union to compel it.

The District Court granted respondent's motion to dismiss the complaint. 168 F. Supp. 702. It held after hearing evidence, much of which went to the merits of the grievance, that the agreement did not "confide in an arbitrator the right to review the defendant's business judgment in contracting out work." *Id.* at 705. It further held that "the contracting out of repair and maintenance work, as well as construction work, is strictly a function of management not limited in any respect by the labor agreement involved here." *Id.* The Court of Appeals affirmed by a divided vote, 269 F.2d 633, the majority holding that the collective agreement had withdrawn from the grievance procedure "matters which are strictly a function of management" and that contracting out fell in that exception. . . .

We held in *Textile Workers v. Lincoln Mills,* 353 U.S. 448, that a grievance arbitration provision in a collective agreement could be enforced by reason of § 301(a) of the Labor Management Relations Act and that the policy to be applied in enforcing this type of arbitration was that reflected in our national labor laws. *Id.* at 456-457. The present federal policy is to promote industrial stabilization through the collective bargaining agreement. *Id.* at 453-454. A major factor in achieving industrial peace is the inclusion of a provision for arbitration of grievances in the collective bargaining agreement.[4]

---

[4] Complete effectuation of the federal policy is achieved when the agreement contains both an arbitration provision for all unresolved grievances and an absolute prohibition of strikes, the arbitration agreement being the *"quid pro quo"* for the agreement not to strike. Textile Workers v. Lincoln Mills, 353 U.S. 448, 455.

Thus the run of arbitration cases, illustrated by *Wilko v. Swan,* 346 U.S. 427, becomes irrelevant to our problem. There the choice is between the adjudication of cases or controversies in courts with established procedures or even special statutory safeguards on the one hand and the settlement of them in the more informal arbitration tribunal on the other. In the commercial case, arbitration is the substitute for litigation. Here arbitration is the substitute for industrial strife. Since arbitration of labor disputes has quite different functions from arbitration under an ordinary commercial agreement, the hostility evinced by courts toward arbitration of commercial agreements has no place here. For arbitration of labor disputes under collective bargaining agreements is part and parcel of the collective bargaining process itself.

The collective bargaining agreement states the rights and duties of the parties. It is more than a contract; it is a generalized code to govern a myriad of cases which the draftsmen cannot wholly anticipate. *See* Shulman, Reason, Contract, and Law in Labor Relations, 68 Harv. L. Rev. 999, 1004-1005. The collective agreement covers the whole employment relationship. It calls into being a new common law — the common law of a particular industry or of a particular plant. As one observer has put it: [6]

". . . [I]t is not unqualifiedly true that a collective-bargaining agreement is simply a document by which the union and employees have imposed upon management limited, express restrictions of its otherwise absolute right to manage the enterprise, so that an employee's claim must fail unless he can point to a specific contract provision upon which the claim is founded. There are too many people, too many problems, too many unforeseeable contingencies to make the words of the contract the exclusive source of rights and duties. One cannot reduce all the rules governing a community like an industrial plant to fifteen or even fifty pages. Within the sphere of collective bargaining, the institutional characteristics and the governmental nature of the collective-bargaining process demand a common law of the shop which implements and furnishes the context of the agreement. We must assume that intelligent negotiators acknowledged so plain a need unless they stated a contrary rule in plain words."

A collective bargaining agreement is an effort to erect a system of industrial self-government. When most parties enter into contractual relationship they do so voluntarily, in the sense that there is no real compulsion to deal with one another, as opposed to dealing with other parties. This is not true of the labor agreement. The choice is generally not between entering or refusing to enter into a

---

[6] Cox, Reflections Upon Labor Arbitration, 72 Harv. L. Rev. 1482, 1498-1499 (1959).

relationship, for that in all probability preexists the negotiations. Rather it is between having that relationship governed by an agreed-upon rule of law or leaving each and every matter subject to a temporary resolution dependent solely upon the relative strength, at any given moment, of the contending forces. The mature labor agreement may attempt to regulate all aspects of the complicated relationship, from the most crucial to the most minute over an extended period of time. Because of the compulsion to reach agreement and the breadth of the matters covered, as well as the need for a fairly concise and readable instrument, the product of negotiations (the written document) is, in the words of the late Dean Shulman,

". . . [A] compilation of diverse provisions: some provide objective criteria almost automatically applicable; some provide more or less specific standards which require reason and judgment in their application; and some do little more than leave problems to future consideration with an expression of hope and good faith." Shulman, *supra* at 1005. Gaps may be left to be filled in by reference to the practices of the particular industry and of the various shops covered by the agreement. Many of the specific practices which underlie the agreement may be unknown, except in hazy form, even to the negotiators. Courts and arbitration in the context of most commercial contracts are resorted to because there has been a breakdown in the working relationship of the parties; such resort is the unwanted exception. But the grievance machinery under a collective bargaining agreement is at the very heart of the system of industrial self-government. Arbitration is the means of solving the unforeseeable by molding a system of private law for all the problems which may arise and to provide for their solution in a way which will generally accord with the variant needs and desires of the parties. The processing of disputes through the grievance machinery is actually a vehicle by which meaning and content are given to the collective bargaining agreement.

Apart from matters that the parties specifically exclude, all of the questions on which the parties disagree must therefore come within the scope of the grievance and arbitration provisions of the collective agreement. The grievance procedure is, in other words, a part of the continuous collective bargaining process. It, rather than a strike, is the terminal point of a disagreement. . . .

"A proper conception of the arbitrator's function is basic. He is not a public tribunal imposed upon the parties by superior authority which the parties are obliged to accept. He has no general charter to administer justice for a community which transcends the parties. He is rather part of a system of self-government created by and confined to the parties. . . ." Shulman, *supra* at 1016.

The labor arbitrator's source of law is not confined to the express provisions of the contract, as the industrial common law — the practices of the industry and the shop — is equally a part of the collective bargaining agreement although not expressed in it. The labor arbitrator is usually chosen because of the parties' confidence in his knowledge of the common law of the shop and their trust in his personal judgment to bring to bear considerations which are not expressed in the contract as criteria for judgment. The parties expect that his judgment of a particular grievance will reflect not only what the contract says but, insofar as the collective bargaining agreement permits, such factors as the effect upon productivity of a particular result, its consequence to the morale of the shop, his judgment whether tensions will be heightened or diminished. For the parties' objective in using the arbitration process is primarily to further their common goal of uninterrupted production under the agreement, to make the agreement serve their specialized needs. The ablest judge cannot be expected to bring the same experience and competence to bear upon the determination of a grievance, because he cannot be similarly informed.

The Congress, however, has by § 301 of the Labor Management Relations Act, assigned the courts the duty of determining whether the reluctant party has breached his promise to arbitrate. For arbitration is a matter of contract and a party cannot be required to submit to arbitration any dispute which he has not agreed so to submit. Yet, to be consistent with congressional policy in favor of settlement of disputes by the parties through the machinery of arbitration, the judicial inquiry under § 301 must be strictly confined to the question whether the reluctant party did agree to arbitrate the grievance or did agree to give the arbitrator power to make the award he made. An order to arbitrate the particular grievance should not be denied unless it may be said with positive assurance that the arbitration clause is not susceptible of an interpretation that covers the asserted dispute. Doubts should be resolved in favor of coverage.[7]

We do not agree with the lower courts that contracting-out grievances were necessarily excepted from the grievance procedure of this agreement. To be sure, the agreement provides that "matters which are strictly a function of management shall not be subject to

---

[7] It is clear that under both the agreement in this case and that involved in American Mfg. Co., *supra* at 564, the question of arbitrability is for the courts to decide. Cf. Cox, Reflections Upon Labor Arbitration, 72 Harv. L. Rev. 1482, 1508-1509 (1959). Where the assertion by the claimant is that the parties excluded from court determination not merely the decision of the merits of the grievance but also the question of its arbitrability, vesting power to make both decisions in the arbitrator, the claimant must bear the burden of a clear demonstration of that purpose.

arbitration." But it goes on to say that if "differences" arise or if "any local trouble of any kind" arises, the grievance procedure shall be applicable.

Collective bargaining agreements regulate or restrict the exercise of management functions; they do not oust management from the performance of them. Management hires and fires, pays and promotes, supervises and plans. All these are part of its function, and absent a collective bargaining agreement, it may be exercised freely except as limited by public law and by the willingness of employees to work under the particular, unilaterally imposed conditions. A collective bargaining agreement may treat only with certain specific practices, leaving the rest to management but subject to the possibility of work stoppages. When, however, an absolute no-strike clause is included in the agreement, then in a very real sense everything that management does is subject to the agreement, for either management is prohibited or limited in the action it takes, or if not, it is protected from interference by strikes. This comprehensive reach of the collective bargaining agreement does not mean, however, that the language, "strictly a function of management," has no meaning.

"Strictly a function of management" might be thought to refer to any practice of management in which, under particular circumstances prescribed by the agreement, it is permitted to indulge. But if courts, in order to determine arbitrability, were allowed to determine what is permitted and what is not, the arbitration clause would be swallowed up by the exception. Every grievance in a sense involves a claim that management has violated some provision of the agreement.

Accordingly, "strictly a function of management" must be interpreted as referring only to that over which the contract gives management complete control and unfettered discretion. Respondent claims that the contracting out of work falls within this category. Contracting out work is the basis of many grievances; and that type of claim is grist in the mills of the arbitrators.[8] A specific collective bargaining agreement may exclude contracting out from the grievance procedure. Or a written collateral agreement may make clear that contracting out was not a matter for arbitration. In such a case a grievance based solely on contracting out would not be arbitrable. Here, however, there is no such provision. Nor is there

---

[8] See Celanese Corp., 33 Lab. Arb. Rep. 925, 941 (1959), where the arbiter in a grievance growing out of contracting out work said:

"In my research I have located 64 published decisions which have been concerned with this issue covering a wide range of factual situations but all of them with the common characteristic — *i.e.,* the contracting-out of work involved occurred under an Agreement that contained no provision that specifically mentioned contracting-out of work."

any showing that the parties designed the phrase "strictly a function of management" to encompass any and all forms of contracting out. In the absence of any express provision excluding a particular grievance from arbitration, we think only the most forceful evidence of a purpose to exclude the claim from arbitration can prevail, particularly where, as here, the exclusion clause is vague and the arbitration clause quite broad. Since any attempt by a court to infer such a purpose necessarily comprehends the merits, the court should view with suspicion an attempt to persuade it to become entangled in the construction of the substantive provisions of a labor agreement, even through the back door of interpreting the arbitration clause, when the alternative is to utilize the services of an arbitrator.

The grievance alleged that the contracting out was a violation of the collective bargaining agreement. There was, therefore, a dispute "as to the meaning and application of the provisions of this Agreement" which the parties had agreed would be determined by arbitration.

The judiciary sits in these cases to bring into operation an arbitral process which substitutes a regime of peaceful settlement for the older regime of industrial conflict. Whether contracting out in the present case violated the agreement is the question. It is a question for the arbiter, not for the courts.

Reversed.

Mr. Justice Frankfurter concurs in the result.

Mr. Justice Black took no part in the consideration or decision of this case. . . .

Mr. Justice Whittaker, dissenting.

Until today, I have understood it to be the unquestioned law, as this Court has consistently held, that arbitrators are private judges chosen by the parties to decide particular matters specifically submitted; that the contract under which matters are submitted to arbitrators is at once the source and limit of their authority and power; and that their power to decide issues with finality, thus ousting the normal functions of the courts, must rest upon a clear, definitive agreement of the parties, as such powers can never be implied. . . . I believe that the Court today departs from the established principles announced in these decisions. . . .

Mr. Justice Brennan, with whom Mr. Justice Harlan joins, concurring.

While I join the Court's opinions in Nos. 443, 360 and 538 [*Warrior & Gulf,* p. 137, *American Manufacturing,* p. 134 *supra,* and *Enterprise Wheel,* p. 148 *infra,* respectively], I add a word in Nos. 443 and 360.

In each of these two cases the issue concerns the enforcement of but one promise — the promise to arbitrate in the context of an agreement dealing with a particular subject matter, the industrial relations between employers and employees. Other promises contained in the collective bargaining agreements are beside the point unless, by the very terms of the arbitration promise, they are made relevant to its interpretation. And I emphasize this, for the arbitration promise is itself a contract. The parties are free to make that promise as broad or as narrow as they wish, for there is no compulsion in law requiring them to include any such promises in their agreement. The meaning of the arbitration promise is not to be found simply by reference to the dictionary definitions of the words the parties use, or by reference to the interpretation of commercial arbitration clauses. Words in a collective bargaining agreement, rightly viewed by the Court to be the charter instrument of a system of industrial self-government, like words in a statute, are to be understood only by reference to the background which gave rise to their inclusion. The Court therefore avoids the prescription of inflexible rules for the enforcement of arbitration promises. Guidance is given by identifying the various considerations which a court should take into account when construing a particular clause — considerations of the milieu in which the clause is negotiated and of the national labor policy. It is particularly underscored that the arbitral process in collective bargaining presupposes that the parties wanted the informed judgment of an arbitrator, precisely for the reason that judges cannot provide it. Therefore, a court asked to enforce a promise to arbitrate should ordinarily refrain from involving itself in the interpretation of the substantive provisions of the contract.

To be sure, since arbitration is a creature of contract, a court must always inquire, when a party seeks to invoke its aid to force a reluctant party to the arbitration table, whether the parties have agreed to arbitrate the particular dispute. In this sense, the question of whether a dispute is "arbitrable" is inescapably for the court.

On examining the arbitration clause, the court may conclude that it commits to arbitration any "dispute, difference, disagreement, or controversy of any nature or character." With that finding the court will have exhausted its function, except to order the reluctant party to arbitration. Similarly, although the arbitrator may be empowered only to interpret and apply the contract, the parties may have provided that any dispute as to whether a particular claim is within the arbitration clause is itself for the arbitrator. Again the court, without more, must send any dispute to the arbitrator, for the parties have agreed that the construction of the arbitration promise itself is for the arbitrator, and the reluctant party has breached his promise by refusing to submit the dispute to arbitration.

In *American,* the Court deals with a request to enforce the "standard" form of arbitration clause, one that provides for the arbitration of "[a]ny disputes, misunderstandings, differences or grievances arising between the parties as to the meaning, interpretation and application of this agreement. . . ." Since the arbitration clause itself is part of the agreement, it might be argued that a dispute as to the meaning of that clause is for the arbitrator. But the Court rejects this position, saying that the threshold question, the meaning of the arbitration clause itself, is for the judge unless the parties clearly state to the contrary. However, the Court finds that the meaning of that "standard" clause is simply that the parties have agreed to arbitrate any dispute which the moving party asserts to involve construction of the substantive provisions of the contract, because such a dispute necessarily does involve such a construction.

The issue in the *Warrior* case is essentially no different from that in *American,* that is, it is whether the company agreed to arbitrate a particular grievance. In contrast to *American,* however, the aribtration promise here excludes a particular area from arbitration — "matters which are strictly a function of management." Because the arbitration promise is different, the scope of the court's inquiry may be broader. Here, a court may be required to examine the substantive provisions of the contract to ascertain whether the parties have provided that contracting out shall be a "function of management." If a court may delve into the merits to the extent of inquiring whether the parties have expressly agreed whether or not contracting out was a "function of management," why was it error for the lower court here to evaluate the evidence of bargaining history for the same purpose? Neat logical distinctions do not provide the answer. The Court rightly concludes that appropriate regard for the national labor policy and the special factors relevant to the labor arbitral process, admonish that judicial inquiry into the merits of this grievance should be limited to the search for an explicit provision which brings the grievance under the cover of the exclusion clause since "the exclusion clause is vague and arbitration clause quite broad." The hazard of going further into the merits is amply demonstrated by what the courts below did. On the basis of inconclusive evidence, those courts found that *Warrior* was in no way limited by any implied covenants of good faith and fair dealing from contracting out as it pleased — which would necessarily mean that *Warrior* was free completely to destroy the collective bargaining agreement by contracting out all the work.

The very ambiguity of the *Warrior* exclusion clause suggests that the parties were generally more concerned with having an arbitrator render decisions as to the meaning of the contract than they were in restricting the arbitrator's jurisdiction. The case might of course be otherwise were the arbitration clause very narrow, or the exclusion clause quite specific, for the inference might then be permissible that the parties had manifested a greater interest in confining the arbitrator; the presumption of arbitrability would then not have the same force and the Court would be somewhat freer to examine into the merits.

The Court makes reference to an arbitration clause being the *quid pro quo* for a no-strike clause. I do not understand the Court to mean that the application of the principles announced today depends upon the presence of a no-strike clause in the agreement.

Mr. Justice Frankfurter joins these observations.

NOTES:

(1) The two preceding cases, together with *United Steelworkers v. Enterprise Wheel & Car Corp. (infra* at p. 399) are familiarly known as the "Steelworkers Trilogy." They have evoked a voluminous literature. *See, e.g.,* Aaron, Arbitration in the Federal Courts: Aftermath of the Trilogy, 9 U.C.L.A. L. Rev. 360 (1962); Gregory, Enforcement of Collective Agreements by Arbitration, 48 Va. L. Rev. 883 (1962); Hays, The Supreme Court and Labor Law — October Term, 1959, 60 Colum. L. Rev. 901 (1960); Meltzer, The Supreme Court, Arbitrability, and Collective Bargaining, 28 U. Chi. L. Rev. 464 (1961); Smith & Jones, The Supreme Court and Labor Dispute Arbitration: The Emerging Federal Law, 63 Mich. L. Rev. 751 (1965); Smith & Jones, The Impact of the Emerging Federal Law of Grievance Arbitration on Judges, Arbitrators, and Parties, 52 Va. L. Rev. 831 (1966); Wellington, Judicial Review of the Promise to Arbitrate, 37 N.Y.U. L. Rev. 471 (1962); Symposium — Arbitration and the Courts, 58 Nw.U. L. Rev. 466, 494, 521, 556 (1963).

(2) Following *American Manufacturing Co.* and *Warrior & Gulf,* the overwhelming trend has been to require arbitration even where, in the court's view, the grievance appears to be frivolous. *See, e.g, IBEW, Local 24 v. Hearst Corp.,* 352 F.2d 957 (4th Cir. 1965), *cert. denied,* 383 U.S. 97 (1966); *Association of Industrial Scientists v. Shell Dev. Co.,* 348 F.2d 385 (9th Cir. 1965); *Brick & Clay Workers v. A.P. Green Fire Brick Co.,* 343 F.2d 590 (8th Cir. 1965). Suprisingly, some courts continue to find a dispute nonarbitrable if they find no merit in the grievant's interpretation of the contract. *See, e.g., Dept. Store Drivers, Local 955 v. Birmingham-Prosser Paper Co.,* 364 F. Supp. 426 (W.D. Mo. 1973) ("the no-strike clause is clear and unnecessary of any interpretation"); *Lodge 2036, IAM v. H.D. Hudson Mfg. Co.,* 331 F. Supp. 361 (D. Minn. 1971). (Union sought arbitration of employer's requirement that employees bear the cost of increased insurance benefits; *held* the provision in the

contract clearly requires the employees to bear any increase in the cost of the program. "It would appear that an arbitrator would have nothing to interpret under this provision.")

Ordinarily, exclusionary clauses must be spelled out plainly and unequivocally. *Carpenters of Denver v. Brady Corp.*, 518 F.2d 1 (10th Cir. 1975); *Retail Clerks, Local 1401 v. Woodman's Food Market, Inc.*, 371 F.2d 199 (7th Cir. 1966); *Mine Workers, Local 12298 v. Bridgeport Gas Co.*, 328 F.2d 381 (2d Cir. 1964). A grievance has been held not arbitrable where specific exclusionary language applied. *Local 13, AFL-CIO v. General Elec. Co.*, 531 F.2d 1178 (3d Cir. 1976); *IUE, Local 787 v. Collins Radio Co.*, 317 F.2d 214 (5th Cir. 1963).

(3) Where an arbitration clause simply provides for arbitration of a few specified types of disputes, but does not expressly exclude other issues from its scope, the courts are likely to hold that the unmentioned categories are excluded from the arbitration clause by clear implication. *See, e.g., Gangemi v. General Elec. Co.*, 532 F.2d 861 (2d Cir. 1976) (company will not be ordered to arbitrate dispute concerning layoff and bumping where arbitration clause was not broad or standard, but provided only for grievances involving disciplinary penalties). *Cook v. Gristede Bros.*, 359 F. Supp. 906 (D.N.Y. 1973) (grievance arising from layoff of employees by virtue of employer's changed method of buying products not subject to mandatory arbitration under arbitration clause applicable exclusively to discharge of employees for just cause).

(4) *Problems On The Arbitrability Of Labor Disputes:* — (a) Despite *Warrior & Gulf's* admonition that "arbitration is a matter of contract and a party cannot be required to submit to arbitration any dispute which he has not agreed to so submit," it is clear that the "Steelworkers Trilogy" require courts to lean heavily towards a finding of arbitrability. In fact, one commentator has argued that the arbitrability of a particular dispute has come to depend not so much on a judicial finding that the parties in fact have agreed to arbitrate the dispute (or would have agreed had they considered the matter), but rather on a legal presumption in favor of arbitrability that can be negated only by an express exclusion or clear implication in the agreement, Goetz, Arbitration After Termination of A Collective Bargaining Agreement, 64 Va. L. Rev. 693, 705 (1977). May the parties to a collective bargaining agreement nullify the *Warrior* presumption of arbitrability? *See IUE v. General Elec. Co.*, 407 F.2d 253, 259 (2d Cir. 1968), *cert. denied,* 395 U.S. 904 (1969).

(b) When the parties to a labor contract have agreed to submit all questions of contract interpretation to the arbitrator, should a court order the parties to arbitrate an issue which the written contract does not address? In *Boeing Co. v. UAW*, 231 F. Supp. 930 (E.D. Pa. 1964), *aff'd,* 349 F.2d 412 (3d Cir. 1965), the court refused to order the company to arbitrate a dispute over the discontinuation of its policy of distributing turkeys to employees at Christmas. The court reasoned that the agreement to arbitrate disputes over the interpretation of contract "provisions" referred to grievances involving a specific provision of the written document. *Accord, Independent Petroleum Workers v. American Oil Co.*, 324 F.2d 903 (7th Cir. 1963), *affirmed* by an equally divided court, 379 U.S. 130 (1964). Can these rulings be squared with the view, endorsed by the Court in *Warrior & Gulf*, that unwritten practices of the industry and the shop are as much a part of the collective bargaining agreement as are its express terms? *See UAW v. Cardwell Mfg. Co.*, 304 F.2d 801 (10th Cir. 1962); *Akron Typographical Union No. 182 v. Beacon Journal Publ. Co.*, 72 L.R.R.M. 2362 (D. Ohio, 1968), *aff'd*, 416 F.2d 969 (6th Cir. 1969), *cert. denied*, 396 U.S. 959 (1969). Of course, the parties might expressly agree to arbitrate only those disputes arising out of specific provisions of a written contract. In such a case a court may properly refuse to order arbitration of a dispute involving an unwritten agreement. *Local 210, Printing Pressman v. Times-World Corp.*, 381 F. Supp. 149 (W.D. Va. 1974); *IUE v. General Elec. Co.*, 407 F.2d 253 (2d Cir. 1968), *cert. denied*, 395 U.S. 904 (1969).

(c) In the absence of an express provision excluding a particular grievance from the scope of a broad arbitration clause, a party resisting a suit to compel arbitration should not prevail unless he can offer "the most forceful evidence of a purpose to exclude the claim from arbitration." *Warrior & Gulf.* What types of evidence may a court properly consider in determining whether a matter is excluded from arbitration? Bargaining history? Past practice of the parties? Consider, for example, the following situation:

The labor agreement between the parties provided, in part, that "controversies arising out of the application or interpretation of this Agreement . . . shall be settled by arbitration. . ." The company contracted out some construction projects at one of its plants. The written bargaining agreement was silent on the subject of contracting out. When the Union brought a § 301 action to compel the company to arbitrate the dispute, the company argued that the dispute was not arbitrable, since it wasn't covered by the Agreement. In resolving whether the dispute arose under the Agreement, may the court properly consider the bargaining history between the parties which indicated unsuccessful attempts by the Union to include in the agreement a provision prohibiting or limiting subcontracting? *See Boiler Makers Local 483 v. Shell Oil Company*, 369 F.2d 526 (7th Cir. 1966), which held that the district court correctly looked to bargaining history to determine the scope of the Agreement (and therefore of the arbitration provision).

See also International Chem. Workers v. Jefferson Lake Sulphur Co., 197 F. Supp 155 (S.D. Tex. 1961); *Communications Workers v. Pacific Northwest Bell Tel. Co.,* 337 F.2d 455 (9th Cir. 1964). *Contra IUE v. General Elec. Co.,* 332 F.2d 485 (2d Cir. 1964).

Although the apparent trend among lower federal courts is to admit evidence of bargaining history to demonstrate the scope and meaning of an arbitration clause, the courts remain sensitive to *Warrior & Gulf's* admonition NOT TO consider the merits of a dispute in the course of interpreting an arbitration clause. *Assoc. Milk Dealers, Inc. v. Milk Drivers, Local 753,* 422 F.2d 546 (7th Cir. 1970). The court must strike a balance between its duty to determine the scope of the promise to arbitrate and the "commandment" that it should not resolve the merits of a dispute while ostensibly deciding the question of arbitrability.

Where an arbitration clause expressly excludes certain types of disputes, *e.g.,* matters strictly a function of management, is it realistic to expect a court to avoid entangling itself in the merits of a dispute? For example, if the company argues that the contracting out of work is strictly a function of management, how can a court determine the validity of this contention without looking to the past practice and bargaining history of the parties? And if such evidence reveals a forty-year practice of unfettered discretion in contracting out work, would not a court be compelled to decide, in the absence of conflicting evidence, that contracting out is "strictly a function of management" and not subject to the arbitral process? If so, the court would simultaneously have resolved the merits of the dispute, *i.e.,* the company has the right to contract out work. On the other hand, should the court refuse to consider such evidence, it may thereby render meaningless the parties' agreement to exclude management's functions from the general arbitration clause. *See Local 13 AFL-CIO v. General Elec. Co.,* 531 F.2d 1178, 1183 (3d Cir. 1976).

(d) May a court refuse to order arbitration of a dispute where it seems that the contract precludes the arbitrator from remedying the alleged contract violation? *See Tobacco Workers, Local 317 v. Lorillard,* 448 F.2d 949 (4th Cir. 1971) (apparent inability of arbitrator to remedy a contract violation did not justify trial court's refusal to compel arbitration; contractual limitations on arbitrator's power to fashion an award did not limit his jurisdiction to hear the dispute); *Accord, Carey v. General Elec. Co.,* 315 F.2d 499 (2d Cir. 1963), *cert. denied,* 377 U.S. 908 (1964).

(e) Are the Trilogy rules on arbitrability binding on arbitrators as well as courts? In a court-ordered arbitration, may the arbitrator subsequently make his own independent determination of arbitrability? *See* Smith and Jones, *supra,* this note (1), Mich. L. Rev. at 761, and 52 Va. L. Rev. at 871-73; Goetz, *supra,* this note (4)(a) 64 Va. L. Rev. at 713-14 (if an arbitrator decides that a dispute is not arbitrable, a court should not overturn this decision unless it does not draw its essence from the collective bargaining agreement).

JOHN WILEY & SONS, INC. v. LIVINGSTON

United States Supreme Court
376 U.S. 543, 84 S. Ct. 909, 11 L. Ed. 2d 898 (1964)

Mr. Justice Harlan delivered the opinion of the Court.

This is an action by a union, pursuant to § 301 of the Labor Management Relations Act . . . to compel arbitration under a collective bargaining agreement. The major questions presented are (1) whether a corporate employer must arbitrate with a union under a bargaining agreement between the union and another corporation which has merged with the employer, and, if so (2) whether the courts or the arbitrator is the appropriate body to decide whether procedural prerequisites which, under the bargaining agreement, condition the duty to arbitrate have been met. Because of the importance of both questions to the realization of national labor policy, we granted certiorari (373 U.S. 908) to review a judgment of the Court of Appeals directing arbitration (313 F.2d 52), in reversal of the District Court which had refused such relief (203 F. Supp. 171). We affirm the judgment below, but, with respect to the first question above, on grounds which may differ from those of the Court of Appeals, whose answer to that question is unclear.

I. District 65, Retail, Wholesale and Department Store Union, AFL-CIO, entered into a collective bargaining agreement with Interscience Publishers, Inc., a publishing firm, for a term expiring on January 31, 1962. The agreement did not contain an express provision making it binding on successors of Interscience. On October 2, 1961, Interscience merged with the petitioner, John Wiley & Sons, Inc., another publishing firm, and ceased to do business as a separate entity. There is no suggestion that the merger was not for genuine business reasons.

At the time of the merger Interscience had about 80 employees, of whom 40 were represented by this Union. It had a single plant in New York City, and did an annual business of somewhat over $1,000,000. Wiley was a much larger concern, having separate office and warehouse facilities and about 300 employees, and doing an annual business of more than $9,000,000. None of Wiley's employees was represented by a union.

In discussions before and after the merger, the Union and Interscience (later Wiley) were unable to agree on the effect of the merger on the collective bargaining agreement and on the rights under it of those covered employees hired by Wiley. The Union's position was that despite the merger it continued to represent the covered Interscience employees taken over by Wiley, and that Wiley was obligated to recognize certain rights of such employees which had "vested" under the Interscience bargaining agreement. Such rights, more fully described below, concerned matters typically covered by collective bargaining agreements, such as seniority status, severance pay, etc. The Union contended also that Wiley was required to make certain pension fund payments called for under the Interscience bargaining agreement.

Wiley, though recognizing for purposes of its own pension plan the Interscience service of the former Interscience employees, asserted that the merger terminated the bargaining agreement for all purposes. It refused to recognize the Union as bargaining agent or to accede to the Union's claims on behalf of Interscience employees. All such employees, except a few who ended their Wiley employment with severance pay and for whom no rights are asserted here, continued in Wiley's employ.

No satisfactory solution having been reached, the Union, one week before the expiration date of the Interscience bargaining agreement, commenced this action to compel arbitration.

II. The threshold question in this controversy is who shall decide whether the arbitration provisions of the collective bargaining agreement survived the Wiley-Interscience merger, so as to be operative against Wiley. Both parties urge that this question is for the courts. Past cases leave no doubt that this is correct. "Under our decisions, whether or not the company was bound to arbitrate, as well as what issues it must arbitrate, is a matter to be determined by the Court on the basis of the contract entered into by the parties." *Atkinson v. Sinclair Refining Co.*, 370 U.S. 238, 241. *Accord, e.g., United Steelworkers v. Warrior & Gulf Navigation Co.*, 363 U.S. 574, 582. The problem in those cases was whether an employer, concededly party to and bound by a contract which contained an arbitration provision, had agreed to arbitrate disputes of a particular kind. Here, the question is whether Wiley, which did not itself sign the collective bargaining agreement on which the Union's claim to arbitration depends, is bound at all by the agreement's arbitration provision. The reason requiring the courts to determine the issue is the same in both situations. The duty to arbitrate being of contractual origin, a compulsory submission to arbitration cannot precede judicial determination that the collective bargaining agreement does in fact create such a duty. Thus, just as an employer has no obligation to arbitrate issues which it has not agreed to arbitrate, so *a fortiori,* it cannot be compelled to arbitrate if an arbitration clause does not bind it at all. . . .

. . . We hold that the disappearance by merger of a corporate employer which has entered into a collective bargaining agreement with a union does not automatically terminate all rights of the employees covered by the agreement, and that, in appropriate circumstances, present here, the successor employer may be required to arbitrate with the union under the agreement.

This Court has in the past recognized the central role of arbitration in effectuating national labor policy. Thus, in *Warrior & Gulf Navigation Co., supra* at 578, arbitration was described as "the substitute for industrial strife," and as "part and parcel of the collective bargaining process itself." It would derogate from "the federal policy of settling labor disputes by arbitration," *United Steelworkers v. Enterprise Wheel & Car Corp.,* 363 U.S. 593, 596, if a change in the corporate structure or ownership of a business enterprise had the automatic consequence of removing a duty to arbitrate previously established; this is so as much in cases like the present, where the contracting employer disappears into another by merger, as in those in which one owner replaces another but the business entity remains the same.

Employees, and the union which represents them, ordinarily do not take part in negotiations leading to a change in corporate ownership. The negotiations will ordinarily not concern the well-being of the employees, whose advantage or disadvantage, potentially great, will inevitably be incidental to the main considerations. The objectives of national labor policy, reflected in established principles of federal law, require that the rightful prerogative of owners independently to rearrange their businesses and even eliminate themselves as employers be balanced by some protection to the employees from a sudden change in the employment relationship. The transition from one corporate organization to another will in most cases be eased and industrial strife avoided if employees' claims continue to be resolved by arbitration rather than by "the relative strength ... of the contending forces," *Warrior & Gulf, supra* at 580.

The preference of national labor policy for arbitration as a substitute for tests of strength between contending forces could be overcome only if other considerations compellingly so demanded. We find none. While the principles of law governing ordinary contracts would not bind to a contract an unconsenting successor to a contracting party,[32] a collective bargaining agreement is not an ordinary contract. " ... [I]t is a generalized code to govern a myriad of cases which the draftsmen cannot wholly anticipate. ... The collective agreement covers the whole employment relationship. It

---

[32] *But cf.* the general rule that in the case of a merger the corporation which survives is liable for the debts and contracts of the one which disappears. 15 Fletcher, Private Corporations § 7121 (rev. ed. 1961).

calls into being a new common law — the common law of a particular industry or of a particular plant." *Warrior & Gulf, supra* at 578-579 (footnotes omitted). Central to the peculiar status and function of a collective bargaining agreement is the fact, dictated both by circumstance, see *id.* at 580, and by the requirements of the National Labor Relations Act, that it is not in any real sense the simple product of a consensual relationship. Therefore, although the duty to arbitrate, as we have said, *supra* at 546-547, must be founded on a contract, the impressive policy considerations favoring arbitration are not wholly overborne by the fact that Wiley did not sign the contract being construed. This case cannot readily be assimilated to the category of those in which there is no contract whatever, or none which is reasonably related to the party sought to be obligated. There was a contract, and Interscience, Wiley's predecessor, was party to it. We thus find Wiley's obligation to arbitrate this dispute in the Interscience contract construed in the context of a national labor policy.

We do not hold that in every case in which the ownership or corporate structure of an enterprise is changed the duty to arbitrate survives. As indicated above, there may be cases in which the lack of any substantial continuity of identity in the business enterprise before and after a change would make a duty to arbitrate something imposed from without, not reasonably to be found in the particular bargaining agreement and the acts of the parties involved. So too, we do not rule out the possibility that a union might abandon its right to arbitration by failing to make its claims known. Neither of these situations is before the Court. . . . In addition, we do not suggest any view on the questions surrounding a certified union's claim to continued representative status following a change in ownership. . . . This Union does not assert that it has any bargaining rights independent of the Interscience agreement; it seeks to arbitrate claims based on that agreement, now expired, not to negotiate a new agreement.[33]

III. Beyond denying its obligation to arbitrate at all, Wiley urges that the Union's grievances are not within the scope of the arbitration clause. . . .

All of the Union's grievances concern conditions of employment typically covered by collective bargaining agreements and submitted

---

[33] The fact that the Union does not represent a majority of an appropriate bargaining unit in *Wiley* does not prevent it from representing those employees who are covered by the agreement which is in dispute and out of which *Wiley's* duty to arbitrate arises. Retail Clerks, Locals, 128 & 633 v. Lion Dry Goods, Inc., 369 U.S. 17. There is no problem of conflict with another union, *cf.* L.B. Spear & Co., 106 N.L.R.B. 687, since *Wiley* had no contract with any union covering the unit of employees which received the former Interscience employees. . . .

to arbitration if other grievance procedures fail. Specific provision for each of them is made in the Interscience agreement. There is thus no question that had a dispute concerning any of these subjects, such as seniority rights or severance pay, arisen between the Union and Interscience prior to the merger, it would have been arbitrable. Wiley argues, however, that the Union's claims are plainly outside the scope of the arbitration clause: first, because the agreement did not embrace post-merger claims, and, second, because the claims relate to a period beyond the limited term of the agreement.

In all probability, the situation created by the merger was one not expressly contemplated by the Union or Interscience when the agreement was made in 1960. Fairly taken, however, the Union's demands collectively raise the question which underlies the whole litigation: What is the effect of the merger on the rights of covered employees? It would be inconsistent with our holding that the obligation to arbitrate survived the merger were we to hold that the fact of the merger, without more, removed claims otherwise plainly arbitrable from the scope of the arbitration clause.

It is true that the Union has framed its issues to claim rights not only "now" — after the merger but during the term of the agreement — but also after the agreement expired by its terms. Claimed rights during the term of the agreement, at least, are unquestionably within the arbitration clause; we do not understand Wiley to urge that the Union's claims to all such rights have become moot by reason of the expiration of the agreement. As to claimed rights "after January 30, 1962," it is reasonable to read the claims as based solely on the Union's construction of the Interscience agreement in such a way that, had there been no merger, Interscience would have been required to discharge certain obligations notwithstanding the expiration of the agreement. We see no reason why parties could not if they so chose agree to the accrual of rights during the term of an agreement and their realization after the agreement had expired. Of course, the Union may not use arbitration to acquire new rights against Wiley any more than it could have used arbitration to negotiate a new contract with Interscience, had the existing contract expired and renewal negotiations broken down.

Whether or not the Union's demands have merit will be determined by the arbitrator in light of the fully developed facts. It is sufficient for present purposes that the demands are not so plainly unreasonable that the subject matter of the dispute must be regarded as nonarbitrable because it can be seen in advance that no award to the Union could receive judicial sanction. *See Warrior & Gulf, supra* at 582-583.

IV. Wiley's final objection to arbitration raises the question of so-called "procedural arbitrability." The Interscience agreement provides for arbitration as the third stage of the grievance procedure.

"Step 1" provides for "a conference between the affected employee, a Union Steward and the Employer, officer or exempt supervisory person in charge of his department." In "Step 2," the grievance is submitted to "a conference between an officer of the Employer, or the Employer's representative designated for that purpose, the Union Shop Committee and/or a representative of the Union." Arbitration is reached under "Step 3" "in the event that the grievance shall not have been resolved or settled in 'Step 2.'" Wiley argues that since Steps 1 and 2 have not been followed, and since the duty to arbitrate arises only in Step 3, it has no duty to arbitrate this dispute. Specifically, Wiley urges that the question whether "procedural" conditions to arbitration have been met must be decided by the court and not the arbitrator.

We think that labor disputes of the kind involved here cannot be broken down so easily into their "substantive" and "procedural" aspects. Questions concerning the procedural prerequisites to arbitration do not arise in a vacuum; they develop in the context of an actual dispute about the rights of the parties to the contract or those covered by it. In this case, for example, the Union argues that Wiley's consistent refusal to recognize the Union's representative status after the merger made it "utterly futile — and a little bit ridiculous to follow the grievance steps as set forth in the contract." Brief, p. 41. In addition, the Union argues that time limitations in the grievance procedure are not controlling because Wiley's violations of the bargaining agreement were "continuing." These arguments in response to Wiley's "procedural" claim are meaningless unless set in the background of the merger and the negotiations surrounding it.

Doubt whether grievance procedures or some part of them apply to a particular dispute, whether such procedures have been followed or excused, or whether the unexcused failure to follow them avoids the duty to arbitrate cannot ordinarily be answered without consideration of the merits of the dispute which is presented for arbitration. In this case, one's view of the Union's responses to Wiley's "procedural" arguments depends to a large extent on how one answers questions bearing on the basic issue, the effect of the merger; *e.g.*, whether or not the merger was a possibility considered by Interscience and the Union during the negotiation of the contract. It would be a curious rule which required that intertwined issues of "substance" and "procedure" growing out of a single dispute and raising the same questions on the same facts had to be carved up between two different forums, one deciding after the other. Neither logic nor considerations of policy compel such a result.

Once it is determined, as we have, that the parties are obligated to submit the subject matter of a dispute to arbitration, "procedural" questions which grow out of the dispute and bear on its final disposition should be left to the arbitrator. Even under a contrary rule, a court could deny arbitration only if it could confidently be said not only that a claim was strictly "procedural," and therefore within the purview of the court, but also that it should operate to bar arbitration altogether, and not merely limit or qualify an arbitral award. In view of the policies favoring arbitration and the parties' adoption of arbitration as the preferred means of settling disputes, such cases are likely to be rare indeed. In all other cases, those in which arbitration goes forward, the arbitrator would ordinarily remain free to reconsider the ground covered by the court insofar as it bore on the merits of the dispute, using the flexible approaches familiar to arbitration. Reservation of "procedural" issues for the courts would thus not only create the difficult task of separating related issues, but would also produce frequent duplication of effort.

In addition, the opportunities for deliberate delay and the possibility of well-intentioned but no less serious delay created by separation of the "procedural" and "substantive" elements of a dispute are clear. While the courts have the task of determining "substantive arbitrability," there will be cases in which arbitrability of the subject matter is unquestioned but a dispute arises over the procedures to be followed. In all such cases, acceptance of Wiley's position would produce the delay attendant upon judicial proceedings preliminary to arbitration. . . .

No justification for such a generally undesirable result is to be found in a presumed intention of the parties. Refusal to order arbitration of subjects which the parties have not agreed to arbitrate does not entail the fractionating of disputes about subjects which the parties do wish to have submitted. Although a party may resist arbitration once a grievance has arisen, as does Wiley here, we think it best accords with the usual purposes of an arbitration clause and with the policy behind federal labor law to regard procedural disagreements not as separate disputes but as aspects of the dispute which called the grievance procedures into play. . . .

Affirmed.

Mr. Justice Goldberg took no part in the consideration or decision of this case.

NOTES:

(1) *Problems on Procedural Arbitrability:* (a) Procedural objections to arbitration commonly include such matters as (A) failure to meet grievance or arbitration time limits specified in the agreement, (B) the res judicata effect of a prior ruling, whether by an arbitrator, a court, or the NLRB, (C) initiation of the grievance

by a party other than the one specified in the agreement, (D) bypassing of a step in the grievance procedure, (E) the right of the party to have more than one grievance heard in the proceeding, (F) the unenforceability of the arbitration clause because of a repudiation of the bargaining agreement or an unreasonable delay in requesting arbitration (laches).

Are all of these kinds of "procedural" issues intertwined with the "merits" as seems to have been assumed by the Court in *Wiley?* Should it make any difference, in disposing of challenges to arbitral jurisdiction before a court, that the agreement states expressly that, for want of meeting a specified procedural requirement, the grievance shall not be arbitrable?

(b) May a court decide questions of procedural arbitrability if there is little or no "intertwining" with the merits of the dispute? *See Tobacco Workers, Local 317 v. Lorillard,* 448 F.2d 949 (4th Cir. 1971) (question of whether grievances were timely filed was for the arbitrator, not the court), in which the court refused to infer from *Wiley's* logic that, where there is no intertwining, a court may decide questions of procedural arbitrability. The various circuits have consistently applied the *Wiley* rule without discussion of whether the procedural questions raised were in fact intertwined with the merits of the underlying dispute. *See e.g. Meat Cutters, Local 405 v. Tennessee Dressed Beef Co.,* 428 F.2d 797 (6th Cir. 1970); *Bealmer v. Texaco, Inc.,* 427 F.2d 885 (5th Cir. 1970), *cert. denied,* 400 U.S. 926 (1970); *Local 595, Machinists v. Howe Sound Co.,* 350 F.2d 508 (3d Cir. 1965); *Trailways, Inc. v. Motor Coach Employees Div. 1318,* 343 F.2d 815 (1st Cir. 1965), *cert. denied,* 382 U.S. 879 (1965).

(c) The procedural question in *Wiley* was "intrinsic" to the labor agreement, *i.e.,* the issue was whether the union's failure to follow certain procedural steps set forth *in the contract* relieved the Company from its duty to arbitrate. Does the *Wiley* rule likewise apply where the procedural question is "extrinsic" to the collective bargaining agreement, *e.g.,* where the issue of untimeliness is based not on a violation of a contractual time limit, but on a failure to give timely notice under the equitable doctrine of laches? In *Operating Engineers Local 150 v. Flair Builders, Inc.,* 406 U.S. 487 (1972), the Supreme Court held that whether a union grievance is barred by laches is a question for the arbitrator to decide on the ground that the agreement to arbitrate "any difference ..." encompassed the issue of laches within its broad sweep. The Court expressly refused to decide whether *Wiley* was limited to cases of "intrinsic" delay or noncompliance. Justice Powell, dissenting, argued that the phrase "any difference" referred only to issues customarily within the scope of a labor agreement and was not intended to include arbitration of an equitable defense asserted against the enforceability of the arbitration clause itself. Powell concluded that the issue of whether delay renders it unfair to enforce the arbitration provision of a contract is neither a question of labor law nor an issue of fact that arbitrators are particularly well qualified to consider.

Compare Drake Bakeries, Inc. v. Bakery Workers Local 50, 370 U.S. 254 (1962), in which the Supreme Court held that the district court properly stayed an employer's action for damages resulting from an alleged one-day strike pending the completion of arbitration. In response to the employer's argument that the union strike amounted to a repudiation of the contract, including the arbitration provision, the Court *decided* that the union had not repudiated the agreement to arbitrate: "Arbitration provisions, which themselves have not been repudiated, are meant to survive breaches of contract, in many contexts, even total breach. . ." Does *Drake* stand for the proposition that a court may properly pass judgment on questions of procedural arbitrability so long as they are "extrinsic" to the labor agreement? *See* Note 10, 370 U.S. at 263. What effect, if any, does *Flair Builders* have on this aspect of *Drake?* -259170r0101 ? The lower federal courts, following *Flair Builders,* have consistently required claims of repudiation to be submitted to the arbitrator. *E.g., Controlled Sanitation Corp. v. District 128, etc.,* 524 F.2d 1324 (3d Cir. 1975), *cert. denied,* 424 U.S. 915 (1976) (allegation of repudiation of agreement to arbitrate amounts to a dispute concerning the application of the labor agreement and is subject to the contract's arbitration clause); *H & M Cake Box, Inc. v. Bakery & Confectionery Workers Local 45,* 493 F.2d 1226 (1st Cir. 1974).

Consider the following criticism of *Flair Builders* and its progeny: The claim that an arbitration provision is unenforceable because of factors extrinsic to the contract, *e.g.,* laches, repudiation, or fraud in the inducement, presents a justiciable question to be decided by a court, not by an arbitrator. The question in such cases is not whether the contractual prerequisites to the invocation of arbitration have been met (clearly a question for the arbitrator under *Wiley*). Rather, the true issue is whether the law, not the contract, excuses the resisting party from performing his promise to arbitrate. Since the issue is one of law, and involves the enforceability rather than the interpretation of a labor agreement, it must necessarily be resolved by a court. Do you agree with this analysis? *See, ILGWU v. Ashland Industries, Inc.,* 488 F.2d 641 (5th Cir. 1974) (Court rather than arbitrator must decide whether labor agreement is unenforceable because of fraud in the inducement).

(2) In *Local 103, Elec. Workers v. RCA Corp.,* 516 F.2d 1336 (3d Cir. 1975), the union sought to enjoin RCA's effort to proceed with arbitration on the ground that arbitration was barred by a provision in the labor contract prohibiting rearbitration of questions that were previously the subject of an arbitration hearing. The court of appeals held that the trial court properly dismissed the action, since it was

for the arbitrator to decide whether the same question had previously been arbitrated within the meaning of the exclusionary clause.

NOLDE BROTHERS, INC. v. BAKERY AND CONFECTIONERY WORKERS UNION, LOCAL 358

United States Supreme Court
430 U.S. 243, 97 S. Ct. 1067, 51 L. Ed. 2d 300 (1977)

Mr. Chief Justice Burger delivered the opinion of the Court.

This case raises the question of whether a party to a collective-bargaining contract may be required to arbitrate a contractual dispute over severance pay pursuant to the arbitration clause of that agreement even though the dispute, although governed by the contract, arises after its termination. Only the issue of arbitrability is before us.

(1) In 1970, petitioner Nolde Brothers, Inc., entered into a collective-bargaining agreement with respondent Local No. 358, of the Bakery and Confectionery Workers Union, AFL-CIO covering petitioner's Norfolk, Va., bakery employees. Under the contract, "any grievance" arising between the parties was subject to binding arbitration. In addition, the contract contained a provision which provided for severance pay on termination of employment for all employees having three or more years of active service. . . . By its terms, the contract was to remain in effect until July 21, 1973, and thereafter, until such time as either a new agreement was executed between the parties, or the existing agreement was terminated upon seven days written notice by either party.

In May 1973, the parties resumed bargaining after the Union advised Nolde, pursuant to § 8(d) of the National Labor Relations Act, 29 U. S. C. § 158(d), of its desire to negotiate certain changes in the existing agreement. These negotiations continued without resolution up to, and beyond, the July 21 contract expiration date. On August 20, the Union served the requisite seven days written notice of its decision to cancel the existing contract. The Union's termination of the contract became effective August 27, 1973.

Despite the contract's cancellation, negotiations continued. They ended, however, on August 31, when Nolde, faced by a threatened strike after the Union had rejected its latest proposal, informed the Union of its decision to close permanently its Norfolk bakery, effective that day. Operations at the plant ceased shortly after midnight on August 31. Nolde then paid employees their accrued wages and accrued vacation pay under the cancelled contract; in addition, wages were paid for work performed during the interim between the contract's termination on August 27 and the bakery's closing four days later. However, the company rejected the Union's demand for the severance pay called for in the collective-bargaining agreement. It also declined to arbitrate the severance pay claim on the ground that its contractual obligation to arbitrate disputes terminated with the collective-bargaining agreement.

The Union then instituted this action . . . under § 301 of the Labor Management Relations Act, 29 U. S. C. § 185, seeking to compel Nolde to arbitrate the severance pay issue. . . . The District Court . . . held that the duty to arbitrate terminated with the contract that had created it.

On appeal, the United States Court of Appeals for the Fourth Circuit reversed. . . . [T]he Court of Appeals concluded that the parties' arbitration duties under the contract survived its termination with respect to claims arising by reason of the collective-bargaining agreement.

(2) In arguing that Nolde's displaced employees were entitled to severance pay upon the closing of the Norfolk bakery, the Union maintained that the severance wages provided for in the collective-bargaining agreement were in the nature of "accrued" or "vested" rights, earned by employees during the term of the contract on essentially the same basis as vacation pay, but payable only upon termination of employment. In support of this claim, the Union noted that the severance pay clause is found in the contract under an article entitled "Wages." The inclusion within that provision, it urged, was evidence that the parties considered severance pay as part of the employees' compensation for services performed during the life of the agreement. In addition, the Union pointed out that the severance pay clause itself contained nothing to suggest that the employees' right to severance pay expired if the events triggering payment failed to occur during the life of the contract. Nolde, on the other hand, argued that since severance pay was a creation of the collective-bargaining agreement, its substantive obligation to provide such benefits terminated with the Union's unilateral cancellation of the contract.

As the parties' arguments demonstrate, both the Union's claim for severance pay and Nolde's refusal to pay the same are based on their differing perceptions of a provision of the expired collective-bargaining agreement. The parties may have intended, as Nolde maintained, that any substantive claim to severance pay must surface, if at all, during the contract's term. However, there is also "no reason why parties could not if they so chose agree to the accrual of rights during the term of an agreement and their realization after the agreement had expired." *John Wiley & Sons v. Livingston*, 376 U.S. 543, 555 (1964). Of course, in determining the arbitrability of the dispute, the merits of the underlying claim for severance pay are not before us. However, it is clear that, whatever the outcome, the resolution of that claim hinges on the interpretation ultimately given the contract clause providing for severance pay. The dispute therefore, although arising *after* the expiration of the collective-bargaining contract, clearly arises *under* that contract.

There can be no doubt that a dispute over the meaning of the severance pay clause during the life of the agreement would have been subject to the mandatory grievance-arbitration procedures of the contract. . . . Here, however, Nolde maintains that a different rule must prevail because the event giving rise to the contractual dispute, *i.e.,* the employees' severance upon the bakery's closing, did not occur until after the expiration of the collective-bargaining agreement.

(3) Nolde contends that the duty to arbitrate, being strictly a creature of contract, must necessarily expire with the collective-bargaining contract that brought it into existence. Hence, it maintains that a court may not compel a party to submit any post-contract grievance to arbitration for the simple reason that no contractual duty to arbitrate survives the agreement's termination. Any other conclusion, Nolde argues, runs contrary to federal labor policy which prohibits the imposition of compulsory arbitration upon parties except when they are bound by an arbitration agreement. In so arguing, Nolde relies on numerous decisions of this Court which it claims establish that "arbitration is a matter of contract and [that] a party cannot be required to submit to arbitration any dispute which he had not agreed so to submit." *United Steelworkers of America v. Warrior & Gulf Navigation Co.,* 363 U.S. 574, 582 (1960); *e.g., Gateway Coal Co. v. United Mine Workers,* 414 U.S. 368, 374 (1974); *John Wiley & Sons v. Livingston,* 376 U.S., at 547; *Atkinson v. Sinclair Refining Co.,* 370 U.S. 238, 241 (1962).

Our prior decisions have indeed held that the arbitration duty is a creature of the collective-bargaining agreement and that a party cannot be compelled to arbitrate any matter in the absence of a contractual obligation to do so. Adherence to these principles, however, does not require us to hold that termination of a collective-bargaining agreement automatically extinguishes a party's duty to arbitrate grievances arising under the contract. Carried to its logical conclusion that argument would preclude the entry of a post-contract arbitration order even when the dispute arose during the life of the contract but arbitration proceedings had not begun before termination. The same would be true if arbitration processes began but were not completed, during the contract's term. Yet it could not seriously be contended in either instance that the expiration of the contract would terminate the parties' contractual obligation to resolve such a dispute in an arbitral, rather than a judicial forum. See *John Wiley & Sons, supra; United Steelworkers of America v. Enterprise Wheel.* 363 U.S. 593 (1960). . . . Nolde concedes as much by limiting its claim of nonarbitrability to those disputes which clearly arise after the contract's expiration.

Our holding in *John Wiley & Sons* is instructive on this matter. There we held that a dispute over employees' rights to severance pay under an expired collective-bargaining agreement was arbitrable even though there was no longer any contract between the parties. ... We thus determined that the parties' obligations under their arbitration clause survived contract termination when the dispute was over an obligation arguably created by the expired agreement. It is true that the union there first sought to arbitrate the question of post-contract severance pay while the agreement under which it claimed such benefits was still in effect. But that factor was not dispositive in our determination of arbitrability. Indeed, that very distinction was implicitly rejected shortly thereafter in *Piano & Musical Inst. Workers, Local 2549 v. W. W. Kimball Co.*, 379 U.S. 357 (1964). . . .

[E]ven though the parties could have so provided, there is nothing in the arbitration clause that expressly excludes from its operation a dispute which arises under the contract, but which is based on events that occur after its termination. The contract's silence, of course, does not establish the parties' intent to resolve post-termination grievances by arbitration. But in the absence of some contrary indication, there are strong reasons to conclude that the parties did not intend their arbitration duties to terminate automatically with the contract. Any other holding would permit the employer to cut off all arbitration of severance pay claims by terminating an existing contract simultaneously with closing business operations.

By their contract the parties clearly expressed their preference for an arbitral, rather than a judicial interpretation of their obligations under the collective-bargaining agreement. Their reasons for doing so, as well as the special role of arbitration in the employer-employee relationship have long been recognized by this Court. . . .

While the termination of the collective-bargaining agreement works an obvious change in the relationship between employer and union, it would have little impact on many of the considerations behind their decision to resolve their contractual difference through arbitration. The contracting parties' confidence in the arbitration process and an arbitrator's presumed special competence in matters concerning bargaining agreements does not terminate with the contract. Nor would their interest in obtaining a prompt and inexpensive resolution of their disputes by an expert tribunal. Hence, there is little reason to construe this contract to mean that the parties intended their contractual duty to submit grievances and claims arising under the contract to terminate immediately on the termination of the contract; the alternative remedy of a lawsuit is the very remedy the arbitration clause was designed to avoid.

It is also noteworthy that the parties drafted their broad arbitration clause against a backdrop of well-established federal labor policy favoring arbitration as the means of resolving disputes over the meaning and effect of collective-bargaining agreements. . . . In order to effectuate this policy. this Court has established a strong presumption favoring arbitrability.

The parties must be deemed to have been conscious of this policy when they agree to resolve their contractual differences through arbitration. Consequently, the parties' failure to exclude from arbitrability contract disputes arising after termination, far from manifesting an intent to have arbitration obligations cease with the agreement, affords a basis for concluding that they intended to arbitrate all grievances arising out of the contractual relationship. In short, where the dispute is over a provision of the expired agreement, the presumptions favoring arbitrability must be negated expressly or by clear implication.

We therefore agree with the conclusion of the Court of Appeals that, on this record, the Union's claim for severance pay under the expired collective-bargaining agreement is subject to resolution under the arbitration provisions of that contract.[8]

Affirmed.

Mr. Justice Stewart, with whom Mr. Justice Rehnquist joins, dissenting.

When a dispute arises between two parties, that dispute is to be settled by the process of arbitration only if there is an agreement between the parties that the dispute will be settled by that means. Yet the Court today says that a union-employer dispute must be settled by arbitration even though the dispute did not even arise until after the contract containing an agreement to arbitrate had been terminated by action of the union, and the employer had closed its business. I think this conclusion is neither required by existing precedent nor based upon any realistic appraisal of the contracting parties' intent. . . .

[T]he duty to arbitrate can arise only upon the parties' agreement to resolve their contractual differences in the arbitral forum. And the presumptive continuation of that duty even after the formal expiration of such an agreement can be justified only in terms of a web of assumptions about the continuing nature of the labor-management relationship and the importance of having

---

[8] Certiorari was neither sought, nor granted, on the question of the arbitrator's authority to consider arbitrability following referral, and we express no view on that matter. Similarly, we need not speculate as to the arbitrability of post-termination contractual claims which, unlike the one presently before us, are not asserted within a reasonable time after the contract's expiration.

available a method harmoniously to resolve differences arising in that relationship. . . .

Those assumptions are wholly inapplicable to this case. The closing of the bakery by the employer-petitioner necessarily meant that there was no continuing relationship to protect or preserve. . . . And the Union's termination of the contract, thereby releasing it from its obligation not to strike, foreclosed any reason for implying a continuing duty on the part of the employer to arbitrate as a *quid pro quo* for the Union's offsetting, enforceable duty to negotiate rather than strike. . . .

Although for these reasons no continuing duty to arbitrate can be presumed in this case in the interest of maintaining industrial peace, it might nevertheless rationally be argued that the arbitration agreement was a term or condition of employment that the employer could not unilaterally change without first bargaining to impasse. . . . The trouble with that argument is that the National Labor Relations Board has rejected the notion that arbitration is a term or condition of employment that by operation of statute continues even after the contract embodying it has terminated. The Board, instead, has viewed arbitration as an obligation that arises solely out of contract, and is favored but not statutorily required as a dispute-resolving mechanism. *See Hilton Davis Chemical Company,* 185 N.L.R.B. 241 (1970). *See also Gateway Coal Co. v. United Mine Workers of America,* 414 U.S. 368.

It is clear, therefore, that neither federal labor law nor the interest of maintaining industrial peace can serve to explain the Court's conclusion that the presumption of arbitrability extends to the facts of this case. . . .

For the reasons I have expressed, I think there was no agreement to arbitrate this dispute. The union had, of course, a clear cause of action under § 301 of the National Labor Relations Act to seek judicial redress against the employer for its failure to meet its severance pay obligations to the employees. . . .

NOTES:

Problems on Post-Termination Duties: (a) Does the post-termination duty to arbitrate established in *Nolde* arise only in the context of rights that survive the contract, *e.g.,* vacation or severance pay? In deciding that the employer was obliged to arbitrate the dispute over post-termination rights to severance and vacation pay, the Fourth Circuit, in the *Nolde* case, qualified its holding as follows: "Our decision only affects those rights, like severance pay, that employees earn and that may or may not 'vest' for future enjoyment — contingent upon a particular event." Is the Fourth

Circuit's distinction between accruable and non-accruable rights meaningful or relevant to a determination of arbitrability? How can a court determine whether a right is accruable, *i.e.,* survives the termination of the contract, without entangling itself in the merits of the underlying substantive dispute? Would the Supreme Court require an employer to arbitrate a dispute over the propriety of a layoff of employees which occurs during the existence of a contract providing for mandatory arbitration of such disputes but where the request for arbitration occurs well after the termination of the contract at a time when no agreement to arbitrate such disputes is in existence? *See generally Minnesota Joint Bd., A.C. Workers v. United Government Mfg. Co.,* 338 F.2d 195, 201 (8th Cir. 1964); *General Tire & Rubber Co. v. Local No. 512, Rubber Workers,* 191 F. Supp. 911, 914 (D. R.I. 1960), *aff'd,* 294 F.2d 957 (1st Cir. 1961).

(b) How long after the termination of a labor agreement does the duty to arbitrate disputes arising under the agreement exist? The dissenters in *Nolde* emphasize that the strong presumption in favor of arbitrability established in the Steelworkers Trilogy, and extended in *Wiley,* was justified, in large part, on the notion that resort to arbitration would minimize industrial strife by promoting the harmonious resolution of differences. Is it proper to impute to the parties, absent forceful evidence to the contrary, an intent to arbitrate disputes which arise at a time when there is no employer-employee relationship to protect? *See generally* Goetz, Arbitration After Termination of a Collective Bargaining Agreement, 64 Va. L. Rev. 693 (1977); Comment, Arbitration Required After Expiration of a Contract, 60 Marq. L. Rev. 1142 (1977).

(c) The employer discharged some employees for misconduct during a strike. The discharge took place during the existence of a new contract which clearly called for arbitration of discharge cases. However, the misconduct, allegedly justifying the discipline, occurred during the interim period between the expiration of the old contract and the execution of a new one. The Union sought to arbitrate during the existence of the new contract. What results? *See Boeing Co. v. I.A.M.,* 381 F.2d 119 (5th Cir. 1967). Would your answer be any different if both the discharge and the request for arbitration occurred in the interim between the expiration of the old contract and the effective date of the new one? *See Proctor & Gamble Independent Union v. Proctor & Gamble Mfg. Co.,* 312 F.2d 181 (2d Cir. 1962), *cert. denied,* 374 U.S. 820 (1963). *See also OCAW, Local 7-210 v. American Maize Products Co.,* 492 F.2d 409 (7th Cir.), *cert. denied,* 417 U.S. 969 (1974).

F. JUDICIAL REVIEW OF ARBITRATION AWARDS

UNITED STEELWORKERS v. ENTERPRISE WHEEL & CAR CORP.

United States Supreme Court
363 U.S. 593, 80 S. Ct. 1358, 4 L. Ed. 2d 1424 (1960)

Mr. Justice Douglas delivered the opinion of the Court.

Petitioner union and respondent during the period relevant here had a collective bargaining agreement which provided that any differences "as to the meaning and application" of the agreement should be submitted to arbitration and that the arbitrator's decision "shall be final and binding on the parties." Special provisions were included concerning the suspension and discharge of employees. The agreement stated:

"Should it be determined by the Company or by an arbitrator in accordance with the grievance procedure that the employee has been suspended unjustly or discharged in violation of the provisions of this Agreement, the Company shall reinstate the employee and pay full compensation at the employee's regular rate of pay for the time lost."

The agreement also provided:

". . . It is understood and agreed that neither party will institute *civil suits* or *legal proceedings* against the other for alleged violation of any of the provisions of this labor contract; instead all disputes will be settled in the manner outlined in this Article III — Adjustment of Grievances."

A group of employees left their jobs in protest against the discharge of one employee. A union official advised them at once to return to work. An official of respondent at their request gave them permission and then rescinded it. The next day they were told they did not have a job any more "until this thing was settled one way or the other."

A grievance was filed; and when respondent finally refused to arbitrate, this suit was brought for specific enforcement of the arbitration provisions of the agreement. The District Court ordered arbitration. The arbitrator found that the discharge of the men was not justified, though their conduct, he said, was improper. In his view the facts warranted at most a suspension of the men for 10 days each. After their discharge and before the arbitration award the collective bargaining agreement had expired. The union, however, continued to represent the workers at the plant. The arbitrator rejected the contention that expiration of the agreement barred reinstatement of the employees. He held that the provision of the agreement above quoted imposed an unconditional obligation on the employer. He awarded reinstatement with back pay, minus pay for a 10-day suspension and such sums as these employees received from other employment.

Respondent refused to comply with the award. Petitioner moved the District Court for enforcement. The District Court directed respondent to comply. 168 F. Supp. 308. The Court of Appeals, while agreeing that the District Court had jurisdiction to enforce an arbitration award under a collective bargaining agreement, held that the failure of the award to specify the amounts to be deducted from the back pay rendered the award unenforceable. That defect, it agreed, could be remedied by requiring the parties to complete the arbitration. It went on to hold, however, that an award for back pay subsequent to the date of termination of the collective bargaining agreement could not be enforced. It also held that the requirement for reinstatement of the discharged employees was likewise unenforceable because the collective bargaining agreement had expired. 269 F.2d 327. . . .

The refusal of courts to review the merits of an arbitration award is the proper approach to arbitration under collective bargaining agreements. The federal policy of settling labor disputes by arbitration would be undermined if courts had the final say on the merits of the awards. As we stated in *United Steelworkers v. Warrior & Gulf Navigation Co., supra* at 574, decided this day, the arbitrators under these collective agreements are indispensable agencies in a continuous collective bargaining process. They sit to settle disputes at the plant level — disputes that require for their solution knowledge of the custom and practices of a particular factory or of a particular industry as reflected in particular agreements.

When an arbitrator is commissioned to interpret and apply the collective bargaining agreement, he is to bring his informed judgment to bear in order to reach a fair solution of a problem. This is especially true when it comes to formulating remedies. There the need is for flexibility in meeting a wide variety of situations. The draftsmen may never have thought of what specific remedy should be awarded to meet a particular contingency. Nevertheless, an arbitrator is confined to interpretation and application of the collective bargaining agreement; he does not sit to dispense his own brand of industrial justice. He may of course look for guidance from many sources, yet his award is legitimate only so long as it draws its essence from the collective bargaining agreement. When the arbitrator's words manifest an infidelity to this obligation, courts have no choice but to refuse enforcement of the award.

The opinion of the arbitrator in this case, as it bears upon the award of back pay beyond the date of the agreement's expiration and reinstatement, is ambiguous. It may be read as based solely upon the arbitrator's view of the requirements of enacted legislation, which would mean that he exceeded the scope of the submission. Or it may be read as embodying a construction of the agreement itself, perhaps with the arbitrator looking to "the law" for help in determining the sense of the agreement. A mere ambiguity in the opinion accompanying an award, which permits the inference that the arbitrator may have exceeded his authority, is not a reason for refusing to enforce the award. Arbitrators have no obligation to the court to give their reasons for an award. To require opinions free of ambiguity may lead arbitrators to play it safe by writing no supporting opinions. This would be undesirable for a well-reasoned opinion tends to engender confidence in the integrity of the process and aids in clarifying the underlying agreement. Moreover, we see no reason to assume that this arbitrator has abused the trust the parties confided in him and has not stayed within the areas marked out for his consideration. It is not apparent that he went beyond the submission. The Court of Appeals' opinion refusing to enforce the reinstatement and partial back pay portions of the award was not based upon any finding that the arbitrator did not premise his award on his construction of the contract. It merely disagreed with the arbitrator's construction of it.

The collective bargaining agreement could have provided that if any of the employees were wrongfully discharged, the remedy would be reinstatement and back pay up to the date they were returned to work. Respondent's major argument seems to be that by applying correct principles of law to the interpretation of the collective bargaining agreement it can be determined that the agreement did not so provide, and that therefore the arbitrator's decision was not based upon the contract. The acceptance of this view would require courts, even under the standard arbitration clause, to review the merits of every construction of the contract. This plenary review by a court of the merits would make meaningless the provisions that the arbitrator's decision is final, for in reality it would almost never be final. This underlines the fundamental error which we have alluded to in *United Steelworkers v. American Manufacturing Co., supra* at 564, decided this day. As we there emphasized, the question of interpretation of the collective bargaining agreement is a question for the arbitrator. It is the arbitrator's construction which was bargained for; and so far as the arbitrator's decision concerns construction of the contract, the courts have no business overruling him because their interpretation of the contract is different from his.

We agree with the Court of Appeals that the judgment of the District Court should be modified so that the amounts due the employees may be definitely determined by arbitration. In all other respects we think the judgment of the District Court should be affirmed. Accordingly, we reverse the judgment of the Court of

Appeals, except for that modification, and remand the case to the District Court for proceedings in conformity with this opinion.

It is so ordered.

Mr. Justice Frankfurter concurs in the result.

Mr. Justice Black took no part in the consideration or decision of this case. . . .

Mr. Justice Whittaker, dissenting. . . .

Once the contract expired, no rights continued to accrue under it to the employees. Thereafter they had no contractual right to demand that the employer continue to employ them, and *a fortiori* the arbitrator did not have power to order the employer to do so; nor did the arbitrator have power to order the employer to pay wages to them after the date of termination of the contract, which was also the effective date of their discharges.

The judgment of the Court of Appeals, affirming so much of the award as required reinstatement of the 11 employees to employment status and payment of their wages until expiration of the contract, but not thereafter, seems to me to be indubitably correct, and I would affirm it.

1. Scope and Standard of Judicial Review

Although the Supreme Court in *Enterprise Wheel* stated that an arbitration award is valid only to the extent that it "draws its essence" from the contract, the Court proceeded to uphold the award even though the arbitrator's opinion did not clearly indicate whether his decision was based on the requirements of "external law" or on a construction of the agreement itself. Evidently, the Court would have held that the arbitrator exceeded his jurisdiction if his award had been predicated on "the law" rather than on the agreement. It reasoned, however, that since the award *might* have been based on the arbitrator's reading, it had to be upheld, because "it is the arbitrator's construction which was bargained for." A "mere ambiguity" concerning the source of arbitral authority was held not to warrant a refusal to enforce the award. Thus, the award was deemed to be within the arbitrator's jurisdiction even though he may not have based it on his construction of the agreement, and even though the Court did not have before it evidence of that very interpretative process for which the parties supposedly bargained. To the same effect, *N&FM Corp. v. United Steelworkers of America,* 524 F.2d 756, 760 (3d Cir. 1975); *Electrical Workers, Local 1260 v. Hawaiian Telephone Co.,* 411 P.2d 134 (Haw. 1966). Isn't this going pretty far? Do these cases mean that an award *without any supporting opinion at all* must be upheld if it could have been based on an interpretation of the agreement? *See, e.g., N&FM Corp., supra* at 759 ("an arbitrator is not required to list his reasons for an award," citing *Enterprise); Bylund v. Safeway Stores, Inc.,* 86 LRRM 2686 (D. Or. 1974) (reasons not required).

If, under *Enterprise Wheel,* courts may not refuse to enforce arbitration awards simply because the arbitrator does not list his reasons therefor, how are they to ensure that the arbitrator did not base his award on impermissible considerations? Apparently, the courts will presume, in the absence of clear evidence to the contrary, that an arbitrator's decision is based on the agreement, as long as an examination of the record before the arbitrator reveals some support for his determinations. *See, e.g., N&FM Corp. v. Steelworkers,* 524 F.2d 756, 759-60 (3d Cir. 1975).

Even where an award is clearly based on an arbitrator's interpretation of the agreement, it may be vacated, if in the courts' opinion, the arbitrator's interpretation was "irrational." *See, e.g., Timken Co. v. Steelworkers,* 482 F.2d 1012 (6th Cir. 1973). *See also Ludwig Honold Mfg. Co. v. Fletcher,* 405 F.2d 1123 (3d Cir. 1969) (award will be upheld if it can "rationally be derived" from the written contract or other manifestations of the parties' intention); *In re Arbitration Between Aloha Motors, Inc. and ILWU, Local 142,* 530 F.2d 848 (9th Cir. 1976) (award will be enforced if it "can be regarded as a plausible interpretation" of the parties' agreement); *UEW v. Peerless Pressed Metal Corp.,* 489 F.2d 768 (1st Cir. 1973) (award will be enforced unless it is "impossible" to construe the agreement as the arbitrator did).

2. Substantive Grounds for Setting Aside an Arbitrator's Award

Under *Enterprise Wheel,* an arbitrator's award must be set aside if the arbitrator is found to have exceeded his authority under the contract, which is both the source and the limit of his power. An arbitrator may exceed his contractual authority in two major respects. First, he may decide a question that is not arbitrable. Second, he may resolve a concededly arbitrable issue in an impermissible manner. For example, the arbitrator may (a) base his decision on an "unwritten agreement" where the contract or stipulation specifically forbids him from doing so; (b) resolve the merits of a dispute on the basis of his view of industrial justice rather than in accordance with the clear dictates of the contract, or (c) fashion a remedy expressly precluded by the agreement.

Moreover, the mere fact that an arbitral award is grounded on the labor contract does not necessarily require a court to enforce it. Thus, the courts have refused to enforce awards which (1) violate public policy or require a party to act illegally, (2) are so ambiguous that the parties are unable to determine what is expected of them, or (3) are the product of an arbitral process tainted with fraud, bias, or serious procedural defects.

Following are cases and problems illustrative of the above principles. It will be a useful exercise to analyze each of these in light of your understanding of the meaning of the Trilogy cases.

a. Exceeding Contractual Authority: Lack of Arbitrability

TEXTILE WORKERS UNION OF AMERICA, AFL-CIO v. AMERICAN THREAD CO., 291 F.2d 894 (4th Cir. 1961). The employer discharged an employee for improper performance of his job after having reprimanded him before on two different occasions for the same offense. The Union, although admitting the guilt of the employee, protested the discharge on the ground that the penalty was too severe. Having failed to settle the grievance, the parties agreed to submit to arbitration the following stipulated issues:

> *Under the terms of the contract and within the limits of those terms, including the restrictions on the power of the arbitrator,* does Grievance 157 allege, and has the union proved, a violation of the contract? If so, and *within the same limitations,* what should be the remedy? (Emphasis supplied by the Court.)

The collective bargaining agreement contained a broad management rights clause including the right to discipline or discharge employees for just cause and reserving to the management "all rights heretofore exercised by or inherent in the Management and not expressly contracted away." Furthermore, the management rights clause declared that "any action by the Company under this Section may be made the subject of collective bargaining and grievance procedure up to but not including arbitration, unless as otherwise hereinafter expressly provided." "Just cause" was described in the Agreement as including the "failure of an employee to properly perform his job in accordance with the Company's standards." The Agreement also contained the following arbitration provisions:

> Disputes, grievances, or disagreements involving application or interpretation of this agreement other than those affecting revision of the wage schedules attached hereto, workloads or work assignments, not satisfactorily adjusted under the Grievance Procedure set out in the preceding section shall be promptly referred to arbitration under the following procedure: . . . .
> It is mutually understood and agreed that the findings and decisions of the arbiter shall be final and binding on both parties hereto. The arbiter shall make *no award affecting a change, modification or addition* to this Agreement and *shall confine himself strictly to the facts submitted in the hearing, the evidence*

before him and the terms of the contract, including any amendments. . . . (Emphasis supplied by the Court.)

The Arbitrator stated that there was no doubt about the employee's guilt but nevertheless held that the offense was not just cause for dismissal. Consequently, he ordered that the discharge be commuted to a disciplinary suspension of one week. The employer refused to comply with the award and the Union brought suit to enforce it. The District Court dismissed the suit for lack of jurisdiction but the Court of Appeals reversed. On remand, the District Court denied enforcement of the award. By a divided vote, the Court of Appeals affirmed, ruling, first, that the arbitrator exceeded his authority and second, that he went beyond and outside the record of the case in formulating his award. Speaking to the first point, the majority observed:

> We are not persuaded that the Supreme Court, in recent cases involving arbitration and the right to enforcement of arbitration agreements, intended that the courts should permit an arbitrator to render decisions which do such violence to the clear, plain, exact and unambiguous terms of the submission and the contract of the contending parties. By Article III the company had the right to discipline *or* discharge employees for just cause, surely a discretionary right, and more particularly when the offense is the "failure of an employee to properly perform his job in accordance with the Company standards," an offense illustratively specified as "just cause" in Article IV, Section I. We find nothing in any section of Article IV or any other provision of the contract to show an intent to expressly contract away the rights reserved to management. The reservation of a right to either discipline or discharge for cause would be wholly ineffective and meaningless if the employer's action, pursuant to such right, is subject to review by an arbitrator on the basis of appropriateness. If the reserved right is construed to mean that the employer can take no disciplinary action in excess of a reprimand, except at its own risk and subject to severe penalties in case an arbitrator should later be of the opinion that some milder action is appropriate, the effect would be that the employer's inherent right which has not been expressly relinquished by contract is no right at all. . . .
>
> . . . When the arbitrator found that Arrowood had permitted a lap to run through, that it was his third offense, that he had received written warnings of the consequence of a third offense, and recognizing the long-standing management policy of discharge for a third offense following written warning, the only possible remaining question was one of appropriateness of the employer's consistent disciplinary practice. That is the question

the arbitrator then undertook to decide and it is that question which we hold to be beyond the terms of the submission and the contract provision for arbitration. If the express limitation contained in Article III (that the employer's exercise of his reserved right to discipline might be made the subject of a grievance and of collective bargaining, *but not of arbitration*) means anything, it means that the employer's established disciplinary practices were not to be upset by an arbitrator on the ground of inappropriateness. Neither the contract nor the submission gave the arbitrator any right to disregard established disciplinary practices, consistently applied, and to dispense his own brand of industrial justice.

With respect to the second ground, the majority stated:

But our decision need not rest on the reasons hereinbefore assigned in support of our conclusion that the arbitrator violated the terms of the contract and exceeded the limits of his authority. There is even a more compelling reason. The arbitrator speculated that Arrowood's offenses were due to mere negligence, or "to a workload so heavy that he could not properly cover it, or to not having his various job duties so lined up in time sequence that he could not cover them." In the absence of an express finding to that effect, we must assume that the arbitrator was not undertaking to base a judgment on "mere negligence." He did, however, disclose the real basis for his determination of the degree of what he had already found to be the employee's "serious offense" and the propriety of the penalty imposed.

It appears from his award that, in another and wholly unrelated arbitration case which involved this same company, a different arbitrator, after determining that the workload was proper under the contract, had found that this company had been remiss in recognizing its responsibilities to train and supervise the "operators in the proper method and schedule of performing the card tender assignment." It is perfectly clear that the arbitrator, without evidentiary support in the instant case, accepted and adopted this finding and decision of the other arbitrator in total disregard of the provisions of Article VII, Section 7, requiring that he confine himself strictly to the facts submitted in the hearing, the evidence before him and the terms of the contract. He went completely outside the record in an obvious effort to find some semblance of support for his award. Thus, in aid of his search for justification of his action, the arbitrator manifested a disregard for the terms of the submission and a determination to exceed, if necessary, the limits of the authority and power conferred upon him. This we cannot approve.

The dissenting judge stated that the grievance concerned the application and interpretation of the Agreement. Citing the 1960 Trilogy, he argued that the arbitrator did not exceed his authority because of the broad scope of the arbitration clause and the absence of any express provision excluding the subject matter of the grievance from arbitration. He further asserted that the arbitrator did not go beyond the record of the case.

NOTES:

(1) In reviewing an arbitrator's determination regarding his/her own jurisdiction to decide an issue, should a court employ the same principle of judicial review that it would, in reviewing his/her decision on the merits? Must an arbitrator's determination that a dispute is or is not arbitrable be upheld if it draws its essence from the labor agreement? *See* Gorman, Basic Text on Labor Law 586-88 (1976) and cases cited therein. Gorman suggests that this narrow standard of review should apply whenever the parties expressly or implicitly present the issue of arbitral jurisdiction to the arbitrator for decision. Several cases, however, state that a court may overrule an arbitrator's finding of arbitrability if it can say with positive assurance that the arbitration clause, upon which the arbitrator bases his authority, does not cover the dispute in question. *Camden Industries Co. v. Carpenters Local Union No. 1688,* 353 F.2d 178, 180 (1st Cir. 1965); *Humble Oil & Refining Co. v. Teamsters Local 866,* 271 F. Supp. 281 (S.D.N.Y. 1967); *Victor Electric Co. v. IBEW,* 411 F. Supp. 338, 343 note 2 (D.R.I. 1976); *Steelworkers v. U.S. Gypsum Co.,* 492 F.2d 713, 732 (5th Cir. 1974). Does the *Warrior & Gulf's* "positive assurance" test invite greater judicial scrutiny of an arbitrator's finding of arbitrability than is required by the "essence of the contract" standard set forth in *Enterprise Wheel?* In *Humble Oil & Refining Co., supra,* the court held that a party does not waive its right to a judicial determination of the question of arbitrability by participating in an arbitration proceeding on the merits. *H.K Porter Co. v. Saw Workers,* 406 F.2d 643, 648-49 (3d Cir. 1969). Of course, questions of procedural arbitrability, *e.g.,* timeliness, are for the arbitrator, *Wiley & Sons v. Livingston, supra,* and his resolution of that issue should be upheld if it is based on a reading of the contract. *N & FM Corp. v. Steelworkers,* 524 F.2d 756 (3d Cir. 1975); *Holly Sugar Corp. v. Distillery Workers Union,* 412 F.2d 899 (9th Cir. 1969); *Yellow Cab. Co. v. Democratic Union,* 398 F.2d 735 (7th Cir. 1968).

(2) Note 4(c), following the *Warrior & Gulf* case, dealt with the reluctance of courts in a proceeding prior to arbitration, to consider bargaining history as evidence of an intention to exclude a dispute from arbitration. However, even those courts which refuse to

consider such evidence in suits to compel arbitration will do so afterwards in a suit to enforce or vacate an award, since the findings of fact regarding the history of the employment relationship, as developed before the arbitrator, have become part of the record of the case. *E.g., Local 719, Bakery Workers v. National Biscuit Co.,* 378 F.2d 918 (3d Cir. 1967). *See also Humble Oil & Refining Co. v. Teamsters Local 866,* 271 F. Supp. 281 (S.D.N.Y. 1967).

(3) In resolving the question of arbitrability, must an arbitrator apply the *Warrior & Gulf* presumption in favor of a finding of arbitrability? In *Hughes Tool Co. & Electrical & Space Technicians, Local 1553,* 36 L.A. 1125 (1960) (grievance held not arbitrable), Arbitrator Benjamin Aaron rejected the contention that an arbitrator must decide the question of arbitrability in accordance with federal principles applicable to courts: "The parties elected to resolve this dispute through arbitration, and the decision rests upon the judgment of a majority of the three arbitrators selected to hear the case. In exercising that judgment, we should not, in my opinion be influenced by any calculation of what a court might do if confronted by the same problem. The dominant theme of the [Steelworkers Trilogy] is that courts typically lack the specialized knowledge, experience, and insight to deal wisely with these types of problems. . . . The temptation to uphold claims of arbitrability solely on the ground that a court would do so in like circumstances must be resisted; for to yield would be to abdicate the assumed independence of judgment based on specialized knowledge and experience upon which the Supreme Court doctrine is predicated." *Accord, Western Electric Co.,* 46 L.A. 1018 (1966). In holding that the grievance was not arbitrable, Arbitrator Dugan declared:

> Finally, as to the union's contention that the Supreme Court's decision in *Warrior* and related cases requires a holding of arbitrability unless the party urging nonarbitrability proves it beyond a shadow of a doubt, an analysis of decisions relied upon by the union show that they involved the approach that a court must have in approaching the problem of arbitrability. They did not involve the approach of an arbitrator in deciding questions of arbitrability. . . .

(4) In the ultimate arbitration of the *Warrior & Gulf* case, Arbitrator J. Fred Holly regarded the issue of arbitrability as the threshold issue before him despite the decision in *Warrior & Gulf.* He concluded, however, that the grievance was arbitrable. 36 L.A. 695 (1961).

> "An intriguing question not actually presented and not expressly considered in these cases is whether, as a matter of federal law, an arbitrator faced with any of the challenges to his jurisdiction or authority presented in these cases [the 1960

Trilogy] is required to decide such an issue the way the Court decided it (*i.e.,* in favor of jurisdiction or authority) or be subject to reversal if his contrary decision should be brought before a court. It has usually been assumed that the arbitrator, despite the Trilogy, has full discretion to decide any issue properly before him. Thus, for example, on facts like those of *Warrior & Gulf* he has the authority to decide whether the grievance protesting subcontracting is arbitrable.

"Actually, we believe it makes no difference in cases like these whether an arbitrator holds the grievance arbitrable and then denies it on the merits (if this should be his conclusion) or dismisses it as non-arbitrable. Either form of decision would have to be predicated on the same basic contractual analysis, namely, that there is no provision in the labor agreement which supports the grievance. The legal and practical results are, therefore, the same, and the point of the matter is that either way the arbitrator writes his opinion he is in fact deciding the merits. For this reason, we doubt that the Court would upset an arbitrator's holding of non-arbitrability." Smith & Jones, The Supreme Court & Labor Dispute Arbitration: The Emerging Federal Law, 63 Mich. L. Rev. 751, 761 (1965).

b. *Exceeding Contractual Authority: Modification of the Agreement*

THE TORRINGTON CO.
and
METAL PRODUCTS WORKERS UNION, LOCAL 1645, UAW, AFL-CIO

45 L.A. 353 (1965)

[For more than 20 years the Company had given time off with pay to vote on election days. This practice was originally initiated by the Company, unilaterally, and had never been provided for in any of the several collective bargaining agreements between the Company and the Union. In December, 1962, while one such agreement was in effect, the Company decided to eliminate the practice. It gave the Union notice of its decision, but also indicated its willingness to bargain about the matter. At that point, however, no bargaining took place. The agreement then in effect was to expire in September, 1963. In April, 1963, the Union filed unfair labor charges against the Company claiming, among other things, that the Company's unilateral change of the established practice of paid time off for voting constituted a Section 8(a)(5) violation of the NLRA. When the charges were last amended, however, this specific claim was omitted. In July, 1963, the NLRB Regional Director dismissed the charges as amended.

Contract negotiations began in August, 1963. At the first negotiating session the Company orally informed the Union that time off for voting would not be paid in the future. At a later meeting, the Union presented its written demands, including a provision for time off with pay for voting. No agreement was reached at that point. On September 26, 1963, the Company proposed the extension of the current agreement with several amendments none of which provided for or mentioned time off with pay for voting. The Union rejected these proposals and called a strike. Negotiations continued during the strike. On October 25, 1963, the Union proposed reinstatement of the expired agreement with certain amendments not, however, including any mention of the matter of time off with pay for voting. No agreement was reached, and the strike continued on through the November, 1963, election. Some of the employees who worked during the strike did not receive pay for voting time.

In January, 1964, agreement was reached on a new contract which, like the preceding agreements, did not contain any provision respecting time off with pay for voting. Subsequently, on 1964 election day the employees were not given time off with pay to vote. A grievance was filed protesting this and the issue was submitted to arbitration. The Company claimed the grievance was not arbitrable, and, in addition, that it should be denied on its merits.

The prior agreement contained the following language respecting an arbitrator's jurisdiction and authority:

"The arbitrator is bound by and must comply with all the terms of this agreement, and he shall not have any power whatsoever to arbitrate away any part of the agreement, nor add to, delete from, or modify, in any way, any of the provisions of this agreement. The Company's decisions will stand and will not be overruled by any arbitrator unless the arbitrator can find that the Company misinterpreted or violated the express terms of the agreement."

The 1964 agreement modified this language, and reads in pertinent part:

"The arbitrator shall be bound by and must comply with all of the terms of this agreement and he shall have no power to add to, delete from, or modify in any way, any of the provisions of this agreement. . . ."]

Kennedy, Thomas, Arbitrator

[The Arbitrator ruled first that the grievance presented an arbitrable claim. He then proceeded to the "merits."]

There was no clause which called for the payment of time off for voting in the earlier labor contracts and there is no such clause in the current contract. However, by 1962 this benefit had become a firmly established practice. It had been available to employees for approximately 20 years. We believe that a *benefit* of this nature, continued as it had been without change over a period of so many years, must be considered to have become an implied part of the contract.

We emphasize that it is a *benefit*. We distinguish between a past practice involving a *benefit* of this type and a past practice involving methods of operation or direction of the working force. In a recent award at the Torrington Company we upheld the company's right to unilaterally change a method of operation. The latter we believe is a right which management clearly has under the management clause in this contract in order to promote efficient operation. On the other hand, we do not believe that the management clause gives to the company the right to discontinue unilaterally a *benefit* which has become an implied part of the contract. In brief, we conclude that the company did have an obligation under the contract to continue to pay for time off for voting until such time as it negotiated a change in the matter. The company recognized its responsibility in this respect when, in its letter of March 8, 1963, it proposed to the union that negotiations on the matter be undertaken.

The union's inclusion of this issue in an unfair labor practice charge and its later withdrawal of it from the charge can have little bearing on this arbitration decision. The union's inclusion of the issue in the charge did indicate that it was aware that the company intended to discontinue this benefit. However, its withdrawal of the issue did not indicate that the union had accepted the company's right to discontinue it. Likewise, the union's action did not foreclose its right to bargain about and to arbitrate this issue. The parties both recognized that it was still a bargainable issue when they included it in their original demands in August, 1963.

It was the company which introduced the matter of pay for time off for voting at the first contract negotiations meeting on August 14, 1963. At that time the Company made it clear that it was insisting on a change in this practice. The union then followed by including the continuance of such time off with pay among its demands. These two conflicting demands evidently remained on the table until September 26.

The company's proposal of September 26, however, in our opinion constituted a significant change in the bargaining position of the parties with respect to this issue. That proposal suggested that the old agreement be extended (until September 27, 1966) except for 22 amendments. No mention was made of time off with pay for voting among the 22 amendments. It may be that the company intended that its earlier oral statement regarding discontinuance of such time off with pay should continue to be considered part of its demands. However, the union had reason to believe that the September 26 proposal meant that the company was dropping its demand for a change in this past practice.

The October 25, 1963, proposal of the union also began with the statement that the "collective bargaining Agreement and the Pension Agreement which expired September 27, 1963 *be reinstated* with the following amendments." There followed then half a dozen or so changes which did not include time off with pay for voting. We believe that the fact that the union did not list this issue among its demands in the October 25 proposal cannot be considered as a withdrawal of the issue by the union and an agreement not to continue this practice. There is no evidence that any union representative ever stated that the union was withdrawing its demand in favor of the company's demand on this issue. In our opinion the company's proposal of September 26 by its failure to mention the company's demand for a change in this practice removed it from the table. Therefore, it was no longer necessary for the union to continue its counter demand. Thus, by October 25 both parties agreed that the old contract was to be continued except for certain changes among which was *not* a change in the practice of giving time off with pay for voting.

The strike continued following the above proposals and on Election Day in November 1963 the company did not give time off with pay for the purpose of voting to its employees who were still coming to work including some bargaining unit employees. Since no contract was in effect at the time, the company was free to change the employee benefits which had been either stated or implied in the earlier contract. We do not find, however, that the failure to provide the benefit under such conditions affected in any way the bargaining position of the parties. It did not create a precedent under a contract.

We have no evidence that the position of the parties on this issue was changed or that the issue was ever discussed after the exchange of the written proposals of September 26 and October 25. We must conclude, therefore, that the final bargaining between the parties did not include an agreement to discontinue the practice of allowing time off with pay for voting — a benefit which had become firmly established by past practice under the old contract. We find, therefore, that the company was in violation of the contract when it refused to pay this benefit to employees on Election Day 1964.

NOTES:

(1) A federal district court vacated the award on the ground that the Arbitrator had exceeded his authority by reading the election day benefit into the new contract. On appeal the Union contended in turn that the Court had exceeded its authority. The Court of Appeals, in a split decision, sustained the District Court [362 F.2d 677 (1966)].

The majority opinion by Chief Judge Lumbard, citing *Warrior & Gulf* of the *1960 Trilogy,* stated that it is now "settled that a grievance is arbitrable 'unless it may be said with positive assurance that the arbitration clause is not susceptible of any interpretation that covers the asserted dispute' " but that "a less settled question is the appropriate scope of judicial review of a specific arbitration award." He noted that "although the arbitrator's decision on the merits is final as to questions of law and fact, his authority is contractual in nature and is limited to the powers conferred in the collective bargaining agreement." Thus, he noted that ". . . a number of courts have interpreted *Enterprise Wheel* [of the 1960 Trilogy] as authorizing review of whether an arbitrator's award exceeded the limits of his contractual authority." The opinion accepted this view, and noted further that ". . . a more exhaustive judicial review of this question is appropriate after the award has been made than before the award in a suit to compel arbitration; in this way the court receives the benefit of the arbitrator's interpretative skills as to the matter of his contractual authority."

The opinion then proceeded, in part:

> We cannot accept this interpretation of the negotiations. In the first place, as Judge Clarie stated, labor contracts generally state affirmatively what conditions the parties agree to, more specifically, what restraints the parties will place on management's freedom of action. While it may be appropriate to resolve a question never raised during negotiations on the basis of prior practice in the plant or industry, it is quite another thing to assume that the contract confers a specific benefit when that benefit was discussed during negotiations but omitted from the contract.
>
> . . . .
>
> The arbitrator's primary justification for reading the election day benefit into the 1964 agreement was that such a benefit corresponded to the parties' prior practice. But in this the arbitrator completely ignored the fact that the company had revoked that policy almost ten months earlier, by newsletter to the employees in December 1962 and by formal notice to the Union in April 1963. It was within the employer's discretion to make such a change since the narrow arbitration clause in the previous collective bargaining agreement precluded resort to arbitration by the Union. And there was no showing that Torrington's announcement was merely a statement of bargaining position and was not a seriously intended change in policy.
>
> In light of this uncontroverted fact, and bearing in mind that the arbitrator has no jurisdiction to "add to" the 1964 agreement, we do not think it was proper to place the "burden" of securing an express contract provision in the 1964 contract

on the company. At the start of negotiations, Torrington announced its intent to *continue* its previous change of election day policy. This was an express invitation to the Union to bargain with respect to this matter. After the Union failed to press for and receive a change in the 1964 agreement, the company was surely justified in applying in November 1964 a policy it had rightfully established in 1962, and had applied in November 1963 (during the strike).

In our opinion, the Union by pressing this grievance has attempted to have "added" to the 1964 agreement a benefit which it did not think sufficiently vital to insist upon during negotiations for the contract which ended a long and costly strike. We find this sufficiently clear from the facts as found by the arbitrator to agree with the district court that the arbitrator exceeded his authority by ruling that such a benefit was implied in the terms of that agreement. . . .

(2) *Problems:* Do you agree with the decision of the Arbitrator on the "merits?" Was he on sound ground in treating the long standing practice concerning pay for voting time as having created a binding obligation? Was he correct in concluding that this was a part of the parties' prior collective bargaining agreements, even though not expressed in any of them? Did his decision have the effect of elevating a past practice to a stature actually more obligatory than a provision expressly contained in a collective bargaining agreement? With respect to this last question, consider what the result would or should have been if the parties' prior agreements had contained an express voting time pay provision, and the subsequent negotiations for the new contract were precisely as indicated by the Arbitrator and the courts (as to proposals and counter-proposals made and as to the silence of the ensuing agreement on the specific point).

One commentator stated that, "The dissent [in Torrington] is, in my view, more faithful to the central thesis of the *Trilogy.* Nevertheless, I would renew an earlier suggestion — that the courts in actions involving the validity of the award should have more responsibility for the merits than in actions to compel arbitration. Unlike the Second Circuit's and Judge Hays' view [Labor Arbitration: A Dissenting View 112 (1966)] that suggestion does not rely on what is, I believe, an unworkable and spurious dichotomy between 'jurisdiction' and 'authority,' but on the following considerations: At the enforcement stage, the court would have the benefit of the arbitrator's expertise in the same way as a court reviewing the decisions of an administrative agency has the benefit of administrative expertise. The suggested approach would, moreover, permit the arbitration process to realize its potential for therapy and would, at the same time, recognize that the award, although therapy for one party, may be poison to the agreement, whose purpose, after all, is to provide a code for both parties rather than a couch for one of them. Beyond those considerations are more important ones that go to the responsible exercise of judicial power. It is, I believe, questionable to require courts to rubber-stamp the awards of private decision-makers when the courts are convinced that there is no rational basis in the agreement for the awards they are asked to enforce. In no other area of adjudication are the courts asked to exercise their powers while they are denied any responsibility for scrutinizing the results they are to enforce. The courts, moreover, exercise such responsibility in areas at least as complex and specialized as labor arbitration, whose mysteries have, I believe, been sometimes exaggerated. In any case, the unique attempt to shrivel judicial responsibility in enforcing arbitration awards is likely to fail because it runs against the grain of judicial tradition. It is thus not surprising that other circuits have adopted an approach similar to that of the Second Circuit." Meltzer, Ruminations About Ideology, Law, and Labor Arbitration, 34 U. Chi. L. Rev. 545, 553-54 (1967). For other comments on the *Torrington* case see Aaron, *Labor Law* (recent decision), 53 Va. L. Rev. 437 (1967); Comment, Labor — Judicial Review of Arbitration — Arbitrator Held Without Authority to Read Implied Term into Collective Bargaining Agreement, 41 N.Y.U.L. Rev. 1220 (1966); Comment, Labor Law — Judicial Review of Arbitrator's Authority to Imply Contractual Conditions, 20 Vand. L. Rev. 182 (1966).

The provision barring arbitral additions to or modifications of "the agreement" is a very common one. Do such provisions necessarily prohibit an arbitrator from basing his decision on sources outside the written agreement? Is it reasonable to interpret anti-modification clauses as mere reiterations of the Supreme Court's statement in *Enterprise* that arbitration awards are enforceable only to the extent that they "draw their essence" from the labor agreement (which, according to *Warrior & Gulf,* encompasses implied obligations.) Wouldn't such an interpretation render anti-modification clauses meaningless?

Most cases appear to embrace the following approach when reviewing arbitration awards: a court may not upset an arbiter's decision unless (1) the arbitrator clearly based his decision upon considerations external to the parties' agreement or (2) the arbitrator's interpretation of the labor agreement is "wholly unreasonable" or "irrational." Cases upholding an award under this standard include *Holly Sugar Corp. v. Distillery Workers,* 412 F.2d 899 (9th Cir. 1969) and *In re Arbitration between Aloha Motors, Inc. and ILWU, Local 142,* 530 F.2d 848 (9th Cir. 1976); *Ludwig Honold Mfg. Co. v. Fletcher,* 405 F.2d 1123 (3d Cir. 1969); *Safeway Stores v. Bakery Workers, Local 111,* 390 F.2d 79 (5th Cir. 1968). Cases vacating arbitration awards include *Timken Co. v. Steelworkers Union,* 482 F.2d 1012 (6th Cir. 1973) and *Amanda Bent Bolt Co. v. UAW Local 1549,* 451 F.2d 1277 (6th Cir. 1971). The existence of a contract provision prohibiting the arbitrator from "altering" the agreement should not be construed as preventing the arbitrator from basing his award upon parol evidence of the parties' intentions, even where his award adds to or seemingly contradicts the written contract. *Torrington, supra,* at 904-6; *Timken Co., supra,* at 1015 note 2. *Cf. Steelworkers Union v. Warrior & Gulf, supra; Aloha Motors, supra.* Nevertheless, such clauses probably increase the likelihood that an award at variance with the written document will be deemed "irrational" and, therefore, unenforceable. *Timken Co., supra; H.K. Porter Co. v. Saw Workers Union 22254,* 333 F.2d 596 (3d Cir.), *cert. denied,* 395 U.S. 964 (1964).

\ (3) Irrespective of a specific restriction on the arbitrator's authority to alter the labor agreement, the courts are obligated, under *Enterprise Wheel,* to vacate awards based on an arbiter's perception of industrial justice rather than on his interpretation of the parties' intentions. In carrying out this obligation, the courts have at times produced seemingly irreconcilable results. *Compare,* for example, *Timken Co. v. Steelworkers Union,* 482 F.2d 1012 (6th Cir. 1973) *with Aloha Motors, Inc. and ILWU Local 142,* 530 F.2d 848 (9th Cir. 1976). In *Timken,* the agreement authorized the employer to discharge employees for "voluntary quitting," defined as an "unauthorized absence of seven consecutive days." The arbitrator ruled that this provision did not permit the employer to discharge an employee who missed one month of work while serving a jail sentence. He reasoned that the voluntary quit provision was intended to apply to employees who voluntarily abandoned their jobs and did not encompass unauthorized absences due to imprisonment. The court reversed on the ground that the arbitrator's interpretation of the contract was "without support in the record" and could not rationally be deduced from the agreement. One judge argued in dissent that the award should have been upheld, since it reflected the arbitrator's understanding of the agreement.

In *Aloha Motors,* the agreement provided (1) that employees would receive sick-leave benefits only if their illness was certified by a physician and (2) that the employer could require, at his expense, an examination by a company physician to confirm the illness. The issue before the arbitrator was whether the employer properly refused to grant sick pay to five employees who obtained a certificate from a physician but refused to be examined by a company doctor. Although the agreement on its face gave the employer complete discretion whether to order such an examination, the arbitrator held that the company rule requiring all employees to be examined by a company doctor, regardless of the circumstances, exceeded the meaning of the agreement. He then ruled that a company examination could be required only where there was a reasonable basis for suspecting abuse of sick leave privileges. The district court vacated the award; however, the Ninth Circuit reversed, holding that the award was a "plausible" interpretation of the contract.

(4) How would you decide the following cases, in light of your understanding of the Steelworkers Trilogy, particularly *Enterprise Wheel?*

(a) The labor agreement between the parties contained the following provisions:

> Whenever the Company determines that a permanent vacancy occurs, or a new job is created, notice of such jobs shall be posted . . .
>
> Employees who have applied for such new jobs and have been assigned to fill such jobs will not be eligible to apply for any other posted job for a period of six months from the date of his transfer into such posted job . . .
>
> When an opening occurs in a higher labor grade and there is no employee with a prior right to such job, such opening will be filled on the basis of skill and ability as the determining factors, with seniority being given full consideration and prevailing when skill and ability are equal . . .

On September 29, 1965, the Company posted the job of Sheet Metal Specialist A, and on the same day Employee *X* applied for and was assigned the job. The next day, September 30, *Y* was hired as a Sheet Metal Specialist A. On November 16, 1965, the Company posted for application the job of Sheet Metal Leader. Both employees *X* and *Y* bid for the job, and the Company awarded *Y* the job. Employee *X* filed a grievance, alleging that he was wrongfully denied the job. The grievance terminated in an arbitration. The Arbitrator upheld the grievance. The Company sought to vacate the award on the ground that it was contrary to the language of the agreement. *What result? See Ludwig Honold Mfg. Co. v. Fletcher,* 275 F. Supp. 776 (E.D. Pa. 1967).

(b) The Company discharged an employee for pilferage. A grievance was filed which terminated in an arbitration. The Arbitrator found the employee guilty but directed that he be reinstated without back pay. The Company sought to vacate the award on the ground that the Arbitrator exceeded his powers. The labor agreement included the following provisions:

> All decisions of the arbitrator shall be limited expressly to the terms and provisions of this Agreement and in no event may the terms of the Agreement be altered, amended or modified by the arbitrator . . . .

> The supervision and control of all operations and the direction of all working forces, which shall include, but not be limited to, the right . . . to suspend or discharge for proper cause . . . shall be vested exclusively in the company. . . .
>
> Proper cause for suspension or discharge shall include, but not be limited to, . . . pilferage . . . .

Should the Company succeed? See Electrical Workers, Local 1260 v. Hawaiian Telephone Co., 411 P.2d 134, 53 L.C. ¶ 11,025 (1966).

c. Exceeding Contractual Authority as to Remedy

Even where an arbitrator concededly has subject matter jurisdiction over a particular dispute, the contract and/or stipulation may expressly or impliedly limit his/her authority to fashion a particular remedy should he find a contract violation. If the arbitrator's award exceeds such limitations upon his authority, it may be vacated by a court under § 301. For example, in *Retail Store Employees' Union Local 782 v. SAV-ON Groceries,* 508 F.2d 500 (10th Cir. 1975), the parties asked the arbitrator to decide whether the Company exercised fairness in not allowing an employee to displace less senior employees. The arbitrator ruled that the company acted improperly, and he awarded the grievant the back pay she would have received but for the Company's action. The Tenth Circuit held that the award was beyond the scope of the arbitrator's authority, since the parties did not explicitly submit to him the issue of back pay. The dissenting judge found this result highly unreasonable, since, in his opinion, the purpose of the submission was not only to determine who was right or wrong, but to achieve a monetary result. To him, the real issue was whether an award of money damages was "within the contemplation of the submission."

A different approach was embraced by the Fifth Circuit in *United Steelworkers of America v. U.S. Gypsum Co.,* 402 F.2d 713 (5th Cir. 1974). The arbitrator concluded that the Company had breached the labor agreement by refusing to negotiate pursuant to a wage reopener clause. Ordinarily, the arbitrator would have ordered the Company to bargain with the union; however, the latter had been decertified for five years when the decision was made. He therefore ordered the Company to pay the union an amount equal to the wage increase the parties would probably have agreed upon had they negotiated. The court flatly rejected the Company's argument that the award was forbidden by the contract, which prohibited the arbitrator from altering its terms in any way: "The nexus between the breach and the reopener clause and the method selected to remedy that breach is sufficient to support the conclusion that the remedy 'draws its essence' from the contract. Gypsum's employees were denied their right to negotiate for increased wages. Relief was given in the form of what they would have received had they negotiated. This remedy is not arbitrary, capricious nor insufficiently grounded in the contract, and it flows logically from the breach of the reopener clause." *Id.* at 731-32. *Accord, Local 369, Bakery Workers Union v. Cotten Back Co. Inc.,* 514 F.2d 1235 (5th Cir. 1975) ("Having found a contract violation [the arbitrator must be free to] fashion a remedial order to bring the parties' actions in conformity with the contract and make reparation for past infringements. A collective bargaining agreement may not specify the relief required for every conceivable contract violation so the arbitrator must often rely on his own experience and expertise in formulating an appropriate remedy. In view of the variety and novelty of many labor-management disputes, reviewing courts must not unduly restrain an arbitrator's flexibility."); *College Hall Fashions v. Philadelphia, etc.,* 408 F. Supp. 722 (E.D. Pa. 1976); *Yellow Cab. Co. v. Democratic Union,* 398 F.2d 735 (7th Cir. 1968).

d. Incompleteness, Ambiguity or Inconsistency

Where the parties cannot agree on how to implement an award because it is incomplete or ambiguous, and neither party can offer a clear and compelling interpretation of the award, the matter ought to be resubmitted for further arbitration. *Bell Aerospace Co. v. Local 516, UAW,* 500 F.2d 921 (2d Cir. 1974) ("The purpose of arbitration is to resolve disputes, not to create new ones. An award which does not fulfill this purpose is [not final and binding]"). *Accord, IBEW, Local 369 v. Olin Corp.,* 471 F.2d 468 (6th Cir. 1972); *Chief Freight Lines v. Local Union No. 886,* 514 F.2d 572 (10th Cir. 1975). What if an arbitration award appears to be irreconcilable with a previous award under the same contract? *See American Sterilizer Co. v. UAW Local 832,* 278 F. Supp. 637 (W.D. Pa. 1968).

e. Violation of Law or Public Policy

Unless the parties otherwise agree, an arbitrator must base his award solely on his interpretation of the labor agreement, not on his understanding of public law or policy. *Enterprise, supra; Teamsters v. Washington Employees,* 557 F.2d 1345 (9th Cir. 1977) (arbitrator may apply state law if parties so request). Not surprisingly, an arbitral award may draw its essence from the contract, and be unassailable on its merits, yet be contrary to law or public policy. Must a court enforce such an award? *See Goodyear Tire & Rubber Co. v. Sanford,* 92 LRRM 3492 (Tex. Ct. Civ. App. 1976) (court vacated award it believed contrary to public policy); *UAW Local 985 v. W.M. Chace Co.,* 262 F. Supp. 114, 118 (E.D. Mich. 1966) (court will not enforce an award which requires a party to commit a crime); *Glendale Mfg.*

Co. v. Local 520, ILGWU, 283 F.2d 936 (4th Cir. 1960), *cert. denied,* 366 U.S. 950 (1961); *Botany Industries, Inc. v. New York Joint Board, Amal. Clothing Workers,* 375 F. Supp. 485 (S.D.N.Y. 1974), vacated on other grounds, 506 F.2d 1246 (2d Cir. 1974). (Court set aside award which was based on what the court found to be an illegal hot cargo provision in violation of § 8e of the NLRA). Did the court in *Botany* invade the province of the NLRB in passing on the unfair labor practice question? *Cf. Carey v. Westinghouse,* 375 U.S. 261 (1964).

f. Procedural Impropriety

In addition to scrutinizing the merits of an arbitrator's decision, courts will screen awards for procedural defects that substantially prejudice the rights of a party to the disputes. The United States Arbitration Act, 9 U.S.C.A. § 1 *et seq.* sets forth four grounds for vacating an arbitration award: corruption or fraud; evident partiality of the arbitrator; prejudicial misbehavior of the arbitrator such as refusing to hear relevant and material evidence; and the arbitrator's failure to make a final and definite award or to act within the powers given him. Several courts have incorporated these provisions into federal labor contract law, pursuant to *Lincoln Mills, supra,* or else have looked to them for guidance. *E.g., Teamsters Local 251 v. Narragansett Co.,* 503 F.2d 309 (4th Cir. 1974); *Allendale Nursing Home v. Joint Board,* 377 F. Supp. 1208 (S.D.N.Y. 1974); *Holodnak v. Avco Corp.,* 381 F. Supp. 191 (D. Conn. 1974), modified on other grounds, 514 F.2d 285 (2d Cir. 1975); *Pietro Scalzetti v. Operating Engineers Local 150,* 351 F.2d 576 (7th Cir. 1965) (specifically applying Arbitration Act); *Ludwig Honold Mfg. Co. v. Fletcher,* 405 F.2d 1123 (3d Cir. 1969) (looking to Act for guidance).

Since the judicial rules of proof, procedure, and evidence do not govern arbitration proceedings, courts are reluctant to second-guess arbitrators on such procedural matters as the admissibility of evidence or the employment of a particular standard of proof. *Compare Amalgamated Meat Cutters, Local 540 v. Neukoff Bros. Packers, Inc.,* 481 F.2d 817 (5th Cir. 1973) (arbitrator may exclude results of polygraph test even though contract gave employer the right to require employees to take the test; also arbitrator may apply a standard of proof even if it is "offensive to judicial thinking") *and Shopping Cart, Inc. v. Food Employees,* 350 F. Supp. 1221 (E.D. Pa. 1972) (arbitrator has discretion to exclude evidence offered after close of hearing), *with Harvey Aluminum v. Steelworkers Union,* 263 F. Supp. 488 (C.D. Cal. 1967) (court may vacate award if exclusion of evidence is technical, unanticipated, and fundamentally unfair) and *Allendale Nursing Home v. Joint Board, supra* (award vacated where arbitrator denied request for continuance after crucial representative of employer became ill).

It is well-settled that an award may be vacated for arbitral partiality, although it is unlikely that a court will upset an award absent clear and convincing evidence of bias. *Brewery Workers v. P. Ballantine & Sons,* 83 LRRM 2712 (D.N.J. 1973). Bias may be revealed by a study of the arbitrator's conduct at the hearing or it may be inferred from a direct, undisclosed personal or business relationship between the arbitrator and one of the immediate parties. *Holodnak v. Avco Corp.,* 381 F. Supp. 191 (D. Conn. 1974), *modified on other grounds* 514 F.2d 285 (2d Cir. 1975) (award vacated where arbitrator was openly hostile toward grievant); *Colony Liquor Distributors, Inc. v. Teamsters Local 669,* 34 App. Div. 2d 1060, 312 N.V.S.2d 403 (1970), *aff'd,* 28 N.Y.2d 596 (1971) (award vacated where arbitrator failed to inform employer that he served as the union's attorney for several years); *Brewery Workers v. P. Ballantine & Sons, supra* at 2723-24 (court refused to vacate award where union did not demonstrate that arbitrator knew of, participated in, or benefited from business dealings his cousin allegedly had with employer prior to rendering the arbitration award).

NOTE:

An arbitrator is clothed with an immunity analogous to judicial immunity against actions brought by either party arising out of the performance of his duties. The same reasons of public policy are applicable; arbitrators must be free from the fear of reprisals by an unsuccessful litigant and be uninfluenced by any fear of consequences for their acts. *Babylon Milk & Cream Co. v. Horovitz,* 151 N.Y.S.2d 221, 26 L.A. 121 (N.Y. Sup. Ct. 1956); *Cahn v. ILGWU,* 311 F.2d 113, 51 LRRM 2186 (3d Cir. 1962); *Hill v. Aro Corp.,* 263 F. Supp. 324, 64 LRRM 2315 (D. Ohio 1967).

Chapter 7

JUDICIAL ENFORCEMENT OF THE ARBITRATION PROCESS

A. ENFORCEMENT OF THE NO-STRIKE OBLIGATION

BOYS MARKETS, INC. v. RETAIL CLERKS LOCAL 770

United States Supreme Court
398 U.S. 235, 90 S. Ct. 1583, 26 L. Ed. 2d 199 (1970)

Mr. Justice Brennan delivered the opinion of the Court.

In this case we re-examine the holding of *Sinclair Refining Co. v. Atkinson,* 370 U.S. 195 (1962), that the anti-injunction provisions of the Norris-LaGuardia Act preclude a federal district court from enjoining a strike in breach of a no-strike obligation under a collective bargaining agreement, even though that agreement contains provisions, enforceable under § 301 (a) of the Labor-Management Relations Act for binding arbitration of the grievance dispute concerning which the strike was called. The Court of Appeals for the Ninth Circuit, considering itself bound by *Sinclair,* reversed the grant by the District Court for the Central District of California of petitioner's prayer for injunctive relief. 416 F.2d 368 (1969). We granted certiorari. . . . Having concluded that *Sinclair* was erroneously decided and that subsequent events have undermined its continuing validity, we overrule that decision and reverse the judgment of the Court of Appeals.

I. In February 1969, at the time of the incidents that produced this litigation, petitioner and respondent were parties to a collective bargaining agreement which provided, *inter alia,* that all controversies concerning its interpretation or application should be resolved by adjustment and arbitration procedures set forth therein and that, during the life of the contract, there should be "no cessation or stoppage of work, lock-out, picketing or boycotts. . . ." The dispute arose when petitioner's frozen foods supervisor and certain members of his crew who were not members of the bargaining unit began to rearrange merchandise in the frozen food cases of one of petitioner's supermarkets. A union representative insisted that the food cases be stripped of all merchandise and be restocked by union personnel. When petitioner did not accede to the union's demand, a strike was called and the union began to picket petitioner's establishment. Thereupon petitioner demanded that the union cease the work stoppage and picketing and sought to invoke the grievance and arbitration procedures specified in the contract.

The following day, since the strike had not been terminated, petitioner filed a complaint in California Superior Court seeking a temporary restraining order, a preliminary and permanent injunction, and specific performance of the contractual arbitration provision. The state court issued a temporary restraining order forbidding continuation of the strike and also an order to show cause why a preliminary injunction should not be granted. Shortly thereafter, the union removed the case to the federal district court and there made a motion to quash the state court's temporary restraining order. In opposition, petitioner moved for an order compelling arbitration and enjoining continuation of the strike. Concluding that the dispute was subject to arbitration under the collective bargaining agreement and that the strike was in violation of the contract, the District Court ordered the parties to arbitrate the underlying dispute and simultaneously enjoined the strike, all picketing in the vicinity of petitioner's supermarket, and any attempts by the union to induce the employees to strike or to refuse to perform their services.

II. At the outset, we are met with respondent's contention that *Sinclair* ought not to be disturbed because the decision turned on a question of statutory construction which Congress can alter at any time. Since Congress has not modified our conclusions in *Sinclair,* even though it has been urged to do so, respondent argues that principles of *stare decisis* should govern the present case.

We do not agree that the doctrine of *stare decisis* bars a reexamination of *Sinclair* in the circumstances of this case. We fully recognize that important policy considerations militate in favor of continuity and predictability in the law. Nevertheless, as Mr. Justice Frankfurter wrote for the Court, "[S]*tare decisis* is a principle of policy and not a mechanical formula of adherence to the latest decision, however recent and questionable, when such adherence involves collision with a prior doctrine more embracing in its scope, intrinsically sounder, and verified by experience." *Helvering v. Hallock,* 309 U.S. 106, 119 (1940). . . . It is precisely because *Sinclair* stands as a significant departure from our otherwise consistent emphasis upon the congressional policy to promote the peaceful settlement of labor disputes through arbitration and our efforts to accommodate and harmonize this policy with those underlying the anti-injunction provisions of the Norris-LaGuardia Act that we believe *Sinclair* should be reconsidered. Furthermore, in light of developments subsequent to *Sinclair,* in particular our decision in *Avco Corp. v. Aero Lodge 735,* 390 U.S. 557 (1968), it has become clear that the *Sinclair* decision does not further but rather frustrates realization of an important goal of our national labor policy.

Nor can we agree that conclusive weight should be accorded to the failure of Congress to respond to *Sinclair* on the theory that congressional silence should be interpreted as acceptance of the decision. The Court has cautioned that "[i]t is at best treacherous to find in congressional silence alone the adoption of a controlling rule of law." *Girouard v. United States,* 328 U.S. 61, 69 (1946). Therefore, in the absence of any persuasive circumstances evidencing a clear design that congressional inaction be taken as acceptance of *Sinclair,* the mere silence of Congress is not a sufficient reason for refusing to reconsider the decision. *Helvering v. Hallock, supra,* at 119-120.

III. From the time *Textile Workers Union v. Lincoln Mills,* 353 U.S. 448 (1957), was decided, we have frequently found it necessary to consider various substantive and procedural aspects of federal labor contract law and questions concerning its application in both state and federal courts. *Lincoln Mills* held generally that "the substantive law to apply in suits under § 301(a) is federal law, which the courts must fashion from the policy of our national labor laws," 353 U.S., at 456, and more specifically that a union can obtain specific performance of an employer's promise to arbitrate grievances. We rejected the contention that the anti-injunction proscriptions of the Norris-LaGuardia Act prohibited this type of relief, noting that a refusal to arbitrate was not "part and parcel of the abuses against which the Act was aimed," *id.,* at 458, and that the Act itself manifests a policy determination that arbitration should be encouraged. *See* 29 U.S.C. § 108. Subsequently in the *Steelworkers Trilogy* [9] we emphasized the importance of arbitration as an instrument of federal policy for resolving disputes between labor and management and cautioned the lower courts against usurping the functions of the arbitrator.

Serious questions remained, however, concerning the role which state courts are to play in suits involving collective bargaining agreements. Confronted with some of these problems in *Charles Dowd Box Co. v. Courtney,* 368 U.S. 502 (1962), we held that Congress clearly intended *not* to disturb the pre-existing jurisdiction of the state courts over suits for violations of collective bargaining agreements. We noted that the

> "clear implication of the entire record of the congressional debates in both 1946 and 1947 is that the purpose of conferring jurisdiction upon the federal district courts was not to displace, but to supplement, the thoroughly considered jurisdiction of the

---

[9] United Steelworkers of America v. American Mfg. Co., 363 U.S. 564 (1960); United Steelworkers of America v. Warrior & Gulf Nav. Co., 363 U.S. 574 (1960); United Steelworkers of America v. Enterprise Wheel & Car Corp., 363 U.S. 593 (1960).

courts of the various States over contracts made by labor organizations." *Id.* at 511.

Shortly after the decision in *Dowd Box,* we sustained, in *Teamsters Local 174 v. Lucas Flour Co.,* 369 U.S. 95 (1962), an award of damages by a state court to an employer for a breach by the union of a no-strike provision in their contract. While emphasizing that "in enacting § 301 Congress intended doctrines of federal labor law uniformly to prevail over inconsistent local rules," *id.* at 104, we did not consider the applicability of the Norris-LaGuardia Act to state court proceedings because the employer's prayer for relief sought only damages and not specific performance of a no-strike obligation.

Subsequent to the decision in *Sinclair,* we held in *Avco Corp. v. Aero Lodge No. 735, supra,* that § 301(a) suits initially brought in state courts may be removed to the designated federal forum under the federal question removal jurisdiction delineated in 28 U.S.C. § 1441. In so holding, however, the Court expressly left open the questions whether state courts are bound by the anti-injunction proscriptions of the Norris-LaGuardia Act and whether federal courts, after removal of a § 301(a) action, are required to dissolve any injunctive relief previously granted by the state courts. *See generally General Electric Co. v. Local Union 191,* 413 F.2d 964 (5th Cir. 1969) (dissolution of state injunction required). Three Justices who concurred expressed the view that *Sinclair* should be reconsidered "upon an appropriate future occasion." 390 U.S. at 562 (Stewart, J., concurring).

The decision in *Avco,* viewed in the context of *Lincoln Mills* and its progeny, has produced an anomalous situation which, in our view, makes urgent the reconsideration of *Sinclair.* The principal practical effect of *Avco* and *Sinclair* taken together is nothing less than to oust state courts of jurisdiction in § 301(a) suits where injunctive relief is sought for breach of a non-strike obligation. Union defendants can, as a matter of course, obtain removal to a federal court, and there is obviously a compelling incentive for them to do so in order to gain the advantage of the strictures upon injunctive relief which *Sinclair* imposes on federal courts. The sanctioning of this practice, however, is wholly inconsistent with our conclusion in *Dowd Box* that the congressional purpose embodied in § 301(a) was to *supplement,* and not to encroach upon, the pre-existing jurisdiction of the state courts. It is ironic indeed that the very provision which Congress clearly intended to provide additional remedies for breach of collective bargaining agreements has been employed to displace previously existing state remedies. We are not at liberty thus to depart from the clearly expressed congressional policy to the contrary.

On the other hand, to the extent that widely disparate remedies theoretically remain available in state, as opposed to federal courts, the federal policy of labor law uniformity elaborated in *Lucas Flour Co.,* is seriously offended. This policy, of course, could hardly require, as a practical matter, that labor law be administered identically in all courts, for undoubtedly a certain diversity exists among the state and federal systems in matters of procedural and remedial detail, a fact which Congress evidently took into account in deciding not to disturb the traditional jurisdiction of the States. The injunction, however, is so important a remedial device, particularly in the arbitration context, that its availability or nonavailability in various courts will not only produce rampant forum-shopping and maneuvering from one court to another but will also greatly frustrate any relative uniformity in the enforcement of arbitration agreements.

Furthermore, the existing scheme, with the injunction remedy technically available in the state courts but rendered inefficacious by the removal device, assigns to removal proceedings a totally unintended function. While the underlying purposes of Congress in providing for federal question removal jurisdiction remain somewhat obscure, there has never been a serious contention that Congress intended that the removal mechanism be utilized to foreclose completely remedies otherwise available in the state courts. Although federal question removal jurisdiction may well have been intended to provide a forum for the protection of federal rights where such protection was deemed necessary or to encourage the development of expertise by the federal courts in the interpretation of federal law, there is no indication that Congress intended by the removal mechanism to effect a wholesale dislocation in the allocation of judicial business between the state and federal courts. *Cf. City of Greenwood v. Peacock,* 384 U.S. 808 (1966).

It is undoubtedly true that each of the foregoing objections to *Sinclair-Avco* could be remedied either by overruling *Sinclair* or by extending that decision to the States. While some commentators have suggested that the solution to the present unsatisfactory situation does lie in the extension of the *Sinclair* prohibition to state court proceedings, we agree with Chief Justice Traynor of the California Supreme Court that "whether or not Congress could deprive state courts of the power to give such [injunctive] remedies when enforcing collective bargaining agreements, it has not attempted to do so either in the Norris-LaGuardia Act or section 301." *McCarroll v. Los Angeles County Dist. Council of Carpenters,* 49 Cal. 2d 45, 61, 315 P.2d 322, 332 (1957), *cert. denied,* 355 U.S. 932 (1958). . . .

An additional reason for not resolving the existing dilemma by extending *Sinclair* to the States is the devastating implications for the enforceability of arbitration agreements and their accompanying no-strike obligations if equitable remedies were not available. As we have previously indicated, a no-strike obligation, express or implied, is the *quid pro quo* for an undertaking by the employer to submit grievance disputes to the process of arbitration. *See Textile Workers Union v. Lincoln Mills, supra,* at 455. Any incentive for employers to enter into such an arrangement is necessarily dissipated if the principal and most expeditious method by which the no-strike obligation can be enforced is eliminated. While it is of course true, as respondent contends, that other avenues of redress, such as an action for damages, would remain open to an aggrieved employer, an award of damages after a dispute has been settled is no substitute for an immediate halt to an illegal strike. Furthermore, an action for damages prosecuted during or after a labor dispute would only tend to aggravate industrial strife and delay an early resolution of the difficulties between employer and union.

Even if management is not encouraged by the unavailability of the injunction remedy to resist arbitration agreements, the fact remains that the effectiveness of such agreements would be greatly reduced if injunctive relief were withheld. Indeed, the very purpose of arbitration procedures is to provide a mechanism for the expeditious settlement of industrial disputes without resort to strikes, lock-outs, or other self-help measures. This basic purpose is obviously largely undercut if there is no immediate, effective remedy for those very tactics which arbitration is designed to obviate. Thus, because *Sinclair,* in the aftermath of *Avco,* casts serious doubt upon the effective enforcement of a vital element of stable labor-management relations — arbitration agreements with their attendant no-strike obligations — we conclude that *Sinclair* does not make a viable contribution to federal labor policy.

IV. We have also determined that the dissenting opinion in *Sinclair* states the correct principles concerning the accommodation necessary between the seemingly absolute terms of the Norris-LaGuardia Act and the policy considerations underlying § 301(a). 370 U.S., at 215. Although we need not repeat all that was there said, a few points should be emphasized at this time.

The literal terms of § 4 of the Norris-LaGuardia Act must be accommodated to the subsequently enacted provisions of § 301(a) of the Labor-Management Relations Act and the purposes of arbitration. Statutory interpretation requires more than concentration upon isolated words; rather, consideration must be given to the total corpus of pertinent law and the policies which inspired ostensibly inconsistent provisions. *See Richards v. United States,* 369 U.S. 1, 11 (1962); *Mastro Plastics Corp. v. NLRB,* 350 U.S. 270, 285 (1956); *United States v. Hutcheson,* 312 U.S. 219, 235 (1941).

The Norris-LaGuardia Act was responsive to a situation totally different from that which exists today. In the early part of this century, the federal courts generally were regarded as allies of management in its attempt to prevent the organization and strengthening of labor unions; and in this industrial struggle the injunction became a potent weapon which was wielded against the activities of labor groups. The result was a large number of sweeping decrees, often issued *ex parte,* drawn on an *ad hoc* basis without regard to any systematic elaboration of national labor policy. See Drivers' Union v. Lake Valley Co., 311 U.S. 91, 102 (1940).

In 1932 Congress attempted to bring some order out of the industrial chaos that had developed and to correct the abuses which had resulted from the interjection of the federal judiciary into union-management disputes on the behalf of management. *See* Declaration of Public Policy, Norris-LaGuardia Act, § 2, 47 Stat. 70 (1932). Congress, therefore, determined initially to limit severely the power of the federal courts to issue injunctions "in any case involving or growing out of any labor dispute. . . ." 47 Stat. 70. Even as initially enacted, however, the prohibition against federal injunctions was by no means absolute. *See* Norris-LaGuardia Act, §§ 7, 8, 9, 47 Stat. 70 (1932). Shortly thereafter Congress passed the Wagner Act, designed to curb various management activities which tended to discourage employee participation in collective action.

As labor organizations grew in strength and developed toward maturity, congressional emphasis shifted from protection of the nascent labor movement to the encouragement of collective bargaining and to administrative techniques for the peaceful resolution of industrial disputes. This shift in emphasis was accomplished, however, without extensive revision of many of the older enactments, including the anti-injunction section of the Norris-LaGuardia Act. Thus it became the task of the courts to accommodate, to reconcile the older statutes with the more recent ones.

A leading example of this accommodation process is *Brotherhood of R.R. Trainmen v. Chicago River & Ind. R.R.,* 353 U.S. 30 (1957). There we were confronted with a peaceful strike which violated the statutory duty to arbitrate imposed by the Railway Labor Act. The Court concluded that a strike in violation of a statutory arbitration duty was not the type of situation to which the Norris-LaGuardia Act was responsive, that an important federal policy was involved in the peaceful settlement of disputes through the statutorily-mandated arbitration procedure, that this important policy was imperiled if equitable remedies were not available to implement it, and hence that Norris-LaGuardia's policy of nonintervention by the federal courts should yield to the overriding interest in the successful implementation of the arbitration process.

The principles elaborated in *Chicago River* are equally applicable to the present case. To be sure, *Chicago River* involved arbitration procedures established by statute. However, we have frequently noted, in such cases as *Lincoln Mills,* the *Steelworkers Trilogy,* and *Lucas Flour,* the importance which Congress has attached generally to the voluntary settlement of labor disputes without resort to self-help and more particularly to arbitration as a means to this end. Indeed, it has been stated that *Lincoln Mills,* in its exposition of § 301(a), "went a long way towards making arbitration the central institution in the administration of collective bargaining contracts."

The *Sinclair* decision, however, seriously undermined the effectiveness of the arbitration technique as a method peacefully to resolve industrial disputes without resort to strikes, lockouts, and similar devices. Clearly employers will be wary of assuming obligations to arbitrate specifically enforceable against them when no similarly efficacious remedy is available to enforce the concomitant undertaking of the union to refrain from striking. On the other hand, the central purpose of the Norris-LaGuardia Act to foster the growth and viability of labor organizations is hardly retarded — if anything, this goal is advanced — by a remedial device which merely enforces the obligation that the union freely undertook under a specifically enforceable agreement to submit disputes to arbitration. We conclude, therefore, that the unavailability of equitable relief in the arbitration context presents a serious impediment to the congressional policy favoring the voluntary establishment of a mechanism for the peaceful resolution of labor disputes, that the core purpose of the Norris-LaGuardia Act is not sacrificed by the limited use of equitable remedies to further this important policy, and consequently that the Norris-LaGuardia Act does not bar the granting of injunctive relief in the circumstances of the instant case.

V. Our holding in the present case is a narrow one. We do not undermine the vitality of the Norris-LaGuardia Act. We deal only with the situation in which a collective bargaining contract contains a mandatory grievance adjustment or arbitration procedure. Nor does it follow from what we have said that injunctive relief is appropriate as a matter of course in every case of a strike over an arbitrable grievance. The dissenting opinion in *Sinclair* suggested the following principles for the guidance of the district courts in determining whether to grant injunctive relief — principles which we now adopt:

"A District Court entertaining an action under § 301 may not grant injunctive relief against concerted activity unless and until it decides that the case is one in which an injunction would be appropriate despite the Norris-LaGuardia Act. When a strike is sought to be enjoined because it is over a grievance which both parties are contractually bound to arbitrate, the District Court may issue no injunctive order until it first holds that the contract *does* have that effect; and the employer should be ordered to arbitrate, as a condition of his obtaining an injunction against the strike. Beyond this, the District Court must, of course, consider whether issuance of an injunction would be warranted under ordinary principles of equity — whether breaches are occurring and will continue, or have been threatened and will be committed; whether they have caused or will cause irreparable injury to the employer; and whether the employer will suffer more from the denial of an injunction than will the union from its issuance." 370 U.S. at 228. (Emphasis in original.)

In the present case there is no dispute that the grievance in question was subject to adjustment and arbitration under the collective bargaining agreement and that the petitioner was ready to proceed with arbitration at the time an injunction against the strike was sought and obtained. The District Court also concluded that, by reason of respondent's violations of its no-strike obligation, petitioner "has suffered irreparable injury and will continue to suffer irreparable injury." Since we now overrule *Sinclair,* the holding of the Court of Appeals in reliance on *Sinclair* must be reversed. Accordingly, we reverse the judgment of the Court of Appeals and remand the case with directions to enter a judgment affirming the order of the District Court.

It is so ordered.

Mr. Justice Marshall took no part in the decision of this case.

Mr. Justice Black, dissenting.
Congress in 1932 enacted the Norris-LaGuardia Act, § 4 of which, 29 U.S.C. § 104, with exceptions not here relevant, specifically prohibited federal courts in the broadest and most comprehensive language from issuing any injunctions, temporary or permanent, against participation in a labor dispute. Subsequently, in 1947, Congress gave jurisdiction to the federal courts in "[s]uits for violation of contracts between an employer and a labor organization." Although this subsection, § 301(a) of the Taft-Hartley Act, 29 U.S.C. § 185(a), explicitly waives the diversity and amount-in-controversy requirements for federal jurisdiction, it says nothing at all about granting injunctions. Eight years ago this Court considered the relation of these two statutes: after full briefing and argument, relying on the language and history of the Acts, the Court decided that Congress did not wish this later statute to impair in any way Norris-LaGuardia's explicit prohibition against

injunctions in labor disputes. *Sinclair Refining Co. v. Atkinson,* 370 U.S. 195 (1962).

Although Congress has been urged to overrule our holding in *Sinclair,* it has steadfastly refused to do so. Nothing in the language or history of the two Acts has changed. Nothing at all has changed, in fact, except the membership of the Court and the personal views of one Justice. I remain of the opinion that *Sinclair* was correctly decided, and, moreover, that the prohibition of the Norris-LaGuardia Act is close to the heart of of the entire federal system of labor regulation. In my view *Sinclair* should control the disposition of this case.

Even if the majority were correct, however, in saying that *Sinclair* misinterpreted the Taft-Hartley and Norris-LaGuardia Acts, I should be compelled to dissent. I believe that both the making and the changing of laws which affect the substantial rights of the people are primarily for Congress, not this Court. Most especially is this so when the law involved is the focus of strongly held views of powerful but antagonistic political and economic interests. The Court's function in the application and interpretation of such laws must be carefully limited to avoid encroaching on the power of Congress to determine policies and make laws to carry them out. . . .

[The concurring opinion of Mr. Justice Stewart is omitted. Mr. Justice White dissented "for the reasons stated in the majority opinion in *Sinclair Refining Co. v. Atkinson.'*]

NOTES:

(1) What if a union strikes over a grievance that it, but not the employer, is entitled to take to final and binding arbitration? *Compare Stroehmann Bros. v. Bakery Workers Local 427,* 315 F. Supp. 647 (M.D. Pa. 1970), *with Avco Corp. v. UAW Local 787,* 459 F.2d 968 (3d Cir. 1972), *and Monongahela Power Co. v. Local 2332, IBEW,* 484 F.2d 1209 (4th Cir. 1973). What if the contract contains a no-strike clause, but no final and binding arbitration provision? *See Operating Engineers v. Trumbull Corp.,* 93 LRRM 2337 (S.D. Fla. 1976) (union is not entitled to TRO restraining the employer from violating the labor agreement, since the contract did not provide for mandatory arbitration; duty to arbitrate will not be implied from no-strike clause and provision for informal discussion of disputes). What if the contract contains a final and binding arbitration clause, but no no-strike clause? *See Gateway Coal Co. v. Mine Workers,* 414 U.S. 368 (1974) (implying a no-strike clause where there was an express provision for mandatory arbitration). *Gateway Coal* held that even a strike against allegedly unsafe conditions could be enjoined, when the union could have arbitrated its grievance that a mining company was retaining foremen who had falsified air-flow records.

Section 502 of the LMRA, which provides that work stoppages because of abnormally dangerous conditions are not "strikes," does not apply in the absence of "ascertainable, objective evidence" of such unsafe conditions.

(2) If a state court issues a temporary restraining order against a strike and picketing which would expire by operation of law after twenty days, what is the effect of the union's removing the action to federal court? Does state or federal law govern the continuing validity of the state court restraining order? *See Granny Goose Foods, Inc. v. Teamsters Local 70,* 415 U.S. 423 (1974), holding that the order could remain in effect no longer than permitted under Federal Rule 65(b), measured from the date of removal. Do the *Boys Markets* criteria and federal procedures for obtaining strike injunctions also bind the state courts? *See generally* Gorman, Basic Text on Labor Law, 615-18 (1976).

(3) Federal Rule of Civil Procedure 65 and sections 7 and 9 of the Norris-La Guardia Act address such matters as the duration of a temporary restraining order, the procedures by which one shall issue, the bond to be posted, and requirements of proof; the Norris-La Guardia requirements are a bit more stringent than those of Federal Rule 65. There is some disagreement as to which procedures govern when a federal court considers a request for a *Boys Markets* injunction. *Compare United States Steel Corp. v. Operating Engineers Local 18,* 69 CCH Lab. Cas. § 12959 (S.D. Ohio 1972) (express application of Rule 65), *with United States Steel Corp. v. UMW,* 456 F.2d 483 (3d Cir. 1972) *and Greyhound Lines, Inc. v. Amalgamated Transit Union, Div. 1384,* 91 LRRM 2456 (9th Cir. 1976), vacated on other grounds, 429 U.S. 807 (1976) (express application of section 7 of the Norris-La Guardia Act). *See generally* Gorman, Basic Text on Labor Law, 615-17 (1976). In *Greyhound Lines,* the 9th circuit also held that a *Boys Markets* injunction may issue even where the plaintiff cannot show that he is likely to prevail on the merits; all that is required is a showing that here is "a genuine dispute with respect to an arbitrable issue."

BUFFALO FORGE CO. v. STEELWORKERS

United States Supreme Court
428 U.S. 397, 96 S. Ct. 3141, 49 L. Ed. 2d 1022 (1976)

[The Buffalo Forge Company operates three separate plant and office facilities in the Buffalo, New York area. The Steelworkers Union has represented the production and maintenance (P&M) employees at these plants for some years. Other locals of the Steelworkers were certified in 1974 to represent the office clerical-technical (O&T) employees of Buffalo Forge at the same three plants. On November 16, 1974, after several months of negotiations looking toward their first collective-bargaining agreement, the O&T employees struck and established picket lines at all three locations. The P&M employees honored the picket lines and stopped work.

The company sued the union under § 301 of the Taft-Hartley Act in Federal District Court for breach of the no-strike clause in the P&M collective agreement, seeking an injunction against the work stoppage. The collective agreement provided for arbitration as follows: "Should differences arise ... as to the meaning and application of the provisions of this Agreement, or should any trouble of any kind arise in the plant, there shall be no suspension of work on account of such differences, but an earnest effort shall be made to settle such differences immediately. . . . In the event the grievance involves a question as to the meaning and application of this Agreement, and has not been previously satisfactorily adjusted, it may be submitted to arbitration upon written notice of the Union or the Company." The District Court found that the P&M employees had engaged in a sympathy action in support of the O&T employees, but held itself forbidden to enjoin it by the Norris-LaGuardia Act. The Court of Appeals affirmed, and the Supreme Court granted certiorari.]

Mr. Justice White delivered the opinion of the Court.

The issue for decision is whether a federal court may enjoin a sympathy strike pending the arbitrator's decision as to whether the strike is forbidden by the express no-strike clause contained in the collective-bargaining contract to which the striking union is a party.

. . . .

As a preliminary matter, certain elements in this case are not in dispute. The Union has gone on strike not by reason of any dispute it or any of its members has with the employer but in support of other local unions, of the same international organization, that were negotiating a contract with the employer and were out on strike. The parties involved here are bound by a collective-bargaining contract containing a no-strike clause which the Union claims does not forbid sympathy strikes. The employer has the other view, its complaint in the District Court asserting that the work stoppage violated the no-strike clause. The contract between the parties also has an arbitration clause broad enough to reach not only disputes between the Union and the employer about other provisions in the contract but also as to the meaning and application of the no-strike clause itself. Whether the sympathy strike the Union called violated the no-strike clause, and the appropriate remedies if it did, are subject to the agreed-upon dispute-settlement procedures of the contract and are ultimately issues for the arbitrator. *United Steelworkers of America v. American Mfg. Co.*, 363 U.S. 564 (1960); *United Steelworkers of America v. Warrior & Gulf Navigation Co.*, 363 U.

S. 574 (1960); *United Steelworkers of America v. Enterprise Wheel & Car Corp.,* 363 U. S. 593 (1960). The employer thus was entitled to invoke the arbitral process to determine the legality of the sympathy strike and to obtain a court order requiring the Union to arbitrate if the Union refused to do so. *Gateway Coal Co. v. United Mine Workers,* 414 U. S. 368 (1974). Furthermore, were the issue arbitrated and the strike found illegal, the relevant federal statutes as construed in our cases would permit an injunction to enforce the arbitral decision. *United Steelworkers of America v. Enterprise Wheel & Car Corp., supra.*

The issue in this case arises because the employer not only asked for an order directing the Union to arbitrate but prayed that the strike itself be enjoined pending arbitration and the arbitrator's decision whether the strike was permissible under the no-strike clause. Contrary to the Court of Appeals, the employer claims that despite the Norris-LaGuardia Act's ban on federal court injunctions in labor disputes the District Court was empowered to enjoin the strike by § 301 of the Labor Management Relations Act as construed by *Boys Markets, Inc. v. Retail Clerks Union, supra.* This would undoubtedly have been the case had the strike been precipitated by a dispute between union and management that was subject to binding arbitration under the provisions of the contract. In *Boys Markets,* the union demanded that supervisory employees cease performing tasks claimed by the union to be union work. The union struck when the demand was rejected. The dispute was of the kind subject to the grievance and arbitration clauses contained in the collective-bargaining contract, and it was also clear that the strike violated the no-strike clause accompanying the arbitration provisions. The Court held that the union could be enjoined from striking over a dispute which it was bound to arbitrate at the employer's behest.

The holding in *Boys Markets* was said to be a "narrow one," dealing only with the situation in which the collective-bargaining contract contained mandatory grievance and arbitration procedures. 398 U. S., at 253. "[F]or the guidance of the district courts in determining whether to grant injunctive relief," the Court expressly adopted the principles enunciated in the dissent in *Sinclair Refining Co. v. Atkinson,* 370 U. S. 195, 228 (1962), including the proposition that:

> " 'When a strike is sought to be enjoined because it is over a grievance which both parties are contractually bound to arbitrate, the District Court may issue no injunctive order until it first holds that the contract *does* have that effect; and the employer should be ordered to arbitrate as condition of his obtaining an injunction against the strike.' " 398 U.S., at 254 (emphasis in *Sinclair*).

The driving force behind *Boys Markets* was to implement the strong congressional preference for the private dispute settlement mechanisms agreed upon by the parties. Only to that extent was it held necessary to accommodate § 4 of the Norris-LaGuardia Act to § 301 of the Labor Management Relations Act and to lift the former's ban against the issuance of injunctions in labor disputes. Striking over an arbitrable dispute would interfere with and frustrate the arbitral processes by which the parties had chosen to settle a dispute. The *quid pro quo* for the employer's promise to arbitrate was the union's obligation not to strike over issues that were subject to the arbitration machinery. Even in the absence of an express no-strike clause, an undertaking not to strike would be implied where the strike was over an otherwise arbitrable dispute. *Gateway Coal Co. v. United Mine Workers, supra; Teamsters Local v. Lucas Flour Co.,* 369 U. S. 95 (1962). Otherwise, the employer would be deprived of his bargain and the policy of the labor statutes to implement private resolution of disputes in a manner agreed upon would seriously suffer.

Boys Markets plainly does not control this case. The District Court found, and it is not now disputed, that the strike was not *over* any dispute between the Union and the employer that was even remotely subject to the arbitration provisions of the contract. The strike at issue was a sympathy strike in support of sister unions negotiating with the employer; neither its causes nor the issue underlying it were subject to the settlement procedures provided by the contract between the employer and respondents. The strike had neither the purpose nor the effect of denying or evading an obligation to arbitrate or of depriving the employer of his bargain. Thus, had the contract not contained a no-strike clause or had the clause expressly excluded sympathy strikes, there would have been no possible basis for implying from the existence of an arbitration clause a promise not to strike that could have been violated by the sympathy strike in this case. *Gateway Coal Co. v. Mine Workers, supra,* at 382.[10]

---

[10] To the extent that the Court of Appeals, 517 F. 2d, at 1211, and other courts, Island Creek Coal Co. v. United Mine Workers, 507 F. 2d 650, 653-654 (CA3), cert. denied, 423 U. S. 877 (1975); Armco Steel Corp. v. United Mine Workers, 505 F. 2d 1129, 1132-1133 (CA4 1974), *cert. denied,* 423 U. S. 877 (1975); Amstar Corp. v. Amalgamated Meat Cutters, 468 F. 2d 1372, 1373 (CA5 1972); Inland Steel Co. v. Local Union No. 1545, UMW, 505 F. 2d 293, 299-300 (CA7 1974), have assumed that a mandatory arbitration clause implies a commitment not to engage in sympathy strikes, they are wrong.

Gateway Coal Co. v. United Mine Workers, *supra,* itself furnishes no additional support for the employer here. In that case, after finally concluding that the dispute over which the strike occurred was arbitrable within the meaning of the arbitration clause contained in a contract which did not also contain a no-strike clause, the Court implied an undertaking not to strike based on Teamsters Local v. Lucas Flour Co., *supra,* and permitted an injunction against the strike based on the principles of *Boys*

Nor was the injunction authorized solely because it was alleged that the sympathy strike called by the Union violated the express no-strike provision of the contract. Section 301 of the Act assigns a major role to the courts in enforcing collective bargaining agreements, but aside from the enforcement of the arbitration provisions of such contracts, within the limits permitted by *Boys Markets,* the Court has never indicated that the courts may enjoin actual or threatened contract violations despite the Norris-LaGuardia Act. In the course of enacting the Taft-Hartley Act, Congress rejected the proposal that the Norris-LaGuardia Act's prohibition against labor-dispute injunctions be lifted to the extent necessary to make injunctive remedies available in federal courts for the purpose of enforcing collective bargaining agreements. *See Sinclair Refining Co. v. Atkinson, supra,* at 205-208, and at 216-224 (dissenting opinion). The allegation of the complaint that the Union was breaching its obligation not to strike did not in itself warrant an injunction. As was stated in the *Sinclair* dissent embraced in *Boys Markets:*

> "[T]here is no general federal anti-strike policy; and although a suit may be brought under § 301 against strikes which, while they are breaches of private contracts, do not threaten any additional public policy, in such cases the anti-injunction policy of Norris-LaGuardia should prevail." *Sinclair Refining Co. v. Atkinson, supra,* at 225.

The contract here at issue, however, also contained grievance and arbitration provisions for settling disputes over the interpretation and application of the provisions of the contract, including the no-strike clause. That clause, like others, was subject to enforcement in accordance with the procedures set out in the contract. Here the Union struck, and the parties were in dispute whether the sympathy strike violated the Union's no-strike undertaking. Concededly, that issue was arbitrable. It was for the arbitrator to determine whether there was a breach, as well as the remedy for any breach, and the employer was entitled to an order requiring the Union to arbitrate if it refused to do so. But the Union does not deny its duty to arbitrate; in fact, it denies that the employer ever demanded

---

Markets. The critical determination in *Gateway* was that the dispute was arbitrable. This was the fulcrum for implying a duty not to strike over that dispute and for enjoining the strike the union had called. Of course, the authority to enjoin the work stoppage depended on "whether the union was under a contractual duty not to strike." 414 U. S., at 380. But that statement was made only preparatory to finding an implied duty not to strike. The strike was then enjoined only because it was over an arbitrable dispute. The same precondition to a strike injunction also existed in *Boys Markets.* Absent that factor, neither case furnishes the authority to enjoin a strike solely because it is claimed to be in breach of contract and because this claim is itself arbitrable.

arbitration. However that may be, it does not follow that the District Court was empowered not only to order arbitration but to enjoin the strike pending the decision of the arbitrator, despite the express prohibition of § 4(a) of the Norris-LaGuardia Act against injunctions prohibiting any person "from ceasing or refusing to perform any work or to remain in any relation of employment." If an injunction could issue against the strike in this case, so in proper circumstances could a court enjoin any other alleged breach of contract pending the exhaustion of the applicable grievance and arbitration provisions even though the injunction would otherwise violate one of the express prohibitions of § 104. The court in such cases would be permitted, if the dispute was arbitrable, to hold hearings, make findings of fact, interpret the applicable provisions of the contract and issue injunctions so as to restore the status quo *ante* or to otherwise regulate the relationship of the parties pending exhaustion of the arbitration process. This would cut deeply into the policy of the Norris-LaGuardia Act and make the courts potential participants in a wide range of arbitrable disputes under the many existing and future collective-bargaining contracts,[12] not just for the purpose of enforcing promises to arbitrate, which was the limit of *Boys Markets,* but for the purpose of preliminarily dealing with the merits of the factual and legal issues that are subjects for the arbitrator and of issuing injunctions that would otherwise be forbidden by the Norris-LaGuardia Act.

This is not what the parties have bargained for. Surely it cannot be concluded here, as it was in *Boys Markets,* that such injunctions pending arbitration are essential to carry out promises to arbitrate and to implement the private arrangements for the administration of the contract. As is typical, the agreement in this case outlines the prearbitration settlement procedures and provides that if the grievance "has not been . . . satisfactorily adjusted," arbitration may be had. Nowhere does it provide for coercive action of any kind, let alone judicial injunctions, short of the terminal decision of the arbitrator. The parties have agreed to grieve and arbitrate, not to litigate. They have not contracted for a judicial preview of the facts and the law. Had they anticipated additional regulation of their relationships pending arbitration, it seems very doubtful that they would have resorted to litigation rather than to private arrangements. The unmistakeable policy of Congress stated in 29 U.S.C. § 173 (d), 61 Stat. 153, is that "Final adjustment by a method

---

[12] This could embroil the district courts in massive preliminary injunction litigation. In 1972, the most recent year for which comprehensive data have been published, more than 21,000,000 workers in the United States were covered under more than 150,000 collective-bargaining agreements. Bureau of Labor Statistics, Directory of National Unions and Employee Assns. 87-88 (1973).

agreed upon by the parties is declared to be the desirable method for settlement of grievance disputes arising over the application or interpretation of an existing collective-bargaining agreement." *Gateway Coal Co. v. United Mine Workers, supra,* at 377. But the parties' agreement to adjust or to arbitrate their differences themselves would be eviscerated if the courts for all practical purposes were to try and decide contractual disputes at the preliminary injunction stage.

The dissent suggests that injunctions should be authorized in cases such as this at least where the violation, in the court's view, is clear and the court is sufficiently sure that the parties seeking the injunction will win before the arbitrator. But this would still involve hearings, findings and judicial interpretations of collective-bargaining contracts. It is incredible to believe that the courts would always view the facts and the contract as the arbitrator would; and it is difficult to believe that the arbitrator would not be heavily influenced or wholly pre-empted by judicial views of the facts and the meaning of contracts if this procedure is to be permitted. Injunctions against strikes, even temporary injunctions, very often permanently settle the issue; and in other contexts time and expense would be discouraging factors to the losing party in court in considering whether to relitigate the issue before the arbitrator.

With these considerations in mind, we are far from concluding that the arbitration process will be frustrated unless the courts have the power to issue interlocutory injunctions pending arbitration in cases such as this or in others in which an arbitrable dispute awaits decision. We agree with the Court of Appeals that there is no necessity here, such as was found to be the case in *Boys Markets,* to accommodate the policies of the Norris-LaGuardia Act to the requirements of § 301 by empowering the District Court to issue the injunction sought by the employer.

The judgment of the Court of Appeals is affirmed.

So ordered.

Mr. Justice Stevens, with whom Mr. Justice Brennan, Mr. Justice Marshall, and Mr. Justice Powell join, dissenting.

A contractual undertaking not to strike is the union's normal *quid pro quo* for the employer's undertaking to submit grievances to binding arbitration. The question in this case is whether that *quid pro quo* is severable into two parts — one which a federal court may enforce by injunction and another which it may not.

Less than three years ago all eight of my Brethren joined in an opinion which answered that question quite directly by stating that whether a district court has authority to enjoin a work stoppage "depends on whether the union was under a contractual duty not to strike." *Gateway Coal Co. v. United Mine Workers,* 414 U.S. 368, 380.

The Court today holds that only a part of the union's *quid pro quo* is enforceable by injunction.[2] The principal bases for the holding are (1) the Court's literal interpretation of the Norris-LaGuardia Act; and (2) its fear that the federal judiciary would otherwise make a "massive" entry into the business of contract interpretation heretofore reserved for arbitrators. The first argument has been rejected repeatedly in cases in which the central concerns of the Norris-LaGuardia Act were not implicated. The second is wholly unrealistic and was implicitly rejected in *Gateway Coal* when the Court held that "a substantial question of contractual interpretation" was a sufficient basis for federal equity jurisdiction. 414 U.S., at 384. That case held that an employer might enforce a somewhat ambiguous *quid pro quo;* today the Court holds that a portion of the *quid pro quo* is unenforceable no matter how unambiguous it may be. With all respect, I am persuaded that a correct application of the reasoning underlying the landmark decision in *Boys Markets, Inc. v. Clerks Union,* 398 U.S. 235, requires a different result.

. . . .

[There follows a detailed review of the rationale in *Boys Markets.*]

The *Boys Markets* decision protects the arbitration process. A court is authorized to enjoin a strike over a grievance which the parties are contractually bound to arbitrate, but that authority is conditioned upon a finding that the contract does so provide, that the strike is in violation of the agreement, and further that the issuance of an injunction is warranted by ordinary principles of equity. These conditions plainly stated in *Boys Markets* demonstrate that the interest in protecting the arbitration process is not simply an end in itself which exists at large and apart from other fundamental aspects of our national labor policy.

On the one hand, an absolute precondition of any *Boys Markets* injunction is a contractual obligation. A court may not order arbitration unless the parties have agreed to that process; nor can the court require the parties to accept an arbitrator's decision unless they have agreed to be bound by it. If the union reserves the right to resort to self-help at the conclusion of the arbitration process, that

---

[2] The enforceable part of the no-strike agreement is the part relating to a strike "over an arbitrable dispute." In *Gateway Coal,* however, my Brethren held that the district court had properly entered an injunction that not only terminated a strike pending an arbitrator's decision of an underlying safety dispute, but also "prospectively required both parties to abide by his resolution of the controversy." *Id.,* at 373. A strike in defiance of an arbitrator's award would not be "over an arbitrable dispute"; nevertheless, the Court today recognizes the propriety of an injunction against such a strike.

agreement must be respected.[16] The court's power is limited by the contours of the agreement between the parties.[17]

On the other hand, the arbitration procedure is not merely an exercise; it performs the important purpose of determining what the underlying agreement actually means as applied to a specific setting. If the parties have agreed to be bound by the arbitrator's decision, the reasons which justify an injunction against a strike that would impair his ability to reach a decision must equally justify an injunction requiring the parties to abide by a decision that a strike is in violation of the no-strike clause.[18] The arbitration mechanism would hardly retain its respect as a method of resolving disputes if the end product of the process had less significance than the process itself.

The net effect of the arbitration process is to remove completely any ambiguity in the agreement as it applies to an unforeseen, or undescribed, set of facts. But if the specific situation is foreseen and described in the contract itself with such precision that there is no need for interpretation by an arbitrator, it would be reasonable to give the same legal effect to such an agreement prior to the arbitrator's decision. In this case, the question whether the sympathy strike violates the no-strike clause is an arbitrable issue. If the court had the benefit of an arbitrator's resolution of the issue in favor of the employer, it could enforce that decision just as it could require the parties to submit the issue to arbitration. And if the agreement were so plainly unambiguous that there could be no bona fide issue to submit to the arbitrator, there must be the same authority to enforce the parties' bargain pending the arbitrator's final decision.

The Union advances three arguments against this conclusion: (1) that interpretation of the collective-bargaining agreement is the exclusive province of the arbitrator; (2) that an injunction erroneously entered pending arbitration will effectively deprive the union of the right to strike before the arbitrator can render his decision; and (3) that it is the core purpose of the Norris-LaGuardia Act to eliminate the risk of an injunction against a lawful strike. Although I acknowledge the force of these arguments, I think they are insufficient to take this case outside the rationale of *Boys Markets.*

The *Steelworkers Trilogy* establishes that a collective-bargaining agreement submitting all questions of contract interpretation to the arbitrator deprives the courts of almost all power to interpret the agreement to prevent submission of a dispute to arbitration or to

---

[16] Associated General Contractors of Illinois v. Illinois Conference of Teamsters, 454 F.2d 1324 (CA7 1972).

[17] In particular, an implied no-strike clause does not extend to sympathy strikes. See *ante,* at n. 10.

[18] The Court recognizes that an injunction may issue to enforce an arbitrator's decision that a strike is in violation of the no-strike clause. . . .

refuse enforcement of an arbitrator's award. *Boys Markets* itself repeated the warning that it was not for the courts to usurp the functions of the arbitrator. And *Gateway Coal* held that an injunction may issue to protect the arbitration process even if a "substantial question of contractual interpretation" must be answered to determine whether the strike is over an arbitrable grievance. In each of these cases, however, the choice was between interpretation of the agreement by the court or interpretation by the arbitrator; a decision that the dispute was not arbitrable, or not properly arbitrated, would have precluded an interpretation of the agreement according to the contractual grievance procedure. In the present case, an interim determination of the no-strike question by the court neither usurps nor precludes a decision by the arbitrator. By definition, issuance of an injunction pending the arbitrator's decision does not supplant a decision that he otherwise would have made. Indeed, it is the ineffectiveness of the damage remedy for strikes pending arbitration that lends force to the employer's argument for an injunction. The court does not oust the arbitrator of his proper function but fulfills a role that he never served.

The Union's second point, however, is that the arbitrator will rarely render his decision quickly enough to prevent an erroneously issued injunction from effectively depriving the union of its right to strike. The Union relies particularly upon decisions of this Court that recognize that even a temporary injunction can quickly end a strike. But this argument demonstrates only that arbitration, to be effective, must be prompt, not that the federal courts must be deprived entirely of jurisdiction to grant equitable relief. Denial of an injunction when a strike violates the agreement may have effects just as devastating to an employer as the issuance of an injunction may have to the union when the strike does not violate the agreement. Furthermore, a sympathy strike does not directly further the economic interests of the members of the striking local or contribute to the resolution of any dispute between that local, or its members, and the employer.[25] On the contrary, it is the source of a new dispute which, if the strike goes forward, will impose costs on the strikers, the employer, and the public without prospect of any direct benefit to any of these parties. A rule that authorizes postponement of a sympathy strike pending an arbitrator's clarification of the no-strike clause will not critically impair the vital interests of the striking local even if the right to strike is upheld, and will avoid the costs of interrupted production if the arbitrator concludes that the no-strike clause applies.

Finally, the Norris-LaGuardia Act cannot be interpreted to immunize the union from all risk of an erroneously issued injunction.

[25] In this case the sympathy strike is in support of a strike by other local unions of the same international. The parties, however, attach no significance to that fact.

Boys Markets itself subjected the union to the risk of an injunction entered upon a judge's erroneous conclusion that the dispute was arbitrable and that the strike was in violation of the no-strike clause. *Gateway Coal* subjected the union to a still greater risk, for the court there entered an injunction to enforce an implied no-strike clause despite the fact that the arbitrability of the dispute, and hence the legality of the strike over the dispute, presented a "substantial question of contractual interpretation." The strict reading that the Union would give the Norris-LaGuardia Act would not have permitted this result.

These considerations, however, do not support the conclusion that a sympathy strike should be temporarily enjoined whenever a collective-bargaining agreement contains a no-strike clause and an arbitration clause. The accommodation between the Norris-LaGuardia Act and § 301(a) of the Labor Management Relations Act allows the judge to apply "the usual processes of the law" but not to take the place of the arbitrator. Because of the risk that a federal judge, less expert in labor matters than an arbitrator, may misconstrue general contract language, I would agree that no injunction or temporary restraining order should issue without first giving the union an adequate opportunity to present evidence and argument, particularly upon the proper interpretation of the collective-bargaining agreement; the judge should not issue an injunction without convincing evidence that the strike is clearly within the no-strike clause.[27] Furthermore, to protect the efficacy of arbitration, any such injunction should require the parties to submit the issue immediately to the contractual grievance procedure, and if the union so requests, at the last stage and upon an expedited schedule that assures a decision by the arbitrator as soon as practicable. Such stringent conditions would insure that only strikes in violation of the agreement would be enjoined and that the union's access to the arbitration process would not be foreclosed by the combined effect of a temporary injunction and protected grievance procedures. Finally, as in *Boys Markets,* the normal conditions of equitable relief would have to be met.

Like the decision in *Boys Markets,* this opinion reflects, on the one hand, my confidence that experience during the decades since the Norris-LaGuardia Act was passed has dissipated any legitimate concern about the impartiality of federal judges in disputes between labor and management, and on the other, my continued recognition of the fact that judges have less familiarity and expertise than

---

[27] Of course, it is possible that an arbitrator would disagree with the court even when the latter finds the strike to be clearly prohibited. But in that case, the arbitrator's determination would govern, provided it withstands the ordinary standard of review for arbitrator's awards. *See* United Steelworkers of America v. Enterprise Wheel & Car Corp., 363 U.S. 593, 597-599.

arbitrators and administrators who regularly work in this specialized area. The decision in *Boys Markets* requires an accommodation between the Norris-LaGuardia Act and the Labor Management Relations Act. I would hold only that the terms of that accommodation do not entirely deprive the federal courts of all power to grant any relief to an employer, threatened with irreparable injury from a sympathy strike clearly in violation of a collective-bargaining agreement, regardless of the equities of his claim for injunctive relief pending arbitration.

Since in my view the Court of Appeals erroneously held that the District Court had no jurisdiction to enjoin the Union's sympathy strike, I would reverse and remand for consideration of the question whether the employer is entitled to an injunction.

NOTES:

UMW Local 1759 struck Cedar Coal Company over an arbitrable issue. Its members picketed the main entrance to nearby mines owned by Cedar but under the jurisdiction of UMW Local 1766, whose members refused to report to work in sympathy with the striking miners. Although there was nothing for Cedar and Local 1766 to arbitrate, any award rendered in a dispute between Cedar and Local 1759 would apparently affect Local 1766. Cedar sought a temporary order restraining Local 1766 from striking. Should it succeed? *See Cedar Coal Co. v. UMW, Local 1766,* 560 F.2d 1153 (7th Cir. 1977) (since (a) the purpose of the strike of Local 1766 was to compel Cedar to concede an arbitral issue to Local 1759, (b) the two locals were both employed by Cedar and bound by the same labor agreement, and (c) Local 1766 adopted 1759's grievance as its own, the *Buffalo Forge* exception to *Boys Markets* was held inapplicable). *Compare Cedar Coal Co. v. UMW,* 560 F.2d 1153 (7th Cir. 1977), *and Zeigler Coal Co. v. Local 1870 UMW,* 566 F.2d 582 (7th Cir. 1977). For additional insight into the problems of applying the rules of *Boys Market* and *Buffalo Forge* to a situation involving sporadic strikes, sympathy walkouts, and refusals to cross picket lines set up by roving pickets, *see Southern Ohio Coal Co. v. UMW,* 551 F.2d 695 (1977).

ATKINSON v. SINCLAIR REFINING CO.

United States Supreme Court
370 U.S. 238, 82 S. Ct. 1318, 8 L. Ed. 2d 462 (1962)

Mr. Justice White delivered the opinion of the Court.

The respondent company employs at its refinery in East Chicago, Indiana, approximately 1,700 men, for whom the petitioning international union and its local are bargaining agents, and 24 of whom are also petitioners here. In early February, 1959, the respondent company docked three of its employees at the East Chicago refinery a total of $2.19. On February 13 and 14, 999 of the 1,700 employees participated in a strike or work stoppage, or so the complaint alleges. On March 12, the company filed this suit for damages and an injection, naming the international and its local as defendants, together with 24 individual union member-employees.

Count I of the complaint, which was in three counts, stated a cause of action under § 301 of the Taft-Hartley Act against the international and its local. It alleged an existing collective bargaining agreement between the international and the company containing, among other matters, a promise by the union not to strike over any cause which could be the subject of a grievance under other provisions of the contract. It was alleged that the international and the local caused the strike or work stoppage occurring on February 13 and 14 and that the strike was over the pay claims of three employees in the amount of $2.19, which claims were properly subject to the grievance procedure provided by the contract. The complaint asked for damages in the amount of $12,500 from the international and the local.

Count II of the complaint purported to invoke the diversity jurisdiction of the District Court. It asked judgment in the same amount against 24 individual employees, each of whom was alleged to be a committeeman of the local union and an agent of the international, and responsible for representing the international, the local, and their members. The complaint asserted that on February 13 and 14, the individuals, "contrary to their duty to plaintiff to abide by such contract, and maliciously confederating and conspiring together to cause the plaintiff expense and damage, and to induce breaches of said contract, and to interfere with performance thereof by the said labor organizations, and the affected employees, and to cause breaches thereof, individually and as officers, committeemen and agents of said labor organizations, fomented, assisted and participated in a strike or work stoppage. . . ."

I. We have concluded that Count I should not be dismissed or stayed. Count I properly states a cause of action under § 301 and is to be governed by federal law. *Local 174 v. Lucas Flour Co.,* 369 U.S. 95, 102-104 (1962); *Textile Workers v. Lincoln Mills,* 353 U.S. 448 (1957). Under our decisions, whether or not the company was bound to arbitrate, as well as what issues it must arbitrate, is a matter to be determined by the Court on the basis of the contract entered into by the parties. . . . We think it unquestionably clear that the contract here involved is not susceptible to a construction that the company was bound to arbitrate its claim for damages against the union for breach of the undertaking not to strike.

While it is quite obvious from other provisions of the contract that the parties did not intend to commit all of their possible disputes and the whole scope of their relationship to the grievance and arbitration procedures established in Article XXVI, that article itself is determinative of the issue in this case since it precludes arbitration boards from considering any matters other than employee grievances. After defining a grievance as "any difference regarding wages, hours or working conditions between the parties hereto or between the employer and an employee covered by the working agreement," Article XXVI provides that the parties desire to settle employee grievances fairly and quickly and that therefore a stated procedure "must be followed." . . .

Article XXVI then imposes the critical limitation. It is provided that local arbitration boards "shall consider only individual or local employee or local committee grievances arising under the application of the currently existing agreement." There is not a word in the grievance and arbitration article providing for the submission of grievances by the company. Instead, there is the express, flat limitation that arbitration boards should consider only employee grievances. Furthermore, the article expressly provides that arbitration may be invoked only at the option of the union. At no place in the contract does the union agree to arbitrate at the behest of the company. The company is to take its claims elsewhere, which it has now done.

The union makes a further argument for a stay. Following the strike, and both before and after the company filed its suit, 14 of the 24 individual defendants filed grievances claiming reimbursement for pay withheld by the employer. The union argues that even though the company need not arbitrate its claim for damages, it is bound to arbitrate these grievances; and the arbitrator, in the process of determining the grievants' right to reimbursement, will consider and determine issues which also underlie the company's claim for damages. Therefore, it is said that a stay of the court action is appropriate.

We are not satisfied from the record now before us, however, that any significant issue in the damage suit will be presented to and decided by an arbitrator. The grievances filed simply claimed reimbursement for pay due employees for time spent at regular work or processing grievances. . . .

The District Court must decide whether the company is entitled to damages from the union for breach of contract. The arbitrator, if arbitration occurs, must award or deny reimbursement in whole or in part to all or some of the 14 employees. His award, standing alone, obviously would determine no issue in the damage suit. If he awarded reimbursement to the employees and if it could be ascertained with any assurance that one of his subsidiary findings was that the 14 men had not participated in a forbidden work stoppage

— the critical issue according to the union's brief — the company would nevertheless not be foreclosed in court since, even if it were bound by such a subsidiary finding made by the arbitrator, it would be free to prove its case in court through the conduct of other agents of the union. In this state of the record, the union has not made out its case for a stay.

For the foregoing reasons, the lower courts properly denied the union's motion to dismiss Count I or stay it pending arbitration of the employer's damage claim.

II. We turn now to Count II of the complaint, which charged 24 individual officers and agents of the union with breach of the collective bargaining contract and tortious interference with contractual relations. The District Court held that under § 301 union officers or members cannot be held personally liable for union actions, and that therefore "suits of the nature alleged in Count II are no longer cognizable in state or federal courts." The Court of Appeals reversed, however, ruling that "Count II stated a cause of action cognizable in the courts of Indiana and, by diversity, maintainable in the District Court."

We are unable to agree with the Court of Appeals, for we are convinced that Count II is controlled by federal law and that it must be dismissed on the merits for failure to state a claim upon which relief can be granted.

Under § 301 a suit for violation of the collective bargaining contract in either a federal or state court is governed by federal law (*Local 174 v. Lucas Flour Co.,* 369 U.S. 95, 102-104 (1962); *Textile Workers Union v. Lincoln Mills,* 353 U.S. 448 (1957)), and Count II on its face charges the individual defendants with a violation of the no-strike clause. After quoting verbatim the no-strike clause, Count II alleges that the 24 individual defendants "contrary to their duty to plaintiff to abide by" the contract fomented and participated in a work stoppage in violation of the no-strike clause. The union itself does not quarrel with the proposition that the relationship of the members of the bargaining unit to the employer is "governed by" the bargaining agreement entered into on their behalf by the union. It is universally accepted that the no-strike clause in a collective agreement at the very least establishes a rule of conduct or condition of employment the violation of which by employees justifies discipline or discharge. . . . The conduct charged in Count II is therefore within the scope of a "violation" of the collective agreement.

As well as charging a violation of the no-strike clause by the individual defendants, Count II necessarily charges a violation of the clause by the union itself. The work stoppage alleged is the identical work stoppage for which the union is sued under Count I and the same damage is alleged as is alleged in Count I. Count II states that the individual defendants acted "as officers, committeemen and agents of said labor organizations" in breaching and inducing others to breach the collective bargaining contract. Count I charges the principal, and Count II charges the agents for acting on behalf of the principal. Whatever individual liability Count II alleges for the 24 individual defendants, it necessarily restates the liability of the union which is charged under Count I, since under § 301(b) the union is liable for the acts of its agents, under familiar principles of the law of agency (see also § 301(e)). Proof of the allegations of Count II in its present form would inevitably prove a violation of the no-strike clause by the union itself. Count II, like Count I, is thus a suit based on the union's breach of its collective bargaining contract with the employer, and therefore comes within § 301(a). When a union breach of contract is alleged, that the plaintiff seeks to hold the agents liable instead of the principal does not bring the action outside the scope of § 301.

Under any theory, therefore, the company's action is governed by the national labor relations law which Congress commanded this Court to fashion under § 301(a). We hold that this law requires the dismissal of Count II for failure to state a claim for which relief can be granted — whether the contract violation charged is that of the union or that of the union plus the union officers and agents.

When Congress passed § 301, it declared its view that only the union was to be made to respond for union wrongs, and that the union members were not to be subject to levy. Section 301(b) has three clauses. One makes unions suable in the courts of the United States. Another makes unions bound by the acts of their agents according to conventional principles of agency law (cf. § 301(e)). At the same time, however, the remaining clause exempts agents and members from personal liability for judgments against the union (apparently even when the union is without assets to pay the judgment). The legislative history of § 301(b) makes it clear that this third clause was a deeply felt congressional reaction against the *Danbury Hatters* case (*Loewe v. Lawlor,* 208 U.S. 274 (1908); *Lawlor v. Loewe,* 235 U.S. 522 (1915)), and an expression of legislative determination that the aftermath (*Loewe v. Savings Bank of Danbury,* 236 Fed. 444 (2d Cir. 1916)), of that decision was not to be permitted to recur. In that case, an antitrust treble damage action was brought against a large number of union members, including union officers and agents, to recover from them the employer's losses in a nation-wide, union-directed boycott of his hats. The union was not named as a party, nor was judgment entered against it. A large money judgment was entered, instead, against the individual defendants for participating in the plan "emanating from headquarters" (235 U.S. at 534), by knowingly authorizing and delegating authority to the union officers to do the acts involved. In the debates, Senator Ball, one of the Act's sponsors, declared that § 301, "by providing that the union may sue and be sued as a legal entity, for a violation of contract, and that liability for damages will lie against union assets only, will prevent a repetition of the *Danbury Hatters* case, in which many members lost their homes" (93 Cong. Rec. 5014). *See also* 93 Cong. Rec. 3839, 6283; S. Rep. No. 105, 80th Cong., 1st Sess. 16.

Consequently, in discharging the duty Congress imposed on us to formulate the federal law to govern § 301(a) suits, we are strongly guided by and do not give a niggardly reading to § 301(b). "We would undercut the Act and defeat its policy if we read § 301 narrowly" (*Lincoln Mills,* 353 U.S. at 456 (1957)). We have already said in another context that § 301(b) at least evidences "a congressional intention that the union as an entity, like a corporation, should in the absence of agreement be the sole source of recovery for injury inflicted by it" (*Lewis v. Benedict Coal Corp.,* 361 U.S. 459, 470 (1960)). This policy cannot be evaded or truncated by the simple device of suing union agents or members, whether in contract or tort, or both, in a separate count or in a separate action for damages for violation of a collective bargaining contract for which damages the union itself is liable. The national labor policy requires and we hold that when a union is liable for damages for violation of the no-strike clause, its officers and members are not liable for these damages. Here, Count II, as we have said, necessarily alleges union liability but prays for damages from the union agents. Where the union has inflicted the injury it alone must pay. Count II must be dismissed. [7]

The case is remanded to the District Court for further proceedings not inconsistent with this opinion.

It is so ordered.

Mr. Justice Frankfurter took no part in the consideration or decision of this case.

Drake Bakeries, Inc. v. Bakery Workers Local 50, 370 U.S. 254, 82 S. Ct. 1346, 8 L. Ed. 2d 474 (1962). The employer was a large bakery. When Christmas and New Year's fell on Friday, it attempted to maintain a supply of fresh goods by rescheduling production so that employees would not work on the Thursdays before the holidays but

---

[7] In reaching this conclusion, we have not ignored the argument that Count II was drafted in order to anticipate the possible union defense under Count I that the work stoppage was unauthorized by the union, and was a wildcat strike led by the 24 individual defendants acting not on behalf of the union but in their personal and nonunion capacity. The language of Count II contradicts the argument, however, and we therefore do not reach the question of whether the count would state a proper § 301(a) claim if it charged unauthorized, individual action.

would work on the following Saturdays. The union claimed the new schedule violated the labor contract. So few employees reported for work on Saturday, January 2 that the company could not operate. The employer promptly sued the union for damages for breach of the no-strike clause. The union sought a stay of the action pending arbitration, and the Supreme Court held such a stay should be granted. The Court distinguished *Atkinson* on the ground that here the arbitration provision did not exclude claims or complaints of the employer but instead permitted either party to refer a matter to arbitration. Moreover, the Court observed that the adjustment procedure broadly applied not only to disputes involving "the interpretation or application of any clause or matter" covered by the contract but also to "any act or conduct or relation between the parties." The Court concluded that this "easily reached the employer's claim against the union for damages caused by an alleged strike in violation of the contract. . . . We can enforce both the no-strike clause and the agreement to arbitrate by granting a stay until the claim for damages is presented to an arbitrator." In response to the employer's argument that the parties could not have intended to arbitrate "so fundamental a matter as a union strike in breach of contract," the Court said: "Arbitration provisions, which themselves have not been repudiated, are meant to survive breaches of contract, in many contexts, even total breach. . . . We do not decide in this case that in no circumstance would a strike in violation of the no-strike clause contained in this or other contracts entitle the employer to rescind or abandon the entire contract or to declare its promise to arbitrate forever discharged. . . . [T]here are no circumstances in this record which justify relieving the company of its duty to arbitrate the consequences of this one-day strike, intertwined as it is with the union denials that there was any strike or any breach of contract at all."

Packing House Workers Local 721 v. Needham Packing Co., 376 U.S. 247, 84 S. Ct. 773, 11 L. Ed. 2d 680 (1964). An employer discharged one employee and as a result 190 others walked out. These employees were also discharged when they failed to return to work. About two months later the union filed grievances over the initial and subsequent discharges. The employer refused to arbitrate, declaring its duty to arbitrate was released by the union's alleged breach of a no-strike clause. When the union sued to compel arbitration, the employer counter-claimed for damages caused by the strike. The Supreme Court held that the alleged violation of the no-strike clause "did not release Needham from its duty to arbitrate the union's claim that employees had been wrongfully discharged."

Drake Bakeries was thought dispositive of the case, even though (1) here the contract did not require the employer to submit its claims to arbitration, and (2) the strike was not merely a one-day work stoppage. The Court went on to say that the employer was not precluded from prosecuting its damage suit on the no-strike clause, but the legal effect of the arbitrator's decision on the court action was left open. The Court also did not decide "whether a fundamental and long-lasting change in the relationship of the parties prior to the demand for arbitration would be a circumstance which, alone or among others, would release an employer from his promise to arbitrate."

NOTES:

(1) *Problem:*
Has the Supreme Court in *Drake* and *Needham* read the "substantial breach" doctrine out of the federal labor contract law being developed under § 301? *See* Summers, Collective Agreementa and the Law of Contracts, 78 Yale L.J. 525 (1969).

In *Steelworkers Local 14055 v. NLRB* (Dow Chem. Co.), 530 F.2d 266 (3d Cir. 1976), *cert. denied,* 429 U.S. 807 (1976) the Court disapproved of a rule which holds that a strike in breach of contract automatically gives the employer the right to terminate the contract, where the company has available to it both legal and contractual remedies short of contract termination.

(2) Individual Liability
The Supreme Court in *Atkinson* did not decide whether an employer could recover money damages from individual union members who engage in an unauthorized (or "wildcat") strike in breach of contract. For a negative view of § 301 damage suits against individual wildcat strikers, *see Sinclair Oil Corp. v. Oil Workers,* 452 F.2d 49 (7th Cir. 1971), *noted in* 86 Harv. L. Rev. 447 (1972). For a contrary view *see Alloy Cast Steel Co. v. Steel Workers,* 429 F. Supp. 445 (N.D. Ohio 1977). Are suits against individuals feasible? How else could an employer protect his economic integrity in the event that the union is held not to be liable for damages resulting from a wildcat strike in breach of the labor agreement? *See generally* Givens, *Responsibility of Individual Employees for Breaches of No-Strike Clauses,* 14 Ind. & Lab. Rel. Rev. 595 (1961); Gould, *The Status of Unauthorized and "Wildcat" Strikes under the NLRB,* 52 Cornell L.Q. 672, 702-04 (1967).

(3) Union Liability in Wildcat Strikes
The Third Circuit has cited two circumstances in which a union may be held financially responsible for damages caused by

unauthorized work stoppage in breach of contract. First, a no-strike undertaking by the union implies an obligation on its part to use "every reasonable means" to prevent and end wildcat strikes. Failure to perform this obligation renders the union liable to the employer for damages proximately resulting therefrom. This obligation is present even where the no-strike agreement is implied pursuant to *Gateway Coal Co. v. UMW*, 414 U.S. 368 (1974). *Eazor Express, Inc. v. Teamsters*, 520 F.2d 951 (3d Cir. 1975), *cert. denied*, 424 U.S. 935 (1976). Second, the union may be liable where its members strike en masse in breach of contract, even though the strike is formally unauthorized. This theory of liability is grounded on the notion that mass action by union members must realistically be regarded as union (union authorized) conduct. *Id.; Foam & Plastic Div. Tenneco Chemicals, Inc. v. Local 401, Teamsters*, 520 F.2d 945, 947-48. (3d Cir. 1975) (court apparently held that where a strike by 90% of union members occurs, the members must realistically be deemed union agents, so that the union is liable for their actions under ordinary agency principles). The Sixth Circuit has refused to accept the proposition that a union may be held responsible for the "mass action of its members in staging an unauthorized strike" or for failure to use its "best efforts" in curtailing one. The union would be liable if it encouraged, condoned or induced the strike, either through action or inaction, including "studied ambivalence." *Peabody Coal Co. v. Local Unions*, 543 F.2d 10, 12 (6th Cir. 1976), *cert. denied*, 430 U.S. 940 (1977); *Southern Ohio Coal Co. v. UMW*, 551 F.2d 695, 699 (6th Cir. 1977).

(4) Punitive Damages

Two district courts have held that an employer may recover punitive damages under § 301 for a strike in breach of contract. *Sidney Wanzer & Sons v. Milk Drivers, Local 753*, 249 F. Supp. 664 (N.D. Ill, 1966), *noted in* 80 Harv. L. Rev. 903 (1967); *Patrick v. I.D. Packing Co., Inc.*, 308 F. Supp. 821 (S.D. Ia. 1969). But a court of appeals has refused to uphold punitive damages under § 301 where an employer violated a contract through a runaway shop. *Shoe Workers, Local 127 v. Brooks Shoe Mfg. Co.*, 298 F.2d 277 (3d Cir. 1962). In *Teamsters, Local 20 v. Morton*, 377 U.S. 252 (1964), the Supreme Court held that punitive damages could not be recovered for peaceful secondary activities forbidden by § 303 of the LMRA. Are the language and policy of § 301 and § 303 distinguishable on this issue? *See generally* Brandwen, *Punitive-Exemplary Damages in Labor Relations Litigation*, 29 U. Chi. L. Rev. 460 (1962), in N.Y.U. Eighteenth Annual Conference on Labor 117 (1966).

B. ENFORCEMENT OF THE DUTY OF FAIR REPRESENTATION IN ARBITRATION

VACA v. SIPES

United States Supreme Court
386 U.S. 171, 87 S. Ct. 903, 17 L. Ed. 2d 842 (1967)

[Owens, a long-time high blood pressure patient, returned from a half-year sick leave to resume his heavy work in a meat-packing plant of Swift & Company. Although Owens' family physician and another outside doctor certified his fitness, the company doctor concluded Owens' blood pressure was too high to permit reinstatement and he was permanently discharged. Owens' union processed a grievance through to the fourth step of the procedure established by the collective bargaining agreement. The union then sent Owens to a new doctor at union expense to "get some better medical evidence so that we could go to arbitration." When this examination did not support Owens' position, the union's executive board voted not to take the grievance to arbitration. Union officers suggested that Owens accept Swift's offer of referral to a rehabilitation center, but Owens declined and demanded arbitration. The union stood by its refusal. Owens thereupon brought a class action in a Missouri state court against petitioners as officers and representatives of the union, alleging that the union had "arbitrarily, [and] capriciously" failed to take his case to arbitration. A jury verdict in his favor was sustained by the Missouri Supreme Court in the amount of $7,000 compensatory and $3,000 punitive damages.]

Mr. Justice White delivered the opinion of the Court.

. . . Although we conclude that state courts have jurisdiction in this type of case, we hold that federal law governs, that the governing federal standards were not applied here, and that the judgment of the Supreme Court of Missouri must accordingly be reversed. . . .

II. Petitioners challenge the jurisdiction of the Missouri courts on the ground that the alleged conduct of the Union was arguably an unfair labor practice and within the exclusive jurisdiction of the NLRB. Petitioners rely on *Miranda Fuel Co.,* 140 N.L.R.B. 181 (1962), *enforcement denied,* 326 F.2d 172 (2d Cir. 1963), where a sharply divided Board held for the first time that a union's breach of its statutory duty of fair representation violates N.L.R.A. § 8(b), as amended. With the NLRB's adoption of *Miranda Fuel,* petitioners argue, the broad pre-emption doctrine defined in *San Diego Building Trades Council v. Garmon,* 359 U.S. 236 (1959), becomes applicable. For the reasons which follow, we reject this argument.

It is now well established that, as the exclusive bargaining representative of the employees in Owens' bargaining unit, the Union had a statutory duty fairly to represent all of those employees, both in its collective bargaining with Swift, *see Ford Motor Co. v. Huffman,* 345 U.S. 330 (1953); *Syres v. Oil Workers,* 350 U.S. 892 (1955), and in its enforcement of the resulting collective bargaining agreement, *see Humphrey v. Moore,* 375 U.S. 335 (1964). The statutory duty of fair representation was developed over 20 years ago in a series of cases involving alleged racial discrimination by unions certified as exclusive bargaining representatives under the Railway Labor Act, *see Steele v. Louisville & N.R.R.,* 323 U.S. 192 (1944); *Tunstall v. Brotherhood of Locomotive Firemen,* 323 U.S. 210 (1944), and was soon extended to unions certified under the N.L.R.A., *see Ford Motor Co. v. Huffman, supra.* Under this doctrine, the exclusive agent's statutory authority to represent all members of a designated unit includes a statutory obligation to serve the interests of all members without hostility or discrimination toward any, to exercise its discretion with complete good faith and honesty, and to avoid arbitrary conduct. *Humphrey v. Moore,* 375 U.S. at 342 (1964). It is obvious that Owens' complaint alleged a breach by the Union of a duty grounded in federal statutes, and that federal law therefore governs his cause of action. *E.g., Ford Motor Co. v. Huffman, supra.*

Although N.L.R.A. § 8(b) was enacted in 1947, the NLRB did not until *Miranda Fuel* interpret a breach of a union's duty of fair representation as an unfair labor practice. In *Miranda Fuel,* the Board's majority held that N.L.R.A. § 7 gives employees "the right to be free from unfair or irrelevant or invidious treatment by their exclusive bargaining agent in matters affecting their employment," and "that Section 8(b)(1)(A) of the Act accordingly prohibits labor organizations, when acting in a statutory representative capacity, from taking action against any employee upon considerations or classifications which are irrelevant, invidious, or unfair." 140 N.L.R.B. at 185. The Board also held that an employer who "participates" in such arbitrary union conduct violates § 8(a)(1), and that the employer and the union may violate §§ 8(a)(3) and 8(b)(2), respectively, "when, for arbitrary or irrelevant reasons or upon the basis of an unfair classification, the union attempts to cause or does cause an employer to derogate the employment status of an employee." *Id.* at 186. . . .

A. In *Garmon,* this Court recognized that the broad powers conferred by Congress upon the National Labor Relations Board to interpret and to enforce the complex Labor Management Relations Act necessarily imply that potentially conflicting "rules of law, of remedy, and of administration" cannot be permitted to operate. 359 U.S. at 242. . . . Consequently, as a general rule, neither state nor federal courts have jurisdiction over suits directly involving "activity [which] is arguably subject to § 7 or § 8 of the Act." *San Diego Building Trades Council v. Garmon,* 359 U.S. at 245.

This pre-emption doctrine, however, has never been rigidly applied to cases where it could not fairly be inferred that Congress intended exclusive jurisdiction to lie with the NLRB. . . . While these exceptions in no way undermine the vitality of the pre-emption rule where applicable, they demonstrate that the decision to pre-empt federal and state court jurisdiction over a given class of cases must depend upon the nature of the particular interests being asserted and the effect upon the administration of national labor policies of concurrent judicial and administrative remedies.

A primary justification for the pre-emption doctrine — the need to avoid conflicting rules of substantive law in the labor relations area and the desirability of leaving the development of such rules to the administrative agency created by Congress for that purpose — is not applicable to cases involving alleged breaches of the union duty of fair representation. The doctrine was judicially developed in *Steele* and its progeny, and suits alleging breach of the duty remained judicially cognizable long after the NLRB was given unfair labor practice jurisdiction over union activities by the L.M.R.A. Moreover, when the Board declared in *Miranda Fuel* that a union's breach of its duty of fair representation would henceforth be treated as an unfair labor practice, the Board adopted and applied the doctrine as it had been developed by the federal courts. See 140 N.L.R.B., at 184-186. Finally as the dissenting Board members in *Miranda Fuel* have pointed out, fair representation duty suits often require review of the substantive positions taken and policies pursued by a union in its negotiation of a collective bargaining agreement and in its handling of the grievance machinery; as these matters are not normally within the Board's unfair labor practice jurisdiction, it can be doubted whether the Board brings substantially greater expertise to bear on these problems than do the courts, which have been engaged in this type of review since the *Steele* decision.

In addition to the above considerations, the unique interests served by the duty of fair representation doctrine have a profound effect, in our opinion, on the applicability of the pre-emption rule to this class of cases. The federal labor laws seek to promote industrial peace and the improvement of wages and working conditions by fostering a system of employee organization and collective bargaining. *See* N.L.R.A. § 1, as amended, 29 U.S.C. § 151. The collective bargaining system as encouraged by Congress and administered by the NLRB of necessity subordinates the interests of an individual employee to the collective interests of all employees in a bargaining unit. *See e.g., J.I. Case Co. v. NLRB,* 321 U.S. 332 (1944). This Court recognized in *Steele* that the congressional grant of power to a union to act as exclusive collective bargaining representative, with its corresponding reduction in the individual rights of the employees so represented, would raise grave constitutional problems if unions were free to exercise this power to further racial discrimination. 323 U.S. at 198-199. Since that landmark decision, the duty of fair representation has stood as a bulwark to prevent arbitrary union conduct against individuals stripped of traditional forms of redress by the provisions of federal labor law. Were we to hold, as petitioners and the government urge, that the courts are pre-empted by the NLRB's *Miranda Fuel* decision of this traditional supervisory jurisdiction, the individual employee injured by arbitrary or discriminatory union conduct could no longer be assured of impartial review of his complaint, since the Board's General Counsel has unreviewable discretion to refuse to institute an unfair labor practice complaint. . . . For these reasons, we cannot assume from the NLRB's tardy assumption of jurisdiction in these cases that Congress, when it enacted N.L.R.A. § 8(b) in 1947, intended to oust the courts of their traditional jurisdiction to curb arbitrary conduct by the individual employee's statutory representative.

B. There are also some intensely practical considerations which foreclose pre-emption of judicial cognizance of fair representation duty suits, considerations which emerge from the intricate relationship between the duty of fair representation and the enforcement of collective bargaining contracts. For the fact is that the question of whether a union has breached its duty of fair representation will in many cases be a critical issue in a suit under L.M.R.A. § 301 charging an employer with a breach of contract. To illustrate, let us assume a collective bargaining agreement that limits discharges to those for good cause and that contains no grievance, arbitration or other provisions purporting to restrict access to the courts. If an employee is discharged without cause, either the union or the employee may sue the employer under L.M.R.A. § 301. Under this section, courts have jurisdiction over suits to enforce collective bargaining agreements even though the conduct of the employer which is challenged as a breach of contract is also arguably an unfair labor practice within the jurisdiction of the NLRB. *Garmon* and like cases have no application to § 301 suits. *Smith v. Evening News Ass'n,* 371 U.S. 195 (1962).

The rule is the same with regard to pre-emption where the bargaining agreement contains grievance and arbitration provisions which are intended to provide the exclusive remedy for breach of contract claims. If an employee is discharged without cause in violation of such an agreement, that the employer's conduct may be an unfair labor practice does not preclude a suit by the union against the employer to compel arbitration of the employee's grievance; the adjudication of the claim by the arbitrator; or a suit to enforce the resulting arbitration award. See *e.g., Steelworkers v. American Mfg. Co.,* 363 U.S. 564 (1960).

However, if the wrongfully discharged employee himself resorts to the courts before the grievance procedures have been fully exhausted, the employer may well defend on the ground that the exclusive remedies provided by such a contract have not been exhausted. Since the employee's claim is based upon breach of the collective bargaining agreement, he is bound by terms of that agreement which govern the manner in which contractual rights may be enforced. For this reason, it is settled that the employee must at least attempt to exhaust exclusive grievance and arbitration procedures established by the bargaining agreement. *Republic Steel Corp. v. Maddox,* 379 U.S. 650 (1965). However, because these contractual remedies have been devised and are often controlled by the union and the employer, they may well prove unsatisfactory or unworkable for the individual grievant. The problem then is to determine under what circumstances the individual employee may obtain judicial review of his breach-of-contract claim despite his failure to secure relief through the contractual remedial procedures. . . .

[W]e think the wrongfully discharged employee may bring an action against his employer in the face of a defense based upon the failure to exhaust contractual remedies, provided the employee can prove that the union as bargaining agent breached its duty of fair representation in its handling of the employee's grievance. We may assume for present purposes that such a breach of duty by the union is an unfair labor practice, as the NLRB and the Fifth Circuit have held. The employee's suit against the employer, however, remains a § 301 suit, and the jurisdiction of the courts is no more destroyed by the fact that the employee, as part and parcel of his § 301 action, finds it necessary to prove an unfair labor practice by the union, than it is by the fact that the suit may involve an unfair labor practice by the employer himself. The court is free to determine whether the employee is barred by the actions of his union representative, and, if not, to proceed with the case. And if, to facilitate his case, the employee joins the union as a defendant, the situation is not substantially changed. The action is still a § 301 suit, and the jurisdiction of the courts is not pre-empted under the *Garmon* principle. This, at the very least, is the holding of *Humphrey v. Moore* with respect to pre-emption, as petitioners recognized in their brief. And, insofar as adjudication of the union's breach of duty is concerned, the result should be no different if the employee, as Owens did here, sues the employer and the union in separate actions. There would be very little to commend a rule which would permit the Missouri courts to adjudicate the Union's conduct in an action against Swift but not in an action against the Union itself.

For the above reasons, it is obvious that the courts will be compelled to pass upon whether there has been a breach of the duty of fair representation in the context of many § 301 breach-of-contract actions. If a breach of duty by the union and a breach of contract by the employer are proven, the court must fashion an appropriate remedy. Presumably, in at least some cases, the union's breach of duty will have enhanced or contributed to the employee's injury. What possible sense could there be in a rule which would permit a court that has litigated the fault of employer and union to fashion a remedy only with respect to the employer? Under such a rule, either the employer would be compelled by the court to pay for the union's wrong — slight deterrence indeed, to future union misconduct — or the injured employee would be forced to go to two tribunals to repair a single injury. Moreover, the Board would be compelled in many cases either to remedy injuries arising out of a breach of contract, a task which Congress has not assigned to it, or to leave the individual employee without remedy for the union's wrong. Given the strong reasons for not pre-empting duty of fair representation suits in general, and the fact that the courts in many § 301 suits must adjudicate whether the union has breached its duty, we conclude that the courts may also fashion remedies for such a breach of duty. . . .

III. Petitioners contend, as they did in their motion for judgment notwithstanding the jury's verdict, that Owens failed to prove that the Union breached its duty of fair representation in its handling of Owens' grievance. Petitioners also argue that the Supreme Court of Missouri, in rejecting this contention, applied a standard that is inconsistent with governing principles of federal law with respect to the Union's duty to an individual employee in its processing of grievances under the collective bargaining agreement with Swift. We agree with both contentions.

A. . . . Quite obviously, the question which the Missouri Supreme Court thought dispositive of the issue of liability was whether the evidence supported Owens' assertion that he had been wrongfully discharged by Swift, regardless of the Union's good faith in reaching a contrary conclusion. This was also the major concern of the plaintiff at trial: the bulk of Owens' evidence was directed at whether he was medically fit at the time of discharge and whether he had performed heavy work after that discharge.

A breach of the statutory duty of fair representation occurs only when a union's conduct toward a member of the collective bargaining unit is arbitrary, discriminatory, or in bad faith. See *Humphrey v. Moore, supra; Ford Motor Co. v. Huffman, supra.* There has been considerable debate over the extent of this duty in the context of a union's enforcement of the grievance and arbitration procedures in a collective bargaining agreement. . . . Some have suggested that every individual employee should have the right to have his grievance taken to arbitration. Others have urged that the Union be given substantial discretion (if the collective bargaining agreement so provides) to decide whether a grievance should be taken to arbitration, subject only to the duty to refrain from patently wrongful conduct such as racial discrimination or personal hostility.

Though we accept the proposition that a union may not arbitrarily ignore a meritorious grievance or process it in perfunctory fashion, we do not agree that the individual employee has an absolute right to have his grievance taken to arbitration regardless of the provisions of the applicable collective bargaining agreement. In L.M.R.A. § 203(d), 29 U.S.C. § 173(d), Congress declared that "Final adjustment by a method agreed upon by the parties themselves is . . . the desirable method for settlement of grievance disputes arising over the application or interpretation of an existing collective bargaining agreement." In providing for a grievance and arbitration procedure which gives the union discretion to supervise the grievance machinery and to invoke arbitration, the employer and the union contemplate that each will endeavor in good faith to settle grievances short of arbitration. Through this settlement process, frivolous grievances are ended prior to the most costly and time-consuming step in the grievance procedures. Moreover, both sides are assured that similar complaints will be treated consistently, and major problem areas in the interpretation of the collective bargaining contract can be isolated and perhaps resolved. And finally, the settlement process furthers the interest of the union as statutory agent and as coauthor of the bargaining agreement in representing the employees in the enforcement of that agreement. . . .

For these same reasons, the standard applied here by the Missouri Supreme Court cannot be sustained. For if a union's decision that a particular grievance lacks sufficient merit to justify arbitration would constitute a breach of the duty of fair representation because a judge or jury later found the grievance meritorious, the union's incentive to settle such grievances short of arbitration would be seriously reduced. The dampening effect on the entire grievance procedure of this reduction of the union's freedom to settle claims in good faith would surely be substantial. Since the union's statutory duty of fair representation protects the individual employee from arbitrary abuses of the settlement device by providing him with recourse against both employer (in a § 301 suit) and union, this severe limitation on the power to settle grievances is neither necessary nor desirable. . . .

B. Applying the proper standard of union liability to the facts of this case, we cannot uphold the jury's award, for we conclude that as a matter of federal law the evidence does not support a verdict that the Union breached its duty of fair representation. . . .

In administering the grievance and arbitration machinery as

statutory agent of the employees, a union must in good faith and in a nonarbitrary manner, make decisions as to the merits of particular grievances. *See Humphrey v. Moore,* 375 U.S. 335, 349-350 (1964); *Ford Motor Co. v. Huffman,* 345 U.S. 330, 337-339 (1953). In a case such as this, when Owens supplied the Union with medical evidence supporting his position, the Union might well have breached its duty had it ignored Owens' complaint or had it processed the grievance in a perfunctory manner. *See* Cox, Rights under a Labor Agreement, 69 Harv. L. Rev., at 632-634. But here the Union processed the grievance into the fourth step, attempted to gather sufficient evidence to prove Owens' case, attempted to secure for Owens less vigorous work at the plant, and joined in the employer's efforts to have Owens rehabilitated. Only when these efforts all proved unsuccessful did the Union conclude both that arbitration would be fruitless and that the grievance should be dismissed. There was no evidence that any Union officer was personally hostile to Owens or that the Union acted at any time other than in good faith. Having concluded that the individual employee has no absolute right to have his grievance arbitrated under the collective bargaining agreement at issue, and that a breach of the duty of fair representation is not established merely by proof that the underlying grievance was meritorious, we must conclude that that duty was not breached here.

IV. In our opinion, there is another important reason why the judgment of the Missouri Supreme Court cannot stand. Owens' suit against the Union was grounded on his claim that Swift had discharged him in violation of the applicable collective bargaining agreement. . . .

The appropriate remedy for a breach of a union's duty of fair representation must vary with the circumstances of the particular breach. In this case, the employee's complaint was that the Union wrongfully failed to afford him the arbitration remedy against his employer established by the collective bargaining agreement. But the damages sought by Owens were primarily those suffered because of the employer's alleged breach of contract. Assuming for the moment that Owens had been wrongfully discharged, Swift's only defense to a direct action for breach of contract would have been the Union's failure to resort to arbitration, *compare Republic Steel Corp. v. Maddox,* 379 U.S. 650 (1965), *with Smith v. Evening News Ass'n,* 371 U.S. 195 (1962), and if that failure was itself a violation of the Union's statutory duty to the employee, there is no reason to exempt the employer from contractual damages which he would otherwise have had to pay. . . . The difficulty lies in fashioning an appropriate scheme of remedies.

Petitioners urge that an employee be restricted in such circumstances to a decree compelling the employer and the union to arbitrate the underlying grievance. It is true that the employee's action is based on the employer's alleged breach of contract plus the union's alleged wrongful failure to afford him his contractual remedy of arbitration. For this reason, an order compelling arbitration should be viewed as one of the available remedies when a breach of the union's duty is proved. But we see no reason inflexibly to require arbitration in all cases. . . .

A more difficult question is, what portion of the employee's damages may be charged to the union: in particular, may an award against a union include, as it did here, damages attributable solely to the employer's breach of contract? We think not. Though the union has violated a statutory duty in failing to press the grievance, it is the employer's unrelated breach of contract which triggered the controversy and which caused this portion of the employee's damages. The employee should have no difficulty recovering these damages from the employer, who cannot, as we have explained, hide behind the union's wrongful failure to act; in fact, the employer may be (and probably should be) joined as a defendant in the fair representation suit, as in *Humphrey v. Moore, supra.* It could be a real hardship on the union to pay these damages, even if the union were given a right of indemnification against the employer. With the employee assured of direct recovery from the employer, we see no merit in requiring the union to pay the employer's share of the damages.

The governing principle, then, is to apportion liability between the employer and the union according to the damage caused by the fault of each. Thus, damages attributable solely to the employer's breach of contract should not be charged to the union, but increases if any in those damages caused by the union's refusal to process the grievance should not be charged to the employer. In this case, even if the Union had breached its duty, all or almost all of Owens' damages would still be attributable to his allegedly wrongful discharge by Swift. For these reasons, even if the Union here had properly been found liable for a breach of duty, it is clear that the damage award was improper.

Reversed.

Mr. Justice Fortas, with whom The Chief Justice and Mr. Justice Harlan join, concurring in the result.

1. In my view, a complaint by an employee that the union has breached its duty of fair representation is subject to the exclusive jurisdiction of the NLRB. It is a charge of unfair labor practice. *See Miranda Fuel Co.,* 140 N.L.R.B. 181 (1962); *Rubber Workers, Local 12,* 150 N.L.R.B. 312, *enforced,* No. 22239 (5th Cir. 1966). As is the case with most other unfair labor practices, the Board's jurisdiction is pre-emptive. . . . There is no basis for failure to apply the pre-emption principles in the present case, and, as I shall discuss,

strong reason for its application. The relationship between the union and the individual employee with respect to the processing of claims to employment rights under the collective bargaining agreement is fundamental to the design and operation of federal labor law. It is not "merely peripheral," as the Court's opinion states. It "presents difficult problems of definition of status, problems which we have held are precisely 'of a kind most wisely entrusted initially to the agency charged with the day-to-day administration of the Act as a whole.' " *Iron Workers v. Perko,* 373 U.S. at 706. Accordingly, the judgment of the Supreme Court of Missouri should be reversed and the complaint dismissed for this reason and on this basis. I agree, however, that if it were assumed that jurisdiction of the subject matter exists, the judgment would still have to be reversed because of the use by the Missouri Court of an improper standard for measuring the union's duty, and the absence of evidence to establish that the union refused further to process Owens' grievance because of bad faith or arbitrarily.

2. I regret the elaborate discussion in the Court's opinion of problems which are irrelevant. This is not an action by the employee against the employer, and the discussion of the requisites of such an action is, in my judgment, unnecessary. The Court argues that the employee could sue the employer under L.M.R.A. § 301; and that to maintain such an action the employee would have to show that he has exhausted his remedies under the collective bargaining agreement, or alternatively that he was prevented from doing so because the union breached its duty to him by failure completely to process his claim. That may be; or maybe all he would have to show to maintain an action against the employer for wrongful discharge is that he demanded that the union process his claim to exhaustion of available remedies, and that it refused to do so. I see no need for the Court to pass upon that question, which is not presented here, and which, with all respect, lends no support to the Court's argument. The Court seems to use its discussion of the employee-employer litigation as somehow analogous to or supportive of its conclusion that the employee may maintain a court action against the union. But I do not believe that this follows. I agree that the NLRB's unfair labor practice jurisdiction does not preclude an action under § 301 against the employer for wrongful discharge from employment. *Smith v. Evening News Ass'n,* 371 U.S. 195 (1962). Therefore, Owens might maintain an action against his employer in the present case. This would be an action to enforce the collective bargaining agreement, and Congress has authorized the courts to entertain actions of this type. But his claim against the union is quite different in character, as the Court itself recognizes. The Court holds — and I think correctly if the issue is to be reached — that the union could not be required to pay damages measured

by the breach of the employment contract, because it was not the union but the employer that breached the contract. I agree; but I suggest that this reveals the point for which I contend: that the employee's claim against the union is not a claim under the collective bargaining agreement, but a claim that the union has breached its statutory duty of fair representation. This claim, I submit, is a claim of unfair labor practice and it is within the exclusive jurisdiction of the NLRB. The Court agrees that "one of the available remedies [obtainable, the Court says, by court action] when a breach of the Union's duty is proved" is "an order compelling arbitration." This is precisely and uniquely the kind of order which is within the province of the Board. Beyond this, the Court is exceedingly vague as to remedy: "appropriate damages or other equitable relief" are suggested as possible remedies, apparently when arbitration is not available. Damages against the union, the Court admonishes, should be gauged "according to the damages caused by its fault" — *i.e.,* the failure to exhaust remedies for the grievance. The Court's difficulty, it seems to me, reflects the basic awkwardness of its position: It is attempting to force into the posture of a contract violation an alleged default of the union which is not a violation of the collective bargaining agreement but a breach of its separate and basic duty fairly to represent all employees in the unit. This is an unfair labor practice, and should be treated as such.

3. If we look beyond logic and precedent to the policy of the labor relations design which Congress has provided, court jurisdiction of this type of actions seems anomalous and ill-advised. We are not dealing here with the interpretation of a contract or with an alleged breach of an employment agreement. As the Court in effect acknowledges, we are concerned with the subtleties of a union's statutory duty faithfully to represent employees in the unit, including those who may not be members of the union. The Court — regrettably, in my opinion — ventures to state judgments as to the metes and bounds of the reciprocal duties involved in the relationship between the union and the employee. In my opinion, this is precisely and especially the kind of judgment that Congress intended to entrust to the Board and which is well within the pre-emption doctrine that this Court has prudently stated. *See* cases cited, *supra,* especially the *Perko* and *Borden* [*Plumber's Union v. Borden,* 373 U.S. 690] cases, the facts of which strongly parallel the situation in this case. *See also Linn v. Plant Guard Workers,* 383 U.S. 53, 72 (1966) (dissenting opinion). The nuances of union-employee and union-employer relationships are infinite and consequential, particularly when the issue is as amorphous as whether the union was proved guilty of "arbitrary or bad-faith conduct" which the Court states as the standard applicable here. In all reason and in all good judgment, this jurisdiction should be left with the Board and not be

placed in the courts, especially with the complex and necessarily confusing guidebook that the Court now publishes. . . .

[The dissenting opinion of Mr. Justice Black is omitted.]

HINES v. ANCHOR MOTOR FREIGHT, INC.

United States Supreme Court
424 U.S. 554, 96 S. Ct. 1048, 47 L. Ed. 2d 321 (1976)

Mr. Justice White delivered the opinion of the Court.

The issue here is whether a suit against an employer by employees asserting breach of a collective-bargaining contract was properly dismissed where the accompanying complaint against the Union for breach of duty of fair representation has withstood the Union's motion for summary judgment and remains to be tried.

I

Petitioners, who were formerly employed as truck drivers by respondent Anchor Motor Freight, Inc. (Anchor), were discharged on June 5, 1967. The applicable collective-bargaining contract forbade discharges without just cause. The company charged dishonesty. The practice at Anchor was to reimburse drivers for money spent for lodging while the drivers were on the road overnight. Anchor's assertion was that petitioners had sought reimbursement for motel expenses in excess of the actual charges sustained by them. At a meeting between the company and the union, Local 377, International Brotherhood of Teamsters (the Union), which was also attended by petitioners, Anchor presented motel receipts previously submitted by petitioners which were in excess of the charges shown on the motel's registration cards; a notarized statement of the motel clerk asserting the accuracy of the registration cards; and an affidavit of the motel owner affirming that the registration cards were accurate and that inflated receipts had been furnished petitioners. The Union claimed petitioners were innocent and opposed the discharges. It was then agreed that the matter would be presented to the joint arbitration committee for the area, to which the collective-bargaining contract permitted either party to submit an unresolved grievance. [2] Pending this hearing, petitioners were

[2] The contractual grievance procedure is set out in Art. 7 of the Central Conference Area Supplement to the National Master Agreement. App. 226-233. Grievances were to be taken up by the employee involved and if no settlement was reached, were then to be considered by the business agent of the local union and the employer representative. If the dispute remained unresolved, either party had the right to present the case for decision to the appropriate joint area arbitration committee. These committees are organized on a geographical area basis and hear grievances in panels made up of an equal number of representatives of the parties

reinstated. Their suggestion that the motel be investigated was answered by the Union representatives' assurances that "there was nothing to worry about" and that they need not hire their own attorney.

A hearing before the joint area committee was held on July 26, 1967. Anchor presented its case. Both the Union and petitioners were afforded an opportunity to present their case and to be heard. Petitioners denied their dishonesty, but neither they nor the Union presented any other evidence contradicting the documents presented by the company. The committee sustained the discharges. Petitioners then retained an attorney and sought rehearing based on a statement by the motel owner that he had no personal knowledge of the events, but that the discrepancy between the receipts and the registration cards could have been attributable to the motel clerk's recording on the cards less than was actually paid and retaining for himself the difference between the amount receipted and the amount recorded. The committee, after hearing, unanimously denied rehearing "because there was no new evidence presented which would justify reopening this case."

There were later indications that the motel clerk was in fact the culprit; and the present suit was filed in June 1969, against Anchor, the Union and its International. The complaint alleged that the charges of dishonesty made against petitioners by Anchor were false, that there was no just cause for discharge and that the discharges had been in breach of contract. It was also asserted that the falsity of the charges could have been discovered with a minimum of investigation, that the Union had made no effort to to ascertain the truth of the charges and that the Union had violated its duty of fair representation by arbitrarily and in bad faith depriving petitioners of their employment and permitting their discharge without sufficient proof.

The Union denied the charges and relied on the decision of the joint area committee. Anchor asserted that petitioners had been properly discharged for just cause. It also defended on the ground that petitioners, diligently and in good faith represented by the Union, had unsuccessfully resorted to the grievance and arbitration machinery provided by the contract and that the adverse decision of the joint arbitration committee was binding upon the Union and petitioners under the contractual provision declaring that "[a] decision by a majority of a Panel of any of the Committees shall be

---

to the collective-bargaining agreement. Cases that deadlocked before the joint area committee could be taken to a panel of the national joint arbitration committee, composed like the area committee panels of an equal number of representatives of the parties to the agreement. If unresolved there, they would be resolved by a panel including an impartial arbitrator. The joint arbitration committee for the Detroit area is involved in this case.

final and binding on all parties, including the employee and/or employees affected." Discovery followed, including a deposition of the motel clerk revealing that he had falsified the records and that it was he who had pocketed the difference between the sums shown on the receipts and the registration cards. Motions for summary judgment filed by Anchor and the Unions were granted by the District Court on the ground that the decision of the arbitration committee was final and binding on the employees and "for failure to show facts comprising bad faith, arbitrariness or perfunctoriness on the part of the Unions." Although indicating that the acts of the Union "may not meet professional standards of competency, and while it might have been advisable for the Union to further investigate the charges . . . ," the District Court concluded that the facts demonstrated at most bad judgment on the part of the Union, which was insufficient to prove a breach of duty or make out a prima facie case against it.

After reviewing the allegations and the record before it, the Court of Appeals concluded that there were sufficient facts from which bad faith or arbitrary conduct on the part of the local Union could be inferred by the trier of fact and that petitioners should have been afforded an opportunity to prove their charges.[4] To this extent the judgment of the District Court was reversed. The Court of Appeals affirmed the judgment in favor of Anchor and the International. . . .

It is this judgment of the Court of Appeals with respect to Anchor that is now before us on our limited grant of the employees' petition for writ of certiorari. 421 U.S. 928 (1975). We reverse that judgment.

II

Section 301 of the Labor Management Relations Act, 29 U.S.C. § 185, provides for suits in the district courts for violation of collective-bargaining contracts between labor organizations and employers without regard to the amount in controversy. This provision reflects the interest of Congress in promoting "a higher degree of responsibility upon the parties to such agreements. . . ."

---

[4] As summarized by the Court of Appeals, the allegations relied on were:

"They consist of the motel clerk's admission, made a year after the discharge was upheld in arbitration, that he, not plaintiffs, pocketed the money; the claim of the union's failure to investigate the motel clerk's original story implicating plaintiffs despite their requests; the account of the union officials' assurances to plaintiffs that 'they had nothing to worry about' and 'that there was no need for them to investigate'; the contention that no exculpatory evidence was presented at the hearing; and the assertion that there existed political antagonism between local union officials and plaintiffs because of a wildcat strike led by some of the plaintiffs and a dispute over the appointment of a steward, resulting in denunciation of plaintiffs as 'hillbillies' by Angelo, the union president." 506 F. 2d 1153, 1156 (CA6 1974).

S. Rep. No. 105, 80th Cong., 1st Sess., 17 (1947). The strong policy favoring judicial enforcement of collective-bargaining contracts was sufficiently powerful to sustain the jurisdiction of the district courts over enforcement suits even though the conduct involved was arguably or would amount to an unfair labor practice within the jurisdiction of the National Labor Relations Board. *Smith* v. *Evening News Ass'n.,* 371 U.S. 195 (1962); *Arkinson* v. *Sinclair Refining Co.,* 370 U.S. 238 (1962); *Local 174, Teamsters Union* v. *Locas Flour Co.,* 369 U.S. 95 (1962); *Charles Dowd Box Co., Inc.* v. *Courtney,* 368 U.S. 502 (1962). Section 301 contemplates suits by and against individual employees as well as between unions and employers; and contrary to earlier indications § 301 suits encompass those seeking to vindicate "uniquely personal" rights of employees such as wages, hours, overtime pay, and wrongful discharge. *Smith* v. *Evening News Ass'n.,* 371 U.S., at 198-200. Petitioners' present suit against the employer was for wrongful discharge and is the kind of case Congress provided for in § 301.

Collective-bargaining contracts, however, generally contain procedures for the settlement of disputes through mutual discussion and arbitration. These provisions are among those which are to be enforced under § 301. Furthermore, Congress has specified in § 203(d), 61 Stat. 153, 29 U.S.C. § 173(d), that "[f]inal adjustment by a method agreed upon by the parties is declared to be the desirable method for settlement of grievance disputes . . . ." This congressional policy "can be effectuated only if the means chosen by the parties for settlement of their differences under a collective-bargaining agreement is given full play." *United Steel Workers* v. *American Mfg. Co.,* 363 U.S. 564, 566 (1960). Courts are not to usurp those functions which collective-bargaining contracts have properly "entrusted to the arbitration tribunal." *Id.,* at 569. They should not undertake to review the merits of arbitration awards but should defer to the tribunal chosen by the parties finally to settle their disputes. Otherwise "plenary review by a court of the merits would make meaningless the provisions that the arbitrator's decision is final, for in reality it would almost never be final." *United Steel Workers* v. *Enterprise Corp.,* 363 U.S. 593, 599 (1960).

Pursuant to this policy, we later held that an employee could not sidestep the grievance machinery provided in the contract and that unless he attempted to utilize the contractual procedures for settling his dispute with his employer, his independent suit against the employer in the District Court would be dismissed. *Republic Steel Corp.* v. *Maddox,* 397 U.S. 650 (1965). *Maddox* nevertheless distinguished the situation where "the union refuses to press or only perfunctorily presses the individual's cliam. . . . See *Humphrey* v. *Moore,* 375 U.S. 335; *Labor Board* v. *Miranda Fuel Co.,* 326 F.2d 132." 379 U.S., at 652 (footnote omitted).

The reservation in *Maddox* was well advised. The federal labor laws, in seeking to strengthen the bargaining position of the average worker in an industrial economy, provided for the selection of collective-bargaining agents with wide authority to negotiate and conclude collective-bargaining agreements on behalf of all employees in appropriate units, as well as to be the employee's agent in the enforcement and administration of the contract. Wages, hours, working conditions, seniority and job security therefore became the business of certified or recognized bargaining agents, as did the contractual procedures for the processing and settling of grievances, including those with respect to discharge.

Necessarily "[a] wide range of reasonableness must be allowed a statutory bargaining representative in serving the unit it represents . . . ." *Ford Motor Co.* v. *Huffman,* 345 U.S. 330, 338 (1953). The union's broad authority in negotiating and administering effective agreements is "undoubted," *Humphrey* v. *Moore,* 375 U.S. 335, 342 (1964), but it is not without limits. Because "[t]he collective bargaining system as encouraged by Congress and administered by the NLRB of necessity subordinates the interests of the individual employee to the collective interests of all employees in a bargaining unit," *Vaca* v. *Sipes,* 386 U.S. 171, 182 (1967), the controlling statutes have long been interpreted as imposing upon the bargaining agent a responsibility equal in scope to its authority, "the responsibility and duty of fair representation." *Humphrey* v. *Moore, supra,* at 342. The union, as the statutory representative of the employees is "subject always to complete good faith and honesty of purpose in the exercise of its discretion." *Ford Motor Co.* v. *Huffman,* 345 U.S., at 338. Since *Steele* v. *Louisville & N. R. Co.,* 323 U.S. 192 (1944), with respect to the railroad industry, and *Ford Motor Co.* v. *Huffman, supra,* and *Syres* v. *Oil Workers Local 23,* 350 U.S. 892 (1955), with respect to those industries reached by the National Labor Relations Act, the duty of fair representation has served as a "bulwark to prevent arbitrary union conduct against individuals stripped of traditional forms of redress by the provisions of federal labor law." *Vaca* v. *Sipes,* 386 U.S., at 182.

Claims of union breach of duty may arise during the life of a contract when individual employees claim wrongful discharge or other improper treatment at the hands of the employer. Contractual remedies, at least in their final stages controlled by union and employer, are normally provided; yet the union may refuse to utilize them or, if it does, assertedly do so discriminatorily or in bad faith. "The problem then is to determine under what circumstances the individual employee may obtain judicial review of his breach-of-contract claim despite his failure to secure relief through the contractual remedial procedures." *Vaca* v. *Sipes, supra,* at 185.

Humphrey v. *Moore, supra,* involved a seniority dispute between the employees of two transportation companies whose operating authorities had been combined. The employees accorded lesser seniority were being laid off. Their grievances were presented to the company and taken by the Union to the joint arbitration committee pursuant to contractual provisions very similar to those now before us. The decision was adverse. The employees then brought suit in the state court against the company, the union and the favored employees, asserting breach of contract by the company and breach of its duty of fair representation by the union. They sought damages and an injunction to prevent implementation of the decision of the joint arbitration committee. The union was charged with dishonest and bad-faith representation of the employees before the joint committee. The unions and the defendant employees asserted the finality of the joint board's decision, if not as a final resolution of a dispute in the administration of a contract, as a bargained-for accommodation between the two parties. The state courts issued the injunction. Respondents argued here that "the decision of the Committee was obtained by dishonest union conduct in breach of its duty of fair representation and that a decision so obtained cannot be relied upon as a valid excuse for his discharge under the contract." *Humphrey* v. *Moore,* 375 U.S., at 342. We reversed the judgment of the state court but only after independently determining that the union's conduct was not a breach of its statutory duties and that the board's decision was not infirm for that reason. Our conclusion was that the disfavored employees had not proved their case: "Neither the parties nor the Joint Committee exceeded their power under the contract and there was no fraud or breach of duty by the exclusive bargaining agent. The decision of the committee, reached after proceedings adequate under the agreement, is final and binding upon the parties, just as the contract says it is." 375 U.S., 331, at 351.

In *Vaca* v. *Sipes, supra,* the discharged employee sued the union alleging breach of its duty of fair representation in that it had refused in bad faith to take the employee's grievance to arbitration as it could have under the contract. In the course of rejecting the claim that the alleged conduct was arguably an unfair practice within the exclusive jurisdiction of the Labor Board, we ruled that "the wrongfully discharged employee may bring an action against his employer in the face of a defense based upon the failure to exhaust contractual remedies, provided the employee can prove that the union as bargaining agent breached its duty of fair representation in its handling of the employee's grievance." 386 U.S., at 186 (footnote omitted). This was true even though "the employer in such a situation may have done nothing to prevent exhaustion of the exclusive contractual remedies . . . ," for "the employer has committed a wrongful discharge in breach of that agreement, a breach which could be remedied through the grievance process . . . were it not for the union's breach of its statutory duty of fair representation . . . ." *Id.,* at 185. We could not "believe that Congress, in conferring upon employers and unions the power to establish exclusive grievance procedures, intended to confer upon unions such unlimited discretion to deprive injured employees of all remedies for breach of contract." Nor did we "think that Congress intended to shield employers from the natural consequences of their breaches of bargaining agreements by wrongful union conduct in the enforcement of such agreements," *Id.,* at 186. At the same time "we conclude[d] that a union does not breach its duty of fair representation . . . merely because it settled the grievance short of arbitration." *Id.,* at 192. "If the individual employee could compel arbitration of his grievance regardless of its merits," that is compel both employers and unions to make full use of the contractual provisions for settling disputes by arbitration, "the settlement machinery provided by the contract would be substantially undermined," for curtailing the "power to settle the majority of grievances short of the costlier and more time-consuming steps" might deter the parties to collective-bargaining agreements from making "provi[sion] for detailed grievance and arbitration procedures of the kind encouraged by L.M.R.A. § 203(d)." *Id.,* at 191, 192. We also expressly indicated that suit against the employer and suit against the union could be joined in one action. *Id.,* at 187.

III

Even though under *Vaca* the employer may not insist on exhaustion of grievance procedures when the union has breached its representation duty, it is urged that when the procedures have been followed and a decision favorable to the employer announced, the employer must be protected from relitigation by the express contractual provision declaring a decision to be final and binding. We disagree. The union's breach of duty relieves the employee of an express or implied requirement that disputes be settled through contractual grievance procedures; if it seriously undermines the integrity of the arbitral process the union's breach also removes the bar of the finality provisions of the contract.

It is true that *Vaca* dealt with a refusal by the union to process a grievance. It is also true that where the union actually utilizes the grievance and arbitration procedures on behalf of the employee, the focus is no longer on the reasons for the union's failure to act but on whether, contrary to the arbitrator's decision, the employer breached the contract and whether there is substantial reason to believe that a union breach of duty contributed to the erroneous outcome of the contractual proceedings. But the judicial remedy in *Humphrey* v. *Moore* was sought after the adverse decision of the joint arbitration committee. Our conclusion in that case was not that the committee's decision was unreviewable. On the contrary, we proceeded on the basis that it was reviewable and vulnerable if tainted by breach of duty on the part of the union, even though the employer had not conspired with the union. The joint committee's decision was held binding on the complaining employees only after we determined that the union had not been guilty of malfeasance and that its conduct was within the range of acceptable performance by a collective-bargaining agent, a wholly unnecessary determination if the union's conduct was irrelevant to the finality of the arbitral process.

In *Vaca* "we accept[ed] the proposition that a union may not arbitrarily ignore a meritorious grievance or process it in a perfunctory fashion," 386 U.S., at 191, and our ruling that the union had not breached its duty of fair representation in not pressing the employee's case to the last step of the grievance process stemmed from our evaluation of the manner in which the union had handled the grievance in its earlier stages. Although "the Union might well have breached its duty had it ignored [the employee's] complaint or had it processed the grievance in a perfunctory manner," "the Union conclude[d] that arbitration would be fruitless and that the grievance should be dismisssed" only after it had "processed the grievance into the fourth step, attempted to gather sufficient evidence to prove [the employee's] case, attempted to secure for [him] less vigorous work at the plant, and joined in the employer's efforts to have [him] rehabilitated." *Id.,* at 914.

Anchor would have it that petitioners are foreclosed from judicial relief unless some blameworthy conduct on its part disentitles it to rely on the finality rule. But it was Anchor that originated the discharges for dishonesty. If those charges were in error, Anchor has surely played its part in precipitating this dispute. Of course, both courts below held there were no facts suggesting that Anchor either knowingly or negligently relied on false evidence. As far as the record reveals it also prevailed before the joint committee after presenting its case in accordance with what were ostensibly wholly fair procedures. Nevertheless there remains the question whether the contractual protection against relitigating an arbitral decision binds employees who assert that the process has fundamentally malfunctioned by reason of the bad-faith performance of the union, their statutorily imposed collective-bargaining agent.

Under the rule announced by the Court of Appeals, unless the employer is implicated in the Union's malfeasance or has otherwise caused the arbitral process to err, petitioners would have no remedy against Anchor even though they are successful in proving the Union's bad faith, the falsity of the charges against them and the breach of contract by Anchor by discharging without cause. This rule would apparently govern even in circumstances where it is shown that a union has manufactured the evidence and knows from the start that it is false; or even if, unbeknownst to the employer, the union has corrupted the arbitrator to the detriment of disfavored Union members. As is the case where there has been a failure to exhaust, however, we cannot believe that Congress intended to foreclose the employee from his § 301 remedy otherwise available against the employer if the contractual processes have been seriously flawed by the union's breach of its duty to represent employees honestly and in good faith and without invidious discrimination or arbitrary conduct.

It is urged that the reversal of the Court of Appeals will undermine not only the finality rule but the entire collective-bargaining process. Employers, it is said, will be far less willing to give up their untrammeled right to discharge without cause and to agree to private settlement procedures. But the burden on employees will remain a substantial one, far too heavy in the opinion of some. To prevail against either the company or the Union, petitioners must show not only that their discharge was contrary to the contract but must also carry the burden of demonstrating breach of duty by the Union. As the District Court indicated, this involves more than demonstrating mere errors in judgment.

Petitioners are not entitled to relitigate their discharge merely because they offer newly discovered evidence that the charges against them were false and that in fact they were fired without cause. The grievance processes cannot be expected to be error-free. The finality provision has sufficient force to surmount occasional instances of mistake. But it is quite another matter to suggest that erroneous arbitration decisions must stand even though the employee's representation by the union has been dishonest, in bad faith or discriminatory; for in that event error and injustice of the grossest sort would multiply. The contractual system would then cease to qualify as an adequate mechanism to secure individual redress for damaging failure of the employer to abide by the contract. Congress has put its blessing on private dispute settlement arrangements provided in collective agreements, but it was anticipated, we are sure, that the contractual machinery would operate within some minimum levels of integrity. In our view, enforcement of the finality provision where the arbitrator has erred is conditioned upon the Union's having satisfied its statutory duty fairly to represent the employee in connection with the arbitration proceedings. Wrongfully discharged employees would be left without jobs and without a fair opportunity to secure an adequate remedy.

Except for this case the Courts of Appeals have arrived at similar conclusions. As the Court of Appeals for the Ninth Circuit put it in *Margetta* v. *Pam Pam Corp.,* 501 F.2d 179, 180 (1974): "To us, it makes little difference whether the union subverts the arbitration process by refusing to proceed as in *Vaca* or follows the arbitration trail to the end, but in doing so subverts the arbitration process by failing to fairly represent the employee. In neither case does the employee receive fair representation."

Petitioners, if they prove an erroneous discharge and the Union's breach of duty tainting the decision of the joint committee, are entitled to an appropriate remedy against the employer as well as the Union. It was error to affirm the District Court's final dismissal of petitioners' action against Anchor. To this extent the judgment of the Court of Appeals is reversed.

So ordered.

Mr. Justice Stevens took no part in the consideration or decision of this case.

[The concurring opinion of Mr. Justice Stewart and the dissenting opinion of Mr. Justice Rehnquist, with whom The Chief Justice joined, are omitted.]

NOTES:

(1) Does the standard of fair representation applied by the Supreme Court appear to be a matter of honesty and subjective good faith, or a matter of reasonableness? A number of cases have stated that negligent conduct by a union does not breach its duty of fair representation. *See e.g., Dente v. Masters, Mates & Pilots Local 90,* 492 F.2d 10 (9th Cir. 1973), *cert. denied* 417 U.S. 910 (1974) (union's delay in processing grievance was at worst negligent; held, no liability); *Bazarte v. United Transp. Union,* 429 F.2d 868 (3d Cir. 1970) (negligence or poor judgment by a union does not breach its duty of fair representation). Nevertheless, some courts, in reliance on *Vaca's* assertion that a union may not process a grievance in a "perfunctory" fashion, have imposed on the union a duty of "meaningful" representation. *See e.g., Holodnak v. Avco Corp.,* 381 F. Supp. 191 (D. Conn. 1977), *modified on other grounds,* 514 F.2d 285 (2d Cir. 1975) (union breached its duty of fair representation during the course of the arbitral process where its attorney neglected to make necessary legal arguments and failed to protect the grievant against "inquisitorial" questioning by the arbitrator); *Figueroa de*

Arroyo v. Sindicato De Trabajadores Packinghouse, 425 F.2d 281 (1st Cir. 1970); *Thompson v. Machinists Lodge 1049,* 258 F. Supp. 235 (E.D. Va. 1966). *See also Griffin v. UAW,* 469 F.2d 181 (4th Cir. 1972).

In *Ruzicka v. General Motors Corp,* 523 F.2d 306 (6th Cir. 1975), the union allowed a deadline for the filing of a grievance to pass without deciding that the claim was without merit, thereby permitting the employer to refuse to arbitrate the grievance. The court held that "such negligent handling of the grievance, unrelated as it was to the merits of [a grievance], amounts to unfair representation. It is a clear example of arbitrary and perfunctory handling of a grievance." Judge McCree, in concurring, cautioned that "arbitrary" and "perfunctory" conduct refers not to negligent actions, but to intentional conduct that is "capricious" or "superficial." He reasoned, however, that "a total failure to act, whether negligent or intentional, is behavior so egregious that, as in the case of bad faith, hostile discrimination, arbitrariness, or perfunctoriness, the union should be held responsible." This test, he noted, would not require the court to second-guess the union on its decisions as to whether a grievance is meritorious enough to warrant arbitration.

(2) To what extent should a union, even if acting honestly, be allowed to sacrifice individual interests for the sake of the group? Should a union be able to trade off or compromise some claims in order to gain concessions on others? Does it make any difference whether the abandoned grievance involves a discharge, minor discipline, seniority, or wages allegedly accrued and owing? In *Union News Co. v. Hildreth,* 295 F.2d 658 (6th Cir. 1961), a lunch counter employing twelve persons suffered unexplained losses of food and money and suspected pilfering by the workers. The employer threatened to fire the entire crew. Rather than have this happen, the union bargained for a trial layoff of five employees. Losses dropped, the layoffs were made final, and the union refused to process a grievance on behalf of one protesting worker, even though there was no direct proof of her dishonesty. Did the union breach its duty of fair representation? (Held, no, since the union had acted honestly to benefit as many employees as it deemed feasible, and there was no showing of "fraud, bad faith, or collusion" by the union in agreeing to the layoffs.) *See also Curth v. Faraday, Inc.,* 401 F. Supp. 678 (E.D. Mich. 1975) (high cost of arbitration and financial difficulty of union warrant union's refusal to arbitrate grievance where it honestly decides, on the basis of rational and objective criteria, that the grievance lacks sufficient merit to justify the expense of arbitration); *Mahnke v. Wisconsin Employment Rel. Commission,* 66 Wis. 2d 524, 225 N.W.2d 617 (1975) (union's decision not to arbitrate based solely on economic considerations might violate its duty of fair representation; such decision must take into account at

least the monetary value of grievant's claim, the effect of the company's action on the employee, and the likelihood of success in arbitration).

(d) In *Dorn v. Meyers Parking System,* 395 F. Supp. 799 (E.D. Pa. 1975), the court held that exhaustion of intraunion remedies was not required where such procedures would be futile. Nor should intraunion appeals be required where the remedy would be inadequate, the union appellate body "might be biased," the internal procedures themselves might be inadequate, or the employee might be prejudiced by the delay involved. Moreover, said the court, the union has the burden of showing (a) that there is a procedure available to union members "reasonably calculated to redress the *particular* grievance complained of," and (b) that such procedure is "generally known to the union membership." *See also Ruzicka v. General Motors Corp.,* 523 F.2d 306, 312 (6th Cir. 1975).

(4) Following *UAW v. Hoosier Cardinal,* 383 U.S. 696 (1966), the federal courts have consistently applied state statutes of limitations in actions against unions for breach of their duty of fair representation. This is so even where the court does not base its jurisdiction for entertaining unfair representation actions on § 301. *Figueroa de Arroyo v. Sindicato De Trabajadores Packinghouse,* 425 F.2d 281 (1st Cir. 1970). There is considerable controversy, however, as to the appropriate type of limitations statute (*e.g., contract vs. tort*) to be applied in such actions. Some courts apply the generally shorter tort limitations statute, even though this may effectively immunize the employer from liability for breaching the labor contract. *Id.; Smart v. Ellis Trucking Co.,* 409 F. Supp. 129, (E.D. Mich. 1976). Other courts have employed the contracts limitation statute, especially where the plaintiff joins the union and employer in a single action. *See Abrams v. Carrier Corp.,* 434 F.2d 1234 (2d Cir. 1970), *cert. denied,* 401 U.S. 1009 (1971); *Butler v. Teamsters Local 823,* 514 F.2d 442 (8th Cir. 1975); *Grant v. Mulvihill Bros. Motor Service, Inc.,* 428 F. Supp. 45 (N.D. Ill. 1975) ("given the primary function of the § 301 suit as a vehicle to redress contract violations, . . . and the interdependence of the employer's contract violation and the union's fiduciary [breach] . . . we feel a single statute of limitations is appropriate"). *See also Tuma v. American Can Co.,* 367 F. Supp. 1178 (D.N.J. 1973).

In a jurisdiction which considers an unfair representation action as sounding in contract, should an employee be allowed to join an employer in a timely action against the union if a direct suit against the employer would be barred by the limitation period? *See Butler v. Teamsters Local 823,* 514 F.2d 442 (8th Cir. 1975), *cert. denied,* 423 U.S. 924 (1975).

(5) Several courts have permitted an employee to recover from the union amounts reasonably expended in attorney's fees and other

costs which would not have occurred but for the union's failure to represent him fairly. *Scott v. Teamsters Union,* 528 F.2d 1244 (6th Cir. 1977); *Emmanuel v. Omaha Carpenters Dist. Council,* 422 F. Supp. 204 (D. Neb. 1976).

The Supreme Court held in *I.B.E.W. v. Foust,* 47 U.S.L.W. 4581 (1979), that punitive damages may not be recovered against a union in a duty of fair representation case. Four members of the Court concurred in the result, preferring not to lay down a *per se* rule.

C. THE DUTY OF A SUCCESSOR EMPLOYER TO ARBITRATE

JOHN WILEY & SONS, INC. v. LIVINGSTON

United States Supreme Court
376 U.S. 543, 84 S. Ct. 909, 11 L. Ed. 2d 898 (1964)

[Read the case again as set forth, *supra* p. 323.]

NOTES:

(1) An unusually comprehensive study of the problems growing out of *Wiley,* as well as of related successorship issues, is presented by Goldberg, The Labor Law Obligations of a Successor Employer, 63 Nw. U.L. Rev. 735 (1969). *See also* Barbash, Feller, Jay & Lippman, The Labor Contract and the Sale, Subcontracting or Termination of Operations, in N.Y.U. Eighteenth Annual Conference on Labor 255, 259, 277, 293, 315 (1966) (four separate papers); Christensen, The Developing Law of Arbitrability, in Southwestern Legal Foundation, Labor Law Developments, Proceedings of the Eleventh Annual Institute on Labor Law 119 (1965); Platt, The NLRB and the Arbitrator in Sale and Merger Situations, in N.Y.U. Nineteenth Annual Conference on Labor 375 (1967); Shaw & Carter, Sales, Mergers and Union Contract Relations, in N.Y.U. Nineteenth Annual Conference on Labor 357 (1967).

(2) The *Burns* case, following, although it is an unfair labor practice case involving the duty to bargain, is included here because of its significance in the development of the law.

NLRB v. BURNS INTERNATIONAL SECURITY SERVICES, INC.

United States Supreme Court
406 U.S. 272, 92 S. Ct. 1571, 32 L. Ed. 2d 61 (1972)

Mr. Justice White delivered the opinion of the Court.

Burns International Security Services, Inc. (Burns), replaced another employer, the Wackenhut Corporation (Wackenhut), which had previously provided plant protection services for the Lockheed Aircraft Service Company (Lockheed) located at the Ontario International Airport in California. When Burns began providing security service, it employed 42 guards; 27 of them had been employed by Wackenhut. Burns refused, however, to bargain with the United Plant Guard Workers of America (the union) which had been certified after an NLRB election as the exclusive bargaining representative of Wackenhut's employees less than four months earlier. The issues presented in this case are whether Burns refused to bargain with a union representing a majority of employees in an appropriate unit and whether the National Labor Relations Board could order Burns to observe the terms of a collective-bargaining contract signed by the union and Wackenhut which Burns had not voluntarily assumed. Resolution turns to a great extent on the precise facts involved here.

I. The Wackenhut Corporation provided protection services at the Lockheed plant for five years before Burns took over this task. On February 28, 1967, a few months before the change-over of guard employers, a majority of the Wackenhut guards selected the union as their exclusive bargaining representative in a Board election after Wackenhut and the union had agreed that the Lockheed plant was the appropriate bargaining unit. On March 8, the Regional Director certified the union as the exclusive bargaining representative for these employees, and on April 29, Wackenhut and the union entered into a three-year collective-bargaining contract.

Meanwhile, since Wackenhut's one-year service agreement to provide security protection was due to expire on June 30, Lockheed had called for bids from various companies supplying these services, and both Burns and Wackenhut submitted estimates. At a pre-bid conference attended by Burns on May 15, a representative of Lockheed informed the bidders that Wackenhut's guards were represented by the union, that the union had recently won a Board election and been certified, and that there was in existence a collective-bargaining contract between Wackenhut and the union. App. 4-5, 126. Lockheed then accepted Burns' bid, and on May 31, Wackenhut was notified that Burns would assume responsibility for protection services on July 1. Burns chose to retain 27 of the Wackenhut guards, and it brought in 15 of its own guards from other Burns locations.

During June, when Burns hired the 27 Wackenhut guards, it supplied them with the membership cards of the American Federation of Guards (AFG), another union with whom Burns had collective bargaining contracts at other locations, and informed them that they must become AFG members to work for Burns, that they would not receive uniforms otherwise, and that Burns "could not live with" the existing contract between Wackenhut and the union. On June 29, Burns recognized the AFG on the theory that it had obtained a card majority. On July 12, however, the UPG demanded that Burns recognize it as the bargaining representative of Burns' employees at Lockheed and that Burns honor the collective-bargaining agreement between it and Wackenhut. When Burns refused, the UPG filed unfair labor practice charges, and Burns responded by challenging the appropriateness of the unit and by denying its obligation to bargain.

The Board, adopting the trial examiner's findings and conclusions, found the Lockheed plant an appropriate unit and held that Burns had violated §§ 8(a)(2) and 8(a)(1) of the Act, 29 U.S.C. §§ 158(a)(2), 158(a)(1), by unlawfully recognizing and assisting the AFG, a rival of the UPG; that it had violated §§ 8(a)(5) and 8(a)(1), 29 U.S.C. §§ 158(a)(5), 158(a)(1), by failing to recognize and bargain with the UPG and by refusing to honor the collective-bargaining agreement which had been negotiated between Wackenhut and UPG.

Burns did not challenge the § 8(a)(2) unlawful assistance finding in the Court of Appeals but sought review of the unit determination and the order to bargain and observe the pre-existing collective-bargaining contract. The Court of Appeals accepted the Board's unit determination and enforced the Board's order insofar as it related to the finding of unlawful assistance of a rival union and the refusal to bargain, but it held that the Board had exceeded its powers in ordering Burns to honor the contract executed by Wackenhut. Both Burns and the Board petitioned for certiorari, Burns challenging the unit determination and the bargaining order and the Board maintaining its position that Burns was bound by the Wackenhut contract, and we granted both petitions, though we declined to review the propriety of the bargaining unit, a question which was presented in No. 71-198. 404 U.S. 822 (1971).

II. We address first Burns' alleged duty to bargain with the union, and in doing so it is well to return to the specific provisions of the Act which both courts and the Board are bound to observe. [The Court quoted from §§ 8(a)(5) and 9.] Because the Act itself imposes a duty to bargain with the representative of a majority of the employees in an appropriate unit, the initial issue before the Board was whether the charging union was such a bargaining represenative.

The trial examiner first found that the unit designated by the regional director was an appropriate unit for bargaining. The unit found appropriate was defined as "[a]ll full-time and regular part-time employees of [Burns] performing plant protection duties as determined in Section 9(b)(3) of the [National Labor Relations] Act at Lockheed, Ontario International Airport; excluding office clerical employees, professional employees, supervisors, and all other employees as defined in the Act." This determination was affirmed by the Board, accepted by the Court of Appeals, and is not at issue here because pretermitted by our limited grant of certiorari.

The trial examiner then found, *inter alia,* that Burns "had in its employ a majority of Wackenhut's former employees," and that these employees had already expressed their choice of a bargaining representative in an election held a short time before. Burns was therefore held to have a duty to bargain, which arose when it selected as its work force the employees of the previous employer to perform the same tasks at the same place they had worked in the past.

The Board, without revision, accepted the trial examiner's findings and conclusions with respect to the duty to bargain, and we see no basis for setting them aside. In an election held but a few months before, the union had been designated bargaining agent for the employees in the unit and a majority of these employees had been hired by Burns for work in an identical unit. It is undisputed that Burns knew all the relevant facts in this regard and was aware of the certification and of the existence of a collective-bargaining contract. In these circumstances, it was not unreasonable for the Board to conclude that the union certified to represent all employees in the unit still represented a majority of the employees and that Burns could not reasonably have entertained a good-faith doubt about that fact. Burns' obligation to bargain with the union over terms and conditions of employment stems from its hiring of Wackenhut's employees and from the recent election and Board certification. It has been consistently held that a mere change of employers or of ownership in the employing industry is not such an "unusual circumstance" as to affect the force of the Board's certification within the normal operative period if a majority of employees after the change of ownership or management were employed by the preceding employer. [Citing cases.]

It goes without saying, of course, that Burns was not entitled to upset what it should have accepted as an established union majority by soliciting representation cards for another union and thereby committing the unfair labor practice of which it was found guilty by the Board. That holding was not challenged here and makes it imperative that the situation be viewed as it was when Burns hired its employees for the guard unit, a majority of whom were represented by a Board-certified union. *See NLRB v. Gissel Packing Co.,* 395 U.S. 575, 609, 610-616 (1969).

It would be a wholly different case if the Board had determined that because Burns' operational structure and practices differed from those of Wackenhut, the Lockheed bargaining unit was no longer an appropriate one. Likewise, it would be different if Burns had not hired employees already represented by a union certified as a bargaining agent, and the Board recognized as much at oral argument. But where the bargaining unit remains unchanged and a majority of the employees hired by the new employer are represented by a recently certified bargaining agent there is little basis for faulting the Board's implementation of the express mandates of § 8(a)(5) and § 9(a) by ordering the employer to bargain with the incumbent union. This is the view of several courts of appeal and we agree with those courts. . . .

III. It does not follow, however, from Burns' duty to bargain that it was bound to observe the substantive terms of the collective-bargaining contract the union had negotiated with Wackenhut and to which Burns had in no way agreed. Section 8(d) of the Act expressly provides that the existence of such bargaining obligation "does not compel either party to agree to a proposal or require the making of a concession." Congress has consistently declined to interfere with free collective bargaining and has preferred that device, or voluntary arbitration, to the imposition of compulsory terms as a means of avoiding or terminating labor disputes. . . .

This Court immediately noted this fundamental theme of the legislation: "[The Act] does not compel any agreement whatever . . . The theory of the Act is that free opportunity for negotiation with accredited representatives of employees is likely to promote industrial peace and may bring about the adjustments and agreements, which the Act in itself does not attempt to compel." *NLRB v. Jones & Laughlin Steel Corp.*, 301 U.S. 1, 45 (1937). *See also NLRB v. American National Insurance Co.*, 343 U.S. 395, 401-402 (1952); *Teamsters Local 357 v. NLRB*, 365 U.S. 667, 676-677 (1961).

Section 8(d), 29 U.S.C. § 158(d), made this policy an express statutory mandate, and was enacted in 1947 because Congress feared that "the present Board has gone very far, in the guise of determining whether or not employers had bargained in good faith, in setting itself up as the judge of what concessions an employer must make and what proposals they may or may not make . . . unless Congress writes into the law guides for the Board to follow, the Board may attempt to carry this process still further and seek to control more and more the terms of collective bargaining agreements." H. R. Rep. No. 245, 80th Cong., 1st Sess., 19-20 (1947).

This history was reviewed in detail and given controlling effect in *H. K. Porter Co. v. NLRB*, 397 U.S. 99 (1970). There this Court, while agreeing that the employer violated § 8(a)(5) by adamantly refusing to agree to a dues checkoff intending thereby to frustrate the consummation of any bargaining agreement, held that the Board had erred in ordering the employer to agree to such a provision:

"While the Board does have power . . . to require employers and employees to negotiate, it is without power to compel a company or a union to agree to any substantive contractual provision of a collective bargaining agreement. . . ." 397 U.S. at 102. . . .

These considerations, evident from the explicit language and legislative history of the labor laws, underlay the Board's prior decisions which until now have consistently held that although successor employers may be found to recognize and bargain with the union, they are not bound by the substantive provisions of a collective-bargaining contract negotiated by their predecessors but not agreed to or assumed by them. [Citing cases.]

The Board, however, has now departed from this view and argues that the same policies which mandate a continuity of bargaining obligation also require that successor employers be bound to the terms of a predecessor's collective-bargaining contract. It asserts that the stability of labor relations will be jeopardized and that employees will face uncertainty and a gap in the bargained-for terms and conditions of employment, as well as the possible loss of advantages gained by prior negotiations, unless the new employer is held to have assumed, as a matter of federal labor law, the obligations under the contract entered into by the former employer. Recognizing that under normal contract principles a party would not be bound to a contract in the absence of consent, the Board notes that in *John Wiley & Sons, Inc. v. Livingston,* 376 U.S. 543, 550 (1964), the Court declared that "a collective bargaining agreement is not an ordinary contract" but is rather an outline of the common law of a particular plant or industry. The Court held in *Wiley* that although the predecessor employer who had signed a collective-bargaining contract with the union had disappeared by merger with the successor, the union could compel the successor to arbitrate the extent to which the successor was obligated under the collective-bargaining agreement. The Board contends that the same factors which the Court emphasized in *Wiley,* the peaceful settlement of industrial conflicts and "protection [of] the employees [against] a sudden change in the employment relationship," *id.,* at 549, require that Burns be treated under the collective-bargaining contract exactly as Wackenhut would have been if it had continued protecting the Lockheed plant.

We do not find *Wiley* controlling in the circumstances here. *Wiley* arose in the context of a § 301 suit to compel arbitration, not in the context of an unfair labor practice proceeding where the Board is expressly limited by the provisions of § 8(d). That decision emphasized "the preference of national labor policy for arbitration as a substitute for tests of strength between contending forces" and held only that the agreement to arbitrate, "construed in the context of national labor law," survived the merger and left to the arbitrator, subject to judicial review, the ultimate question of the extent to which, if any, the surviving company was bound by other provisions of the contract. *Id.* at 549, 551.

Wiley's limited accommodation between the legislative endorsement of freedom of contract and the judicial preference for peaceful arbitral settlement of labor disputes does not warrant the Board's holding that the employer commits an unfair labor practice unless he honors the substantive terms of the pre-existing contract. The present case does not involve a § 301 suit; nor does it involve the duty to arbitrate. Rather, the claim is that Burns must be held bound by the contract executed by Wackenhut, whether Burns has agreed to it or not and even though Burns made it perfectly clear that it had no intention of assuming that contract. *Wiley* suggests no such open-ended obligation. Its narrower holding dealt with a merger occurring against a background of state law which embodied the general rule that in merger situations the surviving corporation is liable for the obligations of the disappearing corporation. See N.Y. Stock Corporation Law § 90 (1951); 15 W. Fletcher, Private Corporations § 7121 (1961 rev. ed.). Here there was no merger, no sale of assets, no dealings whatsoever between Wackenhut and Burns. On the contrary, they were competitors for the same work, each bidding for the service contract at Lockheed. Burns purchased nothing from Wackenhut and became liable for none of its financial obligations. Burns merely hired enough of Wackenhut's employees to require it to bargain with the union as commanded by § 8(a)(5) and § 9(a). But this consideration is a wholly insufficient basis for implying either in fact or in law that Burns had agreed or must be held to have agreed to honor Wackenhut's collective-bargaining contract.

We agree with the Court of Appeals that the Board failed to heed the admonitions of the *H. K. Porter* case. Preventing industrial strife is an important aim of federal labor legislation, but Congress has not chosen to make the bargaining freedom of employers and unions totally subordinate to this goal. When a bargaining impasse is reached, strikes and lockouts may occur. This bargaining freedom means both that parties need not make any concessions as a result of government compulsion and that they are free from having contract provisions imposed upon them against their will. Here, Burns had notice of the existence of the Wackenhut collective-bargaining contract, but it did not consent to be bound by it. The source of its duty to bargain with the union is not the collective-bargaining contract but the fact that it voluntarily took over a bargaining unit that was largely intact and that had been certified within the past year. Nothing in its actions, however, indicated that Burns was assuming the obligations of the contract, and "allowing the Board to compel agreement when the parties themselves are unable to agree would violate the fundamental premise on which the Act is based — private bargaining under governmental supervision of the procedure alone, without any official compulsion over the actual terms of the contract." *H. K. Porter v. NLRB,* 397 U.S. at 108.

We also agree with the Court of Appeals that holding either the union or the new employer bound to the substantive terms of an old collective-bargaining contract may result in serious inequities. A potential employer may be willing to take over a moribund business only if he can make changes in corporate structure, composition of the labor force, work location, task assignment, and nature of supervision. Saddling such an employer with the terms and conditions of employment contained in the old collective-bargaining contract may make these changes impossible and may discourage and inhibit the transfer of capital. On the other hand, a union may have made concessions to a small or failing employer that it would be unwilling to make to a large or economically successful firm. The congressional policy manifest in the Act is to enable the parties to negotiate for any protection either deems appropriate, but to allow the balance of bargaining advantage to be set by economic power realities. Strife is bound to occur if the concessions which must be honored do not correspond to the relative economic strength of the parties.

The Board's position would also raise new problems, for the successor employer would be circumscribed in exactly the same way as the predecessor under the collective-bargaining contract. It would seemingly follow that employees of the predecessor would be deemed employees of the successor, dischargeable only in accordance with provisions of the contract and subject to the grievance and arbitration provisions thereof. Burns would not have been free to replace Wackenhut's guards with its own except as the contract permitted. Given the continuity of employment relationship, the pre-existing contract's provisions with respect to wages, seniority rights, vacation privileges, pension and retirement fund benefits, job security provisions, work assignments and the like would devolve on the successor. Nor would the union commit a § 8(b)(3) unfair labor practice if it refused to bargain for a modification of the agreement effective prior to the expiration date of the agreement. A successor employer might also be deemed to have inherited its predecessor's pre-existing contractual obligations to the union which had accrued under past contracts and which had not been discharged when the business was transferred. "[A] successor may well acquire more liabilities as a result of *Burns* than appear on the face of the contract." Finally, a successor will be bound to observe the contract despite good-faith doubts about the union's majority during the time that the contract is a bar to another representation election. Ranch-Way, Inc., 183 N.L.R.B. No. 116 (1970). For the above reasons, the Board itself has expressed doubts as to the general applicability of its *Burns* rule.

In many cases, of course, successor employers will find it advantageous not only to recognize and bargain with the union but also to observe the pre-existing contract rather than to face uncertainty and turmoil. Also, in a variety of circumstances involving a merger, stock acquisition, reorganization, or assets purchase, the Board might properly find as a matter of fact that the successor had assumed the obligations under the old contract. *Cf. Oilfield Maintenance Co., Inc.,* 142 N.L.R.B. 1384 (1963). Such a duty does not, however, ensue as a matter of law from the mere fact than [that] an employer is doing the same work in the same place with the same employees as his predecessor, as the Board had recognized until its decision in the instant case. See cases cited *supra,* at 284. We accordingly set aside the Board's finding of a § 8(a)(5) unfair labor practice insofar as it rested on a conclusion that Burns was required to but did not honor the collective-bargaining contract executed by Wackenhut.

IV. It therefore follows that the Board's order requiring Burns to "give retroactive effect to all the clauses of said [Wackenhut] contract and, with interest of 6 percent, make whole its employees for any losses suffered by reason of Respondent's [Burns'] refusal to honor, adopt and enforce said contract" must be set aside. We note that the regional director's charge instituting this case asserted that "on or about July 1, 1967, Respondent unilaterally changed existing wage rates, hours of employment, overtime wage rates, differential for swing shift and graveyard shift and other terms and conditions of employment of the employees in the appropriate unit . . . ," App. 113, and that the Board's opinion stated that "[t]he obligation to bargain imposed on a successor-employer includes the negative injunction to refrain from unilaterally changing wages and other benefits established by a prior collective-bargaining agreement even though that agreement had expired. In this respect the successor-employer's obligations are the same as those imposed upon employers generally during the period between collective-bargaining agreements." App. 8-9. This statement by the Board is consistent with its prior and subsequent cases which hold that whether or not a successor employer is bound by its predecessor's contract, it must not institute terms and conditions of employment different from those provided in its predecessor's contract, at least without first bargaining with the employees' representative. *Overnite Transportation Co.,* 157 N.L.R.B. 1185 (1966), *enforced sub nom. Overnite Transportation Co. v. NLRB,* 372 F.2d 765 (4th Cir.), *cert. denied,* 389 U.S. 838 (1967); *Valleydale Packers, Inc.,* 162 N.L.R.B. 1486 (1967), *enforced sub nom. NLRB v. Valleydale Packers, Inc.,* 402 F.2d 768 (5th Cir. 1968); *Michaud Bus Lines, Inc.,* 171 N.L.R.B. 193 (1968); *Emerald Maintenance, Inc.,* 188 N.L.R.B. No. 139 (1971). Thus, if Burns, without bargaining to impasse with the union, had paid its employees on and after July 1 at a rate lower than Wackenhut had paid under its contract or otherwise provided terms and conditions of employment different from those provided in the Wackenhut collective-bargaining agreement, under the Board's view, Burns would have committed a § 8(a)(5) unfair labor practice and would be subject to an order to restore to employees what they had lost by this so-called unilateral change. *See Overnite Transportation Co., supra; Emerald Maintenance, Inc., supra.*

Although Burns had an obligation to bargain with the union concerning wages and other conditions of employment when the union requested it to do so, this case is not like a § 8(a)(5) violation where an employer unilaterally changes a condition of employment without consulting a bargaining representative. It is difficult to understand how Burns could be said to have *changed* unilaterally any pre-existing term or condition of employment without bargaining when it had no previous relationship whatsoever to the bargaining unit and, prior to July 1, no outstanding terms and conditions of employment from which a change could be inferred. The terms on which Burns hired employees for service after July 1 may have differed from the terms extended by Wackenhut and required by the collective-bargaining contract, but it does not follow that Burns changed *its* terms and conditions of employment when it specified the initial basis on which employees were hired on July 1.

Although a successor employer is ordinarily free to set initial terms on which it will hire the employees of a predecessor, there will be instances in which it is perfectly clear that the new employer plans to retain all of the employees in the unit and in which it will be appropriate to have him initially consult with the employees' bargaining representative before he fixes terms. In other situations, however, it may not be clear until the successor employer has hired his full complement of employees that he has a duty to bargain with the union, since it will not be evident until then that the bargaining representative represents a majority of the employees in the union as required by § 9(a) of the Act, 29 U.S.C. § 159(a). Here, for example, Burns' obligation to bargain with the union did not mature until it had selected its force of guards late in June. The Board quite properly found that Burns refused to bargain on July 12 when it rejected the overtures of the union. It is true that the wages it paid when it began protecting the Lockheed plant on July 1 differed from those specified in the Wackenhut collective-bargaining agreement, but there is no evidence that Burns ever unilaterally changed the terms and conditions of employment it had offered to potential employees in June after its obligation to bargain with the union became apparent. If the union had made a request to bargain after Burns had completed its hiring and if Burns had negotiated in good faith and had made offers to the union which the union rejected, Burns could have unilaterally initiated such proposals as the opening terms and conditions of employment on July 1 without committing an unfair labor practice. *Cf. NLRB v. Katz.,* 369 U.S. 736, 745 n. 12 (1962); *NLRB v. Fitzgerald Mills Corp.,* 313 F.2d 260, 272-273 (2d Cir.), *cert. denied,* 375 U.S. 834 (1963); *NLRB v. Southern Coach & Body Co.,* 336 F.2d 214, 217 (5th Cir. 1964). The Board's order requiring Burns to make whole its employees for any losses suffered by reason of Burns' refusal to honor and enforce the contract, cannot therefore be sustained on the ground that Burns unilaterally changed existing terms and conditions of employment, thereby committing an unfair labor practice which required monetary restitution in these circumstances.

Affirmed.

Mr. Justice Rehnquist, with whom The Chief Justice, Mr. Justice Brennan, and Mr. Justice Powell join, concurring in No. 71-123 and dissenting in No. 71-198.

Although the court studiously avoids using the term "successorship" in concluding that Burns did have a statutory obligation to bargain with the union, it affirms the conclusions of the Board and the Court of Appeals to that effect which were based entirely on the successorship doctrine. Because I believe that the Board and the Court of Appeals stretched that concept beyond the limits of its proper application, I would enforce neither the Board's bargaining order nor its order imposing upon Burns the terms of the contract between the union and Wackenhut. I therefore concur in No. 71-123 and dissent in No. 71-198. . . .

The rigid imposition of a prior existing labor relations environment on a new employer whose only connection with the old employer is the hiring of some of the latter's employees and the performance of some of the work which was previously performed by the latter, might well tend to produce industrial peace of a sort. But industrial peace in such a case would be produced at a sacrifice of the determination by the Board of the appropriateness of bargaining agents and of the wishes of the majority of the employees which the Act was designed to preserve. These latter principles caution us against extending successorship, under the banner of industrial peace, step by step to a point where the only connection between the two employing entities is a naked transfer of employees. . . .

Burns acquired not a single asset, tangible or intangible, by negotiation or transfer from Wackenhut. It succeeded to the contractual rights and duties of the plant protection service contract with Lockheed not by reason of Wackenhut's assignment or consent, but over Wackenhut's vigorous opposition. I think the only permissible conclusion is that Burns is not a successor to Wackenhut. . . .

To conclude that Burns was a successor to Wackenhut in this situation, with its attendant consequences under the Board's order imposing a duty to bargain with the bargaining representative of Wackenhut's employees, would import unwarranted rigidity into labor-management relations. The fortunes of competing employers inevitably ebb and flow, and an employer who has currently gained production orders at the expense of another may well wish to hire employees away from that other. There is no reason to think that the best interests of the employees, the employers, and ultimately of the free market are not served by such movement. Yet inherent in the expanded doctrine of successorship which the Board urges in this case is the notion that somehow the "labor relations environment" comes with the new employees if the new employer has but obtained orders or business which previously belonged to the old employer. The fact that the employees in the instant case continued to perform their work at the same situs, while not irrelevant to analysis, cannot be deemed controlling. For the rigidity which would follow from the Board's application of successorship to this case would not only affect competition between Wackenhut and Burns, but would also affect Lockheed's operations. In effect, it would be saddled, as against its competitors, with the disadvantageous consequences of a collective-bargaining contract unduly favorable to Wackenhut's employees, even though Lockheed's contract with Wackenhut was set to expire at a given time. By the same token, it would be benefited, at the expense of its competitors, as a result of a "sweetheart" contract negotiated between Wackenhut and its employees. From the viewpoint of the recipient of the services, dissatisfaction with the labor relations environment may stimulate a desire for change of contractors. *E.g., Tri-State Maintenance Corp. v. NLRB* [408 F.2d 171 (D.C. Cir. 1969)]; 76 Labor Rel. Rep. 230 (1971). Where the relation between the first employer and the second is as attenuated as it is here, and the reasonable expectations of the employees equally attenuated, the application of the successorship doctrine is not authorized by the Labor Management Relations Act.

This is not to say that Burns would be unilaterally free to mesh into its previously recognized Los Angeles County bargaining unit a group of employees such as were involved here who already have designated a collective-bargaining representative in their previous employment. Burns' actions in this regard would be subject to the commands of the Labor Management Relations Act, and to the regulation of the Board under proper application of governing principles. The situation resulting from the addition of a new element of the component work force of an employer has been dealt with by the Board in numerous cases, and various factors are weighed in order to determine whether the new workforce component should be itself a separate bargaining unit, or whether the employees in this component shall be "accreted" to the bargaining unit already in existence. *See e.g., NLRB v. Food Employers Council, Inc.,* 399 F.2d 501 (9th Cir. 1968); *Northwest Galvanizing Co.,* 168 N.L.R.B. 26 (1967). Had the Board made the appropriate factual inquiry and determinations required by the Act, such inquiry might have justified the conclusion that Burns was obligated to recognize and bargain with the union as a representative for its employees at the Lockheed facility.

But the Board, instead of applying this type of analysis to the union's complaints here, concluded that because Burns was a "successor" it was absolutely bound to the mold which had been fashioned by Wackenhut and its emplyees at Lockheed. Burns was thereby precluded from challenging the designation of Lockheed as an appropriate bargaining unit for a year after the original cerification. 61 Stat. 144, 29 U.S.C. § 159(c)(3).

I am unwilling to follow the Board this far down the successorship road, since I believe to do so would substantially undercut the principle of the free choice of bargaining representatives by the employees and designation of the appropriate bargaining unit by the Board which are guaranteed by the Act.

NOTE:

Problems: Does *Burns* foreshadow the eventual demise of *Wiley*, or are the two cases genuinely distinguishable? If so, on what basis? Because *Wiley* was a § 301 contract action and *Burns* a § 8(a)(5) unfair labor practice proceeding? Because *Wiley* dealt only with the duty to arbitrate, and not with the ultimate question of the survival of any substantive terms of the preexisting contract? Because the relationships between the "predecessor" and the "successor" employers were different in the two cases? Do the two decisions vary in their attitudes toward the nature of the collective agreement, and toward the values to be promoted in industrial relations? For contrasting views on these and other questions, see Abodeely, *The Effect of Reorganization, Merger, or Acquisition on the Appropriate*

Bargaining Unit, 39 Geo. Wash. L. Rev. 488 (1971); St. Antoine, *Judicial Caution and the Supreme Court's Labor Decisions, October Term, 1971,* ABA Section of Labor Relations Law, 1972 Proceedings 4, 5-11 (1973); Slicker, *A Reconsideration of the Doctrine of Employer Successorship — A Step Toward a Rational Approach,* 57 Minn. L. Rev. 1051 (1973); Swerdlow, *Freedom of Contract in Labor Law: Burns, H. K. Porter, and Section 8(d),* 51 Texas L. Rev. 1 (1972); Comment, *Contract Rights and the Successor Employer: The Impact of Burns Security,* 71 Mich. L. Rev. 571 (1973); Note, *Contractual Successorship: The Impact of Burns,* 40 U. Chi. L. Rev. 617 (1973).

HOWARD JOHNSON CO. v. HOTEL & RESTAURANT EMPLOYEES DETROIT LOCAL JOINT BOARD

United States Supreme Court
417 U.S. 249, 94 S. Ct. 2236, 41 L. Ed. 2d 46 (1974)

[The Grissom family operated a restaurant and motor lodge under franchise from Howard Johnson, a corporation. Howard Johnson purchased the personal property used in the restaurant and motor lodge from the Grissoms, but they retained the realty, leasing it to the corporation. After hiring only nine of its predecessor's 53 employees, Howard Johnson commenced operation of the establishment with a complement of 45. It refused to recognize the union that had bargained collectively with the Grissoms, and it refused to assume any obligations under the existing labor agreements. The union sued both the Grissoms and Howard Johnson under § 301 to require them to arbitrate the extent of their obligations to the Grissom employees. The Grissoms admitted a duty to arbitrate, but Howard Johnson denied any such duty. The District Court held that Howard Johnson was required to arbitrate the extent of its obligations to the former Grissom employees, and the Court of Appeals affirmed.]

Mr. Justice Marshall delivered the opinion of the Court:

Both courts below relied heavily on this Court's decision in *John Wiley & Sons* v. *Livingston,* 376 U.S. 543 (1964). In *Wiley,* the union representing the employees of a corporation which had disappeared through a merger sought to compel the surviving corporation, which had hired all of the merged corporation's employees and continued to operate the enterprise in a substantially identical form after the merger, to arbitrate under the merged corporation's collective-bargaining agreement. As *Wiley* was this Court's first experience with the difficult "successorship" question, its holding was properly cautious and narrow:

> "We hold that the disappearance by merger of a corporate employer which has entered into a collective bargining

agreement with a union does not automatically terminate all rights of the employees covered by the agreement, and that, in appropriate circumstances, present here, the successor employer may be required to arbitrate with the union under the agreement." *Id.,* at 548.

Mr. Justice Harlan, writing for the Court, emphasized "the central role of arbitration in effectuating national labor policy" and preventing industrial strife, and the need to afford some protection to the interests of the employees during a change of corporate ownership. *Id.,* at 549.

The courts below recognized that the reasoning of *Wiley* was to some extent inconsistent with our more recent decision in *NLRB* v. *Burns International Security Services,* 406 U.S. 272 (1972). Burns was the successful bidder on a contract to provide security services at a Lockheed Aircraft plant, and took a majority of its employees from the ranks of the guards employed at the plant by the previous contractor, Wackenhut. In refusing to enforce the Board's order finding that Burns' failure to honor the substantive provisions of the collective-bargaining agreement negotiated with Wackenhut was an unfair labor practice, we emphasized that freedom of collective bargaining — " 'private bargaining under governmental supervision of the procedure alone, without any official compulsion over the actual terms of the contract' " — was a " 'fundamental premise' " of the federal labor laws, *id.,* at 287, quoting *H. K. Porter Co.* v. *NLRB,* 397 U.S. 99, 108 (1970), and that it was therefore improper to hold Burns to the substantive terms of a collective-bargaining agreement which it had neither expressly nor impliedly assumed. *Burns* also stressed that holding a new employer bound by the substantive terms of the preexisting collective-bargaining agreement might inhibit the free transfer of capital, and that new employers must be free to make substantial changes in the operation of the enterprise. 406 U.S., at 287-288.

The courts below held that *Wiley* rather than *Burns* was controlling here on the ground that *Burns* involved an NLRB order holding the employer bound by the substantive terms of the collective-bargaining agreement, whereas this case, like *Wiley,* involved a § 301 suit to compel arbitration. Although this distinction was in fact suggested by the Court's opinion in *Burns,* see *id.,* at 285-286, we do not believe that the fundamental policies outlined in *Burns* can be so lightly disregarded. In *Textile Workers* v. *Lincoln Mills,* 353 U.S. 448 (1957), this Court held that § 301 of the Labor Management Relations Act authorized the federal courts to develop a federal common law regarding enforcement of collective- bargaining agreements. But *Lincoln Mills* did not envision any freewheeling inquiry into what the federal courts might find to be the most desirable rule, irrespective of congressional pronouncements. Rather, *Lincoln Mills* makes clear that this federal common law must be "fashion[ed] from the policy of our national labor laws." *Id.,* at 456 Mr. Justice Douglas described the process of analysis to be employed:

> "The Labor Management Relations Act expressly furnishes some substantive law. It points out what the parties may or may not do in certain situations. Other problems will lie in the penumbra of express statutory mandates. Some will lack express statutory sanction but will be solved by looking at the policy of the legislation and fashioning a remedy that will effectuate that policy." *Id.,* at 457.

(It would be plainly inconsistent with this view to say that the basic policies found controlling in an unfair labor practice context may be disregarded by the courts in a suit under § 301, and thus to permit the rights enjoyed by the new employer in a successorship context to depend upon the forum in which the union presses its claims. Clearly the reasoning of *Burns* must be taken into account here.)

(We find it unnecessary, however, to decide in the circumstances of this case whether there is any irreconcilable conflict between *Wiley* and *Burns*.) We believe that even on its own terms, *Wiley* does not support the decision of the courts below. The Court in *Burns* recognized that its decision "turn[ed] to a great extent on the precise facts involved here." 406 U.S., at 274. The same observation could have been made in *Wiley,* as indeed it could be made in this case. In our development of the federal common law under § 301, we must necessarily proceed cautiously, in the traditional case-by-case approach of the common law. Particularly in light of the difficulty of the successorship question, the myriad factual circumstances and legal contexts in which it can arise, and the absence of congressional guidance as to its resolution, emphasis on the facts of each case as it arises is especially appropriate. The Court was obviously well aware of this in *Wiley,* as its guarded, almost tentative statement of its holding amply demonstrates.

When the focus is placed on the facts of these cases, it becomes apparent that the decision below is an unwarranted extension of *Wiley* beyond any factual context it may have contemplated. Although it is true that both *Wiley* and this case involve § 301 suits to compel arbitration, the similarity ends there. *Wiley* involved a merger, as a result of which the initial employing entity completely disappeared. In contrast, this case involves only a sale of some assets, and the initial employers remain in existence as viable corporate entities, with substantial revenues from the lease of the motor lodge and restaurant to Howard Johnson. Although we have recognized that ordinarily there is no basis for distinguishing among mergers, consolidations, or purchases of assets in the analysis of successorship problems, see *Golden State Bottling Co.* v. *NLRB*, 414 U.S. 168, 182-183, n. 5 (1973), we think these distinctions are relevant here for two reasons. First, the merger in *Wiley* was conducted "against a background of state law that embodied the general rule that in merger situations the surviving corporation is liable for the obligations of the disappearing corporation," *Burns*, 406 U.S., at 286, which suggests that holding Wiley bound to arbitrate under its predecessor's collective-bargaining agreement may have been fairly within the reasonable expectations of the parties. Second, the disappearance of the original employing entity in the *Wiley* merger meant that unless the union were afforded some remedy against Wiley, it would have no means to enforce the obligations voluntarily undertaken by the merged corporation, to the extent that those obligations vested prior to the merger or to the extent that its promises were intended to survive a change of ownership. Here, in contrast, because the Grissom corporations continue as viable entities with substantial retained assets, the Union does have a realistic remedy to enforce their contractual obligations. Indeed, the Grissoms have agreed to arbitrate the extent of their liability to the Union and their former employees; presumably this arbitration will explore the question whether the Grissoms breached the successorship provisions of their collective-bargaining agreements, and what the remedy for this breach might be.

Even more important, in *Wiley* the surviving corporation hired *all* of the employees of the disappearing corporation. Although, under *Burns*, the surviving corporation may have been entitled to make substantial changes in its operation of the enterprise, the plain fact is that it did not. As the arbitrator in *Wiley* subsequently stated:

> "Although the Wiley merger was effective on October 2, 1961, the former Interscience employees continued to perform the same work on the same products under the same management at the same work place as before the change in the corporate employer." *Interscience Encyclopedia, Inc.,* 55 Lab. Arb. 210, 218 (1970).[4]

The claims which the union sought to compel Wiley to arbitrate were thus the claims of Wiley's employees as to the benefits they were

---

[4] Subsequently, the Interscience plant was closed and the former Interscience employees were integrated into Wiley's work force. The arbitrator, relying in part on the NLRB's decision in *Burns,* held that the provisions of the Interscience collective-bargaining agreement remained in effect for as long as Wiley continued to operate the former Interscience enterprise as a unit in substantially the same manner as prior to the merger, but that the integration of the former Interscience employees into Wiley's operations destroyed this continuity of identity and terminated the effectiveness of the bargaining agreement. 55 Lab. Arb., at 218-220.

entitled to receive in connection with their employment. It was on this basis that the Court in *Wiley* found that there was the "substantial continuity of identity in the business enterprise," 376 U.S., at 551, which it held necessary before the successor employer could be compelled to arbitrate.

Here, however, Howard Johnson decided to select and hire its own independent work force to commence its operation of the restaurant and motor lodge. [5] It therefore hired only nine of the 53 former Grissom employees and none of the Grissom supervisors. The primary purpose of the Union in seeking arbitration here with Howard Johnson is not to protect the rights of Howard Johnson's employees; rather, the Union primarily seeks arbitration on behalf of the former Grissom employees who were *not* hired by Howard Johnson. It is the Union's position that Howard Johnson was bound by the pre-existing collective-bargaining agreement to employ all of these former Grissom employees, except those who could be dismissed in accordance with the "just cause" provision or laid off in accordance with the seniority provision. . . .

What the Union seeks here is completely at odds with the basic principles this Court elaborated in *Burns.* . . .

Clearly, *Burns* establishes that Howard Johnson had the right not to hire any of the former Grissom employees, if it so desired. [8] The Union's effort to circumvent this holding by asserting its claims in a § 301 suit to compel arbitration rather than in an unfair labor practice context cannot be permitted.

---

[5] It is important to emphasize that this is not a case where the successor corporation is the "alter ego" of the predecessor, where it is "merely a disguised continuance of the old employer." Southport Petroleum Co. v. NLRB, 315 U.S. 100, 106 (1942). Such cases involve a mere technical change in the structure or identity of the employing entity, frequently to avoid the effect of the labor laws, without any substantial change in its ownership or management. In these circumstances, the courts have had little difficulty holding that the successor is in reality the same employer and is subject to all the legal and contractual obligations of the predecessor. See Southport Petroleum Co. v. NLRB, supra; NLRB v. Herman Bros. Pet Supply, 325 F. 2d 68 (CA6 1963); NLRB v. Ozark Hardwood Co., 282 F. 2d 1 (CA8 1960); NLRB v. Lewis, 246 F. 2d 886 (CA9 1957).

[8] See Crotona Service Corp., 200 N. L. R. B. 738 (1972). Of course, it is an unfair labor practice for an employer to discriminate in hiring or retention of employees on the basis of union membership or activity under § 8(a)(3) of the National Labor Relations Act, 29 U.S.C. § 158(a)(3). Thus, a new owner could not refuse to hire the employees of his predecessor solely because they were union members or to avoid having to recognize the union. See NLRB v. Burns International Security Services, 406 U.S. 272, 280-281, n. 5 (1972); K. B. & J. Young's Super Markets v. NLRB, 377 F. 2d 463 (CA9), cert. denied, 389 U.S. 841 (1967); Tri State Maintenance Corp. v. NLRB, 132 U.S. App. D. C. 368, 408 F. 2d 171 (1968). There is no suggestion in this case that Howard Johnson in any way discriminated in its hiring against the former Grissom employees because of their union membership, activity, or representation.

We do not believe that *Wiley* requires a successor employer to arbitrate in the circumstances of this case. ⁹ The Court there held that arbitration could not be compelled unless there was "substantial continuity of identity in the business enterprise" before and after a change of ownership, for otherwise the duty to arbitrate would be "something imposed from without, not reasonably to be found in the particular bargaining agreement and the acts of the parties involved." 376 U.S., at 551. This continuity of identity in the business enterprise necessarily includes, we think, a substantial continuity in the identity of the work force across the change in ownership. The *Wiley* Court seemingly recognized this, as it found the requisite continuity present there in reliance on the "wholesale transfer" of Interscience employees to Wiley. *Ibid.* This view is reflected in the emphasis most of the lower courts have placed on whether the successor employer hires a majority of the predecessor's employees in determining the legal obligations of the successor in § 301 suits under *Wiley.* This interpretation of *Wiley* is consistent also with the Court's concern with affording protection to those employees who are in fact retained in "[t]he transition from one corporate organization to another" from sudden changes in the terms and conditions of their employment, and with its belief that industrial

---

⁹ The Court of Appeals stated that "[t]he first question we must face is whether Howard Johnson is a successor employer," 482 F. 2d, at 492, and, finding that it was, that the next question was whether a successor is required to arbitrate under the collective-bargaining agreement of its predecessor, *id.,* at 494, which the court found was resolved by *Wiley.* We do not believe that this artificial division between these questions is a helpful or appropriate way to approach these problems. The question whether Howard Johnson is a "successor" is simply not meaningful in the abstract. Howard Johnson is of course a successor employer in the sense that it succeeded to operation of a restaurant and motor lodge formerly operated by the Grissoms. But the real question in each of these "successorship" cases is, on the particular facts, what are the legal obligations of the new employer to the employees of the former owner or their representative? The answer to this inquiry requires analysis of the interests of the new employer and the employees and of the policies of the labor laws in light of the facts of each case and the particular legal obligation which is at issue, whether it be the duty to recognize and bargain with the union, the duty to remedy unfair labor practices, the duty to arbitrate, etc. There is, and can be, no single definition of "successor" which is applicable in every legal context. A new employer, in other words, may be a successor for some purposes and not for others. See Golden State Bottling Co. v. NLRB, 414 U.S. 168, 181 (1973); International Assn. of Machinists v. NLRB, 134 U.S. App. D.C. 239, 244, 414 F. 2d 1135, 1140 (1969) (Leventhal, J., concurring); Goldberg, The Labor Law Obligations of a Successor Employer, 63 Nw. U. L. Rev. 735 (1969); Comment, Contractual Successorship: The Impact of *Burns,* 40 U. Chi. L. Rev. 617, 619 n. 10 (1973).

Thus, our holding today is that Howard Johnson was not required to arbitrate with the Union representing the former Grissom employees in the circumstances of this case. We necessarily do not decide whether Howard Johnson is or is not a "successor employer" for any other purpose.

strife would be avoided if these employees' claims were resolved by arbitration rather than by " 'the relative strength . . . of the contending forces.' " *Id.,* at 549, quoting *United Steelworkers* v. *Warrior & Gulf Navigation Co.,* 363 U.S. 574, 580 (1960). At the same time, it recognizes that the employees of the terminating employer have no legal right to continued employment with the new employer, and avoids the difficulties inherent in the Union's position in this case. This holding is compelled, in our view, if the protection afforded employee interests in a change of ownership by *Wiley* is to be reconciled with the new employer's right to operate the enterprise with his own independent labor force.

Since there was plainly no substantial continuity of identity in the work force hired by Howard Johnson with that of the Grissoms, and no express or implied assumption of the agreement to arbitrate, the courts below erred in compelling the Company to arbitrate the extent of its obligations to the former Grissom employees. Accordingly, the judgment of the Court of Appeals must be

Reversed.

[The dissent of Mr. Justice Douglas is omitted.]

NOTES:

(1) Consider the following problems in light of the Supreme Court's holding and rationale in Howard Johnson;

(a) How much room for the application of *Wiley* in successorship cases remains after *Howard Johnson*? Are courts as well as the Board precluded from imposing contractual obligations on a recalcitrant "successor?" *See Bartenders & Culinary Workers Union, Local 340 v. Howard Johnson Co.,* 535 F.2d 1160, 1163-65 (9th Cir. 1976). Or has *Wiley* merely been restricted to cases in which the new employer retains a majority of his predecessor's employees? If so, isn't *Wiley* practically a dead letter, since an employer may unilaterally avoid any obligations under his predecessor's agreement simply by refusing to hire a majority of his predecessor's employees (subject to § 8(a)(3)'s prohibition against discrimination in hiring on the basis of union membership)?

(b) Why should the number of employees retained by an employer determine whether he is obligated to honor obligations or correct violations of his predecessors' contract?

(c) What alternatives to arbitration or a breach of contract suit against the "successor" does a union have after *Howard Johnson*?

(2) What happens if the successor has an outstanding contract with a second union at the same time he hires a majority of his

predecessor's employees? *Compare McGuire v. Humble Oil & Ref. Co.*, 355 F.2d 352 (2d Cir. 1966), *noted* in 66 Colum. L. Rev. 967 (1966) *and IAM v. Howmet Corp.*, 466 F.2d 1249 (9th Cir. 1972) *with Monroe Sander Corp. v. Livingston*, 377 F.2d 6 (2d Cir. 1967). *See* Gorman, Basic Text on Labor Law 578-80 (1976).

Chapter 8

RELATION OF ARBITRATION TO UNFAIR LABOR PRACTICES AND OTHER PUBLIC LAW ISSUES

A. THE PROBLEM

Although most judges and commentators either accept or pay lip service to the notion that arbitration is the most efficient means by which parties to a labor agreement can resolve their *contractual* grievances, they have long questioned the wisdom and propriety of allowing arbitrators to resolve issues of public law rather than (or in addition to) contractual matters. The same questions have been raised by arbitrators themselves, who have frequently been confronted with questions of external law that often seem inextricably linked with the contractual matters before them.

The materials which follow deal with the issues and considerations that come into play in cases where terms and conditions of employment are regulated by public law, *i.e.,* legislation, administrative regulations, and decisional law, as well as by a collective bargaining agreement. Because of the growing amount of state and federal regulation of employment relations, there is bound to be a great deal of overlap between contractual and statutory issues. For example, the parties to a labor agreement may include (1) a clause prohibiting discrimination on the basis of sex or race paralleling Title VII of the 1964 Civil Rights Act, (2) wage agreements, which are also subject to the requirements of the Fair Labor Standards Act (FLSA), (3) a provision dealing with health and safety conditions on the jobsite similar to the requirements of the Occupational Safety and Health Act of 1970, and so on. Among the most important questions that will be considered are as follows: (1) What should be the relationship between private grievance arbitration and public law? (2) Should courts or other tribunals defer to arbitration awards or to labor agreements that provide for binding grievance arbitration? (3) Should labor arbitrators look to public law in interpreting private contracts? (4) Should parties attempt to incorporate public law in their collective bargaining agreements? (5) Will the development of public law governing employment relations diminish the role of labor arbitration?

B. CONCURRENT JURISDICTION OF THE BOARD, THE COURTS, AND ARBITRATORS

Carey v. Westinghouse Electric Corp., 375 U.S. 261, 84 S. Ct. 401, 11 L. Ed. 2d 320 (1964). IUE was the certified bargaining representative of "all production and maintenance employees" at the plant where the controversy arose; "salaried, technical" employees were specifically excluded. IUE and Westinghouse were parties to an agreement which provided for arbitration of unresolved disputes, including those involving the "interpretation, application or claimed violation" of the Agreement. IUE filed a grievance asserting that certain employees represented by Westinghouse Independent Salaried Unions (Federation) were performing production and maintenance work. Federation represented a bargaining unit of "all salaried, technical" employees; from this unit "all production and maintenance employees" were excluded. Westinghouse refused to arbitrate, claiming the controversy concerned a representation matter within the exclusive jurisdiction of the National Labor Relations Board, although the Board's jurisdiction had not, in fact, been invoked. IUE petitioned the Supreme Court of New York for an order compelling arbitration, but such order was refused on the ground urged by Westinghouse. This decision was affirmed on appeal through the New York appellate courts. The Supreme Court, in an opinion by Mr. Justice Douglas, with Justices Black and Clark dissenting, reversed and held that the dispute should go to arbitration.

The Court held that, whether the dispute was jurisdictional or representational in nature, the availability of recourse to the NLRB did not preclude contract arbitration. In reaching this conclusion, the Court relied upon *Smith v. Evening News Ass'n,* 371 U.S. 195 (1962), in which it had been held that the existence of a remedy under the NLRA for an unfair labor practice did not bar individual employees from seeking damages for breach of a duplicative provision in a collective bargaining agreement. The opinion stated: "We think the same policy considerations are applicable here. . . ."

A second issue in the case arose out of the fact that "only one of the two unions involved in the controversy has moved the state courts to compel arbitration." Therefore, as the Court further stated, "unless the other union intervenes, an adjudication of the arbiter might not put an end to the dispute." The Court did not regard this fact as an obstacle to proceeding with the arbitration.

NOTES:

(1) Following the decision in the principal case, the Employer filed several motions before the NLRB which sought, among other things,

the clarification of the units represented by the Federation. The Board postponed the hearings on the motions pending the outcome of the arbitration between the Employer and the IUE. In the arbitration proceeding, *Westinghouse Electric Corp.,* 45 L.A. 161 (1965), the arbitrator, I. Robert Feinberg, sustained the IUE's claim in part to the extent that the Employer was directed to recognize the IUE as the bargaining representative of technicians found performing production and maintenance works. The rest of the technicians remained in the unit represented by the Federation. In "splitting" the technicians, the arbitrator used primarily the job descriptions as the basis for his award. When the NLRB resumed hearings on the motions, it granted the motion to clarify the Federation's unit and dismissed the others. The Board refused to accept as dispositive the arbitral award because all the parties involved were not before the arbitrator. Consequently, according to the Board, the ultimate issue of representation could not be decided by the arbitrator through an interpretation of the contract but could be resolved only through the use of Board criteria for unit determinations. While giving "some consideration to the award," the Board proceeded to make a different unit allocation by the use of such criteria as bargaining history, integration of the operations, and the possible adverse effect of splitting the employees. *Westinghouse Electric Corp.,* 162 N.L.R.B. No. 81 (1967).

(2) In *Plumbers, Local 525 v. Reynolds Electrical & Engineering Co.,* 380 F.2d 474 (9th Cir. 1967), the Court of Appeals, in a *per curiam* decision, held that pending an NLRB decision on an employer's unfair labor practice charge against a union, the action to compel arbitration of a grievance filed by the union must be stayed. The Court found that the subject matter of the grievance and the unfair labor practice complaint related to the same issue; hence, according to the Court, the disposition by the NLRB of the complaint in favor of the employer would leave nothing to be decided in the arbitration.

But see Machinists, Aeronautical Industrial District, Lodge 751 v. Boeing Co., 65 L.R.R.M. 2950 (W.D. Wash. 1967), where a district court held that the possibility that the employer might be subject to charges of unfair labor practice was no basis for denying arbitration since such a possibility would not arise until the arbitrator decides in favor of the union, and in that event such award, if contrary to law, could be reviewed in courts.

(3) For comments on *Carey* see Smith & Jones, *The Supreme Court and Labor Dispute Arbitration: The Emerging Federal Law,* 63 Mich. L. Rev. 751, 753, 768-71 (1965); Smith & Jones, *The Impact of the Emerging Federal Law of Grievance Arbitration on Judges, Arbitrators, and Parties,* 52 Va. L. Rev. 831, 865 (1966).

(4) For a spirited debate on the capacity of an arbitrator to induce

(or strong-arm) the second union into an arbitration in a *Carey* situation see Jones, *Autobiography of a Decision: The Function of Innovation in Labor Arbitration, and the "National Steel" Orders of Joinder and Interpleader,* 10 U.C.L.A. L. Rev. 987 (1963); Bernstein, *Nudging and Shoving All Parties to a Jurisdictional Dispute Into Arbitration: The Dubious Procedure of National Steel,* 78 Harv. L. Rev. 784 (1965); Jones, *On Nudging and Shoving the National Steel Arbitration Into a Dubious Procedure,* 79 Harv. L. Rev. 327 (1965); Jones, *Sequel in the Evolution of the Trilateral Arbitration of Jurisdictional Labor Disputes — The Supreme Court's Gift to Embattled Employers,* 15 U.C.L.A.L. Rev. 877 (1968); Jones, *An Arbitral Answer to a Judicial Dilemma: The Carey Decision and Trilateral Arbitration of Jurisdictional Disputes,* 11 U.C.L.A.L. Rev. 327 (1964).

(5) Under the Railway Labor Act, the National Railroad Adjustment Board is authorized (and required) to summon the disputing unions before it in order to dispose of all claims to work assignments in a single proceeding. *Transportation-Communication Employees Union v. Union Pac. R.R.,* 385 U.S. 157 (1966).

(6) In considering the 1947 revisions of the NLRA, Congress rejected the proposal that breaches of collective bargaining agreements should be made unfair labor practices, and, instead, left the enforcement of the labor agreement to the "usual processes of law," and made express provision for such enforcement in § 301 of the LMRA. H.R. Conf. Rep. No. 510, 80th Cong., 1st Sess. 42 (1947). But labor agreements invariably include one or more provisions which, arguably, duplicate or overlap provisions in the NLRA. Examples are the "recognition" clause, which could be said to be the contractual counterpart of the statutory "duty to bargain," the related definition of the "bargaining unit" (which often is in the precise language of an NLRB certification), a provision prohibiting discrimination against employees because of union affiliation or activities (paralleling one of the NLRA proscribed unfair labor practices), or "hot cargo" type of provisions. Contractual enforcement of these and other provisions is typically through the arbitration process, or, if not, through court proceedings initiated pursuant to § 301 of the LMRA.

It is accepted NLRB doctrine that an employer's unilateral change in working conditions, without affording the union an opportunity to bargain, is a violation of § 8(a)(5) of the NLRA. But where a collective bargaining agreement is in effect, that agreement obviously is the standard of many if not all working conditions prevailing for the bargaining unit. Moreover, § 8(d) makes it part of the duty to bargain to refrain from a strike or lockout to "terminate or modify" a contract prior to its expiration date.

NLRB v. C & C PLYWOOD CORP.

United States Supreme Court
385 U.S. 421, 87 S. Ct. 559, 17 L. Ed. 2d 486 (1967)

Mr. Justice Stewart delivered the opinion of the Court.

The respondent employer was brought before the National Labor Relations Board to answer a complaint that its inauguration of a premium pay plan during the term of collective agreement, without prior consultation with the union representing its employees, violated the duties imposed by §§ 8(a)(5) and (1) of the National Labor Relations Act. The Board issued a cease-and-desist order, rejecting the claim that the respondent's action was authorized by the collective agreement. . . .[34]

In August 1962, the Plywood, Lumber, and Saw Mill Workers, Local No. 2405 was certified as the bargaining representative of the respondent's production and maintenance employees. The agreement which resulted from collective bargaining contained the following provision:

"Article XVII

"WAGES

"A. A classified wage scale has been agreed upon by the Employer and Union, and has been signed by the parties and thereby made a part of the written agreement. The Employer reserves the right to pay a premium rate over and above the contractual classified wage rate to reward any particular employee for some special fitness, skill, aptitude or the like. The payment of such a premium rate shall not be considered a permanent increase in the rate of that position and may, at the sole option of the Employer, be reduced to the contractual rate. . . ."

The agreement also stipulated that wages should be "closed" during the period it was effective and that neither party should be obligated to bargain collectively with respect to any matter not specifically referred to in the contract. Grievance machinery was established, but no ultimate arbitration of grievances or other disputes was provided.

Less than three weeks after this agreement was signed, the respondent posted a notice that all members of the "glue spreader" crews would be paid $2.50 per hour if their crews met specified biweekly (and later weekly) production standards, although under

---

[34] The NLRB's order directed respondent to bargain with the union upon the latter's request and similarly to rescind any payment plan which it had unilaterally instituted.

the "classified wage scale" referred to in the above quoted Art. XVII of the agreement, the members of these crews were to be paid hourly wages ranging from $2.15 to $2.29, depending upon their function within the crew. When the union learned of this premium pay plan through one of its members, it immediately asked for a conference with the respondent. During the meetings between the parties which followed this request, the employer indicated a willingness to discuss the terms of the plan, but refused to rescind it pending those discussions.

It was this refusal which prompted the union to charge the respondent with an unfair labor practice in violation of §§ 8(a)(5) and (1). The trial examiner found that the respondent had instituted the premium-pay program in good-faith reliance upon the right reserved to it in the collective agreement. He, therefore, dismissed the complaint. The Board reversed. Giving consideration to the history of negotiations between the parties, as well as the express provisions of the collective agreement, the Board ruled the union had not ceded power to the employer unilaterally to change the wage system as it had. For while the agreement specified different hourly pay for different members of the glue spreader crews and allowed for merit increases for "particular employee[s]," the employer had placed all the members of these crews on the same wage scale and had made it a function of the production output of the crew as a whole.

In refusing to enforce the Board's order, the Court of Appeals did not decide that the premium-pay provision of the labor agreement had been misinterpreted by the Board. Instead, it held the Board did not have jurisdiction to find the respondent had violated § 8(a) of the Labor Act, because the "existence . . . of an unfair labor practice [did] not turn a good-faith dispute as to the correct meaning of the provisions of the collective bargaining agreement. . . ." 351 F.2d at 228.

The respondent does not question the proposition that an employer may not unilaterally institute merit increases during the term of a collective agreement unless some provision of the contract authorizes him to do so. See *NLRB v. J.H. Allison & Co.,* 165 F.2d 766 (6th Cir. 1948), *cert. denied,* 335 U.S. 814 (1948). *Cf. Beacon Piece Dyeing Co.,* 121 N.L.R.B. 953 (1958). The argument is, rather, that since the contract contained a provision which *might* have allowed the respondent to institute the wage plan in question, the Board was powerless to determine whether that provision *did* authorize the respondent's action, because the question was one for a state or federal court under § 301 of the Act.

In evaluating this contention, it is important first to point out that the collective bargaining agreement contained no arbitration clause. [35]   The contract did not provide grievance procedures, but the end result of those procedures, if differences between the parties remained unresolved, was economic warfare, not "the therapy of arbitration." *Carey v. Westinghouse Corp.,* 375 U.S. 261, 272 (1964). Thus, the Board's action in this case was in no way inconsistent with its previous recognition of arbitration as "an instrument of national labor policy for composing contractual differences." *International Harvester Co.,* 138 N.L.R.B. 923, 926 (1962), *aff'd sub nom., Ramsey v. NLRB,* 327 F.2d 784 (7th Cir. 1964), *cert. denied,* 377 U.S. 1003 (1964).

The respondent's argument rests primarily upon the legislative history of the 1947 amendments to the National Labor Relations Act. It is said that the rejection by Congress of a bill which would have given the Board unfair labor practice jurisdiction over all breaches of collective bargaining agreements shows that the Board is without power to decide any case involving the interpretation of a labor contract. We do not draw that inference from this legislative history.

When Congress determined that the Board should not have general jurisdiction over all alleged violations of collective bargaining agreements and that such matters should be placed within the jurisdiction of the courts, it was acting upon a principle which this Court had already recognized:

"The Railway Labor Act, like the National Labor Relations Act, does not undertake governmental regulation of wages, hours, or working conditions. Instead it seeks to provide a means by which agreement may be reached with respect to them." *Terminal Railroad Ass'n v. Brotherhood of Railroad Trainmen,* 318 U.S. 1, 6 (1943). To have conferred upon the National Labor Relations Board generalized power to determine the rights of parties under all collective agreements would have been a step toward governmental regulation of the terms of those agreements. We view Congress' decision not to give the Board that broad power as a refusal to take this step.

But in this case the Board has not construed a labor agreement to determine the extent of the contractual rights which were given the union by the employer. It has not imposed its own view of what the terms and conditions of the labor agreement should be. It has done no more than merely enforce a statutory right which Congress considered necessary to allow labor and management to get on with the process of reaching fair terms and conditions of employment — "to provide a means by which agreement may be reached." The

---

[35] The Court of Appeals in this case relied upon its previous decision in Square D Co. v. NLRB, 332 F.2d 360 (9th Cir. 1964). But *Square D* involved a collective agreement that provided for arbitration. *See* Note, *Use of an Arbitration Clause,* 41 Ind. L.J. 455, 469 (1966).

Board's interpretation went only so far as was necessary to determine that the union did not agree to give up these statutory safeguards. Thus, the Board, in necessarily construing a labor agreement to decide this unfair labor practice case, has not exceeded the jurisdiction laid out for it by Congress.

This conclusion is re-enforced by previous judicial recognition that a contractual defense does not divest the Labor Board of jurisdiction. For example, in *Mastro Plastics Corp. v. NLRB,* 350 U.S. 270 (1956), the legality of an employer's refusal to reinstate strikers was based upon the Board's construction of a "no strike" clause in the labor agreement, which the employer contended allowed him to refuse to take back workers who had walked out in protest over his unfair labor practice. The strikers applied to the Board for reinstatement and back pay. In giving the requested relief, the Board was forced to construe the scope of the "no strike" clause. This Court, in affirming, stressed that the whole case turned "upon the proper interpretation of the particular contract . . . ." 350 U.S. at 279. Thus, *Mastro Plastics* stands squarely against the respondent's theory as to the Board's lack of power in the present case.

If the Board in a case like this had no jurisdiction to consider a collective agreement prior to an authoritative construction by the courts, labor organizations would face inordinate delays in obtaining vindication of their statutory rights. Where, as here, the parties have not provided for arbitration, the union would have to institute a court action to determine the applicability of the premium pay provision of the collective bargaining agreement. [36]   If it succeeded in court, the union would then have to go back to the Labor Board to begin an unfair labor practice proceeding. It is not unlikely that this would add years to the already lengthy period required to gain relief from the board. Congress cannot have intended to place such obstacles in the way of the Board's effective enforcement of statutory duties. For in the labor field, as in few others, time is crucially important in obtaining relief. *Amalgamated Clothing Workers v. Richman Bros. Co.,* 348 U.S. 511, 526 (1955) (dissenting opinion).

The legislative history of the Labor Act, the precedent interpreting it, and the interest of its efficient administration thus all lead to the conclusion that the Board had jurisdiction to deal with the unfair

---

[36] The precise nature of the union's case in court is not readily apparent. If damages for breach of contract were sought, the union would have difficulty in establishing the amount of injury caused by respondent's action. For the real injury in this case is to the union's status as bargaining representative, and it would be difficult to translate such damage into dollars and cents. If an injunction were sought to vindicate the union's contractual rights, the problem of the applicability of the Norris-LaGuardia Act would have to be faced. . . . Thus, it may be that the only remedy in court which would be available to the union would be a suit for declaratory judgment, assuming such a suit in these circumstances would be maintainable under state or federal law.

labor practice charge in this case. We hold that the Court of Appeals was in error in deciding to the contrary.

The remaining question, not reached by the Court of Appeals, is whether the Board was wrong in concluding that the contested provision in the collective agreement gave the respondent no unilateral right to institute its premium pay plan. In reaching this conclusion, the Board relied upon its experience with labor relations and the Act's clear emphasis upon the protection of free collective bargaining. We cannot disapprove of the Board's approach. For the law of labor agreements cannot be based upon abstract definitions unrelated to the context in which the parties bargained and the basic regulatory scheme underlying that context. See Cox, The Legal Nature of Collective Bargaining Agreements, 57 Mich. L. Rev. 1 (1958). Nor can we say that the Board was wrong in holding that the union had not foregone its statutory right to bargain about the pay plan inaugurated by the respondent. For the disputed contract provision referred to increases for "particular employee[s]," not groups of workers. And there was nothing in it to suggest that the carefully worked out wage differentials for various members of the glue spreader crew could be invalidated by the respondent's decision to pay all members of the crew the same wage.

The judgment is accordingly reversed and the case is remanded to the Court of Appeals with directions to enforce the Board's order.

Reversed and Remanded.

NOTE:

Would the result in the principal case have been different if the collective-bargaining agreement had contained a provision for final and binding arbitration? If so, on what theory? Does an arbitration clause constitute an agreement to channel collective bargaining in a particular way, or a waiver of a statutory right to bargain? *See, e.g., Timken Roller Bearing Co. v. NLRB,* 161 F.2d 949 (6th Cir. 1947); *Square D Co. v. NLRB,* 332 F.2d 360 (9th Cir. 1964). If so, why wasn't a similar agreement or waiver found in the contract in the principal case, which provided for a grievance procedure and, presumably, permitted a court suit if necessary to resolve disputes? In *NLRB v. Huttig Sash & Door Co.,* 377 F.2d 964 (8th Cir. 1967), a court of appeals, relying on *C & C Plywood,* upheld the Board's jurisdiction to find an employer guilty of an unfair labor practice in unilaterally reducing wages, even though the contract contained an arbitration clause.

NLRB v. Acme Industrial Co., 385 U.S. 432, 87 S. Ct. 565, 17 L. Ed. 2d 495 (1967). A collective bargaining agreement provided that if plant equipment was moved to another location, employees subject as a result to layoff or reduction in grade could transfer under certain conditions to the new location. The contract also contained a grievance procedure culminating in binding arbitration. When the union discovered that certain machinery was being removed from the employer's plant, it filed contract grievances and requested information about the dates of the move, the destination of the equipment, the amount of machinery involved, the reason for the transfer, and the new use to be made of the equipment. The employer replied it had no duty to furnish this information since no layoffs or reductions had occurred within the five-day time limit for filing grievances. The NLRB ruled the employer had refused to bargain in good faith, observing that the information sought was "necessary in order to enable the Union to evaluate intelligently the grievances filed" and pointing out that the agreement contained no "clause by which the Union waives its statutory right to such information." The Supreme Court upheld the Board's order. The "duty to bargain unquestionably extends beyond the period of contract negotiations and applies to labor-management relations during the term of an agreement." Moreover, the Board did not have to await an arbitrator's determination of the relevancy of the information before enforcing the union's statutory rights under § 8(a)(5). The Board "was not making a binding construction of the labor contract. It was only acting upon the probability that the desired information was relevant, and that it would be of use to the union in carrying out its statutory duties and responsibilities. . . . Thus, the assertion of jurisdiction by the Board in this case in no way threatens the power which the parties have given the arbitrator to make binding interpretations of the labor agreement."

NLRB v. STRONG

United States Supreme Court
393 U.S. 357, 89 S. Ct. 541, 21 L. Ed. 2d 546 (1969)

Mr. Justice White delivered the opinion of the Court.

The Roofing Contractors Association of Southern California, of which respondent was then a member, negotiated a collective bargaining contract with the Roofers Union effective August 15, 1963, establishing compensation levels for the employees of member firms for the next four years. On August 20, 1963, respondent sought to withdraw from the multiple employer bargaining association which had negotiated this agreement. He then refused repeated demands from the union that he sign the contract. At length, the union filed unfair labor practice charges with the National Labor Relations Board, which found that respondent's refusal to sign the contract which had been negotiated on his behalf by the Association was a violation of §§ 8(a) (5) and (1) of the National Labor Relations Act, 29 U.S.C. §§ 158 (a)(5) and (1). The Board ordered respondent to sign the contract, cease and desist from unfair labor practices, post notices, and "[p]ay to the appropriate source any fringe benefits provided for in the above described contract." 152 N.L.R.B. 9, 14 (1965). The Court of Appeals enforced the Board's order except as it required the payment of fringe benefits. That part of the order, the Court of Appeals said, "is an order to respondent to carry out provisions of the contract and is beyond the power of the Board." 386 F.2d 929, 933 (1967). . . .

Believing the remedy provided by the Board was well within its powers, we reverse the judgment of the Court of Appeals. Section 10(c) of the Act empowers the Board when it adjudicates an unfair labor practice to issue "an order requiring such person to cease and desist from such unfair practice, and to take such affirmative action including reinstatement of employees with or without back pay, as will effectuate the policies of this Act." . . . This grant of remedial power is a broad one. It does not authorize punitive measures, but "[m]aking the workers whole for losses suffered on account of an unfair labor practice is part of the vindication of the public policy which the Board enforces." *Phelps Dodge Corp. v. NLRB*, 313 U.S. 177, 197 (1941). Back pay is one of the simpler and more explicitly authorized remedies utilized to attain this end.

Here the unfair labor practice was the failure of the employer to sign and acknowledge the existence of a collective bargaining agreement which had been negotiated and concluded on his behalf. There is no dispute that respondent withdrew from the Roofing Contractors Association too late to escape the binding force of the agreement it had negotiated for him, supplanting previous agreements which had been negotiated in the same way. Nor, in light of the obligation of an employer bargaining in good faith to sign a contract reducing agreed terms to writing, *H. J. Heinz Co. v. NLRB*, 311 U.S. 514, 524-526 (1941), is it argued that respondent's failure to sign the agreement was not an unfair labor practice. The judgment of the Board in these respects is not now challenged. The remedy ordered by the Board included a direction to pay the fringe benefits which would have been paid had the employer signed the agreement and thereby recognized his legal obligations which had matured during the collective bargaining process. This is no more than the Act and cases like *Phelps-Dodge* plainly authorize.

The challenge of the employer, in brief, is that ordering the payment of fringe benefits reserved in the contract inserts the Board into the enforcement of the collective bargaining agreement, contrary to the policy and scheme of the statute. [4] Admittedly, the

---

[4] The fact that the payments in question here did not constitute direct pay to the employees is irrelevant in our view of this case. Whether the payments were made to the employees, who then contributed them to union trust funds in the form of higher union dues, or whether as here they passed straight from the employer to the trust funds, the final result is the same. And it is just as much in the interest of "effectuat[ing] the policies of this Act," and of making the employees whole, to require the payments in either case.

Board has no plenary authority to administer and enforce collective bargaining contracts. Those agreements are normally enforced as agreed upon by the parties, usually through grievance and arbitration procedures, and ultimately by the courts. But the business of the Board, among other things, is to adjudicate and remedy unfair labor practices. Its authority to do so is not "affected by any other means of adjustment or prevention that has been or may be established by agreement, law, or otherwise. . . ." § 10(a), 61 Stat. 146, 29 U.S.C. § 160(a). Hence, it has been made clear that in some circumstances the authority of the Board and the law of the contract are overlapping, concurrent regimes, neither pre-empting the other. *NLRB v. C & C Plywood Corp.,* 385 U.S. 421 (1967); *Carey v. Westinghouse Electric Corp.,* 375 U.S. 261, 268 (1964); *Smith v. Evening News Assn.,* 371 U.S. 195, 197-198 (1962); *Teamsters Local 174 v. Lucas Flour Co.,* 369 U.S. 95, 101, n.9 (1961). Arbitrators and courts are still the principal sources of contract interpretation, but the Board may proscribe conduct which is an unfair labor practice even though it is also a breach of contract remediable as such by arbitration and in the courts. *Smith v. Evening News Assn.,* 371 U.S. 195, 197-198 (1962). It may also, if necessary to adjudicate an unfair labor practice, interpret and give effect to the terms of a collective bargaining contract. *NLRB v. C & C Plywood Corp.,* 385 U.S. 421 (1967).

Bearing more precisely on this case, the Board is expressly invited by the Act to determine whether an employer has refused to bargain in good faith and thereby violated § 8(a)(5) by resisting "the execution of a written contract incorporating any agreement reached if requested by either party. . . ." § 8(d), 61 Stat. 142, 29 U.S.C. § 158(d); *H. J. Heinz Co. v. NLRB,* 311 U.S. 524-526 (1941). The Board is not trespassing on forbidden territory when it inquires whether negotiations have produced a bargain which the employer has refused to sign and honor, particularly when the employer has refused to recognize the very existence of the contract providing for the arbitration on which he now insists. To this extent the collective contract is the Board's affair, and an effective remedy for refusal to sign is its proper business.

Firing an employee for union membership may be a breach of contract open to arbitration, but whether it is or not, it is also an unfair labor practice which may be remedied by reinstatement with back pay under § 10(c) even though the Board's order mandates the very compensation reserved by the contract. Cf. *NLRB v.*

Great Dane Trailers, Inc., 388 U.S. 26 (1967); *Mastro Plastics Corp. v. NLRB,* 350 U.S. 270 (1956); *Wallace Corp. v. NLRB,* 323 U.S. 248 (1944).

The case before us is little, if any, different. The act of refusing to sign the collective bargaining agreement may not have been a breach of contract, but it was an unfair practice. Once adjudicated, it could be remedied by a Board order requiring payment of those fringe benefits which would have been paid had the employer signed and acknowledged the contract which had been duly negotiated on his behalf. The judgment of the Court of Appeals is reversed.

It is so ordered.

Mr. Justice Black concurs in the reversal of the Court of Appeals' judgment, but he would direct that the case be remanded to the Board for it to determine whether to submit to arbitration in accord with the contract.

[The dissenting opinion of Mr. Justice Douglas is omitted.]

NOTE:

In *NLRB v. Huttig Sash & Door Co.,* 377 F.2d 964 (8th Cir. 1967), the court of appeals, relying on *C & C Plywood,* upheld the Board's jurisdiction to find an employer guilty of an unfair labor practice in unilaterally reducing wages, even though there was an arbitration clause in the contract. Subsequently, the Board has held that the availability of contract grievance procedures has not precluded the union from asserting a right to bargain about changes even where the contract contained a "zipper clause." For example, in *Unit Drop Forge Division,* 171 N.L.R.B. No. 73 (1968), the contract provided,

> The company and the union for the life of this agreement, each voluntarily and unqualifiedly waives the right and each agrees that the other shall not be obligated, to bargain collectively with respect to any subject or matter referred to, or covered in this agreement, or with respect to any subject or matter not specifically referred to or covered in this agreement even though such subject or matter may not have been within the knowledge or contemplation of either or both of the parties at the time that they negotiated or signed this agreement.

A majority of the Board concluded that the language of the "zipper clause" was not sufficiently clear and unmistakable to enable the employer to change the operations on its loading platform and eliminate an incentive rate position without bargaining first.

C. DEFERRAL TO ARBITRATION BY THE NATIONAL LABOR RELATIONS BOARD

1. The Spielberg Doctrine: Post-Arbitral Deferral

In the leading case of *Spielberg Mfg. Co.*, 112 NLRB 1080, 1082 (1955), the Board set forth three general conditions under which it would give "recognition" to an arbitrator's award: "[T]he proceedings appear to have been fair and regular, all parties had agreed to be bound, and the decision of the arbitration panel is not clearly repugnant to the purposes and policies of the Act."

a. Fair and Regular Proceedings

Spielberg has been applied to decisions of grievance resolution tribunals and other than neutral arbitrators, such as the decision of a joint panel consisting of an equal number of employer and union representatives. *United Parcel Service*, 232 NLRB No. 179, 96 LRRM 1288 (1977). *But see, IBEW, Local 367*, 230 NLRB No. 12, 96 LRRM 1182 (1977). The Board may or may not defer to an arbitrator's award where a party to the Board proceeding was absent from the Arbitration proceeding. *Compare Raley's Supermarkets,* 143 NLRB 256 (1963) (Board deferred under *Spielberg* where, although petitioner was not represented at arbitration hearing, its position was identical with that of the employer, who vigorously asserted its position in the arbitration proceeding); *with Horn & Harvard Co.,* 173 NLRB 1077 (1968), *enforced,* 439 F.2d 674 (2d Cir. 1971) and *Retail Clerks Union* (Esgro, Inc.), 206 NLRB 931 (1973). Similarly, the Board has refused to defer to an arbitration award that does not bind all affected parties. *T.I.M.E.-DC, Inc.,* 225 NLRB 1175 (1976). The Board will not defer to an arbitration award if the charging party's interests conflicted with those of his representative at the arbitration proceeding. *Longshoremen (ILWU) Local 27,* 205 NLRB 1141 (1973), *enforced,* 514 F.2d 481 (9th Cir. 1975); *Jo-Jo Management Corp.,* 225 NLRB 1133 (1976).

b. Repugnance to the Purposes and Policies of the Act

At least two courts of appeals have upheld Board refusals to defer to arbitration awards which it considered repugnant to the purposes and policies of the Act. *Dries & Krump Mfg. Co. v. NLRB,* 544 F.2d 320 (7th Cir. 1976),*enforcing* 221 NLRB 309 (1975); *Hawaiian Hauling Service, Ltd. v. NLRB,* 545 F.2d 674 (9th Cir. 1976), enforcing 219 NLRB 765 (1975). Cases in which the Board has found an arbitrator's award repugnant to the Act and not entitled to recognition under *Spielberg,* include *Douglas Aircraft Co.,* 234 NLRB No. 80, 97 LRRM 1242 (1978) (award penalized employee for exercising statutory right to file unfair labor practice charge); *Shippers Dispatch, Inc.,* 223 NLRB 439 (1976) (award denied grievance of employee who claimed employer discriminated against him because of his use of grievance procedure); *Dries & Krump Mfg. Co. v. NLRB,* 221 NLRB 309 (1975), *enforced,* 544 F.2d 320 (7th Cir. 1976) (award ruled against grievant who was discharged for engaging in protected concerted activity).

In addition, the Board will not defer to arbitration awards which involve issues solely within the Board's province or which involve violations of certain sections of the Act, even if the issues have clearly been presented to the arbitrator. *E.g., Williams Transportation Co.,* 223 NLRB No. 125, 96 LRRM 1597 (1977) (Board declined to defer to arbitration award which resolved questions of accretion to a bargaining unit and union representation); *Filmation Associates,* 227 NLRB 1721 (1974) (3-2) (*Spielberg* will not be applied to issues involving discrimination against employees because they filed unfair labor practice charges — § 8(a)(4) — since such issues are solely within the Board's province to decide). *See also General American Transportation Co.,* 228 NLRB 808 (1977) (A Board majority indicated that the *Collyer* prearbitral deferral doctrine would no longer be applied in cases involving alleged violations of §§ 8(a)(1), 8(a)(3), 8(b)(1)(A), and 8(b)(2). However, Member Murphy (then Chairman), who cast the swing vote, indicated that she would defer under *Spielberg* to an arbitration award involving the above sections where all of the parties, including the affected employee, have voluntarily submitted their dispute to arbitration. By contrast, she would not compel an unwilling party to go to arbitration if that party charges that his Section 7 rights have been violated).

NOTE:

A newspaper company discharged a pressman, Bowlen, for neglect of duty. In protest, the pressmen on the next shift refused to work. There is conflicting evidence as to whether a union officer, Ellis, led the work stoppage or tried to get the men back to work. The company discharged the pressmen, including Ellis, for striking in breach of the collective agreement. An arbitrator upheld the discharges, including that of Ellis, in an unfair labor practice proceeding, should the NLRB defer to the arbitration award, under the *Spielberg* doctrine? Held: Yes. *Kansas City Star Co.,* 236 NLRB No. 119, 98 LRRM 1320 (1978). Note the dissent as to Ellis by two Board members, finding that he was engaged in protected activity, and the concurring opinion by newly-appointed Member Truesdale, criticizing the dissenters for making a *de novo* review of the evidence.

c. The Congruence of Issues and Competence Requirements

In refining the *Spielberg* doctrine, the Board has since held that it would not defer to an arbitration award unless the issue presented to the Board in an unfair labor practice proceeding was both presented to and considered by the arbitrator. *Raytheon Co.,* 140 NLRB 883 (1963), *vacated on other grounds,* 326 F.2d 471 (1st Cir. 1964); *Airco Industrial Gases,* 195 NLRB 676 (1972); *Yourga Trucking Inc.,* 197 NLRB 928 (1972) (party asserting that the Board should give controlling effect to an arbitration award has the burden of proving that the issue of "improper motivation" for discharge of an employee was presented to and resolved by the arbitrator).

Subsequently, in *Electronic Reproduction Service Corp.,* 213 NLRB 758 (1974), the Board, in a 3-2 decision, overruled *Airco* and *Yourga* and adopted a principle akin to collateral estoppel: henceforth the Board will defer under *Spielberg* where the unfair labor practice issues could have been litigated before the arbitrator, regardless of whether in fact they were so litigated. The majority's reasoning went as follows:

> As mentioned previously, in deciding *Spielberg* and *Collyer,* the Board sought to discourage dual litigation and forum shopping by encouraging the parties to employ initially the contractual procedures for dispute settlement which they have created (*Collyer*), and to permit the dispute resolution achieved through those procedures to stand in the absence of procedural irregularity or statutory repugnancy (*Spielberg*). Thus the purpose of both *Collyer* and *Spielberg* is to encourage, require, and generally to honor the utilization of contractual procedures where "a set of facts . . . presents not only an alleged violation of the Act but also an alleged breach of the collective-bargaining agreement.

> If (under *Spielberg* and *Collyer*) we are to continue to encourage, require, and generally honor the use of available grievance and arbitration procedures to achieve dispute settlement, we ought not encourage either party to withhold from those voluntary procedures full information or relevant evidence on issues scheduled for discussion in the grievance procedure or for hearing by an arbitrator.

> Upon further examination of our decisions in *Airco* and *Yourga* in the light of cases such as the instant one, we are persuaded that the application of the principles established therein is proving deleterious to the contractual dispute settling process by encouraging just such a withholding of clearly relevant evidence.

> For in discharge and discipline cases the basic contractual issue is whether or not the grievant has been disciplined or discharged for just cause. It is of course obvious that "just cause" does not include illegal or discriminatory reasons. Indeed, a showing that the true reason for the discipline or discharge was a

discriminatory one negates any employer claim that the discharge or discipline was "for just cause." Arbitrators have repeatedly so held, and have recognized clearly their responsibilities in this area. Arbitrator Saul Wallen noticed in *Hoague-Sprague Corporation,* 48 LA 19 (1967), at page 23:

"Thus this Board policy, known as the Spielberg doctrine, places on arbitrators an especial responsibility, in a case where an allegation of discrimination appears to be other than wholly capricious, to make certain that Management's actions are completely free of discriminatory taint and, it seems to us, to resolve doubts on this score in favor of upholding the purposes of the Act."

If the result of [*Airco*] and *Yourga* tends, as it apparently did in the instant case, artific[i]ally to separate the issue of just cause from the issue of discrimination, then the contractual efforts at dispute settlement are rendered less likely to resolve the dispute and, surely, less likely to provide "a quick and fair means for the resolution of the dispute." Instead such an artificial separation of issues seems likely to lead, as it did herein, to piecemeal litigation in which a party may well perfer [prefer] to have "two bites of the apple," trying part of the discharge case before the arbitrator but holding back evidence material to its claim so as to be able to pursue the matter in yet another proceeding before this Board . . .

We are not unmindful, however, of the fact that there may be unusualy [unusual] circumstances under which it is not reasonable to expect or require a full litigation of these issues in the grievance and arbitration process . . .

In *Monsanto Chemical Co.,* 130 NLRB 1097 (1961), the arbitrator's award specifically declined to pass on the issues regarded by the arbitrator as statutory rather than contractual. In *Raytheon* [*Co.,* 140 NLRM 883 (1963), vacated on other grounds, 326 F.2d 471 (1st Cir. 1964),] the facts indicated that both parties were

in agreement that certain statutory issues should be excluded from the arbitration proceeding. We have no power or authority, of course, to require unwilling arbitrators to consider issues which they deliberately exclude from the scope of their awards. Nor do we have the power or authority, to prevent parties, by agreement, from restricting the arbitrator's authority and thus to exclude from their voluntary dispute settlement procedures any issues which they do not deem appropriate for resolution therein.

But we are satisfied from our view of such arbitration cases as have been cited, supra, that the usual and normal practice of parties to collective agreements is to submit to the arbitrator the central issues of the justness or unjustness of the discipline or discharge and that it is the normal practice of parties to submit, and of arbitrators to consider as relevant (and in proper circumstances controlling), evidence of unfairness or unjustness arising out of antiunion discrimination of the type which we consider in cases arising under Section 8(a)(3) of our Act.

Accordingly, we believe the better application of the underlying principles of *Collyer* and *Spielberg* to be that we should give full effect to arbitration awards dealing with discipline or discharge cases, under *Spielberg,* except when unusual circumstances are shown which demonstrate that there were bona fide reasons, other than a mere desire on the part of one party to try the same set of facts before two forums, which caused the failure to introduce such evidence at the arbitration proceeding.

[In footnote 18, the Board made clear that the *Monsanto* and *Raytheon* cases were examples of "unusual circumstances" in which its collateral estoppel principle would not be applicable.]

Fanning and Jenkins, dissenting in part, strongly opposed the majority's holding and rationale:

The *Collyer* majority has now eliminated from *Spielberg* the requirement that, for the Board to defer to an arbitrator's award, the award must have determined the same statutory issue presented to the Board.

Now it becomes the burden of the party seeking correction of an alleged violation of the Act to show that the arbitrator did not decide the statutory issue, and next, or perhaps now, that the arbitrator could not have decided the issue regardless of whether it was presented to him.

This means, of course, that the Board for all practical purposes will no longer decide any part of a case which has been or could have been decided by an arbitrator who has issued an award. . . .

We continue to think that Congress meant that statutory violations should be found if they exist, and remedied if found, and by this Board to which Congress entrusted the responsibility.

Arbitration is essentially alien to determination of public rights. Arbitrators have no expertise in the interpretation of the Act. The Board does. The arbitrator is bound to give effect to the collective-bargaining agreement, whatever might be its inconsistency with the law. And public rights cannot be left unvindicated, if the Act is to afford equal protection and uniform application. It is only the requirement of Spielberg that the arbitration award decide the statutory violation, and decide it not incorrectly, that permitted deferral of public rights to arbitration at all. The majority has now eliminated this requirement.

However desirable and fruitful may be the arbitration of private rights, the reasoning is not transferrable to public rights. As we have previously observed, public rights cannot be the "plaything of private treaty." We have heretofore set forth, in our dissents in *Collyer* and its descendants down that slippery slope, the reasons in the structure of the Act, in its legislative history, and in its purpose and policy why arbitration of violations of the Act cannot satisfy the statute. Those reasons apply even more forcefully when under the guise of deferral to arbitration the violations may never be considered.

Prior to *Electronic Reproduction Service*, the Supreme Court had tacitly approved NLRM deferral under *Spielberg*. *NLRB v. C & C Plywood Corp.*, 385 U.S. 421 (1967); *Carey v. Westinghouse Electric Corp.*, 375 U.S. 261 (1964). *See also Machinists, District Lodge 87 v. NLRB*, 530 F.2d 849 (9th Cir. 1976) (upholding Board's deferral under *Spielberg)* and *IBEW Local 715 v. NLRB*, 494 F.2d 1136 (D.C. Cir. 1974) (specifically endorsing *Spielberg).* Recently, however, two circuit courts of appeals, while acknowledging the Board's power in an unfair labor practice proceeding to give controlling effect to a prior arbitration award, have held that the Board may not so defer unless the original *Spielberg* standards, plus two additional requirements, are met: (1) The arbitrator must have *clearly decided* the unfair labor practice issue on which the Board is later urged to give deference; and (2) resolution of that issue must be within the arbitrator's "competence." *Banyard v. NLRB*, 505 F.2d 342 (D.C. Cir. 1974) (decided one month before the *Electronic Reproduction* decision); *Stephenson v. NLRB*, 550 F.2d 535 (9th Cir. 1977) (specifically rejecting *Electronic Reproduction's* extension of *Spielberg).*

In *Banyard*, the D.C. Circuit reversed two NLRB decisions which had given controlling effect to arbitral decisions, even though there was no showing that the contractual issues considered by the arbitrators were "congruent" with the unfair labor practice issues before the Board. In one of the cases, the court stressed that it could not sanction the Board's deferral because of the

> uncertainty over whether the standard applied by the [arbitrator] to the contractual issue before it is the correct standard to be applied to the statutory issue before the Board . . . [The court was concerned that the Board might have resolved the issue differently.]

Our approval of the Board's deferral under *Spielberg* of statutory issues to arbitral resolution along with contractual issues is conditioned upon the *resolution* (emphasis added) by the arbitral tribunal of congruent statutory and contractual issues. . . . If in the present case the [arbitrator] applied to the issue before it a standard correct under the contract but not under judicial interpretation of section 502 [29 U.S.C. § 143], then it cannot be said that the statutory issue was decided by the [arbitrator]. In that event the Board's abstention goes beyond deferral and approaches abdication." 505 F.2d at 348.

Banyard's significance was amplified by the Ninth Circuit's ruling in *Stephenson v. NLRB, supra,* which held that the NLRB improperly deferred to an arbitration award, since the evidence failed to establish that the arbitration panel clearly decided the unfair labor practice issue. As in *Banyard,* the court tacked onto *Spielberg* the additional requirements that, before deferral will be held proper, the arbitrator (1) must have *"clearly decided"* the unfair labor practice issue before the Board and (2) must have been *competent* to do so. It then proceeds to explain its understanding of the terms "clearly decided" and "competent." "Clearly decided," stated the court, means that the arbitrator must deal specifically with the statutory issue. "Merely because the arbitrator is presented with a problem that involves both contractual and unfair labor practice elements does not necessarily mean that he will adequately consider the statutory issue, and merely because he considers the statutory issue does not mean that he will enforce the rights of the parties pursuant to and consistent with the Act. The 'clearly decided' requirement is designed to enable the Board and the courts to fairly test the standards applied by the arbitrator against those required by the Act." 94 LRRM 3224, note 4 at 3226. This test may be satisfied, absent a written memorandum by the arbitrator, where there is "substantial and definite proof that the unfair labor practice issue and evidence were expressly presented to the arbitrator and the arbitrator's decision indisputably resolves the issue in a manner entirely consistent with the Act . . ." Conversely, the test will not be met where there is no proof that the unfair labor practice issue or evidence was ever presented to the arbitrator or his decision is ambiguous as to the resolution of the statutory question.

According to the court, an arbitrator is "competent" to decide the unfair labor practice issue only where its resolution turns on an interpretation of the contract, so that the statutory and contractual issues are congruent. In addition, the arbitrator is competent to resolve unfair labor practice charges which involve mainly factual rather than statutory issues. "[In short], the 'competence' requirement requires the Board to ascertain the underlying issues in the unfair labor practice charge and to determine whether arbitral expertise and institutional competence justify deferral to arbitration of the particular dispute." [Citing *Alexander v. Gardner Denver,* 415 U.S. 36, 57 (1974) (*infra* this chapter).] Unless the statutory issue is "so concomitant" with the contractual issue that the latter disposes of the former, the Board, in the courts' opinion, may not defer under *Spielberg,* since to do so amounts to an abdication of its authority to decide unfair labor practice questions.

NOTES:

(1) *Problem:* Do *Banyard* and *Stephenson* require the arbitrator to decide a contract dispute in accordance with his understanding of how the Board or a court would decide the case? Doesn't *Enterprise Wheel & Car, supra,* preclude the arbitrator from basing his award on his reading of enacted legislation or decisional law? Is there a need in deferred cases to require an arbitrator to resolve "statutory" issues when, under *Spielberg,* the Board will refuse to acknowledge his award if it is clearly repugnant to the Act?

(2) Board decisions subsequent to *Electronic Reproduction* make clear that the Board will not defer to an award under *Spielberg* unless the issues resolved by the arbitrator also dispose of the unfair labor practice question before the Board, *Kroger Co.,* 226 NLRB 512 (1976). In *Clara Barton Terrace Convalescent Center,* 225 NLRB 1028 (1976), a Board majority declined to defer under *Spielberg* where the arbitrator upheld a grievant's discharge on contractual grounds "without once examining the [statutory] protections accorded by [the] Act." Although the Board also found the award "repugnant to the act," since it penalized the grievant for exercising statutorily protected rights, it emphasized that *the arbitrator did not consider the statutory question,* and that therefore his award did not satisfy the *Spielberg* standards.

2. The Collyer Doctrine — Pre-arbitral Deferral

COLLYER INSULATED WIRE

National Labor Relations Board
192 N.L.R.B. 837 (1971)

The complaint alleges and the General Counsel contends that Respondent violated Section 8(a)(5) and (1) of the National Labor Relations act, as amended, by making assertedly unilateral changes in certain wages and working conditions. Respondent contends that its authority to make those changes was sanctioned by the collective-bargaining contract between the parties and their course of dealing under that contract. Respondent further contends that any of its actions in excess of contractual authorization should properly have been remedied by grievance and arbitration proceeding, as provided in the contract. We agree with Respondent's contention that this dispute is essentially a dispute over the terms and meaning of the contract between the Union and the Respondent. For that reason, we find merit in Respondent's exceptions that the dispute should have been resolved pursuant to the contract and we shall dismiss the complaint.

I. The Alleged Unilateral Changes

Respondent manufactures insulated electrical wiring at its plant in Lincoln, Rhode Island. The Union has represented Respondent's production and maintenance employees under successive contracts since 1937. The contract in effect when this dispute arose resulted from lengthy negotiations commencing in December 1968 and concluding with the execution of the contract of September 16, 1969. The contract was made effective from April 1, 1969, until July 2, 1971.

Respondent's production employees have historically been compensated on an incentive basis. The contract provides for a job evaluation plan and for the adjustment of rates, subject to the grievance procedure, during the term of the contract. Throughout the bargaining relationship, Respondent has routinely made adjustments in incentive rates to accommodate new or changed production methods. The contract establishes non-incentive rates for skilled maintenance tradesmen but provides for changes in those rates, also, pursuant to the job evaluation plan, upon changes in or additions to the duties of the classifications. The central issue here is whether these contract provisions permitted certain midcontract wage rate changes which Respondent made in November 1969.

A. *The Rate Increase for Skilled Maintenance Tradesmen:* Since early 1968, Respondent's wage rates for skilled tradesmen have not been sufficiently high to attract and retain the numbers of skilled maintenance mechanics and electricians required for the efficient operation of the plant. The record clearly establishes, and the Trial Examiner found, that other employers in the same region paid "substantially higher rates than those paid by Respondent." In consequence, the number of skilled maintenance workers had declined from about 40 in January 1968 to about 30 in mid-1969, and Respondent had been unable to attract employees to fill the resulting vacancies.

During negotiations, Respondent several times proposed wage raises for maintenance employees over and above those being negotiated for the production and maintenance unit generally. The Union rejected those proposals and the contract did not include any provision for such raises. It is clear, nevertheless, that the matter of the skill factor increase was left open, in *some* measure, for further negotiations after the execution of the agreement. The parties sharply dispute, however, the extent to which the matter remained open and the conditions which were to surround further discussions. The Union asserts, and the Trial Examiner found, that the Union was willing, and made known its willingness, to negotiate further wage adjustments only on a plantwide basis, consistent with the job evaluation system. Respondent insists that it understood the Union's position to be that wage increases for maintenance employees only might still be agreed to by the Union after the signing of the contract, if such increases could be justified under the job evaluation system.

At monthly meetings following conclusion of the contract negotiations, Respondent and the Union continued to discuss the Respondent's desire to raise the rates for maintenance employees. Finally, on November 12, 1969, Respondent informed the Union that five days thence, on November 17, Respondent would institute an upward adjustment of 20 cents per hour. The Union protested and restated its desire for a reevaluation of all jobs in the plant. Respondent's representative agreed to consider such an evaluation on a plantwide basis, upon union agreement to the increase for the skilled tradesmen. The Trial Examiner found that the Union did not agree. The rate increase became effective November 17, 1969.

B. *Reassignment of Job Duties:* One of the production steps, the application of insulating material to conductor, is accomplished through the operation of extruder machines. The insulating material, in bulk, is forced to and through the extruder die by a lare worm gear. Each change in the type of insulation used on an extruder requires that the worm gear be removed and cleaned of insulation remaining from the previous production run. The removal, cleaning, and replacement of the worm gear is performed approximately once each week and requires approximately 40 minutes to one hour for each operation. Prior to November 12, 1969, the worm gear removal and cleaning had been performed by a team of two maintenance machinists. On November 12, Respondent directed that future worm gear removals would be performed by a single maintenance machinist with the assistance of the extruder machine operator and helper.

C. *Rate Increases for Extruder Operators:* Respondent's third change, also effective November 17, 1969, produced a rate increase for extruder operators. It had been Respondent's practice to adjust the straight time earnings of extruder operators by a factor representing the amount of time during an eight-hour shift when the extruder was in continuous operation. Under that system, for example, an operator who maintained his machine in continuous operation for eight hours was paid for 10 hours' work. This incentive factor has never been fixed by the contract and Respondent had, in the past, changed the rate for various reasons. This system of compensation operated somewhat to the detriment of first- and third-shift employees in that third-shift employees incurred the non-productive time required to shut down production at the end of each week, and the first-shift employees incurred that required for starting operations each Monday. That perceived inequity had stimulated numerous union requests for adjustment. Respondent sought to obviate this problem by computing the operating time on a weekly basis for each machine, determining the average incentive factor for all three shifts, and computing pay for that average. In making this change, Respondent gave the assurance that no operator would suffer any loss of pay by virtue of the revision. This was accomplished, in part, by raising the previous maximum 10.0 incentive factor to a range of from 10.3 to 10.6 hours' pay for continuous operation.

Another adjustment in computation related to a pair of extruder machines which were equipped with dual extruder heads so that each machine performed a dual insulation function. Respondent had previously paid a 5-percent premium to operators of these machines. On November 17, this premium was adjusted upward to 7-½ percent.

Finally, on February 16, 1970, in response to another complaint by the Union, Respondent restudied the rate on two extruders, pursuant to its contractual duty, and raised the incentive factor for those machines from 10.3 to 10.5 pay hours.

II. Relevant Contract Provisions

The contract now in effect between the parties makes provision for adjustment by Respondent in the wages of its employees during the contract term. Those provisions appear to contemplate changes in rates in both incentive and nonincentive jobs. Thus, article IX, section 2, provides:

"The Corporation agrees to establish rates and differentials of pay for all employees according to their skill, experience and hazards of employment, and to review rates and differentials from time to time. The Corporation agrees to pay all operators their average earnings for samples and unusual processes; untimed portions of already rated jobs will be paid for at an allowed pay hour of 8.8 and adjustment in pay will be made after the rate is fully established. It is agreed that untimed portions of already rated jobs will be studied within a maximum of one work week. In the event that this time limit is not met, the worker will receive his average hourly rate starting as of the first day. However, no change in the general scale of pay now in existence shall be made during the term of this Agreement. This Article IX is applicable to the general wage scale, but shall not be deemed to prevent adjustments in individual rates from time to time to remove inequalities or for other proper reasons."

Further evidence of the contractual intent to permit Respondent to modify job rates subject to review through the grievance and arbitration procedures is found in article XIII, section 3, paragraph b, covering new or changed jobs. That paragraph provides that the Union shall have seven days to consider any new rating established by the Company and to submit objections. Thereafter, even absent Union agreement, it vests in the Company authority to institute a new pay rate. The Union, if dissatisfied, may then challenge the propriety of the rate by invoking the grievance procedure which culminates in arbitration.

Finally, the breadth of the arbitration provisions makes clear that the parties intended to make the grievance and arbitration machinery the exclusive forum for resolving contract disputes. By article IV of the contract the parties agree that the grievance machinery "shall be adopted for any complaint or dispute . . . which may arise between any employee or group of employees and the Corporation. . . ." That intent is further evidenced by the no-strike, no-lockout provision, article XI, which declares, in part: "All questions, disputes or controversies under this Agreement shall be settled and determined solely and exclusively by the conciliation and arbitration procedures provided in this Agreement. . . ." A grievance is defined as any controversy between an employee and his supervisor or any controversy between the union and the Respondent involving "the interpretation, application or violation of any provision of this agreement or supplement thereto." The arbitration clause, article V, provides that "any grievance" may be submitted to an impartial arbitrator for decision and that the decision of the arbitrator "shall be final and binding upon the parties" if not contrary to law. . . .

IV. Discussion

We find merit in Respondent's exceptions that because this dispute in its entirety arises from the contract between the parties, and from the parties' relationship under the contract, it ought to be resolved in the manner which that contract prescribes. We conclude that the Board is vested with authority to withhold its processes in this case, and that the contract here made available a quick and fair means for the resolution of this dispute including, if appropriate, a fully effective remedy for any breach of contract which occurred. We conclude, in sum, that our obligation to advance the purposes of the Act is best discharged by the dismissal of this complaint.

In our view, disputes such as these can better be resolved by arbitrators with special skill and experience in deciding matters arising under established bargaining relationships than by the application by this Board of a particular provision of our statute. The necessity for such special skill and expertise is apparent upon examination of the issues arising from Respondent's actions with respect to the operators' rates, the skill factor increase, and the reassignment of duties relating to the worm gear removal. Those issues include, specifically: (a) the extent to which these actions were intended to be reserved to the management, subject to later adjustment by grievance and arbitration; (b) the extent to which the skill factor increase should properly be construed, under article IX of the agreement, as a "change in the general scale of pay" or, conversely, as "adjustments in individual rates ... to remove inequalities or for other proper reason;" (c) the extent, if any, to which the procedures of article XIII governing new or changed jobs and job rates should have been made applicable to the skill factor increase here; and (d) the extent to which any of these issues may be affected by the long course of dealing between the parties. The determination of these issues, we think, is best left to discussions in the grievance procedure by the parties who negotiated the applicable provisions or, if such discussions do not resolve them, then to an arbitrator chosen under the agreement and authorized by it to resolve such issues.

The Board's authority, in its discretion, to defer to the arbitration process has never been questioned by the courts of appeals, or by the Supreme Court. Although Section 10(a) of the Act clearly vests the Board with jurisdiction over conduct which constitutes a violation of the provisions of Section 8, notwithstanding the existence of methods of "adjustment or prevention that might be established by agreement," nothing in the Act intimates that the Board must exercise jurisdiction where such methods exist. On the contrary in Carey v. Westinghouse Electric Corporation, 375 U.S. 261, 271 (1964), the Court indicated that it favors our deference to such agreed methods. . . .

In an earlier case, *Smith v. Evening News Ass'n*,[4] the Supreme Court had likewise observed that, "the Board has, on prior occasions, declined to exercise its jurisdiction to deal with unfair labor practices in circumstances where, in its judgment, federal labor policy would best be served by leaving the parties to other processes of the law." As in *Carey v. Westinghouse,* the decision carries a clear implication that the Court approved the informed use of such discretion.

The policy favoring voluntary settlement of labor disputes through arbitral processes finds specific expression in Section 203(d) of the LMRA. . . .

And of course disputes under Section 301 of the LMRA called forth from the Supreme Court the celebrated affirmation of that national policy in the *Steelworkers trilogy.*[5]

---

[4] 371 U.S. 195 (1962).
[5] 363 U.S. 564, 574, 593 (1960).

Admittedly neither Section 203 nor Section 301 applies specifically to the Board. However labor law as administered by the Board does not operate in a vacuum isolated from other parts of the Act, or, indeed, from other acts of Congress. In fact the legislative history suggests that at the time the Taft-Hartley amendments were being considered, Congress anticipated that the Board would "develop by rules and regulations, a policy of entertaining under these provisions only such cases . . . as cannot be settled by resort to the machinery established by the contract itself, voluntary arbitration. . . ." [7]

The question whether the Board should withhold its process arises, of course, only when a set of facts may present not only an alleged violation of the Act but also an alleged breach of the collective-bargaining agreement subject to arbitration. Thus, this case like each such case compels an accommodation between, on the one hand, the statutory policy favoring the fullest use of collective bargaining and the arbitral process and, on the other, the statutory policy reflected by Congress' grant to the Board of exclusive jurisdiction to prevent unfair labor practices.

We address the accommodations required here with the benefit of the Board's full history of such accommodations in similar cases. From the start the Board has, case by case, both asserted jurisdiction and declined, as the balance was struck on particular facts and at various stages in the long ascent of collective bargaining to its present state of wide acceptance. Those cases reveal that the Board has honored the distinction between two broad but distinct classes of cases, those in which there has been an arbitral award, and those in which there has not.

In the former class of cases the Board has long given hospitable acceptance to the arbitral process. In *Timken Roller Bearing Company*[8] the Board refrained from exercising jurisdiction, in deference to an arbitrator's decision, despite the fact that the Board could otherwise have found that an unfair labor practice had been committed. . . .

In those cases in which no award had issued, the Board's guidelines have been less clear. At times the Board has dealt with the unfair labor practice, and at other times it has left the parties to their contract remedies. . . .

Jos. Schlitz Brewing Company,[12] is the most significant recent case in which the Board has exercised its discretion to defer. The underlying dispute in *Schlitz* was strikingly similar to the one now before us. In *Schlitz* the respondent employer decided to halt its production line during employee breaks. That decision was a departure from an established practice of maintaining extra

---

[7] S. Rep. No. 105, 80th Cong., 1st Sess. 23 (1947).

[8] 70 N.L.R.B. 500 (1946).

[12] 175 N.L.R.B. No. 23 (1969).

employees, relief men, to fill in for regular employees during breaktime. The change resulted in, among other things, elimination of the relief man job classification. The change elicited a union protest leading to an unfair labor practice proceeding in which the Board ruled that the case should be "left for resolution within the framework of the agreed upon settlement procedures." The majority there explained its decision in these words:

"Thus, we believe that where, as here, the contract clearly provides for grievance and arbitration machinery, where the unilateral action taken is not designed to undermine the Union and is not patently erroneous but rather is based on a substantial claim of contractual privilege, and it appears that the arbitral interpretation of the contract will resolve both the unfair labor practice issue and the contract interpretation issue in a manner compatible with the purposes of the Act, then the Board should defer to the arbitration clause conceived by the parties. . . ."

The circumstances of this case, no less than those in *Schlitz,* weigh heavily in favor of deferral. Here, as in *Schlitz,* this dispute arises within the confines of a long and productive collective-bargaining relationship. The parties before us have, for 35 years, mutually and voluntarily resolved the conflicts which inhere in collective bargaining. Here, as there, no claim is made of enmity by Respondent to employees' exercise of protected rights. Respondent here has credibly asserted its willingness to resort to arbitration under a clause providing for arbitration in a very broad range of disputes and unquestionably broad enough to embrace this dispute.

Finally, here, as in *Schlitz,* the dispute is one eminently well suited to resolution by arbitration. The contract and its meaning in present circumstances lie at the center of this dispute. In contrast, the Act and its policies become involved only if it is determined that the agreement between the parties, examined in the light of its negotiating history and the practices of the parties thereunder, did not sanction Respondent's right to make the disputed changes, subject to review if sought by the Union, under the contractually prescribed procedure. That threshold determination is clearly within the expertise of a mutually agreed-upon arbitrator. In this regard we note especially that here, as in *Schlitz,* the dispute between these parties is the very stuff of labor contract arbitration. The competence of a mutually selected arbitrator to decide the issue and fashion an appropriate remedy, if needed, can no longer be gainsaid.

We find no basis for the assertion of our dissenting colleagues that our decision here modifies the standards established in *Spielberg* [112 N.L.R.B. 1080 (1957)] for judging the acceptability of an arbitrator's award. . . .

As already noted, the contract between Respondent and the Union unquestionably obligates each party to submit to arbitration any dispute arising under the contract and finds [binds] both parties to the result thereof. It is true, manifestly, that we cannot judge the regularity or statutory acceptability of the result in an arbitration proceeding which has not occurred. However, we are unwilling to adopt the presumption that such a proceeding will be invalid under *Spielberg* and to exercise our decisional authority at this juncture on the basis of a mere possibility that such a proceeding might be unacceptable under *Spielberg* standards. That risk is far better accommodated, we believe, by the result reached here of retaining jurisdiction against an event which years of experience with labor arbitration have now made clear is a remote hazard.

Member Fanning's dissenting opinion incorrectly characterizes this decision as instituting "compulsory arbitration" and as creating an opportunity for employers and unions to "strip parties of statutory rights."

We are not compelling any party to agree to arbitrate disputes arising during a contract term, but are merely giving full effect to their own voluntary agreements to submit all such disputes to arbitration, rather than permitting such agreements to be side-stepped and permitting the substitution of our processes, a forum not contemplated by their own agreement.

Nor are we "stripping" any party of "statutory rights." The courts have long recognized that an industrial relations dispute may involve conduct which, at least arguably, may contravene both the collective agreement and our statute. When the parties have contractually committed themselves to mutually agreeable procedures for resolving their disputes during the period of the contract, we are of the view that those procedures should be afforded full opportunity to function. The long and successful functioning of grievance and arbitration procedures suggests to us that in the overwhelming majority of cases, the utilization of such means will resolve the underlying dispute and make it unnecessary for either party to follow the more formal, and sometimes lengthy, combination of administrative and judicial litigation provided for under our statute. At the same time, by our reservation of jurisdiction, *infra,* we guarantee that there will be no sacrifice of statutory rights if the parties' own processes fail to function in a manner consistent with the dictates of our law. This approach, we believe, effectuates the salutary policy announced in *Spielberg,* which the dissenting opinion correctly summarizes as one of not requiring the "serious machinery of the Board where the record indicates that the parties are in the process of resolving their dispute in a manner sufficient to effectuate the policies of the Act."

We are especially mindful, finally, that the policy of this nation to avoid industrial strife through voluntary resolution of industrial disputes is not static, but is dynamic. The years since enactment of

Section 203 (d) have been vital ones, and the policy then expressed has helped to shape an industrial system in which the institution of contract arbitration has grown not only pervasive but, literally, indispensable. The Board has both witnessed and participated in the growth, a complex interaction where the growth of arbitration in response to Congress' will has called forth and nurtured gradually broader conceptions, of the basic policy. The Supreme Court which in *Lincoln Mills,* first upheld the enforceability of agreements to arbitrate disputes has recently, in *Boys Markets, Inc. v. Retail clerks,*[16] suggested that arbitration has become "the central institution in the administration of collective bargaining contracts." After *Boys Market* it may truly be said that where a contract provides for arbitration, either party has at hand legal and effective means to ensure that the arbitration will occur. We believe it to be consistent with the fundamental objectives of federal law to require the parties here to honor their contractual obligations rather than, by casting this dispute in statutory terms, to ignore their agreed-upon procedures.

V. Remedy

Without prejudice to any party and without deciding the merits of the controversy, we shall order that the complaint herein be dismissed, but we shall retain jurisdiction for a limited purpose. Our decision represents a developmental step in the Board's treatment of these problems and the controversy here arose at a time when the Board decisions may have led the parties to conclude that the Board approved dual litigation of this controversy before the Board and before an arbitrator. We are also aware that the parties herein have not resolved their dispute by the contractual grievance and arbitration procedure and that, therefore, we cannot now inquire whether resolution of the dispute will comport with the standards set forth in *Spielberg, supra.* In order to eliminate the risk of prejudice to any party we shall retain jurisdiction over this dispute solely for the purpose of entertaining an appropriate and timely motion for further consideration upon a proper showing that either (a) the dispute has not, with reasonable promptness after the issuance of this decision, either been resolved by amicable settlement in the grievance procedure or submitted promptly to arbitration, or (b) the grievance or arbitration procedures have not been fair and regular or have reached a result which is repugnant to the Act.

[The concurring opinion of MEMBER BROWN is omitted.]

MEMBER FANNING (dissenting) . . . .

I agree with the Trial Examiner that the wage increases for skilled

---

[16] 398 U.S. 235, 252 (1970).

employees only and the related worm gear change were proper subjects for collective bargaining and that Respondent violated Section 8(a)(5) and (1) of the Act by instituting these changes unilaterally.

In a novel decision with far-reaching implications a majority of this Board in the instant case refuses even to consider the alleged unfair labor practices concluding merely that the Board's "obligation to advance the purposes of the Act is best discharged by the dismissal of this complaint." The majority's refusal to assert the authority granted to it by Congress under Section 10 (a) of the Act is based solely on the ground that the collective-bargaining agreement between the Union and the Respondent contains a standard grievance arbitration procedure, culminating in binding arbitration.

Admittedly, the Union or any of its members had a contractual right to institute grievance with respect to the Respondent's changes and to secure the benefit of an eventual ruling by an arbitrator. No such grievances have been filed in this case and there is no indication that the charging party or its members voluntarily desire to do so. Contrary to the majority, the arbitration provision does not make it clear that the parties intended "to make the grievance and arbitration machinery the exclusive forum for resolving contract disputes." Section 1, article IV, of the contract sets forth the procedure for "any complaint or dispute," as noted by the majority, but further provides that the grievance procedure is "subject to the rights of individual employees as provided for in the Labor-Management Act of 1947." Under article V (arbitration) the parties further agreed that "The arbitration shall be held under the Voluntary Labor Arbitration Rules of the American Arbitration Association and the parties agree that the decision of the arbitrator shall be final and binding upon the parties, *providing such award will not conflict with any rules or regulations or laws of the Federal Government....*" (Emphasis supplied.) Moreover, section 3, article IV, of the contract specifically provides that grievances not presented or advanced within the time limits set forth in sections 1 and 2 "shall be deemed to be settled and shall not be reprocessed." The time limits for the resolution of grievances with respect to these unilateral changes have passed and, so far as the collective-bargaining agreement is concerned, those putative grievances must be deemed to be settled.

Clearly then the effect of the majority's decision is a direction to the parties to arbitrate a grievance which is no longer contractually arbitrable. The complaint is dismissed, but jurisdiction is retained, presumably to give the Union an opportunity to file a grievance under a time-expired contractual provision, with the implicit threat to the Respondent that the Board will assert jurisdiction, upon a proper motion, if Respondent is unwilling now to submit to arbitration. The majority's insistence that the parties' statutory rights cannot be adjudicated in this case except through the authority of an arbitrator verges on the practice of compulsory arbitration. Historically, in this country voluntarism has been the essence of private arbitration of labor disputes. Neither Congress nor the courts have attempted to coerce the parties in collective bargaining to resolve their grievances through arbitration. Compulsory arbitration has been regarded by some as contrary to a free, democratic society. Collective-bargaining agreements, such as the one in the instant case, give aggrieved parties the *right* to file grievances and to present their disputes to an arbitrator. The element of compulsion has been deliberately omitted. To establish the principle, as a matter of labor law, that the parties to a collective-bargaining agreement must, in part, surrender their protection under this statute as a consequence of agreeing to a provision for binding arbitration of grievances will, in my view, discourage rather than encourage the arbitral process in this country. Many may decide they cannot afford the luxury of such "voluntary" arbitration. . . .

The effect of the majority's decision in the instant case is clearly a reversal of the established *Spielberg* line of cases. In the future applicable standards for review of arbitration awards will not be followed. Neither the existence of an actual award, the fairness of the arbitrator's opinion or its impingement upon the policies of the Act will be considered by the Board in dismissing complaints of this nature. Under the majority's accommodation theory even consideration of the nature and scope of the alleged unfair labor practices, as set forth in . . . *Joseph Schlitz, supra,* will not receive the Board's attention. The impact of the majority's decision may be said to go beyond compulsory arbitration. For it means that in the future the Board will not concern itself with the *fact* or the *regularity* of the arbitral process, but will strip the parties of statutory rights merely on the *availability* of such a procedure.

The majority does not frame the primary issue in this case in terms calculated to resolve a particular dispute in a particular case. Rather, a new standard for the nonassertion of jurisdiction is announced, embracing a whole class of employers who have entered into contracts with unions containing a grievance-arbitration clause. In the future, complaints based upon such disputes, without regard to the seriousness of the alleged unfair labor practices, may not be litigated before this Board. . . .

Congress has said that arbitration and the voluntary settlement of disputes are the preferred method of dealing with certain kinds of industrial unrest. Congress has also said that the power of this Board to dispose of unfair labor practices is not to be affected by any other method of adjustment. Whatever these two statements mean, they do not mean that this Board can abdicate its authority wholesale. Clearly there is an accommodation to be made. The majority is so anxious to accommodate arbitration that it forgets that the first duty of this Board is to provide a forum for the adjudication of unfair labor practices. We have not been told that arbitration is the only method; it is one method.

We have recently been told by the Supreme Court that preemption in favor of this Board still exists. It is therefore inappropriate, to say the least, for us to cede our jurisdiction in all cases involving arbitration to a tribunal that may, and often does, provide only a partial remedy.

[The dissenting opinion of MEMBER JENKINS is omitted.]

NOTES:

(1) In *Roy Robinson Chevrolet,* 228 N.L.R.B. 828 (1977), then-Chairman Betty Murphy voted with Members Penello and Walther to follow the *Collyer* doctrine and defer to arbitration in a case involving the employer's alleged violation of Section 8(a)(5) in unilaterally closing down the body shop part of his auto dealer operations. *But* in *General American Transportation Corp.,* 228 N.L.R.B. 808 (1977), she voted with Members Fanning and Jenkins in refusing to defer to arbitration. The opinion written by Members Fanning and Jenkins continued their total opposition to the *Collyer* deferral doctrine. Chairman Murphy explained why, in cases like the *General American* case involving an alleged discriminatory discharge of an individual employee, she would refuse to defer to arbitration:

> In cases alleging violations of Section 8(a)(5) and 8(b)(3), based upon conduct assertedly in derogation of the contract, the principal issue is whether the complained-of conduct is permitted by the parties' contract. Such issues are eminently suited to the arbitral process, and resolution of the contract issue by an arbitrator will, as a rule, dispose of the unfair labor practice issue. On the other hand, in cases alleging violations of Section 8(a)(1), 8(a)(3), 8(b)(1)(A), and 8(b)(2), although arguably also involving a contract violation, the determinative issue is not whether the conduct is permitted by the contract, but whether the conduct was unlawfully motivated or whether it otherwise interfered with, restrained, or coerced employees in the exercise of the rights guaranteed them by Section 7 of the Act. In these situations, an arbitrator's resolution of the contract issue will not dispose of the unfair labor practice allegation. Nor is the arbitration process suited for resolving employee complaints of discrimination under Section 7. . . .

The effect of the *General American* case is thus to overrule *National Radio Co.,* 198 NLRB 527, 1718 (1972) and other cases involving alleged unfair labor practices infringing upon individual employee rights under Section 7.

(2) As member Murphy indicated in *General American Transportation Co.,* she will continue to defer under *Collyer* in § 8(a)(5) cases. Where, however, a complaint alleges a violation of a section of the Act which she will not defer to arbitration, in addition to a § 8(a)(5) charge, member Murphy will not fragmentize the complaint by deferring only the § 8(a)(5) charge. *Texaco, Inc.* 233 NLRB No. 43, 96 LRRM 1534 (1977). *See also National Rejectors Industries,* 234 NLRB No. 34, 97 LRRM 1142 (1978) (NLRB will not defer to arbitration where it is alleged that the employer violated §§ 8(a)(3) and 8(a)(5) of the Act, in view of the Board's majority ruling in *General American Transport Co.* and the fact that the § 8(a)(3) and § 8(a)(5) charges are "inextricably" linked).

(3) If the unfair labor practice charge alleges that there is no stable collective bargaining relationship, or that the conduct of the respondent constitutes a repudiation of the contract grievance machinery or bargaining relationship, the Board will probably not defer under *Collyer. Texaco, Inc., supra* (employer penalized employees for filing contract grievances); *Wabash Asphalt Co., Inc.,* 224 NLRB 820 (1976) (employer refused to hire employees from union hiring hall because of their previous use of grievance machinery); *Mountain States Constr. Co.,* 203 NLRB 1085 (1973); *St. Joseph's Hospital,* 233 NLRB No. 168, 97 LRRM 1212 (1977) (NLRB will not defer under *Collyer* where it is alleged that employer violated § 8(a)(5) of the Act by refusing union's request for information relevant to the arbitration of a grievance, since such conduct interferes with the contract's grievance machinery).

The Board has also refused to defer under *Collyer* where the aggrieved employee's interests were in apparent conflict with the interests of the union as well as of the employer. *Operating Engineers Union, Local 18,* 227 NLRB 1477 (1976). It is unclear whether the Board will defer to arbitration panels which are composed of an equal number of employer and union representatives. *Compare IBEW, Local 367,* 230 NLRB No. 12, 96 LRRM 1182 (1977) (prearbitral deferral improper because of potential conflict of interests) *with United Parcel Service,* 232 NLRB No. 179, 96 LRRM 1288 (1977) (Board deferred to arbitration award).

(4) Deferral under *Collyer* is not available to parties unwilling to arbitrate or unwilling to waive the procedural defense that the grievance was not timely filed. *Pilot Freight Carriers, Inc.,* 224 NLRB 341, 1338 (1976); *Firestone Tire & Rubber Co.,* 219 NLRB 492 (1975). Nor will the Board defer to prospective arbitration where not all of the interested parties before it in the unfair labor practice proceeding are able to participate in the arbitration proceeding, *e.g.,*

Masters, Mates & Pilots (Seatrain Lines, Inc.), 220 NLRB 164 (1975) (several interested parties were not signatories to the contract providing for arbitration). *But cf., Croatian Fraternal Union,* 232 NLRB No. 162, 97 LRRM 1209 (1977) (NLRB defers to prospective arbitration even though union claims it is unable to undertake the costs of arbitration); *Operating Engineers Union, Local 18, supra.*

Similarly, the Board will not defer to prospective arbitration unless it concludes that the issue involved is "arguably" covered by the contract's arbitration provision: *United States Steel Corp.,* 223 NLRB 1246 No. 183, 92 LRRM 1158 (1976); *Graphic Arts Union CS&M Rotogravure Service),* 222 NLRB 280 (1976).

(5) The NLRB has refused to defer under *Collyer* where the issue before it did not, in its opinion, involve questions of contract interpretation or was otherwise unsuitable for arbitral resolution. *Atlas Tack Corp.,* 226 NLRB 222 (1976); *Retail Clerks, Local 588 (Raley's),* 224 NLRB 1638 (1976); *United States Steel Corporation, supra* (no written contract provision applicable to the dispute in question).

The courts of appeals have consistently upheld the Board's authority to defer exercise of its jurisdiction pending arbitration. *Machinists, Lodge 700 v. NLRB,* 525 F.2d 237 (2d Cir. 1975); *IBEW, Local 2188 v. NLRB,* 494 F.2d 1087 (D.C. Cir.), *cert. denied,* 419 U.S. 835 (1974); *Provision House Workers v. NLRB,* 493 F.2d 1249 (9th Cir.), *cert. denied,* 419 U.S. 828 (1974). The Supreme Court indicated its approval of the *Collyer* doctrine in *Arnold Co. v. Carpenters District Council,* 417 U.S. 12 (1974). Justice Brennan, writing for a unanimous court, stated that the "Board's position [in *Collyer*] harmonizes with Congress' articulated concern that '[f]inal adjustment by a method agreed upon by the parties is ... the desirable method for settlement of grievance disputes arising over the application or interpretation of an existing collective bargaining agreement. ...' § 203(d) of the LMRA, 29 U.S.C. § 173(d)." 417 U.S. at 17.

Although the courts of appeals have rejected the contention that deferral under *Collyer* constitutes an illegal abdication of its duty to remedy unfair labor practices, they will scrutinize deferrals to determine whether the Board has *abused its discretion* in deciding that deferral to arbitration furthers the fundamental aims of the NLRA. *E.g., Machinists, Lodge 700 v. NLRB, supra; IBEW, Local 2188 v. NLRB, supra.* In the latter case, the court of appeals for the D.C. Circuit articulated its understanding of the limitations on the Board's discretion to stay its hand pending arbitration:

> We read the *Collyer* doctrine as a balancing rule which requires deferral to arbitration only where a balance of both supporting and antagonistic policies favors deferral. The operation of this balancing process is demonstrated by the *Collyer* opinion itself.

There the Board considered five factors bearing upon the probable effectiveness of arbitration to advance Federal labor policy:

1. The history and quality of the parties' collective bargaining relationship;
2. The absence of anti-union animus;
3. Willingness of the respondent party to arbitrate;
4. The scope of the arbitration clause;
5. Suitability of the dispute to resolution by arbitration.

In *Collyer* all of these considerations favored deferral. Elaborating on the fifth point, the Board noted that the factual bases of the statutory claim and of the contractual dispute were so intertwined that resolution of the contractual issue by arbitration might be dispositive of the statutory (unfair labor practice) issue. . .

This congruence between the contractual dispute and the overlying unfair labor practice charge is significant. If it were not present, the Board's abstention might have constituted not deference, but abdication.

Our endorsement of the *Collyer* rule would be incomplete without one further comment. While the Board's promise to overrule arbitration awards which are irregular or repugnant to the Act is a necessary condition to the legality of pre-arbitral deferrals, it is not a sufficient one. Put another way, the fact that any ultimate award must conform to the policies of the Act does not guarantee that deferral itself is consistent with the Act. Pre-arbitral deferral might constitute an effective denial of any remedy if, for example, arbitration of the dispute would impose an undue financial burden upon one of the parties. Dismissal of the complaint in such a case would be contrary to the policies of the Act although all other criteria for application of the *Collyer* doctrine are met. Deferral might also be unjustified where it prevents an orderly exposition of the law in question. Successive arbitration awards could produce a variety of ad hoc solutions to the same problem, all consistent with the Act, but no uniform rule. In such circumstances further abstention by the Board might be contrary to Federal labor policy." 494 F.2d at 1090-91.

D. ARBITRATION AND PUBLIC LAW ISSUES

1. Deference to Arbitration Awards

ALEXANDER v. GARDNER-DENVER COMPANY

United States Supreme Court
415 U.S. 36, 94 S. Ct. 1011, 39 L. Ed. 2d 147 (1974)

MR. JUSTICE POWELL delivered the opinion of the Court.

This case concerns the proper relationship between federal courts and the grievance-arbitration machinery of collective-bargaining agreements in the resolution and enforcement of an individual's rights to equal employment opportunities under Title VII of the Civil Rights Act of 1964, 42 U.S.C. § 2000e *et seq.* Specifically, we must decide under what circumstances, if any, an employee's statutory right to a trial *de novo* under Title VII may be foreclosed by prior submission of his claim to final arbitration under the nondiscrimination clause of a collective-bargaining agreement.

I. In May 1966, petitioner Harrell Alexander, Sr., a black, was hired by respondent Gardner-Denver Company (the "company") to perform maintenance work at the company's plant in Denver, Colorado. In June 1968, petitioner was awarded a trainee position as a drill operator. He remained at that job until his discharge from employment on September 29, 1969. The company informed petitioner that he was being discharged for producing too many defective or unusable parts that had to be scrapped.

On October 1, 1969, petitioner filed a grievance under the collective-bargaining agreement in force between the company and petitioner's union, Local No. 3029 of the United Steelworkers of America (the "union"). The grievance stated: "I feel I have been unjustly discharged and ask that I be reinstated with full seniority and pay." No explicit claim of racial discrimination was made.

Under Art. 4 of the collective-bargaining agreement, the company retained "the right to hire, suspend or discharge [employees] for proper cause." Art. 5, § 2 provided, however, that "there shall be no discrimination against any employee on account of race, color, religion, sex, national origin, or ancestry," and Art. 23, § 6(a) stated that "[n]o employee will be discharged, suspended or given a written warning notice except for just cause." The agreement also contained a broad arbitration clause covering "differences aris[ing] between the Company and the Union as to the meaning and application of the provisions of this Agreement" and "any trouble aris[ing] in the plant." Disputes were to be submitted to a multi-step grievance procedure, the first four steps of which involved negotiations between the company and the union. If the dispute remained unresolved, it was to be remitted to compulsory arbitration. The company and the union were to select and pay the arbitrator, and his decision was to be "final and binding upon the Company, the Union, and any employee or employees involved." The agreement further provided that "[t]he arbitrator shall not amend, take away, add to, or change any of the provisions of this Agreement, and the arbitrator's decision must be based solely on an interpretation of the provisions of this Agreement." The parties also agreed that there "shall be no suspension of work" over disputes covered by the grievance-arbitration clause.

The union processed petitioner's grievance through the above machinery. In the final prearbitration step, petitioner raised, apparently for the first time, the claim that his discharge resulted from racial discrimination. The company rejected all of petitioner's claims, and the grievance proceeded to arbitration. Prior to the arbitration hearing, however, petitioner filed a charge of racial discrimination with the Colorado Civil Rights Commission, which referred the complaint to the Equal Employment Opportunity Commission on November 5, 1969.

At the arbitration hearing on November 20, 1969, petitioner testified that his discharge was the result of racial discrimination and informed the arbitrator that he had filed a charge with the Colorado Commission because he "could not rely on the union." The union introduced a letter in which petitioner stated that he was "knowledgeable that in the same plant others have scrapped an equal amount and sometimes in excess, but by all logical reasoning I . . . have been the target of preferential discriminatory treatment." The union representative also testified that the company's usual practice was to transfer unsatisfactory trainee drill operators back to their former positions.

On December 30, 1969, the arbitrator ruled that petitioner had been "discharged for just cause." He made no reference to petitioner's claim of racial discrimination. The arbitrator stated that the union had failed to produce evidence of a practice of transferring rather than discharging trainee drill operators who accumulated excessive scrap, but he suggested that the company and the union confer on whether such an arrangement was feasible in the present case.

On July 25, 1970, the Equal Employment Opportunity Commission determined that there was not reasonable cause to believe that a violation of Title VII of the Civil Rights Act of 1964, 42 U.S.C. § 2000e et seq., had occurred. The Commission later notified petitioner of his right to institute a civil action in federal court within 30 days. Petitioner then filed the present action in the United States District Court for the District of Colorado, alleging that his discharge resulted from a racially discriminatory employment practice in violation of § 703(a)(1) of the Act. See 42 U.S.C. § 2000e-2(a)(1).

The District Court granted respondent's motion for summary judgment and dismissed the action. 346 F. Supp. 1012 (1971). The court found that the claim of racial discrimination had been submitted to the arbitrator and resolved adversely to petitioner.[4] It then held that petitioner, having voluntarily elected to pursue his grievance to final arbitration under the nondiscrimination clause of the collective-bargaining agreement, was bound by the arbitral decision and thereby precluded from suing his employer under Title VII. The Court of Appeals for the Tenth Circuit affirmed *per curiam* on the basis of the District Court's opinion. . . .

We granted petitioner's application for certiorari. . . . We reverse.

II. . . . Even in its amended form, . . . Title VII does not provide the Commission with direct powers of enforcement. The Commission cannot adjudicate claims or impose administrative sanctions. Rather, final responsibility for enforcement of Title VII is vested with federal courts. The Act authorizes courts to issue injunctive relief and to order such affirmative action as may be appropriate to remedy the effects of unlawful employment practices. 42 U.S.C. § 2000e-(5)(f) and (g). Courts retain these broad remedial powers despite a Commission finding of no reasonable cause to believe that the Act has been violated. *McDonnell Douglas Corp. v. Green*, [411 U.S. 792,] 798-799. Taken together, these provisions make plain that federal courts have been assigned plenary powers to secure compliance with Title VII.

In addition to reposing ultimate authority in federal courts, Congress gave private individuals a significant role in the enforcement process of Title VII. Individual grievants usually initiate the Commission's investigatory and conciliatory procedures. And although the 1972 amendment to Title VII empowers the Commission to bring its own actions, the private right of action remains an essential means of obtaining judicial enforcement of Title VII. 42 U.S.C. § 2000e-5(f)(1). In such cases, the private litigant not only redresses his own injury but also vindicates the important congressional policy against discriminatory employment practices. . . .

Pursuant to this statutory scheme, petitioner initiated the present action for judicial consideration of his rights under Title VII. The District Court and the Court of Appeals held, however, that petitioner was bound by the prior arbitral decision and had no right to sue under Title VII. Both courts evidently thought that this result

---

[4] In reaching this conclusion, the District Court relied on petitioner's deposition acknowledging that he had raised the racial discrimination claim during the arbitration hearing. 346 F. Supp. 1012, 1014.

was dictated by notions of election of remedies and waiver and by the federal policy favoring arbitration of labor disputes, as enunciated by this Court in Textile Workers Union v. Lincoln Mills, 353 U. S. 448 (1957), and the Steelworkers Trilogy.[6] . . . We disagree.

III. Title VII does not speak expressly to the relationship between federal courts and the grievance-arbitration machinery of collective-bargaining agreements. It does, however, vest federal courts with plenary powers to enforce the statutory requirements; and it specifies with precision the jurisdictional prerequisites that an individual must satisfy before he is entitled to institute a lawsuit. In the present case, these prerequisites were met when petitioner (1) filed timely a charge of employment discrimination with the Commission, and (2) received and acted upon the Commission's statutory notice of the right to sue. 42 U.S.C. §§ 2000e-5(b), (e), and (f). See *McDonnell Douglas Corp. v. Green, supra,* 411 U. S. at 798. There is no suggestion in the statutory scheme that a prior arbitral decision either forecloses an individual's right to sue or divests federal courts of jurisdiction.

In addition, legislative enactments in this area have long evinced a general intent to accord parallel or overlapping remedies against discrimination. In the Civil Rights Act of 1964, 42 U.S.C. § 2000e *et seq.,* Congress indicated that it considered the policy against discrimination to be of the "highest priority." *Newman v. Piggie Park Enterprises, Inc.,* [390 U. S. 400,] 402. Consistent with this view, Title VII provides for consideration of employment-discrimination claims in several forums. See 42 U.S.C. § 2000e-5(b) (EEOC); 42 U.S.C. § 2000e-5(c) (state and local agencies); 42 U.S.C. § 2000e-5(f) (federal courts). And, in general, submission of a claim to one forum does not preclude a later submission to another. See 42 U.S.C. §§ 2000e-5(b) and (f); *McDonnell Douglas Corp. v. Green, supra.* Moreover, the legislative history of Title VII manifests a congressional intent to allow an individual to pursue independently his rights under both Title VII and other applicable state and federal statutes. The clear inference is that Title VII was designed to supplement, rather than supplant, existing laws and institutions relating to employment discrimination. In sum, Title VII's purpose and procedures strongly suggest that an individual does not forfeit his private cause of action if he first pursues his grievance to final arbitration under the nondiscrimination clause of a collective-bargaining agreement.

---

[6] United Steelworkers v. American Mfg. Co., 363 U. S. 564 (1960); United Steelworkers v. Warrior & Gulf Navigation Co., 363 U. S. 574 (1960); United Steelworkers v. Enterprise Wheel & Car Corp., 363 U. S. 593 (1960).

In reaching the opposite conclusion, the District Court relied in part on the doctrine of election of remedies. That doctrine, which refers to situations where an individual pursues remedies that are legally or factually inconsistent, has no application in the present context. In submitting his grievance to arbitration, an employee seeks to vindicate his contractual right under a collective-bargaining agreement. By contrast, in filing a lawsuit under Title VII, an employee asserts independent statutory rights accorded by Congress. The distinctly separate nature of these contractual and statutory rights is not vitiated merely because both were violated as a result of the same factual occurrence. And certainly no inconsistency results from permitting both rights to be enforced in their respectively appropriate forums. The resulting scheme is somewhat analogous to the procedure under the National Labor Relations Act, as amended, where disputed transactions may implicate both contractual and statutory rights. Where the statutory right underlying a particular claim may not be abridged by contractual agreement, the Court has recognized that consideration of the claim by the arbitrator as a contractual dispute under the collective-bargaining agreement does not preclude subsequent consideration of the claim by the National Labor Relations Board as an unfair labor practice charge or as a petition for clarification of the union's representation certificate under the Act. *Carey v. Westinghouse Corp.,* 375 U. S. 261 (1964). *Cf. Smith v. Evening News Assn.,* 371 U.S. 195 (1962). There, as here, the relationship between the forums is complementary since consideration of the claim by both forums may promote the policies underlying each. Thus, the rationale behind the election of remedies doctrine cannot support the decision below.

We are also unable to accept the proposition that petitioner waived his cause of action under Title VII. To begin, we think it clear that there can be no prospective waiver of an employee's rights under Title VII. It is true, of course, that a union may waive certain statutory rights related to collective activity, such as the right to strike. *Mastro Plastics Corp. v. NLRB,* 350 U. S. 270 (1956); *Boys Markets, Inc. v. Retail Clerks Union,* 398 U. S. 235 (1970). These rights are conferred on employees collectively to foster the processes of bargaining and properly may be exercised or relinquished by the union as collective-bargaining agent to obtain economic benefits for unit members. Title VII, on the other hand, stands on plainly different ground; it concerns not majoritarian processes, but an individual's right to equal employment opportunities. Title VII's strictures are absolute and represent a congressional command that each employee be free from discriminatory practices. Of necessity, the rights conferred can form no part of the collective-bargaining process since waiver of these rights would defeat the paramount congressional purpose behind Title VII. In these circumstances, an employee's rights under Title VII are not susceptible to prospective waiver. *See Wilko v. Swan,* 346 U.S. 427 (1953).

The actual submission of petitioner's grievance to arbitration in the present case does not alter the situation. Although presumably an employee may waive his cause of action under Title VII as part of a voluntary settlement, mere resort to the arbitral forum to enforce contractual rights constitutes no such waiver. Since an employee's rights under Title VII may not be waived prospectively, existing contractual rights and remedies against discrimination must result from other concessions already made by the union as part of the economic bargain struck with the employer. It is settled law that no additional concession may be exacted from any employee as the price for enforcing those rights. *J. I. Case Co. v. Labor Board,* 321 U.S. 332, 338-339 (1944).

Moreover, a contractual right to submit a claim to arbitration is not displaced simply because Congress also has provided a statutory right against discrimination. Both rights have legally independent origins and are equally available to the aggrieved employee. This point becomes apparent through consideration of the role of the arbitrator in the system of industrial self-government. As the proctor of the bargain, the arbitrator's task is to effectuate the intent of the parties. His source of authority is the collective-bargaining agreement, and he must interpret and apply that agreement in accordance with the "industrial common law of the shop" and the various needs and desires of the parties. The arbitrator, however, has no general authority to invoke public laws that conflict with the bargain between the parties. . . . If an arbitral decision is based "solely on the arbitrator's view of the requirements of enacted legislation," rather than on an interpretation of the collective-bargaining agreement, the arbitrator has "exceeded the scope of his submission," and the award will not be enforced. [*Steelworkers v. Enterprise Wheel & Car Corp.,* 363 U.S. 593, 597 (1960).] Thus the arbitrator has authority to resolve only questions of contractual rights, and this authority remains regardless whether certain contractual rights are similar to, or duplicative of, the substantive rights secured by Title VII.

IV. The District Court and the Court of Appeals reasoned that to permit an employee to have his claim considered in both the arbitral and judicial forums would be unfair since this would mean that the employer, but not the employee, was bound by the arbitral award. In the District Court's words, it could not "accept a philosophy which gives the employee two strings to his bow when the employer has only one." . . . This argument mistakes the effect of Title VII. Under the *Steelworkers Trilogy,* an arbitral decision is final and binding on the employer and employee, and judicial review is limited as to both.

But in instituting an action under Title VII, the employee is not seeking review of the arbitrator's decision. Rather, he is asserting a statutory right independent of the arbitration process. An employer does not have "two strings to his bow" with respect to an arbitral decision for the simple reason that Title VII does not provide employers with a cause of action against employees. An employer cannot be the victim of discriminatory employment practices. *Oubichon v. North American Rockwell Corp.,* 482 F.2d 569, 573 (9th Cir. 1973).

The District Court and the Court of Appeals also thought that to permit a later resort to the judicial forum would undermine substantially the employer's incentive to arbitrate and would "sound the death knell for arbitration clauses in labor contracts." . . . Again, we disagree. The primary incentive for an employer to enter into an arbitration agreement is the union's reciprocal promise not to strike. As the Court stated in *Boys Markets, Inc. v. Retail Clerks Union,* 398 U.S. 235, 248 (1970), "a no strike obligation, express or implied, is the *quid pro quo* for an undertaking by an employer to submit grievance disputes to the process of arbitration." It is not unreasonable to assume that most employers will regard the benefits derived from a no-strike pledge as outweighing whatever costs may result from according employees an arbitral remedy against discrimination in addition to their judicial remedy under Title VII. Indeed, the severe consequences of a strike may make an arbitration clause almost essential from both the employees' and the employer's perspective. Moreover, the grievance-arbitration machinery of the collective-bargaining agreement remains a relatively inexpensive and expeditious means for resolving a wide range of disputes, including claims of discriminatory employment practices. Where the collective-bargaining agreement contains a nondiscrimination clause similar to Title VII, and where arbitral procedures are fair and regular, arbitration may well produce a settlement satisfactory to both employer and employee. An employer thus has an incentive to make available the conciliatory and therapeutic processes of arbitration which may satisfy an employee's perceived need to resort to the judicial forum, thus saving the employer the expense and aggravation associated with a lawsuit. For similar reasons, the employee also has a strong incentive to arbitrate grievances, and arbitration may often eliminate those misunderstandings or discriminatory practices that might otherwise precipitate resort to the judicial forum.

V. Respondent contends that even if a preclusion rule is not adopted, federal courts should defer to arbitral decisions on discrimination claims where: (i) the claim was before the arbitrator; (ii) the collective-bargaining agreement prohibited the form of discrimination charged in the suit under Title VII; and (iii) the arbitrator has authority to rule on the claim and to fashion a remedy.[17] Under respondent's proposed rule, a court would grant summary judgment and dismiss the employee's action if the above conditions were met. The rule's obvious consequence in the present case would be to deprive the petitioner of his statutory right to attempt to establish his claim in a federal court.

At the outset, it is apparent that a deferral rule would be subject to many of the objections applicable to a preclusion rule. The purpose and procedures of Title VII indicate that Congress intended federal courts to exercise final responsibility for enforcement of Title VII; deferral to arbitral decisions would be inconsistent with that goal. Furthermore, we have long recognized that "the choice of forums inevitably affects the scope of the substantive right to be vindicated." *U. S. Bulk Carriers v. Arguelles,* 400 U. S. 358, 359-360 (1971) (Harlan, J., concurring). Respondent's deferral rule is necessarily premised on the assumption that arbitral processes are commensurate with judicial processes and that Congress impliedly intended federal courts to defer to arbitral decisions on Title VII issues. We deem this supposition unlikely.

Arbitral procedures, while well suited to the resolution of contractual disputes, make arbitration a comparatively inappropriate forum for the final resolution of rights created by Title VII. This conclusion rests first on the special role of the arbitrator, whose task is to effectuate the intent of the parties rather than the requirements of enacted legislation. Where the collective-bargaining agreement conflicts with Title VII, the arbitration must follow the agreement. To be sure, the tension between contractual and statutory objectives may be mitigated where a collective-bargaining agreement contains provisions facially similar to those of Title VII. But other facts may still render arbitral processes comparatively inferior to judicial processes in the protection of Title VII rights. Among these is the fact that the specialized competence of arbitrators pertains primarily to the law of the shop, not the law of the land. *United Steelworkers of America v. Warrior & Gulf Navigation Co.,* 363 U. S. 574, 581-583. Parties usually choose an arbitrator because they trust his knowledge and judgment concerning the demands and norms of industrial relations. On the other hand, the resolution of statutory or constitutional issues is a primary responsibility of courts, and judicial construction has proven especially necessary with respect to Title VII, whose broad language frequently can be given meaning only by reference to public law concepts.

Moreover, the fact-finding process in arbitration usually is not equivalent to judicial fact-finding. The record of the arbitration

[17] Brief of Respondent, at 37. Respondent's proposed rule is analogous to the NLRB's policy of deferring to arbitral decisions on statutory issues in certain cases. See Spielberg Manufacturing Co., 112 N.L.R.B. 1080, 1082 (1955).

proceedings is not as complete; the usual rules of evidence do not apply; and rights and procedures common to civil trials, such as discovery, compulsory process, cross-examination, and testimony under oath, are often severely limited or unavailable. *See Bernhardt v. Polygraphic Co.,* 350 U.S. 198, 203 (1956); Wilko v. Swan, 346 U. S. 427, 435-437 (1953). And as this Court has recognized, "[a]rbitrators have no obligation to the court to give their reasons for an award." *United Steelworkers of America v. Enterprise Wheel & Car Corp.,* 363 U.S. 593, 598. Indeed, it is the informality of arbitral procedure that enables it to function as an efficient, inexpensive, and expeditious means for dispute resolution. This same characteristic, however, makes arbitration a less appropriate forum for final resolution of Title VII issues than the federal courts.

It is evident that respondents' proposed rule would not allay these concerns. Nor are we convinced that the solution lies in applying a more demanding deferral standard, such as that adopted by the Fifth Circuit in *Rios v. Reynolds Metals Co.,* 467 F.2d 54 (1972). As respondent points out, a standard that adequately insured effectuation of Title VII rights in the arbitral forum would tend to make arbitration a procedurally complex, expensive, and time-consuming process. And judicial enforcement of such a standard would almost require courts to make *de novo* determinations of the employees' claims. It is uncertain whether any minimal savings in judicial time and expense would justify the risk to vindication of Title VII rights.

A deferral rule also might adversely affect the arbitration system as well as the enforcement scheme of Title VII. Fearing that the arbitral forum cannot adequately protect their rights under Title VII, some employees may elect to bypass arbitration and institute a lawsuit. The possibility of voluntary compliance or settlement of Title VII claims would thus be reduced, and the result could well be more litigation, not less.

We think, therefore, that the federal policy favoring arbitration of labor disputes and the federal policy against discriminatory employment practices can best be accommodated by permitting an employee to pursue fully both his remedy under the grievance-arbitration clause of a collective-bargaining agreement and his cause of action under Title VII. The federal court should consider the employee's claim *de novo*. The arbitral decision may be admitted as evidence and accorded such weight as the court deems appropriate.[21]

_____

[21] We adopt no standards as to the weight to be accorded an arbitral decision, since this must be determined in the court's discretion with regard to the facts and circumstances of each case. Relevant factors include the existence of provisions in the collective-bargaining agreement that conform substantially with Title VII, the degree of procedural fairness in the arbitral forum, adequacy of the record with

The judgment of the Court of Appeals is

Reversed.

NOTES:

Is the rationale of *Gardner-Denver* limited to Title VII cases? Should a grievant be allowed to circumvent contractual grievance procedures whenever he asserts a statutory, as well as a contractual right? Put another way, to what extent does statutory regulation of the employment relationship displace arbitration as the primary means for resolving labor disputes?

The full impact that *Gardner-Denver* will have on labor arbitration is not yet clear. In *Electronic Reproduction Service Corp.,* 213 NLRB 758 (1974), an NLRB majority made clear that it would continue to defer under *Spielberg* (and *Collyer*) despite *Gardner-Denver.* The Board stressed that, while the Civil Rights Act was designed primarily to protect individuals from discrimination in employment on the basis of race, religion, sex, or national origin, the NLRA's prohibitions of unfair labor practices are only an integral part of a comprehensive regulatory scheme designed to promote industrial peace. As a preferred means of minimizing industrial strife, arbitration was said to deserve more accommodation under the procedures of the NLRA than it does under those of the Civil Rights Act. *But cf., General American Transportation Corp.,* 228 NLRB 808 (Murphy, concurring) (NLRB will defer under *Collyer,* only in §§ 8(a)(5) and 8(b)(3) refusal to bargain cases; Section 7 rights of individual employees *should* be enforced in governmental, rather than private forums).

The impact of *Gardner-Denver* on arbitration under other federal regulatory schemes is also unclear. Several cases, however, suggest that *Gardner-Denver* should not apply in full force whenever federal statutory rights are involved. For example, in *Gateway Coal Co. v. United Mine Workers,* 414 U.S. 368 (1974) (see especially the dissenting opinion of Douglas, J.), the Supreme Court held arbitrable a dispute over mine safety, despite the existence of pervasive federal regulations governing working and environmental conditions in coal mines. *Compare Satterwhite v. United Parcel Service, Inc.,* 496 F.2d

---

respect to the issue of discrimination, and the special competence of particular arbitrators. Where an arbitral determination gives full consideration to an employee's Title VII rights, a court may properly accord it great weight. This is especially true where the issue is solely one of fact, specifically addressed by the parties and decided by the arbitrator on the basis of an adequate record. But courts should ever be mindful that Congress, in enacting Title VII, thought it necessary to provide a judicial forum for the ultimate resolution of discriminatory employment claims. It is the duty of courts to assure the full availability of this forum.

448 (10th Cir. 1974) (employees' right to sue under the Fair Labor Standards Act is foreclosed by prior submission of his claim to final arbitration) and *Union De Tronquistas, Local 901 v. Flagship Hotel Corp.,* 554 F.2d 8 (1st Cir. 1977) (arbitrator's interpretation of Puerto Rico administrative regulation held final and binding) *with Leone v. Mobil Oil Corp.,* 523 F.2d 1153 (D.C. Cir. 1975) (employee need not pursue contractual grievance remedies before suing under FLSA); *U.S. Bulk Carriers, Inc. v. Arguelles,* 400 U.S. 351 (1971) (seamen could sue in federal court for wages under 46 U.S.C. § 596 without invoking contractual grievance and arbitration procedures); *Thompson v. Iowa Beef Packers, Inc.,* 185 N.W.2d 738 (Ia. 1971), *cert. denied,* 405 U.S. 228 (1972) (Supreme Court declined to review ruling by Iowa Supreme Court that *Arguelles, supra,* applies to FLSA suits); and *Brennan v. Alan Wood Steel Co.,* 3 OSHC 1654 (E.D. Pa. 1975) (court refused to defer to arbitrator's ruling in a § 11(c)(1) discrimination proceeding under OSHA).

2. Public Law Issues in Arbitration

FELLER, "THE COMING END OF ARBITRATION'S GOLDEN AGE," in PROCEEDINGS OF THE 29TH ANNUAL MEETING, NATIONAL ACADEMY OF ARBITRATORS 97 (1976)

Essential to the Golden Age of Arbitration was the proposition that the rights of employees and employers with respect to the employment relationship are governed by an autonomous, self-contained system of private law. That system consists of a statute, the collective bargaining agreement, and an adjudicatory mechanism, the grievance and arbitration machinery, integral with the statute and providing only the remedial powers granted, expressly or impliedly, in the statute.

. . . [C]ourts seem to have sensed that labor arbitration is really a system of government. Indeed, you could say that what the courts have done is to treat that system of government as another jurisdiction, to whose judgments they must give full faith and credit when the tribunals had jurisdiction to enter those judgments, that is, when, as required by the *Steelworkers* trilogy, the judgments derived from the collective agreements. It is irrelevant whether the court would have reached the same conclusion.

. . .

Thus the very special status that courts have awarded arbitrators has little to do with speed or informality or, indeed, the special expertise of arbitrators. The status derives from a not always explicitly stated recognition that arbitration is not a substitute for judicial adjudication, but a part of a system of industrial self-governance.

The Golden Age of Arbitration, then, is the era of industrial self-governance. It is that period when the parties to the employment relationship look to their own machinery, including both arbitration and, where so provided, the strike, to resolve their problems; when a worker who believes he has been wronged because he has been denied a promotion or the wage he was entitled to, or because he was discharged improperly, would turn exclusively to that private machinery; and when an employer could, equally, assume that his actions with respect to the employment relationship were final unless rectifiable through the arbitration machinery or, when permitted, by the use of economic force. The law enforced by the courts — which I shall hereafter refer to as the external law to distinguish it from the negotiated rules governing the employment relationship — was irrelevant to such a system until 1947, when Congress passed Section 301, and Section 301, it turned out, served simply to enforce compliance with it.

I have, deliberately, somewhat overstated the autonomous and self-sufficient nature of the arbitration system. It has never been entirely autonomous. There have always been both state and federal laws regulating the employment relationship. There was always, of course, the National Labor Relations Act. But its essential role was mainly procedural, not substantive: to protect the process by which these governance mechanisms were developed and administered and to prohibit practices which would undermine or defeat it, or which — as in the case of closed-shop or hot-cargo agreements — were regarded as socially undesirable. The Act did not, and does not, except in a peripheral way, govern the substantive conditions of employment. Other laws did, but their importance was minimal because those laws were, and were intended to be, minimal standards. Such governmental regulation as the requirement that overtime be paid for work over 40 hours in a week, or provisions such as the state laws requiring that wages be paid at stated intervals, and in money, had very little impact on the relationships created by collective bargaining.

Hence it could be said, not with 100-percent accuracy but with substantial correctness, that the sole source of law in industries in which the grievance and arbitration machinery was well established was the collective agreement. The principal impact of state and federal legislation was upon those industries in which collective bargaining was not established, or at least not well established, and in which, therefore, the institution of labor arbitration was similarly, and consequentially, not established.

This was, truly, the Golden Age of Arbitration. That age began during or immediately after World War II. The beginning of its end can be dated to the 1960s, when we began to have an increasing quantity of substantive federal regulations of the terms and conditions of employment. In 1963 we had the Equal Pay Act, in 1964 Title VII of the Civil Rights Act, in 1970 the Occupational Safety and Health Act and, as well, Title III of the Consumer Credit Protection Act limiting the right of an employer to discharge because of garnishment. In 1974, we had ERISA, the Employee Retirement and Income Security Act, and the problems created by the inter-relationships between that act and collective bargaining agreements are just beginning to be felt. For a period we had wage controls under the Economic Stabilization Act, and we may have them again. Other statutory regulation will undoubtedly be proposed. . . .

The statutory development must do so, in the simple sense, because the introduction of public law as a source of individual employee rights, and the existence of public adjudicative and remedial bodies to vindicate those rights, necessarily undermine the hegemony of the collective bargaining agreement and the unitary — or almost unitary — system of governance under the agreement of which the institution of arbitration and its special status are the products. Arbitration is not an independent force, but a dependent variable, and to the extent that the collective agreement is diminished as a source of employee rights, arbitration is equally diminished.

That is, I think, so obvious as not to need saying. What does need saying is that this is the least of the problems. Far greater is the problem created by two facts. One is that the questions arising under the public, external law and the questions arising under collective bargaining agreements, which it is the function of grievance arbitration to decide, cannot be separated into nicely segmented compartments. The second is that the parties, or one of them, anxious to maintain the hegemony of the collective agreement, may force into the arbitration process questions of adjudication under the public law, sometimes — as in the case of the NLRB — with the active assistance of the public agency charged with enforcement of that law. I perhaps should add a third factor: the tendency of some arbitrators to reach out, without agreement from the parties, to engage in the process of public-law adjudication, a tendency which in the end, I think, can only be fatal to the posture, and the pretensions, of the arbitration profession.

. . .

. . . [T]o the extent that the arbitrator decides disputed questions of external law, he necessarily relinquishes his right to claim immunity from review by the bodies that external law has established as the ultimate deciders of what that law means and how it is to be applied in particular situations. By applying the external law, the arbitrator ceases to be part of an autonomous adjudicatory system and transposes himself into another kind of adjudicatory system. If you will allow me to push my previous analogy a bit further — his judgments are no longer entitled to "full faith and credit" because, rather than being an adjudicator in a foreign jurisdiction, the arbitrator becomes more like a lower court whose decisions are subject to review by higher courts. Further, it seems probable that once undertaken, review can scarcely be limited to decisions on the issues of external law.

. . .

It follows that the preservation of the autonomy and freedom from review which arbitration has enjoyed requires the abjuration of any authority to decide any disputed questions of external law.

Having laid down a principle which I think essential to the maintenance of the special status of arbitration, I must now confess that the goal may not be achievable in any case because of the first two factors I mentioned earlier: (1) the interrelated nature of disputed issues under an agreement and the external law, and (2) the desire of the parties to use the arbitration process to dispose of extra-agreement issues.

. . .

If — and again I emphasize the *if* — it is desirable to maintain the special status which arbitration has achieved as part of an autonomous foreign adjudicatory system, arbitrators can try to arrest this trend. To do so they should, insofar as they can, adhere to the Meltzer view and should certainly not volunteer to adjudicate questions of the external law on the Howlett theory that that law is necessarily embodied in the collective agreement.

But adherence by arbitrators to this narrow view of their function will not preserve the Golden Age. . . . The parties can, if they want to, make it quite explicit that they want the arbitrator to decide the rights of the parties not only under the agreement, but under the applicable external law. An arbitrator is, after all, the servant of the parties, and if they make it clear that they want what must inevitably be an advisory opinion from him in the hope that, when rendered, it will resolve the dispute and no one will seek to contest in court, he must oblige.

Second, and probably more important, whichever way arbitrators respond when they have a choice, their status is necessarily impaired. That status derived, as I said at the beginning, from the existence of an autonomous system of governance of the employment relationship. The statutory enactments of the past few years, and in particular the enactment of Title VII, have made it clear that society is not satisfied with the results of that autonomous system of governance. It was not satisfied, to pick a minor but apt example, that the question of whether a garnishment should be the occasion for discharge was being satisfactorily handled through the collective bargaining process. As a result we have, and I suspect we increasingly will have, alternate standards to govern particular aspects of the employment relationship and alternate forums to adjudicate compliance with those standards. This would create few problems for the arbitration process if the questions posed under these publicly imposed standards were clearly separable and unrelated to questions arising under collective agreements. But it is abundantly clear that the questions are intimately related in a variety of ways. The questions may be duplicative. . . . Or the collective agreement may arguably conflict with the standards of the external law, as in the unpaid maternity-leave cases. Or the answer to the question under the collective agreement may provide the essential datum for resolution of the question under the external law, as in *Mastro Plastics* or *C & C Plywood,* cases in which whether an unfair labor practice had occurred depended on whether a question was covered, or a right waived, by the collective agreement.

There are three solutions to the problem created by the existence of two sets of adjudicatory bodies and two sets of standards. One is to have the arbitrator decide all the questions under both standards, with the unfortunate consequences that I have suggested. The second is to bifurcate the litigation and develop a system of law in which the Labor Board or the courts would defer to arbitration whenever issues arise implicating questions under a collective bargaining agreement and then resume, or first accept, jurisdiction over the remaining statutory issues, using the arbitration decision as datum not subject to review. This alternative seems cumbersome, unlikely of achievement, and not even certain to solve the problem.

The third possibility is to have the Board or the court, or whoever decides the external law question, decide also what the collective bargaining agreement means. If arbitrators abjure decision on questions of external law, I think this last alternative is the one most likely to occur, and it can be disastrous for the parties. If I shudder at how arbitrators have handled external law questions, I scarcely can describe to you my reaction on reading Labor Board decisions construing collective bargaining agreements!

The first alternative will inevitably diminish the status of arbitration as a final and virtually unreviewable process. But the second and third may be more damaging to the sound development of employment relationships than the diminution of the status of arbitration which will follow from the first.

To sum the matter up, there is simply no satisfactory solution to the problem. The Golden Age of Arbitration was essentially premised on the fact that, for most of the important aspects of the employment relationship, the sole source of authority was the collective bargaining agreement. Insofar as that premise ceases to be correct, the institution of arbitration must suffer in one way or another.

Once that result is accepted as inevitable, it may very well be that the better course is not the abjuration of decision on the external law which I earlier urged as desirable in the interest of preserving arbitration's freedom from review. Arbitration exists to serve the interests of the parties, not the arbitrators. And the fact that the parties sometimes use words in their agreements which require arbitrators to decide external law questions, and the fact that they almost never rewrite their agreements so as to withdraw issues from the scope of arbitration when they become subject to adjudication in other forums, should tell us something. So, too, should the apparent acceptance by some parties of *Collyer,* which results in such arbitral statements as "I have authority to resolve the claim of unfair' labor practice in spite of the pending Board proceeding." There may be, and on balance I think there probably are, great advantages to both unions and employers in attempting to resolve their problems at home, even those involving the external law, and, therefore, keeping the grievance and arbitration procedures open to all sorts of claims, even those that ultimately may be subject to final adjudication elsewhere. The necessary result of their doing so may be that arbitrators become primary but not necessarily final adjudicators. But it may also be that, given the alternatives, that result is healthier for their ongoing relationships than the increasing resort to external tribunals as primary adjudicators. After all, a lot of arbitration decisions, even ones that you or I or the courts might regard as erroneous, the parties accept. If they do, their problem is solved. And this channeling of disputes through what Justice Brandeis, quoting Justice Story, referred to as "domestic forums" may have advantages for the ongoing relationship of the parties even if the effect is, in the end, the loss of the insulation from review which arbitrators enjoyed in the Golden Age.

ST. ANTOINE, "JUDICIAL REVIEW OF LABOR ARBITRATION AWARDS," 75 Mich. L. Rev. 1137 (1977)

. . . [S]ome [commentators] worry about the validity and finality of arbitral awards and argue that arbitrators should seek guidance from statutory law in order to reduce the likelihood of challenge in the courts. Others examine arbitrators' professional credentials and conclude they are not up to the task of construing statutes, even if the courts would permit them to do it. Still others stress the undoubted role of the arbitrator as part and parcel of the ongoing collective bargaining process and insist that insofar as arbitrators embark upon the totally different mission of statutory interpretation, their awards will lose the deference traditionally accorded them by the courts.

. . .

. . . [E]xcept for certain considerations of basic public policy . . . it is the parties themselves, unions and employers, who should supply the answers to the questions that have so beset the arbitration profession throughout the past decade. As interested bystanders, arbitrators are entitled to suggest to the parties what answers they might regard as wisest and most prudent. But once we have accepted an arbitral assignment in a given case, our own views should be irrelevant. The parties' views, as best we can discern them, should control.

Put most simply, the arbitrator is the parties' officially designated "reader" of the contract. He (or she) is their joint *alter ego* for the purpose of striking whatever supplementary bargain is necessary to handle the anticipated unanticipated omissions of the initial agreement. Thus, a "misinterpretation" or "gross mistake" by the arbitrator becomes a contradiction in terms. In the absence of fraud or an overreaching of authority on the part of the arbitrator, he is speaking for the parties, and his award *is* their contract. That is what the "final and binding" language of the arbitration clause says. In sum, the arbitrator's award should be treated as though it were a written stipulation by the parties setting forth their own definitive construction of the labor contract.

This thesis that the arbitrator is a contract "reader" helps clarify the proper scope of judicial review of an arbitrator's decision. The explanation of the courts' deference to arbitral awards is not to be found in some unique element of the collective bargaining process. The real explanation is simpler, more profound, and more conventional. Courts will ordinarily enforce an arbitral award because it is part of the parties' contract, and, with certain well-recognized limitations, courts are in the business of enforcing contracts. The doctrine that the arbitrator's decision is "final and binding" is qualified in several respects, as I shall discuss later. But, as the parties have given the arbitrator the task of reading the contract, the court need have no qualms about enforcing an award that appears to the court to be at odds with the parties' agreement.

. . .

Recognition of the arbitrator as the parties' official "reader" of the contract — no more and no less — would also enable us to dispose of many of the conundrums that have plagued the National Academy over the last decade. It clearly would resolve the perennial question of what the arbitrator should do when confronted with an irreconcilable conflict between the parties' agreement and "the law." With a right good conscience, he should follow the contract. After all, he is not responsible for "enforcing" an illegal or invalid contract. Only courts can enforce contracts. All the arbitrator is asked for is a definitive parsing of the parties' own agreement regarding the matter in dispute — or, more realistically, of the putative agreement they would have reached if they had ever anticipated the issue that has now arisen. This preference for contract over "law" also seems supported by *Enterprise Wheel*'s declaration that an arbitrator exceeds the scope of his submission if he bases his decision on his view of the "requirements of enacted legislation." Furthermore, the notion of arbitrator as contract reader permits of no distinction between an award *upholding* conduct contrary to law and an award *ordering* conduct contrary to law. In either instance, the arbitrator's mandate is plain: tell the parties (and the courts) what the contract means and let them worry about the legal consequences.

I do not wish to appear perverse in urging arbitrators to engage in the futility of rendering unenforceable awards. But as I stated at greater length elsewhere, the law is often not all that clear. The parties may hotly dispute not only the legality of a particular interpretation of a contract clause, but also the intended meaning of that clause. One party may be prepared to pursue the legal question through the courts. But first he wants a definitive ruling from the arbitrator on the meaning of the clause in issue. I feel he is entitled to such a ruling, uncluttered by the arbitrator's speculations about the law.

On the other hand, there is obviously a situation in which the arbitrator is entitled or even mandated to draw upon statutory or decisional sources in fashioning his award. That is when the parties call for it, either expressly or impliedly. If a contract clause, such as a union security provision, plainly tracks certain statutory language, an arbitrator is within his rights in inferring that the parties intended their agreement to be construed in accordance with the statute. Similarly, the parties may explicitly agree that they will abide by the arbitrator's interpretation of a statute whose meaning is in dispute between them. In each of these instances, I would say that technically the arbitrator's award implements the parties' agreement to be bound by his analysis of the statute, rather than by the statute itself. That distinction may have significant practical implications, as we shall see in a moment. There may be cogent reasons to avoid saddling arbitrators with the burden of statutory construction, but unless unions and employers are persuaded to refrain from imposing this responsibility, the reasons are beside the point. The choice is made by the parties, not the arbitrators. The only recourse for an adamantly objecting arbitrator is to decline such appointments.

Treating the arbitrator as the parties' designated reader of the contract enables us to resolve the thorny problem of the weight to be given an arbitrator's statutory construction. It has previously been assumed, by others as well as by me, that insofar as an arbitrator's award construes a statute, it is advisory only, and the statutory question will be examined de novo if the award is challenged in the courts. I no longer think this is the necessary result. As between the parties themselves, I see no impediment to their agreeing to a final and binding arbitral declaration of their statutory rights and duties. Obviously, if an arbitrator's interpretation of an OSHA requirement did not adequately protect the employees or violated some other basic public policy, a court would not be bound by it. But if the arbitrator imposed more stringent requirements, I would say the award should be enforced. The parties agreed to that result, and their agreement should be accorded the same finality as any other arbitration contract.

Whatever damage may be done to the pristine purity of labor arbitration by this increased responsibility for statutory interpretation, I consider an expanded arbitral jurisdiction inevitable. Such recent statutes as Title VII of the Civil Rights Act of 1964, the Pension Reform Act (ERISA), and OSHA are so interwoven in the fabric of collective bargaining agreements that it is simply impracticable in many cases for arbitrators to deal with contractual provisions without taking into account statutory provisions. Since I believe that, as between the parties, the arbitrator's rulings on the law should have the same finality as his rulings on the contract, I conclude, in contrast to the foreboding of my friend Professor Feller, that we are actually entering a new "golden age" for the arbitration process.

EDWARDS, "LABOR ARBITRATION AT THE CROSSROADS: THE COMMON LAW OF THE SHOP V. EXTERNAL LAW," 1977 Arb. J. 65 (1977)

[Professor Feller's] thesis is deceptively simple but grossly misleading. [His] argument begins with the premise that arbitration derives its subject matter from collective bargaining. Where public regulation of employment relations increases, he suggests, collective bargaining must decrease; the need for arbitrators will decrease proportionately. And, he says, if arbitrators get into the interpretation of public law, they will undermine the status and future of their profession. Arbitrators, he implies, must watch passively as their traditional base of activity dwindles; if they move beyond that base, they will hasten the demise of their unique role.

Feller's argument falters for three reasons: First, the magnitude of the increase in public regulation of employment relations is not so great as he implies, and its impact is not so persuasive. Second, it is not at all clear that an increase in public legislation brings a decrease in disputes for arbitrators to resolve. And third, it is entirely possible for arbitration to expand to deal with certain issues of public law.

With the noticeable exception of Title VII, the external laws cited by Professor Feller have yet to reduce the significance of collective bargaining and labor arbitration. In situations where unions are present as the exclusive bargaining agent, most terms and conditions of employment are still defined pursuant to collective bargaining and not pursuant to external law. The FLSA, OSHA and ERISA have, for the most part, established *minimum* standards as opposed to substantial substantive regulations or benefit provisions. As a consequence, most unions use these laws to establish a benefit floor in collective bargaining.

NOTE:

For a further discussion of the arbitrator and public law issues, particularly in employment discrimination cases, *see* Part Four, Chapter 19, *infra,* at p. 1049.

PART THREE

THE SUBJECT MATTER
OF COLLECTIVE BARGAINING
AGREEMENTS

Chapter 9

MANAGEMENT RIGHTS AND UNION SECURITY

The problems that arise out of the tension between management's "prerogative" to control its operation and the union's desire to obtain security for its members is an appropriate point of departure. In the broadest sense, the entire book deals with balancing of management and employee interests. In Part One, for example, the materials indicate that the collective bargaining process itself resulted as a compromise between unilateral determination of the terms and conditions of employment by either management or unions. The role of third party neutrals in achieving this balance through the arbitration process was considered in Part Two. Now once again the issue will be considered in the materials by discussing contractual attempts to deal with management rights and union security.

In this part the materials will focus on the content of labor agreements as drawn from actual contracts, arbitration and judicial decisions, and, to some extent, upon the voluminous literature in the field. It is not practical, however, to deal exhaustively with this material. It is hoped that by this presentation the student may become acquainted with the agenda of some of the subjects that confront the negotiator in reaching agreement and drafting a contract.

The materials that follow are intended to illustrate the significance of drafting skills in general. Specifically, the student is asked to consider how the parties attempt to reach a compromise by the use of "management rights" clauses, "union security," "no-strike" and "grievance procedure" provisions. In addition, the student should consider how each subsequent subject treated in Part Three of the materials affects the balance of management rights and union security.

A. MANAGEMENT RIGHTS

1. Reserved Rights Doctrine

C. C. KILLINGSWORTH, MANAGEMENT RIGHTS REVISITED, in ARBITRATION AND SOCIAL CHANGE, PROCEEDINGS OF THE TWENTY-SECOND ANNUAL MEETING OF THE NATIONAL ACADEMY OF ARBITRATORS 1, 3-13, 19 (Somers ed. 1969)[1]

. . . .

I have spoken of the "pristine" version of the management's reserved rights doctrine. The dictionary says "pristine" means "in the original version," "uncorrupted." The importance of the adjective will shortly be apparent. The best statement of this pristine version is found in a paper which Jim Phelps, then of Bethlehem Steel, presented at an Academy meeting in 1956.[2] Here are the key passages from Jim's paper:

> When we speak of the term "management's rights" . . . we are referring to the residue of management's pre-existing functions which remains after the negotiation of a collective bargaining agreement. In the absence of such an agreement, management has absolute discretion in the hiring, firing, and the organization and direction of the working forces, subject only to such limitations as may be imposed by law. . . . [E]xcept as management has agreed to restrict the exercise of its usual functions, it retains the same rights which it possessed before engaging in collective bargaining . . . this view is . . . the only one that gives full recognition to the realities of the collective bargaining relationship. In general, the process of collective bargaining involves an attempt by a labor union to persuade an employer to accept limitations upon the exercise of certain of his previously unrestricted managerial rights. To the extent that the union is unsuccessful in persuading an employer to agree to a particular demand, management's rights remain unlimited.

Jim went on to make it clear that he emphatically rejected the notion that there could be any "implied obligations" on management in a labor agreement. He was highly critical of a passage in an arbitration

---

Note: Footnotes from quoted material have been renumbered and bracketed.

[1] Reprinted with permission of the publisher. Copyright © 1970 by the Bureau of National Affairs, Inc.

[2] James C. Phelps, *Management's Reserved Rights: An Industry View,* MANAGEMENT RIGHTS AND THE ARBITRATION PROCESS, PROCEEDINGS OF THE NINTH ANNUAL MEETING, NATIONAL ACADEMY OF ARBITRATORS 117 (Washington, D.C., BNA 1956).

decision that he had recently received, which included the following dictum:

"Conceivably, in rare and unusual situations, local or departmental management might be guilty of such extreme abuse of managerial authority that its action could be reviewed in arbitration."

Jim denounced this view as "heresy." The essence of his position simply was that, as to all matters not governed by the *specific* terms of the agreement, management retains sole, unlimited discretion; and arbitrators have no jurisdiction whatever to review management's exercise of that discretion.

Some of my arbitrator colleagues have subsequently expressed doubts to me that Jim really said what the printed record shows he said, and others have questioned whether his views were really typical of management representatives generally. My answer to these arbitrators always is that I have heard the doctrine of management's reserved rights expounded in identical terms by many other advocates. Let me add two brief reminders for emphasis: Owen Fairweather's statement of the doctrine at last year's meeting was that management retains those rights not limited "by some *specific* provision of the labor agreement." It would be an injustice to Owen to assume that his choice of the phrase "specific provision," was inadvertent. Moreover, Russ Smith and Dallas Jones in their survey found evidence of rather widespread management efforts to strengthen the management's rights clause of their labor agreements, most generally by writing in the pristine version of the reserved rights concept — in other words, attempts to prevent the arbitrator from relying in any way on the implied obligations doctrine.

In my opinion, the pristine reserved rights concept has two fundamental weaknesses. In the first place, it rests on a highly unrealistic view of the employer's situation in the absence of a labor agreement but with a union representing his employees. In the second place, I believe that the United States Supreme Court has, in effect, rejected the concept.

The reserved rights concept necessarily rests on the view (in Jim Phelps' words) that, in the absence of a labor agreement, "management has absolute discretion in the hiring, firing, and the organization and direction of the working forces, subject only to such limitations as may be imposed by law." Now there may be some basis in legal doctrine for arguing that the employer has the "right" — for example — to abolish a long-established incentive system, or to cut wages by 25 percent, in the absence of any contractual obligation to maintain either.[3] As a nonlawyer, I would not quarrel with the many

[3] The National Labor Law (as interpreted) places certain constraints on the employer where a union is the accredited bargaining agent; but for the sake of simplicity in exposition, we ignore such statutory constraints.

distinguished lawyers who have defended that proposition. But as a labor economist, I would insist that having the legal "right" to do something is not necessarily the same thing as having "absolute discretion" to do it. When we speak of "absolute discretion," we refer to a situation in which there are absolutely no external constraints on choice. The basic fallacy of the reserved rights doctrine lies in its equating a putative "right" to take action with "absolute discretion" to take action. What this doctrine relies upon is the fact that the law does not constrain the employer's discretion. What the doctrine ignores is the existence of an important countervailing right, the right of the employees to go on strike. This right, which has been protected by federal law since 1935, quite frequently and powerfully constrains the employer's discretion.

What we have here, I suggest, is a basic difference between legal analysis and economic analysis. At the risk of considerable oversimplification, one might say that a major concern of the law is analysis of rights and duties under given circumstances, while a major concern of economics is the analysis of human behavior under given circumstances. In particular, economics is concerned with the behavior that is induced by the rational pursuit of self-interest. The law may tell me that I have a "right" to offer my new house for sale at a price three times what I just paid for it; but economics tells me that I am not likely to sell it for any more than is currently being paid for comparable houses in the neighborhood. I have complete control over the asking price, but the prospective buyer has complete control over his offer; and the selling price may be different from either the asking price or the first offer. My legal right to determine the asking price does not give me a right to compel the buyer to agree to pay it. Each of us — the buyer and the seller — has only an uncertain and contingent control over the selling price. If a sale is to take place, then in the typical case, the actual selling price must represent an accommodation of conflicting interests rather than a unilateral determination. The law may tell the employer that he has the unlimited right to direct the work force in the absence of a labor agreement; but the labor economist tells him that this unlimited right is worthless if he cannot recruit or retain a work force on the terms that he is offering. In a free market, the right of either party to a proposed transaction to say "no deal" imposes real constraints on the discretion of the other party.

Collective bargaining is a process that cuts across the domains of both law and economics. Trying to explain the bargaining process, or its product, the labor agreement, in exclusively legal or exclusively economic terms is a prolific source of error. In a later section of this address I will undertake an analysis of the bargaining process and the labor agreement which attempts to encompass economic reality as well as legal theory. The point of emphasis here simply is that the "reserved rights" scenario is highly unrealistic when it portrays the employer coming to the bargaining table with a monopoly of power, and with absolute discretion over every aspect of employment conditions. There are, in reality, many constraints on the employer's discretion with regard to employment conditions, and not in the least of these is the employees' right to strike. In the absence of a labor agreement with a no-strike clause, everything that an employer might seek to do about employment conditions is subject to a strike to compel him not to do it, or to undo whatever he has done. In most situations, the employees' right to strike makes the employer's actual control over employment conditions only partial and contingent; and by the same token, the employees and their union have an uncertain and contingent control over the terms of employment. In modern collective bargaining, some managements do possess absolute discretion over certain subjects; but where they do, the real source of that absolute discretion is not the absence of a labor agreement, but the presence of one which includes a no-strike clause.

This point brings us to the second fundamental weakness of the pristine reserved rights doctrine. I think it is reasonably clear that the United States Supreme Court has definitively rejected this doctrine in the now-famous *Warrior and Gulf* case. . . .[4]

The necessary implication of the order to arbitrate is that the Court rejected the view that the lack of any explicit provision in the agreement covering subcontracting necessarily gave management complete control over that matter. That *was* the view of the lower courts, and their judgment was reversed. I do not think that it is reading too much into the case to say that the Court held, in effect, that to find out what the functions of management are, you have to interpret the agreement, and you have to interpret its silence as well as its language; silence alone cannot automatically be taken to give management unfettered discretion; and since the parties had agreed to arbitrate questions of interpretation, the courts should not undertake the job of the arbitrator.

The pristine reserved rights doctrine holds that silence in a labor agreement can have only one meaning, and this view was accepted by the lower courts in the *Warrior and Gulf* case. By reversing the lower courts, the Supreme Court was necessarily holding that silence in a labor contract may have more than one meaning.

. . . .

The arbitrator interprets an agreement rather than a statute; but it is essential for him, if he is to perform his task properly, to begin with an understanding of the nature and the dynamics of collective bargaining. My most fundamental criticism of the reserved rights

---

[4] United Steelworkers v. Warrior & Gulf Nav. Co., 363 U.S. 574 (1960).

doctrine is that it presents an unrealistic picture of the bargaining process, and therefore offers a seriously misleading guide to the interpretation of the collective bargaining agreement; by concluding that silence in the agreement can have only one meaning, the doctrine greatly oversimplifies. The arbitrator must begin with the understanding that the bargaining process involves two parties, each of whom has a somewhat uncertain, contingent control over the terms and conditions of employment. Each party needs the assent of the other in order to make his control over particular terms and conditions fully effective. So bargaining is a process of give and take on both sides. Each side gives as much as it thinks it safely can in some areas in order to get the consent of the other side in other areas. The compelling force in this process is that mutual agreement is absolutely essential for the welfare of both parties.

The essence of the matter is that collective bargaining is a process of seeking ways and means to accommodate goals and objectives and values which in some respects and on certain subjects are sharply in conflict. [5]   The company, generally speaking, has as its most basic goal the achievement of efficiency; and freedom to change the way things are being done is usually essential to efficiency. The union, generally speaking, has as its most basic goal the achievement of security for employees; and maintenance of the status quo is generally important, if not essential, to employee security. Now obviously the objectives of the company and the union may vary somewhat from one subject to another, but this does not alter the basic analysis. The outcome of the bargaining process normally is that on certain subjects, under certain circumstances, the parties agree that the "efficiency" objective will dominate; and that on other subjects, under other circumstances, the "security" objective will dominate.

It is not always good tactics to spell out in language that everybody can understand just what the accommodation is. Sometimes union negotiators will reluctantly accept a principle but will balk at stating it baldly in the agreement, and the same is true of company negotiators. After all, the agreement must usually be "sold" both to the executive suite and to the shop, and you can have a degree of clarity on some matters that interferes with the selling process. Furthermore, it is simply impossible to anticipate the detailed circumstances of all future problems. And sometimes the parties are unable to agree at all on a matter and simply decide to ignore it with the hope that it will not come up during the life of the agreement.

---

[5] I have developed this point at greater length in an article, *Cooperative Approaches to Problems of Technological Change,* in ADJUSTING TO TECHNOLOGICAL CHANGE 61-94, INDUSTRIAL RELATIONS RESEARCH ASS'N (Gerald G. Somers, Edward L. Cushman & Nat Weinberg eds., Harper & Row, 1963).

The product of this delicate process of finding accommodations is a document that can be fully understood only if the process is understood. Some of the parties' understandings are expressed in deliberately ambiguous language. Sometimes the understandings are only implied by the language of the agreement. Sometimes matters about which the parties clearly have a mutual understanding or shared assumptions are not mentioned at all in the formal agreement. Finally, the difficulties of interpretation may be compounded because the agreement is written by people without training or experience in the art of draftsmanship.

. . . .

One final word, addressed to those who retain unshaken their belief in the pristine reserved rights of management doctrine. If you wish to insure that silence in your agreement will always be interpreted to mean that management has unfettered discretion, you have a choice of means to that end. You can follow the example already set in a number of agreements in the past few years, as reported by Russell Smith and Dallas Jones.[6] You can — if you can get your collective bargaining partner to agree to it — write that rule of interpretation into your agreement. You can say that management functions are limited only by specific provisions of the agreement, and that no implied obligations are intended. I am confident that any competent arbitrator would follow that rule of interpretation if it were clearly stated in the agreement. There is another avenue open to you. I have already said that I speak only for myself today, and I have also assured you that there will be some members of the Academy — and non-member arbitrators as well — who will disagree with my position. I am sure that you will have no trouble finding them if you look for them. . . .

2. "Management Rights" Provisions

BNA's survey of 400 out of 5,000 sample contracts kept on file indicate that all but 4 contained management (and union) rights provisions.[1] This has been consistent throughout the past decade, but there is a trend to include contract clauses which limit management actions in specific areas such as supervisory performance (in 57% of contracts surveyed), subcontracting (in 40% of contracts surveyed), technological change (in 19% of contracts surveyed), and plant relocation (in 17% of contracts surveyed).[2]

---

[6] Russell A. Smith & Dallas L. Jones, *The Impact of the Emerging Federal Law of Grievance Arbitration on Judges, Arbitrators, and Parties,* 52 Va. L. Rev. 831, 888-89 (1966).

[1] 2 C.B.N.C. § 65:1-4 (1/16/75).

[2] *Id.*

Bruno Stein, Director of the Institute of Labor Relations at New York University, indicates the importance of these provisions in arbitration.[3]

The arbitrator, of course, is a creature of the contract. In most cases, he must rely on contract clauses that have at least a tenuous relationship to the issue before him. Only on occasion is he given the history of the agreement so that he may interpret the meaning of a disputed clause. No wonder that all the textbooks — including those written by arbitrators — stress the importance of a clearly written agreement that includes everything that the parties consider relevant. If the parties followed this advice, the frequency and cost of arbitration might well be reduced.

But the parties cannot always follow this advice. For one thing, the need to reach agreement may make it necessary to leave some things vague. For another thing, problems arise that were not foreseen by one side or another at the time of the negotiations. No contract can cover all possibilities. Hence the need for grievance procedures and arbitrators.

Morris Stone writes of the technological radicalism of management versus the job conscious conservatism of the union.[1] It is management that initiates change — radical change — in the work place and elsewhere. The change comes from new products and new methods of production. The changes affect employees in many ways: in wages, work load, in the quality of work life and — perhaps most important — in the very livelihood of workers in the bargaining unit. No wonder that unions must resist change. In the long run, the fruits of higher productivity may lead to higher wages, lower prices and even more jobs. However, displaced workers live in the short run, and look to the collective bargaining agreement for some protection.

It is noteworthy, however, that the union does not seek to manage. This task remains in the hands of management. The union may seek to restrict certain managerial actions, but it does not — in this country — see its role as co-partner in the managerial function. Thus the employer's right to manage is implicitly acknowledged by the union, even in the absence of a management rights clause in the agreement.

One of the perennial needs of management is to increase productivity — to get more output from a given set of inputs of labor and capital. In the absence of a union, this *right* is

---

[3] Stein, "Management Rights and Productivity," 32 Arb. J. 270 (1977). Reprinted with permission of publisher c 1977 American Arbitration Association.

[1] Morris Stone, *Managerial Freedom and Job Security* (New York: Harper & Row, 1964), p. 239.

unrestricted, except for relevant laws on labor standards. Its *power* to do so (as Stone reminds us) was always restricted by what the labor market would tolerate; after all, a totally demoralized work force is not likely to be very productive. In any event, the advent of labor unions put *formal* restrictions on management power and management rights.

The theory that emerged after the rise of unions in the thirties and forties was that management retained all rights not specifically ceded in the agreement. As a practical matter, what arbitrators came to accept was the modified residual rights theory: [2] modifications include, *inter alia,* 1) that management prerogatives be exercised in a reasonable and rational form; 2) that the intent of an action be not to subvert the letter or spirit of the agreement; and 3) that long-established practices are not easily discontinued.

Although the theory suggests that management rights clauses are unnecessary, they are now as common as the recognition clause. Most management attorneys insist on them, and rarely encounter resistance any more. Indeed some standard management rights clauses in the boilerplate of contracts are essentially drafted by unions. The underlying management reason for including the clause is that it won't hurt, and maybe it will help. It certainly eases the arbitrator's task when making an award sustaining the employer's position, an award that he would — in all probability — have made in the absence of a management rights clause.

Turning from theory to practice, a quick survey of arbitration awards which touch upon productivity issues showed, not suprisingly, that the majority were won by management, with or without reference to a management rights clause. This tells us that the theory indeed conforms to practice.

. . . .

[He concludes that the importance of these provisions are as follows:]

1) The modified residual rights theory continues to have great weight in the absence of specific contract language that modifies a management right to effectuate productivity changes.

2) Management rights clauses in the contract are handy pegs for arbitrators who need a contract clause on which to hang an award. When there are cogent reasons to award otherwise, arbitrators will do so. In other words, a management rights clause is an important safety measure for management, but not a universal guarantee. It may yield to conflicting language in the body of the contract or to a very well-established past practice

which is, in effect, part of the body of rights guaranteed by the collective agreement.

3) New methods of production that are designed to increase productivity can raise problems that were not always anticipated by the parties when they signed the contract. In the absence of specific language covering such problems, it may become necessary to infer the respective rights of the parties from other contract language or from what may reasonably have been the intent of the parties.

4) There may be times when the arbitrator is not best suited for solving a technological problem. If the employer is the best judge of how to run the plant, *and* if the impact of change contravenes the rights established in the contract, then one possible course of action may be to compel the parties to work out the problem themselves. The arbitrator can do this by the use of an interim award which keeps the scope of the bargaining narrowed to the issue at hand. However, he must be prepared to render an award on unresolved issues; this is a responsibility that cannot be avoided once he takes jurisdiction.

5) There are exceptions to all rules, including the rule that there is no general rule where a management initiative to change productivity conflicts with past practice. There is a great challenge here to the parties to draft clear contract language if they want to avoid the uncertainty of an arbitration that may resemble a lottery. The best thing that can be said is that clear contract language will end to prevail over vaguely established practices.

6) Finally, the arbitrator is not a substitute for the bargaining process. His job is to complement the process, and to flesh out the bare bone of the agreement. Not only is he a creature of the agreement, but the agreement is also the tool with which he works. The better the tool, the better his work will be, and the less you will need him.

NOTE:

Problem: Consider the following tripartite Board's arbitration decision in light of Messrs. Killingsworth's and Stein's comments. Did they adopt a "pristine" view of management rights? Since the Board did impose a "reasonable and rational" test, would you recommend that Article I in the Agreement should be redrafted to limit future grievances?

In the Matter of the Arbitration Between

NORTHWEST AIRLINES
      AND
BROTHERHOOD OF RAILWAY,
AIRLINE AND STEAMSHIP
CLERKS, FREIGHT HANDLERS,   (UNPUBLISHED AWARD)
EXPRESS AND STATIONED
EMPLOYEES

Hearing Held November 9, 1976

Before the Board:

Richard I. Bloch
Impartial Chairman

Robert Schon
Company-Appointed Member

Raymond T. Thayer
Union-Appointed Member

OPINION

Facts

Grievant is a Transportation Agent for the Company, stationed in Spokane, Washington. On May 16, 1975 he submitted a written request that he be permitted to grow a beard. The request was denied. Subsequently, L. grieved, contending that the Company's regulations forbidding beards were unreasonable. The matter was submitted to the Joint System of Adjustment established by the parties.

Union Position

The Union claims there is no reasonable justification for the rule. In denying employees the right to grow beards, it says, the Company violates the United States Constitution, Title VII of the Civil Rights Act and the Collective Bargaining Agreement.

Company Position

The Company notes that the dispute concerns unilaterally-established Company policy. Since it involves no breach of the Labor Agreement, the Company says the matter is not arbitrable.

On the merits, the Company contends the rule is reasonably related to maintenance of a broadly-based image of acceptability to the traveling public. It denies that the rule is either discriminatory or unreasonable.

Relevant Contract Provisions and Regulations

ARTICLE I
PURPOSE OF AGREEMENT

The purpose of this Agreement is, in the mutual interest of the Company and of the employees, to provide for the operation of the services of the Company under methods which will further to the fullest extent possible the safety of air transportation, the efficiency of operation, and the continuity of employment under conditions of reasonable hours, proper compensation, and reasonable working conditions. For the advancement of this purpose, the Company and Union agree to cooperate fully, both individually and collectively. Subject to conditions specified elsewhere in this [Agreement], the Union recognizes the right and the responsibility of the Company to direct its own affairs, to direct and to supervise all employees, to reduce or increase forces and otherwise determine the necessary number of employees, to discipline and discharge employees for cause, to transfer, to promote and demote employees.

ARTICLE II
SCOPE—EMPLOYEES AFFECTED

These articles shall govern the hours of service, wages and working conditions of clerical, office, fleet and passenger service employees of Northwest Airlines, Inc., . . . The Company and Union agree that there will be no discrimination against any employee or applicant for employment because of race, creed, color, national origin, or sex.

ARTICLE XVI
DISCIPLINE AND GRIEVANCES

(a) *Grievances.* Any employee having a grievance, the cause of which arises out of the interpretation or application of any of the terms of this Agreement, shall have such grievance considered in accordance with the following procedure: . . .

ARTICLE XXVIII
SYSTEM BOARD OF ADJUSTMENT

. . . (d) The Board shall have jurisdiction over disputes between any employee covered by this Agreement and the Company growing out of grievances or out of interpretation or application of any of the terms of this Agreement. The jurisdiction of the Board shall not extend to proposed changes in rates of pay, rules or working conditions covered by this Agreement or any amendment hereto.

PERSONAL GROOMING REGULATIONS

... 14. *Airport Passenger Service Personnel*
...   f. *Hair Grooming*
        (1) Male Employees
        May wear hair styles currently acceptable within the business community and are expected to have their hair trimmed every two to three weeks.
        May not wear long or full hair styles which allow the hair to fall over the ears, forehead or shirt collar while performing assigned duties.
        May wear close-cropped sideburns trimmed straight down without curving onto the cheek.
        May not grow beards or goatees except when approved by the manager in connection with local celebrations.
        May wear close-cropped mustaches which do not extend beyond or around the sides of the mouth.
        (2) Female Employees
        Must wear hair in a style which is attractive and fashionably acceptable which keeps the hair *in place* throughout the work shift.
        May wear wigs of sufficient quality to meet the criteria established here.
        May not wear styles which allow the hair to fall onto the shoulder or over the face at any time while performing assigned duties.
        May wear long hair styles provided it is pulled back and secured at the back of the neck with a black grosgrain ribbon.
        May not use hair combs or pins which are visible.
        May not wear hair styles which protrude excessively from the sides or top of the head.

Issue

  Did the Company violate the Collective Bargaining Agreement when it denied grievant permission to grow a beard?

ANALYSIS

Arbitrability

The Company initially contends the matter is not arbitrable. Among other things, it notes that the contract contains no specific clause over which a question of "interpretation or application" [1] could arise. Additionally, it claims that, since this case stems merely from the denial of an employee's request to grow a beard and not in the context of disciplinary action taken for having grown one, the matter is premature.

The Company's claim as to arbitrability, raised here for the first time, lacks merit. The Company acknowledges that had grievant grown the beard, it would have disciplined him. By contractual agreement, disciplinary matters may be grieved and arbitrated.

In addition, the issues surrounding this dispute are clearly established and would scarcely be better defined in the context of discipline. Grievant has here acted reasonably, consistent with the oft-stated axiom "obey now, grieve later." Under all the circumstances, to deny arbitrability would be merely to promote a more serious, and otherwise avoidable, dispute.

Merits

At the outset, certain comments are in order concerning what this case is not. This is not a matter concerning sanitation or safety, nor is there any question as to an agent's ability to perform his assignments as well with beard as without. Cases dealing with those issues are to be distinguished. Similarly, there is, in this instance, no question of compelling personal necessity submitted as grounds for waiving otherwise unchallenged regulations. Nor does this case involve unequal application or sporadic enforcement of the rule. It is stipulated that the no-beard regulation consistently applies to all employees having substantial public contact. Nor is this a case of vague or somehow ambiguous regulations tending to promote inequitable application. Issued rules clearly forbid male employees from growing beards or goatees except under circumstances not relevant here.

The respective positions of the parties, then, are relatively basic: the employee wants to grow a beard; the employer wishes to enforce its rule prohibiting it.

The Union claims that such rule so infringes on this employee's personal rights as to amount to a regulation which is not only unreasonable but also unconstitutional and illegal under the Civil Rights Act.

The Company seeks to justify the beard regulation on the basis of

---

[1] Article XVI(a), *supra* p. 506.

the conservative image it wishes to portray to the general public — an image which, it believes, is compromised by bearded public representatives.

Having carefully considered the parties' positions and the rather imposing array of case discussions and related materials, the Board concludes, for the reasons which follow, that the contested rule is not improper.

The Constitution

Nowhere in the collective bargaining agreement have these parties indicated an intent to imbue the System Board of Adjustment with authority to consider grievances on the basis of the United States Constitution. Article XVI(a) establishes the internal dispute settlement procedure, including arbitration, for a grievance "the cause of which arises out of interpretation or application of any of the terms of this Agreement, . . ." Article XXVIII(d) states:

> The Board shall have jurisdiction over disputes between any employee covered by this Agreement and the Company growing out of grievances or out of interpretation or application of any of the terms of this Agreement . . .

Taken together, these sections rather clearly limit the Board to the terms and conditions of the collective bargaining agreement. Whether, therefore, this question might somehow be considered a constitutional infringement need not be and is not considered herein.

The Civil Rights Act

Title VII of the Civil Rights Act is not expressly incorporated in this labor agreement, but Article II states the parties' understanding that:

> . . . there will be no discrimination against any employee or applicant for employment because of race, creed, color, national origin or sex.

Given this, it is not unreasonable to consult Title VII caselaw for guidance.

The Union says that, since the rule affects only men, it is discriminatory on the basis of sex. That approach, however, is not compelling in this instance.

The reference books overflow with discussions on hair-length-as-sex-discrimination. Nowhere, however, has this Board determined any clear support for the proposition that a 'no-beard' rule amounts, *per se*, to sex discrimination. It is true that the contested rule affects men only. In light of the United States Supreme Court's recent decision in *General Electric Co. v. Gilbert,* however, one may not conclude that this alone is sufficient to warrant a finding of sex discrimination.

The essential question in this case, and the one to which this opinion now turns, is whether the contested regulation may be seen on balance as reasonable or whether, instead, the impact on the employee's private life is so substantial as to outweigh the employer's business interest.

Is the Rule Reasonable?

Inherent in the Company's right to manage is the right to promulgate reasonable work rules, the breach of which may subject an employee to discipline. Requisite just cause would be lacking for discipline stemming from enforcement of an untenable rule. Generally, the regulation must be reasonably linked to the employment relationship. That a rule is somehow work-related, however, does not mean it is invulnerable to challenge. If the rule extends far beyond the work arena so as to substantially encroach upon an individual's private life, it risks being considered as overly broad and not founded on reason. Each case must, of course, be judged on its own facts. In the final analysis, the reasonableness of a disputed rule must be tested by means of a weighing process which scrutinizes the degree of personal infringement in light of the demonstrated necessity for the rule itself.

As noted by Arbitrator Rolf Valtin,[13] "Arbitrators will scrutinize the need which Management asserts for hair and beard regulations. Hair an l beard regulations are not accepted as a matter of unilateral managerial discretion. They must meet the test of reasonableness." [14]

> Whether or not any particular hair-and-beard rule meets the test of reasonableness depends on a number of considerations. The nature of the industry plays the most significant role. Sub-criteria are: health or safety factors, the employee's exposure or non-exposure and the legitimacy of the particular image concern which the company is expressing.[15]

Arbitration decisions in this area are numerous and responses have varied considerably. To some extent, this in itself is evidence that each case must be decided on the facts peculiar to it.

On the one hand, because a work rule has an incidental effect on private life does not, of itself, supply grounds for its abolition. A number of such requirements impact our lives to varying degrees. And, as indicated above, it is by no means a novel proposition in

---

[13] *See* Hair and Beards in Arbitration, in the Proceedings of the 25th Meeting of the National Academy of Arbitrators (1973); p. 235.

[14] *Id.* at 239.

[15] *Id.* at 251.

arbitration that an employer may adopt rules with respect to overall dress and appearance, assuming they are reasonably related to the business.

Some grooming rules, of course, are essentially confined to the individual's work life and would hardly be vulnerable to challenge. Thus, this airline's requirement with respect to white shirts, checked ties or various uniform regulations present none of the problems inherent in the instant case.

But some rules are not so clearly confined to employment parameters. For example, male employees' hair styles are to be "currently acceptable within the business community." Men are expected to have their hair trimmed every two to three weeks. Mustaches must not extend beyond or around the sides of the mouth. These regulations, not challenged here, intrude to some extent on personal preference and private life.

But even assuming Union acceptance of such regulations, is there cause to distinguish beards? Are they less offensive to the public? Do they have more import on a personal level? It is difficult to draw rational lines between 'degrees of intrusion.' One would be hard-pressed to logically justify why an individual's personal interest in a beard should be greater than, say, in a "Fu Manchu" mustache or long hair, both of which are prohibited but which are not here in dispute. Nevertheless, there is a point beyond which personal constraints simply become excessive and the rule, though work-related, must be seen as unwarranted.

No evidence was introduced either in support of the Company's claim of offensiveness or the Union's challenge. Admittedly, however, the evidentiary burdens in this particular case would be enormous and it is not clear that even the most extensive data would resolve the question. Even assuming beards would be unappealing to various commuters; whether, given time and scheduling requirements, this would necessarily alter their choice of airlines and whether such reaction would have any demonstrable impact on the Company's business would be left, most probably, to conjecture.[17]

Of one fact amidst a substantial degree of guesswork the Board is willing to take notice — a beard may fairly be considered, even today, as out of step with a purely conservative image. And, to the airline industry in general and to Northwest Airlines in particular, image is abundantly important. In a business where competitors supply the same services with essentially the same equipment and for about the same price, this is no surprise. To be sure, the method of promoting the chosen image varies among airlines. But whether overall virtues

---

[17] Herein one may infer what is admittedly idle speculation by the Chairman that a beard might be seen as an attractive feature. [Some described the Impartial Chairman's appearance at the arbitration as hirsute! — Eds.]

are extolled in terms of timeliness of service, quality of food, color, size, shapes or even names of planes, there can be little question that public image, to an airline, is a vital and consistent consideration.[18]

The Union, for its part, notes that times are changing. The Board agrees. Surely, beards are no longer equated *per se* with social radicalism or even with some sort of symbolic speech. It may be safely said that, in 1976, beards are essentially a matter of style and fashion.[19]

But that is just the point, for in perspective, the question here is properly viewed as whether, in the context of competing interests, it is the personal or professional image which shall control.

Considering the nature of this Company's concerns in this industry and balancing them against the desire of this grievant to sport facial adornment, the conclusion is that the contested rule may not be regarded as unreasonable. Conceivably, one may not agree that a well-groomed, albeit bearded, agent could not serve as a readily-acceptable Company representative. Moreover, one may arguably be unmoved by the conservative image adopted by the Company. Surely, however, the choice of image remains with the Company. The issue for arbitral concern is whether the contested rule, while promoting Company policy, does so at such great cost to personal prerogatives as to be, on balance, unreasonable. As indicated, the finding here is that it does not. This is not to suggest, as a general premise, that the individual's concern for image is inherently less important than the Company's. It is to say that, given

---

[18] A *caveat,* however, is in order. The Company rests its case on its belief that a bearded agent would offend certain members of the traveling public. One may assume that certain travelers would be offended. On the other hand, they might also be affected by an agent who is bald, black or blonde. This opinion should in no sense be read as lending validity to management decisions based on such characteristics.

[19] Said Arbitrator Valtin (see n. 13, *supra*):

I admit to some difficulty in viewing Hair and Beards as an area representing a conflict of vital rights on either side. And I think that the passions which have accompanied the discussions of long hair, sideburns and beards — with reference to the work place or outside — have been excessive. (At 237).

Relating a beard case he had presided over, the Arbitrator stated:

I was not very impressed with either party's presentation. As I listened to Management's exaggerated claims of safety hazards and interference with efficiency (allegedly because fellow employees were gawking rather than working, something which would surely fade as beards ceased to be spectacles) my inner voice said "why in the hell can't you let him wear it?" and as I listened to the grievant's tale of how much the beard meant to him — mostly, it appeared, because he was one in a group of friends all of whom were bearded — my inner voice said "Why in the hell can't you shave it off?" Indeed, I subsequently vocalized the questions in private conversations with each of the parties. The difficulty was that neither side shared my perspective and that neither side felt it could reasonably give in. (At 237).

the clash between these two concerns in this particular case, there is sufficient justification for the rule to sustain it.

In sum, the Board finds that the disputed rule has not been shown to have been either unreasonably constructed or improperly applied. The clear prohibition against beards applies to all personnel with significant public contact. Despite grievant's desire to grow a beard as a matter of personal preference, in this instance, that wish must bow to the clear policy of the employer to project a highly conservative stance. It may not be said that the Company's reliance on the such image as appealing to a broadly-based segment of the community is misplaced or that it is obviously unreasonable to assume that beards will detract from that image. For these reasons, the grievance must be denied.

AWARD

The grievance is denied.

B. UNION SECURITY

1. Federal and State Laws

There are now basically four types of specific union security provisions: the union shop, the modified union shop, the agency shop and dues checkoff. "Closed shop" clauses, which require that an employee become and remain a member of the union as a condition of employment, have since the Taft-Hartley amendments of 1947 become illegal for all intents and purposes. The proviso to 29 U.S.C. § 158(a)(3), Section 8(a)(3), reads:

"PROVIDED, That nothing in this Act, or in any other statute of the United States, shall preclude an employer from making an agreement with a labor organization (not established, maintained, or assisted by any action defined in section 8(a) of this Act as an unfair labor practice) to require as a condition of employment membership therein on or after the thirtieth day following the beginning of such employment or the effective date of such agreement, whichever is the later, (i) if such labor organization is the representative of the employees as provided in section 9(a), in the appropriate collective bargaining unit covered by such agreement when made, and (ii) unless following an election held as provided in section 9(e) within one year preceding the effective date of such agreement, the Board shall have certified that at least a majority of the employees eligible to vote in such election have voted to rescind the authority of such labor organization to make such an agreement: PROVIDED FURTHER, That no employer shall justify any discrimination

against an employee for nonmembership in a labor organization
(A) if he has reasonable grounds for believing that such
membership was not available to the employee on the same
terms and conditions generally applicable to other members, or
(B) if he has reasonable grounds for believing that membership
was denied or terminated for reasons other than the failure of
the employee to tender the periodic dues and the initiation fees
uniformly required as a condition of acquiring or retaining
membership."

As indicated, the Act also provides that an employee can no longer
be required to meet any obligation of union membership other than
by tender of reasonable initiation fees and dues, uniformly imposed,
as a condition of employment. This means that as a matter of federal
law all employees could by a union security clause be required to pay
their way, because: "Congress recognized that in the absence of a
union security provision, 'many employees sharing the benefits of
what unions are able to accomplish by collective bargaining will
refuse to pay their share of the cost.' " [4]

However, in 29 U.S.C. § 164(b), Section 14(b),[5] Congress
expressly authorized the states to legislate rules governing union
security agreements. The Supreme Court has limited the
construction of this section to the regulation of *security
arrangements* — the "actual negotiation and execution of a type of
agreement prohibited by Section 14(b)." [6]

Pursuant to Section 14(b),

"Right-to-work laws," prohibiting a union shop, requiring
membership as a condition of employment, are in effect in 20
states: Alabama, Arizona, Arkansas, Florida, Georgia, Iowa,
Kansas, Louisiana, Mississippi, Nebraska, Nevada, North

---

[4] NLRB v. General Motors, 373 U.S. 734, 740-41 (1963); In 29 U.S.C. § 158(f),
Section 8(f), an exception is made in the case of employers engaged primarily in
the building and construction industry which permits provisions that would
otherwise be unlawful. The circumstances and provisions that are permitted are as
follows: (1) the majority status of the union has not been established under the Taft
Act before the agreement is made; (2) the agreement requires membership in the
union as a condition of employment after the seventh day following employment
or the effective date of the agreement, whichever is later; (3) the agreement requires
the employer to notify the union of opportunities for employment with the employer
or gives the union an opportunity to refer qualified applicants for such employment;
and (4) the agreement specifies minimum training or experience qualifications for
employment or provides for priority in opportunities for employment based upon
length of service with the employer, in the industry, or in the geographical area.

[5] Section 14(b) — Nothing in this Act shall be construed as authorizing the
execution or application of agreements requiring membership in a labor
organization as a condition of employment in any State or Territory in which such
execution or application is prohibited by State or Territorial law.

[6] Retail Clerks Local 1625 v. Schermerhorn, 373 U.S. 746, 757 (1963).

Carolina, North Dakota, South Carolina, South Dakota, Tennessee, Texas, Utah, Virginia, and Wyoming. Indiana's right-to-work law was repealed in 1965.

In all but seven of the right-to-work states listed above, the agency shop is clearly outlawed. The exceptions are Arizona, Florida, Kansas, Nevada, North Dakota, South Dakota, and Texas.

Regulatory legislation is in effect in several states that have no right-to-work laws. In Colorado at least three-fourths of the employees must vote their approval of union security clauses, while Wisconsin law requires that a majority of the employees in the bargaining unit and two-thirds of those actually voting must approve such a clause. In Connecticut, Hawaii, Michigan, New York, and Pennsylvania, closed shops or union shop contracts may be entered into only by majority unions. Maryland law declares union-security agreements to be against public policy and not enforceable by the courts, but no penalties are specified.[7]

2. Forms of Union Security Provisions

a. Union Shop

A union shop clause requires that an employee as a condition of employment become a member of the union within a stipulated period, usually thirty days, after being hired or after the effective date of the collective bargaining agreement, whichever is later. Sixty-three percent of all contracts negotiated in the private sector are estimated to contain union shop provisions which means that this is the most prevalent form of union security.[8]

A typical union shop provision will provide that:

> The Company agrees that employees now in the bargaining unit shall on and after thirty (30) days from the signing of this Agreement, and employees employed after the signing of this Agreement shall on and after thirty (30) days from the date of their employment, become and remain members of the Union as a condition of continued employment provided that nothing herein shall be interpreted to cause a violation of the Labor-Management Relations Act of 1947 or any other applicable law. (The Bendix Corporation *and* Auto Workers; exp. 4/77) [9]

---

[7] 2 C.B.N.C. § 87:12 (10/21/76).
[8] *Id.*
[9] 2 C.B.N.C. § 87:61 (2/12/76).

b. Modified Union Shop

The membership requirement in a union shop clause may be modified by providing exemptions for certain groups of employees. The modified union shop is subject to the Taft-Hartley limitations under Section 8(b)(3), as modified in Section 14(b). This type of provision is estimated to be found in 11% of all agreements.[10] The most common among these provisions are the ones that require union membership of all employees except those who were not members on or before the contract's effective date. This type of clause is referred to as a "maintenance of membership" provision because it requires that once an employee becomes a member of a union he must continue to be a member as a condition of employment. There is no requirement, however, that an employee initially become a member. Maintenance of membership agreements are permitted under the Taft-Hartley Act, although they are prohibited in those states with right-to-work laws.

For example, a simple maintenance of membership clause will require that:

> All employees who on the effective date of this agreement are members of the Union in good standing by payment of monthly dues in accordance with its Constitution and By-Laws, and all employees who become members after that date shall, as a condition of employment, maintain their membership in the Union in good standing for the duration of this agreement. (Union Oil Co. and Oil Workers; exp. 1/77) [11]

c. Agency Shop

An agency shop clause requires that an employee as a condition of employment pay an amount equal to the periodic union dues uniformly required as a condition of acquiring or retaining membership. The agency shop is legal under the Taft-Hartley Act, but is prohibited by most state right-to-work laws.

It is estimated that agency clauses appear in 9% of all collective bargaining agreements.[12] A typical clause may read:

> Each employee covered by this Agreement who fails voluntarily to acquire or maintain membership in the Union shall be required as a condition of employment, beginning on the 30th day following the beginning of such employment or March 1, 1966, whichever occurs later, to pay to the Union a service charge as a contribution toward the administration of this Agreement

---

[10] Id.
[11] 2 C.B.N.C. § 87:141 (3/25/76).
[12] 2 C.B.N.C. § 87:1 (1/16/75).

and the representation of such employees. The service charge shall be in the same amount and payable at the same time as the Union's regular dues, exclusive of initiation fees. . . . (National Steel Corp., Weirton Steel Div. *and* Steel Workers; exp. 8/77) [13]

d. Check-Off Provisions

Collection of membership dues is accomplished by the union soliciting employees directly, or by the employer deducting them from payroll. Section 302 of the Taft-Hartley Act permits collection of dues through payroll deduction — "check-off" — provided (1) it is voluntary; (2) the employee executes a written authorization; and (3) the authorization is irrevocable for not more than one year or the term of the contract whichever is shorter. Automatic renewal is permissible provided the dues deduction authorization explicitly permits the employee to revoke the authorization within a certain period prior to its nominal expiration date. Deductions may include periodic union dues, initiation fees and certain assessments, but not fines nor back dues past a certain period. Despite the substantive and procedural problems this raises in drafting such provisions appear in 86% of all contracts.[14] Although not technically considered as such, the dues checkoff is, as a practical matter, a form of union security and will be so considered for the purposes of this chapter.

NOTES:

(1) The following clauses are illustrative of the agenda items involved in check-off provisions:

Example 1 [15]

Check-off Deductions Permitted —
. . . the Company, during the life of this Agreement, will deduct from the wages of Union members their Union initiation fee and their monthly Union dues. . . . (Sperry Rand Corp., Vickers, Inc. Div. *and* Electrical Workers (IUE); exp. 12/67)

Example 2 [16]

Upon assignment in writing from an employee in the bargaining unit, in a manner and substance agreed upon by BIW and the Union, BIW shall: (a) Deduct his initiation fee out of wages earned and due. (b) Deduct his periodic monthly dues out of wages earned in and due for the current month in BIW employ. (c) Transmit all monies so deducted to the Union which will issue to the BIW its official receipt

---

[13] 2 C.B.N.C. § 87:121 (4/22/76).
[14] 2 C.B.N.C. § 87:1 (1/16/75).
[15] 2 C.B.N.C. § 87:401.
[16] 2 C.B.N.C. § 87:402.

therefor when paid. (Bath Iron Works Corp. *and* Shipbuilding Workers; exp. 4/70)

Example 3 [17]

I hereby assign to Local Union No. —, International Union, from any wages earned or to be earned by me as your employee, the sum of $— per month and initiation fees and assessments, or such amount as may hereafter be established by the union and become due to it, as my membership dues in said union. (Authorization submitted to Department of Justice for ruling as to legality)

Example 4 [18]

Revocability of Authorizations —

The Company will withhold dues due the Union upon presentation of a signed order by the individual employee; it is understood, however, that the employee has a right to withdraw the order, at his own discretion, at any time. (Marquette Cement Mfg. Co. *and* Cement, Lime & Gypsum Workers; exp. 5/67)

Example 5 [19]

I reserve the right to revoke this authorization during the two-week period preceding the next anniversary date of the Agreement. The authorization shall renew itself thereafter from year to year, subject each year to revocation during the two-week period preceding the anniversary date. . . . (Wall Paper Mfg. Industry *and* Paper Mill Workers; exp. 5/68)

Automatic Renewal —

Example 6 [20]

. . . I agree and direct that this assignment, authorization and direction shall be automatically renewed, and shall be irrevocable for successive periods of one (1) year each or for the period of each succeeding applicable collective agreement between the Company and the Union, whichever shall be shorter, unless written notice is given by me to the Company and the Union not more than twenty (20) days and not less than ten (10) days prior to the expiration of each period of one (1) year, or of each applicable collective agreement between the Company and the Union whichever occurs sooner. (General Motors Corp. *and* Auto Workers; exp. 9/67)

(2) *Problem:* The Company and the Union have a "check-off" agreement similar to that provided in *Example 1, supra.* However, for 15 years the Company has allowed an amount checked off which was $2.00 a month in excess of that authorized by employee cards

[17] *Id.*
[18] 2 C.B.N.C. § 87:402.
[19] 2 C.B.N.C. § 87:413.
[20] *Id.*

which were similar to *Example 3, supra.* The $2.00 constitutes the individual employee's premium necessary to cover him under a group insurance plan arranged for by the Union. The policy provides life insurance and cash hospitalization benefits, and becomes effective on the first day of the calendar month during which the premium is collected.

The Union periodically advertises the group policy on the Company's bulletin board indicating an enrollment plan for November 15th to December 31st, although new employees have 60 days from the date of their employment to enroll. The Insurance Company cannot cancel the policy, but the insurance of any member ceases automatically 31 days after the due date of any premium for which the member fails to make the required contribution. A like "grace period" is provided to the Union for nonpayment. However, under the Union's insurance application, once the premium is collected from a member it becomes the property of the Insurance Company.

An increase in Union dues brought the management's attention to the fact that the amounts checked off employee's wages, which varied from $3.00 to $19.79 (dues varied according to the amount of wages), was $2.00 over the "authorized" amount. The Company requested a breakdown showing "regular union dues," and advised the Union why. The Union complied, and at the same time submitted new authorization cards covering the $2.00 insurance premium which the company refused to honor under the contract.

In a grievance filed by the Union, the Company contends that the $2.00 is not covered under "initiation fee and . . . monthly Union dues." It contends that it was unaware of the insurance plan which was not in existence when the check-off plan was initiated.

The Union alleges that management had constructive knowledge of all information contained on its bulletin board, and was actually aware of the plan. The Union further adduces evidence that during negotiations, it had asked the Company to bear part of the premium expense which it had refused to do.

As Arbitrator, would you sustain the Union's grievance for continued check-off for insurance premiums? *Compare Southwestern Bell Telephone Co.,* 38 L.A. 693 (R. A. Smith, 1962) *with Globe-Democrat Publishing Co.,* 41 L.A. 65 (R. A. Smith, 1963).

3. Other Forms of Union Security

Although management rights provisions are generally contained in a specific provision or are implied through some form of management rights doctrine, provisions relating to union security are found throughout the contract, for example in seniority provisions for union officers. Like management rights, union rights may also be implied.

Most labor agreements contain "recognition clauses," and due to the National Labor Relations Act the language used is fairly routine. The employer is required by the Act to recognize representatives designated or selected by the majority of employees in a unit appropriate for such purposes as the exclusive representative of all employees in such a unit.[21] Thus, the union's authority and scope is fixed by law. However, the use of such clauses raises a question as to what implications are contained in a provision that describes the bargaining unit and establishes the union's status. For example, do the parties intend by the inclusion of the recognition clause in the contract to incorporate, as if by reference, all past and future NLRA doctrinal developments concerning the scope of the duty to bargain? By way of example, does such a clause limit management's right to change its own rules? Consider the following arbitration decision.

UNITED PAPERWORKERS INTERNATIONAL UNION, AFL-CIO, LOCAL 1553 AND INTERBAKE FOODS, INC.

DONALD P. ROTHSCHILD, Arbitrator (FMCS), October 10, 1977.
77-2 LAB. ARB. AWARDS (CCH) ¶ 8524

BACKGROUND: The facts of this grievance may be simplified as follows:

On June 8, 1976, Interbake Foods, Inc. of the Southern Biscuit Company (hereinafter "Company") promulgated a rule concerning overtime work on Saturdays whereunder: (Company Exhibit 1)

Beginning June 17, 1976, the following rules concerning overtime on Saturday will be in effect.

1. Each employee desiring to volunteer for work must sign the sheet or he cannot work.

2. Each employee must work a full 8 hours shift to begin at 7:00 o'clock (AM) unless agreed otherwise with the Superintendent of Maintenance. Exceptions may be made for emergencies or unusual circumstances.

3. Anyone who doesn't show up for work after having signed will not be allowed to work for the next two Saturdays for which work is scheduled.

All craftsmen must sign the sheet for Saturday work as follows:
First shift must sign by Friday noon.
Second shift must sign by end of shift Thursday.
Third shift must sign by end of shift Friday.

---

[21] 29 U.S.C. §§ 158(a)(5), 159(a), Section 8(a)(5) and 9(a).

The United Paperworkers International Union (AFL-CIO), Local 1553 (hereinafter "Union") acceded to the rationale for, and the operation of, the overtime rule.

During the period from June 17, 1976 until February 19, 1977, both parties adhered to the rule; and, in point of fact, [N.] (hereinafter "grievant") had on one occasion been prevented from working for two consecutive Saturdays for failing to show up for work after having signed up for Saturday overtime. Furthermore, on another occasion (sometime around August, 1976), the grievant asked for overtime work even though he had not signed up in compliance with the "overtime rule," and he was denied the opportunity because the Company is determined to enforce the rule.

However, on February 19, 1977, the Company permitted [H.], an electrician, to work Saturday overtime even though it was known that he had not complied with the sign up provisions of the overtime rule, because a binindicator, which was essential to the normal operation of the plant, was not operating and the Company Supervisor wanted [H.] to work on it even though there were other electricians who were properly signed for work under the overtime rule.

A grievance was filed protesting the violation of the overtime rule, but the circumstances surrounding the filing are in direct dispute. The Union alleges that grievant was told that [H.], whom he had not seen at work in the morning was allowed to work without previously signing up as required by the overtime rule; and that sometime around 2 p.m., grievant went to see [J.], Shop Steward for the Repair and Maintenance Department to complain. The Union maintains that [J.] went to see [B.], Maintenance Supervisor for the Company, about 2:45 p.m., and was told that since [H.] had worked the Saturday overtime shift, [J.] would have to complain to [R.], Plant Engineer. Grievant testified that he saw [J.] talking to [B.], and that he went to see [R.], Monday, February 21st when he arrived at work in the afternoon to grieve, and when he learned Company was not going to pay him for work he had previously been denied because he failed to comply with overtime rule, he filed complaint in a timely fashion.

The Company, on the other hand, states that when [H.] arrived at work on Saturday morning and asked if he could work without prior sign up, [B.] asked the other employees in the office (including the other electricians) if it was alright [sic] that [H.] worked that day, and they all agreed. Accordingly, [B.] let [H.] work because if the binindicator had remained out of operation the plant would have to be shut down, and the other employees who were present did not object. The Company states that no employee was denied work that day including grievant because [H.] was permitted overtime.

Issues

1. Did the Union adhere to Step 1 of the Grievance Procedures, Section 13.2 in filing this grievance, i.e. timely filing?
2. Did the Company subvert its bargaining relationship with the Union by the misapplication of its "overtime rule"?
3. Did the Union "stir up" a grievance because of the Company's misapplication of its "overtime rule"?
4. Should grievant be granted overtime pay due to the Company's misapplication of its "overtime rule"?

Union Position

The Union's position can be summarized as being that the Company must apply its own rules consistently to Union employees, and that it cannot vary these rules by dealing with individual employees outside of the bargaining context. Since the grievant had been denied work for non-compliance with the overtime rule and another employee had been granted overtime although he did not comply, the Union asks that the Company compensate grievant for the overtime work wrongfully denied.

Company Position

The Company's threshold position is that the Union did not file the grievance in a timely fashion, and therefore the arbitrator does not have jurisdiction over the subject matter of the dispute. Secondly, the Company contends that even though it was a mistake to allow a violation of the overtime rule, no employee was injured by that mistake; and, indeed, the other employees working that day "encouraged" the mistake. Finally, the Company argues that grievant should not be entitled to profit from an incident that occurred six months prior to the instant grievance.

Further, the Company alleges that no complaint was filed about [H.] on February 19, 1977; and that although [J.] may have been in [B.'s] office, they did not discuss grievant's complaint. The Company states that it was not until February 22, 1977 that it was aware of any complaint about Saturday overtime, and that no grievance was filed until February 22, 1977 which was untimely, and that it denied the grievance from steps two through four of the grievance procedure for this reason.

Relevant Contract Provisions

13.2 Should any employee present a grievance in connection with his work, or should differences arise between the Company and the

Union with reference to any provision of this Agreement, there shall be no suspension of work on account of such differences, but the same shall be settled in the following manner and order, to-wit:

. . . .

13.3 In the event the dispute shall not have been settled through the procedures set forth in Section 13.2, either party shall have the right to refer it to an arbitrator selected by the Federal Mediation and Conciliation Service; provided, however, that no grievance shall be subject to arbitration unless it shall have been referred to the Federal Mediation and Conciliation Service within thirty-five (35) calendar days and from the date of the Company's decision in Step 4.

13.6 No settlement between an employee and foreman shall establish a precedent as to principles or policies binding either the Company or the Union.

2.1 The Company recognizes United Paperworkers International Union, AFL-CIO, as the exclusive collective bargaining agent for the employees covered by the Agreement.

5.2 Time and one-half shall be paid for time worked:

5.2.1 In excess of forty (40) hours in one work week;

. . . .

5.2.3 On Saturdays "as such" to the first and second shifts;

5.10 In case of scheduled overtime, the name and seniority date of the least senior employee who is scheduled to work in each department shall be posted in that department. Any employee who has sufficient seniority to be entitled to such scheduled overtime work but who is inadvertently excluded from such overtime opportunity shall have no right to complain unless he notifies his foreman at least two (2) hours prior to the end of his regular shift immediately preceding the scheduled overtime.

[For the purposes of this chapter the procedural questions are omitted.]

. . . .

[Merits]

2. When one looks at the merits of this arbitration it is obvious as Company counsel ably argued, that there are serious issues of principle involved in this grievance. Since the Company has admitted error, by far the most expeditious, not to mention inexpensive, way of handling the complaint would have been for it to have paid grievant for the 8 hours of overtime requested. But there is more at issue to both parties than this payment which led to this arbitration.

The Union argues and its President, [C.], testified that a foreman and employee cannot agree to change policies or waive the terms of rules. Whether Section 13.6, cited by the Union, is apposite to the issues of this case — namely whether an agreement between the Maintenance Supervisor and employees *before* any dispute arises is covered by this Section, it is an established principle that when a Company recognizes a Union as the *exclusive* collective bargaining agent for the employees covered by the Agreement (Section 2.1), it may not ignore that recognition by negotiating directly with the employees thereby avoiding the Union. Circumvention of the Union is the basis of this argument, and why the Union argues that the Company was improperly discriminating among its employees.

However, the Union has failed to persuade the arbitrator that the Company intended to subvert the bargaining relationship or was guilty of intentionally discriminating against grievant. The Company has admitted violating its rule, and the agreement by other employees to this violation is of no significance to that violation. It should be noted that the issue of whether any of the assenting employees should be permitted to grieve was withdrawn from this arbitrator. The Company persuaded the arbitrator that [H.'s] selection to work overtime in violation of their overtime rule was clearly a matter of expedience, as testified to by [B.]. Although expedience is no justification for violation of a rule, neither is it indicative of an intent to subvert the Union or discriminate against another employee.

3. In the same candor, and motivated by the Union's summation, suggesting that the Company "feels it is being sandbagged by the Union," it appears the matter of principle referred to by Company counsel is that this arbitration was caused by the Company's mistake "being chased by a grievance." In other words, the Company is accused of believing that this grievance was an afterthought. Just as the arbitrator is not persuaded that the Company intended to avoid its bargaining relationship, neither does it appear that the Union's purpose was to "stir up" a grievance based on the Company's mistake. It is not difficult to believe grievant's testimony that he was angered by the Company's inconsistent application of its overtime rule, particularly in light of the fact that he had twice been adversely affected by the strict application of that rule. Moreover, the Union's attempt to represent grievant in this complaint does not amount to "stirring up" a grievance. The Union has an obligation to see that its members are fairly treated under an Agreement.

Insofar as the issues of "principle" that are involved in this grievance, the arbitrator agrees with the Union that the Company must bargain with the Union under the Agreement, but is not persuaded that the Company intended to do otherwise on the basis of this grievance. The arbitrator is in agreement with the Company that excessive use of the grievance procedure, particularly arbitration, is detrimental to sound labor relations and expensive, but is not persuaded that the Union was "stirring up" grievances on the basis of this dispute.

4. The matters of principle being disposed of still leaves the arbitrator with the basic issue of overtime pay requested by grievant. The arbitrator denies this remedy, because grievant did not work the overtime, and to award any pay for the denial, occurring some six months prior to the instant grievance, would indeed be a "penalty" as characterized by the Union Representative. Since this arbitrator has not found any malice in the Company's action, it seems inequitable to allow an employee to profit from a matter of expedience; such a remedy seems particularly inappropriate when grievant himself might have suffered from a shut down of regular operations had not the binindicator been repaired. Finally, the length of time between grievant's denial of overtime work and the Company's violation of its own rule — 6 months, is too long a period to use for giving a remedy to be conducive to sound labor relations, for it would supply incentive to filing grievance disputes in the hopes of obtaining financial gain, rather than negotiating settlements for the purpose of resolving disputes.

Award

1. As to whether grievance was timely filed, the arbitrator takes substantive jurisdiction of the subject matter of the grievance.

2. As to claim that the Company subverted its bargaining relationship with the Union by misapplication of its "overtime rule," the grievance is denied.

3. There is no evidence that the Union stirred up a grievance because of the Company's misapplication of the overtime rule.

4. As to the remedy of granting grievant overtime pay because of the Company's misapplication of the overtime rule, it is denied.

NOTES:

Problem: Why did the Union consider a single incident of changing a rule, with the concurrence of all employees present, a "serious issue" of union security? Should this issue be left to the implication of a "recognition clause," or should there be a separate provision in the contract covering this problem? What does the *Interbake Foods* case say about the importance of arbitration to union security?

C. RIGHTS AND DUTIES OF BOTH PARTIES LEADING TO SECURITY

1. No-Strike/No-Lockout Provision

Just as managements and unions may attempt to preserve their rights by contract, they may agree to restrict them. Such restrictions appear, in one form or another, in most labor agreements. They may take the form of a provision that the agreement is not to conflict with other agreements or existing laws. Management may agree not to subcontract unilaterally, displace employees, change production methods or automate, close or move plants, at least without prior consultation with the union. As in the case of managements, unions may restrict their rights. The most common example of such limitations are "no-solicitation" and "no-distribution" provisions. However, the most significant of all limitations on rights are the "no-strike" and "no-lockout" provisions.

No-strike and lockout provisions appear in over 90% of collective bargaining agreements.[22] Although no-strike pledges appear in slightly more contracts in BNA's sample than no-lockout pledges, the trend is increasing in both instances.[23] In both types of provisions the language can be either "unconditional," a ban on interference with normal production during the term of the contract; or "conditional," which permits interruption under specified conditions. For example, in a *conditional no-strike provision,* the ban is most commonly lifted after exhaustion of the grievance procedure or when an impasse is reached in a renegotiation of a contract.[24] In the case of a conditional no-lockout provision, the ban may be waived after a grievance procedure has been exhausted, or where the union has refused to submit a dispute to arbitration, or has violated an arbitration award.[25]

Typical unconditional no-strike/no-lockout provisions will read as follows:

Example 1 [26]

The Union agrees that it will not cause, authorize, or sanction, nor permit its members to cause or take part in, any sit-down, stay-in, or slow-down, in any department, or any strike or stoppage of any of the Company's operations or any curtailment of work or restriction of or interference with production or any picketing of the Company's premises during the term of this agreement. (Du Pont

---

[22] 2 C.B.N.C. § 77:1 (3/27/75).
[23] *Id.*
[24] *Id.*
[25] 2 C.B.N.C. § 77:3 (1/2/75).
[26] 2 C.B.N.C. § 77:51 (5/20/76).

of Canada Limited, Maitland Works *and* Chemical Workers; exp. 4/77)

Example 2[27]

The Company agrees that it will not cause a lockout of employees during the life of this Agreement. It is understood and agreed that a lockout means a voluntary cessation of operations of the Company to prevent employees from working. (Coca-Cola Co. *and* Farm Workers; exp. 7/78)

The language in conditional bans, as indicated, varies according to their purpose.

NOTES:

Problem: As indicated in Chapter 7 of this book, in *Boys Markets, Inc. v. Retail Clerks Local 770,* 398 U.S. 90 (1970), the Supreme Court held that an injunctive remedy will lie to enforce a no-strike obligation where the collective bargaining agreement contains a mandatory grievance adjustment or arbitration procedure. However, in *Buffalo Forge Co. v. Steelworkers,* 428 U.S. 397 (1976), the court limited the application of the injunctive power where the issue for the arbitrator was whether the union violated a no-strike provision by engaging in a sympathy strike called by the union. The dissent suggested that injunctions should be authorized where the no-strike ban against sympathy strikes is clear and the parties seeking the injunction would win in arbitration. Would the following provision satisfy such a test?

> ... The Union is not in favor of sympathetic strikers and will do everything honorable to avoid them.... (Food Employees Council, Inc. *and* Teamsters; exp. 4/78).[28]

Draft a clause which you believe would satisfy the dissent's test. Does the language in your proposed clause justify Mr. Justice White's fear that the dissent's test would involve the federal courts in deciding the contractual dispute at the preliminary injunction stage rather than in arbitration?

2. Grievance Procedures

As stated in Part Two of this book, arbitration is usually the terminal step in a grievance procedure. In a minority of labor agreements, binding arbitration may not be provided for, and in many cases the subject matters governed by the grievance and arbitration process are not co-extensive.

---

[27] 2 C.B.N.C. § 77:425 (9/23/76).
[28] 2 C.B.N.C. § 77:35 (11/4/76).

A "grievance" traditionally is a complaint alleging a violation of some provision of the labor agreement. Almost all contracts include a procedure for handling "grievances." However, some do not define the term but simply provide the procedure. Statements detailing the scope of grievances — including complaints over wages, hours, working conditions, discipline, discharge and interpretation of the application of the contract — may be broad, or may detail the subject matter with specificity. Some provisions exclude specified subjects from the grievance procedure, such matters as the selection or assignment of supervisors which are peculiarly within management's prerogative.

A well drafted grievance procedure should include at least the following agenda items:

1. Scope of the procedure;
2. The "who," "how," "when" and "where" grievance procedures are initiated;
3. Grievance time limits;
4. Investigation of grievances;
5. Steps in grievance procedures;
6. Representation;
7. Direct and indirect cost; and
8. Appeals from one stage to the next.

NOTE:

Problem: Consider the following three step grievance procedure which is followed by arbitration: [29]

ARTICLE XI

COLLECTIVE BARGAINING AND ADJUSTMENT OF GRIEVANCES

SECTION 1. UNION COMMITTEE

The Union shall select a committee of not to exceed twenty (20) from the employees represented by it for the purpose of bargaining collectively with the Company, which committee shall be known as the Union Committee. The Union shall furnish the Company with a list of the members of this committee and shall give twenty-four (24) hours' notice of any change therein.

SECTION 2. FIELD REPRESENTATIVE

The Union may appoint a representative at any time to serve in conjunction with the Union Committee and to call in a representative of the District on any case at any time.

---

[29] Reprinted with permission of B.N.A.

SECTION 3. SHOP STEWARDS

The Union may designate a Shop Steward for each shift in a department. No person shall hold the office of Shop Steward unless he is a regular employee of the Company and is regularly assigned to the department which he represents.

No person shall have or exercise any of the authorities, powers, or duties of a Shop Steward, Committeeman, or Field Representative in dealing with the Company unless and until written notice of his appointment signed by the Union, revoking a prior appointment, if any, shall have been filed with the Personnel Department.

No employee of the Company shall collect dues or carry on any Union organizational activities on Company property during working time.

SECTION 4. GRIEVANCE PROCEDURE

Shop Stewards and members of the Union Committee shall be permitted to adjust grievances or complaints during working hours without loss of pay, provided, however, that no Shop Steward or member of the Union Committee shall leave his regular work for the purpose of adjusting grievances or complaints without first reporting to and obtaining the permission of his Foreman. Such permission will be granted unless it interferes with production or any important operation in progress at that time. Upon entering a department other than his own, a Shop Steward or member of the Union Committee must first report to the Foreman of such department stating his reason for being there. Time spent in handling grievances or complaints shall not be unreasonable or excessive.

(a) Should any difference or grievance arise between the Company and the Union or any employee in the unit, as to the meaning and/or application of this Agreement, the procedure of settlement shall be in the following order and manner:

(1) Between the Division Vice President, Chief Steward, Shop Steward and aggrieved employee and the Foreman and/or Supervisor of the department involved and/or his representative; failing an adjustment in this manner.

(2) Between the International Representative or Representatives and the Union Committee and the aggrieved and the Manager Employee Relations and/or his representatives; failing an adjustment in this manner.

(3) Between the Union Committee and a representative or representatives of the International Union and the Vice President of the Company and/or his designated representative or representatives.

(b) It is the intention of both parties to expedite the handling and settlement of grievances. Neither party shall deliberately delay the settlement of grievances in any stage of the procedure.

No grievance shall be considered (1) unless the cause thereof shall have occurred within twenty (20) calendar days next preceding the date the grievance is submitted to the Foreman or (2) unless the cause thereof occurs during the aggrieved's absence due to vacation or sickness and the grievance is submitted within twenty (20) calendar days after his return to work.

The grievance shall be heard in the first step within a period of three (3) days from the time the grievance is called to the attention of the Foreman of the department involved. The Company shall give its first step answer within three (3) days of the hearing. The Union shall have three (3) days to appeal the Company's answer in the first step.

The grievance shall be heard in the second step within a period of ten (10) days from the time of the Union's appeal. The Company shall give its second step answer within three (3) days of the hearing. The Union shall have seven (7) days to appeal the Company's answer in the second step.

The grievance shall be heard in the third step within a period of thirty (30) days from the time of the Union's appeal. The Company shall give its third step answer within three (3) days of the hearing. The Union shall have thirty (30) days to appeal the Company's answer in the third step.

Except by mutual agreement none of the foregoing steps in the grievance procedure shall be extended or by-passed. The grievance shall be reduced to writing by the aggrieved employee or Shop Steward before it is submitted and considered in the first step.

A grievance shall be settled on the basis of the Company's last answer unless, in the case of the first two steps, it is appealed by the Union to a subsequent step within the time limits above set forth after receiving the Company's answer and unless, in the case of the third step, it is appealed by the Union to arbitration within thirty (30) days after receiving the Company's answer.

SECTION 5. COMPENSATION FOR GRIEVANCE MEETINGS

The Company agrees to pay at straight time or overtime, whichever is applicable, members of the Union Grievance Committee, Shop Stewards and other employees whose presence is required, either by the Company or the Union at Grievance Meetings dealing with matters in Article XI, Section 4 of the Agreement and held through mutual consent of both parties for time spent in such grievance meetings during the hours when the above employees would be working. Paid attendance shall be limited to those members of the Union Grievance Committee and Shop Stewards of the department concerned with the matter to be discussed, and no more than two (2) other employees from said department.

In case his entire department works overtime after the completion of the regular hours and he is still held in the meeting, he will receive the overtime of the department.

On emergencies, breakdowns and call-ins, and other emergency work as defined in Article III of this Agreement, the attendance of the above mentioned employees will rest with the discretion of the Foreman or the Supervisor.

SECTION 6. ARBITRATION

If a grievance shall not have been settled through the foregoing procedure, then either party may within thirty (30) days give the other party notice of its desire to submit the grievance to Arbitration. The parties shall select the arbitrator within ten (10) days of such notice but if the parties are unable to agree on a selection the arbitrator shall be selected through the American Arbitration Association. The Arbitrator will follow and be bound by the rules of procedure adopted by the American Arbitration Association.

The Arbitrator shall fix a time, and a place for a hearing upon reasonable notice to each party. After such hearing the Arbitrator shall promptly render a decision which shall be binding upon both parties but the Arbitrator shall have no power to render a decision which adds to, subtracts from or modifies this Agreement; the decision shall be confined to the meaning of the contract provision which give rise to the dispute.

The parties to the arbitration shall bear equally the expenses of the Arbitrator and the rental, if any, of the place of arbitration. All other expenses attendant to arbitration will be borne by the party incurring them, including the expenses of any witnesses called by such party.

For what type of company and union would such a procedure be appropriate? For example, would this be appropriate for a small or large company, an industrial or craft union? Should such a provision be used where there is a high incidence of grievances? Is this procedure appropriate in both an urban and/or rural workplace? *See* Chapters 23 through 26 in S. Slichter, J. Healy and R. Livernash, The Impact of Collective Bargaining on Management (1960).

Chapter 10

DISCIPLINE AND DISCHARGE

"Industrial discipline" logically follows the introductory material concerning "management rights and union security." The subject illustrates the labor relations cycle of management establishing the requirements and standards to which employees must conform; the union challenge to unilateral exercise of management's prerogative; and, through the process of negotiation or contract administration, participation in the development and application of work rules. Professors Slichter, Healy and Livernash state that "few areas of personnel policy have been more significantly affected by collective bargaining than management's administration of employee discipline." [1] They contend that union influence on disciplinary procedures and policies has resulted in: (1) management appreciation of the value of forthright disciplinary policy; (2) management development and publication of reasonable rules and regulations governing employee conduct; (3) uniformity in the administration of these rules; (4) greater care by management in investigating cases of misbehavior due to grievance review; (5) development of orderly and sophisticated procedures for administering discipline (*e.g.,* progressive discipline); (6) molding management's attitudes toward constructive training; and (7) improved management policy.[2]

These improvements in the employment area of discipline and discharge have come about through curtailment of management's right to terminate employment by contractual provision. Management will usually agree with the union that it should be required, contractually, to submit its decisions concerning employee discipline to review through the grievance procedure, including arbitration. Thus, most collective bargaining agreements provide some kind of express restriction on management's right to discipline and discharge. Such contract provisions have one thing in common — they recognize a right of management to discipline or discharge employees for "cause." If the contract does not specify what constitutes "cause," it is obvious that the determination of what is "cause" can be made light in the mores of the industrial community. Other contracts enumerate specific grounds for discipline. Such causes can be divided into three categories: (1) employee conduct directly related to his work performance (absenteeism,

---

[1] S. Slichter, J. Healy & E. Livernash, THE IMPACT OF COLLECTIVE BARGAINING ON MANAGEMENT 624 (1960).

[2] *Id.* at 625-26.

insubordination, negligence); (2) employee conduct which indicates a default as a member of the employer-employee community (fighting, theft or employee or community property, disloyalty); and (3) employee conduct affecting the community at large, regardless of whether it occurs on or off plant premises (violation of civil and criminal law which affects recognized employer interests).

Whether the collective bargaining agreement provides discipline and discharge must be for "just cause" and/or specified grounds, management's interpretation is going to be challenged. A significant, if not the greatest, percentage of grievances involves disciplinary or discharge penalties assessed by management.[3] This chapter will attempt to present the key issues involved in the agenda items of discipline and discharge.

A. THE AGENDA ITEMS

1. Plant Rules

Since current industrial discipline operates through contractual limitations on management rights, it is generally recognized that management is authorized to make and to post any plant rules that are not inconsistent with the collective bargaining agreement.[4] As Arbitrator Robert C. Knee, Jr. indicated in *Tappan Appliance Group,* 64 L.A. 1269, 1271-72 (1975):

> It is a basic accepted principle of arbitral law that the management of a plant reserves to it any and all rights relating to running a business except as specifically excepted by the labor agreement or by statute. As Arbitrator Harry Dworkin put it in Cleveland Newspaper Publications Association, 51 LA 1174, 1181:
>
> > "It is axiomatic that an employer retains all management rights not expressly forbidden by statutory law in the absence of a collective bargaining agreement. When a collective bargaining agreement is entered into, these management rights are given up only to the extent evidenced in the agreement."
>
> The prevailing view among arbitrators dealing with all phases of plant management and rights pertaining thereto is that announced here. Absent any restriction in a labor contract and any binding past practice, management retains the right to transfer employees and make temporary job assignments. "The

---

[3] F. Elkouri & E. Elkouri, HOW ARBITRATION WORKS 610 (3d ed. 1973) [hereinafter cited as HOW ARBITRATION WORKS].

[4] BUREAU OF NAT'L AFFAIRS, LABOR RELATIONS EXPEDITER, LABOR RELATIONS REPORTER 217 [hereinafter cited as BNA, LRX].

authority of management to conduct methods of operation and to direct the work-force, including the right to make changes, if these do not violate some right of the employees under their written agreement, is recognized." ARYSNCO, Inc. and O.C. & A.W.I.W.U. Local 8-417 70-1 ARB § 8414 (I. B. Scheiber). "Thus, this basic right to assign work, control productivity and the like pervades all facets of running the plant in the absence of bad faith on the part of the Company, statutory provisions, or agreed-to language in the labor agreement which indicates management has modified or negotiated such rights." Borg-Warner Corp., Mandel-Schebler Div. and International Union A.I.W. of A. Local 979, 71-1 ARB § 8112 (Harry G. Erbs). Of course underpinning this principle announced herein is the basic right of the union to grieve any questions it may have concerning the reasonableness or any question concerning violation of the labor agreement vis-a-vis the exercise of such management's rights.

On the other hand, as Arbitrator Robert G. Williams explained in *S & S Corp.,* 62 L.A. 883, 886 (1973),

> If the Labor Agreement in this case had limited the right of the Company to unilaterally establish rules then the Point System would have been a violation. For example, in Weatherproof Co. and International Association of Machinists and Aerospace Workers, Local 847, 46 LA 53 (1966). Arbitrator Traynn held that the employer violated the agreement which required mutual consent for the new rules when it unilaterally installed an attendance point system. Union representatives may negotiate, a contract provision authorizing the adoption of plant rules only by mutual agreement. Such a provision cannot be created by an arbitrator, however. This position is consistent with numerous reported arbitration awards. See 53 LA 140; 52 LA 923; 52 LA 484; 51 LA 1110; 43 LA 337; 44 LA 224; 44 LA 733; 47 LA 1065; 49 LA 848; 40 LA 386; 32 LA 1025; 31 LA 865 and cases cited therein.

Nor does the challenge to plant rules as a basis for discipline end with an inquiry into the relevant contract provisions. Clauses may be challenged if arbitrary, unfair or discriminatory, or even vague and ineffective.[5] Even reasonable rules which are specific have been held unenforceable if they have not been brought to the attention of employees, infringe unduly upon an employee's privacy, or are applied discriminatorily.[6] But, the threshold inquiry always relates to the collective bargaining agreement.

---

[5] *See* BNA, LRX §§ 24, 25, pp. 217-18 for numerous arbitration citations.
[6] *Id.*

2. Contract Provisions

Discipline and discharge clauses vary widely from contract to contract.

> *Example 1*[7]
> It is the policy of the Company to base the discharge of an employee on just cause ... (Standard Brands, Inc., and Meat Cutters; exp. 5/76).

> *Example 2*[8]
> It is agreed that warning, disciplinary layoff, or discharge of an employee must be based on evidence that is clear and must be occasioned by a substantial, not merely technical, commission of a wrongful act and that full reason for such warning, suspension or discharge shall be recorded and stated in writing to the Union. Causes for immediate discharge are:

a. Gross insubordination.

b. Endangering self or other employees through violation of published safety rules.

c. Willful violation of the terms of this Agreement.

d. Conviction of a felony.

e. Leaving the premises while on duty without obtaining permission of supervisors.

f. Deliberate destruction or removal of the Company's or other employees' property.

g. Fighting or physical violence.

h. Deliberately recording false information on employment applications or physical examination forms.

i. Falsification of attendance records.

j. Participating in, instigating, fomenting, actively supporting or giving leadership to an illegal strike, walk-out, slow-down, stay-away or other form of strike contrary with the terms and conditions of this contract.

When an employee is discharged, he shall have the right to contact his Steward or if his Steward is not available, some other Union official who is available, before leaving the plant, in order to present his side of the matter if he wishes to do so.

Causes for warning, suspension and ultimate discharge are:

k. Inefficient work of such low standard as to cause operating losses to the Company.

l. Bringing or having intoxicants on the Company's premises.

m. Abuse of the use of alcoholic beverages, causing interference with productive efficiency.

---

[7] 2 C.B.N.C. § 40:11 (12/2/76).
[8] 2 C.B.N.C. § 40:12.

n. Reporting for duty under the influence of intoxicants.

o. Smoking in prohibited areas.

p. Dishonesty of a type other than that stated in sub-paragraphs f, h, and i, above.

q. Deliberately falsifying production records.

r. Habitual failure to report for duty or failure to give notice of intent to be late or absent or absence without justifiable cause.

s. Running, scuffling, horseplay or throwing things.

t. Garnishment of wages. First warning after third garnishment in any one year period, second warning and three days layoff after fourth, subject to discharge after fifth garnishment in that period.

Warnings shall be administered in accordance with the following schedule:

First Offense — Warning in writing.
Second Offense — Warning in writing and three days layoff.
Third Offense — Discharge.

The above offenses shall not accumulate or be held against the offending employee for more than one year from the date the offense is committed. Notice of any disciplinary action taken by the Company shall be mailed to the residence of the local Union President and will contain the full reason for which such disciplinary action was taken, such notice to be mailed not later than one (1) working day following such warning, suspension, or discharge. A copy shall be handed to the Chief Steward and to the employee, if possible. (National Carbon Coated Paper Co. *and* Local 1032, United Papermakers and Paperworkers)

In between these "extremes" are many hybrid variations. A good method of selecting the appropriate provisions for a specific contract is to use a checklist of subjects in order to determine which subjects should be included for disciplinary and discharge provisions.

Checklist [9]

Absence from work, absenteeism
Accident record
Age: compulsory retirement
Alcohol: possession or use
Assault on management personnel
Attack on company product
Automation: elimination or combination of jobs

---

[9] *See* BNA, Labor Relations, Reporter, Master Index for sample provision citations.

Bankruptcy of employee
Boycott activity: consumer boycott; attack on company product
Business competition with employer
Coffee breaks: plant rule violations
Communist activities: refusal to testify
Competition with employer: work for competitors, conflict of interest
Complaints by customers
Conflict of interest
Contagious disease
Criminal prosecution or conviction
Criminal record
Damage suit against employer or customer
Damage to or loss of materials
Disability
   In general
   Doctor's certificate: refusal to give
   Physical examinations: refusal to submit
Discourtesy to or demands by patrons or customers
Dishonesty, theft
Disloyalty to employer
Disloyalty to government
Dissatisfaction: criticism of management
Drugs and other intoxicants, use or possession of
Early quitting
False statements
Falsification of application or work records
Fellow employees: demand by
Fighting, troublemaking
Filing unfair practice charges
Firearms: possession of on company property
Gambling
Garnishment of wages
Grievances: presentation
Handbill distribution attacking employer's product
Hazardous work: refusal to perform
Holiday work: refusal of
Horseplay
Impeding production
Incompetency, inefficiency
Individual employment contracts: refusal to sign
Insubordination
Intoxication: use or possession of liquor
Jail sentence: absence due to
Law violations
Leave of absence: overstaying leave

Leaving plant or work place
Loafing
Low production
Machines, damage to
Material shortage
Medical examination: refusal to submit to
Mental illness
Moonlighting
Name calling
  In general
  By strikers or pickets
Negligence
New standards: failure to meet
Obscene conduct
Off-duty or off-premises misconduct
Outside work: dual jobs
Overtime: refusal to work overtime
Performance: unsatisfactory
Personal appearance
Physical disability
Picket-line observance
Plant rule violations
Profanity
Reduction or redistribution of work
Refusal to submit to physical examinations or give doctor's
  certificate
Reinstatement and back pay
Refusal to testify: suspected security risks
Sabotage
Safety rules: violation
Security clearance: denial of
Sickness, absence due to
Sleeping on job
Slowdowns
Smoking
Solicitation of union members, no solicitation rule
Strikes
Successive violations, progressive discipline
Talking
Tardiness
Theft
Threats or violence
Time card: punching another's
Traffic violations
Troublemaking
Union activity on company time or property

Union insignia: display of
Wage demands: presentation of
Work assignments: refusal of
Work for business competitor
Work jurisdiction disputes

It is important to note that most disciplinary clauses provide procedural steps to be followed in order to insure due process, as well as progressive discipline to be applied for each offense. Procedural aspects will be covered later in this chapter. However, more needs to be said about "just cause" as ground for discipline and discharge.

NOTES:

(1) *Negligence:* How does the factor of "negligence" bear on just cause for discipline in accident cases? In discussing highway accident cases generally, Arbitrator Adolph Koven said in *Kaiser Sand & Gravel,* 50 L.A. 571 (1968):

Arbitrators are ordinarily reluctant to disturb disciplinary discharges in accident cases if it means the return to the highway of an employee who may be dangerous to himself, to others, and where the legal and financial interests of the Company are potentially at stake. Within the framework of this basic consideration, discharges have generally been upheld where such factors as the following were clearly present: (1) *Numerous accidents and/or poor past records:* Four accidents in ten months, and a driving record significantly worse than other drivers' records *Standard Oil Company of California,* 30 LA 213); Six accidents in three years (*Ward Baking Co.,* 8 LA 837); Five accidents within one year (*Chevy Chase Dairy,* 8 LA 897); An extremely bad past record and one serious accident (*Hudson County Bus Owners' Association,* 3 LA 786); A serious pattern of speeding which caused a third accident (*Schreiver Trucking,* 5 LA 430); Seven accidents within five years with progressively deteriorating accident record (*Kroger Co.,* 24 LA 48); (2) *Special factors:* Company's business involved the transportation of dangerous loads so that discharge was justified of employee with four accidents (*Mitchell Bros. Truck Lines,* 48 LA 953; 67-1 ARB 8247); Company engaged in hauling of materials of an inflammable nature (*Coastal Tank Lines, Incorporated,* 64-3 ARB 8914); (3) *Gross negligence or willful or wanton conduct:* The grievant was found to be guilty of gross negligence and his record showed eight misconduct warnings in the last year and one-quarter, seven of these warnings being within the last seven months (*Charleston Transit Company,* 63-2 ARB 8613).

On the other hand, the penalty of discharge has been set aside and reinstatement ordered (usually without back pay) under the following circumstances: (1) *Negligence not conclusively shown:* In *Safe Bus Co., Inc.,* 21 LA 457, though the grievant had a second accident in six months, that accident was the result of "a moment of inadvertence" and not "willful misconduct or gross negligence"; (2) *No danger to the public:* "There is nothing to suggest that (the grievant) will endanger the public if he continues to drive a bus" (*Safe Bus Co., Inc.,* op. cit.); (3) *Ordinary Negligence:* Ordinary negligence is to be distinguished from gross negligence or willful or wanton conduct and discharge of truck driver overruled on this basis (*American Synthetic Rubber Corporation,* 46 LA 1161; 66-2 ARB 8627); reinstatement ordered though evidence of negligence was present (*Boston & Maine Transportation Co.,* 5 LA 3; *Southeastern Greyhound Lines,* 6 LA 913; *Mason & Dixon Lines,* 9 LA 775; *Pacific Greyhound Lines,* 30 LA 830); (4) *Special Conditions:* In *Our Own Bakeries,* 36 LA 537, the grievant was reinstated after his second serious accident in six months on the basis that the evidence was not completely clear as to fault because of poor driving conditions and because the doubt should be resolved in his favor since, implicitly if not explicitly, drivers were expected to drive in bad weather.

(2) *Problem:* With these factors in mind and using the checklist draft a detailed provision with grounds for discipline and discharge of transit company drivers.

(3) *Just Cause:* As Robert P. Brecht pointed out in *Penn-Drive Cement Corp.,* 29 L.A. 451, 457 (1957),

The arbitrator is ordinarily given substantial leeway in determining what is meant by just cause in cases of dismissal. He is, however, obviously enjoined from being arbitrary in his determination. In testing the reasonableness of the Company's cause in the present case, the arbitrator has been guided by certain generally accepted principles or criteria. Their truth and relevancy are so self-evident as to need no justification.

a. The determination of reasonable cause must be made as of the time when the disciplinary action was taken. Theoretically, time should be made to stand still. Since this is impossible and since the arbitration process itself takes time, every effort must be made to eliminate from consideration any variables of experience that followed after the disciplinary action.

b. A discharge or disciplinary action that is originally based on capricious or arbitrary considerations cannot be possibly claimed to be based on just or reasonable cause because events subsequent to that action seemed to prove it right. The element of corroboration is irrelevant. Only if the facts as they existed at the time of discharge lead to reasonable inferences in support of that discharge can the conclusions based on those inferences be said to comprise just or reasonable cause.

c. A discharge or disciplinary action cannot be said to be based on reasonable or just cause if, after it is taken on impulse, a search for reasons is made that seemingly would justify the action. This is a form of rationalizing disciplinary action that is completely unjustified.

d. Just or reasonable cause for work severance must rest on the employee's failure in his job relations and not on the personal preference or predilections of his superiors. Thus a boss's sense of moral outrage is of no relevancy unless the immorality of the employee disturbs any or all of the varied relations associated with his work.

e. The search for justifiable causes may not properly intrude upon the personal life of the employee. There are, of course, possible exceptions to this generalization. For instance, if *upon investigation* the Company finds that a job feud was transferred from the Plant into the personal home of an employee, a crisis point has evidently developed which makes very real the risk of a renewal of that feud back on the job. Again, if *upon due investigation* it is found that an employee's off-job outburst was one of a series of such outbursts increasing in frequency and intensity, a further demonstration of a highly unstable emotional pattern, it might be concluded that his continuance on the job is indefensibly risky. Further, even a first occurrence of berserkness might *upon investigation* be determined to be the forerunner of future emotional instability which could make that employee a grave job risk. The role of investigation before action is stressed in all three exceptions to the general rule.

In drafting a "just cause" provision it is significant that this is a term of art, and not necessarily to be equated with "cause," or "reasonable cause," or other variation. In fact, this is a term which a definition is likely to enhance without destroying flexibility. Whether or not an arbitrator concludes that a "just cause" provision is to be read literally or implied into a contract, it is clear that she/he will require the parties to be put to their proofs.[10]

---

[10] HOW ARBITRATION WORKS, *supra* note 3 at 621-47.

B. BURDEN OF PROOF

1. Just Cause

GORSKE, BURDEN OF PROOF IN GRIEVANCE ARBITRATION, 43 Marquette Law Review 135, 147-55 (1959) [11]

DISCHARGE AND DISCIPLINE CASES

A. *Proof of "Just Cause" for Discharge. . . .*

Arbitrators have almost invariably held that the burden of proving "just cause" is on the employer. As will appear from an examination of the cases, this is burden of proof in the strict sense; in addition, arbitrators have held consistently that the employer bears the initial "burden of proceeding with the evidence."

Various rationales are utilized by arbitrators to justify the imposition of burden of proof in the strict sense upon the employer. These are at least six in number: 1) since discharge is the most severe penalty an employer can impose, being the equivalent of "economic capital punishment," he must bear the burden of justifying such a serious move; 2) since the reasons for the employer's disciplinary action are peculiarly within his own knowledge, he must carry the burden of demonstrating their adequacy, otherwise the employee would be unreasonably obligated to prove the "universal negative," *i.e.,* that he was guilty of no offense of any kind at any time; 3) it is "consistent with the American tradition that a person should not be considered a wrong-doer until proof establishes his guilt"; 4) the imposition of the burden of proof on the employer is justifiable as merely an "extension of scientific management to industrial relations"; 5) the existence of "just cause" for discharge is in the nature of an affirmative defense, therefore the burden rests on the party asserting it; 6) a "just cause" provision in the agreement, in view of circumstances peculiar to industrial relations, "requires the Company, when challenged, to retrace the [disciplinary] process and convince an impartial third person that the facts acted upon warranted the action taken." . . .

Whatever the rationale adopted, whether any or all of the above six arguments are accepted, it seems quite clear that the universal rule in grievance arbitration is that the employer must carry the burden of proof of "just cause" in a discharge case. This unanimity is rather heartening, and suggests that, even in a field so amorphous as industrial relations, some principles have such obvious validity that they will be accepted and applied with uniformity by a wide variety of personalities in a great diversity of situations. The consistency of arbitral opinion on this point seems to suggest the

---

[11] Reprinted with permission of the publisher. Copyright © 1959 by the Marquette Law Review, Marquette University Law School.

existence of an emerging and evolving system of industrial jurisprudence.

B. Burden of Showing Propriety or Impropriety of the Extent of Discipline

While arbitrators agree on the location of the burden of proving "just cause," this unanimity does not extend to other burden of proof problems connected with discharge cases. For example, there is not complete agreement on where the burden of proving the propriety or excessiveness of disciplinary penalty lies. Some arbitrators state simply that

". . . once the employer has successfully established bases for discharge, the burden shifts to the union to demonstrate that the penalty of discharge is too severe."

A rather imposing number of arbitrators reach the same result in a more sophisticated and indirect fashion:

> Where an employee has violated a rule or engaged in conduct meriting disciplinary action, it is primarily the function of management to decide upon the proper penalty. If management acts in good faith upon a fair investigation and fixes a penalty not inconsistent with that imposed in other like cases, an arbitrator should not disturb it. The only circumstances under which a penalty imposed by management can be rightfully set aside by an arbitrator are those where discrimination, unfairness, or capricious and arbitrary action are proved — in other words, where there has been abuse of discretion.

Since arbitrariness, discrimination or caprice cannot be assumed without proof, the practical effect of this approach is to require the union to bear the burden of proving that these factors are in the case. In other words, under this approach, once management has shown an employee to be guilty of an offense, the burden shifts to the union to show that the penalty was assessed in an arbitrary, discriminatory or capricious manner. It is then the union's task to bring in evidence concerning the employee's seniority, his previous good conduct, his skill and utility as a workman, his family status (where such is relevant), any inconsistencies of management in disciplining employees for offenses of this type, and any other mitigating circumstances. The union, then, under this approach bears the risk of non-persuasion.

The contrary rule involves this principle: where the contract forbids discharge without "just cause," the employer has the burden of proving "just cause" *for the discharge.* In other words, he must prove that "the punishment fits the crime." The corollary of this proposition is that an admitted offense might well constitute "just cause" for some kind of discipline, but not "just cause" for discharge. As one arbitrator puts it, in a 1950 decision:

In a discharge case, when the collective agreement between the parties protects employees against discharge where there is not "proper cause," it is well accepted that the burden of justifying the discharge or other discipline is upon the employer. *This involves the necessity on the employer of showing both the infraction of some established rule of employee conduct and the propriety of the disciplinary action taken,* in this case, of discharge. (Emphasis added)

From this point of view, the employer has the obligation of showing that the penalty assessed was just and proper under all the circumstances, and was consistent with disciplinary action taken in other cases.

It can be argued that neither of these positions, nakedly stated, is completely valid. The point of view which places on the union the burden of proving excessiveness of the penalty fails to take account of the fact that not all breaches of discipline warrant extreme penalties. To say that an employer need only prove some act of misconduct, and that the union must then produce evidence to show that the discipline was improper ignores the commonly accepted proposition that there must be some proportion between the punishment and the offense. Indeed, no one would argue that an employer, merely by showing a trivial tardiness by an employee, could thus shift to the union the burden of showing the excessiveness of a penalty of discharge.

On the other hand, when the employer has produced evidence sufficient to establish the commission of an act of misconduct prima facie meriting discharge, he should not be required to go further, and show that there are no mitigating circumstances sufficient to affect the result. The more reasonable view would seem to be that the union should bear the burden of proving such circumstances. Indeed, it is usually in by far a better position to do so, since presumably it knows the precise grounds for its claim of excessiveness. For example, if the union claims that the discipline imposed is inconsistent with the degree of discipline imposed in other like cases, it should be required to show which cases it has in mind and the fact that they actually are similar to the one in dispute. Any other procedure would, in effect, require the employer to prove the "universal negative," a result of undesirability equal to that in cases in which such is required of the union in proving lack of just cause. . . .

2. Quantum of Proof

CANNON ELECTRIC CO.
28 L.A. 879 (1957)

Jones, Edgar A., Arbitrator. . . .

Decision in this case involves consideration of the quantum of proof required to sustain a discharge based upon the managerial right set forth in a collective bargaining agreement to discharge for "just cause."

Because of the impact of a discharge upon the employee affected some arbitrators insist that the facts necessary to sustain a company's action must be so proven as to put their existence "beyond any reasonable doubt." Others hold that it will suffice if the evidence relied upon by management is "clear and convincing" or persuades by a preponderance even though it may not so dispose of all the possibilities inherent in the situation as reasonably to eliminate alternative explanations not warranting discharge. Finally, a few arbitrators apparently hold that the standard to be applied is whether in any case what management did was reasonable at the time and in the circumstances in which the action was taken, a standard which both effectively shifts to the grievant the demonstration that management's action was in fact unreasonable and also substantially rewrites the "just cause" provision to one of "apprehension of just cause by management." That last approach causes the focus to shift from the justice of the total situation to the reasonableness of the subjective judgment of management irrespective of the actual fact; if the principle be valid, a discharge based upon mistaken perception would be upheld so long as the mistake of management was a reasonable one in the circumstances, despite manifest injustice to the employee.

The ultimate utility in our society of labor-management grievance arbitration is the institutionalizing of industrial due process. At its optimum operation it is a means whereby employees and supervisors alike may be assured of objective judgment subject (as in courts) only to the vagaries of perception and understanding by an impartial third person, but one who (unlike courts) specializes in the understanding and resolution of this particular kind of dispute involving as it does a collective bargaining agreement with its continuing relationship of the disputants. The Parties, here and typically, have refrained from attempting either to establish a detailed schedule of "just" causes for discipline or to detail a procedure, including standards of proof, whereby justice may be sought in an arbitration hearing. . . .

It is often said, sometimes uncritically, that discharge is the economic equivalent of capital punishment. Yet it is clear that in an area where there is a shortage of the particular skills possessed by the discharged employee competitive labor conditions may well largely (aside from seniority) redress the injustice of a mistaken or unjust discharge. Perhaps in such a case the application by an arbitrator of either the "clear and convincing" or the "reasonable apprehension" standards of proof would protect the rights of the grievant. But where the local labor situation means an employee is not readily employable elsewhere, or where, as here, discharge is based upon an allegation involving moral turpitude which, if upheld, will blackball the discharged employee elsewhere, a rigorous standard of proof seems applicable. The consequences foreseeable to the affected employee are then so drastic as indeed to be tantamount to economic capital punishment. In the context of a moral turpitude discharge, therefore, protection of an innocent employee against the injustice of industrial blackmailing and social ostracism demands the most careful and exacting scrutiny to assure that the facts alleged as the basis for the discharge actually exist. That kind of scrutiny is embodied by the community in its criminal law under a standard which is phrased to require that guilt be demonstrated beyond any reasonable doubt in the mind of the trier of facts by facts and their necessary inferences.

In this case, applying that standard, the Arbitrator is compelled to reinstate Mrs. Christie because of significantly improper procedures utilized by the Company preliminary to the discharge and significant evidentiary weakness in the Company's proof of the alleged falsification of incentive records by Grievant.

GORSKE, BURDEN OF PROOF IN GRIEVANCE ARBITRATION, 43 Marquette Law Review 135, 161-65 (1959)

DISCHARGE AND DISCIPLINE CASES

Quantum of Proof Required in Discipline Cases

The general rule in civil litigation is that the party who carries the burden of proof on a particular issue must prove the point by a "preponderance of the evidence." This means that he must introduce evidence sufficient to convince the tribunal of the actual truth of the proposition urged, so that actual belief exists in the mind of the tribunal notwithstanding any doubts that may linger there; it is more than quantitative probability, and requires at least sufficient evidence to remove the matter from the realm of conjecture.

On the other hand, in criminal prosecutions, the state is required to prove guilt "beyond a reasonable doubt" or "to a moral certainty"; this means such proof "as satisfies the judgment and consciences of the jury, as reasonable men, that the crime charged has been committed by the defendant, and so satisfies them as to leave no other reasonable conclusion possible." When the commission of a crime is directly brought into issue in a civil case, the prevalent American view (contrary to the rule in England) is that such need only be proved by a preponderance of the evidence, or by "satisfactory and convincing" evidence. It need not be proved beyond a reasonable doubt.

Since arbitration is in the nature of a civil proceeding, we should expect to find the requirement that parties prove their claims and affirmative defenses by a preponderance of the evidence, regardless of their particular nature. But such is not uniformly the case: indeed, there is much confusion and conflict in the reported cases on the subject. Most of this conflict is found in cases involving discipline.

In discipline involving misconduct which is not also a violation of the criminal law, there is a fair amount of agreement that the offense need not be proved by more than a preponderance of the evidence, or some similar standard. The same rule has been held to apply in the case of minor crimes, not involving moral turpitude. However, even in some cases in which there is no question of criminality, arbitrators have held that proof beyond a reasonable doubt was required to sustain a discharge, principally because of the economic effect of the discharge upon the employee.

In cases involving misconduct which is at the same time a serious crime, arbitrators have differed with respect to the standard of proof required. In some instances, the arbitrator has recognized that arbitration is in the nature of a civil, not a criminal proceeding, and has required that the charge be proved by a preponderance of the evidence, or the equivalent. In other cases, the arbitrator has simply stated that when such a charge is made, the employer has a greater obligation of proof than in the usual discharge case.

However, a number of arbitrators have held that criminal standards of proof are required in discharge cases where a crime of moral turpitude, such as theft, is charged. In one case, the arbitrator required that a charge of pilferage be "demonstrated conclusively." In several other cases, arbitrators have held that charges of theft and similar offenses be proved beyond a reasonable doubt. This standard has also been applied in what may be non-criminal cases, where an element of dishonesty is involved, e.g., falsification of timekeeping records. Because of the informality of arbitral procedure, one arbitrator has held that the standard of proof in theft cases is even higher than the criminal court standard for the same kind of case.

The rationale of the cases holding that criminal misconduct must be proved beyond a reasonable doubt is based in part upon the same reasoning that has led arbitrators to impose the burden of proof on employers in discharge cases generally. The principal argument relied on is that discharge is the equivalent of "economic capital punishment," and represents the most severe penalty an employer can impose. This belief, combined with the certainty that "the social effects upon and the stigma attaching to an employee found guilty of a criminal offense are far greater than those attaching to an employee guilty of a non-criminal offense," has made arbitrators understandably conscious of a social responsibility not to regard such charges lightly. Professor Murphy has developed an interesting comparison between discharge for criminal misconduct and prosecution for crime:

> The effects of a finding of guilt in a charge of stealing in a judicial proceeding are generally in terms of fine, imprisonment or probation or suspended sentence; the result is generally loss of property (fine) or liberty (imprisonment or probation). . . . The effects in a finding of guilt in an arbitration proceeding are generally loss of job (corresponding to the property loss), or loss of liberty (as where the guilty person is penalized but kept on a job under probationary rules which restrict his liberty), or loss of freedom to get another job (to the extent that future employers will not hire one who has previously been discharged as a thief).

Professor Murphy also points out similarities in the degree of social stigma which will accrue upon a finding of guilt in each type of tribunal.

The conclusion that misconduct of criminal proportions must be proved by evidence beyond a reasonable doubt is a somewhat questionable one, however. It is possible to argue that most of the similarities that Professor Murphy emphasizes exist between cases of this type and criminal prosecutions are not entirely significant. It is probably possible to fit many other kinds of disciplinary (or even non-disciplinary) discharge into the same pattern. For example, a discharge for extreme disloyalty to the employer (disclosure of trade secrets) can probably be compared to a criminal prosecution on most of the grounds cited above, yet it would probably not be required of the employer that he prove the offense beyond a reasonable doubt. As pointed out above, the standard of proof in civil litigation when commission of a crime is directly in issue is proof by a preponderance of the evidence. It can be forcefully argued that no higher standard should be used in the quasi-civil procedure of grievance arbitration. An employer who could successfully sue an employee for an intentional conversion of the employer's property should probably not be required to retain the individual in his employ merely because a case cannot be proved beyond a reasonable doubt. Where an employer can show by a fair preponderance of the evidence that an employee is guilty of a theft, the employer should, perhaps, not be required to run the continued risk of the employee's dishonest tendencies merely because there exists some possibility of the employee's innocence. In this connection it is interesting to note that the courts uniformly hold that misconduct sufficient for the disbarment of an attorney need not be proved beyond a reasonable doubt, but only by a preponderance of the evidence.

On the other hand, the argument that proof beyond a reasonable doubt should be required because of the social stigma attaching to a discharge for theft or like offense is a potent one. In answer, it is probably not sufficient to point out that the courts in civil cases involving similar issues do not reach this conclusion. Indeed, in fraud cases a somewhat higher degree of proof is required than in ordinary cases. Furthermore, even in a civil court case, when a charge is made that a party has committed a crime, some account must be taken of the natural reluctance of the trier of fact to sustain such a charge unless the evidence is quite satisfactory. What is perhaps a better argument against the use of the "beyond a reasonable doubt" standard of proof in grievance arbitration cases is that it is simply inappropriate. In a proceeding which is hoped to be relatively free of at least the more distasteful legal technicalities, it is somewhat disquieting to encounter one of the most rigid legal concepts extant. The better view would seem to be that in order to prove a charge of theft or the like, the employer should be required to produce evidence sufficient to convince the arbitrator of the justness of the charge. It is conceivable that this kind of standard will vary with the seriousness of the case, but this result is inevitable in any event.

NOTE:

Problem: Grievant was discharged for allegedly attempting arson on company property on the basis of an affidavit of one plant guard and the testimony of another, who admitted on cross examination that he didn't like grievant. Although the affidavit and the testimony both positively identified grievant as the culprit, the guard who testified said that he observed grievant from 100 yards away at night after the affiant guard called for help when he observed grievant throw what appeared to be a lighted object into the trash bin. However, grievant testified that he was picketing on another street with other strikers at the time alleged. Even though no serious damage occurred to employer's property, the plant manufactures a highly inflammable product.

The Company maintains that it had "just cause" within the meaning of the contract to discharge the grievant for violation of the following rule:

> "It is recognized that the following factory rules are in effect and that any violation of them by an employee shall justify the Company in imposing the penalty of suspension or discharge.
>
> . . . .
>
> "D. Willfull destruction, damage or stealing of any Company property. . . ."

As arbitrator, write a decision in the case based upon your notion of the proper "burden" and "quantum" of proof appropriate for this case. *Compare Greyhound Lines-West*, 61 L.A. 45 (Block 1973) *with Imperial Glass Corp.*, 61 L.A. 1180 (Gibson 1973). *Compare* Arbitrator Russell Smith's observations on granting of proof in *Kroger Co.*, 25 L.A. 906, 908 (1955). *See also Dunlop Tire & Rubber Corp.*, 64 L.A. 1099 (Mills 1975).

C. PROGRESSIVE DISCIPLINE

Actually, there is a second area of proof which concerns the issue of once guilt is established whether the punishment assessed by management should be upheld or modified. There are numerous factors involved in evaluating penalties such as: (1) the nature of the offense; (2) fairness and due process; (3) post-discharge conduct; (4) double jeopardy; (5) grievant's past record; (6) length of service with the company; (7) knowledge of rules; (8) lax enforcement of rules; (9) unequal or discriminatory treatment; and (10) joint fault.[12] However, the basic issue involves the nature of discipline in the industrial setting.

1. The Theory of Corrective Discipline

G. N. ALEXANDER, CONCEPTS OF INDUSTRIAL DISCIPLINE, in MANAGEMENT RIGHTS AND THE ARBITRATION PROCESS, PROCEEDINGS OF THE NINTH ANNUAL MEETING OF THE NATIONAL ACADEMY OF ARBITRATORS 76, 79-81 (McKelvey ed. 1956) [13]

. . . .

To turn from the philosophical to the practical, the second concept I wish to describe is one known as "corrective discipline." I don't know where the term was first coined, and I am not aware that anyone has written an essay attempting comprehensively to explain it. My experience with the concept occurred principally at General Motors Corporation under its National Agreement with the United Automobile Workers. Under that agreement, you should understand, the umpire is given "full discretion" in cases of violation of the shop rules. As a means of explaining to the parties what would probably happen in future cases, the various holders of that office have over a period of ten years or more restated and defined what is meant by "corrective discipline."

Most simply put, the principle of corrective discipline requires that management withhold the final penalty of discharge from errant employees until it has been established that the employee is not likely

---

[12] HOW ARBITRATION WORKS, *supra* note 3 at 630-47.

[13] Reprinted with permission of the publisher. Copyright © 1956 by the Bureau of National Affairs, Inc.

to respond favorably to lesser penalty. To draw an analogy from the criminal law, corrective discipline is somewhat like an habitual offender statute. It presupposes that the primary purpose of punishment is to correct wrongdoing rather than to wreak vengeance or deter others. Corrective discipline assumes that the employer as well as the employee gains more by continuing to retain the offender in employment, at least for a period of future testing, than to cut him from the rolls at the earliest possible moment. In view of the high cost of turnover of factory employees, there is considerable logic in this point of view. To paraphrase Hamlet, it may be better to live with, and adjust to, known evils than to flee from them into the possibility of unknown evils. To discharge an employee with considerable experience with his employer because of minor violations of the shop rules does not necessarily mean that the evil is wiped out. If a continuing level of employment is assumed, the discharged employee must be replaced with another. Normal hiring procedures provide little if any guarantee that the new hire will be a perfect citizen or that, on balance, his capabilities and behavior traits will be better than those of the employee discharged.

Within the general concept of "corrective discipline," there are many variations. At General Motors, it is customary to include any and all violations of the shop rules in determining whether it fairly appears that the employee is incorrigible. At other companies, to my knowledge, it is customary only to evaluate penalties for offenses identical or similar to the one currently in dispute. At General Motors, it is not customary to set up an exact scale of frequency of wrongdoing as determinative of the question of incorrigibility. At other companies, to my knowledge, specific schedules of increasingly severe penalties are promulgated or agreed upon as the basis for making a determination as to when discharge is proper. At General Motors, it has been customary, by and large, to precede discharges based upon the principle of corrective discipline by a severe penalty layoff of 30 or 60 days.

Corrective discipline is not simply a device to postpone or defeat discharges. In some circumstances, it works to the disadvantage of employees as compared to other methods of imposing discipline. In some factories, to my knowledge, minor misconduct, such as loitering, is punishable only by mild penalties, no matter how often the offense is repeated. Under corrective discipline, an employee who persists in wasting time or loitering in the face of several penalties of increasing severity for such misconduct may justifiably be discharged for an additional offense of the same nature.

One argument occasionally advanced in defense of employee wrongdoers is that, once a man has suffered a penalty for misconduct, he had "paid his debt to society" and thereafter is free from stigma because of previous misconduct. Corrective discipline does not accept this argument as valid. It responds with the proposition, which in my opinion has greater validity, that management is entitled to have an obedient and cooperative working force and ought not be subjected to the necessity for retaining in its employ persons who over a period of time demonstrate by their conduct that they cannot accommodate themselves to reasonable shop rules.

Corrective discipline imposes upon management a twofold burden of firmness and patience. It requires front line supervision to adopt a reasonably firm attitude against minor violations and not to let them pass by frequently with simple admonition or complete oversight. Where the principle is properly applied, management is obligated to demonstrate that the employee has been put on notice, by penalties of increasing severity, that his course of conduct was not being condoned. It does not permit supervisors to go back to their "little black books" and advance, as grounds for present discharge, misconduct of earlier occurrence which was not taken note of and properly punished at the time.

On the other hand, corrective discipline requires of front line supervision that it be patient and that, even though an employee's behavior is aggravating and provocative, the employee be dealt with objectively and not discharged because of anger or desire to retaliate. This twofold obligation of patience and firmness sometimes traps line supervision when its actions are under review by an arbitrator. Supervision desiring to be patient may find itself overruled on the basis of an overshow of leniency. Supervision desiring to be firm may find itself reversed on the grounds that it was not patient enough. Such instances, in my experience, are rare, however, particularly where the arbitrator restrains himself in reviewing management's exercise of its disciplinary power to considerations of reasonableness and practicability. There is a hazard if the concept of the arbitrator attempts to set a fixed pattern which must be compiled with irrespective of individual circumstances.

The fundamental precept of corrective discipline is that "actions speak louder than words." By this I mean that supervision's admonition of an employee in words is less significant in appraising the employee's degree of incorrigibility than the penalty — mild, moderate, or severe — which supervision assesses at the time the admonition is given. Verbal warnings frequently repeated but unsupported by lost-time penalties seldom command the respect which is needed for observance of the rules.

2. Procedural Due Process Prior to Arbitration

BABCOCK & WILCOX CO.

41 L.A. 862 (1963)

Dworkin, Harry J., Arbitrator

. . . .

The substantive issue presented by this grievance is whether the grievant was discharged for just cause. A procedural issue is raised by the union as to whether the company adhered to the contract provisions governing the procedure applicable to suspension and discharge of employees for violation of their obligations, and for misconduct. The grievant is classified as a "Cold Draw Operator." He has held employment tenure with the company for approximately nine years. He was absent from his scheduled work days on January 11, 12, 14 and 15, 1963. On January 16th the grievant was given an initial five day suspension, which was converted to a discharge following a grievance meeting on January 18. Management then advised the grievant and union representatives that the five day preliminary suspension was being converted to discharge for excessive absenteeism. The union protested the discharge penalty, as distinguished from the suspension, and appealed the grievance to arbitration. . . .

Pertinent Provisions of Contract

Section XV of the Collective Bargaining Agreement, sets forth the following procedure in "Discharge Cases":

In the exercise of its rights as set forth in Section III, the Corporation agrees that a member of the Union shall not be peremptorily discharged from and after the date hereof, but that in all instances in which the Corporation may conclude that an employee's conduct may justify suspension or discharge, he shall be first suspended. Such initial suspension shall be for not more than five (5) calendar days. During this period of initial suspension the employee may, if he believes that he has been unjustly dealt with, request a hearing and a statement of the offense before his department head with an assistant grievance committeeman, or grievance committeeman present, as he may choose, or the General Superintendent, or the Manager of the plant with or without the member or members of the Grievance Committee present, as he similarly may choose. At such hearing, the facts concerning the case shall be made available to both parties. After such hearing, the Corporation may conclude whether the suspension shall be converted into discharge, or dependent upon the facts of the case, that such suspension may be extended or revoked. If the suspension is revoked, the employee shall be returned to employment and receive full compensation at his regular rate of pay for the time lost but in the event a disposition shall result in either affirmation or extension of the suspension or discharge of the employee, the employee may within five (5) days after such disposition allege a grievance which will be handled in accordance with the procedure of Section XVII — Adjustment of Grievances. Final decision on all suspension or discharge cases shall be made by the Corporation within five (5) days from the date of filing of the grievance, if any. Should it be determined by the Corporation or by an umpire in accordance with step five of the grievance procedure that the employee has been discharged or suspended unjustly, the Corporation shall reinstate the employee and pay full compensation at the employee's regular rate of pay for the time lost.

In addition to the terms of the labor agreement, the union submitted in evidence the "General Instructions," effective October 4, 1954, which provides in part as follows:

Certain other conditions not of a contractual nature were discussed, and the following were agreed to:
#3—A uniform policy of penalties:
(a)—First offense—Warn or Dismiss *
(b)—Second offense—1 day or Dismiss *
(c)—Third offense—2 days or Dismiss *
(d)—Fourth offense—Dismiss
                    (* Depending on offense)

All penalties based on a 12-month period. All entries on an employee's Personnel Card, either good or bad, to be signed by the employee, the steward, and the foreman.

Position of Union

. . . .

The union vigorously protests the procedure of the company in failing to apprise the grievant of the fact that his initial suspension would be followed by discharge. Under these circumstances the employee was reasonably led to believe that the five day suspension was the full extent of the disciplinary penalty. An employee preliminarily suspended for consideration of discharge should be advised of management's intention to invoke the discharge penalty. Notice of discharge was not conveyed to the grievant until January 19, the day following the grievance meeting.

The union therefore reasons that the discharge penalty was improper and that the mitigating circumstances surrounding his four day absence were not taken into account; further, the union maintains that the discharge should be vacated and nullified by reason of the failure of the company to follow the prescribed procedure requiring notice to an employee of liability for discharge, at the time of the initial suspension.

Position of Company

. . . .

The company claims that it substantially complied with the requirements of the contract with regard to the procedure in discharge cases. The grievant was suspended for five days on January 16, during which suspension the union requested a grievance meeting, which was held on January 18. During the course of the meeting the company made it clear that the grievant would be discharged, which decision was made effective on the following day.

The company asserts that when the grievant was suspended on January 16, he was fully aware that discharge was then under consideration. Under the terms of the contract, a discharge penalty requires a five day initial suspension. This procedure is provided for in order that an opportunity may be accorded all of the interested parties for a full hearing and a review of the case. During the period of the suspension, management reviewed the grievant's absentee record and determined that the situation was intolerable, and that consideration of his record warranted termination of employment. The company represents that due to the grievant's "insufferable attendance record" just cause was presented warranting discharge, and that the contract procedure has been observed to the letter.

Opinion of Arbitrator

. . . .

The next question presented is whether the company adhered to the requirements of Section XV applicable to discharge cases. In considering this issue, the evidence establishes that on January 16, the grievant, in the presence of his committeeman, was given a five day disciplinary suspension for chronic absenteeism. On that occasion the suspension was not accompanied by any clear indication that he was subject to discharge. At the grievance meeting on January 18, supervision informed the union following a discussion that the decision had been made to convert the suspension to discharge, which was made effective on the following date. A reading of the language of Section XV, provides that an employee shall not be "peremptorily discharged" and that "he shall be first suspended."

The express purpose of the initial suspension is to permit the employee to request a hearing for the purpose of a full consideration of the matter. It is contemplated that the facts concerning the case shall then be fully made available to both parties. After such hearing, the company is authorized to determine whether "the suspension shall be converted into discharge," or whether the suspension shall be continued or revoked as the facts of the case may warrant.

The arbitrator concludes from an analysis of the language of Section XV that the contracting parties intended that an employee be accorded notice of the intention to discharge at the time of the initial suspension. In light of the tenor and import of the language, and viewing the provision in its totality, the arbitrator concludes that an employee is entitled to be fully apprised of the anticipated penalty at the time of the preliminary five day suspension. In the absence of such notification, an employee may reasonably conclude that the suspension is the extent of the penalty which is contemplated.

In the instant case, the first clear notice of the intention to convert the suspension to a discharge was in the form of an announcement made during the grievance meeting on January 19. Under these circumstances, the union contends that a full penalty was applied, and that the procedure was improper. It is claimed, therefore, that the company has in effect applied two successive penalties, for the same offense. The arbitrator feels that the contract language contemplates that an employee be informed at the outset of the initial suspension of the probable application of the discharge penalty after further consideration of the case. There is some merit to the union's claim that if an employee is suspended pending discharge consideration, he is entitled to receive a written notice to the effect that he is "suspended pending consideration of discharge."

The arbitrator observes that the contract lacks clarity and that the language should more clearly spell out that the employee is being suspended subject to discharge, or, that the suspension is the extent of the disciplinary action intended. The evidence indicates that the company had previously adhered to the procedure of notifying an employee at the time of his initial suspension that he may be subject to discharge. In the instant case, the company neglected to so inform the grievant, thereby departing from the established practice and procedure. The arbitrator is aware of the fact that the grievant made inquiry at the time of his suspension as to whether discharge was being considered, however, supervision simply informed him that under the contract it could do no more than suspend him for five days.

The arbitrator feels that under the contract language, the employee should be made fully aware of his situation at the time of the initial suspension. The notification at the time of the grievance meeting that management had decided to convert the suspension into discharge, does not conform to the contract requirement. An award will therefore be issued which the arbitrator deems to be consistent with the facts and the contract provisions.

Award

The arbitrator finds that the grievant had an excessive and chronic record of absenteeism, and that the circumstances made him subject to corrective discipline;

In light of the evidence presented, a penalty of suspension is deemed to be more reasonable and proper to correct the employee's deficiencies, prior to the consideration of the discharge penalty;

The company neglected to observe the requirements of the contract in that it failed to inform the grievant at the time of his initial five day suspension that the disciplinary action was subject to further consideration for the purpose of discharge;

It is therefore awarded that the discharge penalty be vacated and converted to a suspension, and that he be reinstated to his job within two days following the receipt of this award.

NOTES:

(1) *Warnings:* Warnings about the penalty for failure to comply are significant in disciplinary action. Reprimands and warnings may be provided for by contract. For example, in *Marathon Electric Mfg. Corp.,* 41 L.A. 515 (J. Shister, 1963) the provision read,

It has been and will continue to be Company policy to issue Warning Notices for Violation of Company rules, Safety practices, careless work and inefficiency. Warning Notices shall be issued for successive violations in accordance with the following procedure:

(1) The Foreman will first verbally advise the employee of the violation in the presence of his Steward.

(2) A written Warning Notice will be issued by the Foreman in the presence of the Steward setting out the violation.

(3) A written Warning Notice will be issued and the employee may be discharged or disciplined.

The Union will be given a copy of said Notices. Warning Notices shall have an expiration date of six (6) months.

Absent contractual provision, how will an arbitrator deal with a company's attempt to discipline without warning? *See Merchants Fast Motor Lines, Inc.,* 41 L.A. 1020 (H. Wren, 1963) (failure to inform employee about the exact nature of the complaint); *Commercial Steel Casting Co.,* 39 L.A. 286 (S. Kates, 1962) (failure to follow long-established custom).

(2) *Clarity of Rules:* It follows, therefore, that clarity of rules is basic to discipline. As one arbitration board stated, "Arbitrators and Arbitration Boards have consistently held that essential to making discharges stand up are (1) very clear instructions; and (2) even more

explicit statements about the penalty for failure to comply," *Micro Precision Gear & Machine Corp.,* 31 L.A. 575 (D. Young, Chm. 1958).

(3) *Prior Review:* Should pre-discharge investigation, even absent contractual requirement, be considered a condition precedent to discipline and discharge? *See Greif Bros. Cooperage Corp.,* 42 L.A. 555 (C. Daugherty, 1964) (failure to investigate deprives an employer of just cause). Arbitrator S. Kates said in *Decor Corp.,* 44 L.A. 389 (1965), where the labor agreement provided that "No employees, except in situations of urgency shall be discharged without a prior review of the facts involved between the Bargaining Committee and Management":

> The evidence is clear that no such prior review occurred. No reason for ignoring the contractual requirement of such review was presented. The evidence failed to establish any "situation of urgency" within the meaning of that language.
>
> Compliance with this review provision, in my opinion, is a condition precedent to any valid discharge from employment in the absence of "situations of urgency." The review requirement is important because, among other things, it tends to diminish the likelihood of impulsive and arbitrary decisions by supervisors and permits tempers to cool and deliberate judgment to prevail; it encourages careful investigation of the facts by both the Company and the Union; it provides an opportunity whereby the accused may be heard; it permits the presentation, sifting and weighing of all relevant factors; it provides an opportunity to measure the proposed penalty against the alleged offense in the light of the grievant's history, the past treatment by the employer of similar offenses, and other relevant circumstances; it permits consideration of apologies, regrets, and other mitigating circumstances; and enables the parties to consider rehabilitation possibilities.
>
> In a real sense, this contractual requirement of a prior review is a part of contractual "due process," without which a discharge must be held premature and wrongful.

What are "situations of urgency" which enable an employer to summarily discharge an employee? *See Henry Vogt Machine Co.,* 46 L.A. 654 (V. Stouffer, 1966) (where employee falsification of physical condition could have made employer liable for injury); *Proto Tool Co.,* 46 L.A. 487 (T. Roberts, 1966) (blackmail by Union Steward).

D. RIGHTS OF THE ACCUSED EMPLOYEE

As *Holodnak v. Avco Corp.,* 381 F. Supp. 191 (D. Conn. 1974), *modified,* 514 F.2d 285 (2d Cir.), *cert. denied* 423 U.S. 892 (1975); *Vaca v. Sipes,* 386 U.S. 171 (1967), and *Hines v. Anchor Motor Freight, Inc.,* 421 U.S. 928 (1976), indicate quite clearly, ordinarily an employee may not challenge a disciplinary and discharge grievance proceeding where the decision was based on a fair hearing. However, where the proceeding has not been fair or regular, or where the employee has been treated in an arbitrary, capricious and discriminatory fashion, or where there is a question about the integrity of the grievance process, the employee has rights that are independent of the employer and the union. Civil rights attorney John Silard explains why:

SILARD, RIGHTS OF THE ACCUSED EMPLOYEE IN COMPANY DISCIPLINARY INVESTIGATION, in PROCEEDINGS OF N.Y.U. 22ND ANNUAL CONFERENCE ON LABOR 217, 219-26 (Christensen & Christensen ed. 1970) [14]

. . .

SOCIAL POLICY

There are weighty arguments favoring increased protection for the suspected employee in employer disciplinary investigations. We have long passed the era of employment fluidity where a worker fired by one employer could simply saddle his horse and settle in the next county in a new job. With modern record keeping and employer cooperation systems the opprobrium of discharge may follow the employee wherever he goes. Moreover, in many callings a man's job is his permanent career. Job seniority is the key to preferred work and wages, and an employee with seniority can ill afford to start afresh with another employer. Accumulated pension rights representing an enormous capital asset for the employee are imperilled if he is discharged and must begin new employment without pension crediting years of service. Thus, it is clear that for the accused or suspected employee very serious consequences may attach to the investigatory processes wherein his guilt and punishment will be determined by the employer, subject only to limited after-the-fact redress through grievance proceedings.

Moreover, the development of fair protections for the suspected employee also promotes the employer's interests. Recent experience teaches that within our massive bureaucracies—governments, corporations, large unions, universities—the rights accorded to the

---

[14] Reprinted with permission of the publisher. Copyright © New York University.

individual member must be a matter of prime concern to the institution itself. At its worst, disregard and disrespect for the individual result in occupation of the dean's office or in the general boycott. But even absent such dramatic testimonial to institutional inhumanity, the damage can be material. The union which remains authoritarian and undemocratic finds its membership and strength diminished. The government agency which tramples civil servants' rights finds its reputation harmed and its hiring potential impaired. The industrial employer who follows the pattern of nineteenth century paternalism with its inevitable concomitant of contempt for the individual worker, breeds discontent which manifests itself in poor production, proliferation of grievances, and ultimately a strike. Thus major interests of employers no less than of individual employees are at stake in the development of fair protections in the prediscipline investigatory process.

ANALOGIES FROM CRIMINAL INVESTIGATION

Established protections for the suspected criminal which are encompassed in our Federal Bill of Rights and congressional legislation include freedom from compulsory or coerced self-incrimination, including the right to remain silent without consequent inference of guilt; the right to counsel; the right to be informed of these rights; and freedom from arbitrary search or seizure of the person or belongings. Each of these areas of protection for the individual accused or suspected of criminal conduct finds its parallel in employee disciplinary investigations and recent arbitrators' rulings have begun tapping the constitutional protections by way of analogy.[5] The analogy should not, of course, obscure some very real differences between an employer's interest in production and government's interest in law enforcement. It is

---

[5] In Thrifty Drug Stores Co., 50 Lab. Arb. 1253 (1968), the question for the arbitrator was whether two grievants discharged for theft who steadfastly denied complicity were guilty of the alleged misconduct. Relying chiefly on Miranda v. Arizona, 384 U.S. 436 (1966), the arbitrator upheld the rights of suspected employees to the assistance of a union representative at company interrogation and to remain silent when accused of conduct constituting crime. Applying those precepts, the arbitrator declined to consider as probative of guilt the refusal of grievants to undergo interrogation in the absence of a union representative; and he also rejected written accusations made against grievants by other employees during company interrogations wherein union representation had similarly been refused.

In Scott Paper Co., 52 Lab. Arb. A. 57 (1969), the grievant was discharged for refusing an order to empty his pockets after an altercation wherein it was reported that grievant had a gun in his pocket. The company order was held unauthorized and the discharge not "for proper cause," because "in the absence of a clear plant rule requiring it, an employee may not be forced to give evidence against himself, or to submit to search of his person, or to disclose the contents of his pockets. . . ."

clear that the employer has investigative needs which transcend punishment of a culpable employee.[6] Thus, in questioning an employee concerning a production stoppage the facts regarding machine malfunction are of importance quite apart from any possible dereliction by the employee. Similarly, employers must often take measures to prevent rather than to punish misconduct. Thus, there may be no preventive means against petty and continuous pilfering other than a daily check of all employees' lunch and tool boxes as they leave the plant. In such circumstances, the appropriate analogy is not so much to the governmental function of criminal investigation as to routine governmental inspection in such areas as customs, mine safety, licensed premises and the like, where the investigation may in fact reveal misconduct but the primary investigative purpose is preventative rather than accusatory.

With due regard to these considerations emerging from the employer's production necessities, it nevertheless remains clear that when the employer has commenced an investigation of individual misconduct there is need for individual protection. It appears that in at least four salient areas some protection for the accused employee is appropriate and desirable.

Right to Silence

A primary question concerns the right to silence by an employee accused or suspected of misconduct, particularly misconduct amounting to crime. Is the employee's silence under questioning "good cause" for employer imposition of sanctions, or at least a factor tending, together with other evidence, to validate discipline or discharge? In the area of government employment this question has evoked considerable litigation in cases where employees declined to state whether or not they had been Communist Party members. The decisions in *Slochower v. Board of Education*,[7] struck down discharge of a teacher from public education employment for invoking the Fifth Amendment, the Court noting that:

> "In practical effect the questions asked are taken as confessed and made the basis of the discharge. No consideration is given to such factors as the subject matter of the questions . . . or justification for exercise of the privilege. It matters not whether

---

[6] The recent decision in Jacobe-Pearson Ford, Inc., 172 N.L.R.B. No. 84 (1968), recognizes that an employer has an interest to determine facts concerning work-flow interruption which may not rise to the level of disciplinary accusation and yet require questioning an employee. The problem there concerned the employee's early cessation of work on the previous day under circumstances were the employer had not yet "committed itself to a disciplinary course of action" and the "potential for disciplinary action was remote."

[7] 350 U.S. 551, 558 (1966).

the plea resulted from mistake, inadvertence, or legal advice conscientiously given, whether wisely or unwisely. The heavy hand of the statute falls on all who exercise their constitutional privilege, the full enjoyment of which every person is entitled to receive."

Subsequent rulings eroded the spirit and holding of *Slochower,*[8] but more recently its authority appears restored by Garrity v. New Jersey,[9] and Spevack v. Klein.[10]

Notwithstanding the government employment cases, in the private sector the accused employee's right to silence without adverse inference has not yet won respect. While the constitutional right of silence is rooted in the humanitarian norm that no person should be forced through his own mouth to provide the basis for his own punishment, in the area of private employment that principle has so far bowed to the "horse sense" argument that an innocent man is likely to declare his innocence. The fact that the accused employee's silence may become grounds for his discharge underlines the special need for providing him competent representation at his interrogation, a question to which this discussion may now appropriately turn.

Assistance of Counsel

A second key protection finding analogy in constitutional principles is the right to representation and assistance of counsel during interrogation. The right to counsel— "not a formality" but "of the essence of justice" [11] is applicable to the interrogation stage of criminal proceedings since the rulings in *Miranda v. Arizona* [12] and *Escobedo v. Illinois.*[13] Until recently, arbitrators have not shown any great inclination to recognize a similar right in employer disciplinary interrogations and, as noted, the Fifth Circuit has recently taken a similar view. But the trend is in the *Escobedo*

---

[8] Lerner v. Casey, 357 U.S. 468 (1958); Beilan v. Board of Educ., 357 U.S. 399 (1958); Nelson v. County of Los Angeles, 362 U.S. 1 (1960). The relationship between the plea of privilege in government loyalty investigations and discharge from private employment has been the subject of litigation. IUE v. General Elec. Co., 127 F. Supp. 934 (D.D.C. 1954), aff'd 231 F.2d 259, *cert. denied* 352 U.S. 872 (1956). See also treatises cited at pp. 425-426 of Emerson, Haber & Dorsen, *Political and Civil Rights in the United States* (3d ed.).

[9] 385 U.S. 493 (1967).

[10] 385 U.S. 511 (1967). Closely related to the right of silence is the question of whether employees may be subjected to lie detector examinations and whether the results are admissible as grounds for discharge. Arbitrators' decisions on this subject are conflicting. See 1965 ABA Section of Labor Relations Law 288-295.

[11] Kent v. United States, 383 U.S. 541, 561 (1966).

[12] 378 U.S. 478 (1964).

[13] 384 U.S. 436 (1966).

direction.[14] In point is a decision by Judge Motley involving the question of the right to counsel in public school disciplinary proceedings. In *Madera v. Board of Education of the City of New York*,[15] the issue involved an administrative regulation barring counsel at a "guidance conference" with the affected school child and his parents, initiated by his teacher's charge of delinquency. The court's thoughtful analysis underlines the vital importance of the right to counsel as an ingredient of the due process hearing required wherever major adverse effect may result from governmental hearings. The ruling was reversed by the Second Circuit in an opinion emphasizing that no material discipline can follow the informal guidance conference and that statements made at such a conference are not subsequently admissible in Family Court or other judicial proceedings.[16]

Surely the interrogation of an accused or suspected employee can have critical effects upon employment and employability. One should not overlook the positive contribution that assistance by the union can make to a fair result. The extent to which a right of assistance by the union or private counsel should apply in employer disciplinary investigations is the issue in *Texaco* analyzed in the last section of this discussion.

Right to Warning

A person officially accused or suspected of misconduct may forfeit his rights at the interrogation stage if he is unaware of those rights. That reality underlies the Supreme Court's ruling in *Miranda v. Arizona*,[17] that, prior to interrogation, due process requires warning the suspect of his right to silence and to the assistance of counsel. At first there was some question whether the *Miranda* warning obligation applied to a suspect not in jail or formal custody, but it now appears that it applies even absent formal arrest or incarceration.[18] In any event, an employee interrogated in the plant or at the company's offices is not in a state of formal arrest but he is surely not free to leave with impunity. No distinction from the rule applicable in police investigations therefore seems in order on the point of custody or deprivation of physical freedom.

The underlying policy objective of *Escobedo* seems fully applicable in the industrial context. If an accused or suspected employee has a right to silence and/or to counsel, it seems appropriate to warn him

---

[14] See N. 5 *supra.*
[15] 267 F. Supp. 356 (S.D.N.Y. 1967).
[16] 386 F.2d 778 (2d Cir. 1967), *cert. denied,* 390 U.S. 1028 (1968).
[17] 384 U.S. 436 (1966).
[18] See Mathis v. United States, 391 U.S. 1 (1968); Orozco v. Texas, 89 S. Ct. 1095 (1969).

of such rights so that he will not surrender them out of ignorance. Indeed, in one respect, interrogation by the employer has a greater in terroram effect than does police questioning. While citizens know that to be punished for a crime they must be formally charged, tried by jury and convicted, employees know that they can be fired on the spot if the employer believes there is cause — subject, at best, to a grievance procedure after the fact. The perceived immediacy of the ultimate penalty which the employer can impose supports the inference that at prediscipline interrogations many employees will surrender their rights through ignorance unless properly notified before the interrogation takes place. On this ground, *Miranda* appears particularly applicable in employer disciplinary investigation.

Search and Seizure

Another important area of concern involves search and seizure of persons and property, which the Fourth Amendment prohibits except upon warrants for probable cause. The goals of personal privacy and freedom from unwarranted intrusion which underlie the Fourth Amendment appear equally applicable in the plant situation. That is not to suggest that a system of warrants or formal authorization must precede an employer's search of a suspected employee's person or possessions. But an employer who conducts such search without proper grounds should be denied recourse to the fruits of his misconduct in subsequent grievance-arbitration proceedings. It seems axiomatic that arbitrators have power to rule that evidence wrongfully obtained does not constitute "good cause" for discipline, and thus provide some limits upon employer privacy intrusions which today go unchecked by any existing legal sanctions.[19]

. . . .

---

[19] A closely related area which has given rise to much recent attention involves wiretapping, eavesdropping, electronic surveillance, and similar intrusions upon privacy and personal relationships. The Fourth Amendment's restrictions now clearly apply to governmental activity in this area. See Berger v. New York, 388 U.S. 41 (1967); Katz v. United States, 389 U.S. 347 (1967). Congress has also enacted certain safeguards which apply equally to private employers, such as the prohibition on tampering with mail and the restrictions on wiretapping and interception of any private oral communication in Section 2511 of the 1968 "Safe Streets Act" (Pub. L. 90-351; 832 Stat. 197).

NATIONAL DISTILLERS & CHEMICAL CORP.

62 L.A. 338 (1974)

Geissinger, Arbitrator: — Grievance No. 40 was filed under date of March 28, 1972 by A—, S—, and T— in pertinent part as follows:

"Unjustly reprimanded & suspended.

"1. Employees did not overextend lunch. Their car wouldn't start.

"2. Employees were not away without permission. They called in and stated their problem.

"3. The employees gave no false statements to the guard: We expect *all* back pay for all time lost, including holidays."

Supervisor's Reprimand and Discharge Report

Under date of March 28, 1972 each of the three grievants received identical Reports:

"REPORT IN DETAIL: As the result of a Suspension Hearing held this date, you are being suspended for the following reasons:

1) For over-extending your lunch period; 2) Being away from the plant during working hours without permission; 3) Giving false statements to the Guard regarding your reason for not returning to work. This suspension covers period 3/24/72 through 4/30/72; you are to return to work on Monday, May 1, 1972 on your regular shift. Any re-occurrence of this type of violation will result in your immediate suspension and discharge. The above suspension is without pay."

Pertinent Contract Provisions

Article V — Discharge does not provide for disciplinary suspension except for a two-day period during investigation of an alleged offense. It requires that discharge must be for just cause. If the discharge is found to be unwarranted the employee must be made whole for all time and rights lost including the suspension during investigation.

The Agreement does not include a Management Rights clause as such. With or without such a clause the Company retains the right to direct the work force and manage the business, including the right to make and enforce reasonable rules and regulations not inconsistent or in conflict with the provisions of the Agreement.

SUPPLEMENTAL AGREEMENT, incorporated in the Agreement, on page 63, provides in part:

PLANT RULES

"The Employer and the Union agree that the working rules and procedure governing the relations between the Employer and the employees now in effect shall be binding upon the Employer, the employees and the Union and shall be faithfully performed by each. Information Book for Plant Employees (Company Rule and Policies) is referred to in this connection."

The Issue

Was the five-week disciplinary suspension imposed on each of the three grievants for just and proper cause?

The Union has stated the issue as "(1) Is the Company justified in suspending for the reasons they have stated? (2) If they are justified, is a five week suspension justifiable? (3) Is the Company justified in establishing a surveillance system away from the plant for purposes of disciplinary action?" (TR 6).

Facts and Background Summarized

The incidents resulting in the disputed disciplinary suspensions took place between 6:45 P.M. and 9:45 P.M. on the night of Thursday, March 23, 1972.

The grievants, A—, S— and T—, employed as Maintenance Men in the deKuyper plant on the second shift, left the plant to take their authorized thirty-minute lunch-break at the Minute Man Lounge approximately one-half mile from the Plant. Thursday is pay-day and employees frequently eat out rather than use the company cafeteria in order to cash their pay checks. There is no contention that leaving the plant during lunch-break is in itself grounds for discipline.

The grievants drove from the plant to the Minute Man in S—'s automobile at approximately 6:45 P.M. and their normal, authorized lunch period therefore would end at approximately 7:15 P.M.

The grievants were observed in the Minute Man by their foreman, Robert Minshall who finished eating and left to return to the plant about 7:00 P.M. At or about 8:25 P.M. a Guard relayed to General Foreman Zinser a call from grievant S— reporting that due to car trouble he, A— and T— would not return to work that evening. Zinser contacted Minshall who questioned the validity of the report and the two supervisors drove to the Minute Man where Minshall identified Staub's car in the parking area. Zinser returned to the plant and called his superior, Assistant Superintendent Rakel who instructed Zinser to meet him at the Minute Man. Zinser arrived first, saw the three grievants at a table inside the Minute Man but did not contact them. Rakel arrived at about 9:00 P.M. and Zinser pointed out S—'s car. Both returned to the plant where Rakel called Safety and Security Director Seilkop, requesting him to go to the Minute Man and make observations. Rakel and Zinser picked up Union Steward Howard and asked him to go with them to the Minute Man to investigate the situation.

While parked opposite the Minute Man and before the arrival of Zinser, Rakel and Howard, at about 9:30 P.M., Seilkop saw the three grievants leave the Minute Man, start Staub's car and drive away. Shortly thereafter Zinser, Rakel and Howard arrived. As they drove in one side of the parking area the grievants, S— driving, entered from the other end. S— stopped, reversed and backed up the street at a high rate of speed on the wrong side against traffic, turned and disappeared.

Rakel, Zinser and Howard, who had observed the above and identified the grievants and the car, returned to the plant. At about 9:45 P.M. the grievants arrived at the plant and were told by Rakel that they were suspended for the reasons given later in the Reprimand and Discharge Report of March 28. The grievants refused to accept the discipline on the night of March 23 on the grounds that they were not at work and were again informed of the suspension when they next reported for work.

. . .

Opinion

The basic issue is whether the grievants were guilty of culpable misconduct and if so was the disciplinary suspension unduly severe. If the grievants were not guilty of culpable misconduct they are, of course, entitled to be made whole.

. . .

Since the grievants were at work on the day in question they were obligated to observe all conditions of employment not in conflict with the Agreement. They were thereby limited to a thirty-minute lunch break unless given proper permission to extend it. If not given such permission they were obligated to return on time or produce a valid and acceptable reason for such failure. In such case the Company had the implied obligation to be fair and reasonable in evaluating the reason. While away from the plant on a limited lunch break they were not relieved of their obligations as employees. They were not absent, sick or scheduled off, but were obligated to complete their regularly scheduled shift unless there was a valid, legitimate reason for not doing so. In the absence of such a reason or excuse, unreasonable over-extension of their lunch period would constitute culpable misconduct justifying discipline.

It also is undisputed that S—, on behalf of himself and the other two grievants, called the Guard at the plant and reported that they would not return to work because of car trouble. This was in accordance with established procedure for giving notice of absence. The mere fact of reporting in or giving notice is not, however, evidence of the validity of the reason given for the absence nor does receipt of the call and transmission of the information received constitute acceptance or approval of the absence. The decision to accept or reject the reason or excuse offered by the reporting employee depends upon the validity or acceptability of the reason. In the incident under consideration the grievants' foreman, having seen the grievants at the Minute Man, was unwilling to accept the offered excuse as valid and took steps to begin an immediate investigation. During the course of investigation events occurred which in the opinion of supervision confirmed the foreman's initial suspicion that S— was not telling the truth when he reported car trouble. Under the circumstances there were reasonable grounds for questioning S—'s report. The situation was such that immediate investigation was necessary. Otherwise the actual facts probably never could be ascertained. In my opinion the action of supervision did not constitute improper "spying and surveillance" as contended by the Union. If the facts were, as stated by S—, investigation would simply confirm them and Company suspicions would have been proved wrong. Further, the investigation occurred during a period of time when the grievants were supposed to be at work and were under obligation to satisfactorily account for their absence. The Company was not trying to "frame" the grievants or otherwise improperly interfere in their private affairs. It is clear from the evidence that the grievants were away from the plant and their jobs without permission at all times after the expiration of their thirty-minute lunch break. From about 7:15 P.M. and after the burden was on them to justify their absence.

. . .

A review of the evidence supports the conclusion that S—'s report to the Guard at 8:25 P.M. that car trouble prevented all three from returning to the plant was incorrect in view of subsequent events. I am willing to concede that there might have been reason for some delay in returning by 7:15 P.M. but am not persuaded that there was justification for failure to return at all. "False" is defined in the dictionary as "not true or correct; erroneous".

The evidence fully supports the finding that all three grievants over-extended their lunch period, were away from the plant without permission, and through S— gave incorrect or erroneous reasons to the Guard. This is without question culpable misconduct justifying discipline.

The remaining question is whether a disciplinary suspension without pay for five weeks was unduly severe in view of the nature of the offense. Past records may not be used to establish guilt but may be used in evaluating the severity of discipline following determination of guilt.

Unrefuted evidence offered by the Company at the hearing establishes that grievants S— and T— were late returning from lunch 45 times over an 81 day period and that they were "docked" accordingly. These two grievants were warned at least twice that a continuation of such conduct would result in disciplinary action. The most recent warning was the day before the incident in question.

A—'s record prior to transfer to the department was satisfactory. Following transfer he fell into the same pattern as S— and T— and on the very day of the incident was warned against chronic over-extension of lunch periods.

At first impression a five-week suspension without pay for the offense charged appears unduly severe. Upon examination of the records of S— and T— it is apparent that progressive discipline in the form of monetary loss, counseling and warnings was having little or no effect. Under the circumstances of this case, involving an aggravated instance of unjustified absenteeism, the penalty does not seem too severe. The totality of the record of chronic over-extension of lunch periods requires the conclusion that a lesser penalty would not serve the purpose of discipline which is to correct rather than to simply punish for the sake of punishing.

Although A— has a much better overall record the evidence supports the finding that he too was falling into a pattern of chronic lateness in returning from lunch. The fact that he was warned of the possible consequences on the same day the incident occurred indicates to me that he was not responding to progressive discipline. Under the circumstances I do not find that he deserved a lesser penalty than S— and T—.

There is no evidence that the Company was arbitrary or improperly discriminatory in assessing the penalty. All the grievants were on notice of the possible consequences if the pattern of over-extension continued. The matter was promptly investigated. The observed conduct of the grievants justifies the conclusion of guilt. I find no evidence of mitigating or extenuating circumstances sufficient to justify a reduction of the penalty.

. . .

AWARD

Grievance denied.

E. POWER OF AN ARBITRATION TO MODIFY PENALTIES

In *Linear, Inc.,* 48 L.A. 319 (1966), Arbitrator Alexander H. Frey said,

> In a discipline case the initial burden is on the employer to prove that the grievant misconducted himself in a manner warranting discipline. If the employer sustains this burden, then the burden shifts to the union to establish, if it seeks to have the

arbitrator award a lesser penalty, that the discipline imposed is overly severe. In other words, once the employer has convinced the arbitrator that *some* penalty is justified, the employer's judgment as to the extensiveness of the penalty should not be decreased unless the union persuades the arbitrator that under the circumstances the penalty is unreasonable.

Under what circumstances is a penalty unreasonable? Arbitrator James Altieri said in *Brewer Drydock Co.,* 43 L.A. 689, 694 (1964) that he had authority to evaluate whether the penalty imposed was disproportionate to the offense committed except where the type of conduct was expressly stated by the contract to be just cause for discharge. In *International Harvester Co.,* 12 L.A. 653 (1949), which involved a discharge for insubordination, Arbitrator McCoy held that the discharge was, under the circumstances, "neither justifiable nor reasonably necessary," and he ordered the discharged employee reinstated with full rights. He stated his test to be,

> In a case of this sort, where a discharge is held unjustifiable, I generally consider the question whether the employee was somewhat at fault and deserved some penalty. My practice has been to determine what maximum penalty might have been upheld had it been imposed by the Company, and to change the discharge to such penalty. The Arbitration Reports disclose that practically all arbitrators, under the usual contract provisions relating to arbitration of disciplinary matters, assert and act upon the assumption of power. In its post-hearing brief, however, this Company contends that under the contract in effect between these parties, the Arbitrator has no power to change a penalty, but that his power is limited to suspending the discharge or setting it aside entirely.
>
> There is undoubtedly some foundation in the wording of the contract for this position. . . . In view of the fact that acceding to this insistence of the Company cannot do injury to the employee, but could prejudice only the Company, if anyone (in such matters as back pay, morale of supervisors, etc.), I have determined that the proper course for me to pursue is to concede without deciding the point. . . .

Compare Davison Chemical Co., 31 L.A. 920 (1959) where Arbitrator Kenneth C. McGuiness made the following comment,

> Grievant was not "singled out" for any arbitrary or capricious discipline and there is no showing of any kind of Company bias, bad faith, favoritism, or discrimination directed toward him. Where proper cause for disciplinary action exists, a penalty imposed in good faith by management should not be disturbed by the arbitrator. It is not for the arbitrator to

substitute his judgment for that of one having proper authority to discharge, where there has been no abuse of discretion or no conduct forbidden by statute or the labor agreement. *S. A. Shenk & Co.,* 26 L.A. 395. None of these factors being present in this case, the Company's action must be upheld.

See West Virginia Pulp & Paper Co., 42 L.A. 1251 (J. Abersold, 1964) for an example of this test being adopted expressly into the contract. In *Michigan Steel Casting Co.,* 6 L.A. 678, 680 (1947), Arbitrator Harry H. Platt indicated that,

... in a case of this type, it is the right of an arbitrator, unless expressly prohibited by contract, not only to determine whether an employee is guilty of wrongdoing which justifies the taking of disciplinary action against him but also whether the discipline meted out is just and fair and reasonable, under all the circumstances of the situation. This, in my opinion, is nothing more than ordinary fairness and is clearly in line with an arbitrator's function, in discharge cases, to frame his decision on broad moral and equitable principles.

In *Kaiser Sand & Gravel,* 49 L.A. 190 (1967), Arbitrator Adolph Koven upheld Mr. Platt's views in holding,

The Company says that the Arbitrator does not have the authority to modify the discharge penalty which was imposed by the Company. We know that many agreements give the arbitrator express authority to modify penalties found to be improper or too severe. Also the agreement may give him such authority by implication (See *McInerney, Spring and Wire Co.,* 21 LA 80, 82). Some agreements expressly limit the arbitrator's authority to modify penalties. Where the agreement fails to deal with the matter, the right of the arbitrator to change or modify penalties found to be improper or too severe may be deemed to be inherent in his power to decide the sufficiency of cause (Platt, "The Arbitration Process in the Settlement of Labor Disputes," 31 J. Am. Jud. Soc. 54, 58; 28 LA 65, 69; 25 LA 634, 637-638; 25 LA 439, 442).

In a letter to Russell Smith, dated September 9, 1949 (quoted here with permission), Arbitrator Platt further expounded his views on this question:

Where a contract reserves to the employer the right to discipline or discharge for cause, I think the logical inference is that the parties meant that the right shall be exercised only when "good," "sufficient," "proper," or "just" cause exists. What is "good," etc., cause is, of course, subject to interpretation in an arbitration case and may depend, in the final analysis, on the arbitrator's background of experience, his training and education, his own or the community's standards of justice and fair treatment, and possibly, too (as Justice Douglas has said of judges in the exercise of the interpretive function), the "genes of the blood stream of his ancestors." In essence, I think that what the parties intend when they adopt a clause such as above indicated, is that discipline will be imposed only when the employee is guilty of misconduct and that in that event, the penalty will be such a one as would appeal to fair-minded persons as just, under all the circumstances of the case, and not disproportionate to the offense.

When a disciplinary action is submitted to me for arbitration, I assume (unless directed otherwise) that the parties want three things done: (1) A review of the case to determine guilt or innocence; (2) a test of the employer's action and the reasonableness of the penalty in the light of the standards, if any, prescribed in the contract or, absent these, then in the light of the parties' past practice and, lacking these, then in the light of the arbitrator's experience in the industrial world and the prevailing standards of justice therein; (3) to make a final and conclusive determination of the pending dispute — a result that can only be achieved by imposing an appropriate penalty, if one is merited, or by holding that no penalty is warranted. (Of course this is not so where the arbitrator is acting under an agreement that expressly prohibits him from passing on the reasonableness of the penalty or under a submission which merely calls for a finding of fact as to the employee's guilt.)

Personally, I can see no valid objection to the foregoing assumptions and they are confirmed by my feeling, based on experience, that most employers want to treat their employees fairly, that they do not wish to abuse their power to discipline, and that they do not mind if their unintended severity is called to their attention and corrected by an arbitrator, provided he explains his reasons for doing so. The objection that in modifying a disciplinary penalty an arbitrator substitutes his judgment for that of the employer seems rather pointless to me. Indeed, an arbitrator also substitutes his judgment for that of the parties when he gives a "reasonable" meaning to an ambiguous clause, despite the protestations of one of the parties that that was not the intended meaning. He also substitutes his judgment for the employer's when he finds, contrary to the employer's belief, that a senior employee has equal or greater ability than the junior employee who displaced him during a layoff. And, he also substitutes his judgment for the employer's when he decides that a discharge was arbitrary and capricious. Of course, I perceive that those who disagree with my position would have no objection if, after holding that the facts in the case warrant the imposition of a penalty but not one as severe as discharge, I were to refer the case back to the employer for assessment of a different penalty. This would indeed perserve for the employer his right to discipline; but would it finally and conclusively settle the dispute between the parties and would it assure acceptance of the new penalty and that there will be no further arbitrations over it? In the interest of a harmonious labor-management relationship and in the interest of an effective arbitration process, I think it is far more preferable that the arbitrator should exercise the right to modify the penalty in the first place.

NOTES:

Problem: In light of the materials on the authority of an arbitrator to modify a penalty, is it not desirable to include specific contract provisions dealing with this question? Do the following examples obviate the issues arising out of an arbitrator's "implied powers"?

Example 7

ARTICLE XI DISCIPLINE

206 *Section A.* Maintenance of discipline is a responsibility of management, but in carrying out that responsibility the Company shall take disciplinary action only for just cause, which shall mean a breach of discipline, and, in addition, shall not exercise manifestly arbitrary managerial judgment in determining what disciplinary action shall be taken.

207 Therefore, in carrying out its responsibility, the Company shall determine (1) whether any breach of discipline has occurred, and (2) what disciplinary action shall be taken in order to maintain discipline. But any complaint that (1) the alleged breach of discipline was not, in fact, committed, or that (2) the exercise of managerial judgment in fixing the disciplinary action was manifestly arbitrary, may be treated as a grievance if the complaint concerns disciplinary action involving demotion, layoff, or discharge, and if the complaint is presented in accordance with the conditions hereinafter set forth.

208 "Breach of discipline" means any act (not authorized by any provision of this agreement) which interferes with the orderly and efficient administration of the Company's business, including (1) any violation of the agreement and (2) any violation of the Company's published rules or regulations, provided, however, that any new rule or

regulation shall not be contrary to the terms of this agreement.

209 "Manifestly arbitrary exercise of managerial judgment" is the fixing of disciplinary action without utilization of rational processes in determining that such disciplinary action was needed as a deterrent to insure the maintenance of discipline, that is, the state of orderly and efficient administration of the Company's business.

210 In imposing discipline on a current charge, the Company will not take into account any prior infractions which occurred more than three years previously.

211 If the referee finds that (1) the alleged breach of discipline was committed, and (2) the Company's exercise of managerial judgment in fixing the disciplinary action was not manifestly arbitrary, he shall affirm the disciplinary action fixed by the Company, except that the referee may modify any portion of the disciplinary action that is in excess of fourteen (14) days if he finds that such action was too severe.

212 If the referee finds (1) that the alleged breach of discipline was not, in fact, committed, or (2) that there had been a manifestly arbitrary exercise of the Company's managerial judgment in fixing the disciplinary action, the referee shall nullify such disciplinary action. (Allis-Chalmers Mfg. Co., West Allis Works *and* Local 248, UAW)

Example 8

(8) The right to hire; promote; discharge or discipline for cause; and to maintain discipline and efficiency of employees, is the sole responsibility of the Corporation except that Union members shall not be discriminated against as such. . . .

(47) The Corporation delegates to the Umpire full discretion in cases of discipline for violation of shop rules, or discipline for violation of the Strikes, Stoppages and Lock-outs Section of the Agreement. (General Motors Corporation *and* UAW)

Assume the discharge provision reads:

If the referee finds that there is "just cause" for discharge, then the discharge will be upheld. However, if the referee finds a lack of just cause, the employee is to be reinstated with back pay.

However, in either case, the referee's authority is limited to the determination of whether "just cause" for discharge exists. If the arbitrator concludes that some cause exists, but not sufficient cause to warrant discharge, what must he do — set aside the penalty altogether or sustain the discharge?

F. BACK-PAY AWARDS

Professor Dallas L. Jones discussed the converse situation — where a discharged grievant is reinstated by the arbitrator.

"RAMIFICATIONS OF BACK-PAY AWARDS IN SUSPENSION AND DISCHARGE CASES," in PROCEEDINGS OF 22ND ANNUAL MEETING OF NAT'L ACADEMY OF ARBITRATORS 163 (Somers ed. 1969).[15]

Problems of back-pay awards in discharge cases stem, of course, from the concept of "just cause"; that is, if an employee is unjustly discharged, he is entitled to reinstatement to his job with full seniority and other benefits, and he must be made whole for the monies lost while separated from his job. The just-cause concept is a mixture of ideas borrowed from contract law, criminal law, and especially modern personnel management. . . .

. . .

Because the American system does provide for reinstatement, a host of problems are created which are not found in other industrial relations systems. Some of these problems concern the maintenance of discipline in the plant: that is, what is the effect upon the discharged employee's behavior when he is reinstated, and what is the impact upon the behavior of other employees? Certainly, as we know, employers often urge that there will be an adverse effect upon plant discipline if an employee is returned to work. Another problem is the impact of reinstatement upon the management-union relationship. There are many facets to this problem, but an important one is certainly the influence which the possibility of reinstatement may have upon the strategies of the parties in dealing with discharge cases. Clearly involved in all of this is whether the employee is reinstated with no back pay, partial back pay, or full back pay. Thus, the appropriate remedy involves many considerations apart from the problem — and this is a not inconsiderable one — of determining the actual amount of back pay if such is awarded. It is my intention to focus upon the first two problems raised, with some attention to the third.

The problems associated with reinstatement are problems which we cannot ignore. Arbitrators have played an important role in shaping industrial discipline in this country. We have insisted upon due process and the corrective approach for the individual. But we also must be concerned with the impact of our actions upon the

---

[15] Reprinted with permission of the publisher. Copyright © 1970 by the Bureau of National Affairs, Inc.

discipline and morale of other employees as part of the total disciplinary system, and one does not have to embrace the views of Justice Douglas to take such a position. It is my belief that arbitrators are concerned with this problem in spite of many accusations to the contrary. That this is so is evident in many decisions, sometimes explicit but more often implicit. I also suspect that most of us, for this reason, at one time or another have wished that we could award back pay without reinstatement! It may very well be that such a remedy is the appropriate one in some cases, but I have yet to hear of the arbitrator who has been so innovative — or should I say fearless?

The Discharge Problem in Statistical Perspective

Before proceeding to discuss the implications of reinstatement and back pay upon the individual and the work group, it may be helpful to place the discharge problem in statistical perspective. Table I presents the discharge cases reported in Volumes 40-49 of BNA's *Labor Arbitration Reports.* Because discharge and discipline cases still constitute the largest single category of cases arbitrated — some 25 percent — and only a small percentage can be reported, the usual caveat that the reported cases may not be representative is in order. It may even have more validity in this instance because there is some evidence to indicate that if all discharge cases were reported, the percentage of cases in which the discharge penalty was upheld would be greater than the 46 percent indicated in Table I.[2] This figure represents, nevertheless, an increase of 2 percentage points over the 1956-1960 period as reported by John Teele and is about the same as the 1951-1956 period as reported by Fred Holly to the Academy in 1957.[3]

---

[2] The author was informed by Joseph Murphy, Vice President, American Arbitration Association, that many of the cases in which discharge is upheld are not reported because they are "run of the mill" cases; that is, cases which present no unusual issues or circumstances.

[3] The table is reproduced from John W. Teele, "The Thought Processes of the Arbitrator," *Arbitration Journal,* 17:2 (1962), p. 87. The Holly report referred to is found in *Critical Issues in Labor Arbitration,* Proceedings of the Tenth Annual Meeting, National Academy of Arbitrators, Jean T. McKelvey, ed. (Washington: BNA Books, 1957), pp. 1-17.

Table I

DISCHARGE CASES, 1963-1967 [1]

	Total cases	Dis-charge upheld	Rein-state-ment ordered	With full back pay	Partial back pay	With-out back pay
Quit or Discharge	35	15	20	6	8	6
Strike Activity, Slowdown	84	50	34	4	7	23
Refusal to Accept Job Assignment	42	19	23	5	6	12
Plant Rules Generally	42	17	25	9	4	12
Physical or Mental Disability	27	9	18	7	6	5
Loafing, Leaving Work	30	15	15	3	7	5
Intoxication	21	10	11	1	3	7
Insubordination	79	32	47	13	14	20
Incompetence, Negligence, Low Production	47	15	32	13	8	11
Gambling	8	4	4	2	0	2
Theft	42	15	27	12	3	12
Falsification of Records	36	20	16	4	3	9
Disloyalty, Moonlighting	15	10	5	2	1	2
Dishonesty	16	5	11	3	4	4
Horseplay	11	5	6	0	2	4
Criminal Prosecution or Conviction	7	2	5	0	1	4

[1] Source: The Bureau of National Affairs, Inc., *Labor Arbitration Reports,* Vols. 40-49, March 1963 — February 1968.

Table I—Contd.

	Total cases	Dis- charge upheld	Rein- state- ment ordered	With full back pay	Partial back pay	With- out back pay
Fighting, Troublemaking	45	16	29	4	7	18
Tardiness	6	4	2	1	1	0
Absenteeism	91	55	36	11	8	17
Miscellaneous	49	20	29	14	3	12
Total	733	338	395	114	96	185
Total (excluding multiple counts) [2]	665	307	358	104	82	172
Total (excluding multiple counts— by percent)	100.0	46.2	53.8	15.6	12.3	25.9
Total of Reinstate- ment cases by percent			100.0	29.1	22.9	48.0

. . .

There can be no doubt, from the data presented, that an arbitral decision reinstating an employee can have unexpected results in terms of both the individual and the work group. The arbitrator's first concern must be to see that the individual receives justice; if he finds that the individual has been unjustly treated, then he must take appropriate action. But one can question how well we have been meeting the problem of insuring justice to the individual as well as dealing with the other problems.

A reading of many arbitral decisions gives one cause to ponder the reasoning which led to the award. One cannot escape the conviction that in many cases of reinstatement without back pay, the basis for reinstating the individual to work was simply the arbitrator's belief, based upon some unknown standard of fair play, that the individual

---

[2] These figures represent the absolute number of cases judged. In contrast to the "total" category these figures take into account the fact that some discharges were for more than one charge.

should have another chance and that such a decision will seemingly harm no one.

NOTES:

Problems: In commenting upon Professor Jones' paper, Patrick Fisher asked the following questions.[16] What are the appropriate answers?

(a) How Should an Ad Hoc Arbitrator Compute Back Pay?

1. If overtime was common during the period of X's absence from the plant, should that be included in the computation?

2. If X was a second-shift employee, should the shift differential be included?

3. If X was the senior bidder, or the only bidder, on a posting for a higher-paying job at the time of his discharge, is he entitled to that higher rate?

4. Should interest be added to the back-pay award?

5. If X had to borrow money to live on during the period of his absence, is he entitled to the 8-percent or 10-percent or 12-percent interest he had to shell out?

6. If X was hospitalized during the period of his absence and thereby failed to collect accident and health benefits which had been negotiated for all employees, should the amount of lost benefits be added to the back-pay award?

(b) Does a Discharged Employee Have a Duty to Seek Other Employment?

1. What if the discharged employee could obtain employment only in a community that is 30 miles away?

2. What if the only employment available is degrading?

3. How about a disc jockey being required to seek alternate employment?

(c) Should the Ad Hoc Arbitrator Direct that Certain Deductions Be Made from the Back-Pay Awards?

1. Should unemployment compensation be deducted?

2. Should earnings from other employment be deducted?

    a. What if X earned more at the new job?

    b. What if X worked at two jobs during his absence?

    c. What if X earned more because he worked overtime?

    d. What if X's total outside earnings were less than the amount of back pay, but the outside earnings still included overtime?

    e. What if X worked Saturdays and Sundays during his absence?

3. Should any union benefits be deducted?

---

[16] *Id.* at 175.

4. If X took employment which required the use of transportation, whereas he had previously walked from home to the employer's plant, should an adjustment be made for the cost of additional travel?

5. What if employment was available locally and X made no effort to obtain it?

Chapter 11

SENIORITY

A. CONTRACT PROVISIONS

"Seniority" provisions appear almost universally in collective bargaining agreements, albeit in a variety of forms. The variation and diversity are due in part to the complexity of the subject in relation to the operations of the employer, in part to the ineptness of the parties in dealing with the subject, and in part to their tendency to use contract language which reflects shop vernacular and thus can be understood only in context and upon becoming familiar with shop usages and practices. Yet it remains true that the seniority provisions give rise to more problems in their application than most other provisions of the contract — most of them foreseeable — and it is of the utmost importance that the parties, in negotiating these provisions, have a clear concept of the purposes for which "seniority" *may* be used, reach agreement on the extent to which it shall be used, and, within the limits of collective bargaining practicalities, write contract provisions which will clearly express their intent.

The negotiation and drafting of seniority provisions should elicit from the parties a high standard of skill and care if the results are to provide a satisfactory basis for serving both the needs of managerial efficiency and a clear set of rules or principles for day-to-day contract administration (assuming, of course, that the parties wish to settle these matters during their initial bargaining rather than "ad hoc" as the questions arise). A "check list" of the principal questions to be considered and answered would include the following:

(1) For what purposes is seniority to be recognized? Reductions in force (layoffs)? Re-employment after layoff? Promotions? Transfers? Shift preferences? Work assignments?

(2) What *kind* of seniority is to be recognized? Company length of service? Plant length of service? Department length of service? Occupational group length of service? Job classification length of service? Some combination of these? May this depend in part on the degree of complexity of the plant and the variety of different occupational skills required in the operation? How does the type of seniority comply with the anti-discrimination proscriptions of federal law?

(3) To what degree shall seniority be made the controlling factor? Entirely controlling? Controlling if the employee has the necessary

job competence? Controlling if relative merit and ability are relatively equal? Not controlling at all, but only a factor to be "considered," along with others?

(4) How shall an employee's seniority standing be determined? Credit, if any, to be given for non-working time (sick leave, layoffs, leave of absence, etc.)? Credit, if any, to be given for time spent outside the bargaining unit (prior to initial agreement, subsequent to initial agreement)? "Super-seniority" for union officers or others?

(5) Under what circumstances shall seniority be lost or forfeited? Resignation? Discharge? Extended layoff or other absence from work? Transfers to jobs outside the bargaining unit? Change in employer status (merger, consolidation, abandonment of facilities, relocation of plant)?

1. Scope

The widespread acceptance of seniority clauses in collective bargaining agreements is evidence of this acceptance by employer and union alike.[1] Actually these clauses comprise a seniority system by which an employee accrues status with respect to promotion, transfer, layoffs and rehire, vis-a-vis other employees in direct relation to the amount of time she/he has been employed in a particular job (job seniority), or department (department seniority), or with an employer (company seniority).

"Seniority" is of great importance to employees. In the labor relations sense, it means the employee's relative length of service, measured in any one or more of a variety of ways, with the employer. The "seniority question," as it typically arises in collective bargaining negotiations, concerns the extent to which preferential treatment shall be given to employees in various job contexts on the basis of their length of service. Is such treatment basically desirable? For example, it may concern a "competitive" advantage vis-a-vis less senior employees in regard to job security and job preferences such as layoff and re-employment, promotions, transfers, work assignments, and overtime distribution. What is the significance of employee attitudes in establishing such preferences?

"Seniority" may also be the basis for obtaining certain "benefits" of employment such as holiday and vacation rights, sick leave and severance pay, pensions, insurance and welfare programs, bonuses and profit sharing as well as other length-of-service benefits including protection against the loss of seniority itself. The materials will concentrate on the uses of seniority in relation to job security and job preference rather than in relation to economic benefit matters.

---

[1] 2 C.B.N.C. § 75:1 (2/27/75).

2. Importance to Unions

The significance of seniority systems to unions cannot be exaggerated. Because the accrual of seniority discourages the worker from changing employment, a seniority system reduces bargaining unit turnover and gives the union a stable constituency. Since clauses which insure benefits and competitive advantages on length of accrued seniority tend to be objective, rather than subjective, they provide stable union members of long duration with incentive to support the union; and they also provide newer union members with an objective rationale for supporting the system.[2] On the other hand, union support for such systems has been subject to criticism.[3] For example, seniority systems tend to prevent younger, more energetic workers from advancing as rapidly as ability and motivation might otherwise allow, and they tend to perpetuate the past effects of discrimination,[4] thus encouraging mediocrity.[5] Nonetheless, unions usually press for extensive recognition of seniority in relation to these matters. Employers typically seek to retain the right to make employee competence and relative fitness and ability the controlling factors at least in the "competitive" or job preference category. This statement implies that management does not ordinarily press for a third alternative — namely, complete managerial discretion, although this kind of prerogative is sometimes successfully sought with respect to some matters. What are the arguments for and against recognition of seniority? Why do unions press for such recognition? Why do they not, instead, insist on securing the contractual right to have employees given job preference on the basis of their relative merit and ability?

3. Importance to Companies

Seniority is not only advantageous to unions and employees. The stability which reduces bargaining unit turnover also provides an employer with a steady, stable core of regular employees. There is credible evidence that workers with substantial seniority are a considerable asset to employers.[6] Furthermore, since seniority

---

[2] *Compare* S. Slichter, J. Healy & E. Livernash, The Impact of Collective Bargaining on Management 104 (1960) [hereinafter cited as Impact of Collective Bargaining] (seniority gives both parties a clear standard to reassure time-based benefits) *with* Healy, The Factor of Ability in Labor Relations, in Arbitration Today, 8th Ann. Proc. of Nat'l Acad. Arb. 45 (1955) [hereinafter cited as Factor of Ability].

[3] *See generally,* G. Bloom & H. Northrop, Economics of Labor Relations (7th ed. 1973).

[4] *See e.g.* Gould, Employment Security, Seniority and Race: The Role of Title VII in the Civil Rights Act of 1964, 13 How. L. J. 1 (1967).

[5] *See e.g.,* Aaron, Reflections on the Legal Nature and Enforceability of Seniority Rights, 75 Harv. L. Rev. 1532 (1962); Factor of Ability, *supra* note 2.

[6] Impact of Collective Bargaining, *supra* note 2 at 104-210.

systems are universally preferred by unions, by agreeing to such systems an employer in effect delegates application of the rules of the workplace to unions thus avoiding many of the subjective issues inherent in meritorious system. Why is this even advantageous to an employer since it leads to the company losing control over its employees? Is there any way that management can maximize efficiency of its employees as they move into higher positions under seniority systems? How can meritocracy and seniority be rationalized?

4. Legal Status

Seniority rights are not inherent in the employment relationship, but are created most frequently by collective bargaining agreements, as previously indicated through seniority systems. It is now clear that seniority rights created by contract give legal rights to employees. As Judge Gibbons explained in *Nedd v. United Mine Workers of America,* 556 F.2d 190, 197 (3d Cir. 1977) in a suit by pensioners for breach of contractual obligations,

> It is settled law that a suit by nonparty trustees to enforce those provisions may be entertained in federal district court by virtue of § 301. It is also settled law that employees, although not formally parties to a collective bargaining agreement, can bring a § 301 suit to enforce its terms. *Smith v. Evening News Ass'n,* 371 U.S. 195, 83 S. Ct. 267, 9 L.Ed.2d 246 (1962). Where the trustee may sue and wrongfully fails to do so, the beneficiary may sue the trustee as well as the party or parties the trustee failed to sue. Thus, the complaint states a non-frivolous cause of action under 29 U.S.C. § 301, which provides for suits in federal court for violation of such contracts.

In addition to Taft-Hartley Act rights, employees also have statutory rights under Title VII of the 1964 Civil Rights Act. Thus, seniority systems create contract rights enforceable in arbitration and the federal courts. As Professor Feller pointed out in his provocative article about arbitrators, their status derives,

> . . . from the existence of an autonomous system of governance of the employment relationship. The statutory enactments of the past few years, and in particular the enactment of Title VII, have made it clear that society is not satisfied with the results of that autonomous system of governance. It was not satisfied, to pick a minor but apt example, that the question of whether a garnishment should be the occasion for discharge was being satisfactorily handled through the collective bargaining process. As a result we have, and I suspect we increasingly will have, alternate standards to govern particular aspects of the employment relationship and alternate forums to adjudicate

compliance with those standards. This would create few problems for the arbitration process if the questions posed under these publicly imposed standards were clearly separable and unrelated to questions arising under collective agreements. But it is abundantly clear that the questions are intimately related in a variety of ways.[7]

5. Seniority and External Law

Professor Feller's thesis deserves careful consideration by students of collective bargaining and labor arbitration. As one of the authors pointed out, this thesis carried to its logical conclusion suggests an inverse relationship between public law and private bargaining. As legislative regulation of employment increases, Feller argues, the possibilities for collective bargaining must decrease.[8] Whether or not one is carried to this extension of logic, it is clear that all the parties to collective bargaining agreements have considered the impact of public law on seniority systems of such significance that it is now the most litigated provisions in employment contracts.[9] Accordingly, we are devoting considerable coverage to the application of external law to the collective bargaining relationship.[10] The nexus of federal law to seniority systems makes this issue primary in this chapter. We will establish how the issue arises under contract, and how federal law has evolved in Part Four. The genesis of the problem arises from the types of seniority established in collective bargaining agreements.

B. TYPES OF SENIORITY SYSTEMS

Seniority rights relate to a specific group. The degree of job security afforded by a seniority system depends on the scope of the unit within which the competitive or benefit seniority right may be exercised. Thus a seniority unit may be industrywide, plantwide, multiplant, departmental, or it may be based upon the bargaining unit, or upon an occupation group or classification, or it may even be a combination of these configurations.[11] Industrywide or straight companywide seniority, which applies to several plants in different localities, is rare. And, where the bargaining unit covers a number

---

[7] Feller, The Coming End of Arbitration's Golden Age, in 29th Ann. Proc. of Nat'l Acad. Arb. 97, 123-24 (Dennis & Somers ed. 1976); *supra* Part Two at p. 483.

[8] Edwards, Labor Arbitration at the Crossroads: The 'Common Laws & the Shop' v. 'External' Law, 32 Arb. J. 65, 66 (1977), *infra* Part Two at p. 491.

[9] Silbergold, Title VII and The Collective Bargaining Agreement: Seniority Provisions Under Fire, 49 Temple L.Q. 288, 322 (1976) [hereinafter cited as Seniority Provisions].

[10] *See* Part Two, Chapter 8 *supra.*

[11] F. Elkouri & E. Elkouri, How Arbitration Works 555 (3d ed. 1973) [hereinafter cited as How Arbitration Works].

of plants, seniority is frequently left to local bargaining.[12] It is not infrequent that the unit in which seniority accumulates is different from that in which it applies so that seniority rights may be limited to a unit narrower from that in which it was acquired.[13] Furthermore, many contracts establish several types of seniority so that departmental seniority, for example, may govern promotions, whereas plant seniority may govern layoffs.[14] These two types of seniority systems — departmental and plant, have engendered considerable conflict with federal anti-discrimination programs. It is important to note, as one author was careful to point out that:

> The seniority provisions of collective bargaining agreements rarely, if ever, expressly discriminate on the basis of race, ethnicity, or sex; rather, informal, unwritten arrangements engaged in by the employer and often condoned by the union result in practices prohibited by Title VII. From a wide variety of these practices reported in Title VII litigation, three common patterns of discrimination emerge. In the first, either separate seniority lists are maintained for white and black workers, the most junior whites enjoying preference in job movements over the most senior blacks, or two job categories are created for identical work, the blacks in one category subordinate to and earning lower wages than whites in the other. In the second pattern, both whites and blacks are allowed to fill lower level positions in a group of functionally related jobs that normally constitute a single production unit or "district," but only whites are permitted to bid for promition to functionally related positions at higher levels in the unit. A similar result is achieved by hiring blacks at lower entry level positions than whites and setting an arbitrary line beyond which blacks cannot advance. In the third and most prevalent pattern, two or more groups of jobs, each having no apparent functional relation to the other, are organized into independent units or lines of progression. Blacks are hired for the less desirable lines of progression, whites for the others. The seniority system in practice prohibits transfer from one line or unit to another or conditions transfer on loss of seniority accrued in the former line and provides for no retention of the wage rate achieved in that line. A discriminatory hiring pattern is a condition precedent to a system reflecting this third pattern.[15]

---

[12] BNA, Labor Relations Expediter, Labor Relations Reporter 662 [hereinafter cited as BNA, LRX].

[13] *Id.* at 623.

[14] *Id.*

[15] Silbergold, Seniority Provisions, *supra* note 9 at 291-92.

It is now beyond debate that Congress intended to eliminate all discriminatory practices accruing after the effective date of Title VII of the Civil Rights Act of 1964, 42 U.S.C. § 2000(e).

1. Departmental Seniority

The first judicial decisions of whether a seniority system violated Title VII, or fell within the statutory exception of section 703(h) of the Act because they were "bona fide" seniority systems, arose over a challenge to departmental (job) seniority.[16] Where promotional or transfer opportunities depend on time spent in a racially segregated departmental seniority system, or where giving up job seniority was the cost of accepting a vacancy in an integrated seniority unit, the federal courts have not hesitated to strike departmental or job seniority systems which they hold unlawfully perpetuate the effects of past discrimination.[17] Relying on a "rightful place" theory for victims of such discrimination, federal courts have effectuated relief by ordering that plantwide seniority be the basis for awarding competitive seniority.[18] While courts have not held that departmental seniority systems inherently violate Title VII and are not bona fide, "plantwide seniority systems have been the remedial touchstone used to eliminate the present effects of past discrimination." [19] Since seniority clauses rarely expressly indicate discriminatory patterns but departmental systems will perpetuate past discriminatory effects, great care must be used in drafting such clauses to insure their "bona fides."

2. Plantwide Seniority

Until 1974, the federal courts were not asked to decide the effects of Title VII on plantwide seniority rights during layoff, as distinguished from promotions and transfers. However, during the prior decade affirmative action programs, mandated under the Civil Rights Act of 1964, had been effective in achieving some employment equality for women, blacks, latins and other

---

[16] See Quarles v. Phillip Morris, Inc., 279 F. Supp. 505 (E.D. Va. 1968); Local 189, Papermakers v. United States, 416 F.2d 980 (5th Cir. 1969), cert. denied, 379 U.S. 919 (1970).

[17] See Note, "Title VII, Seniority Discrimination and the Incumbent Negro," 80 Harv. L. Rev. 1260 (1967); Note; "Employment Discrimination and Title VII of the Civil Rights Act of 1964," 84 Harv. L. Rev. 1109 (1971).

[18] See Local 189, Papermakers v. United States, 416 F.2d 980, 988 (5th Cir. 1969); see also Carey v. Greyhound Bus Co., 500 F.2d 1372 (5th Cir. 1974); J.D. Thornton v. East Texas Motor Freight, 497 F.2d 416 (6th Cir. 1974); Pettway v. American Cast Iron Pipe Co., 494 F.2d 211 (5th Cir. 1974); Johnson v. Goodyear Tire & Rubber Co., 491 F.2d 1364 (5th Cir. 1974); United States v. N.L. Indus., 479 F.2d 354 (8th Cir. 1973); Long v. Georgia Kraft Co., 450 F.2d 557 (5th Cir. 1971); United States v. Bethlehem Steel Corp., 446 F.2d 652 (2d Cir. 1971).

[19] Seniority Provisions, supra note 9, at 304.

minorities.[20] The 1970's "recession," like any contracting economic situation, cuts into these gains because of the LIFO-type plantwide seniority systems (last person hired is first to be layed off and last to be recalled).[21] Such competitive layoff and rehire seniority provisions detracted from the employment gains realized by minorities and women under Title VII affirmative action plans. The legal questions raised were whether the plantwide seniority system as utilized in layoff and rehire, constituted an unlawful employment practice under Title VII, or whether the system challenged was a bona fide seniority system under Section 703(h)? [22] In addition, the everpresent issue of appropriate remedies also faced the federal courts.

Although there was some indication that the federal courts might reject a plantwide seniority system that perpetuated past discrimination in layoffs and rehire,[23] it is now fairly settled that the use of a LIFO-type plantwide seniority clause is a bona fide system under Section 703(h).[24] However, it is also apparent that affirmative action programs are part of the objectives of Title VII. The oversimplified distinction has been made that affirmative action concerns "hiring and not firing." In any event, draftspersons should be aware of the employment history of the decade between 1964 and

---

[20] See Comment, Title VII and Seniority Systems: Back to the Foot of the Line?, 64 Ky. L.J. 114 (1975); Comment, Sex Discrimination in Employment: What Has Title VII Accomplished For the Female? 9 U. Rich. L. Rev. 149 (1971).

[21] See e.g. Stacy, Title VII Seniority Remedies in a Time of Economic Downturn, 28 Vand. L. Rev. 487 (1975).

[22] 42 U.S.C. § 2000e-2(h) (1970 and Supp. IV 1974), provides in part: "Notwithstanding any other provision of this subsection, it shall not be an unlawful employment practice for an employer to apply different standards of compensation, or different terms, conditions, or privileges of employment pursuant to a bona fide seniority or merit system which measures earnings by quantity or quality of production or to employees who work in different locations, provided that such differences are not the result of an intention to discriminate because of race, color, religion, sex, or national origin . . . ." The section also regulates the use of ability tests by employers. Discrimination on the basis of religion, sex, and national origin, if these factors are bona fide occupational qualifications, and discrimination for reason of communist party membership or national security is also excepted from Title VII, 42 U.S.C. §§ 2000e-2(e)-(g) (1970 and Supp. IV 1974).

[23] See Watkins v. USW Local 2369, 369 F. Supp. 1221 (E.D. La. 1974). However, the Court of Appeals reversed the District Court in 516 F.2d 41 (5th Cir. 1975) holding that Title VII did not prohibit the use of plantwide seniority to determine layoffs.

[24] See Jersey Central Power & Light Co. v. Local 327, IBEW, 508 F.2d 687 (3d Cir. 1975); See also note, Civil Rights Title VII, 41 Duquesne L. Rev. 475 (1975); For general discussion and description of seniority systems see Cooper & Sobol, Seniority and Testing Under Fair Employment Laws: A General Approach to Objective Criteria of Hiring and Promotions, 82 Harv. L. Rev. 1589 (1969); Gould, Employment Security, Seniority and Race: The Role of the Title VII of the Civil Rights Act of 1964,13 How, L.J. 1 (1967); 84 Harv. L. Rev. 1109, 1156-58 (1971).

1974, and the litigation which ensued, which we cover in Part Four of this book, when drafting plantwide seniority systems.

C. DETERMINATION OF SENIORITY

1. Calculation

When does seniority begin to accrue? Will seniority be retroactive to the hiring date after a trial period? What will be the effect of absence during and after probationary periods? What will be the relative seniority of employees hired on the same day? Do part-time employees fall under seniority provisions of the contract? If seniority is to be determined by "continuous service," just what is meant by this term? Will the seniority list be determinative? The answers to these questions may vary, depending upon the purpose of the seniority provision. As previously indicated, "seniority" may be used (1) to determine employee benefits — vacation and holiday pay, automatic wage increases, retirement rights, etc., or (2) an employee's rights vis-a-vis other employees — layoff and recall, promotions, shift preferences, etc. "Seniority standing" may turn on which type of use was contemplated.

NOTES:

Problems: (a) *Purpose:* As an employer if you could unilaterally establish the seniority clause in a contract, would you adopt the following language to determine "competitive" seniority? If not, how would you change it? Make your answer specific.

> Seniority shall be calculated from the date of first employment following a break in continuous service in accordance with the following provisions: provided, however, that the effective date of employment prior to the date of this Agreement shall be the date of first employment or reemployment after any break which constituted a break in service under the practices in effect at the time the break occurred or as such practices were otherwise specifically agreed upon.
>
> There shall be no deduction for any time lost, which does not constitute a break in continuous service, where the employee was: (1) on military leave of absence; (2) on any other authorized leave of absence; (3) absent from the Plant because of accident or illness for a period not in excess of one year, provided the employee presents satisfactory evidence to substantiate his claim; (4) laid off for a period of less than twelve months; or (5) spent time in a position outside the bargaining unit as a result of a transfer or promotion from the bargaining unit.

Continuous service shall be broken when: (1) an employee quits; (2) an employee is discharged, provided that if the employee is rehired within six months, the break in continuous service shall be removed; or (3) the plant, department, or subdivision thereof is permanently shut down, provided that if the employee is rehired within two years, or, if greater, a period equal to his length of continuous service during such absence up to a maximum of two years; and he shall retain his accumulated continuous service at commencement of such absence over two years, whichever is less.

(b) *Continuous Service:* Consider the question of whether half-days worked on Saturdays should be counted as full working days. For example, if an employee was laid off after 43 days and two-half days and the probationary period for new employees was 45 days (after which seniority was retroactive to date of hiring), upon rehire should the employee's seniority date be his original date of hire or should his probationary period begin anew? *See P. M. Northwest Co.,* 42 L.A. 961 (D. Lyons, 1964); *Convey-All Corp.,* 41 L.A. 169 (S. Kates, 1963). *Compare Northeast Airlines, Inc.,* 37 L.A. 741 (S. Wolff, 1961). For an interpretation of continuous service where "benefit seniority" is involved see *Peerless Laundries, Inc.,* 40 L.A. 129 (M. Lugar, 1963); *Interstate Bakeries Corp.,* 36 L.A. 1412 (C. Anrod, 1961).

(c) *Contemporaneous Hiring:* As arbitrator resolve the following problem and specify the basis for your decision. *C* was recalled from layoff before *B.* They had been hired five years previously, and both employees were hired on the same day. On their date of hire, *B* had worked the 7:00 a.m. to 3:00 p.m. shift, and *C* had worked the 3:00 p.m. to 11:00 p.m. shift. The Union claims that the shifts worked should control their relative seniority, and that *B* should have been recalled first. The Company claims that both employees have equal seniority, and that it had discretion to choose which employee to recall first. There is no contract provision directly relevant. The seniority clause provides that "seniority shall be determined by the seniority list." *B* proceeds *C* on the list, but the Company claims that the only reason for the order in this case is because the list is alphabetical. *See Linde Co.,* 32 L.A. 568 (C. Duff, 1959); *Mallory-Sharon Metals Corp.,* 33 L.A. 60 (H. Dworkin, 1959) (time cards punched in at same minute for same job classification and labor grade).

(d) *Superseniority:*

Note: In a recent BNA study over 40% of the labor agreements examined provided special seniority standing for union officials. Superseniority of union officials must be distinguished from exemptions from seniority rules. The union official given superseniority is still subject to the mechanics of the seniority provisions. He is merely placed in a seniority position higher than the position he would have if calculated by his "natural" seniority. Exemptions completely remove the employee involved from the mechanics of the seniority provisions. Exemptions are frequently made for efficiency considerations and managements often reserve the right to exclude specially skilled employees from the effect of seniority provisions. Disabled employees may be excluded or the contract may allow the employer to ignore seniority in times of temporary or emergency layoff.

What is the rationale for such provisions? Would you hold for the Company or the Union in the following situation? Why?

As a result of an unusual situation, it was necessary to have an employee open some crates and help inspectors on a Saturday in addition to working the normal five eight-hour days (Monday-Friday). The employee who normally performs this work was given the assignment. The following Monday, a Union steward employed as a power saw operator learned of the overtime and filed a grievance claiming that he, as shop steward, had top seniority and should have been given the assignment. The collective bargaining agreement provided in pertinent part,

> Stewards, while serving as such, shall have top seniority standing. Stewards shall be given preference of employment in the Department in which he works as long as there is work available in the Department which he is capable of handling. Upon expiration of his term of office as steward, he or she shall revert to his regular seniority standing.

Union Position — The Union contends that the Agreement gives a steward top seniority and preference of employment in work in his department as long as he is capable of handling it. The work performed, the Union claims, requires only the ability to open crates and read. Accordingly, since the steward was able to read and available for work, he should have been permitted to perform the job.

Company Position — The Company contends that since the employee who was given the work normally did the job and was familiar with the materials to be inspected, the assignment was legal and proper. Further, the Company argues, it is not required by the Agreement to assign jobs to the steward with which he is not completely familiar, because "superseniority" provisions are simply designed to afford stewards a degree of protection from layoff during time of work force reduction. *Compare Graham Engineering Co.,* 32 L.A. 445 (H. Wissner, 1959) *with Fabricon Products,* 41 L.A. 275 (T. Roberts, 1963). *See Rola Division,* 40 L.A. 675 (C. McCoy, 1963) for method of obviating problem by contract.

For other problems arising out of the interpretation of superseniority clauses *see Line Materials Industries,* 46 L.A. 1106 (E. Teple, 1966) (shift representation); *New York Shipbuilding Corp.,* 43 L.A. 741 (D. Crawford, 1964) (transfer); *Chrysler Corp.,* 42 L.A. 1019 (J. Stashower, 1964) (shift preference); *Airco Chemical,* 42 L.A. 941 (J. Altieri, 1964) (status after steward loses election); *Rex Windows,* 41 L.A. 606 (P. Lohoczky, 1964) (duty to notify company of steward's status).

2. Promotion, Transfer and Demotion

The term "promotion" usually means upward movement to a better job, or at least a higher rating in the same job. However, care should be taken to distinguish a promotion from a transfer because promotions often involve transfers, and each may involve separate rights, duties and obligations. Conversely, the meaning of demotion is clear, but the right to demote is often not expressly provided for by contract and is sometimes held to be included under the general authority of a management rights clause.[25]

NOTES:

(1) *Problem:* The collective bargaining agreement between the Company and the Union contains the following provisions:

Seniority, Promotions and Layoffs

1. In selecting men for promotion, demotion or the filling of vacancies, the Company will apply the principle of seniority, based on length of service of any regular employee in the plant covered by this agreement, provided employee's physical condition, training, general ability and other essential job requirements qualify the oldest employee in seniority to properly fill the job. Any deviation from the principle of seniority shall first be made the subject of a conference between Management and the Workmen's Committee before the job is permanently filled, subject to the grievance procedure as outlined in Article 5 of this agreement in the event of a disagreement.

2. Vacancies will be posted on a plant bulletin board with qualifications defining the skill and experience required. Any employee wishing to be considered as an applicant should fill out an application form furnished by the office. The posting will remain on the Bulletin Board for a period of five (5) days during which time applications must be returned to the Company office. The successful applicant will be assigned to the job on the sixth

---

[25] How Arbitration Works, *supra* note 11 at 526-39.

day and begin work on that day or at his first regularly scheduled work period thereafter. Employees on authorized leave of absence shall have three (3) days after the expiration of such leave within which to bid for the job before it is finally filled.

Union Position — The Union contends that under the contract the Company was required to post for bid as job "vacancies" each individual job within the classification "Warehouseman," for example, "Hopper Car Loaders," "Lift Truck Operators," "Printing Press Operators," etc.

Company Position — The Company contends that it was required to post only the fact of a vacancy within the classification as a whole, and that it had the right to make "work assignments" to such jobs as those listed above within the classification of "Warehouseman" without regard to the limitations included in the provisions above.

As arbitrator, which position would you uphold? Why? *See Columbian Carbon Co.,* 27 L.A. 769 (P. Herbert, 1956).

(2) This problem, along with many others which might be cited, illustrates the difficulties which can arise from the use of the terms "vacancy," "promotion," "transfer," and "job" without mutual understanding (and contractual specification) of the meaning of these terms in the context of a "seniority" provision. In relation to this problem, the uppermost managerial "interest" doubtless is freedom to make work assignments, or, in broader terms, freedom to direct the work force. The employee (union) interest is in securing work opportunities and preferences for "senior" employees. In considering these interests, is there a substantial basis for differentiating between the selection of an employee to be upgraded from one classification to another, and the selection of an employee for a preferred work station or work assignment within the classification or in another classification which carries the same rate of pay? If a "vacancy" develops in a given classification at a particular work station or "job," should this be treated as a vacancy for seniority purposes, or should management have the right, initially, to reshuffle employees within the same (or an equivalent) classification, and be obligated, only thereafter, to make available a "job" in the classification for seniority bidding purposes?

(3) In *Uniflow Mfg. Co.,* 27 L.A. 367 (J. Shister, 1956), the contract defined seniority as including "the right to transfer from one job to another." Nevertheless, the arbitrator held that this did not give an employee in a particular classification the right to continue on a particular work assignment. *See Pittsburgh Plate Glass Co.,* 30 L.A. 981 (P. Kelliher, Chm., 1958); *Bethlehem Steel Co.,* 30 L.A. 550 (F. Uible, 1958). However, in *Glamorgan Pipe & Foundry Co.,* 44 L.A. 10 (D. Crawford, 1965), relying on provision making seniority and ability controlling "in cases of promotions, demotions, new jobs

created, filling of vacancies," the arbitrator held that an employee may exercise seniority in lateral transfers to vacant jobs.

In *Continental Oil Co.,* 8 L.A. 170 (P. Carmichael, Chm., 1947), there was involved the following unusual kind of contract provision: "The Company subscribes generally to the principle of seniority; that is, the oldest employee in length of service, if qualified, shall be entitled to priority in promotions and other seniority rights and privileges, including the right to more desirable jobs within the same classification." Does such a provision give a senior employee the right to bump at any time into a preferred job held by a junior employee? *See Vickers Inc.,* 49 L.A. 961 (W. Seinsheimer, 1967) (senior employee seeking lateral transfer over junior employee approved for promotion). Such a right would not be contemplated by the more typical kinds of seniority provisions. *See Ford Motor Co.,* 3 L.A. 863 (H. Shulman, 1946); *Pennsylvania Salt Mfg. Co.,* 3 L.A. 205 (J. C. Short, Chm., 1946).

Suppose a "job" within a given classification is upgraded in rate of pay. Should the incumbent thereupon become subject to being bumped by a senior employee? In *Detroit Edison Co.,* 7 L.A. 361 (D. Wolff, Chm., 1947), the contract provided that "in promotions of employees covered by this Agreement to positions within the same bargaining unit, seniority and qualifications shall govern." The arbitrator held that this provision did not require the Company to open upgraded jobs for competitive bidding unless the senior employee was simultaneously being laid off.

How would you analyze the question of the right to exercise seniority in the matter of shift preference? Is a job opportunity on a preferred shift (*e.g.,* a day shift) a "promotional" opportunity? Such cases as *Darling & Co.,* 44 L.A. 718 (J. Doyle, 1965) and *Kuhlman Electric Co.,* 19 L.A. 199 (H. Platt, 1952), suggest that the usual answer would be in the negative, and that specific contract language would be required in order to impel a different result (as in *Western Electric Co., Inc.,* 19 L.A. 908 (V. S. Carroll, 1953) and *International Harvester Co.,* 19 L.A. 812 (C. Emery, 1953)). However, in *Cameron Iron Works, Inc.,* 23 L.A. 51 (A. Ralston, Chm., 1954), the Board stated that while a preferred shift is not a "promotion" in normal, accepted usage, where the practice indicates otherwise, it should be given effect. It noted, incidentally, that a shift preference could be a "promotion," under dictionary definition, as being a "preferment."

3. The Weighting of the Seniority Factor: Seniority Versus Ability

J. HEALY, THE FACTOR OF ABILITY IN LABOR RELATIONS, in ARBITRATION TODAY, PROCEEDINGS OF EIGHTH ANNUAL MEETING OF NATIONAL ACADEMY OF ARBITRATORS 45 (BNA, McKelvey ed. 1955) [82]

There is a growing conviction expressed by many persons that the ability of an individual employee is no longer of much significance in determining his status. The policies developed through collective bargaining are attacked on the ground that there is no incentive for a man to use his initiative when he is restricted in advancement by seniority rules and practices, that seniority provisions make it difficult, if not impossible, for the young, ambitious employee to move ahead rapidly on the basis of merit or performance.[83] From these assumptions the further, dark conclusion is drawn that productive efficiency will be impaired and society's material standards will suffer.

It is surprising that our researches into the field of labor relations have progressed so far without any systematic and empirical analysis designed to test the validity of these pessimistic views. A review of the literature suggests that there has been too much preoccupation (in research endeavors) with the principle of seniority and far too little attention given to the factor of employee ability. Given our knowledge of the field at this time, to what extent can we make even informed guesses concerning the answers to the following questions:

1. Does individual employee ability play little or no part in determining his economic and social role in the work community?

2. If the ability factor is of less significance, is this to be attributed largely to the emphasis upon seniority under union policies and collective bargaining agreements?

3. To what extent is there a correlation between an employee's length of service and ability?

4. What meaning is to be given to the concept of ability? Obviously it is a word of many meanings and many dimensions. To what extent should the meaning employed in personnel policy and collective bargaining vary from one situation to another? Should the test of ability mean one thing in deciding lay-offs, another in making promotions or wage increases within rate ranges, and still another in deciding whether an employee is unfit for continued employment?

---

[82] Reprinted with permission of publisher. Copyright © 1955 by the Bureau of National Affairs, Inc.

[83] *Individual Initiative in Business* at 150 (G.H. Allen ed., Harvard University Press, 1950).

5. Is it proper to differentiate between types of industries or between types of jobs in deciding what weight shall be assigned to employee ability?

6. Is recognition of individual employee ability a strong motivating force, one which stimulates a man to greater effort and nurtures initiative? Is it a stronger psychological force than recognition of a man's length of service?

7. Finally, what evidence is there that the growth of the seniority principles — if it has been at the expense of the ability determinant — has harmed industrial efficiency?

These are only a few of the questions which must be answered before we can affirm or deny the generalizations of those who claim that present day labor relations policies tend to destroy individual initiative. Several months ago a research project was started on this subject at the Harvard Business School.... [S]ome of the observations presented in this paper cannot even be dignified by the label of "tentative conclusions." They are defended only on the terms expressed by Montaigne, when he said:

All I say is by way of discourse, and nothing by way of advice. I should not speak so boldly if it were my due to be believed.

. . . .

One of the major difficulties encountered by management in its attempt to preserve the ability criterion is the inherent vagueness of any contract expression to describe the criterion. The isolated terms of "ability," "qualifications," "qualified to do the work," "satisfactory experience" and the many others now used in layoff and promotion clauses mean many things to many people. The relatively precise meaning of seniority, by comparison, gives it an immediate advantage. . . .

In the early days of collective bargaining management could use the word "ability" with little fear of its being watered down by grievance discussions or by an arbitration decision. Many contracts specified that the determination of the relative abilities of employees, particularly in the making of promotions, was the exclusive judgment of management and only if the judgment was clearly discriminatory could it be subject to challenge.

In a real sense management was the "master" of the meaning of the word "ability," and the word meant just what management chose it to mean at any given time. Indeed, this very mastery of the meaning undoubtedly contributed to the present low status of the ability factor. To illustrate: one of the most interesting cases discovered in the historical analysis of contracts was that of a Company and Union which had incorporated the following promotion clause in their initial bargaining agreement in 1943:

> In all cases of promotion of employees from one classification to another, the factor of ability, as determined solely by management, shall govern. If in management's judgment the ability of the men under consideration is relatively equal, seniority shall govern.

Presumably the clause worked reasonably well until 1945 when the Union charged discrimination by the Company in the exercise of its judgment. The Company had promoted a junior employee to the position of fireman, first class, even though a senior applicant had some part-time satisfactory experience on the job. The Union argued that in other promotions, such experience was given considerable weight by management. The Company agreed, but said that in this case it could not be satisfied by demonstrated ability to do the specific work in question; it was more concerned with a man's potential promotability to an engineer's position. In essence, it was admitting to the use of two different meanings of the word "ability." Rightly or wrongly, the arbitrator found this to be discriminatory application of the clause and the Company's decision was reversed. In the 1946 contract all references to management's sole exercise of judgment as to ability were deleted.

More and more the parties jointly have become masters of the meaning of the word ability, and if the relationship pattern is that of cooperation or accommodation — to use Dr. Selekman's helpful categories — disputes are infrequent. But even this optimistic evidence is misleading and should not be interpreted to mean that the ability factor necessarily is better protected in such an atmosphere. One industrial relations director is quoted as saying:

> The Union is constantly pressing for more consideration for seniority. The infrequency of union grievances on this score is misleading. Actually, operating management gives in to the union pressure many times, because of the difficulty of proving greater ability and in order to avoid a fight with the union. I'm convinced that in many of our promotions seniority gets more consideration than either merit or ability — the clause in the contract notwithstanding.

Perhaps to an even greater extent arbitrators have become the true masters of the meaning of this word "ability" as used in the contract clauses. It is suggested cautiously that the influence of arbitration awards helps to explain the continued decline in the consideration of ability.

First, there is a tendency among arbitrators — whose jurisdiction to decide the question of relative abilities is established by the contract — to join with the Union on the overemphasis of seniority, even though seniority is to govern only when ability is relatively equal. This is understandable, given the objective quality of seniority vis-a-vis the normally subjective nature of the ability measurement. One always feels more secure with the tangible and familiar guides.

Second, arbitrators have tended to transfer the locus of the burden of proof to management, perhaps far more than the contract language intended it to be transferred.

Third, there are those arbitration opinions which lend to standard language an interpretation which would frustrate the most well-intentioned management. To illustrate: it has been held that unless an employee is proved to be "head and shoulders" above the senior employee in ability, he is not entitled to promotion under a clause which reads:

> In the advancement of employees to higher paid jobs when ability, merit and capacity are equal, employees with the longest seniority will be given preference.

Others have held that "ability" can only be measured or tested by an actual trial period on the promotional job, irrespective of complete contract silence on this right and an absence of past practice implying such right. These predilections of arbitrators — as word masters — do not provide a favorable climate for the employee ability factor.

GENERAL MOTORS CORP.
and
UNITED AUTOMOBILE WORKERS

Umpire Decision No. B-52 (1941)

Taylor, George W., Umpire

This case concerns a grievance, presented by Employe M. on August 15, 1941, which reads: "I charge Company with violation of National Agreement P. P. 63 by rating No. 130416 as reliefman when he does not have the seniority I do and I too have been rated as reliefman and can do the work." A hearing on the matter was held in Detroit December 8, 1941.

Nature of Case

On August 4, 1941, a reliefman vacancy occurred on the first shift of Plant No. 3 in Group No. 20 which includes the Spring Housing job and the King Pin Support job. Employe T. was selected to fill the vacancy. The present grievance represents a claim of Employe M. that, in accordance with Paragraph 63, his seniority and previous experience entitle him to the reliefman's job in question.

Management notes that the Spring Housing and the King Pin Support jobs have not been in regular production since 1938 and are now operated in order to supply service parts. Employes are used interchangeably between the two operations and the reliefman is also required to be able to work on both types of work. The relief job in question was not in operation at the time of the discussions of the case in the earlier steps of the grievance procedure, but the Union "requests that M. be placed in line for the job so that when work is resumed he will be made the reliefman."

The previous experience of T. on this work includes service as a reliefman on the King Pin Support job when it was in production as a separate job. He has had other service as a reliefman in Group No. 20 but no significant experience as a reliefman on the Spring Housing job. Altogether T. has had about twenty months' experience as a reliefman and he has a seniority date of 11/21/30.

The claimant in this case, Employe M., served as a reliefman on the Spring Housing job when it was in regular production but has apparently had no experience as a reliefman on the King Pin Support job. His experience as a reliefman totals approximately eleven months and his seniority date is 3/12/24.

Corporation Position

Management is of the opinion that T. has better qualifications than M. to fill the reliefman vacancy. Of the 16 machines included in the King Pin Support job, T. is said to have set up 14 and to have operated all sixteen. Of the 17 operations on the Spring Housing job, T. has set up 15 and has operated 16 of them. Management has weighed T.'s experience which is said to provide him with better qualifications as compared to M. who, it is claimed, has not set up any of the sixteen machines in the King Pin Support job and has only operated eight of them. Of the Spring Housing machines, management reports that M. has had set-up experience on ten and operating experience on thirteen of them.

The selection of an employe for transfer to the vacancy in question had to take into account, states management, the necessity for interchanging employes between two types of work. It is said, therefore, that the best qualified candidate for the reliefman's job would be the one who was most familiar with the various jobs. T.'s longer and wider experience as a reliefman on both the King Pin Support job and later in Group No. 20 is appraised by management as giving him superior qualifications, as compared to M., for the job to which he was promoted. The selection of T., contends management, was a proper exercise of management's responsibility as outlined in Paragraph 63 of the June 3, 1941 Agreement.

Union Contention

The Union, in its brief, recognized that the relief job in question requires a considerable versatility to do various operations and that only a few men have such all-around experience because the jobs are for past model service rather than for current model production.

It is contended by the Union, however, that M. was not only better qualified to fill the reliefman's vacancy but had greater seniority than T. In its brief, the Union expresses its belief that, under Paragraph 63, "when a promotion is to be made, the agreement implies that the employe with the longest seniority shall be the first considered and in the event he can do the job adequately, he is to be given the promotion without the personality comparisons usually made in promoting men."

The Union contends, then, that M. was entitled to selection for the reliefman's vacancy and that he should "be placed in line for the job so that when work resumed he will be made the reliefman."

Comments and Decision of the Umpire

Paragraph 63 of the June 3, 1941 Agreement provides, in part, "The transferring of employes is the sole responsibility of the management. In the advancement of employes to higher paid jobs when ability, merit and capacity are equal, employes with the longest seniority will be given preference."

There have been marked difficulties in the effort satisfactorily to apply this clause. It is difficult to define, let alone evaluate, such intangible factors as "merit and capacity." The Union certainly errs in its present argument, however, that the clause specifies preference to the employe with most seniority and gives him a right to promotion "in the event he can do the job adequately." Since such an interpretation would give importance to seniority irrespective of relative "ability and capacity," the approach of the local Union is obviously not in accordance with Paragraph 63 as written.

Under Paragraph 63 seniority becomes the determining factor in a selection for promotion only as between employes whose "ability, merit and capacity are equal." In order to attribute a reasonable meaning to the clause, it must be recognized that (1) the relative ability, merit and capacity of individual employes cannot be precisely evaluated; (2) these factors in one employe's work will be differently rated by different supervisors because their appraisal involves personal judgment; (3) seniority is, however, a definite factor that can readily be measured; (4) in making a selection for certain promotions, under this clause, management may properly proceed by designating several men whose ability, merit and capacity are considered by management to be equal. The seniority factor can then be applied in making the choice of the individual who is to be promoted.

In considering employes for promotion under Paragraph 63, it may be that an employe's record is so outstanding that he is "head and shoulders" above any other possible candidate. In such cases, he is entitled to promotion irrespective of seniority and, if necessary, management should have no difficulty in pointing out his superior qualifications. Unless such an individual is available for promotion, Paragraph 63 can properly be effectuated by management's selection of several employes who are competent to fill the job and whose "ability, merit and capacity" are considered by management to be approximately equal. From the several candidates adjudged by management to be approximately equal in "ability, merit and capacity," it would then become possible to effectuate Paragraph 63 by selecting for promotion that individual in the group who has the greatest seniority.

Such a procedure follows Paragraph 63 in recognizing that qualifications of several employes are often approximately equal and in recognizing the compelling importance of seniority in such cases. The Umpire must assume that the parties sought to give compelling importance to seniority as respects certain promotions or Paragraph 63 would have been written in different terms. It is emphasized that, under such a procedure, management retains the sole responsibility for designating the employes who are to be promoted.

How would such a procedure be applied to the facts of the present case? Management has made its choice as between T. and M. principally on the basis of the relative number of machines on the relief job, that had been previously operated by each of these men. To be sure, this is a factor that is important because of the nature of the job. The relative ability of these men in operating such jobs is, however, a considerably different factor and the mentioned experience has little to do with merit and capacity. It is the opinion of the Umpire that the evidence does not show that T. had the outstanding "ability, merit and capacity" for the job in question.

It is to be noted that the reliefman job is not now being operated. This provides an opportunity to apply the above-outlined procedure when it resumes operation. At that time, the job should again be considered as a vacancy. If a review of the qualifications of the candidates for the job shows that one is "head and shoulders" above all others, not only in experience but in ability, merit and capacity, it is in conformance with Paragraph 63 for management to assign him to the job. If such an individual is not available, management may designate two or three employes who are competent to take the assignment and who are considered by management as being approximately equal as respects ability, merit and capacity. The individual assigned to the vacancy should be the one in the group who holds the greatest seniority.

Decision

1. In order to give meaning to Paragraph 63 as written, and in order to preclude the nullification of the seniority factor mentioned in it, the following procedure may well be followed:

(a) An outstanding employe, "head and shoulders" above others in ability, merit and capacity, is entitled to promotion irrespective of seniority considerations. If necessary, management should have no difficulty in pointing out the factors that account for his superior qualifications.

(b) When such an outstanding employe is not available, management may select several employes whose "ability, merit and capacity" are adjudged by management to be approximately equal. The individual in the group with greatest seniority may then be selected for the promotion. Such an approach reserves to management the right to make selections for promotion while giving proper weight to the seniority factor mentioned in Paragraph 63.

2. In the present case, the evidence does not support a conclusion that T. was the one employe with superior ability, merit and capacity to perform the job in question.

3. Since the relief job in question is not now in operation, it is ruled that it should be considered a vacancy when it is resumed. It is then to be filled in conformance with the principles developed by this decision.

4. It is emphasized that the procedure outlined by this decision is but one of the ways in which Paragraph 63 as written may be effectuated. This procedure cannot be applied retroactively, nor is it the only procedure that is to be followed in cases of future promotions. It is set forth, not to establish an inflexible precedent in such cases, but as one of the ways by which Paragraph 63 may be applied in a practical and equitable manner.

GENERAL MOTORS CORP.
and
UNITED AUTOMOBILE WORKERS

Umpire Decision No. C-315 (1945)

Seward, Ralph T., Umpire

This grievance raises the question as to whether Local Management properly applied the provisions of Paragraph 63 of the National Agreement in promoting Employe C. to the position of Checker in the Parts Warehouse in preference to either of the two complainants, F.T. and N.

There is little dispute over the essential facts in the case. In July, 1944, Management determined that two additional Checkers were needed in the Warehouse. The following six employes from the Warehouse seniority list were found in line for consideration:

Name	Seniority Date
E.	8/29/28
R.	2/9/34
F.T.	3/12/34
N.	3/12/34
W.T.	3/12/34
C.	3/16/34

Management determined that Employe W.T. stood head and shoulders above the other five employes in ability, merit and capacity and promoted him to one of the two Checker vacancies. This promotion was not protested by any of the other employes.

Management alleges that it then reviewed the qualifications of the remaining five employes and decided that Employes E. and C. were approximately equal in merit, ability and capacity, for promotion to the Checker job and that they were definitely superior to the remaining three. As Employe E. had the highest seniority the vacancy was first offered to him. When he declined, the job was offered to C. who accepted.

As may be noted from the above table, Employe C. was junior in seniority to the other five employes. The Union alleges that Employes F.T. and N. were at least the equal of C. in ability, merit and capacity, and that in view of their greater seniority one of them should have received the promotion. Because of their experience as Packers in the Parts Warehouse, the Union claims, both F.T. and N. are thoroughly conversant with the various parts which the Checker must identify and with their locations. It is emphasized, moreover, that he is superior to C. in education, as he holds a degree in Engineering from the Newark Technical College.

In reply, Management points out that C. had experience as an Unloader in the Export Department in 1928 and 1929; that he worked as an Export Material Handler in 1934 and 1935; that he was a Material Handler in the Parts Warehouse from 1935 to 1940; and that he served as a Stock Picker from 1940-1944. It emphasizes particularly this latter experience, since a Stock Picker must work in all parts of the Warehouse, become familiar with the wide variety of parts handled, and learn the procedure followed in filling orders. Though Employe E. had spent far more time as a Packer than as a Stock Picker, it was felt that his general ability and intelligence coupled with his six years of greater experience made him approximately the equal of Employe C. Employes F.T. and N., on the other hand, had spent most of their time between 1934 and 1942 as Parts Dippers in the Enamel Room. From May, 1942, until the present they were assigned to the packing of parts for shipment. Management asserts, moreover, that even if the experience factor is discounted, F.T. and N. have shown a lack of initiative and of ability to carry out job assignments without close supervision which would make it impossible to consider them the equals of either E. or C.

On the record in this case the Umpire must hold that no violation of Paragraph 63 has been established. In a case of this sort the burden of proof is upon the Union to show that Management's judgment of the relative ability, merit and capacity of the employes was faulty. It has not sustained that burden here. The Umpire cannot discount the greater experience of both C. and E. in handling parts in the Warehouse, or hold that this factor is necessarily overcome by the fact that F.T. holds a degree in an unrelated educational field, or by the alleged fact that both F.T. and N. have proven diligent workmen on the jobs they have been given to perform.

It is true, of course, that no two employes can be found who are the exact equal of each other in all the elements of experience, skill, diligence, and intelligence, that are covered by the contractual phrase "ability, merit and capacity." For that reason this Office has required that when no employe stands "head and shoulders" above his fellows, "Management may select several employes whose ability, merit and capacity are adjudged by *Management* to be *approximately* equal. The individual in the group with the greatest seniority may then be selected for promotion." By prescribing only *approximate equality* for the group under consideration, prior Umpires clearly believed that Management should not be allowed to defeat the purposes of Paragraph 63 by relying on differences in skill and ability which are minor and unsubstantial. On the other hand, by leaving the selection of this group to Management, the Umpires clearly indicated that the initial judgment of ability, merit and capacity was a Management function and was not to be overturned save upon clear proof of error. In the instant case, the Union's showing has not been sufficient to offset the presumption in favor of Management's judgment. The grievance must accordingly be dismissed.

Decision

The grievance is dismissed.

NOTE:

In *General Motors Corp.,* Umpire Decision No. E-305 (1949), Umpire Gabriel N. Alexander summarized the pertinent prior GM decisions as follows:

It is now clearly established that one proper method of

effectuating Paragraph 63(a) is for Management to take a group of employes who are approximately equal in ability, merit and capacity and therefrom select the longest seniority employe for promotion. (Decision B-52.) Where Management follows this procedure, it is incumbent on the Union to show clearly that it erred in omitting others from such group. (Decision C-315.) With the exception of an isolated remark in Decision B-204, in no case has the Umpire ruled or indicated that the grouping of employes approximately equal in ability, merit and capacity is the *only* proper method of applying Paragraph 63(a). Where Management does not follow such procedure, however, and promotes a single employe out of line of seniority, it assumes the obligation of showing that such employe is not merely slightly better qualified than longer seniority employes, but that he is "head and shoulders" above all others. (Decision B-52.) Such outstanding qualifications should be evidenced by "precise reasons," "citation of instances," "production records" and/or "Supervisors' ratings." (Decision B-69.) Management likewise should evaluate "length of machine experience," "variety of machines operated" and "productive ability on machines." (Decision B-204.) The bare opinion of Supervisors, unsupported by an objective factual showing, will not sustain a challenged promotion. (Decisions B-100, E-232.) Potential ability for further promotion is a proper factor to consider where Management in good faith promotes for training purposes with an eye towards subsequent promotion to Supervisory jobs. (Decisions B-55 and C-319.)

In *General Motors Corp.,* Umpire Decision No. F-160 (1950), S. was protesting the promotion of C. to the job of Utility Man on the grounds that S. had greater seniority than C. and as much merit, ability, and capacity to perform the job as C. One issue in contention was whether the job was merely routine, as contended by the Union. On the relevance of this matter, Umpire Alexander stated:

> The distinction is important, even critical, for the following reasons: The evidence suggests strongly that there is little if any difference between C. and S. as to their ability to operate the several machines in Department 11. On the other hand, there is objective evidence which indicates that C. is significantly superior to S. ("head and shoulders" above him) in the other factors. C. has on other occasions performed satisfactorily as a Foreman. He has been in Department 11 about three years. Grievant has been in the department only nine months. Moreover, and the Umpire is impressed by this, Grievant has stated frankly that he is not desirous of assuming the responsibilities of a "boss." If the job to which promotion was made is found to be as Management describes it, the Umpire is

of the opinion that the choice of C. was proper. But contrariwise if the job is only routine.

On the question of the nature of the job, the Umpire held with the Company.

The "head and shoulders" doctrine has now gone beyond General Motors. *See, e.g., Dewey & Almy Chemical Co.,* 25 L.A. 316 (1955); *San Francisco News-Call Bulletin,* 34 L.A. 271 (1960). Is this doctrine, in part, a question of burden of proof?

In *Dayton Power & Light Co.,* 28 L.A. 624 (1957), the question was whether the Company had improperly applied Article VII, Section 2 of the contract (a typical "weak" seniority provision in relation to promotions) in filling the job of "Second Class Repairman-Machinist." Among other things, the Union objected to the fact that the Plant Manager had instructed the foreman to select the "best man" for the job. Arbitrator Carl A. Warns, Jr., although holding with the Company on other grounds, stated, "There can be no serious quarrel with the Union's argument ..." that such instructions "did not follow the requirements of Article VII, Section 2." Do you agree?

G. N. ALEXANDER, SENIORITY PROVISIONS IN ARBITRATION, PROCEEDINGS, 1950 UNIVERSITY OF MICHIGAN LAW SCHOOL SUMMER INSTITUTE ON "THE LAW AND LABOR-MANAGEMENT RELATIONS" 240-42

. . . Another interesting type of issue that frequently arises in seniority cases is the conflict between "seniority," in any one of the three senses which I have mentioned (and I do not think the differentiation among them is important here), and "ability" ("ability, merit and capacity," as it is called in the General Motors Agreement). This conflict is to be seen under various circumstances in connection with promotions, transfers, or job assignments, or layoffs and recalls. The Union stresses seniority. Management emphasizes ability and efficiency. The agreement probably represents a verbal compromise around which the conflict continues. It may be valuable to develop two concepts of "ability" in this area. First, a concept of absolute or minimum "ability," which may be required of every employee as a condition of holding down a job. Using the term in that sense, I know of no responsible union which ever contended that seniority entitled a man to a job he was "unable" to do. The second usage is a comparative one. Here the question is one of "relative ability" as between two or more employees with reference to a particular job.

In some instances the only conflict is over the question of whether an employee can perform a job in a "good and workmanlike" manner, to borrow a phrase from the law. Regardless of how well someone else can do the job, can this employee perform it well enough to allow him to exercise his seniority rights to it? This is usually the issue in disputes over order of layoff or recall.

In other instances, usually where promotions or transfers are involved, the emphasis is apt to be on who among several employees of varying seniority, can *best* do the job. This involves the concept of relative ability and creates the necessity of making a choice in a highly subjective area. I suspect there exists some confusion in thinking (certainly confusion in writing collective agreements) between the concept of absolute ability as a condition of holding a job and the concept of relative ability in the fields of promotions and transfers.

Finally, as Professor Killingsworth said, the question of who is to make the decision in disputes over ability in either the absolute or relative sense is an intriguing recurring problem of jurisdiction in seniority cases. Shall it be the arbitrator's whole judgment? Or shall it be management's whole judgment, subject to review by the arbitrator for discrimination, bias, or essential fairness? I think that any answer to this problem almost defies verbalization for practical purposes. In other words, I don't know how you can set up a rule either by decision or by agreement that will provide an exact standard for disposition of disputes. It seems to me that there can be no such thing as a self-operating or self-executing agreement clause in the matter of balancing ability and seniority. I do not know how you can, in words, state a rule that will enable judgment to be made and sustained for various sets of facts on this question. Whether you say management's decision in the absence of abuse or bias or discrimination shall be final, or whether you say that the arbitrator may decide the question afresh, when the cases get tough, when the facts are close and the arguments are well presented, the arbitrator has an extremely difficult problem in deciding mixed questions of ability and seniority. No one has yet, to my knowledge, devised a workable rule that will settle all these cases on a purely objective basis. In Shulman and Chamberlain, Cases on Labor Relations, there is an interesting record of some contract negotiations on the subject, which point up the necessity for exercising judgment in these matters. Once granted, that in this, as well as in many other aspects of industrial affairs, final action may properly turn upon human judgment, then at least the result in a specific case takes proper relationship to the over-all industrial relations picture. No constitution was ever written, no will was ever written, no contract was ever written, which was perfectly clear at all times and under all circumstances. I think no seniority clause will ever be written that will be completely self-executing.

Recognizing the imperfections of negotiations and draftsmanship, and with the realization that ultimately human judgment must prevail as the final determinant in specific cases, a strong argument can be made to support voluntary grievance arbitration as the method of resorting to such judgment.

NOTES:

Problem: What kind of "evidence" of ability or relative ability may appropriately be considered by management, or presented to an arbitrator, in cases involving the application of seniority provisions to layoffs, promotions, etc.? Consider the following:

(a) *The Opinion of Supervisors:* In *Ford Motor Co.,* 2 L.A. 374 (1945), Umpire Harry Shulman stated,

> A supervisor's testimony that he honestly believes one employee to be superior to another . . . is certainly a factor to be considered [by the Umpire]. It is not, however, either conclusive or sufficient. The supervisor must be prepared to state the basis for his belief and to support it, not by repeated assertion but by specific and understandable evidence — evidence which relates to capacity for the job in question, not merely to the employee's general character. . . .

Is the question of the weight of supervisory judgments affected by the issue of whether the burden of proof (in an arbitration case) is upon the employer or the union, and the further question of how the standard for arbitral review is formulated? *See Lockheed-Georgia Co.,* 42 L.A. 1301 (F. Flannagan, 1964); *International Minerals & Chemical Corp.,* 42 L.A. 47 (A. Koven, 1964). What is the impact of supervisory opinion if the arbitrator applies, in a given case, the proposition that a managerial decision on relative ability must be accepted unless it is shown to be arbitrary, capricious, or discriminatory? *Compare Christy Vault Co.,* 42 L.A. 1093 (A. Koven, 1964) *with Pacific Gas & Electric Co.,* 23 L.A. 556 (A. Ross, Chm., 1954).

(b) *Use of Tests or Examinations:* Where two employees vying for promotion have relatively equal abilities except that a junior employee scores better on written examination than a senior employee, may the employer promote the junior employee on the basis of his testing ability under the standard seniority clause? *Compare United States Steel Corp.,* 49 L.A. 1160 (C. McDermott, 1967) *with Glass Containers Mfrs. Institute,* 47 L.A. 217 (H. Dworkin, 1966). *See generally* Note, *Use of Tests in Promotions Under Seniority Provisions,* 21 Vand. L. Rev. 100 (1967).

However, the Supreme Court stated in *Griggs v. Duke Power Co.,* 401 U.S. 424, 431 (1971), that Title VII proscribes practices that are fair in form, but discriminate against minorities in operation. How can the employer insure that testing is "job related"? *See* Cooper & Sobol, "Seniority and Testing Under Fair Employment Laws: A General Approach to Objective Criteria of Hiring and Promotion," 82 Harv. L. Rev. 1598, 1602 (1969).

(c) *Other Factors:* Where the contract requires that vacancies be filled with the senior bidder provided he is reasonably qualified to do the work, may an employer reject a bid of an otherwise qualified senior bidder who has been disciplined for excessive absence from work? *Compare Emhart Mfg. Co.,* 43 L.A. 946 (B. Turkus, 1964) *with Waller Bros. Stone Co.,* 34 L.A. 852 (H. Dworkin, 1960).

D. CIRCUMSTANCES UNDER WHICH SENIORITY IS LOST, FORFEITED OR CREDITED

Interruptions in Employment Status

There are many events that may cause an interruption in an employee's active employment, including sick leave, personal leave, layoff, absenteeism, military leave, and union or company business leave. These events take the employee away from his everyday work without, normally, severing the employment relationship. Discharge and resignation terminate the employment relationship but a rehire within a stipulated period of time may call specific contract provisions into effect.

Contract provisions deal with the problem of seniority during layoff in many different ways. Seniority may be accumulated indefinitely, may be accumulated for a period equal to past service, may be accumulated for a fixed period and then retained, may be accumulated for a fixed period and then forfeited, may be retained for a fixed period and then lost, may be retained for a period tied to length of service, may be conditioned upon a showing of periodic availability, or may be lost through failure to respond to recall. A provision may combine more than one of the foregoing.

A Prentice-Hall study of labor contracts lists the following as events which will cause the loss of seniority.[88]

Event	Percent of contracts studied
Voluntary quit	81%
Discharge	80%
Failure to return from layoff when called (2-30 days)	68%
Layoff longer than a specified time (6 mo.-3 years)	65%
Absence without notice (2-7 days)	47%
Failure to return from a leave of absence	38%
Acceptance of employment during leave of absence	11%

[88] P-H, Industrial Relations — Union Contracts and Collective Bargaining 54:404 (Prentice-Hall, Inc.).

1. Voluntary Quitting or Discharge

Although the majority of contracts provide for a loss of seniority in the event of voluntary quitting, it is not easy to ascertain when this situation arises. For example, even though an employee who signs a termination slip the day after angrily leaving plant stating dissatisfaction with a new wage rate (*see e.g., FMC Corp. Recreational Vehicle Div.,* 62 L.A. 222 (Sarbarino 1974), does it follow that an employee who signs a similar statement prepared by a private detective when accused of taking company property has voluntarily resigned? *Compare Emge Packing Co.,* 61 L.A. 250 (Getman 1973) (constructive discharge) *with Concord Fabrics Inc.,* 57 L.A. 1200 (Turkus 1971) (voluntary resignation).

What is a "constructive discharge"? For example when an employee is given a choice between resigning or being discharged and resigns, is this a "constructive discharge"? *See e.g., Southern California Edison Co.,* 51 L.A. 869 (Mc Naughton 1968) and *Albertson's Inc.,* 65 L.A. 1042 (Christopher 1975). Can effective drafting dispose of this problem? Consider the case of a longtime employee who has temper tantrum and walks out of plant announcing she/he has quit when precipitous action is due to personal problems. *See e.g., General Tire & Rubber Co.,* 51 L.A. 206 (Amis 1968).

2. Layoffs

FIRESTONE TIRE & RUBBER CO.
and
UNITED RUBBER WORKERS, LOCAL 154

61 L.A. 136 (1973)

SENIORITY DATE

The Issue

Rentfro, Arbitrator: — Did the Company violate Article VI (Seniority) of the Agreement when it failed to credit the Grievant, L—, with service for seniority purposes for the eight months and 15 days he was laid off from March 14, 1957 to November 29, 1957? If so, to what relief is he entitled?

Relevant Contractual Provisions

ARTICLE VI

SENIORITY

(a) Seniority is continuous service with the Employer, compiled by time actually spent on the payroll, plus properly approved absences.

(e) Seniority will be broken only for the following reasons:

1. When an employee quits.

2. When an employee has been discharged for cause.

3. When an employee is absent three (3) consecutive days without report, unless the reason for not reporting is excusable.

4. When a laid-off employee fails to notify the Employer of intention to return to work within three (3) days after notice has been sent to him by the Employer to his latest address as shown on the books of the Employer. Employees shall be recalled by phone and/or registered letter.

5. Failure to renew a leave of absence.

6. An employee who is proved to have been employed elsewhere during an unauthorized absence from work, shall be considered as having terminated his employment.

7. Lay-off in excess of one year.

Statement of the Case

There is no dispute between the parties over the basic facts in this case. The dispute involves the interpretation and application of the collective bargaining agreement, particularly Article VI, *Seniority*.

The Grievant, L. —, was originally hired by the Company on August 16, 1955. Some correspondence and records erroneously refer to the date of August 6, rather than August 16, which is conceded to be the correct date. He was released or laid off on March 13, 1957, due to a reduction in personnel. He remained in layoff status for a period of 8 months and 15 days until November 29, 1957, when he was rehired or recalled from layoff. The terminology used on Company records indicates a "Separation Notice" dated March 13, 1957, showing that Grievant was "released" because of a "reduction in personnel." An "Employment Notice," with "Rehire" written in, dated November 29, 1957, indicates that he was "rehired" on that date to replace an employee who had resigned.

At that time Grievant was given a continuous service seniority date as of the date of "rehire," November 29, 1957. Eleven years later, June 10, 1968, the Operating Manager of the Company requested a correction in L—'s seniority date from November 29, 1957 to April 1, 1956, stating that "he was first employed at the shop from 8/6/55 to 3/57, and then was rehired 11/29/57, but this time was not taken into consideration at the time of rehire." Apparently no action was taken to correct the date at that time.

The issue of L—'s seniority date was next raised by the Assistant Manager in February, 1970, in connection with his vacation eligibility. The Labor Relations Office in Akron investigated the matter and by memo to the Denver shop dated February 19, 1970, set forth the Company position and a corrected date. That memo is set forth in pertinent part below:

"Referring to your memo of February 12, 1970, to P. E.

DuCharme regarding subject employee's service date, we have the following information:

1. Hired: 8-6-55
2. Released: 3-13-57
3. Re-hired: 11-29-57

An examination of the contracts in effect from 1955 through 1957 contains the same wordage as is in the present contract regarding seniority and termination of service.

It appears that when L. — was rehired 11-29-57, he was recalled to work as a result of having been released and retaining recall rights. Thus, his service date was moved up to reduce his service for the time he was laid off, and the date of 4-1-56 was used thereafter. Actually, he was off 8 months and 16 days; and the correct service date should be 4-22-56; but if 4-1-56 has been used previously as his service date, I would continue to use it.

Actually, when the man was released 3-13-57 under certain circumstances such as quitting and discharge, he could have lost his previous service and his rehire date of 11-29-57 would be his new service date. But this apparently was not the case. . . .''

As a result of the above memo, the seniority records of L— were subsequently adjusted to 4/22/56. As of 6/27/72, a Personnel Transaction Record was processed showing a service date of 4/22/56.

The matter was reopened by the filing of the grievance in this case on October 31, 1972. L— charged a violation of Article VI, Section (e) (7). The grievance stated:

"L— was hired on 8/6/55 and was laid off 3/14/55 for 8 months and 15 days, and was reinstated at which time wasn't given credit for seniority during time of layoff. His present seniority is 4/21/56."

Action requested: "That L— be given credit on seniority list for the 8 months and 15 days of layoff."

The Company answered the grievance as follows:

"Per Article VI section (a) 'Seniority is continuous service with the Employer, compiled by time actually spent on the payroll, plus properly approved absences.' It is our determination that lay-off is not a properly approved absence. Grievance denied."

. . . .

Discussion and Conclusions

The answer to the issue in dispute involves a determination of what the contract provides in the way of seniority for employees. The rights of the Grievant in this case exist only to the extent that they are spelled out and provided for in the contract. In other words:

"whatever seniority rights employees have exist only by virtue of the agreement that is in existence between the union and the employer. Such seniority rights depend wholly upon the contract. They arise out of the contract. Before a collective bargaining contract is in existence, there are no seniority rights." (See 4 LA 52)

Since seniority, length of service, and their concomitant rights are creatures of contract, it is necessary always to look first to the contract in determining the length of service. An employee's seniority date or standing may be affected by service outside the unit, and by periods of time he is on layoff. He may lose or retain previously earned seniority, or continue to accumulate seniority while on layoff or while working outside the unit, depending on the wording of the collective bargaining agreement. Special provision may be made that an employee transferred out of the seniority unit or laid off continues to accumulate seniority, or retains seniority already earned.

In this case, the Union says that the language of the agreement means that L— retained seniority already earned and continued to accumulate seniority during the time he was laid off; and that his seniority date should therefore be his date of hire, August 16, 1955. The Company says that the agreement does not provide either for the retention of seniority already earned at the time of layoff or for accumulation of seniority during the period of layoff. However, Company policy has been to credit a rehired or recalled employee with his retained seniority if he is rehired or recalled within one year.

After a thorough consideration of the clear contract language, and all the evidence presented in this case, the Arbitrator is persuaded that the position of the Company must prevail. For example, article VI, section (d) clearly sets forth the intention of the parties in case an employee transfers outside the bargaining unit. It says, he "shall accumulate seniority while on such work." No such provision is made for the employee who is laid off not on the active payroll.

It is significant that the Company and the Rubber Workers Union saw fit to provide for this situation in the Master Plants Agreement, though it has not been specifically dealt with in the agreement in this case. In 1952 the Master Plant Agreement defined seniority as "continuous service at a local plant computed by the time actually spent on the active payroll of that plant plus approved absence". This is substantially the same as the language used in the Denver agreement. Under that language, an employee did not accumulate seniority while on lay off.

In 1954, the Master Plant Agreement was amended to provide for the accumulation of seniority while on layoff under certain conditions: It now provides as follows:

(h)(1) A laid-off employee with three (3) months' seniority but less than two (2) years' seniority when laid off, if rehired within two (2) years from date of layoff, shall receive credit for seniority held at time of layoff, plus seniority credit for time laid off not to exceed his seniority held at time of layoff.

(2) A laid-off employee with two (2) years or more seniority when laid off, if rehired shall receive credit for seniority held at time of layoff, plus seniority credit for time laid off not to exceed two (2) years.

(3) An employee laid off after attaining seniority status shall, with respect to recall rights, be deemed to have accumulated seniority during layoff for a period equal to his seniority held at time of layoff, but in no case more than two (2) years.

If the parties to the Agreement in this case had intended that a laid-off employee continue to accumulate seniority while on layoff, they would have so provided in the language of the contract. They did so provide in Article VI, section (d). The Company and the Union did so provide in the Master Plants Agreement. Nothing in the instant Agreement provides that an employee gets seniority credit for time laid off. The Arbitrator cannot add to the Agreement.

Recognizing this, the Union argues essentially two points: (1) a layoff is a "properly approved absence" within the meaning of Article VI, section (a); and, (2) since the Grievant's seniority was not "broken" by being on layoff in excess of a year, he did not lose the 8 months layoff time as part of his continuous service. The Arbitrator is convinced that neither argument can be sustained.

First, a layoff is a layoff; it is not an approved absence from work. An approved absence contemplates a situation in which the employee is expected to be at work unless he has approval for not being there, such as in the case of a holiday, vacation, funeral leave or illness. An approved absence can develop only at a time an employee is scheduled to work. On layoff, an employee is removed from the payroll. Layoff time is not "time actually spent on the payroll," and is not an "approved absence" as that term is used in the contract.

Secondly, Article VI, section (e) describes those circumstances under which an employee's seniority is "broken." This means completely lost — wiped out, so that if he is rehired he starts as a new employee. This section does not mean that an employee accumulates seniority while on a layoff of less than a year. It only implies, at least, that if the layoff is less than a year, the employee does not lose what he had; because his seniority is not broken. If recalled within a year, as in this case, he picks up the continuous service on the payroll which he had prior to leaving the active payroll and going on layoff.

AWARD

The Company did not violate Article VI of the Agreement when it failed to credit the Grievant, L—, with service for seniority purposes for the period of time he was on layoff. The grievance must be denied.

NOTE:

In *Creamery Package Mfg. Co.,* 31 L.A. 917 (B. Turkus, 1964), the contract expressly stated that an employee would lose all seniority after 18 months of layoff. The Company reinstated an employee after more than 18 months of layoff and granted the employee his original date of hire. Three seniority lists were published by the Company and accepted by the Union before the Company discovered its mistake. The Company was not allowed to change the employee's original date of hire. The arbitrator relied on a sort of estoppel theory; neither the Company nor other employees had grieved within a reasonable period of time and the employee concerned, by remaining on the job, had relied on the seniority lists as being accurate.

In *Armco Steel Corp.,* 39 L.A. 1029 (S. Kates, 1962), the Company decided to close one plant and expand another. Employees at the plant to be closed were given a choice between taking severance pay or being placed on the layoff-rehire list. Some of the employees who had chosen severance pay, rather than go on layoff, were later rehired. The arbitrator upheld the Company's right to give these employees their original date of hire as their seniority date. This placed some of them in a better seniority position than employees who had chosen to go on layoff rather than terminate their employment and accept severance pay. All the laid-off employees had been recalled before any of the severance-pay employees were rehired. The employees who had chosen severance pay were covered by the Contract, "if the employee is rehired within two years the break in continuous service shall be removed." It is not clear whether the laid-off employees accumulated seniority while on layoff. If they did not, would you have chosen layoff rather than severance pay?

In *Mansfield Tire & Rubber Company,* 40 L.A. 285 (V. Stouffer, 1963), two employees were considered by the Company as having lost ten years of seniority each when they failed to notify the Company of a change of address while on layoff. The Company had recalled the employees by sending a registered letter to their addresses of record. When the employees failed to appear within a contractually agreed period of time, the Company terminated their employment. The arbitrator reinstated both employees and granted them seniority as of the day they notified the Company of their new addresses. *Compare American Radiator & Standard Sanitary Corp.,* 36 L.A. 541 (A. Russell, 1961).

When eligibility for severance pay and vacation time are at stake — "benefit" seniority — the factors considered are often different.

See e.g., Chicago Pneumatic Tool Co., 34 L.A. 321 (R. Feinberg, 1961); *Great Atlantic & Pacific Tea Co.,* 43 L.A. 1 (B. Turkus, 1964).

3. Absences

NOTES:

(1) *Problem:* Grievant had been granted a leave of absence for union business in 1960. This leave was extended for one year. In June, 1962, grievant requested another leave of absence for union business which was granted by the Company. During this second leave, grievant was appointed International Representative and did not return to work upon the expiration of this second one-year period. The Company sent grievant a letter informing him that his seniority was being terminated for failure to notify the Company within the time provided for by contract to return to work after a leave of absence of one year. The following contract provisions are relevant:

ARTICLE X—LEAVE OF ABSENCE

Sec. 1. An Employee may be granted a leave of absence without pay upon request for good and valid reasons. Such leave of absence shall be limited to three months unless a further extension is agreed upon by the Company and Union. In any event, leaves of absence without pay and extensions thereof shall not exceed one year.

Sec. 2. At the request of the Union, a leave of absence without pay may be granted to two employees, or such greater number as may be agreed upon by the Company and the Union to permit such employees to hold office in the Union or to be a delegate of the Local to any Union activity.

ARTICLE XV — SENIORITY

. . . .

Sec. 9. An employee shall lose his seniority rights if, (a) he quits his job . . . (f) he fails to report for work at the termination of an authorized leave of absence, unless a satisfactory reason is given in writing to the Company within seven days after he is due to report. An employee who loses his seniority rights . . . shall be considered as having quit his job.

Would you sustain the Company's action in light of Article X, Section 2? *See U.S. Industrial Chemical Co.,* 36 L.A. 400 (E. Teple, 1961). What if the grievant had returned to work two weeks after he was due to report, but had not notified the Company of his intention to return to work? *See E. F. Hauserman Co.,* 42 L.A. 1076 (J. Klein, Chm., 1964). *Compare Ball Brothers,* 36 L.A. 767 (H. Dworkin, 1961) *with Quick Manufacturing Inc.,* 43 L.A. 54 (E. Teple, 1964).

Even though contracts commonly provide that employees on sick leave accumulate or retain seniority, may seniority be retained or accumulated indefinitely? *See Kurtz Brothers, Inc.,* 43 L.A. 678 (C. Duff, 1964).

(2) *Rehiring:* Grievant was hired in December, 1951, but discharged for good cause on June 14, 1955. He was rehired on October 13, 1955. On November 1, 1957, the Company and Union executed a collective bargaining agreement containing the following seniority provisions:

A. Definition and Application

Sec. 92 — The parties recognize that position opportunity and security should increase in proportion to length of continuous service. It is therefore agreed that in all cases of vacancy, promotion, transfer, layoff, termination, and rehiring after layoff or termination, seniority shall apply and shall be defined as length of service plus ability to do the job.

Sec. 93 — Company seniority shall be applicable for purposes of vacation, severance pay, pensions and interplant transfers.

B. Termination of Seniority

Sec. 94 — An employee's seniority will be terminated by (1) voluntarily quitting the service or discharge, (2) absence due to termination or leave of absence (unless renewed), either of which continued for more than six months.

C. Seniority Lists

Sec. 96 — Representatives of the Company and representatives of the Union shall, as soon as possible after the signing of the Agreement, list the employees and decide upon an official seniority list. For the purpose of this list, length of service shall be the total service of the employee in all office and clerical positions. A copy of this list shall be furnished the representatives of the Union and shall be kept up to date as changes occur.

The Union claims that the grievant's seniority on the list shall run from December, 1951 under Section 94(2). However, the Company maintains that his seniority should run from October 13, 1955, because no collective bargaining agreement was in effect at the time of his rehiring and the grievant agreed with the Company to this effect privately at this date. Which position is correct? Why? *See Blaw-Knox Co.,* 33 L.A. 124 (B. Reid, 1959).

4. Mergers, Shutdowns, Successor Companies, Plant Relocation

As one attorney correctly noted,

> Sales and acquisitions of business ordinarily involve legal obligations under various labor laws, contractual obligations under union collective bargaining agreements, and practical considerations — all of a highly complex nature, seriously affecting both seller and buyer.[26]

Indeed, we raise many issues arising from Supreme Court litigation in such situations in Part Two of this book.[27] A concurrent issue arising from such business transactions is the termination or continuation of seniority rights of employees working under collective bargaining agreements. The European Economic Community Commission has recommended that the seniority an employee enjoyed with his old employer be transferred to his new employer.[28] Indeed, one federal court held in *Zdanok v. Glidden,* 288 F.2d 99 (2d Cir. 1961), that a seniority provision in a collective bargaining agreement vests and is effective beyond the life of the agreement.[29] And another, that seniority rights "follow the worker" to different geographical areas on transfer as part of the

---

[26] Spelfogel, A Corporate Successor's Obligation to Honor His Predecessor's Labor Contract: The Howard Johnson Case, 25 Labor L. J. 298 (1974). *See also* Note, Collective Bargaining Agreements — Arbitration Required After Expiration of Contract, 60 Marq. L. Rev. 1142 (1977) for discussion of the recent case of Nolde Bros., Inc. v. Local 358, Bakery & Confectionary Workers Union, 97 S. Ct. 1067 (1977). *Compare* Note, The Bargaining Obligations of Successor Employers 88 Harv. L. Rev. 759 (1975) *with* Aaron, Reflections on the Legal Nature and Enforceability of Seniority Rights, 75 Harv. L. Rev. 1532 (1964).

[27] *Supra* Part Two, p. 207.

[28] Bartlett, "Employees' Right in Mergers and Takeovers: EEC Proposals and the American Approach, 25 Int'l & Comp. L.Q. 621, 637 (1976).

[29] 90 A.L.R.2d 965 (2d Cir.), *cert. denied on this issue,* 368 U.S. 814 (1961), *rev'd,* Local 1251, Int'l U. of V.A., A & A.I.W. v. Robertshaw Controls Co., 405 F.2d 29 (2d Cir. 1968). This decision provoked considerable adverse comment, *see e.g.* Aaron, Reflections on the Legal Nature and Enforceability of Seniority Rights, 75 Harv. L. Rev. 1532 (1962); Lowden, Survival of Seniority Rights Under Collective Agreements: Zdanok v. Glidden Co., 48 Va. L. Rev. 291 (1962) [author is attorney for appellee in the present case]; Turner, Plant Removals and Related Problems, 13 Lab. L.J. 907 (1962); Note, Labor Law Problems in Plant Relocation, 77 Harv. L. Rev. 1100, 1117-21 (1964); Note, Industrial Mobility and Survival of Seniority — What Price Security?, 36 S. Cal. L. Rev. 269 (1963); 61 Colum. L. Rev. 1363 (1961); 40 Texas L. Rev. 721 (1962). But see, e.g., Blumrosen, Seniority Rights and Industrial Change: Zdanok v. Glidden Co., 47 Minn. L. Rev. 505 (1963); 110 U. Pa. L. Rev. 458 (1962). See also Panel Discussion, Plant Removals and Related Problems, 13 Lab. L.J. 914-22 (1962); Seminar, Plant Removals and Subcontracting of Work, 14 Lab. L.J. 366-79 (1963); articles cited in Zdanok v. Glidden Co., 327 F.2d 944, 952 n.11 (2d Cir.), *cert. denied,* 377 U.S. 934, 84 S. Ct. 1338, 12 L. Ed. 2d 298 (1964).

operations.[30] Although the latter case has received more jurisprudential support than the former, it is fair to say as Judge Hays said for the second circuit in reversing *Zdanok*:

> We are persuaded that the reasoning of the majority opinion in the *Glidden* case was erroneous and that that erroneous reasoning led to an incorrect result. For example, the basic proposition of the opinion, that seniority is a vested right, finds no support in authority, in logic or in the socio-economic setting of labor-management relations. Seniority is wholly a creation of the collective agreement and does not exist apart from that agreement. The incidents of seniority can be freely altered or amended by modification of the collective agreement. *Ford Motor Co. v. Huffman,* 345 U.S. 330, 73 S. Ct. 681, 97 L. Ed. 1048 (1953). In giving seniority a conceptual status apart from the provisions of the collective agreement and the intentions of the parties the *Glidden* opinion seriously misconceived the nature of the employment relationship and dealt "a blow to labor-management relations." [31]

Many arbitrators have followed this rationale.[32] In *Interscience Encyclopedia, Inc.,* 55 L.A. 210, 221-22 (1970), arbitrator Benjamin Roberts reasoned that:

> The Union has urged that the Arbitrator find that not only did all rights of the former Interscience employees including seniority, accrue until the expiration date of the Agreement but continued even after its fact expiration date. It asserted that, "seniority rights are property rights and the mere expiration of an agreement cannot take away that property right, so long as the employee remained in the employ of the Employer." In the court proceedings the Union had relied upon a Second Circuit Court decision in *Zdanok v. Glidden* (288 F.2d 99, 47 LRRM

---

[30] Oddie v. Ross Gear & Tool Co., 195 F. Supp. 826 (E.D. Mich. 1961), *modified,* 305 F.2d 143 (6th Cir.) *cert. denied,* 371 U.S. 941 (1962).

[31] Local 1251, Int'l U. of V.A., A & A.I.W. v. Robertshaw Controls Co., 405 F.2d 29 (2d Cir. 1968).

[32] Labor arbitrators have refused to follow the *Glidden* decision. *See* Empire Textile Corp., 44 Lab. Arb. 979, 984-85 (Scheiber, 1965) ("Glidden, whose effective life was short, has proven to be, under sound law, an unsafe guide and a dim beacon"); Paragon Bridge & Steel Co., 44 Lab. Arb. 361, 369 (Casselman, 1965) ("No courts or authorities in the field have been found who attribute any remaining vitality to [the *Glidden* case]"); Sivyer Steel Casting Co., 39 Lab. Arb. 449, 454-55 (Howlett, 1962); United Packers, Inc., 38 Lab. Arb. 619 (Kelliher, 1962). *See also* International Shoe Co. v. International Ass'n of Machinists, 66-2 CCH Lab. Arb. Awards § 8621 (McCoy, 1966); Marsh Wall Products v. Carpenters Local 2288, 65-2 CCH Lab. Arb. Awards § 8774 (Kagel, 1965); H.H. Robertson Co., 37 Lab. Arb. 928, 932 (Duff, 1962). Local 1251, Int'l U. of V.A., A. & A.I.W. v. Robertshaw Controls Co., 405 F.2d 29, 32 (2d Cir. 1968).

2865, 2nd Cir., 1961) in support of the proposition that at least seniority rights survived the termination of an agreement and the relocation of a plant.

However, in *Procter and Gamble Independent Union v. Procter and Gamble Manufacturing Co.* (312 F.2d 181, 51 LRRM 2752, 2nd Cir., 1962), the *Glidden* case was limited by that Court to its facts, and finally was expressly overruled by the Second Circuit sitting en banc in *Local 1251, UAW v. Robertshaw Controls Co.* (405 F.2d 29, 68 LRRM 2671, 2nd Cir., 1968). In the latter case the Second Circuit pointed out that the *Glidden* case not only failed to generate general acceptability but had lost most of its authority in the Second Circuit, citing the restricting *Procter and Gamble* decision. The Second Circuit went on to express what I believe to be the accurate view of seniority rights in its contractual context, as follows:

"For example, the basic proposition of the opinion that seniority is a vested right, finds no support in authority, in logic or in the socio-economic setting of labor-management relations. Seniority is wholly a creation of the collective agreement and does not exist apart from that agreement. . . . In giving seniority a conceptual status apart from the provision of the collective agreement and the intentions of the parties the *Glidden* opinion seriously misconceived the nature of the employment relationship and dealt a 'blow to labor management relations'."

As the Company noted, this decision that formally interred the *Glidden* holding, amply disposed of the Union's claim of "vested" seniority rights, despite the Union's continued insistence that the *Glidden* theory is basically sound and "very much alive." The odd award the Union cited holding that after a collective bargaining agreement has expired, the relationship between employer and employee is that of an individual employment contract, whose standards should be the provisions of the expired contract as a realistic basis for interpreting these individual agreements, hardly fits the instant case (and without comment on its validity for general applicability). This theory would perpetuate rights that exist solely by virtue of the collective bargaining agreement even after that agreement lost its force and effect. In the Wiley plant, it would carve out an elite minority group for discriminate treatment after January 12, 1962 based on an Agreement that did not represent the will of the larger industrial community that had no part in its writing and had never been represented by the bargaining agent that negotiated it. It not only would be unreasonable and inequitable but wholly impracticable.

The Union has urged that as a practical matter Wiley could

comply with the several sections of Article VI (Seniority) to give
the first opportunity in promotion to the senior employee
(Section 6.2), and to follow this principle in a reduction of forces,
subject to qualification and ability to perform the work (Section
6.3), and particularly in view of Wiley's grant of past service
credit to the former Interscience employees. This is but another
form of seeking to "vest" seniority rights beyond January 12,
1962. It also would have "the tail wagging the dog." It would
impose the minority's terminated contract as negotiated by a
union nonrepresentative of the majority upon the latter and an
Employer who is not under any duty to bargain with that Union
or to comply with the terminated contract. The fact that the
seniority system may be followed by Wiley without difficulty
would not be a reason to make it compulsory as a matter of law
or contract.

OTTO MILK CO. and MILK AND ICE CREAM SALESMEN, DRIVERS AND DAIRY EMPLOYEES, LOCAL 205

51 L.A. 408 (1967)

Facts

Duff, Arbitrator: — Otto Milk Company acquired all the capital
stock of Suburban on November 1, 1965, and Thomas Otto is the
owner of all of the capital stock of OMC. Each company has
maintained a separate corporate existence, and each has a separate
milk dealer's license issued by the Pennsylvania Milk Control
Commission. OMC has been engaged in the business of processing
and packaging milk and dairy products and selling them at wholesale
prices. Suburban has been engaged in processing and packaging the
same type of products for retail home delivery. Each maintained its
own separate plant, equipment and fleet of trucks. Both firms have
separate but identical contracts with the Union. The OMC Plant is
on Smallman Street within the City of Pittsburgh, and Suburban's
Plant is located on Camp Horne Road, several miles outside of
Pittsburgh.

Shortly after the purchase of all of the capital stock of Suburban
by OMC, employees of both companies requested the officers of the
Union to determine whether a sale or merger had occurred under
Article IV, Section 8 of the Labor-Management Agreements. A
preliminary investigation was made by the Union, and Union
counsel, in a letter dated January 10, 1966, expressed the opinion
that although the sale of stock changed the ownership of Suburban,
it did not destroy Suburban as a separate legal entity. Union counsel
expressed the conclusion that "both groups of employees are
members of separate bargaining units with separate seniority rights",
and he recommended that the issue be submitted to arbitration. No
further action was taken on the pending grievances at that time.

New Contracts were entered into on May 1, 1967 between the Union and the Companies. The economic relationship between the companies gradually changed, and the employees of both companies demanded a definite answer to their seniority problem.

Further meetings were held between Union Counsel and representatives of the companies and additional information was obtained. In a letter dated June 26, 1967, Union Counsel summarized the operational changes that had occurred, and again recommended that the entire matter be submitted to arbitration.

Another grievance was filed on September 25, 1967. By its letter dated October 18, 1967, the Union requested arbitration and the companies agreed. The present arbitration was then arranged.

Applicable Contract Provisions

Article IV

Seniority

Section 2 — Departmental Seniority

Employees under this Agreement shall have Companywide departmental seniority rights when layoffs become necessary."

Section 8 — Merger and Sales

In the event any of the plants of the Employer covered by this Agreement are discontinued or are merged with other plants of the Employer, the employees involved shall retain their full seniority subject to the following conditions and regulations.

In the event the Employer sells his entire operation or any part thereof covered by this agreement to another employer, the employees covered by this agreement shall retain one-half (½) of their seniority, providing they have been in the employ of the Company being purchased for at least two full years. Such employees shall replace only the youngest employees, by seniority, of the Company's main plant or branch plant.

. . . .

Discussion

In the resolution of any dispute by arbitration, the decision must draw its essence from the pertinent Collective Bargaining Agreements. Article IV, Section 8 contains various provisions that are applicable when there has been a joining together of two or more business firms, both of which are parties to an Agreement with this Union. In the event that a firm merges with another, or becomes part of a cooperative, the employees retain their full seniority rights. If a sale of the entire operation to another employer (covered by this Agreement) takes place, the employees retain only one-half of their seniority. It is important to inquire what type of combination took place. The parties agree that in the present case the purchase of all of the capital stock of Suburban by OMC was not the purchase of an "entire operation" within the intendment of Article IV, Section 8. The language concerning "sale" was not meant to cover stock transactions, but it refers to the purchase of physical assets of a plant, which thereby eliminates the former productive unit.

The key to the present dispute is the meaning of the following language: "In the event the Employer covered by this Agreement merges with another Employer, or becomes part of a cooperative ..." Clearly, the present case does not involve the formation of a co-operative association. The crucial question is whether a merger exists within the intendment of Article IV, Section 8. Black's Law Dictionary, Fourth Edition, 1951, defines the generic term "merger" as follows:

> "The fusion or absorption of one thing or right into another; generally spoken of a case where one of the subjects is of less dignity or importance than the other. Here the less important ceases to have an independent existence ..."

The same Dictionary defines the word "merger" as used in Corporate Law as follows:

> "The union of two or more corporations by the transfer of property of all to one of them, which continues in existence, the others being swallowed up or merged therein ... It differs from a consolidation wherein all the corporations terminate their existence and become parties to a new one ..."

In the present situation, the two Companies are still recognized as separate corporations for all legal and tax purposes. They continue to have separate corporate charters, different names, separate licenses from the Milk Control Commission, and keep separate books of account. In addition, the Management of each Company desires and intends to keep OMC and Suburban as separate legal entities.

It may be that this combination of firms is, in a strictly legal sense, a partnership of corporation. However, in Arbitration we have no authority to adjudicate the strict legal status of these companies nor is it necessary, in order to correctly interpret Article IV, Section 8, to do so. In interpreting the meaning of the term "merger" within the intendment of Article IV, Section 8, we shall determine only economic relationships that affect Labor-Management relations. It is the function of Courts to determine legal status of business units. Seniority rights of employees are determined not by abstract legal rights, but by economic reality. We interpret the word "merger" as used in Article IV, Section 8 to mean a fusion or absorption of two individual business enterprises into one for all purposes relative to Labor-Management relations. In the present case, we must determine whether there has been an economic merger, and leave the determination of strictly legal concepts to the forum which has jurisdiction.

It would serve no useful purpose to repeat in full the complex facts of the present case. In our judgment, many factors indicate an economic merger of OMC and Suburban. Thomas Otto is the owner of all the capital stock of OMC, which firm now owns all the capital stock of Suburban. OMC and Suburban have the same corporate officers. George Pfeil is the General Manager of both companies, and their business policies are determined by the same individuals. Both companies have the same headquarters, use the same headquarters personnel, and have one central telephone exchange. The Labor Agreements of both companies are negotiated and administered by the same persons who determine uniform labor policies and settle labor disputes and grievances. Legal counsel, accounting personnel, and other staff personnel of the companies are the same. All milk used for manufacturing, processing and packaging by both companies is purchased from the same supplier, and is received and distributed from the same receiving stations. Among the public manifestations that these companies are closely inter-related, are that all products have the same label and symbol, and all trucks and equipment carry the same insignia and name. In public hearings before governmental agencies, both companies are represented by the same officials.

There is an exchange of operating functions between the parties. About August, 1966, all paper packaging equipment was removed from Suburban, and therefore OMC packaged all products in plastic and paper that was distributed by either company. All milk in glass containers is processed and bottled by Suburban for both companies. The removal of the packaging equipment from Suburban resulted in a loss of eight jobs at Suburban. At the time of the Arbitration Hearing, new paper packaging equipment was on order, and apparently paper packaging was to be resumed at Suburban. In the actual operation of the companies, there has been the closest type of cooperation in production and in labor policy.

The evidence strongly indicates that what economic function is assigned to each firm depends upon what will yield the greatest net profit for the combination, rather than what will profit each firm. In our judgment, most economic incidents related to Labor-Management matters indicate a blending or consolidation of the two firms into one. We, therefore, find as a fact that what originally was two separate productive units has, in effect, been merged into one, although the corporate integrity of each appears to have been retained for legal and tax purposes which are not relevant to the present proceedings.

Where the blending of economic units has obliterated borderlines and have fused into one consolidated enterprise, it constitutes a merger within the intendment of Article IV, Section 8. This close economic relationship has a direct impact on seniority. One illustration will suffice. When all packaging of milk in paper cartons was discontinued by Suburban in August, 1966, eight employees were displaced, and these employees were hires at OMC as new employees. There now is under consideration a transfer of some paper packaging back to Suburban. Perhaps these same employees, who became new employees at OMC and worked there for more than one year at their former job of paper packaging, again will be displaced. If they follow the work back to Suburban, they again will be new employees (at Suburban). In such a case, seniority benefit rights, such as paid vacations, and competitive status seniority rights would be lost. If employees of both OMC and Suburban are placed on an integrated seniority list, either corporation that is party to the economic merger then freely may transfer productive functions back and forth between the companies without adversely affecting the seniority status of employees of either firm. In our judgment, this latter result protects valuable seniority rights of employees within the intendment of Article IV, Section 8.

We must resolve the question of when the present economic merger occurred. On November 1, 1965, OMC first acquired all of Suburban's capital stock. Thereafter, gradual changes took place in regard to economic cooperation between the companies. These transitional changes took place gradually, and it is difficult to pin-point when the actual economic merger was perfected. Because the evidence is not full and complete as to when each move was made, we must be somewhat arbitrary in our assessing when the transition was completed. The opinion of Union's counsel dated January 10, 1966, concluded that "separate bargaining units with separate seniority rights" existed at that time. However, later developments changed the nature of the economic relationship. At the Arbitration Hearing on December 5, 1967, the evidence indicated that the economic merger within the meaning of that term in Article IV, Section 8, was then completed. Our Award will arbitrarily establish December 1, 1967 as the date when the seniority lists will be merged.

. . . .

AWARD

The companies are hereby directed to consolidate the seniority lists of Otto Milk Company and Suburban on the basis of length of service with either of the companies as of December 1, 1967.

NOTE:

In *Superior Products Co.,* 42 L.A. 517 (R. A. Smith, 1964) the plant closed down was within fifteen minutes of the plant taking on the closed plant's production. The arbitrator stated the equities involved and the mechanics of the solution:

Certain facts seem to me to be especially significant in this case. The contemplated action will not involve the establishment of a new plant at a location not mentioned in the existing Agreement, or of a new type of operation. Rather, it will involve a consolidation of the operations of the Goddard and Lyndon plants at the Goddard Plant, both covered by the Agreement. Moreover, the consolidation will not involve simply an expansion of a kind of operation theretofore conducted previously only at the Lyndon Plant. Distinctive products have been produced at the two plants. With the shutting down of the Lyndon Plant, the machine production of smaller dimension pipe, which has been that plant's principal activity, will not be discontinued; instead, it will be added to the activities of the Goddard Plant as a new function.

The plants are fairly close together, and the employees of both are covered by the Master Agreement. The Lyndon and Goddard plant employees have developed their seniority rights in the context of distinctive types of operations. Beyond question, the "equities" of the situation demand that these equities be reorganized if this can be done on the basis of some reasonable interpretation of the Agreement. A gross injustice would result if either group should be able, as the result of an application of the seniority provisions of the Agreement, to gain or lose at the expense of the other.

It seems to me this kind of result can be avoided, and a proper and equitable result achieved, by considering what the term "plant," as used in Article V, Section 1, should mean upon the consolidation of the two operations at the Goddard Plant. At that point there will be but one manufacturing plant of the Company covered by the Agreement, and seniority rights, as to persons employed there, obviously will be confined to that plant. However, since the plant will be a consolidation of the previously distinctive operations of the two plants, located within a few miles of each other, it seems to me the term "plant," as used in Article V, Section 1, should be construed, upon such consolidation, as establishing, insofar as practicable, two seniority groups, one relating to the type of operation previously performed at the Lyndon Plant and the other relating to the type of operation previously performed at the Goddard Plant. This kind of result could be regarded as inconsistent with the Agreement only on the theory that Article V, Section 1, was intended to confine seniority to a single plant location regardless of the circumstances. But this not only begs the question, but is not supported specifically by the collective bargaining history. It seems to me to be perfectly reasonable to derive from the use of the concept of "plant" seniority in the Agreement the basic intent to grant seniority rights related to the types of plant operations then existing, and not to resume or assume that the parties contemplated the eradication of seniority rights through the consolidation of then existing plant operations.

This conclusion is confined to the particular facts presented (although the same conclusion would be reached, in all probability, if the Company were to shut down both the Goddard and the Lyndon plants and consolidate their operations [*i.e.,* transfer them] to another location in close proximity to the existing plants). I do not base my conclusion on certain judicial rulings that seniority rights "vest" in the individual employees involved, and hence may not be destroyed even though a collective agreement or collective bargaining rights on behalf of such employees cease to exist. [*Zdanok v. Glidden Co.,* 288 F.2d 99, 47 LRRM 2865 (C.A.2d, 1961); *Oddie v. Ross Gear & Tool Co.,* 195 F. Supp. 826, 48 LRRM 2586 (D.C. Mich., 1961), *reversed,* 305 F.2d 143, 50 LRRM 2763 (C.A. 6th, 1962)]. Basically, and subject to the fiduciary obligations which inhere in the collective bargaining relationship, it is my view that seniority rights arise by virtue of the collective bargaining agreement, and are subject to disposition and modification by the collective bargaining representatives. In the instant case I consider that my task has been to construe the agreement to which the parties are subject. This I have done.

Mechanics of Solution

III. It follows the foregoing analysis that, upon the consolidation of the kinds of operations hitherto performed at the two plants, employees on the seniority roster of the Lyndon Plant should be accorded a preferential right to be employed on those kinds of operations theretofore performed only at the Lyndon Plant, and that the employees on the seniority roster of the Goddard Plant should be accorded a preferential right to be employed on those kinds of operations theretofore performed only at the Goddard Plant. This will doubtless require that such operations be identified and that separate seniority lists be maintained. In effect, this will be somewhat similar to the "departmental" seniority which existed under the master agreements prior to 1961. New employees will be in one seniority group or the other, depending on the job.

I recognize that there are some employees (*e.g.,* truck drivers and maintenance personnel, and perhaps others) whose work intrinsically could be associated with the type of operation performed at either plant. Upon the consolidation, the number of employees from each plant who fill these jobs should be in the same proportion as the number of such employees previously in active employment status at each plant prior to the consolidation bore to the total of such employees at both plants. They should be added to the separate seniority rosters in the same proportion."

. . .

In *Lagomarcino-Grupe Co.*, 43 L.A. 453 (H. Davey, 1964) a result opposite to that of the principal case was reached. Employees of Company *A* lost all seniority when rehired at Company *B* after *A* had been closed down. The arbitrator stated that *A* and *B* could be regarded as one from a labor relations view; the same union had contracts with both companies. But the absence of any contract provision allowing the seniority lists to be merged prevented the employees of *A* from carrying their seniority to *B* when rehired.

When the employees of the closed plant are non-union and those at the plant now hiring are unionized, different policies enter the picture. In *Paramount Die Casting Co.*, 38 L.A. 741 (G. Alexander, 1962), the arbitrator held that seniority was to be from date of original hire at the terminated plant regardless of the non-union status of those employees. The decision was based on the contract provision defining seniority. The term continuous service was used but was not limited to continuous service within the bargaining unit.

The equities involved change when a *purchaser* relocates after the expiration of the contract which bound the predecessor employer. *S. B. Penick & Co.*, 43 L.A. 798 (B. Turkus, 1964). The purchaser's good faith in offering severance pay, crediting seniority for benefits, and allowing seniority to accrue from date of acquisition rather than date of hire were considered and the employees were not allowed credit from their original dates of hire. In *Madison-White Motors Inc.*, 41 L.A. 759 (A. Anderson, 1963), seniority was held to be date of original hire when the plant was purchased and relocated.

In *Graphic Arts Ass'n of Michigan,* 40 L.A. 1089 (H. Platt, 1963), an agreement made by the Company and the Union concerning the seniority rights of employees involved in a purchase of one company by another was held not to be binding on the employees unless ratified by the Union members. Employees' seniority was held to be date of original hire when the change incurred by purchase was in name only. *P. M. Northwest Co.,* 42 L.A. 961 (D. Lyons, 1964).

It is important to determine the exact nature of the transaction involved. In *Associated Brewing Co.,* 40 L.A. 680 (M. Kahn, 1963), the arbitrator stated that if the transaction had been a plant shutdown rather than a merger the employees would have been placed at the bottom of the seniority list of the new plant pursuant to the practice in the community.

Chapter 12

WAGES AND HOURS

Unless otherwise specified, "wages" will be used in its broadest sense as any emolument of employment including fixed compensation (salaries) and payment for stated intervals of work (money wages), as well as other forms of compensation (wage supplements) which will be separately treated. Obviously, wages are not only clearly encompassed within the normal area of collective barbaining, but are a major and continuing concern. The subject, however, is extremely complex, both in the underlying theoretical considerations and in the practicalities of bargaining. It is an area of bargaining where specialists like business and labor economists, actuaries, and auditors and accountants, computer technologists and systems analysts, and tax experts supply the necessary expertise.

Due to the limitations of space and the requirements for interdisciplinary skills, this chapter can only touch on the major issues involved in the wage and hour provisions of collective bargaining agreements. In fact, the pedagogical purpose of this section is to alert personnel working in the field of the necessity of obtaining experts from other disciplines to assist in the negotiation, drafting, and administration of wage and hour contract provisions. For example, the reader should refer back to the subsection dealing with the use of economic data in negotiations (Chapter 3 of this book). A few of the significant economic problems involved in the use of this data in the negotiation of "wages" may be noted, although they are beyond the scope of this volume. For example, in what manner do "market forces" shape an individual's wages? What role do these forces play in determining wages within an industry and in setting the "general wage level"?[1] If economic variables are important, is it the labor market or the product market which determines wages?[2] Do unions make a difference in wage determination? Although there is some agreement about the short-range impact of unionization, there is much disagreement about the long-range aspects.[3] Are unions primarily motivated by

---

[1] For a detailed examination *see* Kerr, Wage Relationship — The Comparative Impact of Market and Power Forces, in The Theory of Wage Determination, Proceedings of International Economic Ass'n 173 (Dunlop ed. 1957).

[2] *Compare* Rees, The Effects of Unions on Resource Allocation, 1963 J. Law & Econ. 69-78 *with* Segal, The Relation Between Union Wage Impact and Market Structure, 78 Q. J. of Econ. 96-114 (Feb. 1964). *See generally* R. Lester, Economics of Labor 255-91 (2d ed. 1964).

[3] For an excellent survey of theories on *"Trade Unionism and Wage Determination," see* A. Gitlow, Labor and Industrial Society 189-97 (rev. ed. 1963).

"wage maximization" for its members?[4] Are wages, hours and working conditions, which are mandatory subjects of bargaining, primarily determined by the relative strength of labor and management?[5]

When "wage economics" are set aside, the collective bargaining issues involve, as major areas, (1) internal wage structures; (2) job classification and wage systems; (3) wage supplements; and (4) hour and premium pay provisions. As previously indicated, although the general wage level is of vital importance to a dynamic economy, in drafting wage and hour provisions the immediate issue is how to resolve basic wage level issues for the limitless variety of workers in our modern industrial society.[6] Such a variety of jobs raises

---

Concerning whether unions have captured a larger share of income for their members, Professors Chamberlain & Kuhn state,

". . . labor economists are in considerable agreement that statistical evidence is not conclusive but rather suggests that the actual impact of unions upon relative earnings is less than might have been expected from theoretical analysis. Ross concluded that in the organizing stages of union growth, union members may enjoy some slight wage advantage, but in general the studies indicate that unions have an almost unnoticeable effect. *See* Arthur Ross, 'The Influence of Unionism upon Earnings,' *Quarterly Journal of Economics,* vol. 62 (1948), pp. 263-286; Arthur Ross and W. Goldner, 'Forces Affecting the Inter-industry Wage Structure,' *Quarterly Journal of Economics,* vol. 64 (1950), pp. 254-281; J. Garbarino, 'A Theory of Inter-industry Wage Structure Variation,' *Quarterly Journal of Economics,* vol. 64 (1950), pp. 283-305; Stephen P. Sobotka, 'Union Influence on Wages: The Construction Industry,' *Journal of Political Economy,* vol. 61 (1953), pp. 127-143; P.E. Sultan, 'Unionism and Wage-Income Ratios: 1929-1951,' *Review of Economics and Statistics,* vol. 36 (1954), pp. 67-73; and H.M. Levinson, *Unionism, Wage Trends, and Income Distributions, 1914-1947,* University of Michigan, Ann Arbor, Mich., 1951, pp. 80-110." N. Chamberlain & J. Kuhn, Collective Bargaining, 343 n.4 (2d ed. 1965).

[4] *See generally* E. Beal & E. Wickersham, The Practice of Collective Bargaining 258-318 (3rd ed. 1967) and Selected Annotated Bibliography at 318-21.

[5] *See* J. Garbarino, Wage Policy and Long-Term Contracts (1962); R. Lester & E. Robie, Wages Under National and Regional Collective Bargaining (1946); A. Rees, The Economics of Trade Unions (1962); L. Reynolds & C. Taft, The Evolution of the Wage Structure (1956); New Concepts in Wage Determination (G. Taylor & F. Pierson eds., 1957); Kerr, *Trade Unionism and Distributive Shares,* 77 Monthly Lab Rev. 148 (Feb. 1954); Levinson, *Unionism, Wage Trends and Income Distribution,* 10 Mich. Bus. Studies No. 4, at 115 (1951); and Slichter, *Do Wage-Fixing Arrangements in the American Labor Market Have an Inflationary Bias?,* 64 Am. Econ. Rev. 322 (1954).

[6] It is probably accurate to state that there are no solidly established, universally accepted criteria on the basis of which the parties to collective bargaining negotiations (or third parties called in as "referees" or "adjudicators") agree in attempting to resolve basic wage level issues. Professor Slichter has listed six criteria, in addition to comparisons of wage rates in the area of industry, which are commonly advanced: (1) the minimum necessities of workers (so-called "minimum budgets"); (2) changes in the cost of living; (3) maintenance of "take-home" pay — which was especially prominent in negotiations during the reconversion period following World War II, when workers faced a reduction of the wartime "overtime" work week;

important questions of how to rationalize: (1) the wage system or structure, and (2) wage rates, including the general wage level, the determination of individual rates, and the problem of wage adjustments during the life of the contract. "Wage systems" run the gamut from "daywork" hourly rates to elaborate individual or group incentive plans. Furthermore, the application of a "wage system" to a specific employee will normally turn on his "job profile" which itself may be very detailed. Even where the system and the profile are simple, the "wage package" will usually include wage supplements which may be complex.[7] As indicated, the wage structure is further complicated by "interim adjustments" of initial wage determinations. These are the important kinds of problems that arise in the negotiation and administration of labor agreements, and, therefore, are the subject matter of this part of the materials.

"Hours" are likewise encompassed within the normal area of collective bargaining, and, of course, are directly related to "wages" as part of the basis upon which is determined the direct economic benefit to the worker which follows from his employment and the direct economic cost of employment to the employer. Provisions for "premium pay" for hours worked under certain specified conditions likewise fall in this category.

A. RATIONALIZING THE INTERNAL PAY STRUCTURE

Establishing wages for specific jobs is a very significant consideration in collective bargaining. In large industrial establishments there may be hundreds of individual wage rates that must be established as part of the overall wage structure. The task of setting these job rates is dynamic because of the rapid changes in job content that result from the introduction of new job operations and technological improvement. This problem is complicated by the fact that specific wages do not normally move as a unit even though they tend to "cluster" into groups because of custom, production process, and specific technology. Specific job rates require a lot of time to "hammer out" individually by negotiation. These factors combine to make it difficult to negotiate specific job rates. Moreover, bargaining usually starts with a wage structure which has been

---

(4) ability (or inability) of the employer to pay higher wages or the same wages; (5) changes in "productivity"; and (6) effect of wage changes in consumer buying power. *See* S. Slichter, Basic Criteria Used in Wage Negotiations (Chi. Ass'n of Commerce 1947). *See also* H. Davey, Contemporary Collective Bargaining 239-43 (2d ed. 1959); Taylor, *Criteria in the Wage Bargain,* N.Y.U. First Annual Conference on Labor 65-88 (1948); and Wiseman, *Wage Criteria for Collective Bargaining,* 9 Ind. & Lab. Rel. Rev. 252 (1956).

[7] In the first half of 1978, fringe benefits were negotiated or revised in 83% of all new contracts. 1 C.B.N.C. § 18:965 (7/13/78).

established unilaterally by management, with the union selecting certain aspects of the structure, such as particular wage rates, for attack.

The use of economic data discussed in Chapter 3 concentrated on bargaining criteria affecting the general level of wages. This does not explain why similar jobs within a plant pay different wages. To answer this question, it is necessary to examine the administrative aspect of assigning labor within a plant and paying in accordance with the assignment. An existing wage structure may arise "hotchpot," on an ad hoc basis, depending on management's need for a particular kind of work and on its pragmatic reaction to the question of the wage rate to be established for certain work in order to obtain employees. The result, given this "process," obviously is a wage structure which very often is internally inconsistent. "Inequitable" wage differences within a plant are the source of a great many grievances that are detrimental to employee moral. This fact, together with union pressure, has encouraged management to evaluate jobs and wage differentials.

1. Union Efforts

As Professor Leonard Burgess states:

> While industrial unions have often pushed for an increase in the entire hourly wage structure, craft unions have usually striven for pay increases in particular jobs, typically among the more highly skilled occupations near the upper end of the wage structure. In still other cases, unions have tried to assist the lowest-paid employees — that is, to push upward the bottom end of the pay scale. Unions have also sought to eliminate pay differentials where they are in violation of the union principle of equal pay for equal work. Typical of these differentials are those based on race or sex. Unions have likewise worked for the elimination of interarea differentials, especially in multiplant corporations. . . .
>
> Union efforts toward a more rational internal company pay structure have taken two principal forms — the effort, through the establishment of union wage scales negotiated in collective bargaining, to set pay rates for particular jobs; and the attempt to put a floor under wages through advocacy of minimum-wage legislation.
>
> While industrial unions have tended to push for increases in the entire structure, craft unions have fought for increases in the few selected occupations with which their memberships were concerned. This difference in programs has lost some of its significance because interjob differentials, measured in percentage terms, have followed a downward trend, and both

types of union have bargained for wage scales that eliminate formal differentials in wage rates having race or sex as a basis. However, *area* differentials remain, craft unions tending to perpetuate them, while industrial unions in nationwide contracts continue to strive to eliminate them.

Union efforts toward a higher minimum wage, as well as toward broadening the scope of the minimum-wage law, have been successful in that they have built a floor under the wage structure for covered employees in enterprises engaged in interstate commerce. Despite adverse employment effects in some situations, the Fair Labor Standards Act has been a factor in improving the lot of the worker.[8]

2. Management Efforts

In recent years business management has accentuated the engineering aspect of work accomplishments, and this has naturally been translated into tying wages to jobs.[9] A very small plant may conceivably operate on the basis of "personal" wage rates for employees, but modern wage administration theory and practice, and, indeed, the practical requirements of any employment situation requiring the use of varied occupational skills, dictate that the work be organized systematically, carefully and classified into types of jobs to be performed. Thus, most employers today use "job classification" and many accompany the classification and labeling of jobs with more or less complete and accurate written "job descriptions," although some employers are content to leave the matter of specific job content to develop in accordance with custom and practice in the plant.

In bargaining, the parties may be content with the classification system currently in effect, or the employer or union may press for major or minor revisions. The employer, will, of course, usually insist that the determination of the organization and flow of the work and the kinds of occupational skills (jobs) needed are a function of management, while conceding the right in the union to negotiate concerning the wage rates to be established for the various jobs or classifications of work. An intimate and detailed knowledge of the content of jobs in question and the use of defensible criteria for "rating" jobs are required for intelligent bargaining on issues of this kind.

In recent years an increasing number of employers are attempting

---

[8] L. Burgess, Wage and Salary Administration in a Dynamic Economy 15, 28 (1968) [hereinafter cited as Wage and Salary Administration].

[9] *See* S. Slichter, J. Healy & E. Livernash, The Impact of Collective Bargaining on Management 559-623 (1960) [hereinafter cited as Impact of Collective Bargaining].

to rationalize their wage structures by comparing the requirements of respective jobs. The method most employers use is job evaluation,[10] which differs only in the procedures used from the concept underlying union thinking about appropriate wage scales. The underlying purpose of these mechanisms remains essentially identical — to provide a measure of the relative value of each job compared to other jobs in the company pay structure.

a. Job Classification and Job Rates

As Professor Burgess describes the process: [11]

Measuring the Relative Worth of a Job

The basic element of all job-evaluation schemes is the job description. For example, the position of general ledger bookkeeper is described in one commercial bank as follows: "Under general supervision, receives and posts entries to General Ledger accounts on Burroughs Posting Machine, prepares daily statements of condition, and compiles several other financial reports. One year of previous bank bookkeeping experience or related work is required."

Note that the emphasis is on the job, not the person who is or will be performing it, and that certain factors that facilitate comparison with other jobs in the same or other banks are identified. For example, the work is done "under general supervision" and "one year of previous bank bookkeeping experience or related work" is called for. These and other such factors are in one way or another considered, no matter what the job-evaluation plan.

The four major methods of job evaluation in use among American companies are job ranking, predetermined grading, point rating, and factor comparison.

Job Ranking. The first method, job ranking, is the simplest of the four and can be developed using relatively brief job descriptions such as the one just examined. In the usual procedure, a job-evaluation committee studies descriptions of the jobs to be evaluated. Each member then ranks each job with a numerical value, 1 being the highest-rated job, 2 the second

---

[10] For job evaluation and procedures see generally, E. Lanham, Job Evaluation (1955); C. Lytle, Job Evaluation Methods (2d ed. 1954); J. Otis & R. Leukart, Job Evaluation (2d ed. 1954); J. Patton, C. Littlefield & S. Self, Job Evaluation (3rd ed. 1963); Baker & True, *The Operation of Job Evaluation Plans,* Industrial Relations Section (Princeton University 1947). *See also* New Concepts in Wage Determination (G. Taylor & F. Pierson eds., 1957), for discussion of impact of "market forces" on job evaluation.

[11] Wage and Salary Administration, *supra* note 8, pp. 31-37. Reprinted with permission of publisher; © 1968 by Harcourt, Brace & World, Inc.

highest, and so on. The average of the rankings for each job is its new ranking. Noteworthy in this method of evaluation is the fact that whole jobs are compared.

Predetermined Grading. While the predetermined-grading method has been used elsewhere, its widest application has been in government service. Under the predetermined-grading or classification method, job descriptions are compared with established grade definitions. For example, under the General Schedule of the U.S. Civil Service, each of hundreds of jobs, ranging in annual pay from $3,305 to $20,000, is assigned one of the eighteen different grades. For example, the grade GS-6 includes:

> all classes of positions the duties of which are (1) to perform under general supervision, difficult and responsible work in office, business, or fiscal administration, or comparable subordinate technical work in a professional, scientific, or technical field, requiring in either case (A) considerable training and supervisory or other experience, (B) broad working knowledge of a special or complex matter, procedure or practice, or of the principles of the profession, art, or science involved, and (C) to a considerable extent the exercise of independent judgment; or (2) to perform other work of equal importance, difficulty, and responsibility, and requiring comparable qualifications.[5]

This grade differs from others below and above it according to subtle gradations in such factors as the difficulty of the work, the type of supervision under which the work is done, the latitude allowed for the exercise of independent judgment, and so on.

By comparing particular job descriptions with such grade definitions one can assign most jobs to one of the eighteen grades. As in the job-ranking method, predetermined grading utilizes a job-evaluation committee. Under this method the highest-ranking and most complex jobs are typically the hardest to assign to a particular grade.

Both job-ranking and predetermined-grading methods are nonquantitative. Although the two methods described next — point and factor comparison — place greater emphasis on quantitative measures, these methods must still rely heavily on committee judgments for success.

Point Rating. Under the point-rating method, a job is assigned points according to the degree that it embraces each of several job factors. In the case of supervisory responsibility, for example, a job with no or very little responsibility (designated degree 1)

---

[5] Classification Act of 1949.

might be assigned 20 points for that factor, while one involving supervision of one to three persons (degree 2) would receive 40 points, and so on. The use of degrees representing a fixed interval or spread of points — for example, 20 points per degree, as in the example above — is meant to compensate for the capriciousness and variability of human judgment. To illustrate: if three members of a job-evaluation committee assigned values of 57, 64, and 61 points for supervisory responsibility, it could be argued that human judgment is not precise enough to justify distinctions so fine. The specification of degrees avoids this difficulty.

Table 3-2 shows a typical point scheme for clerical and supervisory workers in an insurance company. It is significant that in the table supervisory responsibility is only one of four kinds of responsibility and that the total number of points for all four can be as high as 370 under this plan. This contrasts with a maximum of 75 points for working conditions and 135 points for education. Also weighted heavily is job knowledge, with a maximum of 310 points. In actual job evaluation, of course, the number of points allotted is determined by the degree assigned to the factor. If the actual weights used are short of the maximum allowable, real weighting may be quite different. For example, even if 75 points are allowable for working conditions, the maximum assigned under actual job evaluation may be only 45 points. Furthermore, the question of how much each factor should be weighted is not an easy one. Even more basic is the selection of the factors. Are they the most important ones for the jobs to be measured? Are they objective? Are the specifications of the degrees clear?

Table 3-2 / Point Scale for Factors Used by an Insurance Company for Clerical and Supervisory Workers

	Points per degree							
Factor	1	2	3	4	5	6	7	8
Education	60	75	90	105	120	135		
Job Knowledge	100	130	160	190	220	250	280	310
Contacts with others	50	70	90	110	130	150		
Responsibility for equipment	50	70	90					
Responsibility for checking errors	70	80	90	100				
Responsibility for records or methods	50	65	80					
Supervisory responsibility	20	40	60	80	100			
Degree supervised	50	75	100					
Working conditions	5	15	25	35	45	55	65	75

Table 3-3 shows how some jobs were rated under the plan discussed. Note that the payroll clerk and the senior machine bookkeeper, with the same point total, are rated higher than the file clerk, despite the latter's more arduous working conditions. The difference is made up of higher ratings on three of the four responsibility factors, but particularly by the rating for job knowledge, which is higher by 180 points. Compared to the payroll clerk and the machine bookkeeper, the secretary to the comptroller gets fewer points on supervisory responsibility but makes up for this in part on degree supervised — there is more general supervision of her actions — and also on factors such as education and job knowledge. The top-rated credit supervisor picks up points on supervisory responsibility as well as on working conditions.

Table 3-3 / Point Ratings for Selected Jobs in an Insurance Company[*]

Factor	File clerk	Payroll clerk	Senior machine book-keeper	Secretary to comptroller	Credit supervisor
Education	75	105	105	135	135
Job Knowledge	100	280	280	310	310
Contacts with others	50	50	50	150	150
Responsibility for equipment	50	90	90	50	50
Responsibility for checking errors	80	100	100	100	100
Responsibility for records or methods	65	65	65	80	65
Supervisory responsibility	20	40	40	20	60
Degree supervised	50	50	50	100	100
Working conditions	45	5	5	5	25
TOTAL	535	785	785	950	995

[*] Calculated on the basis of the point scheme shown in Table 3-2.

Factor Comparison Under the factor-comparison method, emphasis is on the factors that make up the job rather than on the job as a whole. Factors typically used are mental requirements, skill, physical requirements, responsibility, and working conditions.[6] Using only a few key jobs, the method attempts to reconcile two often conflicting types of judgment: the ranking of a job by successive factors and the allocation of the total hourly pay rate for each job among components of each factor.

---

[6] For details of the method see Eugene J. Benge, *Job Evaluation and Merit Rating* (Deep River, Conn.: National Foremen's Institute, 1941).

Table 3-4 / Final Average Factor Rankings for Eight Key Jobs

	Factor				
Job	Mental require- ments	Skill	Physical require- ments	Respon- sibility	Working conditions
Senior draftsman	3	4	8	3	8
Machinist	4	3	6	4	7
Maintenance electrician	2	2	4	2	5
Tool and die maker	1	1	5	1	6
Shipping clerk	5	5	3	5	3
Order filler	6	6	7	6	4
Material-handling laborer	8	7	1	7	1
Janitor	7	8	2	8	2

The ranking of jobs by factors for a typical situation is shown in Table 3-4. While the number would be larger in an actual case, the eight key jobs which are listed in the table from highest paid to lowest paid, are enough to illustrate the method. The jobs chosen were believed to be "on the market" — being neither overpaid nor underpaid — and significant with respect to the company's job structure. In discussing the job-ranking method earlier in this chapter we showed how the evaluation committee studied each job, with judgments pooled and averaged. In the factor-comparison method the same thing is done, but separately for each factor rather than for the job as a whole. The data in the table are the final average rankings.

The next step, illustrated in the columns of Table 3-5, is to make a tentative allocation of a portion of the hourly rate among each of the five factors. For example, of the $2.94 rate for the maintenance electrician, the job-evaluation committee finally designated 82 cents as the value of the mental requirements factor. In constructing the new value table, the allocated money values must add across to the hourly rate and must keep the same order shown in the earlier factor-ranking table (Table 3-4). Because of these conflicting requirements, the two jobs of senior draftsman and machinist, which appear in the factor-ranking table, had to be omitted in the value table. In the factor-ranking table, the tool and die maker ranks higher on every factor than the draftsman or the machinist but has a lower hourly pay rate. The same is also true for the maintenance electrician as compared to the draftsman. These conflicts made it necessary to omit two of these four jobs from the value table. The order-filler job, which also appears in the factor-ranking table but not in the value table, was omitted because the value apportionment necessary to satisfy the matrix resulted in money values for some factors that appeared unrealistic in light of the job description.

Table 3-5 / Money Values by Factor for Five of the Jobs Ranked in Table 3-4

| Job | Hourly rate | Value per factor | | | | |
		Mental require- ments	Skill	Physical require- ments	Respon- sibility	Working conditions
Maintenance electrician	$2.94	$0.82	$.0.80	$0.40	$0.76	$0.16
Tool and die maker	2.89	0.88	0.84	0.30	0.82	0.05
Shipping clerk	2.37	0.29	0.29	0.75	0.29	0.75
Material-handling laborer	2.08	0.05	0.12	0.90	0.11	0.90
Janitor	1.81	0.06	0.05	0.83	0.05	0.82

With the data so far adduced one can construct value scales for each of the five factors, as shown in Figure 3-1. Note that, although the scale for each factor extends from 90 cents to zero, the actual spread of values ranges from as wide as 90 cents to 5 cents for working conditions and to as narrow as 90 cents to 30 cents for physical requirements. The scales are not limited as was the case under the point system, with its fixed number of points for each degree. Under the factor-comparison scheme, the scales are far more flexible, and the addition of a new job to the scale requires only job-to-job comparisons with key jobs under each factor. The totals under each factor are then added across to get the hourly rate for the new job. Obviously, the more jobs that are added to the scales, the easier the process becomes; it is getting started that is difficult.

Aside from the greater flexibility of scales, the factor-comparison method has certain other advantages over the point system. The weighting is less arbitrary, being influenced jointly by both the job-ranking process and the spread of money values. The problem of conversion of points to money is eliminated, for the factor-comparison method gives results directly in terms of money rates. On the other hand, it can be argued that there is too much identification with existing money rates and, thus, too strong a tendency to tailor a scheme to present pay levels. This can be overcome by the use of a modification of the per cent method, which develops a system of factor scales using points instead of money values. Use of this approach requires conversion of final point totals into money rates to develop the wage structure in the same way as under the point system.

Figure 3-1 Factor-Comparison Scale for Five Jobs

Scale	MENTAL	SKILL	PHYSICAL	RESPONSIBILITY	WORKING CONDITIONS
$.90	—TOOL AND DIE MAKER		—LABORER		—LABORER
		—TOOL AND DIE MAKER			
	—ELECTRICIAN		—JANITOR	—TOOL AND DIE MAKER	—JANITOR
.80		—ELECTRICIAN		—ELECTRICIAN	
			—CLERK, SHIPPING		—CLERK, SHIPPING
.70					
.60					
.50					
.40			—ELECTRICIAN		
.30			—TOOL AND DIE MAKER		
	—CLERK, SHIPPING	—CLERK, SHIPPING		—CLERK, SHIPPING	
.20					
					—ELECTRICIAN
		—LABORER		—LABORER	
.10					
	—JANITOR				
	—LABORER	—JANITOR		—JANITOR	—TOOL AND DIE MAKER
0					

b. Reclassification

The establishment of job classifications and wage rates payable for the work called for by the respective classifications presupposes that employees will be classified (and paid) properly for the work they do. A continually recurring question during the life of a collective agreement is whether or not given employees are properly classified. Literally hundreds, perhaps thousands, of arbitration cases have presented this kind of issue for decision, and arbitrators are faced with the problem of determining the proper criteria to be used in making their decisions.

INTERNATIONAL HARVESTER CO.

14 L.A. 53 (1950)

Seward, Ralph T., Arbitrator

Early in January, 1949, Mrs. Eileen Breslin, a "Secretary-Stenographer" in the Material Scheduling Department of the Company's West Pullman Works, left her job on a leave of absence and was replaced by Miss Grace Adduci, the grievant. Management took this occasion to reclassify the job from "Secretary-Stenographer" to "Advanced Stenographer," the classification which Miss Adduci had previously held. In this grievance, the Union claims that this downward reclassification was improper and asks that it be annulled. Since, in effect, this would be a holding that Miss Adduci had been promoted to a higher rated classification, the Union asks that she receive a ten percent increase, effective as of the date she replaced Mrs. Breslin, in accordance with Article XII, Section 5(d) of the Agreement.

Job Description

The negotiated job description for the "Secretary-Stenographer" classification reads:

"Perform difficult and confidential clerical and stenographic work for a department head, requiring a course in shorthand and typewriting and previous satisfactory clerical and stenographic experience, duties include receiving and relaying telephone calls, giving personal attention to special confidential assignments and personal appointments, performing miscellaneous clerical tasks, relieving department head of detail matters; and performing related work as assigned."

The negotiated job description of the "Advanced Stenographer" classification reads:

"Take and transcribe accurately varied and rapid dictation. Must be generally familiar with business organization and office routine. Duties may include the filing of letters and other material and/or the performance of a variety of related clerical duties."

Company's Position

The Company states that when the Material Scheduling Department was first established several years ago, the Company placed Mrs. Breslin's job in the "Secretary-Stenographer" classification in the belief that she would be working primarily as the secretary to a department head and that in that capacity she would be required to perform "difficult and confidential clerical and stenographic work" and to give "personal attention to special confidential assignments and personal appointments" within the meaning of the "Secretary-Stenographer" job description. It developed, however, that Mr. Berkery, the head of the Material Scheduling Department, had little or no work that required a confidential secretary. Instead of working exclusively for Mr. Berkery, Mrs. Breslin took dictation from all clerical personnel in the Department and handled departmental routines, such as the maintenance of a tickler file, the typing of reports on departmental forms, the matching and filing of correspondence, the preparation of stencils or dittos, the recording of phone calls, etc.

In September, 1948, the Company decided that the job was overclassified and communicated this opinion to the Union. Knowing that Mrs. Breslin was going to leave at the first of the year, however, the Company chose not to reclassify the job immediately but to wait until her departure. The Company states further that when Mrs. Breslin returns her job will be left in the "Advanced Stenographer" classification but that she will receive her former rate as an "overrate."

Union's Position

The Union contends that as Miss Adduci is admittedly doing all of the work which Mrs. Breslin had done, she has a right to the same classification. It asserts, in the first place, that since no attempt was made to reclassify the job during the three and a half years that Mrs. Breslin performed it, the Company should be held to be estopped from reclassifying it now that Miss Adduci has replaced her.

In the second place, the Union claims that the job properly belongs in the "Secretary-Stenographer" classification. Miss Adduci keeps records of tardiness and absenteeism in the department which are confidential. She takes and relays phone messages. She keeps a vacation chart and makes up vacation notices for the employees in the department and performs whatever other secretarial duties are requested of her by Mr. Berkery. In the opinion of the Union, these duties clearly fall within the "Secretary-Stenographer" job description and are not mentioned even by implication in the "Advanced Stenographer" description.

As no contractual violation has been shown in this case, the grievance must be denied.

NOTES:

(1) Although it is generally agreed, as the instant case indicates, that an erroneous classification may be corrected, the circumstances under which it may be changed are subject to dispute. Umpire Harry

Shulman stated in *Ford Motor Company and UAW,* Opinion A-100 (1944):

I have previously said that it may never be too late to correct an erroneous classification so long as it continues to be erroneous. The passage of time does not by itself necessarily turn an erroneous classification into a right one. But it must be remembered that classifications and rights are not created by nature. They do not have fixed characteristics which are the same in all plants and at all times. Rates and classifications are established by the parties. They are what the parties say they are. They may differ from plant to plant or from year to year. Their characteristics are entirely within the control of the parties.

Now in an organized shop, the classifications and rates may be established by written agreement following collective bargaining. They may be established through negotiation without a written agreement. Or they may be unilaterally installed by the employer and accepted by the union. The acceptance, in turn, may be communicated in writing or orally. Or the acceptance may be manifested merely by non-verbal action, that is, by not protesting and by working under the installed classification and rate for a long enough time to justify the inference that they are mutually regarded as satisfactory and established. Classifications and rates established in any of these ways govern the parties' relations. But they are not immutable. They may be changed at any time in the same ways. And when so changed, the new supplants the old.

The passage of time, then, is of itself not significant. What is significant is the question whether, during that time, the parties have effected a change — by written agreement, by oral expression, or by mutual understanding or acceptance manifested in other ways. Of course, to the extent that an agreement may limit the manner in which changes are to be made as, for example, by written communication only or by specified individuals, such limitations must be respected.

Again, some classifications are established with detailed descriptions of their coverage. Others have only a title and no description of their coverage. In either case, the meaning of the words is frequently subject to dispute. Here again, the passage of time does not of itself fix that meaning. But the parties' actions during such time may resolve the possible disputes and fix the meaning. And their action may be verbal or it may be non-verbal. It may consist merely of acquiescence in a situation, without protest, over such a period of time as to warrant the inference that it is actually accepted as proper.

The important inquiry, then, is whether the classification is right or wrong at the time of challenge in view of the total situation, that is, in view of all that the parties have done. Obviously this involves a question of fact to which each case may provide a different answer. There can be no inflexible rule for all cases, except the rule that each case must be approached sensibly and with the same purpose and method. Beyond that the answer in each case must depend on its own facts.

In *Lockheed Aircraft Corporation,* 23 L.A. 804 (J. Gaffey, 1954), the arbitrator held that employees were not entitled to be reclassified to a higher classification even though they were performing the duties of employees previously classified in the higher-rated classification, because their negotiated job descriptions covered the work. Even where job descriptions are not as specific, if the union does not protest doing such work, an arbitrator may require the union to correct the alleged error in negotiations with the company. *See Pan American Petroleum Corp.,* 21 L.A. 541 (W. McCoy, 1946). On the other hand, even where a contract permits an employer to reclassify, subsequent statements and/or actions may preclude him from doing so. *See International Harvester Co.,* 17 L.A. 98 (R. Forrester, 1951) (negotiator's statement that only a "few" employees would be downgraded erroneous).

(2) *Problems:* Grievants, "Plant Electricians," sought to be reclassified as "Powerhouse Electricians" in order to obtain twenty percent higher wages paid the latter. The job descriptions were identical except that the higher-rated job required the electricians to "install, repair and maintain high voltage equipment." Grievants adduced evidence, uncontroverted by the Company, that (a) both groups had the same level of background experience and qualifications; (b) the "Powerhouse Electricians" spent only one percent of their working time on high voltage equipment and (c) from time to time "Plant Electricians" had worked on high voltage equipment on a temporary basis. Would you reclassify grievants? Why? *Compare International Harvester Co.,* 9 L.A. 965 (J. Lohman, 1948) *with Consolidated Vultee Aircraft Corp.,* 7 L.A. 55 (E. Hale, 1947) *and Florida Power & Light Company,* 14 L.A. 392 (A. R. Marshall, Chm., 1950). Would you allow the employer to adduce evidence that as a practical matter he had assigned only qualified employees as "Powerhouse Electricians" who had worked around the Company's high voltage equipment for at least two years? *See Warren City Mfg. Co.,* 7 L.A. 202 (B. Abernathy, 1947).

c. New or Changed Jobs

Another item which should be on the negotiator's agenda is the problem that, during the life of the contract, it may become necessary or desirable to add new jobs and new classifications (because, for example, of changed procedure or technology) or to change the content of established job classifications. Sometimes the parties, deliberately or otherwise, fail to make any reference to this contingency in the contract. Obviously, the better course is to anticipate the problem and provide for it in the contract, but such provisions require drafting skill due to the contingent nature of future changes. The threshold issue in such cases is whether changes in job description and/or classification can be made unilaterally in the exercise of a management prerogative or whether they must be made by mutual agreement. This question may arise in the absence of contractual provisions or where the contract does not fully cover the subsequent developments.

(1) Unilateral Action

In *Square D Co.,* 46 L.A. 39, 43 (1966), Arbitrator John Day Larkin stated that,

> Changes in methods of operation unless restricted by the agreement, are properly within the prerogatives of management. (*Goodyear Tire & Rubber Co.,* 6 LA 681; *Modern Bakeries, Inc.,* 39 LA 939; and *Hershey Chocolate Corp.,* 17 LA 268.)
>
> The right to establish new jobs, eliminate obsolete jobs, or to combine jobs and classifications, has been recognized as being a part of management's rights where not expressly limited by the parties' agreement. (30 LA 444; 16 LA 955; 25 LA 188; and 8 LA 1040.) Also, it has been recognized generally that, in the absence of contractual restrictions, management may abolish two job classifications and establish a new classification following a technological change in equipment. (*Great Lakes Corp.,* 19 LA 797; *Hewett-Robbins, Inc.,* 30 LA 81.) The same is true where there has been a change in the product, as in the case now before the Arbitrator.

On the other hand, Charles Reynard reasoned in *Pan-Am Southern Corp.,* 25 L.A. 611 (1955) that, "an employer's act of recognizing a union and entering into a contract with it necessarily carries with it, in addition to a surrender of power to deal with any other agent, an obligation to refrain from making major changes in employment conditions and circumstances without consulting with the union." He distinguished those situations where an employer made "minor changes in the methods of conducting his business." Moreover, as Arbitrator Platt indicated in *Copco Steel & Engineering Co.,* 6 L.A. 156 (1947):

> Under the terms of the contract between the parties which recognizes the union "as the sole collective bargaining agency for the employees of the company" . . . as well as under the law

of the land (National Labor Relations Act . . .), an employer is obligated to bargain with the representatives of his employees with respect to changes in wages, hours, and working conditions. *Whittier Mills Co. v. N.L.R.B.*, 111 F(2d) 474. . . . This requirement to bargain clearly includes a situation where, after a contract is entered into, a new or different job is introduced into the plant for which a new rate is to be established. Indeed, collective bargaining does not end with the execution of a contract; the employer's duty to bargain continues during the entire life of the contract, and a breach of this duty during the term of the contract is, in effect, a violation of the contract.

The mere existence of a relevant contract provision is not always dispositive of issues arising out of an employer's unilateral action. Where the contract provided that when job descriptions are changed, "the job description and job evaluation will be reviewed by the company and the union," the arbitrator held the the employer was not *required* to negotiate with or secure agreement from the union with respect to changes in job description, *Diamond Crystal Salt Co.,* 41 L.A. 510 (F. Uible, Chm., 1963). Is the reason obvious? On the other hand, where the contract contained fairly detailed job descriptions but no explicit statement of how this affected management's right to make changes in operational procedures, Arbitrator James Healy held that changes in job content of existing classifications must be negotiated. *Sperry Gyroscope Company,* 30 L.A. 507 (1948). What do these two cases indicate about drafting provisions in regard to "job descriptions" ?

It does not follow that arbitrators will deal with issues arising from "job classification" in the same manner as problems arising from "job descriptions." For example, in a situation where the contract did not expressly freeze classifications, Arbitrator W. McCoy stated that the weight of authority was to imply that the parties intended mutual agreement in regard to classification and wage rates, *Esso Standard Oil Co.,* 19 L.A. 569 (1952). Even where the contract expressly permitted an employer to establish new classifications when there was a substantial change in job content, Arbitrator Autrey held that the company had to prove that here was actually a substantial change before his unilateral action would be sustained, *Bienville Furniture & Mfg. Co.,* 42 L.A. 697 (1964). However, in *VR/Wesson Co.,* 48 L.A. 339 (H. Davey, Chm., 1967) where the contract provided that job classification and wage rates were to be maintained "unless changed by mutual consent of the parties," it was held that this did not preclude the employer from unilaterally creating new job classifications which did not affect existing classifications. Is this decision inconsistent with the prior two cases?

NOTES:

(1) What is the consequence of holding that the rate for a new or changed job as well as other effects on working conditions — *e.g.,* seniority, working hours, and the like — are subject to negotiation? Must an employer withhold making the change until the process of bargaining has been completed? If the parties fail to agree, what then? Is a matter subject to the grievance procedure, including arbitration, when a contract provides that such procedure is limited to disputes concerning the "interpretation or application of the agreement"? What is the authority of an arbitrator in regard to establishing an appropriate wage rate for a new job where the contract provides that "all disputes, differences or grievances which are not satisfactorily settled are subject to binding arbitration"?

(2) *Problem:* In light of the materials and questions raised above, evaluate each of the following contract provisions suggested during negotiations from the points of view of management and union respectively. As a third party neutral, which provisions would be the easiest to construe in arbitration? In this latter respect, what revisions would you make to obviate potential problems?

Example 1

(a) When Management establishes new jobs or positions for which no applicable salary or salary range has been approved,

(b) When Management materially changes job or position responsibilities, or

(c) When Management consolidates jobs or positions,

Management will develop an appropriate occupational salary or salary range for the new or materially modified job or position by the regular procedure in effect in the Company. The appropriate occupational salary or salary range developed will be fully explained to the office grievance committeeman whose agreement thereto will be requested. In the event Management and the office grievance committeeman fail to reach an agreement as to the new or modified occupational salary or salary range, such occupational salary or salary range may be established by Management and the Union may carry the grievance, if any, through all steps of the contract procedure established for the settlement of grievances including arbitration, to determine whether the rate of pay received by employees involved in such occupational salary or salary range is proper, based upon the duties, responsibilities, and the working conditions of the positions involved as compared with the duties, responsibilities, and the working conditions of other salaried positions within the collective bargaining unit. (*Crucible Steel Co.* and *United Steelworkers of America, CIO*)

Example 2

When new jobs are placed in production and cannot be properly placed in existing classifications by mutual agreement, Management will set up a new classification and a rate covering the job in question, and will designate it as temporary.

The temporary rate for such job and a copy of the temporary rate and classification name will be furnished to the Shop Committee.

As soon as possible after machinery and other equipment have been installed, and, in any event, within 30 calendar days after a production employee has been placed on the job, the Shop Committee and the Management shall negotiate the rate and classification, and when negotiations are completed, such classification and rate shall become a part of the local wage agreement, and the negotiated rate, if higher than the temporary rate shall be applied retroactively to the date the production employee started on the job, except that retroactive payment shall in no event exceed 120 calendar days. (*General Motors Corporation* and *United Electrical, Radio, and Machine Workers, CIO*)

Example 3

There shall be a continuing Joint Job Evaluation Committee consisting of ten persons, five designated by the Union and five by the Employer. The Employer's Salary and Wage Administrator shall act as Secretary of the Joint Job Evaluation Committee. When a new job is established, the Secretary will develop a job description and evaluate such job by using the Joint Job Evaluation Manual. The job description and evaluation of new jobs shall be submitted for approval to the Joint Job Evaluation Committee.

The Employer's and the Union's designees on the Joint Job Evaluation Committee shall each vote as a unit on any matter that comes before the Committee. In the event of disagreement on any matter before the Committee, including the question of whether a new job has been or should be established, the matter shall be finally determined by arbitration under the arbitration machinery set forth elsewhere in this Agreement. Such other rules and regulations for the procedure of the Joint Job Evaluation Committee shall be mutually developed by the parties as the necessity therefor arises. *(Sperry Gyroscope Co. and United Electrical, Radio, and Machine Workers, CIO)*

(2) Change in Production Methods

When production methods are changed by improved procedures including technological change, revision of job description and/or classification may be desirable or necessary. The question then arises whether such changes may be made unilaterally by management or must be negotiated. In such determinations, existing contract provisions are critical. Frequently, the parties will make provision for the creation of "new jobs." When a change occurs, the issue will then arise whether a "new job" has been created which involves an evaluation of changes in the nature of the work involved as well as the ultimate product. *Compare Wallace & Tiernan, Inc.,* 39 L.A. 801 (H. Dworkin, 1962) (changed procedures involving same object not new job) *and Magnavox Co.,* 35 L.A. 662 (J. Willingham, 1960) (where no new skills required no new work) *with Peerless Wire Goods Co.,* 49 L.A. 202 (D. Lewis, 1967) (change from manual to automatic process is new job notwithstanding same result). If a job rate is arrived at by "job evaluation," what significance attaches to a change in several of the "factors" of evaluation in determining whether a new job has been created? *See Peerless Wire Goods Co., supra.*

A subsidiary issue of great importance is the effect that changes in production methods have on the work force — for example, elimination of jobs by automation. In the absence of express contract provisions, whether such changes must be negotiated first is not clear. *Compare Oswald Jaeger Baking Co.,* 42 L.A. 945 (P. Marshall, Chm., 1964) (employer has right to make unilateral decision) *with Marble Cliff Quarries Co.,* 47 L.A. 396 (H. Dworkin, 1966) (company must negotiate decision). On the other hand, a clause providing that an employer has the "right to relieve employees from duty because of lack of work, or for other legitimate reasons," has been interpreted to mean that the employer was not required to staff all classifications, *Simoniz Co.,* 32 L.A. 115 (R. W. Fleming, 1959). Provisions authorizing shutdowns, however, have been held not to encompass the elimination of job classifications due to technological improvement even where the decision to do so was made in good faith. *See Marble Cliff Quarries, supra. Compare Great Atlantic & Pacific Tea Co.,* 43 L.A. 353 (M. Volz, 1964) where *reassignment* of an employee to a lower classification due to a change in production methods was permitted without negotiation in the absence of a relevant contract provision because it was not done in bad faith. Even where unilateral termination of jobs is permitted under the contract, an employer may still have to negotiate with the union in regard to new classifications and rates for "new jobs" which may result in mitigating the hardship. *See, e.g., Phoenix Closures, Inc.,* 49 L.A. 874 (J. Sembower, 1967).

NOTE:

Problem: The operation which is involved in this dispute is part of the Company's process for producing great quantities of "screw-on bottle caps." The grievants are Threader Operators who worked at the machines which put the threads on the caps, and whose duty it was to prevent "jams," watch the level of threaded caps on the production lines, and report any machine malfunction. Before the instant grievance, one Threader Operator was assigned to each of the Company's thirty machines until the Company installed automatic controls on the threading machines which utilize electric eyes or pneumatic sensors to stop the machines if caps begin to pile up. At this point the Company unilaterally reduced the number of operators to one for every three machines, and switched the duty of reporting malfunctions to the Machine Operators. The Union is asking that the twenty discharged Threader Operators be reemployed at their old jobs or reassigned with back pay, and that the Machine Operators' job be reclassified. The following contract provisions are relevant:

Article X — Automation

Sec. 1 — Employees who have completed their initial probationary periods shall not be laid off as a result of technological change or automation except that, as provided in (2) herein, employees may accept severance pay on a voluntary basis.

Sec. 2 — In the event it is necessary, in the opinion of the Company, to reduce the number of employees in any classification because of technological change or automation, the reduction shall take place by attrition and/or reassignment of employees in the "affected classification" (the term "affected classification" means both the classifications immediately affected by technological change or automation and all other classifications progressively affected).

Sec. 3 — The Company and Union agree that every reasonable effort shall be made to reduce the impact of loss of employment due to technological change and automation. The Company further agrees to meet with the Union for the purpose of considering the manner in which such changes or improvements may be installed with the least adverse effect on employment opportunities.

Assuming that you, as arbitrator, have jurisdiction over the dispute, would you hold for the Union? What is the threshold issue in analyzing the Company's change in process in light of the contract provisions? *Compare Mackay Radio & Telegraph Co.,* 42 L.A. 612 (A. Koven, 1964) *with Birmingham News Co.,* 49 L.S. 1018 (H. Platt, 1967). *See also Los Angeles Herald Examiner,* 45 L.A. 860 (S. Kadish, 1965).

(3) Appropriate Wage Rate

In considering the relationship between new wage rates and new or changed jobs, a primary distinction should be made between "permanent" and "temporary" transfers. If the transfer is "permanent," a "major" increase in job content will give rise to a commensurate increase in wages. *See National Cash Register Co.,* 40 L.A. 565 (P. Prasow, 1963) (wage increase granted because of greater individual effort); *Weyerhaeuser Co.,* 37 L.A. 323 (H. Dworkin, 1961) (adjusted rate based on increased work load, skill, responsibility and effort); *Robertshaw-Fulton Controls Co.,* 32 L.A. 308 (R. Emerick, Chm., 1959) (greater machine demands). Where skill, physical effort and responsibility remain the same — "minor change" — a wage increase will not be evoked simply because of change in process. *See United States Ceramic Tile Co.,* 35 L.A. 113 (W. Seinsheimer, 1960) (insufficient change in job duties); *Johnson Bronze Co.,* 32 L.A. 216 (S. Wood, 1959) (no appreciable difference in job "factors"). The converse situation, however, is not necessarily true where the job content is diminished or where an employee is transferred due to elimination of a job, that wages will be automatically lowered. *See Davis Co.,* 41 L.A. 932 (J. Holly, 1963) (no right to reduce wage rate after job eliminated since reduction not based on poor performance); *Morgan Engineering Co.,* 36 L.A. 257 (E. Teple, 1960) (employee entitled to maximum rate of new classification or former rate whichever is lower). Furthermore, where jobs are combined, it does not follow that the wage rate will parallel combination of duties. *See, e.g., U.S. Slicing Machine Co.,* 41 L.A. 1076 (J. Willingham, 1963) (employer had right to offer sum less than equivalent of labor grade increment).

On the other hand, where the job transfer is temporary, generalizations about arbitration decisions become attenuated. For example, where an employee temporarily participated in work of a higher rated category, Arbitrator S. Kates held that whether he was entitled to the higher wage depended on actual work done and whether he was a full-time or part-time employee, *Perfection Biscuit Co.,* 49 L.A. 1095 (1967). *See Paul Mueller Co.,* 40 L.A. 780 (R. Bauder, 1963) (for time actually spent); *Courtaulds, Inc.,* 32 L.A. 643 (W. McCoy, 1959) (maximum classification pay rate earned by regular job holders). *Compare Kroger Co.,* 35 L.A. 480 (R. Howlett, 1960) (not entitled to additional pay where employee regularly performed added duties); *Gulf States Utilities Co.,* 43 L.A. 491 (P. Herbert, Chm., 1964) (additional duties contemplated in contract). Where an employee temporarily participated in a lower-rated job, Arbitrator M. Joseph held that he was entitled to overtime computed on the basis of his regular rate, *Mesta Machine Co.,* 35 L.A. 374 (1960).

In some cases arbitrators view the issue as one of balancing wage rates. *See Parker Co.,* 60 L.A. 473 (Edwards 1973) (higher pay to bring grievants to same level denied); and *Penn Dye & Finishing Co.,* 41 L.A. 193 (Abersold 1962) (transfer with "red circled rate" denied). *Compare American Federation of Gov't Employees,* CCH 72-2 ARB ¶ 8467 (Rothschild 1977) (a public sector case where arbitrator ordered discontinuance of series of temporary transfers at lower rates).

B. WAGE SYSTEMS

Once a job has been classified, the manner in which employees assigned to do the job are to be compensated, the type of "wage system" used — single rate, rate range, measured daywork, piecework, incentive, profit sharing and deferred wages — must be considered. Basically, these break down into two groups — those wages which are primarily a function of the amount of time spent on the job (fixed rates), or those, that reflect the worker's contribution to productivity (incentive rates). The choice between these two depends on a host of considerations. For example, as technology advances, production will generally depend on increased "machine work" and less "employee effort." As machines exert a greater degree of control over the rate of production, there is less need for incentive wages. In a highly automated industry, employees will have little or no opportunity to exert control over production, and therefore, less need for incentive systems to encourage them to increase production. However, incentives may be used to elicit a high degree of cooperation and joint effort with management. This idea of making partners of employees has led to the creation of imaginative profit-sharing plans. However, this concept is tempered by two countervailing considerations: (1) the unions' fear that workers may be co-opted into management, and (2) management's attitude that incentive systems mean greater union involvement, may have a "deadening" effect on supervision, and create a built-in resistance to further technological change.

Whichever labor-pricing wage system is agreed to, it is expected to motivate both employers and wage earners toward the best allocation and application of human resources. At the same time, the wage system is expected to maintain stability and to encourage continued growth in our economy. The recent economic fluctuation due to "stagflation" (recession-unemployment-inflation) has brought pressure on the selection of wage systems in order to permit rising scales of living for workers. The student in studying the specific systems is advised to take into account such considerations.

1. Forms of Wage Payments

In the introduction, we stated that the term "wages" would be used in its broad, generic sense — synonymous with all types of compensation for work. However, in any technical discussion of wages and hours, it is necessary to distinguish wage rates from salaries and from earnings. For example, "earnings" normally refer to the end-product of salaries or wage rates and hours. Whereas, "wage rates" are the amount paid employees on an hourly (time) or a piece (unit) rate. "Salaries" are payments calculated and paid on a longer-term basis than wages. Therefore, the form of wage rate must be defined with specificity in the collective bargaining agreement.

In addition, another form of employee compensation is wage rate or salary supplements, which are commonly called "fringe benefits." Actually, as previously indicated, the Chamber of Commerce reports that as of 1975 the costs of these employee benefits, including those required by law, average 35.48% of payroll in 1975 or almost $2.00 per payroll hour.[12] Because of the dollar amounts involved in these salary supplements, it is probably a misnomer to refer to them as "fringes." [13]

Incentive pay systems (which include piecework since earnings are tied to effort) appear in many variations. They run the gamut from the landmark 1948 General Motors/United Automobile Workers settlement which instituted an "annual improvement factor" that ties wages to the growth of the economy as a whole [14] to the Bedaux system which relates extra pay to extra output.[15] They may also include a variety of profit sharing plans.[16]

The point being made is that the variation in forms of wage payments utilized throughout this country is enormous. Limitations of space preclude even a survey of the various wage provisions. Instead, this chapter illustrates the scope of wage and hour clauses, and identifies issues that are likely to arise from pay practices and procedures.

---

[12] 1 C.B.N.C. § 10:401 (11/4/76).

[13] *See e.g.,* D. Allen, Fringe Benefits: Wages or Social Obligations (1964) [hereinafter cited as Fringe Benefits].

[14] *See* J. Henderson, Creative Collective Bargaining 61-63 (Healy ed. 1965).

[15] U.S. Dep't of Labor, Employer Expenditures for Selected Supplementary Compensation Practices for Production and Related Workers in Manufacturing Industries (BLS Bull. 1428, April 1965).

[16] *See e.g.,* 2 C.B.N.C. § 93:971 (6/29/78); American Motors and UAW plan expiring Sept. 1978; and Kaiser — United Steelworkers Plan, Wage and Salary Administration, *supra* note 8 at 123-25.

2. Rate Ranges and Single Rates [17]

Well over one-half of union members are paid a fixed amount per specific time period spent at work.[18] The "fixed rate" system has the advantage to an employer of simplicity in accounting procedure and administration. In addition, employees may prefer a wage that is not directly related to output. On the other hand, a fixed rate makes it more difficult for an employer to project "unit costs," without knowing output, and reward individual effort. In what type of industry would you expect to find "fixed rates" used extensively? Such a system may include a "single rate" wage or a "range" of wage rates for each classification. Where a "rate range" is used, the ranges may *"overlap"* to offer a larger number of "wage grades," facilitate transfers, and accommodate the imprecise distinctions that actually exist between different wage ranges. They may *"abut"* to minimize the number of grades and simplify both the employer's administration and employee expectations. Or there may be a *"gap"* between ranges to provide incentive for promotion between one grade and another. What are the arguments for and against the use of rate ranges, instead of fixed rates, from the employer and employee points of view?
The employee's "merit," length of service or both. In such a system a number of problems have developed due to imprecise contract language and the obvious importance of paying higher wages from the standpoint of all parties concerned.

NOTES:

(1) In *International Harvester,* 13 L.A. 809 (R. Seward, 1949) where the contract provided that employee movement within an established rate range "shall be fair and reasonable, due consideration being given to all proper factors," and a distinction was drawn between lower-rated jobs where the range was narrow and higher-rated jobs where the spread was substantial, the arbitrator indicated that, in the case of the former, little more than "satisfactory" performance should be required for the employee to move to the top of the range; but in the case of the latter, more latitude should be permitted for management to require excellence of performance. Under what circumstances would you expect a union to agree to a large "spread" in rate ranges with movement based solely on merit? When do you expect management to agree to make pay increases automatic? See H. Davey, Contemporary Collective

---

[17] *Compare* Wage and Salary Administration, *supra* note 8 at 39-51, *with* Impact of Collective Bargaining *supra* note 9 at 597-623.
[18] *See* M. Wortman & C. Randle, Collective Bargaining 337 (3d ed. 1966).

Bargaining 264-64 (2d ed. 1959); S. Torff, *Collective Bargaining* 179-81 (1953). Would you anticipate that the trend is toward "merit" or "automatic" progression? What is the significance of decisions upholding increases for "satisfactory" as distinguished from "exceptional" performance? See *The Impact of Collective Bargaining on Management, supra* footnote 9 at 602-06 (1960).

(2) Although management at one time generally assumed that the subject of merit increases within established rate ranges was exclusively a "management function" [see L. H. Hill & C. R. Hook, Jr., *Management at the Bargaining Table* 125 (1945)], *NLRB v. J. H. Allison,* 165 F.2d 766 (6th Cir.), *cert. denied,* 335 U.S. 814 (1948) established the principle that "merit increases" is a mandatory subject of collective bargaining. Where a contract does not expressly exclude the issue, arbitral review of management decisions regarding merit increases was held established under the *Steelworkers Trilogy* cases in *Dahlstrom Mfg. Corp.,* 39 L.A. 90 (C. Duff, 1961).

(3) *Problems:* (a) Where the contract provides that "Company approval of all increases will be based on merit," what showing by the Union will be necessary to reverse a company decision? *Compare Sommers & Adams Co.,* 6 L.A. 283 (D. Whiting, 1947) *with Burger Iron Co.,* 39 L.A. 799 (R. McIntosh, 1962). If language provided that "approval of all increases will be based on merit to be judged by management," would this change the result? *See Atlas Imperial Diesel Engine Co.,* 3 L.A. 1 (G. Gorder, 1946).

(b) Where contract provided that "automatic progression was limited to job rate," can employer unilaterally grant merit increases up to that rate? *Compare General Electric Co.,* 64 L.A. 765 (Schmertz 1975) *with H.K. Porter Co., Inc.*, 55 L.A. 593 (McDermott 1970).

3. Incentive Rates

Incentive wage systems arose from the "management movement" at the end of the nineteenth century which attempted to improve productivity in industrial plants by reducing "factory wastes" — inefficiency, reduced output, and employee ill will — resulting from wage-output discrepancies. Frederick Taylor, "the father of scientific management," conceptualized that the "one best way" for a worker to do his job could be discovered by studying his procedures. For example, the "proper sequence" of a job can be determined by making a "motion study" of the elements of a worker's repetitive operations. After the "proper sequence" is ascertained, a "time study" is used to determine how many units of production each worker should turn out using average effort, in a unit of time, by using the "proper sequence." Once allowances are made for set-up time, breakdowns, fatigue, and personal needs, a rate is applied that gives a worker an incentive to produce at above average effort. Many unions have traditionally opposed "incentive rates" on the grounds that employers use such systems to "speed up" production which results in employee overstrain, fatigue and ill health. They allege that "work stoppages" arise from "sweating labor" and from machine breakdowns and shortage of materials. Further, they challenge the "scientific" precision of evaluating output premised on standardized methods of work and materials. Although employers generally favor the concept of increasing productivity at lower unit costs and rewarding increased efforts, some view incentive systems with less than complete enthusiasm. Employers point out the problems of quality control, difficulties and cost of administration, and resultant eradication of differentials between earnings of incentive and nonincentive or even supervisory employees.[19]

However, although the traditional notion of incentive pay was to offer an extra reward for extra effort, today's incentive payments include bonuses and profit-sharing on the basis of circumstances beyond an individual employee's own effort. Although bonuses and profit-sharing plans might technically fit under wage supplements, "they are treated in the national accounts as part of wages and salaries rather than as supplements." [20] Under this broader usage of the term, many collective bargaining agreements provide bonuses for all, or large groups of employees, small work groups or individual workers.

Incentive wage plans are widely variant in American industry. Basically, they divide into "straight piece-rate" and "modified piece-rate" systems. Typically, they are either "individual" or "group," depending upon whether or not it is feasible to attempt to measure the output of the individual worker. The most common form of incentive plan is the "piecework" system under which employees are paid a designated amount or "price" per piece or unit produced. This system may employ a straight piece rate as the basis of pay, or may use this method in combination with some form of "guarantee" on an hourly or daily basis. The various kinds of plans which are related to the performance of the individual worker can be used only when the worker, with his tools and other equipment, is turning out a product or performing an operation on a product without the assistance of other workers. Many types of operations,

---

[19] S. Torff, Collective Bargaining: Negotiations and Agreements 188-89. *See generally* H. Davey, Contemporary Collective Bargaining ch. 11 (2d ed. 1959); T. Kennedy, Union Policy and Incentive Wage Methods (1944); C. Lytle, Wage Incentive Methods (rev. ed. 1942); F. Moore, Manufacturing Management chs. 27, 29, 30 (3rd ed. 1961); S. Slichter, J. Healy & E. Livernash, The Impact of Collective Bargaining on Management ch. 17 (1960); S. Torff, Collective Bargaining: Negotiations and Agreements ch. 12 (1953); American Management Ass'n, *Planning and Administering Effective Incentives,* Production Series No. 172 (1947).

[20] Wage and Salary Administration, *supra* note 8 at 121.

however, involve the joint contribution of a number of employees working as a group or team. An example would be an assembly line using a number of work stations when the product moves at a fixed speed from one station to the next. If an incentive system is to be used in such cases, it must be one which takes account of the total output of the group.

It is obvious that any incentive system which measures the individual or group output against some "standard" makes the establishment of the job standard a basic and critical factor. The problem is to determine what would be "normal" production — *i.e.,* the amount which will be produced while working at a normal or non-incentive pace. Is there "one best way" of working? What if actual experience prompts the worker to find a better way? Which worker should be studied? Any worker or a skilled worker? For how long? Such a determination is commonly made by an actual "time study" of each job as it is introduced in the plant. How should the results be analyzed? By weighted mean, median or mode? Another more sophisticated approach to such analysis is the development of so-called "standard data" based on past experience in timing job elements or movements. However, job timing, by whatever method used, involves an element of judgment known as "performance rating," since the time-study man must necessarily pass judgment in each instance on the question of whether the operator whose times are being studied is performing at a rate above or below "normal" and apply a factor based on this judgment. This, of course, introduces an element of subjectivity into the process, and is another basis for the union charge that time study is not scientific. Time study also requires that certain so-called "allowances" be made in the determination of standard times to take account of the fact that the worker does not engage in actual productive work throughout the whole of each day, or, for reasons of fatigue, cannot maintain the same pace throughout the day. This means that "down time" resulting from taking care of "personal relief," or obtaining tools, or waiting for machine set-up or parts, etc. must be taken into account. The worker, therefore, must be given credit for these elements in his work day, and this likewise introduces a factor of judgment on the part of the time study man who may be an outsider. In addition to objections arising out of the "subjective" aspect of time and motion studies, unions fear unemployment which may arise from scientific methods which lessen skill, disregard the "human factor" by regarding labor as an appendage of a machine, and reduce the employees' bargaining power. Furthermore, even where an appropriate standard is arrived at, what "wage rate" is to be applied? How are wages to be assessed? What is the impact of market forces on the wage structure? What is the significance of an existing internal wage structure? Perhaps the impediments raised to the establishment of incentive rates indicated by these questions demonstrate the reason for the modern trend toward "non-individualizing" incentives. Once the parties in collective bargaining agree on the installation or continuance of some kind of incentive wage system, the question arises of the extent to which the contract will deal with the numerous problems that arise in the administration of the system. The employer typically will try to maintain freedom to operate the plan without union intervention. The union will ordinarily attempt to include in the agreement limitations on this kind of freedom. The consequences of problems arising under these provisions are vividly illustrated by a Brookings Institution study of "demoralized" incentive plans.[21] In the study the authors point out that a "demoralized wage incentive plan" is not just a poorly-functioning plan; but encompasses substantial inequities in earnings and effort, a growing average incentive yield or bonus, a declining average level of effort, and a high proportion of "off-standard" payment and time. They indicate that a serious demoralization involves poor union-management relations, high rates of grievances, and a continuous use of wildcat strikes and slowdowns. As the authors indicate,

> "Substantial demoralization of an incentive plan results in an unstable situation. It leads eventually to abandonment, revision, or catastrophe. Abandonment or revision may be reasonably smooth or it may be accompanied by major difficulties." [22]

It is important, therefore, that the major agenda items which ought to be on the bargaining table for discussion should include at least the following:

    a. Establishment of Incentive Rates
    b. Revision of Incentive Rates
    c. Changes from One System to Another
    d. Use of Grievances in Administration of Incentive Systems
    e. Other Wage Plans

---

[21] Impact of Collective Bargaining, *supra* note 9 at 497-503.
[22] *Id.* at 503.

a. *Establishment of Incentive Rates*

DEERE & COMPANY
and
INTERNATIONAL UNION, UNITED AUTOMOBILE, AEROSPACE & AGRICULTURAL IMPLEMENT WORKERS OF AMERICA & ITS LOCALS

Agreement (expires 1 Oct. 1970)

[This illustrative and fairly complete contract provision is included to demonstrate a well drafted incentive plan, and, in part, because the plan includes an attempt to describe for the employee the operation of the "standard hour" plan. *Eds.*]

Outline of Plan

Part I — Standard Hour Incentive Plan

A. The Standard Hour Incentive Plan is operated on the principle that the normal non-incentive performance expected of average employees skilled in their assigned tasks is 100% performance.
B. Performance beyond 100% is compensated for on a one-for-one principle and potential earnings on incentive work time where the operator is not limited or restricted by process or machine time is expected to average thirty (30) percent above occupational rate.
C. The unit of measurement in this Standard Hour Incentive Plan is standard hours per 100 pieces or units.
   1. Standard hours per 100 pieces or units is the unit of time measuring the quantity of work that must be produced in order to earn the equivalent of the occupational rate.
   2. "Standard hours per 100 pieces or units" are referred to as "incentive standards" or "standards."
D. To compute incentive earnings under this Plan the following steps are required. First, multiply the production in pieces or units on each operation by the appropriate standard to arrive at earned hours. Earned hours are then multiplied by the occupational rate to calculate incentive earnings.

How to Figure Earnings on the Standard Hour Incentive Plan

1st Step

No. of Pieces Produced	X Multiply	Inc. Std. Expressed in Std. Hrs. Per 100 Pcs.	= Equals

2nd Step

Hours Earned	X Multiply	Occupational Rate	= Money Earned

E. The standard hours per 100 pieces or units are established from time study or from data (either standard data or plant data) at the level of 100% performance as explained in Part II, and include the allowances explained in Parts III, IV, and V.

F. The incentive earnings of an employee on any given job will be in proportion to his rate of production, except that the minimum pay for incentive employees shall be the occupational rate as set forth in "1" below.

   1. The employee is guaranteed earnings for the day equal to hours worked times the occupational rate or rates appropriate for the work performed during the day.

G. Where an incentive standard is found to be in error due to arithmetical errors in calculation of the incentive standard or clerical errors in the transferring and posting of the incentive standard, such errors shall be corrected.

H. When standard hours per 100 pieces or units for an operation are to be changed on the basis of changes in the operation, time studies may be made of the complete operation, but any revision either by the time study or by the application of data shall apply only to the changed or affected part of the operation.

I. There shall be no ceiling on earnings.

Part II — Performance Rating

A. It is recognized that it is impractical to select an operator to be time studied who will be the average skilled operator. It is also recognized that any operator may possess varying degrees of skill on various work elements and also may work with varying degrees of performance during the time study.

B. It is a principle of this Plan to adjust observed time to normal time. The time study engineer through special training and experience adjusts the observed time by means of factors (as illustrated below) applied from observation of the work elements performed by the employee.

C. These factors will be shown on the time study according to a scale in which 100% indicates normal performance, 105%, 110%, 115%, etc., would indicate progressively higher performance while 95%, 90%, 85%, etc., would indicate lower performance. If the actual time in decimal minutes of an element is given a performance rating of 110%, it means that in computing his study the time study engineer will increase the actual minutes 10% to arrive at the normal time for the operation. Actual time with a 90% performance rating will be reduced to 90% of the actual time to arrive at the normal time.

D. Where time values are established by time study, the performance rating will be made during the observation and the time study engineer will, upon request, indicate the performance rating to the employee.

Part III — Personal and Fatigue

A. Standard hours per 100 pieces or units include percentage factors to provide for necessary personal and fatigue delays. Because an individual tends to recuperate from fatigue during time taken from work for personal needs, it is impossible to separate the allowance for personal needs from the allowance for fatigue where both are present. Therefore, these are combined into one percentage factor.

B. The personal and fatigue percentage factors cover such items as rest or recuperation, the fifteen (15) minute short lunch and rest period, getting a drink, preparing the Daily Work Record, using the toilet, etc. The minimum personal and fatigue percentage factor applied on work elements (not on waiting time) is 10% and provides approximately 44 minutes per eight (8) hour day.

C. The personal and fatigue percentage factor covers the general range of motions included in work elements for factory operations and is based on experience and judgment as conditioned by the findings of various tests and experiments made to determine fatigue factors adequate for an average operation. Beginning with a minimum of 10%, the personal and fatigue percentage factors increase depending upon the type of work being performed.

D. This minimum of 10% coupled with a minimum of 3% job delay equals a minimum delay factor of 13.3% on any work element.

Part IV — Operator Waiting Time (Machine or Process)

A. The amount of time that an operator must wait for his machine(s) or process(es) after he has completed the work that can be performed during the machine element or process cycle of the operation may be computed by either the Inherent Delay Formula or the Work Assignment Factor Formula.

1. *Inherent Delay*

The Formula:

Inherent   Machine   (Std. Min.)
Delay   =   Element or x * 1.08 minus "R" Work Element Time
(I.D.)   Process Cycle   **1.30
           Time "MT"

*The Machine Element or Process Cycle Time and the "R" Work Element Time must be converted to standard minutes. To convert Machine Element or Process Cycle Time to standard minutes, it is multiplied by 1.08. Since there is limited fatigue in a machine element or process cycle time, only an 8% personal and fatigue percentage is allowed instead of the 10% minimum personal and fatigue percentage factor for work elements mentioned under Personal and Fatigue.

**The application of this Inherent Delay formula provides for incentive earnings on work elements performed during the running time of the machine or process. When an operator performs work elements ("R" Work Element Time) during the running time of the machine or process ("MT" Machine Element or Process Cycle Time) the time to be subtracted from the Machine Element or Process Cycle standard minutes will be the sum of the "R" Work Elements Time (Std. Minutes) divided by 1.30. This gives the operator an extra allowance for the work he performs during the Machine Element or Process Cycle. An allowance of 10% is added to the inherent delay to provide a minimum incentive possibility of 110%. The total standard minutes is then the sum of the total standard work minutes and inherent delay minutes.

2. *Work Assignment Factor*

The Work Assignment Factor primarily provides a guide in scheduling combination work assignments that will most fully utilize the operator's time and thereby eliminate or reduce operator's waiting time. The Work Assignment Factor allows a continuation of incentive opportunity if one or more of the machines in a battery becomes inoperable or if a combination of operations is changed for any reason, including the assignment to it of one or more untimed operations.

The sum of the Work Assignment Factors subtracted from 1.00 is the percentage of operator waiting time in a particular combination assignment.

The Formula:

Work Assignment = "D" + "R"
Factor   1.30   x .9 ("UF")
                        ─────────────
                         "D" + "MT"   x 1.08
                        ─────────────
                            1.30

Part V — Job Delay

A. Job delays refer to unmeasurable, miscellaneous work or interruptions not directly related to the number of pieces or units produced. Each such delay which equals or exceeds six (6) minutes (.1 of an hour) will be paid for at the occupational rate of the job being performed provided the delay is recorded on the Daily Work Record, or other approved form, and is approved by the foreman. Job delays of less than six (6) minutes are not accumulative throughout the day.

B. The job delay factor is applied to the total standard minutes in determining the standard hours per 100 pieces or units for an operation. These factors are used to compensate for job delays of less than six (6) minutes.

1. The following list illustrates the types of delays covered by these job delay factor percentages. This list, of necessity, does not include all delays but illustrates the type of delays covered by our job delay factors.

(a) Change from one operation to the next; contact foreman, clerks, inspectors, etc. about job; check orders and order stock; prepare and arrange work area and material; remove or replace protective equipment; put on and remove items such as apron, gloves, glasses, leggings, paint protection, etc.; start or stop equipment; get and check supplies, tools, prints, etc.; check work and equipment; sort, count, and record parts; punch job clock and/or record time, get tools, job, trucks, tractor, stock, oiler, supplies, etc.; move skids, change loads.

(b) Attention to equipment and process — Adjust and make minor repairs to tools and equipment; get oil, oil equipment; mechanical or electrical difficulties; add coolant, thinners, and processing materials; check and maintain set-up — alignment of jigs, fixtures, gauges, resetting stops; remove shavings.

(c) Start or end of shift — Start or stop equipment; open and close windows; turn lights on and off; clear right of way; get and check equipment; clean equipment and work place.

2. These job delay percentage factors have been determined through detailed delay studies on a large number of factory operations and from knowledge gained through years of

experience. Where an operator runs a single machine, the job delay factor amounts to four percent, in most cases, and where an operator tends machines in battery or operates two units, such as a furnace and press, the job delay factor amounts to six percent, in most cases.

C. Elements of work and/or interruptions that occur at a frequency directly related to the number of pieces or units produced but do not occur each cycle are not covered by the job delay factor and should be handled as follows:
1. Prorate the time for the element(s) into the incentive standard for the operation, if:
(a) The occurrence covered by the element(s) requires less than six (6) minutes (7.80 standard minutes) to perform, or
(b) The occurrence occurs at least once per shift.
2. Establish a separate incentive standard for the occurrence, if:
(a) Six (6) minutes (7.80 standard minutes) or more is required by the occurrence and it occurs less than once per shift.
3. Pieces or units produced refer to the unit covered by the incentive standard such as productive pieces or assemblies, setups, job changes, etc.
4. The occurrence referred to in this Paragraph C may be made up by an element(s) of work as referred to above or an interruption as referred to above or by a combination of such an element of work and such an interruption if they occur in sequence.

Part VI — Terminology with Definitions

Combination work assignments are described as:

I. *Batteries*

A. *Machine Tool Batteries*
Two or more machine tools operated by one operator as a combination work assignment. At least one of the machine tools must continue the machining cycle while the operator works or waits at the other machine tool or performs any other work.

B. *Other Batteries*
1. Where the operator of a machine tool performs work at a machine or performs any other work during the machine tool machining cycle.
2. Where the operator of a machine performs work at at another machine or performs any other work during the machine cycle.
3. Where the operator of processing equipment performs work at a machine or performs any other work during the processing cycle time.

II. *Other Combination Work Assignments*

Where one operator performs two or more operations, none of which continues its machining or processing cycle while the operator works at the other operations.

"MT" Machine Element or Process Cycle Time: Elapsed running time for the machine or process controlled elements.

"R" Work Element Time: Standard time in minutes for the elements of work that may be performed during the running time of the machine or process.

"D" Work Element Time: Standard time in minutes for the elements of work that must be performed while the machine or process cannot be in operation.

(I.D.) Inherent Delay: The amount of time in standard minutes that an operator must wait for his machine or process after he has completed the work that can be performed during the machine element or process cycle of the operation.

"WAF" Work Assignment Factor: The percentage that the manual work is of the floor-to-floor cycle modified by the utilization factor.

"UF" Utilization Factor: Compensates for the additional operator waiting time which results from two or more machines being ready to be serviced simultaneously or of no machine being ready to be serviced because of variations in the floor-to-floor cycle time of the different operations run in the combination.

Machine Tool: A non-portable power-driven machine for milling, planing, turning, grinding, boring, drilling, sawing, or otherwise changing the material or parts by removing metal in the form of chips, fragments, spiral shavings or the like.

Machine (Other Than Machine Tools): A non-portable power-driven device for cutting, shearing, punching, straightening, forming, or otherwise working on and modifying material or parts.

Processing Equipment: Powered equipment that subjects material or parts to a process or treatment in the course of manufacture that is not intended to change the size or shape of the material or part. Examples are heat treat furnaces, wheelabrators and flow coat painting.

NOTE:

Problem: "Downtime": The existing labor agreement provides:

1. The determination of piece rates is a function of management. Piecework earnings shall be calculated on a daily basis. No piecework employees will be paid less than the basic hourly rate for the piecework job times the number of hours worked on such piecework job in any given day.

2. Workers employed on piece rated jobs who lose production for as much as thirty minutes, during their shift, due to no fault of their own, because of machinery breakdown, shortage of materials, power interruption, and the like, shall be paid for all time lost at their "regular rate" based on their previous full day worked, provided they are kept on the job.

The Union claims that grievants suffered a loss of earnings for several weeks while the machines they worked on were shut down for cleaning, and that in each instance the shutdown was for more than thirty minutes. The Company denied the grievance because (a) all claimants had earned over the base rate for the days when the shutdown occurred; (b) when the base rate was figured, allowance was made for cleaning the machines as "down time"; and (c) cleaning was a "shutdown" and not a "breakdown." Are the Company's grounds sound in light of the above contract provisions? *Compare Goodyear Clearwater Mills, Inc.,* 8 L.A. 653 (W. McCoy, 1947) *with Armour & Co.,* 9 L.A. 899 (H. Gilden, 1948). *See Stubnitz Spring Division,* 46 L.A. 557 (V. Stouffer, 1966) for an example of how "down time" is computed.

If you were to sustain the Union's grievance presented in the problem, would you award the employees their "average incentive earnings" for the previous day as their "regular rate"? *Compare Peoria Malleable Castings Co.,* 43 L.A. 722 (J. Sembower, 1964) *with Armour & Co.,* 5 L.A. 641 (C. Kerr, 1946). One authority has argued that "average earnings" provisions can never be justified, because they endanger the long run health of an incentive system. Do you agree? What are the contrary arguments?

b. Revision of Incentive Rates

Revision of rate structures conceptually breaks down into two major subdivisions. The first deals with "permanent" revision of wage rates; the second, with "temporary" changes that occur when incentive-rated employees are temporarily transferred to "non-incentive" work.

(1) Permanent Revision

Changes in production methods create pressure to revise wage rates. Where the contract was silent on the right of the company to change an incentive rate upon the installation of new machinery, Arbitrator Dudley Whiting said, ". . . all impartial authorities agree that a change in production method or equipment is cause for a restudy and rate adjustment," *Reliance Mfg. Co.,* 3 L.A. 677 (1946). In *A.C.L. Haase Co.,* 17 L.A. 472 (W. Townsend, 1951), the contract provided: "As thus increased, the wage rates of all employees covered by this agreement shall continue to remain in effect without change for the remainder of the term covered by this agreement." However, the arbitrator still permitted readjustment reasoning that the effect of the change was to establish a new job classification which did not constitute a change in wage rates applicable to previously established job classifications. The legal rationale of this decision was that where two parties enter into a contract with the mutual assumption of the existence of a basic fact (method of operation), a change which eliminates this fact discharges the contract (allows for rescission of the contract provision). What is the significance of management's right to establish wage rates initially? *See United States Steel Corp.,* 39 L.A. 4 (S. Garrett, Chm., 1962); *National Lock Co.,* 18 L.A. 459 (B. Luskin, 1952). Does it follow that where changed methods result in increased productivity without increased employee effort, an employer may unilaterally reduce rates or increase standards? *See Thor Power Tool,* 32 L.A. 383 (P. Prasow, 1959) (reduction of piece rates); *Libbey-Owens Ford Glass Fibres,* 31 L.A. 662 (D. Crawford, 1958) (change of standards). *Compare Monarch Machine Tool,* 38 L.A. 1068 (W. Seinsheimer, 1962) (strong management rights clause permits employer to combine certain operations) *with John Deere Tractor Co.,* 2 L.A. 469 (C. Updegraff, 1954) (employer not permitted to assign one man work formerly done by two). Changes in job content are sometimes minute and as such *de minimis,* but cumulatively, may be "substantial." *See Maytag Co.,* 18 L.A. 164 (P. Kelliher, 1952), applying a 4% criterion to such changes. Even though prospective drafting may limit such problems, the impact of "past practice" on wage revision should be kept in mind. *See A. O. Smith Corp.,* 40 L.A. 1107 (P. Lehoczky, Chm., 1963) (employer precluded from recapturing technological improvements); *John Deere Waterloo Tractor Works,* 18 L.A. 276 (H. Davey, 1952) (unilateral decision to stop payment requires substantial justification).

In addition to changes in production methods, pressure for permanent revision of wages may arise from either an initial mistake in the time study or application of the wrong rate. For example, Arbitrator Sidney Cahn allowed revision where the employer did not properly evaluate the machine operator's skill in making the time study in *Singer Mfg. Co.,* 32 L.A. 640 (1959). B. Meredith Reid similarly allowed revision even where the operators had separately evaluated handicraft skills, *O. Hommel Co.,* 45 L.A. 999 (1965). Adjustment will be allowed due to error in computation. *See Wooster Sportswear Co.,* 45 L.A. 1015 (H. Dworkin, 1965) (overpayment for several months); *Orr & Sembower Inc.,* 43 L.A. 33 (J. Seidenberg, 1964) (inadvertent arithmetical mistakes); *The Raytheon Co.,* 39 L.A. 640 (P. Pigors, 1962) (correction permitted after 27 months).

(2) Temporary Revisions

When an employee is mandatorily transferred to a non-incentive job, the issues are whether the employer had a right to make the transfer, and of greater relevance here, what the rate of pay should be. Whether such transfers are permitted will turn on specific contract language. *See Bucyrus-Erie Co.,* 37 L.A. 681 (J. Blair, 1961) (contract did not require that incentive worker be assigned only to incentive jobs). In addition to specific provisions, the rate at which he will be paid may turn on the longevity of the transfer [*Cameo Curtains of New Bedford,* 34 L.A. 488 (A. Zack, 1960)], and whether such transfers are for the employer's convenience [*International Shoe Co.,* 35 L.A. 265 (J. Larkin, 1960)].

NOTE:

Problem. The relevant contract provision provided that,

> Employees performing non-incentive work in a department which is performing on an incentive basis, shall participate in the incentive plan on the basis of average group incentive earnings when said employees are required to feed materials directly to production workers; this work having a definite bearing upon the production performance of the group. All other employees shall be paid at the base hourly rate.

The Company takes the position that no employees should be entitled to participate in "group incentives" under the contract unless they are engaged in "hand-to-hand feeding" with incentive workers. Accordingly, it has denied a grievance of two groups of employees. The first group is engaged in "banking" raw materials on tables in proximity to the incentive workers who process such materials. The normal "bank" provides incentive workers with sufficient materials to do four hours work. The second group of employees takes sufficient material from the "bank" and places it on the incentive workers' benches to keep them busy for thirty minutes. However, neither group hands the material directly to incentive workers. As arbitrator, would you sustain the Company's denial? *See Chris-Craft Industries,* 45 L.A. 955 (A. Koven, 1965).

c. Changes From One Incentive System to Another

The administration of incentive plans can lead to many grievances. As arbitrator Ralph Seward noted in *Bethlehem Steel Co.* 31 L.A. 20 (1958),

> An incentive plan can hardly encourage an employee to increase his production, if he does not understand it; if he does

not know what standards he should meet or how accurately his time is being recorded; if he sees no clear relationship between his output and his earnings or feels that his efforts are being nullified by the poor performance of others. In the opinion of the Umpire, however, these Union complaints have to do, not with the design of the plan, but rather with its administration. The time standards themselves are not complex. The confusion has arisen because the employees were not always informed what the standards were before they started work.

NOTES:

Problem: (a) *Changes from One Incentive System to Another:* What if a contract provision authorizes the employer to *cancel* the incentive plan and the employer *changes systems* which results in a substantial downward revision of employee earnings? Does the change fall within the provision? *Compare Bucyrus-Erie Co.,* 39 L.A. 193 (P. Marshall, 1962) *with American Welding & Mfg. Co.,* 45 L.A. 812 (H. Dworkin, 1965) (where contract provided "all existing incentive plans to remain in effect absent mutual agreement" and a unilateral change resulted in wage improvement).

(b) *Change from Incentive to Fixed Rate System:* The employer installed new equipment which resulted in a substantial change in job duties and greatly increased productivity without a commensurate increase in employee effort. The employer unilaterally took the employees involved off the "incentive plan" and switched them to an "hourly rate" which did not decrease their earnings. However, the union filed a grievance under the following contract provision:

> "Where new or changed conditions result from either improved methods or changes in methods, equipment, or manufacturing processes, the Company shall adjust existing incentives or shall establish new incentive plans."

Should the Union's grievance be sustained? *Compare Carrollton Mfg. Co.,* 47 L.A. 1157 (C. Duff, 1966) *with American Radiator & Standard Sanitary Corp.,* 38 L.A. 991 (P. Herbert, Chm., 1962). *See International Harvester Co.,* 21 L.A. 124 (D. Cole, 1953) where the contract was silent as to changes in systems.

(c) *Change from Fixed Rate to Incentive System:* The employees had been paid on a fixed rate basis as provided for two of the three year term of the contract. However, the contract was silent as to the right of the employer to change from one system to another except for a "reopener provision" which stated that the employer could reopen the agreement upon 60-day notice to the Union. After giving the Union the appropriate notice, the employer unilaterally terminated the fixed rate system, and established an incentive plan which provided for higher wages for increased production but guaranteed the existing rate as a minimum. The Union filed a grievance contending that the notice provision was intended to insure joint negotiations of any change in system which the employer institutes. Should the Union's grievance be sustained? *Compare Ingersoll Rand Co.,* 42 L.A. 965 (D. Scheiber, 1964) *with Waukesha Bearing Corp.,* 33 L.A. 831 (M. Slavenye, Chm., 1959).

d. Use of Grievances in Administration of Incentive Systems

OWEN FAIRWEATHER, COLLECTIVE BARGAINING AND INCENTIVE SYSTEMS[23]

The maintenance of a sound incentive system is often essential to the company's survival. In many industries the competitive advantage of one company over the others is only found in the effectiveness of its incentive program. If such a company's incentive program gets out of gear, costs will "go to pieces" and the company starts to sink competitively.

From the viewpoint of our national economy the maintenance of sound incentive systems is equally important. If the attack by labor unions develops pressures which, when brought to bear against incentive programs, causes them to break down, the productivity per hour of our industrial system will go down. Stated another way, this is the same thing as saying that the maintenance of good incentive systems is one of the essentials to the maintenance of a high national standard of living.

In plants where employees work under incentives, the establishment of incentive standards is the activity around which much of the day-to-day labor relations problems revolve. This is perfectly natural. The incentive standards determine the compensation which the employee receives and the effort he must put forth. Employees naturally desire to receive more pay for less work — this is an understandable human motivation. Unfortunately, however, we find the labor unions will cater to this natural desire and charge that incentive systems are designed to "get more work" for less pay and hence are "speed ups" unfair to the employee. . . .

All thoughtful managements who operate plants with incentive systems know all this and attempt to adopt for themselves a plan to protect their system from the injury which could result if those who attack the system can turn their attacks into destructive restrictions. Let us look at some of these efforts by managements and attempt to appraise their effectiveness.

---

[23] Address before the Industrial Management Society 18th Annual Clinic, Nov. 10-12, 1954, Chicago, Illinois.

Plan 1: *Reserving to Management the Final Determination over Incentive Standards*

One position that managements often take can be stated something like this:

> We establish the incentive standards. The Union can't promise us extra effort upon the part of each individual employee. The incentive standard provides an earnings opportunity over and above the wage structure which we negotiated with the Union. Hence, incentive standards are something personal between the company and the individual employee. If the individual employee doesn't believe the standard is fair, he, or the Union can file a grievance on his behalf, but such grievance cannot go to arbitration. Since we, the management, are providing this "extra" earnings, we should have the final say.

The Union representatives say in turn

> If that is the position you take, we want the right to strike if you don't establish an incentive rate to our satisfaction.

Management might then say quietly to itself:

> The employees won't strike over every incentive standard which we establish. If we can keep the final say, we will, in fact, keep control of our incentive system.

The unions, at least many of them, don't disagree with such a view. Many unions don't believe incentive disputes should be submitted to arbitration. Such unions, however, want to retain a specific right to strike over such disputes. Particularly is such a position typical of the UAW-CIO. The UAW's position is used to illustrate union attitudes toward incentive systems and the handling of incentive disputes because when it comes to incentive problems it is likely the most sophisticated large union as it represents employees in many metal fabricating plants where incentives of all types are used extensively.

However, the union's basic reasons for not desiring to arbitrate incentive standards are somewhat different from those of the management. First, the union wants to bargain over incentive rates. Solomon Barkin, a very articulate union spokesman, who is Research Director of the Textile Workers Union, CIO noted the contrast between the union and the management approach when he said:

> Unions and workers seek to ... be in a position to secure additional wage concessions in the negotiation of work standards.

Management tends to be in a better bargaining position if the standards are predetermined and a fixed wage relationship set for different levels of application.

Unions, therefore, prefer to retain opportunities for negotiations on the individual job.

If a dispute can go to arbitration, a pattern of decision might be established which might limit its ability to "bargain up" incentive standards. Retaining the right to bargain and if need be to strike over incentive rates disputes permits more "gains" to be made, the union believes, and gains are needed to maintain a cohesive interest in the union.

The difficulty with this "retention of final control" approach to the protection of an incentive system is that it surrounds the incentive system with an atmosphere of contest. "The employee must 'take it' or strike" position, which may not be expressed but is still the underlying fact, confronts the employees with a dilemma. They feel trapped. The creation of such a dilemma surrounds the system with emotional tensions which are not conducive to the development of the truly correct attitudes toward incentive compensation. These tensions can build up and can become very deep seated. The Union can then stimulate these tensions and beliefs simply by using slogan phrases such as "speed up," "chiseling," "man killing rates" and so forth with the result that the attitude of the employees toward the incentive system disintegrates even more.

Under such a plan the company might stay in the "driver's seat" for a period of time. However, when collective bargaining time rolls around again, the union will be in a better position to build up a strike pressure and bring it to bear at the conference table to obtain restrictive contract clauses. If the management concedes the restrictions, the battle to protect the incentive system will be over. The refusal to submit incentive disputes to arbitration — a position adopted to keep the incentive ship afloat — may cause the frustrations that build into destructive pressures which when released may ultimately cause the incentive ship to sink.

Plan 2. *A Willingness to Arbitrate Incentive Disputes May Actually Protect the Incentive System*

We have as the other alternative the idea that we should submit incentive disputes to arbitration. When a company is willing to do this it can counteract the sloganized attacks of "speed up" and "chiseling" by replying: "Let's find out if what you say is true; we will submit the question in dispute to an impartial outsider."

However, to the suggestion that incentive disputes be arbitrated, many managements will reply: "The whole idea seems all right — but few of the recognized arbitrators are industrial engineers and the union wouldn't agree to arbitrate such disputes before an industrial engineer from a management consulting firm. Since we couldn't find an industrial engineer who was mutually acceptable, we don't think we should submit our incentive disputes to arbitration."

Such belief seems reasonable on the surface, but a fundamental and deep-seated problem is revealed by such a position. If a management believes that it cannot convince an impartial arbitrator of the fairness of an incentive standard because he is not an industrial engineer, it is admitting that it can't convince just ordinary fair-minded people that an incentive standard is fair. If that is true, how can management convince its employees and the union leaders who are not trained industrial engineers that an incentive standard or its incentive system is fair? That really puts the question.

The Proof of the Fairness of an Incentive Rate

The question is: Do managements have techniques which are good enough to convince all comers that its incentive system is fair and that an individual incentive standard has been correctly established? If managements have those techniques, then it should be in a position to prove that it has been fair and should be willing to agree to submit incentive disputes to lay arbitrators — lay in the sense that they are not industrial engineers.

Companies that have taken this step — have agreed to submit incentive disputes to arbitration — which they have done after some soul searching and worry, have immediately set about to develop the methods of proof which would be needed to establish the fairness of an incentive standard in an arbitration case. They have also re-inspected much more critically the provision of their labor agreement. As their techniques improve and the labor agreement provisions become more sound in theory and clearer in language, they find that their ability to "sell" incentive standards to employees and to the union leaders increases and thereupon the need to resort to arbitration to resolve incentive disputes actually diminishes.

Our task, therefore, is to examine some of the provisions of labor agreements concerning incentive rate establishment, not so much in detail but in concept, and then to consider some of the methods of proof that can be used if a dispute over an incentive standard reaches arbitration.

NOTE:

It should be noted that there are other attitudes about the use of arbitration in the administration of incentive plans. *See* Davis, *Incentive Problems,* in Management Rights and the Arbitration Process, Proceedings of Ninth Annual Meeting of National Academy of Arbitrators 50-53 (McKelvey ed. 1956), for discussion of different views.

e. Other Wage Plans [24]

The incentive systems previously discussed generally are designed to directly reward an individual employer or group of employees for unit increases in output. There are, however, a number of other plans which aim at spurring productivity by promising increased wages, but which depart from the typical incentive system by providing formal channels for union-management cooperation and by giving all workers a greater wage return as the company's overall competitive posture improves. Space precludes coverage of the myriad "bonus-type" wage plans. J. Henderson, Creative Collective Bargaining (Healy ed. 1965) discusses many types of wage systems. Where the employee's reward is based on factors beyond the company's competitive posture, we will cover the plans either under the following subsection [C] or the subsection [D] on wage supplements.

C. CONTRACTUAL PROVISIONS FOR UNIFORM ADJUSTMENTS IN RATES ON WAGE COVERS

After the parties agree in collective bargaining negotiations on the general wage level and structure and on interclassification differentials, they should, if they are well advised, consider next the desirability of incorporating in their agreement provisions which will spell out their rights with respect to wage questions which may arise during the life of the agreement. To settle upon a given wage rate level and system is to dispose of the essentials of the wage problem in the framework of facts existing at the time. But, conditions may change, and, in any case, problems may arise concerning the application of the wage system to individual employees. Accordingly, a most important function of an advisor to either party in negotiations is to anticipate the kinds of problems which can arise and to assist in reaching a satisfactory agreement on the disposition of such problems. Four methods of dealing with mid-contractual wage levels will be discussed — Deferred Wage Increases, Wage Reopeners, Cost-of-Living Provisions, and Annual Improvement Factor Provisions.

---

[24] *See* M. Wortman & C. Randle, Collective Bargaining 139-42, 446-48; S. Slichter, J. Healy & E. Livernash, The Impact of Collective Bargaining on Management 864-78. For an excellent discussion of labor-management cooperation *see* D. McGregor, The Human Side of Enterprise (1960).

One question which should be faced is whether the contract should make wage rates "firm" for its duration (*e.g.*, by use of "zipper clause") or should provide for the possibility of interim changes in the wage level. Obviously, the length of the contract term will be an important consideration. "Long term" contracts (for three or more years) are fairly common, and frequently — perhaps usually — contain some kind of provision for interim readjustment of the wage level. Such provisions are especially likely to be included to take account of the fact that the parties otherwise lose the opportunity to seek a normal periodic reassessment of the question of the wage level in relation to those criteria deemed relevant. The union is likely to be the moving party in the demand for provisions for interim adjustment, especially in a period of rising prices.

1. Deferred Wage Increases

The most common method of settling these issues is to provide for deferred wage increases — *i.e.*, increases to take effect at a specified time or times during the life of the agreement. As BNA states:

> Provision for general wage increases during the life of the contract remains of prime importance at the bargaining table. The cost-of-living escalator, often in combination with specified deferred increases, is increasingly common in almost all industries as the wage reopener has declined in favor.
>
> . . . .

Provisions For Wage Adjustment

(Frequency Expressed as Percentage of Contracts *)

	Deferred Increases	Cost-of-Living Increases	Reopeners
Overall Frequency	88	36	8
Manufacturing	91	43	8
Nonmanufacturing	81	20	7

* Many contracts contain more than one type of provision

Deferred increases, such as annual improvement factors and productivity increases, were provided in 87 percent of contracts in effect in 1970 and 88 percent in 1973. Deferred increases are provided in 91 percent of manufacturing contracts and in 81 percent of nonmanufacturing.

Ninety-four percent of deferred increases become effective at the beginning of the second year or, if more than one is provided, at yearly intervals. Five percent are granted on a semi-annual basis. The rest are effective at quarterly intervals or are granted at widely varying intervals.

The amount of increase is specified in almost all contracts (99 percent) that provide deferred increases. A small number require the employer to pay wages paralleling those paid by major employers in similar industries in the area.[25]

In fact, the median deferred wage increase perpetuated for 1978 is 6%.[26] In 1977 the deferred wage figure amounted to almost 37 cents per hour.[27]

2. Wage Reopeners

As indicated, if the parties desire more flexibility to protect themselves against unforeseen changes in conditions, they may expressly provide for mid-contractual wage negotiations by the use of wage reopener provisions. However, such clauses have given way to deferral wage increases combined with cost-of-living provisions. Where used, the parties should consider the following agenda items:

    a. Notice and no-strike requirements;
    b. Circumstances that trigger reopener provision; and
    c. Scope of negotiation after reopening.

3. "Cost-of-Living" Provisions

Cost-of-Living" provisions appear in over one-third of all contracts, which indicates a substantial increase in the last decade.[28] Mr. John Zalusky, an AFL-CIO economist explained why: [29]

> **Every day in recent years,** the American worker has been confronted by inflation. The paycheck doesn't go as far as it did when his union negotiated the new pay rate. Since most workers have limited means of dealing with inflation, in the short run, they must cut their standard of living or win an increase in pay. One of the ways American workers have developed to cope with inflation is to have escalator or cost-of-living clauses negotiated into their contracts to increase their pay as prices go up.
>
> Escalator clauses are not a new idea. They first appeared in printing and clothing industry labor agreements after World War

---

[25] 2 C.B.N.C. § 93:1 (2/13/75).
[26] 1 C.B.N.C. § 18:507.
[27] *Id.*
[28] 2 C.B.N.C. § 93:2 (2/13/75).
[29] Zalusky, "AFL-CIO Analysis of Cost-of-Living Clauses," *in* 1 C.B.N.C. § 16:31 (4/8/76). Reprinted with permission of Publisher BNA © 1976.

I. These clauses died out during the late 1920s and were not renewed during the Depression of the 1930s or World War II. However, immediately following World War II workers were trying to catch up with rapid inflation and the escalator clause was again brought to national attention.

The auto industry settlements of 1948 and 1950 were of national interest for a number of reasons, but the major points in them were the long-term agreement, the annual improvement factor, or productivity adjustment, and the cost-of-living or escalator clause.

Cost-of-living adjustments alone, even if they restored all lost wages, would not be enough to provide a worker with a share of our improving standard of living. For this reason productivity increases were included with the escalator clauses in the long-term auto agreements negotiated after World War II. Workers wanted and the auto companies agreed that they were entitled to a share in the benefits of increasing productivity. A contract with only an escalator clause would only be trying to retain the buying power of negotiated wages. This concept of escalator wage adjustments plus productivity increases is still used today.

The 1948 auto agreements were also for two years, in contrast to the one-year contracts prevalent at that time. The bargain was that long-term agreements had to protect the worker against inflation. One of the basic ways of doing this was to adjust wages after prices changed.

When the escalator clause was negotiated in the auto industry agreement of 1948, the National Industrial Conference Board, a business research organization, reported that over 75 percent of the 313 contracts it analyzed were for one year or less. Only one was for three years.

The idea of long-term agreements caught on. Contract terms increased until in 1975 nearly 90 percent of the major industrial agreements are for three or more years. Less than 5 percent are one-year agreements. The average term of contracts negotiated during 1975 was 27.6 months. Employers prefer long-term agreements because they provide stable labor-management relations over a number of years, instead of yearly renegotiations. Escalator clauses help make long-term agreements acceptable.

Escalator clauses in major union contracts covered about 10 percent of the workers by 1950. By 1959, 50 percent of workers were covered by such terms under major agreements covering 1,000 or more workers. As prices stabilized during the early 1960s, the number of escalator clauses declined. By 1966, only 20 percent of workers under major agreements were covered by them. During that period, many unions traded escalator provisions for other improvements, such as fringe benefits.

As prices increased more rapidly during the late 1960s, the number of workers covered by escalators increased. By the end of 1975, 6 million workers — or 59 percent of those under major agreements — were covered by escalator clauses. This is the largest number and percentage of workers ever to share the benefits of escalator clauses.

This actually understates the total number covered. Bureau of Labor Statistics (BLS) figures cover only workers under major agreements of 1,000 or more workers in private industry. Estimates of escalator clause coverage in other agreements in early 1975, based on a BLS sampling, are that an additional 800,000 — about 20 percent — of the workers in smaller manufacturing units are covered. Private nonmanufacturing coverage is estimated at 700,000, or 17 percent.

. . . .

By the end of 1975, the estimated total number of union members covered by escalator clauses was 8.5 million — with varying effectiveness in how well they protect the buying power of wages.

The workers' yield in wage adjustments relative to the changes in the cost of living is directly tied to the specific escalator clause in their contract and these clauses are as varied as the human imagination and the pressures of collective bargaining can make them.

Looking at the yield of the various parts of these clauses is not passing judgment on the whole agreement of which they are a part. Each agreement is negotiated in a total economic and social arena that gives it shape. Cost-of-living clauses are only a part of the total picture of the agreement.

The essential element of an escalator clause is some measure of changes in living costs. Most escalator clauses use the national Consumer Price Index (CPI) prepared by the BLS. However, about 10 percent of the major agreements use the index for a particular city. The choice is due to industry patterns or identity with a community of interest. Some big agreements, including members in Canada, combine the CPI for the United States with the Statistics of Canada CPI.

In any clause, the pay increase depends on which base years are used. At present, the index in which 1967 is the base year equalling 100 is the most commonly used.

The CPI is adjusted to a new base about once every 10 years. Data are currently published or are available for the base years

1935-39, 1947-49, 1957-59 and 1967. In 1980, a new base year will probably be established in which 1977 will equal 100.

The index base year is the point in time from which that index' price changes are measured. If 1967 were the base of 100, an index value of 160 in 1975 meant that the "average" urban wage earner would have paid $160 for items costing $100 in 1967, an increase of 60 percent. At the same time, the 1957-59 index would have been about 186, or an 86 percent increase in prices over the 1957-59 base period.

If a contract provides a 1 cent increase in wages for each 0.4 point change in the index — and the quarter from December 1973 to the end of February 1974 is used as an example — the result would be an hourly wage increase of 13 cents on the 1957-59 base, compared to 11 cents on the 1967 base. This difference can be considerable over a three-year agreement. This does not mean that it is better to use 1957-59, but only that this relationship to wage adjustments must be borne in mind.

Generally, the more current base year is a better approach when renegotiating an escalator clause. However, when the base year is changed, the relationship between index points and cents per hour should also be changed. Trying to use an older index base is difficult because it requires adjustment and may be hard to obtain locally.

The method of directly relating wage changes to index changes has a great impact on worker wage adjustment — for example, the difference between a 0.2 or 0.3 point change in the index will result in a 1 cent change in wages. The escalator wage payment system is the most obvious component and generally the most hotly contested issue when negotiating these clauses. This direct index point change to cents per hour across the board wage adjustment is the most common method of relating the CPI to wages.

4. Annual Improvement Factor Provisions

The 1967 version of the so-called "productivity" or "annual improvement factor" provision was introduced in the auto industry in the GM-UAW negotiations of 1948. The contract of 1948 provided for certain wage increases, including a cost-of-living adjustment, effective May 29, 1948, and also provided for "a further increase of 3 cents per hour for an improved standard of living" to be made in base rates on May 29, 1949. (See 22 LRRM 18) The agreement also included a cost-of-living "escalator" provision. The GM-UAW formula consists of two parts — an escalator clause as discussed in the last subsection, and the annual improvement factor which is a wage-productivity adjustment. Since, as labor economist Zilinsky points out, the escalator clause is intended to adjust money wages to offset any changes in prices, the additional purpose of the annual improvement factor is intended to increase an employee's real hourly wage.

In a book prepared for the Brookings Institution about long-term wage policy, Joseph W. Garbarino summarizes the economic theory underlying the "most interesting" GM-UAW wage formula as follows:

> The GM exposition of the economics of the wage formula, as recorded in the literature on the subject, might be recapitulated as follows: Increases in productivity can be expected in the future that will permit the standard of living of the population to increase. These increases should be realized through higher incomes, including higher wage rates. If real wages are raised at the same average rate as productivity increases, there should be no increase in unit costs and no need for prices to rise. Since real wages are to be raised, money wages must be adjusted to offset price changes and to provide for the real wage increase through the improvement factor. Considering the economy as a whole, this wage policy is neutral in its effects on prices since unit costs are assumed not to increase as a result of operation of the improvement factor. By itself the annual improvement factor increase would not bring the escalator into operation. If inflation arises from some other source, there is no obvious reason why the burden should fall on the workers, and through their organizations they would probably effectively resist a reduction in their real wages anyway. The primary effect of the cost-of-living adjustment is thus to minimize the social conflict involved in adjusting to non-wage-induced inflation. The improvement factor for its part provides for the orderly adjustment of living standards to increases in productivity in an equitable and economically desirable way and permits the negotiation of long-term labor contracts, which contribute to industrial peace and social stability.[30]

The "Annual Improvement Factor Provisions" would seem to be in the national interest by tying interim wage increases to "productivity," analogous to "wage guidelines." However, like the "guidelines," it has evoked vigorous criticisms, both in terms of theory and practicality; see Sibson, "Productivity as a Standard for Wage Determination," 3 Lab. L.J. 187 (1952); Hazlitt, Delusions of "Productivity," NEWSWEEK, Feb. 11, 1952, at 74; and Clark Kerr, writing in a symposium in Harvard Review of Economics and Statistics, November, 1949, at 299. The issue of wages, productivity and inflation remains one of the significant issues of our time.

---

[30] J. Garbarino, Wage Policy and Long-Term Contracts 25 (1962) [hereinafter cited as Wage Policy].

D. "FRINGE" BENEFITS

"Wage supplements," more popularly known as "fringe benefits," comprise a significant percentage of total employee benefits — ranging between 14% and 35% of employee payroll in all industries, according to two survey studies of the subject.[31] The growth and prevalence of wage supplements can be divided into two time periods. During the early 1930's, the major wage supplement was employer contribution to Workmen's Compensation, while in the late 30's, it was Old-Age, Survivors, Disability and Health Insurance ("social security"). The public aspect of the movement toward increased fringe benefits grew out of the exigencies of the depression. The second category, "collectively bargained" private pensions, was a product of the economic climate of the war, and saw its most rapid growth in the late 1940's and throughout the 50's. During World War II and the Korean War, government wage stabilization policies limited union "money" demands in collective bargaining, and the emphasis shifted to fringe benefits.

In this same period, the fringe benefit movement had quietly transformed our concept of wages to include a whole host of social benefits.[32] From the employer's vantage, tax deductions allow the employer to establish and maintain such programs at relatively low costs due to the high rate of corporate taxation. The need for such benefits in industry arises from a combination of factors, including the great population shift from rural to urban areas (dependency on cash income), increased life expectancy of workers (greater percentage of elderly in total population), and the decrease in number of elderly who are gainfully employed (increase in percentage of elderly people unemployed).[33] A milestone in the modern pension movement is the case of *Inland Steel Co. v. NLRB,* 170 F.2d 247 (7th Cir. 1948), *cert. denied,* 336 U.S. 960 (1949), in which the court held that retirement and pension plans were "wages" under the National Labor Relations Act, and, therefore, constituted a mandatory subject for bargaining under Sections 8(a)(5), 9(a). As long as productivity continues high, there may be no end to the list of benefits included in collective bargaining. The U.S. Department of Labor categorizes wage supplements into five categories as follows:

---

[31] *Compare* U.S. Dep't of Labor, Employee Compensation in The Private Nonfarm Economy 1974, BLS Bull. No. 1963, p. 2 [hereinafter cited as Employee Compensation] *with* U.S. Chamber of Commerce, Employee Benefits by Type of Payment, 1 C.B.N.C. § 10:401 (11/4/76).

[32] Wage Policy, *supra* note 30.

[33] M. C. Bernstein, The Future of Private Pensions 4 (1964).

Table 1. Employee Compensation, private nonfarm economy, 1974 [34]

Industry and compensation item	All employees		
	Percent of compensation	Dollars per hour	
		All hours	Work hours
All industries			
Total compensation	100.0	$5.87	$6.33
Pay for time worked	78.2	$4.59	$4.95
Straight-time pay	76.3	4.48	4.83
Premium pay	1.9	.11	.12
Overtime, weekend, and holiday work	1.7	.10	.10
Shift differentials	.3	.02	.02
Paid leave (except sick leave)	6.0	.35	.38
Vacations	3.4	.20	.22
Holidays	2.3	.13	.14
Civic and personal leave	.2	.01	.01
Employer payments to vacation and holiday funds	.1	.01	.01
Employer expenditures for retirement programs .	8.1	.47	.51
Social security	4.4	.26	.28
Private plans	3.7	.22	.23
Employer expenditures for life insurance and health benefit programs [2]	4.9	.29	.31
Life, accident, and health insurance	3.3	.19	.21
Sick leave	.7	.04	.04
Workers' compensation	1.0	.06	.06
Employer expenditures for unemployment benefit programs	1.1	.06	.07
Unemployment insurance	.9	.06	.06
Severance pay	(1)	(1)	(1)
Severance pay funds and supplemental unemployment benefits funds	.1	(1)	(1)
Nonproduction bonuses	1.5	.09	.09
Savings and thrift plans	.2	.01	.01
Wages and salaries (gross payroll)	86.3	5.07	5.46
Supplements to wages and salaries	13.7	.81	.87

It is important to note that these figures assume that

> [w]ages and salaries include all direct payments to workers. They consist of pay for time worked; pay for vacations, holidays, sick leave, and civic and personal leave; severance pay; and nonproduction bonuses. Supplements to wage and salaries include all employer expenditures for compensation other than wage and salaries. They consist of expenditures for retirement programs (including direct pay to pensioners under pay-as-

---

[34] Employee Compensation, *supra* note 31, table 1 at 8.

you-go private pension plans); expenditures for life insurance and health benefit programs (except sick leave); expenditures for unemployment benefit programs (except severance pay); payments to vacation and holiday funds; and payments to savings and thrift plans.[35]

On the other hand, the U.S. Chamber of Commerce categorizes wage supplements into five different categories: [36]

Employee Benefits by Type of Payment, 1975

Type of benefit	Total, all companies	Total, all manu- facturing	Total, all nonmanu- facturing
Total employee benefits as per cent of payroll	35.4	36.1	34.4
1. Legally required payments (employer's share only)	8.0	8.8	6.9
a. Old-Age, Survivors, Disability and Health Insurance	5.7	5.8	5.4
b. Unemployment Compensation	1.0	1.2	0.8
c. Workmen's compensation (including esti- mated cost of self-insured)	1.2	1.7	0.6
d. Railroad Retirement Tax, Railroad Unem- ployment and Cash Sickness Insurance, state sickness benefits insurance, etc.**	0.1	0.1	0.1
2. Pension and other agreed-upon payments (em- ployer's share only)	11.6	11.6	11.4
a. Pension plan premiums and pension pay- ments not covered by insurance type plan (net)	5.5	4.9	6.4
b. Life insurance premiums, death benefits, accident and medical insurance premi- ums, hospitalization insurance, etc. (net)	5.2	6.1	3.8
c. Salary continuation or long term disability ...	0.2	0.2	0.2
d. Dental insurance premiums	0.1	0.1	0.1
e. Discounts on goods and services purchased from company by employees	0.2	*	0.3
f. Employee meals furnished by company	0.2	0.1	0.3
g. Miscellaneous payments (compensation payments in excess of legal requirements, separation or termination pay allowances, moving expenses, etc.)	0.2	0.2	0.3

[35] *Id.,* note 344 at 10.

[36] 1 C.B.N.C. § 10:401 (11/4/76). Even when these figures are adjusted for dissimilar bases, they are irreconcilable. For a strong criticism of the Chamber of Commerce wage supplement studies, see AFL-CIO, Collective Bargaining Report Vol. 1, No. 3, at 17-18.

   *Less than 0.05%

   **Figure shown is considerably less than legal rate, as most reporting companies had only a small proportion of employers covered by tax

Type of benefit	Total, all companies	Total, all manufacturing	Total, all nonmanufacturing
3. Paid rest periods, lunch periods, wash-up time, travel time, clothes-change time, get-ready time, etc.	3.6	3.7	3.5
4. Payments for time not worked	10.1	10.1	10.3
a. Paid vacations and payments in lieu of vacation	5.2	5.4	4.8
b. Payments for holidays not worked	3.3	3.5	3.2
c. Paid sick leave	1.2	0.8	1.8
d. Payments for State or National Guard duty, jury, witness and voting pay allowances, payments for time lost due to death in family or other personal reasons, etc.	0.4	0.4	0.5
5. Other items	2.1	1.9	2.3
a. Profit-sharing payments	1.1	1.1	1.1
b. Contributions to employee thift plan	0.3	0.2	0.4
c. Christmas or other special bonuses, service awards, suggestion awards, etc.	0.4	0.4	0.4
d. Employee education expenditures (tuition refunds, etc.)	0.1	0.1	0.2
e. Special wage payments ordered by courts, payments to union stewards, etc.	0.2	0.1	0.2
Total employee benefits as cents per payroll hour	193.2	191.3	195.8
Total employee benefits as dollars per year per employee	3984	3954	025

The Chamber of Commerce has expanded these categories to encompass discounts on goods and services furnished by companies; employee meals; rest periods, lunch periods, washup time, travel time and clothes-change time; employee education expenditures; and payments to union stewards. Although the two sets of figures proceed from different assumptions, they both provide a graphic illustration of the relative importance of wage supplements.[37]

BNA indicates that:

Fringe benefits were initiated or revised in 84 percent of the 1,979 contracts reported in 1977, compared to 78 percent in 1976. A breakdown of these benefits shows that revisions in insurance plans were the most frequently negotiated in 1977 contracts, compared to 63 percent in 1976.

The most commonly changed insurance benefits were sickness and accident, 30 percent; life, 27 percent; major medical, 22

[37] See U.S. Dep't of Labor, Problems in Measurement of Expenditures on Selected Items of Supplementary Employee Remuneration, Manufacturing Establishments, 1953, B.L.S. Bull. No. 1186 (1956).

percent; dental, 19 percent; hospital, 13 percent; optical, 10 percent; accidental death and dismemberment, disability and surgical, 7 percent; maternity, 6 percent; and prescription drugs, 3 percent.

Pension plans were changed in 57 percent of 1977 contracts, compared to 52 percent in 1976. Those specifying new benefit amounts provided average monthly benefits of $10.65 ($9.20 in 1976) per year of service in manufacturing contracts and $14.37 ($11.07 in 1976) in nonmanufacturing-excluding-construction contracts.

Holidays were changed in 37 percent of 1977 contracts compared to 32 percent in 1976. Those contracts specifying the exact number provided an average of 11 holidays per year.

Vacations were revised in 29 percent of 1977 and 1976 contracts. Supplemental unemployment benefit plans were changed in 7 percent of 1977 contracts, compared to 2 percent in 1976.

Severance pay plans were revised in 2 percent of 1977 contracts, hours were changed in 1 percent, and legal services were provided in fewer than 1 percent.[38]

The ten-year median wage increases including figures by industry appear as follows: [39]

---

[38] 1 C.B.N.C. § 18:959 (1/12/78).
[39] 1 C.B.N.C. § 18:957 (1/26/78).

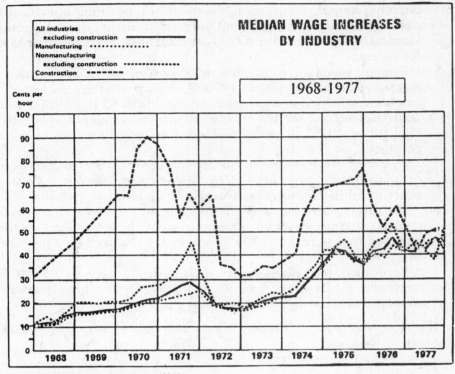

* 1968-69 Construction median calculated on annual basis
† Insufficient data available for 4th quarter construction median

According to Labor Department Statistics, the elements of compensation were divided during this approximate period as illustrated in Chart 2:

The elements of compensation as a percent of total compensation, selected years, 1966-74

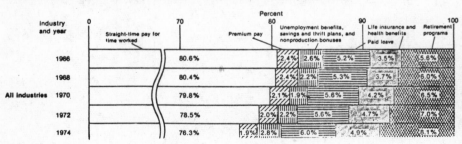

Although these figures corroborate the significance of wage supplements, space limitation requires substantial pruning and allows only cursory treatment of the subject matter. We have selected "paid leave time" for coverage in this chapter,[40] and private pension

---

[40] As indicated the U.S. Department of Labor breaks out wage supplements on the basis of *non-direct* payments to workers, except for sick-leave pay. The U.S. Chamber of Commerce includes this category as a wage supplement on the basis

plans for coverage in the next. However, even these two subjects are too massive for definite coverage. Therefore, the approach taken in these materials is to indicate the more important agenda items for collective bargaining. Wherever practicable, we attempt, in addition, to indicate or illustrate some of the more common or important problems through the use of arbitration decisions or otherwise.

1. Pay for Leave Time: Holiday, Vacation, and Sick Leave

a. Holiday Pay Provisions

In discussing the historical background of holiday pay, Arbitrator Robert L. Howard said in *Carson Electric Co.,* 24 L.A. 667 (1955),

> The matter of holiday pay for holidays not worked, as well as premium pay for work done on holidays, has had an interesting and important history.
>
> At a time when hourly and daily paid wage earners were not given holiday pay of either type, it became common for salaried employees paid on a monthly or weekly basis to receive their regular weekly or monthly salary without deduction for any holiday on which the business was closed and no work was done. This was a recognition that the employee involved should not suffer a loss in pay because management closed its business for a holiday. This plan which applied to executive and administrative employees gradually came to be rather generally extended to the so-called white collar and clerical employees paid on a weekly or monthly basis, to prevent loss of pay due to the holiday, with no thought of giving pay for a holiday not falling within the work week, although the six day week was then common and the problem could not arise.
>
> Such plans almost universally had no application to hourly or daily wage earners.
>
> It was only after union representation and collective bargaining agreements became the order of the day that any plan for holiday pay came to be extended to the wage earner or production worker on any widespread scale. In many instances the purpose merely to protect the employees from loss in take-home pay due to the plant being closed for a holiday was made obvious by express language in the contract.
>
> The following types of provisions, or some variation thereof, were frequently used:
>
> (1) "Employees who have had (stipulated) continuous service shall be paid for time lost by reason of the following holidays occurring on a work day."
>
> (2) "Straight time pay shall be paid for the following holidays not worked, provided they fall on or are observed on regularly

that it is payment for time not worked. Since we view "fringes" as part of the Wages and Hours Chapter, we take no position in this dispute.

scheduled work days," or "within the regularly scheduled work week."

(3) "The following holidays shall be granted without loss in pay."

(4) "An employee will receive pay for holidays not worked only if his work schedule is such that he would have worked on that day but for its·being a holiday."

More recently, collective bargaining has brought about an almost universal recognition of holiday pay for holidays not worked and added provisions for premium pay for holidays worked, not merely to prevent loss in take-home pay, but as a so-called fringe benefit in the nature of a part of the over-all wage picture.

Negotiated provisions of this latter nature are usually substantially like that in the contract here involved, providing that employees, commonly with some eligibility requirement, shall receive straight time pay for the following holidays not worked, plus a provision for premium pay for holidays worked, with no reference to whether they do or do not fall within the regular work week.

Although there are still labor agreements which do not provide for paid unworked holidays, the numbers are fast declining.[41] The observance of holidays, whether national, state, local, legal or religious is generally recognized in the form of a contract clause providing pay for unworked, or premium pay for worked holidays.

CHECKLIST FOR HOLIDAY PAY PROVISIONS

I. HOLIDAYS TO BE RECOGNIZED AND OBSERVED
  a. How are holidays defined?
     (1) By national or local observance
     (2) Selected by management or employees
  b. What is length of time observed?
     (1) Number of hours
     (2) Specific day from one point of time to another
  c. What if holidays fall on non-working time?
     (1) Saturdays or Sundays — including provision for selection in combination with long weekend
     (2) Shutdowns
     (3) In conjunction with birthday-holiday provision

---

[41] *See* U.S. Dep't of Labor, Prevalence of Holiday Provisions in Major Union Contracts, 1961, Monthly Lab. Rev. 522 (May 1962); 2 C.B.N.C. § 57:285; P-H, Union Contracts and Collective Bargaining ¶ 53,492.

d. What if holidays fall on scheduled work days? What provision
   is made for working and restriction on work during holidays?
   (1) Management right to schedule work
   (2) Work bans
   (3) Emergencies
   (4) Maintenance versus production work

II. ELIGIBILITY FOR HOLIDAY PAY
   a. What is extent of coverage?
      (1) Part-time employees
      (2) Temporary work force
      (3) Probationary employees
      (4) Suspended workers
   b. What are "attendance"/"work requirements"?
      (1) Required hours of work before and/or after holiday
      (2) Forfeiture for failure to be available
   c. What are provisions for work and non-work related absenteeism
      and tardiness?
      (1) Necessity of excuse (written permission for illness)
      (2) Time limit for leave of absence
      (3) Layoff: distinctions for temporary and permanent layoff
      (4) Impact of strike — legal or unauthorized strikes, refusal
          to cross picket line, and non-striking employees' refusal to
          cross picket line
      (5) Vacations and other leaves of absence

III. PAY
   a. What rate is to be paid for holidays?
      (1) Where no work—
          (a) Average earned rate
          (b) Hourly rate
          (c) Piecework rate
          (d) With or without wage differentials
      (2) If worked—
          (a) Time and one half
          (b) Double or triple time
          (c) Incentive and overtime pay included or excluded

(1) Designation and Observance of Paid Holidays

In considering the problem of a holiday which fell on a
nonscheduled work day, absent contractual provision, Arbitrator
John Caraway reasoned in *Woodward Wight & Company, Ltd.,* 33
L.A. 494, 496-97 (1959),

This dispute arises from the fact that a holiday, the Fourth of
July, fell on a Saturday during 1959. It is one of six designated
holidays under Article VI, Section F., of the Contract. The

holiday falls outside the regular work week delineated in Article VI, Section A.1, which is Monday through Friday, inclusive.

The Company and the Union have given much consideration to the purpose of holiday pay both in argument at the hearing as well as in their written briefs. It is the contention of the Company that holiday pay is the grant of time off without penalty in compensation if the holiday fell during the regular work week. This is sometimes referred to as the "level pay check theory." *See Standard Grocery Company,* 7 L.A. 745. The Union maintains that holiday pay is in the nature of extra compensation, one of the "fringe benefits" of the Contract. There are arbitration decisions supporting this theory. *Reliable Optical Co.,* 7 L.A. 257. In this case, however, there was no evidence introduced relating to the intent of the negotiators of the holiday pay clause as to the purpose they had in mind. Hence, the arguments of both the Company and the Union have limited evidentiary value in determination of the issue.

. . . .

Resolution of this question must be determined from the language of the agreement. It, however, does not provide for this situation. There is no provision that pay will be given only if the holiday falls within the regular work week. Similarly, the Contract lacks any clause providing for pay to be given if the holiday falls on a day not normally a work day. The pertinent part of the Contract is:

Article VI, Section F. — "The following holidays shall be observed as paid holidays at the regular rate of pay for eight (8) hours:

New Year's Day	Mardi Gras Day
Fourth of July	Labor Day
Thanksgiving Day	Christmas Day

provided said employee is available for work the regular scheduled work day preceding and following said holiday."

The Arbitrator in discharging his duties has the mandate not to add to, amend, or subtract from the provisions of the agreement. It is his function to apply the terms of the Contract to the factual situation and make an award on that basis.

The language of the Contract is clear and positive. It provides that six named holidays shall be paid at the regular rate of pay for eight hours. The only qualification is that the employee be available for work the regular scheduled work day preceding and following the holiday. There is no requirement that the holiday fall within the regular scheduled work week. Article VI, Section F., is totally devoid of any reference to the phrase "regular work week." The Arbitrator cannot interpolate into the holiday pay clause language which is not there. Further, the holiday pay clause makes no exceptions for Saturdays or Sundays. It only guarantees two hours pay, in addition to the regular holiday pay if the employee must work on the named holiday. The Contract language is not restrictive enough to limit holiday pay for the designated holidays to those falling only during the regular work week.

The Company argues that an employee would receive excessive pay where a holiday falls on a Saturday and he is required to work, as he gets Saturday premium pay as well as his holiday pay. To prevent such a result, Article VI, Section F., could have been drafted as to restrict holiday pay only to instances where the holiday fell during the regular work week.

Arbitral awards regarding this issue are less than uniform. *Compare* the principal case and *Courier-Citizen Co.,* 42 L.A. 269 (C. Myers, 1964) *with Milwaukee Linen Supply Co.,* 23 L.A. 392 (A. Anderson, 1954) and *Premium Beverages, Inc.,* 22 L.A. 806 (H. Seligson, 1954).

(2) Eligibility Requirements for Holiday Pay

In cases involving the issue of whether the work requirement has been complied with, the ultimate decision may hinge on the way in which the work requirement is stated. For illustrative cases involving different forms of contractual phraseology *see Peerless Mfg. Co.,* 38 L.A. 746 (L. Larson, 1962) ("worked day before" meant day scheduled for individual employee to work, including overtime); *Greif Bros. Cooperage Corp.,* 35 L.A. 389 (L. Crane, 1960) ("scheduled work day" need not be normal or regular work day); *Iroquois Gas Corp.,* 25 L.A. 764 (H. Somers, 1955) ("actually worked on his scheduled work day" includes pre-arranged Saturday overtime); *Hinde & Dauch Paper Co.,* 22 L.A. 505 (J. McCormick, 1954) ("regular scheduled working day" means Monday through Friday inclusive); and *Armour & Co.,* 9 L.A. 338 (H. Gilden, 1948) ("day before and day after holiday" includes Sunday after Saturday holiday so employee who did not work Monday following was *not* disqualified from receiving holiday pay). Should an arbitrator use a theory of liberal statutory construction based on a view that holidays are part of the negotiated economic package? *See Watkins Trucking, Inc.,* 48 L.A. 1101 (J. Klein, 1967).

NOTES:

Problems: (a) *Part-day absences:* The agreement in dispute provided as a work requirement that,

"The employee must have worked the last scheduled work day prior to and the next scheduled work day after such holiday with the employee's regular work schedule."

On December 31, the day before the New Year's holiday, grievant left his job after working only about half of the 8 hours scheduled time, because he had also worked the afternoon of December 24th, at which time he told his supervisor he would only work a half-day on the 31st. The employer refuses to pay grievant's holiday pay on the ground that he did not fulfill the work requirement.

Union Contention — The agreement does not require an employee to work the entire day prior to a holiday in order to qualify for the holiday allowance. The agreement provides that the employee must have worked the day prior, but it says nothing about working the whole day. Under the terms of the agreement, and in accordance with the common parlance understood in the plant, the term "work day" refers to the 24 hour period beginning when an employee starts work. The term "shift" refers to the actual 8 hour work period plus lunch time. Since no one is expected to work 24 hours at a stretch, the word "day" in the provision does not refer to a certain number of hours. Furthermore, to interpret the provision as meaning the entire shift adds to the contract, which is beyond the contractual power of the arbitrator.

Company Contention — The term "scheduled work day" means a full shift of 8 hours as this is the basic number of hours expected to be worked in a work day. The Union's interpretation of the agreement would rewrite the work requirement provision [which states that "the employee must have worked the last scheduled work day prior" to . . . such holiday] to read "the employee must have worked *on* the last scheduled work day prior" to a holiday. The arbitrator has no authority to add the word "on" in the provision, because the arbitration clause prohibits him from adding to the terms of the agreement. Furthermore, employees cannot be permitted to decide when they will and will not work. Grievant was aware of the heavy work load, and yet, he deliberately left his job without a satisfactory reason.

As Arbitrator, how would you resolve the issue? *Compare General Electric Co.,* 32 L.A. 769 (P. Kleinsorge, 1959) *with Standard Bag Co.,* 45 L.A. 1149 (C. Summers, 1965). Would your decision be different if grievant had been denied holiday pay for reporting late for work? What if grievant was also laid off for his action? *Compare McInerney Spring & Wire Co.,* 11 L.A. 1195 (R. A. Smith, 1948) *with Celotex Corp.,* 33 L.A. 517 (H. Dworkin, 1961). What is the significance of the employee's "intent" in work requirement cases? *See Zion Industries, Inc.,* 41 L.A. 414 (J. Larkin, 1963); *National Rejectors, Inc.,* 28 L.A. 390 (E. Cheit, 1957); and *Lake City Malleable, Inc.,* 25 L.A. 753 (G. Hayes, 1956).

(b) *Excused and unexcused absences:* Suppose the agreement contains the usual work requirements for holiday pay, and provides no exceptions. Is an employee who fails to comply with the requirement because of illness which prevented him from working entitled to holiday pay? Does it make any difference whether the absence is excused? *Compare L. Grossman & Sons, Inc.,* 19 L.A. 347 (H. Parkman, 1952) *with John Deere Waterloo Tractor Works,* 19 L.A. 287 (H. Davey, 1952).

What if the agreement conditions the payment of holiday pay upon the employees' working the last day before and the first day after the holiday "unless his failure to work is by reason of proven sickness or accident or because of death in the immediate family?" How would you decide a grievance if an employee did not work on the first day after a holiday because he attended his daughter's tonsillectomy? *Compare D. L. Auld Co.,* 38 L.A. 507 (E. Teple, 1962) *with Lignum-Vitae Products Corp.,* 9 L.A. 852 (A. Lesser, Jr., 1948). If grievant's excuse was based on a fire that occurred in her home, would you support employer's denial of holiday pay on the ground that she did not suffer any bodily injury from the fire, and was not covered by the term "accident" in the agreement? *See Branch River Wool Combing Co.,* 18 L.A. 34 (M. Copelof, 1952).

(3) Other Circumstances Affecting Eligibility for Holiday Pay

(a) LAYOFFS

Arbitrators are in disagreement over the question of whether laid-off employees are entitled to receive holiday pay when the agreement is silent on the matter. *Compare Nat'l Metal Spinners Ass'n,* 25 L.A. 341 (Shapiro 1954) and *Weinman Pump Mfg. Co.,* 44 L.A. 481 (D. Leach, 1965) (inappropriate to enforce fringe benefit where contract language ambiguous at best) *with Muter Co.,* 37 L.A. 103 (S. Wood, 1961) (layoff did not terminate grievant's status as employee) *and George Otto Boiler Co.,* 37 L.A. 47 (P. Garman, 1961) (contract requires work only on last regularly scheduled workday).

NOTE:

Problem: On May 19th, the employer, who was a member of a multi-employer bargaining association shut down his plant and laid off all the employees when the Union struck two of the association's members.' The strike was settled a few months later, and the employer reinstated all the laid-off employees. The Union subsequently demanded holiday pay for Memorial Day on behalf of the employees. The employer refused to pay alleging that the work requirement was not fulfilled by the employees. The labor agreement contained the following holiday clause:

> To be entitled to holiday pay, the employee must work his regularly scheduled work day preceding and following the holiday. However, the employee shall receive his holiday pay even though, at the instance of the employer, he has been directed not to work the scheduled work day. . . .
>
> An employee covered by the terms of this Agreement laid off or terminated less than fifteen calendar days prior to a holiday shall receive pay for that holiday at the time of lay-off or termination.

If you were the arbitrator, how would you decide? Why? Would it make any difference if the shutdown was economically motivated? *Compare Publishers' Ass'n of New York City,* 40 L.A. 140 (B. Turkus, 1963) *with Intermountain Operators League,* 26 L.A. 149 (S. Kadish, 1956) *infra.*

If the labor agreement includes employees who have worked within a short time of the holiday even if they are laid off, is an employer liable for holiday pay if he ceases doing business permanently? *Compare Shipley Wholesale Drug Co.,* 48 L.A. 915 (S. Kates, 1967) *with Ohringer Home Furniture Co.,* 33 L.A. 477 (H. Pollack, 1959) (permanently laid off employees).

(b) STRIKES

In *Intermountain Operations League,* 26 L.A. 149 (1956), Arbitrator Sanford Kadish considered whether striking employees were entitled to holiday pay where the collective bargaining agreement provided for holiday pay for those who have been laid off or terminated within fifteen days of the holiday. He concluded that:

> I am not suggesting that this clause by its terms automatically disentitles these employees from holiday pay. It does not, as I pointed out above. But it is significant as an indicia of the intent of the parties on the subject of eligibility for holiday pay in the situation where work is not being performed during the period

in which the holiday falls. The clause manifests that the parties gave consideration to the problem of holiday pay for those in this situation. Of all the possible instances of such situation — voluntary quitting, striking, absence on leave, absence due to sickness, etc., — the parties chose to designate only two in which to declare employees eligible for holiday pay despite their not working, namely, layoffs and terminations within fifteen days. It seems to me a fair negative inference that by expressly including only two named instances of such situations the parties must be taken to have intended not to include all other instances of such situations, including that where the employees are not working because they are on strike.

NOTES:

Problems: (a) *Non-striking employees:* In the principal case, the second issue involved the eligibility of employees who were locked out by the non-struck members of the league. Are they entitled to holiday pay? Under a contract which required work on the last scheduled day before and the first scheduled day after a holiday "unless failure to work is due to sickness, death in the family or similar good cause," are employees who report for work and are sent home because of an illegal strike by some fellow employees, entitled to holiday pay? *Compare Bethlehem Steel Co.,* 23 L.A. 141 (R. Seward, 1954) *with Phoenix Steel Corp.,* 44 L.A. 927 (D. Crawford, 1965). Should it make any difference if the strike involves employees from a different bargaining unit? *See Kansas City Bakery Employers Labor Council,* 25 L.A. 91 (J. Walsh, 1955).

(b) *Refusal to cross a picket line:* The labor agreement contains the usual "work before and work after the holiday" requirement for eligibility to holiday pay. It also provides that, "it is understood that each employee shall use his own prerogative to respect or not to respect a bona-fide picket line of another union without fear of recourse or penalty on the part of the Union or on the part of the Employer." If some employees refuse to cross a picket line set up by another Union representing a different bargaining unit while others do, are they entitled to their holiday pay? *Compare Stockton Automotive Ass'n,* 25 L.A. 687 (A. Whitton, 1955) *with Fisher Scientific Co.,* 28 L.A. 616 (B. Reid, 1957).

(c) *Illegal or unauthorized strike:* Assuming that the "work requirement" for holiday pay has been complied with, may an employer, nevertheless, withhold holiday pay on the ground that the strike was illegal or unauthorized? Where the strike is a material breach of the no-strike clause may the employer withhold holiday pay on the ground that he is excused for performance of the terms of the holiday provisions because of the breach? *Compare American*

Brake Shoe Co., 40 L.A. 673 (B. Reid, 1963) *and Continental Can Co.,* 31 L.A. 558 (M. Schmidt, 1958) *with National Lead Co. of Ohio,* 32 L.A. 865 (C. Schedler, 1959).

(d) *Vacations and Leaves of absence:* Grievant, entitled to one week's vacation, took his week beginning July 1st and was due to return on July 8th, but did not return until Tuesday July 9th. Grievant did not ask to be off on July 8th, nor did he report that he would not be in for work. The Union contends that grievant is entitled to the holiday pay despite his failure to work Monday, July 8th. The contract reads in pertinent part:

> Para. 6 — In the event that an employee takes his vacation during a week that contains one of the eight holidays mentioned above [including July 4th], he is to be paid his normal vacation pay for the week plus the holiday pay.
>
> Para. 7 — In order to be eligible for holiday pay an employee must report for work on his scheduled work day immediately preceding and following the holiday.

Does the work test preclude grievant from getting his holiday pay? *Compare Streitman Supreme Bakery of Cincinnati,* 41 L.A. 621 (Suagee, 1963) *with Alside Inc.,* 42 L.A. 75 (Teple, 1964).

b. Vacation Pay

"Vacation pay" and "holiday pay" as wage supplements provided for by collective bargaining agreements have many similarities. Both are contained in the overwhelming majority of union agreements. Since both "fringes" are part of the wage package and are often negotiated instead of a wage increase of a greater amount, the "cost" aspects of both are usually dealt with in the contract. Accordingly, provisions dealing with "eligibility," "rate of pay" and "scheduling" are common to both, as the following checklist reveals, and the issues that arise are analogous.

CHECKLIST FOR VACATION PAY PROVISIONS

I. ELIGIBILITY FOR VACATION PAY
  a. How is eligibility determined?
    (1) Length of service by years, months, weeks or hours
    (2) Part of time lost for illness, sick leave, injury, leave of absence, layoff, strike, shutdown, etc., computed as time worked for purpose of vacation
    (3) Effect of time spent in contract negotiation, grievances, arbitration proceedings, union conventions, etc., on time worked

(4) Credit for civic duties, e.g., military service, courtroom service, draft board service, voting, etc.

(5) Forfeiture for time lost

(6) Impact of absence prior and subsequent to vacation

b. What are minimum work requirements during antecedent period?

(1) Service required — years, months, weeks, hours, pay periods, or a percentage of working days or available shifts

(2) Impact of absences prior and subsequent to vacation

(3) Proration of vacation pay for failure to meet minimum work requirements (full time and part time) for: layoffs, strikes, discontinuance of business, sick leave, death, discharge, quit or retirement, sale, merger or other combination

c. Is vacation pay an accrued right?

II. COMPUTATION OF VACATION PAY

a. How is rate of pay to be determined?

(1) Straight time, incentive, or other

(2) Spread over weekly period, percentage of earnings of past year, or other

(3) Computed for individual employee, majority of employees, or plant

(4) Period of computation

(5) Cut off date for computation

(6) Cost-of-living adjustment

(7) Compensation for holidays or overtime scheduling occurring during vacation

b. Can an employee elect vacation pay as a bonus in lieu of a vacation?

III. SCHEDULING VACATIONS

a. Who determines vacation schedules?

(1) Company — unilaterally or after consultation

(2) By negotiation

(3) Union vacation committee or review board

(4) Provision for grievance resolution or alternate date

b. What are criteria for vacation preferences?

(1) Seniority

(2) Service needs of company

c. What is permissible timing for vacations?

(1) In conjunction with plant closing at employer's discretion

(2) Split vacations

(3) For inventory

(4) During school vacations

(5) Effect of holidays during vacations

(6) Substituted for other time off — short work, random sick leave

IV. POSTPONEMENT, CARRY-OVER AND ACCUMULATION
   a. Who has authority to postpone vacation?
   b. Can employee carry over vacation time?
   c. Can employee accumulate vacation time and take consecutively?

V. EXTENDED VACATIONS
   a. Can employer extend vacations to avoid layoffs?
      (1) Extend vacations against estimated retirement date
   b. Who determines how extended vacations shall operate?
      (1) Eligibility of skilled and non-skilled employees in department
      (2) Scheduling (interference with normal vacations)
      (3) Effect of other compensation earned during extended vacations
      (4) Periodic reevaluation

Generally, the length of an employee's vacation is keyed to his length of service, and is now usually considered to be an "earned" or "accrued" right. Absent contractual provision otherwise, do these rights accrue for service less than the prescribed period? Does this depend upon the kind of contract? Suppose there is no pro-rata provision? Arbitrator John Hogan reasoned in *Bachman Uxbridge Worsted Corp.,* 23 L.A. 597, 601-02 (1954),

> [Vacation pay] . . . is earned pay in the form of deferred wages. To deny the employees who have worked the time specified in the contract the right to their amount of vacation pay would improperly withhold money due them as part of the bargain which settled the contract when vacation pay was bargained into it. The amount of vacation pay due the employees is based on the amount of time they worked. For example, less is accrued by those who have worked six months than by those who have worked one year.
>
> . . . .
>
> The fact that other arbitrators, as well as courts of law have ruled that vacation pay represents an earned right in the form of deferred wages does not in itself mean that the ruling should be for the Union in this particular case. The decision would still depend on the specific contract terms involved. Nor does the fact that vacation pay has been awarded in cases where plants have been liquidated and where the vacation clause required continuous employment up to the vacation period mean that the ruling should necessarily be for the Union here. The Company is right in arguing that each case must be taken on its own merits, viewed in the light of its particular facts and judged within the

four corners of the specific contract involved. The Arbitrator has followed this principle. The terms of the vacation clause in the particular contract strongly supports the principle of vacation pay as an earned right based on amount of work performed during the vacation year. And I find no clause in this specific agreement which denies this right or prohibits the application of the general rule that vacation pay is part of wages and is an earned right.

Furthermore, it is not the long line of previous decisions that is determinative. It is the validity of the reasoning behind the principle that vacation pay is a part of wages that is determinative. The reasoning is clear. Modern collective bargaining is not confined to wage rates and job conditions. The money items involving a cost to the employer often include important fringe items such as vacation pay, holiday pay, insurance, pensions and other items. The total bargain involves a total money cost to the employer composed of all these benefits. Wages may be traded for "fringes," "fringes" for wages. Vacation pay or holiday pay is often negotiated instead of a wage increase or a wage increase of greater amount. A dollar bargained is still a dollar whether it is paid as wages for work performed or in lieu of wages during the vacation period. It is an accrued right in either case.

Indeed the impetus to the expansion of vacation with pay clauses in modern collective bargaining contracts occurred during the last half of the period of wage stabilization in World War II when allowable wages had been granted and the parties substituted vacations with pay for wage increases since wage increases were no longer possible or possible to only a very limited extent. Thus vacations with pay were granted in lieu of wages. The reasoning behind the principle that vacations with pay are part of the money-package bargained and are thus a right, the amount of which depends on specific contract terms, is clear. . . .

(1) Eligibility for Vacation Pay

Arbitrators are often called upon to construe contract provisions governing employee eligibility for vacation pay. A common clause provides that to be eligible, a worker must be "in the employ of the employer" on a date specified by the contract. How an arbitrator interprets such a clause is critical to the rights of employees who are on the company payroll but, due to layoff,[42] strike activities,[43]

---

[42] See, e.g., Whittet-Higgens Co., 15 L.A. 13 (Healy, 1949).

[43] Compare Vickers, Inc., 27 L.A. 251 (R.A. Smith, 1951) with Kroger Co., 42 L.A. 247 (J. Larkin, 1964) and Mobile Oil Co., 42 L.A. 102 (E. Forsythe, 1973).

illness,[44] or death,[45] are not actually at work on the date specified. *See Amory Mills, Inc.,* 11 L.A. 211 (1948).

The concept of vacation pay as an earned, accrued right raises significant implications for disputes arising over an interruption of an employment relationship, whether voluntary or involuntary, which should be considered in the negotiating and drafting of vacation pay provisions. One possible method of solving many of these issues is to pay employees on a pro-rata basis for the time actually worked during the year in which the vacation would have been taken. This would mean that an employee who worked six months during the year and was laid off, for example, would be eligible for one-half of the vacation pay she/he would have received had she/he worked the entire year. Arbitrator John Hogan used this solution in the *Bachman Uxbridge Worsted Corp.* case *supra.*

In prorating, it is important to note that two dates are significant — the period of time worked and the cut-off date for determining that period. It is also necessary to distinguish vacations earned for prior year's service and the accrual of rights during the current year. Yet, surprisingly enough, many contracts fail to mention a cut-off date for determining eligibility; *see Charles Mundt & Sons Co.,* 17 L.A. 732 (E. Levy, 1951). Furthermore, it is advisable that eligibility provisions should stipulate whether "continuous service" is required in computing eligibility. *Compare Button Corp.,* 12 L.A. 13 (E. Stein, 1949) (absent contract provision employees directed to be paid for aggregate service regardless of reason for break in employment) *with General Cable Corp.,* 20 L.A. 505 (R. Montgomery, 1953) (past practice indicates that employees' service must be continuous where contract silent).

NOTES:

Discharge: Although many contracts contain an exclusionary clause in the case of discharge (and quit) such as, "Employees who quit or are discharged for cause before [cut-off date] of the contract year shall not be eligible for vacation pay, under this article," others are silent on the matter. Does it follow in these cases, absent contractual provision to the contrary, that vacation pay should be prorated as an accrued right? *Compare Patterson Steel Co.,* 45 L.A. 783 (L. Autrey, 1965) (where discharged employee held within scope of provision providing for proration to "terminated employees") *with United States Steel Corp.,* 33 L.A. 560 (H. Gilden, 1959) ("layoff" does not cover "disciplinary suspension").

---

[44] *Compare* San Francisco Publishers Ass'n, 46 L.A. 260 (Burns, 1965) *with* Iron Fireman-Webster Inc., 43 L.A. 303 (Dworkin, undated).

[45] *Compare* Burnham Corp., 46 L.A. 1129 (Feinberg, 1966) *with* Bethlehem Steel Corp., 47 L.A. 258 (Seward, 1966).

Does this result change where the employee has quit or retired? *See Heiner's Bakery,* 45 L.A. 1167 (Mullin, 1965). *Compare Pana Refining Co.,* 47 L.A. 193 (D. Traynor, 1966) (employee must fully complete eligibility period before receiving vacation pay) *with Foster Refrigeration Corp.,* 39 L.A. 241 (J. Altieri, 1962) (employee entitled to pro-rata share where contract provided each employee entitled to vacation pay who was employed on June 30th).

Problems: (a) How should vacation rights be determined when an employer shuts down its business? Should employees be entitled to prorated vacation pay in such situations because involuntary termination was different from "discharge or voluntary quit" cases; *see Shipley Wholesale Drug Co.,* 48 L.A. 915 (1967); *Wamsutta Mills Inc.,* 34 L.A. 158 (Hogan, 1959) (since vacation pay is "additional wages earned," the employer must expressly exclude it or owe vacation pay on termination) *with Cricket Shop of Cedarhurst,* 49 L.A. 895 (1967) (strictly construing "eligibility period" to deny vacation pay). Which policy is apposite in the next problem?

(b) The contract provides, *inter alia,* that "in the case of sale, merger, consolidation or other combination of operations," employees will not carry seniority to a successor company, but will be placed in order of their former seniority at the foot of the seniority list at the successor company. It goes on to provide, however, that such employees will be given vacations based on "total service" with the predecessor and successor companies.

When the company at which grievant worked ceased processing materials on which he worked and entered into an agreement with a supplier company to hire its employees as vacancies occurred at the supplier company, grievant was hired. Grievant alleges that he is entitled to vacation pay based on his "total service" with both companies under the provision listed above. Do you agree? *Compare Sidney Wanzer & Sons, Inc.,* 46 L.A. 426 (D. Dolnick, 1966) *with Sanborn's Motor Express, Inc.,* 44 L.A. 346 (S. Wallen, 1965).

(2) Vacation Pay and How It Is Measured

(a) COMPUTATION OF VACATION PAY

Vacation eligibility clauses should be very closely tied in with the method of paying for vacations. The reason for this can be demonstrated by considering the respective rights of two hypothetical employees under the following eligibility clauses:

Example 1

Employees who have been in the service of the Company for at least three months as of August 1 of the vacation year and who have a total actual working record of at least seventy-five percent

(75%) of their scheduled working hours during the preceding twelve-month period, or such shorter period as they may have been employed, shall be entitled to vacation with pay as follows:
. . . .

Example 2

Each employee entitled to . . . a one week vacation shall receive an amount equal to two percent of said employee's total earnings for the twelve months' period ending the last day of the last work week in May. . . . However, a minimum of forty hours vacation pay and eighty hours vacation pay, respectively, shall be paid to any employees eligible for a one week vacation or a two week vacation under this Section, and who has worked a minimum of nine hundred (900) hours in the qualifying year, as set forth in the above paragraphs.

Employee *A* was sick for four (4) months during the qualifying year, while employee *B* was laid off for all except one month during the year which he worked. What are the respective rights of each under Example 1 and 2? Which of the above provisions is the most liberal from the employee's standpoint? Is there any reason to set up an eligibility requirement provision in hours rather than days, as was done in Example 2?

(b) DIFFERENT METHODS OF COMPUTATION

Vacation pay is frequently based on straight-time hourly earnings but may include overtime, shift premiums and incentive payments. Normally the two elements involved in computation are the number of hours to be paid for and the pay basis. For example, the usual method of computation for vacation pay for workers who are paid on an hourly rate is the regular or straight-time hourly rate in effect at the time the vacation begins multiplied by the scheduled weekly hours of work. If the rate at the time of vacation is atypical, a "predominant rate" may be used. If payment has been on an incentive basis, vacation pay may result from "averaging." [46] However, another method of computing vacation pay, which is applicable to an employee either on an hourly or incentive rate, is to provide a specified percentage of his earnings for the year preceding the vacation. For example, the employee may be entitled to two percent (2%) of his earnings for a week of vacation leave, and four percent (4%) for two weeks vacation. Some agreements guarantee a minimum amount of pay for each week of vacation. This means that there are at least four different ways of computing vacation pay — either straight time or incentive earnings can be used

---

[46] A. L. Gitlow, Labor and Industrial Society 486-88 (rev. 3d. 1963).

as the base and these can be spread over either a weekly period or a percentage of the earnings of the past year. Depending on which combination of these is used, very different results can be reached. Consider the following examples.

Example 1

Hourly employees who, on June 15, have 1 year, but less than two years, of continuous service shall be eligible for one week's vacation with pay. Hourly employees, who, on June 15th, have two years or more of continuous service shall be eligible for two weeks' vacation with pay.

Vacation pay shall be computed by multiplying the number of hours in the regularly scheduled work-week by the straight-time hourly rate of pay but shall, in no event, be less than forty nor more than forty-eight hours pay. All normal deductions shall be deducted from vacation pay. The same principle shall be followed in computing vacation pay for straight time employees.

Example 2

Employees who have completed one year of service with the Company shall be granted one week's vacation at straight time pay. The number of days' pay for vacation week, shall be equal to the average of the number of shifts worked during the ten weeks' period immediately preceding vacation.

Example 3

In any calendar year during the term of this Agreement or any extension thereof, the Company will grant vacations to employees who are employed on July 1st, having continuous service to that date, in accordance with the following schedule:

Years of Service	No. of Weeks	Payment Amount
15 or more	3	6% or 120 hrs.
10 but less than 15	2	5% or 100 hrs.
5 but less than 10	2	4% or 80 hrs.
3 but less than 5	1	3% or 60 hrs.
1 but less than 3	1	2% or 40 hrs.

The payment amounts indicated above are in terms of percent of the employee's straight time earnings for the twelve month period prior to July 1st or for the number of hours listed at the employee's base hourly rate. The amount which is the greater will be paid.

Example 4

Piece-workers or employees working on a similar basis will receive vacation money determined by the average hourly earning rate for the four-week period preceding the last week worked (excluding overtime, time spent at hourly rate, and time spent on work to which the employee has been temporarily transferred if his rate is less than on his regular job) and the scheduled workweek in effect at the time of vacation.

Hourly-pay workers will receive vacation money determined by their hourly rate in effect immediately prior to vacation and the scheduled workweek in effect at the time of vacation (excluding overtime, and the time spent on work to which the employee has been temporarily transferred, if the rate is less than on his regular job).

Example 5

Each employee who has a minimum of one year's service with the present or original employer shall be eligible to participate, provided he has not quit or changed employers of his own volition.

Each employee who has one year's service, as outlined above, will be eligible for one week's vacation with pay. Vacation pay will be two percent (2%) of his gross earnings for the preceding calendar year.

Each employee who has five or more years' service, as outlined above, will be eligible for two weeks' vacation with pay. Vacation pay will be four percent (4%) of his gross earnings for the preceding calendar year.

One of the interesting problems, presented by Examples 4 and 5, is whether to include the computation of vacation pay in the case of incentive workers. Vacation pay is supposedly meant to compensate the employee who is on vacation at the same level he would be on if working. On the other hand, incentive earnings are only paid to employees who expend extra effort. Obviously the employee on vacation is not "earning" an incentive wage, but not paying him at such a level would penalize him for taking a vacation. If the premise is accepted that vacations are an earned right, it can be argued that all year while the employee is making incentive earnings, he is earning that much more vacation pay.

In principle is it preferable to compute vacation pay at the present weekly rate or as a percentage of the preceding year's earnings? For an employee who was paid at the same rate all year there would be no difference between a percentage calculation and a weekly figure based on present earnings since 2% of 50 weeks (excluding vacation time) is one week's pay. A percentage figure would seem to make more sense if the employees were under an incentive system since there is more likelihood of wide differences from week to week in take home pay. However, in Example 3 this system is applied to straight time workers. In their case, such an application means that for any raises received over the past year they would get only a percentage of that raise in their vacation pay. Using the "accrued vacation pay" theory, this would seem to be a logical result since the workers were earning less pay and hence less vacation pay earlier in the year when they were paid at the lower rate. However, paying on a percentage basis results in the employee "losing" money during vacation, since his take home pay during vacation won't include his entire raise, and will, therefore, be less than the weeks immediately preceding the vacation. Although these are basic issues in selecting a method of computation of vacation pay, when they are applied to an employment context cost-analysis may affect the parties' attitudes as to which pay variation should be adopted.

(3) Wage Payments in Lieu of Vacations

Where an employer reschedules vacation of an employee for business reasons, may the employer reschedule rather than pay employee in lieu of vacation, even if it is inconvenient to employee? *Compare International Paper Co.,* 65 L.A. 572 (Moore 1975) *with Sanitas Window Cleaner Co.,* 12 L.A. L58 (Donnely 1949).

(4) Scheduling of Vacations

How should management draft a clause so that it might have plant-wide shutdown for a vacation period if it desires? *See Hondaille Industries Inc.,* 61 L.A. 958 (Rill 1973); *Wyman-Gordon Co.,* 51 L.A. 561 (Rauch 1968); *and Tenneco Chemicals Inc.,* 51 L.A. 699 (Williams 1968). *Compare Sherwin-Williams Co.,* 18 L.A. 934 (Kelliher 1952) holding otherwise where contract provided:

"Vacations as far as possible will be granted at the time most desired by the employee, however, the right to allot the vacation period is reserved by the Company to insure the orderly operation of the plant, and the vacation must be taken during the twelve (12) month period following the date of qualification and shall not be consecutive nor cumulative. Every eligible employee will be notified of his vacation allowance and period at least thirty (30) days in advance. Employees receiving vacations will receive vacation pay from the Company at the beginning of their vacation period, if desired by the employee."

(a) *Advance Notice:* Sometimes the employer does not give proper advance notice to the employees about vacation schedules. Even if the contract is silent, it is better policy to give adequate notice of vacation assignments, as a matter of employee relations, so that they can make advance plans. In *Bethlehem Steel Co.,* 11 L.A. 629 (1948), Arbitrator M. Shipman disallowed cancellation of a vacation three days before vacation was scheduled to begin. *Compare General American Transportation Co.,* 15 L.A. 481 (1950) where Arbitrator Kelliher held that an employer was not required to give more notice than the day preceding the beginning of the employee's vacation.

(b) *Postponement, Carry-Over, Accumulation and Extended Vacations:* The contract should provide for other contingencies in scheduling vacations. For example, although many contracts prohibit postponement, carry-over, and accumulation of vacation time,[47] some flexibility may be desirable to meet emergency situations.

Furthermore, traditional concepts of granting vacations for rest and relaxation are expending to include vacations for sabbaticals and to avoid periodic layoffs or anticipate retirement. For examples of such plans *see* CBNC, Collective Bargaining Negotiations and Contract Provisions, Vol. 2, 91:325-431 (BNA).

c. Paid Sick Leave

The two prevalent ways of protecting employees against income loss arising from illness are "sickness and accident insurance" (listed by the Department of Labor under "private welfare plans") and "paid sick leave." This protection is distinguished from Workmen's Compensation protection (listed by the Department of Labor under "legally required insurance programs") which covers on-the-job accidents and illnesses. The major differences between the two "private" plans are that where insurance is used, it is almost always purchased from a private carrier, while sick leave is almost invariably paid directly by the employer. Moreover, while insurance seldom provides full salary, paid sick leave (sometimes after a specified waiting period) normally does pay full salary for a contractual time period. According to Labor Department statistics, paid sick leave amounts only to .5% of total employer expenditures for wages. Without attempting any detailed coverage, the following items are significant in negotiating "paid sick leave" plans.

CHECKLIST FOR SICK LEAVE PROVISIONS

I. ELIGIBILITY REQUIREMENTS FOR SICK LEAVE PAY
    a. Who are excluded from receiving sick leave pay?
        (1) Temporary, casual or part-time employees
        (2) Employees on layoff
        (3) Employees who caused accident by willful and/or unlawful acts

---

[47] 2 C.B.N.C. § 91:151.

b. Is a doctor's certificate required?
  (1) During disability
  (2) On return to work
  (3) After a certain period of illness
  (4) While being attended to by a licensed physician or surgeon (required)
  (5) Notice to company as alternative
c. Do employees receive time off for unused sick leave?
d. Do employees have to make up hours?
e. What is the effect of sick leave on other time off?
  (1) Holiday pay
  (2) Layoff, leave of absence, strike

II. DURATION OF PAID SICK LEAVE
  a. How is the length of time to be paid computed?
    (1) Relate to length of service by hours or days
    (2) Uniform (for eligible employees)
    (3) Use of previous year's sick leave time
    (4) No time limit
  b. Is sick leave pay to be accumulated?
    (1) Prohibition
    (2) Limitations
    (3) Unlimited

III. RATE OF PAY DURING SICK LEAVE
  a. How is the rate of pay during sick leave to be computed?
    (1) Full pay for specified time
    (2) Full pay for specified time period and partial pay for additional time period
    (3) Partial pay throughout
    (4) Prorated with Workmen's Compensation payments
  b. Is there a waiting period prior to payment?
    (1) Days or weeks
    (2) Scaled to length of service — overtime and non-overtime employees included
    (3) None
  c. When is payment made?
    (1) Advances on sick leave pay

IV. UNUSED SICK LEAVE PAY
  a. Are employees paid for unused sick leave pay?
    (1) Limited accumulation
    (2) Excess over eligibility limit
    (3) Annually at base rate
    (4) On termination of employment

V. ABUSES
  a. How can sick leave pay abuses be curbed?
    (1) Required proof of illness

(2) Review board
(3) Disciplinary action
(4) Compensation returned

2. Retirement Plans

Fringe benefits under the U.S. Department of Labor and U.S. Chamber of Commerce nomenclature include retirement programs. After pay for time worked, retirement programs constitute the largest element of compensation — about 8.1% or 51 cents per work hour.[48]

Table 10. Retirement programs: Percent of total compensation.[49]

Employee group, compensation item, and industry	Average expenditures		Total	That had no expend- itures
	All establish- ments	Establish- ments that had expend- itures [1]		
All employees				
Retirement programs:				
All industries	8.1	8.1	100	—
Manufacturing	8.4	8.4	100	—
Nonmanufacturing	7.9	7.9	100	—
Social security:				
All industries	4.4	4.4	100	—
Manufacturing	4.3	4.3	100	—
Nonmanufacturing	4.4	4.4	100	—
Private plans:				
All industries	3.7	4.8	100	34
Manufacturing	4.0	4.6	100	17
Nonmanufacturing	3.5	4.9	100	41

Although these materials do not cover Social Security, the 1977 amendments made clear that there will be substantial increases in contributions and benefits for the next decade, 42 U.S.C.A. § 401 _et seq._ (1978 Supp.).[50]

a. Private Plans

A Labor Department 1974 study indicates:

Higher paid workers are more likely than lower paid workers to have their social security coverage augmented through private retirement plans — pension plans, deferred profit-sharing plans, or both. In manufacturing, for example, 78

---

[48] Employee Compensation, _supra_ note 31 at 8.
[49] Id. at 21.
[50] _See e.g.,_ R. Ball, Social Security Today and Tomorrow (1978); J. Pechman, H. Aaron, M. Taussig, The Objectives of Social Security, in J. T. Elow, Comm. Subcomm. on Fiscal Policy, 90th Cong., 1st Sess. 5-20 (H. Comm. Print 1967).

percent of nonoffice workers and 86 percent of office workers were in establishments having expenditures for private retirement plans, while in nonmanufacturing, where earnings are generally lower, only 69 percent of office and 48 percent of nonoffice workers were in such establishments. Unlike expenditures for social security, those for private plans increased as a percent of compensation as wages and salaries increased.[51]

Table 25 shows the breakdown to be:

Table 25. Private retirement plans by establishment total compensation level, private nonfarm economy, 1974 [52]

Employee group, industry, and establishment average total compensation level per work hour	Percent distribution of employment in all establishments	Establishments that had expenditures for—					
		Any plans		Contributory plans		Noncontributory plans	
		Employees as a percent of employment at the compensation level	Expenditures as a percent of total compensation	Employees as a percent of employment at the compensation level	Expenditures as a percent of total compensation	Employees as a percent of employment at the compensation level	Expenditures as a percent of total compensation
Office employees							
All industries:							
All levels	100	73	5.6	17	4.2	56	6.0
Under $4.00	8	25	2.8	6	2.5	19	2.9
$4.00 to $4.99	12	69	4.4	15	3.7	54	4.6
$5.00 to $5.99	13	68	4.0	15	3.7	52	4.1
$6.00 to $6.99	12	72	4.8	17	5.7	55	4.5
$7.00 to $7.99	12	82	4.7	19	3.6	63	5.0
$8.00 to $8.99	12	82	5.1	27	3.8	55	5.7
$9.00 to $9.99	11	77	5.3	26	4.4	51	5.8
$10.00 to $10.99	5	86	6.2	16	5.4	70	6.3
$11.00 to $11.99	4	95	6.5	29	4.1	66	7.4
$12.00 to $12.99	2	86	7.5	4	2.4	82	7.7
$13.00 to $13.99	2	96	6.4	9	3.8	86	6.7
$14.00 and over	6	75	7.8	1	5.4	74	7.8
Manufacturing:							
All levels	100	86	5.6	18	4.5	68	5.8
Under $4.00	1	32	2.9	25	2.8	7	3.5
$4.00 to $4.99	4	73	3.6	7	2.9	66	3.7
$5.00 to $5.99	7	63	3.7	6	3.4	57	3.8
$6.00 to $6.99	10	79	5.7	29	8.6	49	4.0
$7.00 to $7.99	14	82	4.7	17	4.2	65	4.8
$8.00 to $8.99	15	91	5.0	14	2.9	77	5.4
$9.00 to $9.99	15	92	4.7	38	4.1	54	5.1
$10.00 to $10.99	11	93	6.2	12	5.1	82	6.4
$11.00 to $11.99	7	95	6.4	22	4.1	74	7.0
$12.00 to $12.99	6	97	7.5	5	2.6	92	7.7
$13.00 to $13.99	6	98	6.0	8	3.6	90	6.2
$14.00 and over	3	69	6.6	4	2.8	65	6.8
Nonmanufacturing:							
All levels	100	69	5.6	17	4.1	52	6.1
Under $4.00	10	25	2.8	5	2.5	20	2.8
$4.00 to $4.99	14	68	4.5	15	3.7	53	4.7
$5.00 $5.99	14	68	4.1	17	3.7	51	4.2
$6.00 to $6.99	13	71	4.5	14	4.2	56	4.6
$7.00 to $7.99	12	82	4.7	19	3.4	62	5.1
$8.00 to $8.99	10	78	5.2	33	4.0	46	5.9
$9.00 to $9.99	10	70	5.7	21	4.7	49	6.2
$10.00 to $10.99	3	78	6.1	20	4.6	58	6.2
$11.00 to $11.99	4	95	6.6	34	4.1	61	7.7
$12.00 to $12.99	1	73	7.4	2	2.0	71	7.6
$13.00 to $13.99	1	91	7.3	12	4.2	79	7.8
$14.00 and over	7	76	7.9	1	6.7	75	7.9

[51] Employee Compensation, *supra* note 31 at 8; *see generally* D. M. Gill, Fundamentals of Private Pensions (3d ed. 1975).

[52] Employee Compensation, *supra* note 31 at 39.

b. *The Employee Retirement Income Security Act of 1974 (ERISA)* [53]

As the Department of Labor explains: [54]

> Private employee benefit plans affect the welfare of millions of workers and their families. The vast assets of such plans have a significant impact on the national economy. Protections and guarantees are provided for employees covered by private employee pension and welfare plans and their beneficiaries by the Employee Retirement Income Security Act of 1974 (ERISA), signed into law on Labor Day, September 2, 1974.

> Responsibility for carrying out the law's provisions is assigned to the U.S. Department of Labor, the Internal Revenue Service of the U.S. Treasury Department, and a new Government corporation named the Pension Benefit Guaranty Corporation, which was created to administer the law's plan termination insurance provisions.

> The law applies to two types of employee benefit plans — pension plans, which provide retirement benefits, and welfare plans, which provide health, accident, etc., benefits. The law does not require any employer to establish a plan, but those that do must meet certain minimum standards. The law also provides that each employed individual not covered by a pension plan other than Social Security may put aside, tax-free, a certain amount of compensation for retirement.

> The purpose of ERISA is to protect the interests of workers who participate in these plans and their beneficiaries — to see that workers are not required to satisfy unreasonable age and service requirements before becoming eligible for pension plan participation (through the participation provisions); to see that persons who work for a specified minimum period under a pension plan are assured of at least some pension at retirement age (through the vesting provisions); to see that the money will be there to pay pension benefits when they are due (through the funding provisions); to see that plan funds are handled prudently (through the fiduciary provisions); to see that employees know their rights under the plans and their obligations (through the reporting and disclosure provisions); to see that spouses of pensioners are given better protection (through the joint and survivor provisions); to see that the benefits of workers in certain defined benefit pension plans are protected in the event of a plan

---

[53] Public Law 93-406, 93d Cong. H.R. 2 (9/2/74); 88 Stat. 829, 29 U.S.C. 1001 *et seq.* (1974).

[54] U.S. Dep't of Labor, Coverage Under Employment Retirement Security Act of 1974 (G.P.O. 219-393 1976).

termination (through the plan termination insurance provisions); and to make the tax laws relative to pensions more equitable (through various provisions of title II under the jurisdiction of the Internal Revenue Service).

Both welfare and pension plans are subject to the reporting and disclosure requirements and the fiduciary standards. The participation, vesting, joint and survivor, funding, and plan termination insurance provisions apply only to certain pension plans.

ERISA is composed of four titles. Title I, administered by the Department of Labor, deals with protection of employee benefit rights. Title II is composed of amendments to the Internal Revenue Code. Title III deals with the division of responsibility between the agencies administering the law. Title IV deals with the plan termination insurance provisions and established the Pension Benefit Guaranty Corporation.

As two counselors of the UAW correctly indicate, ERISA "profoundly affects the collective bargaining of employee benefit plans." [55] They explain:

The Act prescribes the minimum requirements an employee benefit plan must satisfy. Further, it defines certain bargaining choices, and provides for alternative means of compliance, variances, and extensions of time, all of which raise bargaining issues. Nonbenefit contract provisions will be affected by ERISA, as will doctrines of successorship and the law of information availability in collective bargaining. Finally, ERISA raises questions of the relationship of its termination provisions to contract terms agreed upon by the parties. Although the changes effected by ERISA are quite significant, the aspects of the bargaining process left unaltered by the Act are equally important. ERISA removes neither the traditional duty of labor and management to bargain over most aspects of employee benefits, nor the parties' obligation to abide by the legally enforceable contract terms to which they have agreed.

The relationship of certain provisions of ERISA to the rights and duties of labor and management outlined in the National Labor Relations Act [²] will be explored and discussed in this Article, and suggestions will be offered for resolution of

---

[55] Fillion and Trebilcock, "The Duty to Bargain Under ERISA," 17 Wm & Mary L. Rev. 251, 251-53, 300-1 (1975). Reprinted with permission of Publisher © 1975.

[²] The Wagner Act, 49 Stat. 449 (1935), as amended by the Taft-Hartley Act, 61 Stat. 136 (1947), comprises the National Labor Relations Act, 29 U.S.C. §§ 151-68 (1970), *as amended,* 29 U.S.C.A. §§ 152, 158 (Supp. 1975) [hereinafter cited as NLRA].

problems inherent in that relationship. As litigation [3] was needed to clarify the connection between contractual grievance arbitration clauses and individual rights under Title VII of the Civil Rights Act of 1964,[4] and the interplay of unfair labor practices and arbitration,[5] judicial guidance ultimately will be required to elucidate the relationship of collective bargaining and resultant contractual rights to the statutory scheme of ERISA.

Although most of the questions for collective bargaining examined in this Article have not yet been answered, labor law practitioners already are encountering new problems resulting from the enactment of ERISA. For example, if benefit plans are rewritten to satisfy the requirements of the Act, the employer's proposed language may omit provisions agreed upon in prior contracts that have given employees rights exceeding ERISA minimum standards.[6] To reap the benefits of ERISA, however, unions cannot be required to relinquish gains previously won in bargaining. The legislative history and the statutory and regulatory structure of ERISA demonstrate that the union need bargain over only those changes required to bring the plan into compliance with the law.

In the area of plan terminations, conflicts already have arisen between determinations of the Pension Benefit Guaranty Corporation, charged with administering the insurance provisions of ERISA, and collective bargaining contract provisions that relate to plan terminations. Divergences occur chiefly over the

---

[3] *See* Rios v. Reynolds Metals Co., 467 F.2d 54 (5th Cir. 1972); Hutchings v. United States Indus., Inc., 428 F.2d 303 (5th Cir. 1970); Dewey v. Reynolds Metals Co., 429 F.2d 324 (6th Cir. 1970), *aff'd by an equally divided Court,* 402 U.S. 689 (1971). The relationship between arbitration and litigation under Title VII was resolved by the Supreme Court in Alexander v. Gardner-Denver Co., 415 U.S. 36 (1974), which held that prior arbitration of a claim under Title VII would not bar trial de novo of that claim in federal court. *See generally* Isaacson & Zifchak, "Fair Employment Forums After Alexander v. Gardner-Denver Co.: Separate and Unequal, 16 Wm. & Mary L. Rev. 439 (1975).

[4] 42 U.S.C. §§ 2000e to 2000e-15 (1970), *as amended,* 42 U.S.C. §§ 2000e to 2000e-17 (Supp. II, 1972).

[5] For example, in Local 55, UAW v. Silver Creek Precision Corp., 89 L.R.R.M. 2922 (W.D.N.Y. 1975), the union was permitted to resort to arbitration over an employer's failure to contribute to a pension plan at the same time that an unfair labor practice charge and a criminal complaint were pursued.

[6] This problem has been increased by the announcement that the Internal Revenue Service will prepare model contract language for compliance with ERISA. The agency was offering the prototype language to employers faced with amending existing plans or establishing new plans. Daily Lab. Rep., Apr. 17, 1975, at A-1. In addition to the inappropriateness of the preparation of such collective bargaining language by the IRS, the action was taken without any recognition of the bargaining duties of employers whose workers are represented by labor unions.

circumstances triggering plan termination, date of termination, the allocation of plan assets upon termination, and the relationship of termination to other issues subject to bargaining. Here, as in plan formulation, if the contract affords better protection to employees than that imposed by the Corporation, the government and judiciary should respect the parties' agreement under the National Labor Relations Act.

The purpose of ERISA, to protect plan participants' and beneficiaries' rights to earned benefits, and that of the National Labor Relations Act, to foster good faith collective bargaining and enforcement of contracts for the peaceful resolution of labor-management disputes, can be accommodated and achieved only by the recognition that ERISA lays down minimum standards for employee benefit plans. Employers and union should remain free to negotiate greater protection for workers than that provided by statute.

They conclude that:

In several major respects, ERISA will have a substantial impact on the collective bargaining process. The Act virtually prescribes minimum contract language, thus limiting the parties' acceptable range of agreement. It requires revisions of employee benefit plans, which often must be negotiated in midterm. Although more information is made freely available to unions, ERISA creates a greater need for detailed information to enable effective bargaining on employee benefits. In addition, because the definition of a successor employer included in the Act differs from that of the Supreme Court, another variable has been introduced into the uncertain status of former and successor employers in relation to incumbent unions.

The changes brought about by ERISA should not obfuscate those areas of labor law that the Act has not altered. The parties still are obligated to bargain over changes in employee benefit plans, and a refusal to bargain will result in the traditional consequences. The scope of the duty to bargain, however, should extend only to those changes necessary to satisfy the Act. Nor does the scheme for plan terminations incorporated in the Act void obligations under a collective bargaining agreement that do not conflict with the Act. Participants' and beneficiaries' rights under a terminated plan are satisfied by Pension Benefit Guaranty Corporation insurance only to the extent of that guarantee; the balance of their pension rights remains enforceable through traditional remedies.

ERISA was enacted to protect participants in collectively bargained plans, as well as in plans formulated by other means. This statutory goal cannot be achieved if the Act is construed to repeal rights and duties in force prior to its enactment. If the parties to a collective bargaining contract reach agreement on standards more protective of employee rights than the provisions of the Act, ERISA should be interpreted to preserve those rights.

NOTE:

Not only does ERISA have a substantial impact on the collective bargaining process, as Fillion and Trebilcock indicate, but it also has major repercussions in the area of labor arbitration. *See* Murphy, "The Impact of ERISA on Arbitration," 32 Arb. J. 123 (1977).

3. Life Insurance and Health Benefits

According to Labor Department statistics, almost all employees covered by collective bargaining agreements have some form of insurance paid for, at least in part, by their employers.[56]

---

[56] Employee Compensation, *supra* note 31 at 23.

Table 12. Life insurance and health benefit programs: Percent of total compensation

Employee group, compensation item, and industry	Average expenditures		Total	That had no no expend- itures
	All establish- ments [1]	Establish- ments that had expend- itures [1]		
All employees				
Life insurance and health benefit programs: [2]				
All industries	4.9	4.9	100	1
Manufacturing	5.9	5.9	100	([3])
Nonmanufacturing	4.4	4.4	100	2
Life, accident, and health insurance:				
All industries	3.3	3.5	100	14
Manufacturing	4.3	4.4	100	3
Nonmanufacturing	2.7	3.0	100	19
Sick leave:				
All industries	.7	.9	100	31
Manufacturing	.6	.7	100	22
Nonmanufacturing	.7	1.0	100	36
Workers' compensation:				
All industries	1.0	1.0	100	5
Manufacturing	.9	.9	100	1
Nonmanufacturing	1.0	1.1	100	6
Office employees				
Life insurance and health benefit programs: [2]				
All industries	4.2	4.2	100	1
Manufacturing	5.0	5.0	100	([3])
Nonmanufacturing	3.8	3.9	100	2
Life, accident, and health insurance:				
All industries	2.8	3.0	100	9
Manufacturing	3.7	3.7	100	3
Nonmanufacturing	2.5	2.7	100	11
Sick leave:				
All industries	.9	1.1	100	20
Manufacturing	.9	1.1	100	15
Nonmanufacturing	.9	1.1	100	22
Workers' compensation:				
All industries	.4	.4	100	7
Manufacturing	.4	.4	100	4
Nonmanufacturing	.4	.4	100	9
Nonoffice employee				
Life insurance and health benefit programs: [2]				
All industries	5.6	5.6	100	2
Manufacturing	6.4	6.4	100	([3])
Nonmanufacturing	5.0	5.1	100	3
Life, accident, and health insurance:				
All industries	3.6	4.0	100	19
Manufacturing	4.7	4.8	100	4
Nonmanufacturing	2.8	3.3	100	27
Sick leave:				
All industries	.5	1.0	100	56
Manufacturing	.4	1.0	100	58
Nonmanufacturing	.5	1.1	100	56
Workers' compensation:				
All industries	1.5	1.5	100	4
Manufacturing	1.2	1.2	100	1
Nonmanufacturing	1.7	1.8	100	6

Sick leave was included as a health benefit rather than as part of paid leave because it is frequently provided in lieu of sickness and accident insurance. Unlike expenditures for retirement programs, those for insurance and health programs were relatively more important for nonoffice workers than for office workers. These expenditures made up 5.6 percent of nonoffice compensation, compared to 4.2 percent for office compensation. However, at 30 cents an hour, expenditures for nonoffice workers were 3 cents less than those for office workers. Only sick leave accounted for a larger proportion of office than of nonoffice compensation. Information about insurance plans must be generalized since the benefits vary greatly.[57] The most common benefit is a group life insurance plan provided in flat amounts for all employees, related to earnings or length of service. Accidental Death and Dismemberment benefits are often equal in amount to life insurance.[58]

As Professor Merton Bernstein points out in his seminal book, The Future of Private Pensions (1964), the advantages of such plans are that they act as a partial substitute for survivor benefits and they cover death from any cause as distinguished from work-related injury. On the other hand, most employees who are covered by pensions are also covered by life insurance, and the size of the benefits are frequently consumed by expenses on the death of the insured.[59] However, each plan should be evaluated on its own merits.

The Bureau of Labor Statistics Table 22 shows the following breakdown of insurance programs:[60]

---

[57] M. C. Bernstein, The Future of Private Pensions 157 (1964).
[58] Id.
[59] Id.
[60] 2 C.B.N.C. § 53:1 (3/13/75).

Table 22. Components of private life, accident, and health insurance, private nonfarm economy, 1974

Employee group, industry, and size of establishment	Percent distribution of employment in all establishments	Life insurance only —		Sickness and accident insurance only —		Hospitalization and medical insurance only —		Life, sickness, and accident insurance only —		Life, hospitalization and medical insurance only —		Sickness and accident insurance only —		Life, sickness, accident, hospitalization, and medical insurance	
		Employees as a percent of employment in the size range	Expenditures as a percent of total compensation	Employees as a percent of employment in the size range	Expenditures as a percent of total compensation	Employees as a percent of employment in the size range	Expenditures as a percent of total compensation	Employees as a percent of employment in the size range	Expenditures as a percent of total compensation	Employees as a percent of employment in the size range	Expenditures as a percent of total compensation	Employees as a percent of employment in the size range	Expenditures as a percent of total compensation	Employees as a percent of employment in the size range	Expenditures as a percent of total compensation
Office employees															
All industries:															
All sizes	100	0.6	1.5	0.1	1.9	0.3	2.7	0.6	1.6	17.8	2.4	0.5	1.8	70.7	3.2
Under 100 employees	46	1.0	1.6	.2	1.9	.5	2.2	1.2	1.6	19.7	2.0	1.0	1.8	56.3	3.0
100 to 499 employees	19	.5	.7	—	—	(¹)	1.1	.1	.7	23.1	2.5	.1	1.7	75.7	2.9
500 or more employees	34	.1	1.8	—	—	.1	4.8	.2	1.6	12.1	3.0	(¹)	1.1	87.4	3.5

4. Income Maintenance

One of three forms of income maintenance — pay guarantees, severance pay or supplemental unemployment benefit (SUB) plans — are found in almost one-half of all labor contracts.[61] The most common clauses provide for severance pay, often called "separation" or "termination" pay. Severance pay is generally available as a result of permanent shutdowns, with the amount frequently tied to prior service and earnings. Some provisions are tied to SUB plans.

Supplemental Unemployment Benefits are the second most common income maintenance provisions.[62] Such plans fall into the common "pooled-fund" system where the benefit arise only in the case of lack of work, or the less common "individual account" system where an employee can draw funds for reasons other than lack of work. These plans are worth consideraing particularly because of their close relationship to Guaranteed Annual Wage Plans (GAW). In Father Becker's worthwhile book, Guaranteed Income for the Unemployed: The Story of SUB (1968), he explains:

> Labor's long-felt interest in a guaranteed annual wage, was given concrete expression toward the end of World War II, when a number of industrial unions, led by the steelworkers, made definite demands on employers for this form of income security. The influential Latimer Report (January 1947) found these demands unrealistic — at least at that time — and suggested instead a plan to supplement the benefits provided by the public program of unemployment insurance. Thus was conceived SUB, one of the more striking examples of social inventiveness in our time.[63]

Father Becker concludes: "As a protection against unemployment, SUB would seem to be a more adequate instrument than either the original proposed guaranteed annual wage or the individual-account plan."

Among the unions negotiating these plans are the UAW, Steelworkers, Rubberworkers, Ladies Garment Workers, IUE, Machinists, Seafarers and Teamsters. As E.H. Beier explains: [64]

> Dissimilar patterns are found in the incidence of benefit disbursement and of contributions during the period. Total benefit payments, as would be expected, varied inversely with the level of business activity. The largest payments occurred in 1961,

---

[61] 2 C.B.N.C. § 53:601 (5/4/75).

[62] 2 C.B.N.C. § 53:601 (8/14/75).

[63] J. Becker, Guaranteed Income for the Unemployed: The Story of Sub 275 (1968).

[64] E.H. Beier, Financing Supplemental Unemployment Benefit Plans, 1969 Monthly Lab. Rev. 31 (Nov. 1969).

the year of heaviest unemployment for most industries with SUB plans, and the smallest occurred in 1964 and 1965, years of relatively high employment. Despite many benefit improvements in the interim, total payments in these 2 years were half as large as those in 1961. However, the amount of contributions was not related as closely to the level of business activity. The employer's financial obligation was almost always related directly to the level of employment, but total contributions in the highest year (1962) exceeded those in the lowest (1961) by less than 50 percent, compared with a difference of more than 100 percent between benefit payments in the highest and lowest years.

Types of funding

Advance funding (the payment of contributions into a trust fund before they are needed) has been used almost without exception. Pay-as-you-go financing could inflict an excessive burden on the employer's working capital, because the number and amount of benefit claims tend to mushroom during slack periods when his earnings are low. However, such benefit experience, plus the fact that certain business risks (*e.g.,* a decline in the demand for the company's products) are not insurable, have also made SUB uninsurable. Consequently, accumulated contributions and the income from their investment are invariably held in a trust fund.

All of the current funding arrangements were developed during the 1950's as SUB arrangements were negotiated. The first plan — that negotiated in 1955 by the Automobile Workers and the Ford Motor Co. — required prompt discharge of the company's entire financial obligation. The full amount of the commitment for each operating period was regularly paid into a general trust fund without any allocation of money to individual participants. This general trust arrangement was subsequently used in plans of the Rubber Workers. Over 1 million employees participated in these plans in 1967.

The funding approach used in multiemployer plans was quite similar to the general trust arrangement used in single employer plans. However, under these pooled funds, the contribution from a number of employers were placed in a single trust fund from which all benefits were paid. There were few such plans, but the largest of them — the Ladies Garment Workers plan — covered over 400,000 workers. Their total coverage in 1967 was approximately a half million workers, or a fifth of all SUB plan participants.

The Steelworkers and companies in the basic steel industry developed another approach of financing. Instead of requiring employers to make regular cash contributions equal to their financial obligation for the previous operating period, their obligation was split into a cash contribution and "contingent liability." The cash portion was placed in a general trust fund. The contingent liability accrual, when added to any other accumulations, measured the employer's commitment to make additional payments if needed to meet benefit claims. In the meantime, the company retained control and use of the funds. About 700,000 workers were covered by plans with this type of arrangement.

The only remaining funding method of any significance required cash contributions that were allocated to the accounts of individual workers,[153] and the participants acquired a vested interest in all contributions made in their behalf. In other words, the balance in an individual's account (*i.e.,* contributions and any income from their investment) was payable when he left the company. The Glass and Ceramic Workers negotiated most of the limited number of such plans. They covered less than 100,000 workers.

Although subsequent negotiations produced some changes in the plans (*e.g.,* in the level of benefits, rate of contribution, or level of maximum financing), the original forms of the funding arrangements have tended to remain unchanged. The cement industry provided the only notable exception, when contingent liability was added in 1967 to most of the plans in that industry.
. . . .

Coverage

Unlike other employee benefits, this product of collective bargaining has not spread to a great variety of industries. In fact, as shown in table 1, the transportation equipment and primary ferrous metals industries accounted for over half of all SUB plan participants throughout the 8-year period studied. This, of course, reflects the pioneering efforts of the Automobile Workers and Steelworkers. But it also underscores the unsuitability of SUB in many situations, the higher priority placed on wages and other benefits, and the limited interest on the part of all but a few unions. Most of the existing plans were negotiated within a 2-year period (1955-56) by the Automobile Workers, Steelworkers, Rubber Workers, and a few other unions. The national plan negotiated in 1960 by the Ladies Garment

---

[153] These plans would not conform with a rigid definition of supplemental unemployment benefits. While employees can draw benefits in time of layoff, they are not integrated with State unemployment insurance benefits.

Workers and employers in the apparel industry accounted for about two-thirds of the growth in coverage since 1956./[154/]

More unions undoubtedly will seek SUB once they have obtained benefits to which they assign higher priorities. However. the lack of growth alsp reflects, at least in part, SUB's unsuitability in some employment situations. Where unemployment is a minor problem, SUB probably is not considered a serious objective of collective bargaining; but where severe unemployment is chronic, its cost could be prohibitive. Furthermore, coverage statistics support the contentions that it is difficult to apply SUB to small groups. Although pooled funding arrangements can help reduce the relatively severe impact that layoffs may have on small companies, in 1967, the plans with under 500 members covered only 2.6 percent of the total, and those with fewer than 4,000 members accounted for about 20 percent of all participants.

The least frequent income maintenance plans — "work or pay guarantees" provide for a specific amount of work or pay for employees with a specified minimum amount of service.[65]

E. HOURS AND PREMIUM PAY PROVISIONS

1. Introduction

Hours of work — This subject is specifically mentioned in Section 8(d) of the National Labor Relations Act as bargaining topic, and most collective agreements deal with it. From the point of view of employees, the bargaining effort will usually be in the direction of spelling out in the contract not only the "normal" work day and workweek, but also specific working schedules. Management may be willing to make specific commitments of these matters; but, on the other hand, it may want to try to preserve some flexibility of scheduling and even the right to reduce (or increase) the "normal" daily or weekly hours of work. Refer to our previous discussion of "management rights" provisions, Chapter 9.

Premium pay — This closely-related subject relates to any payment above standard rates for hours worked where the premium is paid, not because of extra effort or production (as under an incentive wage system), but because of an onerous characteristic of the particular schedule or of working on the particular day. Premium pay provisions exist in many forms, the most commonplace of which are "overtime" rates for daily or weekly hours worked beyond the

---

[154] Social Security Bulletin, April 1965, p. 5.
[65] 2 C.B.N.C. § 53:1 (3/13/75).

normal daily and weekly schedules, and premium pay for work on holidays and weekends.

Legislation — The negotiating problem with respect to hours of work and premium pay assumes a knowledge of related statutory provisions. Every state, for example, has legislation applying to such matters as hours and conditions of work for women and children, for which the State Law volumes of the labor law loose-leaf services should be consulted. At the federal level, in addition to special legislative regulation of working hours for transportation employees, there are a number of statutes regulating the labor standards of government contractors, some of which require the payment of overtime compensation for work over 8 hours in one day or over 40 hours in one week:

> Davis-Bacon Act of 1931, 46 Stat. 1491, as amended, 40 U.S.C. secs. 276a to 276a-7;
>
> Walsh-Healey Public Contracts Act of 1936, 49 Stat. 2036, as amended, 41 U.S.C. secs. 35-46;
>
> Service Contract Act of 1965, Public Law 89-286, 41 U.S.C. secs. 351-57;
>
> Work Hours Act of 1962, Public Law 87-581, 40 U.S.C. secs. 321-26.

But by far the most important federal legislation regulating hours and premium pay, so far as the average employer is concerned, is the Fair Labor Standards Act of 1938, 29 U.S.C. § 201 *et seq.* as amended, and as supplemented by the Portal-to-Portal Act of 1949. 61 Stat. 84, 29 U.S.C. §§ 251-262. An acquaintance with the basic provisions of these Acts, and familiarity with the application of their "overtime" provisions, is essential background for the lawyer who engages or advises in collective bargaining and contract administration. Detailed information can be obtained conveniently from the "wage and hour" volumes of one of the labor law loose-leaf services and from the Interpretive Bulletins on Overtime Compensation published by the U.S. Department of Labor (Title 29, Parts 778, 785, and 790 of the Code of Federal Regulations). The following materials are intended as a brief introduction to the subject.

2. The Fair Labor Standards Act (29 U.S.C., secs. 201-219)

The text of the Act is set out in the Statutory Appendix to Smith, Merrifield, and St. Antoine, Labor Relations Law, 5th edition, pp. 100-20; and G. Ginsburg, Federal Labor Standards (2d ed. 1976). The coverage of the Act is as follows:

> (1) Regulations imposed
> > (a) Minimum wage provisions (Statutory references; Sections 6 and 3(m))

(b) "Overtime" provisions (Statutory references: Sections 7 and 3(o))

(c) Child labor provisions (Statutory references: Sections 12 and 3(*l*))

(2) Coverage
 (a) In general (Statutory references: Sections 6, 7, and 12)
 (b) Exemptions
  (i) From the wage and hour provisions (Statutory references: Sections 13(a), (d) and (f))
  (ii) From the overtime provisions (Statutory references: Sections 13(b), (e) and 14)
  (iii) From the child labor provisions (Statutory reference: Section 13(c))

(3) Enforcement (Statutory references: Sections 11, 15, 16 and 17)

The application of these provisions to wages and hours, however, is beyond the scope of these materials. For in depth coverage, we recommend Cases & Materials on Federal Labor Standards (2d ed.) by Professor Gilbert J. Ginsburg (G.W. University 1976).

3. Hours Provisions in Collective Agreements

Example 1

Eight hours per day and forty hours per week shall be the standard number of hours of work. Such workweek shall be Monday to Friday inclusive. (General Cable Corporation *and* IBEW, Local Union B-868)

Example 2

A normal workweek of forty (40) hours, consisting of five (5) eight (8) hour days, will prevail. This shall not be construed as a guarantee of hours of work per day or per week. [Borg & Beck Division, Borg-Warner Corporation *and* UAW (AFL-CIO)]

Example 3

Section 22 — Hours of Work
 (a) The workday shall be from 8:00 A.M. to 8:00 A.M. the following day.
 (b) The workweek shall be from 8:00 A.M. Monday to 8:00 A.M. the following Monday.
 (c) The normal working hours for the day shift shall be from 8:00 A.M. to 4:00 P.M.
 (d) The normal working hours for the afternoon shift shall be from 4:00 P.M. to 12:00 midnight.

(e) The normal working hours for the midnight shift shall be from 12:00 midnight to 8:00 A.M.

(f) The normal working hours for day workers shall be from 8:00 A.M. to 4:30 P.M., with 30 minutes out for a lunch period.

Section 23 — Odd Schedule

(This section recognized "that some work is of a nature that requires odd schedules," and such schedule is defined as one which does not conform to the "normal" schedules set forth in Section 22. Provision is made for the method of filling such schedules.)

By departmental agreement odd schedules of less than 30 days duration may be instituted.

Odd schedules of more than 30 days duration may be instituted upon approval of the Bargaining Committees. . . . [Dow Corning Corporation *and* Local 12934, District 50, United Mine Workers of America]

Example 4

The regularly scheduled workweek shall consist of forty (40) hours, eight (8) hours each day, from Monday to Friday, inclusive, except that the regular workweek of the regular No. 3 shift in departments other than the power plant and other similar continuous operations shall commence on Sunday night and end on Friday morning, and will not necessarily consist of forty (40) hours. It is agreed, however, that this provision is not intended to prevent the Company from scheduling work in addition to the regularly scheduled workday and workweek. . . .

The established starting times on workshifts shall not be changed without at least twenty-four (24) hours' prior notice to, discussion with and assent by the Shop Chairman.

If a general reduction of plant hours throughout the factory below forty (40) hours a week appears imminent, the Company will discuss the matter with the Union before putting into effect a general work schedule of less than forty (40) hours per week, provided, however, that no regular work schedule of thirty-two (32) hours per week shall be continued for more than six (6) successive weeks without the consent of the Shop Committee, and no regular work schedule of less than thirty-two (32) hours per week shall be instituted without the prior consent of the Shop Committee. [*American Seating Company* and *Local 135, UAW (AFL-CIO)*]

NOTES:

(1) Collective agreements typically provide for a "normal" or "standard" work day of 8 hours and a workweek of 40 hours, although in a substantial number of industries or plants the contract

calls for a shorter (or longer) workday or workweek. *See* U.S. Department of Labor, Bull. No. 1251, Premium Pay for Night, Weekend, and Overtime Work in Major Union Contracts (1959); H. Cohany & D. Weiss, Hours of Work and Overtime Provisions in Union Contracts, 1958 Monthly Lab Rev. 133-41.

(2) *Problems:* (a) Is it necessary or desirable to specify in the contract the period which will comprise the workday and workweek? Consider, in this connection, the implications of the Fair Labor Standards Act. *See Calumet & Hecla, Inc.,* 42 L.A. 25 (R. Howlett, 1963).

(b) Does the contractual specification of the workweek or workday, as in Example 1, *supra,* constitute a guarantee that employees will be given the specified number of hours of work per week or day? *See Wausau Iron Works,* 22 L.A. 473 (M. Slavney, 1954); *American Agricultural Chemical Co.,* 18 L.A. 625 (G. A. Dash, 1952).

(c) If a contract specifies a "regular" workweek of 40 hours spread over a specified five-day period (*e.g.,* Monday through Friday, as in Example 4, *supra*), is the employer precluded from scheduling employees regularly for 40 hours of work during a different five-day period, such as Monday through Saturday, excluding Wednesday? *See General Cable Corp.,* 15 L.A. 343 (S. Cahn, 1950); *Westinghouse Air Brake Co.,* 12 L.A. 307 (P. Lehoczky, 1949); *Pacific Press, Inc.,* 20 L.A. 871 (C. Spaulding, Chm. 1953).

(d) If a contract specifies the *hour* when the workday or workweek begins (*e.g.,* 7:00 A.M. Monday), but says nothing about employee work *schedules,* does it follow that the employer may not establish a regular work schedule beginning at an earlier or later hour (*e.g.,* for the day shift)? *See Western Automatic Machine Screw Co.,* 12 L.A. 38 (A. Horvitz, 1949).

(e) If a contract is (1) silent on employee work schedules, or (2) specifies "normal working hours" (as in Example 3, *supra*), is the employer precluded from changing normal work schedules? *See Standard Oil Co.,* 21 L.A. 243 (C. Kerr, 1953); *Wheeling Steel Corp.,* 21 L.A. 35 (M. Shipman, 1953); *Robertshaw-Fulton Controls Co.,* 21 L.A. 436 (S. Wolff, 1953).

(f) In cases involving departure from the normal workweek, what is the relevance of (1) the "reserved rights" theory, (2) the specificity of the management rights clause, (3) past practice of adhering to the normal workweek, and (4) the employer's motive in making the change? *See* the *Calumet & Hecla* case, *supra,* and *Universal Food Corporation,* 44 L.A. 226 (P. Hebert, 1965).

4. Premium Pay Provisions

"Premium pay" provisions exist in great variety and most collective agreements contain several of them. Since they provide rates of compensation in excess of the normal or regular rates, they are a cost item to the employer and an economic benefit item to the employee. Industry or area patterns and practices are likely to be influential in the determination of the kinds of provisions included in the agreement. Our purpose in this section is to provide a skeletal picture of the more common kinds of provisions (although it should not be assumed that all of those referred to will be found in most agreements). Some indication will be given of the problems of interpretation and application presented by these provisions. These should suggest some of the matters of which negotiators should take account in their bargaining and drafting of premium pay provisions.

a. "Overtime" Premiums

"Overtime at the rate of one and one-half (1½) times regular rate of pay shall be paid for hours worked in excess of eight (8) hours in any one day or forty (40) hours in any one week."

The recognition of hours worked daily or weekly in excess of the standard as premium or "overtime" hours is very common. The example quoted above presupposes, of course, 8 hours and 40 hours as the normal workday and workweek, respectively. The example appears to be a simple, unambiguous, and straightforward statement. Yet there are problems.

(1) What is the "day" or "week" within the meaning of this provision? Is is desirable to be specific about this? What are the possible definitions?

(a) Suppose the contract defines the workweek as being Monday through Sunday, and the daily overtime provision calls for payment of overtime for hours worked in excess of 8 in any 24-hour period (a fairly common type of provision). If an employee works on Sunday of one week on a weekly overtime basis from 4:00 P.M. to midnight, and then reports in on his regular shift the following morning (Monday) and works from 8:00 A.M. to 4:00 P.M., may he legitimately claim daily "overtime" for all the hours worked by him on Monday? Should this result be permitted? What kind of contract language would produce a contrary result?

(b) Suppose the contract defines the workday as the 24-hour period beginning with the employee's normal shift, and either expressly or because nothing is stated to the contrary the workweek is the calendar week. Does the end of the workweek also end the workday for employees working on the last shift in the week, even though the 24-hour period from the beginning of their shift has not expired? The arbitration cases are not unanimous on this point. *Cf. International Harvester Co.* 17 L.A. 29 (R. Seward, 1951); *Evans Products Co.,* 19 L.A. 457 (1952). In the latter case Arbitrator Harry H. Platt made use of an official ruling under the Walsh-Healey Act to find that the end of the workweek terminated the last day of the workweek. In 1956 the Administrator of the Act redefined the terms "workday" and "workweek" with the result that each day, including the last in the workweek, will be exactly 24 hours. Obviously, the lesson to contract negotiators is to anticipate this kind of problem and make their intentions clear.

(c) Some contracts vary the daily and weekly overtime provisions by specifying the employee's standard or normal working hours as "straight time" and providing that any hours worked outside such hours shall be "overtime." Such a provision would obviate any contractual claim for daily overtime in the example cited in (a), *supra.* (*See E. I. DuPont De Nemours & Co., Inc.,* 8 L.A. 425 (A. Horvitz, 1947).) The statutory question under the Walsh-Healey Act, if applicable, would still exist.

Contract provisions of this type involve other problems, however. What should the result be, as to overtime liability, if the employee deliberately or otherwise comes late to work on his regular schedule, and then is kept on an equal amount of time beyond his normal quitting time? If the negotiators agree that, in such circumstance, the employee should not be entitled to daily overtime, what contract language might they use to accomplish this result? *See Allied Master Painters Association,* 3 L.A. 854 (I. Weinzweig, 1944); *Haddon Craftsmen, Inc.,* 24 L.A. 493 (J. Brandschain, 1955).

(d) A provision such as that referred to in (c) would produce the result that an employee working a long stretch of hours (on emergency repairs, for example) would alternate between "overtime" and "straight time" hours. Suppose, for example, an employee begins work on his regular shift Monday at 8:00 A.M. and works 30 continuous hours. How would he be paid, assuming such a contract provision? If the parties, in anticipation of such a situation, consider this to be an inequitable result, what alternative contract solution might be used? What would you think of a provision requiring "overtime" for all hours worked consecutively in excess of the first 8 hours? What about the possibility that the employer might attempt to avoid some part of his overtime liability by sending the employee home after each period of 8 hours, then recalling him to resume 1 or 2 hours later?

(e) Think also of the problem of "swing" shifts, where the regular work schedule (as on continuous operations) calls for rotating schedules set up in such a way that, periodically, an employee assigned to a particular cycle, has to swing from a day to an afternoon shift, an afternoon to a night shift, or a night to a day shift in a given 24-hour period, and thus works, during such period, 16 continuous hours. If the parties do not intend that overtime should be paid for the second 8 hours worked in this situation, what kind of language might they use to accomplish this? *See Ohio Steel Foundry Co.,* 8 L.A. 580 (C. Hampton, 1947).

(2) Are there problems in determining the employee's "regular rate of pay" which must, under the contract, be used as the base for the overtime rate? Some of the kinds of problems which may arise are illustrated below.

(a) Suppose the employee's "overtime" work is in a job classified either higher or lower in rate of pay than the employee's regularly assigned job. Or suppose the employee is regularly on an incentive job and is transferred on overtime to an hourly rated job which pays less than the employee's normal incentive earnings. Would the determination of his premium rate be affected by the fairly common type of contract provision providing that, in the case of temporary transfers, the employee shall receive (as his base rate) the higher of the two rates? Such a provision is placed in the contract, of course, in contemplation of transfer during regular working hours. Should it make a difference whether the overtime assignment was voluntary or at the Company's request? See Volco Brass & Copper Company, 11 L.A. 1154 (I. Feinberg, 1948); International Harvester Company, 12 L.A. 650 (W. McCoy, 1949); International Harvester Company, 13 L.A. 933 (W. McCoy, 1949); Robertshaw-Fulton Controls Company, 12 L.A. 836 (A. R. Marshall, 1949); Deere & Co., 45 L.A. 879 (P. Davis, 1965).

In East Weymouth Wool Scouring Company, 5 L.A. 706 (S. Wallen, 1946), the contract required payment of "time and one-half the regular rate of pay . . . for all overtime work. . . ." Arbitrator Saul Wallen stated that the generally accepted interpretation would be that the premium rate should be based on the regular rate for the particular job done on an overtime basis. In this instance, however, he concluded that the ordinary meaning had been qualified by the past practice of paying overtime on the basis of the employee's "regular" rate of pay. He stated: ". . . the most equitable solution would be for employees in a higher-rated classification who are called in on Saturdays to perform work in a lower-rated classification to be paid at the rate of time and one-half the employee's weighted average rate for the week. This would mean, for example, that a shipper who has worked 40 hours during the week at the rate of $1.09 and who is called in to do a laborer's work for eight hours on Saturday would receive eight hours' pay for the work performed on Saturday at time and one-half the average of the shipper's rate and the laborer's rate weighted by the number of hours worked at each. Thus, in the example given, his work on Saturday would be compensated for at time and one-half based on an hourly rate of $1.07. (40 hours times $1.09 plus 8 hours times $.97 divided by 48 hours times 1½ times 8 equals pay for Saturday.)" See also Union Carbide Nuclear Co., 41 L.A. 224 (J. Gorsuch, 1963).

Consider also Gulf Oil Corporation, 30 L.A. 411 (J. Carraway, 1958). An employee volunteered to work overtime in a lower-rated job when the scheduled employee failed to report for work and the employee who held the job on the preceding shift refused to double over. The arbitration Board found *nothing* in the contract which pertained to the problem. So the Board turned to the "common law" of the plant and found that, in the past, an employee received overtime based on the job rate instead of his regular rate unless the Company and the Union agreed otherwise.

(b) Other kinds of problems likewise arise with respect to the determination of the employee's "regular" rate. How is such rate computed in the case of incentive workers? Or in the case of salaried workers who work a fluctuating work week? Must extra compensation which the employee has already received during a given workweek (or to which he is entitled), such as premium pay for daily overtime, Saturday or Sunday work, or work on a holiday, be averaged into the weekly earnings from which the employee's rate is determined for weekly overtime purposes? These of course, are types of problems involving the Fair Labor Standards Act. But they may likewise arise as matters of contract interpretation. Would it be desirable, at least from the employer's point of view, to spell out in the contract that the provisions of the FLSA, insofar as pertinent, shall apply in determining questions relating to the "regular rate" for weekly overtime purposes?

b. Off-Day Work Premiums

Contracts frequently provide that work performed on the employee's normal days of rest shall be compensated at a premium rate. Thus, where the normal weekly schedule is Monday through Friday, the contract may call for time and one-half for work done on Saturday and double time for work done on Sunday. In some contracts the premium rate will be payable for work performed on the sixth or seventh consecutive days worked in the workweek. These provisions, like the "40 and 8" provisions, sometimes present interpretative problems.

(1) What period of time comprises "Saturday," or "Sunday" or the sixth or seventh consecutive days where the contract fails to define these terms specifically?

(a) Suppose a plant has a three-shift working schedule (*e.g.,* 8:00 A.M to 4:00 P.M.; 4:00 P.M. to 12:00 midnight; 12:00 midnight to 8:00 A.M.), Monday through Friday, the final shift consisting of the period 12:00 midnight Friday to 8:00 A.M. Saturday. Is this final shift, then, regularly a premium pay shift? Set these three schedules up one hour, so that the final shift begins at 11:00 P.M. Friday and extends to 7:00 A.M. Saturday. Arbitration decisions differ on the treatment of this type of situation. *Compare illustratively, Fabricon Products,* 27 L.A. 221 (C. Spaulding, 1956); *North American Aviation, Inc.,* 16 L.A. 892 (M. Komaroff, 1951). In *Bauer Bros., Inc.,* 21 L.A. 529 (L.

Brown, 1953), the employee worked from 11:00 P.M. Saturday until 11:00 A.M. Sunday. His shift would normally have ended at 7:00 A.M. Sunday. Arbitrator Leo Brown held that none of the hours worked after Saturday midnight deserved the Sunday premium, since ". . . the hours worked from 7:00 A.M. to 11:00 A.M. on Sunday . . . were, for overtime purposes, worked on Saturday. . . ." Do you agree?

(b) Would problems such as those considered in (a) be obviated if the parties were to define the workday as the 24-hour period beginning with the start of an employee's shift, or as the 24-hour period beginning with the start of the day shift? For a case illustrating the former type of provision *see Continental Can Co., Inc.,* 26 L.A. 536 (P. Carmichael, 1956). For cases illustrating the latter type of provision *see Bird & Sons, Inc.,* 27 L.A. 605 (A. Hoban, 1956), and *Kentile, Inc.,* 31 L.A. 642 (D. Karnblum, 1958). In *Bird* the "payroll day" was defined as the period 7:00 A.M. to 7:00 A.M. The Arbitrator concluded that all hours worked from 11:00 P.M. Sunday to 7:00 A.M. Monday warranted the Sunday double time premium. In *Kentile* the contract provided that the workday "as used solely for the purpose of computing Saturday, Sunday and holiday overtime premiums, is a twenty-four (24) hour period beginning at 8:00 A.M. of the Saturday, Sunday, or holiday." The Arbitrator held that work on Monday from 7:30 A.M. to 8:00 A.M. did not require payment of the Sunday premium. He stated:

> It must be remembered that the contract definition of an "established work day" in the context of this grievance is for the purpose only of "computing Saturday, Sunday and holiday *overtime* premiums" (Section A, Art. 6). Standing alone it thus begs a key question presented by this grievance: Is "start up" work *per se* really "*overtime*" work? Differently phrased, the question is whether this early time must be regarded as added on to the work time of the previous day and week or considered part of the work time of the ensuing day and week. In the unequivocal terms of the plant practice and giving the word "overtime" its normative meaning in industrial relations, the question must be answered in the negative; the expedient construction asked for by the Union really calls for "special premium pay" and not "overtime premiums."

Was there a distinguishing factor in these cases? In *Bird* the employee began working on Sunday whereas in *Kentile* the employee began working on Monday. If this seems a valid distinction, consider *Corn Products Refining Co.,* 18 L.A. 311 (H. Gilden, Chm., 1952), where the Board of Arbitration required Sunday premium pay for 1½ hours worked prior to the employee's normal starting time Monday morning.

(2) One purpose of week-end (or other off-day) premium pay provisions is to recognize the inequity of interrupting the employee's normal leisure time. Obviously, such interruption may be as serious to the employee who had made plans for a week-end trip whether the Saturday or Sunday work assignment is for 1 hour or 16 hours. Taking account of this fact, contracts sometimes guarantee the employee a minimum number of Saturday or Sunday hours of work (or pay) in the event of a "call-in." In *Hampden Sales Ass'n, Inc.,* 12 L.A. 62 (J. Hill, 1949), the contract provided: "Employees who work on Saturday shall be guaranteed a minimum of five and a third (5⅓) hours of work at time and a half." An employee worked 8 hours on Saturday and the employer argued that he had to pay time and one-half only for the first 5⅓ hours worked. Was the argument valid, where the contract also (in the same section) provided for weekly overtime? How might the contract language be clarified so as to avoid this kind of problem of interpretation?

(3) Where a plant has some kinds of necessarily continuous operations (for example, a steel mill, an oil refinery, or an electric utility), the parties often recognize that week-end premiums are not payable in the case of employees on "continuous" work. Whether particular work is "continuous" sometimes present some difficulty. *See,* for example, *Sheet Glass Co.,* 5 L.A. 127 (M. Copelof, 1946) — watchmen held to be on continuous work, but not janitors; laborers held to be on such work if doing maintenance work but not if called in on Sundays to non-maintenance work. *See also Virginia Oak Tanneries, Inc.,* 8 L.A. 378 (R. Latture, 1947). *Ford Motor Co.,* 7 L.A. 119 (H. Shulman, 1946), involved employees who operated mills which, on occasions, operated around the clock, and on other occasions only 2 shifts per day, 7 days per week. Arbitrator Harry Shulman distinguished these situations. In *Stanolind Pipe Line Co.,* 10 L.A. 426 (R. Bauder, 1948), the term "continuous operation" was held to encompass *all* 7-day operations, even those performed only on 1 shift per day. How does this strike you? Could some of these problems be met by providing, in lieu of straight week-end premiums, premiums for the sixth or seventh consecutive day worked in the workweek? Or by providing for an exception from week-end premium pay in the case of employees whose workweek begins on some day other than Monday?

c. Holiday Premiums

Holiday premium pay is commonly provided for in collective agreements (along with compensation for unworked holidays). The contract will (or should), of course, specify the days which are to be considered holidays. Obviously, the problems considered above with respect to off-day premium pay provisions apply equally in the case of holiday provisions. Others may also arise.

(1) Absent specific contract language either excluding or including employees on continuous operations from the benefits of the holiday provisions, what should be the result? In *Fulton-Sylphon Co.,* 8 L.A. 993 (L. Greene, 1947), the Arbitration Board held that guards and firemen were entitled only to their straight time rate on the grounds (a) that it is to be presumed that, in the case of such employees, their regular rate reflects, as a job characteristic, the necessity of working when others had the holiday off with pay, and (b) the underlying rationale of a holiday premium is to penalize the employer for undertaking productive work on a holiday, and this consideration has no application to plant protective work. *Cf. E. C. Cummings Leather Co.,* 8 L.A. 1052 (A. Myers, 1947), where the opposite result was reached on the ground that the purpose of holiday pay provisions is "to compensate the employee for the inconvenience of being deprived of the holiday. . . ."

(2) Pay for an *unworked* holiday is often made contingent on the employee's working the last scheduled day before and after the holiday. Suppose a contract so provides (and, also provides for holiday premium pay for holidays worked), and that an employee works the day after a given holiday, as well as *on* the holiday, but not on the day preceding the holiday. Does this provide the employer with a defense against a claim for holiday premium pay? *See Stroh Brewery Co.,* 26 L.A. 573 (1956), where Arbitrator M. S. Ryder answered in the negative.

(3) Determination of the rate of pay for holiday time worked sometimes presents special difficulties.

(a) Suppose a contract contains the following provisions:

(1) All regular full-time employees . . . shall be paid for eight (8) hours, at their regular rate of pay, for each of the holidays set forth in Paragraph (17) (a). . . .

(2) Double the regular rate of pay shall be paid for all hours worked on a holiday.

In such case is the employee who works 8 hours on a holiday entitled to double time or triple time for such hours worked? *See M. M. Mades Co., Inc.,* 16 L.A. 442 (M. Copelof, 1951) where the decision was for triple time. *Cf. Menasco Mfg. Co.,* 22 L.A. 564 (P. Prasow, 1954); *contra, Weaver Mfg. Division of Dura Corp.,* 39 L.A. 1262 (H. Davey, 1962).

(b) Suppose the contract cited in (a) also provides for payment of daily overtime at time and one-half, and the employee works 12 hours on a holiday. How is his compensation for the day to be computed? Compare the material on pyramiding in section e., *infra.*

d. Other Premiums

In addition to the fairly typical premium pay provisions which have been considered above, many contracts contain other kinds of premiums related to work characteristics. Some of these are indicated below.

(1) *Split-shift premiums.* This premium would be paid to employees whose working hours are separated by free time. A restaurant employee, for example, might be regularly scheduled to work 10:00 A.M. to 2:00 P.M. and 4:00 P.M. to 8:00 P.M. In recognition of this, the contract might provide for payment of an extra sum per day to such employee.

(2) *Part-time work premiums.* This premium would be paid to employees working less than a full schedule during the week. A summer resort employee, for example, might be scheduled to work only on week-ends. The contract might provide an extra weekly payment to such an employee.

(3) *Night-work premiums.* Contracts often provide for an increment per hour above the standard hourly rate for employees working night shifts.

(4) *Shift differentials.* Contracts often provide for an increment per hour above the standard hourly rate for a classification in the case of employees in the classification who do "shift" work (*i.e.,* work on rotating and shifting work schedules).

(5) *"Call-out" pay.* Contracts often provide for payment of a minimum number of hours of pay to employees who are called out for work outside their normal work schedules, regardless of the number of hours actually worked.

(6) *Onerous or hazardous work premiums.* This premium would be paid to employees for performing work more dangerous or objectionable than their normal work. For example, a maintenance employee who spends half of his shift cleaning the inside of a gasoline storage tank might be paid an extra 25¢ per hour.

(7) *Increased work load premiums.* This premium would be paid to employees who are required to perform more work than their job normally requires. For example, an employee in a painting crew who had to double his output because the crew was temporarily shorthanded might be paid an extra 25¢ per hour.

e. Pyramiding of Overtime and Other Premium Payments

MILFORD CO. OF CALIFORNIA

22 L.A. 249 (1954)

Aaron, Benjamin, Chairman of the Board of Arbitration. . . .

Issue

Although the parties did not execute a formal submission agreement, they agreed informally at the hearing that the sole issue submitted to the Board of Arbitration is the following:

> Under the collective bargaining agreement between the parties what is the proper rate of pay for a warehouse employee for hours in excess of eight, when his regular tour of duty (eight hours) extends beyond 6:00 P.M.?

Having reviewed and considered the entire record in this case, the Board of Arbitration makes the following

Award

Under the collective bargaining agreement between the parties, the proper rate for a warehouse employee for hours in excess of eight, when his regular tour of duty (eight hours) extends beyond 6:00 P.M. is one and one-half times the hourly wage rate established for his classification in Article XI of the said agreement.

Chairman's Opinion

In this case the parties have requested a decision in the nature of a declaratory judgment of their respective rights under several related provisions of their collective bargaining agreement. These provisions are as follows:

ARTICLE XI — MINIMUM WAGE SCALE (establishing fixed hourly
rates for four specified classes of employees)

ARTICLE X — OVERTIME

Overtime shall be paid for all employees who work in excess of eight (8) hours in any one (1) day, or in excess of forty (40 hours in any one (1) week, at the rate of time and one-half (1½) the regular rate of pay as established in these Articles. All emergency work and all inventory work, extending over the regular forty (40) hours of any one (1) calendar week as specified in Article IX shall be classed as overtime. All Saturday work shall be paid at the rate of time and one-half and Sunday work shall be paid at the rate of double time.

Article XIII — Extra Shift and Night Work Payment

When the Employer elects to work more than one (1) shift, he may do so, starting time of said shift to be at the option of the Employer.

An employee whose regular tour of duty necessitates his or her working between the hours of 6:00 P.M. on any one (1) day and 6:00 A.M. of the following day shall be entitled to time and one-half (1½) the regular rate of pay as established in these articles.

The problem to be decided arises from a special situation: one in which an employee is given a regular tour of duty (eight hours) which extends beyond 6:00 P.M. It is mutually agreed that for all time after 6:00 P.M., but within this eight-hour period, the employee must be paid 1½ times the hourly rate he receives for work performed prior to 6:00 P.M. The sole issue to be determined is the rate he should be paid for work after 6:00 P.M. in excess of eight hours.

The facts are not in dispute. During the period from June 8 to September 26, 1953, the Company assigned four men alternatively in pairs to a regular tour of duty from 11:30 A.M. to 8:00 P.M. with one-half hour off for lunch. On a number of occasions during that period the men in question worked shifts of from 9½ to 12½ hours. The Company paid them the same rate for hours in excess of eight as for hours under eight but after 6:00 P.M., that is, 1½ times the rate paid for hours worked prior to 6:00 P.M.

The Union protested, contending that all hours worked in excess of eight should be paid for at 2¼ times the rate paid for work prior to 6:00 P.M., that is, 1½ times the rate paid for hours under eight worked after 6:00 P.M. No more work of this type was scheduled after the Union filed its grievance.

The collective bargaining agreement is industry-wide. There appears to be no precedent governing the practice in question. While each party to this proceeding maintains that its position merely reflects the original intention of the negotiators, evidence to that effect is lacking. In any case, the Board of Arbitration must find the intention of the parties in the language of the agreement.

The term "regular rate of pay" is nowhere defined in the agreement. It appears, however, in identical phrases in both Article X and Article XIII. In Article X overtime is defined as 1½ times "the regular rate of pay as established in these Articles"; the same phrase is used as noted above, in Article XIII to define the rate of pay for work between 6:00 P.M. and 6:00 A.M.

The Company contends that there is only one regular rate of pay, namely, the classification rate established in Article XI. The Union argues that the regular rate changes with the circumstances, and that the regular rate for work after 6:00 P.M. is 1½ times the classification rate established in Article XI.

The Company also maintains that the night penalty payment has no bearing on the normal computation of overtime, citing as an analogy work performed on Saturday which is designated in Article X as a special overtime day. According to the Company, warehousemen working on Saturday have consistently been paid 1½ times the classification rate established in Article XI, whether they worked more or less than eight hours. To this argument the Union responds that the Saturday situation is inapposite, because the regular workweek established in Article IX is Monday through Friday, and Saturday is not part of a regular tour of duty.

Our concern is limited to the meaning of "regular rate" as it appears in Article X, for the problem here involved concerns only *overtime pay.* The language of Article XIII, therefore, is relevant only to the extent that it defines the conditions under which this particular problem can arise; for it does not refer to overtime work as such. One effect of Article XIII, however, is to deprive the Saturday pay analogy cited by the Company of its force. Saturday work is designated as overtime work in Article X, and since no other premium rate applies, the regular rate can only be the classification rate established in Article XI. It merely begs the question to assume that the same thing is true in cases of night work, which is paid for at a premium rate other than overtime during the regular shift.

It was suggested by the Union that a logical extension of the Company's argument could lead to the payment of a single rate for statutory overtime, in violation of the Fair Labor Standards Act. No such possibility occurs in the situation here involved, but the reference to the statute is important. In 1949 Congress enacted certain amendments to FLSA to become effective January 26, 1950, more than a year prior to the execution of the first collective agreement between these parties in which Article XIII appeared. Section 7(d) of P. L. 393 provided in part as follows:

> As used in this section the "regular rate" at which an employee is employed shall . . . not be deemed to include —. . . .
> (7) extra compensation provided by a premium rate paid to the employee, in pursuance of an applicable employment contract or collective-bargaining agreement, for work outside of the hours established in good faith by the contract or agreement as the basic, normal, or regular workday (not exceeding eight hours) or workweek (not exceeding forty hours), where such premium rate is not less than one and one-half times the rate established in good faith by the contract or agreement for like work performed during such workday or workweek.

The legislative history of this provision makes it clear that it was intended to offset the effect of the decision of the United States Supreme Court in *Bay Ridge Operating Co. v. Aaron,* 334 U.S. 446

(1948) [8 WH Cases 20], requiring the payment of statutory overtime rates for work already paid for at a time and one-half premium rate. While the facts of that case were distinguishable from those here involved, the problem was essentially the same. The statutory amendment quoted above does not preclude these parties from agreeing upon an arrangement requiring payment in the manner contended for by the Union; but it is clear that in the absence of such an agreement, set forth in clear and unmistakable language, the Company would not have to pay for over-time work after 6:00 P.M. at a rate in excess of 1½ times the classification rate established in Article XI. A majority of the Board of Arbitration does not read the language of Article X and XIII as expressing an agreement to include the night work premium in the regular rate for purposes of computing overtime pay. Accordingly, we find in favor of the Company's position in the instant case.

NOTES:

(1) There must be hundreds of combinations of premium pay provisions which could be potentially pyramided. Arbitrators are constantly confronted with new variations on the old theme. Innumerable contract clauses attempt to prohibit or limit pyramiding. Even provisions basically the same produce different results. For example, *compare White House Milk Co., Inc.,* 29 L.A. 45 (A. Anderson, 1957) *with* the *Hudson Paper* case, *supra.* On the same point of premium pay for Sunday work plus over-time pay for hours over 40 in the workweek, *compare Safeway Stores, Inc.,* 45 L.A. 1163 (H. Atkins, 1965) *with Southern Clays, Inc.,* 31 L.A. 784 (H. Dworet, 1958). On the question of pay for work on a holiday plus overtime pay for work over 40 hours in the workweek, *compare Hawaiian Pineapple Co., Ltd.,* 30 L.A. 324 (W. Cobb, 1958) and *Hilo Transportation & Terminal Co.,* 33 L.A. 541 (H. Barr, 1959) *with Gorton-Pew Fisheries,* 16 L.A. 365 (S. Wallen, 1951). Prepare for class discussion a check-list of issues which might arise because of the pyramiding problem. Then use your list to determine the adequacy of the following anti-pyramiding clauses:

Example 1

Time worked in excess of eight (8) hours in any twenty-four (24) hour period or in excess of forty hours in any pay period week will be compensated at the rate of time and one-half. Over-time hours paid on a daily basis shall not be included in paying for overtime on a weekly basis. (Goodyear Tire & Rubber Co. *and* Rubber Workers)

Example 2

When two (2) or more types of overtime compensation are

applicable to the same hours of work, only one, the higher, will be paid. In no case will there be a duplication or pyramiding of daily and weekly overtime or of any other overtime compensation. (Borg-Warner Corp., Norge Div. *and* Allied Industrial Workers)

Example 3

Section 9 (Article X). "Overtime at the rate of one and one-half (1½) times his regular rate will be paid to an employee for all hours worked in excess of eight (8) hours in any twenty-four (24) hour period or for all hours worked in excess of forty (40) hours within the workweek, whichever method of computation provides at the end of the workweek the greater total pay to the employee."

Section 15 (Article X). "Overtime or premium payments shall not be duplicated for the same hours under any of the terms of this Agreement, and to the extent that hours are compensated for as overtime or premium under one provision they shall not be counted as hours worked in determining overtime or premium compensation under the same or any other provision, except as specifically provided therefor."

Section 1 (Article X). "Definitions:

"*Workday* means the 24-hour period beginning at 12:00 midnight.

"*Workweek* means the 7-day period beginning at 12:00 midnight on Sunday. . . ."

(Goodyear Atomic Corporation *and* United Plant Guard Workers)

(2) *Problem:* The Company has three shifts, each lasting eight hours, for rotating shift employees: Day shift, 8:00 A.M. to 4:00 P.M.; afternoon shift, 4:00 P.M. to 12:00 midnight; night shift, 12:00 midnight to 8:00 A.M. However, shift employees are required to report for work 30 minutes early on each shift for "preliminary" activities, for which they are compensated, so that their normal work-day is 8½ hours. The problem concerns the proper overtime compensation of rotating shift employees whose shift is changed periodically from the afternoon to the night shift. During the first week in which such change occurs, these employees work from 3:30 P.M. to 12:00 midnight on Monday, Tuesday, and Wednesday. Thursday and Friday they are scheduled off. On Saturday they are changed to the night shift, so report at 11:30 P.M. Friday night and work until 8:00 A.M. Saturday morning. Similarly, they work the next night from 11:30 P.M. to 8:00 A.M. Sunday. During the ensuing week they work 5 consecutive night shifts (from 11:30 P.M. to 8:00 A.M.) beginning Sunday night at 11:30 P.M. How many hours at the overtime rate are to be paid during each of these weeks? (Assume the contract provisions are those in Example 3, *supra.*)

5. Duty to Work Overtime (Employer's Right to Require It)

Where contract gives the Company the sole right to determine the starting and quitting time and the number of hours to be worked subject to other rights and regulations in the contract which included a direction that the employer take into account the service requirements and preferences of the employees when assigning overtime, is there a duty to work overtime if an employee objects to working over 8 hours a day or 40 hours a week? Does the employer have an absolute right to require an employee to work overtime without consulting the unions? *Compare Southwestern Bell*, 61 L.A. 202 (Wolff 1973) *with Ford Motor Co.,* 11 L.A. 1158 (Shulman 1948).

NOTES:

In *General Tire & Rubber Co.,* 6 L.A. 918 (C. Hampton, 1947), it was held that maintenance men could be required to work in excess of the regularly scheduled workweek in order to perform emergency work or work which could not be done without interrupting the flow of production, despite the Union's contention that overtime work was optional, since maintenance employees are recognized in industry generally as being subject to call for overtime work, within reason. In *Dortch Stove Works, Inc.,* 9 L.A. 374 (W. McCoy, 1948) where the contract did not expressly provide whether overtime work was to be optional or mandatory, it was ruled that such work was to be regarded as mandatory because (1) to hold otherwise would be to subject the Company unreasonably to operational waste, and (2) the practice in the plant and in the industry (foundry operations), was to regard overtime as obligatory.

In *Connecticut River Mills, Inc.,* 6 L.A. 1017 (S. Wallen, 1947), the contract provided:

> The eight (8) hour day and forty (40) hour week, commencing Monday, at 12:01 A.M., and ending Friday (inclusive), shall be in effect without revision during the term of this contract. Time and one-half shall be paid for all work done in excess of eight (8) hours in any day or forty (40) hours in any one week, and overtime paid for on a daily basis shall not be duplicated on a weekly basis.

An employee was discharged for refusing to work overtime hours on a Saturday. Arbitrator Saul Wallen held that "once 40 hours of service has been rendered, the obligation imposed by the contract has been met," and that "to rule otherwise would be to render meaningless the provision of Article I, Section 1, which makes the union the collective bargaining agent with respect to hours of employment."

In *Huron Portland Cement Co.,* 9 L.A. 735 (H. Platt, 1948), the contract contained the customary recognition and management clauses, and also the following:

ARTICLE V — WAGES

B. The regular workweeks shall be established by the Company and shall average not less than forty-two (42) hours per week over periods of four weeks. An Employee who has worked overtime shall not be laid off during the remainder of the week for the purpose of offsetting such overtime.

ARTICLE VI — HOURS AND OVERTIME .

A. The regularly scheduled workweek shall begin and end at 6:00 A.M. on Sunday for all departments.

B. For the purpose of computing overtime, eight hours shall constitute a day's work. All time over eight hours in any one day, and all time over forty hours in one workweek shall be paid at the rate of time and one-half. . ."

Four employees were given disciplinary layoffs, for refusing to work beyond their regular shifts in an emergency and filed grievances. Arbitrator Harry H. Platt upheld the Company. He found nothing in the quoted provisions, nor in the recognition clause, which operated to restrict the employer in scheduling overtime work. He said, moreover, that his decision was not in conflict with that rendered in the *Connecticut River Mills* case, *ante,* because the Arbitrator there had "found that (1) by explicit language in the collective bargaining agreement, the hours of employment were fixed on a daily and weekly basis, . . . and (2), the contract provided that the above hours of employment 'shall be in effect without revision during the term of this contract.' " Was Arbitrator Platt on sound ground in attempting to differentiate his case?

For other cases in which the arbitrator seemed to take the view expressed by Arbitrator Wallen *see: National Electric Coil Co.,* 1 L.A. 468 (P. Lehoczky, 1945); *Campbell Soup Co.,* 11 L.A. 715 (L. Tyree, 1948); and *A. D. Julliard & Co., Inc.,* 17 L.A. 606 (D. Muggs, 1951). For cases taking the view expressed by Arbitrator Platt *see: Deere & Co.,* 11 L.A. 561 (C. Updegraff, 1948); *Great Lakes Spring Corp.,* 12 L.A. 779 (P. Kelliher, 1949); *Carnegie-Illinois Steel Corp.,* 12 L.A. 810 (R. Seward, Chm., 1949); *Nebraska Consolidated Mills Co.,* 13 L.A. 211 (M. Copelof, 1949); *Flour Mills of America, Inc.,* 20 L.A. 564 (A. Reeves, 1952); *United States Potash Co.,* 34 L.A. 470 (M. Beatty, 1960); *General Portland Cement Co.,* 35 L.A. 193 (G. Bradley, 1960). For a particularly interesting discussion of the problem, taking into account the bargaining history on the issue, *see*

General Electric Co., 31 L.A. 403 (J. Healy, 1958). The implied condition of reasonableness of the employer request for overtime work may well attach in most instances where the right to require such work is upheld. *See Sunbeam Electric Co.,* 41 L.A. 834 (D. Helfand, 1963). For an instance in which this condition was expressly stated *see Texas Co.,* 14 L.A. 146 (H. Gilden, 1949). Likewise, it may be found in a particular case that the employee's refusal, even of a reasonable employer request, was excusable. *See, e.g., Sylvania Electric Products, Inc.,* 24 L.A. 199 (R. Brecht, 1954). In *Ford Motor Co.,* 11 L.A. 1158 (1948) Arbitrator Harry Shulman held that employee does not have right to reject overtime, but his/her refusal "might be justified."

Problem: If the contract either expressly or properly interpreted permits employee refusal of overtime work requests, but an employee accepts in advance an overtime request, and then, without notice, does not appear, is he subject to discipline? *See Campbell Soup Co.,* 13 L.A. 373 (L. Tyree, 1949); and *Douglas Aircraft Co.,* 20 L.A. 331 (I. Bernstein, 1953).

6. Right to Overtime Work (Employer's Duty to Distribute It)

PITTSBURGH PLATE GLASS CO.

32 L.A. 622 (1958)

Sembower, John F., Chairman.

The above grievances all have a common denominator in that they involve interpretation of the following clauses of the Contract between the parties:

ARTICLE XI—HOURS AND OVERTIME Section 4

... The Company will endeavor to divide overtime equitably among regularly scheduled qualified employees within a department who regularly perform such work.

. . . .

OVERTIME (Supplement Effective—February 13, 1956)

2. On overtime for a particular occupation, the Company will attempt to divide the overtime equitably among those employees regularly scheduled and qualified, first choice being given to the employees low in overtime occupying the block job, and if not available, to those employees in the higher block jobs having previous experience.

In each of these twelve grievances the Union complains that the Company did not give the overtime to the "low man," as compared with the employee who actually worked the overtime. The term "low man" refers to an employee whose total of accumulated overtime hours is lower at the time in question than that of the man who worked.

In addition to the basic issue in each instance, these grievances each present "variations on the basic theme," and therefore each will be considered separately in the light of its particular facts.

But to save reiteration and redundancy in the discussion of each grievance, it is desirable for certain basic determinations to be made at the outset which apply to all the grievances, and then to employ these as criteria in working out each specific answer.

In general, the Company takes the position that the two agreement clauses establish "a rule of reason" (R. 102), based upon the contention that "if the intent of the parties here was the lowest man in time invariably get this overtime, there was certainly a clear and more concise way of saying it than to use words like 'the Company will endeavor to divide overtime equitably. . . .' " (R. 102) The issue between the parties is clearly drawn when the union responds (R. 101) that, ". . . it certainly wasn't intended . . . by this contract that the whole thing be left vague, that the employer unilaterally judge as to when an equitable result can be reached. When do you balance up? Do you balance up within a week? Do you balance up within two weeks? Do you balance up within a year? Or do you balance up within ten weeks?"

So the Board must decide between those two positions, and if possible, by its answer create a sort of template to be laid over the facts in each particular grievance as a guide to answering each specific question.

There is another basic issue that is generic to all these grievances, and that concerns the remedy to be applied, if and when it appears that the overtime has been allocated improperly. The Company argues that in such an eventuality this Board should require that the resultant disparity in overtime hours be corrected at the earliest possible time by affording the successful grievant an opportunity to work it out, and that to do otherwise is to inflict a penalty without the Agreement. The Union, on the other hand, contends that the overtime to which the grievant is entitled was that which occurred at the time the grievance arose, and that time "lost" in this manner is time that is gone over the dam, so to speak; hence that the remedy is to direct that the grievant be compensated for the overtime he should have worked but of which he was deprived. We must decide this question.

"Rule of Reason"

In weighing the persuasive arguments presented by both parties in behalf of their positions on the foregoing issues, reference has been had to reported decisions of leading arbitrators. It is stressed, however, that these are in no wise viewed as controlling precedents, because in arbitration we do not follow what the lawyer knows as the doctrine of *stare decisis,* or "let the decision stand." They are mentioned only to let the parties see examples of the logic adopted in reaching as fair and generally acceptable a decision as possible. A good deal can be said, of course, in favor of following as consistent a course as is feasible in the arbitration decisions within a given plant, and this is a legitimate consideration in weighing past rules in the Greensburg plant. However, with this in mind, we also have endeavored in each instance to reach a conclusion which stands on its own feet in the light of the applicable clauses of the contract and the particular facts.

Now as to the first of the foregoing issues — whether overtime must invariably be given to the "low man" — it is seen from reference to reported arbitration decisions that contract clauses providing for overtime to be equalized "as far as practicable" (29 L.A. 534 and 26 L.A. 540); providing for overtime to be equalized "to the best ability of the supervisor" (30 L.A. 536), and providing that "Co. will endeavor to divide overtime equitably" (28 L.A. 100 and the instant contract), are quite common throughout industry. Without exception among the reported awards, arbitrators have interpreted the clause to provide for more or less flexibility in the distribution of overtime. *See:* 3 L.A. 560, 4 L.A. 161, 7 L.A. 564, 16 L.A. 613, 17 L.A. 798, 18 L.A. 205, 18 L.A. 876, 21 L.A. 622, 22 L.A. 144, 24 L.A. 717, 28 L.A. 754, 29 L.A. 534, 30 L.A. 536.

However, while flexibility has been recognized, it also has been taken into account the rule that the general aim of the agreement is for overtime to be equalized, albeit qualified by the Company's doing so with some latitude, and that this imposes a duty upon the Company to meet an appropriate test of diligence under the particular circumstances of each instance. Indeed, in Grievances 57-18 and 56-20 here at Greensburg, decided by Arbitrator B. Meredith Reid, this was the approach that was adopted. Thus, the Company's suggestion that "a rule of reason" should apply, finds support not only among arbitration awards generally but also in this plant. It follows, of course, that the so-called "rule" must be applied to each individual set of facts, and consequently that will be done in the specific instances presented to this Board.

Remedy

As to the second of the broad issues, a serious question is presented as to whether the remedy, when and if it is found that the Company has failed to meet the test of due diligence in the distribution of overtime, is to be the awarding of pay to the grievant for the time not worked, or whether he simply is to be given the opportunity to work the next available overtime.

The Company's suggestion that it be merely required to give the successful grievant the next, or an early, opportunity to work overtime finds very little support in the reasoning of arbitrators considering this problem either throughout industry generally or in the cases decided heretofore involving the instant parties. In 16 L.A. 613, *Diamond Alkali Co.,* the arbitrator held that the requirement was only that overtime be equalized over a period of time, and that in that case there was no showing that the employer had failed to do so. A sort of middle ground was reached by the Arbitrator Joseph Shister, 27 L.A. 634, *Goodyear Atomic Corp.,* when he ruled that as considerable time had passed since the disparity in overtime distribution was brought to light by the filing of the grievance, pay should be awarded if the Company had not yet equalized it. In 24 L.A. 168, *Celanese Corp. of America,* the arbitrator permitted the Company to offer the aggrieved employee the first opportunity to make up time lost, since the contract did not specify any method for correcting such errors and the evidence showed that both methods had been used in the past in that plant. These are the reports supporting, at least in part, the view that granting an opportunity to do the next overtime available is sufficient.

The overwhelming predominance of view expressed by arbitrators, however, is in favor of granting pay for the overtime lost. *See:* 12 L.A. 389, *Corn Products Refining Co.;* 14 L.A. 970, *Hayes Mfg. Corp.;* and 15 L.A. 608, *Republic Oil Refining Co.* In 19 L.A. 690, *Bridgeport Brass Co.,* the arbitrator, in effect, adopted both remedies for he compensated those employees affected by the violation in the amount of average overtime earnings each would have received had overtime been distributed equally, and then directed the Company also to offer them an opportunity in the future to work the same number of overtime hours as other employees have worked.

Several theories are followed in support of granting back pay at overtime rates. In 26 L.A. 540, *Bendix Aviation Corp.,* Arbitrator Peter M. Kelliher, construing a contract providing that overtime be equalized "within a classification on a shift insofar as practicable," ruled: "It is the Company's position that all that it is required to do under the language of Section 6 is to equalize the overtime. . . . The Company's remedy would not prevent violations of the Collective Bargaining Agreement. A right is of no value unless an adequate remedy exists. The Company cannot 'create' work."

In 17 L.A. 721, *Phillips Chemical Co.,* the arbitrator rejected the suggestion that a proper remedy would be to afford the employees an opportunity in the future to make up lost time, holding that the employee is entitled to compensation "on a principle of damages, not earnings, and his right to compensation arose at the instant that the contract was breached." Both of these holdings partake of a penalty theory and while they certainly are respectable authority for such a proposition, it is our view in this instance that it is better to avoid a penalty concept and instead to settle upon a violation of contract theory.

For one thing, the idea of inflicting a penalty, besides being distasteful on a number of scores, introduces troublesome considerations when the error is inadvertent and innocent. For instance, in 15 L.A. 589, *Monsanto Chemical Co.,* the arbitrator found that the grievant was not offered overtime "due to an honest error," and then was offered the next overtime assignment, which he was unable to accept because of another engagement. The arbitrator ruled that "the responsibility for administration of the practice of rotating overtime work is management's and it must pay for its mistakes, however understandable such mistakes may be." In 7 L.A. 564, *Ingersoll-Rand Co.,* the arbitrator found that although the Company's mistake in not giving grievant the opportunity to work overtime was inadvertent, the employer in fact had ample time to notify the employee to report and therefore the employee was entitled to back pay instead of merely the opportunity to make up time lost.

In 26 L.A. 469, *Standard Lime & Cement Co.,* Arbitrator Harry J. Dworkin construed a contract providing specifically, "It is recognized that overtime cannot always be offered to the man entitled to the same at the time overtime is needed, but the Company will attempt insofar as practical to equalize the same during the one (1) year term of this contract," and he ruled:

> The right and privilege of performing overtime work is to be exercised at the time it arises and may not be substituted by a later assignment. . . . The fact that the overtime assignment section does not specify any penalty against the Company in the case of failure to assign overtime to the proper employee is of no significance since the section expressly affords a right and the remedy in the event of a violation is inherent in the grievance procedure. . . . With reference to alleged past practice, in accordance with which an employee deprived of overtime is given an equal amount of overtime at a later date, such is not controlling, since past practice may not be employed to vary the clear and express language of the contract.

In 28 L.A. 100, *Standard Oil Company* (Indiana), Arbitrator James A. Doyle ruled that in the absence of a provision for a specific period of time within which to measure equality of overtime opportunities among qualified employees, a contract calling for equal distribution of overtime requires the employer to distribute overtime equally on a day-to-day basis. In that instance the Contract said that the Company shall "endeavor" to distribute overtime equally, and added the express proviso: "It is understood that overtime cannot be distributed in any group with mathematical exactness."

Arbitrator Doyle observed that "payment at the overtime rate is well-recognized." He cited 13 L.A. 839, *U.S. Rubber Co.,* where the arbitrator stated:

> Affording an employee an opportunity to make up improperly lost hours at a later date is not an adequate remedy. He is entitled to work those hours at the time they are available, not at a later time more convenient to the employer. Furthermore, there always remains the possibility of termination of an employee between the time he is improperly denied available hours and the time when the employer decides to make additional hours available to him. *See also Phillips Chemical Co.,* 17 L.A. 721.

Arbitrator B. Meredith Reid here at Greensburg, in two awards (Grievances 57-18 and 56-20) holding that overtime should have been given to the grievants, awarded pay at time and a half, so that it might be said that the practice in that regard already has been established under the instant contract, but we have gone into considerable detail to show that in this instance the Board has not reached a casual decision on this important matter, but instead has given it especially careful study in an effort to reach a fair conclusion in accord primarily with the contract and practice here, but also in accord with industry generally where similar or analogous contract provisions prevail and have been construed.

Accordingly, in deciding the following group of grievances, the Board is guided by the foregoing principles, to wit: that in each instance "a rule of reason" will be applied to test whether, under the circumstances, the Company met the test of the Contract for proper allocation of the overtime, and then if it is found that the Company erred, the grievant will be granted pay for the overtime he lost.

Grievance No. 57-15

Grievant worked the 4 p.m. to midnight shift and went home. He claims that when a vacancy developed on the subsequent 8 a.m. to 4 p.m. shift, he should have been called in to work the first four hours of the shift instead of one Falkosky, who had worked the 12 midnight to 8 a.m. and had more accumulated overtime than the grievant, being held over to work the said first four hours.

Although under a strict application of overtime distribution, the grievant was entitled to be called in, the impracticality of doing so appears on the face of the work schedule. It would have necessitated the grievant's working his regular shift of 4 p.m. to midnight, then rousing himself to make the 8 a.m. shift the next morning so that he could work four hours, and finally returning four hours later to resume his regular shift. Since this would place an unreasonable demand upon a man by completely disrupting his personal schedule and rest for twenty-four hours, the Company did the reasonable thing, and the grievance must be denied.

Award

Grievance denied.

NOTE:

See also Singer Manufacturing Co., 35 L.A. 526 (S. Cahn, 1960), and *Virginia-Carolina Chemical Co.,* 42 L.A. 238 (L. Kesselman, 1964).

Where the overtime assignment is made to a person outside of the group in which, by contract, the overtime is to be "equalized," is there any room for a remedy other than back pay? For a negative answer *see Bendix Aviation Corp.,* 26 L.A. 540 (P. Kelliher, 1956), and *United States Pipe & Foundry Co.,* 30 L.A. 172 (H. Dworet, 1958).

Arbitrators have disagreed on the question whether, in the event of an improper assignment of overtime *within* the group in which it is to be equalized, the remedy should be back pay to the by-passed employee or advancing him on the overtime priority list.

"Finally, the Union asserts that the Company's proposed remedy of overtime employment for these grievants would pose a conflict with the provisions of Section XIII(M) of the contract, reading, 'The Company will divide overtime as equally as practicable among the Employees in their respective classifications.' In this respect the Union says that in order to provide such overtime employment, there must, of course, be work available; and if such work is available the quoted provision requires that it be assigned on an equitable basis. If persons other than these grievants were entitled to the overtime, it would violate the contract to award it to these men; and, on the other hand, if these grievants happened to be entitled to it, they should be given the work by reason of such entitlement, not by way of recoupment for a violation of the seniority provisions of the contract." Back pay was therefore awarded. *International Paper Co.,* 31 L.A. 494 (1958), Charles A. Reynard, Chairman of Board.

"We now come to the matter of McConnell. It follows from the preceding analysis that he should have been given an overtime turn on March 3, 1956. But it does not automatically follow, as the Union argues, that he therefore be compensated for time lost. On the one hand, retroactive compensation for overtime lost is tantamount to payment for work not done; and that could spell an undue burden on the Company. On the other hand, an error in overtime allocation can be equitably rectified by providing a corresponding amount of overtime for the aggrieved employee, *provided* such overtime is provided within a reasonable time from the date of the error; for the failure to include the proviso of a reasonable time limit would impose an undue burden on the employee." *Goodyear Atomic Corporation,* 27 L.A. 634 (1956), Joseph Shister, Arbitrator.

Is a middle position between these views possible? Suppose the employer offers the by-passed employee a "made" overtime opportunity equivalent in number of hours, *i.e.,* an overtime assignment which would not otherwise have been provided to anyone. *See Refinery Employees Union v. Continental Oil Co.,* 268 F.2d 447 (5th Cir. 1959). In this case, by the way, the question was not whether this kind of remedy would be appropriate, but, rather, whether the arbitrator had any jurisdiction *at all* with respect to the matter of remedy where the contract made arbitrable only issues concerning "the interpretation or performance of this agreement." The holding? The question of remedy was not arbitrable; hence the employer could not be compelled to arbitrate in a suit brought by the Union under Section 301 of the Taft-Hartley Act. Compare our discussion of issues of arbitrability and the judicial process *supra,* Part Two, Chapter 6, p. 283.

Chapter 13

COLLECTIVE BARGAINING AGREEMENTS AND THE OCCUPATIONAL SAFETY AND HEALTH ACT (OSHA) OF 1970

A. NEED FOR OSHA

The Occupational Safety and Health Act of 1970 [1] was enacted in response to the ever-increasing loss of human resources directly attributable to industrial diseases and accidents. As one prominent union attorney pointed out: [2]

The vital statistics have been repeated all to [too] often. In excess of 14,000 deaths and 2.2 million disabling injuries reported each year were directly traceable to the American workplace.[2] In 1970 the United States Public Health Service reported 390,000 new cases of occupational disease annually.[3] Unfortunately, these staggering numbers just begin to tell the story. A recent study commissioned by the Government disclosed that every year at least 25 million serious injuries and deaths are unaccounted for [4] because of deficiencies in industry's reporting techniques — intentional or inadvertent.

The long term of implications of occupational diseases even continuing at present levels are virtually beyond comprehension, especially since over 80 million employees spend in excess of one-third of their daily existence in a workplace environment. As early as 1967 the Surgeon General of the United States reported that a study [5] of 1,700 representative industrial plants disclosed that sixty-five percent of the workers were potentially exposed

---

[1] 29 U.S.C. §§ 651-678 (1970).

[2] Cohen, OSHA and the Workplace Environment: An Unfulfilled Promise, in 27th N.Y.U. Lab. Conf. 213, 214-15 (1975).

[2] The economic impact of occupation diseases and accidents is likewise overwhelming. In the report accompanying the House bill which [led] to the enactment of OSHA, Congress noted that as of 1970 "over 11.5 billion dollars are wasted on lost wages and the annual loss to the gross national product is over 8 billion dollars. Ten times as many man-days are lost from job-related disabilities as from strikes, and days of lost productivity through accidents and illnesses are ten times greater than the loss from strikes. . . ." Rep. No. 91-1291, 91th Con., 2dn Sess., 14-15 (1970).

[3] Ibid.

[4] United States Department of Health, Education and Welfare-Environmental Health Problems (G.P.O. 1970).

[5] See note 2 supra.

to toxic materials or harmful physical agents. According to that study, industry adequately protected only one quarter of the workers exposed to toxic agents. The long period frequently experienced between initial exposure to deadly materials and the actual onset of disease required prompt, affirmative steps to prevent the situation from deteriorating further. The involuntary act of merely breathing was understood for the first time in our history as posing a "mind-boggling" threat to workers. In this atmosphere of urgency, OSHA was finally passed.

Yet, instead of dealing with the many health hazards of the workplace — dust, fumes, gases, noises, chemical and toxic substances — state laws concentrated on the tort concept in Workmen's Compensation law of paying those who fall victim to industrial dangers. The federal government also defaulted in this area. For example, the recent revelation about the health hazards of asbestos dust were known to government health authorities in the 1930's, but nothing was even done!

B. CONGRESSIONAL RESPONSE: PROVISIONS OF THE ACT

U.S. Dept of Labor, ALL ABOUT OSHA, Program and Policy Series: OSHA 2056 (GPO 1976-201-445)

THE ACT'S COVERAGE

In general, coverage of the Act extends to all employers and their employees in the 50 States, the District of Columbia, Puerto Rico, the Canal Zone, and all other territories under Federal Government jurisdiction.

As defined by the Act, an employer is any "person engaged in a business affecting commerce who has employees, but does not include the United States or any State or political subdivision of a State." Therefore, under the Act's coverage come employers and employees in such varied fields as construction, longshoring, argiculture [agriculture], law and medicine, charity and disaster relief, organized labor, and private education. Such coverage includes religious groups to the extent that they employ workers for secular purposes.

The following are not covered under the Act:
- Self-employed persons;
- Family owned and operated farms; and
- Workplaces already protected by other Federal agencies under other Federal statutes.

But even when another Federal agency is authorized to regulate safety and health working conditions in a particular industry, if it does not do so in specific areas, the OSHA regulations will apply. As OSHA develops effective safety and health standards of its own, standards issued under the following law administered by the Department of Labor are superseded: the *Walsh-Healey Act,* the *Service Contract Act,* the *Construction Safety Act,* the *Arts and Humanities Act,* and the *Longshoremen's and Harbor Workers' Compensation Act.*

STANDARDS [3]

The general duty clause of the Act states that each employer "shall furnish to each of his employees employment and a place of employment which are free from recognized hazards that are causing or are likely to cause death or serious physical harm to his employees."

In carrying out its duties under the Act, OSHA is responsible for promulgating legally enforceable standards. OSHA standards may require conditions, or the adoption or use of one or more practices, means, methods or processes reasonably necessary or appropriate to protect workers on the job. It is the employer's responsibility to become familiar with the standards applicable to their establishments and to assure that employees have and use personal protective gear and equipment required for safety. Even in cases where OSHA has not promulgated specific standards, employers are responsible for following the intent of the Act's general duty clause.

STANDARDS DEVELOPMENT

OSHA can begin standards-setting procedures on its own initiative, or on petitions from other parties, including the Secretary

---

[3] OSHA standards fall in three major categories — General Industry, Maritime, and Construction. Free single copies of the standards in each category may be obtained from local OSHA offices. The *Federal Register* is one of the best sources of information on standards, since all OSHA standards are published in the *Federal Register* when adopted, as are all other amendments, corrections, insertions, or deletions. The *Federal Register* is available in many public libraries. Annual subscriptions are available from the Superintendent of Documents, U.S. Government Printing Office, Washington, D.C. 20402, for $50 (prepaid). In addition, to assist the public in keeping current with OSHA standards, the OSHA Subscription Service was developed. This service provides all standards, interpretations, regulations, and procedures in easy-to-use loose-leaf form, punched for use in a three-ring binder. All changes and additions are issued for an indefinite period of time. The service is available from the Superintendent of Documents only and is not available from OSHA or from the Department of Labor. Individual volumes of the OSHA Subscription Service are available as follows:

Volume I.	General Industry Standards and Interpretations
Volume II.	Maritime Standards and Interpretations
Volume III.	Construction Standards and Interpretations
Volume IV.	Other Regulations and Procedures
Volume V.	Field Operations Manual

of Health, Education, and Welfare; the National Institute for Occupational Safety and Health (NIOSH); [4] State and local governments; and nationally-recognized standards-producing organization; employer or labor representatives; or any other interested person.

STANDARDS ADOPTION

Once OSHA has developed plans to propose, amend, or delete a standard, it publishes these intentions in the *Federal Register* as a "Notice of Proposed Rulemaking." The notice will include the terms of the new rule and provide a specific time (at least 30 days from the date of publication, occasionally 60 days or more) for the public to respond to it.

Interested parties who submit written arguments and pertinent evidence may request a hearing on the proposal when none has been announced in the notice. When such a hearing is requested, OSHA must schedule one, and must publish, in advance, the time and place for it in the *Federal Register*.

Within 60 days after the close of the comment period or public hearing, OSHA must publish its ruling in the *Federal Register*, along with the full, final text of any standard amended or adopted and the date the new ruling will become effective.

EMERGENCY TEMPORARY STANDARDS

Under certain conditions, OSHA is authorized to set emergency temporary standards which take effect immediately. OSHA must first determine that workers are in grave danger due to exposure to toxic substances or new hazards. Then, OSHA publishes an emergency temporary standard in the *Federal Register* where it also serves as a proposed permanent standard. It is then subject to the usual procedure for adopting or rejecting a permanent standard, except that a final ruling must be made within 6 months.

APPEALING STANDARDS

No decision on a permanent standard is ever reached without due consideration of the argument and data received from the public in written submissions and at hearings. However, if any affected party, employer, or employee believes that a final standard or rule is too burdensome, or is inadequate, or does not reflect the record in the case, an appeal may be made (within 60 days of the rule's publication) to the U.S. Circuit Court of Appeals for the circuit in which the objector lives or has his or her principal place of business. Filing an

---

[4] The Act established NIOSH, an agency of the Department of Health, Education, and Welfare (HEW), to conduct research and recommend standards for various safety and health problems.

appeals petition, however, will not delay the enforcement of a standard, unless the Court of Appeals specifically orders it.

VARIANCES

Employers may make application to OSHA for a variance from a standard or regulation if they lack the means to readily comply with it, or if they can prove that their facilities or methods of operation provide employees protection that is "at least as effective as" that required by OSHA.

Temporary Variance

A temporary variance may be granted to an employer who cannot comply with a standard or regulation by its effective date, due to unavailability of personnel, materials or equipment, or because the necessary construction or alteration of facilities cannot be completed in time.

The employer must demonstrate to OSHA that he or she is, nevertheless, taking all available steps to safeguard employees in the meantime, and that the employer has put in force an effective program for coming into compliance with the standard or regulation as quickly as possible.

A temporary variance may be granted for a period of up to 1 year. It is renewable twice, each time for 6 months. Application for a temporary variance must identify the standard or portion of a standard from which the variance is requested and the reasons why the employer cannot comply with the standard. The application must be supported by representations from experts with first-hand knowledge of the facts. The employer must document those measures he or she has taken and will take (including dates) to protect workers from the hazards and to come into compliance with the standard itself.

The employer must certify that he or she has informed the workers of the variance application, that a copy of it has been given to the employees' authorized representative, and a summary of the application has been posted wherever notices are normally posted. The employees must also have been informed that they have the right to request a hearing on the application.

A temporary variance will not be granted to any employer who simply cannot afford to pay for the necessary alterations, equipment, or personnel. But the Act does provide for economic assistance to small business employers through long-term loans from the Small Business Administration.

Permanent Variance

A permanent variance (exemption from a particular standard) may be granted to an employer who can prove his or her own conditions, practices, means, methods, operations, or processes provide a safe and healthful workplace as effectively as would compliance with the standard.

In making a determination, OSHA weighs the employer's evidence and arranges an inspection and a hearing where appropriate. If OSHA finds the request to be valid, it will prescribe a permanent variance detailing the employer's specific exceptions and responsibilities under the ruling.

When applying for a permanent variance, the employer must inform his or her employees of the application and of their right to request a hearing. Within 6 months after a permanent variance has been issued, employees may petition OSHA to modify or revoke it. OSHA also may do this of its own accord.

Interim Order

So that an employer may receive consideration to continue to operate under existing conditions until a variance decision is made, he or she may apply to OSHA for an interim order. Application for an interim order may be made either at the same time of, or after, application for a variance. Statements of fact and arguments as to why order should be granted may be included in the interim order application.

If OSHA denies the interim order request, the employer will be promptly notified of the reason for denial.

If the interim order is granted, the employer and other parties concerned will be served with a copy of the order, and the terms of the order will be published in the *Federal Register.* The employer must inform his or her employees of the order by giving a copy to the authorized employee representative and by posting a copy of the order wherever notices are normally posted.

Experimental Variance

If an employer is participating in an experiment to demonstrate or validate new job safety and health techniques, and that experiment has been approved by either the Secretary of Labor or the Secretary of Health, Education, and Welfare, a variance may be granted to permit the experiment. In such instances, the employer is not required to inform his or her employees when the request is made.

Other

In addition to temporary, permanent, and experimental variances, the Secretary of Labor also may find certain variances justified when the national defense is impaired.

PUBLIC PETITIONS

OSHA continually reviews and redefines its safety and health standards because industrial technology and safety and health knowledge are still developing. Therefore, employers and employees should be aware that, just as they may petition OSHA for the development of standards, they may also petition OSHA for standards modification or revocation.

RECORDKEEPING AND REPORTING

Before the Act became effective, no centralized and systematic method existed for monitoring the occupational safety and health problem. Statistics on job injuries and illnesses were collected by some States and by some private safety and health organizations; national figures were based on not altogether reliable projections. With OSHA regulations came the first basis for consistent, nation-wide procedures — a vital requirement for gauging the problem and attempting to solve it.

OSHA requires employers of eight or more employees to maintain records of occupational injuries and illnesses as they occur. Employers with seven or fewer employees must keep such records also, when selected by the Bureau [of] Labor Statistics (BLS) to participate in periodic statistical surveys.

What is considered to be an occupational injury or illness? An occupational injury is any injury such as a cut, fracture, sprain, or amputation which results from a work-related accident or from exposure involving a single incident in the work environment. An occupational illness is any abnormal condition or disorder, other than one resulting from an occupational injury, caused by exposure to environmental factors associated with employment. Included are acute and chronic illnesses which may be caused by inhalation, absorption, ingestion, or direct contact with toxic substances.

All occupational injuries and illnesses *must* be recorded if they result in:

- Death (must be recorded regardless of the length of time between the injury and death and regardless of the length of the illness);
- One or more lost workdays;
- Restriction of work or motion;
- Transfer to another job; or
- Medical treatment (other than first aid).

INJURY AND ILLNESS RECORDS [5]

Employers must keep injury and illness records for each establishment. An establishment is defined as a "single physical location where business is conducted or where services are performed." An employer whose employees work in dispersed locations must keep his or her records at the place where the employees report for work each workday. In some situations, employees do not report to work at the same place each day. In that case, records must be kept at the place from which they are paid or at the base from which they operate.

KEEPING EMPLOYEES INFORMED

In addition to safety and health standards and recordkeeping duties, employers [are] responsible for keeping their employees informed about OSHA and about the various safety and health matters with which they are involved. OSHA requires that each employer post certain materials at a prominent location in the workplace. These include:

- *Job Safety and Health Protection* (workplace poster, OSHA 2203) informing employees of their rights and responsibilities under the Act. Besides displaying the workplace poster, the employer must make copies of the Act and copies of OSHA rules and regulations relevant to the workplace available to employees upon request.
- *Summaries of petitions for variances* from standards or recordkeeping procedures.
- *Copies of OSHA citations* for violations of standards. These must remain posted for 3 days, or until the violations are abated, whichever is longer.
- *Summary of Occupation Injuries and Illnesses* (OSHA No. 102) which must be posted within one month of the close of the year, and remain posted for at least thirty days.

Occasionally, OSHA standards or NIOSH research activities will require an employer to measure and record employee exposure to potentially harmful substances. Employees have the right (in person or through their authorized representative) to be present during the measuring and to examine the records kept of the results.

Each employee or former employee has the right to see his or her own examinations records, and must be told by the employer if the exposure to hazardous substances has exceeded the levels set by standards. The employee also must be told what corrective measures, if any, are being taken.

---

[5] If an on-the-job accident occurs which results in the death of an employee or in the hospitalization of five or more employees, the employer must (by law) report the accident, in detail, to the nearest OSHA office within 48 hours.

WORKPLACE INSPECTION

Authority to Inspect

In order to enforce its standards and regulations, OSHA is authorized under the Act to conduct workplace inspections. Every establishment covered by the Act is subject to inspection by OSHA compliance safety and health officers, who are chosen for their knowledge and experience in the occupational safety and health fields, and trained rigorously in OSHA standards and in recognition of the hazards they cover.

Under the Act, "upon presenting appropriate credentials to the owner, operator, or agent in charge," an OSHA compliance officer is authorized to:

- Enter without delay and at reasonable times any factory, plant, establishment, construction site, or other area, workplace, or environment where work is performed by an employee of an employer; and to
- Inspect and investigate during regular working hours and at other reasonable times, and within reasonable limits and in a reasonable manner, any such place of employment and all pertinent conditions, structures, machines, apparatus, devices, equipment, and materials therein and to question privately any such employer, owner, operator, agent, or employee.

If an employer refused to admit an OSHA compliance officer, or if an employer attempts to interfere with the inspection, the Act allows for appropriate legal action.

NOTE:

On May 23, 1978, the Supreme Court ruled that a warrantless search of work area of any employment facility within OSHA's jurisdiction for safety hazards and violations of OSHA regulations violated the Fourth Amendment, *Marshall v. Barlow's Inc.,* 98 S. Ct. 1816 (1978). Speaking for the Court, Mr. Justice White stated:

> The critical fact in this case is that entry over Mr. Barlow's objection is being sought by a Government agent. Employees are not being prohibited from reporting OSHA violations. What they observe in their daily functions is undoubtedly beyond the employer's reasonable expectation of privacy. The Government inspector, however, is not an employee. Without a warrant he stands in no better position than a member of the public. What is observable by the public is observable, without a warrant, by the Government inspector as well. The owner of a business has not, by the necessary utilization of employees in his operation, thrown open the areas where employees alone are permitted to

the warrantless scrutiny of Government agents. That an employee is free to report, and the Government is free to use, any evidence of noncompliance with OSHA that the employee observes furnishes no justification for federal agents to enter a place of business from which the public is restricted and to conduct their own warrantless search. 98 S. Ct. at 1821-22.

Accordingly, OSHA's authority to inspect is delimited by this case.

U.S. Dept. of Labor, ALL ABOUT OSHA, Program and Policy Series: OSHA 2056 (GPO 1976-201-445) [Continued]

Inspection Process

Prior to an inspection, the compliance officer becomes familiar with as many relevant facts as possible about the workplace, taking into account such things as the history of the establishment, the nature of the business, and the particular standards most likely to apply. Preparing for the inspection also involves selecting appropriate equipment for detecting and measuring fumes, gases, toxic substances, noise, etc.

INSPECTOR'S CREDENTIALS

An inspection begins when the OSHA compliance officer arrives at the establishment. He or she displays official credentials and asks to meet an appropriate employer representative. Employers should always insist upon seeing the compliance officer's credentials.

An OSHA compliance officer carries U.S. Department of Labor credentials bearing his or her photograph and a serial number that can be verified by phoning the nearest OSHA office. Anyone who tries to collect a penalty or to promote the sale of a product or service is not an OSHA compliance officer.

OPENING CONFERENCE

The compliance officer then explains the purpose of the visit, the scope of the inspection, and the standards that apply. The employer will be given copies of applicable safety and health standards as well as a copy of any employee complaint that may be involved. If the employee has so requested, his or her name will not be revealed.

The employer is asked to select an **employer representative** to accompany the compliance officer during the inspection tour.

An authorized **employee representative** also is usually given the opportunity to accompany the compliance officer during the inspection. If the employees at the workplace are represented by a recognized bargaining representative, the union ordinarily will designate the employee representative who will accompany the compliance officer. Similarly, if there is a plant safety committee, the employee members of that committee will designate the employee representative (in the absence, that is, of a recognized bargaining representative). Where neither employee group exists, the employee representative may be selected by the employees themselves, but not by the compliance officer or the employer.

The Act does not require that there be an employee representative for each inspection. However, where there is no authorized employee representative, the compliance officer must consult with a reasonable number of employees concerning safety and health matters in the workplace.

INSPECTION TOUR

After the opening conference, the compliance officer and the accompanying representatives then proceed through the establishment, inspecting work areas for compliance with OSHA standards.

The route and duration of the inspection are determined by the compliance officer. While talking with employees, the compliance officer makes every effort to minimize any work interruptions by avoiding peak operational time whenever possible. The compliance officer observes conditions, consults with employees, and may take photos (for record purposes), make instrument readings, and examine records to the extent considered appropriate.

Trade secrets observed by the compliance officer must and will be kept confidential. An inspector who releases confidential information without authorization is subject to a $1,000 fine and/or 1 year in jail. The employer may require that the employee representative have confidential clearance for any area in question.

Employees are consulted during the inspection tour. The compliance officer may stop and question workers, in private if necessary, about safety and health conditions and practices in their workplaces. *Each employee is protected, under the Act, from discrimination for exercising his or her rights.*

An employee who believes he or she has been discriminated against, discharged, demoted, or otherwise penalized because he or she requested an inspection, or because he or she exercised any other right under the Act may file a complaint with OSHA within 30 days.

If OSHA determines, upon investigation, that an employee complaint is valid and that the employee has indeed been discriminated against for exercising his or her rights under the Act, the Secretary of Labor may bring action against the employer or seek relief for the employee concerned (which may take the form, when appropriate, of reinstatement with back pay). OSHA will notify the employee of its decision within 90 days of the filing of the complaint.

Posting and recordkeeping are checked. The compliance officer will inspect records of deaths, injuries, and illnesses which the employer is required to keep. He or she will check to see that the annual summary of occupational injuries and illnesses has been posted and that the OSHA workplace poster (OSHA 2203) is prominently displayed. Where records of employee exposure to toxic substances and harmful physical agents have been required, they are also examined.

Some apparent violations detected by the compliance officer can be corrected immediately. When they are corrected on the spot, the compliance officer records such corrections in order to help in judging the employer's good faith in compliance. Even though corrected, however, the apparent violations may still serve as the basis for a citation and/or notice of proposed penalty. *(For cases where imminent danger situations are detected, see·p. 15).*

Coverage for the inspection tour may be part or all of an establishment, even if the inspection resulted from a specific complaint, fatality, or catastrophe.

. . .

CITATIONS AND PENALTIES

Citations Issued by the Area Director

After the compliance officer reports to his or her OSHA office, the area director determines what citations, if any, will be issued, and what penalties, if any, will be proposed.[6]

Citations inform the employer and employees of the regulations and standards which have been violated, and of the time set for their abatement. The employer will receive citations and notices of proposed penalties by certified mail. The employer must post a copy of each citation at or near the place the violation occurred, for 3 days or until the violation is abated, whichever is longer.

APPEALS PROCESS

Appeals by Employees

If an inspection was initiated due to an employee complaint, the employee or authorized employee representative has the right to request an informal review of any OSHA decision not to issue a citation.

Employees may not contest citations, but they may contest the time set by a citation for the abatement of a hazardous condition. Within 15 working days of the employer's receipt of the citation, the

---

[6] There are four categories of violations that may be found during an inspection: (1) de minimis; (2) non-serious; (3) serious; and (4) imminent danger. The penalty imposed on a violator will vary on the basis of the type of violation committed, ranging from the issuance of a "notice of violation" with no fine to as much as $10,000 and 6 months imprisonment.

employee may submit a written objection to OSHA. He or she should also inform the employer that this was done. The OSHA area director will forward the employee's objection to the Occupational Safety and Health Review Commission (independent and not a part of the U.S. Department of Labor).

Employees have the right to request an informal conference with OSHA to discuss any other issues raised by an inspection, citation, notice of proposed penalty, or employer's notice of intention to contest.

Appeals by Employers

When issued a citation or notice of proposed penalty, an employer may request an informal meeting with OSHA's area director to discuss the case.

If the employer decides to contest the citation, the time set for abatement, or the proposed penalty, he or she has 15 working days from the time the citation and proposed penalty are received in which to notify the OSHA area director. This written notification is called a "Notice of Contest."

A copy of the Notice of Contest must be given to the employees' authorized representative. If any or all of the affected employees are not represented by a recognized bargaining agent, a copy of the Notice must be posted in a prominent location of the workplace, or else served personally upon each nonunion employee.

Posted copies of the Notice must inform employees that they have a right to participate in Review Commission procedures and that they must identify themselves to the Commission or Hearing Examiner before or at the beginning of the hearing.

NOTICE OF CONTEST

There is no specific format for the Notice of Contest. However, it must clearly identify the employer's basis for filing — the citation, notice of proposed penalty, abatement period, or notification of failure to correct violations. The Notice must also identify, by name and address, the employees or employee representatives who have been personally served with a copy, as well as the address where the Notice has been posted.

REVIEW PROCEDURE

If the Notice of Contest has been filed within the required 15 working days, the OSHA area director forwards the case to the independent Occupational Safety and Health Review Commission. The Commission assigns the case to an administrative law judge.

The judge may investigate and disallow the contest if it is found to be legally invalid, or a hearing may be scheduled to be held in a public place as close as possible to the employer's workplace. The employer and the employees have the right to participate in the hearing; the Review Commission does not require that they be represented by attorneys.

Once the administrative law judge has ruled, any party to the case may request a further review by the Review Commission itself. Any of the three commissioners also may, at his own motion, bring a case before the Commission for review. If the Commission issues its own ruling, that ruling may itself be appealed to the U.S. Circuit Court of Appeals for the circuit in which the case arose.

. . .

OSHA-APPROVED STATE PLANS

The Act requires OSHA to encourage the States to develop and operate their own job safety and health programs, which must be "at least as effective as" the Federal program. Once a State plan is approved, OSHA funds 50 percent of its operating costs.

To gain OSHA approval, a State must demonstrate that within 3 years it will meet all the steps necessary to become at least as effective as the Federal program, by providing adequate legislation, administration, standards-setting, enforcement and appeals procedures, and a sufficient number of competent enforcement personnel. During this interim period, OSHA closely monitors the State program, and retains its own authority to enforce Federal standards in the State.

. . .

Employers and employees should find out if their State has submitted a plan for OSHA approval, and if so, become familiar with it. State safety and health standards under approved plans must keep pace with OSHA standards, and State plans must guarantee employer and employee rights as does OSHA.

Any interested person who finds inadequacies or other problems in the administration of his or her State's safety and health program may file a specific complaint with the regional administrator for OSHA in the region where the State is located. The complainant's name is kept confidential. OSHA investigates all such complaints, and where complaints are found to be valid, requires appropriate corrective action on the part of the State as a condition for continued plan approval.

. . .

EMPLOYER RESPONSIBILITIES AND RIGHTS

Employers have certain responsibilities and rights under the Occupational Safety and Health Act of 1970. The checklists which follow provide a review of many of these.

Responsibilities

As an employer, you must:

- Meet your general duty responsibility to provide a hazard-free workplace and comply with the occupational safety and health standards, rules, and regulations issued under the Act.
- Be familiar with mandatory OSHA standards and make copies available to employees for review upon request.
- Inform all employees about OSHA.
- Examine workplace conditions to make sure they conform to applicable safety and health standards.
- Remove or guard hazards.
- Make sure employees have and use safe tools and equipment (including personal protective equipment) and that such equipment is properly maintained.
- Use color codes, posters, labels, or signs to warn employees of potential hazards.
- Establish or update operating procedures and communicate them so that employees follow safety and health requirements for their own protection.
- Provide medical examinations when required by OSHA standards.
- Report to the nearest OSHA office, **within 48 hours,** the occurrence of any employment accident which is fatal to one or more employees or which results in the hospitalization of five or more employees.
- Keep OSHA-required records of work-related injuries and illnesses, and post the annual summary during the entire month of February each year. (This applies to employers with eight or more employees.)
- Post, at a prominent location within the workplace, the OSHA poster (OSHA 2203) informing employees of their rights and responsibilities. (In States operating OSHA-approved job safety and health programs, the State's equivalent poster and/or OSHA 2203 may be required.)
- Cooperate with the OSHA compliance officer by furnishing names of authorized employee representatives who may be asked to accompany the compliance officer during the inspection. (If none, the compliance officer will consult with a reasonable number of employees concerning safety and health in the workplace.)
- Not discriminate against employees who properly exercise their rights under the Act.
- Post OSHA citations of apparent violations of standards or of the general duty clause at or near the worksite involved. Each citation, or copy thereof, shall remain posted until the violation

has been abated, or for 3 working days, whichever is longer.
- Abate cited violations within the prescribed period.

Rights

As an employer, you have the right to:

- Seek advice and off-site consultation as needed by writing, calling, or visiting the nearest OSHA office. (OSHA will not inspect merely because an employer requests assistance.)
- Be active in your industry association's involvement in job safety and health.
- Request and receive proper identification of the OSHA compliance officer prior to inspection of the workplace.
- Be advised by the compliance officer of the reason for an inspection.
- Have an opening and closing conference with the compliance officer.
- File a Notice of Contest with the nearest OSHA area director within 15 working days of receipt of a notice of citation and proposed penalty.
- Apply to OSHA for a temporary variance from a standard if unable to comply because of the unavailability of materials, equipment, or personnel to make necessary changes within the required time.
- Apply to OSHA for a permanent variance from a standard if you can furnish proof that your facilities or method of operation provide employee protection that is at least as effective as that required by the standard.
- Take an active role in developing job safety and health standards through participation in OSHA Standards Advisory Committees, through nationally recognized standards setting organizations, and through evidence and views presented in writing or at hearings.
- Avail yourself, if you are a small business employer, of long-term loans through the Small Business Administration (SBA) to help bring your establishment into compliance, either before or after an OSHA inspection.
- Be assured of the confidentiality of any trade secrets observed by an OSHA compliance officer during an inspection.

EMPLOYEE RESPONSIBILITIES AND RIGHTS

Although OSHA does not cite employees for violations of their responsibilities, each employee "shall comply with all occupational safety and health standards and all rules, regulations, and orders issued under the Act" that apply to his or her own actions and conduct on the job.

Responsibilities

As an employee, you should:
- Read the OSHA poster at the jobsite.
- Comply with all applicable OSHA standards.[7]
- Follow all employer safety and health rules and regulations, and wear or use prescribed protective equipment while engaged in work.
- Report hazardous conditions to the supervisor.
- Report any job-related injury or illness to the employer, and seek treatment promptly.
- Cooperate with the OSHA compliance officer conducting an inspection if he or she inquires about safety and health conditions in your workplace.
- Exercise your rights under the Act in a responsible manner.

Rights

As an employee, you have the right to:
- Review copies of any of the OSHA standards, rules, regulations, and requirements that the employer should have available at the workplace.
- Request information from your employer on safety and health hazards in the area, on precautions that may be taken, and on procedures to be followed if an employee is involved in an accident or exposed to toxic substances.
- Request (in writing) the OSHA area director to conduct an inspection if you believe hazardous conditions or violation of standards exist in your workplace.
- Have your name withheld from your employer, upon request to OSHA, if you file a written and signed complaint.
- Be advised of OSHA actions regarding your complaint and have an informal review, if requested, of any decision not to make an inspection or not to issue a citation.
- File a complaint to OSHA within 30 days if you believe you have been discriminated against, discharged, demoted, or otherwise penalized because of asserting an employee right under the Act, and be notified by OSHA of its determination within 90 days of filing.
- Have the authorized employee representative where you work accompany the OSHA compliance officer during the inspection tour.
- Respond to questions from the OSHA compliance officer, particularly if there is no authorized employee representative accompanying the compliance officer.

---

[7] *See* Note, Employee Noncompliance with OSHA Safety Standards, 90 Harv. L. Rev. 1041 (1977).

- Observe any monitoring or measuring of hazardous materials and have the right of access to records on those materials, as specified under the Act.
- Request a closing discussion with the compliance officer following an inspection.
- Submit a written request to the National Institute for Occupational Safety and Health (NIOSH) for information on whether any substance in your workplace has potential toxic effects in the concentrations being used, and have your name withheld from your employer if you so request.
- Object to the abatement period set in the citation issued to your employer by writing to the OSHA area director within 15 working days of the issuance of the citation.
- Be notified by your employer if he or she applies for a variance from an OSHA standard, testify at a variance hearing, and appeal the final decision if you disagree with it.
- Submit information or comment to OSHA on the issuance, modification, or revocation of OSHA standards, and request a public hearing.

C. IMPACT ON COLLECTIVE BARGAINING

In 1976, the Bureau of Labor Statistics examined 1,724 major collective bargaining agreements for safety and health provisions primarily concerned with preventing or minimizing occupational accidents or illnesses, as well as provisions for accident procedures, physical examinations, job protection for employees disabled on the job, and hazard pay premiums in bargaining units covering 1,000 workers or more, or almost all agreements of this size in the United States, excluding those of railroads, airlines, and government. The contracts covered about 7.9 million workers, or nearly half the total estimated to be under collective bargaining agreements in the industries studied. Of these, 908 agreements, covering more than 3.8 million workers, were in manufacturing, and 816, covering more than 4 million workers, were in nonmanufacturing. All agreements were in effect in mid-1974, with the majority remaining in effect during 1975 and later.

Its findings were that:

> MOST MAJOR collective bargaining agreements in high-risk industries refer at least briefly to safety and health. According to studies by the Bureau of Labor Statistics of 503 selected agreements in force before January 1, 1971, and their successor agreements which took effect at least a year later, such references increased slightly after the Occupational Safety and Health Act of 1979 (OSHA) went

into effect in mid-1971. (See table 1.) Although the minimum time separating the two sets of data was 1 year, the average elapsed time was much greater, since many of the newer agreements did not go into effect until mid-1972 and later.

Nearly all the agreements surveyed made some reference to safety and health or related topics, but few of the general types of health and safety provisions appeared in even half the contracts. (See table 2.) Nearly all the types of provisions became more numerous after OSHA went into effect, but the changes were generally slight or moderate. More significant changes may be antipated over longer periods.[8]

Appendix table 1. Major agreements containing safety and health provisions, selected industries, before and after 1971

Industry	All agreements studied			Agreements with safety and health provisions			
	Number	Workers covered before 1971	Workers covered after 1971	Number covered 1971	Workers before before 1971	Number after 1971	Workers covered after 1971
All selected industries	503	1,651.7	1,811.1	476	1,582.4	487	1,767.3
Selected manufacturing	221	648.8	670.9	205	616.4	208	635.3
Food and kindred products	44	121.6	126.5	38	110.6	40	117.8
Textile mill products	15	48.8	41.8	14	47.5	13	33.3
Apparel and related products	33	209.3	234.4	28	195.2	29	221.6
Lumber and wood products	10	16.9	18.1	8	13.4	8	13.8
Furniture and fixtures	11	17.8	18.0	9	15.4	10	16.8
Paper and allied products	33	66.9	61.0	33	66.9	33	61.0
Leather tanning and finishing	1	1.0	1.0	1	1.0	1	1.0
Stone, clay, and glass products	12	24.6	21.5	12	24.6	12	21.5
Primary metals foundries	8	12.0	13.5	8	12.0	8	13.5
Fabricated metals products	16	28.7	25.8	16	28.7	16	25.8
Machinery, except electrical	37	98.9	107.0	37	98.9	37	107.0
Electrical machinery	1	2.5	2.5	1	2.5	1	2.5
Selected nonmanufacturing	282	1,003.0	1,140.2	271	966.0	279	1,132.0
Mining	1	1.1	1.1	1	1.1	1	1.1
Construction	254	858.8	951.4	244	825.8	252	944.8
Transportation	24	135.3	181.0	23	132.4	23	179.4
Wholesale trade	3	6.8	6.8	3	6.8	3	6.8

NOTE: Figures include all agreements containing safety provisions and related provisions on accidents, sanitation, physical examinations, or job protections for occupationally disabled employees but do not include agreements referring only to hazard pay differentials. "Before 1971" refers to agreements in effect before Jan. 1, 1971. "after 1971" refers to agreements which went into effect on or after Jan. 1, 1972. Because of rounding, sums of individual items may not equal totals.

[8] U.S. Dept. of Labor, Major Collective Bargaining Agreements: Safety and Health Provisions 74, BLS Bull. No. 1425-16, (1976).

Appendix table 2. General provisions referring to safety and health in major agreements, before and after 1971 [9]

Provision	Before 1971		After 1971	
	Agreements	Workers covered	Agreements	Workers covered
All agreements studied	503	1,651.7	503	1,811.1
Total referring to safety and health	476	1,582.4	487	1,767.3
General policy statements	200	551.2	219	607.3
Union-management cooperation pledges [1]	98	286.4	107	317.2
Safety committees [2]	109	329.8	124	434.5
Joint safety committees	93	273.1	108	362.3
Safety inspections	63	270.2	77	342.8
Employer pledges of compliance with law	204	751.6	259	1,002.0
Employee compliance with safety rules or laws [3]	197	660.5	246	871.0
Discipline for noncompliance	88	298.1	124	491.6
Employee rights with regard to safety	112	438.5	134	542.1
Union rights with regard to safety	75	292.5	82	383.6
Safety equipment [4]	262	831.6	291	1,116.9
Sanitation provisions	247	847.5	252	1,034.7
Physical examinations [5]	104	309.9	107	401.8
Accident procedures or compensation	300	925.4	324	1,085.9

[1] Excludes pledges in agreements that also establish a joint safety committee.

[2] Includes 2 agreements before and 4 after 1971 in which the committee had functions in addition to safety.

[3] Includes a few agreements requiring only that the employee work in a safe manner.

[4] Generally, safety equipment is to be furnished by the employer. A few agreements require employees to pay all or a part of the cost of specified items.

[5] Includes only those agreements providing for physical examinations to be given at company expense.

D. GOALS AND ACHIEVEMENTS

It is well known that OSHA's methodology and achievements have been subjected to continuing criticism. As Senator Hughes stated in oversight hearings conducted in 1972:

> Enactment of this law in 1970 represented the first real Federal commitment to protecting the safety and health of some 60 million workers and marked an end to the shameful history of Government neglect of on-the-job hazards.
>
> Its passage and signing were accompanied by great hopes that through a coordinated effort involving health and safety research, programs of education and training, establishment of effective standards, and firm but fair enforcement procedures, we would begin a meaningful attack on the 14,500 deaths, the more than 2 million disabling injuries, and the hundreds of thousands of occupational illnesses that occur in the workplace each year.
>
> However, during the 15 months that have elapsed since the act's effective date, there is scarcely a Senate office that has not

---

[9] *Id.* at 76.

been besieged with complaints concerning the act's administration.[10]

In Robert Steward Smith's study of OSHA — "Its goals and its achievements" for the American Enterprise Institute, he concludes that "all tests made suggest that the Target Interest of the Program has had a negligible effect on work injury rates." [11] He recommends that:

(1) The goal of absolute safety, qualified only by cost considerations in the most extreme cases, should be rejected. Because this goal apparently is supported by congressional intent and judicial decisions, OSHA will have to rely on changing the attitudes of Congress or the judiciary so that a goal can be adopted more consistent with promoting the general welfare. Perhaps the best way for OSHA to provoke a serious discussion of goals is to adhere rigidly to a benefit-cost framework in setting standards — as suggested in the case of noise control — and use the resulting conflict to state the case for more rational goals.

(2) The standard-setting approach to occupational safety should be repealed and replaced by a program which sets moderate fines on each injury, to be paid by the victim's employer. The fines should be moderate, because there is no evidence that occupational safety is grievously underprovided by employers.

(3) The largest social gains can be achieved by focusing OSHA's resources on the area of occupational health, where a standards approach must be maintained. OSHA can, however, also increase social welfare by publicizing what is known or suspected about the causes of occupational disease.

(4) The criterion for any standard must be, "would the beneficiaries be willing to pay the costs of this standard if they were fully informed as to the hazards involved?" This criterion underlies the use of benefit-cost analysis, and must be used to prevent the diminution of social welfare from "too little" (as in the case of asbestos hazards) or "too much" (as in the case of the seat belt interlock system) protection against risk. According to this criterion, it is very doubtful that either noise standard OSHA was considering in 1975 will do anything but reduce social welfare.

(5) According to the criterion in (4), it is quite likely that standards should vary across industries. The "equal protection"

---

[10] Implementation of the Occupational Safety and Health Act, 1972: Hearings Before the Subcomm. on Labor of the Senate Comm. on Labor and Public Welfare, 92nd Cong., 2d Sess. 1 (1972).

[11] R. Smith, The Occupational Safety and Health Act: The Goals and Its Achievements, (AEI 1971).

argument is neither cogent nor consistent with the goal of promoting social welfare — unless, for some reason, administrative or enforcement costs of industry-specific standards are enormous.

(6) Targeting high-risk industries for highest inspection priorities will not necessarily prove productive. In fact, given the lack of measured effectiveness of the Target Industry Program and the lack of correlation between injury and compliance rates, OSHA's variant of the "worst-first" approach to inspections must be seriously questioned. It is possible that targeting the high-risk firms within an industry would be more productive.[12]

Less conservative approaches to OSHA's goals have also been critical of its administration.[13] Consider the following "note."

NOTES:

(1) In writing about the "Impact of OSHA on Collective Bargaining," in Proc. of N.Y.U. 27th Ann. Conf. on Labor 267, Wayne T. Brooks, an OSHA consultant stated: "The Act contemplates that the employer has a complete knowledge of workplace as follows: 'Each employer shall promptly notify any employee who has been or is being exposed to toxic material or harmful physical agents — at levels exceeding those prescribed in applicable standards — and inform such employee of corrective action being taken.' OSHA § 8 (c) (3). Much of the whole subject is identifiable with wages, hours and terms and conditions of employment. This fact adds another dimension to the decision making process and suggests even further questions of joint committees, grievance and arbitration procedure, jurisdiction of an arbitration panel or [an] national labor relations board.

In each detail of employment practice OSHA will be recognized. Consider the employment questionnaire and physical examination. What is their purpose? Are they solely concerned with a hire-step inside, or are they a factor to assist in assigning the employee and helping him to select training and work most compatible with his biological strengths and weaknesses? It has been predicted that the industrial physician will become the career guidance counselor in the future."

He then raised the following problems about employment policy. *Id.* at 265-69.

(2) *Problems:* (a) How will a company's employment policies reflect the requirements of OSHA? What are the social, moral and

---

[12] *Id.* at 84-85.

[13] *See, e.g.,* OSHA and the Workplace Environment, note 2, *supra,* at 220-23.

company liability consequences of a policy when an applicant for employment appears physically sound, but is a (an):

> black male, age twenty, who has sickle cell anemia;
>
> person, age 35, who had 5 years exposure to asbestos 10 years ago;
>
> person, age 40, who had 5 years exposure to any known human carcinogen 10 years ago, or to experimental-animal carcinogens;
>
> person, age 45, who had 5 years exposure to vinyl chloride 15 years ago;
>
> person, age 40, who had 10 years exposure to welding fumes;
>
> person, age 25, who has exzema [eczema] and chronic dermatitis;
>
> epileptic under treatment control;
>
> post-recovered cardiac;
>
> "former" alcoholic or drug user;
>
> person, any age, handicapped by loss of member or sight or hearing?

(b) Do employers' physicians think about the health effects of smoking?

(c) How accommodative and flexible are work methods, job assignments, job content and pay practices? Does work simplification, seniority, equal pay for equal work preclude an accommodation to a biological abnormality, or avoid aggravating a previously existing condition?

(d) These questions exist because of the extension of the life span, the reduction of infant mortality, the expansion of welfare rolls, more precise diagnostic techniques and more effective cures, the need to provide employment for and not to discriminate against handicapped thereby keeping them off welfare rolls, and because of OSHA. Read the article *Annals of Industry,* Paul Brodeur, *The New Yorker* (series of five articles — Oct. 30, Nov. 5, Nov. 12, Nov. 19, Nov. 26, 1973), and game-play the role of the various management representatives, the union representatives, and the various physicians involved. What would have been your advice as a consultant?

PART FOUR
DISCRIMINATION IN EMPLOYMENT

Chapter 14

BACKGROUND

A. EMPLOYMENT DISCRIMINATION IN THE UNITED STATES

Discrimination on the basis of race, color, sex, religion and national origin has always been pervasive in the United States. The early days of this country saw the introduction of slavery and the decimation of the Native American population. Colonists who came here to escape religious persecution in Europe persecuted others because of their differing religious views. Women were denied the right to vote and, if married, the right to dispose of their own property. Each successive immigrant group faced barriers such as the signs proclaiming that "No Irish Need Apply." During World War II, United States citizens of Japanese heritage were uprooted from their homes and businesses and held in government camps for the duration of the war. Today, thousands of Blacks and Spanish surnamed Americans remain crowded in ghettos, deprived of equal access to decent education, employment, and housing. Many Native Americans still live in poverty on reservations; and women still have not achieved equality under the law.

One of the most persistent problems of discrimination in the United States is the denial of equal employment opportunities because of some personal characteristic, usually unalterable, which is irrelevant to the performance of the job. Race, color, sex, national origin, religion, age, or handicap are the most frequently encountered bases of discrimination in employment. Although discrimination can manifest itself in many ways, the courts have recognized certain definite patterns of discrimination as proscribed by existing legislation.

First, and most obvious, is the *differential treatment* of persons on the basis of their race, sex, age or other personal characteristics. Refusing to hire Blacks for sales positions, channelling Spanish surnamed Americans into janitorial jobs, and paying women workers on an assembly line a lower hourly wage than men workers doing substantially similar work are all examples of differential treatment. Differential treatment can originate from personal prejudices of employers, traditional practices at a particular worksite, or stereotypical ideas of the capabilities of a given class of employees. The origins of differential treatment are unimportant in most circumstances. If the basis for the discrimination is prohibited by legislation, differential treatment is almost always unlawful.

777

A less obvious form of discrimination occurs where an employment practice is even-handed in its application, but has a *disparate effect* on a protected class of employees. For example, where an employer uses criteria for employment which are not shown to be necessary to the performance of a particular job, and which have the effect of excluding a protected class of people, the courts have held that unlawful discrimination exists. The fact that the employer did not intend to discriminate is irrelevant. Thus, if an employer required a high school diploma for employment in a factory, and significantly fewer Blacks than Whites in the relevant labor market area had high school diplomas, a disproportionate number of Blacks would be excluded from jobs in the factory. In this situation, the employer would have the burden of showing that a high school diploma was in fact necessary to the performance of those jobs. It would not be enough to show that a certain level of intellectual capacity was necessary to perform the job because a person might have the necessary intellectual skills without having a high school diploma.

An exception to this principle occurs if the disparate effect is a result of the application of a bona fide seniority system. The Supreme Court has held that "an otherwise neutral, legitimate seniority system does not become unlawful under Title VII simply because it may perpetuate pre-Act discrimination." Further, the Court held that "Section 703(h) [of Title VII] on its face immunizes all bona fide seniority systems, and does not distinguish between the perpetuation of pre- and post-Act Discrimination." This holding overruled a doctrine developed in the lower courts which found present discrimination where a seniority or transfer system effectively locked members of a protected class into less desirable jobs in which they had been placed as a result of pre-Act discrimination.

An employer's failure to make reasonable accommodation to the requirements of an employee's religion or handicap also may result in a finding of discrimination, unless the employer can demonstrate that undue hardship would result. To avoid conflict with the Establishment Clause of the First Amendment, the Court has narrowly construed the Title VII requirement of reasonable accommodation to an employee's religious practices. Similarly, under regulations promulgated pursuant to the Rehabilitation Act of 1973, a federal contractor has a duty to accommodate to an employee's physical or mental handicaps, "unless the contractor can demonstrate that such an accommodation would impose an undue hardship on the conduct of the contractor's business." Although this regulation was modelled after the section of Title VII requiring accommodation to religious practice, it presents no problem of constitutional conflict which would necessitate a narrow construction.

B. THE EFFECTS OF EMPLOYMENT DISCRIMINATION

The economic impact of employment discrimination is profound. In 1976 the median income for all full-time year-round workers in the United States was $11,723 but Black workers had a median income of $9,032, only about 75 percent of White worker's income of 12,098. Although much has been said about the improvement of the economic position of Black families in recent years, the overall income gap between Black and White families widened during the first half of the 1970's. The income ratio between Black and White families in 1970 was 0.61. By 1976 the ratio had increased to 0.59.

The problem of race bias is compounded by the fact of the continually high rate of unemployment among Black workers. For example, the seasonally adjusted unemployment rate for all workers in August 1977 was 7.1%; for Black workers the unemployment rate was 15.5%, the highest such rate since 1954. However, the official unemployment statistics do not take into account the "hidden unemployed," those workers who have become so discouraged by their inability to find jobs that they have dropped out of the labor market altogether. Because of the problems of discrimination, a large number of discouraged workers are Black. Thus, the actual percentage of unemployed Black workers is often much greater than is reflected in the official statistics.

The low income and high unemployment among Black workers indicated above has resulted in a disproportionate number of Black families falling below the poverty line. In 1976 9.4% of all families had incomes below the poverty level, but 27.9% Black families were living in poverty, compared to 7.1% of White families.

Employment opportunities for Blacks have been further limited by the severe problem of teenage unemployment. This problem was highlighted in a report by the Vocational Foundation, Inc., in New York City, entitled, "To Be Young, Black and Out of Work," published in *The New York Times Magazine,* October 23, 1977, p. 39; the report observes, in part, that:

> There are nearly two million unemployed teenagers in America, black and white, constituting nearly one-fifth of the labor force between the ages of 15 and 19. In the ghettos, however, minority youth have an official unemployment rate of 44 percent — and the Urban League suggests the real number is 60 percent. . . . For minority youth, these are the years of a great depression, far worse in its impact on them than any depression that the country as a whole has ever encountered.
>
> The most disturbing aspect of inner-city joblessness is its recent emergence as a radically separate phenomenon, with a life of its own, relatively unaffected both by the progress of black

people in general and by conditions among other young people. As recently as the mid-1950's, black and white teen-agers had approximately the same unemployment levels, and the blacks often showed rates of labor-force participation higher than those of whites. Today, however, after 20 years of black economic progress and political gains, unemployment among black teen-agers is almost two and a half times that of white teen-agers, while their labor-force participation has sunk to only 75 percent of the white level. These figures mean that since the early 50's, black teen-age unemployment has risen about three times faster annually than white unemployment. . . .

One reason [for these figures] is that many black youths are in a trap that they do not fully understand, and that the government "manpower" programs fail to address. That trap is a Catch 22 employment system that excludes inner-city youth even while it prohibits discrimination against their race. In place of the bigotry of race has arisen a new bigotry of schooling, based on a series of half-truths about the link between education and work, that demean our schools and stultify our personnel policies. Characterized by a worship of credentials, this system has created a schoolmarm meritocracy that blocks every route up the ladder with the stern rule: You cannot pass if you cannot parse, if you cannot put the numbers in the right boxes at the requisite speed, if you cannot perform in the accustomed academic mode.

Impelled by government and corporate personnel policies, the credential-worshipping system, year by year, has the effect of downplaying performance on the job and exalting effort on the test; this has the effect of protecting schooled but shiftless members of the middle class from the competition of unschooled but aggressively hardworking poor people.

The system depreciates the assets of diligence, determination and drive to get ahead that have launched other groups into the middle class, and that every detailed study has shown to be most important to productivity. And it exalts the assets of the advantaged classes — schooling, testing, computing — that are often irrelevant to productivity in most jobs.

Another example of the severe economic impact of discrimination is the reduced income of women workers. In 1974, about seventy percent of all women workers were either single, widowed, divorced, separated or married to men making less than $10,000 per year. Yet in 1976 the median incomes for full-time year-round workers by race and sex were: White males: $14,272; Black males: $10,222; White females: $8,376; Black females: $7,831. Thus, the incomes of White women were only about 59% of those of White men and 82% of those of Black men. Black women, with a double burden of discrimination, had incomes only about 55% of those of White men and 77% of those of Black men. Women also have a higher rate of unemployment than men. In August 1977, the seasonally adjusted unemployment rate was 8.3% for women and 6.3% for men. Like Blacks, women of all races also have a disproportionate number of discourged workers who no longer are represented in the official unemployment statistics. One result of the low economic position of women workers is that over half of the children in the United States who are living in poverty live in households where a woman is the sole wage earner.

The income disparities mentioned above result in part from the segregation of jobs by race, sex, or national origin. Women and minorities traditionally have been channelled into certain jobs, both by employers and by societal expectations. Jobs held by minority workers have historically tended to be dirty, dangerous, menial, and low-paid, although the patterns of minority employment may vary with the composition of the work force or the history of employment at a given worksite. Thus, an employer in New York may hire Puerto Ricans to do janitorial work, whereas an employer in Atlanta would hire Blacks. Similarly, for many years the steel industry channelled Black workers into the dirtiest, hottest jobs in steel mills, whereas White workers were channelled into more desirable jobs with greater upward mobility.

Women have also been confined to certain jobs in the workplace. Although some traditionally "female jobs" have had a greater range of required educational or training levels than those jobs traditionally held for minority workers, the structure of women's employment has tended to be much more uniform throughout the workforce. Thus, until recently, women have tended to be clerical workers, nurses, teachers and household workers regardless of the geographical location of the employer. Such job segregation has resulted in artificially depressed wage rates for traditionally female jobs when compared to traditionally male jobs with similar levels of required skills, education, experience and responsibility. Further, a study conducted in 1977 showed that "women spend less time at work in non-work activities . . . and work harder while at work . . . Accordingly, male-female wage differences are proportionately larger when hours are adjusted for non-work time."

Job channelling and segregation also severely limit the opportunities of minority and women workers to choose jobs in which they have the most interest and ability. Equally, it restricts the opportunity of society as a whole to benefit from the most effective development and utilization of essential human resources.

NOTE:

For further and more comprehensive data concerning the effects of employment discrimination, *see generally* EEOC, Equal Employment Opportunity Report — 1974 (Research Report No. 50, 1976); U.S. Dept. of Commerce, The Social and Economic Status of the Black Population In The United States 1974 (Special Studies Series P-23, No. 54, July 1975); U.S. Dept. of Commerce, Characteristics of the Population Below The Poverty Level: 1975 (Series P-60, No. 106, June 1977); U.S. Dept. of Commerce, Money Income In 1975 of Families and Persons In The United States (Series P-60, No. 105, June 1977); U.S. Dept. of Labor Women's Bureau, Women In the Labor Force — Annual Averages 1975-1976 (Feb. 1977); U.S. Dept. of Labor, Labor Force Developments: Third Quarter 1977 (Bureau of Labor Statistics, Oct. 17, 1977); U.S. Dept. of Commerce, Money Income and Poverty Status of Families and Persons in the United States: 1976 (Series P-60, No. 107, Sept. 1977); U.S. Dept. of Labor, Why Women Work (July 1976); U.S. Dept. of Labor Women's Bureau, The Earnings Gap Between Women and Men (Oct. 1976); U.S. Dept. of Labor Women's Bureau, Women In The Labor Force — July 1976-1977 (August 1977); U.S. Dept. of Labor Women's Bureau, Minority Women Workers: A Statistical Overview (1977); U.S. Dept. of Labor Women's Bureau, Women Workers Today (1976); U.S. Dept. of Labor Women's Bureau, Unemployment In Recessions: Women and Black Workers (April 1977); National Urban League, Black Families in the 1974-75 Depression (Research Dept., July 1975); Stafford and Duncan, The Use of Time and Technology By Households In the United States (Univ. of Michigan, Dept. of Economics, July 1977); Edwards, *Race Discrimination In Employment: What Price Equality?* in Civil Liberties and Civil Rights (Univ. of Illinois Press, 1977) (see in particular the extensive bibliography and statistical charts on pp. 126-44); U.S. Commission on Civil Rights, *To Eliminate Employment Discrimination,* Vol. V in The Federal Civil Rights Enforcement Effort — 1974 (July 1975); Becker, The Economics of Discrimination (2d ed., Univ. of Chicago Press, 1971); Oaxaca, *Theory and Measurement in the Economics of Discrimination,* and Butler & Heckman, *The Government's Impact on the Labor Market Status of Black Americans: A Critical Review,* in Equal Rights and Industrial Relations (IRRA, 1977), Thurow, *The Economic Progress of Minority Groups,* Challenge (March-April 1976), p. 20.

C. THE DEVELOPMENT OF MODERN EQUAL EMPLOYMENT OPPORTUNITY LAW

J. E. JONES, JR., THE DEVELOPMENT OF MODERN EQUAL EMPLOYMENT OPPORTUNITY AND AFFIRMATIVE ACTION LAW: A BRIEF CHRONOLOGICAL OVERVIEW, 20 Howard L.J. 74, 75-82 (1977)*

For a brief discussion of modern equal employment law, February, 1941, is a convenient beginning point. At that time, A. Philip Randolph, President of the predominantly black Brotherhood of Sleeping Car Porters, convened a conference of top black leaders from which emerged the organization of the March on Washington Movement.[6]

Then this nation was preparing for the War to Make the World Safe for Democracy, and its employment practices, as well as other aspects of life in America, revealed a most embarrassing contradiction. The government's use of democratic symbols in its efforts to unify the country and to wage psychological warfare upon the axis nations sharply illuminated the contrast between ideals and reality.

While the upturn in the economy increasingly placed a strain upon the manpower resources of the country, engaged in both production and the raising of an army, Blacks were on the industrial sidelines. A. Philip Randolph, President of the Brotherhood of Sleeping Car Porters, threatened a massive march on Washington unless the President did something about employment discrimination by war contractors.[7] President Roosevelt, after unsuccessful attempts to dissuade Randolph, and recognizing the possibility of international reaction to such demonstration, issued Executive Order 8802 [8] establishing a Fair Employment Practices Committee (FEPC) in the Office of Production and Management.[9]

Probably the most significant thing about the FEPC established by that Executive Order was its mere existence. It prohibited discrimination by war contractors and provided a mechanism for the investigation and processing of complaints, although such sanctions as might have existed were unmentioned and at best vague. Its legality rested upon two presidential prerogatives: 1) the power, as administrative head of the executive branch of government, to set conditions under which the government would do business and 2)

---

* Reprinted with permission of publisher. Copyright 1977 by the Howard University Law Journal.

[6] *See* Sumner and Rosen, *The CIO Era, 1935-1955,* in The Negro and the American Labor Movement, (J. Jacobson ed.) (1968).

[7] *See* D. Lockhart, Toward Equal Employment, (1968).

[8] Exec. Order No. 8802, 6 Fed. Reg. 3,109 (June 25, 1941).

[9] *See* L.C. Kesselman, The Social Politics of FEPC (1948).

the power as commander-in-chief to assure adequate supplies for military forces.[10]

Since Executive Orders of the President, validly issued, have the force and effect of law, they remain on the books until repealed or amended by a succeeding President. However, whether they remain operative in fact is a matter of administration rather than legality. Each succeeding President has either left in place the apparatus of his predecessor, amended it to suit his own concepts, or issued new orders directed to the same end.[11]

After 1941, no novel concepts or initiatives emerged from such presidential programs until the issuance by the late John F. Kennedy of Executive Order 10925 in April of 1961.[12]

But before discussing the contribution of that modern Executive Order, a brief discussion of the judicial developments of the '50s and the '60s which set the stage for modern initiatives is needed.

The Supreme Court of the United States, in *Steele v. Louisville and Nashville Railroad Co.,*[13] enunciated the duty of fair representation and determined that Negro firemen might be entitled to both injunctive relief and damages against a union, operating under the Federal Railway Labor Act, for breach of that duty. The Court declared that as long as the union presumed to act as the statutory representative, it could not refuse to perform the duty which was inseparable from the power of representation conferred upon it by the law. It went on to assert that in making collective bargaining contracts the union was required to represent non-union or minority union members of the craft or class without hostile discrimination, fairly and impartially, and in good faith.[14] In *Wallace Corp. v. National Labor Relations Board,*[15] the Supreme Court applied this duty of fair representation to unions operating under the National Labor Relations Act (NLRA).

As with so many ground-breaking principles, the brave potential of the duty of fair representation has not been realized.[16] The doctrine has retained its legal vigor although the extent to which it has provided practical relief for minorities is questionable. Perhaps it has a greater future than it has had a past, as will be seen in a moment in the discussion of the breach of the duty of fair representation as an unfair labor practice under the NLRA.

---

[10] *Id.* at 15 n. 31.

[11] *See* Norgren and Hill, Toward Fair Employment (1964).

[12] Exec. Order No. 10925, 26 Fed. Reg. 1,977 (1961).

[13] 323 U.S. 192 (1944).

[14] *Id.* at 204.

[15] 323 U.S. 248 (1944).

[16] *See* Herring, *The Fair Representative Doctrine: An Effective Weapon in Union Discrimination?,* 24 Md. L. Rev. 113 (1964).

Another significant development of the '40s was the passage by eight states of fair employment practices measures. These early state laws established agencies with a range of powers from full cease and desist authority to only the power to conciliate. Wisconsin passed a law in 1945, but failed to provide it with any teeth until 1957.[17]

The most significant developments during the '50s undoubtedly occurred in areas like housing, public accommodations, and schools — areas in which there existed an element of state action which put such conduct in the reach of the Constitution.[18] Except for the duty of fair representation discussed above, lawyers and courts did not perceive that the employment relationship was readily within the state action scope. Moreover, the Supreme Court had earlier determined that the Reconstruction Era Civil Rights Act did not reach private discrimination.[19]

Brown v. Board of Education,[20] was the culmination of almost 60 years of litigation seeking to vindicate the constitutional principle of equality. The declaration that school segregation was inherently unequal sounded the death knell for the doctrines of separate but equal in all of its many manifestations, and gave impetus to increased efforts to eradicate all vestiges of racial discrimination from our society.

No one but Mrs. Rosa Parks knows if that Court decision had anything to do with her decision on December 1, 1955 to refuse to move to the back of the bus in Montgomery, Alabama. But the subsequent bus boycott launched Martin Luther King to fame and martyrdom. In February, 1960, four college freshmen from the all-black North Carolina A & T College sat down at a five-and-dime lunch counter, and sit-ins began and proliferated. On May 4, 1961, the Congress of Racial Equality (CORE) sponsored freedom rides. Reactions to the marches, sit-ins and freedom rides exposed the nation to acts of treachery and tragedy which shocked its conscience and gave momentum to the civil rights activities which continued

---

[17] *See* Comment *Labor Law — Union Membership Denied on the Basis of Racial Discrimination,* 1958 Wis. L. Rev. 294; *see also Wisconsin's Fair Employment Act: Coverage, Procedures, Substance, Remedies,* 1975 Wis. L. Rev. 695.

[18] The fourteenth amendment provides that "[n]o state shall make or enforce any law which shall . . . deny to any person within its jurisdiction the equal protection of the laws." Plaintiffs challenging alleged discrimination under the equal protection clause must therefore prove some *state* action, or in some recent cases, at least a nexus of state involvement with private action or exercise of a governmental function by a private party. *See generally,* C.L. Black, Jr., Foreword: *'State Action', Equal Protection and California's Proposition 14,* 81 Harv. L. Rev. 69 (1967); *Jackson v. Metropolitan Edison Co.,* 419 U.S. 345 (1974).

[19] *See U.S. v. Hodges,* 203 U.S. 1 (1906).

[20] 347 U.S. 483 (1954); *See also* L. Lomax, The Negro Revolt, Chapter 8 (1962).

until the late '60s. The fruits of that activity are multiple laws and forums, including:

1. Executive Order 10925, issued by John F. Kennedy in April of 1961, which spawned the modern affirmative action concept, and Executive Order 11246, which resulted in the creation of the Office of Federal Contract Compliance in the Department of Labor;
2. Phase Two of the Duty of Fair Representation — the "Brave New World of Miranda" [21] — and its progeny, which found the Labor Board declaring breach of duty of fair representation to be an unfair labor practice;
3. Congress at last — the passage of the Civil Rights Act of 1964; and
4. The Civil Rights Act of 1866 — "Its Hour Come Round At Last." [22]

The modern Executive Order program, launched by John F. Kennedy, contributed two things of great importance, both of which are bothersome: 1) enforcement; and 2) affirmative action. The Order placed the primary responsibility for enforcing compliance upon the contracting agencies and thus proliferated a multiplicity of agency involvement. Although the contracting agency has primary authority, the Department of Labor (DOL) may exercise the enforcement function. The Labor Department has tried to "thin the crowd" by assigning primary enforcement responsibility by a Standard Industrial Classification Code. Under that arrangement, if the respondent is a school or hospital, the Department of Health, Education, and Welfare (HEW) will be the primary enforcement agency, irrespective of the federal agency with which the contractor may be doing business. However, the contractor will be subject to the rules and regulations of both HEW and DOL. They are supposed to be substantially consistent, but it should be remembered that a multiplicity of laws as well as a multiplicity of tribunals is destructive to uniformity.

The Executive Order requirement to take affirmative action to insure equal employment opportunity is a positive undertaking, required without a determination of prior guilt. It is a remedial concept which "sounds in equity" and is, therefore, subject to the broadest of interpretations. However, as of 1975, the only significant employment case law on the dimensions of affirmative action

---

[21] Sovern, *Race Discrimination and the National Labor Relations Act: The Brave New World of Miranda,* 16 Annual N.Y.U. Conference on Labor 3, 7 (1963).

[22] Kohl, *The Civil Rights Act of 1866 — Its Hour Come Round At Last,* 55 Va. L. Rev. 272 (1969).

involved the construction industry, about which more will be said in a moment.

41 C.F.R./Part 60-2, the Affirmative Action regulations for nonconstruction contractors, sets forth the requirements and procedures of the Department of Labor. These agency rules and regulations are entitled to requisite judicial deference, but they have not been suficiently subject to litigation to give a view of their acceptability to the courts. This may be explained by the paucity of occasions on which the federal agencies have enforced these rules by the sanctions of cancellation of present contracts or debarment from future contract awards.

In 1962, in *Miranda Fuel Co.*,[23] a nonracial case, and in 1964 in *Hughes Tool Co.*,[24] the NLRB interpreted the Taft-Hartley Act to prohibit, as an unfair labor practice, union breaches of the duty of fair representation. Since the duty covers all of the union's collective bargaining relationships, the possibilities of duplication with Title VII of the Civil Rights Act of 1964 are legion. However, since unions are generally not contractors or subcontractors with the federal government, there is little direct overlap with the federal Executive Order program. Unions may, however, by conduct in breach of this duty, interfere with an employer's efforts to comply with the Executive Order and thereby be subject to legal action.[25]

At least one federal court of appeals concluded, as a matter of law, that an employer could be guilty of an unfair labor practice by engaging in a policy of racial discrimination, and the Supreme Court declined to review that decision.[26]

Contrary to most other developments in labor law, the tardy assumption of unfair labor practices jurisdiction for breach of the duty of fair representation by the Labor Board did not preempt the field to the exclusion of direct court action.[27]

Title VII of the Civil Rights Act of 1964, prohibited job discrimination on the basis of race, religion, national origin, and sex for covered employers, unions, and employment agencies in industries affecting commerce. At the same time, Congress preserved state and local laws not inconsistent therewith. It has also been determined that other federal laws were not affected by the Act.[28]

---

[23] 140 N.L.R.B. No. 7.

[24] 147 N.L.R.B. No. 66; *see also Jubilee Manufacturing Co.*, 202 N.L.R.B. No. 2 (1973), applying the duty of fair representation to sex.

[25] *See Local 12, Rubber Workers Union v. National Labor Relations Board*, 368 F.2d — (5th Cir. 1966), *cert. denied*, 389 U.S. 837.

[26] *Packinghouse Workers v. N.L.R.B.*, 416 F.2d 1126 (D.C. Cir. 1969), *cert. denied*, 396 U.S. 903 (1969); *see also WACO v. Emporium*, 420 U.S. 50 (1975), text accompanying note 23 at 988.

[27] *See Vaca v. Sipes*, 386 U.S. 171 (1967).

[28] *See Johnson v. Railway Express*, 421 U.S. 454 (1975).

This, then, was deliberate proliferation of laws and agencies by action of the Congress. The 1972 amendments,[29] which extended the law by including federal, state and local government employees in its protection, rather than thinning the crowd, gave the Equal Employment Opportunity Commission (EEOC) the authority to enforce Title VII in the federal courts. And, although the U.S. Department of Justice was excluded from the enforcement action against private persons, Congress empowered the Attorney General to sue the states, and preserve the plaintiff's right to sue by his own attorney.

Prior to the 1972 amendments, the Supreme Court resuscitated the Reconstruction Era civil rights statues as applied to private acts of discrimination. It had long been the conventional wisdom that 42 U.S.C. §§ 1981, 1982 and 1983 required an element of state action as they were based on the fourteenth amendment to the United States Constitution.[30] In 1968, the Supreme Court in *Jones v. Alfred Mayer Co.,*[31] breathed new life into these old civil rights statutes. Declaring that the congressional authority for the enactment of that legislation stems from the thirteenth amendment, which does not require state action, the Court held that § 1982 barred all racial discrimination, private as well as public. It specifically reversed a prior case, *Hodges v. U.S.,* which had given a restrictive interpretation to 42 U.S.C. § 1981 regarding the right to make and enforce contracts.

In summary, plaintiffs and respondents in the mid-1970's find themselves facing a plethora of options, each with attendant risks:
1. Possible administrative remedies and court enforcement through federal agencies under the Executive Order program;
2. Title VII, and enforcement in the federal district court triggered by EEOC and or the aggrieved party;
3. the National Labor Relations Board and its administrative process;
4. the courts, federal or state, under the doctrine of the duty of fair representation, which when coupled with an action under § 301 of the National Labor Relations Act may involve both employers and unions;
5. the Federal Courts under 42 U.S.C. §§ 1981, 1983, 1985;
6. the state agencies and the state courts under state law;
7. local ordinances and local agencies; and, finally,
8. arbitration under union-management contracts.

The above laundry list excludes other laws such as the Equal Pay Act,

---

[29] Equal Employment Opportunity Act of 1972, 86 Stat. 103, March 24, 1972.
[30] *See The Slaughter House Cases,* 83 U.S. 36 (1873); *The Civil Rights Cases,* 109 U.S. 3 (1883); *see also Hodges v. U.S.,* 203 U.S. 1 (1905).
[31] 392 U.S. 409 (1972).

acts relating to veterans and the handicapped, federal revenue sharing, tax laws, the Age Discrimination Act, and the like.[32]

BELTON, TITLE VII OF THE CIVIL RIGHTS ACT OF 1964: A DECADE OF PRIVATE ENFORCEMENT AND JUDICIAL DEVELOPMENTS, 20 St. Louis Univ. L.J. 225, 226-27, 229-40, 301-4 (1976).*

I. INTRODUCTION AND BACKGROUND

Title VII of the Civil Rights Act of 1964 [2] established for the first time a comprehensive federal law to assure equality of employment opportunity in the private sector by making unlawful practices and devices that discriminate on the basis of race, sex, national origin, or religion. The enactment of Title VII on July 2, 1964, represented a twenty-year struggle by civil rights advocates.[3] The prevailing

---

[32] Equal Pay Act (an amendment to the Fair Labor Standards Act, 29 U.S.C. § 201 *et seq.,* especially 29 U.S.C. § 206(d)); *see generally* Murphy, *Female Wage Discrimination: A Study of the Equal Pay Act 1963-1970,* 39 U. Cin. L. Rev. 615 (1970).

Internal Revenue Code: *see generally* Blumberg, *Sexism in the Code,* 21 Buffalo L. Rev. 49 (1971); Bittker and Kaufman, *Taxes and Civil Rights: 'Constitutionalizing' the I.R.C.,* 82 Yale L.J. 51 (1972); *McGlotten v. Connally,* 338 F. Supp. 448 (D.D.C. 1972).

Revenue sharing: 31 U.S.C. § 1242 (State and Local Fiscal Assistance Act of 1972: (Nondiscrimination Provision); *see also U.S. v. City of Chicago,* 395 F. Supp. 329 (N.D. Ill. 1975).

Handicapped: 29 U.S.C. § 793, 794 (Rehabilitation Act of 1973; *see also* 5 U.S.C. § 7153).

Veterans: 38 U.S.C. § 2011 *et seq.* (Vietnam Era Veterans Adjustment Act of 1974).

Age discrimination: 29 U.S.C. § 621 *et seq.; see generally,* Note, *Age Discrimination in Employment,* 50 N.Y.U. L. Rev. 924 (1975); *Constitutionality of Mandatory Retirement,* 9 Clearinghouse Review 761 (1976); Note, *Proving Discrimination Under the Age Discrimination in Employment Act,* 17 Ariz. L. Rev. 495 (1975); Note, *Age Discrimination in Employment: Available Federal Relief,* 11 Colum. J.L. & Soc. Prob. 281 (1975).

* Reprinted with permission of publisher. Copyright 1976 by the Saint Louis University Law Journal.

[2] 42 U.S.C. §§ 2000e to 2000e-15 (1970), *as amended,* The Equal Employment Opportunity Act of 1972, 42 U.S.C. §§ 2000e to 2000e-17 (Supp. IV, 1974) [hereinafter cited as Title VII or the Act]. For a discussion of some of the more significant changes made by the 1972 amendments, see notes 522-44 and accompanying text *infra.* For a more detailed discussion of the 1972 amendments, see Sape & Hart, *Title VII Reconsidered: The Equal Employment Opportunity Act of 1972,* 40 GEO. WASH. L. REV. 824 (1972).

[3] *See* Vaas, *Title VII: Legislative History,* 7 B.C. IND. & COM. L. REV. 431 & n.2 (1966). For a discussion of the history of federal and state efforts to remedy discrimination in employment prior to the enactment of Title VII, *see* Jenkins, *Study of Federal Effort to End Job Bias: A History, A Status Report, and a Prognosis,* 14 How. L.J. 259, 264-82 (1968). *See generally* M. SOVERN, LEGAL RESTRAINTS ON RACIAL DISCRIMINATION IN EMPLOYMENT, 9-17 (1966) [hereinafter cited as SOVERN].

attitude about Title VII, as finally enacted, was that, in effect, the civil rights movement had suffered a defeat.[4] Congress had deleted the cease and desist provisions in earlier versions of the bill and had vested enforcement authority in the courts. Moreover, the Democratic Leadership Conference had agreed to a number of compromises to facilitate the passage of the 1964 Civil Rights Act.[5]

The Act, as originally passed, established the following three instrumentalities of enforcement: The aggrieved individual;[6] the Equal Employment Opportunity Commission (EEOC or Commission);[7] and the Attorney General.[8] The EEOC, the agency established to enforce Title VII, was considered to be a "toothless tiger" [9] because its only enforcement authority was through "informal methods of conference, conciliation, and persuasion." [10] Governmental power to enforce the Act was vested in the Attorney General by the authorization of "pattern and practice" suits.[11] The burden of the enforcement of Title VII, however, has been borne largely by individually aggrieved "private attorneys general" [12] through private litigation. . . .

---

[4] *See* Berg, *Equal Employment Opportunity under the Civil Rights Act of 1964,* 31 Brooklyn L. Rev. 62, 96-97 (1965) [hereinafter cited as Berg]; A. Blumrosen, Black Employment and the Law, 57-58 (1971) [hereinafter cited as Black Employment].

[5] *See* Berg, *supra* note 4, at 66-67; Black Employment, *supra* note 4, at 57.

[6] Title VII §§ 706 (b), (f)(1), 42 U.S.C. §§ 2000e-(5)(b), (f)(1) (1970).

[7] *Id.*

[8] Title VII § 707, 42 U.S.C. § 2000e-6 (1970). Responsibility for "pattern and practice" suits has been transferred to the EEOC under the 1972 amendments, but the Attorney General is given responsibility for cases against governmental units. Title VII § 706(f)(1), 42 U.S.C. § 2000e-5(f)(1) (Supp. IV, 1974), *amending* Title VII § 706(e), 42 U.S.C. § 2000e-5(e) (1970).

[9] Black Employment, *supra* note 4, at 59. One scholar characterized the EEOC as a "poor enfeebled thing" because Congress gave "it the power to conciliate but not to compel." Sovern, supra note 3, at 205.

[10] Title VII § 706(a), 42 U.S.C. § 2000e-5(a) (1970). The EEOC was granted enforcement authority under the 1972 amendments. Title VII § 706(f)(1), 42 U.S.C. § 2000e-5(f)(1) (Supp. IV, 1974), *amending* Title VII § 706(e), 42 U.S.C. § 2000e-5(e) (1970).

[11] Title VII § 707(a), 42 U.S.C. § 2000e-6(a) (1970). The 1972 amendments to Title VII established a new General Counsel's office within the EEOC to handle its new enforcement authority and litigation responsibility. Title VII § 705(b)(1), 42 U.S.C. § 2000e-4(b)(1) (Supp. IV, 1974), *amending* Title VII § 705, 42 U.S.C. § 2000e-4 (1970). In addition, the new office of the General Counsel of the EEOC was given the authority for the "pattern and practice" suits previously vested in the Attorney General. Title VII § 707(c), 42 U.S.C. § 2000e-6(c) (Supp. IV, 1974), *amending* Title VII § 707, 42 U.S.C. § 2000e-6 (1970).

[12] The "private attorney general" concept was first articulated by the Supreme Court in Newman v. Piggie Park Enterprises, Inc., 390 U.S. 400 (1968), a case arising under Title II of the Civil Rights Act of 1964, 42 U.S.C. §§ 2000a *et seq.* (1970). The concept has since been applied to private plaintiffs in Title VII cases. *See, e.g.,* Albemarle Paper Co. v. Moody, 422 U.S. 405, 413-15 (1975); Lea v. Cone Mills

Individual and class actions were filed under Title VII as early as October, 1965.[22] Despite some earlier adverse decisions by the district courts, [23] it became clear after several years of litigation that in light of the broad wording of the Act and the receptivity of the courts [24] persons victimized by employment discrimination would have some measure of success. The efforts by opponents of the Act to undermine its effectiveness by stripping the EEOC of enforcement power turned out to be a significant benefit for the victims of discrimination. Enforcement of the Act was left, in large part, to aggrieved individuals rather than timid bureaucrats appointed for short terms [25] and subject to political and budgetary pressures from hostile congressional committees and vested interest groups. Ten years of vigorous, aggressive, and protracted litigation, [26] however, have demonstrated that Title VII can be a powerful agent to redress employment discrimination.[27] . . .

Corp., 438 F.2d 86, 88 (4th Cir. 1971); Jenkins v. United Gas Corp., 400 F.2d 28 (5th Cir. 1968).

[22] The first private case filed under Title VII, *Brinkley v. The Great Atl. and Pac. Tea Co.*, Civil No. 1107 (E.D.N.C., filed Oct. 18, 1965), was brought as a class action. In addition to the Title VII claim, *Brinkley* alleged jurisdiction under § I of the Civil Rights Act of 1866, 42 U.S.C. § 1981 (1970).

[23] *See, e.g.*, Griggs v. Duke Power Co., 292 F. Supp. 243 (M.D.N.C. 1968), *aff'd in part, rev'd in part*, 420 F.2d 1225 (4th Cir. 1970), *rev'd in part*, 401 U.S. 424 (1971); Phillips v. Martin Marietta Corp., 1 CCH EMPL. PRAC. DEC. ¶ 9906 (M.D. Fla. 1968), *aff'd*, 411 F.2d 1 (5th Cir. 1969), *vacated and remanded*, 400 U.S. 542 (1971); Ward v. Firestone Tire & Rubber Co., 260 F. Supp. 579 (W.D. Tenn. 1966). *Cf.* Mengelkoch v. Industrial Welfare Comm'n, 284 F. Supp. 956 (C.D. Cal. 1968), *appeal dismissed for want of juris.*, 393 U.S. 83 (1968); Coon v. Tingle, 277 F. Supp. 304 (N.D. Ga. 1967).

[24] It has been suggested that Title VII plaintiffs benefitted from a favorable judicial climate toward racial matters that developed in the wake of litigation generated by Brown v. Board of Educ., 347 U.S. 483 (1954). D. BELL, RACE, RACISM AND AMERICAN LAW 753 (1973) [hereinafter cited as BELL]; Fiss, *The Fate of An Idea Whose Time Has Come: Antidiscrimination Law in the Second Decade After Brown v. Board of Education*, 41 U. CHI. L. REV. 742 (1974).

[25] The EEOC consists of five Commissioners who serve five year terms on a staggered basis. Commissioners are appointed by the President, subject to the consent of the Senate. One Commissioner, designated by the President to serve as Chairman, is responsible for the administrative operations of the Commission. Title VII § 705, 42 U.S.C. § 2000e-4 (Supp. IV, 1974), *amending* Title VII § 705, 42 U.S.C. § 2000e-4 (1970). *See* BELL, *supra* note 24, at 753.

[26] The plaintiffs in Albemarle Paper Co. v. Moody, 422 U.S. 405 (1975), filed their charges with the EEOC in May, 1966; the United States Supreme Court issued its decision in June, 1975. Further proceedings in the lower courts could conceivably consume several more years. Similarly, in Pettway v. American Cast Iron Pipe Co., 494 F.2d 211 (5th Cir. 1974), the complaint was filed in the district court in May, 1966. Following a decision by the district court, the Fifth Circuit reversed nine years later. As of this time, further proceedings in the district court have not been concluded. *See also* Gamble v. Birmingham S. R.R., 514 F.2d 678, 680 (5th Cir. 1975).

[27] There had been a long history of laws and executive orders at the federal and state levels prior to Title VII that established public policy against discrimination

II. THE BEGINNING: ELIMINATING PROCEDURAL ROADBLOCKS

The first several years of litigation under Title VII were chiefly devoted to settling procedural questions concerning the requirements for the filing of charges with the EEOC and the conditions precedent to the filing of complaints in the federal courts. As a result of this early litigation, the victim of discrimination bears the primary responsibility for enforcement through private action. The basic statutory scheme of private enforcement requires the filing of a charge under oath with the EEOC by the person claiming to be aggrieved [30] The Act directs the EEOC to make an investigation of the charge. Upon a finding of reasonable cause to believe the charge is true, the EEOC is directed to try to eliminate the unlawful practice through voluntary conciliation.[31] If the EEOC is unable to obtain voluntary compliance, it notifies the aggrieved person and informs him that he may within the time allowed by the statute bring a civil action in the appropriate federal district court.[32]

A. Jurisdictional Prerequisites

One of the first issues raised in the initial series of Title VII cases was whether it is necessary for the EEOC to investigate a charge and attempt voluntary conciliation before suit could be filed. Plaintiffs and the EEOC successfully argued that a Title VII plaintiff is required to satisfy only two requirements under the Act before

---

in employment. *See generally* SOVERN, *supra* note 3; Bonfield, *The Origin and Development of American Fair Employment Practice Legislation,* 52 IOWA L. REV. 1043 (1967). Proceedings under these earlier laws and orders, however, proved to be generally ineffective to deal with the problems of employment discrimination. *See* BLACK EMPLOYMENT, *supra* note 4, at 9-27; Hill, *Twenty Years of State Fair Employment Practice Commissions: A Critical Analysis with Recommendations,* 14 BUFFALO L. REV. 22 (1964).

[30] Title VII § 706(b), 42 U.S.C. § 2000e-5(b) (Supp. IV, 1974), *amending* Title VII § 706(a), 42 U.S.C. § 2000e-5(a) (1970). A Commissioner may file a charge under the Act and, prior to the 1972 amendments, an action could thereafter be brought "by any person whom the charge alleges was aggrieved by the alleged unlawful employment practice." Title VII § 706(e)(2), 42 U.S.C. § 2000e-5(e)(2) (1970). If the alleged unlawful employment practice occurs in a state or municipality that has a local law prohibiting the alleged practice, the EEOC must defer to the state or local agency for a period defined by the Act. Title VII § 706(c) to (d), 42 U.S.C. §§ 2000e-5(c) to (d) (Supp. IV, 1974), *amending* § 706(b) to (c), 42 U.S.C. §§ 2000e-5(b) to (c) (1970).

Labor unions have been held to be "persons aggrieved" within the meaning of Title VII. Pulp Workers Local 186 v. Minnesota Mining and Mfg. Co., 304 F. Supp. 1284 (N.D. Ind. 1969); Chemical Workers Union v. Planters Mfg. Co., 259 F. Supp. 365, 367 (M.D. Miss. 1966). Shareholders of a corporation, however, are not. Foust v. Transamerica Corp., 391 F. Supp. 312 (N.D. Cal. 1975).

[31] Title VII § 706(b), 42 U.S.C. § 2000e-5(b) (Supp. IV, 1974), *amending* Title VII § 706(a), 42 U.S.C. § 2000e-5(a) (1970).

[32] Title VII § 706(f)(1), 42 U.S.C. § 2000e-5(f)(1) (Supp. IV, 1974), *amending* Title VII § 706(e), 42 U.S.C. § 2000e-5(e) (1970).

seeking relief in federal court.[33] First, he must have filed a timely charge with the EEOC.[34] Secondly, he must have initiated an action in federal court within the time allowed by the statute after receipt of the "notice of right to sue" letter from the EEOC.[35] A contrary ruling by the courts on this issue [36] may well have frustrated aggressive private enforcement of the Act. The EEOC, even now, more than ten years after its establishment, has a backlog of unprocessed charges in excess of 90,000,[37] and it generally takes

---

[33] McDonnell Douglas Corp. v. Green, 411 U.S. 792, 798 (1973); Beverly v. Lone Star Lead Constr. Corp., 437 F.2d 1136 (5th Cir. 1971); Dent v. St. Louis-San Francisco Ry., 406 F.2d 399 (5th Cir. 1969); Johnson v. Seaboard Air Line R.R., 405 F.2d 645 (4th Cir. 1969), *cert. denied sub nom.* Pilot Freight Carriers, Inc. v. Walker, 394 U.S. 819 (1969).

[34] Title VII § 706(e), 42 U.S.C. § 2000e-5(e) (Supp. IV, 1974), *amending* Title VII § 706(d), 42 U.S.C. § 2000e-5(d) (1970), provides that a charge must be filed with the EEOC within 180 days of the alleged unlawful employment practice, except with respect to a claim occurring in a state or local municipality with a fair employment agency. In such a jurisdiction, the aggrieved person has 300 days within which to file the charge with the EEOC. For fuller discussion of relationship between the 180 and 300 day filing periods in deferral states, see Eighth Circuit Review, 20 St. Louis U. L.J. 421 (1976), *infra.*

[35] Plaintiffs now have ninety days in which to file an action in federal district court after receipt of the statutory notice. Title VII § 706(f)(1), 42 U.S.C. § 2000e-5(f)(1) (Supp. IV, 1974).

Some plaintiffs have filed the notice of right to sue with the district court either without complying with FED. R. CIV. P. 8 or without petitioning the court for the appointment of counsel and leave to commence the action within the appropriate limitations period. Some courts have applied the statutory limitations strictly, pointing out that such filings do not comply with the Federal Rules or the statute. *See, e.g.,* Harris v. National Tea Co., 454 F.2d 307, 312 (7th Cir. 1971); Brady v. Bristol Myers Co., 332 F. Supp. 995, 998-99 (E.D. Mo. 1971), *rev'd on other grounds,* 459 F.2d 621 (8th Cir. 1972). Most courts, however, have refused to apply the statutory limitations so strictly. *See, e.g.,* Harris v. Walgreen's Distrib. Center, 456 F.2d 588, 592 (6th Cir. 1972); Reyes v. Missouri-Kansas-Texas R.R., 53 F.R.D. 293, 296 (D. Kan. 1971); Rice v. Chrysler Corp., 327 F. Supp. 80, 84 (E.D. Mich. 1971); Prescod v. Ludwig Indus., 325 F. Supp. 414, 416 (N.D. Ill. 1971); McQueen v. E.M.C. Plastic Co., 302 F. Supp. 881, 884-85 (E.D. Tex. 1969); Witherspoon v. Mercury Freight Lines Inc., 1 CCH EMPL. PRAC. DEC. ¶ 9975 (S.D. Ala. 1968).

[36] Because of the absence of clear legislative history regarding whether the duties of investigation and conciliation imposed upon the EEOC were intended to be mandatory or only directory, courts could have adopted a construction advanced by either plaintiffs or defendants. Defendants urged that the use of the word "unable" in § 706(e), 42 U.S.C. § 2000e-5(e) (1970), implied that the duty to resolve complaints by informal conciliation imposed by § 706(a), 42 U.S.C. § 2000e-5(a) (1970), had to be fully performed by the EEOC before a civil action could be instituted. In Johnson v. Seaboard Air Line R.R., 405 F.2d 645 (4th Cir. 1968), *cert. denied sub nom.* Pilot Freight Carriers, Inc. v. Walker, 394 U.S. 198 (1969), the court noted that both plaintiff and defendant could find support for their positions on the conciliation issue in the legislative history.

[37] *See* Ewald, *supra* note 29, at 116-17; Singer, *Employment Report: Internal Problems Hamper EEOC Anti-Bias Effort,* NATION J. REP. 1226 (August 17, 1974).

nearly two years from the date of the filing of a charge for the EEOC to complete its administrative proceedings.[38]

Defendants have raised a myriad of other jurisdictional objections in an effort to impede the private enforcement of Title VII. These objections were raised ostensibly to protect the conciliation process. Virtually every step in the EEOC enforcement procedure has been asserted as a jurisdictional prerequisite to private enforcement.[39] The courts, however, have given a liberal interpretation to the procedural requirements under the Act. They have held that the EEOC need not have made a finding of reasonable cause prior to the filing of a suit.[40] A charge need not have been made under oath at the time of the original filing with the Commission.[41] Furthermore, it is not necessary that a charge be served on the respondent prior to suit.[42]

B. Timeliness

Some defendants have also urged that a complaint should be dismissed if not filed in court within a limited time after the filing of a charge with the EEOC. This argument was based on section 706(e) of the Act, which gave the EEOC a maximum of sixty days for investigation and conciliation, after which time an aggrieved party was notified that he had thirty days to file suit.[43] Courts have

---

[38] See H.R. Rep. No. 238, 92d Cong., 1st Sess. 61 (1971); Arey v. Providence Hosp., 55 F.R.D. 62, 68 (D.C. Cir. 1972).

[39] See, e.g., Love v. Pullman Co., 404 U.S. 522 (1972); Crosslin v. Mountain State Tel. & Tel. Co., 400 U.S. 1004 (1971); Sanchez v. Standard Brands, Inc., 431 F.2d 455 (5th Cir. 1970); Hebert & Reischel, supra note 29, at 458-78.

The EEOC has promulgated liberal and streamlined procedural regulations for its administrative process. 29 C.F.R. §§ 1601.1 to 1601.59 (1974). These regulations, issued pursuant to Title VII § 713, 42 U.S.C. § 2000e-12(a) (1970), have been upheld by the courts. See, e.g., Robinson v. Lorillard Corp., 444 F.2d 791, 800-01 (4th Cir.), cert. dismissed, 404 U.S. 1006 (1971); Sanchez v. Standard Brands, Inc., supra.

[40] McDonnell Douglas Corp. v. Green, 411 U.S. 792, 798-99 (1973).

[41] Blue Bell Boots, Inc. v. EEOC, 418 F.2d 355 (6th Cir. 1969); Georgia Power Co. v. EEOC, 412 F.2d 462 (5th Cir. 1969); Choate v. Caterpillar Tractor Co., 402 F.2d 357 (7th Cir. 1968). The EEOC procedural regulations provide that the verification of the charge may be made after the 180 day filing requirement in Title VII § 706(e), 42 U.S.C. § 2000e-5(e) (Supp. IV, 1974). 29 C.F.R. § 1601.11(b) (1974).

[42] Johnson v. I.T.T. Indus., Inc.. 323 F. Supp. 1258 (N.D. Miss. 1971); Logan v. General Fireproofing Co., 309 F. Supp. 1096 (W.D.N.C. 1969), rev'd, 521 F.2d 881 (4th Cir. 1971); Holliday v. Railway Express Co., 306 F. Supp. 898 (N.D. Ga. 1968). But under the 1972 amendments the EEOC is required to "serve a notice of the charge [on the respondent] within ten days" of the filing of the charge with the Commission. Title VII § 706(b), 42 U.S.C. § 2000e-5(b) (Supp. IV, 1974).

[43] Title VII § 706(e), 42 U.S.C. § 2000e-5(e) (1970), as amended, Title VII § 706(f)(1), 42 U.S.C. § 2000e-5(f)(1) (Supp. IV, 1974). Although this section allowed thirty days within which the EEOC should complete the administrative

rejected this argument [⁴⁴] and other similar jurisdictional challenges [⁴⁵] on the ground that it would be unnecessarily harsh to interpret the statutory language in a way that could penalize aggrieved parties for the Commission's administrative delays.[⁴⁶] A restrictive interpretation of the Act would be in derogation of the interests of those whom the Act is designed to protect.[⁴⁷] It is a well established rule, however, that the complaint must be filed in the district court within thirty (now ninety) [⁴⁸] days of receipt of the notice of right to sue.[⁴⁹] In only a few cases have the courts found compelling extenuating circumstances sufficient to waive the requirement of the timely filing of a complaint in the district court.[⁵⁰]

The courts have made a distinction between an alleged violation deemed to be "continuing" and one deemed to be a "completed act" for determining whether the ninety (now 180) [⁵¹] day requirement for the filing of a charge with the EEOC has been met.[⁵²] If the act

---

processing of a charge, the EEOC extended the period to an automatic sixty days because of its heavy caseload. 29 C.F.R. § 1601.25(a) (1971). *See* Arey v. Providence Hosp., 55 F.R.D. 62, 69 (D.D.C. 1972).

[⁴⁴] Cunningham v. Litton Indus., 413 F.2d 887 (9th Cir. 1969); Miller v. International Paper Co., 408 F.2d 283, 285-86 (5th Cir. 1969); Pullen v. Otis Elevator Co., 292 F. Supp. 715, 717 (N.D. Ga. 1968).

[⁴⁵] *See* Hebert & Reischel, *supra* note 29; Note, *Developments in the Law — Employment Discrimination and Title VII of the Civil Rights Act of 1964*, 84 HARV. L. REV. 1109, 1198-1216 (1971) [hereinafter cited as *Developments — Title VII*].

[⁴⁶] *See* Miller v. International Paper Co., 408 F.2d 283, 290 (5th Cir. 1969).

[⁴⁷] *See* Graniteville Co. v. EEOC, 438 F.2d 32 (4th Cir. 1971).

[⁴⁸] Title VII § 706(f)(1), 42 U.S.C. § 2000e-5(f)(1) (Supp. IV, 1974) (ninety days), *amending* Title VII § 706(e), 42 U.S.C. § 2000-5(e) (1970) (thirty days). *See* Goodman v. City Prod. Corp., 425 F.2d 702 (6th Cir. 1970). *See also* Johnson v. Railway Express Agency, Inc., 421 U.S. 454 (1975).

[⁴⁹] The time within which a plaintiff must file his complaint in federal court does not begin to run until actual receipt of the notice of right to sue from the EEOC; it does not run until either the date upon which notice was mailed by the EEOC or upon which delivery was made to plaintiff's mailing address. Franks v. Bowman Transp. Co., 495 F.2d 398, 404-405 (5th Cir. 1974), *cert. granted*, 420 U.S. 989 (1975) (*see* Addendum); Tuft v. McDonnell Douglas Corp., 517 F.2d 1301 (8th Cir. 1975), *cert. denied*, 44 U.S.L.W. 3394 (U.S. Jan. 12, 1976) (No. 75-627); Gates v. Georgia-Pacific Corp., 492 F.2d 292 (9th Cir. 1974).

[⁵⁰] *See* Austin v. Reynolds Metals Co., 2 CCH EMPL. PRAC. DEC. ¶ 10, 179 (E.D. Va. 1970) (filing of suit letter with the court sufficient to meet the timely filing requirement); McQueen v. E.M.C. Plastic Co., 302 F. Supp. 881 (E.D. Tex. 1969); Witherspoon v. Mercury Freight Lines, Inc., 1 CCH EMPL. PRAC. DEC. ¶ 9976 (S.D. Ala. 1968). But the parties cannot consent to extend the time for filing suit. Hinton v. CPC Int'l, Inc., 520 F.2d 1312 (8th Cir. 1975).

[⁵¹] Title VII § 706(d), 42 U.S.C. § 2000e-5(d) (1970) (ninety days), *as amended*, Title VII § 706(e), 42 U.S.C. § 2000e-5(e) (Supp. IV, 1974).

[⁵²] *See, e.g.,* Gates v. Georgia-Pacific Corp., 492 F.2d 292, 294 (9th Cir. 1974); Macklin v. Specter Freight Sys., Inc., 478 F.2d 979, 987 (D.C. Cir. 1973); Belt v. Johnson Motor Lines, Inc., 458 F.2d 443, 444 (5th Cir. 1972); Cox v. U.S. Gypsum Co., 409 F.2d 289, 290 (7th Cir. 1969).

is construed to be "continuing" — a discriminatory seniority system, for example — the charge may be filed with the EEOC at any time. If it is a completed act — a discharge or a refusal to hire — it is mandatory that the charge be filed within time set out in section 706(e).[53]

C. Specificity of Charge

Many persons who file charges with the EEOC are untutored in the technicalities of the law and may not be able to articulate fully their grievances or even be aware of the full panoply of discriminatory practices against them and others similarly situated.[54] Defendants have seized upon the statement of the discrimination alleged in the charge to argue that the scope of the allegations in a complaint should be limited by the content of the charge filed with the EEOC. Courts have adopted the rule, however, that a complaint may allege any kind of employment discrimination like or related to the claims contained in the charge or growing out of the charge during its pendency before the EEOC.[55] This rule is consistent with the liberal construction the courts have given to the other procedural and jurisdictional issues. A more exacting rule would have required many uneducated, illiterate, and impecunious Title VII plaintiffs to seek legal counsel prior to filing of a charge with the EEOC; [56] a less exacting rule would have circumvented the statutory requirements because Title VII contemplates that no issue can be the subject of a civil action until it has first been presented to the EEOC.[57]

---

[53] *See* cases cited note 52 *supra*. Ordinarily a refusal to hire is not deemed to be a continuing violation. Molybdenum Corp. v. EEOC, 457 F.2d 935, 936 (10th Cir. 1972). *See also* Tippett v. Liggett & Meyers Tobacco Co., 316 F. Supp. 292, 295-96 (1970).

[54] In Willis v. Chicago Extruded Metals Co., 375 F. Supp. 362 (N.D. Ill. 1974), the court observed the following:

[T]he Civil Rights Act is designed to protect those who are least able to protect themselves. Complainants to the EEOC are seldom [represented by] lawyers. To compel the charging party to specifically articulate in a charge filed with the Commission the full panoply of discrimination which he may have suffered may cause the very persons Title VII was designed to protect to lose that protection because they are ignorant of or unable to thoroughly describe the discriminatory practices to which they are subjected.

Id. at 365 (footnotes omitted). *Accord,* Gamble v. Birmingham S. R.R. Co., 514 F.2d 678, 689 (5th Cir. 1975); Graniteville Co. v. EEOC, 438 F.2d 32, 38 (4th Cir. 1971); Sanchez v. Standard Brands, Inc., 431 F.2d 455, 463 (5th Cir. 1970).

[55] *See* Tipler v. E.I. duPont, 443 F.2d 125, 131 (6th Cir. 1971); Sanchez v. Standard Brands, Inc., 431 F.2d 455 (5th Cir. 1970); King v. Georgia Power Co., 295 F. Supp. 943, 947 (N.D. Ga. 1968).

[56] *See* Sanchez v. Standard Brands, Inc., 431 F.2d 455, 466 (5th Cir. 1970).

[57] *See, id.* at 467. *See generally* Alexander v. Gardner-Denver Co., 415 U.S. 36 (1974); McDonnell Douglas Corp. v. Green, 411 U.S. 792 (1973).

D. Overlapping Procedures

The existence of overlapping and parallel federal, state, and arbitral bases and procedures for eliminating employment discrimination [58] has generated a number of procedural issues. The Act is conspicuously silent on the relationships among the various procedures available to remedy employment discrimination.[59] The Supreme Court has noted, however, that despite the comprehensiveness of Title VII "the legislative history . . . manifests a congressional intent to allow an individual to pursue independently his rights under both Title VII and other applicable federal and state statutes." [60] Many of the arguments advanced by defendants to emasculate the effectiveness of the Act were based on the existence of overlapping remedies. In cases involving railroad employees, for example, it was asserted that complainants must first follow the procedures created by the Railway Labor Act before a Title VII suit could be filed in federal court.[61] Similarly it was argued that proceedings must be initiated before the National Labor Relations Board [62] or that procedures under collective bargaining agreements [63] must be exhausted prior to the filing of charges with the EEOC. These arguments have been unequivocally rejected.[64]

---

[58] Title VII is only one of many remedial schemes available for redressing employment discrimination, although it has been the basis primarily relied upon to redress unlawful employment practices during the past decade. Other bases for attacking employment discrimination include the following: Equal Protection Clause, U.S. CONST., amend. XIV, § 2; Civil Rights Act of 1866, 42 U.S.C. § 1981 (1970); Executive Order 11246, *as amended by* Executive Order No. 11375, 3 C.F.R. 169 (1974); Equal Pay Act of 1963, 29 U.S.C. § 206(d) (1970); National Labor Relations Act, 29 U.S.C. §§ 141-68 (1970); and various state and local human right and fair employment laws. For a discussion of the various remedies and sanctions for employment discrimination see SOVERN, note 3 *supra;* Hebert & Reischel, note 29 *supra;* Peck, *Remedies for Racial Discrimination in Employment: A Comparative Evaluation of Forums,* 46 WASH. L. REV. 455 (1971).

[59] *See* Alexander v. Gardner-Denver Co., 415 U.S. 36, 47-49 (1974).

[60] *Id.* at 48. A final judgment in a state proceeding does not deprive a plaintiff of his right to seek relief in federal court under Title VII. Baptiste v. Furnco Constr. Co., 503 F.2d 447 (7th Cir. 1974); Cooper v. Philip Morris, Inc., 464 F.2d 9 (6th Cir. 1972); Voustis v. Union Carbide Corp., 452 F.2d 889 (2d Cir. 1971).

[61] *E.g.,* Norman v. Missouri-Pacific R.R., 414 F.2d 73 (8th Cir. 1969); Hayes v. Seaboard Coastline R.R., 46 F.R.D. 49, 55 (S.D. Ga. 1968).

[62] Evans v. Local 2127 IBEW, 313 F. Supp. 1354 (N.D. Ga. 1969); Austin v. Reynolds Metals Co., 2 CCH EMPL. PRAC. DEC. ¶ 10, 179 (E.D. Va. 1970). *Cf.* Rubber Workers Local 12 v. NLRB, 368 F.2d 12, 24 (5th Cir. 1966), *cert. denied,* 389 U.S. 837 (1967). For a discussion of the relationship between Title VII and the NLRA see Note, The Inevitable Interplay of Title VII and the National Labor Relations Act: A New Role for the NLRB, 123 U. PENN. L. REV. 158 (1974).

[63] Culpepper v. Reynolds Metals Co., 421 F.2d 888, 892-93 (5th Cir. 1970); Bowe v. Colgate-Palmolive Co., 416 F.2d 711 (7th Cir. 1969).

[64] *See* cases cited notes 62-63 *supra;* Hebert & Reischel, note 29 *supra,* at 463-64.

The most significant litigation on the matter of overlapping remedies has arisen in the following two contexts: First, the relationship between Title VII and grievance-arbitration procedures under collective bargaining agreements; and secondly, the relationship between Title VII and section 1981 of the Civil Rights Act of 1866.[65]

(1) Grievance-Arbitration Procedures

. . . .

In the *Alexander v. Gardner-Denver Co.*[74] case the Court granted certiorari to "decide under what circumstances, if any, an employee's statutory right to a trial *de novo* under Title VII may be foreclosed by prior submission of his claim to final arbitration under the nondiscrimination clause of a collective-bargaining agreement." [75] A unanimous Court held that an employee who alleges his discharge was racially motivated is entitled to pursue his claim under Title VII even though it has already been rejected by an arbitrator in a grievance proceeding brought by a union. . . .

It is now clear that district courts must consider all Title VII claims *de novo,* for as the Supreme Court said in *Alexander,*

> The purpose and procedures of Title VII indicate that Congress intended federal courts to exercise final responsibility for enforcement of Title VII. . . .[79]
>
> . . . .
>
> . . . But courts should be ever mindful that Congress, in enacting Title VII, thought it necessary to provide a judicial forum for the ultimate resolution of discriminatory employment claims. It is the duty of courts to assume the full availability of this forum.[80]

Although the Court held that Title VII cases must be considered *de novo*, it also noted that an arbitral decision may be admitted into evidence and accorded such weight as the district court deems appropriate; however, the Court specifically declined to adopt standards to govern the weight to be accorded an arbitral decision.[81] . . .

---

[65] 42 U.S.C. § 1981 (1970) [hereinafter referred to as section 1981].

[74] 415 U.S. 36 (1974).

[75] *Id.* at 38.

[79] *Id.* at 56.

[80] *Id.* at 60 n.21. The Court specifically rejected the holding of Rios v. Reynolds Metals Co., 467 F.2d 54 (5th Cir. 1972), which had adopted a deferral rule. 415 U.S. at 58-59.

[81] *Id.* at 60 & n.21. For a discussion of the significant problems raised for arbitrators by *Alexander* see EDWARDS, ARBITRATION OF EMPLOYMENT DIS-

(2) Section 1981

Another significant Supreme Court decision on procedural matters is *Johnson v. Railway Express Agency, Inc.* [87] which concerned the relationship between Title VII and section 1981. The issue in *Johnson* was whether the timely filing of a charge with the EEOC tolls the running of the statute of limitations applicable to an action based upon the same facts instituted under section 1981. The Court held that Title VII and section 1981 provide separate and independent remedies and thus there can be no tolling of the statute of limitations for the section 1981 claim because of the timely filing of the EEOC charge.[88] . . .

Johnson is also significant because, for the first time, the Court recognized that section 1981 affords a federal remedy against employment discrimination.[90] An individual who establishes a claim under section 1981 is entitled to both equitable and legal relief, including compensation and, under certain circumstances, punitive damages.[91] At the same time, *Johnson* and another recent Supreme Court decision, *Alyeska Pipeline Service Co. v. The Wilderness Society,* [92] cast doubt upon the practical viability of section 1981 as an employment discrimination remedy. In *Alyeska,* the Court held that attorney's fees cannot be awarded to successful private litigants on a "private attorney general theory" absent specific statutory authorization.[93] Such fees may be recovered only where a common fund is recoverable or in the rare case where the court finds that defendant has acted in bad faith.[94] Thus, the absence of a reasonable expectation of attorney's fees in an action based solely on section 1981 will probably discourage such suits. In addition, because many employment discrimination claimants do not seek legal assistance until after receipt of a notice of right to sue from the EEOC, claimants will often be precluded from bringing a section 1981 action by the statutory time limitation on filing such a claim. . . .

CRIMINATION CASES: AN EMPIRICAL STUDY, PROCEEDINGS OF THE TWENTY-EIGHTH ANNUAL MEETING OF THE NATIONAL ACADEMY OF ARBITRATORS (BNA 1975) and Comment, *Reliance on Arbitral Awards in Title VII Suits: Implications of Alexander v. Gardner-Denver and Public Employment Cases,* 20 ST. LOUIS U. L.J. 366 (1976), *infra.*

[87] 421 U.S. 454 (1975).
[88] *Id.* at 462-67.
[90] 421 U.S. 454, 460 & n.6.
[91] *Id.* at 460.
[92] 421 U.S. 240 (1975).
[93] *See id.* at 269.
[94] *Id.* at 245.

VI. The Equal Employment Opportunity Act of 1972

A. Scope of Title VII Coverage Expanded

Several significant changes were brought about by the amendments to Title VII that were enacted as the Equal Employment Opportunity Act of 1972.[522] More employees may now file charges with the EEOC and, if necessary, proceed to federal district court. Employers with only fifteen employees are now subject to Title VII.[523] Moreover, the previous exemption for educational institutions has been deleted; thus, employees and applicants for employment in teaching, administrative, and clerical positions in both private and public school systems are now covered by the Act.[524]

Congress also expanded the definition of "employer" to include the entire field of public employment under Title VII.[525] . . .

B. Enforcement Powers of the EEOC

Enforcement powes granted to the EEOC by the 1972 amendments enable it to bring civil actions against non-governmental employers with whom conciliation has proved unsatisfactory [531] and to initiate prosecution in "pattern and practice" suits following the filing of a charge by a person allegedly aggrieved or by an EEOC Commissioner.[532] To date, however, the potential of this amendment has not been realized. The case by case approach that has been the backbone of the enforcement of equal employment

---

[522] 42 U.S.C. §§ 2000e to 2000e-17 (Supp. IV, 1974).

[523] Title VII § 701(b), 42 U.S.C. § 2000e-(b) (Supp. IV, 1974), amending Title VII § 701(b), 42 U.S.C. § 2000e-(b) (1970).

[524] Title VII § 702, 42 U.S.C. § 2000e-1 (Supp. IV, 1974), amending Title VII § 702, 42 U.S.C. § 2000e-1 (1970).

[525] Title VII §§ 701(a), (b), 42 U.S.C. §§ 2000e-(a), (b) (Supp. IV, 1974), amending Title VII §§ 701(a), (b), U.S.C. §§ 2000e-(a), (b) (1970), defines an "employer" as a "person," and "person" includes governments, governmental agencies, and political subdivisions. Employment discrimination in federal employment is covered by Title VII § 717, 42 U.S.C. § 2000e-16 (Supp. IV, 1974), and is an entirely new section under Title VII. Actions against the federal agencies are governed in federal court by the same provisions of Title VII as are applicable to cases involving private, state, and local defendants. Title VII § 717(d), 42 U.S.C. § 2000e-16(d) (Supp. IV. 1974). The EEOC does not have enforcement authority over claims against federal agencies. This administrative enforcement authority is vested in the United States Civil Service Commission. Title VII § 717(b), 42 U.S.C. § 2000e-16(b) (Supp. IV, 1974).

[531] Title VII § 706(f)(1), 42 U.S.C. § 2000e-5(f)(1) (Supp. IV, 1974), amending Title VII § 706(e), 42 U.S.C. § 2000e-5(e) (1970).

[532] Title VII §§ 707(c), (d), 42 U.S.C. §§ 2000e-6(c), (d) (Supp. IV, 1974). See EEOC v. Cleveland Mills Co., 502 F.2d 153 (4th Cir.), cert. denied, 420 U.S. 946 (1974).

legislation during the past decade is time-consuming,[533] expensive,[534] and often frustrating.[535] Even successful suits brought as class actions affect only an insubstantial number of blacks or women and are usually limited to a single location or a

---

[533] For example: Plaintiffs in Albemarle Paper Co. v. Moody, 422 U.S. 405 (1975), filed their charges with the EEOC in May, 1966. The trial commenced in July, 1971 — almost five years after the complaint was filed — and the district court entered its decision on the merits in November, 1971, 4 F.E.P. Cas. 561 (E.D.N.C. 1971). Appeal proceedings consumed more than a year. After the decision of the panel in the Fourth Circuit, 474 F.2d 134 (4th Cir. 1973), defendants petitioned for and were granted an *en banc* hearing. Supplemental briefs were filed by all the parties and the case was subsequently argued before the *en banc* court. After the *en banc* argument, but before a decision, the Fourth Circuit, pursuant to 28 U.S.C. § 1254(3), certified to the Supreme Court the question whether senior circuit judges who are members of the originally assigned panel that heard the case are authorized to participate in the determination to rehear that case *en banc;* the Supreme Court ruled that senior judges are not so authorized. Moody v. Albemarle Paper Co., 417 U.S. 622 (1974). Defendants then filed petitions for writ of certiorari; the petitions were granted in December, 1974. The Supreme Court issued its decision in June, 1975. Further proceedings in the lower courts could conceivably consume several more years.

Similarly, in Pettway v. American Cast Iron Pipe Co., 494 F.2d 211 (5th Cir. 1974), the complaint was filed in the district court in May, 1966. The district court dismissed the complaint on the ground that plaintiffs had failed to exhaust their administrative remedies before the EEOC. An appeal ensued and the dismissal was reversed *sub nom.* Dent v. St. Louis-San Francisco Ry., 406 F.2d 399 (5th Cir. 1969). During the appeal on the exhaustion issue, one of the named plaintiffs (Wrenn) was discharged for filing a letter charge with the EEOC containing allegedly false and malicious statements about defendant. The district court upheld the discharge and the Fifth Circuit reversed. 411 F.2d 998 (1969). Before the trial on the merits in 1971, plaintiffs sought and obtained an injunction against the racially discriminatory organizational structure of the defendant. 332 F. Supp. 811 (N.D. Ala. 1970). After trial on the merits the district court entered an adverse ruling against plaintiffs on all issues except attorney's fees. 8 CCH EMPL. PRAC. DEC. ¶ 9474 (N.D. Ala. 1972). The Fifth Circuit reversed in a lengthy and comprehensive opinion. 494 F.2d 211 (1974). As of this time, further proceedings in the district court have not been concluded — more than nine years after the complaint was filed.

One federal judge who has heard a number of employment discrimination cases commented that "almost every corporation, large and small, has been hit with one or more class actions claiming discrimination. Each of these cases, where thousands of employees are involved, require[s] months just to hear the evidence." Edenfield, *The Role of the Federal Courts, Past, Present and Future,* 7 CUMB. LAWYER 2 (Nov. 1972). *See* Gamble v. Birmingham S. R.R., 514 F.2d 678, 680 (5th Cir. 1975).

[534] *See* Maslow, *The Bonhomie of the Plaintiff Bar,* 4 JURIS DOCTOR, No. 8, at 31 (Sept. 1974); *Allowance of Attorney Fees in Civil Rights Actions,* 7 COLUM. J.L. & SOC. PROB. 381, 383 (1971).

[535] *See, e.g.,* Pettway v. American Cast Iron Pipe Co., 411 F.2d 998 (5th Cir. 1969) (one of the named plaintiffs discharged while case on appeal for sending a letter to EEOC containing allegedly false and malicious statements about the defendant employer); Pennsylvania v. Operating Engineers Local 542, 347 F. Supp. 268 (E.D. Pa. 1972) (injunction against a course of conduct designed to intimidate, harass, and preclude class from pursuing claim). *See generally* Spurlock, *Proscribing Retaliation Under Title VII,* 8 IND. L. REV. 453 (1975).

single plant of a company that may have plants and operations in many locations.[536] Recent efforts by federal agencies to negotiate industrywide affirmative action plans [537] indicate an approach that could achieve equal employment without the necessity of protracted private litigation. But rather than complementing the efforts of private enforcement, these plans have resulted in a diversion of efforts into collateral litigation [538] because of the adverse impact these plans may have upon the rights of private individuals.[539]

C. Procedural Changes

The 1972 amendments also added new procedural requirements.[540] The time limits for filing a charge with the EEOC [541] and the time within which to file suit in federal court [542]

---

[536] The defendant in Griggs v. Duke Power Co., 401 U.S. 424 (1971), has a number of plants and operations throughout the states of North and South Carolina, yet the decision affected only thirteen black employees of defendant at its facility located in Draper, North Carolina. One court has described AT&T as a "colossal conglomerate comprised of twenty-four subsidiary companies and, when viewed together as a unit, constitutes the largest single private employer in the country." EEOC v. A.T.&T. Co., 365 F. Supp. 1105, 1108 n.1 (E.D. Pa. 1973). A decision in a case brought by private plaintiffs, Leisner v. New York Tel. Co., 358 F. Supp. 359 (S.D.N.Y. 1973), although certified as a class action, will affect only an extremely small number of women in the Bell system. In Nance v. Union Carbide Corp., 397 F. Supp. 436, 439 (W.D.N.C. 1975), defendant had operations in all fifty states, but the decision was limited to its Charlotte, North Carolina facilities. Compare Danner v. Phillips Petroleum Co., 447 F.2d 159 (5th Cir. 1971) with Sprogis v. United Airlines, Inc., 444 F.2d 1194 (7th Cir.), cert. denied, 404 U.S. 991 (1971), on the question whether a court can enter a judgment, the effects of which will benefit a class, in an action not brought as a class action.

[537] See United States v. Allegheny-Ludlum Indus., Inc., 517 F.2d 826 (5th Cir. 1975), petition for cert. filed, 44 U.S.L.W. 3429 (U.S. Jan. 15, 1976) (No. 75-1008); EEOC v. A.T.&T. Co., 365 F. Supp. 1105 (E.D. Pa. 1973); Kilberg, Current Civil Rights Problems in the Collective Bargaining Process: The Bethlehem and AT&T Experiences, 27 VAND. L. REV. 81 (1974); Kilberg, Progress and Problems in Equal Employment Opportunity, 24 LAB. L.J. 651 (1973).

[538] See United States v. Allegheny-Ludlum Indus., Inc., 517 F.2d 836 (5th Cir. 1975), petition for cert. filed, 44 U.S.L.W. 3429 (U.S. Jan. 15, 1976) (No. 75-1008); Rogers v. United States Steel Corp., 508 F.2d 152 (3rd Cir. 1975); Martini v. Republic Steel Corp., 9 CCH EMPL. PRAC. DEC. ¶ 10,084 (N.D. Ohio 1975).

[539] See N.Y. Times, April 14, 1974, at 1, col. 4.

[540] Title VII §§ 706(a) to (f)(1), 42 U.S.C. §§ 2000e-5(a) to 5(f)(1) (Supp. IV, 1974), amending Title VII §§ 706(a) to (f), 42 U.S.C. §§ 2000e-5(a) to 5(f)(1) (1970).

[541] Title VII § 706(e), 42 U.S.C. § 2000e-5(e) (Supp. IV, 1974). The time within which to file a charge with the EEOC has been extended from ninety days to 180 days. In Davis v. Valley Distrib. Co., 522 F.2d 827 (9th Cir. 1975), the court held that a claim that may have been barred under the ninety day rule can be saved under the 180 day rule under the 1972 amendment.

[542] Title VII § 706(f)(1), 42 U.S.C. § 2000e-5(f)(1) (Supp. IV, 1974). The time within which a charging party may file a complaint in the appropriate federal district court has been extended from thirty days to ninety days. The time for the filing of the complaint in federal court does not begin to run until the plaintiff actually

have been extended. These changes should provide more opportunity for an allegedly aggrieved employee to pursue his rights. Moreover, a charge may now be filed "by or on behalf of a person claiming to be aggrieved. . . ." [543] In addition, the EEOC must now "accord substantial weight to final findings . . . made by State or local authorities in proceedings commenced under State or local law. . . ." [544]

Overall, the 1972 amendments have expanded the scope of employers covered by Title VII, liberalized the time restraints for the filing of charges, and strengthened the federal agency charged with the responsibility of overseeing enforcement of the Act.

NOTES:

(1) Title VII has been the subject of a host of commentaries. *See, e.g.,* A. Blumrosen, Black Employment and the Law (1971); Cooper & Sobel, *Seniority and Testing Under Fair Employment Laws: A General Approach to Objective Criteria of Hiring and Promotion,* 82 Harv. L. Rev. 1598 (1969); Edwards, *Race Discrimination in Employment: What Price Equality?* in Civil Liberties & Civil Rights (Univ. of Ill. Press, 1977); Edwards & Zaretsky, *Preferential Remedies for Employment Discrimination,* 74 Mich. L. Rev. (Nov. 1975); Edwards, *Labor Arbitration At The Crossroads: The "Common Law of the Shop" Versus External Law,* 32 Arbitration Journal (June 1977); Ewald, *Public and Private Enforcement of Title VII of the Civil Rights Act of 1964 — A Ten Year Perspective,* 7 Urban L. Ann. 101 (1974); Fiss, *A Theory of Fair Employment Laws,* 38 U. Chi. L. Rev. 235 (1971); Gardner, *The Development of the Substantive Principles of Title VII Law: The Defendant's View,* 26 Ala. L. Rev. 1 (1973); Gardner, *The Development of the Meaning of Title VII of the Civil Rights Act of 1964,* 23 Ala. L. Rev. 451 (1971); Gould, Black Workers in White Unions (Cornell Univ. Press, 1977); Gould, *Employment Security, Seniority and Race: The Role of Title VII of the Civil Rights Act of 1964,* 13 How. L.J. 1 (1967); Gould, *Seniority and the Black Worker: Reflection on Quarles and Its Implications,* 47 Tex. L. Rev. 1039 (1969); Hebert & Reischel, *Title VII and the Multiple Approaches to Eliminating Employment*

---

receives an appropriate notice from the EEOC. *See* Plunkett v. Roadway Express, Inc., 504 F.2d 417 (10th Cir. 1974); Franks v. Bowman Transp. Co., 495 F.2d 398, 403-406 (5th Cir. 1974), *cert. granted on other grounds,* 420 U.S. 989 (1975). For a discussion of what constitutes appropriate notice from the EEOC, or the so-called "two letter" problem see DeMatteis v. Eastman Kodak Co., 520 F.2d 409 (2d Cir. 1975); Tuft v. McDonnell Douglas Corp., 517 F.2d 1301 (8th Cir. 1975), *cert. denied,* 44 U.S.L.W. 3394 (U.S. Jan. 12, 1976) (No. 75-627).

[543] Title VII § 706(b), 42 U.S.C. § 2000e-5(b) (Supp. IV, 1974).

[544] *Id.*

Discrimination, 46 N.Y.U.L. Rev. 449 (1971); IRRA, Equal Rights and Industrial Relations (1977); Hill, *The Equal Employment Opportunity Acts of 1964 and 1972: A Critical Analysis of the Legislative History and Administration of the Law,* 2 Ind. Rel. L.J. 1 (Spring 1977); Kanowitz, *Sex-Based Discrimination in American Law III: Title VII of the Civil Rights Act of 1964 and the Equal Pay Act of 1963,* 20 Hastings L.J. 305 (1968); Kilberg, *Progress and Problems in Equal Employment Opportunity,* 24 Lab. L.J. 651 (1973); Larson, *The Development of Section 1981 as a Remedy for Racial Discrimination in Private Employment,* 7 Harv. Civ. Rights-Civ. Lib. L. Rev. 56 (1972); Lopatka, *A 1977 Primer on the Federal Regulation of Employment Discrimination,* 1977 Ill. L.F. 69 (1977); Miller, *Sex Discrimination and Title VII of the Civil Rights Act of 1964,* 51 Minn. L. Rev. 877 (1967); Sape & Hart, *Title VII Reconsidered: The Equal Employment Opportunity Act of 1972,* 40 Geo. Wash. L. Rev. 824 (1972); Schlei & Grossman, Employment Discrimination Law (BNA, Inc. 1976); Spurlock, *Proscribing Retaliation Under Title VII,* 8 Ind. L. Rev. 453 (1975); Edwards, *The Coming of Age of the Burger Court: Labor Law Decisions of the Supreme Court During the 1976 Term,* 19 Boston Coll. L. Rev. 1 (1977); Smith, Employment Discrimination Law (Bobbs-Merrill 1978).

(2) *REORGANIZATION OF EQUAL EMPLOYMENT OPPORTUNITY PROGRAMS*
Reorganization Plan No. 1 of 1978

Prepared by the President and transmitted to the Senate and the House of Representatives in Congress assembled, February 23, 1978, pursuant to the provisions of Chapter 9 of Title 5 of the United States Code.

EQUAL EMPLOYMENT OPPORTUNITY

Section 1. *Transfer of Equal Pay Enforcement Functions.*

All functions related to enforcing or administering Section 6 (d) of the Fair Labor Standards Act, as amended, (29 U.S.C. 206 (d)) are hereby transferred to the Equal Employment Opportunity Commission. Such functions include, but shall not be limited to, the functions relating to equal pay administration and enforcement now vested in the Secretary of Labor, the Administrator of the Wage and Hour Division of the Department of Labor, and the Civil Service Commission pursuant to Sections 4 (d) (1); 4 (f); 9; 11 (a), (b) and (c); 16 (b) and (c) and 17 of the Fair Labor Standards Act, as amended, (29 U.S.C. 204 (d) (1); 204 (f); 209; 211 (a), (b) and (c); 216 (b) and (c) and 217) and Section 10 (b) (1) of the Portal-to-Portal Act of 1947, as amended, (29 U.S.C. 259).

Section 2. *Transfer of Age Discrimination Enforcement Functions.*

All functions vested in the Secretary of Labor or in the Civil Service Commission pursuant to Sections 2, 4, 7, 8, 9, 10, 11, 12, 13, 14, and 15 of the Age Discrimination in Employment Act of 1967, as amended, (29 U.S.C. 621, 623, 626, 627, 628, 629, 630, 631, 632, 633, and 633a) are hereby transferred to the Equal Employment Opportunity Commission. All functions related to age discrimination administration and enforcement pursuant to Sections 6 and 16 of the Age Discrimination in Employment Act of 1967, as amended, (29 U.S.C. 625 and 634) are hereby transferred to the Equal Employment Opportunity Commission.

Section 3. *Transfer of Equal Opportunity in Federal Employment Enforcement Functions.*

(a) All equal opportunity in Federal employment enforcement and related functions vested in the Civil Service Commission pursuant to Section 717 (b) and (c) of the Civil Rights Act of 1964, as amended, (42 U.S.C. 2000e-16 (b) and (c)), are hereby transferred to the Equal Employment Opportunity Commission.
(b) The Equal Employment Opportunity Commission may delegate to the Civil Service Commission or its successor the function of making a preliminary determination on the issue of discrimination whenever, as a part of a complaint or appeal before the Civil Service Commission on other grounds, a Federal employee alleges a violation of Section 717 of the Civil Rights Act of 1964, as amended, (42 U.S.C. 2000e-16) provided that the Equal Employment Opportunity Commission retains the function of making the final determination concerning such issue of discrimination.

Section 4. *Transfer of Federal Employment of Handicapped Individuals Enforcement Functions.*

All Federal employment of handicapped individuals enforcement functions and related functions vested in the Civil Service Commission pursuant to Section 501 of the Rehabilitation Act of 1973 (29 U.S.C. 791) are hereby transferred to the Equal Employment Opportunity Commission. The function of being co-chairman of the Interagency Committee on Handicapped Employees now vested in the Chairman of the Civil Service Commission pursuant to Section 501 is hereby transferred to the Chairman of the Equal Employment Opportunity Commission.

Section 5. *Transfer of Public Sector 707 Functions.*

Any function of the Equal Employment Opportunity Commission concerning initiation of litigation with respect to State or local government, or political subdivisions under Section 707 of Title VII of the Civil Rights Act of 1964, as amended, (42 U.S.C. 2000e-6) and all necessary functions related thereto, including investigation, findings, notice and an opportunity to resolve the matter without contested litigation, are hereby transferred to the Attorney General, to be exercised by him in accordance with procedures consistent with said Title VII. The Attorney General is authorized to delegate any function under Section 707 of said Title VII to any officer or employee of the Department of Justice.

Section 6. *Transfer of Functions and Abolition of the Equal Employment Opportunity Coordinating Council.*

All functions of the Equal Employment Opportunity Coordinating Council, which was established pursuant to Section 715 of the Civil Rights Act of 1964, as amended, (42 U.S.C. 2000e-14), are hereby transferred to the Equal Employment Opportunity Commission. The Equal Employment Opportunity Coordinating Council is hereby abolished.

Section 7. *Savings Provision.*

Administrative proceedings including administrative appeals from the acts of an executive agency (as defined by Section 105 of Title 5 of the United States Code) commenced or being conducted by or against such executive agency will not abate by reason of the taking effect of this Plan. Consistent with the provisions of this Plan, all such proceedings shall continue before the Equal Employment Opportunity Commission otherwise unaffected by the transfers provided by this Plan. Consistent with the provisions of this Plan, the Equal Employment Opportunity Commission shall accept appeals from those executive agency actions which occurred prior to the effective date of this Plan in accordance with law and regulations in effect on such effective date. Nothing herein shall affect any right of any person to judicial review under applicable law.

Section 8. *Incidental Transfers.*

So much of the personnel, property, records and unexpended balances of appropriations, allocations and other funds employed, used, held, available, or to be made available in connection with the functions transferred under this Plan, as the Director of the Office of Management and Budget shall determine, shall be transferred to the appropriate department, agency, or component at such time or times as the Director of the Office of Management and Budget shall provide, except that no such unexpended balances transferred shall be used for purposes other than those for which the appropriation was originally made. The Director of the Office of Management and Budget shall provide for terminating the affairs of the Council abolished herein and for such further measures and dispositions as such Director deems necessary to effectuate the purposes of this Reorganization Plan.

Section 9. *Effective Date.*

This Reorganization Plan shall become effective at such time or times, on or before October 1, 1979, as the President shall specify, but not sooner than the earliest time allowable under Section 906 of Title 5 of the United States Code.

COMPARISON OF CURRENT AND PROPOSED ALLOCATION

OF EQUAL EMPLOYMENT AUTHORITIES

CURRENT DISPERSED RESPONSIBILITY		EQUAL EMPLOYMENT AUTHORITIES		PROPOSED CONSOLIDATION	
Agency	Program	Discrimination Covered	Employers Covered	Agency	Timing
EEOC	Title VII	Race, Color, Religion, Sex, National Origin	Private and Public Non-Federal Employers and Unions	EEOC	
Labor (Wage and Hour)	Equal Pay Act, Age Discrimination Act	Sex, Age	Private and Public Non-Federal Employers and Unions	EEOC	July 1979 July 1979
Civil • Service Commission	Title VII, Executive Order 11478, Equal Pay Act, Age Discrimination Act, Rehabilitation Act	Race, Color, Religion, Sex, National Origin, Age, Handicapped	Federal Government	EEOC	October 1978
EEOC •	Coordination of All Federal Equal Employment Programs	. . . .	. . . .	EEOC	July 1978
Labor (OFCCP)	Vietnam Veterans Readjustment Act, Rehabilitation Act	Veterans Handicapped	Federal Contractors	•	
Commerce Defense Energy EPA GSA HEW HUD Interior SBA DOT Treasury	Executive Orders 11246, 11375	Race, Color, Religion, Sex, National Origin	Federal Contractors	Labor (OFCCP)	October 1978
Justice	Title VII, Executive Order 11246, Selected Federal Grant Programs	Race, Color, Religion, Sex, National Origin Varied	Public Non-Federal Employers Federal Contractors and Grantees	Justice	No Change

• A number of Federal grant statutes include a provision barring employment discrimination by recipients based on a variety of grounds including race, color, sex, and national origin. Under the reorganization plan, the activities of these agencies will be coordinated by the EEOC.

Chapter 15

THE BASIC PROSCRIPTION AGAINST DISCRIMINATION

A. UNDER TITLE VII

1. Job-Related Conditions of Employment

GRIGGS v. DUKE POWER CO.

United States Supreme Court
401 U. S. 424 (1971)

MR. CHIEF JUSTICE BURGER delivered the opinion of the Court.

We granted the writ in this case to resolve the question whether an employer is prohibited by the Civil Rights Act of 1964, Title VII, from requiring a high school education or passing of a standardized general intelligence test as a condition of employment in or transfer to jobs when (a) neither standard is shown to be significantly related to successful job performance, (b) both requirements operate to disqualify Negroes at a substantially higher rate than white applicants, and (c) the jobs in question formerly had been filled only by white employees as part of a longstanding practice of giving preference to whites.

Congress provided, in Title VII of the Civil Rights Act of 1964, for class actions for enforcement of provisions of the Act and this proceeding was brought by a group of incumbent Negro employees against Duke Power Company. All the petitioners are employed at the Company's Dan River Steam Station, a power generating facility located at Draper, North Carolina. At the time this action was instituted, the Company had 95 employees at the Dan River Station, 14 of whom were Negroes; 13 of these are petitioners here.

The District Court found that prior to July 2, 1965, the effective date of the Civil Rights Act of 1964, the Company openly discriminated on the basis of race in the hiring and assigning of employees at its Dan River plant. The plant was organized into five operating departments: (1) Labor, (2) Coal Handling, (3) Operations, (4) Maintenance, and (5) Laboratory and Test. Negroes were employed only in the Labor Department where the highest paying jobs paid less than the lowest paying jobs in the other four "operating" departments in which only whites were employed. Promotions were normally made within each department on the basis of job seniority. Transferees into a department usually began in the lowest position.

809

In 1955 the Company instituted a policy of requiring a high school education for initial assignment to any department except Labor, and for transfer from the Coal Handling to any "inside" department (Operations, Maintenance, or Laboratory). When the Company abandoned its policy of restricting Negroes to the Labor Department in 1965, completion of high school also was made a prerequisite to transfer from Labor to any other department. From the time the high school requirement was instituted to the time of trial, however, white employees hired before the time of the high school education requirement continued to perform satisfactorily and achieve promotions in the "operating" departments. Findings on this score are not challenged.

The Company added a further requirement for new employees on July 2, 1965, the date on which Title VII became effective. To qualify for placement in any but the Labor Department it became necessary to register satisfactory scores on two professionally prepared aptitude tests, as well as to have a high school education. Completion of high school alone continued to render employees eligible for transfer to the four desirable departments from which Negroes had been excluded if the incumbent had been employed prior to the time of the new requirement. In September 1965 the Company began to permit incumbent employees who lacked a high school education to qualify for transfer from Labor or Coal Handling to an "inside" job by passing two tests — the Wonderlic Personnel Test, which purports to measure general intelligence, and the Bennett Mechanical Comprehension Test. Neither was directed or intended to measure the ability to learn to perform a particular job or category of jobs. The requisite scores used for both initial hiring and transfer approximated the national median for high school graduates.

The District Court had found that while the Company previously followed a policy of overt racial discrimination in a period prior to the Act, such conduct had ceased. The District Court also concluded that Title VII was intended to be prospective only and, consequently, the impact of prior inequities was beyond the reach of corrective action authorized by the Act.

The Court of Appeals was confronted with a question of first impression, as are we, concerning the meaning of Title VII. After careful analysis a majority of that court concluded that a subjective test of the employer's intent should govern, particularly in a close case, and that in this case there was no showing of a discriminatory purpose in the adoption of the diploma and test requirements. On this basis, the Court of Appeals concluded there was no violation of the Act.

The Court of Appeals reversed the District Court in part, rejecting the holding that residual discrimination arising from prior employment practices was insulated from remedial action. The Court of Appeals noted, however, that the District Court was correct in its conclusion that there was no showing of a racial purpose or invidious intent in the adoption of the high school diploma requirement or general intelligence test and that these standards had been applied fairly to whites and Negroes alike. It held that, in the absence of a discriminatory purpose, use of such requirements was permitted by the Act. In so doing, the Court of Appeals rejected the claim that because these two requirements operated to render ineligible a markedly disproportionate number of Negroes, they were unlawful under Title VII unless shown to be job related. We granted the writ on these claims.

The objective of Congress in the enactment of Title VII is plain from the language of the statute. It was to achieve equality of employment opportunities and remove barriers that have operated in the past to favor an identifiable group of white employees over other employees. Under the Act, practices, procedures, or tests neutral on their face, and even neutral in terms of intent, cannot be maintained if they operate to "freeze" the status quo of prior discriminatory employment practices.

The Court of Appeals' opinion, and the partial dissent, agreed that, on the record in the present case, "whites register far better on the Company's alternative requirements" than Negroes.[6] 420 F. 2d 1225, 1239 n. 6. This consequence would appear to be directly traceable to race. Basic intelligence must have the means of articulation to manifest itself fairly in a testing process. Because they are Negroes, petitioners have long received inferior education in segregated schools and this Court expressly recognized these differences in *Gaston County v. United States,* 395 U. S. 285 (1969). There, because of the inferior education received by Negroes in North Carolina, this Court barred the institution of a literacy test for voter registration on the ground that the test would abridge the right to vote indirectly on account of race. Congress did not intend by Title VII, however, to guarantee a job to every person regardless of qualifications. In short, the Act does not command that any person be hired simply because he was formerly the subject of discrimination, or because he is a member of a minority group. Discriminatory preference for any group, minority or majority, is

[6]In North Carolina, 1960 census statistics show that, while 34% of white males had completed high school, only 12% of Negro males had done so. U. S. Bureau of the Census, U. S. Census of Population: 1960, Vol. 1, Characteristics of the Population, pt. 35, Table 47.

Similarly, with respect to standardized tests, the EEOC in one case found that use of a battery of tests, including the Wonderlic and Bennett tests used by the Company in the instant case, resulted in 58% of whites passing the tests, as compared with only 6% of the blacks. Decision of EEOC, CCH Empl. Prac. Guide, ¶ 17,304.53 (Dec. 2. 1966). See also Decision of EEOC 70-552, CCH Empl. Prac. Guide, ¶ 6139 (Feb. 19, 1970).

precisely and only what Congress has proscribed. What is required by Congress is the removal of artificial, arbitrary, and unnecessary barriers to employment when the barriers operate invidiously to discriminate on the basis of racial or other impermissible classification.

Congress has now provided that tests or criteria for employment or promotion may not provide equality of opportunity merely in the sense of the fabled offer of milk to the stork and the fox. On the contrary, Congress has now required that the posture and condition of the job-seeker be taken into account. It has — to resort again to the fable — provided that the vessel in which the milk is proffered be one all seekers can use. The Act proscribes not only overt discrimination but also practices that are fair in form, but discriminatory in operation. The touch-stone is business necessity. If an employment practice which operates to exclude Negroes cannot be shown to be related to job performance, the practice is prohibited.

On the record before us, neither the high school completion requirement nor the general intelligence test is shown to bear a demonstrable relationship to successful performance of the jobs for which it was used. Both were adopted, as the Court of Appeals noted, without meaningful study of their relationship to job-performance ability. Rather, a vice president of the Company testified, the requirements were instituted on the Company's judgment that they generally would improve the overall quality of the work force.

The evidence, however, shows that employees who have not completed high school or taken the tests have continued to perform satisfactorily and make progress in departments for which the high school and test criteria are now used. The promotion record of present employees who would not be able to meet the new criteria thus suggests the possibility that the requirements may not be needed even for the limited purpose of preserving the avowed policy of advancement within the Company. In the context of this case, it is unnecessary to reach the question whether testing requirements that take into account capability for the next succeeding position or related future promotion might be utilized upon a showing that such long-range requirements fulfill a genuine business need. In the present case the Company has made no such showing.

The Court of Appeals held that the Company had adopted the diploma and test requirements without any "intention to discriminate against Negro employees." 420 F. 2d, at 1232. We do not suggest that either the District Court or the Court of Appeals erred in examining the employer's intent; but good intent or absence of discriminatory intent does not redeem employment procedures or testing mechanisms that operate as "built-in headwinds" for minority groups and are unrelated to measuring job capability.

The Company's lack of discriminatory intent is suggested by special efforts to help the undereducated employees through Company financing of two-thirds the cost of tuition for high school training. But Congress directed the thrust of the Act to the *consequences* of employment practices, not simply the motivation. More than that, Congress has placed on the employer the burden of showing that any given requirement must have a manifest relationship to the employment in question.

The facts of this case demonstrate the inadequacy of broad and general testing devices as well as the infirmity of using diplomas or degrees as fixed measures of capability. History is filled with examples of men and women who rendered highly effective performance without the conventional badges of accomplishment in terms of certificates, diplomas, or degrees. Diplomas and tests are useful servants, but Congress has mandated the commonsense proposition that they are not to become masters of reality.

The Company contends that its general intelligence tests are specifically permitted by § 703 (h) of the Act. That section authorizes the use of "any professionally developed ability test" that is not "designed, intended *or used* to discriminate because of race . . . ." (Emphasis added.)

The Equal Employment Opportunity Commission, having enforcement responsibility, has issued guidelines interpreting § 703 (h) to permit only the use of job-related tests. The administrative interpretation of the Act by the enforcing agency is entitled to great deference. See, *e. g., United States v. City of Chicago,* 400 U. S. 8 (1970); *Udall v. Tallman,* 380 U. S. 1 (1965); *Power Reactor Co. v. Electricians,* 367 U. S. 396 (1961). Since the Act and its legislative history support the Commission's construction, this affords good reason to treat the guidelines as expressing the will of Congress.

Section 703 (h) was not contained in the House version of the Civil Rights Act but was added in the Senate during extended debate. For a period, debate revolved around claims that the bill as proposed would prohibit all testing and force employers to hire unqualified persons simply because they were part of a group formerly subject to job discrimination. Proponents of Title VII sought throughout the debate to assure the critics that the Act would have no effect on job-related tests. Senators Case of New Jersey and Clark of Pennsylvania, comanagers of the bill on the Senate floor, issued a memorandum explaining that the proposed Title VII "expressly protects the employer's right to insist that any prospective applicant, Negro or white, *must meet the applicable job qualifications.* Indeed, the very purpose of Title VII is to promote hiring on the basis of job qualifications, rather than on the basis of race or color." 110 Cong. Rec. 7247. (Emphasis added.) Despite these assurances, Senator

Tower of Texas introduced an amendment authorizing "professionally developed ability tests." Proponents of Title VII opposed the amendment because, as written, it would permit an employer to give any test, "whether it was a good test or not, so long as it was professionally designed. Discrimination could actually exist under the guise of compliance with the statute." 110 Cong. Rec. 13504 (remarks of Sen. Case).

The amendment was defeated and two days later Senator Tower offered a substitute amendment which was adopted verbatim and is now the testing provision of § 703 (h). Speaking for the supporters of Title VII, Senator Humphrey, who had vigorously opposed the first amendment, endorsed the substitute amendment, stating: "Senators on both sides of the aisle who were deeply interested in Title VII have examined the text of this amendment and have found it to be in accord with the intent and purpose of that title." 110 Cong. Rec. 13724. The amendment was then adopted. From the sum of the legislative history relevant in this case, the conclusion is inescapable that the EEOC's construction of § 703 (h) to require that employment tests be job related comports with congressional intent.

Nothing in the Act precludes the use of testing or measuring procedures; obviously they are useful. What Congress has forbidden is giving these devices and mechanisms controlling force unless they are demonstrably a reasonable measure of job performance. Congress has not commanded that the less qualified be preferred over the better qualified simply because of minority origins. Far from disparaging job qualifications as such, Congress has made such qualifications the controlling factor, so that race, religion, nationality, and sex become irrelevant. What Congress has commanded is that any tests used must measure the person for the job and not the person in the abstract.

The judgment of the Court of Appeals is, as to that portion of the judgment appealed from, reversed.

MR. JUSTICE BRENNAN took no part in the consideration or decision of this case.

NOTES:

(1) In *Gregory v. Litton Systems, Inc.,* 472 F.2d 631, 5 FEP Cas. 267 (9th Cir. 1972), it was held that an employer's use of arrest records as an employment criterion may be unlawful under Title VII if the use of such records is not shown to be job related and the employment practice has an adverse discriminatory impact on racial minorities. In a similar ruling, in *Johnson v. Pike Corp. of America,* 332 F. Supp. 490, 495 (C.D. Cal. 1971), the court, in considering the

legality of a dismissal of a Black employee who had an excessive number of wage garnishments, stated:

> Where the discrimination shown results, not from disparate treatment, but from the foreseeable effect of a policy neutral on its face, *Griggs* indicates that under some circumstances the policy may be justified by a showing of "business necessity." Such a showing is an affirmative defense on which the defendant has the burden of proof. In the present case, defendant corporation has argued that Rule 6 is justified on a number of grounds. Specifically, the defendant has argued that the dismissal policy is justified because of the expense and time attendant to responding to attachments and garnishments by various sections of the company's management and clerical staffs, because of the annoyance and time involved in answering letters and telephone calls from its employees' creditors, and, finally, because garnishments result in a loss of efficiency on behalf of the employee whose wages have been garnisheed.

> The exact boundaries and contours of the phrase "business necessity" are still uncertain. The court, in Local 189, United Papermakers and Paperworkers v. United States, *supra,* stated that the policy or practice must be "essential to the safe and efficient operation" of the business. 416 F.2d at 989. In *Griggs,* the Court stated that a permissible practice must be one which can be shown to be "related to job performance" or "measuring job capability."

> If the defendant's justifications of Rule 6 are examined in light of the Supreme Court's definition of business necessity, they are not sufficient. The sole permissible reason for discriminating against actual or prospective employees involves the individual's capability to perform the job effectively. This approach leaves no room for arguments regarding inconvenience, annoyance or even expense to the employer. While the argument that wage garnishment results in a loss of efficiency by the employee is entitled to consideration, the court cannot correlate wage garnishment with work efficiency. Certainly the argument that an employee whose wages are being partially withheld for the benefit of his creditors will apply himself less enthusiastically to his work is at its best only speculative. If he is an unproductive worker, he may be terminated because he is unproductive, but not for a supposedly causal relationship which has the effect of being racially discriminatory.

> It might be argued that *Griggs* should not be followed since the question whether business necessity includes expense and inconvenience to the employer was not presented to the Supreme Court. While there may be in many situations a clear

distinction between business necessity relating to job capability and business necessity relating to the employer's expense and inconvenience, it is submitted that the Court in *Griggs* intended the definition therein outlined to be exclusive. The Court liberally construed Title VII in order to implement the congressional directive that members of minority groups be insured equal opportunity in employment. All attempts to depart from this mandate must be carefully scrutinized. The Court has stated that the only permissible reason for tolerating discrimination is "business necessity" which is "related to job performance." The ability of the individual effectively and efficiently to carry out his assigned duties is, therefore, the only justification recognized by the law.

See also *Wallace v. Debron Corp.,* 494 F. 2d 674 (8th Cir. 1974).

(2) A widely followed test for determining "business necessity" was delineated by the court in *Robinson v. Lorillard Corp.,* 444 F.2d 791 (4th Cir. 1971). There it was held that:

The test is whether there exists an overriding legitimate business purpose such that the practice is necessary to the safe and efficient operation of the business. Thus, the business purpose must be sufficiently compelling to override any racial impact; the challenged practice must effectively carry out the business purpose it is alleged to serve; and there must be available no acceptable alternative policies or practices which would better accomplish the business purpose advanced, or accomplish it equally well with a lesser differential racial impact.

(3) Some scholars have criticized the expanded application of this rigid business necessity test to cover "pure effects" discrimination cases. In Lopatka, *A Primer on the Federal Regulation of Employment Discrimination,* 1977 Ill. L. F. 69, 85-86, the author rejects the holdings in *Johnson v. Pike Corp. of America* and *Wallace v. Debron* with the following comment:

The courts read the job-relatedness requirement of *Griggs,* which was enunciated as a touchstone for education requirements and employment tests, to mean that an employer may use an increase in efficiency to justify a practice only if the increase was related to the ability of an employee to carry out his assigned duties. Because the employer's administrative expense and inconvenience in responding to garnishments was unrelated to the garnisheed employees' job performance, the courts refused even to consider the employer's administrative expense and inconvenience. Thus, the only argument the courts would consider was that garnishments result in the loss of employee efficiency. One court dismissed this argument as speculative, but the other court remanded the case for a factual determination. The arbitrary refusal of these courts to consider an employee's total productivity, which includes not only his performance on the job but also other costs to his employer, is difficult to justify. If expanded, this approach, for example, might require an employer to subsidize travel costs of minority employees from their urban homes to the employer's suburban plant.

Is this a valid criticism?

(4) *Problems*: In light of *Griggs* and the other cases discussed above, how would you answer the following questions:

(a) Can an employer refuse to hire a Black job applicant for a sales job in an all-White neighborhood if it is well known that most of the White residents have a strong bias against Blacks?

(b) Can an employer fire a Black salesperson who is assigned to an all-White neighborhood and is unable to meet company sales quotas due to race bias within the neighborhood?

(c) An employer has a policy of rejecting any applicants who have been convicted of anything more serious than a minor traffic offense. Is this a violation of Title VII, since the practice disqualifies disproportionately more Black applicants than White applicants and is not justified by business necessity? Green v. Missouri Pac. R. R., 523 F.2d 1290 (8th Cir. 1975).

(d) If the *substantive* provisions of Title VII do indeed apply to government employees, is there any reason why a government employee would bring a charge of employment discrimination now under the Fifth or Fourteenth Amendments after the Supreme Court decision in *Washington v. Davis, infra*? Is it fair to say that the substantive reach of Title VII is vastly greater than the constitutional guarantee of equal protection as defined in *Washington v. Davis*?

(5) Employees of the federal government may challenge employment discrimination only under § 717 of the Civil Rights Act of 1964, but they are entitled to a full trial de novo when they do so instead of a review of the administrative record. *Brown v. GSA*, 12 FEP Cas. 1361 (U.S. 1976); *Chandler v. Roudebush*, 12 FEP Cas. 1368 (U.S. 1976).

(6) In *Fitzpatrick v. Bitzer*, 96 S. Ct. 2666 (1976), the Court upheld the portion of the 1972 Amendments to Title VII which extended coverage of the Act to state employees. The Court ruled that Congress had properly acted to protect state employees from employment discrimination pursuant to Section 5 of the Fourteenth

Amendment. The Court then ruled that the Eleventh Amendment did not bar an award of retroactive retirement benefits and attorneys fees for individuals who proved that a state retirement system discriminated against them because of their sex. However, the Court noted in passing, in footnote 11, that "apart from their claim that the Eleventh Amendment bars enforcement of the remedy established by Title VII..., respondents do not contend that the substantive provisions of Title VII as applied here are not a proper exercise of congressional authority under § 5 of the Fourteenth Amendment." It is not clear whether the Court meant to suggest by this comment that such an argument might be entertained in the future.

2. EEOC Suits, Class Actions and Remedies Under Title VII

NOTES:

(1) In *Occidental Life Insurance Co. v. EEOC,* 97 S. Ct. 2447, 45 U.S.L.W. 4752 (1977), the Supreme Court ruled that federal law does not impose a 180-day limitation on the EEOC's authority to sue under Title VII. The Court also ruled that such actions by the EEOC are not governed by any State statute of limitations.

(2) In *East Texas Motor Freight System v. Rodriguez,* 97 S. Ct. 1891, 52 L. Ed. 2d 453 (1977), the Supreme Court held that the Court of Appeals erred in certifying as a class action a suit brought by three city truck drivers who alleged discrimination by their employer and the Teamsters Union in prohibiting transfer to "over-the-road" (line) jobs, because it was evident by the time the case reached the Court of Appeals that the three named plaintiffs lacked the qualifications to be hired as line drivers and hence were not members of the class they purported to represent. Furthermore, each named plaintiff stipulated that he had not been discriminated against with respect to his initial hire. In the light of that stipulation they were hardly in a position to mount a class-wide attack on the no-transfer rule and seniority system on the ground that these practices perpetuated past discrimination and locked minorities into the less desirable jobs to which they had been discriminatorily assigned. Two other indications that they would not "fairly and adequately protect the interests of the class" were (1) their failure to move for class certification prior to trial and (2) the conflict between their demand for a merger of the city and line-driver collective-bargaining units and a vote by members of the class rejecting such a merger. The judgment of the Court of Appeals was, accordingly, vacated.

(3) The Sixth Circuit is prepared to award back pay and retroactive seniority under Title VII to rejected job applicants, *Meadows v. Ford Motor Co.,* 510 F.2d 939 (6th Cir. 1975), but not punitive damages, *EEOC v. Detroit Edison Co.,* 515 F.2d 301 (6th Cir. 1975). The same court, in appropriate circumstances, would hold a successor employer liable for the Title VII violations of a predecessor. *EEOC v. MacMillan Bloedel Containers, Inc.,* 503 F.2d 1086 (6th Cir. 1974).

(4) The court in *Patterson v. American Tobacco Co.,* 535 F.2d 257 (4th Cir. 1976), *cert. denied,* 425 U.S. 944 (1976) said that in order to carry out the policies of the *Albemarle* case, *infra:*

> [B]ack pay must be allowed an employee from the time he is unlawfully denied a promotion, subject to the applicable statute of limitations, until he actually receives it. Some employees who have been victims of discrimination will be unable to move immediately into jobs to which their seniority and ability entitle them. The back pay award should be fashioned to compensate them until they can obtain a job commensurate with their status. This may be accomplished by allowing back pay for a period commencing at the time an employee was unlawfully denied a position until the date of judgment, subject to the applicable statute of limitations. This compensation should be supplemented by an award equal to the estimated present value of lost earnings that are reasonably likely to occur between the date of judgment and the time when the employee can assume his new position. . . . Alternatively, the court may exercise continuing jurisdiction over the case and make periodic back pay awards until the workers are promoted to the jobs their seniority and qualifications merit.

(5) The Supreme Court held, in *United Air Lines v. McDonald,* 14 FEP Cases 1711 (1977), that a stewardess who was a member of a putative class that a federal district court had refused to certify should have been allowed to intervene in a Title VII action, after entry of final judgment incorporating a settlement, for the purpose of taking an appeal challenging denial of class-action certification, even though the motion to intervene was filed nearly three years after the denial of certification, where the motion was filed within the time period in which persons who brought the action could have taken an appeal challenging denial of certification.

(6) As a remedy for past discriminatory practices and relying heavily upon *Franks, infra,* the Court of Appeals for the Third Circuit approved a consent decree which provided an "affirmative action override" as to promotions which would take precedence over the seniority provisions of the collective bargaining agreement. *EEOC v. American Telephone and Telegraph Co.,* 14 FEP Cases 1210 (3d

Cir. 1977). The court approved the decree even though it would give relief to minority persons and women who were not identifiable victims of specific past discrimination. The employer being a major government contractor, the consent decree rested both on Title VII of the Civil Rights Act and on Executive Order 11246.

How is the proper balance to be struck between the national labor policy in favor of collective bargaining agreements, including seniority, and the national policy in favor of eliminating the present effects of past discrimination? Consider the existing caselaw under the section dealing with "Preferential Remedies," *infra.*

B. UNDER SECTION 1981

McDONALD v. SANTA FE TRAIL TRANSPORTATION CO.

United States Supreme Court
427 U.S. 273, 96 S. Ct. 2574, 49 L. Ed. 2d 493 (1976)

MR. JUSTICE MARSHALL delivered the opinion of the Court.

Petitioners L. N. McDonald and Raymond L. Laird brought this action in the United States District Court for the Southern District of Texas seeking relief against Santa Fe Trail Transportation Co. (Santa Fe) and International Brotherhood of Teamsters Local 988 (Local 988), which represented Santa Fe's Houston employees, for alleged violations of the Civil Rights Act of 1866, 42 U. S. C. § 1981, and of Title VII of the Civil Rights Act of 1964, 42 U. S. C. § 2000e *et seq.,* in connection with their discharge from Santa Fe's employment. The District Court dismissed the complaint on the pleadings. The Court of Appeals for the Fifth Circuit affirmed. In determining whether the decisions of these courts were correct, we must decide, first, whether a complaint alleging that white employees charged with misappropriating property from their employer were dismissed from employment, while a black employee [Jackson] similarly charged was not dismissed, states a claim under Title VII. Second, we must decide whether § 1981, which provides that "[a]ll persons . . . shall have the same right . . . to make and enforce contracts . . . as is enjoyed by white citizens . . ." affords protection from racial discrimination in private employment to white persons as well as nonwhites.

I

. . . We reverse.

II

Title VII of the Civil Rights Act of 1964 prohibits the discharge of "any individual" because of "such individual's race," § 703(a)(1), 42 U. S. C. § 2000e-2(a)(1). Its terms are not limited to discrimination against members of any particular race. Thus, although we were not there confronted with racial discrimination against whites, we described the Act in *Griggs v. Duke Power Co.,* 401 U. S. 424, 431 (1971), as prohibiting "[d]iscriminatory preference for *any* [racial] group, *minority or majority"* (emphasis added). Similarly the EEOC, whose interpretations are entitled to great deference, *Griggs v. Duke Power Co.,* 401 U. S., at 433-434, has consistently interpreted Title VII to proscribe racial discrimination in private employment against whites on the same terms as racial discrimination against nonwhites, holding that to proceed otherwise would

> "constitute a dereliction of the Congressional mandate to eliminate all practices which operate to disadvantage the employment opportunities of any group protected by Title VII, including Caucasians." EEOC Decision No. 74-31, 7 FEP 1326, 1338 CCH EEOC Decisions ¶ 6406, p. 4084 (1973).

This conclusion is in accord with uncontradicted legislative history to the effect that Title VII was intended to "cover all white men and white women and all Americans," 110 Cong. Rec. 2579 (remarks of Rep. Celler) (1969), and create an "obligation not to discriminate against whites," *id.,* at 7218 (memorandum of Sen. Clark). See also *id.,* at 7213 (memorandum of Sens. Clark and Case); *id.,* at 8912 (remarks of Sen. Williams). We therefore hold today that Title VII prohibits racial discrimination against the white petitioners in this case upon the same standards as would be applicable were they Negroes and Jackson white.[8]

Respondents contend that, even though generally applicable to white persons, Title VII affords petitioners no protection in this case, because their dismissal was based upon their commission of a serious criminal offense against their employer. We think this argument is foreclosed by our decision in *McDonnell Douglas Corp. v. Green* [411 U.S. 792 (1973)]. . . . The Act prohibits *all* racial discrimination in employment, without exception for any group of particular employees, and while crime or other misconduct may be a legitimate basis for discharge, it is hardly one for racial discrimination. Indeed,

---

[8] . . . Santa Fe disclaims that the actions challenged here were any part of an affirmative action program, see Brief for Respondent Santa Fe, at 19 n. 5, and we emphasize that we do not consider here the permissibility of such a program, whether judicially required or otherwise prompted. . . .

the Title VII plaintiff in *McDonnell Douglas* had been convicted for a non-trivial offense against his former employer. It may be that theft of property entrusted to an employer for carriage is a more compelling basis for discharge than obstruction of an employer's traffic arteries, but this does not diminish the illogic in retaining guilty employees of one color while discharging those of another color.

At this stage of the litigation the claim against Local 983 must go with the claim against Santa Fe, for in substance the complaint alleges that the Union shirked its duty properly to represent McDonald, but instead "acquiesced and/or joined in" Santa Fe's alleged racial discrimination against him. Local 988 argues that as a matter of law it should not be subject to liability under Title VII in a situation, such as this, where some but not all culpable employees are ultimately discharged on account of joint misconduct, because in representing all the affected employees in their relations with the employer, the Union may necessarily have to compromise by securing retention of only some. We reject the argument. The same reasons which prohibit an employer from discriminating on the basis of race among the culpable employees apply equally to the Union; and whatever factors the mechanisms of compromise may legitimately take into account in mitigating discipline of some employees, under Title VII race may not be among them.

Thus, we conclude that the District Court erred in dismissing both petitioners' Title VII claims against Santa Fe, and petitioner McDonald's Title VII claim against Local 988.

III

Title 42 U. S. C. § 1981 provides in pertinent part that "[a]ll persons within the jurisdiction of the United States shall have the same right in every State and Territory to make and enforce contracts . . . as is enjoyed by white citizens . . . ." We have previously held, where discrimination against Negroes was in question, that § 1981 affords a federal remedy against discrimination in private employment on the basis of race, and respondents do not contend otherwise. *Johnson v. Railway Express Agency,* 421 U. S. 454, 459-460 (1975). See also *Runyon v. McCrary,* 427 U.S. 160 (1976); *Jones v. Alfred H. Mayer Co.,* 392 U. S. 409 (1968). The question here is whether § 1981 prohibits racial discrimination in private employment against whites as well as nonwhites.

While neither of the courts below elaborated its reasons for not applying § 1981 to racial discrimination against white persons, respondents suggest two lines of argument to support that judgment. First, they argue that by operation of the phrase "as is enjoyed by white citizens," § 1981 unambiguously limits itself to the protection of nonwhite persons against racial discrimination. Second, they contend that such a reading is consistent with the legislative history of the provision, which derives its operative language from § 1 of the Civil Rights Act of 1866, Act of April 9, 1866, c. 31, § 1, 14 Stat. 27. See *Runyon v. McCrary, Tillman v. Wheaton-Haven Recreation Assn.,* 410 U.S. 431, 439 (1973). The 1866 statute, they assert, was concerned predominantly with assuring specified civil rights to the former Negro slaves freed by virtue of the Thirteenth Amendment, and not at all with protecting corresponding civil rights of white persons.

We find neither argument persuasive. Rather, our examination of the language and history of § 1981 convinces us that § 1981 is applicable to racial discrimination in private employment against white persons.

First, we cannot accept the view that the terms of § 1981 exclude its application to racial discrimination against white persons. On the contrary, the statute explicitly applies to "*all* persons" (emphasis added), including white persons. See, *e.g., United States v. Wong Kim Ark,* 169 U. S. 649, 675-676 (1898). While a mechanical reading of the phrase "as is enjoyed by white citizens" would seem to lend support to respondents' reading of the statute, we have previously described this phrase simply as emphasizing "the racial character of the rights being protected," *Georgia v. Rachel,* 384 U. S. 780, 791 (1966). In any event, whatever ambiguity there may be in the language of § 1981 ... is clarified by an examination of the legislative history of § 1981's language as it was originally forged in the Civil Rights Act of 1866.

[The court then made a detailed examination of the legislative history of the 1866 act.]

This cumulative evidence of congressional intent makes clear, we think, that the 1866 statute, designed to protect the "same right . . . to make and enforce contracts" of "citizens of every race and color" was not understood or intended to be reduced by Congressman Wilson's amendment, or any other provision, to the protection solely of nonwhites. Rather, the Act was meant, by its broad terms, to proscribe discrimination in the making or enforcement of contracts against, or in favor of, any race. Unlikely as it might have appeared in 1866 that white citizens would encounter substantial racial discrimination of the sort proscribed under the Act, the statutory structure and legislative history persuades us that the Thirty-ninth Congress was intent upon establishing in the federal law a broader principle than would have been necessary simply to meet the particular and immediate plight of the newly freed Negro slaves. And while the statutory language has been somewhat streamlined in reenactment and codification, there is no indication that § 1981 is intended to provide any less than the Congress enacted in 1866 regarding racial discrimination against white persons. *Runyon v. McCrary*. Thus, we conclude that the District Court erred in dismissing petitioners' claims under § 1981 on the ground that the protection of that provision are [is] unavailable to white persons.

The judgment of the Court of Appeals for the Fifth Circuit is reversed, and the case is remanded for further proceedings consistent with this opinion.

So ordered.

MR. JUSTICE WHITE and MR. JUSTICE REHNQUIST join Parts I and II of the Court's opinion, but for the reasons stated in MR. JUSTICE WHITE's dissenting opinion in *Runyon v. McCrary*, 427 U.S. 160 (1976), cannot join Part III since they do not agree that § 1981 is applicable in this case. To that extent they dissent.

NOTES:

(1) In general, the courts have held that § 1981 prohibits discrimination based on race or alienage, but not discrimination based on sex. *See, e.g., Guerra v. Manchester Terminal Corp.,* 498 F.2d 641 (5th Cir. 1974) (unlike Title VII, § 1981 can be used to remedy employment discrimination against aliens); *League of Academic Women v. Regents of University of California,* 343 F. Supp. 636 (N.D. Cal. 1972) (Congress did not intend § 1981 to cover sex discrimination). Several courts have permitted an action to be brought under § 1981 on the basis of national origin where the plaintiff is Spanish surnamed, but have usually denied such actions where other national origins are involved. *See, e.g., Sabala v. Western Gillette, Inc.,* 516 F.2d 1251 (5th Cir. 1975) (protection extended to Mexican-Americans); *Maldonado v. Broadcast Plaza, Inc.,* 10 FEP Cas. 839 (D. Conn. 1974) (protection extended to Puerto Ricans); *Budinsky v. Corning Glass Works,* 425 F. Supp. 786 (D. Pa. 1977) (protection denied to plaintiff of Slavic origin).

(2) Because the Civil Rights Act of 1866 contains no federal statute of limitations, the Supreme Court has held that federal district courts should apply the most appropriate state statute, except in those cases where such application would be inconsistent with the federal policy underlying § 1981. *Johnson v. Railway Express Agency,* 421 U.S. 454 (1975). For a method of determining which state statute is most appropriate, *see Shaw v. Garrison,* 545 F.2d 980 (5th Cir. 1977). Does the application of state law encourage "forum shopping" by plaintiffs bringing an action under § 1981?

(3) In *Johnson v. Railway Express Agency, supra,* the Court also held that the remedies available under § 1981 and under Title VII are "separate, distinct and independent." Because § 1981 does not have the burdensome procedural requirements of Title VII, it may

afford relief in cases where the statute of limitations under Title VII has run, where there are fewer than fifteen employees, or in other instances where the action might be barred under Title VII.

C. UNDER THE CONSTITUTION OF THE UNITED STATES

WASHINGTON v. DAVIS

United States Supreme Court
426 U.S. 229, 96 S. Ct. 2040 (1976)

MR. JUSTICE WHITE delivered the opinion of the Court.

This case involves the validity of a qualifying test administered to applicants for positions as police officers in the District of Columbia Metropolitan Police Department. The test was sustained by the District Court but invalidated by the Court of Appeals. We are in agreement with the District Court and hence reverse the judgment of the Court of Appeals.

I

This action began on April 10, 1970, when two Negro police officers filed suit against the then Commissioner of the District of Columbia, the Chief of the District's Metropolitan Police Department and the Commissioner of the United States Civil Service Commission. An amended complaint, filed December 10, alleged that the promotion policies of the Department were racially discriminatory and sought a declaratory judgment and an injunction. The respondents Harley and Sellers were permitted to intervene, their amended complaint asserting that their applications to become officers in the Department had been rejected, and that the Department's recruiting procedures discriminated on the basis of race against black applicants by a series of practices including, but not limited to, a written personnel test which excluded a disproportionately high number of Negro applicants. These practices were asserted to violate respondents' rights "under the due process clause of the Fifth Amendment to the United States Constitution, under 42 U. S. C. § 1981 and under D. C. Code § 1-320."

According to the findings and conclusions of the District Court, to be accepted by the Department and to enter an intensive 17-week training program, the police recruit was required to satisfy certain physical and character standards, to be a high school graduate or its equivalent and to receive a grade of at least 40 on "Test 21," which is "an examination that is used generally throughout the federal service," which "was developed by the Civil Service Commission not the Police Department" and which was "designed to test verbal ability, vocabulary, reading and comprehension." 348 F. Supp., at 16.

The validity of Test 21 was the sole issue before the court on the motions for summary judgment. The District Court noted that there was no claim of "an intentional discrimination or purposeful discriminatory actions" but only a claim that Test 21 bore no relationship to job performance and "has a highly discriminatory impact in screening out black candidates." 348 F. Supp., at 16. Petitioners' evidence, the District Court said, warranted three conclusions: "(a) The number of black police officers, while substantial, is not proportionate to the population mix of the city. (b) A higher percentage of blacks fail the Test than whites. (c) The Test has not been validated to establish its reliability for measuring subsequent job performance." *Ibid.* This showing was deemed sufficient to shift the burden of proof to the defendants in the action, petitioners here; but the court nevertheless concluded that on the undisputed facts, respondents were not entitled to relief. The District Court relied on several factors. Since August 1969, 44% of the new police force recruits had been black; that figure also represented a proportion of blacks on the total force and was roughly equivalent to 20-29-year-old blacks in the 50-mile radius in which the recruiting efforts of the Police Department had been concentrated. It was undisputed that the Department had systematically and affirmatively sought to enroll black officers many of whom passed the test but failed to report for duty. The District Court rejected the assertion that Test 21 was culturally slanted to favor whites and was "satisfied that the undisputable facts prove the test to be reasonably and directly related to the requirements of the police recruit training program and that it is neither so designed nor operated to discriminate against otherwise qualified blacks."

. . .

Having lost on both constitutional and statutory issues in the District Court, respondents brought the case to the Court of Appeals claiming that their summary judgment motion, which rested on purely constitutional grounds, should have been granted. The tendered constitutional issue was whether the use of Test 21 invidiously discriminated against Negroes and hence denied them due process of law contrary to the commands of the Fifth Amendment. The Court of Appeals, addressing that issue, announced that it would be guided by Griggs v. Duke Power Co., 401 U.S. 424 (1971), a case involving the interpretation and application of Title VII of the Civil Rights Act of 1964, and held that the statutory standards elucidated in that case were to govern the due process question tendered in this one. 168 U. S. App. D. C. 42, 512 F. 2d 956 (1975). The court went on to declare that lack of discriminatory intent in designing and administering Test 21 was irrelevant; the critical fact was rather that a far greater proportion of blacks — four times as many — failed the test than did whites. This disproportionate impact, standing alone and without regard to whether it indicated a discriminatory purpose, was held sufficient to establish a constitutional violation, absent proof by petitioners that the test was an adequate measure of job performance in addition to being an indicator of probable success in the training program, a burden which the court ruled petitioners had failed to discharge. That the Department had made substantial efforts to recruit blacks was held beside the point and the fact that the racial distribution of recent hirings and of the Department itself might be roughly equivalent to the racial makeup of the surrounding community, broadly conceived, was put aside as a "comparison [not] material to this appeal.". . .

II

Because the Court of Appeals erroneously applied the legal standards applicable to Title VII cases in resolving the constitutional issue before it, we reverse its judgment in respondents' favor. Although the petition for certiorari did not present this ground for reversal, our Rule 40(1)(d)(2) provides that we "may notice a plain error not presented"; and this is an appropriate occasion to invoke the rule.

As the Court of Appeals understood Title VII,[10] employees or applicants proceeding under it need not concern themselves with the employer's possibly discriminatory purpose but instead may focus solely on the racially differential impact of the challenged hiring or promotion practices. This is not the constitutional rule. We have never held that the constitutional standard for adjudicating claims of invidious racial discrimination is identical to the standards applicable under Title VII, and we decline to do so today.

The central purpose of the Equal Protection Clause of the Fourteenth Amendment is the prevention of official conduct discriminating on the basis of race. It is also true that the Due Process Clause of the Fifth Amendment contains an equal protection component prohibiting the United States from invidiously

[10] Although Title VII standards have dominated this case, the statute was not applicable to federal employees when the complaint was filed, and although the 1972 amendments extending the title to reach government employees were adopted prior to the District Court's judgment, the complaint was not amended to state a claim under that title, nor did the case thereafter proceed as a Title VII case. Respondents' motion for partial summary judgment, filed after the 1972 amendments, rested solely on constitutional grounds; and the Court of Appeals ruled that the motion should have been granted. . . .

discriminating between individuals or groups. Bolling v. Sharpe, 347 U.S. 497 (1954). But our cases have not embraced the proposition that a law or other official act, without regard to whether it reflects a racially discriminatory purpose, is unconstitutional solely because it has a racially disproportionate impact.

. . . . Wright v. Rockefeller, 376 U.S. 52 (1964), upheld a New York congressional apportionment statute against claims that district lines had been racially gerrymandered. The challenged districts were made up predominantly of whites or of minority races, and their boundaries were irregularly drawn. The challengers did not prevail because they failed to prove that the New York legislature "was either motivated by racial considerations or in fact drew the districts on racial lines"; the plaintiffs had not shown that the statute "was the product of a state contrivance to segregate on the basis of race or place of origin." 376 U.S., at 56, 58. The dissenters were in agreement that the issue was whether the "boundaries . . . were purposefully drawn on racial lines." 376 U.S., at 67.

The school desegregation cases have also adhered to the basic equal protection principle that the invidious quality of a law claimed to be racially discriminatory must ultimately be traced to a racially discriminatory purpose. That there are both predominantly black and predominantly white schools in a community is not alone violative of the Equal Protection Clause. The essential element of *de jure* segregation is "a current condition of segregation resulting from intentional state action . . . the differentiating factor between *de jure* segregation and so-called *de facto* segregation . . . is *purpose* or *intent* to segregate." Keyes v. School District No. 1, 413 U.S. 189, 205, 208 (1973). See also *id.,* at 199, 211, 213. The Court has also recently rejected allegations of racial discrimination based solely on the statistically disproportionate racial impact of various provisions of the Social Security Act because "the acceptance of appellant's constitutional theory would render suspect each difference in treatment among the grant classes, however lacking the racial motivation and however rational the treatment might be." Jefferson v. Hackney, 406 U.S. 535, 548 (1972).

This is not to say that the necessary discriminatory racial purpose must be express or appear on the face of the statute, or that a law's disproportionate impact is irrelevant in cases involving Constitution-based claims of racial discrimination. A statute, otherwise neutral on its face, must not be applied so as invidiously to discriminate on the basis of race. Yick Wo v. Hopkins, 118 U.S. 356 (1886). It is also clear from the cases dealing with racial discrimination in the selection of juries that the systematic exclusion of Negroes is itself such an "unequal application of the law . . . as to show intentional discrimination." *Akins v. Texas, supra,* at 404. Smith v. Texas, 311 U.S. 128 (1940); Pierre v. Louisiana, 306 U.S.

354 (1939); Neal v. Delaware, 103 U.S. 370 (1881). . . . With a prima facie case made out, "the burden of proof shifts to the State to rebut the presumption of unconstitutional action by showing that permissible racially neutral selection criteria and procedures have produced the monochromatic result." [citing cases.]

Necessarily, an invidious discriminatory purpose may often be inferred from the totality of the relevant facts, including the fact, if it is true, that the law bears more heavily on one race than another. It is also not infrequently true that the discriminatory impact — in the jury cases for example, the total or seriously disproportionate exclusion of Negroes from jury venires — may for all practical purposes demonstrate unconstitutionality because in various circumstances the discrimination is very difficult to explain on nonracial grounds. Nevertheless, we have not held that a law, neutral on its face and serving ends otherwise within the power of government to pursue, is invalid under the Equal Protection Clause simply because it may affect a greater proportion of one race than of another. Disproportionate impact is not irrelevant, but it is not the sole touchstone of an invidious racial discrimination forbidden by the Constitution. Standing alone, it does not trigger the rule. McLaughlin v. Florida, 379 U.S. 184 (1964), that racial classifications are to be subjected to the strictest scrutiny and are justifiable only by the weightiest of considerations.

[Here follows a discussion of Palmer v. Thompson, 403 U.S. 217 (1971), and Wright v. Council of the City of Emporia, 407 U.S. 451 (1972), which indicate that in certain circumstances racial impact of a law, rather than discriminatory purpose, may be the critical factor invalidating the law.]

Both before and after *Palmer v. Thompson,* however, various Courts of Appeals have held in several contexts, including public employment, that the substantially disproportionate racial impact of a statute or official practice standing alone and without regard to discriminatory purpose, suffices to prove racial discrimination violating the Equal Protection Clause absent some justification going substantially beyond what would be necessary to validate most other legislative classifications. The cases impressively demonstrate that there is another side to the issue; but, with all due respect, to the extent that those cases rested on or expressed the view that proof of discriminatory racial purpose is unnecessary in making out an equal protection violation, we are in disagreement.

As an initial matter, we have difficulty understanding how a law establishing a racially neutral qualification for employment is nevertheless racially discriminatory and denies "any person equal protection of the laws" simply because a greater proportion of Negroes fail to qualify than members of other racial or ethnic groups. Had respondents, along with all others who had failed Test 21, whether white or black, brought an action claiming that the test denied each of them equal protection of the laws as compared with those who had passed with high enough scores to qualify them as police recruits, it is most unlikely that their challenge would have been sustained. Test 21, which is administered generally to prospective government employees, concededly seeks to ascertain whether those who take it have acquired a particular level of verbal skill; and it is untenable that the Constitution prevents the government from seeking modestly to upgrade the communicative abilities of its employees rather than to be satisfied with some lower level of competence, particularly where the job requires special ability to communicate orally and in writing. Respondents, as Negroes, could no more successfully claim that the test denied them equal protection than could white applicants who also failed. The conclusion would not be different in the face of proof that more Negroes than whites had been disqualified by Test 21. That other Negroes also failed to score well would, alone, not demonstrate that respondents individually were being denied equal protection of the laws by the application of an otherwise valid qualifying test being administered to prospective police recruits.

Nor on the facts of the case before us would the disproportionate impact of Test 21 warrant the conclusion that it is a purposeful device to discriminate against Negroes and hence an infringement of the constitutional rights of respondents as well as other black applicants. As we have said, the test is neutral on its face and rationally may be said to serve a purpose the government is constitutionally empowered to pursue. Even agreeing with the District Court that the differential racial effect of Test 21 called for further inquiry, we think the District Court correctly held that the affirmative efforts of the Metropolitan Police Department to recruit black officers, the changing racial composition of the recruit classes and of the force in general, and the relationship of the test to the training program negated any inference that the Department discriminated on the basis of race or that "a police officer qualifies on the color of his skin rather than ability." 348 F. Supp., at 18.

Under Title VII, Congress provided that when hiring and promotion practices disqualifying substantially disproportionate numbers of blacks are challenged, discriminatory purpose need not be proved, and that it is an insufficient response to demonstrate some rational basis for the challenged practices. It is necessary, in addition, that they be "validated" in terms of job performance in any one of several ways, perhaps by ascertaining the minimum skill, ability or potential necessary for the position at issue and determining whether the qualifying tests are appropriate for the selection of qualified applicants for the job in question. However this process proceeds, it involves a more probing judicial review of, and less deference to, the seemingly reasonable acts of administrators and executives than is appropriate under the Constitution where special racial impact, without discriminatory purpose, is claimed. We are not disposed to adopt this more rigorous standard for the purposes of applying the Fifth and the Fourteenth Amendments in cases such as this.

A rule that a statute designed to serve neutral ends is nevertheless invalid, absent compelling justification, if in practice it benefits or burdens one race more than another would be far reaching and would raise serious questions about, and perhaps invalidate, a whole range of tax, welfare, public service, regulatory, and licensing statutes that may be more burdensome to the poor and to the average black than to the more affluent white.

Given that rule, such consequences would perhaps be likely to follow. However, in our view, extension of the rule beyond those areas where it is already applicable by reason of statute, such as in the field of public employment, should await legislative prescription. . . .

III

We also hold that the Court of Appeals should have affirmed the judgment of the District Court granting the motions for summary judgment filed by petitioners and the federal parties. Respondents were entitled to relief on neither constitutional nor statutory grounds.

The District Court . . . assumed that Title VII standards were to control the case, identified the determinative issue as whether Test 21 was sufficiently job related and proceeded to uphold use of the test because it was "directly related to a determination of whether the applicant possesses sufficient skills requisite to the demands of the curriculum a recruit must master at the police academy." 348 F. Supp., at 17. The Court of Appeals reversed because the relationship between Test 21 and training school success, if demonstrated at all, did not satisfy what it deemed to be the crucial requirement of a direct relationship between performance on Test 21 and performance on the policeman's job.

We agree with petitioners and the federal parties that this was error. The advisability of the police recruit training course informing the recruit about his upcoming job, acquainting him with its demands, and attempting to impart a modicum of required skills seems conceded. It is also apparent to us, as it was to the District Judge, that some minimum verbal and communicative skill would be very useful, if not essential, to satisfactory progress in the training regimen. Based on the evidence before him, the District Judge concluded that Test 21 was directly related to the requirements of the police training program and that a positive relationship between the test and training-course performance was sufficient to validate the former, wholly aside from its possible relationship to actual performance as a police officer. This conclusion of the District Judge that training-program validation may itself be sufficient is supported by regulations of the Civil Service Commission, by the opinion evidence placed before the District Judge, and by the current views of the Civil Service Commissioners who were parties to the case. Nor is the conclusion foreclosed by either *Griggs* or *Albemarle Paper Co. v. Moody,* 422 U. S. 405 (1975); and it seems to us the much more sensible construction of the job-relatedness requirement.

The District Court's accompanying conclusion that Test 21 was in fact directly related to the requirements of the police training program was supported by a validation study, as well as by other evidence of record; and we are not convinced that this conclusion was erroneous.

The federal parties, whose views have somewhat changed since the decision of the Court of Appeals and who still insist that training-program validation is sufficient, now urge a remand to the District Court for the purpose of further inquiry into whether the training-program test scores, which were found to correlate with Test 21 scores, are themselves an appropriate measure of the trainee's mastership of the material taught in the course and whether the training program itself is sufficiently related to actual performance of the police officer's task. We think a remand is inappropriate. The District Court's judgment was warranted by the record before it, and we perceive no good reason to reopen it, particularly since we were informed at oral argument that although Test 21 is still being administered, the training program itself has undergone substantial modification in the course of this litigation. If there are now deficiencies in the recruiting practices under prevailing Title VII standards, those deficiencies are to be directly addressed in accordance with appropriate procedures mandated under that Title.

The judgment of the Court of Appeals accordingly is reversed.

MR. JUSTICE STEVENS, concurring.

While I agree with the Court's disposition of this case, I add these comments on the constitutional issue discussed in Part II and the statutory issue discussed in Part III of the Court's opinion.

The requirement of purposeful discrimination is a common thread running through the cases summarized in Part II. These cases include criminal convictions which were set aside because blacks were excluded from the grand jury, a reapportionment case in which political boundaries were obviously influenced to some extent by racial considerations, a school desegregation case, and a case involving the unequal administration of an ordinance purporting to prohibit the operation of laundries in frame buildings. Although it may be proper to use the same language to describe the constitutional claim in each of these contexts, the burden of proving a prima facie case may well involve differing evidentiary considerations. The extent of deference that one pays to the trial court's determination of the factual issue, and indeed, the extent to which one characterizes the intent issue as a question of fact or a question of law, will vary in different contexts.

Frequently the most probative evidence of intent will be objective evidence of what actually happened rather than evidence describing the subjective state of mind of the actor. For normally the actor is presumed to have intended the natural consequences of his deeds. This is particularly true in the case of governmental action which is frequently the product of compromise, of collective decisionmaking, and of mixed motivation. It is unrealistic, on the one hand, to require the victim of alleged discrimination to uncover the actual subjective intent of the decisionmaker or, conversely, to invalidate otherwise legitimate action simply because an improper motive affected the deliberation of a participant in the decisional process. A law conscripting clerics should not be invalidated because an atheist voted for it.

My point in making this observation is to suggest that the line between discriminatory purpose and discriminatory impact is not nearly as bright, and perhaps not quite as critical, as the reader of the Court's opinion might assume. I agree, of course, that a constitutional issue does not arise every time some disproportionate impact is shown. On the other hand, when the disproportion is as dramatic as in *Gomillion* or *Yick Wo,* it really does not matter whether the standard is phrased in terms of purpose or effect. Therefore, although I accept the statement of the general rule in the Court's opinion, I am not yet prepared to indicate how that standard should be applied in the many cases which have formulated the governing standard in different language.

My agreement with the conclusion reached in Part II of the Court's opinion rests on a ground narrower than the Court describes. I do not rely at all on the evidence of good-faith efforts to recruit black police officers. In my judgment, neither those efforts nor the subjective good faith of the District administration, would save Test 21 if it were otherwise invalid.

There are two reasons why I am convinced that the challenge to Test 21 is insufficient. First, the test serves the neutral and legitimate purpose of requiring all applicants to meet a uniform minimum standard of literacy. Reading ability is manifestly relevant to the police function, there is no evidence that the required passing grade was set at an arbitrarily high level, and there is sufficient disparity among high schools and high school graduates to justify the use of a separate uniform test. Second, the same test is used throughout the federal service. The applicants for employment in the District of Columbia Police Department represent such a small fraction of the total number of persons who have taken the test that their experience is of minimal probative value in assessing the neutrality of the test itself. That evidence, without more, is not sufficient to overcome the presumption that a test which is this widely used by the Federal Government is in fact neutral in its effect as well as its "purpose" as that term is used in constitutional adjudication.

My study of the statutory issue leads me to the same conclusion reached by the Court in Part III of its opinion. . . .

NOTES:

(1) Although *Washington v. Davis* involved a claim under the Due Process Clause of the Fifth Amendment, a large number of constitutional claims of employment discrimination have been brought by state or local government employees under the Civil Rights Act of 1871, 42 U.S.C.A. § 1983. *See, e.g., Johnson v. Branch,* 364 F.2d 177 (4th Cir. 1966). Section 1983 states that:

> Every person who, under color of any statute, ordinance, regulation, custom, or usage, or any State or Territory, subjects, or causes to be subjected, any citizen of the United States or other person within the jurisdiction thereof to the deprivation of any rights, privileges, or immunities secured by the Constitution and laws, shall be liable to the party injured in an action at law, suit in equity, or other proper proceeding for redress.

(2) In *Monell v. Department of Social Services,* 17 FEP Cas. 873 (1978), the Supreme Court ruled that municipalities, school boards and other local government units are "persons" within the meaning of § 1983 and, thus, may be sued for monetary, declaratory or injunctive relief thereunder. The decision in *Monell* overturns the Court's 1961 decision to the contrary in *Monroe v. Pape,* 365 U.S. 167.

In defining the potential liability of governmental units, the Court in *Monell* stated that:

> Our analysis of the legislative history of the Civil Rights Act of 1871 compels the conclusion that Congress *did* intend municipalities and other local government units to be included among those persons to whom § 1983 applies.[54] Local

---

[54] There is certainly no constitutional impediment to municipal liability. "The Tenth Amendment's reservation of nondelegated powers to the State is not implicated by a federal-court judgment enforcing the express prohibitions of unlawful state conduct enacted by the Fourteenth Amendment." Milliken v. Bradley,

governing bodies,[55] therefore, can be sued directly under § 1983 for monetary, declaratory, or injunctive relief where, as here, the action that is alleged to be unconstitutional implements or executes a policy statement, ordinance, regulation, or decision officially adopted and promulgated by that body's officers. Moreover, although the touchstone of the § 1983 action against a government body is an allegation that official policy is responsible for a deprivation of rights protected by the Constitution, local governments, like every other § 1983 "person," by the very terms of the statute, may be sued for constitutional deprivations visited pursuant to governmental "custom" even though such a custom has not received formal approval through the body's official decisionmaking channels. As Mr. Justice Harlan, writing for the Court, said in Adickes v. S.H. Kress & Co., 398 U.S. 144, 167-168 (1970): "Congress included custom and usage [in § 1983] because of persistent and widespread discriminatory practices of State officials. ... Although not authorized by written law, such practices of state officials could well be so permanent and well settled as to constitute a 'custom or usage' with the force of law."

On the other hand, the language of § 1983, read against the background of the same legislative history, compels the conclusion that Congress did not intend municipalities to be held liable unless action pursuant to official municipal policy of some nature caused a constitutional tort. In particular, we conclude that a municipality cannot be held liable *solely* because it employs a tortfeasor — or, in other words, a municipality cannot be held liable under § 1983 on a *respondeat superior* theory.

. . .

We conclude, therefore, that a local government may not be sued for an injury inflicted solely by its employees or agents. Instead, it is when execution of a government's policy or custom,

---

433 U.S. 267, 291 (1977); see Ex parte Virginia, 100 U.S. 339, 347-348 (1880). For this reason, National League of Cities v. Usery, 426 U.S. 833, 22 WH Cases 1064 (1976), is irrelevant to our consideration of this case. Nor is there any basis for concluding that the Eleventh Amendment is a bar to municipal liability. See e. g., Fitzpatrick v. Bitzer, 427 U.S. 445, 456, 12 FEP Cases 1586 (1976); Lincoln County v. Luning, 133 U.S. 529, 530 (1890). Our holding today is, of course, limited to local government units which are not considered part of the State for Eleventh Amendment purposes.

[55] Since official capacity suits generally represent only another way of pleading an action against an entity of which an officer is an agent — at least where Eleventh Amendment considerations do not control analysis — our holding today that local governments can be sued under § 1983 necessarily decides that local government officials sued in their official capacities are "persons" under § 1983 in those cases in which, as here, a local government would be suable in its own name.

whether made by its lawmakers or by those whose edicts or acts may fairly be said to represent official policy, inflicts the injury that the government as an entity is responsible under § 1983. Since this case unquestionably involves official policy as the moving force of the constitutional violation found by the District Court, see pp. 1-2, and n. 2, supra, 17 FEP Cases, p. 874, we must reverse the judgment below. In so doing, we have no occasion to address, and do not address, what the full contours of municipal liability under § 1983 may be. We have attempted only to sketch so much of the § 1983 cause of action against a local government as is apparent from the history of the 1871 Act and our prior cases and we expressly leave further development of this action to another day.

(3) *Adickes v. S.H. Kress & Co.,* 398 U.S. 144 (1970), held "that a 'custom or usage' for purposes of § 1983 requires state involvement and is not simply a practice which reflects longstanding social habits, generally observed by the people in a locality"; it "must have the force of law by virtue of the persistent practices of state officials."

(4) In *Geduldig v. Aiello,* 417 U.S. 484 (1974), the Supreme Court upheld California's disability insurance program which did not cover disabilities resulting from normal pregnancy. After noting that the State's disability insurance program was wholly supported by employee contributions and that between 90% and 103% of the revenues collected were paid out each year, the Court stated (417 U.S. at 495-97):

Particularly with respect to social welfare programs, so long as the line drawn by the State is rationally supportable, the courts will not interpose their judgment as to the appropriate stopping point. "[T]he Equal Protection Clause does not require that a State must choose between attacking every aspect of a problem or not attacking the problem at all." Dandridge v. Williams, 397 U.S. 471, 486-87 (1970).

The State has a legitimate interest in maintaining the self-supporting nature of its insurance program. Similarly, it has an interest in distributing the available resources in such a way as to keep benefit payments at an adequate level for disabilities that are covered, rather than to cover all disabilities inadequately. Finally, California has a legitimate concern in maintaining the contribution rate at a level that will not unduly burden participating employees, particularly low-income employees who may be most in need of the disability insurance. These policies provide an objective and wholly non-invidious basis for the State's decision not to create a more comprehensive insurance program than it has. There is no evidence in the record that the selection of the risks insured by the program worked to discriminate against any definable group or class in terms of the aggregate risk protection derived by that group or class from the program. There is no risk from which men are protected and women are not. Likewise, there is no risk from which women are protected and men are not.

D. UNDER EXECUTIVE ORDER 11,246

LOPATKA, A 1977 PRIMER ON THE FEDERAL REGULATION OF EMPLOYMENT DISCRIMINATION, ILL. L.F. 69, 121-25 (1977) (footnotes omitted)

Executive Order (E.O.) 11,246 prohibits federal government contractors and subcontractors from engaging in the same types of discrimination that Title VII condemns more generally. Unlike Title VII, however, E.O. 11,246 requires contractors to "take affirmative action to ensure that applicants are employed, and that employees are treated during employment, without regard to their race, color, religion, sex or national origin." Regulations of the Labor Department's Office of Federal Contract Compliance Programs (OFCCP) generally subject contractors and subcontractors with contracts exceeding $10,000 to the requirements of E.O. 11,246 and implementing regulations. . . .

The Secretary of Labor has issued regulations that effectively make goals and timetables an aspect of the E.O. 11,246 affirmative action obligation. Although the affirmative action language of E.O. 11,246 does not explicitly include the controversial goal requirement, Department of Labor regulations specify that one term in every government contract must require the contractor to comply with all the rules, regulations, and relevant orders of the Secretary of Labor. Under regulations of the Secretary, nonconstruction contractors and subcontractors with contracts of $50,000 or more and with 50 or more employees, must submit a written affirmative action compliance program for each of their establishments within 120 days from the beginning of a contract, whether or not an establishment is involved in the particular contract. The regulations require that employers with contracts or first tier subcontracts of $1 million or more prepare the program and complete a compliance review prior to the award of the contract. In the affirmative action program the regulations require the contractor to undertake comprehensive "utilization" analyses of his own workforce that basically involve several types of statistical comparisons between the participation of women and minorities in the contractor's various job groups and the representation of women and minorities in the area labor pool. If a disparity exists in the utilization of minorities or females in any job group, the regulations would invoke automatically the goals and timetables obligation to rectify the underutilization. Although the proposed regulations state that the goals and timetables are designed to eliminate the disparity on a specific time schedule and that the procedures are "result oriented," they also manage to state that the use of goals "is not intended and should not be used to discriminate. . . ."

. . . .

The Department of Labor, through compliance agencies, monitors the compliance of contractors with their commitments by enforcing detailed reporting obligations and compliance reviews. In addition to the compliance reviews, under revised regulations, the Department of Labor may discover a contractor's failure to meet commitments when an individual or public interest group on behalf of an anonymous class files a complaint with the appropriate agency or with the director of the OFCCP. The OFCCP or the compliance agency first seeks rectification of any deficiency through conciliation. If the conciliation approach is unsuccessful, the OFCCP or compliance agency may seek administratively to enjoin the violations and obtain relief for the affected persons. Failure by a contractor to comply with such an administrative order may invoke the E.O. 11,246 sanctions of cancellation, termination, suspension, or debarment. The OFCCP or the compliance agency also may refer complaints to the Justice Department or, in cases of discrimination, to the EEOC for litigation. Although E.O. 11,246 does not specifically so provide, one district court has ruled that the Justice Department may recover back pay on behalf of victims of discrimination, basing such authority on § 209(a)(2) of E.O. 11,246, which refers to "appropriate proceedings" by the Justice Department on referral by the Secretary of Labor.

Plaintiffs may obtain limited private judicial enforcement of E.O. 11,246 obligations. Although the present state of the law apparently does not allow an individual or social action group to sue an employer directly for violating an affirmative action obligation either on a third party beneficiary theory or on an implied cause of action theory, one case indicates receptivity to the implied cause of action theory. Two other cases hold that an individual or a private organization may bring a mandamus action to compel the agency responsible for enforcing an employer's affirmative action obligations to initiate enforcement action.

NOTES:

(1) A number of commentators have criticized the affirmative action requirement under Executive Order 11246 as being largely ineffective. See Donegan, *The Philadelphia Plan: A Viable Means of Achieving Equal Opportunity In The Construction Industry or More Pie In The Sky?* 20 Kan. L. Rev. 195 (1972); *Jones, Federal Contract Compliance in Phase II — The Dawning of the Age of Enforcement of Equal Employment Obligations,* 4 Ga. L. Rev. 756 (1970); Edwards & Zaretsky, *Preferential Remedies For Employment Discrimination,* 74 Mich. L. Rev. 1 (1975); United States Commission on Civil Rights, The Federal Civil Rights Enforcement Effort — 1974 (July 1975).

(2) On September 29, 1969, the Labor Department put into effect its revised "Philadelphia Plan," under which federal contractors in the Philadelphia area would have to make good faith efforts to meet specific percentage "goals" for minority group employment in six construction trades. In *Contractors Ass'n of Eastern Pennsylvania v. Shultz,* 442 F.2d 159 (3d Cir. 1971), *cert. denied,* 404 U.S. 854 (1971), the plan was upheld against constitutional attack on due process and equal protection grounds, and was found to be neither violative of Title VII of the Civil Rights Act nor inconsistent with the NLRA. The court viewed the program as an appropriate requirement of "affirmative action" to eliminate racial discrimination in employment, as called for by Executive Order 11246, and a proper exercise of Presidential authority. *See also Southern Illinois Builders Ass'n v. Ogilvie,* 471 F.2d 680, 5 FEP Cas. 229 (7th Cir. 1972).

(3) In *Weber v. Kaiser Aluminum & Chemical Corp.,* 16 FEP Cas. 1 (1977), *cert. granted,* 99 S. Ct. 608 (1978), the Fifth Circuit ruled unlawful an affirmative action plan, voluntarily adopted by an employer and union, to increase the number of minorities in the company's craft training program. In an effort to comply with Executive Order 11246, the employer had agreed that 50% of all employees selected for craft training would be Black. Senior White employees sued under Title VII to prevent the company from giving preference to junior Black employees. The court ruled that since the employer had not discriminated against Blacks in the past, the affirmative action plan adopted by the parties violated Title VII because it discriminated against the White plaintiffs. The court also noted that the Black workers who were preferred by the affirmative action plan were not themselves victims of any past discrimination. The court specifically stated, over the strong dissent of Judge Wisdom, that:

[W]e are unable to harmonize the more explicit language of section 703(d) [in Title VII], which specifically prohibits racial classification in admission to on-the-job training programs, with the affirmative action imposed here. If Executive Order 11246 mandates a racial quota for admission to on-the-job training by Kaiser, *in the absence of any prior hiring or promotion discrimination,* the executive order must fall before this direct congressional prohibition.

(4) The Fifth Circuit went one step further in *United States v. East Texas Motor Freight System,* 16 FEP Cas. 163 (1977), where it was held that "the Executive Order imposes obligations on government contractors and subcontractors designed to eliminate employment discrimination of the same sort to which Title VII is directed." The court decision seems to make it clear that no greater relief may be had under the Executive Order than would be available under Title VII. This ruling could have the the effect of substantially nullifying current OFCCP regulations which do not require any finding of discrimination before affirmative action goals and timetables are imposed.

(5) See discussion of the *Bakke* case in Notes at pp. 997-1000, *infra.*

Chapter 16

EVIDENCE OF DISCRIMINATION UNDER TITLE VII

A. BURDEN OF PROOF

McDONNELL DOUGLAS CORP. v. GREEN

United States Supreme Court
411 U.S. 803 (1973)

MR. JUSTICE POWELL delivered the opinion of the Court.

The case before us raises significant questions as to the proper order and nature of proof in actions under Title VII of the Civil Rights Act of 1964.

Petitioner, McDonnell Douglas Corporation, is an aerospace and aircraft manufacturer headquartered in St. Louis, Missouri, where it employs over 30,000 people. Respondent, a black citizen of St. Louis, worked for petitioner as a mechanic and laboratory technician from 1956 until August 28, 1964 when he was laid off in the course of a general reduction in petitioner's work force.

Respondent, a long-time activist in the civil rights movement, protested vigorously that his discharge and the general hiring practices of petitioner were racially motivated. As part of this protest, respondent and other members of the Congress on Racial Equality illegally stalled their cars on the main roads leading to petitioner's plant for the purpose of blocking access to it at the time of the morning shift change. . . .

On July 2, 1965, a "lock-in" took place wherein a chain and padlock were placed on the front door of a building to prevent the occupants, certain of petitioner's employees, from leaving. Though respondent apparently knew beforehand of the "lock-in," the full extent of his involvement remains uncertain.

Some three weeks following the "lock-in," on July 25, 1965, petitioner publicly advertised for qualified mechanics, respondent's trade, and respondent promptly applied for re-employment. Petitioner turned down respondent, basing its rejection on respondent's participation in the "stall-in" and "lock-in." Shortly thereafter, respondent filed a formal complaint with the Equal Employment Opportunity Commission, claiming that petitioner had refused to rehire him because of his race and persistent involvement in the civil rights movement, in violation of §§ 703(a) (1) and 704(a) of the Civil Rights Act of 1964. 42 U.S.C. §§ 2000e-2(a)(1) and

2000e-3(a). The former section generally prohibits racial discrimination in any employment decision while the latter forbids discrimination against applicants or employees for attempting to protest or correct allegedly discriminatory conditions of employment.

The Commission made no finding on respondent's allegation of racial bias under § 703(a) (1), but it did not find reasonable cause to believe petitioner had violated § 704(a) by refusing to rehire respondent because of his civil rights activity. After the Commission unsuccessfully attempted to conciliate the dispute, it advised respondent in March 1968, of his right to institute a civil action in federal court within 30 days.

On April 15, 1968, respondent brought the present action, claiming initially a violation of § 704(a) and, in an amended complaint, a violation of § 703(a) (1) as well. The District Court dismissed the latter claim of racial discrimination in petitioner's hiring procedures on the ground that the Commission had failed to make a determination of reasonable cause to believe that a violation of that section had been committed. The District Court also found that petitioner's refusal to rehire respondent was based solely on his participation in the illegal demonstrations and not on his legitimate civil rights activities. The court concluded that nothing in Title VII or § 704 protected "such activity as employed by the plaintiff in the 'stall-in' and 'lock-in' demonstrations."

On appeal, the Eighth Circuit affirmed that unlawful protests were not protected activities under § 704(a), but reversed the dismissal of respondent's § 703(a) (1) claim relating to racially discriminatory hiring practices, holding that a prior Commission determination of reasonable cause was not a jurisdictional prerequisite to raising a claim under that section in federal court. The court ordered the case remanded for trial of respondent's claim under § 703(a) (1).

In remanding, the Court of Appeals attempted to set forth standards to govern the consideration of respondent's claim. The majority noted that respondent had established a prima facie case of racial discrimination; that petitioner's refusal to rehire respondent rested on "subjective" criteria which carried little weight in rebutting charges of discrimination; that though respondent's participation in the unlawful demonstrations might indicate a lack of a responsible attitude toward performing work for that employer, respondent should be given the opportunity to demonstrate that petitioner's reasons for refusing to rehire him were merely pretextual. In order to clarify the standards governing the disposition of an action challenging employment discrimination, we granted certiorari. . . .

I. We agree with the Court of Appeals that absence of a Commission finding of reasonable cause cannot bar suit under an appropriate section of Title VII and that the District Judge erred in dismissing respondent's claim of racial discrimination under § 703(a)(1). Respondent satisfied the jurisdictional prerequisites to a federal action (i) by filing timely charges of employment discrimination with the Commission and (ii) by receiving and acting upon the Commission's statutory notice of the right to sue. 42 U.S.C. §§ 2000e-5(a) and 2000e-5(e). The Act does not restrict a complainant's right to sue to those charges as to which the Commission has made findings of reasonable cause, and we will not engraft on the statute a requirement which may inhibit the review of claims of employment discrimination in the federal courts. The Commission itself does not consider the absence of a "reasonable cause" determination as providing employer immunity from similar charges in a federal court, 29 CFR § 1601.30, and the courts of appeal have held that, in view of the large volume of complaints before the Commission and the nonadversary character of many of its proceedings, "court actions under Title VII are *de novo* proceedings and . . . a Commission's 'no reasonable cause' finding does not bar a lawsuit in the case." Robinson v. Lorillard Corp., 444 F.2d 791, 800 (4th Cir.); Beverly v. Lone Star Lead Construction Corp., 437 F.2d 1136 (5th Cir.); Flowers v. Local 6, Laborers International Union of North America, 431 F.2d 205 (7th Cir.); Fekete v. U. S. Steel Corp., 424 F.2d 331 (3d Cir.).

Petitioner argues, as it did below, that respondent sustained no prejudice from the trial court's erroneous ruling because in fact the issue of racial discrimination in the refusal to re-employ "was tried thoroughly" in a trial lasting four days with "at least 80%" of the questions relating to the issue of "race." Petitioner therefore requests that the judgment below be vacated and the cause remanded with instructions that the judgment of the District Court be affirmed. We cannot agree that the dismissal of respondent's § 703(a)(1) claim was harmless error. It is not clear that the District Court's findings as to respondent's § 704(a) contentions involved the identical issues raised by his claim under § 703(a)(1). The former section relates solely to discrimination against an applicant or employee on account of his participation in legitimate civil rights activities or protests, while the latter section deals with the broader and centrally important question under the Act of whether, for any reason, a racially discriminatory employment decision has been made. Moreover, respondent should have been accorded the right to prepare his case and plan the strategy of trial with the knowledge that the § 703(a)(1) cause of action was properly before the District Court. Accordingly, we remand the case for trial of respondent's claim of racial discrimination consistent with the views set forth below.

II. The critical issue before us concerns the order and allocation of proof in a private, single-plaintiff action challenging employment discrimination. The language of Title VII makes plain the purpose of Congress to assure equality of employment opportunities and to eliminate those discriminatory practices and devices which have fostered racially stratified job environments to the disadvantage of minority citizens. Griggs v. Duke Power Co., 401 U.S. 424, 429 (1971). . . .

There are societal as well as personal interests on both sides of this question. The broad, overriding interest, shared by employer, employee, and consumer, is efficient and trustworthy workmanship assured through fair and racially neutral employment and personnel decisions. In the implementation of such decisions, it is abundantly clear that Title VII tolerates no racial discrimination, subtle or otherwise.

In this case respondent, the complainant below, charges that he was denied employment "because of his involvement in civil rights activities" and "because of his race and color." Petitioner denied discrimination of any kind, asserting that its failure to re-employ respondent was based upon and justified by his participation in the unlawful conduct against it. Thus, the issue at the trial on remand is framed by those opposing factual contentions. The two opinions of the Court of Appeals and the several opinions of the three judges of the court attempted, with a notable lack of harmony, to state the applicable rules as to burden of proof and how this shifts upon the making of a prima facie case. We now address this problem.

The complainant in a Title VII trial must carry the initial burden under the statute of establishing a prima facie case of racial discrimination. This may be done by showing (i) that he belongs to a racial minority; (ii) that he applied and was qualified for a job for which the employer was seeking applicants; (iii) that, despite his qualifications, he was rejected; and (iv) that, after his rejection, the position remained open and the employer continued to seek applicants from persons of complainant's qualifications. In the instant case, we agree with the Court of Appeals that respondent proved a prima facie case. . . . Petitioner sought mechanics, respondent's trade, and continued to do so after respondent's rejection. Petitioner, moreover, does not dispute respondent's qualifications and acknowledges that his past work performance in petitioner's employ was "satisfactory."

The burden then must shift to the employer to articulate some legitimate, nondiscriminatory reason for respondent's rejection. We need not attempt in the instant case to detail every matter which fairly could be recognized as a reasonable basis for a refusal to hire. Here petitioner has assigned respondent's participation in unlawful conduct against it as the cause for his rejection. We think that this suffices to discharge petitioner's burden of proof at this stage and to meet respondent's prima facie case of discrimination.

The Court of Appeals intimated, however, that petitioner's stated reason for refusing to rehire respondent was a "subjective" rather than objective criterion which "carries little weight in rebutting charges of discrimination." . . . This was among the statements which caused the dissenting judge to read the opinion as taking "the position that such unlawful acts as Green committed against McDonnell would not legally entitle McDonnell to refuse to rehire him, even though no racial motivation was involved. . . ." Regardless of whether this was the intended import of the opinion, we think the court below seriously underestimated the rebuttal weight to which petitioner's reasons were entitled. Respondent admittedly had taken part in a carefully planned "stall-in," designed to tie up access and egress to petitioner's plant at a peak traffic hour. Nothing in Title VII compels an employer to absolve and rehire one who has engaged in such deliberate, unlawful activity against it. In upholding, under the National Labor Relations Act, the discharge of employees who had seized and forcibly retained an employer's factory buildings in an illegal sit-down strike, the Court noted pertinently:

> "We are unable to conclude that Congress intended to compel employers to retain persons in their employ regardless of their unlawful conduct — to invest those who go on strike with an immunity from discharge for acts of trespass or violence against the employer's property. . . . Apart from the question of the constitutional validity of an enactment of that sort, it is enough to say that such a legislative intention should be found in some definite and unmistakable expression." NLRB v. Fansteel Corp., 306 U.S. 240, 255 (1939).

Petitioner's reason for rejection thus suffices to meet the prima facie case, but the inquiry must not end here. While Title VII does not, without more, compel rehiring of respondent, neither does it permit petitioner to use respondent's conduct as a pretext for the sort of discrimination prohibited by § 703(a)(1). On remand, respondent must, as the Court of Appeals recognized, be afforded a fair opportunity to show that petitioner's stated reason for respondent's rejection was in fact pretextual. Especially relevant to such a showing would be evidence that white employees involved in acts against petitioner of comparable seriousness to the "stall-in" were nevertheless retained or rehired. Petitioner may justifiably refuse to rehire one who was engaged in unlawful, disruptive acts against it, but only if this criterion is applied alike to members of all races.

Other evidence that may be relevant to any showing of pretextuality includes facts as to the petitioner's treatment of respondent during his prior term of employment, petitioner's reaction, if any, to respondent's legitimate civil rights activities, and petitioner's general policy and practice with respect to minority employment. On the latter point, statistics as to petitioner's employment policy and practice may be helpful to a determination of whether petitioner's refusal to rehire respondent in this case conformed to a general pattern of discrimination against blacks. Jones v. Lee Way Motor Freight, Inc., 421 F.2d 245 (10th Cir. 1970); Blumrosen, Strangers in Paradise: Griggs v. Duke Power Co., and the Concepts of Employment Discrimination, 71 Mich. L. Rev. 59, 91-94 (1972). In short, on the retrial respondent must be given a full and fair opportunity to demonstrate by competent evidence that the presumptively valid reasons for his rejection were in fact a coverup for a racially discriminatory decision.

The court below appeared to rely upon *Griggs v. Duke Power Co., supra,* in which the Court stated: "If an employment practice which operates to exclude Negroes cannot be shown to be related to job performance, the practice is prohibited." *Id.* at 431. But *Griggs* differs from the instant case in important respects. It dealt with standardized testing devices which, however neutral on their face, operated to exclude many blacks who were capable of performing effectively in the desired positions. *Griggs* was rightly concerned that childhood deficiencies in the education and background of minority citizens, resulting from forces beyond their control, not be allowed to work a cumulative and invidious burden on such citizens for the remainder of their lives. *Id.* at 430. Respondent, however, appears in different clothing. He had engaged in a seriously disruptive act against the very one from whom he now seeks employment. And petitioner does not seek his exclusion on the basis of a testing device which overstates what is necessary for competent performance, or through some sweeping disqualification of all those with any past record of unlawful behavior, however remote, insubstantial or unrelated to applicant's personal qualifications as an employee. Petitioner assertedly rejected respondent for unlawful conduct against it and, in the absence of proof of pretextual or discriminatory application of such a reason, this cannot be thought the kind of "artificial, arbitrary, and unnecessary barrier to employment" which the Court found to be the intention of Congress to remove. *Griggs,* p. 431.

III. In sum, respondent should have been allowed to amend his complaint to include a claim under § 703(a)(1). If the evidence on retrial is substantially in accord with that before us in this case, we think that respondent carried his burden of establishing a prima facie case of racial discrmination and that petitioner successfully rebutted that case. But this does not end the matter. On retrial respondent must be afforded a fair opportunity to demonstrate that petitioner's assigned reason for refusing to re-employ was pretextual or discriminatory in its application. If the District Judge so finds, he must order a prompt and appropriate remedy. In the absence of such a finding, petitioner's refusal to rehire must stand.

The cause is hereby remanded to the District Court for reconsideration in accordance with this opinion.

NOTES:

(1) On remand, the Eighth Circuit affirmed the judgment of the District Court in favor of the defendant. *Green v. McDonnell Douglas Corp.,* 528 F.2d 1102 (1976).

(2) In considering questions pertaining to the burden of proof under Title VII, it is also essential to review the Supreme Court's decisions in: *Griggs v. Duke Power Co.,* 401 U.S. 424 (1971); *Albemarle Paper Co. v. Moody,* 422 U.S. 405 (1975); *International Brotherhood of Teamsters v. United States,* 97 S. Ct. 1843 (1977); *Hazelwood School District v. United States,* 433 U.S. 299, 97 S. Ct. 2736, 45 U.S.L.W. 4882 (1977); and *Dothard v. Rawlinson,* 433 U.S. 321, 97 S. Ct. 2720, 45 U.S.L.W. 4888 (1977). The latter three cases underscore the importance of statistics and relevant labor market populations in employment discrimination cases.

B. DISCRIMINATORY SENIORITY SYSTEMS

INTERNATIONAL BROTHERHOOD OF TEAMSTERS v. UNITED STATES
T.I.M.E.-D.C., INC. v. UNITED STATES

United States Supreme Court
431 U.S. 324, 97 S. Ct. 1843, 52 L. Ed. 2d 396 (1977)

MR. JUSTICE STEWART delivered the opinion of the Court.

This litigation brings here several important questions under Title VII of the Civil Rights Act of 1964. . . . The issues grow out of alleged unlawful employment practices engaged in by an employer and a union. The employer is a common carrier of motor freight with nationwide operations, and the union represents a large group of its employees. The District Court and the Court of Appeals held that the employer had violated Title VII by engaging in a pattern and practice of employment discrimination against Negroes and Spanish-surnamed Americans, and that the union had violated the Act by agreeing with the employer to create and maintain a seniority system that perpetuated the effects of past racial and ethnic discrimination. In addition to the basic questions presented by these two rulings, other subsidiary issues must be resolved if violations of Title VII occurred — issues concerning the nature of the relief to which aggrieved individuals may be entitled.

The central claim ... was that the company had engaged in a pattern or practice of discriminating against minorities in hiring so-called line drivers. Those Negroes and Spanish-surnamed persons who had been hired, the Government alleged, were given lower paying, less desirable jobs as servicemen or local city drivers, and were thereafter discriminated against with respect to promotions and transfers.[3] In this connection the complaint also challenged the seniority system established by the collective-bargaining agreements between the employer and the union. The Government sought a general injunctive remedy and specific "make whole" relief for all individual discriminatees, which would allow them an opportunity to transfer to line-driver jobs with full company seniority for all purposes.

The cases went to trial [4] and the District Court found that the Government had shown "by a preponderance of the evidence that

---

[3] *Line drivers,* also known as over-the-road drivers, engage in long-distance hauling between company terminals. They compose a separate bargaining unit at T.I.M.E.-D.C. Other distinct bargaining units include *servicemen;* who service trucks, unhook tractors and trailers, and perform similar tasks; and *city operations,* composed of dockmen, hostlers, and city drivers who pick up and deliver freight within the immediate area of a particular terminal. All of these employees were represented by the petitioner International Brotherhood of Teamsters.

[4] Following the receipt of evidence, but before decision, the Government and the company consented to the entry of a Decree in Partial Resolution of Suit. The consent decree did not constitute an adjudication on the merits. The company agreed, however, to undertake a minority recruiting program; to accept applications from all Negroes and Spanish-surnamed Americans who inquired about employment, whether or not vacancies existed, and to keep such applications on file and notify applicants of job openings; to keep specific employment and recruiting records open to inspection by the Government and to submit quarterly reports to the District Court; and to adhere to certain uniform employment qualifications respecting hiring and promotion to line driver and other jobs.

The decree further provided that future job vacancies at any T.I.M.E.-D.C. terminal would be filled first "[b]y those persons who may be found by the Court, if any, to be individual or class discriminatees suffering the present effects of past discrimination because of race or national origin prohibited by Title VII of the Civil Rights Act of 1964." Any remaining vacancies could be filled by "any other persons," but the company obligated itself to hire one Negro or Spanish-surnamed person for every white person hired at any terminal until the percentage of minority workers at that terminal equaled the percentage of minority group members in the population of the metropolitan area surrounding the terminal. Finally, the company agreed to pay $89,500 in full settlement of any backpay obligations. Of this sum, individual payments not exceeding $1,500 were to be paid to "alleged individual and class discriminatees" identified by the Government.

The Decree in Partial Resolution of Suit narrowed the scope of the litigation, but the District Court still had to determine whether unlawful discrimination had occurred. If so, the Court had to identify the actual discriminatees entitled to fill future job vacancies under the decree. The validity of the collective-bargaining contract's seniority system also remained for decision, as did the question whether any discriminatees should be awarded additional equitable relief such as retroactive seniority.

T.I.M.E.-D.C. and its predecessor companies were engaged in a plan and practice of discrimination in violation of Title VII . . . ." [5] The court further found that the seniority system contained in the collective-bargaining contracts between the company and the union violated Title VII because it "operate[d] to impede the free transfer of minority groups into and within the company." Both the company and the union were enjoined from committing further violations of Title VII.

With respect to individual relief the court accepted the Government's basic contention that the "affected class" of discriminatees included all Negro and Spanish-surnamed incumbent employees who had been hired to fill city operations or serviceman jobs at every terminal that had a line-driver operation. All of these employees, whether hired before or after the effective date of Title VII, thereby became entitled to preference over all other applicants with respect to consideration for future vacancies in line-driver jobs. Finding that members of the affected class had been injured in different degrees, the court created three subclasses. Thirty persons who had produced "the most convincing evidence of discrimination and harm" were found to have suffered "severe injury." The court ordered that they be offered the opportunity to fill line-driver jobs with competitive seniority dating back to July 2, 1965, the effective date of Title VII. A second subclass included four persons who were "very possibly the objects of discrimination" and who "were likely harmed," but as to whom there had been no specific evidence of discrimination and injury. The court decreed that these persons were entitled to fill vacancies in line-driving jobs with competitive seniority as of January 14, 1971, the date on which the Government had filed its system-wide lawsuit. Finally, there were over 300 remaining members of the affected class as to whom there was "no evidence to show that these individuals were either harmed or not harmed individually." The court ordered that they be considered for line-driver jobs ahead of any applicants from the general public but behind the two other subclasses. Those in the third subclass received no retroactive seniority; their competitive seniority as line drivers would begin with the date they were hired as line drivers. The court further decreed that the right of any class member to fill a line-driver vacancy was subject to the prior recall rights of laid-off line drivers, which under the collective-bargaining agreements then in effect extended for three years.

The Court of Appeals for the Fifth Circuit agreed with the basic conclusions of the District Court: that the company had engaged in

---

[5] The District Court's Memorandum Decision in United States v. T.I.M.E.-D.C., Inc., Civ. No. 5-868 (Oct. 19, 1972), is not officially reported. It is unofficially reported at 6 FEP Cases 690 and 6 EPD ¶ 8979.

a pattern or practice of employment discrimination and that the seniority system in the collective-bargaining agreements violated Title VII as applied to victims of prior discrimination. United States v. T.I.M.E.-D.C., Inc., 517 F.2d 299. . . . The appellate court held, however, that the relief ordered by the District Court was inadequate. Rejecting the District Court's attempt to trisect the affected class, the Court of Appeals held that all Negro and Spanish-surnamed incumbent employees were entitled to bid for future line-driver jobs on the basis of their company seniority, and that once a class member had filled a job, he could use his full company seniority — even if it predated the effective date of Title VII — for all purposes, including bidding and layoff. This award of retroactive seniority was to be limited only by a "qualification date" formula, under which seniority could not be awarded for periods prior to the date when (i) a line-driving position was vacant, *and* (2) the class member met (or would have met, given the opportunity) the qualifications for employment as a line driver. Finally, the Court of Appeals modified that part of the District Court's decree that had subjected the rights of class members to fill future vacancies to the recall rights of laid-off employees. Holding that the three-year priority in favor of laid-off workers "would unduly impede the eradication of past discrimination," id., at 322, . . . the Court of Appeals ordered that class members be allowed to compete for vacancies with laid-off employees on the basis of the class members' retroactive seniority. Laid-off line drivers would retain their prior recall rights with respect only to "purely temporary" vacancies.

The Court of Appeals remanded the case to the District Court to hold the evidentiary hearings necessary to apply these remedial principles. We granted both the company's and the union's petitions for certiorari to consider the significant questions presented under the Civil Rights Act of 1964, 425 U. S. 990.

II

In this Court the company and the union contend that their conduct did not violate Title VII in any respect, asserting first that the evidence introduced at trial was insufficient to show that the company engaged in a "pattern or practice" of employment discrimination. The union further contends that the seniority system contained in the collective-bargaining agreements in no way violated Title VII. If these contentions are correct, it is unnecessary, of course, to reach any of the issues concerning remedies that so occupied the attention of the Court of Appeals.

A

Consideration of the question whether the company engaged in a pattern or practice of discriminatory hiring practices involves controlling legal principles that are relatively clear. The Government's theory of discrimination was simply that the company, in violation of § 703(a) of Title VII, regularly and purposefully treated Negroes and Spanish-surnamed Americans less favorably than white persons. The disparity in treatment allegedly involved the refusal to recruit, hire, transfer, or promote minority group members on an equal basis with white people, particularly with respect to line-driving positions. The ultimate factual issues are thus simply whether there was a pattern or practice of such disparate treatment and, if so, whether the differences were "racially premised," McDonnell Douglas Corp. v. Green, 411 U. S. 792, 805 n. 18, ...[15]

As the plaintiff, the Government bore the initial burden of making out a prima facie case of discrimination. Albemarle Paper Co. v. Moody, 422 U.S. 405, 425 . . . ; McDonnell Douglas Corp. v. Green, supra, at 802, ... And, because it alleged a systemwide pattern or practice of resistance to the full enjoyment of Title VII rights, the Government ultimately had to prove more than the mere occurrence of isolated or "accidental" or sporadic discriminatory acts. It had to establish by a preponderance of the evidence that racial discrimination was the company's standard operating procedure — the regular rather than the unusual practice.

We agree with the District Court and the Court of Appeals that the Government carried its burden of proof. As of March 31, 1971, shortly after the Government filed its complaint alleging systemwide discrimination, the company had 6,472 employees. Of these, 314 (5%) were Negroes and 257 (4%) were Spanish-surnamed Americans. Of the 1,828 line drivers, however, there were only 8 (0.4%) Negroes and 5 (0.3%) Spanish-surnamed persons, and all of

---

[15] "Disparate treatment" such as alleged in the present case is the most easily understood type of discrimination. The employer simply treats some people less favorably than others because of their race, color, religion, sex, or national origin. Proof of discriminatory motive is critical, although it can in some situations be inferred from the mere fact of differences in treatment. . . .

Claims of disparate treatment may be distinguished from claims that stress "disparate impact." The latter involve employment practices that are facially neutral in their treatment of different groups but that in fact fall more harshly on one group than on another and cannot be justified by business necessity. . . . Proof of discriminatory motive, we have held, is not required under a disparate impact theory. Compare, e.g., Griggs v. Duke Power Co., 401 U. S. 424, 430-432, . . . with McDonnell Douglas Corp. v. Green, 411 U. S. 792, 802-806, . . . See generally Schlei & Grossman, Employment Discrimination Law 1-12 (1976); Blumrosen, Strangers in Paradise: Griggs v. Duke Power Co. and the Concept of Employment Discrimination, 71 Mich. L. Rev. 59 (1972). Either theory may, of course, be applied to a particular set of facts.

the Negroes had been hired after the litigation had commenced. With one exception — a man who worked as a line driver at the Chicago terminal from 1950 to 1959 — the company and its predecessors *did not employ a Negro on a regular basis as a line driver until 1969.* And, as the Government showed, even in 1971 there were terminals in areas of substantial Negro population where all of the company's line drivers were white. A great majority of the Negroes (83%) and Spanish-surnamed Americans (78%) who did work for the company held the lower-paying city operations and serviceman jobs, whereas only 39% of the nonminority employees held jobs in those categories.

The Government bolstered its statistical evidence with the testimony of individuals who recounted over 40 specific instances of discrimination. Upon the basis of this testimony the District Court found that "[n]umerous qualified black and Spanish-surnamed American applicants who sought line-driving jobs at the company over the years had their requests ignored, were given false or misleading information about requirements, opportunities, and application procedures or were not considered and hired on the same basis that whites were considered and hired." Minority employees who wanted to transfer to line-driver jobs met with similar difficulties.

The company's principal response to this evidence is that statistics can never in and of themselves prove the existence of a pattern or practice of discrimination, or even establish a prima facie case shifting to the employer the burden of rebutting the inference raised by the figures. But, as even our brief summary of the evidence shows, this was not a case in which the Government relied on "statistics alone." The individuals who testified about their personal experiences with the company brought the cold numbers convincingly to life.

In any event, our cases make it unmistakably clear that "[s]tatistical analyses have served and will continue to serve an important role" in cases in which the existence of discrimination is a disputed issue. Mayor of Philadelphia v. Educational Equality League, 415 U.S. 605, 620. See also McDonnell Douglas Corp. v. Green, supra, at 805, ... Cf. Washington v. Davis, 426 U.S. 229, 241-242, ... We have repeatedly approved the use of statistical proof, where it reached proportions comparable to those in this case, to establish a prima facie case of racial discrimination in jury selection cases, see, e.g., Turner v. Fouche, 396 U.S. 346; Hernandez v. Texas, 347 U.S. 475; Norris v. Alabama, 294 U.S. 587. Statistics are equally competent in proving employment discrimination. We caution only that statistics are not irrefutable; they come in infinite variety and, like any other kind of evidence, they may be rebutted. In short, their usefulness depends on all of the surrounding facts and circumstances. See, e.g., Hester v. Southern R. Co., 497 F.2d 1374, 1379-1381, . . . (CA5).

In addition to its general protest against the use of statistics in Title VII cases, the company claims that in this case the statistics revealing racial imbalance are misleading because they fail to take into account the company's particular business situation as of the effective date of Title VII. The company concedes that its line drivers were virtually all white in July 1965, but it claims that thereafter business conditions were such that its work force dropped. Its argument is that low personnel turnover, rather than post-Act discrimination, accounts for more recent disparities. It points to substantial minority hiring in later years, especially after 1971, as showing that any pre-Act patterns of discrimination were broken.

The argument would be a forceful one if this were an employer who, at the time of suit, had done virtually no new hiring since the effective date of Title VII. But it is not. Although the company's total number of employees apparently dropped somewhat during the late 1960's, the record shows that many line drivers continued to be hired throughout this period, and that almost all of them were white. To be sure, there were improvements in the company's hiring practices. The Court of Appeals commented that "T.I.M.E.-D.C.'s recent minority hiring progress stands as a laudable good faith effort to eradicate the effects of past discrimination in the area of hiring and initial assignment." 517 F.2d, at 316. . . . But the District Court and the Court of Appeals found upon substantial evidence that the company had engaged in a course of discrimination that continued well after the effective date of Title VII. The company's later changes in its hiring and promotion policies could be little comfort to the victims of the earlier post-Act discrimination, and could not erase its previous illegal conduct or its obligation to afford relief to those who suffered because of it. Cf. Albemarle Paper Co. v. Moody, supra, at 413-423, ...

The District Court and the Court of Appeals, on the basis of substantial evidence, held that the Government had proved a prima facie case of systematic and purposeful employment discrimination, continuing well beyond the effective date of Title VII. The company's attempts to rebut that conclusion were held to be inadequate. For the reasons we have summarized, there is no warrant for this Court to disturb the findings of the District Court and the Court of Appeals on this basic issue. . . .

B

The District Court and the Court of Appeals also found that the seniority system contained in the collective-bargaining agreements between the company and the union operated to violate Title VII of the Act.

For purposes of calculating benefits, such as vacations, pensions, and other fringe benefits, an employee's seniority under this system runs from the date he joins the company, and takes into account his total service in all jobs and bargaining units. For competitive purposes, however, such as determining the order in which employees may bid for particular jobs, are laid off, or are recalled from layoff, it is bargaining-unit seniority that controls. Thus, a line driver's seniority, for purposes of bidding for particular runs and protection against layoff, takes into account only the length of time he has been a line driver at a particular terminal. The practical effect is that a city driver or serviceman who transfers to a line-driver job must forfeit all the competitive seniority he has accumulated in his previous bargaining unit and start at the bottom of the line-drivers' "board."

The vice of this arrangement, as found by the District Court and the Court of Appeals, was that it "locked" minority workers into inferior jobs and perpetuated prior discrimination by discouraging transfers to jobs as line drivers. While the disincentive applied to all workers, including whites, it was Negroes and Spanish-surnamed persons who, those courts found, suffered the most because many of them had been denied the equal opportunity to become line drivers when they were initially hired, whereas whites either had not sought or were refused line-driver positions for reasons unrelated to their race or national origin.

The linchpin of the theory embraced by the District Court and the Court of Appeals was that a discriminatee who must forfeit his competitive seniority in order finally to obtain a line-driver job will never be able to "catch up" to the seniority level of his contemporary who was not subject to discrimination.[27] Accordingly, this continued, built-in disadvantage to the prior discriminatee who transfers to a line-driver job was held to constitute a continuing violation of Title VII, for which both the employer and the union who jointly created and maintained the seniority system were liable.

The union, while acknowledging that the seniority system may in some sense perpetuate the effects of prior discrimination, asserts that

----

[27] An example would be a Negro who was qualified to be a line driver in 1958 but who, because of his race, was assigned instead a job as a city driver, and is allowed to become a line driver only in 1971. Because he loses his competitive seniority when he transfers jobs, he is forever junior to white line drivers hired between 1958 and 1970. The whites, rather than the Negro, will henceforth enjoy the preferable runs and the greater protection against layoff. Although the original discrimination occurred in 1958 — before the effective date of Title VII — the seniority system operates to carry the effects of the earlier discrimination into the present.

the system is immunized from a finding of illegality by reason of § 703(h) of Title VII, ...

It argues that the seniority system in this case is "bona fide" within the meaning of § 703(h) when judged in light of its history, intent, application, and all of the circumstances under which it was created and is maintained. More specifically, the union claims that the central purpose of § 703(h), is to ensure that mere perpetuation of *pre-Act* discrimination is not unlawful under Title VII. And, whether or not § 703(h) immunizes the perpetuation of *post-Act* discrimination, the union claims that the seniority system in this case has no such effect. Its position in this Court, as has been its position throughout this litigation, is that the seniority system presents no hurdle to post-Act discriminatees who seek retroactive seniority to the date they would have become line drivers but for the company's discrimination. Indeed, the union asserts that under its collective-bargaining agreements the union will itself take up the cause of the post-Act victim and attempt, through grievance procedures, to gain for him full "make whole" relief, including appropriate seniority.

The Government responds that a seniority system that perpetuates the effects of prior discrimination — pre- or post-Act — can never be "bona fide" under § 703(h); at a minimum Title VII prohibits those applications of a seniority system that perpetuate the effects on incumbent employees of prior discriminatory job assignments.

The issues thus joined are open ones in this Court.[28] We considered § 703(h) in Franks v. Bowman Transportation Co., 424 U.S. 747, 12 FEP Cases 549; but there decided only that § 703(h) does not bar the award of retroactive seniority to job applicants who seek relief from an employer's post-Act hiring discrimination. We stated that "the thrust of [§ 703(h)] is directed toward defining what is and what is not illegal discriminatory practice in instances in which the post-Act operation of a seniority system is challenged as

---

[28] Concededly, the view that § 703(h) does not immunize seniority systems that perpetuate the effects of prior discrimination has much support. It was apparently first adopted in Quarles v. Phillip Morris, Inc., 279 F. Supp. 505, . . . (ED Va.). The court there held that "a departmental seniority system *that has its genesis in racial discrimination* is not a *bona fide* seniority system." Id., at 517, . . . (first emphasis added). The Quarles view has since enjoyed wholesale adoption in the Courts of Appeals. See, e.g., Local 189, United Paperworkers v. United States, 416 F.2d 980, 987-988, . . . (CA5); United States v. Sheet Metal Workers Local 36, 416 F.2d 123, 133-134, n. 20, . . . (CA8); United States v. Bethlehem Steel Corp., 446 F.2d 652, 658-659, . . . (CA2); United States v. Chesapeake & Ohio R. Co., 471 F.2d 582, 587-588, . . . (CA4). Insofar as the result in Quarles and in the cases that followed it depended upon findings that the seniority systems were themselves "racially discriminatory" or had their "genesis in racial discrimination," 279 F. Supp., at 517, . . . the decisions can be viewed as resting upon the proposition that a seniority system that perpetuates the effects of pre-Act discrimination cannot be bona fide if an intent to discriminate entered into its very adoption.

perpetuating the effects of discrimination occurring prior to the effective date of the Act." 424 U.S., at 761, 12 FEP Cases, at 554-555. Beyond noting the general purpose of the statute, however, we did not undertake the task of statutory construction required in this case.

(1)

Because the company discriminated both before and after the enactment of Title VII, the seniority system is said to have operated to perpetuate the effects of both pre- and post-Act discrimination. Post-Act discriminatees, however, may obtain full "make whole" relief, including retroactive seniority under Franks v. Bowman, supra, without attacking the legality of the seniority system as applied to them. Franks made clear and the union acknowledges that retroactive seniority may be awarded as relief from an employer's discriminatory hiring and assignment policies even if the seniority system agreement itself makes no provision for such relief.[29] 424 U.S., at 778-779, ... Here the Government has proved that the company engaged in a post-Act pattern of discriminatory hiring, assignment, transfer, and promotion policies. Any Negro or Spanish-surnamed American injured by those policies may receive all appropriate relief as a direct remedy for this discrimination.[30]

---

[29] Article 38 of the National Master Freight Agreement between T.I.M.E.-D.C. and the International Brotherhood of Teamsters in effect as of the date of the systemwide lawsuit provided:

"The Employer and the Union agree not to discriminate against any individual with respect to his hiring, compensation, terms or conditions of employment because of such individual's race, color, religion, sex, or national origin, nor will they limit, segregate or classify employees in any way to deprive any individual employee of employment opportunities because of his race, color, religion, sex, or national origin."

Any discrimination by the company would apparently be a grievable breach of this provision of the contract.

[30] The legality of the seniority system insofar as it perpetuates post-Act discrimination nonetheless remains at issue in this case, in light of the injunction entered against the union. ... Our decision today in United Airlines v. Evans, ... is largely dispositive of this issue. Evans holds that the operation of a seniority system is not unlawful under Title VII even though it perpetuates post-Act discrimination that has not been the subject of a timely charge by the discriminatee. Here, of course, the Government has sued to remedy the post-Act discrimination directly and there is no claim that any relief would be time-barred. But this is simply an additional reason not to hold the seniority system unlawful, since such a holding would in no way enlarge the relief to be awarded. See Franks v. Bowman, 424 U.S., at 778-779. ... Section 703(h) on its face immunizes all bona fide seniority systems, and does not distinguish between the perpetuation of pre- and post-Act discrimination.

(2)

What remains for review is the judgment that the seniority system unlawfully perpetuated the effects of *pre-Act* discrimination. We must decide, in short, whether § 703(h) validates otherwise bona fide seniority systems that afford no constructive seniority to victims discriminated against prior to the effective date of Title VII, and it is to that issue that we now turn.

The primary purpose of Title VII was "to assure equality of employment opportunities and to eliminate those discriminatory practices and devices which have fostered racially stratified job environments to the disadvantage of minority citizens." McDonnell Douglas Corp. v. Green, supra, at 800, ... See also Albemarle Paper Co. v. Moody, supra, at 417-418; Alexander v. Gardner-Denver Co., 415 U.S. 36, 44, . . . ; Griggs v. Duke Power Co., supra, at 429-431, ... To achieve this purpose, Congress "proscribe[d] not only overt discrimination but also practices that are fair in form, but discriminatory in operation." Griggs, 401 U.S., at 431, ... Thus, the Court has repeatedly held that a prima facie Title VII violation may be established by policies or practices that are neutral on their face and in intent but that nonetheless discriminate in effect against a particular group. General Electric Co. v. Gilbert, 429 U.S. 125, 137, . . . ; Washington v. Davis, 426 U.S. 229, 246-247, . . . ; Albemarle Paper Co. v. Moody, supra, at 422, 425, . . . ; McDonnell Douglas Corp. v. Green, supra, at 802, n. 14, . . . ; Griggs v. Duke Power Co., supra.

One kind of practice "fair in form, but discriminatory in operation" is that which perpetuates the effects of prior discrimination.[32] As the Court held in Griggs, supra: "Under the Act, practices, procedures, or tests neutral on their face, and even neutral in terms of intent, cannot be maintained if they operate to 'freeze' the status quo of prior discriminatory employment practices." 401 U.S., at 430, ...

Were it not for § 703(h), the seniority system in this case would seem to fall under the Griggs rationale. The heart of the system is its allocation of the choicest jobs, the greatest protection against layoffs, and other advantages to those employees who have been line drivers for the longest time. Where, because of the employer's prior

---

[32] Asbestos Workers Local 53 v. Vogler, 407 F.2d 1047 . . . (CA5), provides an apt illustration. There a union had a policy of excluding persons not related to present members by blood or marriage. When in 1966 suit was brought to challenge this policy, all of the union's members were white, largely as a result of pre-Act, intentional racial discrimination. The court observed; "While the nepotism requirement is applicable to black and white alike and is not on its face discriminatory, in a completely white union the present effect of its continued application is to forever deny to negroes and Mexican-Americans any real opportunity for membership." 407 F.2d, at 1054. . . .

intentional discrimination, the line drivers with the longest tenure are without exception white, the advantages of the seniority system flow disproportionately to them and away from Negro and Spanish-surnamed employees who might by now have enjoyed those advantages had not the employer discriminated before the passage of the Act. This disproportionate distribution of advantages does in a very real sense "operate to 'freeze' the status quo of prior discriminatory employment practices." Ibid. But both the literal terms of § 703(h) and the legislative history of Title VII demonstrate that Congress considered this very effect of many seniority systems and extended a measure of immunity to them.

Throughout the initial consideration of H. R. 7152, later enacted as the Civil Rights Act of 1964, critics of the bill charged that it would destroy existing seniority rights. The consistent response of Title VII's congressional proponents and of the Justice Department was that seniority rights would not be affected, even where the employer had discriminated prior to the Act. An interpretative memorandum placed in the Congressional Record by Senators Clark and Case stated:

"Title VII would have no effect on established seniority rights. Its effect is prospective and not retrospective. Thus, for example, *if a business has been discriminating in the past and as a result has an all-white working force, when the title comes into effect the employer's obligation would be simply to fill future vacancies on a non-discriminatory basis.* He would not be obliged — or indeed, permitted — to fire whites in order to hire Negroes, or to prefer Negroes for future vacancies, or, once Negroes are hired, to give them special seniority rights at the expense of the white workers hired earlier." 110 Cong. Rec. 7213 (1964) (emphasis added).[35]

A Justice Department statement concerning Title VII, placed in the Congressional Record by Senator Clark voiced the same conclusion:

"Title VII would have no effect on seniority rights existing at the time it takes effect. If for example, a collective bargaining contract provides that in the event of layoffs, those who were hired last must be laid off first, such a provision would not be affected in the least by Title VII. *This would be true even in the case where owing to discrimination prior to the effective date of the title, white workers*

---

[35] Senators Clark and Case were the "bipartisan captains" responsible for Title VII during the Senate debate. Bipartisan captains were selected for each title of the Civil Rights Act by the leading proponents of the Act in both parties. They were responsible for explaining their title in detail, defending it, and leading discussion on it. See 110 Cong. Rec. 6528 (1964) (remarks of Sen. Humphrey); Vass, Title VII: Legislative History, 7 B. C. Ind. & Com. L. Rev. 431, 444-445 (1966).

had more seniority than Negroes." Id., at 7207 (emphasis added). [36]

While these statements were made before § 703(h) was added to Title VII, they are authoritative indicators of that section's purpose. Section 703(h) was enacted as part of the Mansfield-Dirksen compromise substitute bill that cleared the way for the passage of Title VII. The drafters of the compromise bill stated that one of its principal goals was to resolve the ambiguities in the House-passed version of H. R. 7152. See, e.g., id., at 11935-11937 (remarks of Sen. Dirksen); id., at 12707 (remarks of Sen. Humphrey). As the debates indicate, one of those ambiguities concerned Title VII's impact on existing collectively bargained seniority rights. It is apparent that § 703(h) was drafted with an eye toward meeting the earlier criticism on this issue with an explicit provision embodying the understanding and assurances of the Act's proponents: namely, that Title VII would not outlaw such differences in treatment among employees as flowed from a bona fide seniority system that allowed for full exercise of seniority accumulated before the effective date of the Act. It is inconceivable that § 703(h), as part of a compromise bill, was intended to vitiate the earlier representations of the Act's supporters by increasing Title VII's impact on seniority systems. The statement of Senator Humphrey, noted in Franks, supra, at 761, . . . confirms that the addition of § 703(h) "merely clarifies [Title VII's] present intent and effect." 110 Cong. Rec. 12723 (1964).

In sum, the unmistakable purpose of § 703(h) was to make clear that the routine application of a bona fide seniority system would not be unlawful under Title VII. As the legislative history shows, this was the intended result even where the employer's pre-Act discrimination resulted in whites having greater existing seniority rights than Negroes. Although a seniority system inevitably tends to perpetuate the effects of pre-Act discrimination in such cases, the congressional judgment was that Title VII should not outlaw the use

---

[36] The full text of the statement is set out in Franks v. Bowman, 424 U.S., at 760 n. 16, ... Senator Clark also introduced a set of answers to questions propounded by Senator Dirksen, which included the following exchange:

"Question. Would the same situation prevail in respect to promotions, when the management function is governed by a labor contract calling for promotions on the basis of seniority? What of dismissals? Normally, labor contracts call for 'last hired, first fired.' If the last hired are Negroes, is the employer discriminating if his contract requires they be first fired and the remaining employees are white?

"Answer. Seniority rights are in no way affected by the bill. If under a 'last hired, first fired' agreement a Negro happens to be the 'last hired,' he can still be 'first fired' as long as it is done because of his status as 'last hired' and not because of his race." 110 Cong. Rec. 7217 (1964). See Franks, supra, at 760 n. 16. . . .

of existing seniority lists and thereby destroy or water down the vested seniority rights of employees simply because their employer had engaged in discrimination prior to the passage of the Act.

To be sure, § 703(h) does not immunize all seniority systems. It refers only to "bona fide" systems, and a proviso requires that any differences in treatment not be "the result of an intention to discriminate because of race . . . or national origin. . . ." But our reading of the legislative history compels us to reject the Government's broad argument that no seniority system that tends to perpetuate pre-Act discrimination can be "bona fide." To accept the argument would require us to hold that a seniority system becomes illegal simply because it allows the full exercise of the pre-Act seniority rights of employees of a company that discriminated before Title VII was enacted. It would place an affirmative obligation on the parties to the seniority agreement to subordinate those rights in favor of the claims of pre-Act discriminatees without seniority. The consequence would be a perversion of the congressional purpose. We cannot accept the invitation to disembowel § 703(h) by reading the words "bona fide" as the Government would have us do.[38] Accordingly, we hold that an otherwise neutral, legitimate seniority system does not become unlawful under Title VII simply because it may perpetuate pre-Act discrimination. Congress did not intend to make it illegal for employees with vested seniority rights to continue to exercise those rights, even at the expense of pre-Act discriminatees.[39]

---

[38] For the same reason, we reject the contention that the proviso in § 703(h), which bars differences in treatment resulting from "an intention to discriminate," applies to any application of a seniority system that may perpetuate past discrimination. In this regard the language of the Justice Department memorandum introduced at the legislative hearings, see supra, at 24, 14 FEP Cases, at 1525, is especially pertinent: "It is perfectly clear that when a worker is laid off or denied a chance for promotion because he is 'low man on the totem pole' he is not being discriminated against because of his race. . . . Any differences in treatment based on established seniority rights would not be based on race and would not be forbidden by the title." 110 Cong. Rec. 7207 (1964).

[39] The legislative history of the 1972 amendments to Title VII, summarized and discussed in Franks, supra, at 764-765, n. 21, 12 FEP Cases, at 556, id., at 796-797, n. 18, in no way points to a different result. As the discussion in Franks indicates, that history is itself susceptible of different readings. The few broad references to perpetuation of pre-Act discrimination or "*de facto* segregated job ladders," see, e.g., S. Rep. No. 92-415, pp. 5, 9 (1971); H. R. Rep. No. 92-238, pp. 8, 17 (1971), did not address the specific issue presented by this case. And the assumption of the authors of the Conference Report that "the present case law as developed by the courts would continue to govern the applicability and construction of Title VII," see Franks, supra, at 765 n. 21, . . ., of course does not foreclose our consideration of that issue. More importantly, the section of Title VII that we construe here, § 703(h), was enacted in 1964, not 1972. The views of members of a later Congress, concerning different sections of Title VII, enacted after this litigation was commenced, are entitled to little if any weight. It is the intent of the Congress that enacted § 703(h) in 1964, unmistakable in this case, that controls.

That conclusion is inescapable even in a case, such as this one, where the pre-Act discriminatees are incumbent employees who accumulated seniority in other bargaining units. Although there seems to be no explicit reference in the legislative history to pre-Act discriminatees already employed in less desirable jobs, there can be no rational basis for distinguishing their claims from those of persons initially denied *any* job but hired later with less seniority than they might have had in the absence of pre-Act discrimination.[40] We rejected any such distinction in Franks, finding that it had "no support anywhere in Title VII or its legislative history," 424 U.S., at 768, ... As discussed above, Congress in 1964 made clear that a seniority system is not unlawful because it honors employees' existing rights, even where the employer has engaged in pre-Act discriminatory hiring or promotion practices. It would be as contrary to that mandate to forbid the exercise of seniority rights with respect to discriminatees who held inferior jobs as with respect to later-hired minority employees who previously were denied any job. If anything, the latter group is the more disadvantaged. As in Franks, " '[i]t would indeed be surprising if Congress gave a remedy for the one [group] which it denied for the other.' " Id., quoting Phelps Dodge Corp. v. NLRB, 313 U.S. 177, 187, ...[41]

The seniority system in this case is entirely bona fide. It applies equally to all races and ethnic groups. To the extent that it "locks" employees into nonline-driver jobs, it does so for all. The city drivers and servicemen who are discouraged from transferring to line-driver jobs are not all Negroes or Spanish-surnamed Americans; to the

---

[40] That Title VII did not proscribe the denial of fictional seniority to pre-Act discriminatees who got no job was recognized even in Quarles v. Philip Morris, Inc., 279 F.Supp. 505, ... (E.D. Va.), and its progeny. Quarles stressed the fact that the references in the legislative history were to employment seniority rather than departmental seniority. 279 F.Supp., at 516, ... In Local 189, United Paperworkers v. United States, 416 F.2d 980, . . . (CA5), another leading case in this area, the court observed: "No doubt, Congress, to prevent 'reverse discrimination' meant to protect certain seniority rights that could not have existed but for previous racial discrimination. For example a Negro who had been rejected by an employer on racial grounds before passage of the Act could not, after being hired, claim to outrank whites who had been hired before him but after his original rejection, even though the Negro might have had senior status but for the past discrimination." 416 F.2d at 994, ...

[41] In addition, there is no reason to suppose that Congress intended in 1964 to extend less protection to legitimate departmental seniority systems than to plant-wide seniority systems. Then as now, seniority was measured in a number of ways, including length of time with the employer, in a particular plant, in a department, in a job, or in a line of progression. See Aaron, Reflections on the Legal Nature and Enforceability of Seniority Rights, 75 Harv. L. Rev. 1532, 1534 (1962); Cooper & Sobol, Seniority and Testing under Fair Employment Laws: A General Approach to Objective Criteria of Hiring and Promotion, 82 Harv. L. Rev. 1598, 1602 (1969). The legislative history contains no suggestion that any one system was preferred.

contrary, the overwhelming majority are white. The placing of line drivers in a separate bargaining unit from other employees is rational, in accord with the industry practice, and consistent with NLRB precedents.[42] It is conceded that the seniority system did not have its genesis in racial discrimination, and that it was negotiated and has been maintained free from any illegal purpose. In these circumstances, the single fact that the system extends no retroactive seniority to pre-Act discriminatees does not make it unlawful.

Because the seniority system was protected by § 703(h), the union's conduct in agreeing to and maintaining the system did not violate Title VII. On remand, the District Court's injunction against the union must be vacated.[43]

III

Our conclusion that the seniority system does not violate Title VII will necessarily affect the remedy granted to individual employees on remand of this litigation to the District Court. Those employees who suffered only pre-Act discrimination are not entitled to relief, and no person may be given retroactive seniority to a date earlier than the effective date of the Act. Several other questions relating to the appropriate measure of individual relief remain, however, for our consideration.

The petitioners argue generally that the trial court did not err in tailoring the remedy to the "degree of injury" suffered by each individual employee, and that the Court of Appeals' "qualification date" formula sweeps with too broad a brush by granting a remedy to employees who were not shown to be actual victims of unlawful discrimination. Specifically, the petitioners assert that no employee should be entitled to relief until the Government demonstrates that he was an actual victim of the company's discriminatory practices; that no employee who did not apply for a line-driver job should be granted retroactive competitive seniority; and that no employee should be elevated to a line-driver job ahead of any current line

---

[42] See Georgia Highway Express, 150 NLRB 1649, 1651, ... "The Board has long held that local drivers and over-the-road drivers constitute separate appropriate units where they are shown to be clearly defined, homogeneous, and functionally distinct groups with separate interests which can effectively be represented separately for bargaining purposes. . . . In view of the different duties and functions, separate supervision, and different bases of payment, it is clear that the over-the-road drivers have divergent interests from those of the employees in the [city operations] unit . . . and should not be included in that unit."

[43] The union will properly remain in this litigation as a defendant so that full relief may be awarded the victims of the employer's post-Act discrimination. Fed. Rule Civ. Proc. 19(a). See EEOC v. MacMillan Bloedel Containers, Inc., 503 F.2d 1086, 1095, . . . (CA6).

driver on layoff status. We consider each of these contentions separately.

A

The petitioners' first contention is in substance that the Government's burden of proof in a pattern or practice case must be equivalent to that outlined in McDonnell Douglas Corp. v. Green, supra. Since the Government introduced specific evidence of company discrimination against only some 40 employees, they argue that the District Court properly refused to award retroactive seniority to the remainder of the class of minority incumbent employees.

In McDonnell Douglas the Court considered "the order and allocation of proof in a private, non-class action challenging employment discrimination." 411 U.S., at 800. . . . We held that an individual Title VII complainant must carry the initial burden of proof by establishing a prima facie case of racial discrimination. On the specific facts there involved, we concluded that this burden was met by showing that a qualified applicant, who was a member of a racial minority group, had unsuccessfully sought a job for which there was a vacancy and for which the employer continued thereafter to seek applicants with similar qualifications. This initial showing justified the inference that the minority applicant was denied an employment opportunity for reasons prohibited by Title VII, and therefore shifted the burden to the employer to rebut that inference by offering some legitimate nondiscriminatory reason for the rejection. Id., at 802, . . .

The company and union seize upon the McDonnell Douglas pattern as the *only* means of establishing a prima facie case of individual discrimination. Our decision in that case, however, did not purport to create an inflexible formulation. We expressly noted that "[t]he facts necessarily will vary in Title VII cases, and the specification . . . of the prima facie proof required from [a plaintiff] is not necessarily applicable in every respect to differing factual situations." 411 U.S., at 802 n. 13, ... The importance of McDonnell Douglas lies not in its specification of the discrete elements of proof there required, but in its recognition of the general principle that any Title VII plaintiff must carry the initial burden of offering evidence adequate to create an inference that an employment decision was based on a discriminatory criterion illegal under the Act.

In Franks v. Bowman Transportation Co., the Court applied this principle in the context of a class action. The Franks plaintiffs proved, to the satisfaction of a district court, that Bowman Transportation Company "had engaged in a pattern of racial discrimination in various company policies, including the hiring, transfer, and discharge of employees." 424 U.S., at 751, ... Despite this showing, the trial court denied seniority relief to certain members of the class of discriminatees because not every individual had shown that he was qualified for the job he sought and that a vacancy had been available. We held that the trial court had erred in placing this burden on the individual plaintiffs. By "demonstrating the existence of a discriminatory hiring pattern and practice" the plaintiffs had made out a prima facie case of discrimination against the individual class members; the burden therefore shifted to the employer "to prove that individuals who reapply were not in fact victims of previous hiring discrimination." 424 U.S., at 772, ... The Franks case thus illustrates another means by which a Title VII plaintiff's initial burden of proof can be met. The class there alleged a broad-based policy of employment discrimination; upon proof of that allegation there were reasonable grounds to infer that individual hiring decisions were made in pursuit of the discriminatory policy and to require the employer to come forth with evidence dispelling that inference.

Although not all class actions will necessarily follow the Franks model, the nature of a pattern or practice suit brings it squarely within our holding in Franks. The plaintiff in a pattern or practice action is the Government, and its initial burden is to demonstrate that unlawful discrimination has been a regular procedure or policy followed by an employer or group of employers. . . . At the initial, "liability" stage of a pattern or practice suit the Government is not required to offer evidence that each person for whom it will ultimately seek relief was a victim of the employer's discriminatory policy. Its burden is to establish a prima facie case that such a policy existed. The burden then shifts to the employer to defeat the prima facie showing of a pattern or practice by demonstrating that the Government's proof is either inaccurate or insignificant. An employer might show, for example, that the claimed discriminatory pattern is a product of pre-Act hiring rather than unlawful post-Act discrimination, or that during the period it is alleged to have pursued a discriminatory policy it made too few employment decisions to justify the inference that it had engaged in a regular practice of discrimination.

If an employer fails to rebut the inference that arises from the Government's prima facie case, a trial court may then conclude that a violation has occurred and determine the appropriate remedy. Without any further evidence from the Government, a court's finding of a pattern or practice justifies an award of prospective relief. Such relief might take the form of an injunctive order against continuation of the discriminatory practice, an order that the employer keep records of its future employment decisions and file periodic reports with the court, or any other order "necessary to ensure the full employment of the rights" protected by Title VII.

When the Government seeks individual relief for the victims of the discriminatory practice, a district court must usually conduct additional proceedings after the liability phase of the trial to determine the scope of individual relief. The petitioners' contention in this case is that if the Government has not, in the course of proving a pattern or practice, already brought forth specific evidence that each individual was discriminatorily denied an employment opportunity, it must carry that burden at the second, "remedial" stage of trial. That basic contention was rejected in the Franks case. As was true of the particular facts in Franks, and as is typical of Title VII pattern or practice suits, the question of individual relief does not arise until it has been proved that the employer has followed an employment policy of unlawful discrimination. The force of that proof does not dissipate at the remedial stage of the trial. The employer cannot, therefore, claim that there is no reason to believe that its individual employment decisions were discriminatorily based; it has already been shown to have maintained a policy of discriminatory decision-making.

The proof of the pattern or practice supports an inference that any particular employment decision, during the period in which the discriminatory policy was in force, was made in pursuit of that policy. The Government need only show that an alleged individual discriminatee unsuccessfully applied for a job and therefore was a potential victim of the proven discrimination. As in Franks, the burden then rests on the employer to demonstrate that the individual applicant was denied an employment opportunity for lawful reasons. See 424 U.S., at 773 n. 32, ...

In Part II-A, supra, we have held that the District Court and Court of Appeals were not in error in finding that the Government had proved a systemwide pattern and practice of racial and ethnic discrimination on the part of the company. On remand, therefore, every post-Act minority group applicant for a line-driver position will be presumptively entitled to relief, subject to a showing by the company that its earlier refusal to place the applicant in a line-driver job was not based on its policy of discrimination.

B

The Court of Appeals' "qualification date" formula for relief did not distinguish between incumbent employees who had applied for line-driver jobs and those who had not. The appellate court held that where there has been a showing of classwide discriminatory practices coupled with a seniority system that perpetuates the effects of that discrimination, an individual member of the class need not show that he unsuccessfully applied for the position from which the class had been excluded. In support of its award of relief to all nonapplicants, the Court suggested that "as a practical matter . . . a member of the affected class may well have concluded that an application for transfer to an all [w]hite position such as [line driver] was not worth the candle." 517 F.2d, at 320, ...

The company contends that a grant of retroactive seniority to these nonapplicants is inconsistent with the make-whole purpose of a Title VII remedy and impermissibly will require the company to give preferential treatment to employees solely because of their race. The thrust of the company's contention is that unless a minority-group employee actually applied for a line-driver job, either for initial hire or for transfer, he has suffered no injury from whatever discrimination might have been involved in the refusal of such jobs to those who actually applied for them.

The Government argues in response that there should be no "immutable rule" that nonapplicants are nonvictims, and contends that a determination whether nonapplicants have suffered from unlawful discrimination will necessarily vary depending on the circumstances of each particular case. The Government further asserts that under the specific facts of this case, the Court of Appeals correctly determined that all qualified nonapplicants were likely victims and were therefore presumptively entitled to relief.

The question whether seniority relief may be awarded to nonapplicants was left open by our decision in Franks, since the class at issue in that case was limited to "identifiable applicants who were denied employment . . . after the effective date . . . of Title VII." 424 U.S., at 750, ... We now decide that an incumbent employee's failure to apply for a job is not an inexorable bar to an award of retroactive seniority. Individual nonapplicants must be given an opportunity to undertake their difficult task of proving that they should be treated as applicants and therefore are presumptively entitled to relief accordingly.

(1)

Analysis of this problem must begin with the premise that the scope of a district court's remedial powers under Title VII is determined by the purposes of the Act. Albemarle Paper Co. v. Moody, supra, at 417, ... In Griggs v. Duke Power Co., supra, and again in Albemarle, the Court noted that a primary objective of Title VII is prophylactic: to achieve equal employment opportunity and to remove the barriers that have operated to favor white male employees over other employees. 401 U.S., at 429-430, . . . ; 422 U.S., at 417, ... The prospect of retroactive relief for victims of discrimination serves this purpose by providing the " 'spur or catalyst which causes employers and unions to self-examine and to self-evaluate their employment practices and to endeavor to eliminate, so far as possible, the last vestiges' " of their discriminatory practices. Albemarle, supra, at 417-418, ... An equally important purpose of the Act is "to make persons whole for injuries suffered on account of unlawful employment discrimination." Id., at 418, ... In determining the specific remedies to be afforded, a district court is "to fashion such relief as the particular circumstances of a case may require to effect restitution." Franks, supra, at 764, ...

Thus, the Court has held that the purpose of Congress in vesting broad equitable powers in Title VII courts was "to make possible the 'fashion[ing] [of] the most complete relief possible,' " and that the district courts have " 'not merely the power but the duty to render a decree which will so far as possible eliminate the discriminatory effects of the past as well as bar like discrimination in the future.' " Albemarle, supra, at 421, 418, ... More specifically, in Franks we decided that a court must ordinarily award a seniority remedy unless there exist reasons for denying relief " 'which, if applied generally, would not frustrate the central statutory purposes of eradicating discrimination . . . and making persons whole for injuries suffered.' " 424 U.S., at 771, . . . , quoting Albemarle, supra, at 421, ...

Measured against these standards, the company's assertion that a person who has not actually applied for a job can *never* be awarded seniority relief cannot prevail. The effects of and the injuries suffered from discriminatory employment practices are not always confined to those who were expressly denied a requested employment opportunity. A consistently enforced discriminatory policy can surely deter job applications from those who are aware of it and are unwilling to subject themselves to the humiliation of explicit and certain rejection.

If an employer should announce his policy of discrimination by a sign reading "Whites Only" on the hiring-office door, his victims would not be limited to the few who ignored the sign and subjected themselves to personal rebuffs. The same message can be communicated to potential applicants more subtly but just as clearly by an employer's actual practices — by his consistent discriminatory treatment of actual applicants, by the manner in which he publicizes vacancies, his recruitment techniques, his responses to casual or tentative inquiries, and even by the racial or ethnic composition of that part of his work force from which he has discriminatorily excluded members of minority groups. When a person's desire for a job is not translated into a formal application solely because of his unwillingness to engage in a futile gesture he is as much a victim of discrimination as is he who goes through the motions of submitting an application.

In cases decided under the National Labor Relations Act, the model for Title VII's remedial provisions, Albemarle, supra, at 419, . . . ; Franks, supra, at 769, . . ., the National Labor Relations Board, and the courts in enforcing its orders, have recognized that the failure to submit a futile application does not bar an award of relief to a person claiming that he was denied employment because of union affiliation or activity. In NLRB v. Nevada Consolidated Copper Corp., 316 U.S. 105, . . . this Court enforced an order of the Board directing an employer to hire, with retroactive benefits, former employees who had not applied for newly available jobs because of the employer's well-known policy of refusing to hire union members. See In re Nevada Consolidated Copper Corp., 26 N.L.R.B. 1182, 1208, 1231. Similarly, when an application would have been no more than a vain gesture in light of employe[e] discrimination, the Courts of Appeals have enforced Board orders reinstating striking workers despite the failure of individual strikers to apply for reinstatement when the strike ended. E.g., NLRB v. Park Edge Sheridan Meats, Inc., 323 F.2d 956, . . . (CA 2); NLRB v. Valley Die Cast Corp., 303 F.2d 64, . . . (CA 6); Eagle-Picher Mining & Smelting Co. v. NLRB, 119 F.2d 903, . . . (CA 8). See also Piasecki Aircraft Corp. v. NLRB, 280 F.2d 575, . . . (CA 3); NLRB v. Anchor Rome Mills, 228 F.2d 775, . . . (CA 5); NLRB v. Lummus Co., 210 F.2d 377, . . . (CA 5). Consistent with the NLRA model, several Courts of Appeals have held in Title VII cases that a nonapplicant can be a victim of unlawful discrimination entitled to make-whole relief when an application would have been a useless act serving only to confirm a discriminatee's knowledge that the job he wanted was unavailable to him. Acha v. Beame, 531 F.2d 648, 656, . . . (CA 2); Hairston v. McLean Trucking Co., 520 F.2d 226, 231-233, . . . (CA 4); Bing v. Roadway Express, Inc., 485 F.2d 441, 451, . . . (CA 5); United States v. N. L. Industries, Inc., 479 F.2d 354, 369, . . . (CA 8).

The denial of Title VII relief on the ground that the claimant had not formally applied for the job could exclude from the Act's coverage the victims of the most entrenched forms of discrimination. Victims of gross and pervasive discrimination could be denied relief precisely because the unlawful practices had been so successful as totally to deter job applications from members of minority groups. A *per se* prohibition of relief to nonapplicants could thus put beyond the reach of equity the most invidious effects of employment discrimination — those that extend to the very hope of self-realization. Such a *per se* limitation on the equitable powers granted to courts by Title VII would be manifestly inconsistent with the "historic purpose of equity to 'secur[e] complete justice' and with the duty of courts in Title VII cases " 'to render a decree which will so far as possible eliminate the discriminatory effects of the past.' " Albemarle Paper Co. v. Moody, supra, at 418, . . .

(2)

To conclude that a person's failure to submit an application for a job does not inevitably and forever foreclose his entitlement to seniority relief under Title VII is a far cry, however, from holding that nonapplicants are always entitled to such relief. A nonapplicant must show that he was a potential victim of unlawful discrimination. Because he is necessarily claiming that he was deterred from applying for the job by the employer's discriminatory practices, his is the not always easy burden of proving that he would have applied for the job had it not been for those practices. Cf. Mt. Healthy City School District Board of Education v. Doyle, 229 U.S. 274. When this burden is met, the nonapplicant is in a position analogous to that of an applicant and is entitled to the presumption discussed in Part III-A, supra.

The Government contends that the evidence it presented in this case at the liability stage of the trial identified all nonapplicants as victims of unlawful discrimination "with a fair degree of specificity," and that the Court of Appeals' determination that qualified nonapplicants are presumptively entitled to an award of seniority should accordingly be affirmed. In support of this contention the Government cites its proof of an extended pattern and practice of discrimination as evidence that an application from a minority employee for a line-driver job would have been a vain and useless act. It further argues that since the class of nonapplicant discriminatees is limited to incumbent employees, it is likely that every class member was aware of the futility of seeking a linedriver job and therefore deterred from filing both an initial and a follow-up application.[52]

---

[52] The limitation to incumbent employees is also said to serve the same function that actual job applications served in Franks: providing a means of distinguishing members of the excluded minority group from minority members of the public at large. While it is true that incumbency in this case and actual applications in Franks both serve to narrow what might otherwise be an impossible task, the status of nonincumbent applicant and nonapplicant incumbent differ substantially. The refused applicants in Franks had been denied an opportunity they clearly sought, and the only issue to be resolved was whether the denial was pursuant to a proven discriminatory practice. Resolution of the nonapplicant's claim, however, requires two distinct determinations: that he would have applied but for discrimination and that he would have been discriminatorily rejected had he applied. The mere fact of incumbency does not resolve the first issue, although it may tend to support a nonapplicant's claim to the extent that it shows he was willing and competent to work as a driver, that he was familiar with the tasks of line drivers, etc. An incumbent's claim that he would have applied for a line-driver job would certainly be more superficially plausible than a similar claim by a member of the general public who may never have worked in the trucking industry or heard of T.I.M.E.-D.C. prior to suit.

We cannot agree. While the scope and duration of the company's discriminatory policy can leave little doubt that the futility of seeking line-driver jobs was communicated to the company's minority employees, that in itself is insufficient. The known prospect of discriminatory rejection shows only that employees who wanted line-driving jobs may have been deterred from applying for them. It does not show which of the nonapplicants actually wanted such jobs, or which possessed the requisite qualifications.[53] There are differences between city and line-driving jobs, for example, but the desirability of the latter is not so self-evident as to warrant a conclusion that all employees would prefer to be line drivers if given a free choice. Indeed, a substantial number of white city drivers who were not subjected to the company's discriminatory practices were apparently content to retain their city jobs.

In order to fill this evidentiary gap, the Government argues that a nonapplicant's current willingness to transfer into a line-driver position confirms his past desire for the job. An employee's response to the court-ordered notice of his entitlement to relief demonstrates, according to this argument, that the employee would have sought a line-driver job when he first became qualified to fill one, but for his knowledge of the company's discriminatory policy.

This assumption falls short of satisfying the appropriate burden of proof. An employee who transfers into a line-driver unit is normally placed at the bottom of the seniority "board." He is thus in jeopardy of being laid off and must, at best, suffer through an initial period of bidding on only the least desirable runs. . . . Nonapplicants who chose to accept the appellate court's *post hoc* invitation, however, would enter the line-driving unit with retroactive seniority dating from the time they were first qualified. A willingness to accept the job security and bidding power afforded by retroactive seniority says little about what choice an employee would have made had he previously been given the opportunity freely to choose a starting line-driver job. While it may be true that many of the nonapplicant employees desired and would have applied for line-driver jobs but for their knowledge of the company's policy of discrimination, the Government must carry its burden of proof, with

---

[53] Inasmuch as the purpose of the nonapplicant's burden of proof will be to establish that his status is similar to that of the applicant, he must bear the burden of coming forward with the basic information about his qualifications that he would have presented in an application. As in Franks, and in accord with Part III-A, supra, the burden then will be on the employer to show that the nonapplicant was nevertheless not a victim of discrimination. For example, the employer might show that there were other, more qualified persons who would have been chosen for a particular vacancy, or that the nonapplicant's stated qualifications were insufficient. See Franks, supra, at 773 n. 32, ...

respect to each specific individual, at the remedial hearings to be conducted by the District Court on remand.[58]

C

The task remaining for the District Court on remand will not be a simple one. Initially, the court will have to make a substantial number of individual determinations in deciding which of the minority employees were actual victims of the company's discriminatory practices. After the victims have been identified, the court must, as nearly as possible, " 'recreate the conditions and relationships that would have been had there been no' " unlawful discrimination. Franks, supra, 424 U.S., at 769. . . . This process of recreating the past will necessarily involve a degree of approximation and imprecision. Because the class of victims may include some who did not apply for line-driver jobs as well as those who did, and because more than one minority employee may have been denied each line-driver vacancy, the court will be required to balance the equities of each minority employee's situation in allocating the limited number of vacancies that were discriminatorily refused to class members.

Moreover, after the victims have been identified and their rightful place determined, the District Court will again be faced with the delicate task of adjusting the remedial interests of discriminatees and the legitimate expectations of other employees innocent of any wrongdoing. In the prejudgment consent decree, see supra, at 3-4, n. 4, . . ., the company and the Government agreed that minority employees would assume line-driver positions that had been discriminatorily denied to them by exercising a first-priority right to job vacancies at the company's terminals. The decree did not determine what constituted a vacancy, but in its final order the trial court defined "vacancy" to exclude any position that became available while there were laid-off employees awaiting an opportunity to return to work. Employees on layoff were given a preference to fill whatever openings might occur at their terminals during a three-year period after they were laid off. The Court of Appeals rejected the preference and held that all but "purely temporary" vacancies were to be filled according to an employee's seniority, whether as a member of the class discriminated against or as an incumbent line driver on layoff. 517 F.2d at 322-324. . . .

---

[58] While the most convincing proof would be some overt act such as a pre-Act application for a line-driver job, the District Court may find evidence of an employee's informal inquiry, expression of interest, or even unexpressed desire credible and convincing. The question is a factual one for determination by the trial judge.

As their final contention concerning the remedy, the company and the union argue that the trial court correctly made the adjustment between the competing interests of discriminatees and other employees by granting a preference to laid-off employees, and that the Court of Appeals erred in disturbing it. The petitioners therefore urge the reinstatement of that part of the trial court's final order pertaining to the rate at which victims will assume their rightful places in the line-driver hierarchy.

Although not directly controlled by the Act, the extent to which the legitimate expectations of nonvictim employees should determine when victims are restored to their rightful place is limited by basic principles of equity. In devising and implementing remedies under Title VII, no less than in formulating any equitable decree, a court must draw on the "qualities of mercy and practicality [that] have made equity the instrument for nice adjustment and reconciliation between the public interest and private needs as well as between competing private claims." Hecht Co. v. Bowles, 321 U.S. 321, 329-330. Cf. Phelps Dodge Corp. v. NLRB, 313 U.S. 177, 195-196, . . . modifying and remanding In re Phelps Dodge Corp., 19 N.L.R.B. 547 . . .; Franks, supra, at 798-799. . . . Especially when immediate implementation of an equitable remedy threatens to impinge upon the expectations of innocent parties, the courts must "look to the practical realities and necessities inescapably involved in reconciling competing interests," in order to determine the "special blend of what is necessary, what is fair, and what is workable." Lemon v. Kurtzman, 411 U.S. 192, 201, 200 (opinion of BURGER, C. J.).

Because of the limited facts now in the record, we decline to strike the balance in this Court. The District Court did not explain why it subordinated the interests of class members to the contractual recall expectations of other employees on layoff. When it made that determination, however, it was considering a class or more than 400 minority employees, all of whom had been granted some preference in filling line-driver vacancies. The overwhelming majority of these were in the District Court's subclass three, composed of those employees with respect to whom neither the Government nor the company had presented any specific evidence on the question of unlawful discrimination. Thus, when the court considered the problem of what constituted a line-driver "vacancy" to be offered to class members, it may have been influenced by the relatively small number of proven victims and the large number of minority employees about whom it had no information. On the other hand, the Court of Appeals redefined "vacancy" in the context of what it believed to be a class of more than 400 employees who had actually suffered from discrimination at the behest of both the company and the union, and its determination may well have been influenced by that understanding. For the reasons discussed in this opinion, neither court's concept was completely valid.

After the evidentiary hearings to be conducted on remand, both the size and the composition of the class of minority employees entitled to relief may be altered substantially. Until those hearings have been conducted and both the number of identifiable victims and the consequent extent of necessary relief have been determined, it is not possible to evaluate abstract claims concerning the equitable balance that should be struck between the statutory rights of victims and the contractual rights of nonvictim employees. That determination is best left, in the first instance, to the sound equitable discretion of the trial court. See Franks v. Bowman, supra, at 779 . . . ; Albemarle Paper Co v. Moody, supra, at 416. . . . We observe only that when the court exercises its discretion in dealing with the problem of laid-off employees in light of the facts developed at the hearings on remand, it should clearly state its reason so that meaningful review may be had on appeal. See Franks, supra, at 774 . . .; Albemarle Paper Co. v. Moody, supra, at 421, n. 14. . . .

For all the reasons we have discussed, the judgment of the Court of Appeals is vacated, and the cases are remanded to the District Court for further proceedings consistent with this opinion.

Mr. Justice Marshall, with whom Mr. Justice Brennan joins, concurring in part and dissenting in part.

I agree with the Court that the United States proved that petitioner T.I.M.E.-D.C. was guilty of a pattern or practice of discriminating against blacks and Spanish-speaking Americans in hiring line drivers. I also agree that incumbent minority-group employees who show that they applied for a line-driver job or that they would have applied but for petitioner's unlawful acts are presumptively entitled to the full measure of relief set forth in our decision last Term in Franks v. Bowman Transportation Co., 424 U.S. 747, . . . (1976). But I do not agree that Title VII permits petitioners to treat non-Anglo line drivers differently from Anglo drivers who were hired by the company at the same time simply because the non-Anglo drivers were prevented by the company from acquiring seniority over the road. I therefore dissent from that aspect of the Court's holding, and from the limitations on the scope of the remedy that follow from it.

As the Court quite properly acknowledges, . . . the seniority provision at issue here clearly would violate Title VII absent § 703(h), . . . which exempts at least some seniority systems from the reach of the Act, Title VII prohibits an employer from "classify[ing] his employees . . . in any way which would deprive or tend to deprive any individual of employment opportunities or otherwise adversely affect his status as an employee, because of such individual's race, color, religion, sex or national origin." 42 U.S.C. § 2000e-2(a)(2).

"Under the Act, practices, procedures or tests neutral on their face and even neutral in terms of intent, cannot be maintained *if they operate to 'freeze' the status quo of prior discriminatory employment practices.*" Griggs v. Duke Power Co., 401 U.S. 424, 429, . . . (1971) (emphasis added). Petitioners' seniority system does precisely that: it awards the choicest jobs and other benefits to those possessing a credential — seniority — which, due to past discrimination, blacks and Spanish-speaking employees were prevented from acquiring. Consequently, "Every time a Negro worker hired under the old segregated system bids against a white worker in his job slot, the old racial classification reasserts itself, and the Negro suffers anew for his employer's previous bias." Local 189, United Papermakers & Paperworkers v. United States, 416 F.2d 980, . . . (CA5 1969) (Wisdom, J.), *cert. denied,* 397 U.S. 919, . . . (1970).

As the Court also concedes, with a touch of understatement, "the view that § 703(h) does not immunize seniority systems that perpetuate the effects of prior discrimination has much support." . . . Without a single dissent, six courts of appeals have so held in over 30 cases, and two other courts of appeals have indicated their agreement, also without dissent. In an unbroken line of cases, the EEOC has reached the same conclusion. And the overwhelming weight of scholarly opinion is in accord. Yet for the second time this Term, see General Electric Co. v. Gilbert, 429 U.S. 125, . . . (1976), a majority of this Court overturns the unanimous conclusion of the courts of appeals and the EEOC concerning the scope of Title VII. Once again, I respectfully disagree.

I

Initially, it is important to bear in mind that Title VII is a remedial statute designed to eradicate certain invidious employment practices. The evils against which it is aimed are defined broadly: "to fail . . . to hire or to discharge . . . *or otherwise to discriminate* . . . with respect to . . . compensation, terms, conditions, or privileges of employment," and "to limit, segregate, or classify . . . *in any way* that would deprive *or tend to deprive* any individual of employment opportunities *or otherwise adversely affect his status.*" 42 U.S.C. § 20003-2(a) (emphasis added). Section 703(h) carves out an exemption from these broad prohibitions. Accordingly, under longstanding principles of statutory construction, the Act should "be given a liberal interpretation . . . [and] exemptions from its sweep should be narrowed and limited to effect the remedy intended." Piedmont & Northern R. Co. v. ICC, 286 U.S. 290, 311-312 (1932); see also Spokane & Inland R. Co. v. United States, 241 U.S. 344, 350 (1916); United States v. Dickinson, 15 Pet. 141, 165 (1841) (Story, J.). Unless a seniority system that perpetuates discrimination falls "plainly and unmistakably within [the] terms and spirit" of § 703(h), A. H. Phillips, Inc. v. Walling, 324 U.S. 490, 493, 5 WH Cases 186 (1945), the system should be deemed unprotected. I submit that whatever else may be true of the section, its applicability to systems that perpetuate past discrimination is not "plainly and unmistakably" clear.

The language of § 703(h) provides anything but clear support for the Court's holding. That section provides, in pertinent part:

> "[I]t shall not be an unlawful employment practice for an employer to apply different standards of compensation, or different terms. conditions or privileges of employment pursuant to a bona fide seniority . . . system . . . *provided that such differences are not the result of an intention to discriminate because of race, color, religion, sex, or national origin. . . .*" (Emphasis added.)

In this case, however, the different "privileges of employment" for Anglos and non-Anglos produced by petitioners' seniority system are precisely the result of prior, intentional discrimination in assigning jobs; but for that discrimination, non-Anglos would not be disadvantaged by the system. Thus if the proviso is read literally, the instant case falls squarely within it, thereby rendering § 703(h) inapplicable. To avoid this result the Court is compelled to reconstruct the proviso to read: "provided that such a seniority system did not have its genesis in racial discrimination, and that it was negotiated and has been maintained free from any illegal purpose." . . .

There are no explicit statements in the legislative history of Title VII that warrant this radical reconstruction of the proviso. The three documents placed in the Congressional Record by Senator Clark concerning seniority all were authored many weeks before the Mansfield-Dirksen amendment containing § 703(h) was introduced. Accordingly, they do not specifically discuss the meaning of the proviso. More importantly, none of the documents addresses the general problem of seniority systems that perpetuate discrimination. Not surprisingly, Congress simply did not think of such subtleties in enacting a comprehensive, path-breaking civil rights act. To my mind, this is dispositive. Absent unambiguous statutory language or an authoritative statement in the legislative history legalizing seniority systems that continue past wrongs, I do not see how it can be said that the § 703(h) exemption "plainly and unmistakably" applies.

II

Even if I were to agree that his case properly can be decided on the basis of inferences as to Congress' intent, I still could not accept the Court's holding. In my view, the legislative history of the 1964 Civil Rights Act does not support the conclusion that Congress intended to legalize seniority systems that perpetuate discrimination, and administrative and legislative developments since 1964 positively refute that conclusion.

A

The Court's decision to uphold seniority systems that perpetuate post-Act discrimination — that is, seniority systems that treat non-Anglos who become line drivers as new employees even though, after the effective date of Title VII, these non-Anglos were discriminatorily assigned to city-driver jobs where they accumulated seniority — is explained in a single footnote. Ante, at 174 n. 30, ... That footnote relies almost entirely on United Airlines v. Evans, ... But like the instant decision, Evans is devoid of any analysis of the legislative history of § 703 (h); it simply asserts its conclusion in a single paragraph. For the Court to base its decision here on the strength of Evans is sheer bootstrapping.

Had the Court objectively examined the legislative history, it would have been compelled to reach the opposite conclusion. As we stated just last Term, "it is apparent that the thrust of [§ 703 (h)] is directed toward defining what is and what is not an illegal discriminatory practice in instances in which the post-Act operation of a seniority system is challenged as perpetuating the effects of discrimination *occurring prior to the effective date of the Act.*"[8] Franks v. Bowman Transportation Co., supra, 424 U.S., at 761, . . . (emphasis added). Congress was concerned with seniority expectations that had developed prior to the enactment of Title VII, not with expectations arising thereafter to the extent that those expectations were dependent on whites benefiting from unlawful discrimination. Thus, the paragraph of the Clark-Case Interpretive Memorandum dealing with seniority systems begins:

"Title VII would have no effect on established seniority rights. *Its effect is prospective and not retrospective.*" 110 Cong. Rec. 7213 (emphasis added).

---

[8] This understanding of § 703 (h) underlies Frank's holding that constructive seniority is the presumptively correct remedy for discriminatory refusals to hire, even though awarding such seniority necessarily disrupts the expectations of other employees.

Similarly, the Justice Department memorandum that Senator Clark introduced explains:

> "Title VII would have no effect on seniority rights existing *at the time it takes effect.* If, for example a collective bargaining contract provides that in the event of layoffs, those who were hired last must be laid off first, such a provision would not be affected . . . by Title VII. This would be true even in the case where *owing to discrimination prior to the effective date of the title,* white workers had more seniority than Negroes. . . . Any difference based on *established* seniority rights would not be based on race and would not be forbidden by the title." Id., at 7202 (emphasis added).

Finally, Senator Clark's prepared answers to questions propounded by Senator Dirksen stated:

> "Question. If an employer is directed to abolish his employment list because of discrimination what happens to seniority?
> "Answer. *The bill is not retroactive,* and it will not require an employer to change existing seniority lists." Id., at 7217 (emphasis added).

For the Court to ignore this history while reaching a conclusion contrary to it is little short of remarkable.

B

The legislative history of § 703 (h) admittedly affords somewhat stronger support for the Court's conclusion with respect to seniority systems that perpetuate pre-Act discrimination — that is, seniority systems that treat non-Anglos who become line drivers as new employees even though these non-Anglos were discriminatorily assigned to city-driver jobs where they accumulated seniority before the effective date of Title VII. In enacting § 703 (h), Congress intended to extend at least some protection to seniority expectations that had developed prior to the effective date of the Act. But the legislative history is very clear that the only threat to these expectations that Congress was seeking to avert was nonremedial, fictional seniority. Congress did not want minority group members who were hired after the effective date of the Act to be given superseniority simply because they were members of minority groups, nor did it want the use of seniority to be invalidated whenever it had a disparate impact on newly hired minority employees. These are the evils — and the only evils — that the opponents of Title VII raised and that the Clark-Case Interpretive

Memorandum addressed. As the Court acknowledges, "there seems to be no explicit reference in the legislative history to pre-Act discriminatees already employed in less desirable jobs." Ante, at 28, ...

Our task, then, assuming still that the case properly can be decided on the basis of imputed legislative intent, is "to put to ourselves the question, which choice is it more likely that Congress would have made," Burnet v. Guggenheim, 288 U.S. 280, 285 (1933) (Cardozo, J.), had it focused on the problem: would it have validated or invalidated seniority systems that perpetuate pre-Act discrimination? To answer that question, the devastating impact of today's holding validating such systems must be fully understood. Prior to 1965 blacks and Spanish-speaking Americans who were able to find employment were assigned the lowest paid, most menial jobs in many industries throughout the Nation but especially in the South. In many factories, blacks were hired as laborers while whites were trained and given skilled positions; in the transportation industry blacks could only become porters; and in steel plants blacks were assigned to the coke ovens and blasting furnaces, "the hotter and dirtier" places of employment. The Court holds, in essence, that while after 1965 these incumbent employees are entitled to an equal opportunity to advance to more desirable jobs, to take advantage of that opportunity they must pay a price: they must surrender the seniority they have accumulated in their old jobs. For many, the price will be too high, and they will be locked-in to their previous positions. Even those willing to pay the price will have to reconcile themselves to being forever behind subsequently hired whites who were not discriminatorily assigned. Thus equal opportunity will remain a distant dream for all incumbent employees.

I am aware of nothing in the legislative history of the 1964 Civil Rights Act to suggest that if Congress had focused on this fact it nonetheless would have decided to write off an entire generation of minority group employees. Nor can I believe that the Congress that enacted Title VII would have agreed to postpone for one generation the achievement of economic equality. The backers of that Title viewed economic equality as both a practical necessity and a moral imperative. They were well aware of the corrosive impact employment discrimination has on its victims, and on the society generally. They sought, therefore, "to eliminate those discriminatory practices and devices which have fostered racially stratified job environments to the disadvantage of minority citizens"; McDonnell Douglas Corp. v. Green, 411 U. S. 792, 800, . . . (1973); see also Griggs v. Duke Power Co., supra, 401 U. S., at 429-430, 431, . . . ; Alexander v. Gardner-Denver Co., 415 U. S. 36, 44, . . . ; and "to make persons whole for injuries suffered on account of unlawful employment discrimination," Albemarle Paper Co. v. Moody, 422 U.

S. 405, 418, . . . (1975). In short, Congress wanted to enable black workers to assume their rightful place in society.

It is of course true that Congress was not willing to invalidate seniority systems on a wholesale basis in pursuit of that goal. But the United States, as the plaintiff suing on behalf of the incumbent minority group employees here, does not seek to overturn petitioners' seniority system. It seeks only to have the "time actually worked in [non-Anglo] jobs [recognized] as the equal of [Anglo] time." Local 189, United Papermakers & Paperworkers v. United States, supra, 416 F. 2d, at 995, . . . within the existing seniority system. Admittedly, such recognition would impinge on the seniority expectations white employees had developed prior to the effective date of the Act. But in enacting Title VII, Congress manifested a willingness to do precisely that. For example, the Clark-Case Interpretive Memorandum . . . makes clear that Title VII prohibits unions and employers from using discriminatory waiting lists, developed prior to the effective date of the Title, in making selections for jobs or training programs after that date. 110 Cong. Rec. 7213 (1964). Such a prohibition necessarily would disrupt the expectations of those on the lists. More generally, the very fact that Congress made Title VII effective shortly after its enactment demonstrates that expectations developed prior to passage of the Act were not considered sacrosanct, since Title VII's general ban on employment discrimination inevitably interfered with the pre-existing expectations of whites who anticipated benefiting from continued discrimination. Thus I am in complete agreement with Judge Butzner's conclusion in his seminal decision in Quarles v. Philip Morris, Inc., 279 F.Supp. 505, 516, . . . (E.D. Va. 1968): "It is . . . apparent that Congress did not intend to freeze an entire generation of Negro employees into discriminatory patterns that existed before the Act."

C

If the legislative history of § 703 (h) leaves any doubt concerning the section's applicability to seniority systems that perpetuate either pre- or post-Act discrimination, that doubt is entirely dispelled by two subsequent developments. The Court all but ignores both developments; I submit they are critical.

First, in more than a score of decisions beginning at least as early as 1969, the Equal Employment Opportunities Commission has consistently held that seniority systems that perpetuate prior discrimination are unlawful. While the Court may have retreated, see General Electric v. Gilbert, 429 U. S. 125, 141-142, . . . (1976), from its prior view that the interpretations of the EEOC are " 'entitled to great deference,' " Albemarle Paper Co. v. Moody, 422 U.S. 405,

431, ... (1975), quoting, Griggs v. Duke Power Co., supra, 401 U. S., at 433 ..., I have not. Before I would sweep aside the EEOC's consistent interpretation of the statute it administers, I would require " 'compelling indications that it is wrong.' " Espinoza v. Farah Manufacturing Co., 414 U. S. 86, 94-95, ... (1973), quoting Red Lion Broadcasting Co. v. FCC, 395 U. S. 367, 381 (1969). I find no such indications in the Court's opinion.

Second, in 1972 Congress enacted the Equal Employment Opportunities Act of 1972, ... amending Title VII. In so doing, Congress made very clear that it approved of the lower court decisions invalidating seniority systems that perpetuate discrimination. That Congress was aware of such cases is evident from the Senate and House Committee reports which cite the two leading decisions, as well as several prominent law review articles. S.Rep. No. 92-415, 92d Cong., 1st Sess., 5 n. 1 (1971); H. R. Rep. No. 92-238, 92d Cong., 1st Sess., 8 n. 2 (1971). Although Congress took action with respect to other lower court opinions with which it was dissatisfied, it made no attempt to overrule the seniority cases. To the contrary, both the Senate and House reports expressed approval of the "perpetuation principle" as applied to seniority systems and invoked the principle to justify the committee's recommendations to extend Title VII's coverage to state and local government employees, and to expand the powers of the EEOC. Moreover, the Section-by-Section Analysis of the Conference Committee bill, which was prepared and placed in the Congressional Record by the floor managers of the bill, stated in "language that could hardly be more explicit," Franks v. Bowman Transportation Co., supra, 424 U. S., at 765 n. 21, ... that, "in any areas where a specific contrary intention is not indicated, it was assumed that the present case law ... would continue to govern the applicability and construction of Title VII." 118 Cong. Rev. 7166, 7564 (1972). And perhaps most important, in explaining the section of the 1972 Act that empowers the EEOC "to prevent any person from engaging in any unlawful employment practice as set forth in section 703 or 704," ..., the Section-by-Section Analysis declared that:

"The unlawful employment practices encompassed by sections 703 and 704 which were enumerated in 1964 by the original Act, *and as defined and expanded by the Courts* remain in effect." Id., at 7167, 7564 (emphasis added).

Only last Term, we concluded that the legislative materials reviewed above "completely answer the argument that Congress somehow intended seniority relief to be less available" than backpay as a remedy for discrimination. Franks v. Bowman Transportation Co., supra, at 765 n. 21, ... If anything, the materials provide an even more complete answer to the argument that Congress somehow intended to immunize seniority systems that perpetuate past discrimination. To the extent that today's decision grants immunity to such systems, I respectfully dissent.

UNITED AIRLINES v. EVANS

United States Supreme Court
431 U. S. 553, 97 S. Ct. 1885, 52 L. Ed. 2d 571 (1977)

[Carolyn Evans resigned from her flight attendant job in 1968 under the United Air Lines rule against married women. She did not file a charge with the EEOC within 90 days of her separation, and hence her claim based on that discriminatory act was barred. Meanwhile, the "no-marriage" rule was eliminated and she was rehired on February 16, 1972, but as a new employee without seniority credit for her past service. She had no claim under the Stewardesses' collective bargaining agreement with United because seniority was lost upon resignation.

She filed charges with EEOC on February 21, 1973 and commenced this suit after receiving a "right-to-sue" letter. The District Court dismissed the action, finding that a claim based on her 1968 separation was time-barred and that she was not suffering from any continuing violation. The Court of Appeals initially affirmed but, after the Supreme Court decided Franks v. Bowman Transportation Company, reversed.]

MR. JUSTICE STEVENS delivered the opinion of the Court.

Respondent recognizes that it is now too late to obtain relief based on an unlawful employment practice which occurred in 1968. She contends, however, that United is guilty of a present, continuing violation of Title VII and therefore that her claim is timely.[9] She advances two reasons for holding that United's seniority system illegally discriminates against her: first, she is treated less favorably than males who were hired after her termination in 1968 and prior to her reemployment in 1972; second, the seniority system gives present effect to the past illegal act and therefore perpetuates the consequences of forbidden discrimination. Neither argument persuades us that United is presently violating the statute.

It is true that some male employees with less total service than respondent have more seniority than she. But this disparity is not a consequence of their sex, or of her sex. For females hired between 1968 and 1972 also acquired the same preference over respondent

[9] Respondent cannot rely for jurisdiction on the single act of failing to assign her seniority credit for her prior service at the time she was rehired, for she filed her discrimination charge with the Equal Employment Opportunity Commission on February 21, 1973, more than one year after she was rehired on February 16, 1972. The applicable time limit in February 1972, was 90 days; effective March 24, 1972, this time was extended to 180 days.

as males hired during that period. Moreover, both male and female employees who had service prior to February 1968, who resigned or were terminated for a nondiscriminatory reason (or for an unchallenged discriminatory reason), and who were later re-employed, also were treated as new employees receiving no seniority credit for their prior service. Nothing alleged in the complaint indicates that United's seniority system treats existing female employees differently from existing male employees, or that the failure to credit prior service differentiates in any way between prior service[s] by males and prior services by females. Respondent has failed to allege that United's seniority system differentiates between similarly situated males and females on the basis of sex.

Respondent is correct in pointing out that the seniority system gives present effect to a past act of discrimination. But United was entitled to treat that past act as lawful after respondent failed to file a charge of discrimination within the 90 days then allowed by § 706(d). A discriminatory act which is not made the basis for a timely charge is the legal equivalent of a discriminatory act which occurred before the statute was passed. It may constitute relevant background evidence in a proceeding in which the status of a current practice is at issue, but separately considered, it is merely an unfortunate event in history which has no present legal consequences.

Respondent emphasizes the fact that she alleged a *continuing* violation. United's seniority system does indeed have a continuing impact on her pay and fringe benefits. But the emphasis should not be placed on mere continuity; the critical question is whether any present *violation* exists. She has not alleged that the system discriminates against former female employees or that it treats former employees who were discharged for a discriminatory reason any differently than former employees who resigned or were discharged for a nondiscriminatory reason. In short, the system is neutral in its operation.[10]

Our decision in Franks v. Bowman Transportation Co., 424 U.S. 747 . . . , does not control this case. In Franks we held that retroactive seniority was an appropriate remedy to be awarded under § 706(g) of Title VII, . . . after an illegal discriminatory act or practice had been proved, id., at 762-768. When that case reached this Court, the issues relating to the timeliness of the charge [11] and the violation

---

[10] This case does not involve any claim by respondent that United's seniority system deterred her from asserting any right granted by Title VII. It does not present the question raised in the so-called departmental seniority cases. See, e. g., Quarles v. Philip Morris, 279 F. Supp. 505, . . . (ED Va. 1968).

[11] The Court of Appeals had disposed of the timeliness issues in Franks, 495 F.2d 398, 405, . . . (CA5 1974).

of Title VII [12] had already been decided; we dealt only with a question of remedy. In contrast, in the case now before us we do not reach any remedy issue because respondent did not file a timely charge based on her 1968 separation and she has not alleged facts establishing a violation since she was rehired in 1972.[13]

The difference between a remedy issue and a violation issue is highlighted by the analysis of § 703 (h) of Title VII in *Franks*. As we held in that case, by its terms that section does not bar the award of retroactive seniority after a violation has been proved. Rather, § 703 (h) "delineates which employment practices are illegal and thereby prohibited and which are not," id., at 758, ...

That section expressly provides that it shall not be an unlawful employment practice to apply different terms of employment pursuant to a bona fide seniority system, provided that any disparity is not the result of intentional discrimination. Since respondent does not attack the bona fides of United's seniority system, and since she makes no charge that the system is intentionally designed to discriminate because of race, color, religion, sex, or national origin, § 703 (h) provides an additional ground for rejecting her claim.

The Court of Appeals read § 703 (h) as intended to bar an attack on a seniority system based on the consequences of discriminatory acts which occurred prior to the effective date of Title VII in 1965, but having no application to such attacks based on acts occurring after 1965. This reading of § 703 (h) is too narrow. The statute does not foreclose attacks on the current operation of seniority systems which are subject to challenge as discriminatory. But such a challenge to a neutral system may not be predicated on the mere fact that a past event which has no present legal significance has affected the calculation of seniority credit, even if the past event might at one time have justified a valid claim against the employer. A contrary view would substitute a claim for seniority credit for almost every claim which is barred by limitations. Such a result would contravene the mandate of § 703 (h).

The judgment of the Court of Appeals is

Reversed.

---

[12] This finding at the District Court was unchallenged in the Court of Appeals, 495 F.2d 398, 402, 403, . . . and was assumed in this Court, 424 U.S., at 750, . . .

In any event we noted in Franks, "[t]he underlying legal wrong affecting [the class] is not the alleged operation of a racially discriminatory seniority system but of a racially discriminatory hiring system." Id., at 758, ...

[13] At the time she was rehired in 1972, respondent had no greater right to a job than any other applicant for employment with United. Since she was in fact treated like any other applicant when she was rehired, the employer did not violate Title VII in 1972. And if the employer did not violate Title VII in 1972 by refusing to credit respondent with back seniority, its continued adherence to that policy cannot be illegal.

Dissenting Opinion

MR. JUSTICE MARSHALL, with whom MR. JUSTICE BRENNAN joins, dissenting.

But for her sex, respondent Carolyn Evans presently would enjoy all of the seniority rights that she seeks through this litigation. Petitioner United Air Lines has denied her those rights pursuant to a policy that perpetuates past discrimination by awarding the choicest jobs to those possessing a credential married women were unlawfully prevented from acquiring: continuous tenure with United. While the complaint respondent filed in the District Court was perhaps inartfully drawn, it adequately draws into question this policy of United's.

For the reasons stated in the Court's opinion and in my separate, dissenting opinion in International Brotherhood of Teamsters v. United States, ... I think it indisputable that absent § 703 (h), the seniority system at issue here would constitute an "unlawful employment practice" under Title VII. ... And for the reasons developed at length in my dissenting opinions in Teamsters, ... I believe § 703 (h) does not immunize seniority systems that perpetuate post-Act discrimination.

The only remaining question is whether Ms. Evans' complaint is barred by the applicable statute of limitations. ... Her cause of action accrued, if at all, at the time her seniority was recomputed after she was rehired. Although she apparently failed to file a charge with the EEOC within 180 days after her seniority was determined, Title VII recognizes that certain violations, once commenced, are continuing in nature. In these instances, discriminatees can file charges at any time up to 180 days after the violation ceases. (They can, however, receive backpay only for the two years preceding the filing of charge with the EEOC.) In the instant case, the violation — treating respondent as a new employee even though she was wrongfully forced to resign — is continuing to this day. Respondent's charge therefore was not time barred, and the Court of Appeals judgment reinstating her complaint should be affirmed.

C. STATISTICAL EVIDENCE

In *Teamsters, supra,* the Supreme Court makes it clear that statistical evidence may be used to make out a *prima facie* case of discrimination in a pattern or practice action brought under Title VII. The Court elaborates on this point, at note 20, with the following observation:

> Statistics showing racial or ethnic imbalance are probative ... because such imbalance is often a tell-tale sign of purposeful discrimination; absent explanation, it is ordinarily to be expected

that nondiscriminatory hiring practices will in time result in a work force more or less representative of the racial and ethnic composition of the population in the community from which employees are hired. Evidence of longlasting and gross disparity between the composition of a work force and that of the general population thus may be significant even though § 703(j) makes clear that Title VII imposes no requirement that a work force mirror the general population.

However, the Court in *Teamsters* cautions "that statistics are not irrefutable; they come in infinite variety and, like any other kind of evidence, they may be rebutted."

HAZELWOOD SCHOOL DISTRICT v. UNITED STATES

United States Supreme Court
433 U.S. 299, 97 S. Ct. 2736 (1977)

MR. JUSTICE STEWART delivered the opinion of the Court.

The petitioner Hazelwood School District covers 78 square miles in the northern part of St. Louis County, Mo. In 1973 the Attorney General brought this lawsuit against Hazelwood and various of its officials, alleging that they were engaged in a "pattern or practice" of employment discrimination in violation of Title VII of the Civil Rights Act of 1964, as amended, 42 U.S.C. § 2000e *et seq.* (1970 & Supp. V). The complaint asked for an injunction requiring Hazelwood to cease its discriminatory practices, to take affirmative steps to obtain qualified Negro faculty members, and to offer employment and give backpay to victims of past illegal discrimination.

Hazelwood was formed from 13 rural school districts between 1949 and 1951 by a process of annexation. By the 1967-1968 school year, 17,550 students were enrolled in the district, of whom only 59 were Negro; the number of Negro pupils increased to 576 of 25,166 in 1972-1973, a total of just over 2%.

From the beginning, Hazelwood followed relatively unstructured procedures in hiring its teachers. Every person requesting an application for a teaching position was sent one, and completed applications were submitted to a central personnel office, where they were kept on file. During the early 1960s the personnel office notified all applicants whenever a teaching position became available, but as the number of applications on file increased in the late 1960s and early 1970s, this practice was no longer considered feasible. The personnel office thus began the practice of selecting anywhere from three to 10 applicants for interviews at the school where the vacancy existed. The personnel office did not substantively screen the applicants in determining which of them to send for interviews, other than to ascertain that each applicant, if selected, would be eligible for state certification by the time he began the job. Generally, those who had most recently submitted applications were most likely to be chosen for interviews.

Interviews were conducted by a department chairman, program coordinator, or the principal at the school where the teaching vacancy existed. Although those conducting the interviews did fill out forms rating the applicants in a number of respects, it is undisputed that each school principal possessed virtually unlimited discretion in hiring teachers for his school. The only general guidance given to the principals was to hire the "most competent" person available, and such intangibles as "personality, disposition, appearance, poise, voice, articulation, and ability to deal with people" counted heavily. The principal's choice was routinely honored by Hazelwood's superintendent and Board of Education.

In the early 1960s Hazelwood found it necessary to recruit new teachers, and for that purpose members of its staff visited a number of colleges and universities in Missouri and bordering States. All the institutions visited were predominantly white, and Hazelwood did not seriously recruit at either of the two predominantly Negro four-year colleges in Missouri. As a buyer's market began to develop for public school teachers, Hazelwood curtailed its recruiting efforts. For the 1971-1972 school year, 3,127 persons applied for only 234 teaching vacancies; for the 1972-1973 school year, there were 2,373 applications for 282 vacancies. A number of the applicants who were not hired were Negroes.[5]

Hazelwood hired its first Negro teacher in 1969. The number of Negro faculty members gradually increased in successive years: six of 957 in the 1970 school year; 16 of 1,107 by the end of the 1972 school year; 22 of 1,231 in the 1973 school year. By comparison, according to 1970 census figures, of more than 19,000 teachers employed in that year in the St. Louis area, 15.4% were Negro. That percentage figure included the St. Louis City School District, which in recent years has followed a policy of attempting to maintain a 50% Negro teaching staff. Apart from that school district, 5.7% of the teachers in the county were Negro in 1970.

Drawing upon these historic facts, the Government mounted its "pattern or practice" attack in the District Court upon four different fronts. It adduced evidence of (1) a history of alleged racially discriminatory practices, (2) statistical disparities in hiring, (3) the standardless and largely subjective hiring procedures, and (4) specific instances of alleged discrimination against 55 unsuccessful Negro applicants for teaching jobs. Hazelwood offered virtually no

---

[5] The parties disagree whether it is possible to determine from the present record exactly how many of the job applicants in each of the school years were Negroes.

additional evidence in response, relying instead on evidence introduced by the Government, perceived deficiencies in the Government's case, and its own officially promulgated policy "to hire all teachers on the basis of training, preparation and recommendations, regardless of race, color or creed." [6]

The District Court ruled that the Government had failed to establish a pattern or practice of discrmination. The court was unpersuaded by the alleged history of discrimination, noting that no dual school system had ever existed in Hazelwood. The statistics showing that relatively small numbers of Negroes were employed as teachers were found nonprobative, on the ground that the percentage of Negro pupils in Hazelwood was similarly small. The court found nothing illegal or suspect in the teacher hiring procedures that Hazelwood had followed. Finally, the court reviewed the evidence in the 55 cases of alleged individual discrimination, and after stating that the burden of proving intentional discrimination was on the Government, it found that this burden had not been sustained in a single instance. Hence, the court entered judgment for the defendants. . . .

The Court of Appeals for the Eighth Circuit reversed. After suggesting that the District Court had assigned inadequate weight to evidence of discriminatory conduct on the part of Hazelwood before the effective date of Title VII, the Court of Appeals rejected the trial court's analysis of the statistical data as resting on an irrelevant comparison of Negro teachers to Negro pupils in Hazelwood. The proper comparison, in the appellate court's view, was one between Negro teachers in Hazelwood and Negro teachers in the relevant labor market area. Selecting St. Louis County and St. Louis City as the relevant area, the Court of Appeals compared the 1970 census figures, showing that 15.4[%] of teachers in that area were Negro, to the racial composition of Hazelwood's teaching staff. In the 1972-1973 and 1973-1974 school years, only 1.4% and 1.8%, respectively, of Hazelwood's teachers were Negroes. This statistical disparity, particularly when viewed against the background of the teacher hiring procedures that Hazelwood had followed, was held to constitute a prima facie case of a pattern or practice of racial discrimination.

In addition, the Court of Appeals reasoned that the trial court had erred in failing to measure the 55 instances in which Negro applicants were denied jobs against the four-part standard for establishing a prima facie case of individual discrimination set out in this Court's

---

[6] The defendants offered only one witness, who testified to the total number of teachers who had applied and were hired for jobs in the 1971-1972 and 1972-1973 school years. They introduced several exhibits consisting of a policy manual, policy book, staff handbook, and historical summary of Hazelwood's formation and relatively brief existence.

opinion in *McDonnell Douglas Corp. v. Green,* 411 U.S. 792, 802, 93 S.Ct. 1817, 1824, 36 L.Ed.2d 668. Applying that standard, the appellate court found 16 cases of individual discrimination, which "buttressed" the statistical proof. Because Hazelwood had not rebutted the Government's prima facie case of a pattern or practice of racial discrimination, the Court of Appeals directed judgment for the Government and prescribed the remedial order to be entered.

The petitioners primarily attack the judgment of the Court of Appeals for its reliance on "undifferentiated work force statistics to find an unrebutted prima facie case of employment discrimination." [12] The question they raise, in short, is whether a basic component in the Court of Appeals' finding of a pattern or practice of discrimination — the comparatively small percentage of Negro employees in Hazelwood's teaching staff — was lacking in probative force.

This Court's recent consideration in *International Brotherhood of Teamsters v. United States,* 431 U.S. 324, 97 S.Ct. 1843, 52 L.Ed.2d 396 of the role of statistics in pattern or practice suits under Title VII provides substantial guidance in evaluating the arguments advanced by the petitioners. See also *Village of Arlington Heights v. Metropolitan Housing Development Corp.,* 429 U.S. 252, at 266, 97 S.Ct. 555, at 564, 50 L.Ed.2d 450; *Washington v. Davis,* 426 U.S. 229, 241-242, 96 S.Ct. 2040, 2048-2049, 48 L.Ed.2d 597. Where gross statistical disparities can be shown, they alone may in a proper case constitute prima facie proof of a pattern or practice of discrimination. *Teamsters, supra,* n. 20 at 339, 97 S.Ct., at 1856.

There can be no doubt, in light of the *Teamsters* case, that the District Court's comparison of Hazelwood's teacher work force to its student population fundamentally misconceived the role of statistics

---

[12] In their petition for certiorari and brief on the merits, the petitioners have phrased the question as follows:

"Whether a court may disregard evidence that an employer has treated actual job applicants in a nondiscriminatory manner and rely on undifferentiated workforce statistics to find an unrebutted prima facie case of employment discrimination in violation of Title VII of the Civil Rights Act of 1964."

Their petition for certiorari and brief on the merits did raise a second question — "[w]hether Congress has authority under Section 5 of the Fourteenth Amendment to prohibit by Title VII of the Civil Rights Act of 1964 employment practices of an agency of a state government in the absence of proof that the agency purposefully discriminated against applicants on the basis of race." That issue, however, is not presented by the facts in this case. The Government's opening statement in the trial court explained that its evidence was designed to show that the scarcity of Negro teachers at Hazelwood "is the result of purpose" and is attributable to "deliberately continued employment policies." Thus here, as in *International Brotherhood of Teamsters v. United States,* 431 U.S. 324, 97 S.Ct. 1843, 52 L.Ed.2d 396, "[t]he Government's theory of discrimination was simply that the [employer], in violation of § 703(a) of Title VII, regularly and purposefully treated Negroes . . . less favorably than white persons." At 307, 97 S.Ct. at 1854.

in employment discrimination cases. The Court of Appeals was correct in the view that a proper comparison was between the racial composition of Hazelwood's teaching staff and the racial composition of the qualified public school teacher population in the relevant labor market.[13]

See *Teamsters, supra,* at 337, 97 S.Ct., at 1855, and n. 17. The percentage of Negroes on Hazelwood's teaching staff in 1972-1973 was 1.4% and in 1973-1974 it was 1.8%. By contrast, the percentage of qualified Negro teachers in the area was, according to the 1970 census, at least 5.7%.[14] Although these differences were on their face substantial, the Court of Appeals erred in substituting its judgment for that of the District Court and holding that the

---

[13] In *Teamsters,* the comparison between the percentage of Negroes on the employer's work force and the percentage in the general areawide population was highly probative, because the job skill there involved — the ability to drive a truck — is one that many persons possess or can fairly readily acquire. When special qualifications are required to fill particular jobs, comparisons to the general population (rather than to the smaller group of individuals who possess the necessary qualifications) may have little probative value. The comparative statistics introduced by the Government in the District Court, however, were properly limited to public school teachers, and therefore this is not a case like *Mayor v. Educational Equality League,* 415 U.S. 605, 94 S.Ct. 1323, 39 L.Ed.2d 630, in which the racial-composition comparisons failed to take into account special qualifications for the position in question. *Id.,* at 620-621, 94 S.Ct., at 1333-1334.

Although the petitioners concede as a general matter the probative force of the comparative work force statistics, they object to the Court of Appeals' heavy reliance on these data on the ground that applicant flow data, showing the actual percentage of white and Negro applicants for teaching positions at Hazelwood, would be firmer proof. As we have noted, see n. 5, *supra,* there was not clear evidence of such statistics. We leave it to the District Court on remand to determine whether competent proof of those data can be adduced. If so, it would, of course, be very relevant. Cf. *Dothard v. Rawlinson,* 433 U.S. 321, 97 S.Ct. 2720, 2727, 52 L.Ed.2d

[14] As is discussed below, the Government contends that a comparative figure of 15.4%, rather than 5.7%, is the appropriate one. . . . But even assuming *arguendo* that the 5.7% figure urged by the petitioners is correct, the disparity between that figure and the percentage of Negroes on Hazelwood's teaching staff would be more than fourfold for the 1972-1973 school year, and threefold for the 1973-1974 school year. A precise method of measuring the significance of such statistical disparities was explained in *Castaneda v. Partida,* 430 U.S. 482, at 496-497, n. 17, 97 S.Ct. 1272, at 1281, 51 L.Ed.2d 493. It involves calculation of the "standard deviation" as a measure of predicted fluctuations from the expected value of a sample. Using the 5.7% figure as the basis for calculating the expected value, the expected number of Negroes on the Hazelwood teaching staff would be roughly 63 in 1972-1973 and 70 in 1973-1974. The observed number in those years was 16 and 22, respectively. The difference between the observed and expected values was more than six standard deviations in 1972-1973 and more than five standard deviations in 1973-1974. The Court in *Castaneda* noted that "[a]s a general rule for such large samples, if the difference between the expected value and the observed number is greater than two or three standard deviations," then the hypothesis that teachers were hired without regard to race would be suspect. *Ibid.*

Government had conclusively proved its "pattern or practice" lawsuit.

The Court of Appeals totally disregarded the possibility that this prima facie statistical proof in the record might at the trial court level be rebutted by statistics dealing with Hazelwood's hiring after it became subject to Title VII. Racial discrimination by public employers was not made illegal under Title VII until March 24, 1972. A public employer who from that date forward made all its employment decisions in a wholly nondiscriminatory way would not violate Title VII even if it had formerly maintained an all-white work force by purposefully excluding Negroes.[15] For this reason, the Court cautioned in the *Teamsters* opinion that once a prima facie case has been established by statistical work force disparities, the employer must be given an opportunity to show "that the claimed discriminatory pattern is a product of pre-Act hiring rather than unlawful post-Act discrimination." 431 U.S., at 360.

The record in this case showed that for the 1972-1973 school year, Hazelwood hired 282 new teachers, 10 of whom (3.5%) were Negroes; for the following school year it hired 123 new teachers, five of whom (4.1%) were Negroes. Over the two-year period, Negroes constituted a total of 15 of the 405 new teachers hired (3.7%). Although the Court of Appeals briefly mentioned these data in reciting the facts, it wholly ignored them in discussing whether the Government had shown a pattern or practice of discrimination. And it gave no consideration at all to the possibility that post-Act data as to the number of Negroes hired compared to the total number of Negro applicants might tell a totally different story.

What the hiring figures prove obviously depends upon the figures to which they are compared. The Court of Appeals accepted the Government's argument that the relevant comparison was to the labor market area of St. Louis County and St. Louis City, in which, according to the 1970 census, 15.4% of all teachers were Negro. The propriety of that comparison was vigorously disputed by the petitioners, who urged that because the City of St. Louis has made special attempts to maintain a 50% Negro teaching staff, inclusion of that school district in the relevant market area distorts the comparison. Were that argument accepted, the percentage of Negro teachers in the relevant labor market area (St. Louis County alone) as shown in the 1970 census would be 5.7% rather than 15.4%.

The difference between these figures may well be important; the disparity between 3.7% (the percentage of Negro teachers hired by

---

[15] This is not to say that evidence of pre-Act discrimination can never have any probative force. Proof that an employer engaged in racial discrimination prior to the effective date of Title VII might in some circumstances support the inference that such discrimination continued, particularly where relevant aspects of the decisionmaking process had undergone little change.

Hazelwood in 1972-1973 and 1973-1974) and 5.7% may be sufficiently small to weaken the Government's other proof, while the disparity between 3.7% and 15.4% may be sufficiently large to reinforce it.[17] In determining which of the two figures — or very possibly, what intermediate figure — provides the most accurate basis for comparison to the hiring figures at Hazelwood, it will be necessary to evaluate such considerations as (i) whether the racially based hiring policies of the St. Louis City School District were in effect as far back as 1970, the year in which the census figures were taken;[18] (ii) to what extent those policies have changed the racial composition of that district's teaching staff from what it would otherwise have been; (iii) to what extent St. Louis' recruitment policies have diverted to the city teachers who might otherwise have applied to Hazelwood;[19] (iv) to what extent Negro teachers employed by the city would prefer employment in other districts such as Hazelwood; and (v) what the experience in other school districts in St. Louis County indicates about the validity of excluding the City School District from the relevant labor market.

---

[17] Indeed, under the statistical methodology explained in *Castaneda v. Partida, supra,* at 496-497, n. 17, involving the calculation of the standard devitaion as a measure of predicted fluctuations, the difference between using 15.4% and 5.7% as the areawide figure would be significant. If the 15.4% figure is taken as the basis for comparison, the expected number of Negro teachers hired by Hazelwood in 1972-1973 would be 43 (rather than the actual figure of 10) of a total of 282, a difference of more than five standard deviations; the expected number of 1973-1974 would be 19 (rather than the actual figure 5) of a total of 123, a difference of more than three standard deviations. For the two years combined, the difference between the observed number of 15 Negro teachers hired (of a total of 405) would vary from the expected number of 62 by more than six standard deviations. Because a fluctuation of more than two or three standard deviations would undercut the hypothesis that decisions were being made randomly with respect to race, *ibid.,* each of these statistical comparisons would reinforce rather than rebut the Government's other proof. If, however, the 5.7% areawide figure is used, the expected number of Negro teachers hired in 1972-1973 would be roughly 16, less than two standard deviations from the observed number of 10; for 1973-1974, the expected value would be roughly seven, less than one standard deviation from the observed value of 5; and for the two years combined, the expected value of 23 would be less than two standard deviations from the observed total of 15. A more precise method of analyzing these statistics confirms the results of the standard deviation analysis. See F. Mosteller, R. Rourke & G. Thomas, Probability with Statistical Applications 494 (2d ed. 1970).

These observations are not intended to suggest that precise calculations of statistical significance are necessary in employing statistical proof, but merely to highlight the importance of the choice of the relevant labor market area.

[18] In 1970 Negroes constituted only 42% of the faculty in St. Louis city schools, which could indicate either that the city's goals were not yet in effect or simply that they had not yet been achieved.

[19] The petitioners observe, for example, that Harris Teachers College in St. Louis, whose 1973 graduating class was 60% Negro, is operated by the city. It is the petitioners' contention that the city's public elementary and secondary schools occupy an advantageous position in the recruitment of Harris graduates.

It is thus clear that a determination of the appropriate comparative figures in this case will depend upon further evaluation by the trial court. As this Court admonished in *Teamsters,* "statistics . . . come in infinite variety . . .. [T]heir usefulness depends on all of the surrounding facts and circumstances." 431 U.S., at 340. Only the trial court is in a position to make the appropriate determination after further findings. And only after such a determination is made can a foundation be established for deciding whether or not Hazelwood engaged in a pattern or practice of racial discrimination in its employment practices in violation of the law.[20]

We hold, therefore, that the Court of Appeals erred in disregarding the post-Act hiring statistics in the record, and that·it should have remanded the case to the District Court for further findings as to the relevant labor market area and for an ultimate determination of whether Hazelwood engaged in a pattern or practice of employment discrimination after March 24, 1972.[21] Accordingly, the judgment is vacated, and the case is remanded to the District Court for further proceedings consistent with this opinion.

It is so ordered.

MR. JUSTICE BRENNAN, concurring.
. . . It is my understanding, as apparently it is MR. JUSTICE STEVENS', *post,* at n. 5, that the statistical inquiry mentioned by the Court, *ante,* at n. 17 and accompanying text, can be of no help to the Hazelwood School Board in rebutting the Government's evidence of discrimination. Indeed, even if the relative comparison market is found to be 5.7% rather than 15.4% black, the applicable statistical analysis at most will not serve to bolster the Government's case. This obviously is of no aid to Hazelwood in meeting *its* burden of proof. . . .

MR. JUSTICE STEVENS, dissenting. . . .
As a matter of history, Hazelwood employed no black teachers until 1969. Both before and after the 1972 amendment making the statute applicable to public school districts, petitioner used a standardless and largely subjective hiring procedure. Since "relevant aspects of the decisionmaking process had undergone little change," it is

---

[20] Because the District Court focused on a comparison between the percentage of Negro teachers and Negro pupils in Hazelwood, it did not undertake an evaluation of the relevant labor market, and its casual dictum that the inclusion of the city of St. Louis "distorted" the labor market statistics was not based upon valid criteria. 392 F.Supp., at 1287.

[21] It will also be open to the District Court on remand to determine whether sufficiently reliable applicant flow data are available to permit consideration of the petitioners' argument that those data may undercut a statistical analysis dependent upon hirings alone.

proper to infer that the pre-Act policy of preferring white teachers continued to influence Hazelwood's hiring practices.

The inference of discrimination was corroborated by post-Act evidence that Hazelwood had refused to hire 16 qualified black applicants for racial reasons. Taking the Government's evidence as a whole, there can be no doubt about the sufficiency of its prima facie case. . . .

II

Hazelwood "offered virtually no additional evidence in response," *ante,* at 303. It challenges the Government's statistical analysis by claiming that the city of St. Louis should be excluded from the relevant market and point out that only 5.7% of the teachers in the county (excluding the city) were black. It further argues that the city's policy of trying to maintain a 50% black teaching staff diverted teachers from the county to the city. There are two separate reasons why these arguments are insufficient: they are not supported by the evidence; even if true, they do not overcome the Government's case.

The defendant offered no evidence concerning wage differentials, commuting problems, or the relative advantages of teaching in an inner-city school as opposed to a suburban school. Without any such evidence in the record, it is difficult to understand why the simple fact that the city was the source of a third of Hazelwood's faculty should not be sufficient to demonstrate that it is a part of the relevant market. The city's policy of attempting to maintain a 50/50 ratio clearly does not undermine that conclusion, particularly when the record reveals no shortage of qualified black applicants in either Hazelwood or other suburban school districts. Surely not *all* of the 2,000 black teachers employed by the city were unavailable for employment in Hazelwood at the time of their initial hire.

But even if it were proper to exclude the city of St. Louis from the market, the statistical evidence would still tend to prove discrimination. With the city excluded, 5.7% of the teachers in the remaining market were black. On the basis of a random selection, one would therefore expect that 5.7% of the 405 teachers hired by Hazelwood in the 1972-1973 and 1973-1974 school years to have been black. But instead of 23 black teachers, Hazelwood hired only 15, less than two-thirds of the expected number. Without the benefit of expert testimony, I would hesitate to infer that the disparity between 23 and 15 is great enough, in itself, to prove discrimination.[5] It is perfectly clear, however, that whatever

[5] After I had drafted this opinion, one of my law clerks advised me that, given the size of the two-year sample, there is only about a 5% likelihood that a disparity this large would be produced by a random selection from the labor pool. If his calculation (which was made using the method described in H. Blalock, Social

probative force this disparity has, it tends to prove discrimination and does absolutely nothing in the way of carrying Hazelwood's burden of overcoming the Government's prima facie case.

Absolute precision in the analysis of market data is too much to expect. We may fairly assume that a nondiscriminatory selection process would have resulted in the hiring of somewhere between the 15% suggested by the Government and the 5.7% suggested by petitioner, or perhaps 30 or 40 black teachers, instead of the 15 actually hired. On that assumption, the Court of Appeals' determination that there were 16 individual cases of discriminatory refusal to hire black applicants in the post-1972 period seems remarkably accurate.

In sum, the Government is entitled to prevail on the present record. It proved a prima facie case, which Hazelwood failed to rebut. Why, then, should we burden a busy federal court with another trial. . . .

NOTES:

(1) Following the tests in the *Griggs* case, the Supreme Court held, in *Dothard v. Rawlinson,* 433 U.S. 321 (1977), that a state's employment practice requiring prison guards to be at least 5'2" tall and 120 pounds weight was prima facie discriminatory against women since it would exclude 44% of U.S. women. The employer made no attempt to show that these requirements were job-related, although the court suggested that a test for strength might have been appropriate for prison guards. On another point, the court upheld an Alabama regulation excluding women from "contact" guard positions in all-male prisons. Although nothing that the bona fide occupational qualification (bfoq) provision of § 703(e) of the Civil Rights Act is "an extremely narrow exception" to the general prohibition of discrimination on the basis of sex, the court found it applicable here, in view of the very real risk of attacks on women guards under the conditions in Alabama prisons which a federal court had stated were characterized by rampant violence and a jungle atmosphere.

(2) *Use of Statistical Evidence:* (a) *Hazelwood,* along with *Teamsters, supra,* were the first significant statements by the Supreme Court concerning the use of statistical evidence in Title VII cases. It is noteworthy that the Court, at footnote 14, in *Hazelwood* seems to adopt the "two or three standard deviations" rule from *Castaneda v. Partida,* 430 U.S. 482 (1977). In *Castaneda* the Court found that a prima facie case of discrimination against

---

Statistics 151-175 (1972)) is correct, it is easy to understand why Hazelwood offered no expert testimony.

Mexican-Americans in jury selection was established, in part because statistics for the pertinent period (1962-1972) showed that, although the county's population was 79.1% Mexican-American, only 39% of the persons summoned for grand jury service were in such class. The Court observed, at footnote 17, that:

> If the jurors were drawn randomly from the general population, then the number of Mexican-Americans in the sample could be modeled by a binomial distribution. . . . Given that 79.1% of the population is Mexican-American, the expected number of Mexican-Americans among the 870 persons summoned to serve as grand jurors over the 11-year period is approximately 688. The observed number is 339. Of course, in any given drawing some fluctuation from the expected number is predicted. The important point, however, is that the statistical model shows that the results of a random drawing are likely to fall in the vicinity of the expected value. . . . The measure of the predicted fluctuations from the expected value is the standard deviation, defined for the binomial distribution as the square root of the product of the total number in the sample (here 870) times the probability of selecting a Mexican-American (0.791) times the probability of selecting a non-Mexican-American (0.209). . . . Thus, in this case the standard deviation is approximately 12. As a general rule for such large samples, if the difference between the expected value and the observed number is greater than two or three standard deviations, then the hypothesis that the jury drawing was random would be suspect to a social scientist. The 11-year data here reflect a difference between the expected and observed number of Mexican-Americans of approximately 29 standard deviations. A detailed calculation reveals that the likelihood that such a substantial departure from the expected value would occur by chance is less than 1 in 10.

In reaching this conclusion, the Court relied on Finkelstein, *The Application of Statistical Decision Theory to the Jury Discrimination Cases,* 80 Harv. L. Rev. 338 (1966); P. Hoel, Introduction to Mathematical Statistics (4th ed. 1971); F. Mosteller, R. Rourke & G. Thomas, Probability with Statistical Applications (2d ed. 1970).

(b) *See generally* Rosenblum, *The Use of Labor Statistics and Analysis in Title VII Cases: Rios, Chicago and Beyond,* 1 Ind. Rel. L.J. 685 (1977); Note, *Beyond the Prima Facie Case In Employment Discrimination Law: Statistical Proof and Rebuttal,* 89 Harv. L. Rev. 387 (1975); Note, *Employment Discrimination: Statistics and Preferences Under Title VII,* 59 Va. L. Rev. 463 (1973); Gastwirth & Haber, *Defining the Labor Market for Equal Employment Standards,* 99 Monthly Lab. Rev. 32 (March 1976); R. Oaxaca, *Theory and Measurement in the Economics of Discrimination,* in Equal Rights and Industrial Relations (I.R.R.A. 1977).

D. DISCRIMINATORY EMPLOYMENT TESTS

ALBEMARLE PAPER CO. v. MOODY

United States Supreme Court
422 U.S. 405, 95 S. Ct. 2362, 45 L. Ed. 2d 280 (1975)

MR. JUSTICE STEWART delivered the opinion of the Court.

These consolidated cases raise two important questions under Title VII of the Civil Rights Act of 1964, 78 Stat. 253, as amended by the Equal Employment Opportunity Act of 1972, 86 Stat. 103, 42 U. S. C. §§ 2000(e): First: When employees or applicants for employment have lost the opportunity to earn wages because an employer has engaged in an unlawful discriminatory employment practice, what standards should a federal district court follow in deciding whether to award or deny backpay? Second: What must an employer show to establish that pre-employment tests racially discriminatory in effect, though not in intent, are sufficiently "job related" to survive challenge under Title VII?

I. The respondents — plaintiffs in the District Court — are a certified class of present and former Negro employees at a paper mill in Roanoke Rapids, North Carolina; the petitioners — defendants in the District Court — are the plant's owner, the Albemarle Paper Company, and the plant employees' labor union, Halifax Local No. 425. In August of 1966, after filing a complaint with the Equal Employment Opportunity Commission (EEOC), and receiving notice of their right to sue, the respondents brought a class action in the United States District Court for the Eastern District of North Carolina, asking permanent injunctive relief against "any policy, practice, custom, or usage" at the plant that violated Title VII. The respondents assured the court that the suit involved no claim for any monetary awards on a class basis, but in June of 1970, after several years of discovery, the respondents moved to add a class demand for backpay. The court ruled that this issue would be considered at trial.

At the trial, in July and August of 1971, the major issues were the plant's seniority system, its program of employment testing, and the question of backpay. In its opinion of November 9, 1971, the court found that the petitioners had "strictly segregated" the plant's departmental "lines of progression" prior to January 1, 1964, reserving the higher paying and more skilled lines for whites. . . . The "racial identifiability" of whole lines of progression persisted until 1968, when the lines were reorganized under a new collective-bargaining agreement. The court found, however, that this reorganization left Negro employees "locked in the lower paying job classifications." . . . The formerly "Negro" lines of progression had been merely tacked on to the bottom of the formerly "white" lines, and promotions, demotions, and layoffs continued to be governed

— where skills were "relatively equal" — by a system of "job seniority." Because of the plant's previous history of overt segregation, only whites had seniority in the higher job categories. Accordingly, the court ordered the petitioners to implement a system of "plantwide" seniority.

The court refused, however, to award backpay to the plaintiff class for losses suffered under the "job seniority" program. The court explained:

> "In the instant case there was no evidence of bad faith non-compliance with the Act. It appears that the company as early as 1964 began active recruitment of blacks for its Maintenance Apprenticeship Program. Certain lines of progression were merged on its own initiative, and as judicial decisions expanded the then existing interpretations of the Act, the defendants took steps to correct the abuses without delay. . . .
>
> "In addition, an award of backpay is equitable remedy. . . . The plaintiff's claim for backpay was filed nearly five years after the institution of this action. It was not prayed for in the pleadings. Although neither party can be charged with deliberate dilatory tactics in bringing this cause to trial, it is apparent that the defendants would be substantially prejudiced by the granting of such affirmative relief. The defendants might have chosen to exercise unusual zeal in having this court determine their rights at an earlier date had they known that back pay would be at issue." . . .

The court also refused to enjoin or limit Albemarle's testing program. Albemarle had required applicants for employment in the skilled lines of progression to have a high school diploma and to pass two tests, the Revised Beta Examination, allegedly a measure of nonverbal intelligence, and the Wonderlic Test (available in alternate Forms A and B), allegedly a measure of verbal facility. After this Court's decision in Griggs v. Duke Power Company, 401 U. S. 424 (1971), and on the eve of trial, Albemarle engaged an·industrial psychologist to study the "job relatedness" of its testing program. His study compared the test scores of current employees with supervisorial judgments of their competence in ten job groupings selected from the middle or top of the plant's skilled lines of progression. The study showed a statistically significant correlation with supervisorial ratings in three job groupings for the Beta test, in seven job groupings for either Form A or Form B of the Wonderlic Test, and in two job groupings for the required battery of both the Beta and the Wonderlic Test. The respondents' experts challenged the reliability of these studies, but the court concluded:

> "The personnel tests administered at the plant have undergone validation studies and have been proven to be job

related. The defendants have carried their burden of proof in proving that these tests are 'necessary for the safe and efficient operation of the business' and are, therefore, permitted by the Act. However, the high school education requirement used in conjunction with the testing requirement is unlawful in that the personnel tests alone are adequate to measure the mental ability and reading skills required for job classifications." . . .

The petitioners did not seek review of the court's judgment, but the respondents appealed the denial of a backpay award and the refusal to enjoin or limit Albemarle's use of pre-employment tests. A divided Court of Appeals for the Fourth Circuit reversed the judgment of the District Court, ruling that backpay should have been awarded and that use of the tests should have been enjoined. 474 F.2d 134. . . .

We granted certiorari because of an evident circuit conflict as to the standards governing awards of backpay and as to the showing required to establish the "job relatedness" of pre-employment tests.

II. Whether a particular member of the plaintiff class should have been awarded any backpay and, if so, how much, are questions not involved in this review. The equities of individual cases were never reached. Though at least some of the members of the plaintiff class obviously suffered a loss of wage opportunities on account of Albemarle's unlawfully discriminatory system of job seniority, the District Court decided that *no* backpay should be awarded to *anyone* in the class. The court declined to make such an award on two stated grounds: the lack of "evidence of bad faith non-compliance with the Act," and the fact that "the defendants would be substantially prejudiced" by an award of backpay that was demanded contrary to an earlier representation and late in the progress of the litigation. Relying directly on Newman v. Piggie Park Enterprises, 390 U. S. 400, the Court of Appeals reversed, holding that backpay could be denied only in "special circumstances." The petitioners argue that the Court of Appeals was in error — that a district court has virtually unfettered discretion to award or deny backpay, and that there was no abuse of that discretion in this case.[8]

Piggie Park Enterprises, supra, is not directly in point. The Court held there that attorneys' fees should "ordinarily" be awarded — *i.e.,* in all but "special circumstances" — to plaintiffs successful in

---

[8] The petitioners also contend that no backpay can be awarded to those unnamed parties in the plaintiff class who have not themselves filed charges with the EEOC. We reject this contention. The courts of appeals that have confronted the issue are unanimous in recognizing that backpay may be awarded on a class basis under Title VII without exhaustion of administrative procedures by the unnamed class members. . . . The Congress plainly ratified this construction of the Act in the course of enacting the Equal Employment Opportunity Act of 1972, Pub. L. 92-261, 86 Sat. 103. . . .

obtaining injunctions against discrimination in public accommodations, under Title II of the Civil Rights Act of 1964. . . . There is of course an equally strong public interest in having injunctive actions brought under Title VII, to eradicate discriminatory employment practices. But this interest can be vindicated by applying the *Piggie Park* standard to the *attorneys' fees* provision of Title VII, 42 U. S. C. § 2000e-5(k), see Northcross v. Board of Education, 412 U. S. 427, 428. For guidance as to the granting and denial of *backpay,* one must, therefore, look elsewhere.

The petitioners contend that the statutory scheme provides no guidance, beyond indicating that backpay awards are within the District Court's discretion. We disagree. It is true that backpay is not an automatic or mandatory remedy; like all other remedies under the Act, it is one which the courts "may" invoke. The scheme implicitly recognizes that there may be cases calling for one remedy but not another, and — owing to the structure of the federal judiciary — these choices are of course left in the first instance to the district courts. But such discretionary choices are not left to a court's "inclination, but to its judgment; and its judgment is to be guided by sound legal principles." United States v. Burr, 25 Fed. Cas. 30, 35 (Marshall, C. J.). The power to award backpay was bestowed by Congress, as part of a complex legislative design directed at an historic evil of national proportions. A court must exercise this power "in light of the large objectives of the Act," Hecht Co. v. Bowles, 321 U. S. 321, 331. That the court's discretion is equitable in nature, see Curtis v. Loether, 415 U. S. 189, 197, hardly means that it is unfettered by meaningful standards or shielded from thorough appellate review. In Mitchell v. DeMario Jewelry, 361 U. S. 288, 292, this Court held, in the face of a silent statute, that district courts enjoyed the "historic power of equity" to award lost wages to workmen unlawfully discriminated against under § 17 of the Fair Labor Standards Act of 1938. The Court simultaneously noted that "the statutory purposes . . . (leaves) little room for the exercise of discretion not to order reimbursement." *Id.* at 296. . . .

The District Court's decision must therefore be measured against the purposes which inform Title VII. As the Court observed in Griggs v. Duke Power Co., *supra,* 401 U. S. at 429-430, the primary objective was a prophylactic one. . . . Backpay has an obvious connection with this purpose. If employers faced only the prospect of an injunctive order, they would have little incentive to shun practices of dubious legality. It is the reasonably certain prospect of a backpay award that "provide[s] the spur or catalyst which causes employers and unions to self-examine and to self-evaluate their employment practices and to endeavor to eliminate, so far as possible, the last vestiges of an unfortunate and ignominous page in this country's history." United States v. N. L. Industries, 479 F.2d 354, 379.

It is also the purpose of Title VII to make persons whole for injuries suffered on account of unlawful employment discrimination. This is shown by the very fact that Congress took care to arm the courts with full equitable powers. For it is the historic purpose of equity to "secur[e] complete justice," Brown v. Swann, 10 Pet. 497, 503; see also Porter v. Warner Holding Co., 328 U. S. 395, 397-398. "[W]here federally protected rights have been invaded, it has been the rule from the beginning that courts will be alert to adjust their remedies so as to grant the necessary relief." Bell v. Hood, 327 U. S. 678, 684. Title VII deals with legal injuries of an economic character occasioned by racial or other anti-minority discrimination. The terms "complete justice" and "necessary relief" have acquired a clear meaning in such circumstances. Where racial discrimination is concerned, "the [district] court has not merely the power but the duty to render a decree which will so far as possible eliminate the discriminatory effects of the past as well as bar like discrimination in the future." Louisiana v. United States, 380 U. S. 145, 154. And where a legal injury is of an economic character,

> "[t]he general rule is, that when a wrong has been done, and the law gives a remedy, the compensation shall be equal to the injury. The latter is the standard by which the former is to be measured. The injured party is to be placed as near as may be, in the situation he would have occupied if the wrong has not been committed." Wicker v. Hoppock, 6 Wall. 94, at 99.

The "make whole" purpose of Title VII is made evident by the legislative history. The backpay provision was expressly modeled on the backpay provision of the National Labor Relations Act. . . . We may assume that Congress was aware that the Board, since its inception, has awarded backpay as a matter of course — not randomly or in the exercise of a standardless discretion, and not merely where employer violations are peculiarly deliberate, egregious or inexcusable. Furthermore, in passing the Equal Employment Opportunity Act of 1972, Congress considered several bills to limit the judicial power to award backpay. These limiting efforts were rejected, and the backpay provision was re-enacted substantially in its original form. . . . As this makes clear, Congress' purpose in vesting a variety of "discretionary" powers in the courts was not to limit appellate review of trial courts, or to invite inconsistency and caprice, but rather to make possible the "fashion[ing] [of] the most complete relief possible."

It follows that, given a finding of unlawful discrimination, backpay should be denied only for reasons which, if applied generally, would not frustrate the central statutory purposes of eradicating discrimination throughout the economy and making persons whole for injuries suffered through past discrimination. The courts of appeals must maintain a consistent and principled application of the backpay provision, consonant with the twin statutory objectives, while at the same time recognizing that the trial court will often have the keener appreciation of those facts and circumstances peculiar to particular cases.

The District Court's stated grounds for denying backpay in this case must be tested against these standards. The first ground was that Albemarle's breach of Title VII had not been in "bad faith." This is not a sufficient reason for denying backpay. Where an employer *has* shown bad faith — by maintaining a practice which he knew to be illegal or of highly questionable legality — he can make no claims whatsoever on the Chancellor's conscience. But, under Title VII, the mere absence of bad faith simply opens the door to equity; it does not depress the scales in the employer's favor. If backpay were awardable only upon a showing of bad faith, the remedy would become a punishment for moral turpitude, rather than a compensation for workers' injuries. This would read the "make whole" purpose right out of Title VII, for a worker's injury is not less real simply because his employer did not inflict it in "bad faith." Title VII is not concerned with the employer's "good intent or absence of discriminatory intent" for "Congress directed the thrust of the Act to the *consequences* of employment practices, not simply the motivation." Griggs v. Duke Power Co., *supra*, 401 U. S. at 432. . . . To condition the awarding of backpay on a showing of "bad faith" would be to open an enormous chasm between injunctive and backpay relief under Title VII. There is nothing on the face of the statute or in its legislative history that justifies the creation of drastic and categorical distinctions between those two remedies.

The District Court also grounded its denial of backpay on the fact that the respondents initially disclaimed any interest in backpay, first asserting their claim five years after the complaint was filed. The court concluded that the petitioners had been "prejudiced" by this conduct. The Court of Appeals reversed on the ground "that the broad aims of Title VII require that the issue of backpay be fully developed and determined even though it was not raised until the post-trial stage of litigation," 474 F.2d at 141.

It is true that Title VII contains no legal bar to raising backpay claims after the complaint for injunctive relief has been filed, or indeed after a trial on that complaint has been had. Furthermore, Fed. Rule Civ. Proc. 54(c) directs that

> "every final judgment shall grant the relief to which the party in whose favor it is rendered is entitled, even if the party has not demanded such relief in his pleadings."

But a party may not be "entitled" to relief if its conduct of the cause has improperly and substantially prejudiced the other party. The respondents here were not merely tardy, but also inconsistent, in demanding backpay. To deny backpay because a *particular* cause has been prosecuted in an eccentric fashion, prejudicial to the other party, does not offend the broad purposes of Title VII. This is not to say, however, that the District Court's ruling was necessarily correct. Whether the petitioners were in fact prejudiced, and whether the respondents' trial conduct was excusable, are questions that will be open to review by the Court of Appeals, if the District Court, on remand, decides again to decline to make any award of backpay. But the standard of review will be the familiar one of whether the District Court was "clearly erroneous" in its factual findings and whether it "abused" its traditional discretion to locate "a just result" in light of the circumstances peculiar to the case, Lagnes v. Green, 282 U. S. 531, 541. On these issues of procedural regularity and prejudice, the "broad aims of Title VII" provide no ready solution.

III. In Griggs v. Duke Power Co., 401 U. S. 424, this Court unanimously held that Title VII forbids the use of employment tests that are discriminatory in effect unless the employer meets "the burden of showing that any given requirement [has] . . . a manifest relation to the employment in question." Id. at 432. This burden arises, of course, only after the complaining party or class has made out a prima facie case of discrimination — has shown that the tests in question select applicants for hire or promotion in a racial pattern significantly different from that of the pool of applicants. See McDonnell Douglas Corp. v. Green, 411 U. S. 792, 802. If an employer does then meet the burden of proving that its tests are "job related," it remains open to the complaining party to show that other tests or selection devices, without a similarly undesirable racial effect, would also serve the employer's legitimate interest in "efficient and trustworthy workmanship." Id. at 801. Such a showing would be evidence that the employer was using its tests merely as a "pretext" for discrimination. Id. at 804-805. In the present case, however, we are concerned only with the question whether Albemarle has shown its tests to be job related. . . .

Like the employer in Griggs, Albemarle uses two general ability tests, the Beta Examination, to test nonverbal intelligence, and the Wonderlic Test (Forms A and B), the purported measure of general verbal facility which was also involved in the Griggs case. Applicants for hire into various skilled lines of progression at the plant are required to score 100 on the Beta Exam and 18 on one of the Wonderlic Test's two, alternate forms.

The question of job relatedness must be viewed in the context of the plant's operation and the history of the testing program. The plant, which now employs about 650 persons, converts raw wood into paper products. It is organized into a number of functional departments, each with one or more distinct lines of progression, the theory being that workers can move up the line as they acquire the necessary skills. The number and structure of the lines has varied greatly over time. For many years, certain lines were themselves more skilled and paid higher wages than others, and until 1964 these skilled lines were expressly reserved for white workers. In 1968, many of the unskilled "Negro" lines were "end-tailed" on to skilled "white" lines, but it apparently remains true that at least the top jobs in certain lines require greater skills than the top jobs in other lines. In this sense, at least, it is still possible to speak of relatively skilled and relatively unskilled lines.

In the 1950's while the plant was being modernized with new and more sophisticated equipment, the company introduced a high school diploma requirement for entry into the skilled lines. Though the company soon concluded that this requirement did not improve the quality of the labor force, the requirement was continued until the District Court enjoined its use. In the late 1950's, the company began using the Beta Examination and the Bennett Mechanical Comprehension Test (also involved in the *Griggs* case) to screen applicants for entry into the skilled lines. The Bennett test was dropped several years later, but use of the Beta test continued.

The company added the Wonderlic Tests in 1963, for the skilled lines, on the theory that a certain verbal intelligence was called for by the increasing sophistication of the plant's operations. The company made no attempt to validate the test for job relatedness, and simply adopted the national "norm" score of 18 as a cut-off point for new job applicants. After 1964, when it discontinued overt segregation of the lines of progression, the company allowed Negro workers to transfer to the skilled lines if they could pass the Beta and Wonderlic Tests, but few succeeded in doing so. Incumbents in the skilled lines, some of whom had been hired before adoption of the tests, were not required to pass them to retain their jobs or their promotion rights. The record shows that a number of white incumbents in high ranking job groups could not pass the tests.

Because departmental reorganization continued up to the point of trial, and has indeed continued since that point, the details of the testing program are less than clear from the record. The District Court found that, since 1963, the Beta and Wonderlic tests have been used in 13 lines of progression, within eight departments. Albemarle contends that at present the tests are used in only eight lines of progression, within four departments.

Four months before this case went to trial, Albemarle engaged an expert in industrial psychology to "validate" the job relatedness of its testing program. He spent a half day at the plant and devised a "concurrent validation" study, which was conducted by plant officials, without his supervision. The expert then subjected the results to statistical analysis. The study dealt with 10 job groupings, selected from near the top of nine of the lines of progression. Jobs were grouped together solely by their proximity in the line of progression; no attempt was made to analyze jobs in terms of the particular skills they might require. All, or nearly all, employees in the selected groups participated in the study — 105 employees in all, but only four Negroes. Within each job grouping, the study compared the test scores of each employee with an independent "ranking" ·of the employee, relative to each of his coworkers, made by two of the employee's supervisors. . . .

For each job grouping, the expert computed the "Phi coefficient" of statistical correlation between the test scores and an average of the two supervisorial rankings. Consonant with professional conventions, the expert regarded as "statistically significant" any correlation that could have occurred by chance only five times, or less, in 100 trials. On the basis of these results, the· District Court found that "[t]he personnel tests administered at the plant have undergone validation studies and have been proven to be job related." Like the Court of Appeals, we are constrained to disagree.

The EEOC has issued "Guidelines" for employers seeking to determine, through professional validation studies, whether their employment tests are job related. 29 CFR Part 1607 (1974). These Guidelines draw upon and make reference to professional standards of test validation established by the American Psychological Association. The EEOC Guidelines are not administrative "regulations" promulgated pursuant to formal procedures established by the Congress. But, as this Court has heretofore noted, they do constitute "[t]he administrative interpretation of the Act by the enforcing agency," and consequently they are "entitled to great deference." Griggs v. Duke Power Co., *supra,* 401 U. S. at 433-434. See also Espinoza v. Farah Mfg. Co., 414 U.S. 86, 94.

The message of these Guidelines is the same as that of the *Griggs* case — that discriminatory tests are impermissible unless shown, by professionally acceptable methods, to be "predictive of or significantly correlated with important elements of work behavior which comprise or are relevant to the job or jobs for which candidates are being evaluated." 29 CFR § 1607.4(c).

Measured against the Guidelines, Albemarle's validation study is materially defective in several respects:

(1) Even if it had been otherwise adequate, the study would not have "validated" the Beta and Wonderlic test battery for all of the skilled lines of progression for which the two tests are, apparently, now required. The study showed significant correlations for the Beta Exam in only three of the eight lines. Though the Wonderlic Test's Form A and Form B are in theory identical and interchangeable measures of verbal facility, significant correlations for one Form but not for the other were obtained in four job groupings. In two job groupings neither Form showed a significant correlation. Within some of the lines of progression, one Form was found acceptable for

some job groupings but not for others. Even if the study were otherwise reliable, this odd patchwork of results would not entitle Albemarle to impose its testing program under the Guidelines. A test may be used in jobs other than those for which it has been professionally validated only if there are "no significant differences" between the studied and unstudied jobs. 29 CFR § 1607.4(c)(2). The study in this case involved no analysis of the attributes of, or the particular skills needed in, the studied job groups. There is accordingly no basis for concluding that "no significant differences" exist among the lines of progression, or among distinct job groupings within the studied lines of progression. Indeed, the study's checkered results appear to compel the opposite conclusion.

(2) The study compared test scores with subjective supervisorial rankings. While they allow the use of supervisorial rankings in test validation, the Guidelines quite plainly contemplate that the rankings will be elicited with far more care than was demonstrated here. Albemarle's supervisors were asked to rank employees by a "standard" that was extremely vague and fatally open to divergent interpretations. Each "job grouping" contained a number of different jobs, and the supervisors were asked, in each grouping, to

"determine which ones [employees] they felt irrespective of the job that they were actually doing, but in their respective jobs, did a better job than the person they were rating against. . . ."

There is no way of knowing precisely what criteria of job performance the supervisors were considering, whether each of the supervisors was considering the same criteria — or whether, indeed, any of the supervisors actually applied a focused and stable body of criteria of any kind. There is, in short, simply no way to determine whether the criteria *actually* considered were sufficiently related to the Company's legitimate interest in job-specific ability to justify a testing system with a racially discriminatory impact.

(3) The company's study focused, in most cases, on job groups near the top of the various lines of progression. In *Griggs v. Duke Power Co., supra,* the Court left open "the question whether testing requirements that take into account capability for the next succeeding position or related future promotion might be utilized upon a showing that such long-range requirements fulfill a genuine business need." 401 U.S. at 432. The Guidelines take a sensible approach to this issue, and we now endorse it:

"If job progression structures and seniority provisions are so established that new employees will probably, within a reasonable period of time and in a great majority of cases, progress to a higher level, it may be considered that candidates are being evaluated for jobs at that higher level. However, where job progression is not so nearly automatic, or the time span is such that higher level jobs or employees' potential may be expected to change in significant ways, it shall be considered that candidates are being evaluated for a job at or near the entry level." 29 CFR § 1607.4(c)(1).

The fact that the best of those employees working near the top of a line of progression score well on a test does not necessarily mean that that test, or some particular cutoff score on the test, is a permissible measure of the minimal qualifications of new workers, entering lower level jobs. In drawing any such conclusion, detailed consideration must be given to the normal speed of promotion, to the efficacy of on-the-job training in the scheme of promotion, and to the possible use of testing as a promotion device, rather than as a screen for entry into low-level jobs. The District Court made no findings on these issues. The issues take on special importance in a case, such as this one, where incumbent employees are permitted to work at even high-level jobs without passing the company's test battery. See 29 CFR § 1607.11.

(4) Albemarle's validation study dealt only with job-experienced, white workers; but the tests themselves are given to new job applicants, who are younger, largely inexperienced, and in many instances nonwhite. The Standards of the American Psychological Association state that it is "essential" that

"[t]he validity of a test should be determined on subjects who are at the age or in the same educational or vocational situation as the persons for whom the test is recommended in practice."

The EEOC Guidelines likewise provide that "[d]ata must be generated and results separately reported for minority or non-minority groups wherever technically feasible." 29 CFR § 1607.5(b)(5). In the present case, such "differential validation" as to racial groups was very likely not "feasible," because years of discrimination at the plant have insured that nearly all of the upper level employees are white. But there has been no clear showing that differential validation was not feasible for lower-level jobs. More importantly, the Guidelines provide:

"If it is not technically feasible to include minority employees in validation studies conducted on the present work force, the conduct of a validation study without minority candidates does not relieve any person of his subsequent obligation for validation when inclusion of minority candidates becomes technically feasible." 29 CFR § 1607.5(b)(1). . . . "[E]vidence of satisfactory validity based on other groups will be regarded as only provisional compliance with the guidelines pending separate validation of the test for the minority groups in question." 29 CFR § 1607.5(b)(5).

For all these reasons, we agree with the Court of Appeals that the District Court erred in concluding that Albemarle had proved the job relatedness of its testing program and that the respondents were consequently not entitled to equitable relief. The outright reversal by the Court of Appeals implied that an injunction should immediately issue against all use of testing at the plant. Because of the particular circumstances of this case, however, it appears that the more prudent course is to leave to the District Court the precise fashioning of the necessary relief in the first instance. During the appellate stages of this litigation, the plant has apparently been amending its departmental organization and the use made of its tests. The appropriate standard of proof for job relatedness has not been clarified until today. Similarly, the respondents have not until today been specifically apprised of their opportunity to present evidence that even validated tests might be a "pretext" for discrimination in light of alternative selection procedures available to the company. We also note that the Guidelines authorize provisional use of tests, pending new validation efforts, in certain very limited circumstances. 29 CFR § 1607.9. Whether such circumstances now obtain is a matter best decided, in the first instance, by the District Court. That court will be free to take such new evidence, and to exercise such control of the company's use and validation of employee selection procedures, as are warranted by the circumstances and by the controlling law.

Accordingly, the judgment is vacated, and these cases are remanded to the District Court for proceedings consistent with this opinion.

It is so ordered.

Mr. Justice Powell did not participate in the consideration or decision of these cases.

NOTE:

Problem: Is Part III of the Supreme Court's opinion in *Washington v. Davis, supra,* consistent with the Court's opinion in *Albemarle*? If not, what is the effect of the *Washington v. Davis* decision on the test set out in *Albemarle*?

E. SEX DISCRIMINATION

PHILLIPS v. MARTIN MARIETTA CORP.

United States Supreme Court
400 U.S. 542, 91 S. Ct. 496, 27 L. Ed. 2d 613 (1971)

PER CURIAM.

Petitioner Mrs. Ida Phillips commenced an action in the United States District Court for the Middle District of Florida under Title VII of the Civil Rights Act of 1964 alleging that she had been denied employment because of her sex. The District Court granted a summary judgment for Martin Marietta (Martin) on the basis of the following showing: (1) in 1966 Martin informed Mrs. Phillips that it was not accepting job applications from women with pre-school age children; (2) as of the time of the motion for summary judgment, Martin employed men with pre-school age children; (3) at the time Mrs. Phillips applied, 70-75% of the applicants for the position she sought were women; 75-80% of those hired for the position, assembly trainee, were women, hence no question of bias against women as such was presented.

The Court of Appeals for the Fifth Circuit affirmed, 411 F.2d 1 (CA5 1969), and denied a rehearing *en banc.* 416 F.2d 1257 (CA5 1969). We granted certiorari. 397 U.S. 960 (1970).

Section 703(a) of the Civil Rights Act of 1964 requires that persons of like qualifications be given employment opportunities irrespective of their sex. The Court of Appeals therefore erred in reading this section as permitting one hiring policy for women and another for men — each having pre-school age children. The existence of such conflicting family obligations, if demonstrably more relevant to job performance for a woman than for a man, could arguably be a basis for distinction under § 703(e) of the Act. But that is a matter of evidence tending to show that the condition in question "is a bona fide occupational qualification reasonably necessary to the normal operation of that particular business or enterprise." The record [before] us, however, is not adequate for resolution of these important issues: See Kennedy v. Silas Mason Co., 334 U.S. 249, 256-257 (1948). Summary judgment was therefore improper and we remand for fuller development of the record and for further consideration.

Vacated and remanded.

MR. JUSTICE MARSHALL, concurring.

While I agree that this case must be remanded for a full development of the facts, I can not agree with the Court's indication that a "bona fide occupational qualification reasonably necessary to the normal operation of" Martin Marietta's business could be established by a showing that some women, even the vast majority, with preschool age children have family responsibilities that interfere with job performance and that men do not usually have such responsibilities. Certainly, an employer can require that all of his employees, both men and women, meet minimum performance standards, and he can try to insure compliance by requiring parents, both mothers and fathers, to provide for the care of their children so that job performance is not interfered with.

But the Court suggests that it would not require such uniform standards. I fear that in this case, where the issue is not squarely before us, the Court has fallen into the trap of assuming that the Act permits ancient canards about the proper role of women to be a basis for discrimination. Congress, however, sought just the opposite result.

By adding the prohibition against job discrimination based on sex to the 1964 Civil Rights Act Congress intended to prevent employers from refusing "to hire an individual based on stereotyped characterizations of the sexes." Equal Employment Opportunity Commission, "Guidelines on Discrimination Because of Sex," 29 CFR § 1604.1 (a) (ii). See Bowe v. Colgate-Palmolive Co., 416 F.2d 711 (CA7 1969); Weeks v. Southern Bell Tel. & Tel. Co., 408 F.2d 228 (CA5 1969). Even characterizations of the proper domestic roles of the sexes were not to serve as predicates for restricting employment opportunity. The exception for "bona fide occupational qualifications" was not intended to swallow the rule.

That exception has been construed by the Equal Employment Opportunity Commission, whose regulations are entitled to "great deference," Udall v. Tallman, 380 U.S. 1, 16 (1965), to be applicable only to job situations that require specific physical characteristics necessarily possessed by only one sex. Thus the exception would apply where necessary "for the purposes of authenticity or genuineness" in the employment of actors or actresses, fashion models, and the like. If the exception is to be limited as Congress intended, the Commission has given it the only possible construction.

When performance characteristics of an individual are involved, even when parental roles are concerned, employment opportunity may be limited only by employment criteria that are neutral as to the sex of the applicant.

DOTHARD v. RAWLINSON

United States Supreme Court
433 U.S. 321, 97 S. Ct. 2720 (1977)

Mr. Justice Stewart delivered the opinion of the Court.

The appellee, Dianne Rawlinson, sought employment with the Alabama Board of Corrections as a prison guard, called in Alabama a "correctional counselor." After her application was rejected, she brought this class suit under Title VII of the Civil Rights Act of 1964, 78 Stat. 253, as amended, 42 U.S.C. § 2000e *et seq.* (1970 ed. and Supp. V), and under 42 U.S.C. § 1983, alleging that she had been denied employment because of her sex in violation of federal law. A three-judge Federal District Court for the Middle District of Alabama decided in her favor. *Mieth v. Dothard,* 418 F.Supp. 1169. . . .

I

At the time she applied for a position as correctional counselor trainee, Rawlinson was a 22-year-old college graduate whose major course of study had been correctional psychology. She was refused employment because she failed to meet the minimum 120-pound weight requirement established by an Alabama statute. The statute also establishes a height minimum of 5 feet and 2 inches.

After her application was rejected because of her weight, Rawlinson filed a charge with the Equal Employment Opportunity Commission, and ultimately received a right to sue letter. She then filed a complaint in the District Court on behalf of herself and other similarly situated women, challenging the statutory height and weight minima as violative of Title VII and the Equal Protection Clause of the Fourteenth Amendment. A three-judge court was convened. While the suit was pending, the Alabama Board of Corrections adopted Administrative Regulation 204, establishing gender criteria for assigning correctional counselors to maximum security institutions for "contact positions," that is, positions requiring continual close physical proximity to inmates of the institution Rawlinson amended her class-action complaint by adding a challenge to regulation 204 as also violative of Title VII and the Fourteenth Amendment.

Like most correctional facilities in the United States, Alabama's prisons are segregated on the basis of sex. Currently the Alabama Board of Corrections operates four major all-male penitentiaries — Holman Prison, Kilby Corrections Facility, G. K. Fountain Correction Center, and Draper Correctional Center. The Board also operates the Julia Tutwiler Prison for Women, the Frank Lee Youth Center, the # 4 Honor Camp, the State Cattle Ranch, and nine Work Release Centers, one of which is for women. The Julia Tutwiler Prison for Women and the four male penitentiaries are maximum security institutions. Their inmate living quarters are for the most part large dormitories, with communal showers and toilets that are open to the dormitories and hallways. The Draper and Fountain penitentiaries carry on extensive farming operations, making necessary a large number of strip searches for contraband when prisoners re-enter the prison buildings.

A correctional counselor's primary duty within these institutions is to maintain security and control of the inmates by continually supervising and observing their activities.[8] To be eligible for consideration as a correctional counselor, an applicant must possess a valid Alabama driver's license, have a high school education or its equivalent, be free from physical defects, be between the ages of 20½ years and 45 years at the time of appointment, and fall between the minimum height and weight requirements of five feet and two inches and 120 pounds, and the maximum of six feet and ten inches and 300 pounds. Appointment is by merit, with a grade assigned each applicant based on experience and education. No written examination is given.

At the time this litigation was in the District Court, the Board of Corrections employed a total of 435 people in various correctional counselor positions, 56 of whom were women. Of those 56 women, 21 were employed at the Julia Tutwiler Prison for Women, 13 were employed in noncontact positions at the four male maximum security institutions, and the remaining 22 were employed at the other institutions operated by the Alabama Board of Corrections. Because most of Alabama's prisoners are held at the four maximum security male penitentiaries, 336 of the 435 correctional counselor jobs were in those institutions, a majority of them concededly in the "contact" classification. Thus, even though meeting the statutory height and weight requirements, women applicants could under Regulation 204 compete equally with men for only about 25% of the correctional counselor jobs available in the Alabama prison system.

II

In enacting Title VII, Congress required "the removal of artificial, arbitrary, and unnecessary barriers to employment when the barriers operate invidiously to discriminate on the basis of racial or other impermissible classification." *Griggs v. Duke Power Co.*, 401 U.S. 424, 431, 91 S. Ct. 849, 853, 28 L.Ed.2d 158. The District Court found that the minimum statutory height and weight requirements that applicants for employment as correctional counselors must meet constitute the sort of arbitrary barrier to equal employment opportunity that Title VII forbids. The appellants assert that the District Court erred both in finding that the height and weight standards discriminate against women, and in its refusal to find that, even if they do, these standards are justified as "job related."

[8] The official job description for a correctional counselor position emphasizes counseling as well as security duties; the District Court found that "correctional counselors are persons commonly referred to as prison guards. Their duties primarily involve security rather than counseling." 418 F.Supp. at 1175.

A

The gist of the claim that the statutory height and weight requirements discriminate against women does not involve an assertion of purposeful discriminatory motive.[11] It is asserted, rather, that these facially neutral qualification standards work in fact disproportionately to exclude women from eligiblity for employment by the Alabama Board of Corrections. We dealt in *Griggs v. Duke Power Co., supra* and *Albemarle Paper Co. v. Moody,* 422 U.S. 405, 95 S.Ct. 2362, 45 L.Ed.2d 280, with similar allegations that facially neutral employment standards disproportionately excluded Negroes from employment, and those cases guide our approach here.

Those cases make clear that to establish a prima facie case of discrimination, a plaintiff need only show that the facially neutral standards in question select applicants for hire in a significantly discriminatory pattern. Once it is thus shown that the employment standards are discriminatory in effect, the employer must meet "the burden of showing that any given requirement [has] . . . a manifest relation to the employment in question." *Griggs v. Duke Power Co.,* 401 U.S., at 432, 91 S.Ct., at 854. If the employer proves that the challenged requirements are job related, the plaintiff may then show that other selection devices without a similar discriminatory effect would also "serve the employer's legitimate interest in 'efficient and trustworthy workmanship.'" *Albemarle Paper Co. v. Moody,* 422 U.S., at 425, 95 S. Ct., at 2375, quoting *McDonnell Douglas Corp. v. Green,* 411 U.S. 792, 801, 93 S.Ct. 1817, 1823, 36 L.Ed.2d 668.

Although women 14 years of age or older comprise 52.75% of the Alabama population and 36.89% of its total labor force, they hold only 12.9% of its correctional counselor positions. In considering the effect of the minimum height and weight standards on this disparity in rate of hiring between the sexes, the District Court found that the 5′2″ requirement would operate to exclude 33.29% of the women in the United States between the ages of 18-79, while excluding only 1.28% of the men between the same ages. The 120-pound weight restriction would exclude 22.29% of the women and 2.35% of the men in this age group. When the height and weight restrictions are combined, Alabama's statutory standards would exclude 41.13% of the female population while excluding less than 1 percent of the male population.[12] Accordingly, the District Court found that Rawlinson had made out a prima facie case of unlawful sex discrimination.

---

[11] *See International Brotherhood of Teamsters v. United States,* 431 U.S. 324, at 335 n. 15, 97 S.Ct. 1843, at 1854.

[12] Affirmatively stated, approximately 99.76% of the men and 58.87% of the women meet both these physical qualifications. From the separate statistics on height and weight of males it would appear that after adding the two together and allowing for some overlap the result would be to exclude between 2.35 and 3.63%

The appellants argue that a showing of disproportionate impact on women based on generalized national statistics should not suffice to establish a prima facie case. They point in particular to Rawlinson's failure to adduce comparative statistics concerning actual applicants for correctional counselor positions in Alabama. There is no requirement, however, that a statistical showing of disproportionate impact must always be based on analysis of the characteristics of actual applicants. See *Griggs v. Duke Power Co.,* 401 U.S., at 430, 91 S.Ct., at 853. The application process might itself not adequately reflect the actual potential applicant pool, since otherwise qualified people might be discouraged from applying because of a self-recognized inability to meet the very standards challenged as being discriminatory. See *International Brotherhood of Teamsters v. United States,* 431 U.S. 324 at 362-369, 97 S. Ct. 1843, 1869-1871. A potential applicant could easily measure her height and weight and conclude that to make an application would be futile. Moreover, reliance on general population demographic data was not misplaced where there was no reason to suppose that physical height and weight characteristics of Alabama men and women differ markedly from those of the national population.

For these reasons, we cannot say that the District Court was wrong in holding that the statutory height and weight standards had a discriminatory impact on women applicants. The plaintiffs in a case such as this are not required to exhaust every possible source of evidence, if the evidence actually presented on its face conspicuously demonstrates a job requirement's grossly discriminatory impact. If the employer discerns fallacies or deficiencies in the data offered by the plaintiff, he is free to adduce countervailing evidence of his own. In this case no such effort was made.

B

We turn, therefore, to the appellants' argument that they have rebutted the prima facie case of discrimination by showing that the height and weight requirements are job related. These requirements, they say, have a relationship to strength, a sufficient but unspecified amount of which is essential to effective job performance as a correctional counselor. In the District Court, however, the appellants produced   no   evidence   correlating   the   height   and   weight

---

of males from meeting the Alabama's statutory height and weight minima. None of the parties has challenged the accuracy of the District Court's computations on this score, however, and the discrepancy is in any event insignificant in light of the gross disparity between the female and male exclusions. Even under revised computations the disparity would greatly exceed the 34% to 12% disparity that served to invalidate the high school diploma requirement in the *Griggs* case. *Griggs v. Duke Power Co.,* 401 U.S., at 430, 91 S.Ct. at 853.

requirements with the requisite amount of strength thought essential to good job performance. Indeed, they failed to offer evidence of any kind in specific justification of the statutory standards.[14]

If the job-related quality that the appellants identify is bona fide, their purpose could be achieved by adopting and validating a test for applicants that measures strength directly.[15] Such a test, fairly administered, would fully satisfy the standards of Title VII because it would be one that "measure[s] the person for the job and not the person in the abstract." *Griggs v. Duke Power Co.,* 401 U.S., at 436, 91 S.Ct., at 856. But nothing in the present record even approaches such a measurement.

For the reasons we have discussed, the District Court was not in error in holding that Title VII of the Civil Rights Act of 1964, as amended, prohibits application of the statutory height and weight requirements to Rawlinson and the class she represents.

III

Unlike the statutory height and weight requirements, Regulation 204 explicitly discriminates against women on the basis of their sex. In defense of this overt discrimination, the appellants rely on § 703(e) of Title VII, which permits sex-based discrimination "in those certain instances where . . . sex . . . is a bona fide occupational qualification reasonably necessary to the normal operation of that particular business or enterprise."

The District Court rejected the bona fide occupational qualification (bfoq) defense, relying on the virtually uniform view of the federal courts that § 703(e) provides only the narrowest of exceptions to the general rule requiring equality of employment

---

[14] In what is perhaps a variation on their constitutional challenge to the validity of Title VII itself, see n. 1, *supra,* the appellants contend that the establishment of the minimum height and weight standards by statute requires that they be given greater deference than is typically given private employer-established job qualifications. The relevant legislative history of the 1972 amendments extending Title VII to the States as employers does not, however, support such a result. Instead, Congress expressly indicated the intent that the same Title VII principles be applied to governmental and private employers alike. See H.R. Rep. No. 92-238, 92d Cong., 1st Sess., p. 17 (1971); S.Rep.No. 92-415, 92d Cong., 1st Sess., p. 10 (1971); U.S. Code Cong. & Admin.News 1972, p. 2137. See also *Schaeffer v. San Diego Yellow Cabs,* 462 F.2d 1002 (CA9). Thus for both private and public employers, "The touchstone is business necessity," *Griggs,* 401 U.S., at 431, 91 S.Ct., at 853; a discriminatory employment practice must be shown to be necessary to safe and efficient job performance to survive a Title VII challenge.

[15] Cf. EEOC Guidelines on Employee Selection Procedures, 29 CFR § 1607. See also *Washington v. Davis,* 426 U.S. 229, 246-247, 96 S.Ct. 2040, 2050-2051, 48 L.Ed.2d 597; *Albemarle Paper Co. v. Moody,* 422 U.S. 405, 95 S.Ct. 2362, 45 L.Ed.2d 280; *Officers for Justice v. Civil Service Commission,* 395 F.Supp. 378 (ND Cal.).

opportunities. This view has been variously formulated. In *Diaz v. Pan American World Airways,* 422 F.2d 385, 388, the Court of Appeals for the Fifth Circuit held that "discrimination based on sex is valid only when the *essence* of the business operation would be undermined by not hiring members of one sex exclusively." (Emphasis in original.) In an earlier case, *Weeks v. Southern Bell Telephone and Telegraph Co.,* 5 Cir., 408 F. 228, 235, the same court said that an employer could rely on the bfoq exception only by proving "that he had reasonable cause to believe, that is, a factual basis for believing, that all or substantially all women would be unable to perform safely and efficiently the duties of the job involved." See also *Phillips v. Martin Marietta Corp.,* 400 U.S. 542, 91 S.Ct. 496, 27 L.Ed.2d 613. But whatever the verbal formulation, the federal courts have agreed that it is impermissible under Title VII to refuse to hire an individual woman or man on the basis of stereotyped characterizations of the sexes, and the District Court in the present case held in effect that Regulation 204 is based on just such stereotypical assumptions.

We are persuaded — by the restrictive language of § 703(e), the relevant legislative history, and the consistent interpretation of the Equal Employment Opportunity Commission [19] that the bfoq exception was in fact meant to be an extremely narrow exception to the general prohibition of discrimination on the basis of sex.[20] In the particular factual circumstances of this case, however, we conclude that the District Court erred in rejecting the State's contention that Regulation 204 falls within the narrow ambit of the bfoq exception.

The environment in Alabama's penitentiaries is a peculiarly inhospitable one for human beings of whatever sex. Indeed, a federal district court has held that the conditions of confinement in the prisons of the State, characterized by "rampant violence" and a "jungle atmosphere," are constitutionally intolerable. *James v. Wallace,* 406 F.Supp. 318, 325 (MD Ala.). The record in the present

[19] The EEOC issued guidelines on sex discrimination in 1965 reflecting its position that "the bona fide occupational qualification as to sex should be interpreted narrowly." 29 CFR § 1604.2(a). It has adhered to that principle consistently, and its construction of the statute can accordingly be given weight. See *Griggs v. Duke Power Co.,* 401 U.S., at 434, 91 S.Ct., at 855; *McDonald v. Santa Fe Trail Transportation Co.,* 427 U.S. 273, 279-280, 96 S.Ct. 2574, 2577-2578, 49 L.Ed.2d 493.

[20] In the case of a state employer, the bfoq exception would have to be interpreted at the very least so as to conform to the Equal Protection Clause of the Fourteenth Amendment. The parties do not suggest, however, that the Equal Protection Clause requires more rigorous scrutiny of a State's sexually discriminatory employment policy than does Title VII. There is thus no occasion to give independent consideration to the District Court's ruling that Regulation 204 violates the Fourteenth Amendment as well as Title VII.

case shows that because of inadequate staff and facilities, no attempt is made in the four maximum security male penitentiaries to classify or segregate inmates according to their offense or level of dangerousness — a procedure that, according to expert testimony, is essential to effective penalogical administration. Consequently, the estimated 20% of the male prisoners who are sex offenders are scattered throughout the penitentiaries' dormitory facilities.

In this environment of violence and disorganization, it would be an oversimplification to characterize Regulation 204 as an exercise in "romantic paternalism." Cf. *Frontiero v. Richardson,* 411 U.S. 677, 684, 93 S.Ct. 1764, 1769, 36 L.Ed.2d 583. In the usual case, the argument that a particular job is too dangerous for women may appropriately be met by the rejoinder that it is the purpose of Title VII to allow the individual woman to make that choice for herself. More is at stake in this case, however, than an individual woman's decision to weigh and accept the risks of employment in a "contact" position in a maximum security male prison.

The essence of a correctional counselor's job is to maintain prison security. A woman's relative ability to maintain order in a male, maximum security, unclassified penitentiary of the type Alabama now runs could be directly reduced by her womanhood. There is a basis in fact for expecting that sex offenders who have criminally assaulted women in the past would be moved to do so again if access to women were established within the prison. There would also be a real risk that other inmates, deprived of a normal heterosexual environment, would assault women guards because they were women.[22] In a prison system where violence is the order of the day, where inmate access to guards is facilitated by dormitory living arrangements, where every institution is understaffed, and where a substantial portion of the inmate population is composed of sex offenders mixed at random with other prisoners, there are few visible deterrents to inmate assaults on women custodians.

The plaintiff's own expert testified that dormitory housing for aggressive inmates poses a greater security problem than single-cell lockups, and further testified that it would be unwise to use women as guards in a prison where even 10% of the inmates had been convicted of sex crimes and were not segregated from the other prisoners.[23] The likelihood that inmates would assault a woman

[22] The record contains evidence of an attack on a female clerical worker in an Alabama prison, and of an incident involving a woman student who was taken hostage during a visit to one of the maximum security institutions.

[23] Alabama's penitentiaries are evidently not typical. The appellees' two experts testified that in a normal, relatively stable maximum security prison — characterized by control over the inmates, reasonable living conditions, and segregation of dangerous offenders — women guards could be used effectively and beneficially. Similarly, an *amicus* brief filed by the state of California attests to that state's success in using women guards in all-male penitentiaries.

because she was a woman would pose a real threat not only to the victim of the assault but also to the basic control of the penitentiary and protection of its inmates and the other security personnel. The employee's very womanhood would thus directly undermine her capacity to provide the security that is the essence of a correctional counselor's responsibility.

There was substantial testimony from experts on both sides of this litigation that the use of women as guards in "contact" positions under the existing conditions in Alabama maximum security male penitentiaries would pose a substantial security problem, directly linked to the sex of the prison guard. On the basis of that evidence, we conclude that the District Court was in error in ruling that being male is not a bona fide occupational qualification for the job of correctional counselor in a "contact" position in an Alabama male maximum security penitentiary.

The judgment is accordingly affirmed in part and reversed in part, and the case is remanded to the District Court for further proceedings consistent with this opinion.

It is so ordered.

MR. JUSTICE REHNQUIST, with whom THE CHIEF JUSTICE and MR. JUSTICE BLACKMUN join, concurring in the result and concurring in part.

I agree with, and join, Parts I and III of the Court's opinion in this case and with its judgment. While I also agree with the Court's conclusion in Part II of its opinion, holding that the District Court was "not in error" in holding the statutory height and weight requirements in this case to be invalidated by Title VII, *ante,* at 2728, the issues with which that part deals are bound to arise so frequently that I feel obliged to separately state the reasons for my agreement with its result. I view affirmance of the District Court in this respect as essentially dictated by the peculiarly limited factual and legal justifications offered below by appellants on behalf of the statutory requirements. For that reason, I do not believe — and do not read the Court's opinion as holding — that all or even many of the height and weight requirements imposed by States on applicants for a multitude of law enforcement agency jobs are pretermitted by today's decision.

I agree that the statistics relied upon in this case are sufficient, absent rebuttal, to sustain a finding of a prima facie violation of § 703(a)(2), in that they reveal a significant discrepancy between the numbers of men, as opposed to women, who are automatically disqualified by reason of the height and weight requirements. The fact that these statistics are national figures of height and weight, as opposed to statewide or pool-of-labor-force statistics, does not seem to me to require us to hold that the District Court erred as a matter of law in admitting them into evidence. . . .

Appellants, in order to rebut the prima facie case under the statute, had the burden placed on them to advance job-related reasons for the qualification. *McDonnell Douglas Corp. v. Green,* 411 U.S. 792, at 802, 93 S.Ct. 1817, at 1824, 36 L.Ed.2d 668 (1973). This burden could be shouldered by offering evidence or by making legal arguments not dependent on any new evidence. The District Court was confronted, however, with only one suggested job-related reason for the qualification — that of strength. Appellants argued only the job-relatedness of actual physical strength; they did not urge that an equally job-related qualification for prison guards is the *appearance* of strength. As the Court notes, the primary job of correctional counselor in Alabama prisons "is to maintain security and control of the inmates . . . ," *ante,* at 2725, a function that I at least would imagine is aided by the psychological impact on prisoners of the presence of tall and heavy guards. If the appearance of strength had been urged upon the District Court here as a reason for the height and weight minima, I think that the District Court would surely have been entitled to reach a different result than it did. For, even if not perfectly correlated, I would think that Title VII would not preclude a State from saying that anyone under 5'2" or 120 pounds, no matter how strong in fact, does not have a sufficient appearance of strength to be a prison guard. . . .

MR. JUSTICE MARSHALL, with whom MR. JUSTICE BRENNAN joins, concurring in part and dissenting in part.

I agree entirely with the Court's analysis of Alabama's height and weight requirements for prison guards, and with its finding that these restrictions discriminate on the basis of sex in violation of Title VII. Accordingly, I join Parts I and II of the Court's opinion. I also agree with much of the Court's general discussion in Part III of the bona fide occupational qualification exception contained in § 703(e) of Title VII.

. . . I must, however, respectfully disagree with the Court's application of the bfoq exception in this case. . . .

Some women, like some men, undoubtedly are not qualified and do not wish to serve as prison guards, but that does not justify the exclusion of all women from this employment opportunity. . . .

What would otherwise be considered unlawful, discrimination against women is justified by the Court, however, on the basis of the "barbaric and inhumane" conditions in Alabama prisons, conditions so bad that state officials have conceded that they violate the Constitution. See *James v. Wallace,* 406 F.Supp. 318, 329, 331 (MD Ala. 1976). To me, this analysis sounds distressingly like saying two wrongs make a right. It is refuted by the plain words of § 706(e). The statute requires that a bfoq be "reasonably necessary to the normal operation of that particular business or enterprise." But no governmental "business" may operate "normally" in violation of the

Constitution. Every action of government is constrained by constitutional limitations. While those limits may be violated more frequently than we would wish, no one disputes that the "normal operation" of all government functions takes place within them. A prison system operating in blatant violation of the Eighth Amendment is an exception that should be remedied with all possible speed, as Judge Johnson's comprehensive order in *James v. Wallace, supra,* is designed to do. In the meantime, the existence of such violations should not be legitimatized by calling them "normal." Nor should the Court accept them as justifying conduct that would otherwise violate a statute intended to remedy age-old discrimination.

The Court's error in statutory construction is less objectionable, however, than the attitude it displays toward women. Though the Court recognizes that possible harm to women guards is an unacceptable reason for disqualifying women, it relies instead on an equally speculative threat to prison discipline supposedly generated by the sexuality of female guards. There is simply no evidence in the record to show that women guards would create any danger to security in Alabama prisons significantly greater than already exists. All of the dangers — with one exception discussed below — are inherent in a prison setting whatever the gender of the guards.

The Court first sees women guards as a threat to security because "there are few visible deterrents to inmate assaults on women custodians." *Ante,* at 2730. In fact, any prison guard is constantly subject to the threat of attack by inmates and "invisible" deterrents are the guard's only real protection. No prison guard relies primarily on his or her ability to ward off an inmate attack to maintain order. Guards are typically unarmed and sheer numbers of inmates could overcome the normal complement. Rather, like all other law enforcement officers, prison guards must rely primarily on the moral authority of their office and the threat of future punishment for miscreants. As one expert testified below, common sense, fairness, and mental and emotional stability are the qualities a guard needs to cope with the dangers of the job. App. 81. Well qualified and properly trained women, no less than men, have these psychological weapons at their disposal.

The particular severity of discipline problems in the Alabama maximum security prisons is also no justification for the discrimination sanctioned by the Court. The District Court found in *James v. Wallace, supra,* that guards "must spend all their time attempting to maintain control or to protect themselves." 406 F.Supp., at 325. If male guards face an impossible situation, it is difficult to see how women could make the problem worse, unless one relies on precisely the type of generalized bias against women that the Court agrees Title VII was intended to outlaw. For example, much of the testimony of appellants' witnesses ignores individual differences among members of each sex and reads like "ancient canards about the proper role of women." *Phillips v. Martin Marietta Corp., supra,* 400 U.S., at 545, 91 S.Ct., at 498. The witnesses claimed that women guards are not strict disciplinarians; that they are physically less capable of protecting themselves and subduing unruly inmates; that inmates take advantage of them as they did their mothers, while male guards are strong father figures who easily maintain discipline, and so on. Yet the record shows that the presence of women guards has not led to a single incident amounting to a serious breach of security in any Alabama institution. And in any event, "Guards rarely enter the cell blocks and dormitories," *James v. Wallace, supra,* 406 F.Supp., at 325, where the danger of inmate attacks is the greatest.

It appears that the real disqualifying factor in the Court's view is "[t]he employee's very womanhood." *Ante,* at 2730. The Court refers to the large number of sex offenders in Alabama prisons, and to "the likelihood that inmates would assault a woman because she was a woman." *Ibid.* In short, the fundamental justification for the decision is that women as guards will generate sexual assaults. With all respect, this rationale regrettably perpetuates one of the most insidious of the old myths about women — that women, wittingly or not, are seductive sexual objects. The effect of the decision, made I am sure with the best of intentions, is to punish women because their very presence might provoke sexual assaults. It is women who are made to pay the price in lost job opportunities for the threat of depraved conduct by prison inmates. Once again, "[t]he pedestal upon which women have been placed has . . . , upon closer inspection, been revealed as a cage." *Sail'er Inn, Inc. v. Kirby,* 5 Cal.3d 1, 20, 95 Cal.Rptr. 329, 341, 485 P.2d 529, 541 (1971). It is particularly ironic that the cage is erected here in response to feared misbehavior by imprisoned criminals.

The Court points to no evidence in the record to support the asserted "likelihood that inmates would assault a woman because she was a woman." *Ante,* at 2730. Perhaps the Court relies upon common sense, or "innate recognition." Brief for Appellants, at 51. But the danger in this emotionally laden context is that common sense will be used to mask the "romantic paternalism" and persisting discriminatory attitudes that the Court properly eschews. *Ante,* at 2729. To me, the only matter of innate recognition is that the incidence of sexually motivated attacks on guards will be minute compared to the "likelihood that inmates will assault" a *guard* because he or she is a *guard.*

The proper response to inevitable attacks on both female and male guards is not to limit the employment opportunities of law-abiding women who wish to contribute to their community, but to take swift and sure punitive action against the inmate offenders. Presumably, one of the goals of the Alabama prison system is the eradication of inmates' antisocial behavior patterns so that prisoners will be able to live one day in free society. Sex offenders can begin this process by learning to relate to women guards in a socially acceptable manner. To deprive women of job opportunities because of the threatened behavior of convicted criminals is to turn our social priorities upside down.

Although I do not countenance the sex discrimination condoned by the majority, it is fortunate that the Court's decision is carefully limited to the facts before it. I trust the lower courts will recognize that the decision was impelled by the shockingly inhuman conditions in Alabama prisons, and thus that the "extremely narrow [bfoq] exception" recognized here, *ante,* at 2729, will not be allowed "to swallow the rule" against sex discrimination. See *Phillips v. Martin Marietta Corp., supra,* 400 U.S., at 545, 91 S.Ct., at 498. Expansion of today's decision beyond its narrow, factual basis would erect a serious roadblock to economic equality for women.

GENERAL ELECTRIC CO. v. GILBERT

United States Supreme Court
429 U.S. 125, 97 S. Ct. 401, 50 L. Ed. 2d 343 (1976)

MR. JUSTICE REHNQUIST delivered the opinion of the Court.

I

As part of its total compensation package, General Electric provides nonoccupational sickness and accident benefits to all employees under its Weekly Sickness and Accident Insurance Plan (the Plan) in an amount equal to 60% of an employee's normal straight-time weekly earnings. These payments are paid to employees who become totally disabled as a result of a nonoccupational sickness or accident. . . . Benefit payments normally start with the eighth day of an employee's total disability (although if an employee is earlier confined to a hospital as a bed patient, benefit payments will start immediately), and continue up to a maximum of 26 weeks for any one continuous period of disability or successive periods of disability due to the same or related causes.

The individually named respondents are present or former hourly paid production employees at General Electric's plant in Salem, Va. Each of these employees was pregnant during 1971 or 1972, while employed by General Electric, and each presented a claim to the company for disability benefits under the Plan to cover the period while absent from work as a result of the pregnancy. These claims were routinely denied on the ground that the Plan did not provide disability-benefit payments for any absence due to pregnancy. Each of the respondents thereafter filed charges with the Equal Employment Opportunity Commission (EEOC) alleging that the refusal of General Electric to pay disability benefits under the Plan for time lost due to pregnancy and childbirth discriminated against her because of sex. Upon waiting the requisite number of days, the instant action was commenced in the District Court. The complaint asserted a violation of Title VII. Damages were sought as well as an injunction directing General Electric to include pregnancy disabilities within the Plan on the same terms and conditions as other nonoccupational disabilities.

The ultimate conclusion of the District Court was that petitioner had discriminated on the basis of sex in the operation of its disability program in violation of Title VII. An order was entered enjoining petitioner from continuing to exclude pregnancy-related disabilities from the coverage of the Plan, and providing for the future award of monetary relief to individual members of the class affected. Petitioner appealed to the Court of Appeals for the Fourth Circuit, and that court by a divided vote affirmed the judgment of the District Court.

Between the date on which the District Court's judgment was rendered and the time this case was decided by the Court of Appeals, we decided *Geduldig* v. *Aiello,* 417 U. S. 484 (1974), where we rejected a claim that a very similar disability program established under California law violated the Equal Protection Clause of the Fourteenth Amendment because that plan's exclusion of pregnancy disabilities represented sex discrimination. The majority of the Court of Appeals felt that *Geduldig* was not controlling because it arose under the Equal Protection Clause of the Fourteenth Amendment, and not under Title VII. . . . We granted certiorari to consider this important issue in the construction of Title VII.

II

Section 703(a) (1) provides in relevant part that it shall be an unlawful employment practice for an employer

"to discriminate against any individual with respect to his compensation, terms, conditions, or privileges of employment, because of such individual's race, color, religion, sex, or national origin," 42 U. S. C. § 2000e-2(a) (1).

While there is no necessary inference that Congress, in choosing this language, intended to incorporate into Title VII the concepts of discrimination which have evolved from court decisions construing the Equal Protection Clause of the Fourteenth Amendment, the similarities between the congressional language and some of those decisions surely indicate that the latter are a useful starting point in interpreting the former. Particularly in the case of defining the term "discrimination," which Congress has nowhere in Title VII defined, those cases afford an existing body of law analyzing and discussing that term in a legal context not wholly dissimilar to the concerns which Congress manifested in enacting Title VII. We think, therefore, that our decision in *Geduldig* v. *Aiello, supra,* dealing with a strikingly similar disability plan, is quite relevant in determining whether or not the pregnancy exclusion did discriminate on the basis of sex. In *Geduldig,* the disability insurance system was funded entirely from contributions deducted from the wages of participating employees, at a rate of 1% of the employee's salary up to an annual maximum of $85. In other relevant respects, the operation of the program was similar to General Electric's disability benefits plan, see 417 U. S., at 487-489.

We rejected appellee's equal protection challenge to this statutory scheme. We first noted:

> "We cannot agree that the exclusion of this disability from coverage amounts to invidious discrimination under the Equal Protection Clause. California does not discriminate with respect to the persons or groups which are eligible for disability insurance protection under the program. The classification challenged in this case relates to the asserted under-inclusiveness of the set of risks that the State has selected to insure." *Id.,* at 494.

This point was emphasized again, when later in the opinion we noted:

> "[T]his case is thus a far cry from cases like *Reed v. Reed,* 404 U. S. 71 (1971), and *Frontiero* v. *Richardson,* 411 U. S. 677 (1973), involving discrimination based upon gender as such. The California insurance program does not exclude anyone from benefit eligibility because of gender but merely removes one physical condition — pregnancy — from the list of compensable disabilities. While it is true that only women can become pregnant, it does not follow that every legislative classification concerning pregnancy is a sex-based classification like those considered in *Reed, supra,* and *Frontiero, supra.* Normal pregnancy is an objectively identifiable physical condition with unique characteristics. Absent a showing that distinctions involving pregnancy are mere pretexts designed to effect an invidious discrimination against the members of one sex or the other, lawmakers are constitutionally free to include or exclude pregnancy from the coverage of legislation such as this on any reasonable basis, just as with respect to any other physical condition.

"The lack of identity between the excluded disability and gender as such under this insurance program becomes clear upon the most cursory analysis. The program divides potential recipients into two groups — pregnant woman and nonpregnant persons. While the first group is exclusively female, the second includes members of both sexes." *Id.,* at 496-497, n. 20.

The quoted language from *Geduldig* leaves no doubt that our reason for rejecting appellee's equal protection claim in that case was that the exclusion of pregnancy from coverage under California's disability-benefits plan was not in itself discrimination based on sex.

We recognized in *Geduldig,* of course, that the fact that there was no sex-based discrimination as such was not the end of the analysis, should it be shown "that distinctions involving pregnancy are mere pretexts designed to effect an invidious discrimination against the members of one sex or the other," *ibid.* But we noted that no semblance of such a showing had been made ... *Geduldig* is precisely in point in its holding that an exclusion of pregnancy from a disability-benefits plan providing general coverage is not a gender-based discrimination at all.

There is no more showing in this case than there was in *Geduldig* that the exclusion of pregnancy benefits is a mere "[pretext] designed to effect an invidious discrimination against the members of one sex or the other." The Court of Appeals expressed the view that the decision in *Geduldig* had actually turned on whether or not a conceded discrimination was "invidious" but we think that in so doing it misread the quoted language from our opinion. As we noted in that opinion, a distinction which on its face is not sex related might nonetheless violate the Equal Protection Clause if it were in fact a subterfuge to accomplish a forbidden discrimination. But we have here no question of excluding a disease or disability comparable in all other respects to covered diseases or disabilities and yet confined to the members of one race or sex. Pregnancy is, of course, confined to women, but it is in other ways significantly different from the typical covered disease or disability. The District Court found that it is not a "disease" at all, and is often a voluntarily undertaken and desired condition, 375 F. Supp., at 375, 377. We do not therefore infer that the exclusion of pregnancy disability benefits from petitioner's plan is a simple pretext for discriminating against women. The contrary arguments adopted by the lower courts and expounded by our dissenting Brethren were largely rejected in *Geduldig.*

The instant suit was grounded on Title VII rather than the Equal Protection Clause, and our cases recognize that a prima facie violation of Title VII can be established in some circumstances upon proof that the *effect* of an otherwise facially neutral plan or classification is to discriminate against members of one class or another. See *Washington* v. *Davis,* 426 U. S. 229, 246-248 (1976), For example, in the context of a challenge, under the provisions of § 703(a) (2), to a facially neutral employment test, this Court held that a prima facie case of discrimination would be established if, even absent proof of intent, the consequences of the test were "invidiously to discriminate on the basis of racial or other impermissible classification," *Griggs* v. *Duke Power Co.,* 401 U. S. 424, 431 (1971). Even assuming that it is not necessary in this case to prove intent to establish a prima facie violation of § 703(a) (1), but cf. *McDonnell Douglas Corp.* v. *Green,* 411 U. S. 792, 802-806 (1973), the respondents have not made the requisite showing the gender-based effects.[14]

As in *Geduldig,* respondents have not attempted to meet the burden of demonstrating a gender-based discriminatory effect resulting from the exclusion of pregnancy-related disabilities from coverage.[15] . . .

As in *Geduldig,* we start from the indisputable baseline that "[t]he fiscal and actuarial benefits of the program . . . accrue to members of both sexes," 417 U. S., at 497 n. 20. We need not disturb the findings of the District Court to note that neither is there a finding, nor was there any evidence which would support a finding, that the financial benefits of the Plan "worked to discriminate against any definable group or class in terms of the aggregate risk protection derived by that group or class from the program," *id.,* at 496. The Plan, in effect (and for all that appears), is nothing more than an insurance package, which covers some risks, but excludes others, see *id.,* at 494, 496-497. The "package" going to relevant identifiable groups we are presently concerned with — General Electric's male and female employees — covers exactly the same categories of risk, and is facially nondiscriminatory in the sense that "[t]here is no risk from which men are protected and women are not. Likewise, there is no risk from which women are protected and men are not." *Id.,* at 496-497. As there is no proof that the package is in fact worth more to men than to women, it is impossible to find any gender-based discriminatory effect in this scheme simply because women disabled

---

[14] Respondents, who seek to establish discrimination, have the traditional civil litigation burden of establishing that the acts they complain of constituted discrimination in violation of Title VII. *Albemarle Paper Co.* v. *Moody,* 422 U. S. 405, 425 (1975); *McDonnell Douglas Corp.* v. *Green,* 411 U. S., at 802. In *Griggs,* the burden placed on the employer "of showing that any given requirement must have a manifest relationship to the employment in question," 401 U. S., at 432, did not arise until discriminatory effect had been shown, *Albemarle, supra,* at 425.

[15] Absent a showing of gender-based discrimination, as that term is defined in *Geduldig,* or a showing of gender-based effect, there can be no violation of § 703(a)(1).

as a result of pregnancy do not receive benefits; that is to say, gender-based discrimination does not result simply because an employer's disability-benefits plan is less than all-inclusive. For all that appears, pregnancy-related disabilities constitute an *additional* risk, unique to women, and the failure to compensate them for this risk does not destroy the presumed parity of the benefits, accruing to men and women alike, which results from the facially evenhanded *inclusion* of risks. To hold otherwise would endanger the common sense notion that an employer who has no disability benefits program at all does not violate Title VII even though the "under inclusion" of risks impacts, as a result of pregnancy-related disabilities, more heavily upon one gender than upon the other. Just as there is no facial gender-based discrimination in that case, so, too, there is none here.

III

We are told, however, that this analysis of the congressional purpose underlying Title VII is inconsistent with the guidelines of the EEOC, which, it is asserted, are entitled to "great deference" in the construction of the Act. The guideline upon which respondents rely most heavily was promulgated in 1972, and states in pertinent part:

> "Disabilities caused or contributed to by pregnancy, miscarriage, abortion, childbirth, and recovery therefrom are, for all job-related purposes, temporary disabilities and should be treated as such under any health or temporary disability insurance or sick leave plan available in connection with employement. . . . [Benefits] shall be applied to disability due to pregnancy or childbirth on the same terms and conditions as they are applied to other temporary disabilities." 29 CFR § 1604.10(b) (1975).

In evaluating this contention it should first be noted that Congress, in enacting Title VII, did not confer upon the EEOC authority to promulgate rules or regulations pursuant to that Title. *Albemarle Paper Co. v. Moody,* 422 U. S. 405, 431 (1975).[20] This does not mean that EEOC guidelines are not entitled to consideration in determining legislative intent, see *Albemarle, supra; Griggs* v. *Duke Power Co., supra,* at 433-434; *Espinoza* v. *Farah Mfg. Co.,* 414 U. S. 86, 94 (1973). But it does mean that courts properly may accord less weight to such guidelines than to administrative regulations

---

[20] The EEOC has been given "authority from time to time to issue . . . suitable procedural regulations to carry out the provisions of this subchapter," § 713(a), 42 U. S. C. § 2000e-12(a). No one contends, however, that the above-quoted regulation is procedural in nature or in effect.

which Congress has declared shall have the force of law, see *Standard Oil Co.* v. *Johnson,* 316 U. S. 481, 484 (1942), or to regulations which under the enabling statute may themselves supply the basis for imposition of liability, see, *e.g.,* § 23(a), Securities Exchange Act of 1934, 15 U. S. C. § 78w(a). The most comprehensive statement of the role of interpretative rulings such as the EEOC guidelines is found in *Skidmore* v. *Swift & Co.,* 323 U. S. 134, 140 (1944), where the Court said:

"We consider that the rulings, interpretations and opinions of the Administrator under this Act, while not controlling upon the courts by reason of their authority, do constitute a body of experience and informed judgment to which courts and litigants may properly resort for guidance. The weight of such a judgment in a particular case will depend upon the thoroughness evidence in its consideration, the validity of its reasoning, it consistency with earlier and later pronouncements, and all those factors which give it power to persuade, if lacking power to control."

The EEOC guideline in question does not fare well under these standards. It is not a contemporaneous interpretation of Title VII, since it was first promulgated eight years after the enactment of that Title. More importantly, the 1972 guideline flatly contradicts the position which the agency had enunciated at an earlier date, closer to the enactment of the governing statute. An opinion letter by the General Counsel of the EEOC, dated October 17, 1966, states:

"You have requested our opinion whether the above exclusion of pregnancy and childbirth as a disability under the long-term salary continuation plan would be in violation of Title VII of the Civil Rights Act of 1964.

"In a recent opinion letter regarding pregnancy, we have stated, 'The Commission policy in this area does not seek to compare an employer's treatment of illness or injury with his treatment of maternity since maternity is a temporary disability unique to the female sex and more or less to be anticipated during the working life of most women employees.' Therefore, it is our opinion that according to the facts stated above, a company's group insurance program which covers hospital and medical expenses for the delivery of employees' children, but excludes from its long-term salary continuation program those disabilities which result from pregnancy and childbirth would not be in violation of Title VII." App. 721-722.

A few weeks later, in an opinion letter expressly issued pursuant to 29 CFR § 1601.30 (1975), the EEOC's position was that "an insurance or other benefit plan may simply exclude maternity as a covered risk, and such an exclusion would not in our view be discriminatory," .... In short, while we do not wholly discount the weight to be given the 1972 guideline, it does not receive high marks when judged by the standards enunciated in *Skidmore, supra.*

There are also persuasive indications that the more recent EEOC guideline sharply conflicts with other indicia of the proper interpretation of the sex-discrimination provisions of Title VII. The legislative history of Title VII's prohibition of sex discrimination is notable primarily for its brevity. Even so, however, Congress paid especial attention to the provisions of the Equal Pay Act, 29 U. S. C. § 206(d), when it amended § 703(h) of Title VII.... Senator Humphrey, the floor manager of the bill, stated that the purpose of the amendment was to make it "unmistakably clear" that "differences of treatment in industrial benefit plans, including earlier retirement options for women, may continue in operation under this bill, if it becomes law," *id.,* at 13663-13664. Because of this amendment, interpretations of § 6(d) of the Equal Pay Act are applicable to Title VII as well, and an interpretive regulation promulgated by the Wage and Hour Administrator under the Equal Pay Act explicitly states:

> "If employer contributions to a plan providing insurance or similar benefits to employees are equal for both men and women, no wage differential prohibited by the equal pay provisions will result from such payments, even though the benefits which accrue to the employees in question are greater for one sex than for the other. The mere fact that the employer may make unequal contributions for employees of opposite sexes in such a situation will not, however, be considered to indicate that the employer's payments are in violation of section 6(d), if the resulting benefits are equal for such employees." 29 CFR § 800.116(d) (1975).

Thus, even if we were to depend for our construction of the critical language of Title VII solely on the basis of "deference" to interpretative regulations by the appropriate administrative agencies, we would find ourselves pointed in diametrically opposite directions by the conflicting regulations of the EEOC, on the one hand, and the Wage and Hour Administrator, on the other. Petitioner's exclusion of benefits for pregnancy disability would be declared an unlawful employment practice under § 703(a)(1), but would be declared not to be an unlawful employment practice under § 703(h).

We are not reduced to such total abdication in construing the statute. The EEOC guideline of 1972, conflicting as it does with earlier pronouncements of that agency, and containing no suggestion that some new source of legislative history had been discovered in the intervening eight years, stands virtually alone. Contrary to it are the consistent interpretation of the Wage and Hour Administrator, and the quoted language of Senator Humphrey, the floor manager of Title VII in the Senate. They support what seems to us to be the "plain meaning" of the language used by Congress when it enacted § 703(a)(1).

The concept of "discrimination," of course, was well known at the time of the enactment of Title VII, having been associated with the Fourteenth Amendment for nearly a century, and carrying with it a long history of judicial construction. When Congress makes it unlawful for an employer to "discriminate ... because of ... sex ...," without further explanation of its meaning, we should not readily infer that it meant something different from what the concept of discrimination has traditionally meant. ...

We therefore agree with petitioner that its disability-benefits plan does not violate Title VII because of its failure to cover pregnancy-related disabilities. The judgment of the Court of Appeals is

Reversed.

MR. JUSTICE STEWART, concurring.

I join the opinion of the Court holding that General Electric's exclusion of benefits for disability during pregnancy is not a *per se* violation of § 703(a)(1) of Title VII, and that the respondents have failed to prove a discriminatory effect. Unlike my Brother BLACKMUN, I do not understand the opinion to question either *Griggs* v. *Duke Power Co.*, 401 U. S. 424, specifically, or the significance generally of proving a discriminatory effect in a Title VII case.

MR. JUSTICE BLACKMUN, concurring in part.

I join the judgment of the Court and concur in its opinion insofar as it holds (a) that General Electric's exclusion of disability due to pregnancy is not, *per se,* a violation of § 703(a)(1) of Title VII; (b) that the plaintiffs in this case therefore had at least the burden of proving discriminatory effect; and (c) that they failed in that proof. I do not join any inference or suggestion in the Court's opinion — if any such inference or suggestion is there — that effect may never be a controlling factor in a Title VII case, or that *Griggs* v. *Duke Power Co.*, 401 U. S. 424 (1971), is no longer good law.

MR. JUSTICE BRENNAN, with whom MR. JUSTICE MARSHALL concurs, dissenting.

The Court holds today that without violating Title VII of the Civil Rights Act of 1964, 42 U. S. C. § 2000e *et seq.*, a private employer may adopt a disability plan that compensates employees for all temporary disabilities except one affecting exclusively women, pregnancy. I respectfully dissent. Today's holding not only repudiates the applicable administrative guideline promulgated by the agency charged by Congress with implementation of the Act, but also rejects the unanimous conclusion of all six Courts of Appeals that have addressed this question. . . .

I

This case is unusual in that it presents a question the resolution of which at first glance turns largely upon the conceptual framework chosen to identify and describe the operational features of the challenged disability program. By directing their focus upon the risks excluded from the otherwise comprehensive program, and upon the purported justifications for such exclusions, the Equal Employment Opportunity Commission, the women plaintiffs, and the lower courts reason that the pregnancy exclusion constitutes a prima facie violation of Title VII. This violation is triggered, they argue, because the omission of pregnancy from the program has the intent and effect of providing that "only women [are subjected] to a substantial risk of total loss of income because of temporary medical disability." Brief for EEOC as *Amicus Curiae* 12.

The Court's framework is diametrically different. It views General Electric's plan as representing a gender-free assignment of risks in accordance with normal actuarial techniques. From this perspective the lone exclusion of pregnancy is not a violation of Title VII insofar as all other disabilities are mutually covered for both sexes. This reasoning relies primarily upon the descriptive statement borrowed from *Geduldig v. Aiello,* 417 U. S. 484, 496-497 (1974): "There is no risk from which men are protected and women are not. Likewise, there is no risk from which women are protected and men are not." *Ante,* at 138. According to the Court, this assertedly neutral sorting process precludes the pregnancy omission from constituting a violation of Title VII.

Presumably, it is not self-evident that either conceptual framework is more appropriate than the other, which can only mean that further inquiry is necessary to select the more accurate and realistic analytical approach. At the outset, the soundness of the Court's underlying assumption that the plan is the untainted product of a gender-neutral risk-assignment process can be examined against the historical backdrop of General Electric's employment practices and the existence or nonexistence of gender-free policies governing the inclusion of compensable risks. Secondly, the resulting pattern of risks insured by General Electric can then be evaluated in terms of the broad social objectives promoted by Title VII. I believe that the first inquiry compels the conclusion that the Court's assumption that General Electric engaged in a gender-neutral risk-assignment process is purely fanciful. The second demonstrates that the EEOC's interpretation that the exclusion of pregnancy from a disability insurance plan is incompatible with the overall objectives of Title VII has been unjustifiably rejected.

II

Geduldig v. Aiello, supra, purports to be the starting point for the Court's analysis. . . .

Considered most favorably to the Court's view, *Geduldig* established the proposition that a pregnancy classification standing alone cannot be said to fall into the category of classifications that rest explicitly on "gender as such," 417 U. S., at 496 n. 20. Beyond that, *Geduldig* offers little analysis helpful to decision of this case. . . .

Geduldig itself obliges the Court to determine whether the exclusion of a sex-linked disability from the universe of compensable disabilities was actually the product of neutral, persuasive actuarial considerations, or rather stemmed from a policy that purposefully downgraded women's role in the labor force. . . .

[I]n reaching its conclusion that a showing of purposeful discrimination has not been made, the Court simply disregards a history of General Electric practices that have served to undercut the employment opportunities of women who become pregnant while employed.[1] Moreover, the Court studiously ignores the undisturbed conclusion of the District Court that General Electric's "discriminatory attitude" toward women was "a motivating factor in its policy," 375 F. Supp. 367, 383 (E.D. Va. 1974), and that the pregnancy exclusion was "neutral [neither] on its face" nor "in its intent." *Id.,* at 382.

Plainly then, the Court's appraisal of General Electric's policy as a neutral process of sorting risks and "not a gender-based discrimination at all," cannot easily be squared with the historical record in this case. The Court, therefore, proceeds to a discussion of purported neutral criteria that suffice to explain the lone exclusion of pregnancy from the program. The Court argues that pregnancy is not "comparable" to other disabilities since it is a "voluntary" condition rather than a "disease." *Ibid.* The fallacy of this argument is that even if "non-voluntariness" and "disease" are to be construed as the operational criteria for inclusion of a disability in General Electric's program, application of these criteria is inconsistent with the Court's gender-neutral interpretation of the company's policy.

For example, the characterization of pregnancy as "voluntary" is not a persuasive factor, for as the Court of Appeals correctly noted, "other than for childbirth disability, [General Electric] had never construed its plan as eliminating *all* so-called 'voluntary' disabilities,"

---

[1] General Electric's disability program was developed in an earlier era when women openly were presumed to play only a minor and temporary role in the labor force. As originally conceived in 1926, General Electric offered no benefit plan to its female employees because " 'women did not recognize the responsibilities of life, for they probably were hoping to get married soon and leave the company.' " App. 958, excerpted from D. Loth, Swope of G. E.: Story of Gerard Swope and General Electric in American Business (1958). . . .

including sport injuries, attempted suicides, venereal disease, disabilities incurred in the commission of a crime or during a fight, and elective cosmetic surgery. 519 F. 2d, at 665. Similarly, the label "disease" rather than "disability" cannot be deemed determinative since General Electric's pregnancy disqualification also excludes the 10% of pregnancies that end in debilitating miscarriages, 375 F. Supp., at 377, the 10% of cases where pregnancies are complicated by "diseases" in the intuitive sense of the word, *ibid.,* and cases where women recovering from childbirth are stricken by severe diseases unrelated to pregnancy.

Moreover, even the Court's principal argument for the plan's supposed gender neutrality cannot withstand analysis. The central analytical framework relied upon to demonstrate the absence of discrimination is the principle described in *Geduldig:* "There is no risk from which men are protected and women are not . . . [and] no risk from which women are protected and men are not." 417 U. S., at 496-497. In fostering the impression that it is faced with a mere underinclusive assignment of risks in a gender-neutral fashion — that is, all other disabilities are insured irrespective of gender — the Court's analysis proves to be simplistic and misleading. For although all mutually contractible risks are covered irrespective of gender, the plan also insures risks such as prostatectomies, vasectomies, and circumcisions that are specific to the reproductive system of men and for which there exist no female counterparts covered by the plan.

III

Of course, the demonstration of purposeful discrimination is not the only ground for recovery under Title VII. Notwithstanding unexplained and inexplicable implications to the contrary in the majority opinion,[6] this Court, and every Court of Appeals now have firmly settled that a prima facie violation of Title VII, whether under § 703(a)(1) or § 703(a)(2), also is established by demonstrating that a facially neutral classification has the *effect* of discriminating against members of a defined class.

General Electric's disability program has three divisible sets of effects. First, the plan covers all disabilities that mutually afflict both

---

[6] The cryptic "but cf." citation to *McDonnell Douglas Corp. v. Green,* 411 U. S. 792 (1973), is perhaps the most mystifying. . . .

Equally unacceptable is the implication in the penultimate paragraph of the opinion, that the Fourteenth Amendment standard of discrimination is coterminous with that applicable to Title VII. Not only is this fleeting dictum irrelevant to the reasoning that precedes it, not only does it conflict with a long line of cases to the contrary, but it is flatly contradicted by the central holding of last Term's *Washington v. Davis,* 426 U. S. 229, 239 (1976): "We have never held that the constitutional standard for adjudicating claims of invidious racial discrimination is identical to the standards applicable under Title VII, and we decline to do so today."

sexes. Second, the plan insures against all disabilities that are male-specific or have a predominant impact on males. Finally, all female-specific and female-impacted disabilities are covered, except for the most prevalent, pregnancy. The Court focuses on the first factor — the equal inclusion of mutual risks — and therefore understandably can identify no discriminatory effect arising from the plan. In contrast, the EEOC and plaintiffs rely upon the unequal exclusion manifested in effects two and three to pinpoint an adverse impact on women. However one defines the profile of risks protected by General Electric, the determinative question must be whether the social policies and aims to be furthered by Title VII and filtered through the phrase "to discriminate" contained in § 703(a)(1) fairly forbid an ultimate pattern of coverage that insures all risks except a commonplace one that is applicable to women but not to men.

As a matter of law and policy, this is a paradigm example of the type of complex economic and social inquiry that Congress wisely left to resolution by the EEOC pursuant to its Title VII mandate. And, accordingly, prior Title VII decisions have consistently acknowledged the unique persuasiveness of EEOC interpretations in this area. These prior decisions, rather than providing merely that Commission guidelines are "entitled to consideration," as the Court allows, *ante,* at 141, hold that the EEOC's interpretations should receive "great deference." . . . [W]hile some eight years had elapsed prior to the issuance of the 1972 guideline, and earlier opinion letters had refused to impose liability on employers during this period of deliberation, no one can or does deny that the final EEOC determination followed thorough and well-informed consideration. Indeed, realistically viewed, this extended evaluation of an admittedly complex problem and an unwillingness to impose additional, potentially premature costs on employers during the decisionmaking stages ought to be perceived as a practice to be commended. It is bitter irony that the care that preceded promulgation of the 1972 guideline is today condemned by the Court as tardy indecisiveness, its unwillingness irresponsibly to challenge employers' practices during the formative period is labeled as evidence of inconsistency, and this indecisiveness and inconsistency are bootstrapped into reasons for denying the Commission's interpretation its due deference.

For me, the 1972 guideline represents a particularly conscientious and reasonable product of EEOC deliberations and, therefore, merits our "great deference." . . . [S]hortly following the announcement of the EEOC's rule, Congress approved and the President signed an essentially identical promulgation by the Department of Health, Education, and Welfare under Title IX of the Education Amendments of 1972. Moreover, federal workers subject to the jurisdiction of the Civil Service Commission now are eligible for maternity and pregnancy coverage under their sick leave program.

These policy formulations are reasonable responses to the uniform testimony of governmental investigations which show that pregnancy exclusions built into disability programs both financially burden women workers and act to break down the continuity of the employment relationship, thereby exacerbating women's comparatively transient role in the labor force. . . . In dictating pregnancy coverage under Title VII, the EEOC's guideline merely settled upon a solution now accepted by every other Western industrial country.

MR. JUSTICE STEVENS, dissenting.

The word "discriminate" does not appear in the Equal Protection Clause. Since the plaintiffs' burden of proving a prima facie violation of that constitutional provision is significantly heavier than the burden of proving a prima facie violation of a statutory prohibition against discrimination, the constitutional holding in *Geduldig v. Aiello,* 417 U. S. 484 (1974), does not control the question of statutory interpretation presented by this case. And, of course, when it enacted Title VII of the Civil Rights Act of 1964, Congress could not possibly have relied on language which this Court was to use a decade later in the *Geduldig* opinion. We are, therefore, presented with a fresh, and rather simple, question of statutory construction: Does a contract between a company and its employees which treats the risk of absenteeism caused by pregnancy differently from any other kind of absence discriminate against certain individuals because of their sex?

An affirmative answer to that question would not necessarily lead to a conclusion of illegality, because a statutory affirmative defense might justify the disparate treatment of pregnant women in certain situations. In this case, however, the company has not established any such justification. On the other hand, a negative answer to the threshold question would not necessarily defeat plaintiffs' claim because facially neutral criteria may be illegal if they have a discriminatory effect. An analysis of the effect of a company's rules relating to absenteeism would be appropriate if those rules referred only to neutral criteria, such as whether an absence was voluntary or involuntary, or perhaps particularly costly. This case, however, does not involve rules of that kind.

Rather, the rule at issue places the risk of absence caused by pregnancy in a class by itself. By definition, such a rule discriminates on account of sex; for it is the capacity to become pregnant which primarily differentiates the female from the male. The analysis is the same whether the rule relates to hiring, promotion, the acceptability of an excuse for absence, or an exclusion from a disability insurance plan. Accordingly, without reaching the questions of motive, administrative expertise, and policy, which MR. JUSTICE BRENNAN so persuasively exposes, or the question of effect to which MR. JUSTICE STEWART and MR. JUSTICE BLACKMUN refer, I conclude that the language of the statute plainly requires the result which the Courts of Appeals have reached unanimously.

NOTES:

(1) In a subsequent case, the Court distinguished between the denial of a benefit to a pregnant worker and the placement of a burden on the worker. Thus, the employer could lawfully refuse to allow a pregnant employee to use accumulated sick leave for maternity purposes, but could not force the employee to forfeit her accumulated seniority when she took a leave of absence for maternity reasons. *Nashville Gas Co. v. Satty,* 46 U.S.L.W. 4026 (1977).

(2) *Problem:* Why does the Court in *Satty* grant any relief if, as stated in *Gilbert,* discrimination based on pregnancy is not sex discrimination under Title VII? Can the decision in *Satty* be reconciled with the decision in *Evans* with regard to the effect of the seniority system on women rehired or returning to work after forced leave?

(3) The courts have uniformly found that state protective laws which restrict the hours or conditions under which women may work are invalid under Title VII. *See, e.g., Rosenfeld v. Southern Pacific Co.,* 444 F.2d 1219 (9th Cir. 1971). Where a state law grants a benefit, such as minimum wages or rest periods, to women only, the courts are in conflict as to whether the law should be invalidated or extended to cover men also. *Compare Hays v. Potlatch Forests, Inc.,* 465 F.2d 1081 (8th Cir. 1972) *with Homemakers, Inc. v. Division of Industrial Welfare,* 509 F.2d 20 (9th Cir. 1974), *cert. denied,* 44 U.S.L.W. 3396 (1976). The EEOC Guidelines, 29 CFR § 1604.2(b)(3) (1975), provide that restrictive state protective laws do not come within the BFOQ provisions of Title VII and that benefits, where provided for women, must be extended to men.

(4) In general, the courts have held that employers may not impose different standards on male and female employees. Thus, it is impermissible for an employer to exclude mothers, but not fathers, from employment. *Phillips v. Martin Marietta Corp.,* 400 U.S. 542 (1971). Similarly, an employer may not terminate female flight attendants upon marriage if male flight attendants are retained. *Sprogis v. United Airlines,* 444 F.2d 1194 (7th Cir. 1971), *cert. denied,* 404 U.S. 991 (1971). An employer's discharge of a pregnant unmarried employee was found to be a violation of Title VII in *Jacobs v. Martin Sweets Co.,* 550 F.2d 364 (6th Cir. 1977). Further, the suspension of a newly-married female employee for her refusal to change her name on personnel forms to that of her husband

constituted a violation of Title VII. *Allen v. Lovejoy,* 553 F.2d 522 (6th Cir. 1977).

An exception to the requirement of equal standards for male and female employees has developed in the area of grooming standards. Where an employer imposes sex-differentiated hair regulations, most circuit courts have held that there is no Title VII violation because hair length is not an immutable characteristic nor is the right to wear it at a given length a fundamental right. *See, e.g., Fagan v. National Cash Register Co.,* 481 F.2d 1115 (D.C. Cir. 1973); *Willingham v. Macon Telegraph Publishing Co.,* 507 F.2d 1084 (5th Cir. 1975) (*en banc*); *Earwood v. Continental Southeastern Lines,* 539 F.2d 1349 (4th Cir. 1976); *Barker v. Taft Broadcasting Co.,* 549 F.2d 400 (6th Cir. 1977).

(5) Two Circuit Courts have held that negative employment consequences resulting from a woman's refusal of her employer's sexual advances constitute a violation of Title VII. *Barnes v. Costle,* 561 F.2d 983 (D.C. Cir. 1977); *Tomkins v. Public Service Electric and Gas Co.,* 16 FEP Cases 22 (3d Cir. 1977).

CITY OF LOS ANGELES v. MANHART

United States Supreme Court
98 S. Ct. 1370, 55 L.Ed.2d 657 (1978)

MR. JUSTICE STEVENS delivered the opinion of the Court.

As a class, women live longer than men. For this reason, the Los Angeles Department of Water and Power required its female employees to make larger contributions to its pension fund than its male employees. We granted certiorari to decide whether this practice discriminated against individual female employees because of their sex in violation of § 703 (a)(1) of the Civil Rights Act of 1964, as amended.

For many years the Department has administered retirement, disability, and death benefit programs for its employees. Upon retirement each employee is eligible for a monthly retirement benefit computed as a fraction of his or her salary multiplied by years of service. The monthly benefits for men and women of the same age, seniority, and salary are equal. Benefits are funded entirely by contributions from the employees and the Department, augmented by the income earned on those contributions. No private insurance company is involved in the administration or payment of benefits.

Based on a study of mortality tables and its own experience, the Department determined that its 2,000 female employees, on the average, will live a few years longer than its 10,000 male employees. The cost of a pension for the average retired female is greater than for the average male retiree because more monthly payments must be made to the average woman. The Department therefore required female employees to make monthly contributions to the fund which were 14.84% higher than the contributions required of comparable male employees. Because employee contributions were withheld from paychecks, a female employee took home less pay than a male employee earning the same salary. . . .

It is now well recognized that employment decisions cannot be predicated on mere "sterotyped" impressions about the characteristics of males or females.[13] Myths and purely habitual assumptions about a woman's inability to perform certain kinds of work are no longer acceptable reasons for refusing to employ qualified individuals, or for paying them less. This case does not, however, involve a fictional difference between men and women. It involves a generalization that the parties accept as unquestionably true: women, as a class, do live longer than men. The Department treated its women employees differently from its men employees because the two classes are in fact different. It is equally true, however, that all individuals in the respective classes do not share the characteristic which differentiates the average class representatives. Many women do not live as long as the average man and many men outlive the average woman. The question, therefore, is whether the existence or nonexistence of "discrimination" is to be determined by comparison of class characteristics or individual characteristics. A "sterotyped" answer to that question may not be the same as the answer which the language and purpose of the statute command.

The statute makes it unlawful "to discriminate against any *individual* with respect to his compensation, terms, conditions or privileges of employment, because of such *individual's* race, color, religion, sex, or national origin." 42 U.S.C. § 2000e-2(a)(1) (emphasis added). The statute's focus on the individual is unambiguous. It precludes treatment of individuals as simply components of a racial, religious, sexual, or national class. . . .

That proposition is of critical importance in this case because there is no assurance that any individual woman working for the Department will actually fit the generalization on which the Department's policy is based. Many of those individuals will not live as long as the average man. While they were working, those individuals received smaller paychecks because of their sex, but they will receive no compensating advantage when they retire. . . .

Even if the statutory language were less clear, the basic policy of the statute requires that we focus on fairness to individuals rather than fairness to classes. Practices which classify employees in terms of religion, race, or sex tend to preserve traditional assumptions about groups rather than thoughtful scrutiny of individuals. The generalization involved in this case illustrates the point. Separate mortality tables are easily interpreted as reflecting innate differences between the sexes; but a significant part of the longevity differential may be explained by the social fact that men are heavier smokers than women.

Finally, there is no reason to believe that Congress intended a special definition of discrimination in the context of employee group insurance coverage. It is true that insurance is concerned with events that are individually unpredictable, but that is characteristic of many employment decisions. Individual risks, like individual performance, may not be predicted by resort to classifications proscribed by Title VII. Indeed, the fact that this case involves a group insurance program highlights a basic flaw in the department's fairness argument. For when insurance risks are grouped, the better risks always subsidize the poorer risks. Healthy persons subsidize medical benefits for the less healthy; unmarried workers subsidize the pensions of married workers; persons who eat, drink, or smoke to excess may subsidize pension benefits for persons whose habits are more temperate. Treating different classes of risks as though they were the same for purposes of group insurance is a common practice which has never been considered inherently unfair. To insure the flabby and the fit as though they were equivalent risks may be more common than treating men and women alike; but nothing more than habit makes one "subsidy" seem less fair than the other.

An employment practice which requires 2,000 individuals to contribute more money into a fund than 10,000 other employees simply because each of them is a woman, rather than a man, is in direct conflict with both the language and the policy of the Act. Such a practice does not pass the simple test of whether the evidence shows "treatment of a person in a manner which but for the person's sex would be different." It constitutes discrimination and is unlawful unless exempted by the Equal Pay Act or some other affirmative justification.

II

Shortly before the enactment of Title VII in 1964, Senator Bennett proposed an amendment providing that a compensation differential based on sex would not be unlawful if it was authorized by the Equal Pay Act, which had been passed a year earlier. The Equal Pay Act requires employers to pay members of both sexes the same wages for equivalent work, except when the differential is pursuant to one of four specified exceptions. The Department contends that the fourth exception applies here. That exception authorizes a "differential based on any other factor other than sex."

The Department argues that the different contributions exacted from men and women were based on the factor of longevity rather than sex. It is plain, however, that any individual's life expectancy is based on a number of factors, of which sex is only one. The record contains no evidence that any factor other than the employee's sex was taken into account in calculating the 14.84% differential between the respective contributions by men and women. We agree with Judge Duniway's observation that one cannot "say that an actuarial distinction based entirely on sex is 'based on any other factor other than sex'. Sex is exactly what it is based on." 553 F.2d, at 588.

We are also unpersuaded by the Department's reliance on a colloquy between Senator Randolph and Senator Humphrey during the debate on the Civil Rights Act of 1964. Commenting on the Bennett Amendment, Senator Humphrey expressed his understanding that it would allow many differences in the treatment of men and women under industrial benefit plans, including earlier retirement options for women. Though he did not address differences in employee contributions based on sex, Senator Humphrey apparently assumed that the 1964 Act would have little, if any, impact on existing pension plans. His statement cannot, however, fairly be made the sole guide to interpreting the Equal Pay Act, which had been adopted a year earlier; and it is the 1963 statute, with its exceptions, on which the Department ultimately relies. We conclude that Senator Humphrey's isolated comment on the Senate floor cannot change the effect of the plain language of the statue itself.

III

The Department argues that reversal is required by *General Electric Co.* v. *Gilbert,* 429 U.S. 125. We are satisfied, however, that neither the holding nor the reasoning of *Gilbert* is controlling.

In *Gilbert* the Court held that the exclusion of pregnancy from an employer's disability benefit plan did not constitute sex discrimination within the meaning of Title VII. Relying on the reasoning in *Geduldig* v. *Aiello,* 417 U.S. 484, the Court first held that the General Electric plan did not involve "discrimination based upon gender as such." The two groups of potential recipients which that case concerned were pregnant women and nonpregnant persons. "While the first group is exclusively female, the second includes members of both sexes." 429 U.S., at 135. In contrast, each of the two groups of employees involved in this case is composed entirely and exclusively of members of the same sex. On its face, this plan discriminates on the basis of sex whereas the General Electric plan discriminated on the basis of a special physical disability.

In *Gilbert* the Court did note that the plan as actually administered had provided more favorable benefits to women as a class than to men as a class. This evidence supported the conclusion that not only had plaintiffs failed to establish a prima facie case by proving that the plan was discriminatory on its face, but they had also failed to prove any discriminatory effect.

In this case, however, the Department argues that the absence of a discriminatory effect on women as a class justifies an employment practice which, on its face, discriminated against individual employees because of their sex. But even if the Department's actuarial evidence is sufficient to prevent plaintiffs from establishing a prima facie case on the theory that the effect of the practice on women as a class was discriminatory, that evidence does not defeat the claim that the practice, on its face, discriminated against every individual woman employed by the Department.[30]

In essence, the Department is arguing that the prima facie showing of discrimination based on evidence of different contributions for the respective sexes is rebutted by its demonstration that there is a like difference in the cost of providing benefits for the respective classes. That argument might prevail if Title VII contained a cost justification defense comparable to the affirmative defense available in a price discrimination suit. But neither Congress nor the courts have recognized such a defense under Title VII.

Although we concluded that the Department's practice violated Title VII, we do not suggest that the statute was intended to revolutionize the insurance and pension industries. All that is at issue today is a requirement that men and women make unequal contributions to an employer-operated pension fund. Nothing in our holding implies that it would be unlawful for an employer to set aside equal retirement contributions for each employee and let each retiree purchase the largest benefit which his or her accumulated contributions could command in the open market.[33] Nor does it call

---

[30] Some *amici* suggest that the Department's discrimination is justified by business necessity. They argue that, if no gender distinction is drawn, many male employees will withdraw from the plan, or even the Department, because they can get a better pension plan in the private market. But the Department has long required equal contributions to its death benefit plan, see n. 19, *supra,* and since 1975 it has required equal contributions to its pension plan. Yet the Department points to no "adverse selection" by the affected employees, presumably because an employee who wants to leave the plans must also leave his job, and few workers will quit because one of their fringe benefits could theoretically be obtained at a marginally lower price on the open market. In short, there has been no showing that sex distinctions are reasonably necessary to the normal operation of the Department's retirement plan.

[33] Title VII and the Equal Pay Act govern relations between employees and their employer, not between employees and third parties. We do not suggest, of course, that an employer can avoid its responsibilities by delegating discriminatory programs to corporate shells. Title VII applies to "any agent" of a covered employer, 42 U.S.C. § 2000e (b), and the Equal Pay Act applies to "any person acting directly or indirectly in the interest of any employer in relation to any employee." 29 U.S.C. § 203 (d). In this case, for example, the Department could

into question the insurance industry practice of considering the composition of an employer's work force in determining the probable cost of a retirement or death benefit plan. Finally, we recognize that in a case of this kind it may be necessary to take special care in fashioning appropriate relief.

IV

The Department challenges the District Court's award of retroactive relief to the entire class of female employees and retirees. Title VII does not require a district court to grant any retroactive relief. A court that finds unlawful discrimination "may enjoin [the discrimination] and order such affirmative action as may be appropriate, which may include, but is not limited to, reinstatement . . . with or without back pay . . . or any other equitable relief as the court deems appropriate." 42 U. S. C. § 2000e-5 (g). To the point of redundancy, the statute stresses that retroactive relief "may" be awarded if it is "appropriate."

In *Albemarle Paper Co. v. Moody,* 422 U. S. 405, the Court reviewed the scope of a district court's discretion to fashion appropriate remedies for a Title VII violation and concluded that "back pay should be denied only for reasons which, if applied generally, would not frustrate the central statutory purposes of eradicating discrimination throughout the economy and making persons whole for injuries suffered through past discrimination." *Id.,* at 421. Applying that standard, the Court ruled that an award of backpay should not be conditioned on a showing of bad faith. *Id.,* at 422-423. But the *Albemarle* Court also held that backpay was not to be awarded automatically in every case. . . .

There can be no doubt that the prohibition against sex-differentiated employee contributions represents a marked departure from past practice. Although Title VII was enacted in 1964, this is apparently the first litigation challenging contribution differences based on valid actuarial tables. Retroactive liability could be devastating for a pension fund. The harm would fall in large part on innocent third parties. If, as the courts below apparently contemplated, the plaintiffs' contributions are recovered from the pension fund, the administrators of the fund will be forced to meet unchanged obligations with diminished assets. If the reserve proves inadequate, either the expectations of all retired employees will be disappointed or current employees will be forced to pay not only for their own future security but also for the unanticipated reduction in the contributions of past employees.

---

not deny that the administrative board was its agent after it successfully argued that the two were so inseparable that both shared the city's immunity from suit under 42 U.S.C. § 1983.

Without qualifying the force of the *Albemarle* presumption in favor of retroactive relief, we conclude that it was error to grant such relief in this case. Accordingly, although we agree with the Court of Appeals' analysis of the statute, we vacate its judgment and remand the case for futher proceedings consistent with this opinion.

MR. JUSTICE BRENNAN took no part in the consideration or decision of this case.

MR. CHIEF JUSTICE BURGER, with whom MR. JUSTICE REHNQUIST joins, concurring in part and dissenting in part.

I join Part IV of the Court's opinion; as to Parts I, II, and III, I dissent. . . .

MR. JUSTICE MARSHALL, concurring in part and dissenting in part.

I agree that Title VII of the Civil Rights Act of 1964, as amended, forbids petitioners' practice of requiring female employees to make larger contributions to a pension fund than do male employees. I therefore join all of the Court's opinion except Part IV. . . .

MR. JUSTICE BLACKMUN, concurring in part and concurring in the judgment.

MR. JUSTICE STEWART wrote the opinion for the Court in *Geduldig v. Aiello,* 417 U. S. 484 (1974), and joined the Court's opinion in *General Electric Co.* v. *Gilbert,* 429 U. S. 125 (1976). MR. JUSTICE WHITE and MR. JUSTICE POWELL joined both *Geduldig* and *General Electric.* MR. JUSTICE STEVENS, who writes the opinion for the Court in the present case, dissented in *General Electric.* 429 U. S., at 160. MR. JUSTICE MARSHALL, who joins the Court's opinion in large part here, dissented in both *Geduldig* and *General Electric.* 417 U. S., at 497, 429 U. S., at 146. My own discomfort with the latter case was apparent, I believe, from my separate concurrence there. 429 U. S., at 146.

These "line-ups" surely are not without significance. The participation of my Brothers STEWART, WHITE, and POWELL in today's majority opinion *should* be a sign that the decision in this case is not in tension with *Geduldig* and *General Electric* and, indeed, is wholly consistent with them. I am not at all sure that this is so; the votes of MR. JUSTICE MARSHALL and MR. JUSTICE STEVENS would indicate quite the contrary.

Given the decisions in *Geduldig* and *General Electric* — the one constitutional, the other statutory — the present case just cannot be an easy one for the Court. I might have thought that those decisions would have required the Court to conclude that the critical difference in the Department's pension payments was based on life expectancy, a nonstigmatizing factor that demonstrably differentiates females from males and that is not measurable on an individual basis. I might have thought, too, that there is nothing arbitrary, irrational, or "discriminatory" about recognizing the objective and accepted (see *ante,* pp. 1, 4, and 19) disparity in female-male life expectancies in computing rates for retirement plans. Moreover, it is unrealistic to attempt to force, as the Court does, an individualized analysis upon what is basically an insurance context. Unlike the possibility, for example, of properly testing job applicants for qualification before employment, there is simply no way to determine in advance when a particular employee will die.

. . .

The Court's distinction between the present case and *General Electric* — that the permitted classes there were "pregnant women and nonpregnant persons," both female and male, *ante,* p. 12 — seems to me to be just too easy. It is probably the only distinction that can be drawn. For me, it does not serve to distinguish the case on any principled basis. I therefore must conclude that today's decision cuts back on *General Electric,* and inferentially on *Geduldig,* the reasoning of which was adopted there, 429 U.S., at 133-136, and, indeed, makes the recognition of those cases as continuing precedent somewhat questionable. I do not say that this is necessarily bad. If that is what Congress has chosen to do by Title VII — as the Court today with such assurance asserts — so be it. I feel, however, that we should meet the posture of the earlier cases head-on and not by thin rationalization that seeks to distinguish but fails in its quest.

I therefore join only Part IV of the Court's opinion, and concur in its judgment.

NOTE:

A retirement plan which required women to retire at age 62 and men at age 65 was held to violate Title VII. *Drewrys Ltd. U.S.A., Inc. v. Bartmess,* 444 F.2d 1186 (7th Cir. 1971), *cert. denied,* 404 U.S. 939 (1971).

F. RELIGIOUS DISCRIMINATION

TRANS WORLD AIRLINES v. HARDISON

United States Supreme Court
432 U.S. 63, 97 S. Ct. 2264 (1977)

MR. JUSTICE WHITE delivered the opinion of the Court.

Section 703(a)(1) of the Civil Rights Act of 1964, Title VII, 42 U.S.C. § 2000e-2(a)(1), makes it an unlawful employment practice for an employer to discriminate against an employee or a prospective employee on the basis of his or her religion. At the time of the events involved here, a guideline of the Equal Employment Opportunity Commission (EEOC), 29 CFR § 1605.1(b), required, as the Act itself now does, 42 U.S.C. § 2000e(j), that an employer, short of "undue hardship", make "reasonable accommodations" to the religious needs of its employees. The issue in this case is the extent of the employer's obligation under Title VII to accommodate an employee whose religious beliefs prohibit him from working on Saturdays.

I

We summarize briefly the facts found by the District Court. 375 F. Supp. 877 (WD Mo. 1974).

Petitioner Trans World Airlines (TWA) operates a large maintenance and overhaul base in Kansas City, Mo. On June 5, 1967, respondent Larry G. Hardison was hired by TWA to work as a clerk in the Stores Department at its Kansas City base. Because of its essential role in the Kansas City operation, the Stores Department must operate 24 hours per day, 365 days per year, and whenever an employee's job in that department is not filled, an employee must be shifted from another department, or a supervisor must cover the job, even if the work in other areas may suffer.

Hardison, like other employees at the Kansas City base, was subject to a seniority system contained in a collective-bargaining agreement [1] that TWA maintains with petitioner International Association of Machinists and Aerospace Workers (IAM). The seniority system is implemented by the union steward through a system of bidding by employees for particular shift assignments as they become available. The most senior employees have first choice for job and shift assignments, and the most junior employees are required to work when the union steward is unable to find enough people willing to work at a particular time or in a particular job to fill TWA's needs.

In the spring of 1968 Hardison began to study the religion known as the Worldwide Church of God. One of the tenets of that religion is that one must observe the Sabbath by refraining from performing

---

[1] The TWA-IAM agreement provides in pertinent part:

"The principle of seniority shall apply in the application of this Agreement in all reductions or increases of force, preference of shift assignment, vacation period selection, in bidding for vacancies or new jobs, and in all promotions, demotions, or transfers involving classifications covered by this Agreement.

. . . . .

"Except as hereafter provided in this paragraph, seniority shall apply in selection of shifts and days off within a classification within a department. . . ." App. 214.

any work from sunset on Friday until sunset on Saturday. The religion also proscribes work on certain specified religious holidays.

When Hardison informed Everett Kussman, the manager of the Stores Department, of his religious conviction regarding observance of the Sabbath, Kussman agreed that the union steward should seek a job swap for Hardison or a change of days off; that Hardison would have his religious holidays off whenever possible if Hardison agreed to work the traditional holidays when asked; and that Kussman would try to find Hardison another job that would be more compatible with his religious beliefs. The problem was temporarily solved when Hardison transferred to the 11 p. m. - 7 a. m. shift. Working this shift permitted Hardison to observe his Sabbath.

The problem soon reappeared when Hardison bid for and received a transfer from Building 1, where he had been employed, to Building 2, where he would work the day shift. The two buildings had entirely separate seniority lists; and while in Building 1 Hardison had sufficient seniority to observe the Sabbath regularly, he was second from the bottom on the Building 2 seniority list.

In Building 2 Hardison was asked to work Saturdays when a fellow employee went on vacation. TWA agreed to permit the union to seek a change of work assignments for Hardison, but the union was not willing to violate the seniority provisions set out in the collective-bargaining contract, and Hardison had insufficient seniority to bid for a shift having Saturdays off.

A proposal that Hardison work only four days a week was rejected by the company. Hardison's job was essential and on weekends he was the only available person on his shift to perform it. To leave the position empty would have impaired Supply Shop functions, which were critical to airline operations; to fill Hardison's position with a supervisor or an employee from another area would simply have undermanned another operation; and to employ someone not regularly assigned to work Saturdays would have required TWA to pay premium wages.

When an accommodation was not reached, Hardison refused to report for work on Saturdays. A transfer to the twilight shift proved unavailing since that scheduled still required Hardison to work past sundown on Fridays. After a hearing, Hardison was discharged on grounds of insubordination for refusing to work during his designated shift.

Hardison, having first invoked the administrative remedy provided by Title VII, brought this action for injunctive relief in the United States District Court against TWA and IAM, claiming that his discharge by TWA constituted religious discrimination in violation of Title VII, 42 U.S.C. § 2000e-2(a)(1). He also charged that the union had discriminated against him by failing to represent him adequately in his dispute with TWA and by depriving him of his right to exercise his religious beliefs. Hardison's claim of religious discrimination rested on 1967 EEOC guidelines requiring employers "to make reasonable accommodations to the religious needs of employees" whenever such accommodation would not work an "undue hardship," 29 CFR § 1605-1, 32 Fed.Reg. 10298 (1967), and on similar language adopted by Congress in the 1972 amendments to Title VII, 42 U.S.C. § 2000e(j).

After a bench trial, the District Court ruled in favor of the defendants. Turning first to the claim against the union, the District Court ruled that although the 1967 EEOC guidelines were applicable to unions, the union's duty to accommodate Hardison's belief did not require it to ignore its seniority system as Hardison appeared to claim.[4] As for Hardison's claim against TWA, the District Court rejected at the outset TWA's contention that requiring it in any way to accommodate the religious needs of its employees would constitute an unconstitutional establishment of religion. As the District Court construed the Act, however, TWA had satisfied its "reasonable accommodation" obligations, and any further accommodation would have worked an undue hardship on the company.

The Eighth Circuit Court of Appeals reversed the judgment for TWA. . . .

II

The Court of Appeals found that TWA had committed an unlawful employment practice under § 703(a)(1) of the Act, 42 U.S.C. § 2000e-2(a)(1), which provides:

"(a) It shall be an unlawful employment practice for an employer—

(1) to fail or refuse to hire or to discharge any individual, or otherwise to discriminate against any individual with respect to his compensation, terms, conditions, or privileges of employment, because of such individual's race, color, religion, sex, or national origin."

The emphasis of both the language and the legislative history of the statute is on eliminating discrimination in employment; similarly

---

[4] The District Court voiced concern that if it did not find an undue hardship in such circumstances, accommodation of religious observances might impose "a priority of the religious over the secular" and thereby raise significant questions as to the constitutional validity of the statute under the Establishment Clause of the First Amendment. 375 F.Supp., at 883, quoting Edwards & Kaplan, Religious Discrimination and the Role of Arbitration Under Title VII, 69 Mich.L.Rev. 599, 628 (1971).

situated employees are not to be treated differently solely because they differ with respect to race, color, religion, sex, or national origin. This is true regardless of whether the discrimination is directed against majorities or minorities. . . .

The prohibition against religious discrimination soon raised the question of whether it was impermissible under § 703(a)(1) to discharge or refuse to hire a person who for religious reasons refused to work during the employer's normal work-week. In 1966 an EEOC guildeline dealing with this problem declared that an employer had an obligation under the statute "to accommodate to the reasonable religious needs of employees . . . where such accommodation can be made without serious inconvenience to the conduct of the business." 29 CFR § 1605.1, 31 Fed.Reg. 8370 (1966).

In 1967 the EEOC amended its guidelines to require employers "to make reasonable accommodations to the religious needs of employees and prospective employees where such accommodation can be made without undue hardship on the conduct of the employer's business." 29 CFR § 1605.1, 32 Fed.Reg. 10298 (1967). The Commission did not suggest what sort of accommodations are "reasonable" or when hardship to an employer becomes "undue".

This question—the extent of the required accommodation — remained unsettled when this Court affirmed by an equally divided Court the Sixth Circuit's decision in *Dewey v. Reynolds Metals Co.,* 429 F.2d 324 (CA6 1970), aff'd by an equally divided Court, 402 U.S. 689, 91 S.Ct. 2186, 29 L.Ed.2d 267 (1971). The discharge of an employee who for religious reasons had refused to work on Sundays was there held by the Court of Appeals not to be an unlawful employment practice because the manner in which the employer allocated Sunday work assignments was discriminatory in neither its purpose nor effect; and consistent with the 1967 EEOC guidelines, the employer had made a reasonable accommodation of the employee's beliefs by giving him the opportunity to secure a replacement for his Sunday work.

In part "to resolve by legislation" some of the issues raised in *Dewey*, 118 Cong.Rec. 706 (1972) (remarks of Sen. Randolph), Congress included the following definition of religion in its 1972 amendments to Title VII:

"The term 'religion' includes all aspects of religious observance and practice, as well as belief, unless an employer demonstrates that he is unable to reasonably accommodate to an employee's or prospective employee's religious observance of practice without undue hardship on the conduct of the employer's business."

Title VII § 701(j), 42 U.S.C. § 2000e(j). The intent and effect of this definition was to make it an unlawful employment practice under

§ 703(a)(1) for an employer not to make reasonable accommodations, short of undue hardship, for the religious practices of his employees and prospective employees. But like the EEOC guidelines, the statute provides no guidance for determining the degree of accommodation that is required of an employer. The brief legislative history of § 701(j) is likewise of little assistance in this regard. The proponent of the measure, Senator Jennings Randolph, expressed his general desire "to assure that freedom from religious discrimination in the employment of workers is for all time guaranteed by law," 18 Cong.Rec. 705 (1972) but he made no attempt to define the precise circumstances under which the "reasonable accommodation" requirement would be applied.

In brief, the employer's statutory obligation to make reasonable accommodation for the religious observances of its employees, short of incurring an undue hardship, is clear, but the reach of that obligation has never been spelled out by Congress or by Commission guidelines. With this in mind, we turn to a consideration of whether TWA has met its obligation under Title VII to accommodate the religious observances of its employees.

III

The Court of Appeals held that TWA had not made reasonable efforts to accommodate Hardison's religious needs under the 1967 EEOC guidelines in effect at the time the relevant events occurred.[11] In its view, TWA had rejected three reasonable alternatives, any one of which would have satisfied its obligation without undue hardship. First, within the framework of the seniority system, TWA could have permitted Hardison to work a four-day week, utilizing in his place a supervisor or another worker on duty elsewhere. That this would have caused other shop functions to suffer was insufficient to amount to undue hardship in the opinion of the Court of Appeals. Second—according to the Court of Appeals, also within the bounds of the collective-bargaining contract—the company could have filled Hardison's Saturday shift from other

---

[11] Ordinarily, an EEOC guideline is not entitled to great weight where, as here, it varies from prior EEOC policy and no new legislative history has been introduced in support of the change. *General Electric Co. v. Gilbert,* 429 U.S. 125, 97 S.Ct. 401, 410-413, 50 L.Ed.2d 343 (1976). But where "Congress has not just kept its silence by refusing to overturn the administrative construction, but has ratified it with positive legislation," *Red Lion Broadcasting Co., Inc. v. FCC,* 395 U.S. 367, 381-382, 89 S.Ct. 1794, 1802, 23 L.Ed.2d 371 (1969) (footnote omitted), the guideline is entitled to some deference, at least sufficient in this case to warrant our accepting the guideline as a defensible construction of the pre-1972 statute, *i.e.,* as imposing on TWA the duty of "reasonable accommodation" in the absence of "undue hardship." We thus need not consider whether § 701(j) must be applied retroactively to the facts of this case.

available personnel competent to do the job, of which the court said there were at least 200. That this would have involved premium overtime pay was not deemed an undue hardship. Third, TWA could have arranged a "swap between Hardison and another employee either for another shift or for the Sabbath days." In response to the assertion that this would have involved a breach of the seniority provisions of the contract, the court noted that it had not been settled in the courts whether the required statutory accommodation to religious needs stopped short of transgressing seniority rules, but found it unnecessary to decide the issue because, as the Court of Appeals saw the record, TWA had not sought, and the union had therefore not declined to entertain, a possible variance from the seniority provisions of the collective-bargaining agreement. The company had simply left the entire matter to the union steward who the Court of Appeals said "likewise did nothing."

We disagree with the Court of Appeals in all relevant respects. It is our view that TWA made reasonable efforts to accommodate and that each of the Court of Appeals' suggested alternatives would have been an undue hardship within the meaning of the statute as construed by the EEOC guidelines.

A

It might be inferred from the Court of Appeals' opinion and from the brief of the EEOC in this Court that TWA's efforts to accommodate were no more than negligible. The findings of the District Court, supported by the record, are to the contrary. In summarizing its more detailed findings, the District Court observed:

> "TWA established as a matter of fact that it did take appropriate action to accommodate as required by Title VII. It held several meetings with plaintiff at which it attempted to find a solution to plaintiff's problems. It did accommodate plaintiff's observance of his special religious holidays. It authorized the union steward to search for someone who would swap shifts, which apparently was normal procedure." 375 F.Supp., at 890-891.

It is also true that TWA itself attempted without success to find Hardison another job. The District Court's view was that TWA had done all that could reasonably be expected within the bounds of the seniority system.

The Court of Appeals observed, however, that the possibility of a variance from the seniority system was never really posed to the union. This is contrary to the District Court's findings and to the record. The District Court found that when TWA first learned of Hardison's religious observances in April, 1968, it agreed to permit the union's steward to seek a swap of shifts or days off but that "the steward reported that he was unable to work out scheduling changes and that he understood that no one was willing to swap days with plaintiff." 375 F.Supp., at 888. Later, in March 1969, at a meeting held just two days before Hardison first failed to report for his Saturday shift, TWA again "offered to accommodate plaintiff's religious observances by agreeing to any trade of shifts or change of sections that plaintiff and the union could work out. Any shift or change was impossible within the seniority framework and the union was not willing to violate the seniority provisions set out in the contract to make a shift or change." 375 F. Supp., at 889. As the record shows, Hardison himself testified that Kussman was willing, but the union was not, to work out a shift or job trade with another employee. App. 76-77.

We shall say more about the seniority system, but at this juncture it appears to us that the system itself represented a significant accommodation to the needs, both religious and secular, of all of TWA's employees. As will become apparent, the seniority system represents a neutral way of minimizing the number of occasions when an employee must work on a day that he would prefer to have off. Additionally, recognizing that weekend work schedules are the least popular, the company made further accommodation by reducing its work force to a bare minimum on those days.

B

We are also convinced, contrary to the Court of Appeals, that TWA cannot be faulted for having failed itself to work out a shift or job swap for Hardison. Both the union and TWA had agreed to the seniority system; the union was unwilling to entertain a variance over the objections of men senior to Hardison; and for TWA to have arranged unilaterally for a swap would have amounted to a breach of the collective-bargaining agreement.

(1)

Hardison and the EEOC insist that the statutory obligation to accommodate religious needs takes precedence over both the collective-bargaining contract and the seniority rights of TWA's other employees. We agree that neither a collective-bargaining contract nor a seniority system may be employed to violate the statute, but we do not believe that the duty to accommodate requires TWA to take steps inconsistent with the otherwise valid agreement. Collective bargaining, aimed at effecting workable and enforceable agreements between management and labor, lies at the core of our national labor policy, and seniority provisions are universally included in these contracts. Without a clear and express indication from Congress, we cannot agree with Hardison and the EEOC that an agreed-upon seniority system must give way when necessary to accommodate religious observances. The issue is important and warrants some discussion.

Whenever there are not enough employees who choose to work a particular shift, . . . some employees must be assigned to that shift even though it is not their first choice. Such was evidently the case with regard to Saturday work; even though TWA cut back its weekend work force to a skeleton crew, not enough employees chose those days off to staff the Stores Department through voluntary scheduling. In these circumstances, TWA and IAM agreed to give first preference to employees who had worked in a particular department the longest.

Had TWA nevertheless circumvented the seniority system by relieving Hardison of Saturday work and ordering a senior employee to replace him, it would have denied the latter his shift preference so that Hardison could be given his. The senior employee would also have been deprived of his contractual rights under the collective-bargaining agreement.

It was essential to TWA's business to require Saturday and Sunday work from at least a few employees even though most employees preferred those days off. Allocating the burdens of weekend work was a matter for collective bargaining. In considering criteria to govern this allocation, TWA and the union had two alternatives: adopt a neutral system, such as seniority, a lottery, or rotating shifts; or allocate days off in accordance with the religious needs of its employees. TWA would have had to adopt the latter in order to assure Hardison and others like him of getting the days off necessary for strict observance of their religion, but it could have done so only at the expense of others who had strong, but perhaps nonreligious reasons for not working on weekends. There were no volunteers to relieve Hardison on Saturdays, and to give Hardison Saturdays off, TWA would have had to deprive another employee of his shift preference at least in part because he did not adhere to a religion that observed the Saturday Sabbath.

Title VII does not contemplate such unequal treatment. The repeated, unequivocal emphasis of both the language and the legislative history of Title VII is on eliminating discrimination in employment, and such discrimination is proscribed when it is directed against majorities as well as minorities. See pp. 2270-2271, *supra.* Indeed, the foundation of Hardison's claim is that TWA and IAM engaged in religious *discrimination* in violation of § 703(a)(1) when they failed to arrange for him to have Saturdays off. It would be anomalous to conclude that by "reasonable accommodation" Congress meant that an employer must deny the shift and job preference of some employees, as well as deprive them of their contractual rights, in order to accommodate or prefer the religious needs of others, and we conclude that Title VII does not require an employer to go that far.

(2)

Our conclusion is supported by the fact that seniority systems are afforded special treatment under Title VII itself. ... 42 U.S.C. § 2000e-2(h). "[T]he unmistakable purpose of § 703(h) was to make clear that the routine application of a bona fide seniority system would not be unlawful under Title VII." *International Brotherhood of Teamsters v. United States,* 431 U.S. 324 at 353, 97 S. Ct. 1843 at 1863, 52 L.Ed.2d 396 (1977). See also *United Air Lines, Inc. v. Evans,* 431 U.S. 553, 97 S.Ct. 1885, 52 L.Ed.2d 571 (1977). Section 703(h) is "a definitional provision; as with the other provisions of § 703, subsection (h) delineates which employment practices are illegal and thereby prohibited and which are not." *Franks v. Bowman Transportation Co., Inc.,* 424 U.S. 747, 758, 96 S.Ct. 1251, 1261, 47 L.Ed.2d 444 (1976). Thus, absent a discriminatory purpose, the operation of a seniority system cannot be an unlawful employment practice even if the system has some discriminatory consequences.

There has been no suggestion of discriminatory intent in this case. "The seniority system was not designed with the intention to discriminate against religion nor did it act to lock members of any religion into a pattern wherein their freedom to exercise their religion was limited. ..."

As we have said, TWA was not required by Title VII to carve out a special exception to its seniority system in order to help Hardison to meet his religious obligations.[14]

---

[14] Despite its hyperbole and rhetoric, the dissent appears to agree with—at least it stops short of challenging—the fundamental proposition that Title VII does not require an employer and a union who have agreed on a seniority system to deprive senior employees of their seniority rights in order to accommodate a junior employee's religious practices. This is the principal issue on which TWA and the union came to this Court. The dissent is thus reduced to (1) asserting that the statute requires TWA to accommodate Hardison even though substantial expenditures are required to do so; and (2) advancing its own view of the record to show that TWA could have done more than it did to accommodate Hardison without violating the seniority system or incurring substantial additional costs. We reject the former assertion as an erroneous construction of the statute. As for the latter, we prefer the findings of the district judge who heard the evidence. Thus, the dissent suggests that through further efforts TWA or the union might have arranged a temporary or permanent job swap within the seniority system, despite the District Court's express finding, supported by the record, that "[t]he seniority provisions ... precluded the possibility of plaintiff's changing his shift." 375 F.Supp., at 884. Similarly, the dissent offers two alternatives—sending Hardison back to Building 1 or allowing him to work extra days without overtime pay—that it says could have

C

The Court of Appeals also suggested that TWA could have permitted Hardison to work a four-day week if necessary in order to avoid working on his Sabbath. Recognizing that this might have left TWA short-handed on the one shift each week that Hardison did not work, the court still concluded that TWA would suffer no undue hardship if it were required to replace Hardison either with supervisory personnel or with qualified personnel from other departments. Alternatively, the Court of Appeals suggested that TWA could have replaced Hardison on his Saturday shift with other available employees through the payment of premium wages. Both of these alternatives would involve costs to TWA, either in the form of lost efficiency in other jobs or as higher wages.

To require TWA to bear more than a *de minimus* [minimis] cost in order to give Hardison Saturdays off is an undue hardship. Like abandonment of the seniority system, to require TWA to bear additional costs when no such costs are incurred to give other employees the days off that they want would involve unequal treatment of employees on the basis of their religion. By suggesting that TWA should incur certain costs in order to give Hardison Saturdays off the Court of Appeals would in effect require TWA to finance an additional Saturday off and then to choose the employee who will enjoy it on the basis of his religious beliefs. While incurring extra costs to secure a replacement for Hardison might remove the necessity of compelling another employee to work involuntarily in Hardison's place, it would not change the fact that the privilege of having Saturdays off would be allocated according to religious beliefs.

As we have seen, the paramount concern of Congress in enacting Title VII was the elimination of discrimination in employment. In the absence of clear statutory language or legislative history to the contrary, we will not readily construe the statute to require an employer to discriminate against some employees in order to enable others to observe their Sabbath.

Reversed.

---

been pursued by TWA or the union, even though neither of the courts below even hinted that these suggested alternatives would have been feasible under the circumstances. Furthermore, Buildings 1 and 2 had separate seniority lists, and insofar as the record shows, a return to Building 1 would not have solved Hardison's problems. Hardison himself testified that he "gave up" his Building 1 seniority when he came to Building 2, App. 104, and that the union would not accept his early return to Building 1 in part "because the problem of seniority came up again." App. 71. We accept the District Court's findings that TWA had done all that it could do to accommodate Hardison's religious beliefs without either incurring substantial costs or violating the seniority rights of other employees. See 375 F.Supp., at 891.

MR. JUSTICE MARSHALL, with whom MR. JUSTICE BRENNAN joins, dissenting.

Today's decision deals a fatal blow to all efforts under Title VII to accomodiate work requirements to religious practices. The Court holds, in essence, that although the EEOC regulations and the Act state that an employer must make reasonable adjustments in his work demands to take account of religious observances, the regulation and Act don't really mean what they say. An employer, the Court concludes, need not grant even the most minor special privilege to religious observers to enable them to follow their faith. As a question of social policy, this result is deeply troubling, for a society that truly values religious pluralism cannot compel adherents of minority religions to make the cruel choice of surrendering their religion or their job. And as a matter of law today's result is intolerable, for the Court adopts the very position that Congress expressly rejected in 1972, as if we were free to disregard congressional choices that a majority of this Court thinks unwise. I therefore dissent. . . .

Chapter 17

PREFERENTIAL REMEDIES

A. UNDER THE CONSTITUTION

PORCELLI v. TITUS

United States Court of Appeals, Third Circuit
431 F.2d 1254 (1970)
Cert. denied, 402 U.S. 944 (1971)

PER CURIAM: The plaintiffs herein, Victor Porcelli et al., ten white teachers employed by the Newark Board of Education, brought suit under the Civil Rights Act alleging that as of May 28, 1968, the defendant, Superintendent of Schools in the City of Newark, Franklyn Titus, acting under color of law for the Newark School System, subjected the plaintiffs to deprivation of their rights, privileges or immunities secured to them by the Constitution of the United States of America. This allegedly was accomplished by the abolition of a promotional list which had been in existence since 1953, which provided for oral and written examinations for anyone wishing to aspire to be principals or vice-principals in the System and which, it was contended by so doing, racially discriminated against whites whose names appeared on the promotional list for appointment. At the time of the abolition or suspension of the said promotional list, the first fifteen thereon had been appointed, but Porcelli, Bigley and Shapiro, plaintiffs herein, though eligible, had not yet been appointed.

The school population in the City of Newark in October, 1961, was 67,134, of which the Negro population was 55.1%. In September, 1968, the total school population was 75,876, with a Negro student population of 72.5%, reflecting an increase in seven years of 8,742 students and a percentage increase of Negro students of 17.4%. During the school year 1967-1968, there were 249 administrative and supervisory positions (superintendents, principals and vice-principals, senior and junior high school principals, etc.), of which 27, or 10% were held by Negroes. On August 22, 1968, only one Negro each for principal and vice-principal was eligible on the promotion list and of the 72 principals in the system none were Negro and 67 vice-principals, 64 were white and 3 Negro.

On February 1, 1967, School Board of the City of Newark entered into a contract with the Teachers Association.[2]

---

[2] Under the terms of the contract, it was required:

"A. The positions of principal, vice principal, head teacher, department chairman and counselor shall be filled in order of numerical ranking from the appropriate list,

Under date of May 28, 1968, defendant Board of Education passed a resolution suspending and abolishing the making of appointments from this list and instead the defendant, Franklyn Titus, Superintendent of the School System in Newark, presented certain recommendations for the appointments of principals, vice-principals, senior and junior high school principals, which the Board adopted, representing a total of 35 white appointments and 20 Negro appointments. The appointments were designated as temporary appointments and the Board was to later review the appointments recommended, the criteria to be used by the Board having not as yet been finalized. In his recommendation to the Board the Superintendent candidly admitted that color was one of the criteria which he utilized, contending that the pattern by which principals, vice-principals and others were appointed reflected an era in 1953, when the promotional list was adopted, and as of 1968, conditions had so changed in the Newark School System that the promotional list had become outmoded by virtue of the changing population, community-wise and in the school system, which had occurred since its adoption.

This action was begun by a motion for summary judgment on the pleading, but the lower court denied it and ordered a full evidentiary hearing at which both sides were heard at great length. Superintendent Titus, one of the defendants, stated as one of his reasons for the abolition of the promotional list the fact that the Newark Public School System, especially in reading, was well below the national norm which obtained throughout the country; that there was such a great imbalance in the principal and vice-principal positions that, in his professional judgment, he felt that by adding a Negro who was qualified to these important positions, thus making the faculty more integrated, would the more readily lend itself to an upgrading of the Public School System in Newark. Although, as has been indicated, color was frankly admitted by all the witnesses for the appellees as being one of the factors in the selection of the principals and vice-principals, and one Simeon Moss, who was the

---

which ranking shall be determined by written and oral examination. Appointments to the position of teacher to assist principal (formerly called Administrative Assistant) shall be made annually on a temporary basis if the Superintendent determines that such a position is necessary or desirable, and all appointments to such position shall be made in order of numerical ranking from the appropriate vice-principal's list if such a list exists.

"B. Such examinations shall be given at regularly scheduled intervals and shall be adequately publicized in every school at least sixty (60) days in advance.

"C. All openings for the positions of supervisor, assistant supervisor and director and all positions hereafter created in new categories not existing shall be adequately publicized in every school at least sixty (60) days before the appointment is made and the qualifications for the positions shall be clearly set forth."

assistant superintendent for elementary education who made the recommendations to the Superintendent for the appointments, stated that color was a prime factor, it was not the only factor, as the procuring of qualified individuals was the real objective.[4] Plaintiffs' position was that this use of color in the selection of principals and vice-principals and the device used to achieve that selection by abolition or suspension of the promotional list was a violation of their Constitutional rights under the Fourteenth Amendment.

With this contention we do not agree. State action based partly on considerations of color, when color is not used per se, and in furtherance of a proper governmental objective, is not necessarily a violation of the Fourteenth Amendment. Proper integration of faculties is as important as proper integration of schools themselves, as set forth in Brown v. Board of Education, 349 U.S. 295 (1955), the thrust of which extends to the selection of faculties. In Kemp v. Beasley, 389 F.2d 178 (1968), the court held, at 189, where race was a consideration in the selection of teachers and faculties, "We reaffirm the principle that faculty selection must remain for the board and sensitive expertise of the School Board and its officials." And, at page 190, "The question thus becomes, when is there such faculty distribution as to provide equal opportunities to all students and to all teachers — whether white or Negro? Students in each school should have the same quality of instruction as in any other school. Every predominantly Negro school should have, wherever possible, substantially as integrated a faculty as the predominantly white school."

Again, in Springfield School Committee v. Barksdale, 348 F.2d 261, 266 (1965), the court stated: "It has been suggested that classification by race is unlawful regardless of the worthiness of the objective. We do not agree. The defendants' proposed action does

---

[4] The findings of fact in the district court opinion, 302 F. Supp. at 732-33, 2 FEP Cases 57, include the following:

"A fair evaluation of the record supports the conclusion that the promotional lists were suspended and the examination system abolished, not simply to appoint Negroes to promotional positions, but to obtain for these positions qualified persons, white or black, whose qualifications were based on an awareness of, and sensitivity to, the problems of educating the Newark school population. . . .

. . . .

"The Court is satisfied that in abolishing the examination procedure, there was no intention on the part of the Board to discriminate against white persons or exclude them from consideration for promotional positions. No inference of any such intention can be gleaned from the record. The testimony of several of the witnesses . . . shows that, despite a desire to provide an avenue for the appointment of more Negro administrators, the ultimate objective of the Board was to promote those persons most qualified to suit the needs of the Newark school system. There is nothing in the record to indicate that the Board was attempting to appoint Negroes in numbers proportionate to the school population."

not concern race insofar as race correlates with proven deprivation of educational opportunity." Further, in United States v. Jefferson County Board of Education, 372 F.2d 836, 895 (1966), it was stated, "As to faculty, we have found that school authorities have an affirmative duty to break up the historical pattern of segregated faculties, the hall-mark of the dual system."

It would therefore seem that the Boards of Education have a very definite affirmative duty to integrate school faculties and to permit a great imbalance in faculties — as obtained on August 22, 1968, when a new plan was proposed to the School Board in Newark for the increasing of qualified Negro administrators — would be in negation of the Fourteenth Amendment to the Constitution and the line of cases which have followed Brown v. Board of Education, supra.

We concur in the carefully considered opinion of Chief Judge Augelli, dated August 14, 1969, wherein he made findings of fact and conclusions of law pursuant to Federal Rule of Civil Procedure 52a (Porcelli v. Titus, 302 F. Supp. 726, 2 FEP Cases 52 (District of New Jersey 1969)). He also entered a final order dismissing the complaint with prejudice on September 17, 1969.

The judgment of the lower court will be affirmed.

CARTER v. GALLAGHER

United States Court of Appeals, Eighth Circuit
452 F.2d 315, 327 (1971)
Cert. denied, 406 U.S. 950 (1972)

On Petition for Rehearing En Banc.

GIBSON, Circuit Judge.

A panel of this court . . . sustained the order and opinion of the Honorable Earl R. Larson, District Court of Minnesota, finding that the employment practices and procedures for determining qualifications of applicants for positions on the Minneapolis Fire Department were racially discriminatory in violation of the Equal Protection Clause of the Fourteenth Amendment and the Civil Rights Act of 1870, 42 U.S.C. § 1981, and approved a number of corrective practices ordered so as to eliminate all racially discriminatory practices; but disapproved that part of Judge Larson's order providing for absolute minority preference in the employment of the next 20 persons to be hired by the department. The case was brought as a class action and relief was extended to minority groups as a class.

The panel opinion, while sustaining most of Judge Larson's findings and orders granting affirmative relief, did not approve of the absolute preference in Fire Department employment to 20 minority persons who met the qualifications for the positions under the revised qualification standards established by the decree and held that the absolute preference order infringed upon the constitutional rights of white applicants whose qualifications are established to be equal or superior to the minority applicants. . . .

A petition for rehearing en banc by the appellees was granted but limited solely to the issue of the appropriate remedy. . . .

The fact of past racially discriminatory practices and procedures in employment by the Fire Department is accepted and clearly evidenced by the fact that of the 535 men in the Fire Department none are from minority groups.[2] We are thus here concerned only with the appropriateness of the remedy ordered by the District Court. The absolute preference of 20 minority persons who qualify has gone further than any of the reported appellate court cases in granting preference to overcome the effects of past discriminatory practices and does appear to violate the constitutional right of Equal Protection of the Law to white persons who are superiorly qualified.

The panel opinion has recognized the illegality of the past practices, has ordered those practices abandoned, and the affirmative establishment of nondiscriminatory practices and procedures. There is, as the panel pointed out, no claim or showing made that the plaintiffs were identifiable members of the class who had made prior applications for employment and were denied employment solely because of race. This latter situation could be remedied immediately by ordering the employment of such persons. However, in dealing with the abstraction of employment as a class, we are confronted with the proposition that in giving an absolute preference to a minority as a class over those of the white race who are either superiorly or equally qualified would constitute a violation of the Equal Protection Clause of the Fourteenth Amendment to the Constitution.

The defendants-appellants point out the mandatory requirements of the Minneapolis City and the Minnesota Veterans' Preference Act (Minnesota Statute § 197.45). These requirements however must give way to the Supremacy Clause of Article 6 of the United States Constitution.

Mr. Justice Black, in speaking for a unanimous court (although Mr. Justice Harlan concurred on the basis of the Fifteenth Amendment rather than on the Fourteenth) in Louisiana v. United States, 380 U.S. 145, 85 S. Ct. 817, 13 L. Ed. 2d 709 (1964), approved the suspension of Louisiana voting laws that had been administered discriminatorily against Negroes and held it was the affirmative duty of the district court to eliminate the discriminatory effects of past practices, stating, "We bear in mind that the court has not merely

---

[2] The total minority population of the Minneapolis area was 6.44 percent in 1970; black population 4.37 percent.

the power but the duty to render a decree which so far as possible eliminate the discriminatory effects of the past as well as bar like discrimination in the future." 380 U.S. at 154, 85 S. Ct. at 822. It is apparent that remedies to overcome the effects of past discrimination may suspend valid state laws. United States v. Mississippi, 339 F.2d 679 (5th Cir. 1964); United States v. Duke, 332 F.2d 759 (5th Cir. 1963).

Admittedly the District Court has wide power sitting as a court of equity to fashion relief enforcing the congressional mandate of the Civil Rights Act and the constitutional guarantees of the Equal Protection of the Law; and clearly, courts of equity have the power to eradicate the effects of past discriminations. Parham v. Southwestern Bell Telephone Co., 433 F.2d 421 (8th Cir. 1971). We are not here concerned with the anti-preference treatment section 703(j) of Title VII of the Civil Rights Act of 1964, 42 U.S.C. § 2000e-2(j) [3] as this class action is predicated under § 1981 of the old Civil Rights Act and the provisions of the Fourteenth Amendment. However, even the anti-preference treatment section of the new Civil Rights Act of 1964 does not limit the power of a court to order affirmative relief to correct the effects of past unlawful practices. United States v. IBEW, Local No. 38, 428 F.2d 144 (6th Cir.), cert. denied, 400 U.S. 943, 91 S. Ct. 245, 27 L. Ed. 2d 248 (1970).

Although this case is not predicated upon Title VII of the Civil Rights Act of 1964 and most of the cases that have dealt with the issue of remedying past discriminatory practices along with prohibiting present discriminatory practices are under that Act, the remedies invoked in those cases offer some practical guidelines in dealing with this issue.

As the panel opinion points out most of these cases deal with discriminations to a specified individual who has been presently discriminated against on account of race, and the remedy is there easily applied as the individual who has been discriminated against

---

[3] 42 U.S.C. § 2000e-2(j) provides as follows:

"Nothing contained in this subchapter shall be interpreted to require any employer, employment agency, labor organization, or joint labor-management committee subject to this subchapter to grant preferential treatment to any individual or to any group because of the race, color, religion, sex, or national origin of such individual or group on account of an imbalance which may exist with respect to the total number or percentage of persons of any race, color, religion, sex, or national origin employed by any employer, referred or classified for employment by any employment agency or labor organization, admitted to membership or classified by any labor organization, or admitted to, or employed in, any apprenticeship or other training program, in comparison with the total number or percentage of persons of such race, color, religion, sex, or national origin in any community, State, section, or other area, or in the available work force in any community, State, section, or other area."

can be presently ordered employed without running into the constitutional questions involved in granting preference to any one class over another. However, in the United States v. Ironworkers Local 86, 443 F.2d 544 (9th Cir. 1971), cert. denied, 404 U.S 984, 92 S. Ct. 447, 30 L. Ed. 2d 367 (1971) the Ninth Circuit approved the district court decree ordering building construction unions to offer immediate job referrals to previous racial discriminatees and also approved a prospective order requiring the unions to recruit sufficient blacks to comprise a 30 percent membership in their apprenticeship programs. This was ordered in Seattle which had a black population of approximately 7 percent. See, United States v. Local No. 86, Int. Ass'n of Bridge S., D. & R. Ironworkers et al., 315 F. Supp. 1202 (W.D. Wash. 1970).

In Local 53 of Int. Ass'n of Asbestos Workers v. Vogler, 407 F.2d 1047 (5th Cir. 1969), the trial court ordered the immediate admission into the union of three Negroes who were racially discriminated against in their application for membership and voided a local membership rule that in effect made the union a self-perpetuating nepotistic group, specifically ordering the union to develop objective criteria for membership and prospectively ordering the alternating of white and Negro referrals.

In United States v. Central Motor Lines, Inc., 325 F. Supp. 478 (W.D.N.C. 1970), the trial court issued a preliminary injunction requiring the motor carrier to hire six Negro drivers "promptly," (apparently within two weeks from the date of the order), and that any future drivers hired were to be in an alternating ratio of one black to one white.

Cases arising from Executive Order #11246, prohibiting all contractors and subcontractors on federally financed projects from discriminating in their employment practices, have also upheld plans which establish percentage goals for the employment of minority workers. See Contractors Association of Eastern Pa. v. Secretary of Labor, 442 F.2d 159 (3d Cir. 1971) (upholding the "Philadelphia Plan" requiring minority employment goals in the construction trades ranging from 19 percent-26 percent); Joyce v. McCrane, 320 F. Supp. 1284 (D.N.J. 1970) (requiring contractors to employ 30 percent-37 minority journeymen).

It is also appropriate to note that precedent from our own Circuit establishes that the presence of identified persons who have been discriminated against is not a necessary prerequisite to ordering affirmative relief in order to eliminate the present effects of past discrimination. In United States v. Sheet Metal Workers Local 36, 416 F.2d 123 (8th Cir. 1969), we required substantial changes in union referral systems. In connection with this holding, Judge Heaney noted:

"We recognize that each of the cases cited in n. 15 to support our position can be distinguished on the ground that in each case, a number of known members of a minority group had been discriminated against after the passage of the Civil Rights Act. Here, we do not have such evidence, but we do not believe that it is necessary. The record does show that qualified Negro tradesmen have been and continued to be residents of the area. It further shows that they were acutely aware of the Locals' policies toward minority groups. It is also clear that they knew that even if they were permitted to use the referral system and become members of the union, they would have to work for at least a year before they could move into a priority group which would assure them reasonably full employment. In the light of this knowledge, it is unreasonable to expect that any Negro tradesman working for a Negro contractor or a nonconstruction white employer would seek to use the referral systems or to join either Local." Id. at 132.

It may also be pointed out that in actions under Title VII of the Civil Rights Act, 42 U.S.C. § 2000e et seq., Congress has specifically granted authority to the trial courts to "order such affirmative action as may be appropriate, which may include . . . *hiring of employees* . . . ." 42 U.S.C. § 2000e-5(g) (emphasis added).

None of the remedies ordered or approved in the above cases involved an absolute preference for qualified minority persons for the first vacancies appearing in an employer's business, in contrast to the remedy ordered in the instant case. The absolute preference ordered by the trial court would operate as a present infringement on those non-minority group persons who are equally or superiorly qualified for the fire fighter's positions; and we hesitate to advocate implementation of one constitutional guarantee by the outright denial of another. Yet we acknowledge the legitimacy of erasing the effects of past racially discriminatory practices. Louisiana v. United States, *supra.* To accommodate these conflicting considerations, we think some reasonable ratio for hiring minority persons who can qualify under the revised qualification standards is in order for a limited period of time, or until there is a fair approximation of minority representation consistent with the population mix in the area. Such a procedure does not constitute a "quota" system because as soon as the trial court's order is fully implemented, all hirings will be on a racially nondiscriminatory basis, and it could well be that many more minority persons or less, as compared to the population at large, over a long period of time would apply and qualify for the positions. However, as a method of presently eliminating the effects of past racial discriminatory practices and in making meaningful in the immediate future the constitutional guarantees against racial discrimination, more than a token representation should be afforded. For these reasons we believe the trial court is possessed of the authority to order the hiring of 20 qualified minority persons, but this should be done without denying the constitutional rights of others by granting an absolute preference.

Ideas and views on ratios and procedures may vary widely but this issue should be resolved as soon as possible. In considering the equities of the decree and the difficulties that may be encountered in procuring qualified applicants from any of the racial groups, we feel that it would be in order for the district court to mandate that one out of every three persons hired by the Fire Department would be a minority individual who qualifies until at least 20 minority persons have been so hired.

Fashioning a remedy in these cases is of course a practical question which may differ substantially from case to case, depending on the circumstances. In reaching our conclusion in the instant case, we have been guided to some extent by the following considerations:

(1) It has now been established by the Supreme Court that the use of mathematical ratios as "a starting point in the process of shaping a remedy" is not unconstitutional and is "within the equitable remedial discretion of the District Court." Swann v. Charlotte-Mecklenburg Board of Education, 402 U.S. 1, 25, 91 S. Ct. 1267, 1280, 28 L. Ed. 2d 554 (1971).

(2) Given the past discriminatory hiring policies of the Minneapolis Fire Department, which were well known in the minority community, it is not unreasonable to assume that minority persons will still be reluctant to apply for employment, absent some positive assurance that if qualified they will in fact be hired on a more than token basis.

(3) As the panel opinion noted, testing procedures required to qualify applicants are undergoing revision and validation at the present time. As the tests are currently utilized, applicants must attain a qualifying score in order to be certified at all. They are then ranked in order of eligibility according to their test scores (disregarding for present purposes the veteran's preference). Because of the absence of validation studies on the record before us, it is speculative to assume that the qualifying test, in addition to separating those applicants who are qualified from those who are not, also ranks qualified applicants with precision, statistical validity, and predictive significance. See generally, Cooper & Sobol, Seniority and Testing under Fair Employment Laws: A General Approach to Objective Criteria of Hiring and Promotion, 82 Harv. L. Rev. 1598, 1637-1669 (1969). Thus, a hiring remedy based on an alternating ratio such as we here suggest will by no means necessarily result in hiring less qualified minority persons in preference to more qualified white persons.

(4) While some of the remedial orders relied on by the plaintiffs and the Government ordered one to one ratios, they appear to be in areas and occupations with a more substantial minority population than the Minneapolis area. Thus we conclude that a one to two ratio would be appropriate here, until 20 qualified minority persons have been hired.

The panel opinion is adopted as the opinion of the court en banc with the exception of that part relating to the absolute preference.

The District Court properly retained jurisdiction pending full implementation of its decree and the remedy. Cause is remanded for further proceedings consistent with this opinion. . . .

[The concurring opinion of MATTHES, Chief Judge, is omitted.]

VAN OOSTERHOUT, Senior Circuit Judge (dissenting).

For reasons stated in Division V of the panel opinion in this case, reported at 452 F.2d 324, I dissent from the en banc mandatory determination that one out of three persons hired by the Fire Department shall be a minority person until at least twenty minority persons are hired. Such provision in my opinion is vulnerable to the same constitutional infirmity as Judge Larson's absolute preference provision. This court's minority preference provision will not discriminate against as many white applicants as Judge Larson's decree but it will still give some minority persons preference in employment over white applicants whose qualifications are determined to be superior under fairly imposed standards and tests.

Employment preferences based on race are prohibited by the Fourteenth Amendment. This case is distinguishable from Swann v. Charlotte-Mecklenburg Board of Education relied upon by the majority in that whites have no right to insist upon segregated schools, while white as well as Black applicants cannot be denied employment on the basis of race.

I agree that a court of equity has broad power to frame an appropriate decree but such power does not extend to establishing provisions which deprive persons of constitutionally guaranteed rights.

Present and future applicants for firemen positions are in no way responsible for past discrimination. Plaintiffs have not shown that any plaintiff now seeking employment has personally suffered as a result of past discrimination by being denied employment over a less qualified white person. Past general racial discrimination against Blacks under the circumstances of this case does not justify unconstitutional present racial discrimination against white applicants. The court should of course go as far as is constitutionally permissible to eliminate racial discrimination in employment of firemen. Substantial steps in that direction have been taken by other provisions of Judge Larson's decree and the panel opinion.

MEHAFFY, Circuit Judge, joins in this dissent.

NOTES:

(1) *Compare NAACP v. Allen,* 493 F.2d 614 (5th Cir. 1974), *with Anderson v. San Francisco School District,* 5 FEP Cas. 362 (N.D. Cal. 1972) (where it was held that "preferential treatment under the guise of 'affirmative action' is the imposition of one form of racial discrimination in place of another.")

(2) In the cases involving quota or preferential hiring, the courts are often faced with the argument of "reverse discrimination" as seen in *Carter* and *Porcelli.* How should the courts deal with this problem? Can it be argued that any remedy which gives a preference to minority job applicants is violative of equal protection? The courts have tended to avoid this constitutional question by limiting preferential hiring orders. Usually, before an order for preferential hiring is issued, there must be a finding of a history of discrimination against a protected group or statistical evidence showing a pattern of gross discrimination; members of the preferred class are required to satisfy job related employment tests; the order is almost always temporary; the order is sometimes conditioned to take account of the availability of the preferred group in the geographic areas nearby the place of employment; and there is usually a finding that other available affirmative relief would be inadequate to overcome the present effects of the existing discrimination. *See generally* Edwards and Zaretsky, *Preferential Remedies for Employment Discrimination,* 74 Mich. L. Rev. 1 (1975).

B. UNDER TITLE VII

FRANKS v. BOWMAN TRANSP. CO., INC.

United States Supreme Court
424 U.S. 727, 96 S. Ct. 1251, 47 L. Ed. 2d 444 (1976)

MR. JUSTICE BRENNAN delivered the opinion of the Court.

This case presents the question whether identifiable applicants who were denied employment because of race after the effective date and in violation of Title VII of the Civil Rights Act of 1964, 42 U. S. C. § 2000e *et seq.,* may be awarded seniority status retroactive to the dates of their employment applications.[1]

Petitioner Franks brought this class action in the United States District Court for the Northern District of Georgia against his former employer, respondent Bowman Transportation Company, and his unions, the International Union of District 50, Allied and Technical

---

[1] Petitioners also alleged an alternative claim for relief for violations of 42 U. S. C. § 1981. In view of our decision we have no occasion to address that claim.

Workers of the United States and Canada and its local, No. 13600,[2] alleging various racially discriminatory employment practices in violation of Title VII. Petitioner Lee intervened on behalf of himself and others similarly situated alleging racially discriminatory hiring and discharge policies limited to Bowman's employment of over-the-road (OTR) truck drivers. Following trial, the District Court found Bowman had engaged in a pattern of racial discrimination in various company policies, including the hiring, transfer, and discharge of employees, and found further that the discriminatory practices were perpetrated in Bowman's collective-bargaining agreement with the unions. The District Court certified the action as a proper class action under Fed. Rule Civ. Proc. 23(b)(2) and, of import to the issues before this Court, found that petitioner Lee represented all black applicants who sought to be hired or to transfer to OTR driving positions prior to January 1, 1972. In its final order and decree, the District Court subdivided the class represented by petitioner Lee into a class of black nonemployee applicants for OTR positions prior to January 1, 1972 (class 3), and a class of black employees who applied to transfer to OTR positions prior to the same date (class 4).

In its final judgment entered July 14, 1972, the District Court permanently enjoined the respondents from perpetuating the discriminatory practices found to exist, and, in regard to the black applicants for OTR positions, ordered Bowman to notify the members of both subclasses within 30 days of their right to priority consideration for such jobs. The District Court declined, however, to grant to the unnamed members of classes 3 and 4 any other specific relief sought, which included an award of backpay and seniority status retroactive to the date of individual application for an OTR position.

On petitioners' appeal to the Court of Appeals for the Fifth Circuit, raising for the most part claimed inadequacy of the relief ordered respecting unnamed members of the various subclasses involved, the Court of Appeals affirmed in part, reversed in part, and vacated in part. 495 F.2d 398. The Court of Appeals held that the District Court had exercised its discretion under an erroneous view of law insofar as it failed to award backpay to the unnamed class members of both classes 3 and 4, and vacated the judgment in that respect. The judgment was reversed insofar as it failed to award any seniority remedy to the members of class 4 who after the judgment of the District Court sought and obtained priority consideration for transfer to OTR positions. As respects unnamed members of class 3 —

---

[2] In 1972, the International Union of District 50 merged with the United Steelworkers of America, AFL-CIO, and hence the latter as the successor bargaining representative is the union respondent before this Court.

nonemployee black applicants who applied for and were denied OTR prior to January 1, 1972 — the Court of Appeals affirmed the District Court's denial of any form of seniority relief. Only this last aspect of the Court of Appeals' judgment is before us for review under our grant of the petition for certiorari. 420 U. S. 989 (1975).

I

[The court held that the case was not moot.]

II

In affirming the District Court's denial of seniority relief to the class 3 group of discriminatees, the Court of Appeals held that the relief was barred by § 703(h) of Title VII, 42 U. S. C. § 2000e-2(h). We disagree. Section 703(h) provides in pertinent part that:

"Notwithstanding any other provision of this title it shall not be an unlawful employment practice for an employer to apply different standards of compensation, or different terms, conditions, or privileges of employment pursuant to a bona fide seniority or merit system . . . provided that such differences are not the result of an intention to discriminate because of race, color, religion, sex, or national origin. . . ."

The Court of Appeals reasoned that a discriminatory refusal to hire "does not affect the bona fides of the seniority system: Thus, the differences in the benefits and conditions of employment which a seniority system accords to older and newer employees is protected as 'not an unlawful employment practice' [by § 703(h)]." 495 F.2d, at 417. Significantly, neither Bowman nor the unions undertake to defend the Court of Appeals' judgment on that ground. It is clearly erroneous.

The black applicants for OTR positions composing class 3 are limited to those whose applications were put in evidence at the trial.[10] The underlying legal wrong affecting them is not the alleged operation of a racially discriminatory seniority system but of a racially

---

[10] By its terms, the judgment of the District Court runs to all black applicants for OTR positions prior to January 1, 1972, and is not qualified by a limitation that the discriminatory refusal to hire must have taken place after the effective date of the Act. However, only post-Act victims of racial discrimination are members of class 3. Title VII's prohibition on racial discrimination in hiring became effective on July 2, 1965, one year after the date of its enactment. Pub. L. 88-352, § 716(a)-(b); 78 Stat. 253. Petitioners sought relief in this case for identifiable applicants for OTR positions "whose applications were put in evidence at the trial." App., at 20a. There are 206 unhired black applicants prior to January 1, 1972, whose written applications are summarized in the record and none of the applications relates to years prior to 1970. App., at 52a, Table VA.

discriminatory hiring system. Petitioners do not ask modification or elimination of the existing seniority system, but only an award of the seniority status they would have individually enjoyed under the present system but for the illegal discriminatory refusal to hire. It is this context that must shape our determination as the meaning and effect of § 703(h).

On its face, § 703(h) appears to be only a definitional provision; as with the other provisions of § 703, subsection (h) delineates which employment practices are illegal and thereby prohibited and which are not. Section 703(h) certainly does not expressly purport to qualify or proscribe relief otherwise appropriate under the remedial provisions of Title VII, § 706(g), 42 U. S. C. § 2000e-5(g), in circumstances where an illegal discriminatory act or practice is found. Further, the legislative history of § 703(h) plainly negates its reading as limiting or qualifying the relief authorized under § 706(g). The initial bill reported by the House Judiciary Committee as H. R. 7152 and passed by the full House on February 10, 1964, did not contain § 703(h). Neither the House bill nor the majority Judiciary Committee Report even mentioned the problem of seniority. That subject thereafter surfaced during the debate of the bill in the Senate. This debate prompted Senators Clark and Case to respond to criticism that Title VII would destroy existing seniority systems by placing an Interpretive Memorandum in the Congressional Record. The Memorandum stated that "Title VII would have no effect on established seniority rights. Its effect is prospective and not retrospective." 110 Cong. Rec. 7213 (1964). Senator Clark also placed in the Congressional Record a Justice Department statement concerning Title VII which stated that "it has been asserted that Title VII would undermine vested rights of seniority. This is not correct. Title VII would have no effect on seniority rights existing at the time it takes effect." 110 Cong. Rec. 7207 (1964).[16] Several weeks

---

[16] The full text of the Statement introduced by Senator Clark pertinent to seniority states:

"First, it has been asserted that Title VII would undermine vested rights of seniority. This is not correct. Title VII would have no effect on seniority rights existing at the time it takes effect. If, for example, a collective bargaining contract provides that in the event of layoffs, those who were hired last must be laid off first, such a provision would not be affected in the least by Title VII. This would be true even in the case where owing to discrimination prior to the effective date of the title, white workers had more seniority than Negroes. Title VII is directed at discrimination based on race, color, religion, sex, or national origin. It is perfectly clear that when a worker is laid off or denied a chance for promotion because under established seniority rules he is "low man on the totem pole" he is not being discriminated against because of his race. Of course, if the seniority rule itself is discriminatory, it would be unlawful under Title VII. If a rule were to state that all Negroes must be laid off before any white man, such a rule could not serve as the basis for a discharge subsequent to the effective date of the title. I do not know how anyone could quarrel with such a result. But, in the ordinary case, assuming that

thereafter, following several informal conferences among the Senate leadership, the House leadership, the Attorney General and others, . . . a compromise substitute bill prepared by Senators Mansfield and Dirksen, Senate majority and minority leaders respectively, containing § 703(h) was introduced on the Senate floor. Although the Mansfield-Dirksen substitute bill, and hence § 703(h), was not the subject of a committee report . . . Senator Humphrey, one of the informal conferees, later stated during debate on the substitute that § 703(h) was not designed to alter the meaning of Title VII generally but rather "merely clarifies its present intent and effect." 110 Cong. Rec. 12,723 (1964) (remarks of Sen. Humphrey). Accordingly, whatever the exact meaning and scope of § 703(h) in light of its unusual legislative history and the absence of the usual legislative materials . . . it is apparent that the thrust of the section is directed toward defining what is and what is not an illegal discriminatory practice in instances in which the post-Act operation of a seniority system is challenged as perpetuating the effects of discrimination occurring prior to the effective date of the Act. There is no indication in the legislative materials that § 703(h) was intended to modify or restrict relief otherwise appropriate once an illegal discriminatory practice occurring after the effective date of the Act is proved — as in the instant case, a discriminatory refusal to hire. . . . We therefore hold that the Court of Appeals erred in concluding that, as a matter of law, § 703(h) barred the award of seniority relief to the unnamed class 3 members.

---

seniority rights were built up over a period of time during which Negroes were not hired, these rights would not be set aside by the taking effect of Title VII. Employers and labor organizations would simply be under a duty not to discriminate against Negroes because of their race. Any differences in treatment based on established seniority rights would not be based on race and would not be forbidden by the title." 110 Cong. Rec. 7207 (1964).

Senator Clark also introduced into the Congressional Record a set of answers to a series of questions propounded by Senator Dirksen. Two of these questions and answers are pertinent to the issue of seniority:

"Question. Would the same situation prevail in respect to promotions, when that management function is governed by a labor contract calling for promotions on the basis of seniority? What of dismissals? Normally, labor contracts call for 'last hired, first fired'. If the last hired are Negroes, is the employer discriminating if his contract requires they be first fired and the remaining employees are white?

"Answer. Seniority rights are in no way affected by the bill. If under a 'last hired, first fired' agreement a Negro happens to be the 'last hired,' he can still be 'first fired' as long as it is done because of his status as 'last hired' and not because of his race.

"Question. If an employer is directed to abolish his employment list because of discrimination, what happens to seniority?

"Answer. The bill is not retroactive, and it will not require an employer to change existing seniority lists." 110 Cong. Rec. 7217 (1964).

III

There remains the question whether an award of seniority relief is appropriate under the remedial provisions of Title VII, specifically, § 706(g).

We begin by repeating the observation of earlier decisions that in enacting Title VII of the Civil Rights Act of 1964, Congress intended to prohibit all practices in whatever form which create inequality in employment opportunity due to discrimination on the basis of race, religion, sex, or national origin, *Alexander v. Gardner-Denver Co.,* 415 U. S. 36, 44 (1974); *McDonnel [McDonnell] Douglas Corp. v. Green,* 411 U. S. 792, 800 (1973); *Griggs v. Duke Power Co.,* 401 U. S. 424, 429-430 (171), and ordained that its policy of outlawing such discrimination should have the "highest priority," *Alexander, supra,* at 47; *Newman v. Piggie Park Enterprises, Inc.,* 390 U. S. 400, 402 (1968). Last Term's *Albemarle Paper Company v. Moody,* 422 U. S. 405 (1975), consistently with the congressional plan, held that one of the central purposes of Title VII is "to make persons whole for injuries suffered on account of unlawful employment discrimination." *Id.,* at 418. To effectuate this "make-whole" objective, Congress in § 706(g) vested broad equitable discretion in the federal courts to "order such affirmative action as may be appropriate, which may include, but is not limited to, reinstatement or hiring of employees, with or without backpay . . . or any other relief as the court deems appropriate." *Ibid.* The legislative history supporting the 1972 Amendments of § 706(g) of Title VII affirms the breadth of this discretion. "The provisions of [§ 706(g)] are intended to give the courts wide discretion exercising their equitable powers to fashion the most complete relief possible. . . . [T]he Act is intended to make the victims of unlawful employment discrimination whole and . . . the attainment of this objective . . . requires that persons aggrieved by the consequences and effects of the unlawful employment practice be, so far as possible, restored to a position where they would have been were it not for the unlawful discrimination." Section-by-Section Analysis of H. R. 1746, accompanying the Equal Employment Opportunity Act of 1972 — Conference Report, 118 Cong. Rec. 7166, 7168 (1972). This is emphatic confirmation that federal courts are empowered to fashion such relief as the particular circumstances of a case may require to effect restitution, making whole insofar as possible the victims of racial discrimination in hiring.[21] Adequate relief may well be denied

---

[21] It is true that backpay is the only remedy specifically mentioned in § 706(g). But to draw from this fact and other sections of the statute any implicit statement by Congress that seniority relief is a prohibited, or at least less available form of remedy is not warranted. Indeed, any such contention necessarily disregards the extensive legislative history underlying the 1972 Amendments to Title VII. The

in the absence of a seniority remedy slotting the victim in that position in the seniority system that would have been his had he been hired at the time of his application. It can hardly be questioned that ordinarily such relief will be necessary to achieve the "make-whole" purposes of the Act.

Seniority systems and the entitlements conferred by credits earned thereunder are of vast and increasing importance in the economic employment system of this Nation. . . . Seniority principles are increasingly used to allocate entitlements to scarce benefits among competing employees ("competitive status" seniority) and to compute noncompetitive benefits ("benefit" seniority). *Ibid.* We have already said about "competitive status" seniority that it "has become of overriding importance, and one of its major functions is to determine who gets or who keeps an available job." *Humphrey*

1972 Amendments added the phrase speaking to "other equitable relief" in § 706(g). The Senate Report manifested an explicit concern with the "earnings gap" presently existing between black and white employees in American society. S. Rep. No. 415, 92d Cong., 1st Sess., 6 (1971). The Reports of both Houses of Congress indicated that "rightful place" was the intended objective of Title VII and the relief accorded thereunder. *Ibid.*; H. R. Rep. No. 238, 92d Cong., 1st Sess., 4 (1971). As indicated, *infra,* at — & n. 28, rightful place seniority, implicating an employee's *future* earnings, job security and advancement prospects, is absolutely essential to obtain this congressionally mandated goal.

The legislative history underlying the 1972 Amendments completely answers the argument that Congress somehow intended seniority relief to be less available to pursuit of this goal. In explaining the need for the 1972 Amendments, the Senate Report stated:

"Employment discrimination as viewed today is a . . . complex and pervasive phenomenon. Experts familiar with the subject now generally describe the problem in terms of 'systems' and 'effects' rather than simply intentional wrongs, and the literature on the subject is replete with discussions of, for example, the mechanics of seniority and lines of progression, perpetuation of the present effect of pre-act discriminatory practices through various institutional devices, and testing and validation requirements." S. Rep., *supra,* at 5. See also H. R. Rep., *supra,* at 8. In the context of this express reference to seniority, the Reports of both Houses cite with approval decisions of the lower federal courts which granted forms of retroactive "rightful place" seniority relief. S. Rep., *supra,* at 5 n. 1; H. Rep., *supra,* at 8 n. 2. (The dissent, *post,* at — n. 18, would distinguish these lower federal court decisions as not involving instances of discriminatory *hiring.* Obviously, however, the concern of the entire thrust of the dissent — the impact of rightful place seniority upon the expectations of other employees — is in no way a function of the specific type of illegal discriminatory practice upon which the judgment of liability is predicated.) Thereafter, in language that could hardly be more explicit, the Conference Report stated:

"In any area where the new law does not address itself, or in any areas where a specific contrary intention is not indicated, it was assumed *that the present case law as developed by the courts would continue to govern the applicability and construction of Title VII."* Section-by-Section Analysis of H. R. 1746, accompanying The Equal Opportunity Act of 1972 — Conference Report, 118 Cong. Rec. 7166 (1972) (emphasis added).

v. Moore, 375 U. S. 335, 346-347 (1964). "More than any other provision of the collective [bargaining] agreement . . . seniority affects the economic security of the individual employee covered by its terms." Aaron, Reflections on the Legal Nature and Enforceability of Seniority Rights, 75 Harv. L. Rev. 1532, 1535 (1962). "Competitive status" seniority also often plays a broader role in modern employment systems, particularly systems operated under collective-bargaining agreements:

"Included among the benefits, options, and safeguards affected by competitive status seniority, are not only promotion and layoff, but also transfer, demotion, rest days, shift assignments, prerogative in scheduling vacation, order of layoff, possibilities of lateral transfer to avoid layoff, 'bumping' possibilities in the face of layoff, order of recall, training opportunities, working conditions, length of layoff endured without reducing seniority, length of layoff recall rights will withstand, overtime opportunities, parking privileges, and, in one plant, a preferred place in the punch-out line." Stacy, 28 Vand. L. Rev., at 490 (footnotes omitted).

Seniority standing in employment with respondent Bowman, computed from the departmental date of hire, determines the order of layoff and recall of employees. Further, job assignments for OTR drivers are posted for competitive bidding and seniority is used to determine the highest bidder. As OTR drivers are paid on a per-mile basis, earnings are therefore to some extent a function of seniority. Additionally, seniority computed from the company date-of-hire determines the length of an employee's vacation and pension benefits. Obviously merely to require Bowman to hire the class 3 victim of discrimination falls far short of a "make-whole" remedy.[27] A concomitant award of the seniority credit he presumptively would have earned but for the wrongful treatment would also seem necessary in the absence of justification for denying that relief. Without an award of seniority dating from the time at which he was discriminatorily refused employment, an individual who applies for and obtains employment as an OTR driver pursuant to the District Court's order will never obtain his rightful place in the hierarchy of seniority according to which these various employment benefits are distributed. He will perpetually remain subordinate to persons who,

-----

[27] Further, at least in regard to "benefit"-type seniority such as length of vacation leave and pension benefits in the instant case, any general bar to the award of retroactive seniority for victims of illegal hiring discrimination serves to undermine the mutually reinforcing effect of the dual purposes of Title VII; it reduces the restitution required of an employer at such time as he is called upon to account for his discriminatory actions perpetrated in violation of the law. See *Albemarle Paper,* 422 U. S., at 417-418.

but for the illegal discrimination, would have been in respect to entitlement to these benefits his inferiors.[28]

The Court of Appeals apparently followed this reasoning in holding that the District Court erred in not granting seniority relief to class 4 Bowman employees who were discriminatorily refused transfer to OTR positions. Yet the class 3 discriminatees in the absence of a comparable seniority award would also remain subordinated in the seniority system to the class 4 discriminatees. The distinction plainly finds no support anywhere in Title VII or its legislative history. Settled law dealing with the related "twin" areas of discriminatory hiring and discharges violative of National Labor Relations Act, 29 U. S. C. § 151 *et seq.,* provides a persuasive analogy. "[I]t would indeed be surprising if Congress gave a remedy for the one which it denied for the other." *Phelps Dodge Corp. v. NLRB,* 313 U. S. 177, 187 (1941). For courts to differentiate without justification between the classes of discriminatees "would be a differentiation not only without substance but in defiance of that against which the prohibition of discrimination is directed." *Id.,* at 188.

Similarly, decisions construing the remedial section of the National Labor Relations Act, § 10(c), 29 U. C. C. § 160(c) — the model for § 706(g), *Albemarle Paper,* 405 U. S., at 419 [29] — make clear that remedies constituting authorized "affirmative action" include an award of seniority status, for the thrust of "affirmative action" redressing the wrong incurred by an unfair labor practice is to make "the employees whole, and thus restor[e] the economic status quo that would have obtained but for the company's wrongful [act]." *NLRB v. J. H. Rutter-Rex Manufacturing Company,* 396 U. S. 258,

---

[28] Accordingly, it is clear that the seniority remedy which petitioners seek does not concern only the "make-whole" purposes of Title VII. The dissent errs in treating the issue of seniority relief as implicating only the "make-whole" objective of Title VII and in stating that "Title VII's 'primary objective' of eradicating discrimination is not served at all. . . ." *Post,* at —. Nothing could be further from the reality — the issue of seniority relief cuts to the very heart of Title VII's primary objective of eradicating present and future discrimination in a way that backpay, for example, can never do. "[S]eniority, after all, is a right which a worker exercises in each job movement in the future, rather than a simple one-time payment for the past." Poplin, Fair Employment in a Depressed Economy: The Layoff Problem, 23 U. C. L. A. L. Rev. 177, 225 (1975).

[29] To the extent that there is difference in the wording of the respective provisions, § 706(g) grants, if anything, broader discretionary powers than those granted the NLRB. Section 10 (c) of the NLRA authorizes "such affirmative action including reinstatement of employees with or without back pay, as will effectuate the policies of this subchapter," 29 U. S. C. § 160(c), whereas § 706(g) as amended in 1972 authorizes "such affirmative action as may be appropriate, which may include, *but is not limited to,* reinstatement *or hiring of employees, with or without back pay . . ., or any other equitable relief as the court deems appropriate."* 42 U. S. C. § 2000e-5(g) (emphasis added).

263 (1969). The task of the NLRB in applying § 10(c) is "to take measures designed to recreate the conditions and relationships that would have been had there been no unfair labor practice." *Local 60, United Brotherhood of Carpenters and Joiners of America, AFL-CIO v. NLRB,* 365 U. S. 651, 657 (1961) (Harlan, J., concurring). And the NLRB has often required that the hiring of employees who had been discriminatorily refused employment be accompanied by an award of seniority equivalent to that which they would have enjoyed but for the illegal conduct. See, *e.g., In re Phelps Dodge Corp.,* 19 N. L. R. B. 547, 600 n. 39, 603-604 (1940), modified on other grounds, 313 U. S. 177 (1941) (ordering persons discriminatorily refused employment hired "without prejudice to their other rights and privileges"); *In re Nevada Consolidated Copper Corp.,* 26 N. L. R. B. 1182, 1235 (1940), enforced, 316 U. S. 105 (1942) (ordering persons discriminatorily refused employment hired with "any seniority or other rights and privileges which they would have acquired, had the respondent not unlawfully discriminated against them"). Plainly the "affirmative action" injunction of § 706(g) has no lesser reach in the district courts. "Where racial discrimination is concerned, 'the district court has not merely the power but the duty to render a decree which will so far as possible eliminate the discriminatory effects of the past as well as bar like discrimination in the future.' " *Albemarle Paper, supra,* at 418.

IV

We are not to be understood as holding that an award of seniority status is requisite in all circumstances. The fashioning of appropriate remedies invokes the sound equitable discretion of the district courts. Respondent Bowman attempts to justify the District Court's denial of seniority relief for petitioners as an exercise of equitable discretion, but the record is its own refutation of the argument.

Albemarle Paper, supra, at 416, made clear that discretion imports not the Court's "inclination, but . . . its judgment; and its judgment is to be guided by sound legal principles." Discretion is vested not for purposes of "limit[ing] appellate review of trial courts, or . . . invit[ing] inconsistency and caprice," but rather to allow the most complete achievement of the objectives of Title VII that is attainable under the facts and circumstances of the specific case. *Id.,* at 421. Accordingly, the District Court's denial of any form of seniority remedy must be reviewed in terms of its effect on the attainment of the Act's objectives under the circumstances presented by this record. No less than with the denial of the remedy of backpay, the denial of seniority relief to victims of illegal racial discrimination in hiring is permissible "only for reasons which, if applied generally, would not frustrate the central statutory purposes of eradicating discrimination throughout the economy and making persons whole for injuries suffered through past discrimination." *Ibid.*

The District Court stated two reasons for its denial of seniority relief for the unnamed class members. The first was that those individuals had not filed administrative charges under the provisions of Title VII with the Equal Employment Opportunity Commission and therefore class relief of this sort was not appropriate. We rejected this justification for denial of class-based relief in the context of backpay awards in *Albemarle Paper,* and for the same reasons reject it here. This justification for denying class-based relief in Title VII suits has been unanimously rejected by the courts of appeals, and Congress ratified that construction by the 1972 Amendments. *Albemarle Paper, supra,* at 414 n. 8.

The second reason stated by the District Court was that such claims "presuppose a vacancy, qualification, and performance by every member. There is no evidence on which to base these multiple conclusions." The Court of Appeals rejected this reason insofar as it was the basis of the District Court's denial of backpay, and of its denial of retroactive seniority relief to the unnamed members of class 4. We hold that it is also an improper reason for denying seniority relief to the unnamed members of class 3.

We read the District Court's reference to the lack of evidence regarding a "vacancy, qualification and performance" for every individual member of the class as an expression of concern that some of the unnamed class members (unhired black applicants whose employment applications were summarized in the record) may not in fact have been actual victims of racial discrimination. That factor will become material however only when those persons apply for OTR positions pursuant to the hiring relief ordered by the District Court. Generalizations concerning such individually applicable evidence cannot serve as a justification for the denial of relief to the entire class. Rather, at such time as individual class members seek positions as OTR drivers, positions for which they are presumptively entitled to priority hiring consideration under the District Court's order,[31] evidence that particular individuals were not in fact victims of racial discrimination will be material. But petitioners here have carried their burden of demonstrating the existence of a discriminatory hiring pattern and practice by the respondents and, therefore, the burden will be upon respondents to prove that individuals who reapply were not in fact victims of previous hiring discrimination. Cf. *McDonnell Douglas Corp. v. Green,* 411 U. S.,

---

[31] The District Court order is silent whether applicants to OTR positions who were previously discriminatorily refused employment must be presently qualified for those positions in order to be eligible for priority hiring under that order. The Court of Appeals, however, made it plain that they must be. 495 F. 2d, at 417. We agree.

at 802; *Baxter v. Savannah Super Refining Corp.,* 495 F.2d 437, 443-444 (CA5), cert. denied, 419 U. S. 1033 (1974).[32] Only if this burden is met may retroactive seniority — if otherwise determined to be an appropriate form of relief under the circumstances of the particular case — be denied individual class members.

Respondent Bowman raises an alternative theory of justification. Bowman argues that an award of retroactive seniority to the class of discriminatees will conflict with the economic interests of other Bowman employees. Accordingly, it is argued, the District Court acted within its discretion in denying this form of relief as an attempt to accommodate the competing interests of the various groups of employees.[33]

We reject this argument for two reasons. First, the District Court made no mention of such considerations in its order denying the seniority relief. As we noted in *Albemarle Paper, supra,* at 421 n. 14, if the District Court declines due to the peculiar circumstances of the particular case to award relief generally appropriate under Title VII, "[i]t is necessary ... that ... it carefully articulate its reasons" for so doing. Second and more fundamentally, it is apparent that denial of seniority relief to identifiable victims of racial discrimination on the sole ground that such relief diminishes the expectations of other, arguably innocent, employees would if applied generally frustrate the central "make-whole" objective of Title VII. These conflicting interests of other employees will of course always be present in instances where some scarce employment benefit is distributed among employees on the basis of their status in the seniority hierarchy. But, as we have said, there is nothing in the language of Title VII, or in its legislative history, to show that Congress intended

---

[32] Thus Bowman may attempt to prove that a given individual member of class 3 was not in fact discriminatorily refused employment as an OTR driver in order to defeat the individual's claim to seniority relief as well as any other remedy ordered for the class generally. Evidence of a lack of vacancies in OTR positions at the time the individual application was filed, or evidence indicating the individual's lack of qualification for the OTR positions — under nondiscriminatory standards *actually applied* by Bowman to individuals who were in fact hired — would of course be relevant. It is true of course that obtaining the third category of evidence with which the District Court was concerned — what the individual discriminatee's job performance would have been but for the discrimination — presents great difficulty. No reason appears, however, why the victim rather than the perpetrator of the illegal act should bear the burden of proof on this issue.

[33] Even by its terms, this argument could apply only to the award of retroactive seniority for purposes of "competitive status" benefits. It has no application to a retroactive award for purposes of "benefit" seniority — extent of vacation leave and pension benefits. Indeed, the decision concerning the propriety of this latter type of seniority relief is analogous, if not identical, to the decision concerning an award of backpay to an individual discriminatee hired pursuant to an order redressing previous employment discrimination.

generally to bar this form of relief to victims of illegal discrimination, and the experience under its remedial model in the National Labor Relations Act points to the contrary. Accordingly, we find untenable the conclusion that this form of relief may be denied merely because the interests of other employees may thereby be affected. "If relief under Title VII can be denied merely because the majority group of employees, who have not suffered discrimination, will be unhappy about it, there will be little hope of correcting the wrongs to which the Act is directed." *United States v. Bethlehem Steel Corp.*, 446 F.2d 652, 663 (CA2 1971).[35]

With reference to the problems of fairness or equity respecting the conflicting interests of the various groups of employees, the relief which petitioners seek is only seniority status retroactive to the date of individual application, rather than some form of arguably more complete relief.[36] No claim is asserted that nondiscriminatee employees holding OTR positions they would not have obtained but for the illegal discrimination should be deprived of the seniority status they have earned. It is therefore clear that even if the seniority relief petitioners seek is awarded, most if not all discriminatees who actually obtain OTR jobs under the court order will not truly be restored to the actual seniority that would have existed in the absence of the illegal discrimination. Rather, most discriminatees even under an award of retroactive seniority status will still remain subordinated in the hierarchy to a position inferior to that of a greater total number of employees than would have been the case in the absence of discrimination. Therefore, the relief which petitioners seek, while a more complete form of relief than that which the District Court accorded, in no sense constitutes "complete relief." Rather, the burden of the past discrimination in hiring is with respect to competitive status benefits divided among discriminatee and nondiscriminatee employees under the form of relief sought. The

---

[35] See also *Volger v. McCarty, Inc.*, 451 F. 2d 1236, 1238-1239 (CA5 1971):

"Adequate protection of Negro rights under Title VII may necessitate, as in the instant case, some adjustment of the rights of white employees. The courts must be free to deal equitably with conflicting interests of white employees in order to shape remedies that will most effectively protect and redress the rights of Negro victims of discrimination."

[36] Another countervailing factor in assessing the expected impact on the interests of other employees actually occasioned by an award of the seniority relief sought is that it is not probable in instances of class-based relief that all of the victims of the past racial discrimination in hiring will actually apply for and obtain the prerequisite hiring relief. Indeed, in the instant case, there appear in the record applications of 166 black applicants who claimed at the time of application to have had the necessary job qualifications. However, the Court was informed at oral argument that only a small number of those individuals have to this date actually been hired pursuant to the District Court's order ("five, six, seven, something in that order") Tr. of Oral Arg., at 23, although ongoing litigation may ultimately determine more who desire the hiring relief and are eligible for it. *Id.*, at 15.

dissent criticizes the Court's result as not sufficiently cognizant that it will "directly implicate the rights and expectations of perfectly innocent employees." *Post,* at —. We are of the view, however, that the result which we reach today — which, standing alone,[38] establishes that a sharing of the burden of the past discrimination is presumptively necessary — is entirely consistent with any fair characterization of equity jurisdiction, particularly when considered in light of our traditional view that "[a]ttainment of a great national policy . . . must not be confined within narrow canons for equitable relief deemed suitable by chancellors in ordinary private controversies." *Phelps Dodge Corp. v. NLRB,* 313 U. S., at 188.

Certainly there is no argument that the award of retroactive seniority to the victims of hiring discrimination in any way deprives other employees of indefeasibly vested rights conferred by the employment contract. This Court has long held that employee expectations arising from a seniority system agreement may be modified by statutes furthering a strong public policy interest. *Tilton v. Missouri Pacific Railroad Co.,* 376 U. S. 169 (1964) (construing §§ 9 (c)(1) and 9 (c)(2) of the Universal Military Training and Service Act of 1948, 50 U. S. C. §§ 459 (c)(1)-(2), which provided that a re-employed returning veteran should enjoy the seniority status he would have acquired but for his absence in military service); *Fishgold v. Sullivan Drydock & Repair Corp.,* 328 U. S. 275 (1946) (construing the comparable provision of the Selective Training and Service Act of 1940). The Court has also held that a collective-bargaining agreement may go further, enhancing the seniority status of certain employees for purposes of furthering public policy interests beyond what is required by statute, even though this will to some extent be detrimental to the expectations acquired by other employees under the previous seniority agreement. *Ford Motor Company v. Huffman,* 345 U. S. 330 (1953). And the ability of the union and employer voluntarily to modify the seniority system to the end of ameliorating the effects of past racial discrimination, a national policy objective

---

[38] In arguing that an award of the seniority relief established as presumptively necessary does nothing to place the burden of the past discrimination on the wrongdoer in most cases — the employer — the dissent of necessity addresses issues not presently before the Court. Further remedial action by the district courts, having the effect of shifting to the employer the burden of the past discrimination in respect to competitive status benefits, raises such issues as the possibility of an injunctive "hold harmless" remedy respecting all affected employees in a layoff situation, Brief of *Amicus Curiae* for Local 862, United Automobile Workers, the possibility of an award of monetary damages (sometimes designated "front pay") in favor of each employee and discriminatee otherwise bearing some of the burden of the past discrimination, *ibid.;* Brief for the United States and the Equal Employment Opportunity Commission as *Amici Curiae,* and the propriety of such further remedial action in instances wherein the union has been adjudged a participant in the illegal conduct. Such issues are not presented by the record before us, and we intimate no view regarding them.

of the "highest priority," is certainly no less than in other areas of public policy interests. . . .

V

In holding that class-based seniority relief for identifiable victims of illegal hiring discrimination is a form of relief generally appropriate under § 706(g), we do not in any way modify our previously expressed view that the statutory scheme of Title VII "implicitly recognizes that there may be cases calling for one remedy but not another, and — owing to the structure of the federal judiciary — these choices are of course left in the first instance to the district courts." *Albemarle Paper, supra,* at 416. Circumstances peculiar to the individual case may of course justify the modification or withholding of seniority relief for reasons that would not if applied generally undermine the purposes of Title VII.[41] In the instant case it appears that all new hirees establish seniority only upon completion of a 45-day probationary period, although upon completion seniority is retroactive to the date of hire. Certainly any seniority relief ultimately awarded by the district court could properly be cognizant of this fact. Amici and the respondent union point out that there may be circumstances where an award of full seniority should be deferred until completion of a training or apprenticeship program, or other preliminaries required of all new hirees. We do not undertake to delineate all such possible circumstances here. Any enumeration must await particular cases and be determined in light of the trial courts' "keen appreciation" of peculiar facts and circumstances. *Albemarle Paper, supra,* at 421-422.

Accordingly, the judgment of the Court of Appeals affirming the District Court's denial of seniority relief to class 3 is reversed, and the case remanded to the District Court for further proceedings consistent with this opinion.

It is so ordered.

MR. JUSTICE STEVENS took no part in the consideration or decision of this case.

---

[41] Accordingly, to no "significant extent" do we "[strip] the district courts of [their] equitable powers." *Post,* at —. Rather our holding is that in exercising their equitable powers, district courts should take as their starting point the presumption in favor of rightful place seniority relief, and proceed with further legal analysis from that point; and that such relief may not be denied on the abstract basis of adverse impact upon interests of other employees but rather only on the basis of unusual adverse impact arising from facts and circumstances that would not be generally found in Title VII cases. To hold otherwise would be to shield "inconsisten[t] and capri[cious]" denial of such relief from "thorough appellate review." *Albemarle Paper,* 422 U. S., at 416, 421.

MR. CHIEF JUSTICE BURGER, concurring in part and dissenting in part.

I concur in the judgment in part and generally with MR. JUSTICE POWELL, but I would stress that although retroactive benefit-type seniority relief may sometimes be appropriate and equitable, competitive-type seniority relief at the expense of wholly innocent employees can rarely, if ever, be equitable if that term retains traditional meaning. More equitable would be a monetary award to the person suffering the discrimination. An award such as "front pay" could replace the need for competitive-type seniority relief. . . . Such monetary relief would serve the dual purpose of deterring the wrongdoing employer or union — or both — as well as protecting the rights of innocent employees. In every respect an innocent employee is comparable to a "holder-in-due-course" of negotiable paper or a bona fide purchaser of property without notice of any defect in the seller's title. In this setting I cannot join in judicial approval of "robbing Peter to pay Paul."

I would stress that the Court today does not foreclose claims of employees who might be injured by this holding from petitioning the District Court for equitable relief on their own behalf.

MR. JUSTICE POWELL, with whom MR. JUSTICE REHNQUIST joins, concurring in part and dissenting in part.

I agree that this controversy is not moot. . . .

I also agree with Part II of the opinion insofar as it determines the "thrust" of § 703(h) of Title VII to be the insulation of an otherwise bona fide seniority system from a challenge that it amounts to a discriminatory practice because it perpetuates the effects of pre-Act discrimination. . . . Therefore, I concur in the precise holding of Part II, which is that the Court of Appeals erred in interpreting § 703(h) as a bar, in every instance, to the award of retroactive seniority relief to persons discriminatorily refused employment after the effective date of Title VII.

Although I am in accord with much of the Court's discussion in Parts III and IV, I cannot accept as correct its basic interpretation of § 706(g) as virtually requiring a district court, in determining appropriate equitable relief in a case of this kind, to ignore entirely the equities that may exist in favor of innocent employees. Its holding recognizes no meaningful distinction, in terms of the equitable relief to be granted, between "benefit"-type seniority and "competitive"-type seniority. The Court reaches this result by taking an absolutist view of the "make-whole" objective of Title VII, while rendering largely meaningless the discretionary authority vested in district courts by § 706(g) to weigh the equities of the situation. Accordingly, I dissent from Parts III and IV.

. . . .

It is true, of course, that the retroactive grant of competitive-type seniority does go a step further in "making whole" the discrimination victim, and therefore arguably furthers one of the objectives of Title VII. But apart from extending the make-whole concept to its outer limits, there is no similarity between this drastic relief and the granting of backpay and benefit-type seniority. First, a retroactive grant of competitive-type seniority usually does not directly affect the employer at all. It causes only a rearrangement of employees along the seniority ladder without any resulting increase in cost. Thus, Title VII's "primary objective" of eradicating discrimination is not served at all, for the employer is not deterred from the practice.

The second, and in my view controlling, distinction between these types of relief is the impact on other workers. As noted above, the granting of backpay and of benefit-type seniority furthers the prophylactic and make-whole objectives of the statute without penalizing other workers. But competitive seniority benefits, as the term implies, directly implicate the rights and expectations of perfectly innocent employees. The economic benefits awarded discrimination victims would be derived not at the expense of the employer but at the expense of other workers. Putting it differently, those disadvantaged — sometimes to the extent of losing their jobs entirely — are not the wrongdoers who have no claim to the Chancellor's conscience, but rather are innocent third parties.

. . . .

The decision whether to grant competitive-type seniority relief therefore requires a district court to consider and weigh competing equities. In any proper exercise of the balancing process, a court must consider both the claims of the discrimination victims and the claims of incumbent employees who, if competitive seniority rights are awarded retroactively to others, will lose economic advantages earned through satisfactory and often long service. If, as the Court today holds, the district court may not weigh these equities much of the language of § 706(e) is rendered meaningless. We cannot assume that Congress intended either that the statutory language be ignored or that the earned benefits of incumbent employees be wiped out by a presumption created by this Court.

. . . .

JERSEY CENTRAL POWER & LIGHT CO. v. IBEW LOCALS 327

United States Court of Appeals, Third Circuit
508 F.2d 687 (1975)

GARTH, Circuit Judge:

This case presents to us, in an unusual procedural context, the difficult question of determining which of two allegedly conflicting contracts is to dictate the plaintiff employer's course of conduct. We must resolve whether in reducing a company's work force an employer is obligated to adhere to collective bargaining agreement provisions requiring layoffs in reverse order of seniority, or whether the employer is obligated to implement the provisions of a conciliation agreement made with the Equal Employment Opportunity Commission (EEOC) to retain among its employees a larger proportion of minority group and female workers. It is agreed among the parties that layoffs in reverse order of seniority will have a disproportionate effect upon minority group and female workers, as they are the most recently hired employees. Despite this consequence, we reverse the judgment of the district court and hold that the provisions of the collective bargaining agreements must govern in this procedural context.

I.A. Procedural History

On July 18, 1974, Jersey Central Power & Light Company ("Company"), the employer, brought the instant action pursuant to 28 U.S.C. §§ 2201, 2202 in the District Court for the District of New Jersey. The Company sought a judgment declaring its rights and obligations under: (1) a collective bargaining agreement between the Company and the Unions, and (2) a conciliation agreement among the EEOC, the Company and the Unions. Named as defendants in the action for declaratory judgment were the Unions, the EEOC, the United States Office of Federal Contract Compliance (OFCC), the United States General Services Administration (GSA) and the New Jersey Division of Civil Rights. The Company presented itself in this litigation as a "neutral" party, taking no position as to which of the two contracts must govern the manner by which a substantial cutback in employment would be effectuated. In this posture, the Company sought guidance from the district court, asserting that economic circumstances required it to lay off substantial numbers of employees. The Company alleged that it could not determine the specific individuals to be affected until the court declared which of the two agreements was to govern the layoff procedure. . . .

The district court denied the motion to dismiss brought by GSA and OFCC and granted partial summary judgment, requiring the Company to lay off employees in a manner inconsistent with the collective bargaining agreement to avoid a reduction in the percentage of females and minority group members in the work force. As such, the district court rejected the Unions' contentions that the collective bargaining provisions (layoff by reverse order of seniority) were to control without modification. . . .

I.B. Facts

The Company is a large public utility operating in New Jersey and engaged in the generation and distribution of electrical power throughout approximately half of that State. As of June 29, 1974, the Company employed 3,859 employees, of whom 2,877 were in the bargaining units represented by the Unions involved in the instant proceeding.

In January 28, 1972, a charge had been filed with the EEOC alleging that the Company and the Unions unlawfully discriminated against women and "minority group persons," in violation of Title VII of the Civil Rights Act of 1964. The EEOC investigated the charge and found reasonable cause to believe that the Company discriminated against minority group persons and females with respect to hiring and job assignments. Thereafter a conciliation agreement was entered into among the Company, EEOC, and the Unions. The conciliation agreement was signed in January, 1974, to be effective from December 3, 1973 through December 3, 1977. The agreement was divided into several sections. Section I — "General Provisions" — provides, *inter alia:*

1. It is understood that this Agreement does not constitute an admission by the Respondents of any violation of Title VII of the Civil Rights Act of 1964, as amended.

2. . . . .

3. The Commission agrees not to sue the Respondents over matters contained in this Agreement subject to Respondent's compliance with the promises and representations contained herein. If the Commission believes that this Agreement has been violated, it shall first attempt to resolve the dispute with the parties; then if no Agreement can be reached, the Commission can seek to enforce this Agreement through the legal process.

4. This waiver by the Commission extends to any matter which is covered by this Agreement. This does not preclude individual Charging Parties, or the Commission itself, from filing charges or suit over new matters or practices which may arise with respect to practices of the Respondents.

5. Respondents agree that all hiring and promotion practices, and any and all other conditions of employment shall be maintained and conducted in a manner which does not discriminate on the basis of race, color, creed, ancestry, religion, sex, national origin, age, place of birth, marital status or liability for services in the armed forces of the United States in violation of Title VII of the Civil Rights Act of 1964, as amended.

Section III of the conciliation agreement ("Recruitment and Hiring Practices") Paragraph 9, obligates the Company to make reasonable efforts to "recruit minorities and females into those craft areas where such jobs are to be filled by new hires, where they have heretofore been under utilized or not employed." Paragraph 10 provides that the minority group persons and female recruits for craft jobs are to be given credit for experience gained in the craft with other employers and may be considered for jobs other than those at the entry level. Paragraph 10 concludes that:

The wages, benefits, other conditions of employment and seniority date of such employee shall be determined in accordance with the provisions of the Collective Bargaining Agreement.

Section IV of the conciliation agreement is entitled "Promotion and Transfer" and establishes a special program for female and minority group Company employees who are to be given preference for promotions and transfers into vacant positions on the basis of their company seniority. Paragraph 2 specifically provides: "For purposes of this Conciliation Agreement vacancies occasioned by layoff . . . shall not be considered as vacancies."

Section V ("Affirmative Action") establishes a five year affirmative action program designed to increase the percentage of minority group and female employees.[18] Among other provisions, the agreement also provides for reporting (Section IX), a modification of the maternity leave policy (Section VI) and certain payments by the Company to employees and others for past discriminatory practices. (Section VII).

The conciliation agreement has no express seniority provision nor does it expressly modify or alter the seniority provisions found in the collective bargaining agreement. Rather, a fair reading of the conciliation agreement reveals that it is primarily concerned with the hiring, promotion and transfer of female and minority group employees.

On December 3, 1973, prior to the execution of the conciliation agreement by the Company, the Unions and EEOC, the Company

---

[18] The percentages to be attained by December 1977, the end of the five year affirmative action plan, and the hiring rate necessary to achieve those percentage goals, are set forth in the conciliation agreement:

	Min %	Hiring Rate %	Fem. %	Hiring Rate %
Officials & Managers	3.0	5.0	5.0	8.0
Professionals	5.0	8.0	5.0	8.0
Technicians	6.0	9.0	3.0	5.0
Sales	3.0	5.0	13.0	20.0
Office Clerical	9.0	14.0	46.0	70.0
Skilled	8.0	12.0	1.0	2.0
Semi-Skilled	19.0	28.0	3.0	5.0
Laborer-Unskilled	24.0	36.0	3.0	5.0
Service Workers	21.0	32.0	31.0	46.0

(Section V, Par. 1).

The primary obligation for achieving these percentages among employees is on the Company, as it, and not the Union, is solely responsible for hiring. . . .

and the Unions entered into a new collective bargaining agreement effective from November 1, 1973 through October 31, 1975. In pertinent part the collective bargaining agreement continues the seniority policies in operation among the bargaining unit employees of the Company. In regard to layoffs, the collective bargaining agreement provides *inter alia:*

. . . .

3.2(a) All layoffs, or demotions occasioned because of falling off or curtailment of work, shall be discussed with the Union two (2) weeks in advance of the layoff and shall be made in order of seniority. No senior employee shall be laid off as long as any work which he can reasonably be expected to do is being performed by an employee junior in point of service.

. . . .

3.3. Employees who have been laid off shall be reinstated to employment as need for their services arises, in the reverse order of their layoff.

3.4. Seniority is defined as length of continuous service with the Company. . . .

These provisions establish a plantwide seniority system for employees with respect to layoffs.

The Company in its pleadings asserts that economic considerations compelled it to announce a layoff of employees in July, 1974. The Company estimates that approximately 400 employees will have been laid off by mid-December, 1974. The Unions required strict adherence by the Company to the seniority provisions of the collective bargaining agreement. The EEOC responded to the Company's layoff plans by indicating that a layoff accomplished by seniority alone would violate the provisions of the conciliation agreement and Title VII of the Civil Rights Act of 1964.

Confronted with two apparently conflicting contracts, the Company instituted this action for declaratory judgment. At about the same time, the Company and the Unions submitted to an expedited arbitration proceeding under their collective bargaining agreement to determine if a layoff of employees in reverse order of seniority would violate the nondiscrimination provision of the collective bargaining agreement. On August 21, 1974, the arbitrator held that a layoff in accordance with the seniority provisions of the collective bargaining agreement would not violate the non-discrimination provision of the same document.

In accordance with the arbitrator's award, on August 23, 1974, the Company commenced the layoff in reverse order of seniority. Layoffs in this manner continued until September 5, 1974 when the district court issued its opinion which, as previously noted, required accommodation with the conciliation agreement.

After the first week of layoffs, statistics provided by the Company indicated that the layoffs had a disproportionate impact upon minority group employment. As of August 30, 1974, one hundred seventy-six (176) employees were identified for layoff or termination, of which 30.7% or 54, were male or female minority group persons. As a result of this first group of *bargaining unit* employees being laid off, the percentage of male and female minority group employees in the *bargaining unit* decreased from 7.9% on July 27, 1974 to 6.4% as of August 30, 1974. With respect to female employees only, however, the initial layoff had no disparate impact. Both before and after the layoff, women constituted 14.6% of the total workforce and 15.2% of the bargaining unit.

Subsequent to the district court's opinion announced on September 5, 1974, the Company began to program the remainder of its layoffs to comply with the district court's directive that the female and minority group employee ratios existing as of July 27, 1974 be maintained throughout the layoff process. The Company continued layoffs pursuant to the district court's directive until October 9, 1974, at which time this Court granted a motion to stay the order of the district court. Since October 9, 1974 the Company has reverted to laying off employees solely by reverse order of seniority. . . .

III. Contract Theory

The district court, viewing the instant proceeding as one requiring the interpretation of contracts only, specifically refused to consider the issue of past employment practices of either the Company or the Unions. Although we agree with the district court that the instant controversy must be analyzed according to the principles of general contract law, see United States v. Seckinger, 397 U.S. at 210; Priebe & Sons, Inc. v. United States, 332 U.S. 407, 411 (1947), we must nevertheless differ with that court's interpretations of the two contracts and, as such, with its issuance of the judgment predicated upon those interpretations.

In interpreting the two contracts before us, we must: first, determine whether or not an express or implied conflict exists as between the provisions of the conciliation agreement and the provisions of the collective bargaining agreement, and, if such a conflict does exist, which of the two contracts is to govern; second, if no such conflict is held to exist, determine if the collective bargaining agreement must nevertheless be modified to accommodate an overriding public policy. The district court followed a similar approach concluding (1) that to the extent that the conciliation agreement conflicts with the collective bargaining agreement, the conciliation agreement prevails; and (2) that the layoffs are not to be accomplished in the manner prescribed by seniority clauses of the collective bargaining agreement, because such a method of layoffs would "frustrate" the objective of the conciliation agreement. We hold both conclusions of the district court to be erroneous as a matter of law.

A. The Two Contracts Do Not Conflict.

In our interpretation of both contracts we are governed solely by federal law. After comparing and contrasting the provisions of the two contracts, we are of the view that no conflict exists with respect to layoffs.

The conciliation agreement has, as its objective, the percentage increase of females and minority group persons among employees. This objective was to be attained by the Company *hiring* a greater percentage of minority group and female workers — not by resort to a system of "artificial" seniority. As such the conciliation agreement sought an increase in the proportion of female and minority group workers by "hires" and not by "fires." It is highly significant to us that the conciliation agreement contains no overall layoff procedures or seniority system. Moreover, the express terms of the conciliation agreement do not attempt to affect, nor can we interpret them to affect, the layoff provisions of the collective bargaining agreement.

The "new hire" method of attaining a higher proportion of female and minority group workers is evident throughout the conciliation agreement. In particular, reference to "new hires" is made in Section III, paragraph 9 of the conciliation agreement, which provides:

Respondent Company shall make a reasonable effort to recruit minorities and females into those craft areas where such jobs are to be filled by new hires, where they have heretofore been underutilized or not employed. To this end, Respondent Company agrees that in *each instance where a job is not to be filled from within, pursuant to the Collective Bargaining Agreement and practices thereunder, reasonable efforts will be made to secure a minority or female as outlined in paragraph 1 of the Affirmative Action portion* of this Agreement. (Emphasis supplied).

Paragraph 1 of the Affirmative Action program, in turn, is confined solely to "new hire" situations:

Respondent Company is presently undergoing its utilization analysis for preparation of its goals and time tables. *The Company agrees to make every reasonable effort to bring its minority and female workforce up to parity by location and EEO-1 categories as openings for new hires occur* and qualified applicants are available within five (5) years. (Emphasis supplied).

We regard the conciliation agreement as unambiguous in its requirements that an increased proportion of females and minority group persons *be hired,* but that *once hired,* workers in these classes be controlled by the terms and conditions of employment as set forth in the collective bargaining agreement. Accordingly, we read the conciliation agreement as not modifying the promotion, transfer or layoff practices established by the collective bargaining agreement once females and minority group persons have been employed. We base this interpretation, in part, on two provisions of the conciliation agreement. As previously noted, in regard to recruitment and hiring practices, section III, paragraph 10, provides:

The wages, benefits, *other conditions of employment and seniority date of such employee* shall be determined in accordance with the provisions of the Collective Bargaining Agreement. (Emphasis supplied).

Moreover, in the context of promotions and transfer practices, section IV, paragraph 2, in pertinent part provides:

"[T]hose male minorities/females who are qualified and who had indicated the desire to transfer shall be given the opportunity to transfer, *using their total length of Company service,* subject to vacancies being available and in a *manner consistent with the current Collective Bargaining Agreement. For purposes of this Conciliation Agreement vacancies occasioned by layoff . . . shall not be considered as vacancies.* (Emphasis supplied).

We thus interpret the conciliation agreement as being consistent with rather than in conflict with the collective bargaining agreement, in that it incorporates the Company seniority system.

EEOC alternatively argues that if not an express, at least an implicit inconsistency exists between the two agreements and that this inconsistency requires a modification of the seniority provisions of the collective bargaining agreement. For EEOC's argument to succeed, it must persuade us that despite the silence of the conciliation agreement respecting overall seniority, we should nonetheless interpret the two contracts as being inconsistent.

First, EEOC contends that where the subject matter is the same in two contracts but the contracts contain terms inconsistent with each other, the later agreement will supersede the earlier agreement. Second, EEOC contends that the Company's agreement to use "best efforts" to have its work force reflect the racial, ethnic and sex composition in the relevant labor market should be given effect as an implicit modification of the seniority provisions. Third, EEOC argues that the objectives of the conciliation agreement (to increase the proportion of female and minority group workers) will be thwarted if effect is given to the seniority provisions of the collective bargaining agreement.

We cannot agree with EEOC's arguments. First, whether or not a subsequent contract is deemed to supersede an earlier contract is a question of the parties' intent to be ascertained from the contracts themselves when they are unambiguous. In order for us to hold that the parties intended the second agreement (here the conciliation agreement) to operate as a substituted contract, the terms of the second contract must be so inconsistent with those of the first that both contracts cannot stand together. Here, we can discern no such intent as the conciliation agreement is completely silent on the issue of overall seniority. Hence, despite its later execution we find no inconsistency, apparent or otherwise, between the two contracts. Accordingly, there is no basis to preclude our sustaining both contracts in full. . . .

Second, the conciliation agreement, section II (Recruitment and Hiring Practices) and V (Affirmative Action Program), requires the Company to use "best efforts" to increase the percentage of female and minority group employees. We do not believe that this undertaking by the Company necessarily modifies by implication a seniority system of layoffs. We interpret the "best efforts" commitment in a context that requires the Company to use its "best efforts" to increase the female and minority group proportion among employees as openings for *new hires* arise. This is completely consistent with the express terms of the conciliation agreement (see infra). Third, with respect to the objective which EEOC claims is defeated if effect is given to the collective bargaining agreement, we believe EEOC has only partially stated the objective of that agreement. As our analysis reveals, the true objective of the conciliation agreement is to increase the percentage of female and minority group employees through "new hires" only. The express language of the conciliation agreement so provides:

"The Company agrees to make every reasonable effort to bring its minority and female work force up to parity . . . as openings for new hires occur and qualified applicants are available within five (5) years."

Section V, paragraph 1. We thus do not agree with EEOC or with the district court that layoffs by reverse order of seniority would unlawfully frustrate this objective.

Hence, we conclude that the two agreements are not in conflict either by their express terms or by implication. We are obliged, nonetheless, to proceed to the question of whether an overriding public policy dictates a modification of the collective bargaining agreement.

B. Public Policy

The district court emphasized that the principal purpose of the conciliation agreement between the Company, the Unions and EEOC was to ensure that at the end of five years the proportion of females and minority group employees would approximate the proportion of those groups in the relevant labor market. The primary basis for the district court's modification of the collective bargaining agreement was the district court's conclusion that insistence on layoff solely according to the collective bargaining agreement would frustrate the purposes of the conciliation agreement.

As our analysis indicates, the district court's conclusion in this respect is without merit. Consequently, we now believe the appropriate inquiry is whether a seniority clause providing for layoffs by reverse order of seniority *must* be modified as being contrary to public policy and welfare. Cf. Restatement, Contracts, § 369, at 671 (1932).

In order to declare the provisions of the collective bargaining agreement (entered into by the parties freely and without evidence of fraud) void as against public policy, the contract terms must be invalid on the basis of clear and distinct legal principles. . . .

Title VII of the Civil Rights Act of 1964 provides Congress' formulation of public policy. Cf. Twin City Pipe Line Co. v. Harding Glass Co., 283 U.S. 353, 357 (1931). By Title VII, Congress in the context of employment discrimination supplanted with its own views any judicial determination of public policy. . . .

Our reading of Title VII reveals no statutory proscription of plant-wide seniority systems. To the contrary, Title VII authorizes the use of "bona fide" seniority systems:

Notwithstanding any other provision of this subchapter, it shall not be an unlawful employment practice for an employer to apply different standards of compensation, or different terms, conditions or privileges of employment pursuant to a bona fide seniority or merit system. . . .

42 U.S.C. § 2000e-2(h). Moreover, we can discern no ". . . definite indications . . . to justify the invalidation of [such] a contract as contrary to that [public] policy." Muschany [v. United States] 324 U.S. [49] at 66. While the legislative history of Title VII is largely uninstructive with respect to seniority rights, it is evident to us that Congress did not intend that a *per se* violation of the Act occur whenever females and minority group persons are disadvantaged by reverse seniority layoffs. . . .

Accordingly, we hold that a seniority clause providing for layoffs by reverse order of seniority is not contrary to public policy and welfare and consequently is not subject to modification by court decree.

IV. Evidentiary Considerations

To this point we have concluded that: (1) the seniority provisions of the Company's collective bargaining agreement are not inconsistent with any provision of the conciliation agreement; and (2) the seniority provisions do not offend public policy.

There remains for our consideration the effect that *evidence* of discrimination may have upon laying off workers in reverse order of seniority. We turn to evidentiary considerations at this juncture because: (1) evidence appears in the record indicating disparate impact on the employment of female and minority group workers, cf. Western Addition Community Org. v. N.L.R.B., 485 F.2d 917 (D.C. Cir. 1973), *cert. granted,* 415 U.S. 912 (1974); and (2) we are obliged to furnish directions to the district court with respect to evidence, if any, it may receive concerning those issues which remain for resolution.

Consequently we must answer the following questions: (1) what evidence, if any, may be adduced in the district court; (2) to what issue is such evidence to be directed? Depending upon the answers to the preceding questions, the ultimate question in this proceeding becomes: assuming, *arguendo,* evidence of past discrimination, is judicial modification permitted of facially neutral plant-wide seniority provisions where these provisions operate to the disadvantage of female and minority group workers?

We are not concerned here with allegations or proof that the Company's plant-wide seniority system is by its express terms and intent presently discriminatory. Nor are we concerned with any charges or proofs that this plant-wide seniority system, which is facially neutral, was intended and designed to disguise present discriminatory practices. The only challenge to the validity of the Company's plant-wide seniority system is that the seniority system, although facially neutral, nevertheless violates Title VII in that it operates to carry forward the effect of prior acts of discrimination. If evidence were to be permitted in support of such a theory, . . . it could, at best, demonstrate that past discrimination occurred, and that the effects of such past discrimination are perpetuated by the present layoff practices under the current plant-wide seniority system. As we explain below, proofs of this nature are without probative value in challenging a bona fide seniority system. We believe that Congress intended to bar proof of the "perpetuating" effect of a plant-wide seniority system as it regarded such systems as "bona fide." Congress, while recognizing that a bona fide seniority system might well perpetuate past discriminatory practices, nevertheless chose between upsetting all collective bargaining agreements with such provisions and permitting them despite the perpetuating effect that they might have. We believe that Congress intended a plant-wide seniority system, facially neutral but having a disproportionate impact on female and minority group workers, to be a bona fide seniority sytem within the meaning of § 703(h) of the Act.

To effectuate this intent, the only evidence probative in a challenge to a plant-wide seniority system would be evidence directed to its bona fide character; that is, evidence directed either to the neutrality of the seniority system or evidence directed to ascertaining an intent or design to disguise discrimination. As such, it is not fatal that the seniority system continues the effect of past employment discrimination. We believe this result was recognized and left undisturbed by Congress in its enactment of § 703 (h) and (j). Although the Congressional statements which we set out were made prior to the adoption of the Act in its final form and therefore were not addressed to the explicit language of § 703(h), these statements nonetheless were directed to the effect of seniority systems with which § 703(h) is concerned. As such, we believe they are of primary assistance in interpreting congressional intent as to seniority systems.

The Interpretive Memorandum of Senators Clark and Case, floor managers for the Title VII bill in the Senate, in pertinent part provided:

Title VII would have no effect on established seniority rights. Its effect is prospective and not retrospective. Thus, for example, if a business has been discriminating in the past and as a result has an all-white working force, when the title comes into effect the employer's obligation would be simply to fill future vacancies on a nondiscriminatory basis. He would not be obliged — or indeed, permitted — to fire whites in order to hire Negroes, or to prefer Negroes for future vacancies, or, once Negroes were hired, to give them *special seniority rights at the expense of the white workers hired earlier.* (However, where waiting lists for employment or training are, prior to the effective date of this title, maintained on a discriminatory basis, the use of such lists after the title takes effect may be held an unlawful subterfuge to accomplish discrimination.) (Emphasis supplied).

110 Cong. Rec. 7213 (April 8, 1964) . . .

Our interpretation of the legislative history of Title VII (i.e., that Congress did not intend the chaotic consequences that would result from declaring unlawful all seniority systems which may disadvantage females and minority group persons, *see, e.g.,* United States v. Jacksonville Terminal Co., 451 F.2d at 445) has been adopted by other courts as well. The Fifth and Seventh Circuits agree with our view of the legislative history even though they considered this question in the more traditional procedural context of a Title VII proceeding. In Waters v. Wisconsin Steel Works, 502 F.2d 1309 (7th Cir. 1974), the Seventh Circuit stated:

An employment seniority system embodying the "last hired, first fired" principle does not of itself perpetuate past discrimination. To hold otherwise would be tantamount to shackling white employees with a burden of a past discrimination created not by them but by their employer. Title VII was not designed to nurture such reverse

discriminatory preferences. Griggs v. Duke Power Co., 401 U.S. 424, 430-31 (1971).
502 F.2d at 1320. . . .

We thus conclude in light of the legislative history that on balance a facially neutral company-wide seniority system, *without more,* is a bona fide seniority system and will be sustained even though it may operate to the disadvantage of females and minority group as a result of past employment practices. If a remedy is to be provided alleviating the effects of past discrimination perpetuated by layoffs in reverse order of seniority, we believe such remedy must be prescribed by the legislature and not by judicial decree.

Having reached this conclusion our analysis is complete. Here, with the meager record before us and considering the manner in which the issues are framed, we need not, and indeed could not, decide whether any different result would obtain in an action brought by an aggrieved party were the requisite burden of proof sustained. . . . What we decide here can obviously affect and bind only the parties present in this litigation. Of the parties before us, none has offered evidence to prove that the seniority provisions are not bona fide.

Having ascertained no basis in the record, or as a matter of law, to sustain the partial summary judgment order of September 23, 1974 as it pertains to the subject of layoffs, we will remand to the district court with directions: (1) to vacate so much of the September 23, 1974 order as is inconsistent with this opinion; and (2) to conduct such further proceedings not inconsistent with this opinion as may thereafter be required.

Each party will bear its own costs.

VAN DUSEN, CIRCUIT JUDGE, concurring:
While concurring in the judgment of the court, I respectfully am unable to agree with the majority's view of (1) the effect of public policy behind Title VII, and (2) the legislative history of that title. . . . Because this case is being remanded and past discrimination may be found on an amplified record in this or a related case, I will state my views briefly. . . .

The importance of this policy [underlying Title VII] has prompted courts to require that labor agreements of various types be modified to effect the ends of Title VII. . . . These modifications were ordered even though the seniority provisions were "neutral on their face, and even neutral in terms of intent," where the effect was "to 'freeze' the status quo of prior discriminatory employment practices." Griggs v. Duke Power Co., 401 U.S. 424, 430 (1971). See also Robinson v. Lorillard, 444 F.2d 791, 796-97 (4th Cir. 1971). The objective criterion of intent and the rationale of these cases apply equally to plant-wide seniority systems where the plant formerly hired on a "whites only" basis. "If the seniority practices struck down . . . were not 'bona fide' within the meaning of section 703(h), because they discriminated on grounds of race, and if former exclusionary practices in those cases established that the present differences in treatment of whites and blacks were the result of 'an intention to discriminate' within the meaning of section 703(h), then, for the identical reasons, section 703(h) does not violate seniority practices in formerly white only plants." Cooper & Sobol, Seniority and Testing Under Fair Employment Law: A General Approach to Objective Criteria of Hiring and Promotion, 82 Harv. L. Rev. 1598, 1629 (1969) (footnotes omitted). It is true that certain cases have indicated that plant-wide seniority systems would be treated differently from job or departmental seniority. Waters v. Wisconsin Steel Works, 502 F.2d 1309, 1318-20 (7th Cir. 1974); Local 189, United Papermakers v. United States, 416 F.2d 980, 994-95 (5th Cir. 1969), *cert. denied*, 397 U.S. 919 (1970). However, the basis for such discrimination has been the court's view of the legislative history of the Act, rather than any conclusion that the principles which required modification of other seniority practices did not apply to plant seniority. I disagree with the interpretation of the legislative history expressed in *Waters* and *Local 189*, as well as by the majority. . . .

I find persuasive the writers who contend that the legislative history indicates that Congress, in enacting Title VII, did not intend to preclude remedies altering plant seniority which perpetuates discrimination. See Watkins v. U.S.W.A., 369 F. Supp. 1221, 1227-29 (E.D. La. 1974), app. pending; Cooper & Sobol, *supra;* Comment, The Inevitable Interplay of Title VII and the National Labor Relations Act: A New Role For the NLRB, 123 U. Pa. L. Rev. 158, 163-64 (1974). But see Note, Business Necessity Under Title VII of the Civil Rights Act of 1964: A No-Alternative Approach, 84 Yale L. J. 98, 100-01 n. 17 (1974).

For these reasons, I disagree with the majority's conclusion . . . that no relief could be forthcoming to an aggrieved party who established that a plant-wide seniority system embodied in the collective bargaining agreement perpetuated past discrimination without providing a subjective discriminatory intent.

NOTES:

(1) The Supreme Court vacated the judgment in the *Jersey Central* case and remanded the case to the Court of Appeals for the Third Circuit for further consideration in light of *Franks v. Bowman Transp. Co., Inc., supra.*

Upon further consideration, the Third Circuit said, 542 F.2d 8 (1976):

Having considered the Supreme Court order, its opinion in Franks v. Bowman, 424 U. S. 727, the . . . briefs and the record, we conclude that parts I—III-A of our 1975 opinion are not inconsistent with the Franks decision. Portions of the balance of our opinion, however, are not in full accord with Franks, which requires that those identifiable individuals who were deprived of job tenure because of Title VII proscribed discrimination must be afforded such "make-whole" relief as the District Court in its discretion deems necessary. In Franks, this mandated their being granted the seniority that would have been theirs had they not suffered discrimination. On the present record, however, no victimized employees—identified or otherwise—are before us.[3]

In Part IV of this Court's Jersey Central opinion, 508 F.2d at 705-10, we construed § 703(h) of Title VII as sanctioning *all* bona fide plant-wide seniority systems. The Supreme Court in Franks, however, chose a more restrictive interpretation. The Court held that § 703(h) is no bar to a claim raised by actual victims of post-Title VII (post-1965) discrimination for retroactive or constructive seniority.

Our previous directive requiring the district court to make findings as to the bona fides of the seniority system remains appropriate. Although the Court in Franks could prohibit layoffs of those employees who, because of discrimination, lack the seniority that would protect them, there is no proof of actual discrimination in the Jersey Central record and we do not know whether there actually are victims of discrimination who could avail themselves of relief such as the constructive seniority authorized by the Franks opinion.[4] In any event, proof of discrimination would be more appropriately presented in a proceeding where the alleged discriminatees, if any, are parties.[5]

---

[3] As the EEOC emphasizes, it had not "received a charge, investigated it, or attempted conciliation." Brief for Appellee EEOC on remand at 26.

[4] We note that footnote 6 on page 14 of the Jersey Central Power & Light brief, filed July 16, states:

An individual not covered by the conciliation agreement is obviously not barred by that agreement from initiating a Title VII procedure, but at the time of settlement all known potential claimants identified by the EEOC were considered and dispositions were made as to them.

[5] Given the peculiar procedural posture of this case, see our earlier opinion 508 F.2d at 691-94, 9 FEP Cases 118-120, we emphasize that in an appropriate case no actual victims of post-1965 discrimination will be precluded from seeking Franks-authorized relief by the district court's resolution of the issues here presented. Other than as may be stated herein, we express no views on any of the issues raised by the parties in their briefs on remand, leaving resolution of those issues to the district court in the first instance.

The judgment of the district court will be vacated and the case remanded to that court for further consideration in light of Franks v. Bowman Transportation Co., Inc., *supra,* and the foregoing opinion.

(2) A court of appeals has ruled that it is improper to "bump" incumbent white employees with less company seniority in an effort to remedy past effects of a discriminatory departmental seniority system. However, the court did award "front pay" which provides discriminatees with a modified compensatory sum until they are placed in their rightful place. In refusing to allow bumping, the court explained: "A primary goal of Title VII is to induce voluntary compliance by employers and unions. . . . Demoting employees, especially those who are not responsible for wrongdoing, undoubtedly would encounter more resistance than deferring their future expectancies." The court feared the domino effect could adversely affect not only those who have done no wrong but also those who may have been the victims of discrimination. *Patterson v. American Tobacco Co.,* 12 FEP Cas. 314 (4th Cir. 1976).

(3) Finding a history of discrimination in the promotion of foremen, the court in *United States v. N. L. Industries, Inc.,* 479 F.2d 354 (8th Cir. 1973), ordered a one-Black-to-one-White hiring ratio until fifteen Blacks (out of one hundred positions) were promoted. However, the court rejected a government request for a recruiting campaign designed to effect a goal of one-third Black hires into office, clerical, and technical positions notwithstanding that there was a history of discrimination in that area. Similarly, in *EEOC v. Detroit Edison Co.,* 515 F.2d 301 (6th Cir. 1975), the court upheld the use of hiring ratios where the district court had found a long history of discrimination against Black job applicants and employees by both the company and the unions involved.

(4) In *Rios v. Steamfitters Local 638,* 501 F.2d 622 (2d Cir. 1974), the Second Circuit held that a remedy embodying an affirmative action program by a union was not prohibited under § 703(j) of Title VII or the equal protection clause of the Federal Constitution. Section 703(j) was only intended to prohibit preferential quota hiring as a means of changing a racial imbalance attributable to causes other than unlawful discrimination. *See also Patterson v. Newspaper Deliverers' Union,* 514 F.2d 767 (2d Cir. 1975), *cert. denied,* 427 U.S. 911.

But compare Cramer v. Virginia Commonwealth Univ., 415 F. Supp. 673 (E.D. Va. 1976), where the court held that a state university which considered and hired only female applicants for a teaching position violated both the Equal Protection Clause of the Constitution and Title VII of the Civil Rights Act. The action violated the Equal Protection Clause because there was no rational basis to consider gender in determining a suitable professor, despite the university's contention that its consideration of sex was rationally related to its intention to comply with state and federal affirmative action guidelines. Title VII was violated since its § 703(j) expressly prohibits preferential treatment on the basis of sex.

(5) An order requiring that a union which had a long record of egregious racial discrimination attain a 29% nonwhite membership by 1981 was sustained, but a racially oriented program for determining admissions to the union apprenticeship program regardless of job-related test results was disapproved in *EEOC v. Sheet Metal Workers, Local 638,* 532 F.2d 821 (2d Cir. 1976).

(6) Section 703(j) was added to the Civil Rights Act of 1964 as a compromise measure to emphasize that the Act would not require employers to achieve or maintain specific racial balances through the use of preferential treatment. However, at no point in the consideration of the Act did the sponsors indicate that temporary preferential remedies could not be used to overcome the effects of past discrimination. In considering the 1972 amendments to the Act, Congress impliedly recognized the importance of preferential remedies by rejecting a number of proposed amendments that would have eliminated their use. Senator Javits, one of the sponsors of the bill, in arguing against an amendment that would have enjoined all federal officials from requiring preferential remedies, pointed out that the amendment would not only eliminate an important judicial remedy for employment discrimination, but would also preclude effective consent decrees and affirmative action under Executive Order 11246. *See* 118 Cong. Rec. 1664 (1972). *See also* 118 Cong. Rec. 1661-76 (1972); 118 Cong. Rec. 4917-18 (1972).

C. AFFIRMATIVE ACTION

1. "Reverse" Discrimination

In the landmark decision of *Regents of the University of California v. Bakke,* 438 U.S. 265, 98 S. Ct. 2733 (1978), the Supreme Court upheld the constitutionality of certain "affirmative action" plans designed to remedy the effects of racial discrimination in university admissions. In *Bakke,* the Medical School of the University of California at Davis had two admissions programs for an entering class of 100 students — a regular admissions program and a special admissions program. A California trial court found that the special admissions program operated as a racial quota, because minority applicants in that program were rated only against one another, and 16 places in the class of 100 were reserved for them. The trial court concluded that the university could not take race into account in making admissions decisions and, therefore, the program was found to violate the Federal and State Constitutions and Title VI of the Civil Rights Act of 1964, 42 U.S.C. § 2000d. On review, the California Supreme Court ruled that the Davis special admissions program violated the Equal Protection Clause. Since Davis could not satisfy its burden of demonstrating that Mr. Bakke, absent the special program, would not have been admitted to medical school, the California Supreme Court ordered his admission to Davis.

In a five-four decision, the Supreme Court affirmed the judgment of the California Supreme Court insofar as it ordered Bakke's admission to Davis and invalidated the Davis special admissions program; however, the judgment of the California Supreme Court was reversed insofar as it prohibited Davis from taking race into account as a factor in future admissions decisions.

Justice Powell providing the swing vote, and announcing the judgment of the Court, concluded that Title VI proscribed only those racial classifications that would violate the Equal Protection Clause if employed by a State or its agencies; racial and ethnic classifications of any sort are inherently suspect and call for the most exacting judicial scrutiny; and, while the goal of achieving a diverse student body is sufficiently compelling to justify consideration of race in admissions decisions under some circumstances, the Davis special admissions program, which foreclosed consideration to white applicants like Bakke, was unnecessary to the achievement of this compelling goal and therefore invalid under the Equal Protection Clause.

The decision of Justice Powell noted that prior cases in which racial preferences had been ordered or sanctioned to remedy the effects of employment discrimination could not be seen to justify the Davis affirmative action plan which established a fixed quota for minority admissions. However, Justice Powell did appear to cite with approval several of the prior employment cases upholding preferential remedies:

> For example, in *Franks v. Bowman Transportation Co.,* 424 U.S. 747 (1975), we approved a retroactive award of seniority to a class of Negro truck drivers who had been the victims of discrimination — not just by society at large, but by the respondent in that case. While this relief imposed some burdens on other employees, it was held necessary 'to make [the victims] whole for injuries suffered on account of unlawful employment discrimination.' . . . The courts of appeals have fashioned various types of racial preferences as remedies for constitutional or statutory violations resulting in identified, race-based injuries to individuals held entitled to the preference. *E.g., Bridgeport Guardians, Inc. v. Civil Service Commission,* 482 F.2d 1333 (2d Cir. 1973); *Carter v. Gallagher,* 452 F.2d 315, *modified on*

rehearing en banc, 452 F.2d 327 (8th Cir. 1972). Such preferences also have been upheld where a legislative or administrative body charged with the responsibility made determinations of past discrimination by the industries affected, and fashioned remedies deemed appropriate to rectify the discrimination. *E.g., Contractors Association of Eastern Pennsylvania v. Secretary of Labor,* 442 F.2d 159 (3d Cir.), *cert. denied,* 404 U.S. 954 (1971).[40]

In the opinion of Justice Powell it is made clear that such remedies which fix preferences for an identifiable class must be done pursuant to specific judicial, legislative or administrative findings:

The State certainly has a legitimate and substantial interest in ameliorating, or eliminating where feasible, the disabling effects of identified discrimination. . . . We have never approved a classification that aids persons perceived as members of relatively victimized groups at the expense of other innocent individuals in the absence of judicial, legislative, or administrative findings of constitutional or statutory violations. . . . After such findings have been made, the governmental interest in preferring members of the injured groups at the expense of others is substantial, since the legal rights of the victims must be vindicated. In such a case, the extent of the injury and the consequent remedy will have been judicially, legislatively, or administratively defined. Also, the remedial action usually remains subject to continuing oversight to assure that it will work the least harm possible to other innocent persons competing for the benefit. Without such findings of constitutional or statutory violations, it cannot be said that the government has any greater interest in helping one individual than in refraining from harming another. Thus, the government has no compelling justification for inflicting such harm.

Justice Powell did add, however, that at least in the academic context, universities may, in the name of academic freedom, "take race into account in achieving the educational diversity valued by the First Amendment." He stated that, "in such an admissions program, race or ethnic background may be deemed a 'plus' in a particular applicant's file, yet it does not insulate the individual from comparison with all other candidates for the available seats." Thus,

---

[40] Every decision upholding the requirement of preferential hiring under the authority of Executive Order 11246 has emphasized the existence of previous discrimination as a predicate for the imposition of a preferential remedy. *Contractors Association, supra; Southern Illinois Builders Assn. v. Ogilvie,* 471 F.2d 680 (7th Cir. 1972); ....

according to Justice Powell, "the applicant who loses out on the last available seat to another candidate receiving a 'plus' on the basis of ethnic background will not have been foreclosed from all consideration for that seat simply because he was not the right color or had the wrong surname."

Justices Brennan, White, Marshall and Blackmun agreed with Justice Powell that affirmative action plans were permissible under the Fourteenth Amendment. However, these four Justices expressed the additional view that the Davis plan should have been upheld as lawful because it was designed to overcome the substantial, chronic minority underrepresentation in the medical profession. In differing with Justice Powell, Justices Brennan, White, Marshall and Blackmun expressed the view that Davis should have been allowed to voluntarily adopt an affirmative action plan including fixed racial preferences (without judicial, legislative or administrative findings) to overcome the effects of past racial discrimination.

Justice Stevens, Chief Justice Burger, Justice Stewart and Justice Rehnquist expressed the view that the Davis special admissions plan violated the statutory mandate of Title VI and, therefore, it was unnecessary to decide whether race can ever be a factor in an admissions policy.

2. Affirmative Action

As discussed in Chapter 11, while discrimination in employment at the hiring stage is proscribed by statute, such unequal treatment in discharging employees is tolerated. *See e.g., Jersey Central Power & Light Co. v. IBEW Locals 327,* 508 F.2d 687 (3d Cir. 1957), vac. U.S. (1976), on remand, 542 F.2d 8 (3d Cir. 1976).

After the *Bakke* decision, many commentators have questioned the continued validity of quotas in the implementation of affirmative action programs designed to overcome the effects of past discriminatory practices. In *EEOC v. American Telephone & Telegraph Co.,* 14 FEP Cases 1210 (3d Cir. 1977), the Court of Appeals for the Third Circuit approved the use of a quota system in the company's affirmative action program embodied in a consent decree with EEOC. Three unions, having negotiated collective bargaining agreements with A.T. & T., challenged the decree as it related to promotion decisions on the grounds that it (1) conflicted with the bargained-for seniority provisions in their agreement; and (2) violated the affected employees' equal protection rights guaranteed by the Federal Constitution. In rejecting both contentions, the Court declared:

> The use of employment goals and quotas admittedly involves tensions with the equal protection guarantee inherent in the due process clause of the Fifth Amendment. But the remedy granted

by the district court is permissible because it seems reasonably calculated to counteract the detrimental effects a particular, identifiable pattern of discrimination has had upon the prospects of achieving a society in which the distribution of jobs to basically qualified members of sex and racial groups is not affected by discrimination. 14 FEP Cases at 1220.

In *Steelworkers v. Weber* (Slip Opinion No. 74-432) decided June 27, 1979, the Supreme Court validated some private, voluntary, race-conscious affirmative action plans. In a 5-2 decision written by Mr. Justice Brennan the Court held that Section 703 of Title VII intended employers and unions to endeavor to eliminate the last vestiges of discrimination in employment. Without establishing the line between permissible and impermissible affirmative action plans, the decision held Kaiser's plan valid because it was a temporary measure, not intended to maintain racial balance nor discharge white workers, but rather implemented to break down the barriers to the employment of black workers in occupations that were traditionally closed to them.

Chapter 18

EMPLOYMENT DISCRIMINATION UNDER OTHER ACTS

A. EMPLOYMENT DISCRIMINATION UNDER THE NATIONAL LABOR RELATIONS ACT

HANDY ANDY, INC.

National Labor Relations Board
228 N.L.R.B. 447 (1977)

[Local 657 of the Teamsters won a decertification election, 108 to 66. The bargaining unit was composed of 211 employees, 58 of whom were Black and 164 of whom were Spanish-surnamed. The employer objected to the Board's issuance of a certification because of the union's alleged discriminatory practices against its members.]

On December 29, 1975, the Board, having determined that this and a number of other cases involving alleged race and sex discrimination on the part of labor organizations presented issues of importance in the administration of the National Labor Relations Act, as amended, scheduled oral argument in this and other cases limited to all issues arising from NLRB v. Mansion House Center Management Corp., 473 F.2d 471 (CA 8th 1973), and Bekins Moving & Storage Co. of Florida, Inc., 211 N.L.R.B. 138 (1974), Members Fanning and Penello dissenting. Oral arguments were heard on February 2, 1976. Amici curiae arguments were also heard at that time. . . .

The Employer contends that the Union's alleged discriminatory practices preclude it from being certified as an exclusive bargaining representative, citing *Bekins Moving & Storage Co. of Florida, Inc.,* supra. As evidence in support of its objection, the Employer relies primarily upon several decisions by the United States Court of Appeals for the Fifth Circuit.[3] In these cases, the court held, inter alia, that certain seniority provisions of the National Master Freight Agreement, to which the Union is a party together with various employers (but not the Employer herein), were unlawful because they perpetuated the effects of the employers' past discrimination.

---

[3] Rodriguez, et al. v. East Texas Motor Freight, Southern Conference of Teamsters and Teamsters Local 657, 505 F.2d 40 (CA 5th, 1974); Herrera et al. v. Yellow Freight System, Inc. 505 F.2d 66 (CA 5th, 1974); Resendis et al. v. Lee Way Motor Freight, Inc. 505 F.2d 69 (CA 5th, 1974).

Consequently, the court found that the Union, by being part to such an agreement, had violated Title VII of the Civil Rights Act of 1964.

The Employer's reliance on *Bekins* is based on the majority's holding in that case that the Board is constitutionally required to consider issues raised by an objection grounded on alleged invidious discrimination prior to issuance of a Board certification of representative. . . . We now conclude that the policies of the Act are better effectuated by considering allegations that a labor organization practices invidious discrimination in appropriate unfair labor practice rather than representation proceedings. Accordingly, for the reasons set forth hereafter, the *Bekins* decision is overruled.

In our view neither the Fifth Amendment to the Constitution nor the National Labor Relations Act, as amended, requires the Board to resolve questions of alleged invidious discrimination by a labor organization before it may lawfully certify the union as the exclusive bargaining representative of employees in an appropriate unit. Indeed, it appears to us that the contrary is true; namely, that the Board is not authorized to withhold certification of a labor organization duly selected by a majority of the unit employees. . . .

The majority in *Bekins* concluded that precertification consideration of alleged invidious discrimination by labor organizations is required by the Fifth Amendment to the Constitution because the Board may not lawfully bestow its certification upon a union which in fact discriminates on the basis of such considerations. The majority stated that, under the principle enunciated by the Supreme Court in Shelley v. Kraemer [7] and subsequent cases,[8] were the Board, as a Federal agency, to confer the benefits of certification on a labor organization which practices unlawful discrimination "the power of the Federal Government would surely appear to be sanctioning, and indeed furthering, the continued practice of such discrimination, thereby running afoul of the due process clause of the fifth amendment."

The foregoing statement misconstrues the "state action" doctrine [10] as defined in Shelley v. Kraemer, supra, and its progeny. In *Shelley,* petitioners were blacks seeking to buy property covered by private restrictive covenants which prohibited occupancy of the covered premises by persons "not of the Caucasian race." The state courts had enforced the covenants and, consequently, had found that petitioner could not obtain valid title. The Supreme Court held that

---

[7] 334 U.S. 1 (1948).

[8] See, e.g., Burton v. Willmington Parking Authority, 365 U.S. 715 (1961); Evans v. Newton, 382 U.S. 296 (1966); Evans v. Abney, 396 U.S. 435 (1970).

[10] Although the equal protection clause does not by its terms apply to the Federal Government, it is well settled that the due process clause of the Fifth Amendment imposes the same restrictions on Federal action that the Fourteenth Amendment imposes on State action. Bolling v. Sharpe, 347 U.S. 497, 499 (1954).

the agreement, standing alone, did not violate any constitutional right of petitioners, emphasizing that: "[T]he principle has become firmly embedded in our constitutional law that the action inhibited by the [equal protection clause] of the Fourteenth Amendment is only such action as may fairly be said to be that of the States. That Amendment erects no shield against merely private conduct, however discriminatory or wrongful.[11] The Court concluded, however, that enforcement of the covenants by state courts was state action subject to the equal protection clause. In so concluding, the Court commented: "It is clear that but for the *active intervention* of the state courts, supported by the full panoply of state power, petitioners would have been free to occupy the properties in question without restraint.

"These are not cases . . . in which the States have merely abstained from action, leaving private individuals free to impose such discriminations as they see fit. Rather, these are *cases in which the States have made available to such individuals the full coercive power of government to deny to petitioners, on the grounds of race or color, the enjoyment of property rights* in premises which petitioners are willing and financially able to acquire and which the grantors are willing to sell." [Emphasis supplied.] [12] Thus, the prohibited state action in Shelley v. Kraemer was the *affirmative enforcement* by the State of a private agreement to discriminate. . . .

Finally, in Moose Lodge No. 107 v. Irvis,[19] a state liquor control agency, in granting liquor licenses, promulgated numerous regulations with which licensees had to comply. One of these required that "[e]very club licensee shall adhere to all of the provisions of its Constitution and Bylaws." [20] Moose Lodge had a provision in its constitution which denied membership to blacks. The trial court had relied on the pervasive regulation of the club's activity by the liquor control board in ruling that the agency was sufficiently implicated with the discriminating club to violate the Fourteenth Amendment. But the Court, in analyzing the amount of government involvement necessary to raise constitutional issues, rejected the trial court's reasoning, noting that "[h]owever detailed this type of regulation may be in some particulars, it cannot be said to in any way *foster* or *encourage* racial discrimination." [21] (Emphasis supplied.) The Court held that only one regulation which had the effect of specifically requiring the club to discriminate was sufficiently involved with the private club's racially discriminatory policy to run

[11] 334 U.S. at 13.
[12] 334 U.S. at 19.
[19] 407 U.S. 163 (1972).
[20] 407 U.S. at 177.
[21] 407 U.S. at 176, 177.

afoul of the Constitution. None of the other regulations governing the operation of Moose Lodge were so entwined with the racial policies as to trigger the equal protection clause, because they did not specifically support the racial discrimination. This distinction, which is of obvious importance, was stated by the Court as follows:

"The Court has never held, of course, that discrimination by an otherwise private entity would be violative of the Equal Protection Clause if the private entity receives any sort of benefit or service at all from the State, or if it is subject to state regulation in any degree whatever. . . . [S]uch a holding would utterly emasculate the distinction between private as distinguished from state conduct. . . . Our holdings indicate that where the impetus for the discrimination is private, the state must have *significantly involved* itself with invidious discriminations [citation omitted] in order for the discriminatory action to fall within the ambit of the constitutional prohibition." [Emphasis supplied.] [23]

Thus, to summarize, while "to fashion and apply a precise formula for recognition of state responsibility under the Equal Protection Clause is an 'impossible task,' " [24] it is clear that governmental bodies cannot be "significantly involved" in discrimination. Such involvement has been found in the past where government "required" private parties to discriminate, "enforced" private discrimination, "authorized" private discrimination, or "fostered and encouraged" discrimination. Thus, the issue is whether a sufficiently close nexus is established between governmental action and actual discrimination by a private party. . . . For the reasons set forth below, we conclude that there is no such nexus between the Board's certification and any discrimination undertaken by a union which has received such a certification.

We recognize, of course, that certification of a labor organization confers substantial benefits. The Board does not, however, by certifying a labor organization, place its imprimatur on all the organization's activity, lawful or otherwise. On the contrary, a certification is neither more nor less than an acknowledgment that a majority of the employees in an appropriate bargaining unit have selected the union as their exclusive bargaining representative. The choice of representative is made by the employees, and may not be exercised by this Board: "For, it must be remembered that, initially, the Board merely provides the machinery whereby the desires of the employees may be ascertained, and the employees may select a 'good' labor organization, a 'bad' labor organization, or no labor

---

[23] 407 U.S. at 173.

[24] Burton v. Willmington Parking Authority, supra, 365 U.S. at 722.

organization, it being presupposed that employees will intelligently exercise their right to select their bargaining representative." [26]

Clearly, certification does not constitute enforcement or even approval of a labor organization's activities, and should not be construed as "state action" restricted by the fifth amendment.

Indeed, a union's status as the bargaining representative gives it no right or authority to establish *hiring* restrictions based on membership restrictions whether or not such membership restrictions are legitimate for other purposes. For, under the Act, it is an unfair labor practice for a labor organization whether or not it is certified, to cause or attempt to cause employers to hire on the basis of membership or nonmembership in a union.... Furthermore, a bargaining representative's right to enter into union-security agreements with employers conditioning continued employment on union membership or payment of agency shop fees is dependent on the availability of membership in the bargaining representative to any employees who choose to join. Similarly, if access to a union hiring hall is limited to union members, the exclusive hiring hall agreement violates the Act. Further, any membership policy of a union which would tend to limit job opportunities for minorities is barred by Title VII of the Civil Rights Act of 1964, as amended. Finally, the duty of fair representation prevents unions from using their bargaining representative powers in a discriminatory manner....

... The Congress has also taken steps to eliminate such discrimination based on race, etc., by enacting Title VII of the Civil Rights Act of 1964, as amended. Title VII, as implemented by the Equal Employment Opportunities Commission, performs the very function — using the same test for discrimination — which the Eighth Circuit Court of Appeals in NLRB v. Mansion House Center Management Corporation [29] would require of the Board. The *Mansion House* court was thus not requiring the Government merely to meet constitutional requirements, but to meet them in a particular way which the court preferred to the methods Congress has chosen....

A logical consequence of the *Bekins* constitutional determination is the conclusion that in their respective areas of authority the Federal agencies have overlapping responsibility for remedying any invidious discrimination by private parties.[32] For example, one

---

[26] Alto Plastics Manufacturing Corp. 136 N.L.R.B. 850, 851 (1962).

[29] 473 F.2d 471 (CA 8th, 1973). In that case, the court held that the remedial machinery of the Act could not be made available to a labor organization which engaged in unlawful racial discrimination.

[32] The *Bekins* conclusion further implies that Congress does not have the power to vest jurisdiction over claims of racial or other invidious discrimination exclusively in a single agency, the Equal Employment Opportunity Commission. This

might argue that the Interstate Commerce Commission may not constitutionally approve a route of a common carrier which engages in discriminatory hiring practices or that the Securities and Exchange Commission is prohibited from approving a prospectus of a corporation which engages in such practices. This argument was recently rejected by the Supreme Court in National Association for the Advancement of Colored People v. Federal Power Commission,[33] in which the Court held that the FPC does not have the authority to promulgate rules prohibiting its regulatees from engaging in discriminatory employment practices, but that the Commission does have authority to consider the consequences of employment discrimination in performing its mandated regulatory functions. In that case, the Court discussed extensively the petitioner's argument that the references to the "public interest" in the Gas and Power Acts authorized "if indeed it did not require" the FPC to promulgate such rules. Rejecting this argument, the Court emphasized that it was necessary to look to the purposes of the Gas and Power Acts and: ". . . that the principal purpose of those Acts was to encourage the orderly development of plentiful supplies of electricity and natural gas at reasonable prices. While there are undoubtedly other subsidiary purposes contained in these Acts, the parties point to nothing in the Acts of their legislative histories to indicate that the elimination of employment discrimination was one of the purposes that Congress had in mind when it enacted this legislation." [35]. . .

Furthermore, as Professor Meltzer of the University of Chicago has noted,[37] "An administrative agency generally does not have jurisdiction to invalidate important elements of its enabling legislation." In Johnson, Administrator of Veterans' Affairs v. Robinson,[38] Mr. Justice Brennan, speaking for the majority of the Court, quoted with approval Mr. Justice Harlan's concurring opinion in Oestereich v. Selective Service System Local Board No. 11, Cheyenne, Wyoming [39] for the proposition that "[a]djudication of the constitutionality of congressional enactments has generally been thought beyond the jurisdiction of administrative agencies." [40] In our view, the *Bekins* majority ignored this principle. . . .

---

conclusion is clearly wholly untenable. See Meltzer, The National Labor Relations Act and Racial Discrimination, 42 U. Chi. L. Rev. 1, 10 (1974).

[33] 425 U.S. 662 (1976).

[35] 425 U.S. at 669, 670.

[37] "The National Labor Relations Act and Racial Discrimination: The More Remedies, the Better?" 42 U. Chi. L. Rev. 1, 20, fn. 93 (1974).

[38] 415 U.S. 361 (1974).

[39] 393 U.S. 233, 242 (1968).

[40] 415 U.S. at 368.

Issuance of a certification to a union which has won a fairly conducted valid election is mandated by the Act. As the dissenters in *Bekins* emphasized: "Congress in § 9(c)(1) directed that '[w]henever a petition has been filed, in accordance with such regulations as may be prescribed by the Board ... the Board *shall* investigate such petition and if it has reasonable cause to believe that a question concerning representation affecting commerce exists *shall* provide for an appropriate hearing. ... If the Board finds upon the record of such hearing that such a question of representation exists, it shall direct an election by secret ballot and shall certify the results thereof.' (Emphasis supplied.) This language is language of requirement...."

We conclude that the *Bekins* doctrine will significantly impair the national labor policy of facilitating collective bargaining, the enforcement of which is our primary function. First, the workers in the unit will be denied the "right guaranteed them by § 7 of the Act to bargain collectively through representatives of their own choosing," which could be the only effective bargaining representative available to them.

Indeed, even a union which practices some unlawful discrimination may be the best one available in the opinion of the workers in the unit, who are given the right to decide for themselves by the Act. Even if minority members of the unit are convinced that the union will fairly represent them, and vote for the union under the *Bekins* approach, a bargaining order may still have to be denied. Yet, the minority workers might not be helped by keeping the union out, since they will then be at the mercy of their employer who has no duty of fair representation to fulfill, who may act to the detriment of *all* the workers, and who may also discriminate against minorities.... Second, employers faced with the prospect of unionization will be provided and have been provided under the Board's *Bekins* doctrine with an incentive to inject charges of union racial discrimination into Board certification and bargaining order proceedings as a delaying tactic in order to avoid collective bargaining altogether rather than to attack racial discrimination.

Not only does the *Bekins* approach impair the national labor policy favoring collective bargaining, but it is ineffective in implementing an antidiscrimination policy. Denying certification and bargaining orders to discriminating unions may seem to be an effective sanction as the status of bargaining representative is the source of a union's power. However, many unions have no need of Board aid to gain or keep the position of bargaining representative. Most unions do not resort to certification elections to establish their majority status, and many unions which are certified would not be harmed by losing their certifications. Entrenched unions, which already have well-established bargaining relationships with employers, need no aid from the Board in maintaining their positions. Powerful unions, which can make effective use of such traditional self-help remedies as striking and picketing to force employers to bargain, have no need for bargaining orders. These powerful and entrenched unions are the ones with the least natural incentive to lower racial barriers, because they do not have to worry about attracting votes at representation elections as the weaker unions must. Thus the *Bekins* remedies fail to reach those unions likely to be the worst offenders. In addition, *Bekins,* by increasing the duration of representation cases, would create problems in applying § 8(b)(7)(C) to picketing by unions whose representational eligibility is being litigated or has been denied by the Board. To prevent a union found ineligible for certification from engaging in recognitional picketing and thereby to secure the representation status unavailable through the Board's usual representation case processes, and to prevent the prospect of a series of election petitions followed by recognitional picketing, the Board would be under pressure to disregard the literal language of § 8(b)(7)(C) by making any recognitional picketing by an ineligible union a violation of that section.

Also, under the majority *Bekins* holding, a labor organization could be denied certification upon the mere presumption that it will fail to discharge its responsibility to represent employees in *this* unit fairly solely because it has failed to represent employees fairly in some *other* bargaining unit, rather than on proof of such dereliction as to unit employees in revocation proceeding. In fact, the Employer herein, in seeking to prevent the issuance of certification, relies upon discriminatory provisions in the Union's contracts in other bargaining units with other employers, contracts to which this Employer has never been a party and which were found to be unlawful solely because they perpetuated the other employers' past discrimination. For the Board to conclude that there will be further unlawful conduct solely on the basis of such evidence is directly contrary to our longstanding policy. Traditionally, as is true of virtually all court and administrative determinations, the Board's findings and remedies apply only to the particular parties before us.[48]

. . . Indeed, it appears that the Employer's purpose is to delay the onset of bargaining, rather than to protect the minority or female employees from actual discrimination by the bargaining representative.

---

[48] Even in cases where the Board has held, prior to an election, that a union was disqualified from representing employees, such finding has been predicated on the labor organization's conflict of interest with employees in the *specific unit* sought. Harlem River Consumers Cooperative, Inc., 191 N.L.R.B. 314 (1971); Bambury Fashions, Inc., 179 N.L.R.B. 447 (1969).

Questions concerning representation must be expeditiously resolved in order to achieve the statutory objective of fostering collective bargaining and assuring stability in labor-management relations. To that end, Congress chose to deny the parties judicial review of representation proceedings and to exempt such proceedings from the strictures of the Administrative Procedure Act. For the same reason, representation questions are decided in nonadversary, factfinding proceedings. The overriding importance of allowing employees to decide as expeditiously as possible whether or not they desire a bargaining representative justifies elimination of those procedural safeguards in representation cases.

This is not to say that the Board will never consider such issues in representation proceedings. Rather, we have and will continue to consider the impact of unlawful discrimination where such consideration is required to preserve the integrity of the Board's own processes. Thus, the Board has long held that it would not apply its contract-bar rules so as to shield collective bargaining agreements which patently discriminate between black and white employees from the challenge of otherwise appropriate election petitions.[50] In reaching this conclusion, the Board specifically recognized that to hold otherwise would be inconsistent with the Supreme Court's condemnation of governmental sanctioning of racially separate groupings.[51] Similarly, in order to insure fairness in Board-conducted elections, the Board has held that an employer's preelection propaganda which constituted "a deliberate, sustained appeal to racial prejudice ... created conditions which made impossible a reasoned choice of a bargaining representative." [52]. ...

It is thus apparent that the Board has considered, and will continue to consider, in representation proceedings the possible impact of clearly existing invidious discrimination within the unit at issue or of appeals to prejudice directed at employees in such unit in cases where an inquiry into these matters is necessary to protect the fairness of the election process.[54] However, because of the essentially nonadversary nature of representation proceedings, we believe that allegations of invidious discrimination should be considered in such proceedings *only* when required to fulfill our primary obligation of protecting employees from interference in exercising their right to select a bargaining representative.

---

[50] Pioneer Bus Company, Inc., 140 N.L.R.B. 54 (1962).

[51] Brown, et al. v. Board of Education of Topeka, et al., 349 U.S. 294 (1954). ...

[52] Sewell Manufacturing Company, 138 N.L.R.B. 66, 70 (1962).

[54] In these cases, however, the Board was not required to resolve factual disputes. Rather, each instance involved evaluation of uncontroverted facts as to possible impact on the election process.

It is thus apparent that issues involving alleged invidious discrimination by a labor organization should be considered in an adversary proceeding in which the accused union is accorded the full spectrum of due process, including particularly the right of judicial review.[55]

... These procedures also accord with the basic procedures required under Title VII, i.e., filing of a charge followed by investigation and, where required, a full court hearing on the merits.

Indeed, as Professor Meltzer observed with respect to the *Bekins* doctrine:

"In addition, the dissenters' approach would avoid the suspension of important rights on the basis of allegations, and thereby would serve the values of the NLRA, Title VII and our legal system generally. Indeed, it is one of the several ironies of *Bekins* that the Board will suspend an important right on the basis of allegations of Title VII violations, while a party charged under that title suffers no legal disability until there is a judicial finding upholding the charge." [57]

We conclude that our statutory function of eliminating invidious discrimination by labor organizations is best served by scrutinizing their activities when they are subject to our adversary procedures and remedial orders. . . .

The duty of fair representation has become the touchstone of the Board's concern with invidious discrimination by unions. For example, it is well established that a labor organization's rejection of an employee's grievance solely because of his or her race breaches the duty of fair representation and violates §§ 8(b)(1)(A), 8(b)(2), and 8(b)(3) of the Act.[64] Similarly, we have held that a union's refusal to process grievances filed to protest an employer's segregated plant facilities constitutes a violation of § 8(b)(1)(A).[65]

In *Galveston Maritime Association, Inc.*,[66] the Board held, again relying on the duty of fair representation, that a union's maintenance of a collective bargaining agreement which allocated work on the

---

[55] We agree with our concurring colleague that all fair representation claims must be adjudicated under § 8(b) of the Act and not as a defense to an 8(a)(5) proceeding or in a representation proceeding.

[57] See Meltzer, supra at p. 24.

[64] Independent Metal Workers Union Local 1 (Hughes Tool Company), 147 N.L.R.B. 1573 (1964).

[65] Local Union 12, United Rubber, Cork, Linoleum & Plastic Workers of America AFL-CIO (The Business League of Gadsden), 150 N.L.R.B. 312 (1964) enfd. 368 F.2d 12 (CA 5th, 1966). The Board specifically noted that the union's refusal to process the grievances was based on its belief that discriminatory job conditions should continue and therefore held that the refusal to process a grievance on that ground violated the duty of fair representation.

[66] Local 1367, Intl. Longshoremen's Assoc., AFL-CIO, et al. (Galveston Maritime Assoc. Inc.), 148 N.L.R.B. 897 (1964), Member Fanning concurring.

basis of race violated §§ 8(b)(1)(A), 8(b)(2), and 8(b)(3) of the Act. The Board premised the 8(b)(2) violation on its conclusion that the establishment, maintenance, and enforcement of discriminatory work quotas based on irrelevant, invidious, and unfair considerations of race and union membership discriminated against employees in violation of § 8(a)(3) of the Act and that, by causing an employer to so discriminate, a union violates § 8(b)(2). In holding that the work allocation violated § 8(b)(3), the Board concluded that "a labor organization's duty to bargain collectively includes the duty to represent fairly," on grounds that collective bargaining agreements which discriminate invidiously are not lawful under the Act and therefore do not meet the good-faith requirements of § 8(d).

The duty of fair representation is not limited to present discrimination, but is also breached by union policies which perpetuate past discrimination. Thus, in *Houston Maritime Association*,[68] the union had a policy prior to September 1963 of refusing to accept black applicants for membership. In the latter part of that month, the union adopted a policy of closing its register of applicants and refusing to accept any further applications regardless of the applicant's race. In addition to finding that the union's new policy violated § 8(b)(1)(A) and § 8(b)(2) of the Act as an attempt to perpetuate past discrimination, the Board found that the employers who had participated in the pattern of unlawful conduct had thereby violated § 8(a)(1) and (3).

While these cases clearly illustrate that we provide a remedy for breach of the duty of fair representation, thereby protecting employees from invidious discrimination by their bargaining representative, other remedies for a union's unlawful discrimination are also available. For example, we have held that a union commits unfair labor practices by attempting to force an employer to continue discriminatory practices even though no breach of the duty of fair representation is involved.[69] Additionally, the Board has, in appropriate cases, revoked the certification of unions which engage in unlawful invidious discrimination.[70]

As the foregoing discussion indicates, the Board has long recognized its obligation to consider issues concerning dis-

---

[68] Houston Maritime Assoc. Inc., and its Member Companies, 168 N.L.R.B. 615 (1967).

[69] Local Union No. 2 of the United Association of Journeymen and Apprentices of the Plumbing and Pipefitting Industry of the United States and Canada, AFL-CIO (Astrove Plumbing and Heating Corp.) 152 N.L.R.B. 1093 (1965), wherein the Board held that a union violated §§ 8(b)(2) and 8(b)(1))A) of the Act by engaging in a walkout in order to protest an employer's attempt to remedy its past discrimination.

[70] Independent Metal Workers Union, Local No. 1 (Hughes Tool Company), supra.

crimination on the basis of race, sex, national origin, or other unlawful invidious, or irrelevant reasons when they are raised in an appropriate context, and we shall continue to do so.[71] However, on the basis of all the foregoing, although we neither approve nor condone discriminatory practices on the part of unions, we hereby overrule *Bekins* as we conclude that the holding of that case is neither mandated by the Constitution nor by the Act and is destructive of the policies embodied in § 9(c) of the Act. We further conclude that issues such as those raised by the Employer herein are best considered in the context of appropriate unfair labor practice proceedings. We do so on the basis of the paramount importance of avoidance of delay in representation cases, the procedural safeguards afforded in unfair labor practice proceedings which are not available in representation proceedings, the somewhat different purposes served by § 8 and § 9 of the Act, and the fact that effective procedures already exist for litigation of the type of discrimination alleged by the Employer herein.

We therefore overrule the Employer's objection and shall certify the Union as the representative of the employees in the unit found appropriate above. . . .

Member WALTHER, concurring:

I agree with my colleagues in the majority that the Employer's objection should be overruled. I agree also with their rationale for doing so to the extent that it is consistent with the views expressed below.

With respect to allegations pertaining to a union's breach of its duty of fair representation, not only do I agree with my colleagues that such claims "should be" considered in an adversary proceeding,

---

[71] Member Fanning notes the dissent's observation in fn. 76 that "Member Fanning has not yet accepted *Miranda*." This is superficially correct. He does not, for the reasons explained in General Truck Drivers, Chauffeurs and Helpers Union Local 692, International Brotherhood of Teamsters, Chauffeurs, Warehousemen and Helpers of America (Great Western Unifreight System), 209 N.L.R.B. 446 (1974). But, as he carefully explained in his concurring opinion in that decision, that does not mean that he — any more than the Board majority — sanctions or condones union misconduct toward employees. He has found violations of § 8(b)(1)(A) in the maintenance of segregated locals, Local 106 Glass Bottle Blowers Association, AFL-CIO (Owens-Illinois, Inc.,) 210 N.L.R.B. 943 (1974), enfd., 520 F.2d 693 (CA 6th, 1975); and of §§ 8(b)(1)(A) and 8(b)(2)in a union's coercive advocation and enforcement of racially discriminatory hiring policies, International Brotherhood of Painters and Allied Trades, Local Union 1066, AFL-CIO (W. J. Siebenoller, Jr., Paint Company), 205 N.L.R.B. 651 (1973). He has, moreover, found breaches of the duty of fair representation to be violations of § 8(b)(1)(A), Truck Drivers, Oil Drivers and Filling Station and Platform Workers Local 705 International Brotherhood of Teamsters, Chauffeurs, Warehousemen and Helpers of America (Associated Transport, Inc.), 209 N.L.R.B. 292 (1974); Local 485, International Union of Electrical, Radio & Machine Workers, AFL-CIO (Automotive Plating Corp.) 170 N.L.R.B. 1234 (1968).

I think that they *must be* considered in such a proceeding. Assuming, as I do, that a proper accommodation between this Board and other governmental agencies (e.g., EEOC) requires us to confine our examination to actual discrimination in the particular unit under consideration, fair representation claims are premature in both representation and § 8(a)(5) certification-test proceedings — for in neither situation has the union yet been afforded an opportunity to represent the unit employees at all, fairly or unfairly. Such claims would, of necessity, have to relate to potential breaches of the duty of fair representation based upon conduct at other locations, an area of inquiry I would not entertain in any Board proceeding. For this reason, and for all of the due process safeguards attendant to our unfair labor practice proceedings mentioned by my colleagues, I conclude that all fair representation claims must be adjudicated under § 8(b) of the Act.

My colleagues in the majority note that, "we have and will continue to consider [in a representation proceeding] the impact of unlawful discrimination where such consideration is required to preserve the integrity of the Board's own processes." To the instances which they cite, I would add yet another: instances in which it can be established through reference to a petitioner's constitution, bylaws, or other written statement of policy, that the petitioner — not an affiliated organization or sister local — restricts access to membership on the basis of race, alienage, national origin, or sex. Should such discrimination be found, I would disqualify the petitioner from access to our election machinery until it can establish that the offensive practices have been eliminated.

The proviso to §8(b)(1)(A), of course, prohibits litigation of membership discrimination claims in an unfair labor practice proceeding. I do not think, however, that the Board should ignore such blatant discrimination. Irrespective of whether we are constitutionally obligated to do so, I would, as a matter of discretion, deny a union which discriminates in this fashion access to our election machinery. In such instances, the discriminatory conduct is open, documented, and pervasive. The step which I recommend it seems to me is, in the words of the majority, "required to preserve the integrity of the Board's own processes." [72]

In the instant case, the Employer alleged discrimination both in the form of exclusionary membership policies and unfair representation. The evidence which was submitted, however, all related to matters falling within the realm of fair representation. No evidence was offered in support of the restrictive membership claim. In these

_____

[72] Since the inquiry would determine the union's qualifications to use our election procedures, appropriate membership discrimination claims would have to be entertained at the outset of the representation procedure, prior to the direction of an election.

circumstances, I agree with my colleagues that the Employer's objection should be overruled. . . .

. . . Member JENKINS, dissenting: Experience of more than 2½ years with the *Bekins* decision has provided no evidence of the delays which the dissenting members envisaged and which constituted a principal basis for their dissent. . . . The Board majority in *Bekins,* of which I was a member, found that such certification "would appear to be sanctioning, and indeed furthering, the continued practice of such discrimination, thereby running afoul of the due process clause of the Fifth Amendment." Nothing has occurred since that decision to undermine the validity of this conclusion. I therefore vigorously disagree with today's contrary holding of my colleagues.

In my colleagues' view the language of § 9(c)(1) requires the Board to certify a union even though its governing instruments (constitution, charter, bylaws, etc.) exclude from its membership black or female employees in the unit or permit black or female employees in the unit to become members only of a segregated local.[74] As a result of the Board's certification, the employer is required to bargain with the union as the exclusive representative of all employees in the unit, minority employees who voted against the union can have no other representation, the union's status as exclusive bargaining representative cannot be challenged for a year, and there is a presumption that its status as exclusive bargaining representative continues after a year. My colleagues acknowledge "that certification of a labor organization confers substantial benefits" but nevertheless assert that these benefits which flow directly from the Board's certification do not support a discriminating union in its invidious discrimination. They do not, and cannot, explain how assistance to the union in the exclusive representation of unit employees does not amount to assistance in the union's discrimination when that representation is conducted in accordance with the union's discriminatory practices. It is no answer that at some uncertain future date, after the union with Board assistance has carried out its discriminatory practices, unfair labor practice proceedings may be instituted which will bring these activities to a halt. The fact of the matter is that until that day comes,

---

[74] I do not mean to suggest that the present case involves this situation, but the effect of the majority's decision is to require certification of such a union by precluding any precertification inquiry into a union's discriminatory practices. In the present case, the objection to certification included the claim that the union excluded "persons from membership on the basis of race, alienage or national origin." Local 657, which was the subject of the Employer's certification objection in this case, has been found accountable for discriminatory practices in establishing seniority rosters in its collective-bargaining agreements with three other employers engaged in similar business in this same area. Rodriguez v. East Texas Motor Freight, supra; Herrera v. Yellow Freight System, Inc., supra; Resendis v. Lee Way Motor Freight, Inc., supra.

if it ever does come, the Board has fostered invidious discrimination by the statutory agent.

The decisions of the Supreme Court leave no room for such Government-supported discrimination. In Steele v. Louisville & Nashville Railroad Co., 323 U.S. 192 (1944), the Supreme Court made clear that the Constitution prohibited a labor organization, which was granted a statutory right to bargain exclusively for employees, from engaging in invidious discrimination in their representation. The decisions of the Supreme Court have repeatedly invalidated action taken by Federal or state agencies which have the effect of furthering, supporting, or assisting discrimination in any form. See, e.g., Bolling v. Sharpe, 347 U.S. 498 (1954); Shelley v. Kraemer, 334 U.S. 1 (1948); Burton v. Wilmington Parking Authority, 365 U.S. 715 (1961). Since the Board's certification grants a discriminating union the right of exclusive representation, together with various concomitant advantages, it seems that my colleagues close their eyes to the facts when they assert that certification does not assist a discriminating union in its discriminatory practices. As the Court stated in NLRB v. Mansion House Center Management Corporation, 473 F.2d 471, 477 (CA 8th, 1973), "Federal complicity through recognition of a discriminating union serves not only to condone the discrimination, but in effect legitimizes and perpetuates such invidious practices. Certainly such a degree of federal participation in the maintenance of racially discriminatory practices violates basic constitutional tenets." . . .

[The majority's] evaluation of the Board's involvement in the union's discriminatory practices is a patent understatement of the significant effects of certification. By certification the union becomes the statutory bargaining agent with statutory rights. Improper interference with the selection of the bargaining representative is the violation of "public, not private, rights." Virginia Electric & Power Co. v. NLRB, 319 U.S. 533, 543 (1943). . . . The invidious discrimination of a discriminating union is practiced in the very areas to which the certification as representative relates. . . . [C]ertification of a union confers the exclusive right to represent all employees in the bargaining unit, the right to be free from challenge for a year, and a presumption that its majority status continues after a year. Without the Board's certification a labor organization does not enjoy the rights of a statutory bargaining agent. Obviously, a union's status as the statutory bargaining agent enhances its position with respect to both the employer and the unit employees. By certifying a union which excludes blacks or women from membership or segregates them in a separate local, the Board directs the employer to bargain exclusively with his discriminating union as representative of the excluded or segregated blacks or women. Minorities do not have a protected right, separate from the certified representative, to engage in concerted activities to protest discrimination by their employer. Emporium Capwell Co. v. Western Addition Community Organization, 420 U.S. 50 (1975). Certification is thus an integral part of the representation function in which the union practices discrimination and is patently direct participation and assistance by a Government agency, contrary to constitutional strictures, in the union's discriminatory representation. . . . The Board's conferring the status of statutory bargaining agent upon a union which engages in invidious discrimination clearly fosters and supports the union's discriminatory practices and this constitutes the Board's involvement in them under the standards which my colleagues acknowledge but contend are not applicable here. As the Supreme Court stated in Burton v. Wilmington Parking Authority, supra, where the state authority merely leased space in a public building to a private restaurant which denied service to blacks, there existed "that degree of state participation and involvement in discriminatory action which it was the design of the Fourteenth Amendment to condemn."

The Board's decisions holding breach of the duty of fair representation to be an unfair labor practice, with which I of course fully agree, are no substitute for the disqualification of a discriminating union in a representation proceeding. The fifth amendment does not permit a Government agency to provide the instrument for practicing discrimination merely because at some uncertain future date the Board may have an opportunity to terminate this discrimination in unfair labor practice proceedings set in motion by the charges of private parties if the General Counsel decides to file a complaint. . . .

The effect of a union's exclusion of blacks or women from membership or their segregation in separate locals may discourage them from seeking or retaining employment with an employer who is compelled by the Board's certification to bargain exclusively with the discriminating union. An employer confronted with a certification may find it expedient to enter into a collective-bargaining agreement with a union which excludes blacks or women from employment. In these situations, the possibility of invidious discrimination being raised as an unfair labor practice is minimized or eliminated. The certification of the Board thus serves as an instrument for the perpetuation of invidious discriminatory practices. It is clear to me, therefore, that the due process clause of the Fifth Amendment requires that certification be denied whenever the evidence establishes that the labor organization's representation in the unit for which it requests certification will be infected with invidious discrimination.

My colleagues contend that certification of a union successful in an election is mandatory under the act and that an administrative agency cannot pass upon the constitutionality of a statute whose obligation is the agency's to administer. This argument is completely devoid of merit. Certainly an agency is not holding a statute unconstitutional when it decides to administer it in a constitutional manner. Direct commands in a statute are impliedly made subject to constitutional limitations. My colleagues would meet the problem of eliminating invidious discrimination by labor organizations through its power in unfair labor practice proceedings to remedy the union's breach of its duty of fair representation. But the National Labor Relations Act nowhere expressly imposes on the statutory bargaining agent a duty of fair representation. This doctrine, first enunciated by the Board in Miranda Fuel Company, Inc., 140 N.L.R.B. 181 (1962), as my colleagues acknowledge, was derived from the Supreme Court's decisions in Steele v. Louisville & Nashville R.R. Co., 323 U.S. 192 (1944); Tunstall v. Brotherhood of Locomotive Firemen & Enginemen, 323 U.S. 210 (1944); and Wallace Corporation v. NLRB, 323 U.S. 248 (1944). In these cases the Supreme Court held that a statutory duty of fair representation by the exclusive bargaining representative must be implied for constitutional reasons. Thus, in attacking the problem of invidious discrimination by reading into the statute a duty of fair representation, my colleagues rely no less on constitutional requirements than they would if they held nondiscrimination to be a condition to certification. Similarly, in Pioneer Bus Company, Inc., 140 N.L.R.B. 54 (1962), the Board took account of constitutional requirements in denying the benefits of its contract-bar doctrine to a discriminating union. And in Independent Metal Workers Union Local 1 (Hughes Tool Company), 147 N.L.R.B. 1573 (1964), the Board relied on constitutional doctrine for its holding that racial segregation in membership by a statutory bargaining representative cannot be countenanced by a Federal agency. *Miranda, Pioneer Bus,* and *Hughes Tool* are relied on approvingly by my colleagues. It is clear that the Board is required to interpret and apply the Act in a manner which will avoid offense to the Constitution and that in doing so it is not adjudicating the constitutionality of congressional enactments.

My colleagues' decision does further violence to constitutional doctrine in its suggestion that a discriminating union which wins an election should be certified because it may be preferred by minority employees as better than no union at all. The majority does not indicate how the minority employees' preference in this respect would be ascertained. Moreover, as to a discriminating union's being preferable to none at all, it might just as readily be claimed that segregated school systems should have been upheld because they were better than none at all and a state might refuse to support a desegregated system. The effect of may colleagues' position is that the Board can properly assist in the perpetuation of discriminatory representation because such representation might be preferred to no representation. No authority is cited for this bizarre suggestion and I am certain none can be found.

The constitutional impediment to certification of a discriminating union forecloses consideration of policy reasons for adopting a procedure which grants certification and postpones determination of disqualifying discrimination to a later date. But even if there were no such impediment, I find to be singularly lacking in substance the reasons advanced by my colleagues for postponing until after certification the determination of invidious discrimination questions. The principal concerns of my colleagues appear to be that employers will seize upon the opportunity to raise questions of discrimination as a device for delaying certification and collective bargaining, that they will present evidence of discrimination of a character that does not establish that the particular local involved will engage in discrimination in the unit for which certification is sought, and that in the certification stage there is no opportunity for an adversary hearing which will permit the question of discrimination to be determined properly.

In attempted support of their argument that employers will use objections to certification based on discrimination as a tool for delaying or avoiding collective bargaining, my colleagues cite as illustrations cases in which the evidence of a labor organization's discriminatory conduct fell far short of establishing that it would engage in discrimination in the unit for which certification was currently being sought. If there is a propensity of employers to submit inadequate evidence of discrimination in support of an objection to certification, this is hardly relevant to the question whether certification should be denied when conclusive evidence of such discrimination is presented. I agree with my colleagues that disqualifying evidence of discrimination must relate to the union's future course of conduct in the unit involved in the representation proceeding and must do more than provide a basis for speculation as to the union's conduct as the certified bargaining representative. My colleagues apparently assume that it is impossible to prove disqualifying discrimination before certification. But certainly where a union's governing instruments require it to exclude minorities from membership or segregate them in separate locals in the unit for which certification is sought, there is irrebuttable evidence of invidious discrimination. What lesser evidence will satisfy the Board is a matter for case-by-case determination. To hold, as my colleagues do, that because some evidence will be insufficient no evidence will be permitted, is a perversion of the administrative process. Nor can it be persuasively maintained that the mere opportunity to present inadequate evidence of discrimination will unduly delay the bargaining process. . . .

My colleagues further claim that determination of an invidious discrimination objection should be made in an adversary proceeding which is not available during the representation stage of a case. This is clearly in error. If a genuine issue of discrimination is presented as an objection to certification after an election, the procedure contemplated by *Bekins* would be to designate a Hearing Officer to conduct a hearing on the question of discrimination and any other objections to the election which involved genuine issues of fact. At this hearing all interested parties would have an opportunity to present evidence, cross-examine witnesses, submit briefs, and, if desired, to participate in oral argument. After the Hearing Officer files his report and recommendations, the parties may file exceptions and briefs with the Board after consideration of which the Board will render its decision. If certification is granted, the employer may obtain judicial review in a court of appeals after the summary judgment finding of an 8(a)(5) violation based upon its refusal to bargain. . . . If certification is denied, a union may obtain judicial review by means of an independent action in a United States District Court. Miami Newspaper Printing Pressmen's Union Local 46 v. McCulloch, 322 F.2d 993 (C.A.D.C. 1963). These opportunities for hearing and review are obviously adversary in character (see *Miami Newspaper* case, *supra* at 998) and meet all the requirements of due process.

NOTES:

(1) In *Emporium Capwell Co. v. Western Addition Community Organization,* 420 U.S. 50 (1975), the Supreme Court ruled that, although national labor policy accords the highest priority to non-discriminatory employment practices, the National Labor Relations Act does not protect concerted activity by minority employees who seek to bypass their union representative and bargain directly with their employer over issues of employment discrimination. The court ruled in effect that if the relief available under Title VII is inadequate, because the legal procedures are too cumbersome or time-consuming, this will not justify dissident employee action taken against an employer to protest against alleged race discrimination. The Court thus concluded that employee interests (at least under the NLRA) may be adequately protected when a union is serving as the employees' exclusive bargaining agent and where a collective bargaining agreement adequately provides for nondiscrimination and makes available a grievance-arbitration procedure to redress employee complaints.

(2) For discussions of employment discrimination cases under the NLRA, *see* Lopatka, *A 1977 Primer on the Federal Regulation of Employment Discrimination,* 1977 Ill. L.F. 125-32; Note, 123 U. Pa. L. Rev. 158 (1974).

B. EQUAL PAY ACT

CORNING GLASS WORKS v. BRENNAN

United States Supreme Court
417 U.S. 188, 94 S. Ct. 2223 (1974)

MR. JUSTICE MARSHALL delivered the opinion of the Court.

These cases arise under the Equal Pay Act of 1963, 77 Stat. 56, § 3, 29 U. S. C. § 206 (d)(1),[1] which added to § 6 of the Fair Labor Standards Act of 1938 the principle of equal pay for equal work regardless of sex. The principal question posed is whether Corning Glass Works violated the Act by paying a higher base wage to male night shift inspectors than it paid to female inspectors performing the same tasks on the day shift, where the higher wage was paid in addition to a separate night shift differential paid to all employees for night work. In No. 73-29, the Court of Appeals for the Second Circuit, in a case involving several Corning plants in Corning, New York, held that this practice violated the Act. 474 F. 2d 226 (1973). In No. 73-695, the Court of Appeals for the Third Circuit, in a case involving a Corning plant in Wellsboro, Pennsylvania, reached the opposite conclusion. 480 F.2d 1254 (1973). We granted certiorari and consolidated the cases to resolve this unusually direct conflict between two circuits, 414 U. S. 1110 (1973). Finding ourselves in substantial agreement with the analysis of the Second Circuit, we affirm in No. 73-29 and reverse in No. 73-695.

I

Prior to 1925, Corning operated its plants in Wellsboro and Corning only during the day, and all inspection work was performed

---

[1] "No employer having employees subject to any provisions of this section shall discriminate, within any establishment in which such employees are employed, between employees on the basis of sex by paying wages to employees in such establishment at a rate less than the rate at which he pays wages to employees of the opposite sex in such establishment for equal work on jobs the performance of which requires equal skill, effort, and responsibility, and which are performed under similar working conditions, except where such payment is made pursuant to (i) a seniority system; (ii) a merit system; (iii) a system which measures earnings by quantity or quality of production; or (iv) a differential based on any other factor other than sex: *Provided,* That an employer who is paying a wage rate differential in violation of this subsection shall not, in order to comply with the provisions of this subsection, reduce the wage rate of any employee."

by women. Between 1925 and 1930, the company began to introduce automatic production equipment which made it desirable to institute a night shift. During this period, however, both New York and Pennsylvania law prohibited women from working at night. As a result, in order to fill inspector positions on the new night shift, the company had to recruit male employees from among its male dayworkers. The male employees so transferred demanded and received wages substantially higher than those paid to women inspectors engaged on the two day shifts. During this same period, however, no plant-wide shift differential existed and male employees working at night, other than inspectors, received the same wages as their day shift counterparts. Thus a situation developed where the night inspectors were all male, the day inspectors all female, and the male inspectors received significantly higher wages.

In 1944, Corning plants at both locations were organized by a labor union and a collective-bargaining agreement was negotiated for all production and maintenance employees. This agreement for the first time established a plant-wide shift differential, but this change did not eliminate the higher base wage paid to male night inspectors. Rather, the shift differential was superimposed on the existing difference in base wages between male night inspectors and female day inspectors.

Prior to June 11, 1964, the effective date of the Equal Pay Act, the law in both Pennsylvania and New York was amended to permit women to work at night. It was not until some time after the effective date of the Act, however, that Corning initiated efforts to eliminate the differential rates for male and female inspectors. Beginning in June 1966, Corning started to open up jobs on the night shift to women. Previously separate male and female seniority lists were consolidated and women become eligible to exercise their seniority, on the same basis as men, to bid for the higher paid night inspection jobs as vacancies occurred.

On January 20, 1969, a new collective-bargaining agreement went into effect, establishing a new "job evaluation" system for setting wage rates. The new agreement abolished for the future the separate base wages for day and night shift inspectors and imposed a uniform base wage for inspectors exceeding the wage rate for the night shift previously in effect. All inspectors hired after January 20, 1969, were to receive the same base wage, whatever their sex or shift. The collective-bargaining agreement further provided, however, for a higher "red circle" rate for employees hired prior to January 20, 1969, when working as inspectors on the night shift. This "red circle" rate served essentially to perpetuate the differential in base wages between day and night inspectors.

The Secretary of Labor brought these cases to enjoin Corning from violating the Equal Pay Act [8] and to collect back wages allegedly due female employees because of past violations. Three distinct questions are presented: (1) Did Corning ever violate the Equal Pay Act by paying male night shift inspectors more than female day shift inspectors? (2) If so, did Corning cure its violation of the Act in 1966 by permitting women to work at night shift inspectors? (3) Finally, if the violation was not remedied in 1966, did Corning cure its violation in 1969 by equalizing day and night inspector wage rates but establishing higher "red circle" rates for existing employees working on the night shift?

II

Congress' purpose in enacting the Equal Pay Act was to remedy what was perceived to be a serious and endemic problem of employment discrimination in private industry — the fact that the wage structure of "many segments of American industry has been based on an ancient but outmoded belief that a man, because of his role in society, should be paid more than a woman even though his duties are the same." S. Rep. No. 176, 88th Cong., 1st Sess., 1 (1963). The solution adopted was quite simple in principle: to require that "equal work will be rewarded by equal wages." *Ibid.*

The Act's basic structure and operation are similarly straightforward. In order to make out a case under the Act, the Secretary must show that an employer pays different wages to employees of opposite sexes "for equal work on jobs the performance of which requires equal skill, effort, and responsibility, and which are performed under similar working conditions." Although the Act is silent on this point, its legislative history makes plain that the Secretary has the burden of proof on this issue, as both of the courts below recognized.

The Act also establishes four exceptions — three specific and one a general catchall provision — where different payment to employees of opposite sexes "is made pursuant to (i) a seniority system; (ii) a merit system; (iii) a system which measures earnings by quantity or quality of production; or (iv) a differential based on any other factor other than sex." Again, while the Act is silent on this question, its structure and history also suggest that once the Secretary has carried his burden of showing that the employer pays workers of one sex

---

[8] The District Court in No. 73-29 issued a broadly worded injunction against all future violations of the Act. The Court of Appeals modified the injunction by limiting it to inspectors at the three plants at issue in that case, largely because of that court's belief that "Corning had been endeavoring since 1966 — sincerely, if ineffectively — to bring itself into compliance." 474 F. 2d 226, 236 (CA2 1973). Since the Government did not seek certiorari from this aspect of the Second Circuit's judgment, we have no occasion to consider this question.

more than workers of the opposite sex for equal work, the burden shifts to the employer to show that the differential is justified under one of the Act's four exceptions. All of the many lower courts that have considered this question have so held, and this view is consistent with the general rule that the application of an exemption under the Fair Labor Standards Act is a matter of affirmative defense on which the employer has the burden of proof.

The contentions of the parties in this case reflect the Act's underlying framework. Corning argues that the Secretary has failed to prove that Corning ever violated the Act because day shift work is not "performed under similar working conditions" as night shift work. The Secretary maintains that day shift and night shift work are performed under "similar working conditions" within the meaning of the Act.[13] Although the Secretary recognizes that higher wages may be paid for night shift work, the Secretary contends that such a shift differential would be based upon a "factor other than sex" within the catchall exception to the Act and that Corning has failed to carry its burden of proof that its higher base wage for male night inspectors was in fact based on any factor other than sex. . . .

We agree with the Second Circuit that the inspection work at issue in this case, whether performed during the day or night, is "equal work" as that term is defined in the Act.[24]

This does not mean, of course, that there is no room in the Equal Pay Act for nondiscriminatory shift differentials. Work on a steady night shift no doubt has psychological and physiological impacts making it less attractive than work on a day shift. The Act contemplates that a male night worker may receive a higher wage than a female day worker, just as it contemplates that a male employee with 20 years' seniority can receive a higher wage than a

---

[13] The Secretary also advances an argument that even if night and day inspection work is assumed not to be performed under similar working conditions, the differential in base wages is nevertheless unlawful under the Act. The additional burden of working at night, the argument goes, was already fully reflected in the plant-wide shift differential, and the shifts were made "similar" by payment of the shift differential. This argument does not appear to have been presented to either the Second or the Third Circuit, as the opinions in both cases reflect an assumption on the part of all concerned that the Secretary's case would fail unless night and day inspection work was found to be performed under similar working conditions. For this reason, and in view of our resolution of the "working condition" issue, we have no occasion to consider and intimate no views on this aspect of the Secretary's argument.

[24] In No. 73-29, Corning also claimed that the night inspection work was not equal to day shift inspection work because night shift inspectors had to do a certain amount of packing, lifting, and cleaning which was not performed by day shift inspectors. Noting that it is now well settled that jobs need not be identical in every respect before the Equal Pay Act is applicable, the Court of Appeals concluded that the extra work performed by night inspectors was of so little consequence that the jobs remained substantially equal.

woman with two years' seniority. Factors such as these play a role under the Act's four exceptions — the seniority differential under the specific seniority exception, the shift differential under the catchall exception for differentials "based on any other factor other than sex."

The question remains, however, whether Corning carried its burden of proving that the higher rate paid for night inspection work, until 1966 performed solely by men, was in fact intended to serve as compensation for night work, or rather constituted an added payment based upon sex. We agree that the record amply supports the District Court's conclusion that Corning had not sustained its burden of proof. As its history revealed, "the higher night rate was in large part the product of the generally higher wage level of male workers and the need to compensate them for performing what were regarded as demeaning tasks." 474 F. 2d, at 233. The differential in base wages originated at a time when no other night employees received higher pay than corresponding day workers, and it was maintained long after the company instituted a separate plant-wide shift differential which was thought to compensate adequately for the additional burdens of night work. The differential arose simply because men would not work at the low rates paid women inspectors, and it reflected a job market in which Corning could pay women less than men for the same work. That the company took advantage of such a situation may be understandable as a matter of economics, but its differential nevertheless became illegal once Congress enacted into law the principle of equal pay for equal work.

III

We now must consider whether Corning continued to remain in violation of the Act after 1966 when, without changing the base wage rates for day and night inspectors, it began to permit women to bid for jobs on the night shift as vacancies occurred. It is evident that this was more than a token gesture to end discrimination, as turnover in the night shift inspection jobs was rapid. The record in No. 73-29 shows, for example, that during the two-year period after June 1, 1966, the date women were first permitted to bid for night inspection jobs, women took 152 of the 278 openings, and women with very little seniority were able to obtain positions on the night shift. Relying on these facts, the company argues that it ceased discriminating against women in 1966, and was no longer in violation of the Equal Pay Act.

But the issue before us is not whether the company, in some abstract sense, can be said to have treated men the same as women after 1966. Rather, the question is whether the company remedied the specific violation of the Act which the Secretary proved. We agree with the Second Circuit, as well as with all other circuits that have had occasion to consider this issue, that the company could not cure its violation except by equalizing the base wages of female day inspectors with the higher rates paid the night inspectors. This result is implicit in the Act's language, its statement of purpose, and its legislative history. . . .

To achieve this end, Congress required that employers pay equal pay for equal work and then specified:

> "*Provided,* That an employer who is paying a wage rate differential in violation of this subsection shall not, in order to comply with the provisions of this subsection, reduce the wage rate of any employee." 29 U. S. C. § 206(d)(1).

The purpose of this proviso was to ensure that to remedy violations of the Act, "[t]he lower wage rate must be increased to the level of the higher." H. R. Rep. No. 309, *supra,* at 3. Comments of individual legislators are all consistent with this view. Representative Dwyer remarked, for example, "The objective of equal pay legislation . . . is not to drag down men workers to the wage levels of women, but to raise women to the levels enjoyed by men in cases where discrimination is still practiced." Representative Griffin also thought it clear that "[t]he only way a violation could be remedied under the bill . . . is for the lower wages to be raised to the higher."

By proving that after the effective date of the Equal Pay Act, Corning paid female day inspectors less than male night inspectors for equal work, the Secretary implicitly demonstrated that the wages of female day shift inspectors were unlawfully depressed and that the fair wage for inspection work was the base wage paid to male inspectors on the night shift. The whole purpose of the Act was to require that these depressed wages be raised, in part as a matter of simple justice to the employees themselves, but also as a matter of market economics, since Congress recognized as well that discrimination in wages on the basis of sex "constitutes an unfair method of competition." Pub. L. 88-38, *supra,* § 2 (a)(5).

We agree with Judge Friendly that

> "In light of this apparent congressional understanding, we cannot hold that Corning, by allowing some — or even many — women to move into the higher paid night jobs, achieved full compliance with the Act. Corning's action still left the inspectors on the day shift — virtually all women — earning a lower base wage than the night shift inspectors because of a differential initially based on sex and still not justified by any other consideration; in effect, Corning was still taking advantage of the availability of female labor to fill its day shift at a differentially low wage rate not justified by any factor other than sex." 474 F. 2d, at 235.

The Equal Pay Act is broadly remedial, and it should be construed and applied so as to fulfill the underlying purposes which Congress sought to achieve. If, as the Secretary proved, the work performed by women on the day shift was equal to that performed by men on the night shift, the company became obligated to pay the women the same base wage as their male counterparts on the effective date of the Act. To permit the company to escape that obligation by agreeing to allow some women to work on the night shift at a higher rate of pay as vacancies occurred would frustrate, not serve, Congress' ends. . . .

The company's final contention — that it cured its violation of the Act when a new collective-bargaining agreement went into effect on January 20, 1969 — need not detain us long. While the new agreement provided for equal base wages for night or day inspectors hired after that date, it continued to provide unequal base wages for employees hired before that date, a discrimination likely to continue for some time into the future because of a large number of laid-off employees who had to be offered re-employment before new inspectors could be hired. . . .

We therefore conclude that on the facts of this case, the company's continued discrimination in base wages between night and day workers, though phrased in terms of a neutral factor other than sex, nevertheless operated to perpetuate the effects of the company's prior illegal practice of paying women less than men for equal work. Cf. *Griggs v. Duke Power Co.,* 401 U. S. 424, 430 (1971).

The judgment in No. 73-29 is affirmed. The judgment in No. 73-695 is reversed and the case remanded to the Court of Appeals for further proceedings consistent with this opinion.

It is so ordered.

MR. JUSTICE STEWART took no part in the consideration or decision of these cases.

THE CHIEF JUSTICE, MR. JUSTICE BLACKMUN, and MR. JUSTICE REHNQUIST dissent and would affirm the judgment of the Court of Appeals for the Third Circuit and reverse the judgment of the Court of Appeals for the Second Circuit for the reasons stated by Judge Adams in his opinion for the Court of Appeals in *Brennan v. Corning Glass Works,* 480 F. 2d 1254 (CA3 1973).

NOTES:

(1) In *Schultz v. Wheaton Glass Co.,* 421 F.2d 259 (3d Cir. 1970), *cert. denied,* 90 S. Ct. 1696, the court ruled that, under the Equal Pay Act, "Congress in prescribing 'equal' work did not require that the jobs be identical, but only that they must be substantially equal.

Any other interpretation would destroy the remedial purposes of the Act." *Id.* at 265.

(2) Although the "substantial equality" test set out in *Wheaton Glass* is widely applied, it is not completely accepted by all circuits. *See Hodgson v. Golden Isles Nursing Homes, Inc.,* 468 F.2d 1256 (5th Cir. 1972). The courts will apply the Act to successive employees in a particular job, as well as to those holding jobs contemporaneously. In all cases, actual job content is the important consideration in determining equal or substantially equal work; the employer's job description does not control. *Brennan v. Victoria Bank & Trust Co.,* 493 F.2d 896 (5th Cir. 1974).

(3) The defense to the Equal Pay Act which permits a "differential based on any factor other than sex" has generated litigation in a variety of situations. In *Hodgson v. Robert Hall Clothes, Inc.,* 473 F.2d 589 (3d Cir. 1972), *cert. denied,* 414 U.S. 866 (1973), the court held that the fact that the profit from the sale of men's clothes was greater than the profit from the sale of women's and children's clothes could justify a wage differential between male and female salespeople.

Although bona fide training programs can justify a wage differential, the courts have required that the programs be concrete, formal, and provide for rotation and placement which are not dependent on manpower needs or job openings. *Schultz v. First Victoria National Bank,* 420 F.2d 648 (5th Cir. 1969); *Hodgson v. Behrens Drug Co.,* 475 F.2d 1041 (5th Cir. 1973), *cert. denied,* 417 U.S. 196 (1973).

In addition, a training program may not be bona fide if qualified women are excluded from the program. *Hodgson v. Security National Bank,* 460 F.2d 57 (8th Cir. 1972).

(4) Section 6 (d)(1) of the Equal Pay Act provides that an employer who is paying a wage differential in violation of the Act may not reduce the wages of any employee in order to eliminate the differential. Thus, courts have required that the employer raise the wages of female employees to the level of male employees performing substantially equal work rather than lower the wages of the male employees. *See, e.g., Corning Glass Works v. Brennan,* 417 U.S. 188 (1974).

(5) The courts have held that the Supreme Court's decision in *National League of Cities v. Usery,* 426 U.S. 833 (1976), does not preclude the application of the Equal Pay Act to state and local governments. *See, e.g., Usery v. Allegheny County Institution District,* 544 F.2d 148 (3d Cir. 1976).

C. AGE DISCRIMINATION IN EMPLOYMENT ACT

USERY v. TAMIAMI TRAIL TOURS, INC.

Fifth Circuit Court of Appeals
531 F.2d 224 (1976)

JOHN R. BROWN, Chief Judge:
We are asked to review the lower court's determination that appellee's (Tamiami) policy of refusing to consider applications of individuals between the ages of 40 and 65 for initial employment as intercity bus drivers is a bona fide occupational qualification (BFOQ) reasonably necessary to the normal operation of its business. . . .

After reviewing the record at length we are convinced that the conclusions of the District Judge were not clearly erroneous. F.R.Civ.P. 52(a). We affirm.

The Proceedings Below

This action was brought by the Secretary of Labor, United States Department of Labor under the provisions of Section 4 of the Age Discrimination in Employment Act of 1967, 29 U.S.C.A. § 621, *et seq.*, seeking to permanently enjoin Tamiami Trail Tours, Inc. from allegedly denying the employment to individuals within the age group protected by the Act [2] and from withholding payment for unpaid wages allegedly due eight individuals (the complaining witnesses herein) because of discrimination against them. In its answer Tamiami admitted that it refused to consider two of the eight complaining witnesses solely on account of their age. With respect to the other six complaining witnesses the defendant contended that it would not have employed them in any event because of reasons other than age. It asserted, however, that such refusal was done pursuant to the BFOQ exemptions provided in § 4(f)(1) of the Age Discrimination in Employment Act of 1967 [5]. . .

---

[2] Section 12 of the Act limits the prohibitions to individuals who are at least 40 years of age but less than 65 years of age. Defendant readily admitted that its practice was to consider and process for employment as intercity bus drivers only individuals between the ages of 25 and 40 (35 prior to January 1, 1970), regardless of the applicant's prior experience or physical condition, and that these age limits were specified in advertisements soliciting applicants placed by it in newspapers.

[5] Section 4(f)(1) provides an exception to the prohibitions against age discrimination which reads in pertinent part:

(f) It shall not be unlawful for an employer . . . —
   (1) to take any action otherwise prohibited under subsection[s] (a) . . . of this section where age is a bona fide occupational qualification reasonably necessary to the normal operation of the particular business, or where the differentiation is based on reasonable factors other than age;

. . . [I]n the District Court's view, Tamiami could sustain its burden of justifying its application of the general rule (i) by showing that it had a factual basis for believing that otherwise its business operations (safety obligations) would be undermined and (ii) by demonstrating that dealing with each applicant over 40 years of age on an individual basis by considering his particular functional ability to perform safely the duties of a driver notwithstanding his age, would be impractical.[8]

In support of its defense, Tamiami produced numerous witnesses who testified that, in their opinion, age was a reasonable and necessary employment qualification for the position of intercity bus driver. Representatives of other bus companies testified that their practice (see note 2, supra) was similar to that of Tamiami and was grounded upon reasons of safety. This testimony set out with painstaking clarity the great lengths to which bus companies go to promote safety. . . .

Introduced also was conflicting expert testimony regarding the effects of the aging process upon the ability to safely perform the duties of bus driver and upon the reliability of an annual or recurringly scheduled full physical examination used as a screening process to detect those physical and sensory changes common to all persons which result from the aging process.

In his findings of fact and conclusions of law, the trial judge characterized the dispute as not being such a case of "arbitrary" age discrimination as contemplated under the Act. The court concluded that the extraordinarily high degree of care required of bus companies in hiring drivers coupled with the fact that the seniority system imposes roughly a 10-year period on the extra board, justified the industry's utilization of an age limitation as the best available tool for screening out unsuitable driver applicants. The Court concluded

---

[8] This test evolved from footnote 5 of our opinion in *Weeks v. Southern Bell Telephone and Telegraph Co.*, 5 Cir., 1969, 408 F.2d 228, involving sex discrimination under the 1964 Civil Rights Act, as an alternative to the main *Weeks* test. We commented:

> It may be that where an employer sustains its burden in demonstrating that it is impossible or highly impractical to deal with women on an individualized basis, it may apply a reasonable general rule.

408 F.2d at 235 n. 5.

The main method of demonstrating a BFOQ discussed in *Weeks* was stated as follows:

> We conclude that the principle of nondiscrimination requires that we hold that in order to rely on the bona fide occupational qualification exception an employer has the burden of proving that he had reasonable cause to believe, that is, a factual basis for believing, that all or substantially all women would be unable to perform safely and efficiently the duties of the job involved.

408 F.2d at 235.

from the evidence that functional age, as distinguished from the chronological age, of a driver applicant over 40 cannot be determined with sufficient reliability to meet the special safety obligations of motor carriers of passengers. Finding (i) that the defendant had demonstrated a factual basis for its belief that all or substantially all men over 40 would be unable to perform safely and efficiently the duties of the job of intercity bus driver and (ii) that the weight of the evidence introduced supported the view that recurring physical examinations and other testing methods are unreliable in detecting certain of the mental and psychological changes inherent with aging such that individual consideration of applicants over 40 would be highly impractical, i. e. untrustworthy, the court entered its judgment for Tamiami. . .

The Act

President Johnson, in his Older American Message of January 23, 1967, recommended the Age Discrimination in Employment Act of 1967, which was transmitted to the Congress by the Secretary of Labor in February of that year. The president's message, in the section on job opportunities, stated —

> Hundreds of thousands, not yet old, not yet voluntarily retired, find themselves jobless because of arbitrary age discrimination. Despite our present low rate of unemployment, there has been a persistent average of 850,000 people age 45 and over who are unemployed. Today more than ¾ of the billion dollars in unemployment insurance is paid each year to workers who are 45 and over. They comprise 27% of all the unemployed. . . . In economic terms, this is a serious — and senseless — loss to a nation on the move. But the greater loss is the cruel sacrifice in happiness and well-being, which joblessness imposes on these citizens and their families. Opportunity must be opened to the many Americans over 45 who are qualified and willing to work. We must end arbitrary age limits on hiring. [113 Cong.Rec. pp. 34743—34744, Dec. 4, 1967.]

Recognizing the seriousness of the problem,[11] Congress enacted the Age Discrimination in Employment Act in 1967 for the express

---

[11] The Congressional findings underlying this purpose are stated in Section 2(a) of the Act:

The Congress hereby finds and declares that —
(1) in the face of rising productivity and affluence, older workers find themselves disadvantaged in their efforts to retain employment, and especially to regain employment when displaced from jobs;
(2) the setting of arbitrary age limits regardless of potential for job

purpose of promoting "employment of older persons based on their ability rather than age" and prohibiting "arbitrary age discrimination." The Act makes it unlawful for employers, employment agencies, and labor organizations to discriminate on the basis of age, against persons between the ages of 40 and 65.[13]

Section 4(f)(1) provides the BFOQ statutory defense to actions brought for violation of the Act under certain restrictive circumstances. Pursuant to its usual practice, the Department of Labor promulgated an Interpretative Bulletin indicating the construction of the Act which it believed correct to be used as an aid for employers and employees to comply with its provisions. With regard to BFOQ, this Bulletin states that "whether occupational qualification will be deemed to be 'bonafide' and 'reasonably necessary to the normal operation of the particular business' will be determined on the basis of all the pertinent facts surrounding each particular situation." The Bulletin further anticipates "that this concept of a bonafide occupational qualification will have limited scope and application" and reiterating, states that "further, as this

---

performance has become a common practice, and certain otherwise desirable practices may work to the disadvantage of older persons;

(3) the incidence of unemployment, especially long-term unemployment with resultant deterioration of skill, morale, and employer acceptability is, relative to the younger ages, high among older workers; their numbers are great and growing; and their employment problems grave;

(4) the existence in industries affecting commerce, of arbitrary discrimination in employment because of age, burdens commerce and the free flow of goods in commerce.

Congressional finding (1) above, with respect to those older Americans displaced from their jobs, was poignantly pointed out by the Director of the Office of Aging of the Department of Health, Education and Welfare when he testified before the Subcommittee on Employment and Retirement Incomes of the Special Committee on Aging, United States Senate:

... It is one of the anomalies, that every time we go in an employer and we say to him, "Tell us who are your most valuable employees," he will almost invariably name his older employees, the people who have been with the company for many years. But if for some reason or another, because of automation or because of change in techniques, those people are thrown out of work, the older person finds the greater difficulty in being employed. (88 Cong., Part I, Dec. 19, 1963, p. 21).

[13] Section 7(b) of the Act provides for enforcement of the Act's provision "in accordance with the powers, remedies, and procedures" provided in §§ 16 (except for the criminal provisions) and 17 of the Fair Labor Standards Act, 29 U.S.C.A. Section 7(b) of the Age Discrimination in Employment Act further provides that any act prohibited by § 4 of the Act shall be deemed to be a prohibited act under § 15 of the Fair Labor Standards Act, and that amounts owing to a person as a result of a violation of the Age Discrimination in Employment Act shall be deemed to be unpaid minimum wages or unpaid overtime compensation for purposes of §§ 16 and 17 of the Fair Labor Standards Act.

is an exception it must be construed narrowly, and the burden of proof in establishing that it applies is the responsibility of the employer . . . which relies upon it." The Bulletin continues on to list as an illustration of a possible bonafide occupational qualification those situations where "federal statutory and regulatory requirements provide compulsory retirement, without reference to the individual's actual physical condition at the terminal age, when such conditions are clearly imposed for the safety and convenience of the public." The Bulletin cites as an example the situation where federal aviation agency regulations do not permit airline pilots to engage in carrier operations as pilots after they reach age 60. (29 C.F.R. § 860.102). . . .

. . . The Bulletin states that "a differentiation based on a physical examination, but not one based on age, may be recognized as reasonable in certain job situations which necessitate stringent physical requirements due to inherent occupational factors such as the safety of the individual employees or of other persons in their charge, or those occupations which by nature are particularly hazardous." It is then stated that "a claim for a differentiation will not be permitted on the basis of an employer's assumption that every employee over a certain age in a particular type of job usually becomes physically unable to perform the duties of that job."

That these interpretations by the agency charged with the enforcement of the statute are entitled to considerable weight is well settled. *Udall v. Tallman,* 1965, 380 U.S. 1, 85 S.Ct. 792, 13 L.Ed.2d 616; *Griggs v. Duke Power Co.,* 1971, 401 U.S. 424, 91 S.Ct. 849, 28 L.Ed.2d 158.

The Industry

Tamiami Trail Tours, Inc. is an intrastate and interstate motor common carrier of passengers and baggage operating under certificates of public convenience and necessity issued by the Interstate Commerce Commission and the Florida Public Service Commission. Founded in 1924 and headquartered in Miami, Florida, Tamiami is the oldest bus company in Florida and today provides bus transportation services for the general public in all of Florida, South and Central Georgia and a portion of Alabama.

With respect to bus drivers, Tamiami follows an industry-wide policy of conducting operations under a seniority system which is embodied in its labor contracts. Under the system there are two general classifications of drivers — those who perform "regular runs" and whose who perform "extra board." Extra board drivers consist of operators who have insufficient seniority to successfully attain a regularly scheduled run.

The Extra Board

The nature of Tamiami's business, and for that matter, that of other major bus companies also, necessitates that they operate with approximately 25 to 30% more drivers than would be required to drive the regularly scheduled runs. Accordingly, bus drivers bid for preferred runs on the basis of seniority. Within Tamiami, the existing seniority system relegates a driver to approximately 7 to 12 years of extra board driving before he has sufficient seniority to bid for and obtain a regular route. In such status, extra board operators are called upon to take up the slack in normal operations and to fill in for regular drivers in the event of vacation, sick leave and the addition of extra buses to regularly scheduled runs where needed. Additionally, these drivers are responsible for Tamiami's charter services which constitute a significant portion of its total operations.

The term "extra board" actually refers to a schedule where the drivers are listed on a first in, first out basis. As a driver completes an assignment and returns to his home terminal, he is then placed at the bottom of the extra board list. As additional assignments (over and above the regularly scheduled runs) are to be made by Tamiami, the extra board man whose name is at the top of the list is designated as the driver. A man on the extra board has no flexibility or freedom of choice concerning his assignments. He must take whatever assignment comes up and complete it, whether it be a two week charter to another state or a one-day sight-seeing tour. With each assignment, the next driver on the extra board moves into the "first out" slot, and so on down the list.

There can be little doubt that, since extra board drivers are on call 24 hours per day, 7 days a week, and must be prepared to go anywhere in the continental United States at any time on short notice, the work is demanding and physically exhausting. Although there is a provision under which a driver must be given two hours notice prior to departure time for short trips, 8 to 24 hours prior notice for longer trips,[16] tight scheduling and unforeseen demands frequently greatly dimish a driver's ability to predict the time of his next assignment. As such, it can hardly be disputed that the unpredictability, coupled with the strains and rigors of extra board driving would almost certainly render an extra board driver's opportunity for a normal home or family life more difficult than that of a driver with a seniority-attained scheduled run.

---

[16] The testimony established that a long trip would be one that will take over 24 hours. Of course, DOT regulations do not permit a driver to drive more than 10 hours following 8 consecutive hours of duty. The regulations forbid a driver from remaining on duty more than 70 hours in any eight consecutive day period.

Governmental Safety Regulation

Motor bus carriers, along with all common carriers, are charged both under considerations of public policy and by the operation of law with exercising an extraordinarily high standard of care for the safety of their passengers. Pursuant to the Interstate Commerce Act [17] as well as other laws, the Bureau of Motor Carriers Safety has issued detailed regulations affecting drivers among other aspects of motor carrier passenger operations (49 C.F.R. Parts 390—396). These regulations prescribe minimum qualifications for the drivers of motor vehicles and minimum standards governing the forms of employment applications, written and road tests to be given, and physical requirements applicable to drivers (49 C.F.R. Part 391). They further impose the rules under which motor vehicles shall be driven (49 C.F.R. Part 392). The hours of service permitted drivers are also set out in detail (49 C.F.R. Part 395) (see note 16, *supra*). That these regulations are minimum standards only is expressly provided —

> Nothing in parts 390—397 of this subchapter prohibits a motor carrier from requiring and enforcing more stringent rules and regulations relating to safety of operation (49 C.F.R. Part 392.1(b))....

Tamiami's Practices

Tamiami, certainly not alone in the busing industry, has paid careful heed to the rigorous federal and state regulations governing such operations. Commendably, their operations for selection of drivers are exercised with the utmost care for insuring the safety of the traveling public. The hiring process at Tamiami begins with a written application form designed to eliminate those applicants who are unqualified [21]....

---

[17] With the passage of the Department of Transportation Act, responsibility for safety regulation was transferred from the Interstate Commerce Commission to the Department of Transportation, 49 U.S.C. 1655. Section 204(a)(1), of the Interstate Commerce Act, 49 U.S.C. 304(a)(1), provides that:

> (a) It shall be the duty of the Commission — (1) To regulate common carriers by motor vehicle as provided in this part, and to that end the Commission may establish reasonable requirements with respect to continuous and adequate service, transportation of baggage and express, uniform systems of accounts, records, and reports, preservation of records, qualifications and maximum hours of service of employees, and safety of operation and equipment.

[21] This is the stage at which the industry-wide practice operates to exclude those applicants above a certain age, in Tamiami's case — those individuals above the age of 40.

... Once hired, the drivers are given recurring physical examinations on an annual basis (although the Department of Transportation requires physical examinations only once every two years). The physical examination given to all applicants and incumbent drivers is extremely thorough and rigorous. ...

Tamiami's training program for new drivers is conducted by their own personnel and lasts approximately six weeks, the bulk of which time is spent in operating the bus under all conditions, including night driving, under the supervision of either an instructor or one of the regular bus drivers who is required to fill out a form evaluating the student's performance. Upon completion of the training course, the student driver is given a comprehensive road test, which requires the examiner to grade the student on 120 different driving skills (parking, steering, stopping, slowing, passing, turning, etc.), using a form prepared by the Department of Transportation. The examiner also grades the student on his alertness and attentiveness, willingness to take instructions and suggestions, degree of nervousness and apprehensiveness, whether the applicant is easily angered, and physical stamina. Tamiami further continuously evaluates its drivers in terms of their job performance, safety record, attitude and physical fitness and, on the basis of these evaluations, may require particular drivers to report for more frequent physical examinations or to undergo periodic retraining.

Throughout its history of operation, Tamiami has compiled an enviable record of safe, accident-free driving mileage and has been recognized within the motor bus industry by many highly coveted safety awards.

The Question

With this as background, the question presented is whether the conclusion of the District Judge that age is a bona fide occupational qualification reasonably necessary to the safe operation of Tamiami Trail Tours, Inc. is clearly erroneous. F.R.Civ.P. 52(a); *Zenith Radio Corp. v. Hazeltine Research,* 1969, 395 U.S. 100, 89 S. Ct. 1562, 23 L.Ed.2d 129; *Chalk v. Beto,* 5 Cir., 1970, 429 F.2d 225. The Government specifically challenges this conclusion on the grounds that (1) the evidence showed conclusory assertions — not the "factual basis" we required in *Weeks* to establish the BFOQ, and (2) that there was insufficient evidence to show that it would be highly impractical to evaluate older driver-applicants on an individual basis. Tamiami, the Government contends, should have been made to compare the accident records of its extra board drivers over 40 with the accident rates of its under 40 extra board drivers in order to carry its burden. The Government suggests that the conclusions of the

District Judge generally represent precisely the stereotypical thinking that the ADEA was designed to prevent.

The Safety Factor And The
Weeks-Diaz Test

We are not the first Circuit to consider this question. In *Hodgson v. Greyhound Lines, Inc.,* 7 Cir., 1974, 499 F.2d 859, *cert. denied sub nom., Brennan v. Greyhound Lines, Inc.,* 1975, 419 U.S. 1122, 95 S.Ct. 805, 42 L.Ed.2d 822, the Seventh Circuit reviewed the even more exclusive hiring policy of Greyhound precluding the employment of intercity bus drivers 35 years or older. The District Judge had determined that Greyhound failed to carry its burden to demonstrate a factual basis for its belief that its policy was reasonably necessary for the safe operation of its business.[23] Although the District Judge relied primarily in our *Weeks* case, the Court of Appeals chose to shift the focus for determining the standards to prove up the defense. In view of the overriding public safety factor not present in *Weeks,* the Seventh Circuit, relying on *Diaz*[24] required Greyhound to demonstrate that the essence of its business would be endangered by hiring drivers who were over 40.

The Seventh Circuit in *Greyhound* concluded that

Greyhound need only demonstrate however a minimal increase in risk of harm for it is enough to show that elimination of the hiring

---

[23] *Hodgson v. Greyhound Lines, Inc.,* N.D.Ill., 1973, 354 F.Supp. 230.
[24] *Diaz v. Pan American World Airways, Inc.,* 5 Cir., 1971, 442 F.2d 385. The Seventh Circuit in *Greyhound* discussed our business *necessity* test as follows:

In analyzing the standard of proof required of Pan American to establish a "bona fide occupational qualification reasonably necessary to the normal operation of that particular business or enterprise," the Fifth Circuit construed the word "necessary" in the Act to require:

[T]hat we apply a business *necessity* test, not a business *convenience* test. That is to say, discrimination based on sex is valid only when the *essence* of the business operation would be undermined by not hiring members of one sex exclusively. (Emphasis in original.) 442 F.2d at 388.

The court proceeded to characterize the essence of the normal operation of an airline stating that: "The primary function of an airline is to transport passengers safely from one point to another." 442 F.2d at 388. In the court's view Pan American could not establish that the employment of male cabin attendants would have any impact on its ability to provide safe transportation and accordingly the court rejected Pan American's defense of bona fide occupational qualification. Pan American's basis for excluding male applicants, that they could not cater to the psychological needs of the passengers as adequately as females, was found to be merely "tangential to the essence of the business involved." 442 F.2d at 388.

Hodgson v. Greyhound Lines, Inc., supra, at 862.

policy might jeopardize the life of one more person than might otherwise occur under the present hiring practice.

499 F.2d at 863.

In reassessing all of the evidence under this revised standard, the Court concluded that Greyhound by demonstrating the rigors of the extra board and the degenerative effects of age upon the human body, plus the statistical evidence showing that the profile of the safest Greyhound driver shows him to be approximately 50 to 56 years of age with 16 to 20 years experience (which he could not acquire if hired after 40) adequately demonstrated that Greyhound's position that elimination of its maximum hiring age would increase the potential risk of harm to its passengers was grounded on an adequate factual basis. The Court therefore held the findings to the contrary to be clearly erroneous.

The *Greyhound* court distinguished *Weeks* on the ground that "the Fifth Circuit was not confronted with a situation where the lives of numerous persons are completely dependent on the capabilities of the job applicant." 499 F.2d at 861-62. The question raised, therefore, is whether the *Weeks* requisite of the BFOQ test should be dropped or modified when the safety factor is present. Though we agree with the *Greyhound* court that the safety of third parties is a factor which cannot be ignored, we believe that this safety factor is already appropriately highlighted within the current framework of the *Weeks-Diaz* test.

In *Weeks* we held that the employer's refusal to hire women for a job that required occasional strenuous activity violated the Title VII prohibition of employment discrimination. In rejecting the employer's assertion of the BFOQ defense, we set out the test for qualification for that defense:

an employer has the burden of proving that he had reasonable cause to believe, that is, a factual basis for believing, that all or substantially all women would be unable to perform safely and efficiently the duties of the job involved.

408 F.2d at 235. However, even when the employer cannot carry this burden, if it demonstrates "that it is impossible or highly impractical to deal with women on an individualized basis, it may apply a reasonable general rule." 408 F.2d at 235 n. 5. *(See* note 8, *supra.)* One method by which the employer can carry this burden is to establish that some members of the discriminated-against class possess a trait precluding safe and efficient job performance that cannot be ascertained by means other than knowledge of the applicant's membership in the class.[26]

---

[26] An example is *Diaz v. Pan American World Airways, Inc.,* 5 Cir., 1971, 442 F.2d 385, *cert. denied,* 404 U.S. 950, 92 S.Ct. 275, 30 L.Ed.2d 267, where the would-be male cabin attendants allegedly would not have been able to comfort the

The second element of the employer's burden under the BFOQ defense was set out in *Diaz*, in which we invalidated the employer's policy of refusing to hire males for jobs as airline cabin attendants. The statutory requirement that the BFOQ be "reasonably necessary" to the operation of the business was construed to limit qualification for the defense to those cases in which "the *essence* of the business operation would be undermined by not hiring members of one sex exclusively." 442 F.2d at 388. We then noted that "[t]he primary function of an airline is to transport passengers safely from one point to another." *Id. See* note 29, *infra.* We held that the employer could not carry its burden under the BFOQ defense because, although most males may not be able to adequately perform the nonmechanical functions of a cabin attendant, this would not undermine the safe transportation of passengers.[27]

It is in the *Diaz* element of the BFOQ defense that the third-party safety factor comes into play. *Diaz* mandates that the job qualifications which the employer invokes to justify his discrimination must be *reasonably necessary* to the essence of his business — here, the *safe* transportation of bus passengers from one point to another. The greater the safety factor, measured by the likelihood of harm and the probable severity of that harm in case of an accident, the more stringent may be the job qualifications designed to insure safe driving. Thus, it is the *Diaz* element rather

---

passengers precisely because they were male. In *Diaz*, however, the second requisite of the BFOQ test (discussed below) was not satisfied.

Because *Weeks* is typical of most cases in which added expense would be incurred by individualized dispositions of employment applications, it should be clear that alleging this expense is insufficient to meet the employer's burden under footnote 5. Indeed, that note concluded as follows: "No [footnote 5] showing was made here; it seems plain that it could not be."

[27] The Seventh Circuit's reliance on *Diaz* and simultaneous rejection of *Weeks* indicates a misapprehension of the rule established by those two cases. *Diaz* was decided in the context of the application of *Weeks* to Pan Am's sex discrimination in the selection of flight attendants. Before we would allow Pan Am to justify its discrimination as a BFOQ under *Weeks,* we held that the duties of the position for which Pan Am found it necessary to discriminate in its hiring must be reasonably *necessary* to the normal operation — the essence — of Pan Am's business, which we defined as the safe transportation of air passengers. Since the nonmechanical duties of a flight attendant, for which Pan Am felt most males were unqualified, were *not* reasonably necessary to the safe transportation of passengers, Pan Am was precluded from justifying its sex discrimination as a BFOQ under *Weeks.* Thus, the *Diaz* requirement of a correlation between the job description and the essence of the business operation is a condition precedent to the application of *Weeks'* BFOQ exception to the ban on hiring discrimination. As such, *Diaz* affirms and elaborates on the *Weeks* rationale. *Diaz* was not an exception to *Weeks* based on the third-party safety factor. It represented an evolution of *Weeks* to cover attempts by employers to discriminate on the basis of job descriptions not related to the essence of the employer's business.

than the *Weeks* element of the BFOQ defense which adjusts to the safety factor.

It is important to understand that once an employer's job qualifications have passed muster under *Diaz,* the *Weeks* element of the BFOQ test does not mandate hiring applicants who do not meet these perhaps stringent qualifications. On the contrary, if all or substantially all members of a class do not qualify, or if there is no practical way reliably to differentiate the qualified from the unqualified applicants in that class, it is precisely then that *Weeks* permits otherwise proscribed class discrimination as a BFOQ. The *Weeks* test does *not* mandate either the hiring of unqualified applicants or applicants whose qualifications cannot be reliably determined, whether or not they are black or female or over 40 years old.

No one has suggested that Tamiami's stringent job qualifications (discussed above at p. 233) for the position of bus driver are either unrelated to the essence of the business or unreasonable in light of the safety risk. Tamiami has unquestionably satisfied the *Diaz* prong of the BFOQ test.

Having overcome this threshold obstacle which tripped Pan Am in *Diaz,* Tamiami faces the second, double-faceted prong of the BFOQ test set out in *Weeks:* whether it had reasonable cause, that is, a factual basis, for believing that all or substantially all persons over 40 would be unable to perform safely and efficiently the duties of the job involved, *or* whether it is impossible or impractical to deal with persons over 40 on an individualized basis.

Tamiami did not attempt to establish a factual basis for believing that substantially all job applicants over 40 years of age would be unable to drive buses safely. It is thus relegated to the "footnote 5" burden in *Weeks* of demonstrating that the passenger-endangering characteristics of over-40-year-old job applicants cannot practically be ascertained by some hiring test other than automatic exclusion on the basis of age.

Trial Court's Findings Supported

Much of the evidence submitted by Tamiami on the BFOQ issue, and relied upon by the District Court, is either irrelevant to the *Weeks* (footnote 5) standard or insufficient to carry Tamiami's burden. . . .

Tamiami, however, did present proof that, if accepted, would satisfy its BFOQ burden under *Weeks* (footnote 5). Tamiami introduced testimony by both medical and transportation experts. In particular the testimony of Dr. Harold Brandaleone, an eminent medical expert in the field of transportation and motor vehicle accidents, was heavily weighted by the Court. Dr. Brandaleone testified that while chronological age could not be isolated as a factor automatically indicating that an individual could not adjust to the rigors of the extra board schedule, medical science could not accurately separate chronological from functional or physiological age. According to him, (1) certain physiological and psychological changes that accompany the aging process decrease the person's ability to drive safely and (2) even the most refined examinations cannot detect all of these changes. In his opinion 40 years of age was by no means an arbitrary cutoff to enable bus companies to screen out such impairments.[31]

In addition to this medical testimony, Tamiami called Dr. Ernest G. Cox, former Safety Director for the Bureau of Motor Carriers in the Interstate Commerce Commission and later Deputy Director of the Bureau of Motor Carrier Safety in the Department of Transportation to explain the strains on intercity drivers and the importance of the driver's relationship to traffic safety. Dr. Cox expressed the unequivocal opinion that the maximum age qualification was essential to the normal and safe operation of intercity bus lines.

Lastly, Tamiami called five of its current drivers — both senior and extra board juniors — to describe their experiences with the driving conditions of the extra board and regular runs. It was clear from their testimony that acquiring enough seniority to get off the extra board was a primary goal of every driver. Despite their experience, the regular run senior drivers emphatically believed that they could not return to the extra board and still maintain the safety of their passengers.

In contrast to Dr. Brandaleone's medical testimony, the Government relied primarily on the rebuttal testimony of Dr. Abraham J. Mirkin, an expert on automotive accidents, who dismissed any relationship between age and one's ability to drive a vehicle safely, and Kenneth Pierson, Dr. Cox' successor as Deputy Director of the Bureau of Motor Carrier Safety of DOT, who believed that the physical examination, training program and road test that all new drivers are subjected to were sufficient to screen out those applicants of any age who would not be qualified to be safe bus drivers.

The key question is whether a sufficient factual basis for Tamiami's case has been demonstrated by the catalogued strains and pressures of the extra board on the drivers who must serve it, the evidence regarding the inevitable physiological degeneration that accompanies age, and in particular the testimony of Dr. Brandaleone

---

[31] Age in itself, Dr. Brandaleone stated, had never statistically been isolated as a factor because its close association with the aging process.

— which the District Judge was entitled to credit fully — that the available tests cannot distinguish those drivers not yet affected by the more crucial age-related accident-causing impairments like loss of stamina, etc. Whatever might have been our finding were we deciding this issue *de novo,* the District Court found that examinations cannot detect the relevant physiological and psychological changes "with sufficient reliability to meet the special safety obligations of motor carriers of passengers." *Hodgson* v. *Tamiami Trial Tours, Inc.,* S.D.Fla., 1972, 4 E.P.D. § 7795, at 6051. This is a finding of fact and, therefore, may not be set aside unless "clearly erroneous." Fed.R.Civ.P. 52(a). Because of the testimony of Dr. Brandaleone, we do not believe the District Court's finding can be so categorized.[32]

Refrain

This interpretaton of *Weeks-Diaz* clarifies the significance of safety to passengers and members of the public. We emphasize safety in busing just as we would in a variety of other industrial areas where safety to fellow employees is of such humane importance that the employer must be afforded substantial discretion in selecting specific standards which, if they err at all, should err on the side of preservation of life and limb. The employer must of course show a reasonable basis for its assessment of risk of injury/death. But it cannot be expected to establish this to a certainty, for certainty would require running the risk until a tragic accident would prove that the judgment was sound. Priceless as is a single life in our concept of the value of human life and our undoubted unwillingness ever to approve a practice which might kill one but not, say, twenty, we think the safety factor should be evaluated in terms of the possibility or likelihood of injury/death.

The ADEA was designed to eliminate unjustifiable age barriers to the competitive job market erected by societal conventions. To fell these barriers, Congress used the tried-and-true tool of a strong presumption against maximum age hiring categories. Against this presumption, however, the employer may vindicate his hiring policies by demonstrating that the contended discrimination is a bona fide occupational qualification that meets the *Weeks-Diaz* standard discussed in this opinion.

AFFIRMED.

---

[32] The Government's suggestion that the "best evidence" here would have been a comparison between Tamiami's extra board post-40 drivers and its pre-40 extra board drivers does not compel a different answer because, insofar as the evidence shows, there are only two senior Tamiami drivers who chose to remain on the extra board apparently for the reason that they did not want to change locale.

JOHN R. BROWN, Chief Judge (concurring specially):

While, as author for the Court, I join fully in the Court's opinion affirming the District Judge and would not detract from it as long as the Court is committed to the proposition that we must decide it here and now, I believe that the ideal resolution here is not an outright affirmance but that the Court seek further information and guidance by requiring DOT, the agency specially vested with the resources to investigate, hear and then decide initially such difficult transportation questions to make its official position known under its primary jurisdiction. I am not concerned that the District Judge based his findings of fact on insufficient evidence but that the Courts have input from all of the best available sources before they decide crucial questions such as this. . . .

NOTES:

(1) *Problem:* Can the decision in *Tamiami Trail Tours* be read to allow discrimination against "older" workers (as a group) who are allegedly less alert or less productive in other job situations? Or does the opinion mostly rest on considerations of safety? Does the court distort the BFOQ test? Is it possible to square the holding in *Tamiami Trail Tours* with the Supreme Court's holding in *Griggs, supra,* that "any tests used must measure the person for the job and not the person in the abstract."

In another bus driver case, *Hodgson v. Greyhound Lines, Inc.,* 499 F.2d 859 (7th Cir. 1974), the court also granted a BFOQ for age because the employer had a rational basis in fact to believe that increased likelihood of risk of harm to passengers would result from hiring drivers over the age of 40. However, in *Houghton v. McDonnell Douglas Corp.,* 553 F.2d 561 (8th Cir. 1977), the court held that the lower court's finding that age constituted a BFOQ for test pilot was clearly erroneous where there was conflicting evidence as to the effect of the aging process on pilots.

(2) *Advertising:* The Age Discrimination in Employment Act (ADEA) prohibits employment advertising which indicates any limitation or preference which disfavors persons between 40 and 64 years of age. Guidelines issued by the Secretary of Labor prohibit the use of terms such as "boy" or "recent college graduate" in help wanted advertising. 29 CFR § 860.92. The regulations also forbid discrimination in advertising within the protected age group, such as "between 45 and 55." The courts have split on upholding these regulations. *Compare Hodgson v. Approved Personnel Service,* 529 F.2d 760 (4th Cir. 1975), *with Brennan v. C/M Mobile, Inc.,* 8 FEP Cas. 551 (S.D. Ala. 1974).

(3) *Defenses:* The ADEA allows employers to plead defenses

based on bona fide seniority systems and on "differentiations based on reasonable factors other than age." 29 U.S.C. § 623(f). Under the regulations issued by the Secretary of Labor, 29 CFR § 860.105 (1968), a bona fide seniority system must accord employees greater rights with length of service, must be communicated to the employees, must be uniformly applied without regard to age, and must not perpetuate pre-ADEA discrimination.

In interpreting differentiations not based on age, the regulations permit the use of physical fitness requirements, evaluations of production quantity and quality and validated employee tests, so long as these factors are uniformly applied and directly related to the performance of the job. 29 CFR § 860.103 (1968). Most courts have upheld the termination of an older worker based on job performance factors, but asserting these factors cannot be a pretext for discrimination based on age. *Surrisi v. Conwed Corp.,* 510 F.2d 1088 (8th Cir. 1975); *Bishop v. Jelleff Associates, Inc.,* 398 F. Supp. 579 (D.D.C. 1974).

(4) *Section Bibliography: See generally: Age Discrimination in Employment,* 50 N.Y.U. L. Rev. 924 (1975); *Employment Discrimination — Age Discrimination of Employment Act of 1967 — bona fide occupational qualification,* 16 Bost. Coll. Ind. & Com. L. Rev. 688 (1975); Gillan, *Federal Age Discrimination in Employment Act Revisited,* 9 Clearinghouse Rev. 761 (1976); *Proving Discrimination Under the Age Discrimination in Employment Act,* 17 Ariz. L. Rev. 495 (1975); *State Deferral of Complaints Under the Age Discrimination in Employment Act,* 51 Notre Dame Law. 492 (1976).

AGE DISCRIMINATION IN EMPLOYMENT ACT AMENDMENTS OF 1978

In May, 1978, Congress enacted amendments to the Age Discrimination in Employment Act of 1967, 29 U.S.C. 631. The Age Discrimination in Employment Act Amendments of 1978 accomplished three things:

1. The Amendments extended the coverage of the Act to age 70. This was a compromise between those who wanted to retain the maximum age of 65 and those who wanted to eliminate all limits.

2. The Amendments prohibit mandatory retirement for employees under age 70. This will go into effect on January 1, 1980 for those employees covered by a collective bargaining agreement, unless the agreement is terminated earlier. There are two exceptions to this provision:

a. Section 12(b) exempts bona fide executive or high policymaking employees who have attained the age of 65, if such employees receive an annual retirement benefit from the employer which equals at least $27,000.

b. Section 12(d) exempts employees who are serving under a contract of unlimited tenure at an institution of higher education if they have attained 65 years of age. However, the Amendments also provide that this exemption is repealed on July 1, 1982.

3. The Amendments make some procedural changes that affect the way an action under the Act is charged and tried:

a. A jury trial is made available for "any issue of fact in any such action for recovery of amounts owing as a result of a violation of this Act, regardless of whether equitable relief is sought by any party in such action." This resolved a conflict among the courts.

b. The statute of limitations may be tolled for up to one year while the Secretary of Labor is attempting conciliation. The Conference Committee indicated, however, that a conciliation attempt was not to be considered a jurisdictional prerequisite. This was also the subject of some dispute among courts.

c. The original Act required an aggrieved person to file a notice of intent to sue with the Secretary of Labor within 180 days after the alleged act of discrimination (or 300 days if a claim was filed with a state agency). After filing the notice of intent to sue, the aggrieved person was required to wait 60 days before filing suit so that the Secretary of Labor would have an opportunity to attempt conciliation. Many courts strictly construed the notice requirement and generalized complaints of age discrimination were held not to comply. The Conference Committee decided to change the requirement of a "notice of intent to sue" to one of a "charge." The Conference Committee Report states that it was intended that this requirement would be satisfied by the filing of a statement which identifies the potential defendant and generally outlines the action which is alleged to be discriminatory. The Report also states that the "charge" requirement is not a jurisdictional prerequisite to bringing an action under the Age Discrimination in Employment Act. Equitable modification for failure of timely filing will be available.

d. Section 14(b) of the original Act provides that when a state has a statute forbidding age discrimination and establishing an administrative agency, no action can be brought under the federal Act before the expiration of sixty days after "proceedings have been commenced under state law, unless such proceedings have been earlier terminated." The Conference Committee referred to a Senate Report which addressed this problem in an attempt to resolve a conflict among courts. In the Report, the Senate Human Resources Committee stated that § 14(b) "does not require that the individual go to the State first in every instance."

4. For a copy of the full text of the Amendments, with "explanatory notes," *see* 46 U.S.L.W. 51-57 (Statute Section, May 9, 1978).

5. Probably the most significant change made to ADEA by the 1978 amendments is the prohibition against mandatory retirement for employees under age 70. Under the law as originally written, an employer was permitted to force the retirement of an employee, without regard to age, so long as the retirement was done pursuant to "the terms of a bona fide seniority system or any employee benefit plan such as retirement, pension, or insurance plan, which [was] not a subterfuge to evade . . . the Act." This provision was confirmed by the Supreme Court in *United Airlines v. McMann,* 46 U.S.L.W. 4043 (Dec. 12, 1977), where it was held that an employer could observe a provision in a retirement plan that allowed for the forced retirement of an employee at age 60. The 1978 amendments alter the result in *McMann.*

6. Although employees can no longer be compelled to retire pursuant to a retirement plan before age 70, the legislative history surrounding the 1978 amendments indicates that employers "will not be required to continue contributions to either defined benefit or defined contribution plans for employees who continue working beyond the plan's normal retirement age." Cong. Record, p. S4450, March 23, 1978.

Chapter 19

ARBITRATION OF EMPLOYMENT DISCRIMINATION CASES

[Refer to *Alexander v. Gardner-Denver Co.,* 415 U.S. 36 (1976), *supra* Chapter 8 at pp. 473 — 482.]

EDWARDS, ARBITRATION OF EMPLOYMENT DISCRIMINATION CASES: AN EMPIRICAL STUDY, in PROCEEDINGS OF THE 28th ANNUAL MEETING OF THE NATIONAL ACADEMY OF ABRITRATORS 59, 70-89 (BNA, Inc. 1976).

. . . Since Gardner-Denver leaves open the issue as to how much weight, if any, should be accorded an arbitral decision, it is important to get more empirical evidence about the capacity of the arbitration process and arbitrators to deal with legal issues arising under Title VII. In an effort to do just this, this writer conducted a survey of all of the U.S. members of the National Academy of Arbitrators in February 1975. The survey questionnaire was sent to 409 persons; 200 arbitrators responded to the questionnaire. (See Appendices A and B attached hereto.) The average age of the responding arbitrators was 49 years, and the range of ages was from 31 to 77 years. The average years of arbitration experience among the respondents was 21 years (with the range being from 4 to 40 years).

The percentage of survey questionnaires returned from each region in the United States was approximately the same. (The lowest percentage was in the southeast region where 40 percent of the arbitrators returned their survey questionnaire; the highest percentage of returns came from the State of Michigan where nearly 63 percent of the arbitrators answered the survey questionnaire.)

The Capacity of Arbitrators to Decide "Legal" Issues in Cases Involving Claims of Employment Discrimination

One of the things that the survey attempted to determine was the extent to which arbitrators are competent to handle "legal" issues in employment discrimination cases. The findings on this score were most interesting.

One of the questions asked of the respondents was whether they had ever read any *judicial* opinions involving a claim of discrimination under Title VII. One respondent appeared to think that the question was incredulous, and he or she asked, "What kind or arbitrator does not" read judicial opinions? The survey results do not indicate what kind of an arbitrator does not read judicial opinions; however, it does indicate that 77 percent of the respondents had read judicial opinions involving claims of discrimination under Title VII at one time or another, 16 percent of the respondents indicated that they had never read any such judicial opinions, and 7 percent of the respondents declined to answer the question.

The arbitrators were also asked whether they regularly read labor advance sheets to keep abreast of current developments under Title VII. On this question, only 52 percent of the respondents indicated that they did read labor advance sheets, nearly 40 percent of the respondents answered that they did not, and 8 percent of the respondents declined to answer the question.

Another question asked the arbitrators was whether they could define "bona fide occupational qualification," "reasonable accommodation/undue hardship," and "preferential treatment" and accurately explain the current status of the law under Title VII with respect to each of these legal terms. It is significant that very few of the respondents felt that they could define these terms without first doing some legal research. Only 14 percent of the respondents indicated that they felt confident that they could accurately define each of the terms and explain the relevant law, 30 percent of the respondents stated that they could make a good "educated guess" but would not certify their answers as being accurate, and nearly 50 percent of the respondents indicated that they would prefer to research the question before answering.

Finally, the arbitrators were asked whether they felt that they were professionally competent to decide "legal" issues in cases involving claims of race, sex, national origin, or religious discrimination. It is extremely noteworthy that, in answer to this question, only about 72 percent of the respondents indicated that they felt professionally competent to decide legal issues in cases involving claims of employment discrimination. Sixteen percent of the respondents answered that they did not feel professionally competent to handle such cases, and 12 percent of the respondents declined to answer the question.

While these statistics raise some troublesome questions about the capacity of arbitrators to decide legal issues in cases involving claims of employment discrimination, they surely do not, without more, prove that arbitrators are incapable of handling such legal matters. There are some additional data from the survey, however, that raise more serious questions with respect to the capacity of arbitrators to decide legal issues in cases involving claims of employment discrimination.

Most of the respondents (83 percent) who indicated that they had never read a judicial opinion involving a claim of employment discrimination also indicated that they did not regularly read labor advance sheets to keep abreast of current developments under Title VII. Yet, 50 percent of this group of respondents nevertheless answered that they felt professionally competent to decide "legal" issues in cases involving claims of race, sex, national origin, or religious discrimination. Similarly, 70 percent of the group of respondents who indicated that they did not regularly read labor advance sheets to keep abreast of current developments under Title VII nevertheless indicated that they felt professionally competent to decide legal questions in cases involving claims of employment discrimination. From these facts, it is obvious that many arbitrators do not believe that these factors are relevant measures of the professional competence of arbitrators to decide legal issues in cases involving claims of employment discrimination.

However, it is interesting to note that 83 percent of the group of respondents who had never read a judicial opinion indicated that they could not define the three legal terms mentioned on the questionnaire without first doing some legal research. Only 13 percent of this group felt that they could make a good "educated guess" about the definition of the three legal terms, and only 3 percent of the group felt that they could do more than give an educated guess.

On this same score, 63 percent of the group of respondents who answered that they did not regularly read labor advance sheets also answered that they could not define the three legal terms without doing some research on the subject. Only 5 percent of this group indicated that they could do more than give an educated guess about the meaning of the legal terms in question.

Only 14 percent of the total group of respondents indicated that they felt that they were both (1) professionally competent to decide legal issues in cases involving claims of employment discrimination, and (2) able to define "bona fide occupational qualification," "reasonable accommodation/undue hardship," and "preferential treatment" without doing any research, and accurately explain the current status of the law with respect to each of these concepts. Of equal significance is the fact that only 18 percent of the group of respondents who felt that they were professionally competent to decide legal issues in employment discrimination cases stated that they could define the three legal terms with something more than a good "educated guess" and without doing any research on the subject. Finally, it is surprising to note that nearly 20 percent of the respondents who indicated that they *could* accurately define each of the three legal terms or make a good "educated guess" on the subject nevertheless indicated that they did *not* feel professionally competent to decide "legal" issues in cases involving claims of employment discrimination.

The question of professional competence would be of little interest if only qualified persons were being selected to hear and decide arbitration cases involving legal issues in connection with claims of employment discrimination. However, the survey data indicate that one half of the respondents who answered that they did not feel professionally competent to decide legal issues in cases involving claims of employment discrimination also answered that they had heard and decided such cases during the past year. Thus, there is no reason to believe that the arbitration-selection processes, as they presently exist, are designed to screen out persons who are not professionally qualified to decide legal issues in cases involving claims of employment discrimination.

It is obvious from the above data that many arbitrators feel that they are competent to handle employment discrimination cases (and to decide related legal issues) even though they are not otherwise knowledgeable about current developments in the law under Title VII. This is shown by the fact that there is no strong statistical relationship between arbitrators' ability to define three oft-cited legal terms (pertaining to the law under Title VII) and arbitrators' personal perceptions about their professional competence to decide "legal" issues in cases involving claims of employment discrimination. In fairness, however, it must be conceded that a great many of the persons who are members of the National Academy of Arbitrators clearly possess the intellectual wherewithall, general expertise in the field of labor and industrial relations, and sufficient "judicial" experience to make them potentially well qualified and highly able to decide most employment discrimination cases (and most "legal" issues associated with such cases). Indeed, many arbitrators are well able to research a "legal" issue, discover the relevant law, and issue a sound decision on the matter. However, it must be recognized that the judgment as to "qualifications" may be viewed as an abstract possibility or as a current reality. The data from the survey would suggest that many arbitrators are potentially, but not actually, well qualified to decide *legal* issues in cases involving claims of employment discrimination at the present time.

The Capacity of the Arbitration Process to Handle Employment Discrimination Cases Involving Legal Issues Cognizable Under Title VII

The problem here is compounded by some additional considerations having to do with the nature of the arbitration process and with the arbitrators' perceptions about their roles in cases involving legal issues. Even if it may be assumed, *arguendo,* that many arbitrators are professionally competent to decide *legal* issues in cases involving claims of employment discrimination, the nature of the arbitration process will often make it impossible, or at best difficult, for such arbitrators to render opinions that effectively resolve legal issues in cases involving claims of employment discrimination. The following facts, based on the evidence from the survey, appear to support this conclusion.

In many cases, lawyers do not appear as advocates for the parties in arbitration proceedings involving claims of employment discrimination. This is not to say that only lawyers are qualified to serve as advocates in arbitration proceedings; quite the contrary, because it is clear that there are many outstanding arbitration advocates on both sides of the table who have never had any legal training. However, it must be assumed that lawyers, because of their professional training, should be better able than nonlawyers to identify and argue about "legal" issues that might be relevant in employment discrimination cases.

The survey results indicate that lawyers represented both the union and the company in only 173 out of 328 employment discrimination cases heard during the period from February 1974 until February 1975 (*i.e.,* 53 percent of all of the cases). Companies were represented by legal counsel in 76 percent of the cases; unions were represented by legal counsel in only 53 percent of the cases. On the basis of these data, and if it can be assumed that legal representation may be an advantage in an arbitration case involving claims of employment discrimination, then it may be concluded that employee-grievants are at least somewhat disadvantaged in approximately 25 percent of these cases where the company has legal representation and the union does not.

One way to overcome this problem might be to allow grievants to appear with their own legal counsel in arbitration cases involving claims of employment discrimination. However, the survey results indicate that this approach was followed in only 9 percent (30 out of 328) of the cases involving claims of employment discrimination heard in arbitration.

It also might be argued that, since employee-grievants are not foreclosed by arbitration from pursuing their legal remedies under Title VII, it should not matter whether they are given legal representation in arbitration. However, the survey results suggest that many of the employment discrimination cases that are decided in arbitration do not subsequently get reheard by the EEOC or by the courts. The evidence received from the arbitrators who responded to the survey reveals that employment discrimination charges had been filed with the EEOC or the courts in only 25 percent (84 out of 328) of all of the employment discrimination cases that were heard in arbitration. This figure may be deceptively low, either because some of the arbitrator respondents were unaware of all of the cases in which grievants filed charges under Title VII or because such charges were filed subsequent to the conclusion of the arbitration proceeding. However, it is nevertheless noteworthy that the number of duplicate charges (involving complaints of employment discrimination which are heard in arbitration and in the courts) does not appear to be nearly as high as some persons have suggested. If these figures are accurate, then they certainly negate the argument advanced by those who oppose the decision in *Gardner-Denver* on the ground that an employee should not get "two bites at the same apple."

Several other important problems were raised in connection with the capacity of the arbitration process to deal with legal issues in employment discrimination cases. One such problem has to do with the nature of the substantive issue that is actually decided by an arbitrator in a case involving a claim of employment discrimination. On this score, it must be recognized that an arbitrator cannot resolve a legal issue, or give due consideration to the relevant law, if the matter is not raised as an issue in arbitration. On this point, the survey results indicate that the relevance of Title VII was raised in only 31 percent (103) of the employment discrimination cases heard in arbitration. Furthermore, company officials argued that the legal precedents under Title VII were relevant and should be considered by the arbitrator in only 12 percent of the cases, and union officials argued in favor of relevance in only 22 percent of all of the employment discrimination cases heard in arbitration.

Another like problem arises because arbitrators only infrequently rely on Title VII and other relevant legal precedents when deciding employment discrimination cases. The evidence from the survey reveals the following: The responding arbitrators indicated that they had actually relied on Title VII legal precedents in only 12.5 percent of all of the employment discrimination cases heard in arbitration; and legal precedents were actually cited in these arbitrators' decisions in only 11 percent of all of the employment discrimination cases heard in arbitration.

Although the survey data indicate that the responding arbitrators ruled in favor of employee-grievants in 34 percent of the cases involving claims of employment discrimination, the arbitrators in these cases usually avoided "legal" issues. In instances in which the grievants won, the arbitrator found that the company or union was guilty of discrimination *under the contract* in only 48 percent of the cases and guilty of discrimination *under the law* in only 21 percent of the cases; no information was furnished with respect to the remaining 31 percent of the cases.

In Footnote 21 in the *Gardner-Denver* decision, the Supreme Court stated that "where an arbitral determination gives full consideration to an employee's Title VII rights, a court may properly accord it great weight." Two of the measures of "full consideration" identified by the Court were "degree of procedural fairness" and "adequacy of the record with respect to the issue of discrimination." Some of the data gleaned from the survey speak to these two considerations.

The evidence from the survey indicates that official transcripts were made in only 43 percent (140) of all of the employment discrimination cases heard in arbitration. Furthermore, the evidence reveals that prehearing and/or posthearing briefs were submitted by both parties in only 52 percent (172) of all of the employment discrimination cases heard in arbitration.

It is also noteworthy that most of the employment discrimination cases decided in arbitration were resolved on the merits. This is clear from the facts that show that in only 11 cases (3.3 percent) did the company or the union argue that the claim of discrimination was not arbitrable under the collective bargaining agreement and in only 16 (4.8 percent) of the cases did the parties' collective bargaining agreement explicitly exclude discrimination claims from arbitration. However, only 25 percent of the responding arbitrators who heard and decided employment discrimination cases last year indicated that they had advised grievants of their statutory rights pursuant to Title VII. While there is no legal requirement that such advice be given by the arbitrator, it would be clear that many grievants who are not so advised, and who are otherwise not represented by counsel, may not realize that arbitration is not the forum of last resort for the resolution of employment discrimination cases.

Finally, and most significantly, it is somewhat amazing to note that many of the responding arbitrators suggested that the quality of the evidence given in employment discrimination cases heard in arbitration was deficient. On this point, the survey questionnaire asked the arbitrators: "In how many of these [employment discrimination] cases did you feel that the record was complete enough so that all of the legal issues under Title VII could have been resolved in a court of law?" In response to this question, the responding arbitrators indicated that the record was complete in only about 55 percent of all the employment discrimination cases heard in arbitration. This fact alone would surely suggest that the courts ought to be very careful before they begin to accord great weight to arbitration opinions involving claims of employment discrimination. This is especially so in light of the evidence here, which indicates that (1) no transcript of the proceedings is made in more than half of the arbitration cases involving claims of employment discrimination, and (2) most of the arbitrators who have heard and decided these cases have admittedly declined to consider and resolve "legal" issues.

Arbitrators' Views Concerning the Role of the Arbitrator in Deciding Employment Discrimination Cases

Whether or not arbitrators are professionally competent to decide legal issues in cases involving claims of employment discrimination, it still must be realized that many arbitrators are loath to decide such issues. For many years, various members of the National Academy of Arbitrators have debated the question dealing with the proper role of the arbitrator in handling "legal" issues in arbitration cases. Several theories have been advanced, most notably by Bernard Meltzer, Robert Howlett, Richard Mittenthal, Theodore St. Antoine, and Michael Sovern. All of these theories were ably summarized by Dean Sovern in a paper entitled "When Should Arbitrators Follow Federal Law?" that was delivered during the 1970 meeting of the National Academy of Arbitrators.[21] While these debates have been healthy academic exercises, they really have not told us much about what arbitrators are actually doing as a group (or what they feel that they ought to be doing) when presented with legal issues in connection with claims of employment discrimination in arbitration. One of the reasons for the current survey was to get better and more accurate empirical data on this subject. The results of the survey on this point are interesting but not surprising.

Nearly two thirds of the responding arbitrators stated that they believed that an arbitrator has no business interpreting or applying a public statute in a contractual grievance dispute. (However, nearly one half of the responding arbitrators did indicate that an arbitrator should be free to *comment* on the relevant law if it appears to conflict with the collective bargaining agreement.) Only one third of all of the responding arbitrators indicated that they believed a collective bargaining agreement must be read to include by reference all public law applicable thereto. In other words, most of the arbitrators rejected the view that an arbitrator should always apply constitutional, statutory, or common law principles to aid in the resolution of contractual grievance disputes.

Nearly all of the responding arbitrators who believed that an arbitrator has no business interpreting or applying a public statute in a contractual grievance dispute conceded that there were certain exceptions to this rule. Of these respondents, 85 percent agreed that an arbitrator may consider and interpret public law in order to avoid compelling a union or a company to do something that is *clearly* unlawful. Ninety-five percent of them agreed that an arbitrator may

---

[21] Michael I. Sovern, "When Should Arbitrators Follow Federal Law?" in *Arbitration and the Expanding Role of Neutrals,* Proceedings of the 23rd Annual Meeting, National Academy of Arbitrators, eds. Gerald G. Somers and Barbara D. Dennis (Washington, BNA Books, 1970), pp. 29-47.

properly refer to the applicable law if it can be found that the parties have intentionally adopted a contract clause pursuant to an existing statute with the object of incorporating the body of public law into the contract. Finally, 97 percent of these respondents agreed that an arbitrator should consider public law when the parties have, by submission, conferred jurisdiction upon him or her to decide the contract issue in light of the applicable federal or state law.

Although most of the responding arbitrators appear to accept the view that an arbitrator generally has no business interpreting or applying a public statute in a contractual grievance dispute, except in limited and exceptional circumstances, the survey results on this point are nevertheless anomalous in certain respects. More than one third of all of the respondents disagreed with the result in the *Gardner-Denver* decision. This figure by itself is not surprising. However, nearly 30 percent of all of the respondents who stated that an arbitrator has no business interpreting or applying public law in a contractual grievance dispute also stated that they disagreed with the opinion in *Gardner-Denver*. This result would appear to be inherently illogical.

Most of the respondents (90 percent) who disagreed with the result in *Gardner-Denver* felt that they were professionally qualified to resolve legal issues in employment discrimination cases. This surely is not surprising, nor is it surprising that these persons would prefer some kind of deferral rule as opposed to the principles stated in the *Gardner-Denver* decision. However, it is curious that nearly 20 percent of the responding arbitrators who stated that they were *not* professionally competent to handle legal issues in employment discrimination cases also stated that they disagreed with the decision in *Gardner-Denver*. This position is surely inherently illogical.

Not only did a substantial majority of the responding arbitrators who disagreed with the decision in *Gardner-Denver* indicate that they felt professionally competent to decide legal issues, but 86 percent of this group also stated that they had read judicial opinions involving claims of employment discrimination and 60 percent of the group stated that they regularly read labor advance sheets to keep abreast of current developments under Title VII. Taken together, these statistics not surprisingly suggest that those persons who are most familiar with the law under Title VII are more inclined to disagree with the result in *Gardner-Denver*.

However, these findings do not negate the data that reveal that only 71 percent of the responding arbitrators felt that they were professionally competent to decide legal issues in cases involving claims of employment discrimination; only 52 percent of the responding arbitrators indicated that they regularly read labor advance sheets to keep abreast of current developments under Title

VII; and only 14 percent of the responding arbitrators felt confident that they could accurately define "bona fide occupational qualification," "reasonable accommodation/undue hardship," and "preferential treatment" and explain the relevant law under Title VII with respect to each of these legal concepts.

Regional Differences

The evidence from the survey reveals some minor, but no significant, distinctions in the attitudes expressed among the arbitrators from different geographic regions in the United States. For example, more than 50 percent of the responding arbitrators from every region in the country felt that they were professionally competent to decide legal issues in employment discrimination cases: The figures ranged from 94 percent in Michigan, 91 percent in the Midwest, 86 percent in the Southeast, 74 percent in the Southwest (including California and Hawaii), 67 percent in the Northeast, and 50 percent in the Northwest (including only Idaho, Washington, and Oregon).

Likewise, the proportional number of employment discrimination cases heard in arbitration appeared to be evenly divided throughout the various regions in the country. Of the respondents from the northeast region, 54 percent indicated that they had heard employment discrimination cases in arbitration during the past year; 50 percent of the respondents from the Southeast and the Northwest had heard such cases; 44 percent of the respondents from the Midwest and the Southwest had heard discrimination cases; and 67 percent of the respondents from Michigan had decided employment discrimination cases.

It is interesting that nearly 53 percent of the respondents from the midwest region indicated that they did not agree with the Supreme Court decision in *Gardner-Denver*. This percentage was nearly 20 points higher than the next highest region. The figure is not surprising, however, when it is coupled with the fact that 91 percent of all of the respondents in the Midwest felt that they were professionally competent to decide issues in cases involving claims of employment discrimination.

Conclusion

There is nothing wrong with arbitrators' deciding cases involving claims of race, sex, national origin, or religious discrimination. For, as the Supreme Court noted in *Gardner-Denver*, "where the collective-bargaining agreement contains a nondiscrimination clause similar to Title VII, and where arbitral procedures are fair and regular, arbitration may well produce a settlement satisfactory to both employer and employee." But it should not be assumed that merely because an arbitrator has heard a case involving a claim of employment discrimination that he has also resolved the underlying "legal" issues that may be posed. The data recovered from the survey strongly militate against any such conclusion.

The evidence as to whether and how many arbitrators are professionally competent to decide legal issues in cases involving claims of employment discrimination is at best mixed. Furthermore, even assuming, *arguendo,* that most arbitrators are professionally competent to decide such issues, the nature of the arbitration process often will not allow for full and adequate consideration of an employee's Title VII rights. Finally, the evidence from the survey suggests that even when arbitrators are professionally competent to decide legal issues and when the arbitration process is adequate to allow for full consideration of legal questions arising pursuant to Title VII, still many arbitrators believe that they have no business interpreting or applying a public statute in a contractual grievance dispute.

Given all of these considerations, the courts should be very wary about reading *Gardner-Denver* too expansively in a manner that might well result in the development of de facto schemes of deferral that effectively foreclose full and complete judicial resolution of employment discrimination claims.

Some of the arbitrators who responded to the survey, and who indicated that they were opposed to the decision in *Gardner- Denver,* argued that they were as competent as many judges to decide legal issues arising pursuant to Title VII. Whether or not this is true is really beside the point. One responding arbitrator put the problem in proper perspective with the following comment: "Subjectively and privately I feel as well qualified as many of the judges writing the decisions; but I would not publicly make this claim, nor would I be eager to assume that responsibility unless the parties explicitly so requested."

Another responding arbitrator commented that the *Gardner-Denver* decision

"permits the arbitrator to confine himself to interpreting the collective bargaining agreement with less strain on his conscience, particularly where the agreement and the law are not congruent, because the grievant now clearly has an alternative tribunal which is not confined to the terms of the collective bargaining agreement. I think this will tend to make many cases much less elaborate since there is no longer any question of meeting all the standards which would be relevant if deferral to arbitration by the courts or EEOC was a possibility."

Arbitrators, unlike judges, are accountable only to the parties and their decisions are rarely subject to close judicial review. The simple fact is that arbitrators are not responsible for developing principles of public law. As the Court in *Gardner-Denver* noted, "the specialized competence of arbitrators pertains primarily to the law of the shop, not the law of the land." Therefore, even if some arbitrators are better qualified than some judges to decide certain legal issues, this still would not militate in favor of a deferral rule in cases involving claims of employment discrimination.

The proper role of the arbitrator, as distinguished from arbitral competence, is the real reason why the Supreme Court should not dilute the *Gardner-Denver* decision in favor of any deferral rule. This point was best stated by Dean Shulman, in his oft-quoted article, "Reason, Contract and Law in Labor Relations," [22] as follows:

> "A proper conception of the arbitrator's function is basic. He is not a public tribunal imposed upon the parties by superior authority which the parties are obliged to accept. He has no general charter to administer justice for a community which transcends the parties. He is rather part of a system of industrial self-government created by and confined to the parties. He serves their pleasure only, to administer the rule of law established by their collective agreement."

A modern-day version of this same idea was stated by one of the arbitrators who responded to the survey and made the following comments:

> "A national public policy on discrimination should and must be developed, under statutes, by public administrative quasi-judicial agencies and courts; not by private persons like me, selected by private parties to decide particular disputes which *they* have. A consistent and uniform body of 'law,' binding on the nation should not be the creation of private decision-makers but of public instrumentalities. Arbitration of labor-management disputes has been successful because of its restricted role. Freight it with the responsiblity of law enforcement and the interpretation of statutes and great harm will be done to the institution as it presently exists.
> "[The *Gardner-Denver* decision] hasn't changed my thinking at all. I was always confident that when the question reached the Supreme Court, an arbitrator's decision on the application of a statute would not (and should not) be binding and final as his decision on the private disputes of parties under their contract. Those whose bowels are in an uproar over *Gardner-Denver* are acting in accordance with Maxim #244 of Publilius Syrus: 'The end justifies the means.' Occasionally this may be so; but there is no insufficient justification in this case. The Court has decided wisely."

---

[22] 68 *Harv. L. Rev.* 999, 1016 (1955).

Appendix A

RESULTS FROM SURVEY QUESTIONNAIRE DEALING WITH ARBITRATION OF EMPLOYMENT DISCRIMINATION CASES SINCE THE ISSUANCE OF THE GARDNER-DENVER DECISION

1. Date when survey questionnaire was sent out: February 3, 1975
2. Deadline for survey replies: April 1, 1975
3. Sample group: All current United States members of the National Academy of Arbitrators
4. Total number of surveys sent out: 409
5. Total number of responses: 200 (49 percent)
6. Responses by region:

Region	No. of Surveys Sent Out	No. of Responses from Region (% of Total Responses)	Percentage of Returns from the Region
Northeast	147	70 (35%)	47.6%
Southeast	78	31 (15.5%)	39.7
Northwest (Idaho, Washington, and Oregon)	7	4 (2%)	57
Midwest	68	37 (18.5%)	54.4
Southwest (including California and Hawaii)	77	37 (18.5%)	48
Michigan	32	20 (10%)	62.5
Unidentified	—	1 (.5%)	
	409	200 (100%)	48.8%

7. Number of years of arbitration experience among respondents: Mean — 21 years / Median — 22 years / Range — 4-40 years
8. Average age of respondents: Mean — 49 years / Median — 51 years
9. Full-time v. part-time status among respondents: Full-time — 61 (33%) / Part-time — 123 (66%)
10. Professional training of respondents: Lawyers — 108 (54%) / Economists — 58 (29%)

	Political Scientists — 14 (7%)
	Industrial Relations — 54 (27%)
	Business — 10 (5%)
	Other — 11 (5.5%)
11. Number of respondents who have read *judicial* opinions involving claims of discrimination under Title VII:	Yes — 154 (77%) No — 31 (16%) NA — 15 (7%)
12. Number of respondents who regularly read labor advance sheets to keep abreast of current developments under Title VII:	Yes — 105 (52.5%) No — 79 (39.5%) NA — 16 (8%)
13. Number of respondents who believe that they can define "bona fide occupational qualification," "reasonable accommodation/undue hardship," and "preferential treatment" (as legal principles arising under Title VII) without doing any research:	Can accurately define terms and explain the relevant law — 28 (14%) Could make a good 60 (30%) "educated guess" Would prefer to research the question — 96 (48%) NA — 16 (8%)

14. Respondents' viewpoints concerning the role of the arbitrator in handling employment discrimination cases:

   a. An arbitrator has no business interpreting or applying a public statute in a contract grievance dispute. If there is an irreconcilable conflict between Title VII and the terms of an agreement, it is the arbitrator's duty to abide by the contract and ignore the law.   28 (14%)

   b. An arbitrator has no business interpreting or applying a public statute or law in a contract grievance dispute. However, an arbitrator should be free to comment on the relevant law, especially if it appears to conflict with the contract.   96 (48%)

    c. A collective bargaining contract must be read to include by reference all public law applicable thereto; hence, an arbitrator should always apply constitutional, statutory, and common law to aid in the resolution of any grievance dispute.   53 (26.5%)

    d. No choice.   4 (2%)

    e. A different choice other than (a), (b), or (c).   3 (1.5%)

15. Number of respondents who selected (a) or (b) above (and thus agreed that an arbitrator has no business interpreting or applying a public statute in a contract grievance dispute) who were willing to modify their positions by one of the following three exceptions:

    a. An arbitrator may consider and interpret public law in order to avoid compelling a company or union to do something that is clearly unlawful.   Yes — 105/124 (85%)   No — 10/124 (8%)

    b. If it can be found that the parties have intentionally adopted a contract clause pursuant to an existing statute, with the object of incorporating the body of public law into the contract, then the arbitrator may properly refer to the applicable statute and any regulations or decisions thereunder in attempting to ascertain the meaning of the contract clause in issue.   Yes — 118/124 (95%)   No — 1/124 (.8%)

    c. An arbitrator should consider public law when the parties have, by submission, conferred jurisdiction upon him or her to decide the contract issue in light of applicable federal or state law.   Yes — 120/124 (97%)   No — 2/124 (1.5%)

16. Number of respondents who heard employment discrimination cases during the 12 months between February 1, 1974 and February 1, 1975:   Yes — 93 (46.5%)   No — 107 (53.5%)

17. Total number of employment discrimination cases heard by respondents: 328
18. Average number of employment discrimination cases heard by all respondents: 1.8
19. Average number of employment discrimination cases heard by respondents who decided employment discrimination cases: 3.52
20. Number of cases involving race discrimination: 231 (70%)
21. Number of cases involving sex discrimination: 86 (26%)
22. Number of cases involving national origin discrimination: 16 (4.8%)
23. Number of cases involving religious discrimination: 5 (1.5%)
24. Number of cases in which there were lawyers representing both the union and the company: 173 (52.7%)
25. Number of cases in which the company was represented by legal counsel: 251 (76.5%)
26. Number of cases in which the union was represented by legal counsel: 174 (53%)
27. Number of cases in which the grievant was represented by legal counsel who was not otherwise associated with the union or the company: 30 (9%)
28. Number of cases in which the grievant had filed a charge of discrimination with the EEOC, or a state civil rights agency or in court: 84 (25%)
29. Number of cases in which the issue of relevance of Title VII was raised: 103 (31%)
30. Number of cases in which the company argued that the legal precedents under Title VII were relevant and should be considered by the arbitrator: 42 (12%)
31. Number of cases in which the union argued that the legal precedents under Title VII were relevant and should be considered by the arbitrator: 72 (22%)

32. Number of cases in which the company argued that the legal precedents under Title VII were irrelevant and should not be considered by the arbitrator: 45 (13.7%)

33. Number of cases in which the union argued that the legal precedents under Title VII were irrelevant and should not be considered by the arbitrator: 18 (5.4%)

34. Number of cases in which the arbitrator actually relied on Title VII precedent in reaching his or her opinion: 41 (12.5%)

35. Number of cases in which the arbitrator actually cited legal precedents under Title VII in the body of his or her arbitration decision: 37 (11%)

36. Number of cases where a transcript of the proceedings was made: 140 (42.6%)

37. Number of cases in which the arbitrator felt that the record was complete enough so that all of the legal issues under Title VII could have been resolved in a court of law: 179 (54.5%)

38. Number of cases in which the arbitrator actually ruled in favor of the grievant: 111 (33.8%)

39. Number of cases in which the arbitrator actually found that the company and/or the union was guilty of race, sex, religious, or national origin discrimination which was prohibited by the collective bargaining agreement: 53/111 (48%)

40. Number of cases in which the arbitrator found the company and/or the union was guilty of race, sex, national origin, or religious discrimination as prohibited by Title VII: 23/111 (20.7%)

41. Number of cases in which both parties submitted prehearing and/or posthearing briefs: 172 (52.4%)

42. Number of cases in which the company or the union argued that the claim of discrimination was not arbitrable under the collective bargaining agreement: 11 (3.3%)

43. Number of cases where the parties' contract explicitly excluded discrimination claims from arbitration: 16 (4.8%)

44. Number of respondents who feel that they are professionally competent to decide *legal* issues in cases involving claims of race, sex, national origin, or religious discrimination:

Yes — 143 (71.5%)
No — 32 (16%)
NA — 25 (12.5%)

45. Number of respondents who agree with the judicial opinion rendered in the *Gardner-Denver* decision:

Yes — 74 (37%)
No — 57 (28.5%)
Qualified yes — 22 (11%)
No opinion — 47 (23.5%)

46. Number of respondents who are now more reticent about deciding employment discrimination cases:

Yes — 23 (11.5%)
No — 125 (62%)
NA — 52 (26%)

47. Number of arbitrators who are now less reticent about deciding employment discrimination cases:

Yes — 5 (2.5%)
No — 127 (63.5%)
NA — 68 (34%)

48. Number of respondents who advised grievants of their statutory rights before the issuance of the *Gardner-Denver* opinion:

Yes — 30 (15%)
No — 120 (60%)
NA — 50 (25%)

49. Number of respondents who would now (since the issuance of the *Gardner-Denver* opinion) advise grievants of their statutory rights:

Yes — 48 (24%)
No — 100 (50%)
NA — 52 (26%)

50. Number of respondents who find that they now spend more time with "legal" issues in employment discrimination cases since the issuance of the *Gardner-Denver* opinion:

Yes — 31 (15%)
No — 78 (39%)
NA — 91 (45.5%)

51. Number of respondents who find that they spend less time with "legal" issues in employment discrimination cases since the issuance of the *Gardner-Denver* opinion:

Yes — 2 (1%)
No — 98 (49%)
NA — 100 (50%)

52. Number of respondents who have found that the parties tend to be better prepared in employment discrimination cases since the issuance of the *Gardner-Denver* opinion:

Yes — 25 (12.5%)
No — 62 (31%)
NA — 113 (56.5%)

NOTE:

There have been some excellent scholarly treatments of the subject of arbitration of employment discrimination cases. Some of the works worth reviewing are: Coulson, *The Polarized Employee — Can Arbitration Bridge The Gap,* Proceedings of the Southwestern Legal Foundation Annual Institute on Labor Law (Oct. 26, 1977); Edwards, *Arbitration of Employment Discrimination Cases: A Proposal for Employer and Union Representatives,* 27 Lab. L.J. 265 (1976); Meltzer, *Labor Arbitration and Discrimination: The Parties' Process and the Public's Purposes,* 43 U. Chi. L. Rev. 724 (1976); Gould, *Labor Arbitration of Grievances Involving Racial Discrimination, 118 U. Pa. L. Rev. 40 (1969); Platt, The Relationship Between Arbitration and Title VII of the Civil Rights Act of 1964,* 3 Ga. L. Rev. 398 (1969); Sovern, *When Should Arbitrators Follow Federal Law?* in Proceedings of the 23rd Annual Meeting of the National Academy of Arbitrators (BNA, Inc. 1970); Shaw, *Comment on "The Coming End of Arbitration's Golden Age"* in Proceedings of the 29th Annual Meeting of the National Academy of Arbitrators (BNA, Inc. 1976); St. Antoine, *Judicial Review of Labor Arbitration Awards: A Second Look At Enterprise Wheel and Its Progeny,* 75 Mich. L. Rev. 1137 (1977); Howlett, *The Arbitrator, The NLRB and the Courts* in Proceedings of the 20th Annual Meeting of the National Academy of Arbitrators (BNA, Inc. 1967); Mittenthal, *The Role of Law In Arbitration* in Proceedings of the 21st Annual Meeting of the National Academy of Arbitrators (BNA, Inc. 1968); Feller, *The Impact of External Law Upon Labor Arbitration* in The Future of Labor Arbitration in America (Amer. Arb. Assoc. 1976); Edwards, *Labor Arbitration At The Crossroads: The "Common Law of the Shop" Versus External Law,* 32 Arb. J. 65 (June 1977).

Index

References are to pages.

A